Douglas Moo's commentary on the Epistle to the Hebrews provides an extremely useful tool for close study of this powerful but enigmatic early Christian text. Rightly recognizing the difficulties and in dialogue with a wide range of scholarship, Moo usefully reviews the basic issues of authorship, date, circumstances, and genre of the text. His detailed analysis pays close attention to the work's rhetorical and grammatical structures and highly suggestive vocabulary. Recognizing Hebrews' complex relationship with Jewish apocalyptic and Hellenistic philosophical discourses, Moo ably guides readers with a basic knowledge of Greek through the complexities of this unique reflection on the significance of Christ's reconciling work. Serious students of the New Testament will welcome this new resource.

—HAROLD ATTRIDGE, Sterling Professor of Divinity,
  Yale University

With appropriate attention both to Hebrews' historical situatedness and to its soaring theology, Doug Moo provides a clear and compelling reading of this unparalleled biblical book. Moo's gift for organizing a complicated text shines forth in the many outlines and charts and the way he patiently walks through all the pieces of the argument allows readers to follow him or see the precise moment in which they might make a different decision. I look forward to putting this adept guide in the hands of many students.

—AMY PEELER, Wessner Chair of Biblical Studies,
  Wheaton College

After having spoken in decades past, in many and various ways, about the Pauline corpus, at the zenith of his career Douglas Moo turned his exegetical prowess and theological acumen to *Ad Hebraeos*, giving New Testament scholars a commentary worthy to be placed alongside its most excellent predecessors.

—RADU GHEORGHITA, professor of biblical studies,
  Midwestern Baptist Theological Seminary

Anyone looking for a well-reasoned and carefully argued interpretation of the Epistle to the Hebrews in the broadly Reformed, evangelical tradition will greatly appreciate the text-focused exegesis and theological applications offered by Moo throughout this commentary.

—DAVID M. MOFFITT, professor of New Testament and early Christianity,
  St. Andrews University

Always clear, concise, and pedagogical, Doug Moo makes it look easy as he takes us by the hand and walks us through all the complexities of this challenging letter. Eschewing easy answers, he weighs the evidence evenhandedly and offers cautious conclusions. With this judicious defense of a traditional Reformed reading of Hebrews, Moo solidifies his reputation as one of the best commentary writers of his generation.

—SIGURD GRINDHEIM, professor of New Testament,
  Western Norway University

HEBREWS

Zondervan Exegetical Commentary on the New Testament

Editorial Board

General Editor
Clinton E. Arnold

Associate Editors
George H. Guthrie

Constantine R. Campbell

Thomas R. Schreiner

Mark L. Strauss

Zondervan Editors
Editorial Advisor: Katya Covrett
Production Editor: Christopher A. Beetham

Consulting Editors
Richard Bewes

Craig Blomberg

Ajith Fernando

David E. Garland

Paul Gardner

Carolyn Custis James

Karen Jobes

David W. Pao

Frank Thielman

Tite Tienou

HEBREWS

ZONDERVAN
Exegetical Commentary
ON THE
New Testament

DOUGLAS J. MOO

CLINTON E. ARNOLD
General Editor

ZONDERVAN ACADEMIC

Hebrews
Copyright © 2024 by Douglas J. Moo

Published in Grand Rapids, Michigan, by Zondervan. Zondervan is a registered trademark of The Zondervan Corporation, L.L.C., a wholly owned subsidiary of HarperCollins Christian Publishing, Inc.

Requests for information should be addressed to customercare@harpercollins.com.

Zondervan titles may be purchased in bulk for educational, business, fundraising, or sales promotional use. For information, please email SpecialMarkets@Zondervan.com.

Library of Congress Cataloging-in-Publication Data

Names: Moo, Douglas J., author.
Title: Hebrews / Douglas J. Moo.
Description: Grand Rapids : Zondervan Academic, [2024] | Series: Zondervan exegetical commentary on the New Testament | Includes bibliographical references and index.
Identifiers: LCCN 2024012269 (print) | LCCN 2024012270 (ebook) | ISBN 9780310244004 (hardcover) | ISBN 9780310168843 (ebook)
Subjects: LCSH: Bible. Hebrews--Commentaries.
Classification: LCC BS2775.53 .M66 2024 (print) | LCC BS2775.53 (ebook) | DDC 227/.8707--dc23/eng/20240512
LC record available at https://lccn.loc.gov/2024012269
LC ebook record available at https://lccn.loc.gov/2024012270

Unless otherwise noted, all Scripture quotations from books other than Hebrews (which in the "Explanation of the Text" sections and the translation diagrams are translations by the author) are taken from The Holy Bible, New International Version®, NIV®. Copyright © 1973, 1978, 1984, 2011 by Biblica, Inc.® Used by permission of Zondervan. All rights reserved worldwide. www.Zondervan.com. The "NIV" and "New International Version" are trademarks registered in the United States Patent and Trademark Office by Biblica, Inc.® • Scripture quotations marked CEB are taken from the Contemporary English Version. Copyright © 1991, 1992, 1995 by American Bible Society. Used by permission. • Scripture quotations marked CSB® are taken from the Christian Standard Bible®, Copyright © 2017 by Holman Bible Publishers. Used by permission. Christian Standard Bible®, and CSB®, are federally registered trademarks of Holman Bible Publishers. • Scripture quotations marked ESV are taken from the ESV® Bible (The Holy Bible, English Standard Version®). Copyright © 2001 by Crossway, a publishing ministry of Good News Publishers. Used by permission. All rights reserved. • Scripture quotations marked KJV are taken from the King James Version. Public domain. • Scripture quotations marked NAB are taken from the *New American Bible*, revised edition. Copyright © 2010, 1991, 1986, 1970 by the Confraternity of Christian Doctrine, Washington, DC. Used by permission of the copyright owner. All rights reserved. No part of the New American Bible may be reproduced in any form without permission in writing from the copyright owner. • Scripture quotations marked NASB are taken from the New American Standard Bible®. Copyright © 1960, 1971, 1977, 1995, 2020 by The Lockman Foundation. Used by permission. All rights reserved. www.lockman.org. • Scripture quoted by permission. Quotations designated (NET©) are from the NET Bible®. Copyright © 1996–2017 by Biblical Studies Press, L.L.C. http://netbible.com. All rights reserved. • The Scripture quotations marked NRSV are taken from the New Revised Standard Version Bible. Copyright © 1989, National Council of the Churches of Christ in the United States of America. Used by permission. All rights reserved. • Scripture quotations marked NLT are taken from the Holy Bible, New Living Translation. © 1996, 2004, 2015 by Tyndale House Foundation. Used by permission of Tyndale House Publishers, Inc., Carol Stream, Illinois 60188. All rights reserved. • Scripture quotations marked RSV are taken from the Revised Standard Version of the Bible. Copyright © 1946, 1952, 1971 National Council of the Churches of Christ in the United States of America. Used by permission. All rights reserved.

Any internet addresses (websites, blogs, etc.) and telephone numbers in this book are offered as a resource. They are not intended in any way to be or imply an endorsement by Zondervan, nor does Zondervan vouch for the content of these sites and numbers for the life of this book.

All rights reserved. No part of this publication may be reproduced, stored in a retrieval system, or transmitted in any form or by any means—electronic, mechanical, photocopy, recording, or any other—except for brief quotations in printed reviews, without the prior permission of the publisher.

Cover design: Tammy Johnson
Interior design: Beth Shagene

Printed in the United States of America

25 26 27 28 29 30 31 32 33 34 35 36 37 38 /TRM/ 19 18 17 16 15 14 13 12 11 10 9 8 7 6 5 4 3 2

Contents

Series Introduction vii

Author's Preface xi

Abbreviations xiii

Introduction 1

Select Bibliography 19

A Note on the Use of Primary Sources 25

Commentary on Hebrews 27

Some Theological Emphases in Hebrews 533

Scripture Index 543

Other Ancient Literature Index 569

Subject Index 573

Author Index 579

Series Introduction

This generation has been blessed with an abundance of excellent commentaries. Some are technical and do a good job of addressing issues that the critics have raised; other commentaries are long and provide extensive information about word usage and catalogue nearly every opinion expressed on the various interpretive issues; still other commentaries focus on providing cultural and historical background information; and then there are those commentaries that endeavor to draw out many applicational insights.

The key question to ask is: What are you looking for in a commentary? This commentary series might be for you if

- you have taken Greek and would like a commentary that helps you apply what you have learned without assuming you are a well-trained scholar.
- you would find it useful to see a concise, one-or two-sentence statement of what the commentator thinks the main point of each passage is.
- you would like help interpreting the words of Scripture without getting bogged down in scholarly issues that seem irrelevant to the life of the church.
- you would like to see a visual representation (a graphical display) of the flow of thought in each passage.
- you would like expert guidance from solid evangelical scholars who set out to explain the meaning of the original text in the clearest way possible and to help you navigate through the main interpretive issues.
- you want to benefit from the results of the latest and best scholarly studies and historical information that help to illuminate the meaning of the text.
- you would find it useful to see a brief summary of the key theological insights that can be gleaned from each passage and some discussion of the relevance of these for Christians today.

These are just some of the features that characterize the new Zondervan Exegetical Commentary on the New Testament series. The idea for this series was refined over time by an editorial board who listened to pastors and teachers express what they wanted to see in a commentary series based on the Greek text. That board consisted of myself, George H. Guthrie, William D. Mounce, Thomas R. Schreiner, and Mark L. Strauss along with Zondervan senior editor at large Verlyn Verbrugge, and former Zondervan senior acquisitions editor Jack Kuhatschek. We also enlisted a board of consulting editors who are active pastors, ministry leaders, and seminary professors to help in the process of designing a commentary series that will be useful to the church. Zondervan senior acquisitions editor Katya Covrett has now been shepherding the process to completion, and Constantine R. Campbell is now serving on the board.

We arrived at a design that includes seven components for the treatment of each biblical passage. What follows is a brief orientation to these primary components of the commentary.

Literary Context

In this section, you will find a concise discussion of how the passage functions in the broader literary context of the book. The commentator highlights connections with the preceding and following material in the book and makes observations on the key literary features of this text.

Main Idea

Many readers will find this to be an enormously helpful feature of this series. For each passage, the commentator carefully crafts a one- or two-sentence statement of the big idea or central thrust of the passage.

Translation and Graphical Layout

Another unique feature of this series is the presentation of each commentator's translation of the Greek text in a graphical layout. The purpose of this diagram is to help the reader visualize, and thus better understand, the flow of thought within the text. The translation itself reflects the interpretive decisions made by each commentator in the "Explanation" section of the commentary. Here are a few insights that will help you to understand the way these are put together:

1. On the far left side next to the verse numbers is a series of interpretive labels that indicate the function of each clause or phrase of the biblical text. The corresponding portion of the text is on the same line to the right of the label. We have not used technical linguistic jargon for these, so they should be easily understood.

2. In general, we place every clause (a group of words containing a subject and a predicate) on a separate line and identify how it is supporting the principal assertion of the text (namely, is it saying when the action occurred, how it took place, or why it took place?). We sometimes place longer phrases or a series of items on separate lines as well.
3. Subordinate (or dependent) clauses and phrases are indented and placed directly under the words that they modify. This helps the reader to more easily see the nature of the relationship of clauses and phrases in the flow of the text.
4. Every main clause has been placed in bold print and pushed to the left margin for clear identification.
5. Sometimes when the level of subordination moves too far to the right—as often happens with some of Paul's long, involved sentences!—we reposition the flow to the left of the diagram, but use an arrow to indicate that this has happened.
6. The overall process we have followed has been deeply informed by principles of discourse analysis and narrative criticism (for the Gospels and Acts).

Structure

Immediately following the translation, the commentator describes the flow of thought in the passage and explains how certain interpretive decisions regarding the relationship of the clauses were made in the passage.

Exegetical Outline

The overall structure of the passage is described in a detailed exegetical outline. This will be particularly helpful for those who are looking for a way to concisely explain the flow of thought in the passage in a teaching or preaching setting.

Explanation of the Text

As an exegetical commentary, this work makes use of the Greek language to interpret the meaning of the text. If your Greek is rather rusty (or even somewhat limited), don't be too concerned. All the Greek words are cited in parentheses following an English translation. We have made every effort to make this commentary as readable and useful as possible even for the nonspecialist.

Those who will benefit the most from this commentary will have had the equivalent of two years of Greek in college or seminary. This would include a semester or two of working through an intermediate grammar (such as Wallace, Porter, Brooks and Winbery, or Dana and Mantey). The authors use the grammatical language that is found in these kinds of grammars. The details of the grammar of the passage, however, are discussed only when it has a bearing on the interpretation of the text.

The emphasis in this section of the text is to convey the meaning. Commentators examine words and images, grammatical details, relevant Old Testament and Jewish background to a particular concept, historical and cultural context, important text-critical issues, and various interpretational issues that surface.

Theology in Application

This, too, is a unique feature for an exegetical commentary series. We felt it was important for each author not only to describe what the text means in its various details, but also to take a moment and reflect on the theological contribution that it makes. In this section, the theological message of the passage is summarized. The authors discuss the theology of the text in terms of its place within the book and in a broader biblical-theological context. Finally, each commentator provides some suggestions on what the message of the passage is for the church today. At the conclusion of each volume in this series is a summary of the whole range of theological themes touched on by this book of the Bible.

Our sincere hope and prayer is that you find this series helpful not only for your own understanding of the text of the New Testament but also as you are actively engaged in teaching and preaching God's Word to people who are hungry to be fed on its truth.

Clinton E. Arnold, general editor

Author's Preface

After spending so much time studying and writing about the apostle Paul, it has been a singular pleasure for me to switch gears and dig into the book of a very different kind of author. I am very grateful to the editors of the ZECNT series and Zondervan publishers for giving me this opportunity—and for their valuable input into the substance of the volume. Here I think especially of Clint Arnold and George Guthrie. And I am especially grateful for their patience, as the original deadline for this commentary receded farther and farther into the past.

Once I knew I would be writing a commentary on Hebrews, I took advantage of every possible opportunity to teach the book: in classes at Wheaton College, in seminars in different parts of the world, in local Sunday School classes. While difficult neatly to quantify, what I learned from these students, pastors, and parishioners over the years has been significant. I have especially enjoyed working with a series of PhD students who wrote on Hebrews under my direction: Gene Smillie at Trinity Evangelical Divinity School and Ben Ribbens, Mike Kibbe, Stephen Wunrow, and Jason Liu at Wheaton College. My thinking about Hebrews has been significantly shaped by their work, as the footnotes in this volume attest. I should also make mention of the contribution of another of my PhD students, Ben Dally, who undertook the labor of transferring my handwritten notes on Hebrews into digital form (anyone who is familiar with my handwriting will understand just how remarkable an achievement this was!).

As always, I am especially grateful to my wife and coworker, Jenny, who not only helped me think through this book in conversation after conversation but who also proofread the volume.

Finally, I should note that I turned this MS over to the publishers in the spring of 2022, so I have been able to interact with books and articles published after that time only sporadically.

Douglas Moo
Emeritus Professor of Biblical Studies
Wheaton College

Abbreviations

AB	Anchor Bible
ABD	*Anchor Bible Dictionary*. Edited by David Noel Freedman. 6 vols. New York: Doubleday, 1992
AcBib	Academia Biblica
ACCS	Ancient Christian Commentary on Scripture
AD	*anno Domini* (in the year of our Lord)
ALGHJ	Arbeiten zur Literatur und Geschichte des hellenistischen Judentums
AnBib	Analecta Biblica
AOTC	Abingdon Old Testament Commentaries
ApOTC	Apollos Old Testament Commentary
AUSS	*Andrews University Seminary Studies*
BBR	*Bulletin for Biblical Research*
BC	before Christ
BCOTWP	Baker Commentary on the Old Testament Wisdom and Psalms
BDAG	Danker, Frederick W., Walter Bauer, William F. Arndt, and F. Wilbur Gingrich. *Greek English Lexicon of the New Testament and Other Early Christian Literature*. 3rd. ed. Chicago: University of Chicago Press, 2000
BDF	Blass, Friedrich, Albert Debrunner, and Robert W. Funk. *A Greek Grammar of the New Testament and Other Early Christian Literature*. Chicago: University of Chicago Press, 1961
BECNT	Baker Exegetical Commentary on the New Testament
BGBE	Beiträge zur Geschichte der biblischen Exegese
Bib	*Biblica*
BibInt	Biblical Interpretation Series
BSac	*Bibliotheca Sacra*
BT	*The Bible Translator*
BTB	*Biblical Theology Bulletin*
BU	Biblische Untersuchungen
BZNW	Beihefte zur Zeitschrift für die neutestamentliche Wissenschaft
CBQ	*Catholic Biblical Quarterly*
CBQMS	Catholic Biblical Quarterly Monograph Series

CC	Continental Commentaries
CCC	*Catechism of the Catholic Church*
CEB	Common English Bible
CJT	*Canadian Journal of Theology*
ConBNT	Coniectanea Neotestamentica or Coniectanea Biblica: New Testament Series
CSB	Christian Standard Bible (2017)
CTJ	*Calvin Theological Journal*
CurBR	*Currents in Biblical Research*
DCH	*Dictionary of Classical Hebrew*. Edited by David J. A. Clines. 9 vols. Sheffield: Sheffield Phoenix Press, 1993–2014
DSSR	*The Dead Sea Scrolls Reader*. Edited by Donald W. Parry and Emanuel Tov. 6 vols. Leiden: Brill, 2004–2005
EB	Echter Bibel
EGGNT	Exegetical Guide to the Greek New Testament
EKKNT	Evangelisch-katholischer Kommentar zum Neuen Testament
ESV	English Standard Version
FRLANT	Forschungen zur Religion und Literatur des Alten und Neuen Testaments
Gk.	Greek
HBS	History of Biblical Studies
HBT	*Horizons in Biblical Theology*
HCSB	Holman Christian Standard Bible
HNT	Handbuch zum Neuen Testament
HNTC	Harper's New Testament Commentaries
ICC	International Critical Commentary
Int	*Interpretation*
JBL	*Journal of Biblical Literature*
JETS	*Journal of the Evangelical Theological Society*
JSJ	*Journal for the Study of Judaism in the Persian, Hellenistic, and Roman Periods*
JSNT	*Journal for the Study of New Testament*
JSNTSup	Journal for the Study of New Testament Supplement Series
JTS	*Journal of Theological Studies*
KEK	Kritisch-exegetischer Kommentar über das Neue Testament (Meyer-Kommentar)
KJV	King James Version
L&N	Louw, Johannes P., and Eugene A. Nida, eds. *Greek English Lexicon of the New Testament: Based on Semantic Domains*. 2nd ed. New York: United Bible Societies, 1989

LD	Lectio Divina
LEH	Lust, Johan, Erik Eynikel, and Katrin Hauspie, eds. *Greek-English Lexicon of the Septuagint*. Rev. ed. Stuttgart: Deutsche Bibelgesellschaft, 2003
LNTS	The Library of New Testament Studies
LSJ	Liddell, Henry George, Robert Scott, Henry Stuart Jones. *A Greek-English Lexicon*. 9th ed. with revised supplement. Oxford: Clarendon, 1996
LXX	Septuagint
MS(S)	manuscript(s)
MT	Masoretic Text
MTS	Marburger Theologische Studien
NA^{28}	*Novum Testamentum Graece*, Nestle-Aland, 28th ed.
NAB	New American Bible
NAC	New American Commentary
NASB	New American Standard Bible
NET	New English Translation
NETS	*A New English Translation of the Septuagint*. Edited by Albert Pietersma and Benjamin G. Wright. New York: Oxford University Press, 2007
NIBC	New International Biblical Commentary
NICNT	New International Commentary on the New Testament
NICOT	New International Commentary on the Old Testament
NIDNTTE	*New International Dictionary of the New Testament Theology and Exegesis*. Edited by Moisés Silva. 5 vols. Grand Rapids: Zondervan, 2014.
NIGTC	New International Greek Testament Commentary
NIV	New International Version
NIVAC	New International Version Application Commentary
NJB	New Jerusalem Bible
NJPS	Tanakh: The Holy Scriptures (published by the Jewish Publication Society [1985])
NKJV	New King James Version
NLT	New Living Translation
NovT	*Novum Testamentum*
NovTSup	Supplements to Novum Testamentum
NRSV	New Revised Standard Version
NSBT	New Studies in Biblical Theology
NT	New Testament
NTL	New Testament Library
NTS	*New Testament Studies*
OT	Old Testament

OTP	*Old Testament Pseudepigrapha*. Edited by James H. Charlesworth. 2 vols. New York: Doubleday, 1983, 1985
OtSt	*Oudtestamentische Studiën*
parr.	parallels
PG	Patrologia Graeca. Edited by J.-P. Migne. 162 vols. Paris, 1857–1886
RNT	Regensburger Neues Testament
RSV	Revised Standard Version
SBLDS	Society of Biblical Literature Dissertation Series
SBLMS	Society of Biblical Literature Monograph Series
SBT	Studies in Biblical Theology
ScrHier	Scripta Hierosolymitana
SNT	Studien zum Neuen Testament
SNTSMS	Society for New Testament Studies Monograph Series
SP	Sacra Pagina
StBibLit	Studies in Biblical Literature (Lang)
STDJ	Studies on the Texts of the Desert of Judah
STI	Studies in Theological Interpretation
StPB	Studia Post-biblica
StudNeot	Studia Neotestamentica
SubBi	Subsidia Biblica
SwJT	*Southwestern Journal of Theology*
TDNT	*Theological Dictionary of the New Testament*. Edited by Gerhard Kittel and Gerhard Friedrich. Translated by Geoffrey W. Bromiley. 10 vols. Grand Rapids: Eerdmans, 1964–1976
THGNT	Tyndale House Greek New Testament (2017)
THKNT	Theologischer Handkommentar zum Neuen Testament
TJ	*Trinity Journal*
TNTC	Tyndale New Testament Commentaries
TOTC	Tyndale Old Testament Commentaries
TynBul	*Tyndale Bulletin*
UBS⁵	*The Greek New Testament*, United Bible Societies, 5th revised ed. (2014)
WA	Weimarer Ausgabe (the Weimar edition of Luther's Works)
WBC	Word Biblical Commentary
WMANT	Wissenschaftliche Monographien zum Alten und Neuen Testament
WTJ	*Westminster Theological Journal*
WUNT	Wissenschaftliche Untersuchungen zum Neuen Testament
ZECNT	Zondervan Exegetical Commentary on the New Testament
ZGNT	Zondervan Greek New Testament
ZNW	*Zeitschrift für die neutestamentliche Wissenschaft und Kunde der älteren Kirche*

Introduction

In the classic movie *The Wizard of Oz*, farm girl Dorothy wakes up in the strange, even bizarre, environment of Oz and exclaims to her dog, "Toto, I don't think we are in Kansas anymore!" Readers of the New Testament may experience a similar sense of dislocation when they encounter the letter to the Hebrews. Of course, each New Testament book has its own perspective and way of communicating. However, if indeed diversity marks our New Testament, Hebrews stands out as "more diverse." We begin with the language. As every student of New Testament Greek knows, moving from the rather simple Greek of John's Gospel to the intricacies of the Greek of Hebrews is like moving from the morning newspaper to James Joyce's *Ulysses*. Hebrews uses many words not found elsewhere in the New Testament. But what makes reading Hebrews especially challenging is the syntax. The author's language lies toward the literary end of the spectrum of ancient Greek style. Another distinctive feature of Hebrews is the sophisticated rhetoric the author uses to argue his case. No other New Testament book comes even close to the style of Hebrews, with its frequent *inclusios*, chiasms, and other stylistic mechanisms. Indeed, one of the chief challenges—and, for those who like this kind of thing, pleasures—is the task of tracing the course of the author's argument. The distinctive Greek style and rhetorical sophistication of Hebrews is matched by its theology. One obvious example: the author uses as the centerpiece of his theological argument the high priesthood of Jesus. Yet no other New Testament book, even in passing, labels Jesus as a priest or high priest. Hebrews's resolute focus on the Old Testament cult and its fulfillment in new-covenant realities sets the letter apart from the theological method and focus of other New Testament books. Hebrews, finally, also follows its own distinctive style of argument. The standard "horizontal" axis of salvation history, with its promise-fulfillment scheme, is supplemented in Hebrews with a vertical axis of earth and heaven, below and above, transitory and stable. Thus, for example, the Old Testament tabernacle is a reflection of the heavenly prototype that God revealed to Moses on Sinai (8:5).

These positive indications of Hebrews's distinctiveness are met, in a sense, by a series of negative factors also. Probably no other New Testament book is more underdetermined in its circumstances of writing than Hebrews. We do not know who the author is, we can't be certain where it was written from, we don't know who the readers were or where they were located, and we can't determine the date of the letter. These matters, of course, are basic to the standard academic historical-critical approach to studying and explaining the New Testament. How are we to proceed when we don't know any of this background information? Our relative ignorance about all these matters means that we are free, in a sense, to read the letter within the parameters of the letter itself. "Historical minimalism" is forced upon us.[1] Moreover, our ignorance about the specifics of Hebrews's origins has a positive side. Christopher Seitz suggests that the underdetermined nature of Hebrews forces us to affiliate the book "in the broadest possible way with the remaining New Testament books as a whole."[2] Because we cannot interpret the text according to a specific historical context, canonical relationships will loom all the larger. Approaches such as the "theological interpretation of Scripture" will become more important than the usual critical reconstructions that, for all their usefulness, can sometimes interfere with our hearing Scripture as a word for God's people today.[3]

Nevertheless, for all the focus we rightly place on theological and canonical reading, the more we can identify the specific circumstances in which Hebrews was written, the more accurate our interpretation will be. In the following paragraphs, then, I will briefly survey some of these issues, though at best these will be good guesses about the details of composition. Our overview will take the form, then, of a listing of more-or-less probable options than of determinative conclusions.[4]

Genre

Hebrews begins like a sermon and ends like a letter. This neat summary, which one can find in any number of commentaries, pretty well answers the genre question. Hebrews launches directly into high theology, and the intricate structure of the book does not in any way mask the clear and obvious hortatory thrust of the book. The author's claim to be writing a "word of exhortation" (τοῦ λόγου τῆς παρακλήσεως, 13:22) confirms the sermonic nature of the book: this language is found elsewhere in the New Testament to describe a synagogue homily (Acts 13:15). As Webster puts it, "Hebrews is an exercise in pastoral eschatology, an exposition of truth directed to

---

1. Ole Jakob Filtvedt, *The Identity of God's People and the Paradox of Hebrews*, WUNT 2/400 (Tübingen: Mohr Siebeck, 2015), 24–27.

2. Christopher R. Seitz, *The Character of Christian Scripture: The Significance of a Two-Testament Bible*, STI (Grand Rapids: Baker Academic, 2011), 132.

3. Jon C. Laansma, "Hebrews: Yesterday, Today, and Future: An Illustrative Survey, Diagnosis, Prescription," in *Christology, Hermeneutics, and Hebrews: Profiles from the History of Interpretation*, ed. Jon C. Laansma and Daniel J. Treier, LNTS 423 (London: T&T Clark, 2012), 1–32.

4. For overviews of the history of Hebrews interpretation, see Craig R. Koester, *Hebrews: A New Translation with Introduction and Commentary*, AB 36 (New York: Doubleday, 2001), 19–54; and, for the early church, Hans-Friedrich Weiss, *Der Brief an die Hebräer*, KEK (Göttingen: Vandenhoeck & Ruprecht, 1991), 115–26.

the correction of practice."⁵ However, if formal epistolary markers are missing at the beginning of Hebrews, they are quite evident at the end (13:18–25). As regularly noted, then, Hebrews is a sermon put into a letter.⁶ These two genre claims raise the question of whether we should think of Hebrews mainly as a sermon to be heard or a letter to be read. However, since the written letter would ultimately be delivered in oral form, we might want to privilege the oral. Following Johnson, then, I will freely mix references to "readers" and "hearers" or "listeners."⁷

Author

The paucity of the data for us to use in reconstructing the circumstances in which Hebrews originated is nowhere clearer or more frustrating than in the attempt to identify the author. The book makes no claim about the author, so our only option is to construct a profile of the writer from the book itself and then see if we can match that profile to a known figure from the early church. As I have noted above, Hebrews is written in very good Greek and its rhetoric is intricately and carefully developed. The author is deeply familiar with the Old Testament, which he quotes in Greek. He uses, in a moderate way, some perspectives typical of the philosophical movement called "Middle Platonism," suggesting that he comes from, or is familiar with, the larger world of Hellenistic thinking. The author's use of a masculine participle to refer to himself in 11:32 justifies our referring to a "he" ("the time is not left for me to tell [διηγούμενον]"). Reference to Timothy in the epistolary conclusion at 13:23 suggests the author may be part of the "Pauline circle."⁸ Finally, the claim that the message of salvation was "confirmed to us by those who heard [the Lord]" (2:3) strongly suggests that the author was not an apostle.

This last point especially makes it unlikely that Paul is the author. To be sure, the early church, after a time of doubt and debate, finally came down on the side of Pauline authorship. The ambivalence is clear in the decisions of the Synod of Hippo

---

5. John Webster, "One Who Is Son: Theological Reflections on the Exordium to the Epistle to the Hebrews," in *The Epistle to the Hebrews and Christian Theology*, ed. Richard Bauckham et al. (Grand Rapids: Eerdmans, 2009), 72.

6. Evidence is lacking for more detailed identifications of genre (e.g., that Hebrews is a *petichta* synagogue homily: see Gabriella Gelardini, "Hebrews, Homiletics, and Liturgical Scripture Interpretation," in *Reading the Epistle to the Hebrews: A Resource for Students*, ed. Eric F. Mason and Kevin B. McCruden [Atlanta: Society of Biblical Literature, 2011], 121–43).

7. Luke Timothy Johnson, *Hebrews: A Commentary*, NTL (Louisville: Westminster John Knox, 2006), 10–11; see also Koester, *Hebrews*, 80–82.

8. This reference, along with other elements in the epistolary postscript, are certainly not strong enough to point to Pauline authorship, as Clare K. Rothschild suggests (she thinks the author is claiming to be Paul, while he clearly was not Paul; so the letter is pseudepigraphical [*Hebrews as Pseudepigraphon: The History and Significance of the Pauline Attribution of Hebrews*, WUNT 2/235 (Tübingen: Mohr Siebeck, 2009)]). In response to Rothschild, see Bryan R. Dyer, "The Epistolary Closing of Hebrews and Pauline Imitation," in *Paul and Pseudepigraphy*, ed. Stanley E. Porter and Gregory P. Fewster, Pauline Studies 8 (Leiden: Brill, 2013), 269–85.

(AD 393) and the Third Council of Carthage (AD 397), which, in their canonical lists, say "thirteen epistles of the Apostle Paul, one epistle of the same [writer] to the Hebrews."[9] Pauline authorship was unambiguously asserted at the Sixth Synod of Carthage in AD 419. Church leaders in the East tended to accept authorship by Paul at a fairly early time. But it was only after Jerome and Augustine accepted Pauline authorship that the claim was widely accepted in the West also. This view is officially enshrined in the KJV, which puts as a heading on Hebrews, "The Epistle of Paul the Apostle to the Hebrews." However, doubts about Paul's authorship were expressed by the Reformers (Luther and Calvin rejected Pauline authorship), and the view that Paul wrote Hebrews has almost disappeared from modern scholarship.[10]

At least a dozen other proposed author identifications have been put forward over the years. Of these, three deserve mention.

Perhaps the earliest clear claim about the authorship of Hebrews comes from Clement of Alexandria (d. AD 215), who claimed that Paul wrote the letter in Hebrew and that Luke then translated it into Greek. Lukan authorship has recently been defended at some length by David Allen in his commentary.[11] Some similarities between the Greek of Luke-Acts and Hebrews are evident, but they are not striking enough to suggest common authorship. Barnabas is identified in Acts as a Levite and as the "son of encouragement" (Acts 4:36), a profile that fits the author of Hebrews, who knows the Levitical system very well and writes a "word of encouragement" (Heb 13:22). The most popular option, however, ever since it was proposed by Luther, has been Apollos. He is introduced to us in Acts 18:24: "Meanwhile a Jew named Apollos, a native of Alexandria, came to Ephesus. He was a learned man, with a thorough knowledge of the Scriptures." This brief profile certainly fits well with what we can surmise about the author of Hebrews. Alexandria was an important center of Greek culture and Hellenistic-Jewish thinking—the kind of place in which, as a "learned man," Apollos could have gained facility in Greek and become acquainted with the kind of Hellenistic perspectives seen in Hebrews. Like the author to the Hebrews, Apollos knew the Scriptures very well.

Of the several candidates for the authorship of Hebrews that have been put forth over the years, Apollos certainly ticks the most boxes.[12] However, as Attridge points out, "Apollos might well be the sort of person who could have composed Hebrews, but too little is known of his specific teaching to allow a positive identification. Surely

---

9. *A History of the Councils of the Church*, ed. William R. Clark et al., vol. 2 (Edinburgh: T&T Clark, 1876), 468.

10. But not entirely; see, fairly recently, David Alan Black, "Who Wrote Hebrews? The Internal and External Evidence Re-examined," *Faith & Mission* 18 (2001): 3–26. See also, earlier but at greater length, William Leonard, *The Authorship of the Epistle to the Hebrews: Critical Problem and Use of the Old Testament* (Rome: Vatican Polyglot, 1939).

11. David L. Allen, *Hebrews*, NAC 35 (Nashville: Broadman & Holman, 2010), 29–61; see also Franz Delitzsch, *Commentary on the Epistle to the Hebrews*, 2 vols. (repr., Minneapolis: Klock & Klock, 1871), 1:18.

12. Some of the scholars who think he is the most likely candidate include, e.g., Ceslas Spicq, *L'Épitre aux Hébreux*, 3rd ed., 2 vols., EB (Paris: Gabalda, 1951, 1953), 1:197–219; Johnson, *Hebrews*, 40–44.

his rhetorical and exegetical skills were not unique in the early Christian movement."[13] Moffatt appropriately warns us of "an irrepresible desire to construct New Testament romances."[14] We need to take heed of the warning of Sherlock Holmes: "It is a capital mistake to theorize before one has data."[15] In the case of Hebrews, we would do well to admit that we do not have the data we need to identify the author.

Our admission of ignorance on this point might raise questions about the place of Hebrews in the canon. Certainly, there was some degree of connection in the early-church discussion of Hebrews between apostolic authorship and canonicity. However, the key criterion of canonicity in the early church was not apostolic authorship but conformity to apostolic teaching.[16] Indeed, the strong imprint that the message of Hebrews stamped on the early church was one of the main motivations for attributing the letter to Paul. As Cockerill puts it, "It is clear that Pauline authorship was defended in order to sustain Hebrews's canonical status. In the end, however, the greatest biblical scholars of the ancient church (Origen, Jerome) affirmed Hebrews's worth and canonical status despite doubts about Pauline authorship."[17]

Destination

Yet another circumstance of Hebrews's origin that we cannot determine is its destination. Some interpreters think that the focus on the cult suggests that the letter was written to Jewish Christians living in Palestine.[18] However, the most popular option, by far, is Rome. Two pieces of data could suggest a Roman destination. First, the earliest Christian document to reveal influence from Hebrews is 1 Clement, a letter written from Rome, probably around AD 96.[19] Second, the epistolary postscript might imply a Roman destination. The author writes, "Those from Italy [οἱ ἀπὸ τῆς Ἰταλίας] send you their greetings" (13:24b). The reason why the author singles out people from Italy may be that the readers of the letter are themselves residents in Italy or Rome; naturally those who know them from having lived among them are anxious to convey their greetings.[20] It must be said, however, that this is not the only

---

13. Harold W. Attridge, *The Epistle to the Hebrews*, Hermeneia (Philadelphia: Fortress, 1989), 4.

14. James Moffatt, *A Criticial and Exegetical Commentary on the Epistle to the Hebrews*, ICC (Edinburgh: T&T Clark, 1924), xx.

15. Arthur Conan Doyle, "A Scandal in Bohemia," in *The Adventures of Sherlock Holmes* (Scholastic Book Services, 1964), 8.

16. See, e.g., David G. Dunbar, "The Biblical Canon," in *Hermeneutics, Authority, Canon*, ed. D. A. Carson and John D. Woodbridge (Grand Rapids: Zondervan, 1986), 295–359.

17. Gareth Lee Cockerill, *The Epistle to the Hebrews*, NICNT (Grand Rapids: Eerdmans, 2012), 6; see also Erich Grässer, *An die Hebräer*, 3 vols., EKKNT 17.1-3 (Neukirchen-Vluyn: Neukirchener, 1990, 1993, 1997), 1:22.

18. Delitzsch, *Hebrews*, 1:18–21; Brooke Foss Westcott, *The Epistle to the Hebrews* (repr., Grand Rapids: Eerdmans, 1973), xxxix–xlii; Philip Edgcumbe Hughes, *A Commentary on the Epistle to the Hebrews* (Grand Rapids: Eerdmans, 1977), 10–19.

19. The clearest evidence of dependence on Hebrews comes in 1 Clem. 36.1–5.

20. Similar language in Acts 18:2 has this sense: Aquila with his wife Priscilla "had recently come from Italy [ἐληλυθότα ἀπὸ τῆς Ἰταλίας]."

way to read this verse: it could also mean that people now living in Italy (perhaps where the author is living) are sending greetings.[21] Nevertheless, I favor the former reading of the verse, which therefore points to a Roman destination for the letter. Even this conclusion, of course, leaves many options open. Was the letter addressed to the entire Roman Christian community, which appears to have been divided into several house churches (as Rom 16 implies) or to only one of these assemblies? The author never refers to a "church [ἐκκλησία]," so we have no clear evidence from the letter on this point.[22] However, the specifics that the author mentions in passages such as 10:32–35 suggest that he has a specific Christian assembly in view.[23]

Date

The author of Hebrews assumes that his readers have been Jesus followers for some time. The author urges his readers to "remember those earlier days after you had received the light" (10:32). The gospel was proclaimed to them, not by the apostles, but by those who had heard the message from the apostles (2:3). One of the fundamental issues the author addresses is spiritual lassitude, "drifting" (2:1), a loss of the readers' original zeal for Christ. It is more likely that this kind of spiritual problem would have arisen only among those who had known Christ for some time. Here our uncertainty about author and destination makes it difficult to translate these general circumstances into specific dates. If, for instance, as I tentatively concluded, the letter is written to Roman Christians, the timing of this letter with respect to Paul's letter to the Romans becomes an issue. Is Hebrews written before Romans or after? Perhaps "after" is the best option. Timothy is with Paul, and apparently a free man, when Paul writes Romans (Rom 16:21). In Hebrews, on the other hand, Timothy has recently been released from prison (13:23). The combined evidence of Acts and the letters of Paul provides much less than a full outline of Timothy's ministry. Yet he is mentioned often enough to make it somewhat questionable that an imprisonment would not have been mentioned. Another key piece of evidence, if the letter was written to Rome, is the fact that the readers have not yet shed their blood for their faith (12:4). This presumes a date before the persecution under Nero that began in AD 64. If, then, we think the letter was written to Rome, a date after 57 but before 64 seems to be indicated. However, as we have seen, a Roman destination cannot be assumed.

If we leave the issue of destination undetermined, the latest date for Hebrews is the early 90s, granted the use of the letter in 1 Clement (see above). Nailing down

---

21. The preposition ἀπό functions to indicate one's current residence in John 11:1 and Acts 10:23, and it should be noted that Acts 18:2, often cited as a parallel to Heb 13:24, uses a verb ("come") that is not found in the Hebrews text.

22. Grässer takes this as one indication that the letter is intended for the church at large rather than for any one assembly (*An die Hebräer*, 1:22–25).

23. E.g., Attridge, *Hebrews*, 9; Koester, *Hebrews*, 74.

a more specific date depends especially on the timing of the letter with respect to the Roman invasion of Palestine in AD 66 and the subsequent destruction of the temple. A number of interpreters contend that this climactic event has no bearing on Hebrews, since the letter focuses all its attention on the Old Testament cultic system. For them, although the author consistently uses the present tense to refer to the cult, this does not assume that the temple must still be standing, since the author never refers to the temple. The destruction of the Jerusalem temple in AD 70 has no bearing on the date of Hebrews. These scholars therefore date Hebrews in the 80s or early 90s.[24] However, while it is true that the letter does not focus on the temple, it is certainly difficult to think that the author could mount the kind of argument he does without any reference to the destruction of the temple, if indeed this had already happened. Indeed, it is possible, though far from certain, that 8:13 looks ahead to the destruction of the temple: "By calling this covenant 'new,' he has made the first one obsolete; and what is obsolete and outdated will soon disappear."[25] Taken together, these data suggest a date before AD 70, whatever the destination of the letter.

Audience and Occasion

Our uncertainty about so many of the circumstances in which Hebrews was written does not seriously affect our ability to interpret the letter. The issue we now tackle, however, has much greater potential to affect our reading of Hebrews. The author "preaches his sermon" in response to a pastoral situation. If we can identify that situation, we will be in better position to interpret what he is saying. The point is an obvious one: all communication has a context; what we write or say is oriented toward and often seriously conditioned by that context. In biblical studies, we often identify the process of relating New Testament teaching to its context as "mirror reading." We treat the text as a mirror that reflects the circumstances and then use those circumstances to refine our interpretation of the text. "Mirror reading" can become a problem, however, when we are overly optimistic about our ability to use the text to reconstruct the context. The situation we deduce, sometimes with questionable basis, becomes a straitjacket that dictates what the text means. Nevertheless, with appropriate caution and humility, some degree of mirror reading is both inevitable and helpful.

---

24. E.g., Raymond E. Brown, *An Introduction to the New Testament* (New York: Doubleday, 1997), 696–97; Weiss, *Der Brief an die Hebräer*, 76–77; Kenneth L. Schenck, *Understanding the Book of Hebrews: The Story behind the Sermon* (Louisville: Westminster John Knox, 2003), 93–98.

25. Interpreters who think this verse is suggestive include Johnson, *Hebrews*, 38–40; F. F. Bruce, *The Epistle to the Hebrews*, rev. ed., NICNT (Grand Rapids: Eerdmans, 1990), 20–22; Barnabas Lindars, *The Theology of the Letter to the Hebrews*, New Testament Theology (Cambridge: Cambridge University Press, 1991), 19–21.

Mirror reading of Hebrews is complicated by two distinctive rhetorical thrusts that mark the letter throughout. On the one hand, the author repeatedly warns the readers about their failure to move ahead in their spiritual journey. On the other hand, he often warns them about the danger of falling back. To illustrate this point, I have gathered below all the relevant exhortations and warnings in Hebrews, with passages about *failing to move ahead* in italics and passages about the <u>danger of falling back</u> underlined.[26]

2:1	<u>"so that we do not drift away"</u>
2:3	"if we ignore so great a salvation"
3:6	*"if indeed we hold firmly to our confidence and the hope in which we glory"*
3:12	<u>"See to it, brothers and sisters, that none of you has a sinful, unbelieving heart that turns away from the living God"</u>
3:13	"so that none of you may be hardened by sin's deceitfulness"
3:14	*"if indeed we hold our original conviction firmly to the very end"*
4:1	"Therefore, since the promise of entering his rest still stands, let us be careful that none of you be found to have fallen short of it"
4:11	<u>"Let us, therefore, make every effort to enter that rest, so that no one will perish by following their example of disobedience"</u>
4:14	"let us hold firmly to the faith we profess"
4:16	"Let us then approach God's throne of grace with confidence"
5:12	"you need someone to teach you the elementary truths of God's word all over again. You need milk, not solid food!"
6:1	"let us move beyond the elementary teachings about Christ and be taken forward to maturity"
6:4–6	"It is impossible for those who have once been enlightened, who have tasted the heavenly gift, who have shared in the Holy Spirit, who have tasted the goodness of the word of God and the powers of the coming age <u>and who have fallen away</u>, to be brought back to repentance. To their loss <u>they are crucifying the Son of God all over again and subjecting him to public disgrace.</u>"
6:9	"we are convinced of better things in your case—the things that have to do with salvation"
6:11–12	*"We want each of you to show this same diligence to the very end, so that what you hope for may be fully realized. We do not want you*

---

26. Jon Laansma divides exhortations in Hebrew into two similar categories (*"I Will Give You Rest": The Rest Motif in the New Testament with Special Reference to Mt 11 and Heb 3-4*, WUNT 2/98 [Tübingen: Mohr Siebeck, 1997], 264–65). The quotations in this list are from NIV.

	to become lazy, but to imitate those who through faith and patience inherit what has been promised."
6:18b–19a	"we who have fled to take hold of the hope set before us may be greatly encouraged. We have this hope as an anchor for the soul, firm and secure."
10:22	"let us draw near to God"
10:23	"Let us hold unswervingly to the hope we profess"
10:24	"let us consider how we may spur one another on toward love and good deeds"
10:25	"not giving up meeting together . . . but encouraging one another"
10:26	<u>"if we deliberately keep on sinning after we have received the knowledge of the truth"</u>
10:29	<u>"who has trampled the Son of God underfoot, who has treated as an unholy thing the blood of the covenant that sanctified them, and who has insulted the Spirit of grace"</u>
10:32	"after you had received the light"
10:35	"So do not throw away your confidence"
10:36	*"You need to persevere so that when you have done the will of God, you will receive what he has promised"*
10:39	<u>"But we do not belong to those who shrink back and are destroyed, but to those who have faith and are saved"</u>
12:1	"let us throw off everything that hinders and the sin that so easily entangles. And let us run with perseverance the race marked out for us"
12:3	"so that you will not grow weary and lose heart"
12:7	"Endure hardship as discipline"
12:12–13	"Therefore, strengthen your feeble arms and weak knees. 'Make level paths for your feet,' so that the lame may not be disabled, but rather healed."
12:14	"Make every effort to live in peace with everyone and to be holy"
12:15	"See to it that no one falls short of the grace of God and that no bitter root grows up to cause trouble and defile many"
12:16	"See that no one is sexually immoral"
12:25	<u>"See to it that you do not refuse him who speaks"</u>
12:25	<u>"if we turn away from him who warns us from heaven"</u>
12:28	"let us be thankful, and so worship God acceptably with reverence and awe"
13:9	"Do not be carried away by all kinds of strange teachings"
13:13	"Let us, then, go to him outside the camp, bearing the disgrace he bore"

What can accurately be labeled the "traditional" view highlights the warnings against falling back, identifying the letter as written to Jewish Christians who are being tempted to turn away from their Christian commitment to embrace again their Jewish heritage as the locus of their religious life.[27] Advocates of this interpretation often identify the persecution that the readers are facing (10:32–34; cf. 12:4–11) as an impetus for this regression.[28] As a "tolerated religion" in the Roman Empire, Judaism would shield its adherents from the persecution that Jesus followers would have been experiencing. The traditional title to the book—"To the Hebrews" (ΠΡΟΣ ΕΒΡΑΙΟΥΣ)—may reflect an early interpretation of the letter along these lines.[29]

An alternative to this construal has been gaining in popularity.[30] Its advocates make two main points. First, the letter, in fact, never warns its readers against regressing to Judaism. The author's concern is not about his readers falling back but about them failing to progress. Second, it is argued that a Jewish-Christian audience is not clear from the letter. As I note above, the title is not original to the letter. Nor does the letter's pervasive argument from the Old Testament require a Jewish audience. As the letter to the Romans reveals, New Testament writers often assume that gentile readers know and appreciate arguments from the Scriptures, perhaps because many of them were "God-fearers" before converting to Christianity (gentiles who attached themselves to Judaism without actually converting to Judaism). Furthermore, it is argued that the author warns his readers in language that would be inappropriate if he were addressing Jewish Christians. In 3:12, for instance, he warns his readers about having "an unbelieving heart that turns away from the living God." Yet Jewish Christians, it is argued, would not be abandoning "the living God" if they reverted

---

27. For this view, see, e.g., Donald Guthrie, *New Testament Introduction*, 3rd ed. (Downers Grove, IL: InterVarsity Press, 1970), 682–87; Bruce, *Hebrews*, 3–9; Lindars, *Theology*, 9–15; William L. Lane, *Hebrews 1–8, Hebrews 9–13*, 2 vols., WBC 47A-B (Dallas: Word, 1991), 1:cxxv–cxxxv. Morna Hooker is unclear: she argues that there is no clear evidence of a falling back into Judaism but later says, "Just as Paul insisted that for gentiles to accept circumcision and obedience to the law would be to make Christ's death of no effect (Gal. 2:21–3:5), so our author, writing in a Jewish context, urges his congregation to recognize that those who continue to offer sacrifices in order to deal with sin are treating Christ's death with contempt and rejecting the covenant established through his death (6:6; 10:29)" (Morna Hooker, "Christ, the 'End' of the Cult," in Bauckham et al., *Epistle to the Hebrews*, 210).

28. Kevin B. McCruden, *Solidarity Perfected: Beneficient Christology in the Epistle to the Hebrews*, BZNW 159 (Berlin: de Gruyter, 2008), 127–31; cf. also Bryan R. Dyer, *Suffering in the Face of Death: The Epistle to the Hebrews and Its Context of Situation*, LNTS 568 (London: T&T Clark, 2017), 21–46.

29. The title, of course, is not original to the letter; it was probably added in the last quarter of the second century (it is found in the early papyrus MS $\mathfrak{P}^{46}$).

30. See, e.g., James W. Thompson, *Hebrews*, Paideia (Grand Rapids: Baker Academic, 2008), 6–10; David A. deSilva, *Perseverance in Gratitude: A Socio-Rhetorical Commentary on the Epistle "to the Hebrews"* (Grand Rapids: Eerdmans, 2000), 2–7; Weiss, *Der Brief an die Hebräer*, 55–60. Schenck sees Hebrews as written to gentiles who have a background steeped in Judaism and who therefore see the destruction of the temple in AD 70 as calling into question their faith (Kenneth L. Schenck, "Hebrews, Homiletics, and Liturgical Scripture Interpretation," in Mason and McCruden, *Reading the Epistle to the Hebrews*, 177; Schenck, *Understanding the Book of Hebrews*, 98–103). Some interpreters do not buy into this whole scenario, but argue for a mixed Jewish/gentile audience (e.g., Paul Ellingworth, *The Epistle to the Hebrews*, NIGTC [Grand Rapids: Eerdmans, 1993], 21–27; Andrew H. Trotter Jr., *Interpreting the Epistle to the Hebrews*, Guides to New Testament Exegesis 6 [Grand Rapids: Baker, 1997], 28–33; Koester, *Hebrews*, 48).

to Judaism.³¹ On this view, then, the ethnic makeup of the audience is unclear, but what is clear is that the author is warning them about a failure to move ahead, not about a reversion to Judaism.

This last argument, however, is not compelling. As F. F. Bruce points out, the claim that falling away from "the living God" could not apply to Jews founders on the fact that the context from which this warning is taken is dealing with Old Testament Israel. "What was possible for Israelites then was equally possible for Israelites now."³² The argument that this warning could not apply to Jewish Christians assumes a rather late date for the "parting of the ways." This phrase has become a popular way to refer to the ultimate separation of Jews and Christians. In New Testament times, it is argued, this parting had not yet taken place: Jesus followers constituted a particular sect within Judaism. However, while we do indeed need to exercise caution about anachronistically reading later stages in Christian history back into early Christianity, I am persuaded that many New Testament texts warrant us speaking of a significant parting from a fairly early date. To make the key point here, then: a New Testament writer in the mid-60s could understandably view Jesus and his sacrifice as the exclusive means of coming into relationship with the "living God," meaning that any other option—including Judaism—would entail a falling away from that God.

The argument for a gentile audience is not, then, compelling. And, positively, I think the case for a Jewish-Christian audience is, in fact, quite strong. Graham Hughes asks a relevant question (two questions, actually): "Why should such a word of exhortation, written to a concrete situation of urgency, demand such a massive structuring and working out of the salvation-historical purposes of God? And why *this particular structure*?"³³ The "particular structure" includes not just positive claims about the fulfillment of Old Testament institutions in Christ but also frequent and strong *negative* claims. Not only has a new covenant arrived, but the old covenant is "obsolete and outdated" (8:13 NIV). Not only does Christ introduce a "better hope," but the "former regulation" was "weak and useless" (7:18–19 NIV). Not only has Jesus offered himself as the final, once-for-all sacrifice, but the old-covenant sacrifices are "fleshly" regulations having to do with external matters (9:10), unable to cleanse the conscience or "take away" sins (10:1, 11). Grace is the means of strengthening the heart, not (OT ritual) "foods" (13:9). True, this argument could possibly be directed solely in a positive direction, enhancing the decisive salvation-historical moment that marks Christ's coming. But it makes better sense if it is also directed, negatively, to those who are tempted to turn back from Christ's high-priestly work to rely again on Jewish institutions.³⁴ Moreover, while the author never in so many words urges

---

31. Similar arguments are made about the rhetoric in 6:1, 4; 13:9.

32. Bruce, *Hebrews*, 6.

33. Graham Hughes, *Hebrews and Hermeneutics: The Epistle to the Hebrews as a New Testament Example of Biblical Interpretation*, SNTSMS 36 (Cambridge: Cambridge University Press, 1979), 28.

34. E.g., D. A. Carson and Douglas J. Moo, *An Introduction*

his readers not to fall back into Judaism, his call to "go to [Jesus] outside the camp" (13:13 NIV) comes close to saying just this.[35]

I conclude, then, that the traditional understanding of Hebrews's origin has a lot to say for it: the author writes to warn Jewish Christians not to fall back into Judaism again.[36] However, while this view must be part of the picture, I am uncertain that it can be made the whole picture. If the author indeed often warns his readers not to fall away, he equally often urges his readers to move ahead. The danger of falling back into Judaism should perhaps be seen as one specific aspect of a more general failure to advance in the faith—a problem that, of course, affects gentiles as well as Jews.[37]

Worldview

In our postmodern world, we have become more aware than ever of the effect of worldview on people's thought and speech. One's assumptions about "the way the world works," while not always, or even usually, formulated consciously, have a powerful impact on our thinking about a range of issues, including, of course, religious issues. The author of Hebrews would not be immune to this influence. Our purpose here, then, is to use the only evidence we have—Hebrews itself—to piece together the basic worldview of the author. The ultimate goal is to lend precision to our interpretation of the letter shaped by that worldview. For the language used in specific texts often functions to communicate ideas within the matrix of the author's worldview. As we engage in this process of identifying worldview, however, caution is needed. It is terribly easy to fall into a circular argument. Text X must mean Y because that text reflects background Z. And we know that background Z is involved because of the language used in text X. While, then, it is almost impossible not to use an interpretive grid drawn from a worldview to exposit Hebrews, we do well to be cautious about imposing such a grid without sufficient warrant in the text itself.

Scholars have identified a variety of worldviews that form the matrix for the teaching of Hebrews.[38] The discovery of the Dead Sea Scrolls in the late 1940s and

---

to the New Testament, 2nd ed. (Grand Rapids: Zondervan, 2005), 610–11; Schenck, *Understanding the Book of Hebrews*, 99–101.

35. Lindars, *Theology*, 9–15; Cockerill, *Hebrews*, 16–23.

36. I should also mention the option (not very popular anymore) that the audience of Hebrews consists of former priests, perhaps influenced by the Essene theology represented in the Dead Sea Scrolls (e.g., Spicq, *L'Epître aux Hébreux*, 1:22–52; P. Hughes, *Hebrews*, 10–15; Matthias Rissi, *Die Theologie des Hebräerbriefs: Ihre Verankerung in der Situation des Verfassers und seiner Leser*, WUNT 2/41 [Tübingen: Mohr Siebeck, 1987], 3–25, 56–59).

37. See esp. Cockerill, *Hebrews*, 16–23; Johnson, *Hebrews*, 33–38.

38. For instance, in his earlier work, Ernst Käsemann saw significant gnostic influence on Hebrews (*The Wandering People of God: An Investigation of the Letter to the Hebrews* [Minneapolis: Augsburg, 1984; original German edition, 1939]; see also Grässer, *An die Hebräer*, 1:25–28). The view has few contemporary advocates. As is generally recognized, Gnosticism is a second-century movement; any apparent "gnostic" perspectives can be explained as components of other first-century movements. For a response to Käsemann, see Otfried Hofius, *Der Vorhang vor dem Thron Gottes: Eine*

the assessment of their theological focus over subsequent years sparked interest in aligning Hebrews with the (probably) Essene movement that gave rise to the scrolls.[39] The Essenes and Hebrews share an interest in an authentic priesthood, accompanied by suspicions about the "official" Old Testament/Jewish cult. Like the author, the Essenes are interested in Melchizedek (as the scroll 11QMelch clearly reveals). However, while some similarities between the teaching of Hebrews and the scrolls certainly exist, these are not specific or numerous enough to justify thinking that our author is primarily oriented to "Essene" ways of thinking.[40]

The contemporary debate about the worldview of Hebrews has taken the form of a series of options that can all be plotted on a line with Middle Platonism at one end and Jewish apocalyptic at the other. Middle Platonism, as its name suggests, is a way of looking at reality that is rooted in the thinking of the famous philosopher of the early fourth century BC. Plato's basic perspective was adopted by his followers in his day and later and, as one would expect, his ideas were developed in various directions over time. Middle Platonism, then, is the name given to the stage of this movement from early in the first century BC up to around the fourth century AD (when Middle Platonism gave way to Neoplatonism). What makes this movement especially interesting for comparison with Hebrews is the quite thorough adoption of Middle Platonism by the first-century Jewish philosopher and theologian Philo. Based in Alexandria, Philo has left us a significant library of his writings, providing abundant data for comparison with Hebrews. Philo generally follows his ultimate mentor Plato in stressing the supremacy of the unseen realm over the reality of our experience.[41] Points of contact with Hebrews are obvious. The author also attaches great importance to the unseen, heavenly realm. It is in that realm that Jesus, our high priest, completes his atoning ministry, offering himself to God as the perfect sacrifice (e.g., 9:24). That ministry is performed, not on earth, but in the heavenly tabernacle (8:5). "Created things" must be removed so that the eternal spiritual kingdom can "remain" (12:25–29 NIV). We new-covenant Christians have not come to a mountain "that can be touched" (12:18 NIV); rather, we look for a "heavenly country" (11:16). In general, it is suggested, the author operates with a basic ontological contrast that is vertical in orientation (this world vs. the world "above") rather than horizontal

---

exegetisch-religionsgeschichtliche Untersuchung zu Hebräer 6,19f. und 10,19f., WUNT 1/14 (Tübingen: Mohr Siebeck, 1972).

39. See esp. Yigael Yadin, "The Dead Sea Scrolls and the Epistle to the Hebrews," in *Aspects of the Dead Sea Scrolls*, ed. Chaim Rabin and Yigael Yadin, ScrHier 4 (Jerusalem: Magnes, 1958), 36–55. See also P. Hughes, *Hebrews*, 10–15.

40. See, e.g., Lincoln D. Hurst, *The Epistle to the Hebrews: Its Background of Thought*, SNTSMS 65 (Cambridge: Cambridge University Press, 1990), 43–66.

41. Plato's fundamental teaching about this point is found especially in *Republic* 509c–521b and *Timaeus* 27C–29D. These texts can be accessed at the Perseus Digital Library (www.perseus.tufts.edu/hopper/). A thorough overview of significant Middle Platonic works is found in Wilfried Eisele, *Ein unschütterliches Reich: Die mittelplatonische Umformung des Prausiegedanken im Hebräerbrief*, BZNW 116 (Berlin: de Gruyter, 2003), 137–368. See also John M. Dillon, *The Middle Platonists: 80 B.C. to A.D. 220* (Ithaca, NY: Cornell University Press, 1996).

(past, present, future). This overall prioritizing of the immaterial over the material, it is argued, aligns Hebrews with the general world of thought found in Philo's writings, a point confirmed by similar vocabulary and similar approaches to the interpretation of the Old Testament. Some scholars, for these reasons, locate Hebrews pretty far toward the Middle Platonism end of the worldview spectrum.[42] Other scholars still recognize the influence of Middle Platonism on the author's world of thought, but locate the author's perspective a bit more toward the middle of the spectrum.[43]

Locating the author's thought too far toward the Middle Platonic end of the spectrum raises questions about the degree to which the author's perspective can fit with the overall perspective of other biblical authors. Scripture as a whole operates with a redemptive-historical scheme, according to which theological meaning is located in the fulfillment of God's past promises in the present and future. Several scholars resist the notion, therefore, that Hebrews reveals any strong influence from Middle Platonism. These scholars argue that Philo and the author of Hebrews use key vocabulary differently and have distinct overall conceptual perspectives.[44] Many who doubt significant Middle Platonic influence highlight the importance of Jewish apocalyptic for the author's worldview.[45] The distinctive "apocalyptic" can conceal more than it reveals, since the meaning of the word and the thought-world it connotes are debated. However, most agree that apocalyptic combines a horizontal focus on promise and fulfillment with a vertical focus on the heavenly realm and its significance for our own world. This combination matches the perspective of Hebrews well. In addition to the evidence of a vertical contrast that we noted above, the author also operates with a strongly temporal orientation: God has revealed himself through his Son in "the last days" (1:2). "The end of the ages" has dawned (9:26). Yet Christians also await a final judgment to come (10:25–31), when Christ will return to culminate salvation (9:28). In keeping with apocalyptic and in contrast to Middle Platonism, the created world continues to be significant for the author.[46] Many apocalyptic works

---

42. See especially, in his earlier work, Spicq, *L'Épître aux Hébreux*, 1:39–91 (the author is a "converted Philonist"); Eisele, *Ein unschütterliches Reich*; James W. Thompson, *The Beginnings of Christian Philosophy: The Epistle to the Hebrews*, CBQMS 13 (Washington, DC: Catholic Biblical Association of America, 1982); Thompson, "What Has Middle Platonism to Do with Hebrews?," in Mason and McCruden, *Reading the Epistle to the Hebrews*, 31–52; Thompson, *Hebrews*.

43. E.g., Johnson, *Hebrews*, 17–21; Kenneth L. Schenck, *Cosmology and Eschatology in Hebrews: The Settings of the Sacrifice*, SNTSMS 143 (Cambridge: Cambridge University Press, 2007), 191; Schenck, "Hebrews, Homiletics, and Liturgical Scripture Interpretation," 186; Weiss, *Der Brief an die Hebräer*, 99–100.

44. See esp. Ronald Williamson, *Philo and the Epistle to the Hebrews*, ALGHJ 4 (Leiden: Brill, 1970); see also Hurst, *Epistle to the Hebrews*, 7–42; C. K. Barrett, "The Eschatology of the Epistle to the Hebrews," in *The Background of the New Testament and Its Eschatology*, ed. W. D. Davies and D. Daube (Cambridge: Cambridge University Press, 1956), 363–93.

45. The focus on Jewish apocalyptic as the key background for Hebrews has become the majority view among scholars. See, for a clear and succinct summary, Benjamin J. Ribbens, *Levitical Sacrifice and Heavenly Cult in Hebrews*, BZNW 222 (Berlin: de Gruyter, 2016), 85–88. See also, e.g., Jody A. Barnard, *The Mysticism of Hebrews: Exploring the Role of Jewish Apocalyptic Mysticism in the Epistle to the Hebrews*, WUNT 2/231 (Tübingen: Mohr Siebeck, 2012).

46. See, e.g., Jon Laansma, "The Cosmology of Hebrews," in *Cosmology and New Testament Theology*, ed. Jonathan T.

also feature visions of worship of God in the heavenly realm, a focus that resembles the author's concern with the ministry of Christ in the heavenly tabernacle.

Identifying Jewish apocalyptic as the most significant factor in the author's worldview has become the dominant view in recent scholarship. I concur with this decision. However, I also disagree with those who prioritize Jewish apocalyptic to the exclusion of Middle Platonism. If Hebrews is not "Philonic," we might view it as "Philonish."[47] If we return to our spectrum analogy once more, then, I locate Hebrews toward the Jewish apocalyptic end but not so far toward that end that influence from Middle Platonism is excluded. What complicates this decision is the fact that, as Koester reminds us, these various streams of intellectual perspectives did not exist in isolation from each other.[48] We may, for instance, account for some or all of the Middle Platonic influence on Hebrews by recognizing that it comes to the author indirectly through some Jewish apocalyptic traditions that have themselves been significantly influenced by Middle Platonic perspectives—perspectives that may, of course, already have been adopted within early Christianity.

In conclusion, the basic redemptive-historical outlook that characterizes Scripture as a whole is found in Hebrews also. The decision of early Christians to recognize the letter's fit with apostolic doctrine and therefore to include it in the canon is fully justified. At the same time, we should not be closed off to the ways that Hebrews, especially with its addition of a vertical axis to the horizontal and its focus on the significance of Christ's heavenly ministry, adds to the richness of biblical teaching on these matters.

Interpretive Assumptions: Canonical Constraints

I want to be explicit about one key methodological approach that colors all my discussion of the theology of this marvelous letter. I approach Hebrews not ultimately as an isolated book to be interpreted purely on its own terms but as a part of the canon of Scripture. This does not mean that I run roughshod over the text of Hebrews in order to make it "fit" with the theology found in other canonical books. To do so would be to rob us of the rich and distinctive message of this book that God has preserved for our benefit. Rather, this principle means that I admit as one "pressure point" in our set of interpretive concerns the apostolic teaching in the rest of the New Testament (and Old!). This principle will become especially obvious in my discussions of perseverance and of the timing and place of Christ's atoning work.

Pennington and Sean M. McDonough, LNTS 355 (London: T&T Clark, 2008), 125–43; Edward Adams, "The Cosmology of Hebrews," in Bauckham et al., *Epistle to the Hebrews*, 122–39.

47. Sean M. McDonough, *Christ as Creator: Origins of a New Testament Doctrine* (Oxford: Oxford University Press, 2009), 195.

48. Koester, *Hebrews*, 63.

Structure and Outline

The rhetorical artistry of the author to the Hebrews reveals itself, among other ways, in the way he organizes his sermon. *Inclusios* (beginning and concluding a section with similar language and/or concepts), chiasms, and other literary devices occur throughout the letter. He introduces key Old Testament texts and then uses their words and imagery to develop his teaching. The very complexity of the letter means that scholars have to choose which of its many literary features to use as a basis for structuring the sermon.[49] Indeed, virtually any attempt to diagram the course of the letter will omit certain features that contribute to its organization.[50]

Following a number of other interpreters,[51] I divide the sermon into three basic parts and use the author's alternation between exposition and exhortation as a helpful organizing principle.

    I. The Exalted Son and a Rest for the People of God (1:1–4:13)
        A. Exordium (1:1–4)
        B. Exposition: The Exalted Status of the Son (1:5–14)
        C. Exhortation: Take Hold of Your Great Salvation (2:1–4)
        D. Exposition: The Humanity of the Son and Its Significance (2:5–18)
            1. The Son of Man of Psalm 8 (2:5–9)
            2. Jesus's Identification with Humans (2:10–18)
        E. Exhortation: Focus on the Faithful Son (3:1–6)
        F. Exhortation: Avoid the Fate of the Wilderness Generation (3:7–4:11)
            1. The Warning from Scripture (3:7–11)
            2. The Disaster of Unbelief (3:12–19)
            3. Entering the Rest (4:1–11)
        G. Exposition: The Power of the Word of God (4:12–13)
    II. Our Great High Priest and His Ministry (4:14–10:31)
        A. Exhortation: Persevere through the Power of Our Exalted High Priest (4:14–16)
        B. Exposition: High Priests and Our High Priest (5:1–10)
        C. Exhortation: Move on to Maturity (5:11–6:20)

---

49. For a history of discussion and various options, see esp. George H. Guthrie, *The Structure of Hebrews: A Text-Linguistic Analysis*, Biblical Studies Library (Grand Rapids: Baker, 1994), 3–40; and see also Brian C. Whitfield, *Joshua Traditions and the Argument of Hebrews 3 and 4*, BZNW 194 (Berlin: de Gruyter, 2013), 2–38.

50. However, Albert Vanhoye's layout is an admirable attempt to capture a lot of these relationships (*The Structure and Message of the Epistle to the Hebrews*, SubBi 12 [Rome: Pontifical Biblical Institute, 1989], 79–109). On the structure of the letter, see also George Guthrie, *Structure of Hebrews*; Cynthia Long Westfall, *A Discourse Analysis of the Letter to the Hebrews: The Relationship between Form and Meaning*, LNTS 297 (London: T&T Clark, 2005).

51. E.g., Cockerill, *Hebrews*, 61; Weiss, *Der Brief an die Hebräer*, 49. My former doctoral student, Ben Mandley, influenced me to adopt this threefold structure.

1. Avoiding Spiritual Stagnation (5:11–6:12)
   a. Growing by Feeding on Solid Food (5:11–6:3)
   b. Warning and Promise (6:4–12)
2. The Dependable Promises of God (6:13–20)

D. Exposition: A High Priest "according to the Order of Melchizedek" (7:1–28)
1. Melchizedek's Supremacy over Abraham (Gen 14:17–20) (7:1–10)
2. The Supremacy and Sufficiency of Our High Priest (Psalm 110:4) (7:11–25)
3. The High Priest Who Is Also the Son (7:26–28)

E. Exposition: The Ministry of Our High Priest (8:1–10:18)
1. Overview: Sanctuary, Sacrifice, and Covenant (8:1–6)
2. A New and Better Covenant (8:7–13)
3. The Earthly Sanctuary and Its Regulations: An Illustration of the New (9:1–10)
4. Eternal Redemption: Heavenly Sanctuary, Decisive Sacrifice, and New Covenant (9:11–28)
5. The Ultimate Sacrifice (10:1–18)

F. Exhortation and Warning: Appropriating the Benefits of Our High Priest's Ministry (10:19–31)
1. Encouragement to Appropriate and Act on Christ's High-Priestly Work (10:19–25)
2. Warning about Rejecting Christ's High-Priestly Work (10:26–31)

III. Exhortation: Follow and Serve the Pioneer of Our Faith through Endurance and Faith (10:32–13:25)
A. Introductory Call to Endurance and Faith (10:32–39)
B. The Nature and Power of Faith Illustrated in Salvation History (11:1–40)
1. The Ancients Commended for the Faith That Sees the Unseen (11:1–7)
2. Faith in the Patriarchal Era (11:8–22)
3. Faith in the Era of the Exodus and Conquest (11:23–31)
4. The Faith of Judges, Prophets, Women, and Martyrs (11:32–38)
5. The Ancients Commended for Faith That Looks to the Future (11:39–40)

C. Run the Race with Endurance, Remembering That You Are Children of God (12:1–17)
D. Coming to Mount Zion and Inheriting the Unshakeable Kingdom (12:18–29)
E. Letter Closing (13:1–25)
1. Concluding Exhortations and Encouragement (13:1–17)
2. Concluding Epistolary Matters (13:18–25)

Select Bibliography

Commentaries

Allen, David L. *Hebrews*. NAC 35. Nashville: Broadman & Holman, 2008.

Attridge, Harold A. *A Commentary on the Epistle to the Hebrews*. Hermeneia. Philadelphia: Fortress, 1989.

Backhaus, Kurt. *Der Hebräerbrief*. RNT. Regensburg: Pustet, 2009.

Bénétrau, Samuel. *L'Épître aux Hébreux*. 2 vols. Vaux-sur-Seine: EDIFAC, 1990.

Braun, Herbert. *An die Hebräer*. HNT 14. Tübingen: Mohr Siebeck, 1984.

Bruce, F. F. *The Epistle to the Hebrews*. Rev. ed. NICNT. Grand Rapids: Eerdmans, 1988.

Buchanan, George Wesley. *To the Hebrews*. AB. Garden City, NY: Doubleday, 1972.

Calvin, John. *The Epistle of Paul the Apostle to the Hebrews and the First and Second Epistles of St. Peter*. Calvin's Commentaries. Grand Rapids: Eerdmans, 1963.

Cockerill, Gareth Lee. *The Epistle to the Hebrews*. NICNT. Grand Rapids: Eerdmans, 2012.

Delitzsch, Franz. *Commentary on the Epistle to the Hebrews*. 2 vols. Edinburgh: T&T Clark, 1871.

deSilva, David. *Perseverance in Gratitude: A Socio-Rhetorical Commentary on the Epistle "to the Hebrews."* Grand Rapids: Eerdmans, 2000.

Ellingworth, Paul. *The Epistle to the Hebrews: A Commentary on the Greek Text*. NIGTC. Grand Rapids: Eerdmans, 1993.

France, R. T. "Hebrews." Pages 17–195 in *The Expositor's Bible Commentary*. Edited by Tremper Longman and David E. Garland. Grand Rapids: Zondervan, 2006.

Grässer, Erich. *An die Hebräer*. 3 vols. EKKNT. Zurich: Benziger, 1990, 1993, 1997.

Guthrie, Donald. *The Letter to the Hebrews*. TNTC. Downers Grove, IL: InterVarsity Press, 1983.

Guthrie, George H. *Hebrews*. NIVAC. Grand Rapids: Zondervan, 1998.

Hagner, Donald A. *Hebrews*. NIBC. Peabody, MA: Hendrickson, 1990.

Harris, Dana M. *Hebrews*. EGGNT. Nashville: Broadman & Holman, 2019.

Hegermann, H. *Der Brief an die Hebräer*. THKNT. Berlin: Evangelische Verlagsanstalt, 1988.

Hughes, Philip Edgcumbe. *A Commentary on the Epistle to the Hebrews*. Grand Rapids: Eerdmans, 1977.

Johnson, Luke Timothy. *Hebrews: A Commentary*. NTL. Louisville: Westminster John Knox, 2006.

Koester, Craig. *Hebrews*. AB. Garden City, NY: Doubleday, 2001.

Laansma, Jon C. *The Letter to the Hebrews: A Commentary for Preaching, Teaching, and Bible Study*. Eugene, OR: Cascade, 2017.

Lane, William. *Hebrews 1–8*. WBC 47A. Waco, TX: Word, 1991.

———. *Hebrews 9–13*. WBC 47B. Waco, TX: Word, 1991.

Long, D. Stephen. *Hebrews*. Belief: A Theological Commentary on the Bible. Louisville: Westminster John Knox, 2011.

Massonnet, Jean. *L'Épître aux Hébreux*. ConBNT. Paris: du Cerf, 2016.

Michel, Otto. *Der Brief an die Hebräer*. KEK. Göttingen: Vandenhoeck & Ruprecht, 1975.

Mitchell, Alan C. *Hebrews*. SP 13. Collegeville, MN: Liturgical Press, 2007.

Moffatt, James. *A Critical and Exegetical Commentary on the Epistle to the Hebrews*. ICC. Edinburgh: T&T Clark, 1924.

Montefiore, Hugh. *A Commentary on the Epistle to the Hebrews*. HNTC. San Francisco: Harper & Row, 1964.

Osborne, Grant R., with George H. Guthrie. *Hebrews Verse by Verse*. Osborne New Testament Commentaries. Bellingham, WA: Lexham, 2021.

Owen, John. *A Commentary on Hebrews*. 1684. Repr., Edinburgh: Banner of Truth, 1991.

Schreiner, Thomas R. *Commentary on Hebrews*. Biblical Theology for Christian Proclamation. Nashville: Holman, 2015.

Spicq, Ceslas. *L'Épître aux Hébreux*. 3rd ed. 2 vols. EB. Paris: Lecoffre, 1952, 1953.

Thompson, James W. *Hebrews*. Paideia. Grand Rapids: Baker, 2008.

Weiss, Hans-Friedrich. *Der Brief an die Hebräer*. KEK. Göttingen: Vandenhoeck & Ruprecht, 1991.

Westcott, Brooke Foss. *The Epistle to the Hebrews*. 1889. Repr., Eugene, OR: Wipf & Stock, 2001.

Witherington, Ben, III. *Letters and Homilies for Jewish Christians*. Downers Grove, IL: IVP Academic, 2007.

Other Works

The following list is far from exhaustive. Readers will have to consult footnotes in conjunction with indices to track down many other books and articles that I reference.

Adams, Edward. "The Cosmology of Hebrews." Pages 122–39 in *The Epistle to the Hebrews and Christian Theology*. Edited by Richard Bauckham, Daniel R. Driver, Trevor A. Hart, and Nathan MacDonald. Grand Rapids: Eerdmans, 2009.

Allen, David M. *Deuteronomy and Exhortation in Hebrews: A Study in Narrative Re-Presentation*. WUNT 2/238. Tübingen: Mohr Siebeck, 2008.

Barnard, Jody A. *The Mysticism of Hebrews: Exploring the Role of Jewish Apocalyptic Mysticism in the Epistle to the Hebrews*. WUNT 2/331. Tübingen: Mohr Siebeck, 2012.

Barrett, C. K. "The Eschatology of the Epistle to the Hebrews." Pages 363–93 in *The Background of the New Testament and Its Eschatology*. Edited by W. D. Davies. Cambridge: Cambridge University Press, 1964.

Bateman, Herbert W., IV, ed. *Four Views on the Warning Passages in Hebrews*. Grand Rapids: Kregel, 2007.

Bauckham, Richard. "The Divinity of Jesus Christ in the Epistle to the Hebrews." Pages 15–36 in *The Epistle to the Hebrews and Christian Theology*. Edited by Richard Bauckham, Daniel R. Driver, Trevor A. Hart, and Nathan MacDonald. Grand Rapids: Eerdmans, 2009.

Bauckham, Richard, Daniel R. Driver, Trevor A. Hart, and Nathan MacDonald, eds. *The Epistle to the Hebrews and Christian Theology*. Grand Rapids: Eerdmans, 2009.

Caird, George B. "Exegetical Method of the Epistle to the Hebrews." *CJT* 5 (1959): 44–51.

―――. "Son by Appointment." Pages 73–81 in *The New Testament Age: Essays in Honor of Bo Reicke*. Vol. 1. Edited by W. C. Weinrich. Macon, GA: Mercer University Press, 1984.

Church, Philip. *Hebrews and the Temple: Attitudes to the Temple in Second Temple Judaism and in Hebrews*. NovTSup 171. Leiden: Brill, 2017.

Cockerill, Gareth Lee. "Melchizedek without Speculation: Hebrews 7:1–25 and Genesis 14:17–24." Pages 128–44 in *A Cloud of Witnesses: The Theology of Hebrews in Its Ancient Contexts*. Edited by Richard Bauckham, Daniel Driver, Trevor A. Hart, and Nathan MacDonald. London: T&T Clark, 2008.

Compton, Jared. *Psalm 110 and the Logic of Hebrews*. LNTS 537. London: Bloomsbury T&T Clark, 2015.

Croy, N. Clayton. *Endurance in Suffering: Hebrews 12:1–13 in Its Rhetorical, Religious, and Philosophical Context*. SNTSMS 98. Cambridge: Cambridge University Press, 1998.

D'Angelo, Mary Rose. *Moses in the Letter to the Hebrews*. SBLDS 42. Missoula, MT: Scholars Press, 1979.

Docherty, Susan E. *The Use of the Old Testament in Hebrews: A Case Study in Early Jewish Bible Interpretation*. WUNT 2/260. Tübingen: Mohr Siebeck, 2009.

Dyer, Bryan R. *Suffering in the Face of Death: The Epistle to the Hebrews and Its Context of Situation*. LNTS 568. London: T&T Clark, 2017.

Easter, Matthew C. *Faith and the Faithfulness of Jesus in Hebrews*. SNTSMS 160. Cambridge: Cambridge University Press, 2014.

Filson, Floyd V. *"Yesterday": A Study of Hebrews in the Light of Chapter 13*. SBT 2/4. Naperville: Allenson, 1967.

Filtvedt, Ole Jakob. *The Identity of God's People and the Paradox of Hebrews*. WUNT 2/400. Tübingen: Mohr Siebeck, 2015.

France, R. T. "The Writer of Hebrews as a Biblical Expositor." *TynBul* 47 (1996): 245–76.

Fuhrmann, Sebastian. *Vergeben und Vergessen: Christologie und Neuer Bund im Hebräerbrief*. WMANT 113. Neukirchen-Vluyn: Neukirchener, 2007.

Gäbel, Georg. *Die Kulttheologie des Hebräerbriefes: Eine Exegetisch-Religionsgeschichtliche Studie*. WUNT 2/212. Tübingen: Mohr Siebeck, 2006.

Gheorghita, Radu. *The Role of the Septuagint in Hebrews: An Investigation of Its Influence with Special Consideration to the Use of Hab 2:3–4 in Heb 10:37–38*. WUNT 2/160. Tübingen: Mohr Siebeck, 2003.

Grässer, Erich. *Der Glaube im Hebräerbrief*. MTS 2. Marburg: Elwert, 1965.

Gray, Patrick. *Godly Fear: The Epistle to the Hebrews and Greco-Roman Critiques of Superstition*. AcBib 16. Atlanta: Society of Biblical Literature, 2003.

Guthrie, George H. *The Structure of Hebrews: A Text-Linguistic Analysis*. Biblical Studies Library. Grand Rapids: Baker, 1994.

Hofius, Otfried. *Katapausis: Die Vorstellung vom endzeitlichen Ruheort im Hebräerbrief*. WUNT 1/11. Tübingen: Mohr Siebeck, 1970.

Hughes, Graham. *Hebrews and Hermeneutics: The Epistle to the Hebrews as a New Testament Example of Biblical Interpretation*. SNTSMS 36. Cambridge: Cambridge University Press, 1979.

Isaacs, Marie E. *Sacred Space: An Approach to the Theology of the Epistle to the Hebrews*. JSNTSup 73. Sheffield: JSOT, 1992.

Jamieson, R. B. *Jesus' Death and Heavenly Offering in Hebrews*. SNTSMS 172. Cambridge: Cambridge University Press, 2019.

Joslin, Barry C. *Hebrews, Christ, and the Law: The Theology of the Mosaic Law in Hebrews 7:1–10:18*. Paternoster Biblical Monographs. Milton Keynes: Paternoster, 2008.

Käsemann, Ernst. *The Wandering People of God: An Investigation of the Letter to the Hebrews.* Minneapolis: Augsburg, 1984.

Kibbe, Michael. *Godly Fear or Ungodly Failure? Hebrews 12 and the Sinai Theophanies.* BZNW 216. Berlin: de Gruyter, 2016.

Kistemaker, Simon J. *The Psalm Citations in the Epistle to the Hebrews.* Amsterdam: Wed. G. van Soest, 1961.

Kurianal, James. *Jesus, Our High Priest: Ps. 110,4 as the Substructure of Heb. 5,1–7,28.* Europäische Hochschulschriften 693. Frankfurt am Main: Lang, 2000.

Laansma, Jon. *"I Will Give You Rest": The Rest Motif in the New Testament with Special Reference to Mt 11 and Heb 3–4.* WUNT 2/98. Tübingen: Mohr Siebeck, 1997.

Laansma, Jon, and Daniel J. Treier, eds. *Christology, Hermeneutics, and Hebrews: Profiles from the History of Interpretation.* LNTS 423. London: T&T Clark, 2012.

Laansma, Jon, George H. Guthrie, and Cynthia Long Westfall, eds. *So Great a Salvation: A Dialogue on the Atonement in Hebrews.* LNTS 516. London: T&T Clark, 2019.

Lee, Gregory W. *Today When You Hear His Voice: Scripture, the Covenants, and the People of God.* Grand Rapids: Eerdmans, 2016.

Lehne, Susanne. *The New Covenant in Hebrews.* JSNTSup 44. Sheffield: JSOT, 1990.

Lindars, Barnabas. *The Theology of the Letter to the Hebrews.* New Testament Theology. Cambridge: Cambridge University Press, 1991.

Loader, William R. G. *Sohn und Hoherpriester: Eine Traditionsgeschichtliche Untersuchung zur Christologie des Hebräerbriefes.* WMANT 53. Neukirchener-Vluyn: Neukirchener, 1981.

Mackie, Scott D. *Eschatology and Exhortation in the Epistle to the Hebrews.* WUNT 2/223. Tübingen: Mohr Siebeck, 2007.

Mason, Eric F. *"You Are a Priest Forever": Second Temple Jewish Messianism and the Priestly Christology of the Epistle to the Hebrews.* STDJ 74. Leiden: Brill, 2008.

McCruden, Kevin B. *Solidarity Perfected: Beneficent Christology in the Epistle to the Hebrews.* BZNW 159. Berlin: de Gruyter, 2008.

McKnight, Scot. "The Warning Passages of Hebrews: A Formal Analysis and Theological Conclusions." *TJ* 13 (1992): 21–59.

Moffitt, David M. *Atonement and the Logic of Resurrection in the Epistle to the Hebrews.* NovTSup 141. Leiden: Brill, 2011.

Peeler, Amy L. *You Are My Son: The Family of God in the Epistle to the Hebrews.* LNTS 486. London: T&T Clark, 2014.

Peterson, David. *Hebrews and Perfection: An Examination of the Concept of Perfection in the "Epistle to the Hebrews."* SNTSMS 47. Cambridge: Cambridge University Press, 1982.

Pierce, Madison N. *Divine Discourse in the Epistle to the Hebrews: The Recontextualization of Spoken Quotations of Scripture.* SNTSMS 178. Cambridge: Cambridge University Press, 2020.

Rascher, Angela. *Schriftauslegung und Christologie im Hebräerbrief.* BZNW 153. Berlin: de Gruyter, 2007.

Rhee, Victor (Sung Yul). *Faith in Hebrews: Analysis within the Context of Christology, Eschatology, and Ethics.* StBibLit 19. Berlin: Lang, 2001. Repr., Eugene, OR: Wipf & Stock, 2019.

Ribbens, Benjamin J. *Levitical Sacrifice and Heavenly Cult in Hebrews.* BZNW 222. Berlin: de Gruyter, 2016.

Richardson, Christopher A. *Pioneer and Perfecter of Faith: Jesus' Faith as the Climax of Israel's History in the Epistle to the Hebrews.* WUNT 2/338. Tübingen: Mohr Siebeck, 2012.

Rissi, Mathias. *Die Theologie des Hebräerbriefs.* WUNT 2/41. Tübingen: Mohr Siebeck, 1987.

Rose, Christian. *Die Wolke der Zeugen: Eine Exegetisch-Traditionsgeschichtliche Untersuchung zu Hebräer 10,32–12,3*. Tübingen: Mohr Siebeck, 1994.

Schenck, Kenneth L. *Cosmology and Eschatology in Hebrews: The Settings of the Sacrifice*. SNTSMS 143. Cambridge: Cambridge University Press, 2007.

———. *Understanding the Book of Hebrews: The Story behind the Sermon*. Louisville: Westminster John Knox, 2003.

Schröger, Friedrich. *Der Verfasser des Hebräerbriefes als Schriftausleger*. BU 4. Regensburg: Friedrich Pustet, 1968.

Small, Brian C. *The Characterization of Jesus in the Book of Hebrews*. BibInt 128. Leiden: Brill, 2014.

Thiessen, Matthew. "Hebrews and the Jewish Law." Pages 183–94 in *So Great a Salvation: A Dialogue on the Atonement in Hebrews*. Edited by Jon C. Laansma, George H. Guthrie, and Cynthia Long Westfall. LNTS 516. London: T&T Clark, 2019.

Thompson, James W. *The Beginnings of Christian Philosophy: The Epistle to the Hebrews*. CBQMS 13. Washington, DC: Catholic Biblical Association of America, 1982.

Vanhoye, Albert. *La Structure Littéraire de L'Épître aux Hébreux*. StudNeot 1. Paris: Desclée de Brouwer, 1962.

———. *The Structure and Message of the Epistle to the Hebrews*. SubBi 12. Rome: Pontifical Biblical Institute, 1989.

Westfall, Cynthia Long. *A Discourse Analysis of the Letter to the Hebrews: The Relationship between Form and Meaning*. LNTS 297. London: T&T Clark, 2005.

Whitfield, Bryan J. "Pioneer and Perfecter: Joshua Traditions and the Christology of Hebrews." Pages 80–87 in *A Cloud of Witnesses: The Theology of Hebrews in Its Ancient Contexts*. Edited by Richard Bauckham, Daniel Driver, Trevor Hart, and Nathan MacDonald. LNTS 387. London: T&T Clark, 2008.

Williamson, Ronald. *Philo and the Epistle to the Hebrews*. ALGHJ 4. Leiden: Brill, 1970.

A Note on the Use of Primary Sources

Unless otherwise noted, I have used *Novum Testamentum Graece* (ed. Kurt Aland, Johannes Karavidopoulos, Carlo M. Martini, and Bruce M. Metzger, 28th ed. [Stuttgart: Deutsche Bibelgesellscaft, 2012]) for my study of Hebrews and other New Testament literature; *Biblia Hebraica Stuttgartensia* (ed. K. Elliger and W. Rudolf, 5th ed. [Stuttgart: Deutsche Bibelgesellscaft, 1997]) for the Hebrew Old Testament; *Septuaginta* (ed. A. Rahlfs [Stuttgart: Deutsche Bibelgesellscaft, 1979]) for the Septuagint; *The Dead Sea Scrolls Reader* (ed. Donald W. Parry and Emanuel Tov, 6 vols. [Leiden: Brill, 2004–2005]) for the Dead Sea Scrolls; the Loeb Classical Library editions for the works of Josephus and Philo; *The New International Version* (2011) for quotations of the Old and New Testaments (unless otherwise noted); *The New Revised Standard Version* (1989) for English translations of the Apocrypha; and *The Old Testament Pseudepigrapha* (ed. J. Charlesworth, 2 vols. [Garden City, NY: Doubleday, 1983, 1985]) for English translations of the Pseudepigrapha.

The translations of Hebrews within the Explanation of the Text sections are my own (see also the translation diagrams). I have cited texts from the Old Testament according to the versification of the English translations, even when the MT or LXX numbering differs, although I often provide the LXX versification when I think it helpful.

CHAPTER 1

Hebrews 1:1–4

Literary Context

Hebrews ends with the kind of material we often find at the conclusion of a New Testament letter: a request for prayer, a benediction, references to coworkers, and greetings (13:18–25). But the beginning of Hebrews lacks the typical elements of letter openings: author and audience identification and greetings. Instead, the author launches into a highly theological celebration of the enormous benefits conferred by the exalted Son of God "in these last days." This immediate plunging of the reader into theological depths is similar to the openings of the Gospel of John (1:1–18) and 1 John (1:1–4). These verses serve as the exordium, as it is known in ancient Greco-Roman rhetoric. According to Witherington, "the function of any exordium was to establish rapport with the audience and to stir their emotions so they would be favorably disposed to receive the rest of the discourse."[1] These verses, however, perform a dual role: while they introduce the letter as a whole, they also function to bracket the first major section of the letter (1:1–4:13); God's "speaking" in the exordium is reprised with the author's description of the word of God in 4:12–13.[2]

The high Christology of verses 2b–3, celebrating the central role of the Son in creation and redemption, is similar to what we find in passages such as Philippians 2:6–11 and Colossians 1:15–20. Those passages are usually thought to incorporate confessional or hymnic material from the early church. The author has likely drawn from the same well of early christological reflection, using those materials to draw a breathtaking picture of the Son of God.[3] Contemplating the greatness of the Son of God, who provided "purification of sins" for us, should stimulate our own emotions and make us eager to see just how the sermonic exposition of these truths will develop.

---

1. Ben Witherington III, *Letters and Homilies for Jewish Christians: A Socio-Rhetorical Commentary on Hebrews, James and Jude* (Downers Grove, IL: InterVarsity Press, 2007), 97.

2. On the identification of 1:1–4:13 as the first major section of the letter, see above, pp. 16–17.

3. For a recent survey of NT christological hymns, see Matthew E. Gordley, *New Testament Christological Hymns: Exploring Texts, Contexts, and Significance* (Downers Grove, IL: IVP Academic, 2018).

> I. **The Exalted Son and a Rest for the People of God (1:1–4:13)**
> ➔ A. **Exordium (1:1–4)**
>   B. Exposition: The Exalted Status of the Son (1:5–14)
>   C. Exhortation: Take Hold of Your Great Salvation (2:1–4)
>   D. Exposition: The Humanity of the Son and Its Significance (2:5–18)
>   E. Exhortation: Focus on the Faithful Son (3:1–6)
>   F. Exhortation: Avoid the Fate of the Wilderness Generation (3:7–4:11)
>   G. Exposition: The Power of the Word of God (4:12–13)
> II. Our Great High Priest and His Ministry (4:14–10:31)
> III. Exhortation: Follow and Serve the Pioneer of Our Faith through Endurance and Faith (10:32–13:25)

Main Idea

The author briefly introduces three of the themes that will dominate his sermon: the immense privilege of believers who live in the new age of fulfillment, the presence of the glorious Son of God at God's right hand in heaven, and the provision for full and final forgiveness of sins by that exalted Son of God.

Translation

Hebrews 1:1-4

1a	manner		In many parts and in many ways	
1b	temporal	God spoke		
1c	temporal		in the past	
1d	recipients		to our ancestors	
1e	location		in the prophets	
2a	time		[but] in these last days	
2b	assertion	**he has spoken**		
2c	recipients		to us	
2d	sphere		in (the) Son,	
2e	assertion		whom	he appointed as heir to all things,
2f	assertion		through whom also	he created the ages of the world
3a	assertion		who	is the radiance of God's glory and
3b	assertion			the representation of his essence,

3c	assertion	supporting all things by his powerful word.
3d	circumstance	Having achieved cleansing for sins,
3e	assertion	he sat down at the right hand of the majesty in the highest realms,
4a	result	becoming as much greater than the angels
4b	comparison	as the name he inherited is greater than theirs.

Structure

The exordium falls into two basic parts: an initial statement about God's climactic "speaking" in the Son (vv. 1-2a) and a lengthy elaboration of the nature and work of that Son (vv. 2b-4). This second section begins with three ontological descriptions of the Son—who the Son *is*—and then moves to a focus on what the Son *does*. This part of the exordium is arranged in chiastic structure:[4]

```
A  whom he appointed as heir to all things,                  appointed messianic heir
   B  through whom also he created the ages of the world     mediates creation of universe
      C  who is the radiance of God's glory                  relationship to the Father
      C' and the representation of his essence,              relationship to the Father
   B' supporting all things by his powerful word.            upholding creation
      (Having achieved cleansing for sins,)                  (secures forgiveness)
A' he sat down at the right hand of the majesty on high      enthroned as Lord
```

The last part of this chiasm is climactic, as the author introduces two elements of the Son's work and position that are critical to his argument: providing cleansing for sin and occupying the exalted position at the Father's right hand. The exordium ends with an announcement of the Son's superiority to the angels (v. 4), a note that creates a transition to the next section.

Exegetical Outline

→ **A. Exordium (1:1–4)**
  1. Inauguration of the Last Days (vv. 1–2a)
  2. The Exalted Son (vv. 2b–4)

---

4. This chiasm is widely recognized, although scholars sometimes differ on the details. See esp. Daniel J. Ebert IV, "The Chiastic Structure of the Prologue to Hebrews," *TJ* 13 (1992): 163–79; John P. Meier, "Structure and Theology in Heb 1:1–14," *Bib* 66 (1985): 168–89; Lane, *Hebrews*, 1:6–7.

Explanation of the Text

1:1 In many parts and in many ways God in the past spoke to our ancestors in the prophets (Πολυμερῶς καὶ πολυτρόπως πάλαι ὁ θεὸς λαλήσας τοῖς πατράσιν ἐν τοῖς προφήταις). Hebrews begins with a reminder that God has revealed himself to the people of Israel in the Old Testament Scriptures. The author displays his literary artistry immediately in this opening verse, an artistry that, indeed, characterizes the exordium as a whole. Attridge claims that "the rhetorical artistry of this exordium surpasses that of any other portion of the New Testament."[5] While impossible to duplicate in English, the author uses five words beginning with *pi* (equivalent to "p" in English) in this statement about God's past revelation. The author refers to God's various ways of "speaking" in the past to set up a comparison with his speaking at the present time (v. 2a). However, we should not therefore minimize this initial claim about the revelation of God in the past—mainly, if not exclusively, in the Old Testament Scriptures. The situation the author addresses requires that he constantly draw his readers' attention to the climactic revelation they have received "in the Son." Yet he clearly and repeatedly also insists on the reality and value of God's prior speaking as well.

The author qualifies God's "speaking" (λαλήσας) in terms of its form, its time, its recipients, and its nature. In form, God spoke "in many parts and in many ways" (πολυμερῶς καὶ πολυτρόπως). Many translations give the former word a temporal meaning (NIV: "at many times"). However, there is not much support for a temporal meaning of this word. It means "various parts," while the second word means "various ways." Interpreters, then, strain to figure out what the distinct meaning of each term might be. However, we may doubt if the author was thinking in these terms. He probably uses both terms for stylistic reasons, extending his alliteration using "p" words and emphasizing the diversity of Old Testament revelation (its many forms—poetry, narrative, etc.—and its many authors). The two terms should be read together as mutually interpreting.[6] "In the past" (πάλαι) brings in the temporal element: it is the era that precedes "the last of these days." The recipients of this varied speaking of God in the past are "the ancestors." The Greek word here is the one that also simply means "father" (πατήρ; see, e.g., "fathers" in ESV). But the word can also refer to a group of people of mixed gender, from previous generations; "ancestors" is a good rendering here (so most translations; see also Heb 3:9; 8:9). Many translations use a possessive pronoun with "ancestors": "*our* ancestors" (e.g., NIV; ESV; NLT). Although the Greek lacks a possessive pronoun, this translation can be justified as a possible connotation of the article. However, the article may be used for other reasons, and we should probably not assume that the author intends to refer to "our ancestors."[7] Finally, and perhaps climactically, the author specifies the nature of God's speaking in the Old Testament: "in the prophets." We are most familiar with the use of "prophet" to denote the great Old Testament fore- and forthtellers, like Isaiah, Jeremiah, and Ezekiel. However,

---

5. Attridge, *Hebrews*, 36.
6. Grässer, *An die Hebräer*, 1:52.
7. The translation here is sometimes thought to have an impact on the question about the audience of Hebrews. "Our ancestors" might imply a Jewish audience, whereas "the ancestors" keeps the matter open. However, as Rom 4 reveals, gentile as well as Jewish Christians can claim the Jewish ancestors as their own. This issue therefore has no bearing on the audience question (Attridge, *Hebrews*, 38).

the scope of the word can be extended to anyone who speaks in God's name (e.g., Moses [Acts 3:21-22] and David [Acts 2:30]). "In the prophets" can also be rendered "through the prophets" (giving ἐν an instrumental force).[8] But it might be that the author wants also to indicate the "location" of God's past revelation, in accordance with the concept of inspiration, whereby God does not simply use people as the instruments of his speaking but puts his word in their hearts and minds for them to transmit to the people. God speaks "in and through" the prophets.[9]

1:2 [but][10] in these last days he has spoken to us in (the) Son, whom he appointed as heir to all things, through whom also he created the ages of the world (ἐπ' ἐσχάτου τῶν ἡμερῶν τούτων ἐλάλησεν ἡμῖν ἐν υἱῷ, ὃν ἔθηκεν κληρονόμον πάντων, δι' οὗ καὶ ἐποίησεν τοὺς αἰῶνας). The God who graciously spoke in the past now speaks finally and decisively in his Son, who is installed as Lord of all and who was instrumental in creating the world. This fresh revelation of God takes place "in these last days" (contrast "in the past"), is directed "to us" (contrast "to the ancestors"), and comes "in (the) Son" (in contrast to "in the prophets").[11] "These last days" (or "the last of these days": ἐσχάτου τῶν ἡμερῶν τούτων) reflects the LXX, which reproduces in Greek a Hebrew phrase that refers to the future age of fulfillment; see Daniel 10:14: "I . . . have come to help you understand what is to happen to your people at the end of days [ἐπ' ἐσχάτου τῶν ἡμερῶν]" (NRSV).[12] With other early Christians (e.g., Acts 2:17; 3:24; 2 Tim 3:1; Jas 5:3; 2 Pet 3:3), the author sees himself and his readers situated in the era of fulfillment that stretches from Christ's first coming to his second.

The heart of the author's claim about God's current speaking—and the key contrast with God's prior speaking—is that this new revelation is "in (the) Son." I put the article in parentheses because it approximates what the author seems be trying to convey in his choice of the Greek phrase here. Clearly, as many texts in Hebrews reveal, there is, for the author, only one Son. So to use an indefinite article in English—"a son"—would seriously mislead us about the author's meaning (though see NRSV; NET; CEB). Since English cannot easily use a noun in this context without any modifier at all—"in Son"—the only real option in English is to make the word definite, either with the article—"*the* Son"—or with a possessive pronoun—"*his* Son" (which is the choice of most English translations: NIV; ESV; NLT; NASB). However, this option may obscure the point our author is making by not using the article: his focus here is not on the Son as a person but on "son" as a way of accentuating the importance of this new revelation. It is not a "prophet" type of speaking but a "son" type of speaking.[13] The speaking God is

---

8. Attridge, *Hebrews*, 38; Lane, *Hebrews*, 1:4.
9. Weiss, *Der Brief an de Hebräer*, 138.
10. Gene Smillie has argued for continuity between vv. 1 and 2, suggesting that the "but" I have used in English (for which there is no exact counterpart in Greek) is unwarranted ("Contrast or Continuity in Hebrews 1.1–2?," *NTS* 51 [2005]: 543–60). However, while he is right to see continuity—it is the same God who speaks in prophets and "in Son"—there is also contrast.
11. "In" (ἐν) is again (as with ἐν in v. 1) more local than instrumental (see, e.g., Webster, "One Who Is Son," 79).
12. This and Jer 23:20 and 25:19 are the only texts that use the singular ἐσχάτου; other texts convey the same point with the plural (e.g., Hosea 3:5b: "they shall come in awe to the LORD and to his goodness in the latter days [ἐπ' ἐσχάτων τῶν ἡμερῶν].")
13. Most grammarians and commentators recognize the qualitative force of the construction: see, e.g., C. F. D. Moule, *An Idiom Book of New Testament Greek* (Cambridge: University Press, 1971), 114; Westcott, *Hebrews*, 7; Ellingworth, *Hebrews*, 93. A similar use of anarthrous υἱός occurs in 5:8: καίπερ ὢν υἱός, "Son though he was" (NIV). This nuance of anarthrous constructions is universally recognized; see, e.g., Daniel B. Wallace, *Greek Grammar Beyond the Basics* (Grand Rapids: Zondervan, 1996), 244–45.

now addressing "us" is in and through his own Son, elevating the significance of this current speaking. This speaking is obviously verbal, but at the same time comes to expression in who the Son is and what the Son does.[14] The author will draw out the practical implications of this definitive speaking in 2:1–4: "we must pay careful attention . . . to what we have heard."

In the middle of verse 2, the author transitions from his focus on God's speaking in the Son to the Son himself. The author describes the Son in seven clauses, which, as I noted above, are arranged in a chiasm.

At the center of the chiasm are two parallel lines focusing on the essence of the Son. At the outside of the chiasm are claims about the elevation of the Son to supreme status over all things. The two intermediate lines (the B and B′ lines) indicate the Son's relationship to creation. One line does not fit neatly into this chiastic arrangement: "having achieved cleansing for sins." The author disrupts his structure in order to foreshadow a central argument of the letter: the Son's elevated status enables him to "purify" or "cleanse" sinful humans.[15]

The sequence of christological assertions in verses 2b–3 follows a logical rather than a chronological order. Thus, "whom he appointed as heir to all things" refers not to a pretemporal appointment of the second person of the Trinity[16] but to the Son's elevation to the "right hand" of the Father after his death and resurrection. As we have seen, this appointing of the Son as heir of all things (A) matches the line in verse 3 about the Son's elevation to the Father's right hand (A′).[17] As Cockerill notes, the move from sonship (v. 2a) to inheritance is a natural one.[18] In this case, that connection has its basis especially in Psalm 2, to which the author is alluding here. In that psalm, which celebrates the appointment of the Israelite king, God proclaims the king is God's "Son" (v. 7) and promises to "make the nations [his] inheritance, the ends of the earth [his] possession" (v. 8). The author quotes Psalm 2:7 in 1:5, and he returns to it later in the letter as well (5:5).

The lack of concern for chronology is evident again when we move from the first to the second christological claim: the Son is the one "through whom also he created[19] the ages of the world." Jesus's role in the act of creation is a staple of the New Testament's high Christology: see, for example, John 1:3; 1 Corinthians 8:6; Colossians 1:16. The logical connection between the Son's appointment as heir of all things and his involvement in creation is not easy to discern. It may be that the Son's role in creating all things might explain how and why he is made the heir of all things. However, rather than using the phrase "all things" from verse 2b, he shifts to the word I have translated "the ages of the world" (αἰῶνας). This somewhat expansive translation is my attempt to capture the two sides of this word: both temporal and spatial. (English translations tend to favor the spatial: "world" [ESV; NET; CEB; NASB] or "universe" [NIV; NLT; CSB]; see, however, NJB: "ages").[20] The temporal

---

14. Kurt Backhaus, *Der Hebräerbrief*, RNT (Regensburg: Pustet, 2009), 83.

15. See, e.g., Attridge, *Hebrews*, 36.

16. As, e.g., Webster thinks ("One Who Is Son," 82); see also Moffatt, *Hebrews*, 5.

17. "Appoint" translates ἔθηκεν, from the verb τίθημι, which has a variety of specific connotations, including, as here, "appoint" ("τίθημι," BDAG 1004, §3). In agreement with the English translations, "all things" is the best rendering of πάντων (e.g., it is neuter rather than masculine ["all persons"]). Koester discerns an "anti-Empire" nuance in the claim here: Jesus, not the emperor, is "heir of all things" (*Hebrews*, 185). However, I am less certain than others that the NT is peppered with anti-empire rhetoric, and there is little to suggest it is present here.

18. Cockerill, *Hebrews*, 92.

19. The Greek verb used here, ποιέω, can refer to the act of creation ("ποιέω," BDAG 839, §1.b).

20. Weiss, *Der Brief an die Hebräer*, 143–44.

connotation of the word is very clear in many of its New Testament occurrences, as in the frequent reference to "this age" (e.g., 1 Cor 1:20; Gal 1:4), sometimes contrasted with "the age to come" (e.g., Matt 12:32; Mark 10:30; Luke 18:30; Eph 1:21). However, the word, even in these texts, takes on more than a simple temporal sense: "this age" and "the age to come" are distinguished not only in time but also in character. The Greek word here then combines the temporal with the spatial; Adams paraphrases it as "the physical cosmos, with the plural perhaps laying emphasis on the succession of eras allotted to it."[21]

1:3 who is the radiance of God's glory and the representation of his essence, supporting all things by his powerful word.[22] **Having achieved cleansing for sins,**[23] **he sat down at the right hand of the majesty in the highest realms** (ὃς ὢν ἀπαύγασμα τῆς δόξης καὶ χαρακτὴρ τῆς ὑποστάσεως αὐτοῦ, φέρων τε τὰ πάντα τῷ ῥήματι τῆς δυνάμεως αὐτοῦ, καθαρισμὸν τῶν ἁμαρτιῶν ποιησάμενος ἐκάθισεν ἐν δεξιᾷ τῆς μεγαλωσύνης ἐν ὑψηλοῖς). The Son shares the very being of God, is active in upholding the world he helped create, and, having accomplished purification for sins, has taken the highest position in heaven. With the first two lines of verse 3, we reach the heart of the author's christological chiasm, where he makes claims about the very nature of the Son.

The "is" in this last clause translates a participle (ὤν), which, in parallel with the two following ones, modifies the verb "sat down" at the end of the verse: "who **being** the radiance . . . and the representation . . . **supporting** all things . . . **having achieved** cleansing . . . he sat down." This structure is further evidence of the author's literary artistry and suggests that the author's main point comes in the indicative verb at the end of the verse: the Son's sitting down at the right hand of God.

"Radiance" translates a rare Greek word (ἀπαύγασμα) that can have either an active or passive meaning: "radiance" or "reflection" (or, as is often illustrated, the difference between the sun, which radiates its own light, and the moon, which reflects the light of the sun). The word occurs only here in the New Testament and only once in the LXX, where the author of Wisdom, referring to wisdom, calls her "a reflection of eternal light, a spotless mirror of the working of God" (Wis 7:26 NRSV). This LXX instance seems to have a passive sense. This passive sense might be reflected in later creedal formulations, as in the Nicene Creed, which describes the Son as "God from God, light from light." However, all three of its occurrences in Philo probably have an active sense, and most of the Greek fathers also gave the word an active sense.[24] We should probably prefer the active sense of "radiance" here then.[25] What the Son radiates is "glory" (δόξα), a word that connotes the awesome splendor

---

21. Adams, "Cosmology of Hebrews," 125. McDonough thinks the author uses the plural to stress that Christ is the creator both of this creation and the new creation (*Christ as Creator*, 200–204). The closest parallel in Hebrews is 11:3, "by faith we discern that the ages were formed by the word of God" (see also 1 Cor 2:7; Eph 3:9; Col 1:26).

22. The phrase τῆς δυνάμεως is qualitative, functioning basically like an adjective (see, e.g., Nigel Turner, *Syntax*, vol. 3 of J. H. Moulton, W. F. Howard, and Nigel Turner, *A Grammar of New Testament Greek*, 4 vols. [Edinburgh: T&T Clark, 1963], 214; and see NIV, NLT, NET etc.).

23. The KJV (and NKJV) "when he had *by himself* purged our sins" reflects a textual variant, either δι' αὐτοῦ (𝔓⁴⁶ D etc.) or δι' ἑαυτοῦ (D² Hᶜ, K, L etc.). But these are suspect as additions elaborating the middle voice of the participle ποιησάμενος (Bruce M. Metzger, *A Textual Commentary on the Greek New Testament*, 2nd ed. [Stuttgart: United Bible Societies, 1994], 592).

24. See Philo, *Creation* 146; *Planting* 50; *Spec. Laws* 4.123. It is probably active also in T. Abraham (A) 16.8.

25. See, e.g., Bruce, *Hebrews*, 48; P. Hughes, *Hebrews*, 41–42; Lane, *Hebrews*, 1:13; Cockerill, *Hebrews*, 94.

of God himself. The author refers to "the essential glory of the Son's eternal person."[26] Most interpreters are convinced that the author draws from Second Temple Jewish teaching about intermediaries in his description of the Son here. Hebrews has several parallels with the Jewish book of Wisdom (quoted above) as well as with Philo, who gives both "wisdom" and "word" (the *logos*) a significant role in mediating between God and humans.[27] Some influence from this tradition is probable; however, the author's teaching about the person of Christ goes beyond the Jewish personification of wisdom and the *logos*. This focus on persons—Father and Son—makes clear that the author presumes here the personal preexistence of the Son.[28]

This extraordinarily high Christology continues in the next assertion: the Son "is the representation of [God's] essence." "Representation" translates a word (χαρακτήρ) that connotes the idea of an impression stamped upon someone by something else. David deSilva usefully cites 4 Maccabees 15.4: "we [parents] impress upon the character [χαρακτήρ] of a small child a wondrous likeness both of mind and of form." So the very nature of God has been stamped on his Son.[29] This concept of "nature" is expressed here by a Greek word (ὑπόστασις) with a variety of meanings, but "inner nature" or "essence" appears to capture the sense here.[30]

After these two assertions about the nature of the Son, the author returns to descriptions of the Son's activity. "Supporting[31] all things by his powerful word" indicates that the Son, who was instrumental in creating the universe (v. 2c), continues his work in sustaining it. What the author says here is similar to the claim in Colossians 1:17b: "in him all things hold together."

As we have seen above, the reference to the Son's securing of "cleansing for sins" in verse 3c introduces a key motif of the letter. While this is the author's only use of "cleansing" (καθαρισμός), he uses other words from this same root to refer to the Son's work in taking care of the human sin problem (καθαρίζω, "cleanse," "purify": 9:14, 22, 23; 10:2; καθαρός, "clean," "pure": 10:22; καθαρότης, "cleansing," "purifying": 9:13). The author's use of these words points to the conceptual world of Old Testament sacrifice that dominates his presentation of Christ's work. Reference to this aspect of Christ's work sits a bit awkwardly with the focus on the exalted role and divine character of the Son in the other lines of this christological chiasm. However, as John Webster comments, the focus of this line is theologically quite appropriate: "what is needed, therefore, if the world is to reach its consummation, are not only conservation and governance but cleansing."[32]

The verb the author uses to describe this act of cleansing (ποιησάμενος) is an aorist middle. The use of the middle of this verb is a known feature of Greek: it combines with an object to indicate the verbal idea of that object. Here, then, we could translate simply "cleansing."[33] The aorist tense of

---

26. P. Hughes, *Hebrews*, 42.
27. Albert Vanhoye, *Situation du Christ: Hébreux 1–2*, LD 58 (Paris: Éditions du Cerf, 1969), 72–74.
28. See, e.g., Amy L. Peeler, *You Are My Son: The Family of God in the Epistle to the Hebrews*, LNTS 486 (London: T&T Clark, 2014), 25–29; contra the doubts of James D. G. Dunn, *Christology in the Making: A New Testament Inquiry into the Origins of the Doctrine of the Incarnation* (Philadelphia: Westminster, 1980), 52–55.
29. DeSilva, *Perseverance in Gratitude*, 89.
30. Delitzsch defines as "the essence or essential ground underlying the phenomenon" (*Hebrews*, 1:50); see also Attridge, *Hebrews*, 44.
31. "Supporting" translates a common Greek verb (φέρω) that has a variety of specific connotations. It often refers to "carrying" something from one place to another.
32. Webster, "One Who Is Son," 89.
33. Maximillian Zerwick and Mary Grosvenor, *A Grammatical Analysis of the Greek New Testament*, 5th ed. (Rome: Biblical Institute Press, 1996), 654.

the participle usually indicates action that takes place before the action of the verb it modifies. Most of our English versions convey this idea here by introducing the word "after"; for example, NIV: "after he had provided purification for sins, he sat down." If we read the sequence of verbs in this way, then the author indicates that the purification of sins takes place *before* the Son takes his place at the right hand of the Father (often called his "session"): "after purifying, he sat down." The author might then imply a reference to the cross, where Christ's sacrifice for sins was made.[34] However, as we will see, Hebrews's presentation of Christ's work takes on an added dimension. While not ignoring the cross (see the repeated references to "death" and "blood" in 9:11–28), he focuses on the moment of Christ's presentation of his sacrifice to the Father in the heavenly realm. It is possible, then, that the aorist participle expresses contemporaneous action: "making purification for sins, he sat down."[35] However, a survey of similar constructions in Hebrews suggests that the usual "antecedent action" is probable, which is perhaps further supported by the shift from the preceding present tense participles (ὤν ["is"], φέρων ["supporting"]) in the context.[36] However, it is still not clear what moment in the work of Christ he refers to: the cross, or Christ's entry into the heavenly sanctuary. Certainly the latter receives a lot of attention in Hebrews and, in the author's scheme, precedes Christ's taking his seat beside the Father.[37]

At the climax of the author's introductory sketch of Christology is the Son's sitting down at the Father's right hand. With this line we reach the end of the chiasm, with the "sitting down" of the Son in heaven matching his appointment as the "heir to all things" (v. 2b). Singling out Christ's "session" for attention, instead of, for instance, Christ's incarnation, death, or resurrection, foreshadows a central theme in the letter. The author consistently appeals to the power and finality of Christ's heavenly ministry to encourage his readers to stay the course. And, as he does here, he often uses the language of Psalm 110:1 to refer to this heavenly ministry (1:13; 8:1; 10:12; 12:2). Indeed, when we note that Psalm 110:4 is cited by our author to justify his "priest according to Melchizedek" theme (see esp. 5:6, 10; 6:20; 7:1–10), one could make the case that Psalm 110 is basic to the development of the letter.[38] The author's two key christological claims are both found here: that Jesus is the royal "Son" and that he is the "high priest" in the order of Melchizedek.[39] The author does not quote Psalm 110:1, but his allusion to this text is clear enough:

---

34. E.g., Koester, *Hebrews*, 188.
35. E.g., Ribbens, *Levitical Sacrifice*, 99.
36. While some instances are disputed, the aorist participle, when it precedes the verb it modifies, tends to express antecedent action in Hebrews (5:9; 6:1, 15; 9:11–12, 19, 28; 10:28, 32, 36; 11:7, 23, 24). Two seem to indicate contemporaneous action (6:13; 12:17a); others are unclear (2:10; 7:3; 11:29, 39; 12:1). The sequence of finite verb + aorist participle is more mixed between antecedent action (2:3; 11:13, 24–25, 30, 31) and contemporaneous action (7:27; 10:24–25; 11:9, 17–19; 12:2, 17b; 13:2); several are unclear (5:9–10; 6:20; 9:12; 11:27). Hebrews 10:12 presents a similar grammatical and substantive issue: "he, having offered [or offering] one sacrifice for sins forever, sat down at the right hand of God" (οὗτος δὲ μίαν ὑπὲρ ἁμαρτιῶν προσενέγκας θυσίαν εἰς τὸ διηνεκὲς ἐκάθισεν ἐν δεξιᾷ τοῦ θεοῦ). The sequence in Heb 9:12b, another controversial text touching on the same issue, is the reverse: indicative verb + aorist participle: "through his own blood he entered once for all into the Most Holy Place, securing [or having secured] eternal redemption" (διὰ δὲ τοῦ ἰδίου αἵματος εἰσῆλθεν ἐφάπαξ εἰς τὰ ἅγια αἰωνίαν λύτρωσιν εὑράμενος).
37. See esp. R. B. Jamieson, *Jesus' Death and Heavenly Offering in Hebrews*, SNTSMS 172 (Cambridge: Cambridge University Press, 2019), e.g., 41. Jamieson further suggests that the author may have Lev 16:30 in view: "for on this day [the Day of Atonement] atonement shall be made for you, to cleanse you; from all your sins you shall be clean before the Lord" (NRSV).
38. Jared Compton, *Psalm 110 and the Logic of Hebrews*, LNTS 537 (London: Bloomsbury T&T Clark, 2015).
39. Otto Michel, *Der Brief an die Hebräer*, KEK, 7th ed. (Göttingen: Vandenhoeck & Ruprecht, 1975), 102.

Ps 110:1: "the Lord says to my lord: 'Sit at my right hand until I make your enemies a footstool for your feet.'" (LXX [109:1]: Εἶπεν ὁ κύριος τῷ κυρίῳ μου Κάθου ἐκ δεξιῶν μου, ἕως ἂν θῶ τοὺς ἐχθρούς σου ὑποπόδιον τῶν ποδῶν σου)

Heb 1:3d: "he sat down at the right hand of the majesty in the highest realms." (ἐκάθισεν ἐν δεξιᾷ τῆς μεγαλωσύνης ἐν ὑψηλοῖς)

The author stresses the exalted position the Son has attained not only by referring to the "right hand" (the place of honor)[40] but also by naming God "the majesty" (τῆς μεγαλωσύνης)[41] and locating God "in the highest realms" (ἐν ὑψηλοῖς).[42]

1:4 becoming as much greater than the angels as the name he inherited[43] is greater than theirs (τοσούτῳ κρείττων γενόμενος τῶν ἀγγέλων ὅσῳ διαφορώτερον παρ᾽ αὐτοὺς κεκληρονόμηκεν ὄνομα). The author finishes his exordium with a claim that the Son is greater than the angels. The author for the first time uses a literary device that will undergird most of his major arguments: *synkrisis*, or "comparison." And the author here introduces for the first time the word that he will use twelve other times to mark this comparison: "greater," or, as it is usually translated, "better" (κρείττων). This verse, in fact, features a double comparison: as compared to the angels, the Son is greater; and the extent to which the Son is greater is compared to the extent to which the Son's name is greater than the angels' name.[44] "Angels" figure prominently in chapters 1–2, usually as foils for the greater significance of the Son (1:5, 6, 7–9, 13–14; 2:2–3, 5, 7, 9, 16; they appear elsewhere in Hebrews only in 12:22; 13:2). Some interpreters think the author brings them in to counter an overemphasis on angels among his readers, perhaps akin to the false teaching that Paul confronts in Colossians.[45] However, the lack of any explicit warning along these lines, along with the fact that the issue of angels is confined to chapters 1–2 (except the non-polemical mentions in 12:22 and 13:2), suggests rather that the author uses them as "measures of ontological status."[46] That is, they are the most exalted beings one could imagine apart from God: asserting the Son's superiority to them therefore accentuates his own status. At the same time, as 2:2–3 reveals, the author is concerned with angels in their role as intermediaries of divine truth.[47]

The author does not, of course, identify the "name" that is greater than the angels' name. Richard Bauckham argues that this name is Yahweh, since no greater name than this can be imagined.[48]

---

40. The Greek word δεξιός, which means "right," can also, without further modifier, mean "right hand" (BDAG 217, §1.b).

41. This word is used as a title of God only in Hebrews in the NT (see also 8:1); while not used as a divine title in the LXX, it is a quality often ascribed to God (Deut 32:3; 2 Kgdms (E 2 Sam) 7:21, 23; 1 Chr 17:19; 29:11; Ps 78:11; 144:3, 6; 150:2; Dan 2:20).

42. As BDAG ("ὑψηλός," 1044, §1) notes, ὑψηλοῖς refers to heaven (see, e.g., NIV), but the word suggests the highest parts of heaven (see 7:26, ὑψηλότερος τῶν οὐρανῶν, "the highest parts of heaven," or perhaps, "the heights that are heaven").

43. "Inherited" translates a verb in the perfect tense (κεκληρονόμηκεν). This tense often focuses on a state of affairs: the author suggests that the "inheriting," while occurring at a moment in time, has enduring consequences.

44. The comparison is expressed with the combination τοσούτῳ . . . ὅσῳ: "by some much . . . than" ("τοσούτος," BDAG 1012, §5).

45. T. W. Manson, "The Problem of the Epistle to the Hebrews," in *Studies in the Gospels and Epistles*, ed. M. Black (Manchester: Manchester University Press, 1962), 242–58.

46. Richard J. Bauckham, *Jesus and the God of Israel: God Crucified and Other Studies on the New Testament's Christology of Divine Identity* (Grand Rapids: Eerdmans, 2008), 240–41; Cockerill, *Hebrews*, 100–101; Koester, *Hebrews*, 200–201.

47. Vanhoye, *Structure and Message*, 48–49; Rissi, *Die Theologie des Hebräerbriefs*, 49–51; Hurst, *Epistle to the Hebrews*, 45–46.

48. Richard Bauckham, "The Divinity of Jesus Christ in the Epistle to the Hebrews," in Bauckham et al., *Epistle to the*

However, granted its prominence in the context (1:2, 5, 8), "Son" is a better candidate.[49] The author says that Jesus "inherited" this name, which brings us to the beginning of the christological chiasm in verse 2b, where we learned that the Son had been appointed "heir to all things." These statements, as we noted in our comments on verse 2, are sometimes interpreted in terms of the pretemporal being of the Son.[50] However, the language more naturally refers to the incarnate career of the one who has eternally been the Son: in a breathtaking turn of affairs, the one who perfectly reflects God's glory and is the very representation of his being "becomes" (γενόμενος).[51]

Theology in Application

God Speaks

We could easily react to the first verse of Hebrews with a "ho hum." Those of us who have been believers for a long time are quite accustomed to owning Bibles (usually several), reading them (often, it is hoped), and hearing teaching from them. So the claim in verse 1 that God has spoken does not seem to be a very big deal. But it is. God spoke with the first human couple in the garden of Eden, but God graciously condescended to continue to speak with humans even after they had rejected his lordship and went their own way. As Hebrews notes, his speaking took many forms. At times he addressed his people quite directly through prophets, who often introduce their teaching by claiming, "Thus says the Lord." But we believe God speaks in more indirect ways also. The Old Testament, we believe, contains words "inspired" by God: "breathed into" his chosen intermediaries (see 2 Tim 3:16). These words were often first expressed orally but at some point were written down for the benefit of future generations. This whole process, from beginning to end, was supervised by God. The writers of the Pentateuch and the historical books speak God's words in and through their own words. Likewise, the psalmists, who movingly express their own strong emotions of lament and praise, speak exactly what God wants them to speak.[52]

Hebrews, 21–22. George H. Guthrie argues that the "name" is "an honor conferred by God on the Messiah as the Davidic heir" ("Hebrews," in *Commentary on the New Testament Use of the Old Testament*, ed. G. K. Beale and D. A. Carson [Grand Rapids: Baker Academic, 2007], 924–25). Delitzsch (*Hebrews*, 1:60) argues that the "name" is a hidden heavenly name expressing Christ's preeminence.

49. So most commentators; e.g., Bruce, *Hebrews*, 50; P. Hughes, *Hebrews*, 51; Attridge, *Hebrews*, 47; Lane, *Hebrews*, 1:17; Koester, *Hebrews*, 181–82. See also R. B. Jamieson, *The Paradox of Sonship: Christology in the Epistle to the Hebrews*, Studies in Christian Doctrine and Scripture (Downers Grove, IL: IVP Academic, 2021), 102–4.

50. See again on v. 4, Webster, "One Who Is Son," 93.

51. Grant Macaskill, *Union with Christ in the New Testament* (Oxford: Oxford University Press, 2013), 180–81.

52. For a recent, wide-ranging exploration of this theme, see D. A. Carson, ed., *The Enduring Authority of the Christian Scriptures* (Grand Rapids: Eerdmans, 2016).

We call the process by which the words of Scripture are fully human and fully divine at the same time *concurrence*. At the risk of stretching the significance of Hebrews 1:1 to the breaking point, I might suggest that the author at least hints as this concurrent process. On the one hand, the "speaking" the author refers to comes in many different forms "in the prophets"—alluding to the human element in this speaking. On the other hand, however, it is God who speaks in and through this process. I may further suggest that the former, human, side of the process justifies careful interpretation of the words of Scripture in their original contexts. However, the divine element in this speaking at the same time underlines the truthfulness and authority of these words. God has spoken. What can humans do but listen carefully, attentively, and obediently?

The One Who Is Son

The author's description of Jesus the Son in verses 2b–3 is one of the mountaintops of New Testament christological teaching. The outer lines of the chiasm in these verses describe the exalted position that the Son occupies, using language and concepts widely distributed in the New Testament (Ps 110:1, to which the author alludes in v. 4, is the most frequently quoted OT text in the NT). The inner lines of this chiasm, however, venture into territory that is shared by only a few other New Testament texts (e.g., John 1:1–18; 1 Cor 8:6; Phil 2:5–11; Col 1:15–20). Here Christ is given a foundational role in the creation of the universe and is described in terms that identify him so closely with God that the implication of his own deity seems to be required. It is often noted that teaching about Christ in the New Testament focuses on understanding who he is by seeing what he has done. However, we should not forget the ontological claims (that is, claims about Christ's essence or nature) that we find in texts such as this one. The language of "son" applied to Jesus here goes beyond the "official" meaning the term is sometimes given—that is, that "son" simply identifies Jesus as the messianic king (see Ps 2:7). In this passage, the Son is the agent of New Testament revelation, the mediator of creation, and one who shares God's character and essence. The eternal Son "becomes" (v. 4); it is the Son who is made heir of all things (v. 2).[53]

Two extremes in interpreting these statements must be avoided. On the one hand, we must be careful not to read later, developed christological reflection into these verses. Our author is writing long before some of the controversies leading to that mature theological development took place. However, on the other hand (and this

---

53. See on this point D. A. Carson, *Jesus the Son of God: A Christological Title Often Overlooked, Sometimes Misunderstood, and Currently Disputed* (Wheaton, IL: Crossway, 2012), 44–62; I. Howard Marshall, *The Origins of New Testament Christology* (Downers Grove, IL: InterVarsity Press, 1990), 111–25.

is, perhaps, the more common error in our day), neither should we minimize the import of these lines for that later christological development. The author makes claims here that are rightly seen as grounding important insights from that later stage of theological reflection.[54]

---

54. See on this point esp. Webster, "One Who Is Son." It might be noted, for instance, that Athanasius repeatedly cites Heb 1:3 in his refutation of Arianism (Frances M. Young, "Christological Ideas in the Greek Commentaries on the Epistle to the Hebrews," in Laansma and Treier, *Christology, Hermeneutics, and Hebrews*, 34).

CHAPTER 2

Hebrews 1:5–14

Literary Context

As we have suggested, Hebrews is a sermon that has been placed into a letter. Ancient letters fall into a simple, three-part pattern: opening, body, and closing. If the exordium (1:1–4) is the opening of the letter to the Hebrews, this passage (vv. 5–14) begins the body of the letter. The author links this body opening to the exordium with the theme of the Son's superiority to the angels. As noted in the previous section, the author repeatedly brings angels into his teaching right through to the end of chapter 2 (1:5, 6, 7–9, 13–14; 2:2–3, 5, 7, 9, 16). We might then label this whole passage something like "The Son's Superiority to the Angels." However, this might be slightly misleading. The author's point is not simply that the Son is greater than the angels. As argued above, the author uses the angels as a foil to proclaim the utter uniqueness of the Son by virtue of his unique relationship to God—and, in 2:5–18, to assert the unique ability of the Son to bring redemption to humans by virtue of his full identification with sinful humans. It is the unique status of Jesus as both God and human that is the focus of these verses.[1] The Old Testament texts that our author cites elaborate three of the key points in the exordium: Christ's identity as the Son (v. 2b = vv. 5–6), Christ's divine nature (v. 3a = vv. 8–9), and Christ's role in creation (v. 3b = vv. 10–12).[2] Moreover, we must attend to the author's explicit rhetorical purpose in asserting Christ's superiority over the angels: the severe consequences of ignoring a revelation that is mediated by the Son, who is also the Lord (2:1–4).

---

1. See Vanhoye, *Situation du Christ*, 119–20.
2. Weiss, *Der Brief an die Hebräer*, 156; Grässer (*An die Hebräer*, 1:71) suggests a similar scheme.

- I. **The Exalted Son and a Rest for the People of God (1:1–4:13)**
  - A. Exordium (1:1–4)
  - ➡ B. **Exposition: The Exalted Status of the Son (1:5–14)**
  - C. Exhortation: Take Hold of Your Great Salvation (2:1–4)
  - D. Exposition: The Humanity of the Son and Its Significance (2:5–18)
  - E. Exhortation: Focus on the Faithful Son (3:1–6)
  - F. Exhortation: Avoid the Fate of the Wilderness Generation (3:7–4:11)
  - G. Exposition: The Power of the Word of God (4:12–13)
- II. Our Great High Priest and His Ministry (4:14–10:31)
- III. Exhortation: Follow and Serve the Pioneer of Our Faith through Endurance and Faith (10:32–13:25)

Main Idea

The unique and exalted status of Jesus (vv. 1–4) is demonstrated by means of a series of Old Testament quotations comparing Jesus to angels. Jesus is identified as the one who is appointed "Son" (vv. 5–7), the one who rules as "God" (vv. 8–9), and the one who, as "Lord," will live and reign forever (vv. 10–12). Jesus has been exalted to the supreme position at "the right hand" of God, in fulfillment of Psalm 110:1 (v. 13).

Translation

Hebrews 1:5–14

5a	explanation	For	
5b	rhetorical question	**to which of the angels did God ever say,**	
5c	content		"You are my son;
5d	parallel		I have today begotten you"? (Ps 2:7)
		and	again,
5e	content		"I will be as a father to him, and
5f	parallel		he will be as a son to me"? (2 Sam 7:14; 1 Chr 17:13)
6a	time	And	when God brings his firstborn into the world,
6b	assertion	**again he says:**	
6c	content		"Let all the angels of God worship him." (Deut 32:43)

Continued on next page.

7a	reference	And	**with respect to the angels, he says,**
7b	content		"He makes his angels spirits
7c	parallel		and makes his servants a fiery flame." (Ps 104:4)
8a	assertion	But	God says to the Son:
8b	content		"Your throne, God, is forever, and
8c	parallel		the scepter of justice is the scepter of your kingdom.
9a	parallel		You have loved righteousness and hated wickedness.
9b	result		Because of this, God, your God, anointed you with the oil of gladness,
9c	result		setting you over your companions." (Ps 45:6–7)
10a	assertion	And	he also says:
10b	content		"You, Lord, in the beginning laid the foundations of the earth, and
10c	parallel		the heavens are the work of your hands.
11a	parallel		They will perish, but you remain;
11b	parallel		they will all wear out like a garment.
12a	parallel		You will roll them up like a cloak;
12b	parallel		like a garment they will be changed.
12c	parallel		But you are the same, and your years will not end." (Ps 102:25–27)
13a	rhetorical question	And	to which of the angels did God ever say:
13b	content		"Sit at my right hand
13c	time		until I place your enemies under your feet"? (Ps 110:1)
14a	rhetorical question	Are	**not the angels merely ministering spirits**
14b	explanation		sent to serve those who are about to inherit salvation?

Structure

This first stage of the author's argument consists of a series of Old Testament quotations, with brief interspersed comments on them. The author quotes seven texts—perhaps deliberately matching the seven lines of his christological chiasm in verses 2b–3.[3] Indeed, the quotations in these verses have strong connections with the exordium. The author amasses Old Testament texts that enable him to proclaim the supreme position of Jesus by means of three key christological titles: "Son" (vv. 5–7), "God" (vv. 8–9), and "Lord" (vv. 10–12). The author, as he often does, uses an *inclusio* to tie the section together: the question "To which of the angels did God ever say . . . ?" appears in both verse 5a and verse 13a. The catena of quotations ends with a full quotation of Psalm 110:1 (v. 13), making another connection with the exordium

---

3. See, e.g., Bauckham, "Divinity of Jesus Christ," 20.

(v. 4) and forming an opening salvo—through a barrage of quotations and allusions to this text—that will mark the argument of the letter.

The comparison of the Son with angels that the author introduced in verse 4 continues to mark these verses. In addition to the questions in verses 5 and 13 noted above, the author quotes two Old Testament texts that refer to angels (vv. 6, 7) and concludes the section with a final reminder of the subordinate status of angels: they are "ministering spirits" (v. 14).

The claim is often made that Hebrews cites Old Testament verses in a kind of "proof-text" fashion, applying the language of Scripture to Christ, whatever that language might have meant in its original setting. Some interpreters attribute this allegedly scattershot approach in this passage to the author's dependence on a "testimony book," a list of Old Testament passages applied to Christ that circulated in the early church.[4] However, while our author certainly interprets and applies the meaning of the Old Testament in light of God's "final word" in his Son (1:2), he also has some contextual basis for the Scripture he cites (see further, the In Depth discussion below). The texts he cites in 1:5–13 provide a good example of this.

First, the opening and closing citations, from Psalms 2:7 and 110:1, respectively, have in common a focus on the elevation of the Israelite king to an exalted status: "You are my Son" is addressed to the one who has been enthroned (Ps 2:6), sitting at the right hand of God (Ps 110:1). Second, the naming of the king as God's Son in Psalm 2:7 has a natural connection to the Lord's prediction about the eternal kingdom over which David's "son" would reign (2 Sam 7:13–14; see v. 5b). Undergirding the application of these texts to Jesus is the widely recognized pattern of Old Testament prophecy, according to which predictions about a historical king ultimately have in view the ultimate king, the Messiah. "Messiah" means "anointed," and the language of anointing is another factor that links two of the texts cited here, Psalm 2:7 (see "the Lord's anointed" in 2:2) and Psalm 45:7 (v. 9). Psalm 45:6–7 (quoted in Heb 1:8–9) is linked to other quotations in the context in at least three ways: as we just mentioned, Psalms 2 and 45 both refer to the Lord's "anointed"; the claim that the Son's throne will "last forever and ever" (Ps 45:6 = Heb 1:8) reminds us of the promise that David's son would reign over an eternal kingdom (2 Sam 7:13 quoted in Heb 1:5b); and the reference to the throne of the Son (Ps 45:6 = Heb 1:8) reflects the installation of God's son as king in Psalm 2:6–7.[5] Finally, Psalm 102:25–27 (quoted in Heb 1:10–12) stresses the eternality of the Son, taking us back to the similar focus in Psalm 45:6 (Heb 1:8): the Son whose throne will "last forever and ever" (Ps 102:24) is the Lord

---

4. E.g., Hugh Montefiore, *A Commentary on the Epistle to the Hebrews*, HNTC (San Francisco: Harper & Row, 1964), 43–44. See the "In Depth" note for discussion of this hypothesis.

5. See, for these connections, John Goldingay, *Psalms 42–89*, vol. 2 of *Psalms*, BCOTWP (Grand Rapids: Baker, 2007), 58; Hans-Joachim Kraus, *Psalms 1–59*, CC (Minneapolis: Fortress, 1993), 455.

"whose years will never end" (102:27 = Heb 1:12).[6] What at first sight, then, might appear as a collection of random quotations appears at closer scrutiny to possess a coherence in terms of focus on key messianic passages that celebrate the exaltation of the Messiah and his intimacy with the God who installs him in his supreme position.

Exegetical Outline

→ **B. Exposition: The Exalted Status of the Son (1:5–14)**
  1. Superior to Angels as Son (vv. 5–7)
  2. Superior to Angels as God (vv. 8–9)
  3. Superior to Angels as Lord (vv. 10–12)
  4. Exaltation (v. 13)
  5. Angels as "Ministering Spirits" (v. 14)

Explanation of the Text

1:5 For to which of the angels did God ever say, "You are my son; I have today begotten you"? And again, "I will be as a father to him, and he will be as a son to me"? (Τίνι γὰρ εἶπέν ποτε τῶν ἀγγέλων, Υἱός μου εἶ σύ, ἐγὼ σήμερον γεγέννηκά σε; καὶ πάλιν, Ἐγὼ ἔσομαι αὐτῷ εἰς πατέρα, καὶ αὐτὸς ἔσται μοι εἰς υἱόν;). The "for" (γάρ) links the following verses to the previous ones, and the specific connection is easy to see: the Son's superiority to the angels will now be elaborated with a series of Old Testament quotations. Angels are sometimes called "sons of God" in the Old Testament (e.g., Gen 6:4, 6 [probably]; Job 1:6; 2:1; 38:7; Ps 29:1; 89:7), but there is only one figure that God calls "my son": the king whom God himself appoints in Psalm 2:7: "I will proclaim the LORD's decree: He said to me, 'You are my son; today I have begotten you.'"[7] This psalm celebrates the installation of the Israelite king (see v. 6) and, in keeping with other ancient Near Eastern peoples, the ruler is called a son of God.[8] The author, along with other Second Temple Jews (see 4Q174 [4QFlor] 1.10–11, 18–19; Pss. Sol. 17.24–30; 18.7) and early Christians (see Matt 3:17; Mark 1:11; Luke 3:22; Acts 4:25–26; 13:33; 2 Pet 1:17; Rev 12:5; 19:15), interpreted this psalm as a reference to the Messiah, an interpretation facilitated by the fact that the king is called the Lord's "anointed" (χριστός; "Christ") in verse 2 of the psalm.[9]

---

6. Despite the argument of L. D. Hurst, the application of this language confirms what the sequence of quotations most naturally suggests: that the one appointed as Son and superior to angels is more than an exalted human ("The Christology of Hebrews 1 and 2," in *The Glory of Christ in the New Testament: Studies in Christology in Memory of George Bradford Caird*, ed. Lincoln D. Hurst and N. T. Wright [Oxford: Clarendon, 1987], 151–64).

7. As he usually does, the author seems to quote from the Old Greek: the LXX wording (which translates the MT accurately) is identical to Hebrews.

8. Peter Craigie labels it a "coronation psalm" (*Psalms 1–50*, WBC 19 [Nashville: Thomas Nelson, 2004], 64). Verse 7 specifically, as John Goldingay puts it, is "a performative declaration of adoption" (*Psalms 1–41*, vol. 1 of *Psalms*, BCOTWP [Grand Rapids: Baker Academic, 2006], 100).

9. In his groundbreaking book, C. H. Dodd identifies Ps 2:7 as one of the "testimonia," key OT texts used by early

The language of "begetting," or "giving birth" (γεννάω), continues the imagery of a royal coronation. The time of this begetting in Hebrews is debated. Many fathers of the church interpret this text in terms of the "eternal generation" of the Son. Other interpreters have naturally thought of the incarnation.[10] However, considering the focus on this event in Hebrews and the probable *inclusio* this proclamation in Hebrews 1:5 forms with Psalm 110:1 in verse 13, the exaltation is probably the moment the author has in view.[11] The Son, of course, has been the Son in one sense through all eternity; but, in another sense, with respect to the work of redemption, the Son is appointed to a new status via resurrection and exaltation (see also Rom 1:3–4).[12] Kenneth Schenck helpfully distinguishes between Jesus's eternal *identity* as the Son and his salvation-historical *role* as Son.[13]

The author quickly adds a second quotation that also uses the father/son relationship to characterize Christ. This quotation is taken from the famous oracle that the Lord delivers to David through the prophet Nathan (2 Sam 7:4–16; 1 Chr 17:3–14). The Lord promises to make David's name great (2 Sam 7:9) and to provide security for his people Israel (vv. 10–11a). David will not be the one to build a "house" for the Lord; rather, the Lord promises to "raise up" David's offspring to build that house. The Lord promises to "establish the throne of his kingdom forever" (v. 13) and goes on to say, "I will be his father, and he will be my son" (v. 14). This prediction has immediate reference to Solomon, David's son, who, of course, builds a "house" (the temple) for the Lord. But, in a manner typical of Old Testament messianic prophecy, the promise made to Solomon the king extends to the ultimate king, the "greater Son of David." In this regard, as with Psalm 2:7, this text was given a messianic application in the Judaism of that time; indeed, 2 Samuel 7:14 is combined with Psalm 2:7 in a messianic sense in a Qumran scroll (4Q174 [4QFlor] 1.10–11). Early Christians interpreted similarly (Luke 1:33; 2 Cor 6:18; Rev 21:7). The author, quoting from the Old Greek, applies this prophecy to Jesus, the Son.

1:6 And when God brings his firstborn into the world, again he says: "Let all the angels of God worship him" (ὅταν δὲ πάλιν εἰσαγάγῃ τὸν πρωτότοκον εἰς τὴν οἰκουμένην, λέγει, Καὶ προσκυνησάτωσαν αὐτῷ πάντες ἄγγελοι θεοῦ). The fact that angels worship the Son is further evidence of his exalted status. The "again" (πάλιν) could go either with the verb "says" (λέγει)—"he says again" (so most English translations)—or with the verb "brings into" (εἰσαγάγῃ)—"he brings again into . . . the world" (NASB; NET). If we translate "bring again into," then the reference could be to the parousia, to Christ's "second" appearance (see Heb 9:28).[14] However, "again" is used in both Judaism and the New Testament elsewhere to connect a series of Old Testament quotations, and this

---

Christians to explain their beliefs (*According to the Scriptures: The Substructure of New Testament Theology* [New York: Charles Scribner's Sons, 1953], 31–32).

10. E.g., Spicq, *L'Épitre aux Hébreux*, 2:16.

11. E.g., Kenneth L. Schenck, "A Celebration of the Enthroned Son: The Catena of Hebrews 1," *JBL* 120 (2001): 472–73 (who thinks all the texts in vv. 5–13 refer to the exalted Christ); Bruce, *Hebrews*, 13; Ellingworth, *Hebrews*, 113–14; Victor (Sung Yul) Rhee, "Christology in Hebrews 1:5–14: The Three Stages of Christ's Existence," *JETS* 59 (2016): 718–19.

12. This christological theme, that "the Son becomes the son," is explored by Jamieson (*Paradox of Sonship*).

13. Kenneth L. Schenck, "Keeping His Appointment: Creation and Enthronement in Hebrews," *JSNT* 66 (1997): 95–100.

14. Westcott, *Hebrews*, 22–23; William R. G. Loader, *Sohn und Hoherpriester: Eine traditionsgeschichtliche Untersuchung zur Christologie des Hebräerbriefes*, WMANT 53 (Neukirchener-Vluyn: Neukirchener, 1981), 24–25.

pattern strongly favors rendering "he says again." This is clear from the fact that the author uses this word to link Old Testament quotations elsewhere (1:5; 2:13; 4:5; 10:30).[15] "Bringing the firstborn into the world" might, then, naturally refer to the incarnation.[16] However, most interpreters think that the author refers to the exaltation of Christ, both because this moment is so central in Hebrews and because it is argued that "world" here (οἰκουμένη) must mean what this word clearly means in 2:5, where the author refers to "the world to come" (τὴν οἰκουμένην τὴν μέλλουσαν).[17] This last argument, however, is not decisive: the fact that the author qualifies the word in 2:5 ("to come") may suggest that the word by itself (as in our v. 6) would have the ordinary meaning "the earth as inhabited area" ("οἰκουμένη," BDAG 699, §1). Indeed, we might question whether the word "world" on its own would have led the readers of Hebrews to think of the new era of redemption: the word always refers elsewhere in the New Testament and LXX to this world. The former argument is a powerful one, however. While, then, I think the decision is much more difficult than many interpreters suggest, we should probably prefer the view that the author here pictures the Son's royal entrance into the new redemptive realm.

Calling the Son the "firstborn" both carries forward the filial imagery so central to this passage and adds a further messianic nuance. "Firstborn" (πρωτότοκος) is used often in a straightforward way to refer to the first person to be born to a set of parents (e.g., Luke 2:7). But because in Israel's culture the firstborn had preeminence and was entitled to a special status as heir, the word was extended to refer to preeminence generally, without reference to physical birth order. We see this usage in Exodus 4:22, which calls Israel God's "firstborn." Particularly relevant to our text is Psalm 89:20–29. In this text, "David my servant" is anointed (v. 20) and calls out to God, "You are my Father" (v. 26). God then promises: "I will appoint him to be my firstborn, the most exalted of the kings of the earth. I will maintain my love to him forever, and my covenant with him will never fail. I will establish his line forever, his throne as long as the heavens endure" (vv. 27–29). The messianic overtones of this passage are clear, as are the allusions to 2 Samuel 7:13–14.[18]

The words quoted in the second part of this verse could come from either a variant Greek version of Deuteronomy 32:43 or from the LXX of Psalm 97:7 (96:7 LXX). The former passage is, frankly, a textual mess, as the footnotes in our English versions reveal. However, we have indirect evidence of a form of the Greek text of this verse identical to Hebrews 1:6b.[19] Psalm 97:7 is similar but uses a second-person imperative instead of

---

15. Most of the English translations take the syntax this way. For "again" used this way, see also John 19:37; Rom 15:10–12; 1 Cor 3:20. Philo also uses the word this way quite often. See Bruce, *Hebrews*, 56; Attridge, *Hebrews*, 55; Lane, *Hebrews*, 1:26.

16. E.g., Attridge, *Hebrews*, 56; Rhee, "Christology," 720–23.

17. See esp. Ardel B. Caneday, "The Eschatological World Already Subjected to the Son: The Οἰκουμένη of Hebrews 1.6 and the Son's Enthronement," in *A Cloud of Witnesses: The Theology of Hebrews in Its Ancient Contexts*, ed. Richard Bauckham et al., LNTS 387 (London: T&T Clark, 2008), 28–39. Madison N. Pierce suggests that οἰκουμενή may refer to the heavenly realm in some psalm texts (Ps 93:1; 96:9–10; 97:4 [LXX 92:1; 95:9-10; 97:4]) (*Divine Discourse in the Epistle to the Hebrews*:

The Recontextualization of Spoken Quotations of Scripture, SNTSMS 178 [Cambridge: Cambridge University Press, 2020], 47–49). Some interpreters (e.g., Lane, *Hebrews*, 1:27; Weiss, *Der Brief an die Hebräer*, 163; Ellingworth, *Hebrews*, 116) discern a typological connection with the "entrance" of the people of Israel into the promised land. But there is insufficient basis for this connection.

18. "Firstborn" (πρωτότοκος) refers to Christ also in Rom 8:29; Col 1:15, 18; cf. Rev 1:5.

19. This Greek text is attested in Odes Sol. 2.43b (a liturgical text drawn from Deut 32): καὶ προσκυνησάτωσαν αὐτῷ πάντες ἄγγελοι θεοῦ (some think that this text is the source for Hebrews [Michael H. Kibbe, *Godly Fear or Ungodly Failure?*

the third-person form found in Hebrews: "do obeisance [προσκυνήσατε] to him, all his angels!" (NETS). Neither Old Testament passage has any obvious messianic reference: Yahweh is the one worshiped by the angels in both texts. All but one of the texts our author quotes in 1:5–13 comes from the Psalms, so we might think that he has quoted here Psalm 97:7 with a minor adaptation. However, Deuteronomy 32, usually called "the Song of Moses," is often quoted in the New Testament, and it is probably a bit more likely therefore that our author quotes from it here.[20] In either case, the author's point is clear: the Son's superiority to the angels is clear from God's call to his angels to worship him. We should not ignore the startling implications of Hebrews's application of this call to worship of the Son: only God is properly the object of worship.

1:7 And with respect to[21] the angels, he says, "He makes his angels spirits and makes his servants a fiery flame" (καὶ πρὸς μὲν τοὺς ἀγγέλους λέγει, Ὁ ποιῶν τοὺς ἀγγέλους αὐτοῦ πνεύματα καὶ τοὺς λειτουργοὺς αὐτοῦ πυρὸς φλόγα). The Old Testament reference to angels as servants again proves the Son's superiority. The author signals that he is continuing to describe angels by beginning this verse with "and" (καί).[22] The Old Testament text comes again from the Psalms, in this case Psalm 104:4 (103:4 LXX). As the context makes clear, the verse is celebrating God's ability to use various parts of the natural world for his own purposes. The NIV translation is representative: "he makes winds his messengers, flames of fire his servants."[23] In the LXX, however, the sequence of words is shifted: it should be translated, "he who makes messengers [or angels] his spirits and his servants a burning fire."[24] The point our author wants to make by citing this verse is not clear. The problem is that two key Greek words each have two different meanings. The word translated "angels" (ἀγγέλους) can also mean "messengers," and the word translated "spirits" (πνεύματα) can also mean "winds." If we accept that the noun with the

---

Hebrews 12 and the Sinai Theophanies, BZNW 216 (Berlin: de Gruyter, 2016), 121–22]). The Hebrew text in 4QDeut is similar. It is quite likely that this Hebrew text, perhaps attested in Odes, was the original text of Deut 32:43 (Cockerill, *Hebrews*, 105–7). See, e.g., the translation in the NLT; and also NRSV; CEB.

20. E.g., David M. Allen, *Deuteronomy and Exhortation in Hebrews: A Study in Narrative Re-Presentation*, WUNT 2/238 (Tübingen: Mohr Siebeck, 2008), 44–52; Radu Gheorghita, *The Role of the Septuagint in Hebrews: An Investigation of Its Influence with Special Consideration to the Use of Hab 2:3–4 in Heb 10:37–38*, WUNT 2/160 (Tübingen: Mohr Siebeck, 2003), 40–43; Ellingworth, *Hebrews*, 118–19; Grässer, *An die Hebräer*, 1:80; Friedrich Schröger, *Der Verfasser des Hebräerbriefes als Schriftausleger*, BU 4 (Regensburg: Pustet, 1968), 50.

21. The Greek behind this English is the preposition πρός, which, as in vv. 8 and 13, might mean "to" (Koester, *Hebrews*, 193). But "concerning" or "about," well-attested meanings for πρός, make better sense here (so most translations; and see Cockerill, *Hebrews*, 108).

22. For the view that καί often indicates simple continuation of thought, see Steven E. Runge, *Discourse Grammar of the Greek New Testament: A Practical Introduction for Teaching and Exegesis*, Lexham Bible Reference Series (Peabody, MA: Hendrickson, 2010), 23–27, 51.

23. As John Goldingay notes, the double noun construction in Hebrew—"his messengers/winds"—means that the second noun indicates "the material from which something is made" (*Psalms 90–150*, vol. 3 of *Psalms*, BCOTWP [Grand Rapids: Baker Academic, 2008], 185).

24. As Wallace points out, the noun with an article will be the direct object in a double accusative construction (*Greek Grammar*, 184). As is often noted, then, the LXX suits the author's argument better than the MT (e.g., Simon Kistemaker, *The Psalm Citations in the Epistle to the Hebrews* [Amsterdam: Free University, 1961], 23–24, 27–28; Schröger, *Der Verfasser des Hebräerbriefes als Schriftausleger*, 262). However, the difference should not be exaggerated, as many do. The only difference between the LXX and the author's version of the quotation comes in the last words. LXX has "a burning fire" (πῦρ φλέγον), while Hebrews has "flames of fire" (πυρὸς φλόγα). The author may have modified his source slightly to create a better match with the plural "servants" (λειτουργούς) (L. Timothy Swinson, "'Wind' and 'Fire' in Hebrews 1:7: A Reflection upon the Use of Psalm 104 (103)," *TJ* 28 [2007]: 219).

article will be the direct object, four options for the translation emerge:[25]

1. "He makes his angels spirits" (NIV; cf. NET; KJV).
2. "He makes his angels winds" (ESV; cf. NRSV; CSB; NLT; NAB; NASB).[26]
3. "He makes his messengers spirits."
4. "He makes his messengers winds."

The last two options suffer from a serious problem: after the introduction to the quotation mentioning "angels," we expect the same Greek word in the quotation to refer to angels also. A decision between the first two options is more difficult. Verse 7 is attached to verses 8–9 in a construction (μέν . . . δέ) that makes clear they are making opposite points. Since verses 8–9 stress the eternal kingdom of the Son, associating the angels with changeable and transitory "winds" would make a lot of sense.[27] However, the author's description of angels as "ministering spirits" (λειτουργικὰ πνεύματα) in verse 14 lends strong support to the other option. The author's use of these two key words (or cognate words) from verse 7 certainly suggests that he picks up this description from the psalm quotation: and only a reference to "spirits" makes sense in verse 14.[28] I think this latter consideration may tilt the scales slightly in favor of translating "spirits" here. In any case, the key point our author makes stands: in contrast to the Son, angels, for all their might and splendor, are, in the last analysis, "servants."

1:8–9 But God says to the Son: "Your throne, God, is forever, and the scepter of justice is the scepter of your kingdom. 9 You have loved righteousness and hated wickedness. Because of this, God, your God, anointed you with the oil of gladness, setting you over your companions" (πρὸς δὲ τὸν υἱόν, Ὁ θρόνος σου ὁ θεὸς εἰς τὸν αἰῶνα τοῦ αἰῶνος, καὶ ἡ ῥάβδος τῆς εὐθύτητος ῥάβδος τῆς βασιλείας σου. 9 ἠγάπησας δικαιοσύνην καὶ ἐμίσησας ἀνομίαν· διὰ τοῦτο ἔχρισέν σε ὁ θεὸς ὁ θεός σου ἔλαιον ἀγαλλιάσεως παρὰ τοὺς μετόχους σου). In contrast to what God says about the angels, the author here tells us what God says to the Son (the δέ at the beginning of v. 8 functions with the μέν in v. 7 to create a contrast).[29] The content of God's speech to the Son comes from Psalm 45:6–7, which, as usual, the author appears to cite from the LXX.[30] Psalm 45 is a royal wedding song.[31] It extols the greatness and goodness of the king (vv. 1–9) before focusing attention on the king's bride (vv. 10–15) and concludes with further praise of the king (vv. 16–17). The quoted text comes amid the initial praise of the king, which, as the quotation shows, takes the form of direct address (the second-person singular is used throughout vv. 2–10). The author was undoubtedly drawn to Psalm 45 because it shares with other texts he cites in this context a focus on the king. There are probably three reasons the author cites these particular verses from the psalm. First, these verses address the king as "God," an important, even climactic, argument for the superiority of the Son to angels. Second, these verses ascribe to

---

25. I therefore eliminate two options that reverse the object/complement relationship: "He uses the spirits for his messengers" (CEB); "appointing the winds his messengers" (NJB). See also Ellingworth, who suggests translating "making winds his angels" (*Hebrews*, 120–21).

26. Lane, *Hebrews*, 1:29.

27. It is not surprising, then, that most commentators support this view; see, e.g., Westcott, *Hebrews*, 25; Attridge, *Hebrews*, 58; Cockerill, *Hebrews*, 108–9.

28. Koester, *Hebrews*, 193–94.

29. The direct address of the Son in vv. 8–9 makes clear that πρός here should be translated "to" (NLT; CSB; CEB; contrast NIV; NRSV; ESV; NET). See, e.g., Koester, *Hebrews*, 194.

30. The relevant verses in the LXX are numbered 44:7–8. The text in Hebrews has only minor stylistic differences from the LXX (e.g., Hebrews adds a καί in the second line in LXX 44:7 and reverses the position of the article in that same line).

31. Goldingay, *Psalms 42–89*, 55.

the king an eternal throne, reminding us of 2 Samuel 7:14 (see Heb 1:5b).³² Third, these verses also use the language of "anointing," which, of course, provides the linguistic basis for "Messiah," "Christ."

The first point needs a brief defense. The New Testament rarely uses the title "God" (θεός) to refer to Christ. Indeed, some scholars claim it never does, arguing that early Christians did not make this kind of direct claim of deity about Christ. This being the case, then, it has been argued that verse 8 does not address the Son as "God"; rather, we should translate "God is your throne" or "your throne is divine."³³ However, in recent years several scholars have argued that the New Testament shows clear evidence of what is called "early high Christology": that Christians began perceiving Christ to be divine quite early in the history of the movement.³⁴ Of course, these scholars are simply reinforcing what most orthodox theologians have argued all along. Certainly, in the case of Hebrews 1:8, the grammatical and contextual arguments for construing "God" as a vocative (as all our English translations do) are quite conclusive.³⁵ As the climax of his argument for the Son's superiority over angels, the author quotes a text that applies the title "God" to the Son.

As I have noted, the author is particularly interested in Psalm 45 because it calls the Son "God," lauds his eternal kingdom, and mentions his "anointing." The other details in the psalm are probably not of particular interest to the author. However, there may be one exception: the claim at the end of the quotation that the anointed one is "above" or "beyond" (παρά) "your companions" (τοὺς μετόχους σου). Our author uses this same Greek word three other times in Hebrews to refer to believers as "partaking" or "participating" in new-covenant benefits (3:1, 14; 6:4; cf. also 12:8). The "companions" Christ is superior to here might, then, be believers, pictured as sharing with Christ in the blessings of his kingdom.³⁶ However, the context might slightly favor a reference to angels.³⁷

1:10–12 And he also says: "You, Lord, in the beginning laid the foundations of the earth, and the heavens are the work of your hands. 11 They will perish, but you remain; they will all wear out like a garment. 12 You will roll them up like a cloak; like a garment they will be changed. But you are the same, and your years will not end" (καί, Σὺ κατ' ἀρχάς, κύριε, τὴν γῆν ἐθεμελίωσας, καὶ ἔργα τῶν χειρῶν σού εἰσιν οἱ οὐρανοί· 11 αὐτοὶ ἀπολοῦνται, σὺ δὲ διαμένεις, καὶ πάντες ὡς ἱμάτιον παλαιωθήσονται, 12 καὶ ὡσεὶ περιβόλαιον ἑλίξεις αὐτούς, ὡς ἱμάτιον

---

32. Kraus notes the parallel between Ps 45:7 and 2 Sam 7:16 (*Psalms 1–59*, 455). He also suggests a parallel between calling the king "God" here and calling him God's "Son" in Ps 2:7 (Heb 1:5a). We might also note that the word "scepter" (ῥάβδος) occurs both in Ps 45:7 and in Ps 2:9, which refers to the king/son ruling all the nations with "an iron scepter" (see Rev 12:5; 19:15). Thompson thinks the focus on "forever" is important, as the author contrasts the eternity of the Son with the transience of angels (*Beginnings of Christian Philosophy*, 134–35).

33. These translations assume that the Greek behind "God" (ὁ θεός) is nominative, functioning as subject—"God is your throne"—or as a predicate noun, with a qualitative force—"Your throne is divine." For the former, see Westcott, *Hebrews*, 25–26; for the latter, see the RSV marginal reading, and its translation of Ps 45:7. OT scholars naturally debate the meaning of Ps 45:7. Goldingay, e.g., translates, "Your throne of God"—that is,

"Your throne is a throne like God's" (*Psalms 42–89*, 53; see also Tremper Longman, *Psalms: An Introduction and Commentary*, TOTC [Downers Grove, IL: IVP Academic, 2014], 202). Kraus, however, defends the vocative reading, noting that, while other ANE cultures described their king as "god," this is the only place in the OT that does so (*Psalms 1–59*, 451–52).

34. See esp. Bauckham, *Jesus and the God of Israel*; N. T. Wright, *Paul and the Faithfulness of God*, 2 vols. (Minneapolis: Fortress, 2013), 2:680–88; Larry W. Hurtado, *One God, One Lord: Early Christian Devotion and Ancient Jewish Monotheism* (London: Bloomsbury T&T Clark, 2015).

35. See esp. Murray J. Harris, *Jesus as God: The New Testament Use of* Theos *in Reference to Jesus* (Grand Rapids: Baker, 1992), 205–27.

36. E.g., Bruce, *Hebrews*, 63; Koester, *Hebrews*, 195.

37. E.g., Attridge, *Hebrews*, 60; Lane, *Hebrews*, 1:30.

καὶ ἀλλαγήσονται· σὺ δὲ ὁ αὐτὸς εἶ καὶ τὰ ἔτη σου οὐκ ἐκλείψουσιν). The Son's exalted status is indicated by his title "Lord," by his role in creation, and by his eternal nature. The "and" (καί) picks up the introductory words in verse 8, signaling that the author is again quoting what God says (see v. 6). We should note that this claim about God himself speaking in the words of this psalm text is typical of the author's view of Scripture. The quotation is again from a psalm, but this time it is not a royal or messianic psalm. Psalm 102 (101 LXX) is a typical lament psalm, opening with the psalmist pouring out his complaint before God (vv. 1–11), followed by an expression of renewed confidence in the Lord who is sovereign over the nations (vv. 12–22). The psalmist again complains in his distress (v. 23) and finishes with a plea that the Lord who controls all of creation would intervene on his behalf (vv. 24–28). The author of Hebrews quotes several lines from this last part of the psalm to identify the Son with the "Lord" who created the universe and who, in contrast to creation, will never perish. There are several differences between the Greek Old Testament and the form of the quotation in Hebrews, but these are probably editorial adaptations to suit the words of the text to their context in Hebrews.[38]

One reason it seems clear that the author is using the LXX is that it uses the title "Lord" (κύριε); there is nothing corresponding in the Hebrew text.[39] This, then, is the first reason why our author cites this particular text: it enables his listeners to complete his trifecta of titles: Christ is "Son" (v. 5), "God" (v. 8), and "Lord." A second reason why this text would have attracted our author's attention is its claim that this Lord "in the beginning[40] laid the foundations of the earth." Here we circle back all the way to the exordium, where the author introduced the Son as the one "through whom . . . he [God] made the universe" (v. 2c). Indeed, this text appears to move one step beyond the claim made in 1:2c. According to this earlier verse, the Son is a mediator of the creative act; it is "through" (διά) him that the universe is made—a claim repeated elsewhere in the New Testament (e.g., John 1:3; 1 Cor 8:6; Col 1:16). Here in 1:10, however, the "Lord," identified with the Son, is the one who creates. As McDonough puts it, then, this text is "perhaps the boldest statement in the entire New Testament concerning Jesus' role in creation."[41] Oscar Cullmann claims that this passage is one of the strongest assertions of Christ's full deity.[42] Of course, the author is not denying the role of the Father in creation, and ultimately we need to recognize that all three persons of the Trinity are involved in creation in various ways. The engagement of all three persons of the Trinity in creation, in a complicated and mysterious process, must be affirmed.

The third, and perhaps most important, reason the author quotes this text is because of its affirmation of the eternality and unchangeableness of the Lord. The earth and the heavens will "perish"; they will "wear out like a garment"; the Lord will "roll them up like a cloak"[43]; they will "be changed." But of the Lord he says, "you remain"; "you are the same, and your years will not end." These contrary

---

38. Kistemaker, *Psalm Citations*, 26–27; Weiss, *Der Brief an die Hebräer*, 167.

39. It is possible, of course, that the LXX is based on a variant Hebrew text that did have "lord" in it (e.g., P. Hughes, *Hebrews*, 67).

40. The Greek is κατ' ἀρχάς, used here as equivalent to ἐν ἀρχῇ (Ellingworth, *Hebrews*, 127).

41. *Christ as Creator*, 205.

42. Oscar Cullmann, *The Christology of the New Testament* (Philadelphia: Westminster, 1963), 98.

43. The language of "rolling up" (the verb is ἑλίξεις, from ἑλίσσω) is not found in the LXX, which refers rather to "change" (ἀλλάξεις, from ἀλλάσσω)—agreeing here with the MT. It is not clear where the author has derived his language: perhaps from a variant Greek text, or perhaps under the influence of Isa 34:4: "All the stars in the sky will be dissolved and the heavens

assertions form a chiasm in verses 11–12, with the outer ends of the passage asserting the unchangeableness of the Lord and the inner lines referring to the transient nature of all created things. As often in the Bible, "earth" and "heavens" (v. 10) is a merism (a literary device that uses a pair of terms to connote a larger whole), referring to the entire created universe. The language that the author uses from the psalm is often thought to indicate a total eradication of created things.[44] However, I am not certain that the text requires this conclusion; in keeping with other New Testament authors, this passage can be read as predicting not an annihilation of the cosmos but its thorough renovation.[45] In any case, the author is not focused here on providing information about the future of the cosmos. The teaching about the mutability of the natural world is designed to set in contrast the immutability of the Son. He rules over a kingdom that will last "forever" (v. 8) as the one whose "years will not end" (v. 12).[46] In what we might identify as yet another *inclusio*, the quotation begins by locating the Son in eternity past—"in the beginning"—and ends with an assertion of his endless future—"your years will not end."[47] The unchanging nature of the Son (7:16), of his work of mediation on behalf of believers (7:23–25), and of the promises that undergird that work (6:17–18) are key emphases in Hebrews, designed to give us "hope," "as an anchor for the soul, firm and secure" (6:19). The author's claim that the Son alone "remains" (using διαμένω) is picked up several times with the cognate verb (μένω): the Son of God "remains a priest forever" (7:3); because Jesus remains, he has "a permanent priesthood" (7:24); believers have possessions that "remain" (10:34); and "what cannot be shaken" remains (12:27). In what might be a grand *inclusio*, embracing most of the letter, the author's claim in our verses 11 and 12, that the Son "remains" and that he "[stays] the same" (σὺ δὲ ὁ αὐτός), is reiterated in the famous words of 13:8: "Jesus Christ is the same yesterday and today and forever."

1:13 And to which of the angels did God ever say, "Sit at my right hand until I place your enemies under your feet"? (πρὸς τίνα δὲ τῶν ἀγγέλων εἴρηκέν ποτε, Κάθου ἐκ δεξιῶν μου, ἕως ἂν θῶ τοὺς ἐχθρούς σου ὑποπόδιον τῶν ποδῶν σου;). The climax of Old Testament evidence about the greatness of the Son in relationship to angels is the invitation to the Son to sit at God's right hand. In an obvious *inclusio*, the author here returns to the introductory language he used to begin this series of quotations in verse 5a: "To which of the angels did God ever say . . . ?" The quotations themselves also form something of an *inclusio*. Both Psalm 2 and Psalm 110 are royal/messianic psalms; and, as Goldingay comments, "Psalm [110] is the twin of Ps. 2."[48] In verse 5a the author quoted Psalm 2:7 to refer to the divine appointment of the Son to

---

rolled up [ἑλιγήσεται] like a scroll; all the starry host will fall like withered leaves from the vine, like shriveled figs from the fig tree." A few MSS in Heb 1:12 read the verb ἀλλάξεις, but the reading is probably secondary, as scribes try to align Hebrews with the LXX (Metzger, *Textual Commentary*, 593).

44. E.g., Edward Adams, *The Stars Will Fall from Heaven: Cosmic Catastrophe in the New Testament and Its World*, LNTS 347 (Edinburgh: T&T Clark, 2007), 183–85; Schenck, *Cosmology and Eschatology*, 124–32; Thompson, *Beginnings of Christian Philosophy*, 136. The notion of a cosmic destruction is often attributed to the author's use of the Platonic contrast between the mutability of created things and the immutability of the spiritual realm—an influence perhaps mediated to the author through Philo (or at least shared between the two).

45. The language in v. 11, "they will perish," appears to be the strongest support for the annihilation view. However, the Gk. word used here (ἀπόλλυμι) need not mean "destroy" or "annihilate" (see, e.g., Douglas J. Moo and Jonathan A. Moo, *Creation Care: A Biblical Theology of the Natural World*, Biblical Theology for Life [Grand Rapids: Zondervan Academic, 2018], 161; and on the larger issue, 146–67).

46. Lane makes this connection (*Hebrews*, 1:30).

47. Kistemaker, *Psalm Citations*, 79.

48. Goldingay, *Psalms 90–150*, 291.

messianic royal rule. Now he quotes Psalm 110:1 to refer to the divine invitation to the Son to assume the highest office in God's kingdom, with all things subjected to him. Occupying the position at God's "right hand"[49] indicates "a real *co-enthronement* of the addressee, that is, a participation in the exercise of YHWH's own royal rule."[50] This notion of dominion and rule is reinforced by the placing of the "enemies" "under the feet"[51] of the Son—an additional link to Psalm 2, which celebrates the king's absolute rule over all the nations (Ps 2:8–9).

Although Psalm 110 is one of the more difficult psalms to interpret, the New Testament appropriation of its opening verse is relatively straightforward. Jesus himself initiated the early Christian use of the verse. After parrying the Jewish leaders' polemical thrusts (Matt 22:15–40), Jesus turns the tables and asks them a question about the Messiah: "Whose son is he?" They respond, "The son of David." Jesus then asks, "How is it then that David, speaking by the Spirit, calls him 'Lord'?" Jesus then quotes Psalm 110:1 to justify this claim: "The Lord [*yhwh*] said to my lord ['*ādōn*]" (Matt 22:41–46; see also Mark 12:35–37; Luke 20:41–44). This interaction suggests that Second Temple Jews were interpreting this verse as a reference to the Messiah, a view Jesus obviously assumes.[52] Early Christians followed Jesus's lead in applying the language of Psalm 110:1 to him, sometimes quoting the verse (Acts 2:33–34) and at other times using the language of "the right hand" or "under his feet" to connote Jesus's exalted status and rule (this application was also first made by Jesus: Matt 26:64; Mark 14:62; Luke 22:69; see also Acts 5:31; 7:55–56; Rom 8:34; 1 Cor 15:25, 27; Eph 1:20; Col 3:1; 1 Pet 3:22). Indeed, Psalm 110:1 is the most often cited Old Testament verse in the New Testament.[53] As we noted in our comments on verse 3, the text plays a central role in the author's argument in this letter.[54] With his formal quotation of the verse here, then, the author returns to the language of verse 3 while at the same time setting before his readers a key building block of his subsequent argument.

1:14 Are not the angels merely ministering spirits sent to serve those who are about to inherit salvation? (οὐχὶ πάντες εἰσὶν λειτουργικὰ πνεύματα εἰς διακονίαν ἀποστελλόμενα διὰ τοὺς μέλλοντας κληρονομεῖν σωτηρίαν;). In contrast to the Son, who initiates salvation, the angels are sent to serve those destined for salvation. The author has used a series of seven Old Testament quotations to reinforce the picture of the Son as an exalted divine figure, a picture first sketched in the exordium (vv. 2b–3). He makes this point by showing that the Son is greater even than the angels, those splendid beings who occupy heaven itself. It is fitting, then, that he concludes this passage with a final reminder of the

---

49. "At my right hand" translates ἐκ δεξιῶν μου, which is what is in the LXX. The noun is neuter plural but means "on the right" or "at the right hand" ("δεξιός," BDAG 217, §1b). There is no difference in meaning between this phrase and the one the author elsewhere uses in quotations and allusions to Ps 110:1, ἐν δεξιᾷ (1:3; 8:1; 10:12; 12:2).

50. Frank-Lothar Hossfeld and Erich Zenger, *Psalms 3: A Commentary on Psalms 101–150*, Hermeneia (Minneapolis: Fortress, 2011), 147.

51. "Under your feet" translates ὑποπόδιον τῶν ποδῶν σου, which again duplicates the LXX. The word ὑποπόδιον means "footstool": the whole phrase means, as BDAG ("ὑποπόδιον," 1040) paraphrases it, "*make someone a footstool for someone*, i.e., subject one pers. to another, so that the other can put a foot on the subject's neck."

52. To be sure, we have little or no direct evidence from Jewish sources dated to the time of Christ that Jews interpreted the verse messianically. But indirect evidence suggests this conclusion (David M. Hay, *Glory at the Right Hand: Psalm 110 in Early Christianity*, SBLMS 18 [Nashville: Abingdon, 1973], 26–33).

53. See Hay, *Glory at the Right Hand*.

54. It is the "unifying thread" (Thompson, "What Has Middle Platonism to Do with Hebrews?," 38; Bauckham, "Divinity of Jesus Christ," 18; and esp. Compton, *Psalm 110*).

subordinate status of angels. They are, he asserts, merely "ministering" spirits.⁵⁵ This phrase echoes the author's quotation of Psalm 104:4 in verse 7b: "he makes his angels spirits [πνεύματα] and makes his servants [τοὺς λειτουργούς] a fiery flame." Their ministry has a particular focus: it is to "serve (εἰς διακονίαν) those who are about to inherit salvation." The word translated "about" (μέλλοντας) comes from a verb that Hebrews often uses to refer to the realities of the eschatological consummation (2:5, 6:5; 10:1, 27; 13:14; see also 8:5; 11:8, 20). Angels are sent by God to serve believers as they await the coming salvation. Salvation in the ultimate sense of final deliverance from sin and death is clear in another text in Hebrews: "Christ was sacrificed once to take away the sins of many; and he will appear a second time, not to bear sin, but to bring salvation to those who are waiting for him" (9:28). Other occurrences of "salvation" language in Hebrews do not clearly refer either to the present or the future (σωτηρία in 2:3, 10; 5:9; 6:9 [cf. 11:7]; σώζω ["save"] in 7:25 [cf. 5:7]).

Theology in Application

Salvation "Already" and "Not Yet"

It may seem odd to some that the author would claim that believers are waiting to inherit salvation. Many of us are used to saying things such as "I was saved as a senior in college." Salvation is something we already possess. There is no problem in speaking this way; the New Testament sometimes also refers to salvation as already experienced. See, for example, Romans 8:24: "in this hope we were saved." However, more often New Testament writers use the language of salvation—"save," "salvation," "Savior"—to refer to the ultimate deliverance from sin and death that we will experience when our bodies are transformed. This perspective is very clear in Romans 13:11b, where Paul reminds the Roman Christians that "salvation is nearer now than when we first believed."

Our experience of salvation therefore follows a pattern that is fundamental to the eschatological perspective of the New Testament. This perspective is based on the nature of God's intervention to fulfill his Old Testament promises about what he would do in the "last times" (the *eschata*, "last things": hence "*eschat*ology"). This fulfillment comes at two decisive moments, one associated with Christ's first coming and another with his second coming. We often rather inelegantly use the contrast of the "already" and the "not yet" to refer to this fundamental framework of God's redemptive work.

---

55. Following most English versions, I use "ministering" to translate the adjective λειτουργικά because this word, and its cognates (λειτουργέω ["serve"], λειτουργία ["service"], and λειτουργός ["servant"]) especially connote ritual and cultic service. All six occurrences of this word in the LXX have this sense (Exod 31:10; 39:12; Num 4:12, 26; 7:5; 2 Chr 24:14); and see, in Hebrews, the occurrences of these cognate words: 8:2, 6; 9:21; 10:11. Philo refers to "ministering angels" (ἄγγελοι λειτουργοί, *Virtues* 74).

As we have seen above, salvation language in Hebrews twice clearly refers to this "not yet" side of our experience (1:14; 9:28). The other occurrences of the language in Hebrews do not clearly refer to either the "already" or the "not yet." Jesus is the "pioneer of [our] salvation" (2:10), the "source of eternal salvation" (5:9); the one who is "able to save completely those who come to God through him" (7:25); he has secured a "great salvation" for us (2:3; see also 6:9). These passages may focus on salvation in general, perhaps in both its present and future aspects. (See comments on these verses for more discussion.) The pattern of eschatological fulfillment we find in Hebrews's use of salvation language extends to other key concepts in his letter as well, where it is often difficult to determine which "moment" he might have in view.

The tension of the already versus the not yet shapes the spiritual reality we believers live in. It is particularly vital to maintain a perspective that keeps these moments in balance. On the one hand, we rejoice in the many blessings we already experience in our union with Christ. We are regenerated, filled with God's Spirit, and put securely on the road to ultimate salvation. On the other hand, we are not yet "glorified," our bodies have not been transformed, we face the reality of physical death (if we die before the Lord's return), and we remain subject to the influence of sin. If we focus on the first "moment" at the expense of the second, we can foolishly imagine that we have already "arrived"; that we can just sit back and enjoy our new status, failing to come to grips with the continuing influence of sin. On the other hand, if we focus on the second "moment" at the expense of the first, we can fall into despair, forgetting to celebrate and live out the decisive change of status that has happened at our conversion.

IN DEPTH: The Old Testament in Hebrews[56]

The author's argument in Hebrews takes the form of an extended interaction with and application of the Old Testament Scriptures.[57] The clearest evidence of this feature of the book comes in its formal quotations, which number around thirty-five.[58] The author quotes the Pentateuch thirteen times; the Historical

---

56. For a survey of this issue, see, e.g., Benjamin J. Ribbens and Michael H. Kibbe, "'He Still Speaks!' The Authority of Scripture in Hebrews," in *Authoritative Writings in Early Judaism and Early Christianity*, ed. Tobias Nicklas and Jens Schröter, WUNT 2/441 (Tübingen: Mohr Siebeck, 2020), 189–207. See also Trotter, *Interpreting the Epistle to the Hebrews*, 190–202; George H. Guthrie, "Hebrews' Use of the Old Testament: Recent Trends in Research," *CurBR* 1 (2003): 271–94; Guthrie, "Hebrews" (2007), 919–95; Dana M. Harris, "The Use of the Old Testament in the Epistle to the Hebrews," *SwJT* 64 (2021): 91–106.

57. Markus-Liborius Hermann argues that the density of interaction with Scripture in Hebrews far exceeds that in any other New Testament book (*Die "Hermeneutische Stunde" des Hebräerbriefes: Schriftauslegung in Spannusngfelder*, HBS 72 [Freiburg: Herder, 2013], 124).

58. The question of which OT references rise to the level of a formal "quotation" and about how to count combined quotations means that scholars end up with different totals, ranging from twenty-nine to thirty-nine (see Gheorghita, *Role of the Septuagint*, 32).

Books once; the Prophets six times; and the Psalms an impressive seventeen times. The regular verbal agreement between the Greek text found in the Old Testament and the Greek text of Hebrews shows that he is using a Greek text that is close to the LXX. It should be stressed that agreement in specifics such as the order of Greek words (which is highly variable in Greek) makes quite clear that there is a literary relationship between Hebrews and the LXX. We have to remember at this point that, technically speaking, the author could not be citing the LXX: the name "Septuagint" designates a form of the Greek text found in the great uncials Alexandrinus (A), Sinaiticus (א), and Vaticanus (B)—and these uncials were produced by Christian scribes in the fourth and fifth centuries CE. However, it is clear that the text form we find in these uncials goes back in time to the first century and earlier, so we can follow most scholars and refer to this developing text form as the LXX.

While the author's quotations generally follow this LXX text quite closely, there are disagreements—most of them minor but a few more substantive.[59] These deviations can be explained in several ways. A few scholars think that the author may have used a Hebrew text in these places.[60] However, most see no clear evidence of the author ever using a Hebrew text. Another explanation is that our author is following the text found in a "testimony book." By this we mean a document that circulated widely in early Christianity, containing a series of Old Testament texts regularly used by Christian apologists and preachers. The appeal to a "testimony book" to explain some phenomena in New Testament quotations of the Old had its defenders early in the twentieth century,[61] but the hypothesis was given fresh impetus when documents of this nature were found among the Dead Sea Scrolls.[62] This hypothesis, however, is now generally dismissed also. However, while we should probably not think of a "testimony *book*," the idea that early Christians identified and regularly appealed to a set of Old Testament texts to explain their faith makes a good deal of sense. C. H. Dodd argued this hypothesis in his well-known book *According*

---

59. Within the LXX tradition, the author's text stands a bit closer to that found in Alexandrinus (Weiss, *Der Brief an die Hebräer*, 173). For a brief overview of (relatively) current LXX studies with reference to Hebrews, see Susan E. Docherty, *The Use of the Old Testament in Hebrews: A Case Study in Early Jewish Bible Interpretation*, WUNT 2/260 (Tübingen: Mohr Siebeck, 2009), 121–32. And for a thorough analysis of the author's quotations and their relationships to various textual traditions, see Gert J. Steyn, *A Quest for the Assumed LXX Vorlage of the Explicit Quotations in Hebrews*, FRLANT 235 (Göttingen: Vandenhoeck & Ruprecht, 2011).

60. The contact of Hebrews with Hebrew texts need not be direct; Laansma, e.g., notes that the author might have been influenced by others who had such contact ("Hebrews: Yesterday, Today, and Future," 11).

61. See esp. J. Rendel Harris, *Testimonies* (Cambridge: Cambridge University Press, 1920); and, for Hebrews, F. C. Synge, *Hebrews and the Scriptures* (London: SPCK, 1959).

62. The documents are 4QTestimonia and 4QFlorilegium.

to the Scriptures, and it is worth noting that, of the fifteen "testimonia" he identified, five are found in Hebrews.[63] We are reminded therefore that, for all the author's exegetical ingenuity, his use of the Old Testament has deep roots in the larger early Christian movement.

The Dead Sea Scrolls have influenced our evaluation of the textual basis of New Testament quotations in another important way. Among these scrolls were found biblical manuscripts with a Hebrew text different than the "official" Masoretic Text but agreeing with the LXX. These discoveries have made clear that several textual traditions, in both Hebrew and Greek, were circulating in the first century.[64] Therefore, places where the author's quotations disagree with the LXX might reflect a Greek textual tradition differing a bit from the LXX. Finally, as is usually the case when one quotes a source, minor differences between the LXX and the author's quotations might be due simply to his own editorial work, adapting the quotations to their context.

The introductions to the quotations in Hebrews say a lot about the author's view of the Old Testament. He never uses the formula familiar from other New Testament books, "as it is written." Instead, the author prefers verbs of speaking. Moreover, the author consistently highlights the divine author, as is evident in chapter 1: "To which of the angels did *God* ever say" (vv. 5a, 13a); "he [God] says" (vv. 6, 7, 8, 10; see also 4:3, 4, 7; 5:5, 6; 6:13; 7:21; 8:8; 10:30; 12:26, 27; 13:5).[65] One quotation is introduced with "the Holy Spirit says" (3:7), and two others indicate that it is the Spirit who reveals truth in Old Testament texts (9:8; 10:15). The quotation of Jeremiah 31:31–34 is attributed to "God" in 8:8 but to the Holy Spirit in 10:15. The focus on the divine speaker in Scripture is reinforced by the author's apparent unconcern about the human and historical aspect of the Old Testament. He mentions a specific human author of Scripture only once (4:7), referring once to "someone" (2:6); twice he introduces a quotation by claiming it is found "somewhere" in the Old Testament (2:6; 4:4). At the same time, the author is happy to claim that Christ himself speaks the words of some Old Testament texts he quotes (2:12–13; 10:5, 30a). The author therefore clearly has a "high" view of Scripture. His focus on the decisive

---

63. Dodd, *According to the Scriptures*, 31–57.

64. This point is emphasized by Georg A. Walser, *Old Testament Quotations in Hebrews: Studies in Their Textual and Contextual Background*, WUNT 2/356 (Tübingen: Mohr Siebeck, 2013), 8–13, and throughout the book.

65. Some of these lack an explicit reference to "God," but the context makes clear that the speaker is God. It should also be noted that several of these texts are, in fact, spoken by God in the OT texts that are cited. In general, it should also be noted that the author engages in what some are calling "prosopological" exegesis, in which the words of Scripture are put on the lips of one divine being, who then addresses another (e.g., 1:5, 8–9, 10–12, 13; 2:12; 5:5, 6; 7:17, 21; 10:5–7). See esp. Pierce, *Divine Discourse*. For another exploration of prosopological exegesis, see Matthew W. Bates, *The Hermeneutics of the Apostolic Proclamation: The Center of Paul's Method of Scriptural Interpretation* (Waco, TX: Baylor University Press, 2012).

nature of God's "new" work in Christ should not obscure this point. The author balances "contrast" with "continuity" in his handling of Scripture.[66]

These quotation introductions underline the "living and active" (4:12) nature of Scripture in our author's viewpoint. Scripture, as the author uses it, speaks directly and immediately to his audience: its words refer to Christ and the spiritual realities he has introduced.[67] A focus on the (past) "written" nature of Scripture in most of the rest of the New Testament gives way to a (present) "speaking" focus.[68] A corollary is often drawn: our author has no interest in the historical context of Scripture. This, however, may be going too far. To claim that God addresses his people directly in Scripture does not necessarily mean that the author has deliberately abandoned the "concursive" view of Scripture, as a text produced equally by God and humans.[69] Moreover, the author at several points indicates his awareness of the historical context of the texts he cites: he knows that the warning about entering God's "rest" (Ps 95:7-11) had its background in the wilderness wandering of the Israelites (Heb 3:16-18) and that it came long after God's original "rest" (Gen 2:2; see Heb 4:3-4, 7); he knows the history of the promise given to Abraham (6:13-14); he refers to the narrative context of the Melchizedek story (Gen 14:18-20; cf. Heb 7:4-10); he notes in 8:5 that Exodus 25:40 was a warning to Moses; and he goes into great detail in describing the Old Testament "heroes of the faith" (Heb 11). These are all quite obvious, but they should be noted lest we think the author reads the Old Testament purely ahistorically. Treier is right: "Hebrews, it seems, freely finds correspondences between past and present generations of God's people that allow for pastoral application and fresh theological insight, without negating the historical particularity of the prior text."[70] This pattern is labeled "typology."[71] Some of these contemporary applications may not exactly match the intention of the text in its original context. As Calvin notes (commenting on the use of Ps 8 in Heb 2:6-8), "it was not the purpose of the apostle to give

---

66. See esp. Jonathan I. Griffiths, *Hebrews and Divine Speech*, LNTS 507 (London: Bloomsbury, 2014), e.g., 61.

67. For this emphasis, see esp. Gene R. Smillie, "'The Word of God' in the Book of Hebrews" (PhD diss., Trinity Evangelical Divinity School, 2000); Gregory W. Lee, *Today When You Hear His Voice: Scripture, the Covenants, and the People of God* (Grand Rapids: Eerdmans, 2016), esp. 196-217; David Peterson, "God and Scripture in Hebrews," in *The Trustworthiness of God: Perspectives on the Nature of Scripture*, ed. Paul Helm and Carl R. Trueman (Grand Rapids: Eerdmans, 2002), 120-22.

68. Hermann, *Die "Hermeneutische Stunde" des Hebräerbriefes*, 125, etc.

69. Some support for this concursive view of inspiration might come from 4:7, where Ps 95:7-8 is attributed to God, who "spoke through David."

70. Daniel J. Treier, "Speech Acts, Hearing Hearts, and Other Senses: The Doctrine of Scripture Practiced in Hebrews," in Bauckham et al., *Epistle to the Hebrews*, 343. See also G. Hughes, *Hebrews and Hermeneutics*, 63-66.

71. Goppelt claims that the many comparisons between old and new in Hebrews are typological and that Hebrews makes more use of typology than any other NT book (Leonhard Goppelt, *Typos: The Typological Interpretation of the Old Testament in the New* [Grand Rapids: Eerdmans, 1982], 176).

an accurate exposition of the words [of Ps 8]. There is nothing improper if he looks for allusions in the words to embellish the case he is presenting."[72]

The author also engages in a kind of "vertical typology," comparing earthly matters to heavenly ones—most famously, in his claims about the tabernacle (8:1–6). It has often been thought that the author is here using the distinctive "image/reality" contrast typical of Platonic philosophy and extensively utilized by Philo of Alexandria. However, comparison with Philo is not really appropriate because the author locates this vertical comparison solidly within an overall horizontal salvation-historical reading of Scripture.[73]

Of course, the influence of the Old Testament on our author's argument goes far beyond quotations. He often alludes to scriptural passages and, most obviously, much of his explicit argument takes the form of an interpretation and application of key Old Testament texts: the meaning and significance of Psalm 8:4–6 (Heb 2:6–9), Psalm 95:7–11, combined with Genesis 2:2 (Heb 3:7–4:11); Psalm 110:4 and Genesis 14:18–20 (Heb 7); the Old Testament provisions for tabernacle, covenant, and sacrifice (8:1–10:18); the "heroes" of the Old Testament (ch. 11); and the giving of the law at Sinai (12:18–21).[74] Schnelle is right: "a theology of the word is the guideline that begins with the prologue of 1:1–4 and proceeds throughout the entire writing."[75] An equally important, but more subtle, influence of the Old Testament on Hebrews is the author's reliance on basic patterns of thinking exhibited in Scripture. For instance, David Allen has persuasively argued for a fundamental "deuteronomic" structure in the way the author presents the divine-human relationship.[76]

In applying these texts to the author's situation, he is following the pattern of other Jewish interpreters of Scripture in his day. The Dead Sea Scrolls have, again, shed fresh light on this process, as we find in several of the scrolls a kind of "this is that" (or *pesher*) approach to Scripture: "this" (what the prophet wrote about) is "that" (what has transpired in the life of the community). Many scholars have compared Hebrews's use of Scripture with these patterns, and there is no question that the author's techniques for appropriating Scripture resemble those of his Jewish contemporaries. However, the author's appropriation of the Old Testament is ultimately rooted in his particular "hermeneutical axioms": fundamental theological convictions about the final "word" that God

---

72. John Calvin, *The Epistle of Paul the Apostle to the Hebrews and the First and Second Epistles of St. Peter*, Calvin's Commentaries (Grand Rapids: Eerdmans, 1963), 22.

73. See, e.g., Gerhardus Vos, *The Teaching of the Epistle to the Hebrews* (Grand Rapids: Eerdmans, 1956), 56–58; Goppelt, *Typos*, 166–68; G. Hughes, *Hebrews and Hermeneutics*, 35–47.

74. See esp. Gheorghita, *Role of the Septuagint*.

75. Udo Schnelle, *Theology of the New Testament* (Grand Rapids: Baker Academic, 2020), 633.

76. Allen, *Deuteronomy and Exhortation*; see also Kibbe, *Godly Fear*, 120–36.

has revealed in his Son (1:1–2), which is authoritatively determinative for the ultimate meaning of Scripture.[77] We do not have evidence, then, that our author labored to study the Old Testament in its original context like a modern exegete might do. However, granted his hermeneutical assumptions about the unity of Scripture and the christological shape of its ultimate meaning, we can justify our author's hermeneutical approach.[78]

Moreover, at the end of the day, what is particularly impressive about the author's appropriation of Scripture is the way he appears to be massively focused on reading the Old Testament in its own right. In contrast to some, we find little evidence of the influence of other Jewish traditions on our author's interpretation of Scripture. He seems to us rather to be working intensely with the Old Testament text itself, discovering in it what he sees as God's own word for his struggling readers.

---

77. For an elaboration of this distinction between "appropriation techniques" and "hermeneutical axioms" with reference to the NT use of the OT, see Douglas J. Moo, *The Old Testament in the Gospel Passion Narratives* (Sheffield: Almond Press, 1983; repr., Eugene, OR: Wipf & Stock, 2008), 5–78.

78. For a broader study of this issue, see Douglas J. Moo and Andrew Naselli, "The Problem of the New Testament's Use of the Old Testament," in Carson, *Enduring Authority*, 702–46.

Chapter 3

Hebrews 2:1–4

Literary Context

As we saw in our discussion of the structure of Hebrews above (pp. 16–17), the author, like a good preacher, has interspersed his exposition with admonition: teaching gives way frequently to preaching. The first of these preaching texts comes in 2:1–4. A "therefore" reveals that the author draws a conclusion here from his exposition of Christ's exalted status and superiority to angels in chapter 1. Obvious verbal and conceptual links with this previous chapter cement this relationship. Our author began his sermon by pointing out that God's previous ways of speaking (using λαλέω) have come to climactic expression in his speaking to us "in [his] Son" (1:1–2a). This same contrast is central to the author's warning in 2:1–4: if failure to obey God's previous speaking, in his law, resulted in punishment, how do believers think they will "escape" if they ignore his final and decisive word? A second connection with the context is the language of "salvation" that concludes chapter 1 (v. 14) and is now used as a way of summarizing the content of God's final word (2:3). Third, the comparison with angels is continued: the superiority of the Son to angels (1:5–14) means that the revelation associated with the Son is greater than the revelation God gave his people through angels (2:2).

I. The Exalted Son and a Rest for the People of God (1:1–4:13)
  A. Exordium (1:1–4)
  B. Exposition: The Exalted Status of the Son (1:5–14)
→ **C. Exhortation: Take Hold of Your Great Salvation (2:1–4)**
  D. Exposition: The Humanity of the Son and Its Significance (2:5–18)
  E. Exhortation: Focus on the Faithful Son (3:1–6)
  F. Exhortation: Avoid the Fate of the Wilderness Generation (3:7–4:11)
  G. Exposition: The Power of the Word of God (4:12–13)
II. Our Great High Priest and His Ministry (4:14–10:31)
III. Exhortation: Follow and Serve the Pioneer of Our Faith through Endurance and Faith (10:32–13:25)

Main Idea

The supreme and final revelation of God's salvation means that God's people must pay careful attention to that revelation.

Translation

Hebrews 2:1–4

1a	inference (from ch. 1)	Therefore	
1b	exhortation	**it is necessary for us**	
1c	content		to pay very careful attention
1d	content		to what we have heard,
1e	purpose		lest we drift away.
2a	basis (for 1)	For	
2b	contrast (with 3a)		if the word . . .
2c	description		that was spoken through angels
2d	assertion		. . . was valid and
2e	parallel (to 2b)		every transgression and act of disobedience received a just penalty,
3a	rhetorical question	**how will we escape**	
3b	condition		if we neglect such a great salvation?
3c	expansion (of 3b)		This salvation,
3d	description		which was first spoken through the Lord,
3e	assertion		has been validated to us
3f	agency		by those who heard him. And
4a	parallel (to 3c–e)		God is testifying to it
4b	means		by signs and wonders and
4c	means		by various miracles and
4d	means		by distributions of the Holy Spirit,
4e	manner		in accordance with God's will.

Structure

This short paragraph falls into three parts. The main point comes in the first verse, where the author exhorts his readers to pay careful attention to what they have heard so that they don't lose their standing with Christ. He grounds this exhortation in one of his typical comparisons (vv. 2–3a): if God punished those who disobeyed his earlier word, how much more will he punish those who ignore God's final word, which speaks of his definitive salvation? Third, he reinforces the greatness of this salvation by reminding his readers of its origin in the Lord, its proclamation by those who heard the Lord, and the miraculous gifts that have accompanied it (vv. 3b–4).

Exegetical Outline

→ **C. Exhortation: Take Hold of Your Great Salvation (2:1–4)**
  1. Exhortation to Pay Attention to God's Final Word (v. 1)
  2. Warning about Neglecting God's Salvation (vv. 2–3a)
  3. The Origin of and Attestation to Salvation (vv. 3b–4)

Explanation of the Text

2:1 Therefore it is necessary for us to pay very careful attention to what we have heard, lest we drift away (Διὰ τοῦτο δεῖ περισσοτέρως προσέχειν ἡμᾶς τοῖς ἀκουσθεῖσιν, μήποτε παραρυῶμεν). Our response to the greatness of the Son should be devoted attention to the message about the Son. With his "therefore" (διὰ τοῦτο) the author ties the exhortation in this verse to his teaching in chapter 1. What the readers have "heard" is nothing less than God's climactic "speaking" in and through his Son (1:2a). The importance of this "speaking" is underlined by the exalted, even divine status of the Son (1:2b–13). What believers need to do, then, is to "pay attention" to this word: to "believe and act upon what is heard."[1] The present tense of the verb behind "pay attention" (προσέχειν) suggests a continual effort to appropriate God's word. We can't know if our author had the text in view as he wrote this, but Deuteronomy 32:46 at any rate indicates the kind of broad-based Old Testament theme that undoubtedly has influenced our author: "[Moses] said to them, 'Take to heart all the words I have solemnly declared to you this day, so that you may command your children to obey carefully all the words of this law'" (see also, e.g., Acts 8:6; 2 Pet 1:19).[2] In translating "pay very careful attention," I understand the comparative adverb the author uses here (περισσοτέρως) to have an elative sense—that is, it simply emphasizes the verbal idea. This interpretation is reflected in the NIV ("pay the most careful attention") and NLT ("listen very carefully").[3] Most translations, however, take the word to have its normal comparative force; for example, ESV: "we must pay much closer attention." In this case, the comparison would presumably be with the readers' current attitude.

By paying careful attention to the word they have already heard, the readers will be kept from "drifting away." We hear now for the first time the pastoral concern that drives the entire argument of

---

1. Moffatt, *Hebrews*, 17.
2. The verb the author uses (προσέχω) is so common in the LXX that it in itself provides insufficient basis to connect the verses.

3. See, e.g., Moffatt, *Hebrews*, 17. On the "elative" use of comparative forms, see, e.g., Heinrich von Siebenthal, *Ancient Greek Grammar for the Study of the New Testament* (New York: Lang, 2019), 201–2.

the letter: the readers by growing lax and careless in their attention to God's word may begin to "drift away" and so, if their course is not reversed, fall away from God's grace in Christ. It is common to think that the author is employing a nautical metaphor at this point: believers need to stay in place (e.g., keep securely tied to the dock) so that they won't drift away (like a rowboat one forgets to tie up for the night).[4] Both Greek words, to be sure, are sometimes applied to the world of boating in this way. However, both words are also used with no reference at all to boats. We may, then, be dealing with a "dead metaphor" here—that is, an original association with a particular conceptual world that is lost over time.[5]

2:2–3a For if the word that was spoken through angels was valid and every transgression and act of disobedience received a just penalty, 3 how will we escape if we neglect such a great salvation? (εἰ γὰρ ὁ δι' ἀγγέλων λαληθεὶς λόγος ἐγένετο βέβαιος καὶ πᾶσα παράβασις καὶ παρακοὴ ἔλαβεν ἔνδικον μισθαποδοσίαν, 3 πῶς ἡμεῖς ἐκφευξόμεθα τηλικαύτης ἀμελήσαντες σωτηρίας). The reason ("for," γάρ) it is important to pay such close attention to "what [they] have heard" is that the word they have heard threatens an even more certain and final punishment than did the Old Testament law. "The word that was spoken through angels" refers, then, to the Old Testament law. No canonical Old Testament text refers to angels as mediators of God's law to his people, but the belief that angels were present at the giving of the law is widespread, and a few texts refer to angelic mediation of the law—including two New Testament texts (Acts 7:53; Gal 3:19).[6] The author introduces the angels to enhance the status of the law and, in light of the argument of chapter 1, it is clear he also has in view the grand comparison in that chapter between angels and the Son. Implicitly he is saying, if the revelation of God "in the past" (1:1) through angels could bring punishment for disobedience, how much greater will be the punishment for those who neglect his climactic revelation "in [his] Son" (1:2a)!

The author describes the law as "valid" (βέβαιος), a word with legal connotations; as the CSB translates, "the message spoken through angels was legally binding."[7] Its formal legal standing means that deviations from its prescriptions were appropriately met with a "penalty" (μισθαποδοσίαν) that was "just" (ἔνδικον)—more legal terminology.[8] The author uses two words to describe these deviations: "transgression" and "act of disobedience." The former (παράβασις) refers to the breaking of a law or commandment one knows one is responsible for, the latter (παρακοή) to any act of disobedience.[9] Some interpreters have tried to find a distinct connotation for each term here,[10] but it is more likely that the author uses two relatively parallel words to enhance his point.

---

4. E.g., Koester, *Hebrews*, 205.

5. Ellingworth, *Hebrews*, 137; Grässer, *An die Hebräer*, 1:100. The case for a nautical flavor in the first word, παρέχω, is hard to make, since it is used many times in the NT and LXX without any such association. The issue is harder to decide in the case of the second verb, παρερ[ρ]υέω, since the verb is rare, and one of the two of its LXX occurrences refers to water (Isa 44:4; see also Prov 3:21; the verb does not occur elsewhere in the NT).

6. The LXX of Deut 33:2 refers to angels appearing with Yahweh when he gave the law to the people. See also, e.g., Jub. 1.27, 29; 2.1.

7. See Lane, *Hebrews*, 1:37; Attridge, *Hebrews*, 65. See also Heb 3:14; 6:19; 9:17.

8. The former word means "recompense," sometimes favorable (as in Heb 10:35 and 11:26), sometimes unfavorable (here). The word ἔνδικος, which occurs only here and in Rom 3:8 in the NT, means "just" or "deserved."

9. The word παράβασις occurs also in Heb 9:15 (see also Rom 2:23; 4:5; 5:14; Gal 3:19; 1 Tim 2:14), while παρακοή occurs in Rom 5:19; 2 Cor 10:6.

10. E.g., it has been suggested that the former has in view sins of commission, the latter sins of omission (Spicq, *L'Epître aux Hébreux*, 67; Attridge, *Hebrews*, 65 [as possible]).

The "if X, how much more Y" logic (often described in the Latin *a minore ad maius*, "from the lesser to the greater") that is so basic to the author's argument surfaces here again with the combination "if [v. 2a] . . . how [v. 3a]." As the Old Testament repeatedly and forcefully makes clear, God did indeed punish failure to obey his law with appropriate and just retribution. After graciously rescuing his people Israel from slavery in Egypt, he gave them his law as a means of securing a life of prosperity in the promised land. The people, however, failed to follow his law, and God was therefore quite "just" to bring the punishment of exile—a punishment he had warned about from the beginning—on the people. Whatever his readers' background (see pp. 7–12), our author clearly assumes they know this history. And that history should strike fear into the hearts of those in his audience who are failing to take God's message in Christ seriously: they can expect, our author implies, serious consequences.[11] The argument here is repeated with even stronger language in 10:28–31:

> Anyone who rejected the law of Moses died without mercy on the testimony of two or three witnesses. How much more severely do you think someone deserves to be punished who has trampled the Son of God underfoot, who has treated as an unholy thing the blood of the covenant that sanctified them, and who has insulted the Spirit of grace? For we know him who said, "It is mine to avenge; I will repay," and again, "The Lord will judge his people." It is a dreadful thing to fall into the hands of the living God.

One unusual feature of verse 3 is the reference to "such a great salvation."[12] Granted the logic of the author's argument, we would have expected here a reference to God's ultimate "word" or "speaking" in his Son: as disobedience of God's first *word* was punished, so ignoring his second and climatic *word* will be punished. In order to preserve a closer parallelism, we might perhaps think the author refers here to "the message of salvation."[13] But it is also possible that, under the influence of verse 14, the author shifts almost unconsciously from the message to that great gift the message ultimately refers to and mediates. The author worries that his readers may be "neglecting" this salvation by forgetting both the incredible gift it truly is and the need to respond to the gift with worship and obedience. The author does not, at least in this text, indicate that his readers are actually guilty of such "neglect"; the participle involved is probably conditional in force: hence the translation "if we neglect" or "if we ignore" in English translations.[14] But the author would not say what he does here if he was not worried that his readers might be heading in this direction.

2:3b–4 This salvation, which was first spoken through the Lord, has been validated to us by those who heard him. And God is testifying to it by signs and wonders and by various miracles and by distributions of the Holy Spirit, in accordance with God's will (ἥτις ἀρχὴν λαβοῦσα λαλεῖσθαι διὰ τοῦ κυρίου ὑπὸ τῶν ἀκουσάντων εἰς ἡμᾶς ἐβεβαιώθη, συνεπιμαρτυροῦντος τοῦ θεοῦ σημείοις τε καὶ τέρασιν καὶ ποικίλαις δυνάμεσιν

---

11. The "penalty" for ignoring God's final word in his Son may not be greater in kind but rather even more certain (Cockerill, *Hebrews*, 120–21). Granted the parallel warnings in Hebrews, what is escaped from here is not discipline but salvation itself. Contra Thomas Kem Oberholtzer, "The Warning Passages of Hebrews, Part 1: The Eschatological Salvation of Hebrews 1:5–2:5," *BSac* 145 (1988): 95–97.

12. "Such a great" translates τηλικαύτης (see also 2 Cor 1:10; Jas 3:4; Rev 16:18).

13. Ellingworth, *Hebrews*, 139.

14. See, e.g., Zerwick and Grosvenor, *Grammatical Analysis*, 656.

καὶ πνεύματος ἁγίου μερισμοῖς κατὰ τὴν αὐτοῦ θέλησιν). The reality of salvation is clear from the message passed on to the readers and confirmed by accompanying Spirit-wrought miracles. In the Greek text, verse 3c is connected to verse 3b with a relative pronoun (ἥτις, which agrees with its antecedent σωτηρίας).[15] However, it is better for English style to start a new sentence, replacing the pronoun with its antecedent to mark the continuity. The purpose of verses 3b–4 is to underscore the reality of salvation by showing how it has been "validated." This verb (ἐβεβαιώθη, from βεβαιόω) is cognate to the adjective "valid" (βέβαιος), which our author applied to the law in verse 2. Just as the law received a "stamp of authenticity" because it was mediated by angels, so also the salvation the author refers to is authenticated by its mediators (v. 3b) and by the miraculous signs that have accompanied it (v. 4). The readers should have no doubt about the reality and significance of the salvation they have experienced.

The author cites three stages in the transmission of salvation. It "was first[16] spoken through the Lord." If we define "spoken" strictly, the reference here could be to the teaching of the earthly Jesus or to his proclamation of the completed work of salvation after his resurrection (Matt 28:18; Luke 24:25–27, 46–47).[17] And the clause following this at the end of verse 3 could suggest this narrow meaning of "speak." However, what is "spoken" here is not the word but "salvation," and this opens the way to think that the verb here (λαλεῖσθαι, from λαλέω) might refer to events that "proclaim" or "reveal" truth. See Hebrews 11:4, where the author claims that Abel, though dead, "still speaks [λαλεῖ]," or 12:24, where he says that "the sprinkled blood" (of Jesus's sacrifice) "speaks [λαλοῦντι] a better word than the blood of Abel." Here, then, the author might refer broadly both to Christ's teaching and to the events of his ministry that secured salvation: "the Son's incarnation, teaching, sacrificial death, exaltation, and session are the origin of this salvation and the content of its proclamation."[18]

The second stage of the proclamation of salvation comes with those "who heard him": the first generation of Christ followers.[19] These early believers, in turn, "validated" this salvation by faithfully passing the message on to the audience of Hebrews (cf. 13:7). This chain of transmission, our author suggests, gives the readers every reason to put their full confidence in the salvation they have experienced and shows how foolish it is for them to neglect it in any way.

In verse 4, the author adds a final "testimony" to the reality and significance of salvation: God himself has "testified to it" by miraculous signs.[20] The author uses a rare double-compound verb to indicate this "testifying" (συνεπιμαρτυρέω), both prefixes, perhaps adding something to the meaning: "the witness of events accompanies (σύν-) and

---

15. The use of the indefinite relative pronoun (instead of the definite relative pronoun ἥ) may connote a qualitative idea, "which is of the nature of" (Grässer, *An die Hebräer*, 1:105), but probably simply is a manifestation of the tendency in Hebrews's day for the indefinite relative to be used as equivalent to the definite (e.g., Wallace, *Greek Grammar*, 344–45).

16. "First" translates a participial clause, ἀρχὴν λαβοῦσα, straightforwardly "taking beginning," which here means "at first" ("ἀρχή," BDAG 137, 1.a). The infinitive λαλεῖσθαι is then to be construed as epexegetic of ἀρχήν.

17. See Koester, *Hebrews*, 210–11, for the former view; Ellingworth, *Hebrews*, 140, for this latter view.

18. Rissi, *Die Theologie des Hebräerbriefs*, 3; Cockerill, *Hebrews*, 121; see also Backhaus, *Der Hebräerbrief*, 107; Grässer, *An die Hebräer*, 1:106.

19. This first generation would, of course, include apostles, but I hesitate to use the word here because the author never mentions them.

20. The author uses a genitive absolute construction, συνεπιμαρτυροῦντος τοῦ θεοῦ, which probably picks up the main focus, "salvation."

adds to (-επι-) the witness of words."²¹ The present form of the participle may also suggest that God's testifying through miracles is continuing in the life of the community.²² These witnessers include, first, "signs and wonders," a phrase that evokes the miracles God performed when he brought his people Israel out of Egypt (e.g., Deut 4:34; 6:22; Ps 135:9; Acts 7:36) and that is taken up again to describe the miracles accompanying the proclamation of the New Testament "exodus" from sin (Acts 2:22, 43; 4:30; 5:12; 14:3; 15:12; Rom 15:19; 2 Cor 12:12).²³ A second, related, means of testimony consists of "various miracles" (ποικίλαις δυνάμεσιν), which are generally similar to the "signs and wonders" the author already mentioned.²⁴ Third, God's testimony to salvation comes through "distributions" (μερισμοῖς) of the Holy Spirit. The reference is probably to what we know from other New Testament passages as "the gifts of the Spirit"; most translations accordingly translate with "gifts" here. All these testifying marks of salvation are given in accordance with God's will. The author will elsewhere mention the miraculous work of God and manifestations of the Holy Spirit to indicate the importance of salvation and the consequent extreme seriousness of neglecting or rejecting it (6:4–5).

Theology in Application

Drifting

As we will see as we move through Hebrews, it is not easy to identify precisely the spiritual problem that the author warns about. Some texts suggest a deliberate decision to renounce the faith. Other texts suggest the problem is a failure to move forward in the Christian life. And still others seem to point to a gradual lessening of spiritual fervor. Hebrews 2:1–4 clearly falls into this last category. The author warns his readers about "neglecting" the salvation they have experienced and urges them to pay very careful attention to the word, lest they "drift away." As we saw in the exegesis, this word is often thought to have a nautical flavor, bringing to our mind's eye the unmoored boat drifting slowly from shore. One suspects that certain practically minded interpreters are prone to see this metaphor here because it preaches so well. Indeed, I have warned my students for years about "homiletical expediency": selecting an interpretation of the text not on the basis of the data but on the basis of which view will preach the best.

So we can't be sure that a nautical metaphor is here. However, whether we think the author is conjuring up boats for us or not, his warning about "drifting away" is clear enough. I suspect that most of us find gradual drifting to be a greater danger

---

21. Ellingworth, *Hebrews*, 141.
22. Lane, *Hebrews*, 1:39.
23. "Signs and wonders" translates σημείοις τε καὶ τέρασιν. The dative of these words, as well as δυνάμεσιν and μερισμοῖς that follow, indicate the means by which God testifies.

24. The word δύναμις is, in fact, often used in parallel to "signs and wonders" (e.g., Acts 2:22; 2 Cor 12:12) or to "signs" (Acts 8:13). Here, however, δυνάμεσιν is grammatically separate from "signs and wonders," the latter two being joined with the particle τε.

to our faith than the temptation to outright apostasy. We live in a world with a bewildering variety of distractions, ranging from the sinful—pornography, greed, lust for power—to the neutral—golf, biking, baking—to the positive—family, yes, even ministry. Each of these holds the potential to keep our attention from being focused on the spiritual. As C. S. Lewis once said, when he hears someone claim that they "are making their way in the world," he fears that what actually is happening is that "the world is making its way in them."[25] The remedy for such drift, our author suggests, is a renewed concentration on the message of salvation that God has transmitted to us.

---

25. C. S. Lewis, *The Screwtape Letters* (New York: Macmillan, 1950), 143.

Chapter 4

Hebrews 2:5–9

Literary Context

In 1:14, the author adds a final comment on the Old Testament quotations of verses 5–13, summing up a key theme of these texts: the angels, subordinate to the Son, are sent to serve "those who will inherit salvation." In 2:1–4, the author turns directly to his audience to express, for the first time, his concern about his readers reaching this ultimate goal of salvation. Now, in 2:5, the author returns to the comparison of the Son and angels that dominated 1:4–13, picking up particularly the language of subordinating "enemies" under the Son's feet from 1:13. Some interpreters think that the comparison is the overall theme of 2:5–18. They point to an *inclusio*, with angels mentioned in both verse 5 and verse 16.[1] However, it should be noted that these verses refer to the angels for quite different purposes. Following the model of 1:3–13, 2:5 asserts the supremacy of the Son over angels. But verse 16 compares angels with humans, not with the Son. This difference in rhetorical purpose suggests that we have here, at most, a literary *inclusio*. Angels appear again in the quotation and application of Psalm 8 in verses 7 and 9, but it is striking that the author does not pick this point up in his application of the text.

I therefore doubt that comparison with angels is the focus of verses 5–18. What they *do* clearly focus on is the humanity and suffering of the Son. In the first part of the passage, verses 5–9, the author uses Psalm 8 to characterize Jesus as the "ultimate human," the one to whom God has subjected all things. In verses 10–18, the author continues to argue that Jesus shares fully in the human condition, qualifying him to become a "merciful and faithful high priest" (v. 17) and enabling him to identify with other humans in their testing (v. 18). Woven into this exposition of Jesus's humanity

---

1. E.g., M. Harris summarizes ch. 1 as "Jesus Superior to Angels as God" and ch. 2 as "Jesus Superior to Angels as Man" (*Jesus as God*, 207). R. T. France ("Hebrews," in *The Expositor's Bible Commentary*, ed. Tremper Longman and David E. Garland [Grand Rapids: Zondervan, 2006], 35) places all of 1:5–2:18 under the heading "Better Than the Angels." See also Vanhoye, *Situation du Christ*, 256; G. Guthrie, *Structure of Hebrews*, 119. Among those who identify the *inclusio* are Lane, *Hebrews*, 1:44; Ellingworth, *Hebrews*, 143; Grässer, *An die Hebräer*, 1:113.

is the suffering he endures as a human (vv. 9, 10, 14). Verse 9 summarizes the central point our author is making in this passage: it is "because he suffered death" that Jesus is "now crowned with glory and honor." The author has painted a picture of the Son in chapter 1 as a glorious, majestic being; he is both "Lord" and "God," the one who is promised victory over all his enemies (Ps 110:1 in v. 13). "How," the readers may well be asking, "do we square this vision with the reality of suffering we are experiencing?" (see 10:32–35; 12:4–13). The sequence of redemptive events in the experience of Jesus, "the pioneer of [our] salvation" (2:10), helps us understand this circumstance. He leads his people through the sequence he himself experienced: suffering that gives way to glory. But of equal (or even more) importance, Jesus provides the way to move through that sequence: his atoning death "break[s] the power of him who holds the power of death" and sets his followers free from "fear of death" (vv. 14, 15).[2]

I. **The Exalted Son and a Rest for the People of God (1:1–4:13)**
   A. Exordium (1:1–4)
   B. Exposition: The Exalted Status of the Son (1:5–14)
   C. Exhortation: Take Hold of Your Great Salvation (2:1–4)
   D. Exposition: The Humanity of the Son and Its Significance (2:5–18)
      1. **The Son of Man of Psalm 8 (2:5–9)**
      2. Jesus's Identification with Humans (2:10–18)
   E. Exhortation: Focus on the Faithful Son (3:1–6)
   F. Exhortation: Avoid the Fate of the Wilderness Generation (3:7–4:11)
   G. Exposition: The Power of the Word of God (4:12–13)
II. Our Great High Priest and His Ministry (4:14–10:31)
III. Exhortation: Follow and Serve the Pioneer of Our Faith through Endurance and Faith (10:32–13:25)

Main Idea

The promise that humans would have everything put under their feet from Psalm 8 is fulfilled in Jesus, the true and ultimate human, who, because of his atoning death, is now "crowned with glory and honor."

---

2. For this general view of 2:5–18, see, e.g., Backhaus, *Der Hebräerbrief*, 112–14; G. Hughes, *Hebrews and Hermeneutics*, 58, 82–83; Westcott, *Hebrews*, 41.

Translation

Hebrews 2:5–9

5a	explanation (of 1:13)	For
5b	assertion	it is not to angels that
5c	object of 5a	**he has subjected the world to come**,
5d	identification	about which we are speaking.
6a	verification (of 5)	And
6b	assertion	**someone somewhere has born witness**
6c	reference	to this point:
6d	rhetorical question	"What is man that you are mindful of him, or
6e	parallel (to 6d)	the son of man that you are concerned about him?
7a	basis (for 6d–e)	You have made him
7b	degree	a little lower than the angels,
7c	manner	with glory and honor
7d	parallel (to 7a)	you have crowned him;
8a	extent (or object)	all things
8b	parallel with 7a, d	you have subjected
8c	location	under his feet." (Ps 8:4–6)
8d	restatement (of 8a–c)	In making everything subject to him,
8e	explanation	**nothing was left**
8f	identification	not subject to him.
8g	contrast (with 8a–c)	But
8h	time	now
8i	assertion	**we do not yet see everything subject to him.**
9a	contrast (with 8d–f)	But
9b	time	for a little while
9c	circumstance	made lower than the angels
9d	assertion	**we see Jesus**,
9e	description	who,
9f	cause	because of the suffering of death
9g	assertion	is crowned
9h	manner	with glory and honor,
9i	purpose (of 9b)	so that . . .
9j	means	by the grace of God
9k	assertion	. . . he might taste death for everyone.

Structure

The passage falls into three obvious parts. Verse 5 uses the concept of "subjection" to link the quotation of Psalm 110:1 in Hebrews 1:13 to the quotation of Psalm 8:4–6 in Hebrews 2:6–8a. The quotation itself, then, is the second part. In the third part, verses 8b–9, the author draws out the meaning of Psalm 8 for Jesus.

Exegetical Outline

➡ **1. The Son of Man of Psalm 8 (2:5–9)**
  a. The Subjection of All Things Not Fulfilled by Angels (v. 5)
  b. The Subjection of All Things Fulfilled in Humans (Ps 8) (vv. 6–8a)
  c. The Subjection of All Things Fulfilled in Jesus, the Ultimate Human (vv. 8b–9)

Explanation of the Text

2:5 For it is not to angels that he has subjected the world to come, about which we are speaking (Οὐ γὰρ ἀγγέλοις ὑπέταξεν τὴν οἰκουμένην τὴν μέλλουσαν, περὶ ἧς λαλοῦμεν). The author returns to his comparison between the Son and angels—only the Son has been installed as vice-regent over the realm of salvation. The connection between this verse and the context, indicated by "for" (γάρ), is not with the immediately preceding verses but with 1:13.[3] In that verse, the author climaxed his series of Old Testament quotations with a pivotal reference to Psalm 110:1: "sit at my right hand until I make your enemies a footstool for your feet." The author picks up the concept of "subjection" from that text and, in keeping with the underlying logic of 1:4–13, reminds us that this subjection was not promised to angels. He does not here complete the idea by identifying the person to whom it *was* subjected, but both the previous and following contexts make clear who that is. What is "subjected," claims the author, is "the world to come" (τὴν οἰκουμένην τὴν μέλλουσαν). As I noted in our comments on 1:6, the Greek word refers to "the inhabited world" and is not used in an eschatological sense anywhere else. The timing of this new world is uncertain, manifesting again the notorious problem of pinning down the focus on the "already" versus the "not yet" in Hebrews's eschatology. If we stress the temporal force of "coming" from the author's perspective, we might conclude that the author thinks of this world as yet future.[4] However, the author uses this same verb (μέλλω) elsewhere to refer to things that are "in the process of fully coming": "the coming age" (6:5); "the good things that are coming" (10:1);

---

3. The conjunction γάρ often creates a connection with material earlier in a discourse or narrative. For Hebrews, see esp. Attridge, *Hebrews*, 69–70n.

4. Ellingworth, *Hebrews*, 146; G. Hughes, *Hebrews and Hermeneutics*, 81–82.

"the city that is to come" (13:14). Probably, then (at the risk of avoiding a decision by affirming both options), the "coming world" has been inaugurated but awaits its consummated state.[5] The Son's dominion has begun (see v. 9) but is not yet absolute, as it one day will be (1 Cor 15:24–28).

2:6–8c And someone somewhere has born witness to this point: "What is man that you are mindful of him, or the son of man that you are concerned about him? 7 You have made him a little lower than the angels, with glory and honor you have crowned him; 8 you have subjected all things under his feet" (διεμαρτύρατο δέ πού τις λέγων, Τί ἐστιν ἄνθρωπος ὅτι μιμνήσκῃ αὐτοῦ, ἢ υἱὸς ἀνθρώπου ὅτι ἐπισκέπτῃ αὐτόν; 7 ἠλάττωσας αὐτὸν βραχύ τι παρ' ἀγγέλους, δόξῃ καὶ τιμῇ ἐστεφάνωσας αὐτόν, 8 πάντα ὑπέταξας ὑποκάτω τῶν ποδῶν αὐτοῦ).[6] The Old Testament claims that human beings have been given a status only slightly lower than the angels, with all things "subjected" to them. The author's apparent disinterest in the original context of Scripture reaches its apex in this introductory formula. The author may implicitly be pointing us to the divine author,[7] or he may want to draw attention to the quotation itself.[8] However, this way of introducing quotations has a precedent in Philo, and it is possible the author simply assumes his readers know the context.[9] The author quotes Psalm 8:4–6 (8:5–7 LXX), following the LXX letter by letter, with the exception that he omits the first part of verse 6 ("you have given him dominion over the works of your hands"). The LXX, in turn, faithfully renders the Hebrew—with one possible exception. As the text quoted above indicates, the author, following his source, claims that the Lord has made humans "a little lower than the angels." In place of LXX "angels," the MT has the customary Hebrew word for "God," 'ĕlōhîm. Several versions therefore translate Psalm 8:5 as "you have made them a little lower than God" (NRSV; see also NLT; CSB; NASB). Yet this plural Hebrew word can also denote "heavenly beings" or "angels"; see NIV: "you have made them a little lower than the angels" (see also ESV, "heavenly beings"). This latter interpretation may be preferable; as Kraus puts it, the psalm is teaching that "human beings have their station, given to them by God in creation, immediately below the heavenly beings that surround Yahweh's royal throne."[10] The LXX "angels," taken over by Hebrews, may then capture the original sense pretty accurately.

Psalm 8 has a substantive and verbal connection to Psalm 110:1: as the latter speaks of the "lord" having enemies made a "footstool for your feet" (LXX ὑποπόδιον τῶν ποδῶν σου), so Psalm 8:6 refers to man/the son of man having all things "subjected under his feet" (πάντα ὑπέταξας ὑποκάτω τῶν ποδῶν αὐτοῦ). This parallelism was observed by others in the early church: these verses are combined also in 1 Corinthians 15:25–28 and 1 Peter 3:22 (see also Eph 1:22; Phil 3:21). Clearly

---

5. Delitzsch, *Hebrews*, 1:102.

6. I have used masculine singular forms to translate equivalent forms in Greek for the purpose of commenting on the text. I would seek a more "gender accurate" translation for other purposes—though the challenge of such a translation that maintains the integrity of the text may be more difficult here than anywhere in Scripture (as the abundance of footnotes in the NIV of these verses attests).

7. Koester, *Hebrews*, 213–14.

8. Delitzsch, *Hebrews*, 1:104 ("like a grand pictured figure in the plainest, narrowest, frame"). It might also be noted that the use of πού when introducing quotations is found in classical and LXX Greek ("πού," BDAG 858, §1).

9. Attridge, *Hebrews*, 70–71. See, e.g., Philo, *Drunkenness* 61: "For someone somewhere says . . ." (my translation; the Greek is εἶπε γάρ πού τις).

10. Kraus, *Psalms 1–59*, 183. For the view that the Hebrew here refers to God, see, e.g., Allen P. Ross, *A Commentary on the Psalms*, 3 vols., Kregel Exegetical Library (Grand Rapids: Kregel, 2011), 1:296.

early believers saw in these texts a prefiguration of the Messiah's universal rule.

In typical Hebrew poetic fashion, Psalm 8 uses "man" and "son of man" in parallel to mean the same thing: a "human being," "human beings in general" (see, e.g., the NIV translation of Ps 8:4). The debated question is how the author to Hebrews read this parallel. In light of the ubiquitous use of "son of man" in the Gospels to refer to Jesus, many interpreters think the author read "son of man" as a direct—or at least an implicit—reference to Jesus. On this view, the application in verse 9 focuses on timing: we do not "yet" see Jesus with everything under his feet. He is reigning, but that reign is largely hidden at the present time.[11] Other interpreters, however, doubt that the author thought "son of man" in Psalm 8 was a direct reference to Jesus. They note that the author does not elsewhere use this phrase as a title for Jesus and that, unlike the Gospel references to Jesus as "Son of Man," the text here does not use articles on either word.[12] On this view, then, the author is quoting the psalm in accordance with its original intent: as a celebration of the status of human beings, given to us when God first created humans "in his image" (Gen 1:26, 28). The force of the author's application would then focus on "Jesus" (v. 9): we don't see humans ruling the universe, but we do see *Jesus* doing so, "crowned with glory and honor."[13] On the whole, I think this second interpretation is preferable. Our author is, then, implicitly identifying Jesus as the representative human, to whom has been given the universal dominion of Psalm 8.[14]

2:8d-9 In making everything subject to him, nothing was left not subject to him. But now we do not yet see everything subject to him. 9 But for a little while made lower than the angels we see Jesus, who because of the suffering of death is crowned with glory and honor, so that by the grace of God he might taste death for everyone (ἐν τῷ γὰρ ὑποτάξαι αὐτῷ τὰ πάντα οὐδὲν ἀφῆκεν αὐτῷ ἀνυπότακτον. νῦν δὲ οὔπω ὁρῶμεν αὐτῷ τὰ πάντα ὑποτεταγμένα· 9 τὸν δὲ βραχύ τι παρ' ἀγγέλους ἠλαττωμένον βλέπομεν Ἰησοῦν διὰ τὸ πάθημα τοῦ θανάτου δόξῃ καὶ τιμῇ ἐστεφανωμένον, ὅπως χάριτι θεοῦ ὑπὲρ παντὸς γεύσηται θανάτου). In verses 8d-9, the author applies the Psalm 8 text to Jesus. His focus, as we have noticed, is the subjection of all things and the related exalted

---

11. See esp. George H. Guthrie and Russell D. Quinn, "A Discourse Analysis of the Use of Psalm 8:4-6 in Hebrews 2:5-9," *JETS* 49 (2006): 235-46; also, e.g., Bruce, *Hebrews*, 72-73; Attridge, *Hebrews*, 72; Jason Maston, "'What Is Man?': An Argument for the Christological Reading of Psalm 8 in Hebrews 2," *ZNW* 112 (2021): 89-104.

I should note that several interpreters take a nuanced approach to this issue, suggesting that, while the author reads "son of man" as a reference to humans in general, the title as a reference to Christ would surely have been known by the author and that it therefore provides a kind of bridge to a christological application. See, e.g., David M. Moffitt, *Atonement and the Logic of Resurrection in the Epistle to the Hebrews*, NovTSup 141 (Leiden: Brill, 2011), 125-27; France, "Hebrews," 50-51 (and, in greater detail, France, "The Son of Man in Hebrews 2:6: A Dilemma for the Translator," in *New Testament Theology in Light of the Church's Mission: Essays in Honor of I. Howard Marshall*, ed. Jon C. Laansma, Grant R. Osborne, and Ray van Neste [Eugene, OR: Cascade, 2011], 81-96); Koester, *Hebrews*, 215-16.

12. Although the strength of this point is considerably mitigated by the fact that the author is quoting a source.

13. Jamieson (*Jesus' Death and Heavenly Offering*, 100-102) notes the importance of the emphatic "Jesus" in support of this view. See also, e.g., Lane, *Hebrews*, 1:47; Cockerill, *Hebrews*, 128; Matthew C. Easter, *Faith and the Faithfulness of Jesus in Hebrews*, SNTSMS 160 (Cambridge: Cambridge University Press, 2014), 35-45. Schenck suggests that the failure of humans to have assumed dominion is the key "problem" that the story of God's plan in Hebrews is designed to solve (*Cosmology and Eschatology*, 44, 54-59).

14. It should be stressed that, as a "representative" human, Jesus does not exhaust the meaning of the dominion spoken of in Ps 8 (and Gen 1). The mandate to "rule" still applies to humans in general. Our author's point is that this mandate is not perfectly fulfilled in any other human.

position ascribed to humans that are finding their fulfillment in Jesus, the quintessential human. In verse 8d, the author makes clear that the "all things" subjected to "him" does, indeed, include everything.[15] In keeping with the "representative human" view I advocated above, I take both pronouns in this half verse—"him . . . him" (αὐτῷ . . . αὐτῷ)—as references to a generic human being, appropriately rendered in some English versions as plurals (NIV; NLT; NRSV; CEB).

The author next identifies the one spoken of in Psalm 8 as "made a little lower than the angels" as Jesus.[16] This is the first occurrence of "Jesus" in the letter. The letter to the Hebrews uses the name "Jesus" absolutely far more often, percentage-wise, than any other New Testament letter (see also 3:1; 4:14; 6:20; 7:22; 10:19; 12:2, 24; 13:12; see also "Jesus Christ" in 10:10; 13:8, 21 and "the Lord Jesus" in 13:20).[17] The author often uses the name when he wants to draw attention to Jesus as human (as here), and, as here, "Jesus" is often introduced in emphatic expressions (the fact that the name appears last in its clause in Greek may suggest this emphasis). If we take the "representative human" interpretation of the author's application of Psalm 8, then the name is indeed emphatic here: we do not see all things subjected to *humans* in general, but we do see *Jesus*. The alternative interpretation focuses not on a shift in subject but on a shift in time. We do "not yet" (οὔπω) see all things subjected to "him" (Jesus), but (by the eyes of faith) we see Jesus in his exalted position, and that exalted status will be manifest to all in the future.[18] As Lane notes, then, the author sees three phases of Christ's existence in Psalm 8: incarnation ("lower than the angels"), exaltation ("crowned with glory and honor"), and final victory ("all things subject to him").[19] While the presence of the "not yet" language provides some basis for this temporal-oriented interpretation, it is odd that our author does not follow through with an explicit reference to the future manifestation of glory. The emphasis seems to be rather on the contrast between the one to whom all things are not now subjected and Jesus, "crowned with glory and honor."

This glory and honor, however, comes only after Jesus had been "made a little lower than the angels"—that is, his earthly existence. In an elaboration of this point, our author claims that the glory Jesus now enjoys came "because of the suffering of death."[20] The author here makes reference to the familiar New Testament humiliation-exaltation sequence. "All those who exalt themselves will be humbled, and those who humble themselves will be exalted" (Luke 18:14b). The most famous christological application of this principle is, of course, Philippians 2:6–11. In that text, as here in Hebrews, exaltation does not simply follow humiliation; the humiliation is *the cause* of the exaltation (διά with accusative is the construction

---

15. The infinitive clause that begins this clause—ἐν τῷ . . . ὑποτάξαι—might be causal (Turner, *Syntax*, 146), but more likely it is elliptical, the full idea being "now when the text I quoted refers to 'all things submitted to him,' it means. . . ." Most English versions use temporal language to make this point; e.g., NIV: "in putting everything under them."

16. "For a little while" translates βραχύ τι, a phrase that could have a spatial sense—see KJV: "made a little lower"—but probably has a temporal sense here in Hebrews—"made for a little time lower"; see, basically, all modern translations and most commentators (although Cockerill, *Hebrews*, 132–33, is an exception: he thinks Hebrews preserves the original spatial sense: the Hebrew of Ps 8:5 [8:6 MT, מְעַט] almost certainly has a spatial sense).

17. "Jesus" on its own, of course, appears everywhere in the Gospels, and also in Acts, especially the earlier chapters.

18. Alone among the translations, NIV does not have a "not yet" or "yet" to represent οὔπω.

19. Lane, *Hebrews*, 1:48.

20. I assume, therefore, that διὰ τὸ πάθημα τοῦ θανάτου (the genitive is expexegetic) modifies ἐστεφανωμένον: "crowned because of the suffering that consists in death."

here in Hebrews; in Phil 2:9, the conjunction διό expresses this relationship). The author then elaborates by briefly alluding to the significance of and reason for Jesus's death: "so that by the grace of God[21] he might taste death for everyone." This clause may depend on "for a little while made lower" or on the whole sequence of christological events in the verse.[22] "Taste death" does not refer to a superficial acquaintance with death; indeed, either one is dead or one is not: it is by nature a binary matter. Rather, it means simply to experience death (NET), to suffer death (see CSB). In using the phrase "for everyone" (ὑπὲρ παντός), the author picks up common New Testament language for the vicarious nature of Jesus's death: it was "on behalf of" (ὑπέρ) others.[23] Many texts elaborate on the exact way Jesus's death positively affects us, and the author will briefly do the same thing in verses 14–15, 17, and extensively later in the letter. But he is obviously not interested here in developing a theology of the atonement. Nevertheless, two aspects of that atoning death are suggested here: it took place through the grace of God, and it was universal in its significance.[24]

Theology in Application

Jesus as Representative Human

Psalm 8, as we have seen, is a song of praise that celebrates the majesty of God. It is framed by the refrain "how majestic is your name in all the earth" (vv. 1, 9). Embedded within this song is a reflection on the nature of human beings within creation (vv. 3–8). These verses clearly pick up the foundational language about the creation of humans in Genesis 1. Psalm 8:6a (which our author does not quote) says, "You have made them [humans] rulers over the works of your hands," and the psalm goes

---

21. An interesting textual variant here is χωρις θεου, "apart from God." It is sparsely supported (one uncial, 0243, one minuscule, 1739), but is intriguing because it is clearly "the more difficult reading," a basic criterion of textual evaluation. It was also known in the early church: see, e.g., Theodore of Mopsuestia, quoted in *Hebrews*, ed. Erik M. Heen and Philip D. W. Krey, ACCS 10 (Downers Grove, IL: InterVarsity Press, 2005), 38–39. No major translation adopts the reading, and it has little support among modern scholars (though see Sebastian Fuhrmann, *Vergeben und Vergessen: Christologie und Neuer Bund im Hebräerbrief*, WMANT 113 [Neukirchener/Vluyn: Neukirchener, 2007], 68–70; Rissi, *Die Theologie des Hebräerbriefs*, 77–78; Christopher A. Richardson, *Pioneer and Perfecter of Faith: Jesus' Faith as the Climax of Israel's History in the Epistle to the Hebrews*, WUNT 2/338 [Tübingen: Mohr Siebeck, 2012], 25–28 [weakly]; Michel [*Der Brief an die Hebräer*, 109–12] thinks the reading is possible).

22. For the former (which I slightly favor), see Lane, *Hebrews* 1:49; for the latter, see Attridge, *Hebrews*, 76; Jean Massonnet, *L'Épître aux Hébreux*, ConBNT (Paris: du Cerf, 2016), 88.

23. See, e.g., Luke 22:20; John 6:51; 11:50–51; Rom 5:8; 8:34; 1 Cor 15:3; Gal 2:20; Titus 2:14.

24. The nature of this significance is, of course, much debated. Some argue that this universalism must be qualified in some way, referring, perhaps, only to the elect (such a view is compatible with the theological position known as "limited atonement"); cf. P. Hughes, *Hebrews*, 93n77: ὑπὲρ παντός here is equivalent to ὑπὲρ ἡμῶν πάντων, "on behalf of all of *us*." The claim that God is bringing "many" sons to glory in v. 10 might support a restrictive meaning. Others insist that the language should be given an unlimited universality, implying that Christ's death was intended to be effective for all humanity. It was popular in the patristic period to understand παντός as a neuter, so that the clause would refer to Christ's redemptive work for all of creation. However, we would expect the plural πάντα had this been our author's intention.

on to enumerate the creatures over which humans have dominion, classifying those creatures in categories similar to Genesis 1:26. The author of Hebrews, of course, is quite narrowly focused on the significance of these verses for the life of Christ, using them to portray his incarnation and subsequent exaltation. This temporal shift is not obvious in Psalm 8, which portrays humans from two sides: a little lower than the angels but also crowned with glory and honor.

Our author, as I have argued, applies Psalm 8 to Christ on the basis of seeing him as a representative, or quintessential, human: Jesus is what a human was truly designed to look like. His sinless life and benevolent, self-giving rule embody the "image of God" in which God created humans. One point to emerge from this is that we need to appreciate the true humanity of Jesus and understand its significance for theology and the life of discipleship (more on this in the next section of the letter). But here I want briefly to note the broader theological basis for the author's identification of Jesus as the ultimate human. Paul exposes the foundation of this interpretation by comparing Christ to Adam. Christ is a "second Adam," obeying where the first Adam disobeyed and thereby reversing the death and devastation the first Adam brought into the world (Rom 5:12–21; 1 Cor 15:39–50). Building on this foundation, Paul can then describe the Christian community as the "new man," in contrast to the "old man," the solidarity of humans in death with Adam (Rom 6:6; Eph 4:19–25; Col 3:9–10; see also Eph 2:15 and 4:13). These texts reveal a "representative human" way of looking at Christ that could serve as the hermeneutical platform for our author's application of Psalm 8 to Christ. What might first appear to be an arbitrary interpretation of the Old Testament text is seen, in a larger theological light, to be a reasonable application of the text.

CHAPTER 5

Hebrews 2:10–18

Literary Context

This paragraph is one of the most difficult to fit into the logical flow of the argument in Hebrews—as is evident from the diverse explanations of its place in the letter. Some view it as an excursus; others as a fundamental text for the rest of the letter.[1] My view leans toward the latter end of the spectrum. On the one hand, therefore, the passage is a kind of "add-on" to verses 5–9, explaining further the identification of Jesus with humans ("made lower than the angels for a little while") and how his death benefits sinful humans (v. 9). However, on the other hand, the passage introduces several words and concepts that are developed later in Hebrews: Jesus as the "pioneer" of our salvation (v. 10; see 12:2); the concept of "perfection" (v. 10; the concept appears again and again in Hebrews); the "sanctifying" or "being made holy" purpose of Christ's death (v. 11; see, e.g., 10:10, 14, 29; 13:12); the solidarity of Christ with sinful humans, enabling him to be a "merciful" high priest (v. 17; see 5:1–10); and, above all, the identification of Jesus as our high priest (v. 17), which becomes the dominant christological and soteriological perspective of the letter. The text therefore elaborates key points from verses 5–9 but also introduces words and concepts that lay the foundation for much that is to come in Hebrews's argument.

As Weiss notes, the paragraph intriguingly combines two different soteriologies, or we might say, theories of atonement: the *"archēgos"* ("pioneer") idea of leading people in triumph over an enemy (vv. 10, 14–15), and the *"archiereus"* ("high priest") idea of providing for forgiveness of sins by sacrifice.[2] To put this in historical theological terms, then, this passage combines perspectives from the "classic" *Christus Victor* view of the atonement along with hints of the "penal substitution" view.

---

1. Koester, e.g., sees 2:10–18 as the first main argument of the letter (*Hebrews*, 224–25).

2. Weiss, *Der Brief an die Hebräer*, 203.

I. **The Exalted Son and a Rest for the People of God (1:1–4:13)**
   A. Exordium (1:1–4)
   B. Exposition: The Exalted Status of the Son (1:5–14)
   C. Exhortation: Take Hold of Your Great Salvation (2:1–4)
   D. Exposition: The Humanity of the Son and Its Significance (2:5–18)
      1. The Son of Man of Psalm 8 (2:5–9)
      2. **Jesus's Identification with Humans (2:10–18)**
   E. Exhortation: Focus on the Faithful Son (3:1–6)
   F. Exhortation: Avoid the Fate of the Wilderness Generation (3:7–4:11)
   G. Exposition: The Power of the Word of God (4:12–13)
II. Our Great High Priest and His Ministry (4:14–10:31)
III. Exhortation: Follow and Serve the Pioneer of Our Faith through Endurance and Faith (10:32–13:25)

Main Idea

By fully identifying with human beings, Jesus through his own sufferings and death has set humans free from their slavery to death and the devil and become a high priest who can finally and forever address humanity's most fundamental problem—namely, sin.

Translation

Hebrews 2:10–18

10a	circumstance	In bringing many sons to glory,
10b	assertion	**it was fitting for him,**
10c	description	because of whom and
10d	description 2	through whom all things exist,
10e	content (of 10b)	to perfect the pioneer of their salvation
10f	means	through sufferings.
11a	basis (for 10)	For
11b	assertion	**the one who sanctifies and**
11c	parallel (to 11b)	**the ones who are sanctified are all from one source.**

11d	result (of 11a–b)	For this reason,
11e	assertion	**he is not ashamed**
11f	content	to call them brothers and sisters.
12a	verification (of 11c–f)	**He says:**
12b	promise 1	"I will declare your name
12c	place 1	among my brothers and sisters,
12d	place 2	in the midst of the assembly
12e	promise 2	I will sing praises to you." (Ps 22:22)
13a	verification (of 11a–b)	And, **again:**
13b	promise	"I will put my trust in him"; (Isa 8:17)
13c	verification (of 11a–b)	and **again:**
13d	result (of 13b)	"Behold, I and the children
13e	identification	whom God has given me." (Isa 8:18)
14a	resumption (of 10)	Therefore
14b	basis (for 14c)	since . . . the children share in blood and flesh,
14c	assertion	**he also likewise partakes of the same things,**
14d	purpose (of 14c)	in order that he . . .
14e	means	through death
14f	sequence 1	. . . might defang the one
14g	identification	who holds the power of death,
14h	description	that is, the devil,
15a	sequence 2	and set free those
15b	identification	who all their lives were held
		in slavery
15c	means	by their fear of death.
16a	explanation (of 14a–15c)	For
16b		surely
16c	assertion	**he does not come alongside** to assist angels
		but
16d	contrast	**comes alongside** to assist the seed of Abraham.
17a	summary (of 10–16)	Therefore
17b	assertion	**he had to be made like his brothers and sisters**
17c	manner	in every way,
17d	purpose 1 (of 17a)	in order that he might become a merciful and faithful high priest
17e	reference	with respect to the things of God
17f	purpose 2 (of 17a)	and so, in turn, he might atone for the sins of the people.
18a	cause (of 18c)	Because he himself suffered
18b	time (of 18a)	when tried,
18c	assertion	**he is able to help those**
18d	identification	who are being tempted/tried.

Structure

As I noted above, there is considerable confusion about just how this paragraph contributes to the movement of the author's sermon. This confusion is the direct result of uncertainty about this paragraph's fundamental focus. Amid the several themes that emerge in these verses, I think the unifying thread is the theme of victory through suffering. The author applies this principle to Christ in verse 10: "it was fitting for him [God] . . . to perfect the pioneer of their salvation *through sufferings*." The salvation our pioneer secures for us is achieved also through the same means: it is "*through death*" that Jesus breaks the power of him who "holds the power of death" (v. 14). As deSilva puts it, "Only by such a path could Jesus become a merciful and capable high priest (2:17–18), and only thus could Jesus take on our most fearsome enemies (death, the devil, 2:14–15)."[3]

The claim in these two roughly parallel texts elaborates the same two points the author made in verse 9: Jesus achieves "glory and honor because he suffered death," and "everyone" receives the benefit of Jesus dying on behalf of them. Reflecting another key theme in verses 5–9, the author then explains how what happened to Jesus can have such benefit for humans in general: Jesus fully shares the nature of human beings (vv. 11–13; cf. v. 16). This gives further reason to view verses 10–18 as an elaboration of the previous paragraph (vv. 5–9). Verses 17–18 offer a transitional conclusion, picking up the theme of Jesus's identification with humans (v. 18; cf. "merciful" in v. 17) and his vicarious suffering and death ("might atone for the sins of the people," v. 17) while also introducing the great christological and soteriological theme that dominates much of the rest of the letter: Jesus is our high priest.[4]

Exegetical Outline

→ **2. Jesus's Identification with Humans (2:10–18)**
   a. Perfection through Suffering Leading to Glory (v. 10)
   b. Jesus's Identification with Humans (vv. 11–13)
   c. Victory over Death and the Devil through Jesus's Death (vv. 14–16)
   d. Transitional Conclusion: Jesus Our Sympathetic High Priest (vv. 17–18)

---

3. *Perseverance in Gratitude*, 113.
4. Greek conjunctions and particles occur so frequently and have so many different functions that they are not always very helpful in identifying the structure of a passage. This paragraph may be something of an exception. After the two somewhat parallel descriptions of the principle of benefit through suffering (vv. 10, 14–15), a γάρ ("for") introduces the important link between Jesus and those he helps (vv. 11–13 and 16). A ὅθεν ("for which reason") then introduces the transitional conclusion (v. 17).

Explanation of the Text

2:10 In bringing many sons[5] to glory, it was fitting for him, because of whom and through whom all things exist, to perfect the pioneer of their salvation through sufferings (Ἔπρεπεν γὰρ αὐτῷ, δι' ὃν τὰ πάντα καὶ δι' οὗ τὰ πάντα, πολλοὺς υἱοὺς εἰς δόξαν ἀγαγόντα τὸν ἀρχηγὸν τῆς σωτηρίας αὐτῶν διὰ παθημάτων τελειῶσαι). As our "pioneer," Jesus has gone ahead of us, securing salvation for us by his suffering. An explanatory "for" (γάρ) connects verses 10–18 to verses 5–9.[6] I have traced the connection between the paragraphs above. Here I might note the way verse 10 explains and develops verse 9. Jesus is now crowned with "glory" and honor because "he suffered death." Verse 10 repeats this point with different language: it was "fitting" for Christ to be made "perfect . . . through sufferings."[7] God is the implied subject in this verse: the three pronouns ("him" and "whom" twice) have God as their antecedent.[8] The verb "perfect" introduces what becomes a key concept in Hebrews, expressed both in the verb, as here (τελειόω), and in several cognate words.[9] As David Peterson has shown in his monograph, "perfection" in Hebrews, at least when applied to Christ, is not ethical but "vocational": it signifies Christ's "qualification" to be the savior of lost and sinful humanity.[10] Christ is described in this clause as "the pioneer of their salvation," and earlier in the verse, his "perfecting" work has specific reference to "bringing many sons to glory."[11] These points reveal a second way

---

5. Even though it is clearly the author's intention to include both men and women in this category, I use "sons" to preserve the cultural connotations of the language: "sons" inherited from their fathers, and, in a sense, we could say that the point in passages like this is that in Christ both men and women can equally share in the dignity and blessings of being "sons."

6. Unlike Greek, English often suggests relationships simply by juxtaposition of content (one does not need an explicit connective to make sense of the two sequential statements, "Take your umbrella. It is raining"). As a result, there are many verses in the NT that feature a Greek conjunction or particle that is not directly translated into English (this is the case here in NIV; NLT; NRSV; CEB). On the flexible meaning of γάρ generally and in Hebrews particularly, see Maximillian Zerwick, *Biblical Greek Illustrated by Examples*, 4th ed., Scripta Pontificii Instituti Biblici 114 (Rome: Pontifical Biblical Institute, 1963), §472–77; Attridge, *Hebrews*, 69–70. The author uses γάρ 90 times in 13 chapters, a rate of 6.9 times per chapter; Paul, in comparison, uses the word 456 times in 87 chapters, a rate of 5.2 times per chapter.

7. As Dyer notes, the plural form παθημάτων, along with the identification of Jesus with human beings in their earthly situation in the context, suggests that the reference, while including death, is wider than that (*Suffering in the Face of Death*, 87).

8. The main verb in the verse, ἔπρεπεν, is an impersonal verb, whose implied subject is put in the dative case (αὐτῷ). Some versions clarify by using "God" in their translations (e.g., NIV; NLT; NRSV). The two parallel prepositional phrases describing God—δι' ὃν τὰ πάντα and δι' οὗ τὰ πάντα ("because of whom are all things," "through whom are all things")—echo Stoic ways of describing God. NT authors adapted this language from their culture to describe the all-encompassing significance of the God of the Bible (see also Rom 11:36: "for from [ἐξ] him and through [δι'] him and for [εἰς] him are all things [τὰ πάντα]").

9. Words from the τελει- root occur fifteen times in Hebrews. The verb occurs with reference to Christ also in 5:9; 7:28; and in reference to believers in 9:9; 10:1, 14; 11:40; 12:23 (it refers to the law in 7:19). The adjective (τέλειος) is used once with reference to believers (5:14) and once with reference to the tabernacle (9:11). The personal noun (τελειωτής, "perfecter") refers once to Christ (12:2). The abstract noun (τελείωσις, "perfection") denotes the full and permanent forgiveness under the new covenant (7:11); and the abstract noun (τελειότης) refers to Christian "maturity" or "perfection" in 6:1. Note also that words from this root refer to the ordination of priests in Leviticus (e.g., 8:33; 16:32).

10. David Peterson, *Hebrews and Perfection: An Examination of the Concept of Perfection in the "Epistle to the Hebrews,"* SNTSMS 47 (Cambridge: Cambridge University Press, 1982), 49–73. Jamieson refers to "eschatological, unsurpassable fulfillment" (*Paradox of Sonship*, 89).

11. The participle in the clause πολλοὺς υἱοὺς εἰς δόξαν ἀγαγόντα ("bringing many sons to glory") is in the accusative because it is indirectly related to the infinitive τελειῶσαι ("perfect").

that verse 10 picks up verse 9. The earlier verse concluded by touching on the way Christ's death is "for everyone." Now the author elaborates. The "glory" Jesus attains is not for him alone; he brings "sons" to glory, the use of "sons" here implying a connection with *the* Son.

This connection is made explicit when Jesus is denoted as "the pioneer of their salvation." The Greek word behind "pioneer" (ἀρχηγός) is debated, as the English translations imply, rendering the word variously as "source" (CSB), "captain" (KJV), "author" (NASB), "leader" (NLT; NAB; NJB), or "founder" (ESV). However, a slight majority prefer "pioneer" (NIV; NET; NRSV; CEB), and I think this is probably the best option.[12] The word has the sense of "initiator" (e.g., Acts 3:15), but often in the sense that the "initiator" brings others along with him. Jesus goes before us on the road of faith (12:2), opening the way to the glory he has already experienced (the occurrences of the word here and in 12:2 may be seen as a grand *inclusio*; see also "source [αἴτιος] of eternal salvation" in 5:9). Many fill out the significance of the word by suggesting that the author has in view the "divine hero," made popular in Hellenistic literature: Jesus descends to earth to rescue humans from their plight and bring them back to heaven with him.[13] However, without denying some influence from this background, it is more likely that our author, as so often, is reflecting on the story of Israel in the wilderness that will play a central role in 3:7–4:11. In this narrative, the scouts who spy out the land are called *archēgoi* (Num 13:2, 3), and the people plead with God to appoint an *archēgos* in place of Moses (Num 14:4).[14] Koester, then, sums it up well: "By calling Jesus the *pioneer* of salvation . . . , the author identifies him as the one who leads people forward, like those who led Israel through the wilderness toward the promised land or through battle to victory. . . . Christ brought salvation, not by avoiding conflict with hostile powers, but by overcoming them and making a way for others to move into the future that God promised them."[15]

2:11 For the one who sanctifies and the ones who are sanctified are all from one source. For this reason, he is not ashamed to call them brothers and sisters (ὅ τε γὰρ ἁγιάζων καὶ οἱ ἁγιαζόμενοι ἐξ ἑνὸς πάντες· δι' ἣν αἰτίαν οὐκ ἐπαισχύνεται ἀδελφοὺς αὐτοὺς καλεῖν). Only by identifying thoroughly with humans could the Son suffer and provide salvation. As I argued above, the author follows a clear pattern in this passage, grounding Christ's saving work for humans in Christ's identification with humans (hence the "for" [γάρ] here). Somewhat unexpectedly, the author expresses this solidarity with the language of "sanctify" (e.g., ESV) or "make holy" (e.g., NIV). Yet for those familiar with the ultimate direction of the author's argument, this language is not at all unexpected. He famously presents Christ's work in cultic categories, a world in which "sanctify" or "make holy" is right at home. The author uses the Greek word that occurs here (ἁγιάζω) five more times to denote the benefit of Christ's sacrifice for believers (9:13; 10:10, 14, 29; 13:12).[16] And, of course, the author

---

12. See, e.g., Massonnet, *L'Épître aux Hébreux*, 89.
13. Stories about the exploits of Heracles (Latinized as "Hercules") in these ways were particularly common. See esp. Lane, *Hebrews*, 1:56–57; Attridge, *Hebrews*, 88; McCruden, *Solidarity Perfected*, 50–67. Others see the influence of Gnosticism (Grässer, *An die Hebräer*, 1:131–33; Weiss, *Der Brief an die Hebräer*, 211–12).
14. Whitfield, *Joshua Traditions*, 249–50.
15. Koester, *Hebrews*, 236. See also Cockerill, *Hebrews*, 138; Moffitt, *Atonement*, 129–30. Each tribal leader sent into the promised land to explore it ahead of the people is called an ἀρχηγός in Num 13:2. The word occurs twenty-eight times in the LXX, usually meaning "leader" or "captain."
16. The author also uses three other cognate words to describe the status of believers: ἅγιος, "holy" (3:1; 6:10; 13:24), ἁγιασμός, "holiness" (12:14), and ἁγιότης, "holiness" (12:10).

has already alerted us to the importance of these cultic associations for his argument (see "purification for sins" in 1:3). "The one who sanctifies" in this verse might refer to God, but the second part of the verse makes it quite clear that the author refers to Jesus, whose death made it possible for sinful humans to be forgiven and thus to enter into the presence of a holy God.

The author emphasizes the oneness between sanctifier and sanctified by claiming that both come "from one source" (ἐξ ἑνός). Defining this source is difficult, partly because the pronoun ("one") could be either masculine or neuter. The two most likely options find expression in English translations: "from one Father" (masculine: see NLT; NRSV; CSB; NASB) or "from one stock, or family" (neuter: NIV; ESV; NET; CEB).[17] While the familial imagery of this text might suggest that "Father" is the most likely option, it is also possible that our author does not intend any one of these options; his point is simply to assert a common origin for both our pioneer Jesus and those he leads to cultic purity.[18] At any rate, this common origin means the Son is "not ashamed" to call them "brothers and sisters" (ἀδελφούς, "brothers," but in this kind of context, referring to men and women equally, better translated as "siblings" or "brothers and sisters" [NIV; NLT; NET; NRSV; CSB; CEB]). Shame was an important concept in the honor/shame culture of the author's world; Jesus's willingness to identify with us shows that he honors us, considering us to be worthy.[19] Perhaps the author hints at the corollary: that believers, in turn, not be ashamed of their pioneer, showing him respect by maintaining a firm confession.[20]

2:12 He says: "I will declare your name among my brothers and sisters, in the midst of the assembly I will sing praises to you" (λέγων, Ἀπαγγελῶ τὸ ὄνομά σου τοῖς ἀδελφοῖς μου, ἐν μέσῳ ἐκκλησίας ὑμνήσω σε). Jesus's willingness to call humans his brothers and sisters is attested by the words of Psalm 22:22, which the author puts on Jesus's lips.[21] We can imagine that the author was drawn to this passage because he was familiar with the early Christian appropriation of this psalm to describe Christ's sufferings. Jesus himself quotes Psalm 22:1 from the cross (Mark 15:34//Matt 27:46), and, taking their lead from Jesus, the evangelists apply other verses from this psalm to Jesus's passion.[22] Only Hebrews quotes from the second, "praise" part of the psalm. The point of the quotation lies in the reference to "my brothers and sisters" (τοῖς ἀδελφοῖς μου).[23] But does the author intend any

---

17. In favor of "Father," or God: e.g., Lane, *Hebrews*, 1:58; deSilva, *Perseverance in Gratitude*, 114; Thomas R. Schreiner, *Commentary on Hebrews*, Biblical Theology for Christian Proclamation (Nashville: Holman, 2015), 98; Dana M. Harris, *Hebrews*, EGGNT (Nashville: Broadman & Holman, 2019), 56; in favor of the neuter "family" or "stock": Witherington, *Letters*, 153; George Guthrie, *Hebrews*, NIVAC (Grand Rapids: Zondervan, 1998), 108. Less likely are: Adam (Moffitt, *Atonement*, 130–31), Abraham (see v. 16: Johnson, *Hebrews*, 97–98; Ellingworth, *Hebrews*, 164–65 [perhaps]).

18. E.g., Attridge, *Hebrews*, 88–89; Koester, *Hebrews*, 229.

19. DeSilva, *Perseverance in Gratitude*, 115.

20. Koester, *Hebrews*, 238.

21. The connection with v. 11b is forged with a participle (λέγων) that depends on the verb ἐπαισχύνεται ("is . . . ashamed").

22. Ps 22:18 in Matt 27:35a//Mark 15:24//Luke 23:34b//John 19:24; Ps 22:16 in Luke 24:39//John 20:25. See Moo, *Old Testament in the Gospel Passion Narratives*, 225–300.

23. The quotation again follows the LXX closely, with the exception of the opening verb: the author replaces LXX διηγήσομαι (from the verb διηγέομαι) with ἀπαγγελῶ. Some suggest that this might be one place where the author works from the Hebrew (K. J. Thomas, "The Old Testament Citations in the Epistle to the Hebrews," *NTS* 11 [1965]: 306), but the author's verb is no closer to the Hebrew than to the LXX (Attridge, *Hebrews*, 90). Ellingworth thinks the author may allude to Ps 78:3–6, where the verb ἀπαγγέλλω appears twice (*Hebrews*, 168). Still others think the author has switched verbs because the one the author uses is better suited to stress Christ's mission (Attridge, *Hebrews*, 90): ἀπαγγελῶ has a stronger sense of "proclaim publicly" than διηγέομαι. None of these explanations can

other part of the quotation to have application to this context? Some interpreters, for instance, think that this text, along with the quotations that follow, are portrayed as the Son's response to the Father's address to the Son in 1:5–14.[24] Attridge argues that the author sees significance in the "assembly" in the second part of the verse. The word for "assembly" (ἐκκλησία) is the common New Testament designation of Christian gatherings for worship (see 12:23), so the author may hint at the context within which human beings can become "sons" related to the Son.[25] Neither suggestion has clear support in the text, however. It may be that the author sees the reference to an "assembly" in which both the Son and sons join as confirmation of their close relationship.[26]

2:13 And, again: "I will put my trust in him"; and again: "Behold, I and the children whom God has given me" (καὶ πάλιν, Ἐγὼ ἔσομαι πεποιθὼς ἐπ᾽ αὐτῷ, καὶ πάλιν, Ἰδοὺ ἐγὼ καὶ τὰ παιδία ἅ μοι ἔδωκεν ὁ θεός). Two further Old Testament quotations reveal the fully human status of the Son. As he has done in chapter 1 (1:5a, 6), the author links a series of Old Testament quotations with "again" (πάλιν). The two quotations actually come from the same Old Testament source: Hebrews 2:13a–b quotes Isa 8:17c, while verse 13c–e quotes the next words in Isaiah, from 8:18a.[27] As is true of the quotation in verse 12, these quotations come from a passage given significant attention by New Testament authors. Isaiah's warning not to "fear what they fear" (Isa 8:12) is echoed in 1 Peter 3:14, and the subsequent exhortation to fear God rather than humans (Isa 8:13) is followed by God's establishing of a "holy place," explained as a "stone that causes people to stumble and a rock that makes them fall" (v. 14). This is one of three "stone" passages (along with Isa 28:16 and Ps 118:22) that are taken up by Jesus and early Christians as references to Christ (Matt 21:42//Mark 12:10//Luke 20:17; Rom 9:33; 1 Pet 2:4–8). As C. H. Dodd points out in his small but influential book *According to the Scriptures*, early Christians seem to have gravitated to a series of key Old Testament passages as they related God's new work in Christ to Old Testament revelation and prophecy.

As he did in his quotation of Psalm 22:22 in verse 12, the author of Hebrews places the words of the text (in this case, the words of Isaiah) on the lips of Jesus. Both quotations reinforce the solidarity of the "one who sanctifies" with the "ones who are being sanctified." Jesus's trust in the Lord reveals his true human nature: as the "pioneer" of salvation, he shows the way to the brothers and sisters who follow him. They, like him, must learn to trust in the Lord in the face of temptations and distractions. "Trust, hope, confidence should be the definitive marks of the believing community in history, and in his participation in this community for a short time Jesus, the Christians' 'brother,' both exemplifies and also elicits such 'faith.'"[28] The second quotation expresses the result of such faith: God gives "children" (παιδία) to Christ, others who

---

be verified; we perhaps have to admit that we don't know why the author changed verbs (and, of course, it is always possible that he was working from a Greek source that is lost to us that had that verb).

24. Cockerill, *Hebrews*, 142.
25. Attridge, *Hebrews*, 90.
26. G. Guthrie, "Hebrews" (2007), 949.
27. The author makes only minor changes to the LXX of Isa 8:17c: he adds an emphatic pronoun (ἐγώ, "I") to the first quotation and, perhaps because of this addition, puts the indicative verb (ἔσομαι) in front of the participle (πεποιθώς, "trust"), reversing the LXX order. His quotation of Isa 8:18a follows the LXX exactly. The language of Isa 8:17c is found also in Isa 12:2 and 2 Sam 22:3, and some interpreters think one of these texts might be the source for the words in Heb 2:13a (or perhaps at least have had some influence; see Ellingworth, *Hebrews*, 169, on Isa 12:2; and Cockerill, *Hebrews*, 144, on 2 Sam 22:3).

28. G. Hughes, *Hebrews and Hermeneutics*, 84.

follow his faith and are therefore joined to him. God's "giving" of children may suggest his initiative and faithfulness in preserving a "remnant" for himself.²⁹

2:14–15 Since therefore the children share in blood and flesh, he also likewise partakes of the same things, in order that he through death might defang the one who holds the power of death, that is, the devil, 15 and set free those who all their lives were held in slavery by their fear of death (ἐπεὶ οὖν τὰ παιδία κεκοινώνηκεν αἵματος καὶ σαρκός, καὶ αὐτὸς παραπλησίως μετέσχεν τῶν αὐτῶν, ἵνα διὰ τοῦ θανάτου καταργήσῃ τὸν τὸ κράτος ἔχοντα τοῦ θανάτου, τοῦτ᾽ ἔστιν τὸν διάβολον, 15 καὶ ἀπαλλάξῃ τούτους, ὅσοι φόβῳ θανάτου διὰ παντὸς τοῦ ζῆν ἔνοχοι ἦσαν δουλείας). The author here resumes the main line of his teaching in this paragraph, asserting again the solidarity of the Son with human beings and the reason for that solidarity: rescue of humans from their plight.³⁰ The basic sentence in these verses is marked by the words "since [ἐπεί] . . . also likewise [καί . . . παραπλησίως]." "The children" (παιδία, referring back to παιδία in v. 13b),³¹ or humans, "share in blood and flesh," and the Son himself (αὐτός) also "partakes of" (μετέχεν)³² these "same things" (τῶν αὐτῶν). Flesh and blood, of course, are the substances that make up a human being, and this pairing often connotes the weakness of humans (Matt 16:17; 1 Cor 15:50; Eph 6:12).³³

While this alignment between "sons" and the Son is the grammatical center of this sentence, our author's emphasis actually emerges in the compound purpose clause in verses 14d–15.³⁴ The Son's assumption of human nature has the purpose of (1) defanging the devil, and (2) setting humans free. The two are related as a sequence of actions: the defeat of the devil leads to humans being set free. Our translation "defang" requires comment. The verb our author uses here (καταργέω) often means "destroy" (so most English versions), but more often means "render powerless" (NASB; see "break the power" in NIV and NLT).³⁵ Here, then, the author might be referring to the devil's ultimate destruction (Rev 20:10). However, in this context, the more likely reference is the penultimate stage of God's redemptive work when, through the atonement for sins provided by our high priest (v. 17), the devil's hold over humans because of their unforgiven sin is broken once for all.³⁶ The author here taps into a broad New Testament conception of Christ's work.³⁷ See, for example, Jesus's promise that "the prince of this world will

---

29. E.g., Attridge, *Hebrews*, 91.

30. The "therefore" (οὖν) at the beginning of v. 14 in this case "serves to resume a subject once more after an interruption" ("οὖν," BDAG 736, §2.a, though it does not list Heb 2:14 in this category). See Attridge, *Hebrews*, 91.

31. The article before παιδία is therefore anaphoric.

32. The verb μετέσχεν is in the aorist tense, in contrast to the perfect-tense verb (κεκοινώνηκεν) the author used to depict the "sharing" of humans in flesh and blood. The author may imply by this shift that what humans in general have "by nature" (emphasizing the stative force of the perfect verb) the Son has only by an act of "assuming" that nature (Lane, *Hebrews*, 1:60). The point is theologically useful, but one fears that too much may be read into the tense shift.

33. The order "blood and flesh" here in Hebrews is a bit unusual (though see Eph 6:12).

34. The ἵνα ("in order that") in the middle of v. 14 has two subjunctive verbs dependent on it: καταργήσῃ ("destroy") in v. 14 and ἀπαλλάξῃ ("set free") at the beginning of v. 15.

35. Paul is especially fond of the verb, using it twenty-five times (it also appears once in Luke; and only here in Hebrews). "Destroy" is the meaning in texts such as 1 Cor 15:26: "the last enemy to be destroyed [καταργεῖται] is death," but it more often means "nullify," "render powerless," as in Rom 6:6 (marginal reading): "our old self was crucified with him so that the body ruled by sin might be rendered powerless [καταργηθῇ]."

36. Jamieson, e.g., translates the verb as "disarm" (*Jesus' Death and Heavenly Offering*, 112–13).

37. This atonement perspective is often labeled the *Christus Victor* view (see, e.g., I. Howard Marshall, "Soteriology in Hebrews," in Bauckham et al., *Epistle to the Hebrews*, 260–61).

be driven out" (John 12:31), and Paul's claims that Christ "disarmed the powers and authorities ... triumphing over them by the cross" (Col 2:15) and that he "has destroyed death" (2 Tim 1:10). The author highlights Jesus's death as the means (διά) by which this defeat of the one who holds the power of death occurred.[38] While, therefore, the author puts a great deal of emphasis on Jesus's high-priestly ministry in the heavenly sanctuary, this verse (and others) make it clear that he also views Jesus's death as a victory over his foes (note also the focus on the subduing of enemies of Ps 110:1 at 1:13 and of Ps 8 at Heb 2:8).

In the second part of his purpose clause, the author continues to celebrate the victory over death won through the Son's own death. The overpowering of the devil, who holds the power of death, means that people can be "set free" (ἀπαλλάξῃ).[39] The author never explicitly says what it is humans are set free from, but the clause describing those who are set free—"who all their lives[40] were held in slavery by their fear of death"—suggests that it is death from which we are set free.[41]

The defeat of the devil and consequent setting free of humans could be seen as the events that lead to the Son, as our "pioneer," leading many sons to glory (v. 10). The imagery of Christ's work in verses 14–15 has, indeed, much in common with verse 10, and the same options for the sources our author might be drawing from in verse 10 are advanced here also. Some see allusion to the Greco-Roman myth of the hero who descends to the underworld to free humans from evil powers.[42] Others think our author is dependent on the Old Testament exodus narrative: Jesus, like Moses, leads his people out of slavery.[43] Again, I am not sure that our author provides adequate basis to conclude that either of these has exercised significant influence on what he says. But one key difference between the Greco-Roman hero and Moses, on the one hand, and Jesus, on the other, is the means by which Jesus overcomes the devil and sets his people free: "through death." This focus on Jesus's suffering and death is, of course, a key motif in this context (see vv. 9, 10).

2:16 For surely he does not come alongside to assist angels but comes alongside to assist the seed of Abraham (οὐ γὰρ δήπου ἀγγέλων ἐπιλαμβάνεται ἀλλὰ σπέρματος Ἀβραὰμ ἐπιλαμβάνεται). The Son has identified with humans so that he might assist the people of God. In our outline of the paragraph above, I advocated a two-part structure, with both

---

38. The διά almost certainly has an instrumental force here, not a spatial one (e.g., "through the realm of death"), as Koester (*Hebrews*, 231) thinks. See, on the general issue, notes on 8:4; 9:13–14. See also Michael H. Kibbe, "Is It Finished? When Did It Start? Hebrews, Priesthood, and Atonement in Biblical, Systematic, and Historical Perspective," *JTS* 65 (2014): 25–61; Jamieson, *Jesus' Death and Heavenly Offering*.

39. The verb is ἀπαλλάσσω, which has several meanings. Only in this verse in the NT does the verb mean "set free," but the meaning is well documented in, e.g., Josephus (*Ant.* 11.270; 13.363). The verb also occurs in Luke 12:58; Acts 19:12. See Fuhrmann, *Vergeben und Vergessen*, 52–54.

40. The Greek behind this phrase is διὰ παντὸς τοῦ ζῆν, in which the infinitive (unusually) functions as the object of διά and is (unusually) modified by a genitive adjective (see BDF §398).

41. Fear of death is often cited in ancient literature as a basic characteristic of human existence, and this fear, of course, continues to hold sway over people in our day.

42. Lane, *Hebrews*, 1:61.

43. David M. Moffit, "Modelled on Moses: Jesus' Death, Passover, and the Defeat of the Devil in the Epistle to the Hebrews," in *Rethinking the Atonement: New Perspectives on Jesus' Death, Resurrection, and Ascension* (Grand Rapids: Baker Academic, 2022), 13–15 (the article was originally published in *Mosebilder: Gedanken zur Rezeption einer literarischen Figur im Frühjudentum, frühen Christentum und der römisch-hellenistischen Literatur*, ed. Michael Sommer et al., WUNT 2/390 [Tübingen: Mohr Siebeck, 2017], 279–97); Koester, *Hebrews*, 240.

parts marked by key assertions of the Son's provision of salvation through suffering (vv. 10, 14–15) followed by elaborations of the Son's solidarity with humans (vv. 11–13, 16). To be sure, a concern with the Son's solidarity with humans does not at first sight seem to be very evident in verse 16. However, I tentatively suggest that at least a muted reference to this effect can be seen in the verb that occurs twice in the verse (ἐπιλαμβάνομαι). The verb could mean simply "come to the assistance of" (English versions tend to use "help" or "be concerned"; and BDAG ["ἐπιλαμβάνομαι," 374, §5] suggests "take an interest in"). However, the verb can sometimes connote the idea of "take someone by the hand," often to help them (see, e.g., Mark 8:23; Luke 9:47; Acts 23:19). The author's one other use of the verb (in a quotation from Jer 31:32 in 8:9) has this sense.[44] The author's choice of this verb, then, might suggest that the "help" the Son offers humans is a help that comes via "taking their part." "The Son has 'taken hold of' this people in the sense that he associates and participates fully in their being."[45]

The reference here to "angels" shows that our author has not wholly abandoned his interest in what is a basic motif in 1:4–14 and 2:5–9. As in 2:5–9, where the author appealed to Psalm 8 to show that God subjected the world to humans rather than to angels, the author compares angels with humans. Yet rather than referring simply to "people," or "brothers and sisters" (v. 11), or "sons" (v. 10), he uses the phrase "seed of Abraham" (σπέρματος Ἀβραάμ; some English translations, recognizing the collective meaning of the word, render "descendants" [NIV; NLT; NRSV; CEB]). The language of "seed of Abraham" and the concept it denotes are widespread in the Old Testament as a way of characterizing the people of God, descendants of Abraham (and the other patriarchs) by biology and promise (e.g., Gen 26:24; 28:4, 13; Exod 33:1; Deut 1:8; Ps 105:6; see John 8:33; Rom 4:13; 9:7–8; Gal 3:16).[46] Our author alludes to this notion in 11:12: "and so from this one man, and he as good as dead, came descendants as numerous as the stars in the sky and as countless as the sand on the seashore." "Seed of Abraham" introduces a specificity in the identity of those the Son has "taken hold of" (and this focus is carried on in v. 17 with its reference to "the people" [τοῦ λαοῦ]).[47] It is the people of God whom the Son has come to help. The author's regular transfer of Old Testament language to depict the New Testament people of God suggests that, like other New Testament authors (e.g., Paul, in Rom 4), the author views descent from Abraham not in biological but in spiritual terms.

2:17 Therefore he had to be made like his brothers and sisters in every way, in order that he might become a merciful and faithful high priest with respect to the things of God[48] and so, in turn, he might atone for the sins of the people (ὅθεν

---

44. The verb is used nineteen times in the NT, often meaning simply "take hold," "seize," "grab hold of," and this is its regular meaning in the LXX as well. Several recent commentators, noting this preponderance of usage, prefer to translate "take hold of" rather than simply "help" (see, e.g., Attridge, *Hebrews*, 94; Koester, *Hebrews*, 232; Cockerill, *Hebrews*, 148–49). Some of the fathers of the church, along with Calvin (*Hebrews*, 32; cf. also P. Hughes, *Hebrews*, 115–18), saw a direct reference to Christ's "assuming" the nature of Abraham's seed.

45. Johnson, *Hebrews*, 102; cf. Vanhoye, *Situation du Christ*, 357–58; Delitzsch, *Hebrews*, 1:139.

46. Some interpreters think the author may have picked this phrase up specifically from Isa 41:8–10, which shares some common themes with Hebrews (see esp. Ellingworth, *Hebrews*, 176; Lane, *Hebrews*, 1:63–64).

47. See esp. Filtvedt, *Identity of God's People*, 66–68 (on this text).

48. The Greek phrase τὰ πρὸς τὸν θεόν is an accusative of respect (BDF 160). The same construction occurs in Heb 5:1; see also 2 Cor 3:4.

ὤφειλεν κατὰ πάντα τοῖς ἀδελφοῖς ὁμοιωθῆναι, ἵνα ἐλεήμων γένηται καὶ πιστὸς ἀρχιερεὺς τὰ πρὸς τὸν θεὸν εἰς τὸ ἱλάσκεσθαι τὰς ἁμαρτίας τοῦ λαοῦ). The Son's human nature enables him to perform his high-priestly work, providing for the forgiveness of sins. We have described verses 17–18 as a "summary transition": these verses draw together the basic teaching of verses 10–16 ("therefore," ὅθεν) at the same time as they introduce key concepts that the author will develop later in the letter.[49] Being "made like his brothers and sisters" reiterates the theme of the solidarity of the Son with "sons" (vv. 11–12, 14a), and the language of "had to be," or "it was necessary" (NLT; ὤφειλεν, "he was obligated") takes us back to the beginning of the paragraph: "it was fitting" that God would use the path of suffering to "perfect" the Son and thus enable him to be our "pioneer" (v. 10).

The connection the author makes in verse 10 between the Son's suffering and the benefit of that suffering for humans (see also v. 9) is reinforced in this verse: being made like his brothers and sisters "in every way" (κατὰ πάντα) has the purpose of preparing the Son to be a "merciful and faithful high priest." The role of Jesus as our high priest becomes the dominating christological focus of the letter—a christological focus that bleeds over significantly into soteriology as well. The issue of just when Jesus "became" a high priest is disputed, and I will tackle this question later in the commentary (see pp. 276–77). However, the atoning work focused on here includes Jesus's earthly ministry (especially his death), so there is some reason to think this verse locates Jesus's high priesthood on earth.[50] There is little, if anything, that we can learn from this verse about this issue. The author's focus is rather on the character of Jesus's high priesthood. The author has paved the way for both descriptions in the teaching of verses 10–16. The full humanity of Jesus prepares him to be a "merciful [ἐλεήμων]" high priest.[51] And the designation of Jesus as a "faithful" (πιστός) high priest may pick up verse 13a, where Jesus proclaims his "faith" or "trust" in God. The two adjectives therefore depict the high priest in relation to humans and to God.[52] "Faithful" probably combines here both the ideas of "reliable" or "trustworthy" and "faithful" in his ministry with respect to God.[53] The transitional force of this verse is not only seen in the introduction of the key title "high priest": the two parallel descriptions also prepare for arguments that follow, "merciful" being developed in 5:1–10 and "faithful" in 3:1–6 (see vv. 2, 5) (thus, perhaps, in intentionally chiastic order).[54]

Becoming a "merciful and faithful" high priest is the immediate purpose of Jesus's full identification with humanity. But that office, in turn, has a further purpose: that he might "atone for the sins of the people." The word translated "atone" comes from a theologically significant and much debated word group, formed with the basic root *hilast-* (ἱλαστ-). A word from this root is used in Hebrews 9:5 (ἱλαστήριον; see also Rom 3:25), while another cognate noun (ἱλασμός) occurs in 1 John 2:2; 4:10.

---

49. The author uses ὅθεν in this "summary" way elsewhere: 3:1; 7:25; 8:3; 9:18; 11:19.

50. Richardson, *Pioneer and Perfecter of Faith*, 28–43.

51. It is possible to take ἐλεήμων as an independent adjective—"he has become merciful and a faithful high priest"—but more likely both adjectives are dependent on ἀρχιερεύς.

52. Weiss, *Der Brief an die Hebräer*, 226.

53. Bruce, *Hebrews*, 88.

54. Albert Vanhoye, *La Structure Littéraire de l'Épître aux Hébreux*, StudNeot 1 (Paris: Desclée de Brouwer, 1962), 81–82; Vanhoye, *Structure and Message*, 24–25. The author may allude to Ps 145 (144 LXX), which describes Yahweh as "gracious and merciful" (οἰκτίρμων καὶ ἐλεήμων, v. 8) and "faithful" (πιστός) to his promises (v. 13).

The verb used here—ἱλάσκομαι—occurs only here and in Luke 18:13 in the New Testament. In the LXX the verb is used thirteen times, usually in the sense of "pardon" or "forgive." Particularly significant for our text are passages in which (as in Heb 2:17) the verb is used with a word referring to sins in the accusative (interestingly, all in the Psalms: 25:11; 65:3; 78:38; 79:9).[55] Psalm 65:3b is typical. Most translations render simply "you forgive our transgressions," but ESV has "you atone for our transgressions" (cf. CSB). The latter translation, using "atone," is overwhelmingly preferred in Hebrews 2:17—and I think rightly so.[56] The verb suggests not only that sins are forgiven but also hints at the mechanism by which they are forgiven. We enter here into the long and acrimonious debate about whether the basic idea is "expiation"[57] or "propitiation."[58] Of course, it makes no sense to say that God "propitiates sins"; with "sins" (τὰς ἁμαρτίας) as the object, "expiate" is probably the main focus. Nevertheless, I think that the word our author uses connotes the whole mechanism of Old Testament atonement, which (I would argue) involves the removal of sins as a barrier between God and humans—and this inevitably in turn involves the appeasing of God's just and necessary wrath against sin.[59]

2:18 Because[60] he himself suffered when tried, he is able to help those who are being tempted/tried (ἐν ᾧ γὰρ πέπονθεν αὐτὸς πειρασθείς, δύναται τοῖς πειραζομένοις βοηθῆσαι). The last verse of the paragraph again draws attention to the benefits conferred on humans made possible by the Son's full identification with humans. The verse has a particularly clear tie with the claim that the Son becomes a *merciful* high priest in verse 17. English versions provide a window into the central interpretive issue in this verse: Is the author referring to "temptation" (NIV; ESV; NET; CSB) or to "testing" (NLT; NRSV; NAB)? The Greek verb, which occurs twice in the verse (πειράζω), can mean either, as can the cognate noun (πειρασμός). The verb occurs three other times in Hebrews: the meaning is debated in 4:15; twice it probably means "test" (3:9; 11:17). The only occurrence of the noun means "test" (3:8). The connection with suffering in this verse favors a reference to "testing": it is a bit more natural to think of someone suffering while undergoing testing than while being tempted.[61] Jesus's "suffering of death" (v. 9), because he withstood the test, brought him glory and honor. At the same time, his suffering enabled him fully to identify with others undergoing similar suffering, and this focus on identification favors a reference to temptation. Perhaps we need not choose between these options: every "test" brings with it a comparable "temptation." The author may have his audience in view here. They have "endured in a great conflict full of suffering" (10:32); they need now to persevere (10:36), which they can do by focusing on Jesus, who "endured the cross, scorning its shame" (12:2).

---

55. In three of these four verses, the underlying Hebrew uses the *k-p-r* root, which is used in several words that have a key bearing on OT atonement theology.

56. E.g., Ribbens, *Levitical Sacrifice*, 211. For the meaning "be merciful toward" here in v. 17, see esp. Fuhrmann, *Vergeben und Vergessen*, 18–30.

57. See, e.g., Attridge, *Hebrews*, 96; Ellingworth, *Hebrews*, 188–89.

58. This debate often focuses on Rom 3:25; see Douglas J. Moo, *The Letter to the Romans*, 2nd ed., NICNT (Grand Rapids: Eerdmans, 2018), 252–57, with bibliography cited there.

59. On Heb 2:17, see Koester, *Hebrews*, 241; Cockerill, *Hebrews*, 151; Ribbens, *Levitical Sacrifice*, 206–11.

60. The Greek behind "because" is ἐν ᾧ, which has a causal meaning here (BDF 219[2]).

61. E.g., Attridge, *Hebrews*, 96; Ellingworth, *Hebrews*, 191.

Theology in Application

The Many Sides of Atonement

The New Testament repeatedly celebrates the fact that God sent his Son to take care of the human problem of sin, and the death that results from that sin. As Paul puts it in his famous summation of the gospel, "what I received I passed on to you as of first importance: that Christ died for our sins according to the Scriptures" (1 Cor 15:3). As this verse implies, Jesus's sufferings on the cross are often the focus of Jesus's work on our behalf. However, the New Testament writers also attribute saving benefit to Jesus's incarnation, sinless life, resurrection, ascension, and heavenly ministry. These various stages in Christ's work, along with the different imagery used to describe the benefits of that work, have given theologians a difficult task when they try to organize and make sense of all this evidence. Over the course of time, at least three key "theories of atonement" have been especially popular. The first is what some call the "classic" theory, which focuses on Jesus's triumph over evil spiritual powers, especially Satan, as the heart of what Jesus came to do. This view is often labeled with the Latin phrase *Christus Victor*. A second model seizes on the imagery of sacrifice that is often associated with Jesus's death in particular: he dies as a sacrificial victim so that people can have their sins forgiven. This sacrificial approach sometimes incorporates a specific view on how Christ's sacrifice "works": in his death, Jesus takes the place of sinful humanity, offering himself in their place as the one who receives the full and final punishment for sins (e.g., "penal substitution"). Finally, some theologians have viewed Jesus more as the example to be followed than as the victim (sacrifice) or victor. In his life of obedience to the Father, an obedience that culminated in his willingness to die on the cross, Jesus provides an example that should stimulate our humble submission to God (the "moral influence" theory).

This overview of "theories of atonement" is necessarily brief and superficial.[62] But I hope it is at least adequate to provide a context in which we can consider and appreciate the contribution of Hebrews 2:10–18 to this discussion. One of the remarkable aspects of this passage is the way it looks at Christ's work from two very different angles. One angle, as we have seen, takes its origin from the ancient world, where the myth of a hero who rescues people by descending into the underworld and conquering their enemies is widespread. So, our author suggests, Jesus "descended" by fully entering into the human condition. He broke the power of the devil, setting humans

---

62. For a brief overview of atonement views, see James Beilby and Paul R. Eddy, eds., *The Nature of the Atonement: Four Views* (Downers Grove, IL: IVP Academic, 2006).

free and leading them to glory (vv. 10, 14–15). But a second angle keeps popping up in our text: it is Jesus's sufferings or death that is the means by which he brings benefit to humans (vv. 10, 14). This focus comes to clearest, though indirect, expression in verse 17, where Jesus is presented as the high priest who "atones" for sin—language that brings clearly into the picture the ritual of Old Testament sacrifice. This passage, therefore, provides evidence for at least two of the traditional atonement theories: *Christus Victor* and sacrifice.[63] More than this: the text also suggests a particular relationship between them. As I have observed, the "victory" of our "hero" Jesus comes via his suffering. This characteristic New Testament emphasis on Jesus's death and its significance distinguishes Jesus from other heroes in the ancient world.

Hebrews 2:10–18, then, suggests that the victory Christ wins comes via his sacrificial death—a death that could, of course, only occur if Christ were fully human (a point of emphasis throughout this passage). As Graham Cole succinctly puts it, "No incarnation, no atonement; but also no atonement, no victory over the evil one."[64]

---

63. Interpreters regularly note these two approaches in this text, but they often imply that the approaches stand in tension with one another (e.g., Weiss, *Der Brief an die Hebräer*, 218–19).

64. Graham A. Cole, *The God Who Became Human: A Biblical Theology of Incarnation*, NSBT 30 (Downers Grove, IL: IVP Academic, 2013), 134. For a similar emphasis on the relationship of atonement and victory, see esp. Henri A. G. Blocher, "*Agnus Victor*: The Atonement as Victory and Vicarious Punishment," in *What Does It Mean to Be Saved? Broadening Evangelical Horizons of Salvation*, ed. John G. Stackhouse Jr. (Grand Rapids: Baker Academic, 2002), 67–91; Jeremy R. Treat, *The Crucified King: Atonement and Kingdom of God in Biblical and Systematic Theology* (Grand Rapids: Zondervan, 2014).

Chapter 6

Hebrews 3:1–6

Literary Context

This paragraph functions as a transition, shifting the focus from the identity of Christ, our divine-human high priest, to the people of God and their need to display unwavering faith in order to enter "rest," the ultimate state of salvation.[1]

On the one hand, then, this paragraph displays a remarkable number of linguistic and conceptual parallels with 1:1–2:18:

"holy brothers and sisters" (3:1)	"brothers and sisters" whom God "makes holy" (2:11, 12)
"partners" (μέτοχοι) (3:1)	"companions" (μέτοχοι) (1:9)
Jesus as "apostle" (3:1)	Jesus as "pioneer" (2:10)
"high priest" (3:1)	"high priest" (2:17)
"Jesus" (3:1)	"Jesus" (2:9)
Jesus as "faithful" (3:2, 6)	Our "faithful" high priest (2:17; cf. 2:13a)
Jesus worthy of "glory" and "honor" (3:3)	Jesus "crowned with glory and honor" (2:9)
"things spoken" [by God] (3:5)	God "speaking" in the Son (1:2); salvation "spoken" in the Lord (2:3)
The Superiority of the Son (1:4–13)	The Superiority of the Son (3:6)[2]

---

1. See, e.g., Grässer, *An die Hebräer*, 1:157. Some interpreters see 3:1–6 as the first stage of a section that runs from here through 5:10 (Spicq, *L'Épître aux Hébreux*, 2:62; Vanhoye, *La Structure Littéraire*, 86–115; Vanhoye, *Structure and Message*, 24–25; Lane, *Hebrews*, 1:68; Ellingworth, *Hebrews*, 68; Massonnet, *L'Épître aux Hébreux*, 99; Rissi, *Die Theologie des Hebräerbriefs*, 13–16); others see it linked with 3:7–4:12(13) (e.g., Whitfield, *Joshua Traditions*, 232–33). See also Laansma, who stresses that the narrative of Num 12–14 stands behind all of Heb 3 ("I Will Give You Rest," 273).

2. See, e.g., Weiss, *Der Brief an die Hebräer*, 240.

The author gathers up many of his key points from the first two chapters as the basis for his exhortation.

At the same time, we also hear some new notes introduced into the developing argument. First, Jesus's superiority is highlighted not in terms of a comparison with angels but in terms of a comparison with Moses. While Moses will not figure prominently in 3:7–4:11 (though see 3:16), his introduction into the author's exposition takes us back to the narrative of Israel's wilderness wandering that is the backdrop for this part of the letter. Second, this narrative also brings to the fore the theme of the people of God, which is a key motif in this paragraph ("house"; see vv. 2, 3, 4, 5, 6). Finally, the author's exhortations to "fix your attention" on Jesus (v. 1) and to "hold fast to our confidence" (v. 6) are echoed in the rest of the letter (see esp. 12:2 for the former; and 3:14; 10:19, 23, 35 for the latter).

I. **The Exalted Son and a Rest for the People of God (1:1–4:13)**
   A. Exordium (1:1–4)
   B. Exposition: The Exalted Status of the Son (1:5–14)
   C. Exhortation: Take Hold of Your Great Salvation (2:1–4)
   D. Exposition: The Humanity of the Son and Its Significance (2:5–18)
   → E. **Exhortation: Focus on the Faithful Son (3:1–6)**
   F. Exhortation: Avoid the Fate of the Wilderness Generation (3:7–4:11)
   G. Exposition: The Power of the Word of God (4:12–13)
II. Our Great High Priest and His Ministry (4:14–10:31)
III. Exhortation: Follow and Serve the Pioneer of Our Faith through Endurance and Faith (10:32–13:25)

Main Idea

Mixing exposition and exhortation, the author urges his readers to fix their attention on Jesus and to be confident in their hope because Jesus, the Son who himself brings into existence the people of God, can be relied on to bring his people to their ultimate goal.

Translation

Hebrews 3:1–6

1a	conclusion (from 1:1–2:18)	Therefore,	
1b	address		holy brothers and sisters,
1c	description		you people who participate in a heavenly calling,
1d	exhortation	**fix your attention on**	**the apostle and**
			high priest of our confession,
1e	identification		Jesus.
2a	description		Jesus is faithful to the one who appointed him,
2b	comparison		just as Moses also was faithful
2c	sphere		in all his house.
3a	expansion (of 2)	For	
3b	assertion	**Jesus is worthy**	**of greater glory**
3c	contrast		than Moses,
3d	comparison (with 3a)		to the same extent that the builder of a house has more honor
3e	contrast		than the house itself.
4a	explanation (of 3)	For	
4b	general	**every house is built by someone,**	
4c	specific	but **the one who builds all things is God**.	
5a	resumption (of 2–3)	Moreover,	
5b	assertion	**Moses**, on the one hand, **was faithful** in all his house (Num 12:7)	
5c	manner		as a servant,
5d	goal		testifying about things yet to be spoken.
6a	contrast (with 5)	But **Christ**	**is faithful**
6b	manner		as the Son over God's house.
6c	encouragement	We belong to this house,	
6d	condition		if we hold fast to our confidence and
6e	parallel (to 6d)		to the hope we boast in.

Structure

The author deploys once again one of his favorite literary devices, the *inclusio*, as he begins and ends on a note of exhortation (vv. 1, 6b). In between, he uses Numbers 12:7 (quoted in v. 5a) to describe Jesus and his relationship to the people of God. We may, in fact, outline the text in terms of three key words from the Numbers text: "faithful" is exposited in verses 1–2, "house" is the key word in verses 3–4, and "servant" is the jumping off point for verses 5–6. The argument can be difficult to follow because the author's logic is, as Ellingworth notes, "episodic rather than linear."[3] But three key ideas, all tied to the language of the quotation from Numbers, emerge. First, underlying the points our author makes is the language of "house," which introduces the idea of the people of God (vv. 2, 3, 4, 5, 6). Second, the author uses the description of Moses from the quotation to make a point of similarity: Jesus, like Moses, is "faithful" (vv. 2, 5, 6). But, third, we also find a point of contrast: Moses is faithful as a "servant," but Jesus is faithful as a "Son," worthy therefore of greater honor and glory than was Moses (vv. 3, 6).

Exegetical Outline

→ **E. Exhortation: Focus on the Faithful Son (3:1–6)**
   1. Exhortation to Fix Attention on Jesus (v. 1)
   2. Jesus and Moses (vv. 2–6a)
   3. Exhortation to Maintain Confidence in Hope (v. 6b)

Explanation of the Text

3:1 Therefore, holy brothers and sisters, you people who participate in a heavenly calling, fix your attention on the apostle and high priest of our confession, Jesus (Ὅθεν, ἀδελφοὶ ἅγιοι, κλήσεως ἐπουρανίου μέτοχοι, κατανοήσατε τὸν ἀπόστολον καὶ ἀρχιερέα τῆς ὁμολογίας ἡμῶν Ἰησοῦν). In light of Jesus's status—greater than the angels, a high priest who identifies with us—we are exhorted to keep our focus on him. The "therefore" (ὅθεν) at the beginning of this verse suggests that the author draws a conclusion from what precedes—in my view (see above), this includes all of 1:1–2:18. Addressing the believers as "holy brothers and sisters" is one of several obvious connections with this previous context. In 2:11, the author refers to believers as "ones being made holy" (ἁγιαζόμενοι), and in 2:11, 12, as "brothers and sisters." A parallel in word but probably not in meaning occurs in the second description of the readers: "you people who participate in a heavenly calling." The word translated "you people who participate in" (μέτοχοι) referred in 1:9 to the "companions" of Christ. The word may have a similar meaning here (see "partner" in NET; NRSV; CEB), but, as our translation suggests, probably means here "those who are participating in."[4] The "calling" (κλῆσις) they participate in is God's act of drawing sinful human beings into relationship with himself; believers are "those who are called" (Heb 9:5).[5] Of course, a key debate in Hebrews is whether this calling is

---

3. Ellingworth, *Hebrews*, 195.
4. Hebrews uses this word three other times with a genitive word following (3:14; 6:4; 12:8), and, in each verse, I think the genitive word specifies the thing or person in which people participate. BDAG ("μέτοχος," 643, §1) notes both options. The word occurs elsewhere in the NT only in Luke 5:7.
5. The noun κλῆσις occurs elsewhere in Rom 11:29; 1 Cor 1:26; 7:20; Eph 1:18; 4:1, 4; Phil 3:14 (ἄνω κλήσεως); 2 Thess

"effectual"—that is, whether it infallibly ensures that those who receive this calling end up at the ultimate goal. Paul, I argue, uses the language in this way, but we should probably refrain from insisting that this must also be the sense it has in Hebrews until more evidence of the author's theological perspective can be marshaled.[6] When the author describes this calling as "heavenly," he might mean that it originates from heaven,[7] that its destination is heaven,[8] or, perhaps best, both.[9]

The author charges those who have been drawn into fellowship with Christ to "fix [their] attention" on "the apostle and high priest of [their] confession."[10] "Fix attention" translates a word (κατανοέω) that can mean "notice, observe," but that more often means "consider," "think carefully about" (see the other occurrence of this verb in Hebrews at 10:24). The author identifies the one we are to pay close attention to at the end of his sentence, thereby highlighting him: "Jesus."[11] Describing Jesus as a "high priest" makes perfect sense in light of the author's introduction of this nomenclature in 2:17. However, nowhere else in Hebrews or anywhere in the New Testament is Jesus called an "apostle" (ἀπόστολος). This word is familiar as a way of referring to "sent out" ministers of the gospel (e.g., 2 Cor 8:23; Phil 2:25) and especially to those special emissaries given a foundational role in the formation of the Christian community ("apostle"; e.g., Acts 1:2, 26; Eph 4:11). The root idea of the word "sent out" suggests that the author may intend to portray Jesus as one sent from God, "in the these last days," to reveal his ultimate message of salvation (see 1:1–2; 2:1–4).[12] Johnson attractively suggests that "as the *Apostolos* is sent by God to deliver the summons from God to humans through the proclamation of the good news, so the *archiereus* is preeminently the one who responds from the side of humans to God."[13] Our author connects this twofold description to his readers by relating them to "our confession" (τῆς ὁμολογίας ἡμῶν). The word "confession" appears at two other important moments in Hebrews's argument (4:14; 10:23), and all three occurrences are debated. On the one hand, the word could have a verbal nuance, captured, for example, in the NIV's "whom we acknowledge" (see also NLT; NET). However, it is perhaps more likely that the word has a more static sense, referring not to the "act of confessing" but to "what is confessed": a doctrinal summary of some kind.[14] The people of God need to take to heart and ponder what they profess with their lips.

1:11; 2 Tim 1:9; 2 Pet 1:10 (all having the same meaning); and the cognate verb occurs in Hebrews in this sense in 5:4; 9:15. See also 2:11; 3:13; 11:8, 18.

6. Note, e.g., Attridge (*Hebrews*, 107) and deSilva (*Perseverance in Gratitude*, 133), who argue that the warnings in Hebrews suggest that "calling" in Hebrews does not "guarantee entrance."

7. Weiss, *Der Brief an die Hebräer*, 242.

8. Grässer, *An die Hebräer*, 1:159. The closest NT parallel may have this sense: the "upward call" (τῆς ἄνω κλήσεως) in Phil 3:14.

9. E.g., Ellingworth, *Hebrews*, 198; Cockerill, *Hebrews*, 158. The author uses "heavenly" five other times (6:4; 8:5; 9:23; 11:16; 12:22).

10. The verb κατανοήσατε is an aorist imperative.

11. As I noted in my comments on 2:9, the author employs the name "Jesus" in this emphatic way several times.

12. See, e.g., Attridge, *Hebrews*, 107. Brian C. Small suggests that the title sums up the presentation of Jesus in chs. 1–2 and "indicates Jesus' authority as one commissioned by God to represent him" (*The Characterization of Jesus in the Book of Hebrews*, BibInt 128 [Leiden: Brill, 2014], 192).

13. Johnson, *Hebrews*, 107. See also Cockerill: "'Apostle' contrasts the Son with Moses as the source of revelation; 'High Priest' anticipates comparison with Aaron as the source of salvation (5:1–10)" (*Hebrews*, 160).

14. See, e.g., Lane, *Hebrews*, 1:75; Attridge, *Hebrews*, 108. I am attaching the genitive τῆς ὁμολογίας ἡμῶν to both ἀπόστολον and ἀρχιερέα, as the single article governing both words might suggest (cf. Delitzsch, *Hebrews*, 1:155).

3:2 Jesus is faithful to the one who appointed him, just as Moses also was faithful in all his house (πιστὸν ὄντα τῷ ποιήσαντι αὐτὸν ὡς καὶ Μωϋσῆς ἐν ὅλῳ τῷ οἴκῳ αὐτοῦ). The author here turns to another comparison, claiming that Jesus, like Moses, was faithful. This verse is connected syntactically to verse 1 with a participle that modifies "Jesus" (ὄντα, "being").[15] English style cannot sustain as many subordinate clauses as Greek can, so it is often best to break up these Greek sentences into several English ones. Most translations use the past tense here (e.g., NIV: "He *was* faithful"), perhaps because the "appointing" of Jesus to his role is in the past (ποιήσαντι, an aorist participle).[16] However, I think it more likely that the author refers here to Jesus's ongoing faithfulness to God, with the powerful implications that his ministry has for the people he represents as high priest (see, e.g., NET: "who is faithful"). See 7:24–25: "Because Jesus lives forever, he has a permanent priesthood. Therefore he is able to save completely those who come to God through him, because he always lives to intercede for them."

The language of "faithful" (πιστός) looks both backward to 2:17—Jesus is a "faithful [πιστός] high priest"—and forward to the quotation of Numbers 12:7 in Hebrews 3:5a—"Moses also was faithful [πιστός] in all his house." Indeed, our author alludes to that verse in the second part of verse 2 as a means of introducing a comparison between Moses and Jesus. A contrast between Moses and Jesus is introduced later in the passage; here, however, the author attributes faithfulness to God equally to both Moses and Jesus. Moses, of course, is a central figure in Old Testament history and, as such, is a subject of extensive comment in Jewish literature. His role as lawgiver is especially prominent. But the author, in this context, appears to be thinking more of Moses's role as the leader of the people from Egypt to the promised land (see 3:16) and his mediatorial role during that fraught journey.

Moses's faithfulness is displayed "in all his house." "His" almost certainly refers to God, the one who, it is implied, appoints Moses (most versions make this clear by referring to "God's house" [e.g., NIV, ESV]). "House" (οἶκος) in this context refers both to the place where people live and the people who live in it.[17] In this verse, the focus is clearly on the people: the "household" (CSB). Here the "household" is the extended family that consists of the people of God. The Old Testament regularly refers to God's people in this way (see, e.g., Heb 8:8 and 10, quoting Jer 31:31, 33), and the church is regularly viewed in the New Testament as an extended family: see, for example, "holy brothers and sisters" in our verse 1. It is also possible that our author has in view 1 Samuel 2:35, which promises that God will "raise up . . . a faithful [LXX πιστός] priest" to take the place of the rejected line of Eli. This priest, the text says, "will do according to what is in my heart and mind. I will firmly establish his priestly house [LXX "faithful house," οἶκον πιστόν], and they will minister before my anointed one always."[18]

---

15. Another possible (though, in our view, unlikely) syntactical option is to view the participle ὄντα as a noun clause dependent on κατανοήσατε. See NRSV: "consider that Jesus, the apostle and high priest of our confession, was faithful."

16. I should make clear that the aorist tense form does not point to a past action; tense in participles has much more to do with "aspect"—how one chooses to portray an action—than time. Rather, a past meaning of the verb is mandated by the meaning of the verb itself: "appoint" is a punctiliar event. On the meaning of "appoint" for ποιέω, see BDAG ("ποιέω," 839, §1.b). Johnson, on the other hand, thinks the verb means "make" or "create" (see 1:2, 7) with reference to Jesus as Son (*Hebrews*, 107).

17. Jared C. Calaway suggests that "house" might allude to the temple/tabernacle, but this is unlikely (*The Sabbath and the Sanctuary: Access to God in the Letter to the Hebrews and Its Priestly Context*, WUNT 2/349 [Tübingen: Mohr Siebeck, 2013], 99–101).

18. E.g., Laansma, *"I Will Give You Rest,"* 269–71.

3:3 For Jesus is worthy of greater glory than Moses, to the same extent that the builder of a house has more honor[19] than the house itself (πλείονος γὰρ οὗτος δόξης παρὰ Μωϋσῆν ἠξίωται, καθ' ὅσον πλείονα τιμὴν ἔχει τοῦ οἴκου ὁ κατασκευάσας αὐτόν). While both were faithful, Jesus is superior to Moses, since he himself is the creator. The logic of verses 3–4 and its link to the context is difficult to sort out. Indeed, if one were to remove verses 3–4, the flow of the passage would apparently be improved: "Jesus was faithful as was Moses [v. 2] . . . but Christ was faithful as a Son and Moses as a servant [vv. 5–6a]." Verses 3–4 diverge from what seems to be this main line of argument with its introduction of the "builder."[20] In my view (which I should note is a minority view), the only way to make satisfactory sense of these verses in their context is to identify Jesus as "the one who builds all things" in verse 4b. Once that move is made, we can then recognize that in verse 3b the author is not citing a general truism but is, in fact, implicitly asking us to identify the "builder" with Jesus and the "house" with Moses.[21] Moses is faithful "in" the house (v. 2); while a leader of the people, he is nevertheless a part of the people, a member of the "household." Jesus, however, is the one who "builds" the house—that is, he is the one who, through his sacrificial death, resurrection, and exaltation to the Father's right hand, brings the "household"—that is, the new-covenant people of God—into existence. The author uses this comparison in verse 3b to construct a larger comparison between "builder-house" and "Jesus-Moses."[22]

It is because Jesus has this role that, despite their being united in faithfulness to their calling and ministry, Jesus is "worthy"[23] of greater glory than Moses.[24] "Glory" (δόξα) was used in the Greco-Roman world to refer to the honor that was so important in that honor/shame culture. However, it also has a rich Old Testament background, where it refers to the (often visible) splendor of God himself. The author is using it in this latter way here, taking us back to critical points in the earlier argument: Jesus is "the radiance of God's glory" (1:3), the one now "crowned with glory and honor" (2:9). Moses, of course, reflects God's glory; after his interaction with the Lord on the mountain, his face was "radiant" with the splendor of the Lord (Exod 34:29–35).[25] Jesus, however, radiates a glory that is intrinsic to him (see our comments on 1:3).

3:4 For every house is built by someone, but the one who builds all things is God (πᾶς γὰρ οἶκος κατασκευάζεται ὑπό τινος, ὁ δὲ πάντα κατασκευάσας θεός). The author confirms the point he made in verse 3 by identifying Jesus as "God" who created all things. The "for" (γάρ), as it often does, introduces an explanatory aside, filling

---

19. "Honor" trasnslates τιμήν, which, for the logic of the verse to work, must be roughly equivalent in meaning to δόξα, "glory."

20. The Greek verb is κατασκευάζω, which can mean "prepare" (e.g., Matt 11:10), but also "build, construct, erect, create" ("κατασκευάζω," BDAG 527–28, §1; see, e.g., Heb 11:7 and 1 Pet 3:20 [both referring to Noah "building" an ark]). It can also mean "furnish" (see Heb 9:2), and some interpreters think this meaning could fit in Heb 3:3 (Cockerill, *Hebrews*, 166).

21. See, e.g., Ellingworth, *Hebrews*, 195–96; Cockerill, *Hebrews*, 165; McDonough, *Christ as Creator*, 209; contra, e.g., Attridge, *Hebrews*, 110; Lane, *Hebrews*, 1:77.

22. The verse-spanning comparison is made with the phrase καθ' ὅσον, "in so far as, inasmuch" ("ὅσος," BDAG 729, §3).

23. The verb translated "is worthy" (ἠξίωται) is in the perfect tense, signifying an enduring state of affairs (on this "stative" force of the tense, see, e.g., Kenneth L. McKay, *A New Syntax of the Verb in New Testament Greek: An Aspectual Approach* [New York: Lang, 1994], 31).

24. The γάρ at the beginning of the verse therefore will have a mildly adversative meaning ("yet" in NRSV; "but" in NLT; CEB; NAB). For more on the uses of γάρ in Hebrews, see footnote on 2:10.

25. The LXX in this passage refers to the radiance on Moses's face with the verb δοξάζω (vv. 29, 30, 35).

in some necessary information to make sense of verse 3.[26] In this case, as I have argued, the author identifies "the builder," Jesus (v. 3b), with God, thereby supplying a compelling reason for him to be worthy of greater glory than Moses.

The author reminds his audience of an obvious point in verse 4b: "every house is built by someone." As the "building" language may suggest, the meaning of οἶκος has probably drifted to the "place" end of the spectrum of the meaning of this word. However, remembering that the verb translated "build" (κατασκευάζω) can mean "create, prepare," a reference to "household" cannot be excluded.

Most interpreters view verse 4c as a simple assertion that God is the one who builds all things—"God" being assumed to refer to God the Father. On this view, the author here is arguing that "Jesus is worthy of more glory than Moses in the same measure as God has more honor than the universe he created."[27] However, as I noted above, this interpretation of the clause makes it very hard to see how it contributes to the ongoing logic of the author's argument. I think Cockerill is right: "failure to accept this verse [4] as confirmation of the Son's divine creatorship leaves it a foreign body in the text."[28] "The one who builds all things" (ὁ δὲ πάντα κατασκευάσας), then, is Jesus, who is identified in this verse as "God."[29] The reason why so many interpreters take the other option is that it simply appears more likely that God the Father would be identified as the builder/creator of all things. Yet a reference to Christ as this universal "builder" is not as unlikely as it might first appear in light of the very high christological claims of chapter 1, where Jesus is identified as the one "through whom he made the universe" (1:2), as "God" (1:8), and as the "Lord" who "laid the foundations of the earth" and whose hands created the "heavens" (1:10). Of course, one must be careful to preserve the distinct roles of Father and Son in creation: the New Testament usually views Christ as the agent through whom God the Father created. Yet, as Hebrews 1:10 shows, the lines between the two are often blurred, so that in a general sense it can be said that creation is the product of the triune God. Jesus, the "builder," is God, and this claim supplies the ultimate reason for Jesus having glory greater than that of Moses.

3:5 Moreover, Moses, on the one hand, was faithful in all his house as a servant, testifying about things yet to be spoken (καὶ Μωϋσῆς μὲν πιστὸς ἐν ὅλῳ τῷ οἴκῳ αὐτοῦ ὡς θεράπων εἰς μαρτύριον τῶν λαληθησομένων). The author here resumes his comparison between Moses and Jesus. In verse 2 his comparison took the form of an "as . . . so also" logic: as Jesus was faithful, so also was Moses. Here, however, the comparison takes the form of a contrast: Moses, on the one hand, was faithful as *a servant* (v. 5), but Christ is faithful as *a Son* (v. 6a).[30]

---

26. Labeling the verse a parenthesis, as ESV (following RSV) punctuates (see, e.g., Zerwick and Grosvenor, *Grammatical Analysis*, 659; Attridge, *Hebrews*, 110), goes too far in "sidelining" the verse (see Jon Laansma, "Hidden Stories in Hebrews: Cosmology and Theology," in Bauckham et al., *Cloud of Witnesses*, 11).

27. Lane, *Hebrews*, 1:77.

28. Cockerill, *Hebrews*, 167; see also Backhaus, *Der Hebräerbrief*, 140.

29. I therefore take ὁ κατασκευάσας ("the one who builds") as the subject and θεός as the predicate. Therefore, with most translations, "the builder of all things is God" rather than "God is the builder of all things" (CEB; NJB; see Ellingworth, *Hebrews*, 206). On determining subject and predicate in this kind of clause, see Wallace, *Greek Grammar*, 42–45. Angela Costley suggests that there might be an allusion to the cosmos in v. 4c (*Creation and Christ: An Exploration of the Topic of Creation in the Epistle to the Hebrews*, WUNT 2/527 [Tübingen: Mohr Siebeck, 2020], 250–51).

30. This contrast is explicitly marked by a μέν ("on the one hand") . . . δέ ("on the other hand") combination.

The author returns here to the language of Numbers 12:7, which he already began using in verse 2. Significant differences in the order of words between Hebrews and the LXX of Numbers 12:7 make it difficult to decide if the author is "quoting" the text (see NIV) or alluding to it. However, the difference is probably not worth debating. What is clear is that all the key words in verse 5a come from the Old Testament text: "faithful in all my/his house," "servant."[31]

The Lord's commendation of Moses in Numbers 12:7 comes in response to Miriam and Aaron's failure to respect Moses's role as mediator between God and the people and as spokesman for God. When God reveals himself to prophets, he speaks in visions and dreams (v. 6), but with Moses, God speaks "face to face" (v. 8). Moses's role as revealer of God's truth in this text fits naturally into the author's focus on the way God has spoken. That past speaking, the author has pointed out, took the form of "prophet-like" speech (Heb 1:1). Yet in the Numbers passage, Moses is seen as a medium of revelation superior to even that of the prophets. Perhaps, then, the author is drawn to the language of Numbers 12:7 in order to highlight the way Jesus's mediatorial role is greater even than that of Moses.[32] Jewish tradition might provide a further stimulus to the author's use of this text. A commentary on Numbers claims that "God calls Moses 'faithful in all his house' and thereby he ranked higher than the ministering angels themselves."[33] We cannot be sure if this Jewish tradition goes back as early as the date of Hebrews, but if it does it would provide another obvious point of contact: Jesus is not only greater than angels (1:3–13; 2:5–9) but also greater than the "one greater than the angels"—that is, Moses. In any case, what is clear is that the author continues to assert the superiority of Christ, as the Son, over any possible contender, however great and important they may have been.

The author adds a phrase that does not derive from his Numbers source: Moses's "service" took the form particularly of his "testifying[34] about things yet to be spoken."[35] The reference is almost certainly to the eschatological events that have unfolded in the ministry of Christ (see 10:1, "the good things that are coming"). The words to be spoken, then, are not words of Moses but the message decisively revealed in the Son, words that Moses in some way "bore witness to."[36] Perhaps the author has in mind the way Moses's faithfulness to God was displayed in his willingness to be mistreated "for the sake of Christ" (Heb 11:24–28).[37]

3:6 But Christ is faithful as the Son over God's house. We belong to this house, if we hold fast[38] to our confidence and to the hope we boast in

---

31. The author reverses the order of words, putting πιστός ("faithful") at the front of the phrase, and he changes the person of the pronoun (from "my" [μου] in the LXX to "his" [αὐτοῦ]) to fit the language to its context. "Servant" translates θεράπων, a word not found elsewhere in the NT but that occurs many times in the LXX, referring, for instance, to Pharaoh's "servants" or "officials" in Exod 4–14. Designating Moses as a "servant" of God is not intended, then, to diminish him but to elevate his status, since he serves the Lord of the universe.

32. E.g., Grässer, *An die Hebräer*, 1:166. Philo portrays Moses as both a mediator and priest (*Moses* 2.160–86).

33. Sifre Num. 110. See Lane, *Hebrews*, 1:73.

34. "Testifying" captures the intent in the Greek εἰς ματύριον, where εἰς has its common sense of indicating the destination or goal of something.

35. "Things yet to be spoken" translates a future passive participle, λαληθησομένων (the only one in the NT; cf. BDF §351.2).

36. Cockerill, *Hebrews*, 168–69.

37. Johnson, *Hebrews*, 110.

38. The majority of MSS (including ℵ, A, 33, 81, 104, 1505, 1739, and 1881) add here the phrase μέχρι τέλους βεβαίαν, "firm until the end." Since this reading occurs in the Majority text, the KJV and NKJV include the phrase "firm [un]to the end." However, no modern English translation includes the words, since they appear to be an interpolation based on the very similar 3:14b (see Metzger, *Textual Commentary*, 595).

(Χριστὸς δὲ ὡς υἱὸς ἐπὶ τὸν οἶκον αὐτοῦ· οὗ οἶκός ἐσμεν ἡμεῖς, ἐάν[39] τὴν παρρησίαν καὶ τὸ καύχημα τῆς ἐλπίδος κατάσχωμεν). Christ's greatness is seen in his status "over" the people of God, and belonging to that people is tied to maintaining confidence in hope. This verse falls obviously into two parts. In the first part, our author completes the contrast he introduced in verse 5b between Moses and Christ at the same time as he brings to an end his exposition of Numbers 12:7 that began in verse 2. In the second part of the verse, our author swings back into the mode of exhortation with which the passage began (v. 1).

Moses's status as a "servant," as I noted, does not demean him but, if anything, elevates him. Yet it is clearly not as great a position as being "the Son." As he has been doing since 1:2, the author uses the multifaceted title "Son" to assert the unique, elevated role of Christ.[40] And not only is Christ the Son in contrast to Moses, the servant; Moses serves "in" (ἐν) the house, while Christ stands "over" (ἐπί) it.

The second part of the verse is at first sight encouraging: "we" (ἡμεῖς) have the inestimable privilege of belonging to this "house," the new-covenant people of God.[41] Yet what dominates in this second part of the verse is not so much this assertion as the condition that follows: we belong to this house only "if[42] we hold fast to our confidence and to the hope we boast in." The verb translated "hold fast" (κατάσχωμεν) comes last in the clause, perhaps for emphasis. Our author uses this same verb to issue a similar encouragement in two other verses: 3:14, "We have come to share in Christ, if indeed we hold our original conviction firmly to the very end"; and 10:23, "Let us hold unswervingly to the hope we profess, for he who promised is faithful." As these texts suggest, the verb connotes the idea of "holding fast" (ESV) or "holding firmly" (NET). The author specifies here two things that believers must hold onto: "confidence" and "the hope we boast in." "Confidence" translates a word (παρρησία) that often refers to boldness in speech (e.g., the apostles desire to "speak the word of God boldly" [Acts 4:31]), but here it refers to a state of confidence, perhaps implicitly to confidence in approaching God and living in his presence (Heb 4:16; 10:19; cf. 10:35; cf. Eph 3:12). As the author's sermon unfolds, of course, he will go into great detail about the basis for the confidence believers can have. The warning here is a kind of "shot across the bow," anticipating the thrust of the author's exhortation that will follow.

The second thing believers need to hold onto is "the hope we boast in." The Greek phrase might at first sight more naturally be translated "boasting in our hope" (ESV) or "pride in our hope" (RSV). This is because the first word in the phrase in Greek is "boasting" (καύχημα), on which depends a genitive phrase (τῆς ἐλπίδος, "of hope"). However, it is not uncommon for phrases of this type to forefront the genitive word and make the first word the modifier.

---

39. The NA[28]/USB[5] reads ἐάν[περ] and is the reading adopted in my comments.

40. This is the first occurrence of "Christ" (χριστός) in Hebrews, a title the author uses eleven other times (a frequency of usage considerably less than we find in Paul). Attridge (*Hebrews*, 111) suggests that "Jesus" in v. 1 and "Christ" in this verse frame the paragraph.

41. Some interpreters think this claim may open up the issue of "supercessionism," the word being widely used in NT academic circles to denote the idea that the church has "taken the place" of Israel. Hebrews, as we will see, has much to contribute to this issue, but I don't think this verse is relevant to it: the author does not indicate any intentional contrast in his use of "we"; he is simply identifying his readers. See, e.g., Weiss, *Der Brief an die Hebräer*, 250.

42. The "if" translates ἐάν[περ] (a combination of ἐάν and πέρ), a rare NT word that means "if indeed," "supposing that" ("ἐάν," BDAG 268, §1.c.γ), perhaps a slightly strengthened form of ἐάν ("ἐάνπερ," LSJ 465). It occurs only in Heb 3:14; 6:3 in the NT and in 2 Macc 3:38 in the LXX.

That seems to be the best option here, resulting woodenly in the translation "hope that has to do with boasting." Since "boasting" is a verbal idea, it then also makes sense to translate with a verb in English: hence "hope in which we glory" (NIV; see also NET; CSB; CEB).[43]

The rhetorical and theological implications of this conditional statement should be briefly noted. What is quite striking here (and in the closely parallel 3:14) is the combination of a protasis ("if" clause) that focuses on the future—"*if* we hold fast"—with an apodosis that uses a present tense—"*then* we belong to God's house" (the perfect tense is used in 3:14, but the semantic effect is similar). It's as if I would say to an athlete, "You are on the team if you continue to score a lot of points." Is one on the team or not? Only future performance will tell.

Transferred into theology, then, present status dependent on future adherence could suggest that one can determine who is *now* among the people of God only by knowing who, *in the future*, will persevere. And this, in turn, might suggest that our author's many severe warnings are not in the mode of "if you do not persevere, you will lose your spiritual benefits," but "if you do not persevere, you were never part of God's household at all."[44] That is, the author is offering a kind of definition of a true believer: it is the one who perseveres (and only that one!) who truly belongs to the household of God. As Bruce puts it, "The doctrine of the final perseverance of the saints has as its corollary the salutary teaching that the saints are the people who persevere to the end."[45] Or, to put it another way, perseverance is not so much the condition that qualifies people to be the "house of God" (for perseverance *follows* this status) but the *evidence* of this already attained status.[46]

The syntax of this sentence (and of 3:14b) certainly makes this interpretation a valid option.[47] However, most interpreters (usually tacitly) understand the logic in this verse (and in 3:14) to be more in the mode of a "consequence-condition" relationship. On this view, the "then" clause has an implicitly future aspect: "belonging to God's house" is a present status that will continue into the future *if* the condition stated in the "if" clause continues to be fulfilled. Cockerill, for instance, translates it as "whose house we are (and continue to be) by virtue of the fact that we hold fast."[48] The semantic relationship presumed in this case can appeal to

---

43. It is possible also to construe the final genitive phrase τῆς ἐλπίδος, "of hope," with παρρησίαν, "confidence," as well as with καύχημα, "boasting": "the confidence and boasting that arise from our hope"; so perhaps NRSV: "the confidence and the pride that belong to hope." The use of articles on both nouns is not at all decisive here, since the words have different genders and a single article could not govern both of them.

44. E.g., Buist Fanning, "A Classical Reformed View," in *Four Views on the Warning Passages in Hebrews*, ed. Herbert W. Bateman IV (Grand Rapids: Kregel, 2007), 207–18; D. A. Carson, "Reflections on Assurance," in *Still Sovereign: Contemporary Perspectives on Election, Foreknowledge, and Grace*, ed. Thomas R. Schreiner and Bruce A. Ware (Grand Rapids: Baker Academic, 2000), 247–76, esp. 267; G. Guthrie, *Hebrews*, 134–36. The clearest textual basis for this thinking is 1 John 2:18–19: "Dear children, this is the last hour; and as you have heard that the antichrist is coming, even now many antichrists have come. This is how we know it is the last hour. They went out from us, but they did not really belong to us. For if they had belonged to us, they would have remained with us; but their going showed that none of them belonged to us."

45. Bruce, *Hebrews*, 94.

46. E.g., Carson: "Hebrews virtually defines true believers as those who hold firmly to the end the confidence they had at first" ("Reflections," 267).

47. Fanning ("Classical Reformed View," 210–11) notes several texts that fall into what Wallace calls an "evidence-inference" semantic relationship (*Greek Grammar*, 683). See, e.g., John 15:14: "You are [ἐστε, present tense] my friends if [ἐάν] you do what I command." Obeying Jesus is evidence (or a "symptom") of being Jesus's friend (see also von Siebenthal, *Ancient Greek Grammar*, 607, who calls this a "consequence-condition/symptom" relationship).

48. Cockerill, *Hebrews*, 172. See also deSilva: "the opportuniy to retain their place" (*Perseverance in Gratitude*, 138); Lane: the audience "must maintain their stance" (*Hebrews*, 1:79).

parallel texts with similar syntax.⁴⁹ The strongest support for this interpretation comes from the larger context: Hebrews is full of exhortations in which the continuing enjoyment of God's blessing is contingent on continuing faithfulness (e.g., 4:11: "let us, therefore, make every effort to enter that rest, so that no one will perish by following their example of disobedience"). The grammatical challenge this interpretation faces is the present tense used in the "then" clause (ἐσμεν). Comparable constructions in the New Testament consistently refer to the *present* or immediate consequence of the protasis.⁵⁰ In other words, the future element suggested by Cockerill and others does not have clear syntactical justification. Indeed, the logic of Cockerill's view seems to demand that the condition be tied to future continuance more than present status. That is, their view seems to suggest a paraphrase something like "we are God's household—and we will continue to be God's household if we hold firmly." However, we can relieve this grammatical problem slightly if we view the present tense as indicating an "ongoing state."⁵¹ On this reading, the author claims that the ongoing state of belonging to the household of God is true "as long as" the condition of "standing firm" is being fulfilled.⁵²

A decision between these options is not easy. The roughly parallel 3:14 might favor the former view. Not only does this verse emphasize the "present state" indicated in the "then clause" by using a perfect tense, but it also speaks in the "if clause" of holding firmly "to the end." This addition makes it harder to understand the protasis as a condition that must *continue to be* fulfilled for the assertion in the apodosis to be true (you continue to be partakers of Christ as long as you hold firmly to the end); rather, it suggests that the apodosis is *now* fulfilled if the assertion in the protasis is true (you are now partakers of Christ if you hold firmly to the end).

At the end of the day, then, these two verses (3:6b and 14) offer only limited help in resolving the question about the relationship between salvation and perseverance. The grammar of the text, as we have seen, is not decisive for one view or the other, and it would in any case be precarious to build a full picture of the situation on two verses.⁵³ However, the rhetorical pattern of "contingency-consequence" that is so ubiquitous in Hebrews suggests the latter interpretation may be closer to the truth: the "if" clause issues a warning/exhortation: we only remain in the state of being God's house if we continue to hold fast.⁵⁴

---

49. See esp. Rom 11:22: "Consider therefore the kindness and sternness of God: sternness to those who fell, but kindness to you, provided that [ἐάν] you continue in his kindness. Otherwise, you also will be cut off." There is no explicit verb in the apodosis ("kindness to you"), but the context presumes a present tense. "Continuing in God's kindness" is clearly here the condition for continuing to experience God's kindness, as the threat at the end of the verse makes clear ("you also will be cut off").

50. I am assuming that the ἐάν[περ] in this verse (and in v. 14) is comparable to ἐάν. There are about sixty-five NT occurrences of conditional sentences using ἐάν that have a present indicative verb in the apodosis. See, e.g., 1 Cor 8:8b: "we are no worse off [ὑστερούμεθα] if we do not eat, and no better [περισσεύομεν] if we do."

51. Wallace, *Greek Grammar*, 521.

52. This logic would seem to fit some of the grammatical and semantic parallels elsewhere in the NT. See especially Rom 11:22, which I note above. Other parallel texts appear to define a status; see, e.g., Rom 8:9: "You, however, are [ἐστέ] not in the realm of the flesh but are in the realm of the Spirit, if indeed [εἴπερ] the Spirit of God lives in you." To have the Spirit within one puts one (by definition) in the realm of the Spirit. Other passages to be considered are John 6:53; 8:31; 13:8b, 17; 15:14; Rom 2:25; 2 Cor 13:5b; Col 1:22–23; 1 John 4:12.

53. Contra Fanning ("Classical Reformed View"), for whom the pattern he discerns in these verses indicates the author's basic perspective on the issue.

54. See esp. Schreiner, *Hebrews*, 119. I prefer not to characterize the logic here as "cause and effect" (as, e.g., B. J. Oropeza suggests ["The Warning Passages in Hebrews: Revised Theologies and New Methods of Interpretation," *CurBR* 10 {2011}: 85]). Wallace's semantic categories need to be expanded or nuanced: the rhetorical pattern of Hebrews—and may other NT texts—is one of "contingency—consequence."

Theology in Application

The Household of God

The household was considered one of the most fundamental and important social entities in the ancient world. Its health, cohesiveness, and good order were considered essential for the well-being of the state. Unlike our modern nuclear family, the ancient household often included extended families as well as house slaves and others who might live and work in the confines of a household. Early Christians quickly appropriated the household to describe the nature of the new people of God. This image of the church is central to the argument of 1 Timothy, as the summary language in 1 Timothy 3:15 indicates: "If I am delayed, you will know how people ought to conduct themselves in God's household, which is the church of the living God, the pillar and foundation of the truth." Like the earthly household, the spiritual household is a collection of very different individuals who need to learn to live and work in harmony. Like the earthly household, the spiritual household requires leaders who maintain good order. And, like the earthly household, the spiritual household needs to establish good relationships with the world it is a part of.

The author to the Hebrews, therefore, has a rich, developing theological tradition to draw from when he portrays believers as brothers and sisters who belong to a household. As I have noted, this tradition extends back into the Old Testament, where "house" language regularly occurs as a way of referring to the people of God. And, as we have also seen, the imagery is complicated by the way the word "house" can refer both to the place where people live as well as to the people themselves. In the Old Testament, this duality is seen in the way "house" can refer to the temple—the place where the people of God gather—as well as to the people.

"House" never refers to a church building or place of worship in the New Testament; as in the New Testament generally, the focus is on the people themselves. Since we know so little about the destination of Hebrews, it is hard to be sure whether his references to "house" in this text refer to individual "house churches" or to the people of God as a whole, who constitute one universal "house." The author's basic theological argument, however, seems to favor this latter reading. We are therefore reminded of the single family, or to put it in Pauline terms, the single "body of Christ," to which everyone who believes belongs. This family, incredibly diverse as it is, is united in being rooted in—indeed, created by—the Son whom everyone in the family acknowledges as their Lord.

Hebrews 3:7–11

Literary Context

As we have seen, Hebrews is unlike any other New Testament letter in shifting repeatedly between exposition and exhortation. These genres have both been on display in the letter so far: exposition in 1:1–14; exhortation in 2:1–4; exposition in 2:5–18; and a mixture of both in 3:1–6. Now our author introduces a long section of exhortation. The material in 3:7–4:11 has an obvious coherence, everything being related more or less directly to the introductory quotation of Psalm 95:7b–11 (94:7b–11 LXX). After the initial full quotation, the author cites portions of the text in 3:15; 4:3, 5, 7. The section falls clearly into three parts: the quotation (3:7–11) and two exhortations grounded in the language of the quotation: 3:12–19, which focuses on the word "today" from the psalm and warns about "unbelief," and 4:1–11, which focuses on the word "rest" and urges the readers to enter that rest (4:1–11). The author beautifully uses the narrative of Israel's pilgrimage from Egypt to the promised land as a warning to his readers. As that earlier generation of the people of God failed to enter God's rest because of unbelief, so the believers the author addresses are in danger of failing to enter the ultimate "rest" God has promised them.[1]

A more difficult question to answer is the place of this passage within the larger argument. One obvious possibility is that 3:7–4:11 is an extended exhortation based on the comparison between Moses and Christ in 3:1–6.[2] The comparison of the two leaders of the people of God morphs naturally into a comparison between the two groups of people they lead. However, while 3:1–6 (with its references to Num 12:7) and 3:7–4:11 are obviously linked in their mutual dependence on the story of Israel's wilderness wandering, the lack of focus on Christ's "leadership," in contrast to that of

---

1. Käsemann, in his influential monograph, argues that the "wandering people of God" theme developed in this section of Hebrews is the organizing concept of the letter (*Wandering People of God*).

2. "Christ is greater than Moses" (3:1–4:13) would then match the alleged "Christ is greater than the angels" theme of 1:5–2:18 (France, "Hebrews," 58). While not necessarily seeing an overarching "Christ greater than Moses" theme, others who view 3:1–4:11 (or 4:13) as a section are Weiss, *Der Brief an die Hebräer*, 237–38; Cockerill, *Hebrews*, 153.

Moses (and Joshua), suggests that "Moses versus Christ" is not the theme of the latter section. The paragraph 3:1–6, however, hints at two themes that follow. First, Christ's faithfulness is implicitly set against the unfaithfulness of the wilderness generation. Second, reference to the people of God (God's "house" in 3:2, 3, 4, 5, 6) and the need for perseverance to attain the goal anticipates the main direction of what follows; see especially the concluding warning: "we belong to this house, if we hold fast to our confidence and to the hope we boast in" (3:6). Hebrews 3:7–4:11 elaborates this "if" clause.[3]

I think it is better, then, to treat 3:7–4:11 as a discrete stage within the author's opening argument in 1:5–4:13.[4] It is an extended exhortation that unpacks the condition the author has introduced in 3:6b: "we belong to this house, if [and only if!] we hold fast to our confidence and to the hope we boast in" (cf. 3:14). The extensive appeal to the narrative of the wilderness generation brings into the open the story that has apparently mildly influenced our author in 2:10–18 (see "pioneer" in v. 10, and our notes there) and served as the clear background in 3:1–6.

> **I. The Exalted Son and a Rest for the People of God (1:1–4:13)**
>   A. Exordium (1:1–4)
>   B. Exposition: The Exalted Status of the Son (1:5–14)
>   C. Exhortation: Take Hold of Your Great Salvation (2:1–4)
>   D. Exposition: The Humanity of the Son and Its Significance (2:5–18)
>   E. Exhortation: Focus on the Faithful Son (3:1–6)
>   F. Exhortation: Avoid the Fate of the Wilderness Generation (3:7–4:11)
>   **1. The Warning from Scripture (3:7–11)**
>   2. The Disaster of Unbelief (3:12–19)
>   3. Entering the Rest (4:1–11)
>   G. Exposition: The Power of the Word of God (4:12–13)
> **II. Our Great High Priest and His Ministry (4:14–10:31)**
> **III. Exhortation: Follow and Serve the Pioneer of Our Faith through Endurance and Faith (10:32–13:25)**

Main Idea

The author cites an Old Testament passage warning about the unbelief that prevents God's people from reaching their intended blessed destiny as a basis for his extended warning and exhortation to his readers.

---

3. Johnson, *Hebrews*, 104–5.

4. Grässer, *An die Hebräer*, 1:173; Lane, *Hebrews*, 1:83.

Translation

Hebrews 3:7–11

7a	inference (from 6d–f)	Therefore,
7b	verification	as the Holy Spirit says:
7c	time	"Today
7d	condition	if you hear his voice,
8a	exhortation	**do not harden your hearts**,
8b	comparison	as happened in the rebellion,
8c	time	on the day of testing
8d	place	in the wilderness,
9a	expansion (of 8b)	where your ancestors tested me in a trial
9b	contra-expectation	even though they saw my works
10a	time	for forty years.
10b	result (of 9a)	Therefore
10c	assertion	**I was angry with that generation and**
10d	parallel	**said**:
10e	time	'Always
10f	content (of 10d)	they are straying from me
10g	sphere	in their hearts,
10h	parallel (to 10f)	they have not known my ways.'
11a	result	So
11b	oath	**I swore in my wrath:**
11c	content	'They shall never enter into my rest.'" (Ps 95:7b–11)

Structure

After an introduction (Heb 3:7a), the author quotes Psalm 95:7b–11 (Heb 3:7b–11).

Exegetical Outline

→ **1. The Warning from Scripture (3:7–11)**
   a. Introduction to the Quotation (v. 7a)
   b. Quotation of Psalm 95:7b–11 (vv. 7b–11)

Explanation of the Text

3:7a Therefore, as the Holy Spirit says (Διό, καθὼς λέγει τὸ πνεῦμα τὸ ἅγιον). The author introduces an Old Testament quotation as the product of the Spirit. The "therefore" (διό) is dependent especially on the last part of verse 6: we are God's house, we belong to his family *if and only if* we firmly hold on to the new status we have been graciously given by God. God's warning to the people of David's day in Psalm 95, reminding them of the disastrous results of unbelief for the people of God in Moses's day, pointedly and evocatively reinforces that warning. The New Testament regularly associates the Holy Spirit with Old Testament revelation (Matt 22:43// Mark 12:36; Acts 1:16; 4:25; 28:25; 1 Pet 1:11). But Hebrews is the only New Testament writer to attribute words of the Old Testament directly and only to the Holy Spirit (see also 10:15; cf. 9:8). The author's mention of the Spirit alone fits with his view of the Old Testament as a word that speaks directly to the people of God of his own day (see "In Depth: The Old Testament in Hebrews" on pp. 54–59) and suits especially well his application of Psalm 95 directly to his audience.

3:7b–11 "Today if you hear his voice,[5] 8 do not harden your hearts, as happened in the rebellion, on the day of testing in the wilderness, 9 where[6] your ancestors tested me in a trial even though they saw my works for forty years. 10 Therefore I was angry with that generation and said: 'Always they are straying from me in their hearts, they have not known my ways.' 11 So[7] I swore in my wrath: 'They shall never enter[8] into my rest'" (Σήμερον ἐὰν τῆς φωνῆς αὐτοῦ ἀκούσητε, 8 μὴ σκληρύνητε τὰς καρδίας ὑμῶν ὡς ἐν τῷ παραπικρασμῷ κατὰ τὴν ἡμέραν τοῦ πειρασμοῦ ἐν τῇ ἐρήμῳ, 9 οὗ ἐπείρασαν οἱ πατέρες ὑμῶν ἐν δοκιμασίᾳ καὶ εἶδον τὰ ἔργα μου 10 τεσσεράκοντα ἔτη διὸ προσώχθισα τῇ γενεᾷ ταύτῃ καὶ εἶπον, Ἀεὶ πλανῶνται τῇ καρδίᾳ, αὐτοὶ δὲ οὐκ ἔγνωσαν τὰς ὁδούς μου, 11 ὡς ὤμοσα ἐν τῇ ὀργῇ μου· Εἰ εἰσελεύσονται εἰς τὴν κατάπαυσίν μου). A long quotation from Psalm 95 uses the "rest" theme from the era of Israel's wilderness wandering as the basis for a renewed exhortation. Psalm 95 (94 LXX) consists of a puzzling mixture of praise and warning.[9] It opens with an invitation to extol the Lord as the God who has created all things and who has graciously adopted Israel as his people. In verse 7a, the psalmist rejoices in the fact that "we are the people of his pasture, the flock under his care." But he then suddenly turns to the warning that our author quotes (vv. 7b–11). In a sense, this movement in the psalm parallels the sequence we find in Hebrews: "we are his house/people"—*if* we hold fast to our confidence (v. 6a) and do not harden our hearts (vv. 7b–11).

---

5. It is not clear whether the Hebrew text of Ps 95:7b should be translated "if you hear" (an ordinary condition: ESV; see Goldingay, *Psalms 90–150*, 95) or "if only you would hear" (an implied exhortation: see NIV and most translations; Frank-Lothar Hossfeld and Erich Zenger, *Psalms 2: A Commentary on Psalms 51–100*, Hermeneia [Minneapolis: Fortress, 2005], 458).

6. The Greek word behind "where" (οὗ) can also be translated "when" (NJB; Zerwick and Grosvenor, *Grammatical Analysis*, 659).

7. "So" translates ὡς, which would often be translated "as." However, the word can have a consecutive sense, which works well here (NIV; NLT; CSB; BDAG ["ὡς," 1105, §4]; Koester, *Hebrews*, 256; Ellingworth, *Hebrews*, 220).

8. The εἰ introducing this clause reflects the Hebrew word *'im*, used to introduce an oath ("εἰ," BDAG 278, §4; "אִם," *DCH* 1:304, §2a; T. Muraoka, *A Syntax of Septuagint Greek* [Leuven: Peeters, 2016], 766–67).

9. This mixture has given rise to suspicions that the psalm is not an original unity; for evaluation and conclusion in favor of unity, see Hossfeld and Zenger, *Psalms 2*, 458–60.

As is his custom, the author appears to take the wording of his quotation from the LXX, or from a Greek text very similar to it. The author makes a few minor stylistic changes.[10] One change, however, is substantive. In both the MT and the LXX, "for forty years" modifies what follows it: "I was angry with that generation for forty years." However, Hebrews, by inserting the inferential particle "therefore" (διό) immediately after the phrase, attaches it to what precedes: "they saw my works for forty years." The author's reference to this text in verse 17—"With whom was he angry for forty years?"—indicates that he knows the original sequence. His change in the quotation has the effect of putting greater stress on the privileges of the people and, consequently, their responsibility: *for forty years* they witnessed the marvelous things God did for his people.[11]

The author's use of Psalm 95 involves a kind of bifocal approach to the Old Testament. The psalmist appeals to the Pentateuchal story of Israel's failure in the wilderness to warn his own generation about the danger of the "hard heart." The story is well-known. With display after display of his power to the Egyptians, God powerfully led his people from slavery in Egypt into the wilderness. Here they received the law from God; here they again saw example after example of God's power and his care for them; and here they constantly "test" God by questioning his power and goodness (see esp. Exod 17:1–7, where both Massah ["testing"] and Meribah ["quarreling"] are mentioned). This questioning reaches its pinnacle at Kadesh (Barnea), where, in a decisive act of rebellion, the people refuse to follow the exhortation of Joshua and Caleb to believe God's promise that they would be able to conquer the land (Num 13:26–14:35; 20:1–21). God therefore condemns that generation to wander in the wilderness until all (except a select few) are dead. The author, after putting this narrative before his readers via the Psalm 95 quotation, uses various specifics from both this narrative and from the psalm to exhort and warn his readers.

Theology in Application

When we think of the wilderness generation, to which our author points with his quotation of Psalm 95, we often use a happy alliteration: "wilderness wandering." The language has biblical precedent: the Old Testament speaks of the Lord expressing his wrath against his people by making them "wander in the wilderness forty years" (e.g., Num 32:13). Since the author draws a comparison between that generation

---

10. Stylistic changes: in place of the LXX verb "tested" (ἐδοκίμασαν), Hebrews has a prepositional phrase, "in testing" (ἐν δοκιμασίᾳ, v. 9a, which is closer to the MT); the author uses a different spelling of two verbal forms (LXX εἴδοσαν ["they saw"] becomes εἶδον in v. 9b; LXX εἶπα ["I said"] becomes εἶπον in v. 10a); the author omits a καί ("and") before the clause "they know my ways" in v. 10b (and adds the postpositive δέ instead). The author follows the LXX in "translating" Hebrew place names: "Meribah" becomes "rebellion" (παραπικρασμῷ) and "Massah" becomes "testing" (πειρασμοῦ, v. 8). The phrase "that generation" (τῇ γενεᾷ ἐκείνῃ) becomes "this generation" (τῇ γενεᾷ ταύτῃ, v. 10). The LXX, however, does not use the word παραπικρασμός ("rebellion") in the Pentateuchal narratives. For an overview and analysis of the textual situation, see, e.g., Pierce, *Divine Discourse*, 142–46.

11. See, e.g., Peter E. Enns, "Creation and Re-Creation: Psalm 95 and Its Interpretation in Hebrews 3:1–4:13," *WTJ* 55 (1993): 273–75. As a way of making "forty years" refer to the same period of time in this verse and in 3:17, Cockerill suggests that the "works" the people saw were the post-Kadesh acts of God's judgment (*Hebrews*, 180–81).

and his audience, it is also popular to use the image of "the wandering people of God" for Hebrews's own theology.[12] If the language is being applied to the spiritual condition of the people, it may not be inappropriate: the author is worried that they have become aimless, that they have lost their spiritual focus, that they are "drifting away" (2:1). But "wandering," which suggests aimless movement, is not appropriate language to describe what the author wants for his audience. God has provided a direct route from the prison of sin people find themselves in to the "rest" he has called them to. We Christians are not called to "wander" but to move confidently and directly toward the rest so that we might "enter in." Our confidence in moving toward this goal is rooted in the fact that our "pioneer," Christ (2:10), has opened this route for us. "Christ perfects pilgrims by taking them on a path he himself walked—without wandering."[13]

---

12. See esp. Käsemann, *Wandering People of God*.

13. Daniel J. Treier, "'Mediator of a New Covenant': Atonement and Christology in Hebrews," in *So Great a Salvation: A Dialogue on Atonement in Hebrews*, ed. Jon C. Laansma, George H. Guthrie, and Cynthia Long Westfall, LNTS 516 (London: T&T Clark, 2019), 115.

Hebrews 3:12–19

Literary Context

In this paragraph (3:12–19) and the following one (4:1–11) the author draws out the implications of Psalm 95:7b–11 (quoted in Heb 3:7b–11) for his readers. In this first stage of exhortation, the author reapplies to his readers the psalmist's warnings against following the wilderness generation in having a "wandering heart" (Ps 95:10; see v. 12) and "a hardened heart" (Ps 95:8; see v. 13). He underscores the seriousness of these warnings by reminding his readers about the time in which they live: the "today" of God's invitation to participate in his final rest—a theme the author will elaborate in 4:1–11. In addition to Psalm 95, the author also clearly reflects language and concepts from the original narrative to which the psalmist alludes. As Laansma says, "The Scriptures are the matrix of Heb 3,7–4,11."[1] Numbers 13:26–14:35 describes the ultimate failure of the people of Israel to trust God's promises and providence. They ignore the warning of Joshua and Caleb not to "rebel against the LORD" (14:9) but rather to "go up and take possession of the land" (13:30). In fear of the powerful people living in that land, the people again "grumble" against the leadership of Moses and Aaron (14:2) and "refuse to believe" in the Lord (14:11). The Lord therefore condemns the entire generation—with the exception of Joshua and Caleb—to wander in the wilderness until they are all dead. "Not one of you [who rebelled] will enter the land" (14:30).

I. **The Exalted Son and a Rest for the People of God (1:1–4:13)**
   A. Exordium (1:1–4)
   B. Exposition: The Exalted Status of the Son (1:5–14)
   C. Exhortation: Take Hold of Your Great Salvation (2:1–4)
   D. Exposition: The Humanity of the Son and Its Significance (2:5–18)
   E. Exhortation: Focus on the Faithful Son (3:1–6)
   F. Exhortation: Avoid the Fate of the Wilderness Generation (3:7–4:11)
      1. The Warning from Scripture (3:7–11)
      2. **The Disaster of Unbelief (3:12–19)**
      3. Entering the Rest (4:1–11)
   G. Exposition: The Power of the Word of God (4:12–13)
II. Our Great High Priest and His Ministry (4:14–10:31)
III. Exhortation: Follow and Serve the Pioneer of Our Faith through Endurance and Faith (10:32–13:25)

Main Idea

The author uses the language of his quotation of Psalm 95:7b–11 to exhort his readers to trust the Lord and not to turn away from him in disobedience.

Translation

Hebrews 3:12–19

12a	address	Brothers and sisters,
12b	warning	**see to it**
12c	content	that there is in none of you an evil unbelieving heart
12d	description	that turns away from the living God.
13a	contrast (with 12b–d)	But
13b	exhortation	**exhort one another**
13c	time	each day—
13d	expansion	as long as it is called "Today"—
13e	purpose (of 13b)	so that none of you will be hardened
13f	means	through the deceitfulness of sin.
14a	aside	For
14b	assertion	**we are partakers of Christ—**

14c	condition		if, indeed, we hold fast to the reality we first possessed
14d	manner		firmly to the end.
15a	resumption (of quote)	As it says,	
15b	time		"Today
15c	condition		if you hear his voice,
15d	exhortation		do not harden your hearts
15e	comparison		as you did in the rebellion." (Ps 95:7-8)
16a	question	**Who were**	**those**
16b	identification		who, having heard, then rebelled?
16c	rhetorical question	**Was it not all those**	
16d	identification		who came out of Egypt
16e	circumstance		through Moses?
17a	question	**With**	**whom was he angry**
17b	time		for forty years?
17c	rhetorical question	**Was it not**	**those**
17d	identification 1		who sinned,
17e	identification 2		whose bodies fell in the wilderness?
18a	question	And **to**	**whom did he swear**
18b	content		that they would never enter his rest
18c	answer	if not	those
18d	identification		who disobeyed?
19a	inference	(from 16–18)	And so
19b	assertion	**we see**	
19c	content		that they were not able to enter
19d	cause		because of unbelief.

Structure

The paragraph again exhibits an *inclusio*, with the key words "see" and "unbelief" found at both the beginning (v. 12) and the end (v. 19). Verses 12–13 take up words from Psalm 95 to warn (v. 12) and encourage (v. 13) the readers. Verse 14a grounds these imperatives with a reminder of the new status believers enjoy—a status, however, that depends on continuing perseverance (v. 14b). The author wraps up this initial section of the paragraph with a further reference to Psalm 95 (v. 15). Verses 16–18 offer a series of questions to bring home to the readers the seriousness of their situation. Using a rhetorical device called *subjectio*, these questions implicitly suggest a comparison between their situation and that of the wilderness generation. This section ends with a comment from the author that summarizes the point he wants his readers to understand: that generation could not "enter" the rest God had offered them "because of their unbelief."

Exegetical Outline

→ **2. The Disaster of Unbelief (3:12–19)**
    a. Exhortations Based on Psalm 95 (vv. 12–15)
    b. Warnings Based on Numbers 14 (vv. 16–19)

Explanation of the Text

3:12 Brothers and sisters, see to it that there is in none of you an evil unbelieving heart that turns away from the living God (Βλέπετε, ἀδελφοί, μήποτε ἔσται ἔν τινι ὑμῶν καρδία πονηρὰ ἀπιστίας ἐν τῷ ἀποστῆναι ἀπὸ θεοῦ ζῶντος). The opening two verses of this paragraph pick up language from Psalm 95 to warn the readers not to follow in the footsteps of the wilderness generation. The author addresses his readers as "brothers and sisters" (ἀδελφοί), a designation he uses rather sparingly (see also 3:1; 10:19; 13:22). The opening verb in the verse is variously translated: "take care" (ESV), "be careful" (NLT), "watch out" (CSB; CEB), "see to it" (NIV; NET). I have opted for this last option because it enables us to preserve in English the obvious *inclusio* with verse 19, where the same Greek verb is used (βλέπομεν, "we see"). The various translations give a good sense of how this verb is used in contexts like this, where the concern is to urge close attention to a particular point (see also Heb 12:25). Luke 8:18 makes especially clear that any notion of seeing in the usual sense of the word is lost when the word is used this way: "see how you hear" (author's translation). The present tense of the verb form here suggests the need for "perpetual vigilance."[2]

What the readers are to "watch out for" is the presence in any of them of "an evil unbelieving heart." The two modifiers of "heart" have different forms: "evil" translates an adjective (πονηρά), while "unbelieving" translates a noun in the genitive ("of unbelief," ἀπιστίας). The two words, however, function similarly, each of them referring to a quality of the heart. "Heart" (καρδία), as is usual in Scripture, refers to the animating center of a person. The whole phrase alludes to the description of the wilderness generation in Psalm 95:10: "always they are straying from me in their hearts." The author adds an additional description of the heart, which takes the form of a Greek infinitive clause (ἐν τῷ ἀποστῆναι ἀπὸ θεοῦ ζῶντος), which can be straightforwardly rendered "in turning away from the living God."[3] The construction often signifies time, but this does not work very well here: "a heart while turning from the living God."[4] We are therefore encouraged to look at other options, the

---

1. Laansma, *"I Will Give You Rest,"* 264.
2. Cockerill, *Hebrews*, 182.
3. Characterizing God as "living" (ζῶντος) is a motif in Hebrews; see also 9:14; 10:31; 12:22. It is not clear, then, whether he uses the phrase here under the influence of Num 14:21, 28 ("as I live," LXX ζῶ ἐγώ). Some interpreters think that referring here to falling away from the living God implies that the readers are gentiles, because Jews would fall away from Christ but not necessarily God. However, the author's radical reconfiguration of "God" in christological terms might very well lead him to think of Jews who abandon Christ as falling away from God as well.
4. BDF §404.3 therefore notes that the construction here has "a sense not purely temporal."

two most likely being that it signifies the result of this evil, unbelieving heart—a heart "leading you to fall away" (ESV)[5]—or that it adds a further description of the heart: it is a heart "that turns away from the living God."[6] This latter option makes best sense. The author adds this description because it captures one of the basic concerns he has for his readers: that they will "fall away" (6:6); "drift away" (2:1); "throw away [their] confidence" (10:35).

3:13 But exhort[7] one another each day—as long as it is called "Today"—so that none of you will be hardened through the deceitfulness of sin (ἀλλὰ παρακαλεῖτε ἑαυτοὺς καθ᾽ ἑκάστην ἡμέραν, ἄχρις οὗ τὸ Σήμερον καλεῖται, ἵνα μὴ σκληρυνθῇ τις ἐξ ὑμῶν ἀπάτῃ τῆς ἁμαρτίας). The combination of address to the readers in general with individual concern in verse 12 continues in more emphatic form in this verse: *all* the readers are to be "exhorting one another"[8] with the purpose that *none* of them would be hardened. The community as a whole is to exercise watchful and loving care for each one of its participants. As Calvin notes, Christian communities must constantly engage in this kind of mutual encouragement: "unless our faith is repeatedly encouraged, it lies dormant; unless it is warmed, it grows cold; unless it is aroused, it gets numb."[9] The concern about hardening applies to the readers the key warning from Psalm 95: "do not harden your hearts" (v. 8). To be "hardened" is to become spiritually insensitive, to close oneself off to the impact of God's word.[10] The instrument of this hardening is "the deceitfulness of sin." This phrase renders a genitive construction (ἀπάτη τῆς ἁμαρτίας) which might mean "deceitfulness that sin possesses" or, perhaps more likely, "the deceitfulness that sin carries out" (a subjective genitive). The NLT captures the sense well: "so that none of you will be deceived by sin and hardened against God."[11] On this reading, the author characterizes sin as a kind of power that actively works to trick people into thinking wrongly about God.[12]

Amid this warning against hardening, the author introduces an aside about "today." This aside is triggered by the reference to "each day" (καθ᾽ ἑκάστην ἡμέραν),[13] which leads the author to think of the emphatic introduction to the warning in Psalm 95: "*Today* if you hear his voice...." The author signals his intention to quote from Psalm 95 by using the article before "today" (τὸ σήμερον):

---

5. Wallace, *Greek Grammar*, 593.

6. Most of the English translations adopt this view; see, e.g., Lane, *Hebrews*, 1:82; Koester, *Hebrews*, 258. The author's three other uses of this construction are not strictly temporal either: 2:8; 3:15; 8:13. The author may have been influenced to use the verb ἀφίστημι by Num 14:9, which warns the people not to be "apostates" (LXX ἀποστάται) from the Lord.

7. Many versions have "encourage one another." The verb παρακαλέω can mean either "encourage" or "exhort." There is little difference between them in this context, "encourage" being a bit milder ("I encourage you to try the cookies"; "I exhort you: stop this misbehavior!").

8. The normally reflexive pronoun ἑαυτούς (here "yourselves") has a reciprocal ("one another," often ἀλλήλους) meaning here (von Siebenthal, *Ancient Greek Grammar*, 208).

9. Calvin, *Hebrews*, 41.

10. The verb is σκληρύνω. Its best-known biblical occurrences come in Exod 4–14, where it describes God's hardening of Pharaoh's heart and Pharaoh's hardening of his own heart (fourteen occurrences). See also, as a typical example of the verb's usage, Isa 63:17: "Why, Lord, do you make us wander from your ways and harden our hearts so we do not revere you?" Apart from references to Ps 95 in the context (3:13, 15; 4:7), the verb occurs elsewhere in the NT only in Acts 19:9; Rom 9:18. Note also the cognate words σκληροκαρδία ("hard of heart") in Matt 19:8 and Mark 10:5; and σκληροτράχηλος ("hard-necked," "stiff-necked") in Acts 7:51. See K. L. Schmidt and M. A. Schmidt, "παχύνω, κτλ," *TDNT* 5:1030.

11. Johnson, *Hebrews*, 117, thinks the genitive is epexegetic: "deceitfulness that is sin."

12. Personifying sin in this way is very common in Paul, especially in passages such as Rom 5–8. See esp. Rom 7:11: "for sin, seizing the opportunity afforded by the commandment, deceived [ἐξηπάτησεν] me, and through the commandment put me to death."

13. The preposition καθ᾽ (κατά) is distributive.

we might paraphrase as "the 'today' from the quotation." This "today" connects the context of the psalmist with that of the author and his readers: both live in the same salvation-historical period, a time when God's voice is being heard and the invitation to enter into his rest by a faithful response to that voice is open. As France puts it, "the early Christians for whom he is writing are not just another generation of Jews, but are the people of the New Exodus."[14] But "as long as" (ἄχρις οὗ) reminds us that this "today" will not last forever: there will come a time when this invitation will no longer be open.[15]

3:14 For we are partakers of Christ—if, indeed, we hold fast to the reality we first possessed firmly to the end (μέτοχοι γὰρ τοῦ Χριστοῦ γεγόναμεν, ἐάνπερ τὴν ἀρχὴν τῆς ὑποστάσεως μέχρι τέλους βεβαίαν κατάσχωμεν). A somewhat parenthetical warning reinforces the point made in verse 6b: belonging to Christ requires perseverance. The sequence of thought in this part of the paragraph is unclear. We might think that this verse grounds verse 13 (or vv. 12 and 13). It could do so by reminding the people not to throw away their current status as "participants in Christ." Or, perhaps more likely, it could reinforce the exhortations of verses 12 and 13 by reminding the readers that it is only those who "hold fast" (negatively, who don't have an "evil unbelieving heart" [v. 12] or don't "harden" themselves [v. 13]) who will enjoy this status. The verse could, then, conclude the first section of the paragraph, with the citation of Psalm 95:7–8 in verse 15 setting the stage for a fresh series of warnings in verses 16–18.[16] However, while certainly having a relationship to what follows, I think that verse 15 has a closer relationship with what precedes, providing a final bracket of references to Psalm 95 around 3:7–15. On this view, then, verse 14 is an aside.[17] However, we should quickly add that labeling a text as an aside in no way diminishes its overall importance. An aside interrupts the sequence of thought, but the very fact an author thinks it necessary to introduce the aside indicates its importance for the larger message.

The importance of the verse for the author's ultimate purpose is indicated by the way it mirrors verse 6, which, like this verse, asserts that the readers presently possess great spiritual benefit—"we belong to this house"—but only "if . . . we hold fast" (ἐάνπερ . . . κατάσχωμεν in both verses) "to our confidence and to the hope we boast in"/"to the reality we first possessed." Belonging to God's house—that is, belonging to God's people—in verse 6 becomes "partakers of Christ" in this verse. The Greek (μέτοχοι . . . τοῦ Χριστοῦ) could mean "partners with Christ" (NET; CEB; see NRSV), especially in light of the focus on believers as "brothers and sisters" with Christ in 2:11.[18] But in the three other texts where the author uses this construction (μέτοχοι with a genitive), the word in the genitive (here τοῦ Χριστοῦ) indicates the thing or person in which someone "shares" or "participates."[19] The author therefore joins with other early Christians

---

14. R. T. France, "The Writer of Hebrews as a Biblical Expositor," *TynBul* 47 (1996): 270.
15. Koester, *Hebrews*, 265.
16. E.g., Koester, *Hebrews*, 261; Ellingworth, *Hebrews*, 225–26.
17. The standard Greek text (NA[28]) uses punctuation to mark v. 14 as an aside and puts a minor paragraph break between vv. 15 and 16. See also, e.g., Attridge, *Hebrews*, 117; Johnson, *Hebrews*, 118; Lane, *Hebrews*, 1:88.

18. E.g., Delitzsch, *Hebrews*, 1:177; Montefiore, *Hebrews*, 78; Koester, *Hebrews*, 260.
19. "Partakers in the heavenly calling" in 3:1; "those who share in the Holy Spirit" in 6:4; and those who "participate in discipline" in 12:8 (my translation). For this meaning, see, e.g., Attridge, *Hebrews*, 117; Ellingworth, *Hebrews*, 226–27.

in describing salvation in terms of a participation in Christ himself (see also, e.g., Rom 6:1–6; Gal 2:19–20; Phil 3:10–11; 1 John 2:28; cf. John 15).

As in verse 6, however, this relationship exists[20] only if we persevere: we must hold fast to "the reality we first possessed." The word we translate as "reality" might also mean "conviction" or "confidence," as many English translations attest (e.g., ESV: "if indeed we hold our original confidence firm to the end").[21] The word used here (ὑπόστασις) has this subjective sense of confidence in two of its five New Testament occurrences (2 Cor 9:4; 11:17) and might also have this sense in one of its three occurrences in Hebrews (11:1; see the notes there). However, as we have seen, the word has an objective sense—"essential reality"—in 1:3, and it might be preferable to give it this meaning here also (e.g., CSB: "if we hold firmly until the end the reality that we had at the start").[22] Our place in the people of God, acquired through participation in Christ, is a solid reality that we are given when we first believe.[23] But this reality is true only for those who hold their original conviction firmly to the end.[24] See, e.g., 1 John 2:24: "See that what you have heard from the beginning remains in you. If it does, you also will remain in the Son and in the Father."

3:15 As it says, "Today if you hear his voice, do not harden your hearts as you did in the rebellion" (ἐν τῷ λέγεσθαι Σήμερον ἐὰν τῆς φωνῆς αὐτοῦ ἀκούσητε, Μὴ σκληρύνητε τὰς καρδίας ὑμῶν ὡς ἐν τῷ παραπικρασμῷ). As I argued in our comments on verse 14, this verse concludes the section that begins in verse 12 (or v. 7). The author comes full circle, citing a fragment of Psalm 95 to remind them of his textual basis.[25] At the same time, however, it also looks forward, since two of the words in the citation—"hear" and "rebellion"—are picked up in verse 16. Verse 15 is therefore a janus, looking both backward and forward.[26]

3:16 Who were those who, having heard, then rebelled?[27] Was it not all those who came out of Egypt through Moses? (τίνες γὰρ ἀκούσαντες παρεπίκραναν; ἀλλ᾽ οὐ πάντες οἱ ἐξελθόντες ἐξ Αἰγύπτου διὰ Μωϋσέως;). The warning in these verses is sharpened by the reminder that those who turned away from God were those who also experienced the miracles of the exodus. Verse 16 marks a shift in the argument. Quotations of Psalm 95 frame the first part of the text, with the exhortations in verses 12 and 13 using language from that text. Beginning in verse 16, the author mixes

---

20. In v. 6, the author uses the present tense—"we belong [ἐσμεν] to this house"—while he uses the perfect here—"we have come to be [γεγόναμεν] partakers of Christ." But, particularly if we think of the perfect tense as indicating a state, the two are very close in meaning. Wallace (*Greek Grammar*, 576) labels this perfect as an "intensive perfect" (focusing on the resultant state of an action); Stanley E. Porter (*Verbal Aspect in the Greek of the New Testament with Reference to Tense and Mood* [New York: Lang, 1989], 269–70) labels it a "timeless perfect."

21. Moffatt, *Hebrews*, 48; see Cockerill, *Hebrews*, 189: "steadfastness."

22. E.g., deSilva, *Perseverance in Gratitude*, 150; Attridge, *Hebrews*, 119.

23. "When we first believe" in this sentence and "[that] we first possessed" in our translation reflect the governing word in a genitive phrase, τὴν ἀρχὴν τῆς ὑποστάσεως. We would normally render such a phrase something like "the beginning of. . . ." However, in contrast to μέχρι τέλους, "until the end," τὴν ἀρχὴν probably refers not to a first stage of the reality but to the reality that we had from the beginning (see, e.g., Koester, *Hebrews*, 260).

24. The Greek word βεβαίαν is a predicative adjective modifying ἀρχήν—"hold to the beginning firm." It is best translated as an adverb.

25. The author introduces the quotation with the infinitive clause ἐν τῷ λέγεσθαι, which we could woodenly render "in the saying." A fair paraphrase here might be "in what has been said" or "as it says" (NET) or "for it is said" (NAB).

26. D. Harris, *Hebrews*, 87.

27. The sequence of first "hearing" and then "rebelling" is signaled by the use of the aorist participle (ἀκούσαντες, "having heard") preceding the verb it modifies.

in allusions to the narrative on which the exhortations of Psalm 95 are based: Numbers 13:26–14:35. Indeed, the author's use of these two texts falls into a pattern, with the first part of verses 16, 17, and 18 alluding to Psalm 95, while the second part of each verse alludes to the Numbers narrative.[28] It is as if the author is expecting his readers to answer his initial questions with the details they know from the narrative. A second shift, one of style, is evident also, the straightforward exhortations and warnings of verses 12–14 giving way to a series of five questions in verses 16–18.

The first question in verse 16 uses the verbal cognate of "rebel" from Psalm 95, with the author using the verbal form cognate to the noun "rebellion" in Psalm 95:8.[29] Those who rebelled, the author claims, were the same people as those who "heard." "Hearing" picks up another key word from Psalm 95—"if you hear his voice" (3:7, 15)—and also an important point the author has made in chapters 1–2: because God has spoken definitively "in the Son" (1:2), it is vital to "pay very careful attention to what we have heard" (2:1). The author responds to this first question about the identity of those who heard and rebelled with a rhetorical question: Was it not "all those who came out of Egypt through Moses?"[30] "Through Moses" (διὰ Μωϋσέως) is an abbreviation for "under Moses's leadership."[31] The peoples' accountability for their refusal to enter the land is a recurring theme in the Numbers narrative; see, for example, Numbers 14:22–23: "Not one of those who saw my glory and the signs I performed in Egypt and in the wilderness but who disobeyed me and tested me ten times—not one of them will ever see the land I promised on oath to their ancestors. No one who has treated me with contempt will ever see it."

3:17 With whom was he angry for forty years? Was it not those who sinned, whose bodies fell in the wilderness? (τίσιν δὲ προσώχθισεν τεσσεράκοντα ἔτη; οὐχὶ τοῖς ἁμαρτήσασιν, ὧν τὰ κῶλα ἔπεσεν ἐν τῇ ἐρήμῳ;). God's anger at the rebellious Israelites was a response to their sin and was poignantly manifested in their death in the wilderness. The author repeats the basic point of verse 16 and again uses wording from Psalm 95 (προσώχθισεν ["was angry"], τεσσεράκοντα ἔτη ["forty years"]). As I noted in my comments on verses 7b–11, "forty years" is connected with "they saw my works" in the author's quotation (vv. 9b–10a) but is linked here, in accordance with the intent of the original text, with "he was angry."[32] God's punishment of the wilderness generation for forty years is mentioned twice in the Numbers 14 narrative (vv. 33, 34), and this same period of time is referred to in later texts (Num 32:13; Deut 2:7; 8:2, 4; 29:5; Neh 9:21; Amos 2:10; 5:25; Acts 7:36, 42; 13:18).

---

28. Lane, *Hebrews*, 1:88; Koester, *Hebrews*, 266.

29. The noun in Ps 95:8 is παραπικρασμός; the verb used here is παραπικραίνω (which occurs only here in the NT). It refers to rebellion against God during the wilderness wanderings in Deut 31:27; Ps 78:8; 105:28; 106:7, 33, 43; Ezekiel, among others, uses this same word to denote the "rebellion" of Israel that led to exile (e.g., 2:3, 5, 6, 7, 8; 3:9, 26, 27).

30. The question is introduced by οὐ, a particle that signals that the question expects a positive answer. This second question in the verse is also preceded by the conjunction ἀλλ' (usually "but"). The difficulty of the word here is signaled by the fact that no English translation represents it. BDAG ("ἀλλά," 45, §2) suggests that it might be a "strong asseveration": "*surely* it was all those who...*.*" Ellingworth, on the other hand, suggests an ellipsis: "*But* [how can you ask?] Was it not all those who...?" (*Hebrews*, 230–31).

31. "διά," BDAG 226, §A.4.a.

32. A few interpreters think that the author may have thought there were two periods of "forty years" (Lane, *Hebrews*, 1:89). But it is more likely that the author views the same period of time from two perspectives: a time when God's blessings are displayed and a time when God's judgment is being enacted. The διό that the author adds to the quotation in v. 10 may, therefore, indicate not a temporal distinction but a conceptual one (G. Guthrie, "Hebrews," 955).

The reference to "bodies" or "corpses" (τὰ κῶλα) that "fell in the wilderness" also comes from Numbers 14:29–30: "In this wilderness your bodies [τὰ κῶλα] will fall [πεσεῖται]—every one of you twenty years old or more who was counted in the census and who has grumbled against me. Not one of you will enter the land I swore with uplifted hand to make your home, except Caleb son of Jephunneh and Joshua son of Nun." Paul alludes to this same sobering display of God's judgment in 1 Corinthians 10:5: "God was not pleased with most of them; their bodies were scattered in the wilderness."[33] This judgment fell because the people "sinned," language that again may reflect the Numbers narrative: after God pronounced judgment on the people, they tried to rectify matters by affirming their intention to take the land after all, confessing, "Surely we have sinned" (14:40).[34] However, God rejects their tardy and undoubtedly insincere promise to obey: they had "turned away" and so the Lord would not be "with them" in this attempt (14:41–43). The author uses these rhetorical questions to suggest a comparison between the wilderness generation and his audience: their sin, if they continue in it, will lead to God's anger and ultimate judgment.[35]

3:18 And to whom did he swear that they would never enter his rest if not those who disobeyed? (τίσιν δὲ ὤμοσεν, μὴ εἰσελεύσεσθαι εἰς τὴν κατάπαυσιν αὐτοῦ εἰ μὴ τοῖς ἀπειθήσασιν;). The author continues to use questions to get his point across. In contrast to verses 16 and 17, where a rhetorical question in the second part of the verses answers the question in the first part of the verses, he now asks a single question that includes within it the answer. But he follows the pattern of using language from Psalm 95 in the first part of the verse and language from Numbers 14 in the second part. The author repeats the word of judgment from the psalm, that the people would "never enter his rest." "Rest" becomes a key motif in 4:1–11, where we will explore its meaning in some detail. For now, it is sufficient to note that it refers to the blessed state the people enjoy when they possess the land God has promised his people.[36] In the second part of the question, the author identifies those who hear this word of judgment as those who "disobeyed" (the verb is ἀπειθέω). This verb occurs in the LXX of Numbers 14:43b: "because you have turned away by disobeying [ἀπειθοῦντες] the Lord, the Lord will also not be among you" (NETS). See also Numbers 11:20, which pronounces judgment on the wilderness people "because you disobeyed the Lord" (NETS again). But perhaps even more important is Deuteronomy 9:23–24, which uses three key terms from verses 12–19: "When the LORD sent you from Kadesh-barnea, saying, 'Go up and occupy the land that I have given you,' you rebelled against ["disobeyed"; LXX ἠπειθήσατε] the command of the LORD your God, neither trusting [οὐκ ἐπιστεύσατε; see Heb 3:19] him nor obeying him ["hearing his voice"; LXX εἰσηκούσατε τῆς φωνῆς αὐτοῦ; see Heb 3:15, 16]. You have been rebellious ["disobedient";

---

33. There is no reason to think that Hebrews borrows directly from Paul in using the wilderness generation as a warning. Rather, it suggests that the narrative was a common early Christian "type" (see τύποι in 1 Cor 10:6; cf. Jude 5) for new-covenant believers. Early Christians reflect the widespread rhetorical use of the story among Jews (e.g., Neh 9:15–17; Ps 106:24–26; CD A 3.6–9; LAB 15).

34. The likelihood of an allusion to Numbers is increased by the fact that the author rarely uses the verb ἁμαρτάνω (only here and 10:26).

35. Verse 17b, like v. 16b, is a question expecting a positive answer (see the οὐχί).

36. The word the author uses, κατάπαυσις, only rarely refers to the land of promise (in addition to Ps 95:11, see also Deut 12:9). The cognate verb, καταπαύω, refers to rest in the promised land in Deut 3:20; 12:10; 25:19; Josh 1:13, 15.

LXX ἀπειθοῦντες] against the LORD as long as he has known you" (NRSV).[37]

3:19 And so we see that they were not able to enter because of unbelief (καὶ βλέπομεν ὅτι οὐκ ἠδυνήθησαν εἰσελθεῖν δι᾽ ἀπιστίαν). The root cause of judgment was unbelief. As most translations recognize, the conjunction that introduces this verse (καί), which often means simply "and," here has a consecutive sense ("so" in most versions).[38] The author draws a conclusion from this paragraph (and especially from vv. 16–18), using two key words from verse 12 to signal that he is wrapping up his argument: "see" (βλέπομεν here; βλέπετε in v. 12) and "unbelief" (ἀπιστίαν here; ἀπιστίας in v. 12). The shift to the first-person plural verb—"*we see*"—returns to the style of exhortation we have seen in verse 14—"*we* are partakers of Christ." The word "unbelief" occurs only here and in verse 12 in Hebrews (and none of its cognates occur in Hebrews). Once again, the author may have the Numbers narrative in view; in 14:11, the Lord addresses Moses: "How long will these people treat me with contempt? How long will they refuse to believe [οὐ πιστεύουσιν] in me, in spite of all the signs I have performed among them?" In light of the cognate "faithful" (πιστός) in 2:17; 3:2, 5, some interpreters want to translate the word here as "faithlessness."[39] However, it is better to align "faithlessness" with "disobedience" as the penultimate failure, while the ultimate failure is "unbelief":[40] the lack of a heartfelt, sincere trust in and commitment to God; to fail to trust God's word and power; to allow difficult circumstances to overwhelm us to the point where we can't follow God to the destiny he wants to bring us to.

Theology in Application

The Power of Stories

Modern studies of human learning and behavior confirm what preachers have always known: telling stories is an especially powerful way to shift perceptions and inculcate values. It is not, then, surprising that God has chosen to communicate his truth to humans by means of stories: most of the Bible, after all, is story or narrative. Of course, we must not take this to the extreme of deprecating other modes of communication. It is popular in some circles, for instance, to criticize or at least downplay the value of "propositions," in which one states truth in simple abstract fashion. The letters of the New Testament communicate mainly by way of such propositions, and we should not ignore their vital importance in forming our thinking and developing our theology.

Even in letters, however, writers will sometimes tell stories, or at least allude to stories, to drive home their teaching. Such is the case in Hebrews 3:7–4:11, where the author buttresses his exhortations to continue on the path of faithful Christian

---

37. Johnson, *Hebrews*, 119.
38. BDF §442.2.
39. E.g., Johnson, *Hebrews*, 119.
40. Cockerill, *Hebrews*, 193–94.

living and his warnings about turning away from God (3:6, 12–14; 4:1, 11) with constant reference to a well-known Old Testament story. Our author introduces this story indirectly through a psalm text (95:7b–11) that alludes to that story. It is the story of the people of God in the era of the exodus. Here are people who vividly see the power of God exercised on their behalf as he works miracles in Egypt, parts the Red Sea, and miraculously provides for his people in the wilderness. Their departure from Egypt had a special destination in view: a land "flowing with milk and honey" that could become a secure place for the people to flourish. At a critical point in this journey, scouts are sent ahead to spy out the land. They bring a mixed report back to the people: the land is, indeed, fertile, but it is inhabited by powerful nations. Faced with this sobering report, most of the people quail in fear and determine not to move forward. As a result of this unbelief in God's promise and power, leading to disobedience of the command to "go up and take the land," the people's pilgrimage becomes a wandering. They are condemned to move about the wilderness until that entire generation (with the exception of Joshua and Caleb) die off. This story clearly had a powerful impact on the people of Israel. The failure of the people in the face of God's call and provision has left its mark on other psalms as well (see esp. Ps 78:8–64, esp. v. 8; 81:1–16; 106:13–33, esp. vv. 24–27).

One of the first sermons I heard after coming to Christ in my early twenties was based on this story. The preacher warned us that we face our own "Kadesh Barneas" (the location of Israel's failure): times of testing when we are tempted to doubt the power and providence of God, when we are in danger of turning away and losing our vital relationship with the living God. That sermon along with the story it is based on has stayed with me powerfully to this day—almost fifty years later. The author to the Hebrews does something similar. By weaving into his exhortation allusions to this story, he brings it before the eyes of his audience, bringing home to them the seriousness of their tendency to wander from "the living God" (3:12). In that earlier time of salvation history, the corpses of the disobedient people "fell in the wilderness" (3:17)—a powerful image of the terrible fate awaiting those who turn away.

Hebrews 4:1–11

Literary Context

This paragraph is the second stage in the author's exhortations based on the quotation of Psalm 95:7b–11 in Hebrews 3:7b–11. The first stage of the author's "mini sermon" on Psalm 95 has a dominant negative flavor, as the author urges his audience not to follow the example of the wilderness generation, who were hardened in unbelief and suffered judgment as a result. This new stage of exhortation, while still including warnings (vv. 1–2, 11b), shifts the focus to the positive. As Koester notes, the author employs Psalm 95 as a "double-edged sword" (see v. 12) that issues strong warnings at the same time as it implies renewed opportunity.[1]

At the risk of imposing a "grand narrative" on the movement of the author's sermon, we might suggest that chapters 2–4 follow the pattern (see v. 11) of Israel's history: enslaved in Egypt, liberated by God's power in the exodus (2:14–15), condemned to wander in the wilderness for forty years (3:7–19). Unlike that generation of Israelites, however, the believers the author addresses have the opportunity to rewrite the ending of the story by grasping God's promise and entering into the rest.[2]

---

1. Koester, *Hebrews*, 275.
2. Koester, *Hebrews*, 276.

- I. **The Exalted Son and a Rest for the People of God (1:1–4:13)**
  - A. Exordium (1:1–4)
  - B. Exposition: The Exalted Status of the Son (1:5–14)
  - C. Exhortation: Take Hold of Your Great Salvation (2:1–4)
  - D. Exposition: The Humanity of the Son and Its Significance (2:5–18)
  - E. Exhortation: Focus on the Faithful Son (3:1–6)
  - F. Exhortation: Avoid the Fate of the Wilderness Generation (3:7–4:11)
    1. The Warning from Scripture (3:7–11)
    2. The Disaster of Unbelief (3:12–19)
    3. **Entering the Rest (4:1–11)**
  - G. Exposition: The Power of the Word of God (4:12–13)
- II. Our Great High Priest and His Ministry (4:14–10:31)
- III. Exhortation: Follow and Serve the Pioneer of Our Faith through Endurance and Faith (10:32–13:25)

Main Idea

God has invited his people to join in his "rest." While an earlier generation forfeited the promise of that rest because of unbelief and disobedience, Christians are now invited to enter into that rest, experiencing the ultimate salvation God has in store for those who believe.

Translation

Hebrews 4:1–11

1a	inference (from 3:19)	Therefore
1b	basis	since the promise of entering his rest remains,
1c	exhortation	**let us fear**
1d	content	lest any one of us be judged
1e	content	to have fallen short of it.
2a	explanation (of 1)	For
2b	assertion	**we also have had good news proclaimed to us**,
2c	comparison	just as they had.

Continued on next page.

2d	contrast (with 2a)	But **the word they heard did not profit them**
2e	cause	because they were not united
2f	description	with those who heard with faith.
3a	explanation (of 2d–f)	For
3b	assertion	**we who believe are those who enter the rest;**
3c	verification	as he says,
3d	oath	"As I swore in my anger:
3e	content	they will never enter my rest," (Ps 95:11)
3f	contrast (with 3c)	even though his works have been done
3g	time	since the foundation of the world.
4a	expansion (of 3f–g)	For
4b	assertion	somewhere **he has spoken**
4c	reference	concerning the seventh day
4d	manner	in this manner:
4e	content	"And God rested
4f	time	on the seventh day
4g	separation	from all his works." (Gen 2:2)
5a	location	And in this place again
5b	assertion	**he says,**
5c	content	"They shall never enter my rest." (Ps 95:11)
6a	inference (from 2–5)	Therefore
6b	basis 1 (for 7a)	since it remains for some to enter it, and
6c	basis 2 (for 7a)	those to whom the good news was formerly proclaimed did not enter
6d	reason	because of disobedience,
7a	assertion	**he again appoints a day,**
7b	identification	"Today,"
7c	means	speaking through David
7d	time	a long time after,
7e	comparison	even as it was said before,
7f	time	"Today
7g	condition	if you hear his voice,
7h	exhortation	**do not harden your hearts.**" (Ps 95:7–8)
8a	basis (for 7a)	For
8b	condition	if Joshua had given them rest,
8c	assertion	**he would not have spoken** about another day
8d	time	after these days.
9a	inference (from 1–8)	So, then,
9b	assertion	**there remains a Sabbath rest**
9c	advantage	for the people of God.
10a	expansion (of 9a)	And

10b	identification	the one who enters into God's rest
10c	assertion	**himself rests** from his works,
10d	comparison	just as God rested from his.
11a	inference (from 2–10)	therefore
11b	exhortation	**Let us ... strive to enter into that rest**,
11c	result	so that no one will fall
11d	instrument	through the same pattern of disobedience.

Structure

Inclusios once again provide the scaffolding for both the paragraph and for the two units within the paragraph.

The paragraph as a whole begins with a hortatory subjunctive—"let us fear" [φοβηθῶμεν]—and reminds the readers that the promise of "entering his rest" is still open. Verse 11, likewise, features a hortatory subjunctive—"let us strive" [σπουδάσωμεν]—and urges the readers to "enter that rest." While there is some debate about the internal structure of this paragraph,[3] most interpreters agree that the "therefore" (οὖν) in verse 6 marks a division into two parts: verses 1–5 and 6–11.[4] Each of these units is also marked out by an *inclusio*: "entering rest" which, as we have seen, is found in verse 1 and occurs again in verse 5. And verses 6–11 are bracketed by references to both "entering" and to warnings about "disobedience" (ἀπείθεια). Each section also features a formal quotation from Psalm 95 at its center (vv. 3, 7).

Allusions to "entering rest," then, are the obvious keynote of the paragraph (vv. 1, 3a, 3b, 5, 6, 10, 11). The language is taken from Psalm 95:11, where it is used in the context of judgment: the sin of the wilderness generation means that they will "never enter my rest." The author infers that the opportunity to experience that rest is still open, since David, centuries after the wilderness wandering, continues to warn about not entering the rest—that is, the "today" of David's time is still the "today" of the readers' context. As this contemporizing of the concept reveals, "rest" is not the promised land. Positively, the author interprets "rest" by bringing in another key Old Testament passage: Genesis 2:2, which speaks of God himself resting on the seventh day after creation (quoted in Heb 4:4, alluded to in vv. 3 and 10). The rest God has promised his faithful people must be eschatological and have a strong spiritual component (see our notes on v. 1).

---

3. E.g., G. Guthrie (*Structure of Hebrews*, 66) views vv. 1–2 as a transitional unit; Cockerill (*Hebrews*, 196) divides the paragraph into two main units, vv. 1–3a and vv. 3b–10; Ellingworth (*Hebrews*, 238) sees a division into three parts, marked by οὖν in vv. 1, 6, and 11.

4. See, e.g., for both this division and the occurrences of *inclusio*, Attridge, *Hebrews*, 123; Lane, *Hebrews*, 1:96; Koester, *Hebrews*, 276.

Exegetical Outline

→ **3. Entering the Rest (4:1–11)**
   a. Exhortation to Enter the Rest (vv. 1–5)
   b. "A Sabbath-Rest for the People of God" (vv. 6–11)

Explanation of the Text

4:1 Therefore since the promise of entering his rest remains, let us fear lest any one of us be judged to have fallen short of it (Φοβηθῶμεν οὖν, μήποτε καταλειπομένης ἐπαγγελίας εἰσελθεῖν εἰς τὴν κατάπαυσιν αὐτοῦ δοκῇ τις ἐξ ὑμῶν ὑστερηκέναι). The author begins explicitly applying the lesson of the wilderness generation to his readers. "Entering rest," taken from Psalm 95:11 is, as we have seen, the thread woven throughout the fabric of this paragraph. The author has echoed the judgment pronounced on the wilderness generation in the Old Testament: "they were not able to enter, because of their unbelief" (3:19). The "therefore" (οὖν), while it might pick up the previous context in general, probably relates especially to this last verse: they were prevented from entering; therefore, we need to be careful lest the same fate befall any of us. The combination of corporate address—"we"—with individual focus—"any one of us"—characterizes the author's exhortations in this context (see 3:12; 4:11). The Christian community is to "fear" or "be careful" (the verb is φοβέομαι) about a person being "judged" to have fallen short of the rest. "Judged" translates a verb (δοκέω) that could also mean "seem" or "appear" (Heb 12:10, 11; see, e.g., ESV; NET; CEB).[5] But the verb can also mean "recognize as," and this stronger sense works well in this verse. The issue is not whether someone might "appear" to fall short but whether they will judged (by God) to have actually fallen short.[6]

The subordinate clause in the sentence, which takes the form of a genitive absolute (καταλειπομένης ἐπαγγελίας), briefly introduces an important note that will sound throughout the passage: the "promise [of entering the rest] is still open."[7] "Promise," which appears here for the first time in the letter, is a concept that plays an important role in the author's sermon (the noun appears again in 6:12, 15, 17; 7:6; 8:6; 9:15; 10:36; 11:9 [twice], 13, 17, 33, 39; the cognate verb in 6:13; 10:23; 11:11; 12:26). "What he [God] has promised" is shorthand for all that God is committed to do for his people (6:12; 10:36; 11:39) and often has a future orientation that matches the usual hortatory perspective of the author: what God promises is utterly certain to come to pass, but much of what he has promised lies ahead of us in the Christian life.

---

5. See Westcott, *Hebrews*, 93.

6. Moffatt, *Hebrews*, 50; Donald Guthrie, *The Letter to the Hebrews*, TNTC (Grand Rapids: Eerdmans, 1983), 111; Attridge, *Hebrews*, 124; Weiss, *Der Brief an die Hebräer*, 275; Koester, *Hebrews*, 269.

7. Ellingworth, *Hebrews*, 238: it is "the essential new idea of this verse, and indeed of this section." "Still open" is the translation that BDAG ("καταλείπω," 521, §4) suggests here. The infinitive clause εἰσελθεῖν εἰς τὴν κατάπαυσιν αὐτοῦ ("to enter into his rest") is the content of the promise.

4:2 For we also have had good news proclaimed[8] **to us, just as they had. But the word they heard**[9] **did not profit them because they were not united with those who heard with faith** (καὶ γάρ ἐσμεν εὐηγγελισμένοι καθάπερ κἀκεῖνοι· ἀλλ᾽ οὐκ ὠφέλησεν ὁ λόγος τῆς ἀκοῆς ἐκείνους μὴ συγκεκερασμένους τῇ πίστει τοῖς ἀκούσασιν). The author here further explains ("for," γάρ) how the promise of rest remains open for his audience: we have heard the "good news" that the wilderness generation also heard. "Good news" is often presented in the New Testament as a distinctive blessing of the new covenant (e.g., Mark 1:1; Rom 1:16).[10] However, in a more general sense, it can also be said that the Old Testament people of God also heard "good news" (e.g., Gal 3:8). The author may be thinking of passages such as Numbers 14:7b–8, which records Joshua and Caleb, after scouting the land, proclaiming to the people, "The land we passed through and explored is exceedingly good. If the LORD is pleased with us, he will lead us into that land, a land flowing with milk and honey, and will give it to us."[11] The emphasis in this first sentence is instructive. Granted the usual application of "good news" language to the time of the new covenant, we might have expected the argument to run "as we have heard good news, so did they."

But the author moves in the opposite direction, arguing from the obvious point that the wilderness generation heard the good news of promised rest to the key point that his audience has also heard this same good news.

God has made the good news of his promised rest available, but the problem is that humans have not rightly responded to this gracious promise. The author reminds his readers once again of the failure of the wilderness generation to "enter" because of their lack of faith. However, while this general point is quite clear, the way the author communicates it is not. The problem is a textual variant in the Greek text. The participle translated "united with" occurs in two different forms in the textual tradition. One form (the nominative συγκεκερασμένος) agrees with "the word they heard," yielding a translation such as we find in NASB: "the *word* they heard did not profit them, because *it* was not united by faith in those who heard."[12] However, most modern scholars think the more likely original reading is a form (the accusative συγκεκερασμένους) that agrees with "those"/"they" (ἐκείνους). In this case, we would translate as I do above: "the word they heard did not profit *them* because *they* were not united with those who heard with faith" (so also most English translations).[13] On this view, which

---

8. The author uses a periphrastic perfect form: ἐσμεν εὐηγγελισμένοι, "we are in a state of having heard the good news" (see Laansma, *"I Will Give You Rest,"* 286).

9. Most interpreters think the genitive in the phrase ὁ λόγος τῆς ἀκοῆς is descriptive: "the word qualified by hearing," "the word they heard" (see 1 Thess 2:13; and, e.g., Moule, *Idiom Book*, 175; Johnson, *Hebrews*, 125). Ellingworth (*Hebrews*, 242), however, construes it to mean "hearing the word" (perhaps an "attributed genitive"). The phrase is difficult to interpret because ἀκοή can mean either "what is heard" or "act of hearing" (each of these options are argued for ambiguous occurrences in Gal 3:2, 5; Rom 10:17).

10. "Good news" language is not, however, significant for the theology of Hebrews. The author uses the verb εὐαγγελίζομαι only elsewhere in 4:6 and never uses the cognate noun εὐαγγέλιον.

11. Whitfield, *Joshua Traditions*, 242.

12. This form of the word is found in the important uncial ℵ, as well as in the minuscule 104 (in slightly different form), and several ancient versions. This reading is supported by, e.g., Grässer, *An die Hebräer*, 1:206; Montefiore, *Hebrews*, 82–83; D. Guthrie, *Hebrews*, 112; Delitzsch, *Hebrews*, 1:190–91. On this view, τῇ πίστει is an instrumental dative (Spicq, *L'Épître aux Hébreux*, 2:81).

13. This reading is found in most MSS, including 𝔓[13] (and perhaps 𝔓[46]); the uncials A B C D K L P Ψ 0243 0278, many minuscules, and the Majority text (𝔐). It is the reading adopted in the NA[28]/UBS[5] as well as in the THGNT. As Metzger points out, this reading has broad geographical support and is also the more difficult reading (*Textual Commentary*, 595).

I slightly prefer, the point is that the bulk of Israelites did not "join" with people such as Joshua and Caleb in their believing response to God's word of promise.[14] Everybody "heard" the good news of the promise ("the word they heard"), but most did not "hear" with faith.

4:3 For we who believe are those who enter the rest; as he says, "As I swore in my anger: they will never enter my rest," even though his works have been done[15] **since the foundation of the world** (εἰσερχόμεθα γὰρ εἰς τὴν κατάπαυσιν οἱ πιστεύσαντες, καθὼς εἴρηκεν, Ὡς ὤμοσα ἐν τῇ ὀργῇ μου, Εἰ εἰσελεύσονται εἰς τὴν κατάπαυσίν μου, καίτοι τῶν ἔργων ἀπὸ καταβολῆς κόσμου γενηθέντων). The initial point this verse makes in its context is clear enough: it is vital to join those who "hear with faith" because ("for," γάρ[16]) it is faith that enables a person to enter into God's rest. At least this is how most interpreters understand the verse. An alternative approach, reflected in the CEB, is to see the opening sentence as focusing on the fact that believers are presently entering the rest: "we who have faith are entering the rest."[17] However, by placing "those who believe" (οἱ πιστεύσαντες) at the end of the clause, the author draws attention to it, suggesting that his focus is on the connection between believing and entering.[18] The present tense of "enter" (εἰσερχόμεθα), then, is best taken in a gnomic sense, without any specific time reference.[19] The quotation of Psalm 95:11 that follows (καθὼς εἴρηκεν[20]), then, supports this opening statement by way of negation. By quoting the final line of judgment, the author invites his readers to recall Psalm 95's negative evaluation of the people who receive the judgment: they are those who "harden themselves," who are "always going astray in their hearts," who do not understand Yahweh's "ways"—they will not enter. To avoid this judgment, then, the opposite attitude is needed—that is, faith.

The second part of verse 3 takes a sudden turn to an apparently unrelated topic, asserting the continuing existence of God's works ever since "the foundation of the world."[21] The introduction of God's "works" (ἔργα) anticipates the quotation of Genesis 2:2 that follows in verse 4 and that the author uses to further elaborate the meaning of "God's rest" from Psalm 95. Most versions translate in a way that suggests the point of this final clause is to assert the completion of God's works: see, e.g., NIV:

---

14. Our translation takes τῇ πίστει ("by faith") as a modal dative modifying τοῖς ἀκούσασιν ("those who heard"): "those who heard in a believing way" (e.g., Cockerill, *Hebrews*, 203). It is possible that "those who heard with faith" includes believing Christians also (Koester, *Hebrews*, 270).

15. The author uses here a genitive absolute: τῶν ἔργων ... γενηθέντων.

16. A good number of manuscripts, however, read οὖν, "therefore," instead of γάρ (ℵ A C 0243. 0278. 81. 104. 365. 1739. 1881. 2464 vg^ms). But γάρ has broad support (𝔓^13.46 B D Ψ 33 𝔐 lat sy^h), and οὖν may reflect assimilation with vv. 1 and 11 (Metzger, *Textual Commentary*, 595–96; Attridge, *Hebrews*, 122).

17. See also, e.g., Montefiore, *Hebrews*, 83; Attridge, *Hebrews*, 126; Lane, *Hebrews*, 1:99; Spicq, *L'Épître aux Hébreux*, 2:81–82; Whitfield, *Joshua Traditions*, 239.

18. The aorist tense of the participle translated "those who believe" (πιστεύσαντες) might at first seem to militate against the gnomic sense of the verb (see below). The aorist, however, might be chosen to put emphasis on the fact of belief rather than on the process of believing.

19. On the gnomic use of the present tense, see, e.g., Wallace, *Greek Grammar*, 523–24. Others think the verb expresses present continuous action, signifying current entrance into rest (Montefiore, *Hebrews*, 83) or progress toward a (yet future) rest (Cockerill, *Hebrews*, 205). And still others give the present tense here a future force (Ellingworth, *Hebrews*, 246).

20. The subject of this verb is not specified. The subject could be "Scripture" (see NJB; Ellingworth, *Hebrews*, 247), but the personal word of judgment makes it more likely that God is the subject (so most versions and commentators).

21. "Foundation" translates καταβολή, which is almost a technical word for "creation" in the NT (Matt 13:35; 25:34; Luke 11:50; John 17:24; Eph 1:4; Heb 9:26; 1 Pet 1:20; Rev 13:8; 17:8). Only once does it not refer to creation (Heb 11:11).

"yet his works have been finished since the creation of the world" (also ESV; NRSV; CSB; CEB). Others, however, think that the contrast between the quotation of Psalm 95 and the last clause ("and yet" [καίτοι][22]) requires a continuous present sense: the works are "still done and being done."[23] However, the author's choice of the perfect tense of the participle translated "have been finished" (γενηθέντων) suggests the nuance of completion.[24] I therefore prefer the usual interpretation: God's works have been in a state of completion ("finished") since the completion of God's creative work. As I suggest above, the author appears to have introduced an inference from Genesis 2:2 before he quotes it. In normal order, then, the argument runs as follows: "God rested on the seventh day from all his works" (v. 4); therefore, "his works have been done since the foundation of the world."

4:4 For somewhere he has spoken concerning the seventh day in this manner: "And God rested on the seventh day from all his works" (εἴρηκεν γάρ που περὶ τῆς ἑβδόμης οὕτως, Καὶ κατέπαυσεν ὁ θεὸς ἐν τῇ ἡμέρᾳ τῇ ἑβδόμῃ ἀπὸ πάντων τῶν ἔργων αὐτοῦ). The rest God now promises his people can be understood better in light of the rest of God on the seventh day. The vague reference to Scripture in the introductory formula—"somewhere" (που)—is something we have already seen in Hebrews (2:6). The text here is, of course, Genesis 2:2, the author quoting one clause from the verse.[25] Many interpreters identify the hermeneutical procedure our author uses as what the early Jewish interpreters labeled *gezerah shawah*, "equal or similar decision." According to this principle, it is legitimate to associate texts of Scripture that use the same or similar wording. Thus "rest" (κατάπαυσις) in Psalm 95:11 invites comparison with Genesis 2:2, where the verbal cognate of this word occurs (κατέπαυσεν).[26] Without dismissing the influence of this hermeneutical principle (which the author uses elsewhere [e.g., see 1:13 and 2:5–6]), it should be noted that it is quite natural to explain "his rest" in Psalm 95 in terms of the most famous text in Scripture that refers to God "resting."[27]

This "rest" of God is not a cessation from "working": as Jesus said, "My Father is always at his work to this very day, and I too am working" (John 5:17b). The "work" that God completes on the seventh day is "the work he had been doing"— that is, the work of creation (note the reference to "the work of creating" at the end of Gen 2:3). God's "rest," then, is not his inactivity but the settled state of regular activity that follows and fulfills his initial work of creating and putting his creation into order. The conclusion our author draws from this text takes advantage of the interpretive approach of his contemporaries, which invests significance in the silence of Scripture. The presentation of the "seventh day" in the creation breaks the pattern of the other six: there is no concluding refrain, "and there was evening, and there was morning—the xth day." This break in the pattern suggests that the seventh day is continuing and that, therefore, the rest of God also continues.[28]

The author has both positive and negative

---

22. A particle used elsewhere in the NT only in Acts 14:17 (καίτοιγε occurs in John 4:2). See BDF #425(1).

23. Johnson, *Hebrews*, 127.

24. A rough paraphrase might be "in the state of having become." Johnson suggests that the use of "from" (ἀπό) rather than "in" or "at" (ἐν) points to a continuous translation of the participle (*Hebrews*, 127). However, "from" is natural if the emphasis is on the continuing state of "having become."

25. The author as usual cites a Greek version very close to the LXX. The only variation is the author's insertion of a reference to God (ὁ θεός), required by his abbreviated quotation.

26. It might be noted that the principle does not work in the Hebrew text, which uses different word groups in each text.

27. Cockerill, *Hebrews*, 206–7; Laansma, *"I Will Give You Rest,"* 67–73.

28. D. Harris, *Hebrews*, 97.

reasons for quoting this text. Negatively, the existence of "rest" since creation shows that the promised land of Canaan cannot exhaust the meaning of rest in Psalm 95.[29] As Backhaus puts it, the author "thinks in a different, vertical and eschatological topography."[30] Positively, Genesis 2:2 opens up the meaning of "rest" to include participation in the divine realm.

4:5 And in this place[31] **again he says, "They shall never enter my rest"** (καὶ ἐν τούτῳ πάλιν, Εἰ εἰσελεύσονται εἰς τὴν κατάπαυσίν μου). After the introduction of Genensis 2:2 into the author's exploration of Old Testament "rest," he reminds us one final time of the original text about "rest": Psalm 95:11. As several interpreters have noted, the resulting sequence in verses 3b–5 falls into a chiasm:

3b   "my rest" (Ps 95:11)
    3c   "works"
        4a   "seventh day"
            4b   "God rested" (Gen 2:2)
        4b   "seventh day" (Gen 2:2)
    4c   "works" (Gen 2:2)
5   "my rest" (Ps 95:11)[32]

In light of the argument of this paragraph, we are now in a position to comment generally about the meaning of "rest" in Hebrews. Several scholars have devoted significant time to the question of the religions-history background that might inform the author's use of the term. Gnosticism, Jewish apocalyptic,[33] and Middle Platonism are among popular suggestions.[34] However, while some parallels with each of these can be discerned, none provides a comprehensive series of parallels sufficient to explain our author's use of the term. Moreover, the very number of suggestions raises serious doubt about these specific identifications.[35] As so often is the case, the author, while probably drawing in certain respects from one or more of these conceptual worlds, appears to be resolutely focused on the Old Testament. In the Old Testament, "rest" connotes, as the English word would suggest, a settled and secure state, whether that state is in the afterlife (see the frequent refrain "*x* rested with his ancestors," e.g., 1 Kgs 2:10) or, often, in a land where enemies have been subdued (e.g., Deut 3:20; 12:9, 10; 25:19; Josh 1:15; 1 Kgs 8:56; and, in hope during the exile, Jer 31:2; 50:34). The motif of God's own rest, from Genesis 2, adds a further dimension, suggesting both that God himself provides for our spiritual state without the need for continued "striving" (v. 11) and that the rest we enjoy involves intimacy with the resting God. This relationship is memorialized in the weekly Sabbath and is, in a sense, "localized" in the temple, which is sometimes called the "resting place" of God (e.g., 1 Chr 28:2; 2 Chr 6:41; Ps 132:8, 14; Isa 66:1; cf. Acts 7:49).[36]

---

29. Ellingworth, *Hebrews*, 247.
30. "Er denkt in einer anderen, vertikalen und endzeitlichen Topographie" (*Der Hebräerbrief*, 158).
31. "This place" translates τούτῳ, which probably refers to "this passage I have been quoting throughout this context" (see NIV: "in the passage above").
32. Laansma, *"I Will Give You Rest,"* 289; see also, e.g., Cockerill, *Hebrews*, 206.
33. Otfried Hofius, *Katapausis: Die Vorstellung vom endzeitlichen Ruheort im Hebräerbrief*, WUNT 1/11 (Tübingen: Mohr Siebeck, 1970), esp. 22–101.

34. One of the most influential suggestions, now generally rejected (though see Grässer, *An die Hebräer*, 1:209–11, 218–19), is that the author derives his basic idea of rest from gnostic speculation (Käsemann, *Wandering People of God*, esp. 67–75, 87–96, 174–82; for a refutation, see Hofius, *Katapausis*).
35. Among those expressing skepticism about locating a particular religious-historical context for the author's rest are Laansma, *"I Will Give You Rest,"* 335–57; Attridge, *Hebrews*, 128; Koester, *Hebrews*, 269.
36. Two main Greek words are used in these texts, κατάπαυσις and its cognates (the word that occurs in Ps 95:11

Of course, the author's understanding of rest is clearly dominated by Psalm 95 and related texts. As deSilva comments, "This repetitive recontextualization of Psalm 95:11 allows 'entering God's rest' to saturate the hearers' minds, replacing any contrary or competing agendas they may have brought to the hearing of this sermon."[37] Psalm 95 leads the author back to the narrative of the failure of the exodus generation. In this story and related texts, "rest" refers to a secure and blessed life in the land of promise (e.g., Deut 3:20; 12:9, 10; 25:19; Josh 1:15)—a rest the people forfeit because of their unbelief. Their failure provides for the author a potent warning for his own audience. Like Israel of old, the people of God the author addresses have experienced the miraculous power of God (Heb 2:4), exercised through their pioneer and high priest (2:10, 17) and directed toward their deliverance. This deliverance, or "salvation" (1:14; 2:3), while already underway, is yet to be consummated. Again, like Israel of old, the Christians the author speaks to are in danger of "drifting away" (2:1), failing to attain what God has promised because of their unbelief and disobedience. "Rest" functions within this narrative to link the destination of Israel in the day of Moses and Joshua with the destination of believers in the day of Christ. The fact that our author refers to "rest" only within 3:7–4:11 makes pretty clear that the term is closely tied to the underlying wilderness wandering narrative (3:11, 18; 4:1, 3, 4, 5, 8, 10, 11).[38]

As a number of interpreters suggest, then, "rest" ultimately must be defined in terms of the other images our author uses to describe the believer's final destiny: "salvation" (1:14; 2:3), "glory" (2:10), "a better, heavenly, homeland" (11:16), the "city to come" (13:14), and an "unshakable kingdom" (12:28).[39] The use of God's own rest from Genesis 2 to refine the concept suggests to many interpreters that the author thinks of this destiny in purely spiritual terms, in opposition to the earthly destiny of Israel.[40] However, I am not sure that all reference to a material element of the rest should be eliminated. The "rest" in Hebrews is certainly not "territorial," as some who identify it with the millennial kingdom argue.[41] But it is not necessarily devoid of all "terrestrial" features. Indeed, there is some reason to think it connotes a "place of rest."[42]

Another issue that divides scholars is the timing of this rest. Some argue that the rest is presently available to, or being experienced by, God's people. This view notes, rightly, that the author's appeal to Genesis 2:2 shows that he thinks of God's rest as continuously existing since the completion of

---

and in Heb 3–4) and ἀνάπαυσις and its cognates. The equivalent Hebrew word is often from the נוח root, but several other Hebrew words stand behind these Greek words. See for a full lexical survey and discussion, Laansma, *"I Will Give You Rest,"* 78–101; *NIDNTTE* 1:284–88. Easter (*Faith and the Faithfulness of Jesus*, 80–81) notes that "entering" language in Hebrews usually has to do with the presence of God.

37. DeSilva, *Perseverance in Gratitude*, 153.

38. The word "rest" (κατάπαυσις) occurs elsewhere outside of Hebrews in the NT only at Acts 7:49, where it refers to the temple. The cognate verb, καταπαύω, occurs only in Acts 14:18. The related words ἀναπαύω and ἀνάπαυσις, in related senses to what we find in Hebrews, occur in Matt 11:28, 29; 12:43; 26:45; Mark 6:31; 14:41; Luke 10:6; 11:24; 1 Pet 4:14; Rev 14:11, 13.

39. See, e.g., Attridge (*Hebrews*, 128): the imagery of rest is in part to be "understood as a complex symbol for the whole soteriological process that Hebrews never fully articulates, but which involves both personal and corporate dimensions." Thompson thinks the author uses "rest," in line with the dualism he perceives throughout Hebrews, as heaven (*Beginnings of Christian Philosophy*, 81–102).

40. E.g., deSilva, *Perseverance in Gratitude*, 166–67; Elllingworth, *Hebrews*, 249; Whitfield, *Joshua Traditions*, 240–41. This focus on the "spiritual" vs. the "material" is often seen as a reflection of the Middle Platonism that many allege has influenced the author.

41. E.g., Walter C. Kaiser Jr., "The Promise Theme and the Theology of Rest," *BSac* 130 (1973): 135–50. DeSilva argues at length against this millennial view (*Perseverance in Gratitude*, 157–63).

42. See, e.g., Hofius, *Katapausis*, 48–50; Laansma, *"I Will Give You Rest,"* 277–83.

the work of creation.[43] This focus on the present experience of rest is usually understood within the framework of the customary New Testament "now and not yet" eschatological framework: the rest believers experience now will be consummated in a final and permanent state of rest.[44] However, while the author probably does assume the continuing existence of God's rest, it is not clear that he thinks believers are now experiencing it. I have argued that verses sometimes used to argue for a present experience of rest are not at all clear on the matter. And I think there are other indications that the author views the rest as a final state that believers will enter only in the future.[45] Especially telling is the description of rest as involving a cessation from "works" that is parallel to God's own resting from his works. If, as seems to be the case, these "works" refer to the constant effort needed to sustain Christian faithfulness, then it is only when the believer reaches his or her final destiny that such "rest" will be attained.

4:6–7 Therefore since it remains for some to enter it, and those to whom the good news was formerly proclaimed did not enter because of disobedience, 7 he again[46] appoints a day, "Today," speaking through David a long time after, even as it was said before, "Today if you hear his voice, do not harden your hearts" (ἐπεὶ οὖν ἀπολείπεται τινὰς εἰσελθεῖν εἰς αὐτήν, καὶ οἱ πρότερον εὐαγγελισθέντες οὐκ εἰσῆλθον δι᾽ ἀπείθειαν, 7 πάλιν τινὰ ὁρίζει ἡμέραν, Σήμερον, ἐν Δαυὶδ λέγων μετὰ τοσοῦτον χρόνον, καθὼς προείρηται, Σήμερον ἐὰν τῆς φωνῆς αὐτοῦ ἀκούσητε, μὴ σκληρύνητε τὰς καρδίας ὑμῶν). "Therefore since" (ἐπεὶ οὖν) marks the transition into the second stage of the argument in verses 1–11. Ellingworth nicely summarizes the sequence of thought:

> God made a promise that his people would one day have access to his own place of rest. The place of rest has been available since the seventh day of creation. The promise cannot be repealed; but it was not fulfilled at the time of the exodus (as v. 8 will confirm); it therefore remains open for some.[47]

The author takes up key language from verses 1–2 to make his point: the exodus generation "had good news proclaimed" (εὐαγγελισθέντες) to them, but they failed to "enter" (εἰσῆλθον) because of their "disobedience" (ἀπείθειαν). The logic of the author's argument appears to assume that there must be "some" who enter God's rest. Perhaps he reasons that God would not allow his rest to exist without people to enjoy it.

What is explicit is that the rest remains open for people to enter into it. The author appeals to

---

43. Philo endorsed such a view; see, e.g., *Cherubim* 26; *Sacrifices* 8.

44. A. T. Lincoln, "Sabbath, Rest, and Eschatology in the New Testament," in *From Sabbath to Lord's Day: A Biblical, Historical, and Theological Investigation*, ed. D. A. Carson (Grand Rapids: Zondervan, 1982), 210–12; Barrett, "Eschatology," 366–72; Scott D. Mackie, *Eschatology and Exhortation in the Epistle to the Hebrews*, WUNT 2/223 (Tübingen: Mohr Siebeck, 2007), 49–54; Lane, *Hebrews*, 1:99; Attridge, *Hebrews*, 128.

45. See also, e.g., Hofius, *Katapausis*, 55–58; Cockerill, *Hebrews*, 198–200; Koester, *Hebrews*, 277; P. Hughes, *Hebrews*, 159. Early Christians, following the lead of Jewish interpreters, sometimes envisaged the future messianic age as the "seventh" day of creation (e.g., Barn. 15). Paul's use of the language of "works" moves in a different sphere, as he (1) denies that works provide a basis for justification and (2) nevertheless insists that works are necessary as the believer works out his or her salvation.

46. "Again" (πάλιν), as in 1:5b, 6, might introduce another OT quotation, but it is much more natural to take it with "appoints" (ὁρίζει): God "appointed" a rest for his people in the days of the exodus; now he appoints another day (Ellingworth, *Hebrews*, 251).

47. Ellingworth, *Hebrews*, 250.

another element in Psalm 95:7b–11 to make this point: it speaks of "today" (σήμερον).⁴⁸ In his grace, God "appointed" a new "day" when the people of God were once again invited to share in the rest of God. This new day, announced by David,⁴⁹ came hundreds of years after God's refusal to allow his people to enter the land of Canaan. The author, by applying the psalm to his readers, effectively announces that the "today" of the psalm applies equally to them. The appointment of this new "day," then, is obviously a great opportunity. However, as the author's renewed quotation of Psalm 95:8 reveals, it also carries a significant responsibility. God has "spoken" in his Son (1:2), and the readers have "heard" (2:1). They must now make sure not to harden their hearts, but to open their hearts to the word by responding in belief.

4:8 For if Joshua had given them rest, he would not have spoken about another day after these days (εἰ γὰρ αὐτοὺς Ἰησοῦς κατέπαυσεν, οὐκ ἂν περὶ ἄλλης ἐλάλει μετὰ ταῦτα ἡμέρας). The author adds another reason ("for," γάρ) to think that "it still remains for some to enter the rest" (v. 6a): Joshua did not lead the people of his day into that rest. The author employs a contrary-to-fact conditional clause (marked by the ἄν in the apodosis) to make his point.⁵⁰ This type of condition uses the logic of "if A, then B; but not B, therefore not A." So here:

If Joshua had led the people into rest (A), God would not have spoken about another "day" (B)

But God did speak about another "day" (not B) (see v. 7)

Therefore: Joshua did not lead the people into rest (not A)

One potential difficulty for this logic is the claim in the latter chapters of Joshua that "the LORD gave them [the people in the land] rest on every side" (Josh 21:44; see also 22:4; 23:1). However, as is well-known, the end of the book of Joshua exhibits a tension in terms of the completion of the conquest. Verses such as I have just cited suggest that the conquest was complete, but others make clear that there was still territory not yet subdued; there are still "nations that remain among" them whose influence the people must resist (23:7; see vv. 12–13).⁵¹ On the one hand, therefore, the book wants to affirm that God had faithfully fulfilled his promise to the people. But, on the other hand, it also blames the people for not finalizing the conquest and thereby achieving full and final rest. As Bruce Waltke summarizes, the end of Joshua "asserts both a successful ending to subduing the land and the beginning of Israel's failed history to retain it."⁵²

"Joshua" translates the Greek Ἰησοῦς, which, of course, is very often translated "Jesus." A few interpreters have suggested that the author intends

---

48. As Backhaus (*Der Hebräerbrief*, 162) notes, "today" is a key word in this section. John Dunnill suggests a possible parallel with the setting of Deuteronomy, a book that also exhorts its audience by referring to a "today" that places the readers in the same situation as the people who first received the law (*Covenant and Sacrifice in the Letter to the Hebrews*, SNTSMS 75 [Cambridge: Cambridge University Press, 1992], 132–36).

49. Our language here of "by David," as well as our translation "through David," understands the preposition in the phrase ἐν Δαυίδ as having an instrumental force and therefore identifies David as the composer of Ps 95. This identification follows the explicit reference to David in LXX Ps 94:1 (David is not referred to in the MT; see Grässer, *An die Hebräer*, 1:213; Attridge, *Hebrews*,

130). Others suggest, however, that the ἐν might be local, "David" being understood as a reference to the "book of David," the Psalms (BDF §219.1; Turner, *Syntax*, 261; Lane, *Hebrews*, 1:94).

50. For a general discussion of this type of conditional sentence ("contrary to fact"), see, e.g., Wallace, *Greek Grammar*, 694–96.

51. See, e.g., Pekka M. A. Pitkänen, *Joshua*, ApOTC (Downers Grove, IL: IVP Academic, 2010), 351–52; Marten H. Woudstra, *The Book of Joshua*, NICOT (Grand Rapids: Eerdmans, 1981), 313–14.

52. Bruce K. Waltke, with Charles Yu, *An Old Testament Theology: An Exegetical, Canonical, and Thematic Approach* (Grand Rapids: Zondervan Academic, 2007), 531.

to refer to Jesus: "Jesus did not give *them* rest; but as for us. . . ."[53] A more plausible view is that the author intends a play on words, suggesting therefore a "Joshua typology." The physical pioneer of the people of God at the time of the exodus has a counterpart in the spiritual pioneer of the new-covenant people of God (see 2:10).[54] The author certainly does little to suggest he is thinking along these lines; however, one might wonder if any group of early Christians could have heard the Greek Ἰησοῦς without thinking of their Savior, the Lord Jesus.

4:9 So, then, there remains a Sabbath rest for the people of God (ἄρα ἀπολείπεται σαββατισμὸς τῷ λαῷ τοῦ θεοῦ). The author draws a conclusion[55] from the several lines of evidence he has amassed about the rest being yet open "today" for believers to enter into it.[56] As I noted above, some interpreters think this text and others in the context point to the rest being presently available. However, I continue to think that the rest that "remains" is a future state promised to believers. Instead of the expected word "rest," the author uses the rare word usually translated in English "Sabbath rest" (σαββατισμός). The word has not yet been found in any writing that predates Hebrews. It is possible, then, though probably unlikely, that he has coined the word.[57] The sparsity of occurrences makes exact definition difficult. Lane, citing occurrences of the word in patristic sources that do not clearly depend on Hebrews, thinks the word has the nuance of festivity and celebration.[58] However, his argument for finding a particular connotation in this word is not altogether convincing: "if it had been the writer's intention to say only 'there remains a Sabbath rest for the people of God,' he could have retained the word κατάπαυσις ["rest"]."[59] Yet, while "rest" is obviously associated with the Sabbath via the author's quotation of Genesis 2:2, the word does not directly connote Sabbath in the way that σαββατισμός does. It might be, then, that he chooses this word simply because it directly links the notions of "rest" and "Sabbath."

What does the author mean by asserting that a "Sabbath rest" remains for God's people? An initial, straightforward reading might suggest that the author asserts the continuing responsibility of Christians to observe a weekly Sabbath.[60] Yet this view not only has great difficulty accounting for other New Testament perspectives on the Sabbath (see below), but it also ignores the way the author has used the language of rest in this context. Rest, as we have seen, refers to the ultimate settled and secure state of

---

53. A. T. Hanson, *Jesus Christ in the Old Testament* (London: SPCK, 1965), 61; J. Michael McKay Jr., "Is Joshua a Type of Christ in Hebrews 4.8? An Assessment of the Referent of Ἰησοῦς," *NTS* 68 (2021): 105–18. The Greek word for "them" (αὐτούς) comes first in the clause, perhaps for emphasis. The fact that the KJV uses "Jesus" here does not indicate that the translators have taken this view; the KJV consistently transliterates names (Ellingworth, *Hebrews*, 253).

54. See Montefiore, *Hebrews*, 85; and especially Richard Ounsworth, *Joshua Typology in the New Testament*, WUNT 2/328 (Tübingen: Mohr Siebeck, 2012), 55–97; Whitfield, *Joshua Traditions*, 246–65; Whitfield, "Pioneer and Perfecter: Joshua Traditions and the Christology of Hebrews," in Bauckham et al., *Cloud of Witnesses*, 80–87. Whitfield thinks further that the "Joshua" of Zech 3 might also figure into the typology. In this he picks up an idea originally suggested by J. R. Harris (*Testimonies*, 51–57).

55. He uses a weak inferential particle, ἄρα, which the versions usually translate "so," "then," or "so then."

56. Verse 9 formally parallels v. 6: both assert that a "rest" of some kind "remains" (ἀπολείπεται).

57. The Greco-Roman moralist Plutarch uses it (*Mor.* 166A), and it is very unlikely that Plutarch would borrow from Hebrews (Attridge, *Hebrews*, 131). Moffatt (*Hebrews*, 53), however, thinks the author may have coined it.

58. Lane, *Hebrews*, 1:101–2. He cites Justin, *Dial.* 23.3; Epiphanius, *Pan.* 30.2.2; *Martyrdom of Peter and Paul*, ch. 1; and *Apostolic Constitutions* 2.36.2. This nuance is advocated by a number of other scholars as well.

59. Lane, *Hebrews*, 1:101.

60. E.g., Samuele Bacchiocchi, *From Sabbath to Sunday: A Historical Investigation of the Rise of Sunday Observance in Early Christianity* (Rome: The Pontifical Gregorian University Press, 1977), 65.

faithful Christians in the consummation of history. "Sabbath," via the author's reflections on Genesis 2:2, simply adds a further connotation to this future rest: it is the eternal Sabbath, when humans, like God after the creation, can rest from their works (v. 10).[61]

4:10 And the one who enters into God's[62] rest himself rests from his works, just as God rested from his (ὁ γὰρ εἰσελθὼν εἰς τὴν κατάπαυσιν αὐτοῦ καὶ αὐτὸς κατέπαυσεν ἀπὸ τῶν ἔργων αὐτοῦ ὥσπερ ἀπὸ τῶν ἰδίων ὁ θεός). This verse might explain why there is a Sabbath rest (v. 9), but more naturally it develops further implications of the Sabbath rest.[63] As I noted in my comments on verse 4, God's resting on the seventh day marked the end of his work of creation. The "work" he does during the time of his ongoing rest is distinct, a working "with" what he has already "worked" by bringing it into existence and giving order to it. The author in this verse compares the works God ceased to do on the seventh day with the works that believers put behind them when they enter God's rest. Those who think the rest is presently available to believers sometimes define the works believers rest from as equivalent to the "dead works" of 6:1 and 9:14—the works people suppose they must perform to enter into relationship with God. Entering the new covenant, however, means that "they cease from their own works so that God may work in them," as Lincoln puts it.[64]

The obvious challenge to this view is the comparison the author makes between the works God rests from and the works "the one who enters" rests from. A comparison is, to be sure, possible; Johnson, for instance, suggests the work that follows creation is a work that flows naturally from the living and powerful God, a work that does not "redress a lack." Believers who enter God's rest, likewise, live out of the power of God that has embraced them and so, like God, no longer work to "redress a lack."[65] Nevertheless, the comparison between God's works and ours functions much better if the works we rest from are the effort and striving involved in living for God in the present era of partial fulfillment. Once we enter the eternal kingdom, our activity, like God's, will flow naturally and inevitably from our identity.[66] This verse, then, asserts a point similar to that in Revelation 14:13: "Then I heard a voice from heaven say, 'Write this: Blessed are the dead who die in the Lord from now on.' 'Yes,' says the Spirit, 'they will rest from their labor [τῶν κόπων αὐτῶν], for their deeds [τὰ ... ἔργα αὐτοῦ] will follow them.'" On this view, then, "the one who enters" (ὁ εἰσελθών) does not denote activity at a particular point in time but identifies, generically, a certain kind of person.[67]

4:11 Let us therefore strive to enter into that rest, so that no one will fall through the same[68] pattern

---

61. E.g., P. Hughes, *Hebrews*, 161–62; Cockerill, *Hebrews*, 210–11; Koester, *Hebrews*, 279.
62. The Greek here is simply the pronoun "his" (αὐτοῦ); but the antecedent is clearly "God" (v. 9) (Bruce, *Hebrews*, 109).
63. The conjunction is the very common γάρ which, as we have seen, denotes several different logical relationships in Hebrews; see the note on 2:10, and, here, Ellingworth, *Hebrews*, 257. The NAB "and" might therefore be a better translation than the "for" found in most translations.
64. Lincoln, "Sabbath, Rest, and Eschatology," 213.
65. Johnson, *Hebrews*, 130.
66. See, e.g., Cockerill, *Hebrews*, 212. Our activity in this era is the product of God's grace and Spirit, but it is far from inevitable—indeed, it is always falling short.

67. The participle is in the aorist. Wallace (*Greek Grammar*, 615) notes that the present tense is more often used with a substantival participle and has a generic force. However, this pattern holds for truly gnomic participles (e.g., "the one who hears"), but does not so obviously apply to participles that denote an activity that is not time-determined. Whitfield (*Joshua Traditions*, 252–53) thinks that "the one who enters" is Jesus. But this does not fit well with the focus on the believer who enters in this context.
68. The author uses an identical adjective (αὐτῷ) to stress the similarity between the disobedience of the wilderness generation and the disobedience he warns his readers away from.

of disobedience (σπουδάσωμεν οὖν εἰσελθεῖν εἰς ἐκείνην τὴν κατάπαυσιν, ἵνα μὴ ἐν τῷ αὐτῷ τις ὑποδείγματι πέσῃ τῆς ἀπειθείας). The author caps off this paragraph by returning to the same point he made at the beginning.[69] In both verse 1 and this verse, he uses a hortatory subjunctive ("let us...") to urge his audience to take advantage of God's offer of rest. As he warns about "falling short" of this goal in verse 1, so he warns here about "falling" by imitating the wilderness generation's example of disobedience. The verb translated "strive" (σπουδάζω) sometimes means "make haste," but in contexts such as this it refers to "zealous effort";[70] versions render it "strive" (ESV; NAB), "make every effort" (NIV; NET; NRSV; CSB; CEB), "do our best" (NLT). The aorist tense of the verb portrays the action simply as something "to be done."[71]

The author again shows his concern for each member of the community by following up the collective "let us" with a reference to "each person" (τις). Several versions suggest that "fall" and "example" work together here; see CSB: "fall into the same pattern of disobedience." However, this combination of Greek words does not occur elsewhere with this meaning.[72] "Fall," then, is used absolutely to mean "be condemned" (see also Rom 11:11, 22; 1 Cor 10:12; perhaps also Rom 14:4),[73] and "same pattern of disobedience" is probably the instrument of this fall, hence the "through" in our translation (also NRSV; NASB; "by" in NIV; ESV; NET; CEB). The author makes explicit the exemplary role of the wilderness generation, even as Paul does also by identifying the people of that era as "types" (τύποι; 1 Cor 10:6; see also τυπικῶς there in v. 11).[74] "Disobedience," finally, denotes the content of the pattern. Putting this all together, we might paraphrase "so that no one will fall because they imitate the same pattern of disobedience that we see in the wilderness generation." "Disobedience" (ἀπείθεια), as we have seen, is one of the author's key words to denote the failure of that generation (4:6).

Theology in Application

A Sabbath Rest for the People of God

"So, then, there remains a Sabbath rest for the people of God" (4:9). As I noted in my explanation of the text, some interpreters think that this claim makes clear that new-covenant believers are to observe a weekly Sabbath. This view takes two

---

69. A few interpreters, however, think the exhortation in v. 11 initiates a new paragraph (e.g., Bruce, *Hebrews*, 111; Westcott, *Hebrews*, 99; Michel, *Der Brief an die Hebräer*, 196). The ESV suggests this arrangement in its paragraph division.

70. G. Harder, "σπουδάζω, κτλ," *TDNT* 7:559. For the meaning "make haste," see 2 Tim 2:15; 4:9, 21; Titus 3:12; for the sense "zealous effort," see Gal 2:10; Eph 4:3; 1 Thess 2:17; 2 Pet 1:10, 15; 3:14.

71. Others suggest that the tense signals entrance into an action ("ingressive") (e.g., D. Harris, *Hebrews*, 101; Lane, *Hebrews*, 1:94).

72. That is, nowhere else do we find the combination "fall" (πίπτω) + "in" (ἐν) to mean "fall into" (Turner, *Syntax*, 257; Ellingworth, *Hebrews*, 258–59).

73. E.g., Lane, *Hebrews*, 1:94. It is possible, though doubtful, that the author is influenced to use this word here because of its occurrence in 3:17, referring to the corpses of the wilderness generation "falling" in the wilderness.

74. The author of Hebrews uses the word ὑπόδειγμα, which occurs in 8:5 and 9:23 to denote the earthly counterpart to the heavenly sanctuary and its trappings. The word refers, as here in v. 11, to OT people or events as "examples" in Jas 5:10 and 2 Pet 2:6; in John 13:15, the word refers to an "example" set by Jesus.

forms. Some argue that Christians should continue to observe the "seventh day," worshiping and resting on Saturday (e.g., Seventh-Day Adventists). Most of those who insist on the observance of a weekly Sabbath think that, while requirements of worship and rest (in some degree, at least) are still incumbent, the day has been moved from Saturday to Sunday in recognition of the resurrection. This shift of day, while never made explicit in the New Testament, seems to be suggested by references to worship activities on "the first day of the week" (Acts 20:7; 1 Cor 16:2)—the day John in the Revelation calls "the Lord's Day" (1:10). However, should we consider this day a "Sabbath"?

Hebrews 4, despite its reference to "Sabbath rest," gives little support to this view, since, as I have argued, "rest" in this context refers to the ultimate destiny of believers in the afterlife. Adding the allusion to "Sabbath" simply identifies that rest with the seventh-day rest of God himself. What do we find when we expand our purview to the New Testament as a whole? Unfortunately, as the continuing controversy among serious students of the Bible suggests, the evidence is not clear-cut. Jesus certainly claimed authority over the Sabbath, an authority manifested in his Sabbath-day healings (Mark 2:23–28 parr.; 3:1–6 parr.; Luke 13:10–17; John 5:1–17; 9:1–31; see esp. Mark 2:28: "the Son of Man is Lord even of the Sabbath"). But did his activity on the Sabbath manifest a permanent shift in view of Sabbath? That point is debated. A bit more light might be shed on the issue in two texts where Sabbath observance is addressed in the letters. In response to false teachers, Paul insists that the believers should not let anyone judge them with respect to "a religious festival, a New Moon celebration or a Sabbath day" (Col 2:16). Paul seems to imply here that observance of the Sabbath is not a requirement for Christians. To be sure, some avoid this conclusion by arguing that Sabbath observance here is prohibited only as it is bound up with the wider false teaching of these heretics.[75] However, the fact that Paul appears to make observance optional, rather than prohibiting it altogether, suggests that he implies it is not incumbent on Christians. Moreover, the language and logic of Colossians 2:17 suggests that the primary problem with Sabbath observance was a failure to reckon with the "fulfillment" of such institutions in the new era of salvation. As Lincoln puts it, "That Paul without any qualification can relegate Sabbaths to shadows certainly indicates that he does not see them as binding and makes it extremely unlikely that he could have seen the Christian first day as a continuation of the Sabbath."[76]

A similar conclusion appears to emerge from Paul's rebuke of the weak and the strong in Romans 14:1–15:13. In 14:5, Paul characterizes the view of each group: "One person considers one day more sacred than another; another considers every day alike. Each of them should be fully convinced in their own mind." The "day" here

---

75. E.g., Bacchiocchi, *From Sabbath to Sunday*, 343–64.
76. A. T. Lincoln, "From Sabbath to Lord's Day: A Biblical and Theological Perspective," in Carson, *From Sabbath to Lord's Day*, 368.

is not explicitly identified as a Sabbath, but it is overwhelmingly probable, granted the Jewish context of this whole discussion, that the most famous Jewish "day," the Sabbath, is in view.

While by no means crystal clear, then, I think that the New Testament teaches that observance of a weekly Sabbath is no longer required of the new-covenant people of God—for both Jewish and gentile Christians, I might add.[77] This issue is bound up ultimately with the wider and also controversial question of the continuing applicability of the law of Moses to Christians: Sabbath observance, after all, is one of the Ten Commandments. I cannot here pursue this larger issue (which I will touch on again in Heb 7). However, I will say that I think that freedom from observing a weekly Sabbath is part and parcel of a larger view of the Mosaic law as no longer directly binding on believers.[78]

To say that believers are not required to observe a weekly Sabbath is not to say that believers are wrong to observe one if they choose to do so. Indeed, while I am convinced that I am not obliged to observe a Sabbath, I have throughout my Christian life followed a very modest form of Sabbath observance. Shortly after my conversion, I became immersed in the life of a devout Christian family through a woman who would eventually become my wife. I learned a lot about what it means to follow Christ from them, and one of their practices was to avoid "normal" work on Sunday. While strange to me at first, I came to recognize the ultimately liberating power of this practice. I did not need to feel guilty about putting my usual work aside to focus on other things on Sunday. For all of our married life, then, my wife and I have avoided, wherever possible, doing our normal "work" on Sunday. To be sure, I often teach or preach, but I avoid study for the purpose of my writing or lecturing. Such a weekly pattern perhaps recognizes the fundamental principle involved in Sabbath. As God sanctified space through his six-day creative "work," so he sanctified time through his seventh-day "rest." A "rest" of some sort (however modest) might be an appropriate way to show our respect for God's lordship over our time even as we anticipate the greater and final "rest" yet to come.

---

77. See esp. on this whole matter, Carson, *From Sabbath to Lord's Day*.

78. See Douglas J. Moo, "The Law of Moses or the Law of Christ," in *Continuity and Discontinuity: Perspectives on the Relationship between the Old and New Testaments: Essays in Honor of S. Lewis Johnson, Jr.*, ed. John S. Feinberg (Westchester, IL: Crossway, 1988), 210–17; idem, "The Law of Christ as the Fulfillment of the Law of Moses: A Modified Lutheran View," in *Five Views on Law and Gospel*, ed. Stanley N. Gundry, Counterpoints (Grand Rapids: Zondervan, 1996), 319–76.

Hebrews 4:12–13

Literary Context

The author seems to break off his train of argument in verses 12–13, which speak generally of the power, penetrating effect, and illuminating impact of God's word. By introducing these verses with "for" (γάρ), the author indicates that this short passage about God's word has some kind of relationship to its context. But what is that relationship? Most interpreters tie these verses closely to 3:7–4:11. This passage, as we have seen, is an extended exhortation based on Psalm 95:7b–11, with Genesis 2:2 brought in to further the argument and with implicit allusions throughout to the narrative of wilderness wandering from Numbers. A reminder of the penetrating power of the word of God and the accountability of people to the God who inspired that word would be an appropriate conclusion to this exhortation.[1] At the same time, we recall that the author began his letter with a focus on the word of God, claiming that God has spoken decisively "in (the) Son" (1:1–2a). It is therefore tempting to see these verses as one part of a grand *inclusio* enclosing the first major stage of the author's argument.[2]

Forcing a choice between these two options would likely impose too rigid an approach to the structure of the author's argument. Both connections are probably intended by the author. Fundamental to the author's whole argument is his assumption about the authority of God's word and its power to transform people. He therefore begins and ends this opening argument with principial claims about that word. These claims about the nature of God's word therefore undergird his argument, with its constant appeal to Scripture (1:5–13; 2:6–8, 12–13; 3:5), and his exhortations (2:1–4; 3:7–4:11).

---

1. E.g., Cockerill, *Hebrews*, 214; Grässer, *An die Hebräer*, 1:226. Most of those who argue for this connection also note the possible relationship with 1:1–2.

2. E.g., Attridge, *Hebrews*, 133; Backhaus, *Der Hebräerbrief*, 169. Another, less likely, option is to take 4:12–13 as the introduction to the following section (Griffiths, *Hebrews and Divine Speech*, 88–89).

I. **The Exalted Son and a Rest for the People of God (1:1–4:13)**
   A. Exordium (1:1–4)
   B. Exposition: The Exalted Status of the Son (1:5–14)
   C. Exhortation: Take Hold of Your Great Salvation (2:1–4)
   D. Exposition: The Humanity of the Son and Its Significance (2:5–18)
   E. Exhortation: Focus on the Faithful Son (3:1–6)
   F. Exhortation: Avoid the Fate of the Wilderness Generation (3:7–4:11)
   ➡ G. **Exposition: The Power of the Word of God (4:12–13)**
II. Our Great High Priest and His Ministry (4:14–10:31)
III. Exhortation: Follow and Serve the Pioneer of Our Faith through Endurance and Faith (10:32–13:25)

Main Idea

Appropriately responding to God's word is vital because God's word is powerful and penetrating, laying open before God the deepest human impulses and emotions. The word of God and the God who speaks in that word are inseparable, so it is ultimately God, the revealer of the heart, to whom we are accountable.

Translation

Hebrews 4:12–13

12a	conclusion (to 3:7–4:11) and basis (for 1:1–4:11)	For
12b	series 1	**the word of God is living** and
12c	series 2	**effective** and
12d	series 3	**sharper**
12e	comparison	than any two-edged sword.
12f	series 4	It pierces to the division of soul and spirit,
12g	parallel	joints and marrow, and
12h	series 5 (and result of 12e)	**it is a judge** of the thoughts and
12i	parallel	attitudes of the heart.
13a	result (of 12)	And
13b	assertion	**no creature is hidden** before him; rather,
13c	contrast	**all things are naked** and
13d	parallel	**exposed** to his eyes,
13e	description	to whom we must give an account.

Structure

In verse 12, the author lists in series five qualities of the word of God; it is

- living,
- effective,
- sharper than any two-edged sword,
- penetrating to the inmost parts of a human,
- and discerning of the thoughts and attitudes of the heart.

His focus shifts to the God who speaks through his word in verse 13, stressing our accountability to the one who is able look deeply into the human heart.

Noting the several words in this passage that the author does not use anywhere else, and the lack of explicit connection with the context, many scholars think the author may here be quoting, or at least leaning on, a semi-poetic tradition.[3]

Exegetical Outline

→ **G. Exposition: The Power of the Word of God (4:12–13)**

Explanation of the Text

4:12 For the word of God is living and effective and sharper than any two-edged sword. It pierces to the division of soul and spirit, joints and marrow, and it is a judge of the thoughts and attitudes of the heart (Ζῶν γὰρ ὁ λόγος τοῦ θεοῦ καὶ ἐνεργὴς καὶ τομώτερος ὑπὲρ πᾶσαν μάχαιραν δίστομον καὶ διϊκνούμενος ἄχρι μερισμοῦ ψυχῆς καὶ πνεύματος, ἁρμῶν τε καὶ μυελῶν, καὶ κριτικὸς ἐνθυμήσεων καὶ ἐννοιῶν καρδίας). The word of God is powerful and penetrating. As I suggested above, the "for" (γάρ) at the beginning of verse 12 forges at least two links with the context: it fittingly concludes the exhortation of 3:7–4:11, focused as it is on the word of God found in Psalm 95, and it harks back to 1:1–2a, bracketing the first stage of the author's argument with a focus on God's word.[4] The link with 3:7–4:11 might suggest that the "word" refers here to the Old Testament Scriptures. However, 1:1–2a (see also 2:1–4) refers to the ultimate expression of God's will in his Son. We should probably, then, choose an expansive referent for God's word here: God's speaking, as it is recorded in the Old Testament

---

3. E.g., Michel, *Der Brief an die Hebräer*, 197.
4. Some think the verse grounds the appeal in v. 11 (e.g., Michel, *Der Brief an die Hebräer*, 191).

Scriptures as well as his speaking in and through his Son—speaking that ultimately found its authoritative form in the canon of the New Testament.⁵ As verse 13 makes explicit, the author in these verses aligns the word of God closely with the person of God. Thus, the fact that the word is "living" (ζῶν) reminds us of the author's ascription of this same quality to God (3:12; 9:14; 10:31; 12:22). The point is that neither God nor his word can be ignored, as if the word he speaks no longer applies or has no power.⁶ This point is underlined with the next adjective, "effective" (ἐνεργής; see also 1 Cor 16:9; Phlm 6). The cognate verb from this word is used with respect to the power of the word in 1 Thessalonians 2:13: "And we also thank God continually because, when you received the word of God, which you heard from us, you accepted it not as a human word, but as it actually is, the word of God, which is indeed at work [ἐνεργεῖται] in you who believe." This idea that God's word is a kind of "speech act," a speaking that infallibly accomplishes what it claims to do, is a familiar Old Testament theme, articulated clearly in the well-known Isaiah 55:11, where God says of his "word": "it will not return to me empty, but will accomplish what I desire and achieve the purpose for which I sent it." This claim brings to clear expression the author's view of the dynamic nature of God's word, a word that speaks directly and powerfully to the author's own contemporaries (see "In Depth: The Old Testament in Hebrews" on pp. 54–59).

In the rest of the verse, the author focuses on one aspect of the word's effectiveness: its ability to "cut through" our outer persona and pretensions to our inmost being. The author puts three clauses or phrases in a series (connected with καί, "and"), but their logical relationship seems clear enough: (1) the word is like a sword (2) that pierces a person right to their inmost being, (3) and as a result discerns that person's innermost thoughts and intentions.

The metaphor of a sword to describe the word of God is found elsewhere in the New Testament (Eph 6:17; Rev 19:15, 21; see also Rev 1:16; 2:12, 16). Two different Greek words are used, the one occurring here (μάχαιρα) often connoting a short sword, or dagger (often carried by Roman soldiers), or even a knife.⁷ However, the word generally in the New Testament denotes a sword of any kind, so the word itself does not help us pin down the specific imagery.⁸ It is tempting to think that our author may again be influenced by his paradigmatic narrative about the wilderness generation, for in Numbers 14:43, coming just after the peoples' rebellion at Kadesh, the Lord warns that the people, should they attack their enemies, will "fall by the sword."⁹ Nor does its qualification as "double-edged" point toward a particular idea; "double-edged sword" seems to have become a stereotyped phrase.¹⁰ Clearly it is the notion of "sharpness" that the author wants to emphasize, supporting his claim that this sword is capable of penetrating or piercing (διϊκνούμενος)¹¹ "to the division of soul and spirit, joints and marrow." The author's choice of these pairs of contrasts has sparked considerable

---

5. See Gene R. Smillie, "Ὁ Λόγος τοῦ Θεοῦ in Hebrews 4:12-13," *NovT* 46 (2004): 339. A few interpreters over the years have thought that "word" (λόγος) might refer to Christ (as in, e.g., John 1:1; 1 John 1:1). However, there is nothing in the context or in Hebrews generally to suggest such a reference.

6. The word of God is described as "living" also in Acts 7:38 and 1 Pet 1:23. Jesus's own words are also called "living" (John 6:63, 68).

7. Smillie suggests the reference is to a surgeon's scalpel, which is used to "open up" a person's body to the searching scrutiny of God ("Ὁ Λόγος τοῦ Θεοῦ"; see also Cockerill, *Hebrews*, 216).

8. The relative rarity of the other word for "sword," ῥομφαία, in the NT (seven occurrences, six of them in Revelation) might further support this.

9. Lane, *Hebrews*, 1:102; Koester, *Hebrews*, 280.

10. See Judg 3:16; Ps 149:6; Prov 5:4; Sir 21:3; Rev 1:16; 2:12.

11. Josephus uses the same verb (διϊκνέομαι) to describe

discussion among interpreters. At the end of the day, the most that I can say with any confidence is that the author probably intended to refer to both the immaterial and material aspects of humans. More important, perhaps, is the fact that these pairs, along with "thoughts and attitudes" at the end of the verse, do not feature natural opposites: theologians might spend a lot of time trying to figure out how the "soul" and the "spirit" differ! What the author is suggesting is that God's word has the ability to discern and differentiate things that are beyond our ability to separate.[12] "God's word can penetrate precisely to those places where human knowledge cannot."[13] As I suggested above, it makes sense to see the final clause as expressing the result of the penetrating power of the word: because it cuts right through to our innermost being, the word is a "judge" of the "thoughts and attitudes of the heart."[14] "Judge" means here has not the sense of condemn but the sense of "make a judgment, discriminate."[15] The word of God, as we read it or hear it read, has the ability to expose our deepest impulses and attitudes.[16]

4:13 And no creature is hidden before him; rather, all things are naked and exposed to his eyes, to whom we must give an account (καὶ οὐκ ἔστιν κτίσις ἀφανὴς ἐνώπιον αὐτοῦ, πάντα δὲ γυμνὰ καὶ τετραχηλισμένα τοῖς ὀφθαλμοῖς αὐτοῦ, πρὸς ὃν ἡμῖν ὁ λόγος). Nothing in our lives is hidden from God, a sober reminder that his judgment will be fair and scrupulous. God sees all things. The author uses another colorless "and" (καί) to introduce this verse. The conjunction in general signals a close connection, but only the context can tell us what the specific connection might be.[17] A few translations use "and" here (ESV; NET; NRSV), while most of them do not use any conjunction. Calvin suggests a causal function—God's word can penetrate to our inmost being *because* God, who speaks in that word, sees everything[18]—but the emphasis might well fall in the other direction: because God's word opens us to examination, all things are laid bare before the God to whom we must give an account. As Koester notes, "The impossibility of avoiding examination by God plays an important role in the rhetorical strategy of Hebrews."[19] This accountability, stated in the last clause of verse 13, is what these verses have been driving toward.

God's ability to see all things is a staple of biblical teaching:

> From heaven the Lord looks down and sees all mankind; from his dwelling place he watches all who live on earth—he who forms the hearts of all, who considers everything they do. (Ps 33:13–15)

---

javelins that did not "penetrate" the bodies of the soldiers they were hurled at (*Ant.* 13.96). The verb occurs only here in the NT and once in the LXX (Exod 26:28).

12. Michael Allen, "Living and Active: The Exalted Prophet in the Epistle to the Hebrews," in Laansma, Guthrie, and Westfall, *So Great a Salvation*, 154.

13. Johnson, *Hebrews*, 134.

14. "Heart" (καρδίας, a genitive form) probably modifies both previous words: ἐνθυμήσεων ("thoughts"; cf. Matt 9:4; 12:25; Acts 17:29) and ἐννοιῶν ("insights," "attitudes"; cf. 1 Pet 4:1 and twelve occurrences in Proverbs [also Wis 2:14; Sus 28]; see D. Harris, *Hebrews*, 106). It is not possible neatly to distinguish their meanings; they work together in a kind of merism to denote a person's basic mindset.

15. The Greek word, κριτικός, is rare, occurring only here in the NT and not at all in the LXX.

16. "Heart," as so often in Scripture, refers not to the seat of our emotions but to our inner being.

17. On καί as signaling "close connection," see Runge, *Discourse Grammar*, 23–27. Stephen H. Levinsohn prefers to speak of an associative or additive function (*Discourse Features of New Testament Greek: A Coursebook on the Information Structure of New Testament Greek*, 2nd ed. [Dallas: SIL International, 2000], 118).

18. Calvin, *Hebrews*, 53.

19. Koester, *Hebrews*, 280.

The realm of the dead is naked before God. (Job 26:6)

He views the ends of the earth and sees everything under the heavens. (Job 28:24)

Therefore judge nothing before the appointed time; wait until the Lord comes. He will bring to light what is hidden in darkness and will expose the motives of the heart. At that time each will receive their praise from God. (1 Cor 4:5)

The author joins his voice to these others: no creature is "invisible" or "hidden" (ἀφανής) before him; everything in the created order is "naked" and "exposed" to him. "Exposed" translates a word (τετραχηλισμένα) whose exact connotation is debated. It is formed with the Greek word for "neck" (τράχηλος) and seems to have here the general idea of "laid bare" ("τράχηλος," BDAG 1014). Some interpreters think the image is of the wrestler whose neck is laid bare to his opponent;[20] others of the sacrificial victim bound for the knife;[21] still others to the patient's neck exposed to the surgeon.[22] We simply do not have enough occurrences of this verb elsewhere to know. What is clear, however, is that the general sense is "total exposure and utter defenselessness."[23]

We have two options for the meaning of the last clause in the verse, depending on how we define λόγος. This word refers to the "word" of God in verse 12, and it would be natural to think it has the same meaning here. If this is so, the clause will mean "about whom we speak."[24] However, all the translations take the second view and, I think, with good reason.[25] On this view, λόγος means "account," and, as I suggested above, the clause then fittingly closes this brief paragraph with a reminder of the "account" we all must give to God. He whose gaze is penetrating and perfect is the one before whom we will have to defend ourselves. No private thought or inclination will be hidden from him.

Theology in Application

Law and Gospel

A time-honored distinction that has been especially central in Lutheran theology is the contrast in God's word between the "law" and the "gospel." Luther claims that "the knowledge of this topic, the distinction between the Law and the Gospel, is necessary to the highest degree; for it contains a summary of all Christian doctrine."[26] Luther is not talking about the law of Moses or the gospel narrowly understood. Rather, these terms describe two contrasting ways that God addresses us throughout

---

20. Ellingworth, *Hebrews*, 265.
21. DeSilva, *Perseverance in Gratitude*, 171.
22. Smillie, "Ὁ Λογος του Θεου"; Cockerill, *Hebrews*, 218.
23. Lane, *Hebrews*, 1:103.
24. The Gk. is πρὸς ὃν ἡμῖν ὁ λόγος: "concerning whom the word [we have just been discussing] is for us." For this view, see, e.g., Griffiths, *Hebrews and Divine Speech*, 82–85.
25. See Bruce, *Hebrews*, 114; Koester, *Hebrews*, 275; Ellingworth, *Hebrews*, 265.
26. Martin Luther, *Luther's Works*, vol. 26, ed. Jaroslav Pelikan (St. Louis, MO: Concordia, 1963), 117 (in an exposition of Gal 2:14).

his word. As Luther puts it elsewhere, "the gospel teaches exclusively what has been given us by God" and the law "what we are to do and give to God."[27]

The author's teaching about God's word in 4:12–13 would clearly be classified as "law." He sets before us the vision of the word as a sword, cutting deeply into our inmost being, exposing to his searching gaze our deepest and most secret thoughts and emotions. A terrifying prospect, if we really take it seriously! Nor is this the only place where our author puts "law" before us. In an effort to stir his audience to action, he repeatedly reminds us that God warns his people against the awful consequences of unbelief and disobedience (e.g., 2:1–4; 3:15–19; 6:4–6, 8; 10:26–31; 12:16–21, 25). Yet, while the severity of some of these passages draws our attention, and theologians endlessly debate their significance, "gospel" passages, in fact, far outnumber "law" passages in Hebrews. The author again and again focuses on God's provision for our need in the exalted Son of God and high priest, Jesus.

We need both "voices" of God in Scripture. "Law" reminds us of the holiness of God and of the holiness we need to stand before him. It prevents us from falling into an "easy believism" that takes God for granted or that treats him as a grandparent who overlooks all the failures and misdeeds of the grandchild. But we certainly also need to hear God's reassuring address to us in the "gospel": the good news that God has provided fully for the free forgiveness of our sins and is constantly at work through his Spirit to bring to us the inestimable comfort of his presence and sovereign purposes.

---

27. "How Christians Should Regard Moses," in *Luther's Works: Word and Sacrament 1*, ed. E. Theodore Bachmann, vol. 35 (Philadephia: Fortress, 1960), 162.

CHAPTER 11

Hebrews: 4:14–16

Literary Context

These verses introduce the second main stage of the author's argument. Verses 12–13, as we have seen, close off the first stage by returning to the theme of God's word with which it began (1:1–2a). In verse 14, the author signals the topic of the long and complex argument at the heart of his sermon by referring to our "great high priest." Of course, the author has mentioned Jesus's high-priestly status earlier in the letter, but only quickly to move on to other topics (2:17; 3:1). From this point on, the identity of Jesus as high priest and his ministry in that role are the constant touchstones of the argument ("high priest" occurs in 4:15; 5:1, 5, 10; 6:20; 7:26–28; 8:1, 3; 9:7, 11, 25; 13:11; "great priest" in 10:21; "priest" in 7:3, 11, 14, 15–17, 20–21, 23; 8:4; 10:11–12). The conclusion of this section is marked both by the point where "high priest"/"priest" language drops out of the letter and by one of the more remarkable *inclusios* in the letter. Note the parallels between this paragraph and 10:19–25:

4:14–16	10:19–25
[14]Therefore, <u>since we have a great high priest</u> [ἔχοντες . . . ἀρχιερέα μέγαν] who has gone through the heavens, Jesus the Son of God,	Therefore, brothers and sisters, since we have <u>confidence</u> [παρρησίαν] to enter the Most Holy Place <u>by the blood of Jesus</u>, [20]by the new and living way that he inaugurated for us through the curtain, that is, his flesh, [21]and <u>(since we have) a great priest</u> [ἔχοντες . . . ἱερέα μέγαν] over the house of God,
let us hold fast to the confession [κρατῶμεν τῆς ὁμολογίας]. [15]For we do not have a high priest who is unable to empathize with our weaknesses, but one who has been tested and tried in every way, just as we are, without sin.	[22]**let us draw near** [προσερχώμεθα] with a sincere heart and the full assurance of faith, with our hearts sprinkled clean from an evil conscience and our bodies washed with pure water. [23]**Let us hold firmly to the confession** [κατέχωμεν τὴν ὁμολογίαν] of our hope without wavering, for faithful is the one who has promised. [24]**And let us consider** one another, with the purpose of stimulating each other to love and good works, [25]not giving up meeting with one another, as is the habit of some, but rather exhorting one another and doing so all the more as you see the day coming near.
[16]**Let us then draw near** [προσερχώμεθα] to the throne of grace with <u>confidence</u> [παρρησίας], so that we may receive mercy and find grace for the time of need.	

In both of these passages, the author cites the theological truth at the heart of his letter—access to God through Jesus's high-priestly ministry—as the basis for exhortations (using the hortatory subjunctive in Greek ["let us . . ."]) to hold firmly to the "confession" and to draw near to God. The text in chapter 10 goes into more detail, as we might expect of a text that rests on the detailed argument of 5:1–10:18. Where this great central section of the letter ends is harder to determine. But 1) the warnings in 10:26–31 are closely tied to the exhortation in 10:19–25, and 2) a shift of vocabulary and focus is evident at 10:32. I therefore place the transition from the second to the third main part of the letter at 10:32. (See notes on 10:19–25; 10:26–31; and 10:32–39 for more detail.)[1]

> I. The Exalted Son and a Rest for the People of God (1:1–4:13)
> II. **Our Great High Priest and His Ministry (4:14–10:31)**
> → **A. Exhortation: Persevere through the Power of Our Exalted High Priest (4:14–16)**
>   B. Exposition: High Priests and Our High Priest (5:1–10)
>   C. Exhortation: Move on to Maturity (5:11–6:20)
>   D. Exposition: A High Priest "According to the Order of Melchizedek" (7:1–28)
>   E. Exposition: The Ministry of Our High Priest (8:1–10:18)
>   F. Exhortation and Warning: Appropriating the Benefits of Our High Priest's Ministry (10:19–31)
> III. Exhortation: Follow and Serve the Pioneer of Our Faith through Endurance and Faith (10:32–13:25)

Main Idea

Because believers are represented before God by a high priest who is nothing less than the Son of God and who has passed through the heavens themselves to accomplish his work, they can approach God with confidence. This confidence is bolstered by the realization that this exalted high priest has entered fully into our tests and temptations and is thereby able to empathize with our own struggles.

---

1. The following are among those who identify 4:14–10:31 (with some variation as to where the section ends) as an integral argument: Cockerill, *Hebrews*, 218; Weiss, *Der Brief an die Hebräer*, 291; Backhaus, *Der Hebräerbrief*, 177; Michel, *Der Brief an die Hebräer*, 204. Most other scholars note the break at 4:14 but limit the section it introduces to 5:10 (Attridge, *Hebrews*, 138; Koester, *Hebrews*, 281) or 7:28. A few attach 4:14 to the previous section, as a kind of *inclusio* with the introduction of high-priest language in 2:17 and 3:1 (Massonnet, *L'Épître aux Hébreux*, 129, 131).

Translation

Hebrews 4:14–16

14a	conclusion (of 1:1–4:13)	Therefore,
14b	basis	since we have a great high priest
14c	identification 1	who has gone through the heavens,
14d	identification 2	Jesus the Son of God,
14e	exhortation	**let us hold fast to the confession.**
15a	basis (for 14d)	For
15b	assertion	**we do not have a high priest**
15c	identification	who is unable to empathize with our weaknesses, but
15d	contrast	one who has been tested
15e	parallel	in every way,
15f	comparison	just as we are,
15g	description	without sin.
16a	inference (from 15)	then
16b	exhortation	**Let us … draw near** to the throne of grace
16c	manner	with confidence,
16d	result	so that we may receive mercy and
16e	parallel	find grace
16f	time	for the time of need.

Structure

This paragraph exhibits a very common "indicative-imperative" pattern. The "indicatives," consisting of theological claims about Jesus, come in verses 14a and 15: the verb "have" (ἔχω) is used in both, as a participle, "having" (ἔχοντες) in verse 14a, and as an indicative in verse 15, "we have" (ἔχομεν). The imperatives are expressed by means of hortatory subjunctives in verses 14b (κρατῶμεν, "let us hold fast") and 16 (προσερχώμεθα, "let us draw near").

Exegetical Outline

→ **A. Exhortation: Persevere through the Power of Our Exalted High Priest (4:14–16)**
   1. The High Priest Who Is the Exalted Son (v. 14a)
   2. Keeping a Firm Grip on the Confession (v. 14b)
   3. The High Priest Who Empathizes with Our Weakness (v. 15)
   4. Coming Near to the God Who Offers Grace and Help (v. 16)

Explanation of the Text

4:14 Therefore, since we have a great high priest who has gone through the heavens, Jesus the Son of God, let us hold fast to the confession (Ἔχοντες οὖν ἀρχιερέα μέγαν διεληλυθότα τοὺς οὐρανούς, Ἰησοῦν τὸν υἱὸν τοῦ θεοῦ, κρατῶμεν τῆς ὁμολογίας). Our continued faithfulness to basic Christian truth is grounded in and motivated by the reality of our heavenly high priest. "Therefore" (οὖν) gathers up the argument of the letter thus far and carries it on to an initial conclusion.[2] However, the author's assumption that the readers will already know about Jesus as high priest ("because we have"—ἔχοντες is an obvious causal participle) points to the earlier texts where Jesus was so identified as a particular focus (2:17 and 3:1). At the same time, the verses provide a preliminary survey of the long argument that lies at the heart of the author's sermon. The author refers often in this argument to Jesus as "high priest" (ἀρχιερεύς), as a "priest" (ἱερεύς), as a "great priest" (once, in 10:21), and, here, as a "great high priest." The somewhat redundant addition of "great" (μέγαν) to "high priest" may imply that Jesus is distinguished from all other priests; however, this combination is not unknown in Judaism, so we should probably not make much of it (e.g., 1 Macc 13:42; Philo, *Dreams* 1.214, 219; 2.183).

The author's particular perspective on Jesus's high priesthood is immediately expressed in his claim that this high priest "has gone through the heavens." Jesus's ministry in heaven itself distinguishes him from all other high priests and indicates the surpassing significance of his work in representing and atoning for sinful humans. My translation follows the Greek quite closely, but some of the translations offer a different understanding of the phrase; note, for example, the NIV's "who has ascended into heaven" (cf. NLT). On this view, the reference is simply to Jesus's exaltation to the heavenly realm. However, the construction the author uses here (the verb διέρχομαι + accusative) has the meaning "pass through" in New Testament Greek.[3] The plural form of "heaven" (τοὺς οὐρανούς), then, will not here, as sometimes in Hebrews, have a singular sense (reflecting the Hebrew word, which is plural with a singular meaning: see 8:1; 12:23, 25). Rather, with "pass through," it refers to the various "layers" of the heavenly realm, as they are referred to often in Judaism and also in the New Testament.

---

2. Weiss, *Der Brief an die Hebräer*, 291.
3. See Luke 19:1; Acts 13:6; 14:24; 15:3, 41; 16:6; 19:1, 21; 20:2; 1 Cor 16:5 (twice); in Acts 12:10, it means "pass by." It seems to be the case that only when the verb is followed by εἰς or ἕως does it mean simply "come" or "arrive" (e.g., Mark 4:35; Luke 2:15).

See, for example, Paul's claim to have been "caught up to the third heaven" (2 Cor 12:2).[4] The author's reference to "passing through the heavens" is probably intended to imply that Jesus left these lower levels of heaven behind in order to penetrate into the highest heaven, where God dwells.[5] This idea seems to be buttressed by 7:26, which claims that Jesus was "exalted above the heavens." As Attridge puts it, "The emphasis is not on the process of passage . . . but on the result—Christ's exalted status"[6] (hence, perhaps, the translations in NIV and NLT).

Picking up key christological points from 1:1–3:6, the author identifies this high priest as "Jesus" (2:9; 3:1), "the Son of God" (1:2, 5a, 5b, 8; 3:6). Indeed, the author's Christology could be pretty well summarized with these three titles: the historical human "Jesus" has been exalted to the royal status of "Son" and, by virtue of that exalted position, now ministers as our heavenly high priest, providing for the full and final forgiveness of our sins.

As I noted in my discussion of structure, this verse falls into the typical New Testament "indicative-imperative" pattern: because Jesus is the kind of high priest the author has described (indicative), we must "hold fast to the confession" (imperative). This exhortation is similar to two earlier such pleas:[7]

> we are his house, if we hold fast [κατάσχωμεν] to our confidence and to the hope we boast in (3:6b)

> we are partakers of Christ—if, indeed, we hold fast [κατάσχωμεν] to the reality we first possessed firmly to the end (3:14)

And I noted above the parallel in 10:23: "let us hold unswervingly [κατέχωμεν] to the confession of our hope." The verb the author uses here in 4:14 is a different one than that found in these other three texts, but its meaning is similar.[8] "Confession" (ὁμολογία) was used already in 3:1, where I argued it meant "what is confessed," a doctrinal summary of some kind. DeSilva here paraphrases it as "the Christian view of reality and the hopes and values it articulates."[9] The author is not, of course, referring to a mere verbal recitation of a creed—although verbal confession, or better, "profession," cannot be ruled out.[10] Rather, he refers to a constant, tenacious commitment to the truth of the faith that will enable believers to maintain their status as the people of God and to exhibit that status in acts of love and obedience.

4:15 For we do not have a high priest who is unable to empathize with our weaknesses, but one who has been tested in every way, just as we are, without sin (οὐ γὰρ ἔχομεν ἀρχιερέα μὴ δυνάμενον συμπαθῆσαι ταῖς ἀσθενείαις ἡμῶν, πεπειρασμένον δὲ κατὰ πάντα καθ᾽ ὁμοιότητα χωρὶς ἁμαρτίας). The humanity of our high priest (ch. 2) means he can fully identify with our needs and problems. The relationship of this verse to verse 14 is not

---

4. Second Temple Jewish writings feature one, three, five, seven, or ten heavens (*NIDNTTE* 3:568).

5. See, e.g., Ribbens, *Levitical Sacrifice*, 100; Koester, *Hebrews*, 282. Some interpreters think "heavens" refers to the material heavens (deSilva, *Perseverance in Gratitude*, 181; Delitzsch, *Hebrews*, 1:219).

6. Attridge, *Hebrews*, 139. The perfect form of the participle διεληλυθότα supports this emphasis: his "passing through" is an abiding truth.

7. To be sure, the author uses a conditional sentence form in 3:6 and 14, but the rhetorical intent is the same.

8. See "κατέχω," BDAG 533, §2.b; the verb occurs only here and in 6:18 in Hebrews.

9. DeSilva, *Perseverance in Gratitude*, 179. See also Lane, *Hebrews*, 1:104; Ellingworth, *Hebrews*, 267.

10. The word ὁμολογία sometimes seems to refer to a verbal "profession" in the NT (see esp. 1 Tim 6:12, 13). "Profess" is better than "confess," because the latter in contemporary English tends to be confined to admission of sin.

clear. The "for" (γάρ) might at first glance suggest that this verse grounds or explains something in verse 14. Yet it is hard to see how a claim about Jesus's sympathy grounds or explains either Jesus's identity as high priest or the exhortation to hold fast to the confession. One option is to see verse 15 as dealing with a possible objection stemming from the stress in verse 14 on Jesus's exalted status: Does his superior status mean that he will prove aloof?[11] Perhaps a better option, however, is to view the conjunction "for" (γάρ) as introducing verses 15–16 as a whole: we are able to "hold fast to the confession" because we are invited to draw near to a throne characterized by grace (v. 16), grace that is displayed in the identification of our high priest with our state of weakness (v. 15).

This identification of Christ with weak human beings reiterates a point that was extensively developed in 2:5–18. The conclusion our author draws from that discussion is that Jesus is a "merciful" high priest, one who "himself suffered when tried" and who thereby is "able to help those who are being tried" (2:17, 18). Verse 15 obviously makes a similar point. Our high priest can sympathize with our weaknesses, for he was tested just as we are tested. "Empathize" (which transliterates the Gk. word used here, συμπαθέω) does not refer simply to an emotional reaction ("feeling sorry" for someone) but to an active identification with people. The only other occurrence of this word in the New Testament is in Hebrews 10:34, where it is rendered in the NET as "shared the sufferings."[12]

The "weaknesses" (ἀσθενείαις) that our high priest sympathizes with probably are spiritual (the word seems to refer to spiritual weaknesses also in 5:2; 7:28; it refers to physical weakness in 11:34). In the second half of the verse, the author shifts from the syntax of negation in the first part of the verse—"we do *not* have a high priest who is *un*able to empathize"—to a positive description—"[we have a high priest] who has been tested in every way, just as we are."[13] The verb I have translated "tested" (πειράζω) is the same one the author used in 2:18, where, as I noted, it is difficult to decide between the meanings "tempt" and "test." I suggested that the author might be intentionally playing on the dual meaning of the word, and I think this is probably the case here as well.[14] To be sure, most translations and commentators think it probably here means "tempt." The qualification "without sin" at the end of the verse might point in this direction, "temptation" and "sin" naturally going together.[15] Moreover, the idea of temptation to sin seems to be implied in the "weakness" of Christ in 5:2. However, this same context also speaks of Jesus "learning obedience from what he suffered" (5:8), which suggests the idea of testing. Moreover, testing also brings with it the temptation to sin. However we translate, the form of the verb (πεπειρασμένον, a perfect participle) suggests the enduring significance of Jesus's experience: his undergoing trials of all kinds (or resisting temptation of all kinds) means he has the ability fully to "identify with" our own experience of these things.

---

11. Lane, *Hebrews*, 1:107; D. Harris, *Hebrews*, 110.

12. The cognate adjective occurs in 1 Pet 3:8. The only LXX occurrence of the verb is in 4 Macc. 5.25: "the Creator of the world in giving us the law has shown sympathy toward us" (NRSV; the cognate noun συμπαθός occurs in 4 Macc. 13.23). See Lane, *Hebrews*, 1:108, 114. McCruden (*Solidarity Perfected*, 103–7) notes the prominence of this motif, which, in his view, contributes to the emphasis on Christ's "philanthropia" in Hebrews.

13. The Gk. uses two parallel adjectival participles: [μὴ] δυνάμενον ("[not] able") and πεπειρασμένον, "having been tested." The negation of the verb "have" (ἔχομεν) governs only the first clause: in an ellipsis typical of Gk., we must read an unnegated "we have" as governing the second part of the verse.

14. See also, e.g., Koester, *Hebrews*, 283; Johnson, *Hebrews*, 140; Attridge, *Hebrews*, 140; Ellingworth, *Hebrews*, 268–69 (as possible). NLT, NRSV, NAB, and NJB, translate it as "test."

15. E.g., Calvin, *Hebrews*, 56.

The author stresses again the identification of Jesus our high priest with the sinful humans he represents: our high priest was "tested in every way, just as we are." Jesus's "empathy," his active coming alongside us, is meaningful and effective because he has experienced the range and extent of the testing we face. The author does not, of course, mean that Jesus has experienced every particular test we face but that he has felt the full strength of testing. "Without sin" at the end of the verse is sometimes thought to limit the kind of temptations or testings Jesus underwent: he was tempted/tested just as we are except for those temptations involving previous sin.[16] However, it more naturally qualifies the degree of his identification with humans: whereas our testing is accompanied by and often results in sin, Jesus remained sinless.

4:16 Let us then draw near to the throne of grace with confidence, so that we may receive mercy and find grace for the time of need (προσερχώμεθα οὖν μετὰ παρρησίας τῷ θρόνῳ τῆς χάριτος, ἵνα λάβωμεν ἔλεος καὶ χάριν εὕρωμεν εἰς εὔκαιρον βοήθειαν). Our high priest's sympathetic coming alongside us in our weakness should give us the confidence to "draw near to the throne of grace with confidence." "Confidence" (παρρησία), as I noted in my comments on 3:6, expresses a key aspect of the theology of Hebrews: Jesus's ministry as high priest gives each believer the boldness to enter God's presence (see also 10:19, 35). Equally if not more important is the verb "draw near" (προσέρχομαι), which ties into the dominant cultic perspective on the work of Christ in Hebrews. As we have seen, this same verb occurs in the twin of this text in 10:19–25 (v. 22; and see also, e.g., 7:25; 10:1; 11:6; 12:18, 22; and 1 Pet 2:4).[17] The "joyful confidence"[18] to draw near to God arises from the finished work of our high priest, who "always lives to intercede" for us (7:25). And since it is the "throne" to which we draw near here, the verb might also have royal associations.[19] Our confidence, or boldness, in drawing near is also stimulated when we recognize that the throne is a throne "characterized by grace."[20] Grace does not have the same integrative role in Hebrews as it does in Paul's theology, but it occurs often enough to show that our author shares with Paul an underlying conviction that God in Christ is fundamentally gracious toward his people, supplying as a free gift all they need to approach and worship God (see also 2:9; 10:29; 12:15; 13:9, 25). This call to draw near has sometimes been interpreted to mean, specifically, "draw near to God in prayer."[21] However, while prayer is certainly included (and "time of need" might suggest such a focus), it is likely that the encouragement is more general: to enter into God's presence.

The purpose (or result) of approaching God's throne of grace will be that we "receive mercy and find grace for the time of need." "Mercy" (ἔλεος)

---

16. Westcott, *Hebrews*, 107.
17. The verb in the LXX often has a prosaic meaning (Joseph's brothers "went up to" the steward of Joseph's house [Gen 43:19]), but it also refers to "drawing near" to God in general (e.g., Exod 16:9; 34:32; Deut 4:11; 5:23; 1 Sam 14:36) and to "drawing near" to the altar or to God in terms of the cult: e.g., Lev 9:7: "Moses said to Aaron, 'Come [πρόσελθε] to the altar and sacrifice your sin offering and your burnt offering and make atonement for yourself and the people; sacrifice the offering that is for the people and make atonement for them, as the Lord has commanded'" (see also Ezek 44:16). In several texts, the focus is negative: certain people are not allowed to "draw near" the altar (Lev 21:17, 21, 23; 22:3; Num 17:5; 18:3, 4, 22). Some interpreters think this "drawing near" may refer to the believers' invitation to enter the heavenly throne room of God (e.g., Scott D. Mackie, "Heavenly Sanctuary Mysticism in the Epistle to the Hebrews," *JTS* 62 [2011]: 77–117).
18. Johnson, *Hebrews*, 140.
19. See 1 Kgs 21:13, 22, 28; Esth 1:14; 5:1; Dan 6:7, 13; 3 Macc. 5.14. See Backhaus, *Der Hebräerbrief*, 186–87.
20. The genitive τῆς χάριτος is probably descriptive.
21. Koester, *Hebrews*, 295. In my early days as a believer, I listened to a radio program that every day used this verse as a call to prayer.

and "grace" (χάριν) are mutually interpreting: it would be fruitless to insist on a neat separation in meaning between the two.[22] What the author means in general is clear enough: when we draw near to God, he graciously gives us whatever we need for the particular situation we face. "Time of need," the default translation, renders a Greek phase that means simply "well-timed help" (εὔκαιρον βοήθειαν).[23] But help that is "well-timed" would appear to refer to help that comes just when it is needed: so "time of need" gets the idea pretty well.

Theology in Application

The Heavens

In verse 14, our author claims that Jesus, our high priest, "passed through the heavens." I argued that he is probably here reflecting a widespread first-century cosmology according to which the immaterial realm is divided into several levels. We find evidence for this view especially in a form of Judaism called apocalyptic, which often features the journey of famous biblical figures into and through the heavens. And, as I noted, Paul seems to suggest a similar view of the cosmos when he refers to his ascension to the "third heaven" (2 Cor 12:2). I have also noted that the matter is complicated by the fact that the plural of the word "heaven" in Greek sometimes simply reflects the plural *form* of the equivalent word in Hebrew—the point being that, while the form of the word might be plural, the meaning of the word might be singular (see, e.g., the NIV on v. 14: "ascended into heaven"). However, there seems to be adequate evidence to indicate that our New Testament authors do speak occasionally of several "heavens." What are we to make of this?

On the one hand, we might conclude that we should adopt this way of thinking about the cosmos: if the Bible refers to more than one heaven, we, as people committed to the authority and truthfulness of Scripture, should adopt that same viewpoint. I have great respect for this attitude toward God's word. However, we should also reckon with the fact that biblical authors sometimes adopted ways of speaking from their culture that they are not necessarily affirming as the way things really are. For instance, the Old Testament is filled with poetic images of the nature and composition of the cosmos that no one today would endorse as the actual reality (e.g., the earth resting on "pillars" [Job 9:6; Ps 75:3]). While we cannot be sure, we might then conclude that references to several immaterial "heavens" may not be intended to teach us "the geography of heaven." The point, rather, is theological: unlike earthly

---

22. The words occur together also in 1 Tim 1:2; 2 Tim 1:2; Titus 1:4 (variant reading); 2 John 3.

23. The adjective εὔκαιρον occurs elsewhere in the NT only in Mark 6:21, where it refers to the "well-timed day" (ἡμέρας εὐκαίρου), or "opportune time" (NIV), for Herodias to exact her revenge on John the Baptist.

high priests, who minister on earth, our high priest Jesus has completed his work in the highest heaven, in the presence of God himself. His work therefore has a decisive finality that goes far beyond what any earthly priest was able to achieve. Moreover, by claiming that Jesus has "passed through" the lower heavens, the author may also be emphasizing the fact that all the "lower" spiritual beings that might be seen to inhabit those heavens have also been pacified, so that we need not fear any accusations that they might bring against us (see Col 2:14–15).

Hebrews 5:1–10

Literary Context

In this paragraph the author begins his exposition about Jesus our high priest. As we have seen, this central theme of the letter is introduced in 4:14–16 with a mixture of teaching and exhortation. This new paragraph elaborates some of the same points we find in this introductory paragraph, especially the focus on the identification of the high priest with the people he represents. Appropriately for a text that is the first stage in the high-priestly exposition, the focus is on the appointment of Jesus to this role.

Direct connection with the material immediately following this paragraph is less obvious, as the author turns from exposition to exhortation and warning (5:11–6:20). Reference to Jesus as high priest is conspicuously absent—at least until we reach the very end of chapter 6, where the author briefly mentions the "priest in the order of Melchizedek" theme he first touches on here in 5:6, 10. Chapter 7, then, is devoted to a full-scale exploration of this theme. The author signals a break in his argument with the summary nature of 7:26–28 and the literary marker in 8:1 ("now the main point of what we are saying is this . . ."). Probably, then, we should view chapters 5–7 as a discrete unit, bounded on both ends by exposition of Jesus as high priest with a long exhortation at its center.[1]

---

1. E.g., G. Guthrie, *Structure of Hebrews*, 92–93; James Kurianal, *Jesus Our High Priest: Ps 110,4 as the Substructure of Heb 5,1–7,28*, European University Studies: Theology 23 (New York: Peter Lang, 2000), 237–53.

I. The Exalted Son and a Rest for the People of God (1:1–4:13)
II. **Our Great High Priest and His Ministry (4:14–10:31)**
   A. Exhortation: Persevere through the Power of Our Exalted High Priest (4:14–16)
   ➡ **B. Exposition: High Priests and Our High Priest (5:1–10)**
   C. Exhortation: Move on to Maturity (5:11–6:20)
   D. Exposition: A High Priest "According to the Order of Melchizedek" (7:1–28)
   E. Exposition: The Ministry of Our High Priest (8:1–10:18)
   F. Exhortation and Warning: Appropriating the Benefits of Our High Priest's Ministry (10:19–31)
III. Exhortation: Follow and Serve the Pioneer of Our Faith through Endurance and Faith (10:32–13:25)

Main Idea

Jesus, the Son of God, has been appointed by God to be a high priest—one uniquely in "the order of Melchizedek." He is like the Aaronic high priests in being appointed and, as a human, being able to empathize with humans in their weakness. He is unlike them, however, in not having the need to offer sacrifices for his own sins.

Translation

Hebrews 5:1–10

1a	explanation (of 4:15)	For
1b	assertion 1	**every high priest** ... is taken from among humans and
1c	assertion 2	... **is appointed** on behalf of humans,
1d	reference	with respect to matters pertaining to God,
1e	purpose	to offer gifts and sacrifices for sins.
2a	assertion 3	He is able to deal gently with people
2b	description	who are ignorant and
2c	parallel	going astray,
2d	basis (for 2a)	since he himself is also enveloped in weakness.
3a	result (from 2d)	And because of this,
3b	assertion	**he is obliged**
3c	content	to offer a sacrifice for sin for himself, just as he does
3d	comparison	for the people.
4a	expansion (of 1b)	And

4b	assertion	**a person does not take this honor**
4c	means	by his own decision; rather,
4d	contrast	he is called by God—
4e	comparison	just as it was in the case of Aaron.
5a	comparison (with 4, and 1–4)	In this same way also
5b	assertion	**Christ did not glorify himself**
5c	purpose	so as to become high priest;
5d	contrast	rather [he was elevated to this rank]
5e	agent	**by the one**
5f	identification	**who said to him:**
5g	content	"You are my son;
5h	restatement	today I have begotten you." (Ps 2:7)
6a	verification (of 5c)	Even as in another passage **he says**:
6b	content	"You are a priest forever
6c	sphere	in the order of Melchizedek." (Ps 110:4)
7a	time	In the days of his flesh,
7b	assertion (referring to 5a)	Christ offered prayers and supplications,
7c	manner	with loud crying and tears
7d	direction	to the one
7e	description	who was able
7f	content	to save him from death; and
7g	sequence (with 7b)	he was heard
7h	reason	because of his reverent piety.
8a	concession	Son though he was,
8b	contra-expectation	**he learned obedience**
8c	source	from the things he suffered.
		And,
9a	antecedent	having been perfected,
9b	assertion	**he became the source of eternal salvation**
9c	advantage	for all who obey him,
10a	result (of 9b)	having been designated
10b	agent	by God
10c	content	as high priest
10d	comparison	according to the order of Melchizedek.

Structure

The passage takes the form of an extended comparison ("in this same way" [οὕτως] in v. 5a) between the Old Testament high priests (vv. 1–4) and the high priesthood of Christ (vv. 5–10). The author arranges the items in this comparison in chiastic order:

The Old Testament high priests:
- A   "offer gifts and sacrifices for sins" (v. 1)
-   B   are "enveloped in weakness" (vv. 2–3)
-     C   do not take this honor on themselves but are called by God (v. 4)

Jesus our high priest:
-     C'   "did not glorify himself . . . rather [God] said to him" (vv. 5–6)
-   B'   "in the days of his flesh . . . learned obedience from the things he suffered" (vv. 7–8)
- A'   "became the source of eternal salvation" (vv. 9–10)[2]

Exegetical Outline

➡ **B. Exposition: High Priests and Our High Priest (5:1–10)**
    1. The Old Testament High Priests (vv. 1–4)
    2. Jesus, Our High Priest (vv. 5–10)

Explanation of the Text

5:1 For every high priest is taken from among humans and is appointed on behalf of humans, with respect to matters pertaining to God, to offer gifts and sacrifices for sins (Πᾶς γὰρ ἀρχιερεὺς ἐξ ἀνθρώπων λαμβανόμενος ὑπὲρ ἀνθρώπων καθίσταται τὰ πρὸς τὸν θεόν, ἵνα προσφέρῃ δῶρά τε καὶ θυσίας ὑπὲρ ἁμαρτιῶν). The author begins his presentation of the high priesthood of Christ by mentioning three aspects of the Old Testament high priesthood. All three are briefly introduced in verse 1 and then elaborated in verses 2–4:

high priests are chosen "from among humans" (vv. 2–3)

high priests are "appointed" (v. 4)

high priests "offer gifts and sacrifices for sins" (v. 3)

The author places special emphasis on the humanity of the priests, a point he will elaborate with respect to Jesus's high priesthood also. This suggests that the "for" (γάρ), while anchoring this new paragraph generally in verses 14–16, might especially explain further the focus on the high priest's "empathy" in verse 15.[3] The word order (in Greek) reinforces this emphasis: "from among humans" (ἐξ ἀνθρώπων) comes first in the sentence. This phrase, which comes immediately before the verb "taken,"[4] has its rhetorical match in "for humans" (ὑπὲρ ἀνθρώπων),

---

2. Most interpreters identify this chiasm, differing over whether it has two, three, four, or five parts (advocating two elements: Grässer, *An die Hebräer*, 1:268; advocating five: Backhaus, *Der Hebräerbrief*, 197; agreeing with our identification of three basic elements, e.g., Lane, *Hebrews*, 111; D. Harris, *Hebrews*, 115).

3. Ellingworth, *Hebrews*, 272; Attridge, *Hebrews*, 142. The γάρ, then, is probably explanatory rather than causal (Grässer, *An die Hebräer*, 1:269). Delitzsch (*Hebrews*, 1:226), on the other hand, thinks that the γάρ covers all of vv. 1–10, as the basis for the imperative "draw near" in 4:16.

which comes immediately after "taken." The rest of the verse elaborates how high priests are appointed "for" or "on behalf of" humans: their appointment generally has to do with "matters pertaining to God,"[5] and, more specifically, is for the purpose of offering "gifts and sacrifices for sins." Interpreters naturally wonder why the author uses two words for sacrifices here. Some posit that he may intend to denote cereal offerings on the one hand and animal offerings on the other.[6] But the phrase here (δῶρά τε καὶ θυσίας) and elsewhere (see 8:3; 9:9) is probably just a way of referring to Old Testament sacrifices in general.[7]

5:2 He is able to deal gently with people who are ignorant and going astray, since he himself is also enveloped in weakness (μετριοπαθεῖν δυνάμενος τοῖς ἀγνοοῦσιν καὶ πλανωμένοις, ἐπεὶ καὶ αὐτὸς περίκειται ἀσθένειαν). This verse continues the description of Old Testament high priests from verse 1.[8] The author has already introduced the theme of compassion with respect to Jesus as high priest (2:17; 4:15); now he traces that quality back to the Old Testament high priests. "Deal gently" translates a word (μετριοπαθέω) used only here in the Greek Bible; it has the connotation of "moderate one's feelings" and sometimes, it seems, to "restrain one's anger."[9] It is common among interpreters to find a difference between this word and the one the author has used to describe Jesus in 4:15; for example, "the ordinary high priest controls his anger, Christ actually sympathizes."[10] The distinction is not clear, however, and we must be wary of finding distinctions between words when the author does not draw any attention to them.

Interpreters have likewise suggested that the author's description of the people with whom high priests deal gently, those "who are ignorant and going astray," may also subtly point to two kinds of sinners: those who sin "in ignorance" and those who sin deliberately (or, as the Old Testament often puts it, "with a high hand").[11] Again, however, we may be pressing the language to mean more than the author intends. The two words he uses (participles in Greek) may produce what we call a hendiadys, when the words modify each other to produce a single idea: here, "those who err through ignorance."[12] The author probably refers to humans in general, who all sin in various ways. The reason the Old Testament high priest can "deal gently" with such people is that he shares their situation: he is also "enveloped in," or "surrounded by," weakness.[13]

---

4. "Taken" translates λαμβανόμενος, from λαμβάνω, a verb usually rendered "take" or "receive." BDAG ("λαμβάνω," 584, §6) suggests "choose" or "select" for the meaning here, which many translations follow (e.g., NIV; ESV; NLT). However, this is the only NT verse that they cite for this meaning, and the focus here seems to be on the "taking" of this person from among the people; see, e.g., Num 8:6: "take [λαβέ] the Levites from among the Israelites and cleanse them" (NRSV). The participle is probably circumstantial, justifying its translation with a finite verb in English.

5. The Greek is τὰ πρὸς τὸν θεόν. The article τά should be construed as an accusative of reference, "with respect to the things," while πρός has a similar meaning (see "πρός," BDAG 875, §3.e.α). The same phrase occurs with the same meaning in 2:17.

6. Westcott, *Hebrews*, 118; Delitzsch, *Hebrews*, 1:227.

7. E.g., Ribbens, *Levitical Sacrifice*, 149; Attridge, *Hebrews*,

143. The phrase our author uses does not occur in the LXX, but the two words δῶρον and θυσία are often found together, often referring to the same thing.

8. It is linked with it syntactically by the participle δυνάμενος, which modifies the main verb in v. 1, "appointed" (καθίσταται).

9. See, e.g., Josephus, *Ant.* 12.128: "one may properly be amazed at the generosity of Vespasian and Titus who acted with moderation [μετριοπαθησάντων] after the wars."

10. Attridge, *Hebrews*, 144.

11. Ellingworth, *Hebrews*, 276; Koester, *Hebrews*, 286.

12. Zerwick and Grosvenor, *Grammatical Analysis*, 662; see also Zerwick, *Biblical Greek*, §184; Bruce, *Hebrews*, 120.

13. The Greek verb here is περίκειμαι, which the author uses again in 12:1, referring to the "cloud of witnesses" that we are "surrounded" by.

5:3 And because of this, he is obliged to offer a sacrifice for sin for[14] **himself, just as he does for the people** (καὶ δι' αὐτὴν ὀφείλει, καθὼς περὶ τοῦ λαοῦ, οὕτως καὶ περὶ αὐτοῦ προσφέρειν περὶ ἁμαρτιῶν). With an "and" (καί), the author adds a further point, stemming from the fact that the high priest is "enveloped in weakness." Since he is a sinner, he must offer a sacrifice for himself at the same time as he offers it for the people in general. The author may have in mind the Day of Atonement ritual, when the requirement for the high priest (Aaron) is to "offer the bull for his own sin offering" (Lev 16:6; cf. v. 11) before he slaughters "the goat for the sin offering for the people" (v. 15). This passage uses basically the same Greek construction in these verses that the author uses to depict the "sin offering" (περὶ τῆς ἁμαρτίας in the LXX; περὶ ἁμαρτιῶν in Hebrews). Moreover, our author uses the Day of Atonement ritual as the key Old Testament sacrificial context for his interpretation of the sacrifice of Christ.[15] However, the same phrase is also used elsewhere to refer to the sin offering, and regulations about the high priest making sacrifices for himself as well as the people also occur in other texts (e.g., Lev 4:3–12; 9:7). So a reference to the Day of Atonement here is not certain.[16] The need for the Old Testament high priests to sacrifice for their own sins becomes an important argument for the superiority of Christ, our high priest, who does not have to make such an offering (Heb 7:27; 9:7).

5:4 And a person does not take this honor by his own decision; rather, he is called by God—just as it was in the case of Aaron (καὶ οὐχ ἑαυτῷ τις λαμβάνει τὴν τιμὴν ἀλλὰ καλούμενος ὑπὸ τοῦ θεοῦ καθώσπερ καὶ Ἀαρών). The author here adds a further piece of information (hence the "and," καί), elaborating the point he made briefly in verse 1: high priests are appointed; they do not choose the profession of high priest. The author uses the present tense to state a general truth.[17]

At the end of the verse, he singles out the first and most famous biblical high priest, Aaron, as an illustration of the principle of appointment (Aaron's appointment as high priest is mentioned in several texts: Exod 28:1; Lev 8:1–36; Num 3:10). High priests in the Second Temple period often combined their priestly duties with political responsibilities, sometimes in ways that severely compromised their priesthood and violated the idea of divine appointment. Our author, however, as is usually the case, is thinking only of the biblical record.

5:5–6 In this same way also Christ did not glorify himself so as to become high priest; rather [he was elevated to this rank] by the one who said to him: "You are my son; today I have begotten you." 6 Even as in another passage he says: "You are a priest forever in the order of Melchizedek"[18] (Οὕτως καὶ ὁ Χριστὸς οὐχ ἑαυτὸν ἐδόξασεν γενηθῆναι ἀρχιερέα ἀλλ' ὁ λαλήσας πρὸς αὐτόν, Υἱός μου εἶ σύ, ἐγὼ σήμερον γεγέννηκά σε· 6 καθὼς καὶ ἐν ἑτέρῳ λέγει, Σὺ ἱερεὺς εἰς τὸν αἰῶνα κατὰ τὴν τάξιν Μελχισέδεκ). "In this same way" (οὕτως) marks the paragraph's transition from the author's brief rehearsal of the circumstances and nature of

---

14. This is one of the many verses in which the preposition περί, used twice here, takes on the connotation of ὑπέρ, "on behalf of," "for" (see Murray J. Harris, *Prepositions and Theology in the Greek New Testament* [Grand Rapids: Zondervan, 2012], 179–80; Moule, *Idiom Book*, 63). See M. Harris also on the use of περὶ ἁμαρτίας/περὶ ἁμαρτιῶν to mean "sin offering" (*Prepositions*, 182–83).

15. Attridge, *Hebrews*, 144.

16. Ribbens, *Levitical Sacrifice*, 152.

17. The verbal forms are λαμβάνει, "take" (cf. λαμβανόμενος in v. 1), and καλούμενος, "being called." This last form is a participle, which may modify the ellided verb λαμβάνει: a person does not *take* the honor; rather he "receives" it, being called by God. See Zerwick and Grosvenor, *Grammatical Analysis*, 662.

18. It is possible that the last phrase in the Hebrew text is not a proper name at all: see, e.g., NJPS: "You are a priest

Old Testament high priesthood (vv. 1–4) to the high priesthood of Christ (vv. 5–10). At the same time, however, the word marks a more specific comparison: as the Old Testament priests did not take the "honor" (τιμή) of this office on themselves (v. 4), so also Christ "did not glorify himself [οὐχ ἑαυτὸν ἐδόξασεν] so as to become high priest" (v. 5).[19]

The author's description of Christ's appointment is an important moment in the author's argument, bringing together the two central christological titles in Hebrews: Son and high priest. At the risk of overgeneralizing, we might even say that these verses function as a hinge in the author's argument, linking 1:1–4:13 with its focus on "Son" to 4:14–10:31, with its focus on "high priest."[20] "Son," as we have seen, has messianic allusions, so the author presents Christ here as a royal priest.[21] "It is the creative combination of royal and priestly dignity in Psalm 110, unique in the Old Testament, which has caught the writers' imagination."[22]

In our author's typical approach, he uses Old Testament quotations to bring the titles to our attention.[23] The author may intend us to read verses 5b–6 as a single sentence; see CSB: "but God who said to him, 'You are my Son; today I have become your Father,' also says in another place, 'You are a priest forever according to the order of Melchizedek'" (see also CEB). This arrangement has the virtue of giving the introductory clause in verse 5 its natural meaning: "the one who said" (English versions often add "God" to clarify the antecedent).[24] However, this reading of the syntax is challenged by the "just as" (καθώς) at the beginning of verse 6 (the CSB does not clearly translate it). So it might be better to view the participle as modifying an assumed verb "he appointed": see NLT: "he was chosen by God, who said to him. . . ." However we construe the details of the syntax, the emphasis falls on verse 6: the author moves *from* God's proclamation of Jesus's sonship *to* the proclamation of his high-priestly status. We will recall that the author has already used Psalm 2:7 to announce Jesus's sonship (1:5). He now introduces the verse that will become the Old Testament linchpin of his exposition of the high priesthood of Jesus, Psalm 110:4 (see also v. 10; 6:20; 7:1–10, 11, 15, 17). I will analyze this text and its background in my comments on 7:1–10. Here I pause to point out an obvious but significant fact: Psalm 110:4 comes just a few verses after the text that our author has already singled out as critical to his argument: Psalm 110:1. It is possible, then, that our author here might reveal the tip of his hermeneutical iceberg. We can imagine him reflecting on Psalm 110:1, a verse both Jesus and his followers applied to himself. That verse expresses a point the author is keen to emphasize: Jesus's exaltation. But, as a good interpreter of the Bible, our author might then have read further into

---

forever, a rightful king by my decree." But this is an unlikely reading of the Hebrew.

19. The Greek construction uses the infinitive γενηθῆναι ("to become [a high priest]") after the verb δοξάζω ("glorify"). The infinitive might express purpose (Ellingworth, *Hebrews*, 281), but more likely is epexegetic: Moule paraphrases "Christ did not take for himself the honor of becoming high priest" (*Idiom Book*, 127). It is tempting to suggest that "honor" (τιμή) in v. 4 and "glorify" in this verse are chosen to match the pairing of "glory and honor" in Ps 8:5, quoted in 2:7 (see also 2:9). But the words are not unusual, and the contexts are very different.

20. G. Guthrie, *Hebrews*, 189.

21. The combination of royal and priestly status reminds some of the way in which the Dead Sea Scrolls posit both a royal Messiah ("Messiah of Judah") and priestly Messiah ("Messiah of Aaron"): see esp. 1QS 9.11 (Yadin, "The Dead Sea Scrolls," 36–55). However, Hebrews's claim that one person combines both messianic and priestly status is quite different than what we find in the Scrolls (Bruce, *Hebrews*, 123).

22. France, "Writer of Hebrews," 261.

23. Both quotations follow the LXX closely. The author's wording of Ps 2:7 is identical to the main LXX tradition (as is the case also in 1:5); his quotation of Ps 110:4 differs from the LXX only in dropping the (unnecessary) copulative, εἶ ("are").

24. "The God who said" interprets ὁ λαλήσας as a substantival participle, a regular function of the participle.

the psalm, noting that the same person addressed as "lord" in verse 1 is installed as a "priest . . . in the order of Melchizedek" in verse 4. Surely, he might have reasoned, this text must also apply to Jesus, thus opening the door for the identification of Jesus as high priest and for speculation about the nature of that high priesthood. An obvious problem for this hermeneutical move is that the author sets up his quotation of Psalm 110:4 not with Psalm 110:1 but with Psalm 2:7. His quotation of that verse, however, as we have seen, is motivated by his desire to connect "Son" with "high priest." I still think, then, that Psalm 110:1 probably lurks in the background as a jumping-off point for the author's identification of Jesus as high priest.

I argued in my exposition of 1:5 that the Father's "begetting" of the Son took place at his exaltation, and the combination of quotations here might suggest that Jesus was also installed as high priest at his exaltation.[25] However, I also noted, with respect to Psalm 2:7 in 1:5, that "the Son, of course, has been the Son in one sense through all eternity; but, in another sense, with respect to the work of redemption, the Son is appointed to a new status via resurrection and exaltation (see also Rom 1:3–4)."[26] It is possible that this same logic applies to Jesus as "high priest": that he was high priest before his exaltation but that his exaltation and entrance into the heavenlies marked a new and vital stage in that ministry.[27]

5:7 In the days of his flesh, Christ offered prayers and supplications, with loud crying and tears to the one who was able to save him from death; and he was heard because of his reverent piety (ὃς ἐν ταῖς ἡμέραις τῆς σαρκὸς αὐτοῦ δεήσεις τε καὶ ἱκετηρίας πρὸς τὸν δυνάμενον σῴζειν αὐτὸν ἐκ θανάτου μετὰ κραυγῆς ἰσχυρᾶς καὶ δακρύων προσενέγκας καὶ εἰσακουσθεὶς ἀπὸ τῆς εὐλαβείας). Christ's full humanity is revealed in his agonizing prayer for deliverance and his steady faithfulness in the way God answered that prayer. With verse 7, the author begins a complex thought that runs through to the end of verse 10:

> Christ (simply "who" [ὅς] in Greek)
>> having offered prayers
>> having been heard
>> being a son
> learned obedience
> and
>> having been perfected
>> became the source of eternal salvation
>>> designated a high priest according to the order of Melchizedek[28]

The need to split up this long and complex sentence to suit English style can obscure the focus that is suggested by the Greek syntax. When we attend to this syntax, we recognize that the heart of this passage comes in verses 8 and 9: he "learned

---

25. E.g., Jamieson, *Jesus' Death and Heavenly Offering*, 28.
26. See also on this, Jamieson, *Paradox of Sonship*.
27. See, for this view, e.g., Cockerill, *Hebrews*, 239. Some scholars, noting the "forever" in the quotation here, emphasize the eternality of Jesus's high priesthood (e.g., Massonnet, *L'Épître aux Hébreux*, 139). I will look at this issue more closely in conjunction with some key texts in ch. 7, but it is possible that the "forever" means "from this time forward" rather than "for all times." Many other scholars emphasize (or assume) Jesus's high-priestly role in his death (e.g., Peterson, *Hebrews and Perfection*, 85).
28. Several aspects of the text in these verses have given rise to the theory that the author is quoting a hymn or hymn-like tradition: the occurrence of a relative pronoun (ὅς, "who") at the beginning, words not used elsewhere in Hebrews, and a certain rhythm created by the sequence of indicative verbs and participles (see, e.g., Weiss, *Der Brief an die Hebräer*, 311). However, disagreement among those who advocate such a tradition over the extent and original form of the tradition does not inspire confidence in the theory (Grässer, *An die Hebräer*, 1:313–14). It is better to think that the author himself has borrowed from the language of the psalms to create a semi-poetic depiction of Christ as the "righteous sufferer" (Backhaus, *Der Hebräerbrief*, 198; Attridge, *Hebrews*, 148).

obedience from the things he suffered" and "became the source of eternal salvation."²⁹ In general, these verses highlight the humanity of Jesus, showing that he fits the mold of an empathetic high priest (4:15) who can "deal gently" with the sins of people (5:2). As Calvin puts it, "If Christ had been untouched by any sorrow, then no consolation would come to us from His sufferings."³⁰ It was through his thorough identification with humans that Christ was "perfected"—that is, fully equipped to be a high priest who could adequately represent sinful humans before a holy God.

As a glance at a Greek or English Bible reveals, verse 7 is especially complicated. The basic thrust of the verse is carried by two Greek participles: "having offered" (προσενέγκας) and "having been heard" (εἰκασουσθείς). The object of the first participle is the phrase "prayers and supplications" (δεήσεις τε καὶ ἱκετηρίας), placed early in the verse. The author denotes the one to whom these prayers are offered as "the one who was able to save him from death" (πρὸς τὸν δυνάμενον σῴζειν αὐτὸν ἐκ θανάτου). Finally, he adds two prepositional phrases, the first indicating the time when the prayers were offered—"in the days of his flesh"—and the second the manner in which he offered the prayers—"with loud crying and tears." The choice of the word "offer" to depict Jesus's prayer characterizes this praying as a priestly activity: the same verb is used in verse 1 to describe the high priest's "offering" of gifts and sacrifices (προσφέρω).³¹ The language our author uses to describe Christ's praying is drawn from the Psalms. One of the most common scenarios in the Psalms is that of a pious Israelite (often David) who is facing persecution and suffering and who cries out to God in his distress. The author uses several words and concepts that are common in these prayers³² to highlight the intensity of Jesus's praying: "prayers,"³³ "supplications,"³⁴ "loud crying,"³⁵ "tears,"³⁶ "the one who was able to save him from death,"³⁷ "he was heard."³⁸ The author therefore portrays Jesus as the quintessential "righteous sufferer," a pious individual crying out to God for deliverance amid

---

29. See, e.g., deSilva, *Perseverance in Gratitude*, 191.
30. Calvin, *Hebrews*, 64.
31. E.g., Lane, *Hebrews*, 1:119; Johnson, *Hebrews*, 146. It is also possible that the author draws attention to the parallel by following the verb in each case with a dual construction: "sacrifices and offerings" on the one hand and "prayers and supplications" on the other. Fuhrmann argues that Jesus's "offering" takes the form of his prayers, and that these prayers consititute the new-covenant sacrifice (*Vergeben und Vergessen*, 110–12).
32. This same language is then picked up in Hellenistic-Jewish writings, which may also have influenced the author (Attridge, *Hebrews*, 148–49; Lane, *Hebrews*, 1:120; deSilva, *Perseverance in Gratitude*, 190–91). See, e.g., Philo's description of prayer in *Heir* 14–29; see also, e.g., 3 Macc. 1.16: "then the priests in all their vestments prostrated themselves and entreated [δεομένων] the supreme God to aid in the present situation and to avert the violence of this evil design, and they filled the temple with cries [κραυγῆς] and tears [δακρύων]" (NRSV).
33. Greek δεήσεις, a word that often connotes petitionary prayer. It occurs twenty-seven times in Psalms.
34. Greek ἱκετηρίας. The word occurs only twice in the LXX, but once along with δέησις (Job 41:3 [LXX 40:27]).
35. The Greek is κραυγῆς ἰσχυρᾶς. The singular κραυγῆς could be a kind of distributive, justifying the translation "cries" in most English versions. I follow BDAG ("κραυγή," 565, §1.a) in taking it as a verbal noun. The word κραυγή occurs five times in Psalms to describe prayer.
36. Greek δακρύων, which occurs five times in Psalms in conjunction with prayer.
37. Psalms often describes pious individuals calling on God to "save" (σῴζω) them (twenty-three times). No prayer in Psalms requests specifically that God would save from death, but salvation from death is sometimes celebrated as the answer to prayer. See, e.g., Ps 116:8: "for you, LORD, have delivered [ἐξείλατο] me from death, my eyes from tears [δακρύων], my feet from stumbling."
38. The Greek verb used here is εἰσακούω, which is the standard verb in the LXX of Psalms to describe God's positive response to prayer (it is used over fifty times this way). See, e.g., Ps 34:6: "This poor man called, and the LORD heard [εἰσήκουσεν] him; he saved him out of all his troubles."

unjust suffering.³⁹ This figure is often identified with David in the Psalms, and the widespread early Christian interpretation of Christ's significance in relation to David's history and the prophecies about him probably lies in the background here.⁴⁰

A more difficult question to answer is what situation in Jesus's life this language describes. An option that springs immediately to mind is Jesus's agonizing prayer in Gethsemane.⁴¹ To be sure, the words our author uses to describe Jesus's praying are not the words used in the Synoptic Gospels' accounts of Gethsemane. However, the author would not likely have had access to the written Gospels, and we can't know to what degree he may have been familiar with oral or written traditions preceding the written Gospels.⁴² Moreover, as we have seen, it is obviously the author's intention to use language from Psalms to situate Jesus's fervent praying in the context of the "righteous sufferer" tradition. The lack of verbal parallels with the Gospels' Gethsemane narratives does not rule out a reference to this experience. Nevertheless, noting the general introduction to verse 7—"in the days of his flesh"—many interpreters think the author refers to Jesus's life or at least his passion as a whole.⁴³ However, it does seem strange that the fervent praying the author describes here would not have some reference to the outstanding episode in Jesus's life when he prayed with this kind of fervor. I therefore adopt a compromise solution: the author refers generally to Jesus's prayer life, but with particular focus on Gethsemane. Bruce, quoting A. E. Garvie, characterizes Jesus's Gethsemane experience as "the most telling illustration" of his fervent praying.⁴⁴

Whether the author refers to Jesus's life generally or to Gethsemane in particular, or some combination of the two, the author's claim that Jesus prayed to the God "who was able to save him from death" and that he was "heard because of his reverent piety" is difficult, for Jesus was not "saved from death": he died on a Roman cross. The problem can be eliminated if we view "who was able to save him from death" as a general description of God rather than as an allusion to what Jesus was praying for.⁴⁵ But this does not seem to be a natural way to read this clause. Another option is to interpret Jesus's being "heard because of his reverent piety" (εἰσακουσθεὶς ἀπὸ τῆς εὐλαβείας)⁴⁶ as referring to the Father's support in enabling Jesus to accept his destiny.⁴⁷ But this interpretation does not do justice

---

39. E.g., Easter, *Faith and the Faithfulness of Jesus*, 157–63.

40. In light of this early Christian appropriation of this tradition, some interpreters think that the author may refer especially to Ps 22, which is central to this tradition, and which the author has quoted in ch. 2. Note, e.g., Ps 22:24: "for he [God] has not despised or scorned the suffering of the afflicted one; he has not hidden his face from him but has listened to his cry for help." See Bruce, *Hebrews*, 128–29.

41. See, e.g., Moffatt, *Hebrews*, 66; Montefiore, *Hebrews*, 97–98; P. Hughes, *Hebrews*, 182; G. Guthrie, *Hebrews*, 189–90; Johnson, *Hebrews*, 145; Peterson, *Hebrews and Perfection*, 86–87.

42. Loader, for instance, thinks that the author used a Gethsemane tradition independent of the Gospels (*Sohn und Hoherpriester*, 104–10).

43. E.g., Christopher A. Richardson, "The Passion: Reconsidering Hebrews 5:7–8," in Bauckham et al., *Cloud of Witnesses*, 51–67; Attridge, *Hebrews*, 148; Ellingworth, *Hebrews*, 286.

44. Bruce, *Hebrews*, 127; see also Cockerill, *Hebrews*, 244; Schreiner, *Hebrews*, 162–63.

45. Lane, *Hebrews*, 1:120.

46. The word εὐλάβεια is rare, occurring only here and in Heb 12:28 in the NT and three times in the LXX. In all three LXX occurrences (Josh 22:24; Prov 28:14; Wis 17:8) it means "fear," "anxiety," and some interpreters think it has this meaning here also, perhaps with reference to Christ's "fear" about bearing God's wrath against sin on the cross (Calvin, *Hebrews*, 65; D. L. Allen, *Hebrews*, 321–22). However, the large majority of interpreters think the word here means what it does in its one other occurrence in Hebrews, "reverence," "piety," "reverent submission," and all the English translations follow suit. See, e.g., M. Harris, *Prepositions*, 65–66; Koester, *Hebrews*, 289; Ellingworth, *Hebrews*, 289–90. The preposition ἀπό that governs this word has a causal force: "heard *because of* his reverence" (BDF §210.1).

47. Peterson, *Hebrews and Perfection*, 92.

to "saved from death." Since this can obviously not mean "saved from entering death," the best option seems to be to interpret it to mean "saved out of [ἐκ] the realm of death." The ultimate answer to Christ's prayer, then, is the resurrection.[48]

Despite uncertainty about several details, the main point in verse 7 is clear enough: Christ is the ultimate "righteous sufferer," crying out to God for deliverance and being heard because of his reverent piety. In the larger argument of 5:1–10, Christ's struggle in prayer makes clear that he identifies fully with human beings, qualifying him to be their "merciful" high priest (2:17–18; 4:15; see 5:2).

5:8 Son though he was, he learned obedience from the things he suffered (καίπερ ὢν υἱός, ἔμαθεν ἀφ᾽ ὧν ἔπαθεν τὴν ὑπακοήν). The Son's humanity is revealed further in the way his suffering deepened his steady reliance on the Father. As I noted in my overview of the long complex thought in verses 7–10, one of its main verbs comes here in verse 7: "he [Christ; see ὅς in v. 7] learned obedience." Learning obedience is another of the author's strong assertions about the full humanity of Christ. He does not, of course, mean that Christ moved from a posture of disobedience to obedience. Rather, he means that Christ's struggle in prayer in the face of his impending death provided the means to test and put into effect his obedience—strengthening it as a muscle is strengthened when it faces resistance. The main clause, "he learned obedience," is modified by a preceding participial clause: "Son though he was" (καίπερ ὢν υἱός). This translation of the clause, found in the NIV and the NAB, is the best way to capture the author's focus in English. As in 1:2, we are otherwise faced with the decision between saying "although he was a son" (ESV; NRSV; NET) or "although he was the Son" (see NLT, CSB: "God's Son"). The former is open to the implication that there is more than one son; the latter puts the emphasis on a concrete identification. Again, as in 1:2, the anarthrous Greek word probably focuses on the quality of the word, and the NIV/NAB rendering captures this well. A few interpreters take this clause with what precedes— "he offers up prayers ... Son though he was"[49]— but most, rightly, take it with what follows (as do the English versions).[50]

A second clause following the main verb provides another example of the author's literary ability. Christ, our author asserts, "learned" (ἔμαθεν) "from the things he suffered" (ἔπαθεν): the assonance created with *emathen/epathen* is obvious. "The things he suffered" undoubtedly has in view Christ's agonizing prayer of verse 7 but includes also, more broadly, the experience of suffering and death generally.

5:9–10 And, having been perfected, he became the source of eternal salvation for all who obey him, 10 having been designated by God as high priest according to the order of Melchizedek (καὶ τελειωθεὶς ἐγένετο πᾶσιν τοῖς ὑπακούουσιν αὐτῷ αἴτιος σωτηρίας αἰωνίου, 10 προσαγορευθεὶς ὑπὸ τοῦ θεοῦ ἀρχιερεὺς κατὰ τὴν τάξιν Μελχισέδεκ). "Learning obedience" contributes to Jesus being

---

48. This is the majority view; see, e.g., Patrick Gray, *Godly Fear: The Epistle to the Hebrews and Greco-Roman Critiques of Superstition*, AcBib 16 (Atlanta: Society of Biblical Literature, 2003), 189–98; Loader, *Sohn und Hoherpriester*, 109–11; Kurianal, *Jesus Our High Priest*, 69–70; Ellingworth, *Hebrews*, 288–89; Johnson, *Hebrews*, 146–47. It is possible that the "death" from which Christ is rescued includes also what I might call "spiritual death": Christ's experience of "the cup" of God's wrath (Bruce L. McCormack, "'With Loud Cries and Tears': The Humanity of the Son in the Epistle to the Hebrews," in Bauckham et al., *Epistle to the Hebrews*, 56).

49. Koester, *Hebrews*, 290.

50. Cockerill (*Hebrews*, 246) thinks it goes both directions.

perfectly qualified to be a high priest in the order of Melchizedek and therefore to be the source of salvation. The "and" (καί) suggests that the author here adds additional information.[51] Semantically, the "and" connects the indicative verbs "he learned" and "he became." Many interpreters rightly note the summary and transitional nature of these verses. Christ's being "perfected," as I noted in our comments on 2:10, refers to his full vocational qualification to be high priest, a motif that the author develops in the following chapters (e.g., 7:28; 10:14). "Source of eternal salvation" sums up Christ's intercessory role as high priest (see 6:9; 9:28). And "priest ... according to the order of Melchizedek," picking up on verse 6, introduces a key point that is developed extensively in chapter 7.[52]

"Became [ἐγένετο] the source of eternal salvation" is syntactically parallel to the main clause "learned obedience" in verse 8. This learning obedience is now interpreted as part of the process by which Jesus is "perfected." This verb in the Greek is an aorist passive participle (τελειωθείς), a form that may suggest that perfecting preceded and opened the way for Christ to become the "source of eternal salvation."[53] This is the only place the author qualifies "salvation" as "eternal." Indeed, this is the only place in the New Testament where salvation is described as eternal, and only one verse in the LXX does so, Isaiah 45:17: "but Israel will be saved by the LORD with an everlasting salvation [σωτηρίαν αἰώνιον]; you will never be put to shame or disgraced, to ages everlasting."[54] One reason the author adds the adjective here, then, may be to draw attention to this text in Isaiah. However, there is nothing obvious in the context of this verse in Isaiah that would draw our author's attention, so I remain uncertain about the significance of any allusion. "Having been designated" (προσαγορευθείς) in verse 10 translates a participle that is in the same form as "having been perfected." While strictly parallel in syntax, the first should be seen as logically prior to the second: it was because he was perfected that he was appointed high priest.

Theology in Application

Christians of orthodox belief throughout the centuries have naturally been keen to defend the deity of Christ. The biblical testimony to Christ's divine status is clear and unambiguous, leading early Christian theologians to conclude that this testimony required believers to affirm that the Son is fully God, sharing "one essence" with the Father (and, of course, with the Spirit as well). The author to the Hebrews, as we have seen, makes a significant contribution to this biblical testimony about Christ's deity (1:2–3, 8; cf. 7:3, 16, 24; 13:8; and the many references to Christ's exaltation to "the right hand" of God). Imbalance, however, is ever the danger in our theology. A zeal to defend Christ's deity can too easily slide into a neglect (or even tacit denial) of

---

51. Levinsohn, *Discourse Features*, 118.
52. See, e.g., Vanhoye, *Structure and Message*, 27–29. Referring to the recipients of salvation as those who "obey" Christ is, however, unusual; this specific language occurs only here in Hebrews (though note 3:18; 4:6, 11; 11:8, 31).
53. "Source" translates αἴτιος, used only four other times in the NT (Luke 23:4, 14, 22; Acts 19:40), where it means "basis" or "grounds."
54. The Greek for "eternal salvation" is a variant reading in "the shorter ending" of Mark.

Christ's true humanity. Again, early theologians were very clear on this point: Christ is both fully divine and fully human.

A distinctive feature of the author's Christology is his ringing endorsement of both Christ's divinity and his humanity. The opening passage in the author's exposition of Jesus's high priesthood provides perhaps the strongest evidence for Jesus's humanity in the letter. The author suggests that Jesus, like every other high priest, is chosen "from among the people" (v. 1) and is subject to weakness (v. 2). Though indeed being the "Son," with all the honor that title connotes, Jesus "learned obedience from the things he suffered" (v. 8). Especially evocative is the author's description of the Son's intense struggle in prayer (v. 7).

I suspect that few of us have heard many sermons on the humanity of Jesus. And yet it is an important point to make, not only theologically but pastorally. Indeed, it is the pastoral significance of Jesus's humanity that is the author's concern. First, because Jesus is human, he can offer himself as a sacrifice, taking the place of other humans. As early theologians put it, "What has not been assumed has not been healed."[55] Jesus needed to "assume," or take on, the full gamut of our humanity in order to heal, by his sacrifice, us humans. Only someone who is mortal can, after all, die as a sacrifice. Second, and this is the author's main point in this context, Jesus's full humanity means that he can empathize with humans, in all our weakness, as he represents us before the divine throne. "He [a high priest in general, but with reference to Christ] is able to deal gently with people who are ignorant and are going astray" (v. 2). The author here repeats a point he has made twice before: "Therefore he had to be made like his brothers and sisters in every way, in order that he might become a merciful and faithful high priest with respect to the things of God and so, in turn, he might atone for the sins of the people. Because he himself suffered when tried, he is able to help those who are being tempted/tried" (2:17–18); "for we do not have a high priest who is unable to empathize with our weaknesses, but one who has been tested in every way, just as we are, without sin" (4:15).

The last phrase in this latter verse is an important qualification with respect to Jesus's humanity. All humans since Adam inevitably sin and are condemned for that sin. The only exception, of course, is Jesus, whose virginal conception means that he did not inherit sin or "original death" from Adam. In all other respects, however, Jesus identifies with humans, experiencing what we experience, feeling the same power of temptation that we all must fight every day. Indeed, as Westcott notes, Jesus has felt the force of temptation more strongly than any other human, since he never gave way to sin.[56] The strength of temptation would therefore have continued

---

55. Gregory of Nazianzus, a fourth-century archbishop of Constantinople and theologian (*Epistle* 101, "Critique of Apollinarius and Apolliniarianism," 32 [https://earlychurchtexts.com/public/gregoryofnaz_critique_of_apolliniarianism.htm]).

56. Westcott, *Hebrews*, 59.

to increase, with no end. Our encouragement to come before "the throne of grace" through our great high priest, Jesus, therefore rests on both sides of his person. As true God, he can offer a sacrifice that has eternal and universal power, and he will always be available to intercede on behalf of his people. As true man, Jesus can fully identify with our predicaments and temptations. We need not fear to bring even our darkest thoughts and actions before him for forgiveness, for he knows them all and can therefore empathize with us.

Hebrews 5:11–6:3

Literary Context

In the course of his introductory paragraph about Jesus as high priest (5:1–10), the author briefly introduces a topic that will be at the heart of his message: Jesus Christ is a priest in "the order of Melchizedek" (5:6, 10). However, while the author has "much to say" about this (5:11), he delays his elaboration of this germinal idea, waiting until chapter 7 to draw out the significance of this Melchizedekian high priesthood. In 5:11–6:20 he prepares for this theologically and scripturally dense exposition by urging his readers to move on in their faith, scolding, warning, and reassuring them along the way. Like a good preacher, the author moves back and forth in his sermon between exposition and exhortation. He has already "interrupted" his exposition twice with exhortations (2:1–4; 3:7–4:13); now he does so again. He signals a return to exposition at the end of this section, reminding us that the one who has entered "behind the curtain" on our behalf is a "high priest forever, in the order of Melchizedek" (6:20).[1]

The internal structure of 5:11–6:20 is marked out by an *inclusio*: the author accuses his audience of being "sluggish" (νωθροί) in hearing in 5:11 and then describes his purpose in exhorting them as preventing them from becoming "sluggish" (νωθροί) in 6:12.[2] The "voice" of the author in this passage is put in the first-person plural: "*we* have much to say" (5:11); "God permitting, *we* will do" (6:3); "*we* speak like this" (6:9); "*we* want each of you" (6:11); "*we* do not want you" (6:12). The use of the "authorial we" throughout this passage is a shift from the author's use of the first-person plural in the earlier chapters to identify with his readers (e.g., "*we* have a

---

1. Vanhoye (*La Structure Littéraire*, 115), thinks that 5:11 is the beginning of the third major part of the letter, extending through 10:39. He characterizes 5:11–6:20 as the "preamble" of this section, focused on Jesus as high priest.

2. Most scholars note this *inclusio* and use it to mark out the paragraphs. However, a few think that a threefold division, 5:11–6:3, 6:4–12, and 6:13–20, does more justice to the content (e.g., Backhaus, *Der Hebräerbrief*, 213).

great high priest" [4:14]).³ This first major part of this section can be further divided into two parts, 5:11–6:3 and 6:4–12.

The second major part of this section, 6:13–20, by contrast, is cast mainly in the third person, pointing to a more expository focus of this section. In fact, without dismissing the useful categorization of large sections of Hebrews as either exposition or exhortation, these two modes of speech are usually intertwined to some degree throughout. This second major part is also marked by a return to the "we of identification" found earlier in the letter ("*we* who have fled for refuge" [6:18]; "*we*" have this "hope" [6:19]) and in this case is more exposition than exhortation. These verses ground the call to faith and patience so that what was promised might be attained through the faithfulness of God to his promises.

I. The Exalted Son and a Rest for the People of God (1:1–4:13)
II. **Our Great High Priest and His Ministry (4:14–10:31)**
    A. Exhortation: Persevere through the Power of Our Exalted High Priest (4:14–16)
    B. Exposition: High Priests and Our High Priest (5:1–10)
    C. Exhortation: Move on to Maturity (5:11–6:20)
        1. Avoiding Spiritual Stagnation (5:11–6:12)
            ➡ **a. Growing by Feeding on Solid Food (5:11–6:3)**
            b. Warning and Promise (6:4–12)
        2. The Dependable Promises of God (6:13–20)
    D. Exposition: A High Priest "According to the Order of Melchizedek" (7:1–28)
    E. Exposition: The Ministry of Our High Priest (8:1–10:18)
    F. Exhortation and Warning: Appropriating the Benefits of Our High Priest's Ministry (10:19–31)
III. Exhortation: Follow and Serve the Pioneer of Our Faith through Endurance and Faith (10:32–13:25)

Main Idea

The author scolds his audience for failing to progress in their spiritual formation and urges them to move ahead to maturity.

---

3. Backhaus, *Der Hebräerbrief*, 216. Wallace (*Greek Grammar*, 396), however, noting that the first explicit first-singular form does not occur until 11:32 and that the audience is asked in 13:18 to pray for "us," suggests that the first-person plural here and elsewhere might imply two authors for the book.

Translation

Hebrews 5:11–6:3

11a assertion 1 (rel. 10c–e)		Concerning this matter we have much to say; and
11b assertion 2		it is hard to explain,
11c reason		since you have become sluggish
11d reference		in hearing.
12a explanation (of 11)	For	
12b concession		although you should by this time be teachers,
12c contra-expectation	**you again have the need**	
12d content		for someone to teach you
12e object		the elementary principles of the oracles of God.
12f assertion	**You**	**need milk** and not
12g contrast		solid food.
13a elaboration (of 12f–g)	For	
13b identification	**anyone who lives on milk . . .**	
13c assertion		**. . . is unacquainted with the message of righteousness;**
13d explanation (of 13b–c)	for **that person is an infant.**	
14a contrast (with 13)	But	
14b assertion	**solid food is for the mature,**	
14c description		who,
14d basis		because of their condition,
14e assertion		. . . have had their faculties trained
14f result		to discern between good and evil.
6:1a inference (from 11–14)	Therefore,	
1b parallel (to 1c)		leaving behind the elementary message about Christ,
1c exhortation	**let us be carried on to maturity,**	
1d explanation		not laying again a foundation of repentance from dead works and
1e list		faith in God,
2a list		teaching about washings,
2b list		the laying on of hands,
2c list		resurrection of the dead, and
2d list		eternal judgment.
3a assertion	And **we will do this,**	
3b condition		if God permits.

Structure

The passages falls into two parts. In the first (5:11–14), the author uses language from the educational philosophy and practice of his day to scold his audience for their failure to progress in their spiritual formation.[4] In the second paragraph (6:1–3), the author urges his audience to forge ahead, seeking a "mature" spiritual status that is built on but moves beyond the fundamental truths they learned in their earlier spiritual experience. The two parts of this passage present, at first sight, a tension, or even a contradiction. In the first part, he suggests that the audience is not ready to move on: they "need milk and not solid food" (5:12). Yet in the second part, he urges his readers to move beyond elementary teachings and to pursue "maturity"; in other words, to feed on solid food rather than milk. The tension is probably to be resolved in terms of rhetoric: the author in 5:11–14 refers to the state of his audience in exaggerated terms in order to shame them into no longer closing their ears to his word of exhortation (5:11).[5]

Exegetical Outline

→ **a. Growing by Feeding on Solid Food (5:11–6:3)**
  i. Rebuke for Spiritual Lassitude (5:11–14)
  ii. Encouragement to Move on to Maturity (6:1–3)

Explanation of the Text

5:11 Concerning this matter we have much to say; and it is hard to explain, since you have become sluggish in hearing (Περὶ οὗ πολὺς ἡμῖν ὁ λόγος καὶ δυσερμήνευτος λέγειν, ἐπεὶ νωθροὶ γεγόνατε ταῖς ἀκοαῖς). The author interrupts his exposition of Jesus as high priest to scold his listeners for their failure to pay appropriate attention to the word. No conjunction or particle joins verse 11 to its previous context (asyndeton), but the author signals his transition into a different mode of speech by the prepositional phrase "concerning which" (περὶ οὗ). The pronoun I translate "this matter" (οὗ) could be masculine, referring back to Melchizedek, obviously viewed in his significance for Christ's high priesthood.[6] However, the author more likely refers to the "matter" or "topic" (NET; CEB) of Christ as

---

4. On this background, see esp. Thompson, *Beginnings of Christian Philosophy*, 17–40.
5. Attridge, *Hebrews*, 157–58; Koester, *Hebrews*, 308; Grässer, *An die Hebräer*, 1:332–33; Backhaus, *Der Hebräerbrief*, 214.

6. Ellingworth, *Hebrews*, 299; Weiss, *Der Brief an die Hebräer*, 330. Richard N. Longenecker suggests that the difficulty our author has in explaining Melchizedek has to do with the fact that his readers are former members of the Qumran sect, where certain views of Melchizedek were already popular ("The

a priest in the order of Melchizedek (the pronoun will then be neuter).[7] As I observed above, the author takes up this topic in chapter 7, and has "much to say" about it.[8] More significantly, the message is "hard to explain" (δυσερμήνευτος, used only here in biblical Greek). This word was sometimes used to refer to things inherently difficult to explain, such as dreams or visions.[9] However, the following clause in this verse makes clear that in this case the difficulty lies more with the hearers than with the subject matter itself. They have become[10] "sluggish in hearing" (νωθροὶ ... ταῖς ἀκοαῖς); and it is for this reason (see the ἐπεί) that the teaching about Melchizedek and Christ is difficult. Here the author touches again on a regular motif in his exhortation: the need to pay careful attention to the message (1:1–2a; 2:14; 4:12–13). The word for "sluggish" (νωθρός) is rare, occurring only here and in 6:12 in the New Testament and three times in the LXX. It is qualified here by "with respect to hearing."[11] The different renderings in the English versions point to the semantic range of the word in this phrase: "dull of hearing" (NASB; ESV); "sluggish in hearing" (NET; NAB); "too lazy to understand" (CSB; see CEB).[12] As I observed above, the occurrence of this word again in 6:12 acts as a framing device around this passage. But comparison with the later verse reveals a problem: in that verse the author claims to be exhorting his listeners so that they do not become "sluggish." Yet the form of the Greek verb in 5:11 (γενόνατε, a perfect) indicates that the author here is accusing them of already being in a state of "sluggishness."[13] Resolution of this apparent contradiction lies in the rhetorical purposes of the author. He is, in effect, seeking to stimulate in them the response, "No, we are not dullards, we are ready to hear what you have to say."[14]

5:12 For although you should by this time be teachers, you again have the need for someone to teach you the elementary principles of the oracles of God. You need milk and not solid food (καὶ γὰρ ὀφείλοντες εἶναι διδάσκαλοι διὰ τὸν χρόνον, πάλιν χρείαν ἔχετε τοῦ διδάσκειν ὑμᾶς τινὰ τὰ στοιχεῖα τῆς ἀρχῆς τῶν λογίων τοῦ θεοῦ καὶ γεγόνατε χρείαν ἔχοντες γάλακτος [καὶ][15] οὐ στερεᾶς τροφῆς). Verses 12–14 elaborate and explain the author's claim in verse 11 that his audience has become "sluggish in hearing."[16] He begins in verse 12 by accusing them of remaining at an elementary stage in their

---

Melchizedek Argument in Hebrews," in *Unity and Diversity in New Testament Theology: Essays in Honor of George E. Ladd*, ed. Robert A. Guelich [Grand Rapids: Eerdmans, 1978], 174).

7. All the English versions go this direction, as do most of the commentators (see, e.g., Attridge, *Hebrews*, 156; Grässer, *An die Hebräer*, 1:320). Johnson (*Hebrews*, 154) thinks the antecedent might be "Christ."

8. The Greek uses an expression known from the classical period on: πολὺς ἡμῖν ὁ λόγος, "our message is great."

9. E.g., Philo uses the word to refer to the "unseen world" (*Dreams* 1.188).

10. The Greek verb here (γεγόνατε) is in the perfect tense, suggesting that the listeners have already entered into this state of "sluggishness" (Ellingworth, *Hebrews*, 301).

11. The dative in the Greek phrase (ταῖς ἀκοαῖς) probably is a dative of reference (Turner, *Syntax*, 220). The plural ἀκοαῖς may be best explained if the word refers to the organs of hearing, "the ears" (the plural of this word usually has this meaning in the NT; see "ἀκοή," BDAG 36, §3). The author here may be influenced by the metaphor of "digging out the ear" that is used in the OT to refer to responsiveness to God's word (e.g., Ps 40:6 [LXX 39:7], quoted in Heb 10:5 with the substitution of "body" for "ear"]; Isa 50:4–5). The refrain in the letters to the seven churches, "whoever has ears, let them hear what the Spirit says to the churches" (Rev 2:7, 11, 17, 29; 3:6, 13, 22; cf. 13:9), makes a similar point, though the Greek word here is οὖς.

12. Peter S. Perry has suggested the translation "unambitious" ("Making Fear Personal: Hebrews 5.11–6.12 and the Argument from Shame," *JSNT* 32 [2009]: 99–125).

13. Ellingworth, *Hebrews*, 301.

14. Attridge, *Hebrews*, 157. See also esp. deSilva, *Perseverance in Gratitude*, 209, 211; Witherington, *Letters*, 203–5.

15. Reading with the NA[28]; the ZGNT omits.

16. The key connective word is "for" (γάρ). The καί (often translated "and") often loses any particular force when it is used with γάρ (see BDF 452(3) on this text, and also D. Harris, *Hebrews*, 128). None of the English translations attempts to render it with a particular English word.

spiritual progress. "Although you should be teachers" translates a participial clause in Greek, with the participle (ὀφείλοντες, "being obliged," "ought") having a concessive force (hence "although" in our translation and in other English versions). The author's claim that they should "by this time"[17] be teachers does not mean that they should have assumed official positions in the church. It is, rather, a way of castigating his listeners for remaining at an elementary stage in their spiritual journey.[18] The first-century Roman philosopher Seneca, for instance, criticizes people who never progress in their own understanding: "How long will you be a learner? From now on be a teacher as well!" (*Epistles* 33.9). Instead of themselves being teachers, his audience is in need of teaching, and teaching of the most elementary kind, learning "again . . . the elementary principles of the oracles of God." The Greek behind this phrase consists of a series of words in the genitive, often rendered in English with the help of the preposition "of": "the principles of the beginning of the oracles of God." "Principles" translates a word (στοιχεῖα) that refers to the basic building blocks or essential components of something; it can denote letters of the alphabet (the "ABCs") or the "elements" of which the universe is made (2 Pet 3:10, 12). Its meaning is hotly debated in two passages in Paul (Gal 4:3, 9; Col 2:8, 20), but pretty clearly here refers to the "basics" (CEB) of Christian instruction. The nuance of this word is accentuated by the addition of a modifying word that means "beginning" (τῆς ἀρχῆς), "the beginning principles," or "the basics—that is, the beginning."[19] These "elementary principles" have to do with "the oracles of God." The reference is clearly to what the author usually calls "the word [λόγος] of God," but he uses a different Greek word here (λογίον) that draws attention to the speaking of those words.[20]

The author adds to his negative portrayal of his audience with the use of another well-known educational metaphor of his day: they "need milk and not solid food."[21] The imagery is quite natural: people who are learning the very basics of a matter are like babies who can be fed only milk. If growth, however, is to occur, humans need to start eating solid food. Both Paul (1 Cor 3:2) and Peter (1 Pet 2:2) use this imagery. Epictetus, a Stoic philosopher who wrote in the early second century AD, rebukes sluggish learners: "Are you not willing, at this late date, like children, to be weaned and to partake of more solid food?"[22] The author addresses his audience as people who have known Christ for some time and should by now have progressed to the point where they should be feeding their souls on solid, nourishing, scriptural truth. Once more, however, we have to allow here for rhetorical exaggeration. Since the author does, in fact, go on to feed his audience the solid food of Christ's being a priest in the order of Melchizedek, he cannot here mean objectively that his audience

---

17. The Greek phrase is διὰ τὸν χρόνον, "because of the time," i.e., "in view of the time that has passed."

18. E.g., Moffatt, *Hebrews*, 70.

19. The former translation takes τῆς ἀρχῆς as a genitive of description, the latter as a genitive of apposition.

20. See Acts 7:38; Rom 3:2; 1 Pet 4:11. It occurs nineteen times in the long celebration of God's word in Ps 119. It usually translates Heb. אמרה.

21. The verb "need" is a reasonable translation of a more cumbersome Greek clause, which uses a periphrastic Greek construction that means "have" (γεγόνατε . . . ἔχοντες; see on this periphrasis with γίνομαι, Turner, *Syntax*, 89), plus the noun χρείαν.

22. *Diatr.* 2.16.39. Another good example is found in Philo, *Agriculture* 9: "But seeing that for babes milk is food, but for grown men wheaten bread, there must also be soul-nourishment, such as is milk-like suited to the time of childhood, in the shape of the preliminary stages of school-learning, and such as is adapted to grown men in the shape of instructions leading the way through wisdom and temperance and all virtue." See the overview in Grässer, *An die Hebräer*, 1:327–29.

can't handle solid theological food. Rather, he is shaming them in order to encourage them to embrace this teaching.[23]

5:13 For anyone who lives on milk is unacquainted[24] with the message of righteousness; for that person is an infant (πᾶς γὰρ ὁ μετέχων γάλακτος ἄπειρος λόγου δικαιοσύνης, νήπιος γάρ ἐστιν). The author develops ("for," γάρ) the metaphor he has used at the end of verse 12. The point the author wants to make in the first part of the verse is hard to pinpoint, the problem being the meaning of the phrase "message of righteousness" (λόγου δικαιοσύνης). The meaning of both words is uncertain. The former (λόγος) has a wide semantic range, the meanings being proposed for this verse being "speech"/"speaking," "reasoning," or "message"/"word."[25] The second word, which qualifies the first in some manner, can refer to "what is right" in a general moral sense or "what is right" in a biblical, theological sense. This latter meaning morphs into a more technical meaning, especially common in Paul: "righteousness" as right standing before God (e.g., Rom 4:1–8). The author's five other uses of this latter word are not very helpful in deciding its meaning here; he uses it once in the sense of "righteous standing" (Noah became the "heir of the righteousness according to faith" [11:7]) and twice in the sense of "right conduct" (1:9; 12:11; cf. possibly 11:33; it also occurs in the "translation" of the name Melchizedek in 7:2).

There are essentially two major directions interpreters take in their definitions of the phrase. On the one hand, some argue that the phrase adds one more description to the educational or philosophical "word game" that the author plays in verses 12–14. It might therefore refer to "speech characterized by righteousness"—that is, the "correct speech" that "infants" (see v. 13b)[26] are incapable of. Others taking this approach give *logos* a more active meaning, suggesting the phrase means "speaking about what is right" or "reasoning about what is right."[27] According to the other major approach, the author here draws a theological inference from the educational/philosophical background he has used to castigate his readers. The phrase might, then, mean "the message about [forensic] righteousness,"[28] "the message about [the life of] righteousness,"[29] or "the message [about Christ our high priest] that enables people to discern righteousness and live righteous lives."[30] Some of these options import more into the phrase than seems appropriate; for example, a reference to forensic righteousness (which plays a negligible role in Hebrews), or to the author's teaching about Jesus as high priest. I think the most straightforward reading, using the meaning each word in the phrase most often has in Hebrews and the natural syntactical connection between them, is "message about righteousness," with "righteousness" referring to the right standard of living.[31] "Righteousness" is broadly applicable, referring to the distinguishing "between good and evil" that the author highlights in verse 14b. However, this "righteousness" receives

---

23. See, again, esp. deSilva, *Perseverance in Gratitude*, 209, 211; Witherington, *Letters*, 203–5; also here Grässer, *An die Hebräer*, 1:325.

24. "Unacquainted" translates a Greek word (ἄπειρος) that occurs only here in the NT (four times in the LXX).

25. The extent of the semantic range can be gauged by the length of the entry for this word in BDAG ("λόγος," 598–601).

26. BDF §165; Delitszch, *Hebrews*, 1:264; Ellingworth, *Hebrews*, 307.

27. For the former, see Attridge, *Hebrews*, 160; for the latter, Koester, *Hebrews*, 302.

28. P. Hughes, *Hebrews*, 191–92. See NJB: "the doctrine of saving justice."

29. G. Guthrie, *Hebrews*, 202–3.

30. Cockerill, *Hebrews*, 258–59.

31. The author often uses λόγος to refer to the "message" of God; and see 6:1: "the message [λόγον] about Christ." As I noted above, two, and perhaps three, of the author's uses of

its ultimate definition in the word of God and the message about Christ.

The last part of the verse adds a further explanation, circling back to the first part of the verse: the person the author describes is unable to discern and do "what is right" because he or she is an "infant" (νήπιος), "feeding on" (μετέχων) milk. As Ellingworth notes, it is a brief restatement: "you see, you are children."[32]

5:14 But solid food is for the mature, who, because of their condition, have had their faculties trained to discern between good and evil (τελείων δέ ἐστιν ἡ στερεὰ τροφή, τῶν διὰ τὴν ἕξιν τὰ αἰσθητήρια γεγυμνασμένα ἐχόντων πρὸς διάκρισιν καλοῦ τε καὶ κακοῦ). In this verse, the author develops his metaphor of milk and solid food, contrasting immature believers who can handle only milk (v. 13) with the mature, who grow in their moral reasoning by feeding on solid food.[33] The author continues to adapt the language of ancient education to make his point about spiritual maturity. Thus, the word for "trained" (γεγυμνασμένα, a participle)[34] is from the verb γυμνάζω, which can readily be recognized as the source of our English words "gymnasium," "gymnastics," and so on. This verb was widely used, in accordance with the meaning of its Greek root word, to mean "exercise naked"—exercise being a central component in the education and training of children.[35] But the word was also widely extended to apply to moral or spiritual training. The author uses this verb again in Hebrews 12:11: "No discipline seems pleasant at the time, but painful. Later on, however, it produces a harvest of righteousness and peace for those who have been trained [γεγυμνασμένοις] by it."[36] The tense of the verb (perfect) focuses on the completion of the process of training. A text from Philo illuminates the author's "language game" in this context: "at an earlier stage, when he [a 'guardian'] was in training [ἐγυμνάζετο], this man was a pupil with another to teach him, but when he became capable of watching and guarding, he obtained the power and position of a teacher [διδασκάλου; cf. Heb 5:12]" (*Worse* 66).

The consistent intake of "solid food" trains believers so that they become "mature" (τελείων). The author's use of this word again draws from ancient educational philosophy; in the passage I quoted above, Philo uses this same word several times to denote the goal of the training process. However, while "mature" is probably the best translation here, contrasting naturally with "infant" in verse 13,[37] the word may also carry connotations of the author's "perfection" motif (see the note on 2:10). The English versions pretty much agree in

---

"righteousness" (δικαιοσύνη) refer to "right behavior" (a use of the noun that is also widespread in the NT and the LXX). Owens argues that the phrase denotes the moral reasoning that leads to maturity and the ability to eat "solid food" (H. P. Owens, "The 'Stages of Ascent' in Hebrews V.11–VI.3," *NTS* 3 [1957]: 244–45).

32. Ellingworth, *Hebrews*, 307.

33. A δέ introduces this verse, which, as we have seen, indicates a "development" in an argument (see the note on 4:13). This development can take the form of a continuation (a weak "and") or a contrast (a weak "but"), the latter being the meaning here.

34. The participle goes with the word αἰσθητήρια ("faculties"), which in turn is the object of the substantival participle ἐχόντων. In a typical "envelope order," this participle picks up the article τῶν earlier in the verse. The words are in the genitive plural because they modify τελείων. Hence, tracing the syntax: "mature people, the ones having faculties trained because of their [mature] condition."

35. Note the cognate γυμνασία, used to describe physical exercise, in 1 Tim 4:8. The basic word using this root is γυμνός, meaning "naked" or "inadequately clothed" (e.g., Matt 25:36; Acts 19:16).

36. See also, in the sense of positive training for "godliness," 1 Tim 4:7; and, with negative results, false teachers who have "hearts trained in greed" (2 Pet 2:14; my translation).

37. E.g., Koester, *Hebrews*, 303.

saying that this training leading to maturity comes "by practice" (NRSV; NET; NAB) or "constant use" (NIV). However, the Greek word here (ἕξιν) probably means "condition" or "capacity" rather than "practice."[38] And in the context, that condition is the state of maturity.[39] It is because of that mature state that these believers are able to discern good and evil (πρὸς διάκρισιν καλοῦ τε καὶ κακοῦ).[40]

6:1 Therefore, leaving behind the elementary message about Christ, let us be carried on to maturity, not laying again a foundation of repentance from dead works and faith in God (Διὸ ἀφέντες τὸν τῆς ἀρχῆς τοῦ Χριστοῦ λόγον ἐπὶ τὴν τελειότητα φερώμεθα, μὴ πάλιν θεμέλιον καταβαλλόμενοι μετανοίας ἀπὸ νεκρῶν ἔργων καὶ πίστεως ἐπὶ θεόν). After using a strong rebuke to try to wake up his readers, the author now exhorts them to move ahead in their faith. At first sight, the connection between the previous paragraph (5:11–14) and this verse is hard to make sense of. In these previous verses, the author appears to be despairing about his audience, criticizing them for still feeding on spiritual milk rather than solid food. How, then, can the author draw as a conclusion from that grim assessment ("therefore," διό) his intention to carry them on to maturity—precisely by *not* focusing on the "milk," the "foundation" they have already put in place? The answer, as I have suggested at a couple of points in our exposition of the last paragraph, lies in the exaggeration that the author employs for rhetorical effect. In 5:11–14, he is not dispassionately diagnosing their spiritual state. Rather, he seeks to shake them out of their lethargy by accusing them of behaving as if they were spiritual infants. He is convinced, in fact, that they are well able to move on to maturity if they will only develop a taste for the "solid food" the author wants to feed them. They need to shrug off their lackadaisical attitude and become mature; "therefore" the author urges them to do this very thing.[41]

The basic framework of this verse imitates a common New Testament pattern, with a negative command followed by a positive. The negative is communicated by means of a participle (ἀφέντες), but the participle in this case is probably semantically equivalent to an imperative verb (hence most English translations render it as "let us leave").[42] This pattern often features the combination of a command to leave sinful behavior behind and to take up right attitudes or behavior. In this case, what the author wants his audience to "leave behind" is not something sinful but "the elementary message about Christ" (τὸν τῆς ἀρχῆς τοῦ Χριστοῦ λόγον).[43]

---

38. See esp. John A. L. Lee, "Hebrews 5:14 and Ἕξις: A History of Misunderstanding," *NovT* 39 (1997): 151–76; and also, e.g., G. Guthrie, *Hebrews*, 203; Ellingworth, *Hebrews*, 309. For the other meaning, see, e.g., deSilva, *Perseverance in Gratitude*, 213 ("constancy"); Lane, *Hebrews*, 1:131.

39. This word is the object of the preposition διά, which, when followed by an accusative word (as here), means "because of."

40. The word διάκρισις can refer to "quarreling" in the NT (Rom 14:1), but here (and in 1 Cor 12:10) means "distinguishing, differentiation" ("διάκρισις," BDAG 231, §1).

41. "There is no alternative (διό) but to press on to maturity" (G. Hughes, *Hebrews and Hermeneutics*, 162).

42. The participle is, in technical terms, circumstantial, becoming in effect parallel in meaning and emphasis to the verb it modifies. The participle is derived from ἀφίημι, which occurs frequently in the NT to refer to "leaving" in a physical sense or to "releasing," whether applied to physical circumstances (e.g., imprisonment) or to spiritual ones (e.g., "forgiving" sins). Particularly relevant here are occurrences of the verb that signal a transition in a speech or discourse (see "ἀφίημι," BDAG 156, §3.b; Koester, *Hebrews*, 303).

43. In this phrase the object of the participle, τὸν ... λόγον ("the message") is modified by τῆς ἀρχῆς ("the beginning"), probably a descriptive genitive ("a message characterized as elementary"; cf. Attridge, *Hebrews*, 162), and by τοῦ Χριστοῦ ("of Christ"). This latter genitive is sometimes interpreted as subjective—"the message proclaimed by Christ" (Attridge, *Hebrews*, 162; Witherington, *Letters*, 209–10; Loader, *Sohn und Hoherpriester*, 83–93)—but is almost certainly objective: "the message about Christ" (NIV; NLT; NET; NRSV; CSB; and see, e.g., Lane, *Hebrews*, 1:131).

Of course, the author is not suggesting that his listeners turn away from this basic message about Christ.⁴⁴ In the second part of the verse, he characterizes this teaching as a "foundation." "In building a house one must never abandon the foundation, but at the same time it is ridiculous to spend all one's time in laying it. A foundation is laid for the sake of the building."⁴⁵ So the author exhorts his readers, with the foundation of the basic message about Christ in place, to move on to "maturity" (τελειότητα). As is the case with τελείων in 5:14, this word is appropriately translated "maturity." But even more than in the former verse, we should probably hear overtones of "perfection" as well: for "perfection" is the goal to which believers are called and the ultimate benefit Christ's sacrifice provides for them (2:10; 7:11; 9:9; 10:1, 4; 11:40; 12:23).⁴⁶

The positive command in the verse takes the form of a hortatory subjunctive. In 5:11, the author used an "authorial we" to refer to himself; here he returns to the "inclusive we," which he has used earlier (e.g., 2:1, 3; 3:6, 14; 4:1-3, 11, 14-16). The exhortation is translated in most versions in the active voice: "let us go on" or "let us move on." Such translations assume the author is using the middle/passive form of the verb (φερώμεθα) in an active sense.⁴⁷ But occurrences of this form elsewhere in the New Testament suggest that it should rather be understood as a passive form, with a passive meaning.⁴⁸ In this case, a rendering such as we find in the NIV is more accurate: "let us . . . be taken forward."⁴⁹ As is often the case in the New Testament, then, we probably have here a "divine passive": a verb in the passive that assumes the agent of the action is God. The exhortation therefore balances, in a manner thoroughly typical of the New Testament, human response and divine enablement.

Moving forward toward maturity means, as we have seen, building on the foundation of basic Christian truth that "those who confirmed" that message originally brought to the audience (2:3). This "foundation" (θεμέλιον) is outlined in verses 1b-2 in three pairs of terms:

"repentance from dead works and faith in God"
　teaching about "washings" and "the laying on of hands"
　　"resurrection of the dead and eternal judgment"

The author's selection of these six items to characterize the spiritual foundation of his audience has sparked considerable discussion. For it does not seem likely that a person would summarize "the elementary message about Christ" without even mentioning Christ. As has regularly been noted, the list has nothing distinctively Christian about it. While certainly not serving as an adequate description of the basic elements of the Jewish faith, these six items could all have been endorsed by certain Jews (such as the Pharisees). Indeed, this "lowest common denominator" factor may explain what our author is doing here. If, as I think, the audience is Jewish, the author may single out theological points that his audience would have endorsed both in their Jewish past and in their initial, distinctively

---

44. Indeed, Lane suggests that ἀφέντες might mean "leave standing" (*Hebrews*, 1:131), but the evidence from the texts he cites for this meaning is not compelling.

45. Calvin, *Hebrews*, 71.

46. E.g., Attridge, *Hebrews*, 163; deSilva, *Perseverance in Gratitude*, 215.

47. See Attridge, *Hebrews*, 162-63.

48. There are five other texts in which this verb, φέρω, could be either middle or passive (the forms are identical). Four of them (Acts 27:15, 17; Heb 9:16; 1 Pet 1:13) have a passive meaning. The fifth (Acts 2:2) is middle with an active intransitive meaning.

49. See, e.g., Lane, *Hebrews*, 1:131; Ellingworth, *Hebrews*, 312; Cockerill, *Hebrews*, 262 (perhaps). While not citing this verse, BDAG ("φέρω," 1051-52, §3) note that this verb in the passive, with the meaning "cause to follow a certain course in direction or conduct," can be translated "be moved, be driven, let oneself be moved"—all passive in sense.

Christian commitments.⁵⁰ While, in my view, "the parting of the ways" between Jews and Christians was well under way at this date (in contrast to the view of many other scholars), Christian truth was deeply rooted in, and often took over, Jewish theological perspectives. These elements common to Judaism and Christianity could, then, justly be labeled an "elementary message about Christ." It is attractive, then, to take one further step and to suspect that the readers were retreating into a focus on these points precisely so that they could avoid being persecuted for distinctively Christian beliefs (see 10:25, 32–35; 12:4; see the introduction).⁵¹

The first two items on the list, "repentance" and "faith," would appear to be a natural pairing. However, while the two terms are used together to summarize the heart of Jesus's call for response (Mark 1:15) and also the preaching of the early Christians (Acts 20:21), they are paired only rarely in the New Testament. One reason for this is that "repentance" on its own sometimes appears to be used broadly to mean "turn around," "be converted" (e.g., Acts 2:38; 3:19; 17:30)—and, in this sense, the word would include the positive response of faith.⁵² In our text, however, "repentance" (μετάνοια) clearly has the more negative nuance we are familiar with: turning away from "dead works." These "dead works" (νεκρῶν ἔργων) are sometimes given a restricted reference, for instance, to the Levitical regulations the author will criticize later on (see 9:10).⁵³ Others, noting the language of conversion elsewhere in the New Testament, suggest that "dead works" might refer especially to idolatry; for example, 1 Thessalonians 1:9 describes how the Thessalonians "turned to God from idols."⁵⁴ However, both here and in the only other text where the author uses the phrase (9:14), it probably refers generally to sins, viewed in terms of the spiritual death that they bring about.⁵⁵ "Faith in God" (πίστεως ἐπὶ θεόν) expresses the positive side of conversion: one moves "from" (ἀπό) dead works "to" (ἐπί) God. The author never specifies a particular object of faith anywhere else; he prefers to speak simply of "faith." We should not make too much, then, of the fact that the author speaks here of "faith in God" rather than "faith in Christ" (as other NT authors regularly do). However, it is certainly possible that he is again seeking to use language that would be at home among both Jews and Christians.⁵⁶

6:2 teaching about washings, the laying on of hands, resurrection of the dead, and eternal judgment (βαπτισμῶν διδαχῆς ἐπιθέσεώς τε χειρῶν, ἀναστάσεώς τε νεκρῶν καὶ κρίματος αἰωνίου). The author adds four more elements to his list describing the "foundation" of the faith. The word "teaching" (διδαχῆς) governs all four items in this conclusion to the list of foundational beliefs and practices.⁵⁷ And "teaching" itself stands in

---

50. E.g., Weiss suggests the list reflects early Christian prebaptismal instruction typical in Jewish missionary preaching (*Der Brief an die Hebräer*, 337).

51. Peterson, *Hebrews and Perfection*, 180; Donald A. Hagner, *Hebrews*, NIBC (Peabody, MA: Hendrickson, 1990), 87; G. Guthrie, *Hebrews*, 205.

52. It is possible that the word has this broader sense in 6:6 (see our notes there). The author uses the word only one other time, to refer to Esau's inability to repent (12:17).

53. Westcott, *Hebrews*, 144; Lane, *Hebrews*, 1:140. Other scholars note texts in which "dead works" are associated with idolatry (e.g., Wis 15:7; see deSilva, *Perseverance in Gratitude*, 216).

54. See deSilva, *Perseverance in Gratitude*, 216.

55. Attridge, *Hebrews*, 164; Ellingworth, *Hebrews*, 314; Koester, *Hebrews*, 304.

56. There is certainly no reason to think that "faith in God" would apply only to gentiles; Koester (*Hebrews*, 305) rightly notes that it applies equally to Jew and gentile.

57. The modern Greek New Testaments (UBS⁵, NA²⁸, and Tyndale House) all read the genitive διδαχῆς. But the accusative διδαχήν is attested in some early and good MSS (e.g., 𝔓⁴⁶, B)

apposition to "foundation," so these four items conclude the survey of basic teaching. The author does not signal by his syntax that these four items fall into two pairs, but the meanings of the terms make this almost certain.

The variety of options in English translations reveal the difficulty of determining what the first word, βαπτισμῶν, refers to: "cleansing rites" (NIV), "washings" (ESV); "baptisms" (NLT); "ablutions" (RSV). A reference to Christian baptism might seem to be an obvious choice, since the Greek word, transliterated, is *baptismōn*.[58] However, the Greek word used here (βαπτισμός) refers to the rite of Christian baptism only one other time in the New Testament (Col 2:12),[59] and the plural form of the word is very difficult to explain if the reference is simply to baptism.[60] The author uses this word one other time, to refer to Jewish ritual washings (9:10), and this is perhaps the most likely meaning here (see also Mark 7:4). This is the view of most interpreters, although scholars divide over whether the author might be including John's baptism and perhaps also Christian baptism in this general category of ritual cleansing rites.[61] I think it likely that the author refers to initiation rites and ritual cleansings that involve water (very widespread in the ancient world), with particular reference to the Christian initiation rite in water. If this is so, then it is natural also to think that the next item, "laying on of hands," refers to a rite of initiation. The apostles laid hands on people to signify the coming of the Holy Spirit upon them (Acts 8:17), sometimes in conjunction with baptism in water. See, for example, Acts 19:5b–6: "They [the disciples of John] were baptized in the name of the Lord Jesus. When Paul placed his hands on them, the Holy Spirit came on them, and they spoke in tongues and prophesied."[62]

If the first pair in this series—repentance and faith—expresses one's basic response to God, and the second—washings and laying on of hands—points to the beginning of one's spiritual journey, then the third—resurrection of the dead and eternal judgment—marks the end of that journey. The doctrine of a final resurrection of the body was a disputed matter in first-century Judaism, but it was probably the majority view among Jews at that time. Our author refers to the "better resurrection" enjoyed by faithful Jews at the time of the Maccabees (11:35; see also 11:19). Christians tied the general resurrection of the righteous to the resurrection of Christ (e.g., 1 Cor 15:20–28).

---

and receives support from a number of scholars (e.g., Moffatt, *Hebrews*, 74–75; Bruce, *Hebrews*, 137; Attridge, *Hebrews*, 155; Lane, *Hebrews*, 1:132; D. Harris, *Hebrews*, 133; Massonnet, *L'Épître aux Hébreux*, 147). It has been suggested that the latter reading would mean that the four items governed by the word in v. 2 would not be part of the foundation. But this does not follow. Either form of the word would appear most naturally to be epexegetic of "foundation." For a brief defense of the reading διδαχῆς, see Metzger, *Textual Commentary*, 596.

58. See Koester, *Hebrews*, 305; Lindars, *Theology*, 66–68.

59. I should note that there is a well-supported variant in this verse, βαπτίσματι, which is from the noun βάπτισμα. This latter word refers often to John's baptism (Matt 3:7; 21:25; Mark 1:4; 11:30; Luke 3:3; 7:29; 20:4; Acts 1:22; 10:37; 13:24; 18:25; 19:3, 4) and to Christian baptism (Rom 6:4; Eph 4:5; 1 Pet 3:21).

60. Although some interpreters find ways of reconciling the plural with a reference to Christian baptism: the author assumes multiple immersions in the ceremony (attested in Tertullian, *Against Praxeas* 26.9; see also Did. 7.3 [if there is no opportunity for immersion, "pour water on the head three times"]); the author refers both to the external ceremony and the internal cleansing (deSilva, *Perseverance in Gratitude*, 218); the author is thinking of many people being baptized.

61. Those who think that Christian baptism is included are, e.g., Moffatt, *Hebrews*, 75; Westcott, *Hebrews*, 145–46; P. Hughes, *Hebrews*, 202; Ellingworth, *Hebrews*, 315. Witherington (*Letters*, 210) thinks the author may intend to contrast John's baptism with Christian baptism.

62. For this interpretation, see, e.g., Attridge, *Hebrews*, 164; Ellingworth, *Hebrews*, 316; Grässer, *An die Hebräer*, 1:340. The laying on of hands also figures in healings (Mark 6:5; 8:23; Luke 4:40; 13:13; Acts 9:17) and in commissionings (Acts 6:6; 13:3; 1 Tim 4:14; 5:22; 2 Tim 1:6).

While the New Testament also teaches a resurrection of all the dead (John 5:28–29), the author here probably refers to the resurrection of the righteous. As, then, the resurrection of the body marks the end of the believer's journey of faith, "eternal judgment" signals the end of human history. Again, the teaching of a general judgment of all humans in the last days was standard in both Judaism and early Christianity. The author labels this judgment "eternal" (αἰωνίου), probably because it has eternal consequences.[63] As resurrection probably connotes a favorable outcome of one's spiritual journey, "eternal judgment" might focus on the negative: the author elsewhere uses judgment language to express God's punishment of sinners (10:27–31; 13:4). However, he also refers to a judgment that all people must face (9:25–27; cf. 4:12; 12:23), so the issue is unclear.[64]

6:3 And we will do this, if God permits (καὶ τοῦτο ποιήσομεν, ἐάνπερ ἐπιτρέπῃ ὁ θεός). The "this" refers back to verse 1: the author is committed to helping his audience be led on to a deeper experience of their faith—to "maturity" or "perfection." He reverts here again to the "authorial we."[65] The qualification "if God permits" (see also Jas 4:15) is not a pious throwaway line: the author recognizes that his ability to stimulate his audience to move on in their faith is very much dependent on God's will and enablement.

Theology in Application

The author's urgent call to his readers to move on to "maturity" in 6:1 is the heart of the long exhortation that runs from 5:11–6:20. As I noted in my comments on that verse, the translation "maturity" for the word the author uses here (τελειότης) is probably appropriate, granted the educational context (see 5:14; and see also, e.g., 1 Cor 14:20). However, cognates of this word occur many other times in Hebrews, and most of these clearly mean "perfection" or "perfect." Thus, as we have seen (see comments on 2:10), the author famously describes Jesus being "perfected" (2:10; 5:9; 7:28), and these texts would not make good sense if the author was referring to Christ becoming "mature." The same is true of the author's claim that the new-covenant era, with the once-for-all sacrifice at its inception, brings "perfection" (7:11; 9:9; 10:1, 14; 11:40; 12:23). Again, "maturity" is clearly not the idea here.

The decision about the translation of this word group throughout the New Testament is often not an easy one. Thus, does Jesus urge his disciples to "be perfect, therefore, as your heavenly Father is perfect" (Matt 5:48 NIV), *or* is he saying that

---

63. Ellingworth, *Hebrews*, 316; cf. Bruce, *Hebrews*, 143.
64. Ellingworth thinks the reference is to the judgment of both the righteous and the unrighteous (*Hebrews*, 316). Cockerill, e.g., thinks that judgment refers to the favorable verdict passed on the righteous (*Hebrews*, 266–67).
65. I take this plural form to refer to the author. However, if we follow a number of MSS and read in place of the indicative ποιήσομεν the (hortatory) subjunctive ποιήσωμεν, then the verb would be plural in meaning (e.g., the uncials A, C, D, P, Ψ, as well as the important minuscules 81, 104, and 1505). If this variant reading is adopted, the verse would frame the brief paragraph with exhortations ("let us [you, my audience, and I] do this [move on to maturity]").

"just as your heavenly Father is complete in showing love to everyone, you also must be complete" (CEB)? Does Paul's ministry have the purpose of presenting people "fully mature" in Christ (Col 1:28 NIV) or "perfect" in Christ (NAB)? Are trials given to us by God to make us "mature" (Jas 1:4 NIV) or "perfect" (ESV)? Arguing for an idea such as "mature" or "complete" is the Old Testament background, where equivalent Hebrew words (especially *tamim*) have this sense. "Perfection," on the other hand, might introduce a kind of ideal that reflects a fundamentally non-biblical way of assessing things.

Another argument for "maturity" is that it sets a target that a person has a realisitic chance of hitting in this life. Calls to a "perfection" that can only be attained after this life offer an impossible ideal that would hardly stimulate people to seek after it. Yet just here may lie the problem with settling for "maturity." In his exposition of James 1:4, F. J. A. Hort warns believers who reach a certain level of maturity against building a platform on which they can rest. That is, once we are convinced we have reached some level of "maturity"—"I am certainly more mature than most of my fellow congregants!"—we might be tempted to call that "good enough."[66] In this regard, then, it might stimulate rather than hinder believers to be reminded that God is satisfied with nothing less than the "perfection" that he himself shares in. This is a goal we will not finally attain in this life. But we should seek to get as close to this goal as we can and never be satisfied with anything less. And, as we pursue it, we should always keep in mind that Jesus himself is the "perfecter" of faith (12:2).

---

66. F. J. A. Hort, *The Epistle of St. James* (London: Macmillan, 1909), 7.

Hebrews 6:4–12

Literary Context

The ministry of Jesus our high priest is the central theological message of Hebrews. The author develops this theme in an extensive and varied argument in 4:14–10:31. He launches this rich, Old Testament-based exposition in 4:14–16, which, along with 10:19–25, "bookends" this exposition. The first stage of this exposition comes in 5:1–10, where he focuses on Jesus as a fully human and merciful high priest. At the same time, this paragraph introduces the author's particular "take" on Jesus's high priesthood: he is a "priest forever in the order of Melchizedek" (5:6). The author will develop this latter point in considerable detail in chapter 7. But before he can do that, he needs to get the full attention of his listeners. This he seeks to do in 5:11–6:20. He has scolded his audience for their contentment with the milk of spiritual teaching when they should by now be feeding on solid food (5:11–14). The author is determined to force-feed them this food (6:1–3). But before he does this, he raises the stakes by warning them about the serious consequences should they refuse this food and turn away from the God who has given them so much (6:4–8). Yet, achieving a balance typical of ancient rhetoric and the author's approach, he goes on immediately to express his confidence about his readers (vv. 9–12)—a confidence resting securely on God's promises (vv. 13–20).

One other aspect of the literary context of this passage should be noted. The warning that our author issues in verses 4–8 is, in fact, only one such warning that our author uses in this letter to stir his readers to attentiveness (see also 2:2–3; 3:7–4:11; 10:26–31; 12:14–17, 25). Indeed, the warning in 10:26–31 is arguably stronger than the one here in chapter 6. However, the text now before us is the traditional locus for discussion of the theological implications of the warning passages, so I will tackle the issue here. Our discussion, however, cannot come to general theological conclusions apart from consideration of these other texts as well. No ultimately satisfactory view of the author's intentions in this passage can be attained without aligning this text with the others.[1]

---

1. A point rightly made by Scot McKnight, "The Warning Passages of Hebrews: A Formal Analysis and Theological Conclusions," *TJ* 13 (1992): 21–59.

Hebrews 6:4–8 is probably the best-known paragraph in the letter and has long been an exegetical and theological battlefield (Luther labeled it a "hard knot"[2]). This is unfortunate, since the passage does not express the most important or characteristic teaching of the letter. This passage played a significant role in early Christian debates over whether those who had been baptized/converted and then fell away from faith could be baptized or restored again. Certain groups (the Montanists in the second century and the Novatians in the third) advocated a rigorous view—no second baptism and no possibility of a "second repentance"! This rigorism was disputed by many other theologians and church leaders, and there is evidence suggesting that some of these leaders questioned the place of Hebrews in the canon precisely because it was seen to teach this view.[3]

Most of us, however, will be familiar with this passage because it has become the poster child in theological battles over eternal security. On one side are those who think that truly regenerate people can lose their place among God's people by rejecting God and his grace (a view often labeled "Arminian," although many scholars who hold this view would not self-identify as Arminians). These interpreters cite this text as key evidence for their view. On the other side are those who are convinced that truly regenerate people are infallibly preserved by God in their state of salvation (the "Calvinist" view). Advocates of this theological perspective (often labeled "eternal security") are on the defensive in their interpretation of this text, for an initial reading of the passage certainly seems to support the Arminian perspective.

I mention this well-known theological debate at the outset because it will inevitably play a role in our analysis of the details of the text. Indeed, it would be foolish to deny that interpreters—including this one!—inevitably bring to the exposition of the text certain theological perspectives.[4] These need not fatally bias our exposition, but they must be frankly acknowledged, and sustained effort must be put forth to avoid being handcuffed by one's theological preferences. At the same time, we must avoid reading later theological issues and perspectives into this first-century letter. We must also remind ourselves that the author is not writing a dispassionate theological treatise but is preaching a passionate sermon designed to move his listeners to a certain course of action. However, when all the appropriate hermeneutical caveats have been

---

2. Martin Luther, "Preface to Hebrews," in Bachmann, *Luther's Works: Word and Sacrament 1*, 395.

3. Both Ambrose (*Repentance* 2.2) and Jerome (*Against Jovinian* 2.3) claim that the "rigorists" cited Hebrews in support of their views. See, e.g., Weiss, *Der Brief an die Hebräer*, 347–49, and cf. Calvin, *Hebrews*, 74. For an overview of the way Heb 6:4–6 was read in the early church, see Patrick Gray, "The Early Reception of Hebrews 6:4–6," in *Scripture and Traditions: Essays on Early Judaism and Christianity in Honor of Carl R. Holladay*, ed. Patrick Gray and Gail R. O'Day, NovTSup 129 (Leiden: Brill, 2008), 321–39.

4. While I therefore admire commentators such as Ellingworth, who insist that we use normal exegetical methods, looking only to the immediate context before looking further afield (*Hebrews*, 317), I question whether it is actually possible (or perhaps even preferable) to do so. See, on this latter point, Laansma, *Hebrews*, 143.

registered, the interpreter of Hebrews 6:4–6, who is seeking to integrate this letter with the witness of other texts in Hebrews and of other New Testament writings, has no choice but to deal with the larger theological question. The New Testament, and indeed Hebrews itself, displays a baffling interplay of apparently absolute assurances about final salvation and stern warnings about falling away. The canonically oriented interpreter simply cannot dodge this issue.

In the interests of full disclosure, then, I should lay my cards on the table: these cards, however, do not at all neatly meld together. Thus, on the one hand, I am basically convinced that what we might label the "Arminian" interpretation has most to be said for it when we limit the parameters of our study to this letter itself. However, on the other hand, I am also convinced that the New Testament, taken as a whole, supports the "Calvinist" conclusion that truly regenerate people will infallibly, by God's grace and power, be saved in the last day. These two conclusions stand in awkward relationship with one another. In the "Theology in Application" section I will attempt to alleviate this awkwardness, at least to some extent.

> I. The Exalted Son and a Rest for the People of God (1:1–4:13)
> **II. Our Great High Priest and His Ministry (4:14–10:31)**
>   A. Exhortation: Persevere through the Power of Our Exalted High Priest (4:14–16)
>   B. Exposition: High Priests and Our High Priest (5:1–10)
>   C. Exhortation: Move on to Maturity (5:11–6:20)
>   1. Avoiding Spiritual Stagnation (5:11–6:12)
>   a. Growing by Feeding on Solid Food (5:11–6:3)
>   **b. Warning and Promise (6:4–12)**
>   2. The Dependable Promises of God (6:13–20)
>   D. Exposition: A High Priest "According to the Order of Melchizedek" (7:1–28)
>   E. Exposition: The Ministry of Our High Priest (8:1–10:18)
>   F. Exhortation and Warning: Appropriating the Benefits of Our High Priest's Ministry (10:19–31)
> III. Exhortation: Follow and Serve the Pioneer of Our Faith through Endurance and Faith (10:32–13:25)

Main Idea

People who have had significant experience of God's new-realm gifts and then decisively reject God and his Son who gave those gifts cannot be restored again to their original spiritual status. Yet the author is hopeful that this warning will not apply to his readers, who have displayed in their lives the fruit of regeneration.

Translation

Hebrews 6:4–12

4a	basis (for 1–3)	For
4b	assertion	**it is impossible . . .**
4c	content	**. . . to renew again to repentance**
4d	object	those
4e	identification 1	who have once been enlightened and
4f	identification 2	who have both tasted the heavenly gift and
4g	parallel	become partakers of the Holy Spirit and
5a	identification 3	who have tasted both the good word of God and
5b	parallel	the powers of the age to come and
6a	identification 4	who then fall away,
6b	basis (for 4b–c)	crucifying the Son of God for themselves and
6c	parallel	disgracing him publicly.
7a	illustration (of 4–6)	For
7b	identification (of 7f)	**land** that drinks from the rain
7c	description	that regularly falls on it and
7d	parallel	produces vegetation useful for those
7e	identification	for whom it is cultivated—
7f	assertion	**this land receives a blessing from God.**
8a	contrast (with 7)	But
8b	condition	if it produces thorns and thistles,
8c	assertion	**it is worthless** and
8d	parallel	**near to being cursed**;
8e	sequence	its end is burning.
9a	contrast (with 4–8)	However,
9b	concession	even though we speak this way, beloved,
9c	contra-expectation	**we are convinced** of better things
9d	reference	concerning you—
9e	description	things having to do with salvation.
10a	basis (for 9c)	For
10b	assertion	**God is not unjust**
10c	result	to forget your work and
10d	parallel	the love
10e	description	you have demonstrated in his name,
10f	expansion (of 10b)	as you have served the saints, and
10g	time	continue to do so.
11a	desire	**Now we desire**
11b	content	that each one of you might show the same zeal
11c	time	up to the end

11d	result (of 11b)	so that you might have the assurance of hope
12a	purpose (of 11)	in order that you might not be sluggish, but
12b	contrast (with 12a)	be imitators of those
12c	identification	who through faith and perseverance inherit
12d	object	what has been promised.

Structure

The passage clearly falls into two main sections. The point of transition from the first to the second is marked by the direct address of the audience as "beloved" (ἀγαπητοί) in verse 9—the only place in the letter the author uses this particular address. Reinforcing this transition is a shift in the way the author is speaking. In verses 4–6, he creates a certain distance from his audience by speaking in the third person: "*those* who have been enlightened," "*they* are crucifying for themselves." Verses 7–8 add an illustration to bring home this warning. Again, the author speaks in the third person: "*land*," "*it*."[5] In verse 9, however, the author, in keeping with the vocative "beloved," shifts to the second person: "We are convinced . . . concerning *you*," "*your* work and . . . love," "each one *of you*," "that *you* might not be sluggish." The third-person forms in verses 4–8 create distance between the author and his audience. This does not mean, however, that he does not have his audience in view. One can use the third person as clear implicit reference to those one addresses. For instance, I might say to my grandchildren, "The child who picks up their toys first gets a popsicle." Nevertheless, the shift in person signals also a shift in rhetoric. In verses 4–8, the author *warns* his audience; in verses 9–12 he *assures* them. The combination of strict warning with warm assurance follows ancient rhetorical convention. An ancient rhetorical handbook recommends after "frank speech" that one should offer "palliation" so that the praise "might free the hearer from wrath and annoyance."[6]

---

5. Wallace (*Greek Grammar*, 393) draws attention to this shift in person, suggesting that it falls into a pattern of using third-person forms in what he labels the "insecure" part of the text.

6. *Rhetorica ad Herennium* 4.37.49 (this work is a first-century BC rhetorical handbook by an unknown author), quoted in Witherington, *Letters*, 219.

Exegetical Outline

→ **b. Warning and Promise (6:4–12)**
  i. Warning (vv. 4–6)
  ii. Illustration (vv. 7–8)
  iii. Reassurance (vv. 9–12)

Explanation of the Text

6:4–6 For it is impossible to renew again to repentance those who have once been enlightened and who have both tasted the heavenly gift and become partakers of the Holy Spirit 5 and who have tasted both the good word of God and the powers of the age to come 6 and who then fall away, crucifying the Son of God for themselves and disgracing him publicly (Ἀδύνατον γὰρ τοὺς ἅπαξ φωτισθέντας, γευσαμένους τε τῆς δωρεᾶς τῆς ἐπουρανίου καὶ μετόχους γενηθέντας πνεύματος ἁγίου 5 καὶ καλὸν γευσαμένους θεοῦ ῥῆμα δυνάμεις τε μέλλοντος αἰῶνος 6 καὶ παραπεσόντας, πάλιν ἀνακαινίζειν εἰς μετάνοιαν, ἀνασταυροῦντας ἑαυτοῖς τὸν υἱὸν τοῦ θεοῦ καὶ παραδειγματίζοντας). The "for" (γάρ) at the beginning of verse 4 is best viewed as connecting all of verses 4–12 with all of verses 1–3: progress toward "maturity" or "perfection" is absolutely needed because failing to progress easily morphs into outright rejection of God's grace—with disastrous consequences.[7]

A single complicated sentence in Greek spans verses 4–6. I have moved a clause from verse 6—"to renew again to repentance" (πάλιν ἀνακαινίζειν εἰς μετάνοιαν)—to the beginning of the translation in order to help the English reader navigate the basic structure of this sentence. This structure is best appreciated when it is laid out in a diagram (see following page).

I add a few notes on this overall structure. "Impossible" (ἀδύνατον) comes first in the sentence, probably for emphasis. We have to wait until verse 6 to discover what is impossible.[8] Before finishing the main verbal idea, the author uses five roughly parallel substantival participles to describe the people to whom this warning applies.[9] The sentence ends with two participles in the present tense, suggesting continuing activity. While it is debated (see below on v. 6), these two verbs probably further explain why it is impossible to restore these people to repentance.

---

7. E.g., Attridge, *Hebrews*, 167; contra, e.g., Grässer, who thinks the link is with v. 3 specifically (*An die Hebräer*, 1:346; cf. also Delitzsch, *Hebrews*, 1:280).

8. The completing word is the infinitive ἀνακαινίζειν ("renew"); it is because the infinitive is the subject of the implied verb "to be"—"to renew is impossible"—that the word ἀδύνατον is in the accusative (an infinitive, while it has no case, is treated as being in the accusative when it is modified).

9. The five participles are all aorist masculine accusative plural. The first four participles, at least, have a complexive aspect; the last, as I will observe in my comments on v. 6, functions differently. The article (τούς) that occurs before the first participle probably governs the next three (and perhaps the next four). While not, then, technically an instance of Granville Sharp's Rule, the single article serves to bind the participles together. As I display in our diagram above, we may find another manifestation of the author's literary touch in the sequence of the first four participles: φωτισθέντας—γευσαμένους—γενηθέντας—γευσαμένους.

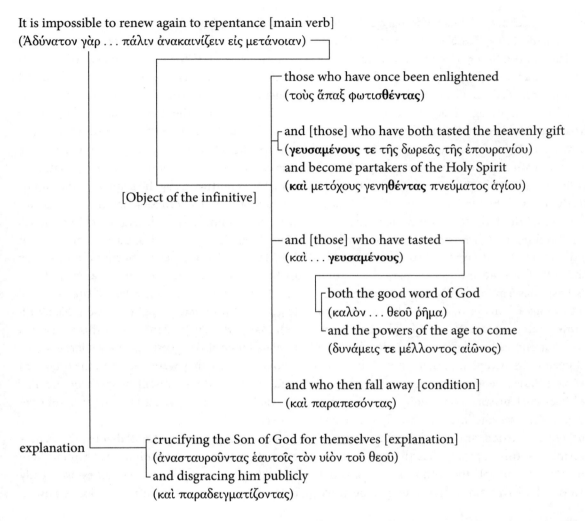

As I have noted, the author puts "impossible" at the beginning of his sentence, probably for emphasis. Uncomfortable with the severity of the fate in store for people who fall away, some interpreters suggest that the claim of "impossible" (ἀδύνατον) might be mitigated by defining the word to mean "difficult" or to restricting the "impossible" to humans' ability (in contrast to God's).[10] Neither option is likely. The word here is not qualified, and the author's other uses of the word suggest it means exactly what our English versions suggest: that restoration to repentance of those who fall away simply cannot take place (6:18; 10:4; 11:6).[11] The first description of the people about whom the

---

10. For the latter, see, e.g., Thomas Kem Oberholtzer, "The Warning Passages in Hebrews, Part 3: The Thorn-Infested Ground in Hebrews 6:4–12," *BSac* 145 (1988): 323; Randall C. Gleason, "The Old Testament Background of the Warning in Hebrews 6:4–8," *BSac* 155 (1998): 84.

11. See, e.g., Attridge, *Hebrews*, 167. A limitation of the subject for whom something might be impossible is naturally expressed with a restrictive phrase: e.g., "with man this is impossible, but not with God" (Mark 10:27).

author is speaking is "those who have once been enlightened" (τοὺς ἅπαξ φωτισθέντας). "Once" translates a word (ἅπαξ) that can have a qualitative force, in which case the completeness of the action might be intended: this word is rightly translated "once for all" in passages that refer to the finality of Christ's sacrifice later in the letter (e.g., 9:26; 10:2).[12] However, the "again" in verse 6 suggests the word is used here with a quantitative force, simply "once" (see 9:7, 27, 28; 12:26, 27). It is debated whether this adverb modifies the first participle in this series or all of them. I think the former is more likely.

I also think that "who have once been enlightened" is intended as an initial summary description, with the following participles elaborating this basic description.[13] The heated battles over the theology of this passage are fully in evidence in interpreters' exegesis of this phrase. Some think that our author describes people who have had deeply significant experiences of God's new-covenant grace, people who are participating in the life of the Christian community, but who have not quite "crossed the line" into a fully regenerate experience. Carried through the entire series of descriptions, this approach has the net result of identifying the people the author is talking about as those who have come so far in their experience of God's good gifts that, should they turn back, they can never be restored to that point of progress toward salvation.[14] To be "enlightened" (the verb is φωτίζω) then, on this view, is to have received and understood the truth of the gospel. The reference is to "illumination" rather than to conversion; see, for example, the description of the "word" in John 1:9: "the true light that gives light [φωτίζει] to everyone was coming into the world." This interpretation is sometimes buttressed by the claim that the author is alluding to the wilderness generation of Israelites who play a central role in the argument in 3:7–4:13. "Enlighten," it is suggested, alludes to the "pillar of fire" that guided the people during their journey to the promised land. See, for example, Psalm 105:39, which refers to this pillar of fire as "a fire to give light [φωτίσαι] at night" (see also Neh 9:12, 19). Many who are convinced that this allusion is intended then also suggest that the wilderness generation, because they were not yet in the promised land, typologically represent people who are also "on their way" to salvation but who have not yet "entered in."[15]

However, others who think that the wilderness generation informs our author's description here argue that the Israelites in the wilderness were truly redeemed.[16] In fact, it is difficult to know how to

---

12. See Koester, *Hebrews*, 313. With this meaning, the unrepeatable nature of Christ's sacrifice might be an important factor in explaining the unrepeatable nature of repentance (Backhaus, *Der Hebräerbrief*, 231; Grässer, *An die Hebräer*, 1:370). See also the compound word ἐφάπαξ (7:27b; 9:12; 10:10).

13. E.g., Weiss, *Der Brief an die Hebräer*, 340; Grässer, *An die Hebräer*, 1:347, 350.

14. This is by far the most popular exegetical option among those who try to reconcile this text with a "Calvinist" view of eternal security. It was given classic expression in the massive Hebrews commentary of the seventeenth-century Puritan theologian John Owen: *A Commentary on Hebrews*, Kindle edition (Banner of Truth, 1991 [1684]), 1576–1603. For particularly clear modern expositions of this viewpoint see, e.g., Philip Edgcumbe Hughes, "Hebrews 6:4–6 and the Peril of Apostasy," *WTJ* 35 (1973): 137–55; Roger Nicole, "Some Comments on Hebrews 6:4–6 and the Doctrine of the Perseverance of the Saints," in *Current Issues in Biblical and Patristic Interpretation*, ed. Gerald F. Hawthorne (Grand Rapids: Eerdmans, 1975), 355–64; Wayne Grudem, "Perseverance of the Saints: A Case Study from Hebrews 6:4–6 and Other Warning Passages in Hebrews," in *The Grace of God, the Bondage of the Will*, ed. Thomas Schreiner and Bruce A. Ware, 2 vols. (Grand Rapids: Baker, 1995), 1:133–81; Fanning, "Classical Reformed View."

15. See esp. David Mathewson, "Reading Heb 6:4–6 in Light of the Old Testament," *WTJ* 61 (1999): 215–16; G. Guthrie, "Hebrews," 962.

16. Randall C. Gleason, "A Moderate Reformed View," in Bateman, *Four Views*, 344–52.

align the movements of the Old Testament wilderness generation onto the stages of New Testament spiritual experience. However, by applying the exhortations and warnings of Psalm 95 to his readers, the author does appear to suggest that the wilderness generation was in a similar spiritual state as his readers. More to the point, however, is the question about whether our author intends to allude to the wilderness generation here. The verb "enlighten" provides only a weak argument for an allusion; the verb (φωτίζω) occurs thirty-nine times in the LXX, and it refers to the pillar of fire only three times. Those who defend an allusion respond that the argument is cumulative: there is an alignment between the series of descriptions here in Hebrews 6 and descriptions of the wilderness generation that confirms the background. However, while there are a few verbal parallels (see, e.g., "heavenly gift" below), they are not enough to confirm the allusion. If the author wanted to draw attention to the parallel, he could easily have used language that is more clearly distinctive of the wilderness generation experience in the Old Testament or that would draw our attention back to 3:7–4:13. But he does not.

We now return, then, to the significance of "who have once been enlightened." The author uses this verb only one other time: "remember those earlier days after you had been enlightened [φωτισθέντες], when you endured a great conflict of suffering" (10:32, my translation). The verb here seems clearly to refer to a genuine Christian conversion experience, and this naturally suggests that it has this meaning also in 6:4.[17] However, one other instance of the verb does not, obviously, give us much data to go by, so any definitive claim about the spiritual status of these people based on this verb alone would be inappropriate.[18]

The next two substantival participles, which are closely related in the Greek,[19] elaborate on what it means to have been "enlightened": these people have also "tasted the heavenly gift" and have "become partakers of the Holy Spirit." It is universally recognized today that the metaphor "taste" does not imply a less than complete experience (e.g., tasting without ingesting); as the parallel in 2:9 demonstrates—Jesus "tasted" death—the word connotes a full experience.[20] Identifying "the heavenly gift" is impossible. Those who think the author's descriptions in this context allude to the

---

17. See, e.g., Koester, *Hebrews*, 313–14; Cockerill, *Hebrews*, 269; Schreiner, *Hebrews*, 183. Many interpreters, sometimes without argument, take "enlightened" to refer to baptism. However, the first occurrence of this kind of language to refer to baptism comes in the second-century apologist Justin Martyr (*First Apology* 61.12; 65.1). If baptism is included, it is as part of a larger spiritual experience (Backhaus, *Der Hebräerbrief*, 229; Grässer, *An die Hebräer*, 1:348; Rissi [*Die Theologie des Hebräerbriefs*, 6] disputes a reference to baptism).

18. Other NT occurrences of φωτίζω do not shed much light on the matter (if I may speak in these terms). None of the nine other occurrences refer to conversion (Luke 11:36; John 1:9; 1 Cor 4:5; Eph 1:18; 3:9; 2 Tim 1:10; Rev 18:1; 21:23; 22:5). The word usually refers either to physical light or to intellectual/ and or spiritual cognition. The latter is the meaning of the cognate noun in both its occurrences (φωτισμός, 2 Cor 4:4, 6). The language of "give light to" as a way of referring to conversion is attested in Jewish literature of the period; see Jos. Asen. 8.10–11: "Lord God of my father Israel, the Most High, the Powerful One of Jacob, who gave life to all (things) and *called (them) from the darkness to the light*, and from the error to the truth, and from the death to the life; you, Lord, bless this virgin, and renew her by your spirit, and form her anew by your hidden hand, and make her alive again by your life, and let her eat your bread of life, and drink your cup of blessing, and number her among your people that you have chosen before all (things) came into being, and let her enter your rest which you have prepared for your chosen ones, and live in your eternal life forever (and) ever" (my emphasis).

19. The combination of particles τε . . . καί suggests the idea of "not only . . . but also" (BDAG s.v. τέ, 2.c; see, on this text, Matthew McAffee, "Covenant and the Warnings of Hebrews: The Blessing and the Curse," *JETS* 57 [2014]: 542–43). The author uses the combination τε . . . καί fourteen times to create this close connection: 2:4, 11; 4:12; 5:1, 7, 14; 6:2 [twice], 19; 8:3; 9:2, 9, 19; 10:33; 11:32.

20. NLT translates "experience." See also Matt 16:28; Mark 9:1; Luke 9:27; John 8:52; 1 Pet 2:3. See "γεύομαι," BDAG 195, §2.

wilderness generation suggest that the "heavenly gift" might connote the manna, described in the Old Testament as "bread from heaven" (Exod 16:4; Ps 78:24; 105:40).[21] Again, I am not convinced of this connection.[22] Those who discern an allusion to baptism in "enlighten" suggest that "tasting the heavenly gift" might refer to participation in the Lord's Supper.[23] However, the author's failure to mention either of the sacraments anywhere else (with the possible exception of 6:2) raises questions about this identification. Perhaps we must be content with a vague identification: the author refers to some kind of spiritual experience—one that is "heavenly" perhaps in the sense that it both comes from heaven and leads those who experience it to heaven.[24] However, considering the close relationship the author suggests between the second and third descriptions (see above), it is also possible that the "heavenly gift" is the Holy Spirit.[25]

Of the five descriptions of the spiritual status of the people the author is here warning, the third is perhaps the strongest: they are "partakers of the Holy Spirit."[26] "Partakers" translates a word (μέτοχος) that the author used in 3:14 to describe believers as "partakers in Christ." The word could in both these texts mean "companions"—with Christ/the Spirit (see the CSB on this verse; and also CEB, "partners with the Holy Spirit"). However, as I note in my comments on 3:14, "participating/sharing in" is the more likely meaning.[27] The early Christians viewed the Holy Spirit as one of the most distinctive blessings of the new covenant (e.g., John 1:17; Rom 8:5–11; Gal 3:1–5). Of course, this understanding of the epochal significance of the Spirit rests on Old Testament prophecies about the "last days" (Joel 2:28–32 [Acts 2:16–21]; Ezek 36:24–32). To claim, then, that people are "partakers of the Holy Spirit" seems to be tantamount to claiming that they are members of the new covenant.[28] To be sure, the salvation-historical significance of the Spirit is not as prominent in Hebrews as it is in Paul and other New Testament writers. The author attributes Scripture to the Spirit (3:7; see 9:8; 10:15) and claims Christ offered himself through "the eternal Spirit" (9:14). More relevant to this text is 10:29, which, in another warning passage, accuses people of insulting the Spirit of grace and, especially 2:4, which speaks of the coming of God's salvation as accompanied by "distributions of the Holy Spirit."

Two more closely related descriptions of the

---

21. E.g., Mathewson, "Reading Hebrews 6:4–6," 217; G. Guthrie, "Hebrews," 962.

22. The wording in Hebrews (τῆς δωρεᾶς τῆς ἐπουρανίου) is not that close to these OT texts (ἄρτον οὐρανοῦ). Neither of the words the author uses—δωρεά and ἐπουράνιος—is used in the LXX to refer to manna (though the verb δίδωμι, "give," is). See on the general issue Cockerill, Hebrews, 272.

23. E.g., Bruce, Hebrews, 146. This view does not necessarily assume that "taste" refers to actual eating.

24. On the gift as general, see Attridge, Hebrews, 170. For "heavenly" in this dual sense, see Grässer, An die Hebräer, 1:350. Attridge (Hebrews, 170) suggests that the use of the genitive for the object of tasting (in contrast to the accusative used after this verb in v. 5) might imply an incomplete experience. But the variation is probably simply stylistic (Ellingworth, Hebrews, 320).

25. Koester, Hebrews, 314.

26. See Rissi, Die Theologie des Hebräerbriefs, 5–6. He notes that "partakers of the Holy Spirit" is at the center of the series and is the only designation not connected (with a τε) to another.

27. It is again suggested that the author is referring to the wilderness generation. Note especially Neh 9:19b–20, where three of the blessings listed in vv. 4b–5 are alleged to have parallels: "by day the pillar of cloud did not fail to guide them on their path, nor the pillar of fire by night to shine on the way they were to take. You gave your good Spirit to instruct them. You did not withhold your manna from their mouths, and you gave them water for their thirst" (see, e.g., Mathewson, "Reading Hebrews 6:4–6," 217–18). However, the language of "partakers of the Spirit" points to a relationship that goes far beyond anything experienced by the wilderness generation. I again think the parallel is too vague to be compelling.

28. Moreover, as Schreiner rightly notes, membership in the new covenant, unlike the old, is granted only to those who have been truly regenerated (Hebrews, 480–81).

people the author is talking about come in verse 5: they have tasted both "the good word of God"[29] and "the powers of the age to come."[30] The first phrase could also be translated "[tasted] that the word of God is good,"[31] and this translation certainly puts the emphasis where we would expect it. However, the parallel clauses suggest that the usual translation makes better sense in context. The language is reminiscent of 1 Peter 2:2–3: "Like newborn babies, crave pure spiritual milk, so that by it you may grow up in your salvation, now that you have tasted that the Lord is good."[32] Perhaps we have here evidence of an early Christian way of referring to Christian experience. The reference is probably to the "word about Christ" (6:1).[33] Both unconverted and converted people can, in perhaps different ways and to different degrees, experience the goodness of God's word, so this description does not contribute much to our decision about the spiritual status of these people.

Nor does the second description in verse 5 help toward this end. "The powers [δυνάμεις] of the age to come" is a way of referring to the miracles that accompanied the inbreaking of the new age of salvation (see 2:4; and also Acts 2:22; 10:38; 19:11; 1 Cor 12:10, 28, 29; 2 Cor 12:12; Gal 3:5—all using δύναμις). Christians experienced various kinds of miracles. However, people from outside the community could also have witnessed these miracles (see, e.g., 1 Cor 14:23–25, which refers to "outsiders" entering the worship service and witnessing prophesying and speaking in tongues). Taken together, then, these five descriptions do not warrant dogmatism in either direction. Osborne overstates the matter on one side: "there is hardly anything to compare with it elsewhere in terms of a brief, creedal-like presentation of the privileges of being a Christian."[34] Grudem takes the opposite extreme: "these experiences are all preliminary to those decisive beginning stages of the Christian life."[35] In my view, however, the assertions that these people have been enlightened (in view of 10:32) and have become "partakers of the Holy Spirit" tip the scales toward the conclusion that these people are genuine Christians.

The fifth participle in this series is grammatically parallel to the first four (it is an aorist masculine plural form), and some interpreters insist that it is also semantically parallel. In addition to being "enlightened," having tasted "the heavenly gift," having become partakers in the Holy Spirit, and having tasted the "good word of God" and "the powers of the age to come," these people have also "fallen away."[36] However, most English translations signal a shift here, many of them by simply adding a "then" to this description; see, for example, ESV: "and then have fallen away" (see also NLT; NET; NRSV; NAB).[37] Some break is justified: while

---

29. "Word" translates the Gk. word ῥῆμα, which the author uses apparently interchangeably with the more common λόγος (the former occurs elsewhere in Hebrews in 1:3; 11:3; 12:19).

30. The author joins the two objects of the participle "tasted" (γευσαμένους) with a τε, again connoting close relationship.

31. On this view, the adjective καλόν is understood predicatively (Moule, *Idiom Book*, 36; D. Harris, *Hebrews*, 137). See also Lane: "the goodness of God's word" (*Hebrews* 1:133). With no articles, one cannot know for certain whether an adjective is attributive—"the good word"—or predicative—"the word is good" (see Wallace, *Greek Grammar*, 310).

32. Peter, in turn, alludes to Ps 34:8: "taste and see that the LORD is good."

33. It is possible that the "good word of God" alludes to promised covenant blessing (McAfee, "Covenant and the Warnings of Hebrews," 540–44).

34. Grant Osborne, "A Classical Arminian View," in Bateman, *Four Views*, 114.

35. Wayne Grudem, "Perseverance of the Saints," in Bateman, *Four Views*, 153.

36. See, e.g., D. L. Allen, *Hebrews*, 347–48; D. Harris, *Hebrews*, 137–38; and cf. Wallace, *Greek Grammar*, 633.

37. Weiss (*Der Brief an die Hebräer*, 345) suggests that the καί has the force of "und dennoch!"—"and yet!"

grammatically parallel to the others, the simple "and fallen away" (καὶ παραπεσόντας) comes with "dramatic abruptness,"[38] signaling a semantic shift. The NJB captures the sense very well: "and yet in spite of this have fallen away." The participle translated "fallen away" (παραπεσόντας, from παραπίπτω), which occurs only here in the New Testament, can denote a simple "sin" or "transgression" (see, e.g., Wis 6:9; 12:2). However, this "falling away" also sometimes refers to a more fundamental and serious turning away from the Lord (Ezek 14:13; 15:8; 18:24; 20:27; 22:4).[39] This kind of outright rejection of God seems to be what is intended here.[40] "This sin, then, is a sin against the light. It is a sin committed, not in ignorance, but in the face of knowledge and even experience of the truth . . . not the sin of those who are 'ignorant and wayward' (Heb 5:2) but of those who 'sin deliberately after receiving the knowledge of the truth' (10:26)."[41]

After the series of five subordinate, participial clauses, the author is finally in a position to complete the main clause he began in verse 4: "it is impossible . . . to renew again to repentance." One of the sometimes underappreciated aspects of this challenging text is the author's choice here of the word "repentance" (μετάνοιαν). We are accustomed to speak of the issue in this passage in terms of salvation (e.g., can a believer lose his or her salvation?), but the author does not use this word or even others that would be common New Testament equivalents to it. It is "repentance" that the people who fall away lose forever. The author uses this word in only two other texts: in 6:1, it heads the list of "foundational" Christian truths; in 12:17, it refers to the state that Esau could not gain because he had rejected his heritage. Neither text suggests that "repentance" would have been a standard way to describe "the state of being a Christian." Nor does the broader New Testament usage suggest such a reference. As we might expect, the word focuses on the human response that leads to spiritual benefits. See, for example, Acts 11:18, where Peter claims that "even to gentiles God has granted repentance that leads to life," and 2 Corinthians 7:10, where Paul refers to "repentance that leads to salvation."[42] The verb "renew" (ἀνακαινίζειν)[43] along with the adverb "again" (πάλιν) make clear that "repentance" is a condition those who fall away forfeit. These people have taken the first step toward forgiveness by repenting (6:1); should they now turn back from that state of repentance, they can never again return to it. It is possible that the peoples' inability to reach again the state of repentance implies that they cannot be baptized again (a divisive issue in the early church, as I noted above) and/or that they cannot be saved. However, it is worthwhile to point out that this text does not speak clearly in these terms.[44] Nevertheless, parallel warning texts do

---

38. Attridge, *Hebrews*, 171.

39. Four of these five verses combine the verb with the cognate noun, παράπτωμα: "fall away in a falling away." The noun παράπτωμα refers to sin in all nineteen of its NT occurrences. Michel notes that the Hebrew word מעל used in these Ezekiel texts is translated in the LXX by both παραπίπτω and ἀφίστημι, which is the word the author uses in 3:12 for "turning away" from God (*Der Brief an die Hebräer*, 243; see also Massonnet, *L'Épître aux Hébreux*, 156).

40. Contra, e.g., D. L. Allen, *Hebrews*, 359–63.

41. P. Hughes, "Hebrews 6:4–6," 148.

42. The word is often used in conjunction with John's ministry and baptism: Matt 3:8, 11; Mark 1:4; Luke 3:3, 8; Acts 13:24; 19:4. See also Luke 5:32; 15:7; 24:47; Acts 5:31; 13:24; 20:21; 26:20; Rom 2:4; 2 Tim 2:25; 2 Pet 3:9. The focus on human response is of course maintained in the cognate verb, μετανοέω (used thirty-four times in the NT, though never in Hebrews).

43. The verb occurs only here in the NT and only five times in the LXX (Ps 39:2; 103:5; 104:30; Lam 5:21; 1 Macc 6:9).

44. Westcott (*Hebrews*, 150) implies an important restriction on the theological significance of this text along these lines. He defines "repentance" as "a complete change of mind consequent upon the apprehension of the true moral nature of things." In this sense, he argues that there can be no second repentance; though there may be, by the gift of God, "a regaining of the lost view with the consequent restoration of the fulness of

speak more clearly in these broadly salvific terms; see especially 10:26: "if we deliberately keep on sinning after we have received the knowledge of the truth, no sacrifice for sins is left." The innate focus on human response in the word strongly suggests that renewal to repentance is "impossible" because decisive rejection of God's grace puts humans in a situation in which they themselves will not sincerely seek it again.[45]

The author finishes his sentence with two parallel adverbial participles: "crucifying the Son of God for themselves" and "disgracing him publicly."[46] In contrast to the aorist participles in verses 4b–5, these are both in the present tense, suggesting that they designate a continuing, open-ended action. The translation of the first verb is debated, the issue being the force of the prefixed preposition (ἀνά). This preposition could have the sense "again," which, it is argued, fits the context well (cf. "renew *again*") (so most English translations).[47] However, the preposition could simply reinforce the movement "upward" that is inherent in the act of crucifixion; the verb might simply mean "crucify" (RSV).[48] Perhaps the former view should be adopted; the Greek fathers, who obviously were much closer to the language of Hebrews than we are, took the verb this way. With this meaning, then, "to themselves" (the dative ἑαυτοῖς) might not mean "to their own detriment" (a dative of disadvantage)[49] but rather "for their own benefit" (a dative of advantage).[50] In other words, for those who have fallen away to seek renewal would be as if they are requiring that Christ be crucified again for their own benefit. But Christ died for sins "once for all": any repetition of his saving act is impossible. The author highlights the enormity of what is involved by referring to "the Son of God," the title the author has used in chapters 1–5 to connote the majesty and dignity of Christ. The second verb brings out the cultural "shame" that was an inherent aspect of crucifixion. This form of execution was not simply a means of killing people; it was also designed to humiliate them, to present the victim to all the world as shameful.[51]

The present tense of these participles has suggested to some interpreters that they have a primarily temporal force: "it is impossible to renew those who fall away *while/as long as* they are crucifying again the Son of God and holding him up to public shame."[52] The "impossibility" is in this way

---

life, but this is different from the freshness of the vision through which the life is first realized."

45. See, e.g., Schreiner, *Hebrews*, 180; Cockerill, *Hebrews*, 276; contra, e.g., Ellingworth, *Hebrews*, 323.

46. These participles modify the implied verbal idea in the main clause "it *is* impossible . . . to renew again to repentance." A few scholars have suggested that the participles refer to those who are trying to renew those who have fallen (Paul Proulx and Alonso Schöckel, "Heb 6,4–6: εἰς μετάνοιαν ἀνασταυροῦντας," *Bib* 56 [1975]: 193–209; Leopold Sabourin, "Crucifying Afresh for One's Repentance," *BTB* 6 [1976]: 264–71). This interpretation has more to be said for it than is usually recognized, since it provides a very natural reading of these participles. However, it faces the probably insuperable objection that these people who are doing the restoring are never actually mentioned (see Attridge, *Hebrews*, 171).

47. See "ἀνασταυρόω," BDAG 72; Lane, *Hebrews*, 1:133; Ellingworth, *Hebrews*, 324; Cockerill, *Hebrews*, 274.

48. BDAG ("ἀνασταυρόω," 72) notes that this is the consistent meaning of the verb outside the NT. The verb does not occur elsewhere in the NT or in the LXX, although it is common in Josephus. For this meaning, see, e.g., Attridge, *Hebrews*, 171; Koester, *Hebrews*, 315; Massonnet, *L'Épître aux Hébreux*, 157.

49. This is the interpretation of most scholars (e.g., Wallace, *Greek Grammar*, 144; Lane, *Hebrews*, 1:133; Backhaus, *Der Hebräerbrief*, 235). See NIV "to their loss"; ESV "to their own harm."

50. See, perhaps RSV: "they crucify the Son of God on their own account"; NET: "they are crucifying the Son of God for themselves all over again."

51. See esp. Witherington, *Letters*, 215.

52. E.g., J. K. Elliott, "Is Post-Baptismal Sin Forgivable?," *BT* 28 (1977): 330–32.

mitigated, and full restoration is possible if those who have fallen away turn back again and cease to "re-crucify" Christ and publicly shame him. Modern interpreters almost unanimously reject this interpretation of the participles, arguing that it would be quite unnecessary to claim that people cannot be restored while they are doing such things. Most therefore view the participles, probably correctly, as causal (note the "since" in ESV; NET; NRSV; NAB; NASB).[53] In effect, these participles then would elaborate just what is involved in the "falling away" in verse 6a. However, I also think that G. Guthrie has a point when he suggests that scholars have sometimes too quickly dismissed the implications of the present tense of these participles.[54] It is going too far to translate simply "as long as" and so remove the force of the warning in these verses. On the other hand, however, even if they have a causal force, the present tense of the participles "might suggest that the current state of apostasy could be abandoned in favor of true Christian repentance."[55]

6:7 For land that drinks from the rain that regularly falls on it and produces vegetation useful for those for whom it is cultivated—this land receives a blessing from God (γῆ γὰρ ἡ πιοῦσα τὸν ἐπ᾽ αὐτῆς ἐρχόμενον πολλάκις ὑετὸν καὶ τίκτουσα βοτάνην εὔθετον ἐκείνοις δι᾽ οὓς καὶ γεωργεῖται, μεταλαμβάνει εὐλογίας ἀπὸ τοῦ θεοῦ). The author urges his audience to respond positively to God's grace, illustrating the spiritual situation with land that receives rain but produces very different results. Steven Runge notes that the conjunction "for" (γάρ) tends to introduce "offline material that strengthens or supports what precedes."[56] The "for" that connects verses 7–8 to verses 4–6 functions in this manner: these new verses "strengthen" the warning in verses 4–6 by making a similar point via an illustration. This illustration takes the form of a contrast between two possible results from the rain that regularly falls on a piece of land: that land might produce useful vegetation or it might produce thorns and thistles. In the former case, God responds with blessing; in the latter case, however, with a curse.

The author's source for this imagery plays a possibly significant role in the overall interpretation of this passage. Verlyn Verbrugge, for instance, argues that the imagery is drawn from Isaiah 5:1–7, where the prophet compares the nation of Israel to a vineyard. The owner prepares and cares for this vineyard, only to find that it produces "bad grapes," "briers and thorns." God therefore threatens to turn the vineyard into a wasteland. Verbrugge then argues that the corporate focus of verses 7–8, based on its allusion to Isaiah 5, flows over also into verses 4–6. The issue in these verses is not the spiritual status of individuals but the state of the covenant community.[57]

As a general explanation of verses 4–8, this interpretation does not stand up to scrutiny. The experiences attributed to the people in verses 4–6 are not easily transferred to a community: the plural forms are clearly individual, not corporate. Moreover, other generally parallel warning texts in Hebrews are also directed to individuals (see, e.g.,

---

53. E.g., J. H. Moulton, *Prolegomena*, vol. 1 of *A Grammar of New Testament Greek*, 4 vols., J. H. Moulton, W. F. Howard, Nigel Turner, 3rd ed. (Edinburgh: T&T Clark, 1908), 230 (though he notes temporal as an option).

54. G. Guthrie, *Hebrews*, 220; see also Massonnet, *L'Épître aux Hébreux*, 157 (?). The present tense of ἀνασταυροῦντας is especially striking, since the verb itself denotes punctiliar action.

55. G. Guthrie, *Hebrews*, 220.

56. *Discourse Grammar*, 52.

57. Verlyn D. Verbrugge, "Towards a New Interpretation of Hebrews 6:4–6," *CTJ* 15 (1980): 61–73.

3:12: "see to it, brothers and sisters, that none of you has a sinful, unbelieving heart that turns away from the living God"). A more fundamental objection to Verbrugge's interpretation has to do with his appeal to Isaiah 5. It is possible that this text figures into the background imagery the author draws from. However, the imagery of land that produces either useless or useful produce is in fact quite widespread, found in various Old Testament texts,[58] Jewish literature,[59] the teaching of Jesus,[60] and the larger Greco-Roman world.[61] Our author, in other words, is using a common image that cannot be traced to any one text.[62]

"Land" (γῆ), then, refers not to *the* land of Israel but to "ground" in a general sense (see NRSV; NET; CSB; CEB). The word is then qualified in three participial clauses in verses 7–8. The first—"that drinks from the rain that regularly falls on it"[63]—makes clear that this land has what it needs to produce a good crop. This imagery illustrates the point the author made in verses 4b–5: the people he refers to have received abundant spiritual resources. God has provided all that is needed for growth toward "maturity"/"perfection" (6:1); the problem lies with people who may not take advantage of those resources. Land that receives abundant rain would be expected to "produce vegetation useful for those for whom it is cultivated."[64] Such land "receives a blessing from God."[65]

6:8 But if it produces thorns and thistles, it is worthless and near to being cursed; its end is burning (ἐκφέρουσα δὲ ἀκάνθας καὶ τριβόλους, ἀδόκιμος καὶ κατάρας ἐγγύς, ἧς τὸ τέλος εἰς καῦσιν). This verse is connected to verse 7 by means of a participle (ἐκφέρουσα) that is in the same form as the two participles in that verse. This participle, then, will also, like these other two, have some relationship to "land" (γῆ) at the beginning of verse 7. We could construe this specific relationship in two ways. First, we might assume a repetition of the noun "earth" at the beginning of verse 8, in which

---

58. Gen 3:17–18, in which God pronounces a "curse" on the ground, resulting in it producing "thorns and thistles" (ἀκάνθας καὶ τριβόλους), might be particularly important (the phrase "thorns and thistles" occurs only in Gen 3:18; Hos 10:8; and Heb 6:8 in the Scriptures). G. Guthrie suggests that Deuteronomy might be the source of much of the imagery ("Hebrews," 963–64): it often refers to land (usually in terms of the promised land) and puts before the people the fundamental choice of curse or blessing. Especially noteworthy is Deut 11:11, since it is the only OT text that uses the verb "drink" (used 272 times in the LXX) with reference to "land": "but the land [γῆ] you are crossing the Jordan to take possession of is a land of mountains and valleys that drinks rain from heaven [ἐκ τοῦ ὑετοῦ τοῦ οὐρανοῦ πίεται ὕδωρ]" (see Mathewson, "Reading Hebrews 6:4–6," 221; McAffee, "Covenant and the Warnings of Hebrews," 539). Cockerill raises legitimate questions about this general line of interpretation, though his criticism of a possible allusion to Deut 11:11 assumes an unfairly high standard for verbal allusion (*Hebrews*, 279).

59. E.g., Philo, *Heir* 204.

60. E.g., the well-known parable of the sower—or, more accurately, the parable of the soils (Mark 4:1–8); note that one type of soil produces "thorns" (v. 7, ἀκάνθας).

61. See, e.g., Quintilian, *Institutes* 5.11.24: "for instance, if you wish to argue that the mind requires cultivation, you would use a comparison drawn from the soil, which if neglected produces thorns and thickets, but if cultivated will bear fruit."

62. Attridge, *Hebrews*, 172. One could also make a case for an allusion to Deut 11:26–28 (Kibbe, *Godly Fear*, 128–29).

63. "Drink" (the verb is πίνω, used here in a present feminine singular nominative participle [in agreement with γῆ]) is elsewhere used as a metaphor for receiving rain; see again esp. Deut 11:11: "but the land [γῆ] you are crossing the Jordan to take possession of is a land of mountains and valleys that drinks [πίνω] rain from heaven."

64. The participle in this second qualifying clause is τίκτουσα, another present nominative feminine singular form that agrees with γῆ. The verb τίκτω normally means "give birth to," but it is often used with reference to land or the earth "producing" crops (e.g., Philo, *Creation* 132: "the earth which gives birth [τικτούσης] to all things").

65. The verb μεταλαμβάνει, "receives," is probably a gnomic present. "From God" translates ἀπὸ τοῦ θεοῦ. The ἀπό may signify the agent of the blessing—"blessed *by* God" (Wallace, *Greek Grammar*, 433)—but probably, as usual, signifies source: the blessing comes "from God."

case the author may be contrasting one piece of ground (v. 7) with another (v. 8). See the NIV, which suggests this reading by repeating the word "land" in a new sentence in verse 8: "but land that produces thorns and thistles. . . ." It is, however, more likely that the participle is a third modifier of "earth" in verse 7. In this case, the two verses refer to the same "land," land that enjoys abundant and regular rain, but land that then produces two different results: "suitable vegetation" on the one hand or "thorns and thistles" on the other. As Lane puts it, "The initial advantage described is the same; it is only the final result that is different."[66] The participle at the beginning of verse 8, then, probably has something of a conditional force (note the "if" in most English versions).

On this view, then, the author illustrates two possible responses to the new-covenant blessings that the people he refers to are experiencing: they can take advantage of these blessings to foster positive spiritual growth, or they can disdain or turn aside from the benefits of those blessings. Verse 8 ends with a description of what happens to the land if it produces thorns and thistles: it is "worthless" (ἀδόκιμος), "near to being cursed" (κατάρας ἐγγύς); its "end is burning" (ἧς τὸ τέλος εἰς καῦσιν). These three descriptions may depict a sequence.[67] The first description uses a Greek word that means "not having stood the test" (ἀδόκιμος). Translators typically choose a word with a similar semantic force that fits the agricultural imagery in this text ("worthless," "useless"). This may be appropriate. But it should be noted that this word is not used with reference to agriculture in the New Testament, LXX, Philo, or Josephus. It is tempting, then, to think that the word functions at the level of application rather than illustration, indicating that the people who do not produce good fruit have "failed the test" and so are in danger of judgment.[68] A "curse," on the other hand, can be pronounced on land, nations, or cities (e.g., Gen 3:17; Isa 64:10 [NETS: "curse"]; Zech 8:13) or on humans (Gal 3:10, 13; 2 Pet 2:14; see also Jas 3:10). The author's construction does not indicate possibility so much as inevitability—"the curse is definitely about to fall on you."[69] The language of "curse," because it occurs so prominently in the concluding chapters of Deuteronomy, may again evoke the history of God's people between the exodus and the entrance into the promised land.

The ultimate destiny (τέλος) of this unfruitful land is "burning" (καῦσιν). George Guthrie is right to remind us that this word applies first of all to the land, or field, which is the topic of this illustration. An immediate application of this language to the destiny of people, then, would ignore the need to "translate" the word from illustration to application.[70] Nevertheless, this reference to "burning" cannot but suggest the notion of judgment. The noun "burning" (καῦσις) does not occur elsewhere in Hebrews, but see 10:27 and 12:29. Particularly relevant to this text in Hebrews may be Deuteronomy 29:18–28:

> Make sure there is no man or woman, clan or tribe among you today whose heart turns away from

---

66. Lane, *Hebrews*, 1:143. See also Cockerill, *Hebrews*, 277.
67. Westcott, *Hebrews*, 153.
68. See the use of ἀδόκιμος in 1 Cor 9:27; 2 Cor 13:5, 6, 7; 2 Tim 3:8; Titus 1:16 (it occurs also in Rom 1:28).
69. The NLT—"the farmer will soon condemn that field"—and NRSV—"on the verge of being cursed"—are therefore better here than the NIV—"in danger of being cursed." The word ἐγγύς normally refers to "nearness" in time or space in the NT. The closest parallels to the occurrence of the word here in 6:8 imply the certain occurrence of an event. The only other occurrence of the word in Hebrews (8:13) suggests inevitability: "what is obsolete and outdated [the "first" covenant] will soon disappear [ἐγγὺς ἀφανισμοῦ]." See also Matt 24:32, 33; 26:18; Mark 13:28, 29; Luke 21:30, 31; John 6:4; Rom 13:11; Phil 4:5; Rev 1:3; 22:10. For this meaning, see, e.g., Attridge, *Hebrews*, 173.
70. G. Guthrie, *Hebrews*, 224.

the LORD our God to go and worship the gods of those nations. . . . When such a person hears the words of this oath and they invoke a blessing on themselves, thinking, "I will be safe, even though I persist in going my own way," they will bring disaster on the watered land as well as the dry. The LORD will never be willing to forgive them; his wrath and zeal will burn against them. All the curses written in this book will fall on them, and the LORD will blot out their names from under heaven. The LORD will single them out from all the tribes of Israel for disaster, according to all the curses of the covenant written in this Book of the Law. Your children who follow you in later generations and foreigners who come from distant lands will see the calamities that have fallen on the land and the diseases with which the LORD has afflicted it. The whole land will be a burning waste of salt and sulfur—nothing planted, nothing sprouting, no vegetation growing on it. It will be like the destruction of Sodom and Gomorrah, Admah and Zeboyim, which the LORD overthrew in fierce anger. All the nations will ask: "Why has the LORD done this to this land? Why this fierce, burning anger?" And the answer will be: "It is because this people abandoned the covenant of the LORD, the God of their ancestors, the covenant he made with them when he brought them out of Egypt. They went off and worshiped other gods and bowed down to them, gods they did not know, gods he had not given them. Therefore the LORD's anger burned against this land, so that he brought on it all the curses written in this book.

In furious anger and in great wrath the LORD uprooted them from their land and thrust them into another land, as it is now.[71]

These texts make clear that our author here in Hebrews is depicting the fate of those who "fall away" (v. 6) as eternal rejection from God's grace and salvation. The notion, then, that the "judgment" faced by these apostates is only disciplinary, involving perhaps "loss of reward," is not well supported in this text or elsewhere in Hebrews.[72]

6:9 However, even though we speak this way, beloved, we are convinced of better things concerning you—things having to do with salvation (Πεπείσμεθα δὲ περὶ ὑμῶν, ἀγαπητοί, τὰ κρείσσονα καὶ ἐχόμενα σωτηρίας, εἰ καὶ οὕτως λαλοῦμεν). The author moves from warning to assurance, marking the rhetorical shift with his address of his readers as "beloved" (ἀγαπητοί, used only here in Hebrews) and with a shift from third-person speech (vv. 4–8) to first ("*we* are convinced," an "authorial plural") and second ("concerning *you*"). As I noted above, this sudden turn in tone is typical of ancient rhetoric.

As is so often the case, the order of clauses in Greek cannot be followed if one is to produce a coherent English translation. In this case, then, the clause that comes last in the verse in Greek is moved to the beginning of the sentence in English: "even though we speak this way" (εἰ καὶ οὕτως λαλοῦμεν). "This way," of course, refers to the stern warning about "falling away" in verses 4–8. The author does

---

71. "Burning" and "fire" are, of course, customary figures of speech for God's judgment in the OT. The language of burning with respect to "thorns and briers" and "forests and fertile fields" refers to God's judgment on Assyria in Isa 10:15–19. See also, e.g., Isa 33:14; 66:24. God's anger is often pictured as "burning" (e.g., Josh 7:1; Isa 5:25; 13:13; 30:27; 42:25; Jer 4:4; 17:4; 21:12).

72. Contra Gleason, "Moderate Reformed View"; D. L. Allen, *Hebrews*, 344–77. These scholars are correct to argue that loss of covenant blessings is the threatened consequence. But *new*-covenant blessing is the forgiveness of sins through the sacrifice of Christ. To lose that "blessing" is to forfeit salvation itself. For the view that what is lost here is temporal rewards (perhaps in the millennium), see Oberholtzer, "Thorn-Infested Ground," 319–28.

not intend to withdraw the warning he has issued by this "mitigation" (*mitigatio*, the technical Latin term for this rhetorical device). Warning and assurance stand side by side, producing a somewhat uncomfortable logical (and *theo*logical) tension.[73] In fact, after his expression of confidence (v. 9) and reasons for it (v. 10), the author turns again to exhortation (vv. 11–12), revealing his continuing concern for the spiritual state and progress of his audience.

The author is convinced of "better things" with respect to his audience—that is, "better" than the curse and burning judgment of verse 8.[74] With this contrast in view, the "better things" might refer to the "blessing" that fruitful land enjoys (v. 7). Another option, however, is that "better things" refer forward to the evidence of the audience's positive spiritual condition (e.g., their "work" and "love," v. 10). However, perhaps the author does not intend a specific referent: these "better things" might be an undefined and vague reference to the various spiritual blessings enjoyed by the audience. Whatever the referent, these "better things" have some relationship, not clearly specified, to "salvation"; for example, "things that have to do with salvation" (NIV); "better things relating to salvation" (NET); "things that go together with salvation" (CEB).[75] The exact relationship depends on whether "salvation" (σωτηρία) refers to the present—"better things that manifest salvation"—or the future—"better things that point to salvation [on the last day]."[76]

6:10 For God is not unjust to forget your work and the love you have demonstrated in his name, as you have served the saints, and continue to do so (οὐ γὰρ ἄδικος ὁ θεὸς ἐπιλαθέσθαι τοῦ ἔργου ὑμῶν καὶ τῆς ἀγάπης ἧς ἐνεδείξασθε εἰς τὸ ὄνομα αὐτοῦ, διακονήσαντες τοῖς ἁγίοις καὶ διακονοῦντες). The author now indicates why ("for," γάρ) he has confidence in his audience. This confidence rests, first, on God's own "faithfulness," expressed here in a litotes (asserting a positive point by using the negative): God is "not unjust" (οὐ . . . ἄδικος).[77] Specifically, he is not unjust in "neglecting" or "overlooking" (cf. ESV)[78] the way the readers have demonstrated the reality of God's work in their lives—namely, through their "work" (ἔργου) and their "love" (ἀγάπης). The singular "work" gathers up in one generic description the various ways in which the readers have been, and continue to be, serving the "saints"—that is, the people of God.[79] The author refers to these practical manifestations

---

73. DeSilva, *Perseverance in Gratitude*, 245.

74. "Better things" translates τὰ κρείσσονα, a neuter plural form of κρείσσων. This word expresses one of the central theological motifs of the letter, highlighting the greatness of God's present provision for his people in comparison with what came before. However, the reference here does not seem to have this same theological connotation.

75. The Greek construction pairs "better things" (τὰ κρείσσονα) with a substantival participle, "having" (ἐχόμενα, a middle form). This participle, in turn, is followed by "salvation" (σωτηρίας, a genitive form). The combination of the verb ἔχω ("have") with a genitive does not occur elsewhere in the NT, but is found in the LXX (Ezek 1:15, 19; 10:9) and in Philo (*Agriculture* 101). The combination has the sense "pertaining to" ("ἔχω," BDAG 422, §11.a).

76. For the future aspect of salvation here, see, e.g., Osborne, "Classical Arminian View," 116. Cockerill, on the other hand, thinks both present and future salvation is intended (*Hebrews*, 281).

77. The word ἄδικος, "unjust," often refers to human sin; when it is used of God, reflecting the OT use of the δικ- root, it refers to God's not being "unfair" or "unfaithful" in his dealings with humans (see Rom 3:5); see also ἀδικία in Rom 9:14.

78. The language of "forget" (the Greek verb is ἐπιλανθάνομαι) with reference to God obviously does not indicate the kind of "senior moments" that the author of this volume is ever more frequently having. It refers to God's choosing not to bring up a particular point, his decision to overlook something, as when God chooses not to "remember" people's sins in the new-covenant economy (8:12; 10:17). See Luke 12:6; also Deut 4:31; Ps 9:12, 17; 13:1; 42:9; 74:19, 23; 77:9; Isa 49:15; Jer 14:9; Lam 5:20.

79. The participles at the end of the verse—the aorist διακονήσαντες and the present διακονοῦντες—therefore

of commitment to God and his people in another assurance text, 10:32–34:

> Remember those earlier days after you had received the light, when you endured in a great conflict full of suffering. Sometimes you were publicly exposed to insult and persecution; at other times you stood side by side with those who were so treated. You suffered along with those in prison and joyfully accepted the confiscation of your property, because you knew that you yourselves had better and lasting possessions.

The second demonstration of the reality of God's work in the lives of these people is their love. This love is tied to "his [God's] name."[80] Many English versions take this to mean that the love is directed toward God (e.g., NIV: "the love you have shown him"), and this might be right. However, the qualifying phrase "in his name" could rather refer to the ultimate goal in the love these people are showing. In this sense, the love could be love *for* other believers, motivated by and directed to God.[81] Calvin notes, rightly, that the "work" and "love" of these believers is not the *cause* of God's mindfulness; these are manifestations of an underlying spiritual relationship that is built on grace.[82]

6:11 Now we desire that each one of you might show the same zeal up to the end so that you might have the assurance of hope (ἐπιθυμοῦμεν δὲ ἕκαστον ὑμῶν τὴν αὐτὴν ἐνδείκνυσθαι σπουδὴν πρὸς τὴν πληροφορίαν τῆς ἐλπίδος ἄχρι τέλους). Having expressed his confidence in his readers, the author now turns back to exhortation. Verses 11–12 are rightly connected to what has come before (the paragraph break comes after v. 12), but the introduction of the motifs of "inheritance" and "hope" anticipate the theme of verses 13–20.[83] The author addresses "each one of you" (ἕκαστον ὑμῶν), showing again that the author's concern is the spiritual condition of individuals rather than the health of the community.[84] The author desires that each of them would show σπουδήν. The semantic range of this word can be appreciated from the spread of words the NIV uses to translate it: "haste" (e.g., "hurried"; Mark 6:25; Luke 1:39); "diligence" (Rom 12:8); "earnestness" (2 Cor 7:11; 8:7, 8); "zeal" (Rom 12:11); "devotion" (e.g., "devoted" in 2 Cor 7:12); "concern" (2 Cor 8:16); "effort" (2 Pet 1:5); "eager" (Jude 3).[85] English translations in this verse display a similar semantic range: "diligence" (NIV; CSB; NASB); "earnestness" (NRSV; ESV); "eagerness" (NET; NAB); "effort" (CEB); "enthusiasm" (NJB). Whichever translation we might choose, the basic

---

probably unpack this word "work." The shift in tense probably has a temporal focus, clearly seen in most English versions (and see BDF §339). However, if "aspect" is more to the fore, then the aorist might refer to a particular work, while the present would refer to regular, continuing forms of "work" (Lane, *Hebrews*, 1:133). The traditional translation "saints" for ἅγιοι is misleading in modern English, since the word usually refers to "super-spiritual" people (e.g., "Saint Teresa"). In the NT, however, the word refers to all God's people (see therefore NIV; NLT; CEB).

80. A relative clause—ἧς ἐνεδείξασθε εἰς τὸ ὄνομα αὐτοῦ— modifies "love" (ἀγάπης). The case of the relative pronoun should technically be accusative (it is the object of the verb), but it is common for such relative pronouns to have their case "attracted" to the case of their antecedent (e.g., Wallace, *Greek Grammar*, 339).

81. The phrase εἰς τὸ ὄνομα does not elsewhere in the NT function as the object of a verb, though its use after πιστεύω ("believe in his name") comes close (e.g., John 1:12). The phrase often functions to describe what accompanies an action (e.g., being "baptized" in name).

82. Calvin, *Hebrews*, 79.

83. Johnson, *Hebrews*, 166.

84. See, e.g., Grässer, *An die Hebräer*, 1:366. The word ἕκαστον is accusative because it functions as the subject of the infinitive ἐνδείκνυσθαι (the infinitive clause, in turn, functions as the object of ἐπιθυμοῦμεν ["we desire"]).

85. Note the use of the cognate verb in 4:11 and our notes there.

meaning of the word is clear enough: the author wants his readers to recapture the zeal for God that their "work" and "love" displayed in the past ("the same zeal"[86]).

Our understanding of the next part of the verse depends on the meaning we give to a Greek word (πληροφορίαν) that can mean either "fullness/fulfillment," or "assurance/confidence."[87] Either meaning is possible in its three other New Testament occurrences (Col 2:2; 1 Thess 1:5; Heb 10:22), and translations go both ways here ("full assurance" in NRSV; ESV; CSB; "fulfillment" in NET; NAB; NJB).[88] However, the meaning "confidence," or something like it, appears to be preferable in each of these verses. If, then, we translate "assurance," the word "hope" (τῆς ἐλπίδος) might indicate the source of that assurance—"the assurance that arises from your hope"—or the object of that conviction—"assurance of what you hope for," as in "the assurance that you will receive what you hope for" (cf. CEB; NIV).[89] I prefer the latter, in which case the NIV captures the sense well: "so that what you hope for might be fully realized."[90] This translation also makes clear the function of this prepositional phrase in the sentence: it expresses the result, or purpose, of the zeal that the readers need to recapture. The verse ends on a note that rings throughout the author's sermon: the need to maintain one's spiritual fervor right up to the time one enters the "rest," the final salvation God has in store for his people (see esp. 3:14).[91]

6:12 in order that you might not be sluggish, but be imitators of those who through faith and perseverance inherit what has been promised (ἵνα μὴ νωθροὶ γένησθε, μιμηταὶ δὲ τῶν διὰ πίστεως καὶ μακροθυμίας κληρονομούντων τὰς ἐπαγγελίας). The author finishes this section of exhortation by spelling out the ultimate goal (ἵνα, indicating purpose) of the zeal for God and the "work" and "love" he calls his people to display (vv. 10, 11). This goal is, negatively, to avoid "sluggishness" and, positively, to take their stand with all those faithful people of God who have inherited what has been promised. The author signals an end to the exhortation that began in 5:11 by using again the same word that occurred there: "sluggish" (νωθροί). In the earlier verse, he accused the readers of being "sluggish in hearing." Now he urges them to avoid becoming (or being) sluggish.[92] The tension between these two texts is easily resolved, as I argued earlier, when we recognize the rhetorical technique of hyperbole the author uses throughout 5:11–14. He exaggerates the spiritual lethargy of his readers in order to shame them into moving forward in their faith. Nor does this key word νωθροί need to be given a different meaning in these two verses.[93] The English "sluggish" gets to the basic sense of the word.

---

86. The author uses αὐτήν as an "identical adjective," marked by its attributive position.

87. For the former, see Attridge, *Hebrews*, 175; Ellingworth, *Hebrews*, 332; Johnson, *Hebrews*, 167; for the latter, Koester, *Hebrews*, 317; Grässer, *An die Hebräer*, 1:368; Grässer, *Der Glaube im Hebräerbrief*, MTS 2 (Marburg: Elwert, 1965); BDAG ("πληροφορία," 827) appears to prefer the latter also.

88. Note also the cognate verb πληροφορέω (Luke 1:1; Rom 4:21; 14:5; Col 4:12; 2 Tim 4:5, 17).

89. In the former case, the genitive would be a source or subjective genitive, and "hope" would mean the activity of hoping. In the latter, the genitive would be an objective genitive, with "hope" having the meaning "what one hopes for."

90. The preposition πρός introduces a result or purpose clause (see "πρός," BDAG 874, §3.c.α,γ, for this meaning).

91. I am taking the phrase ἄχρι τέλους with the main verb of the sentence—see NIV: "to show this same diligence to the very end"—rather than with the immediately preceding clause—"to have the full assurance of hope until the end" (ESV).

92. The author's use of the verb γίνομαι (here in the aorist subjunctive) makes it uncertain whether we should translate "become" or simply "be" (γίνομαι means both, and particularly in the non-indicative moods, often serves in place of εἰμί).

93. Contra, e.g., Ellingworth, who thinks the formal equivalence of the two is not matched by semantic equivalance (*Hebrews*, 333).

In 5:11 the author is more specific in indicating that this sluggishness pertains to their hearing. Here he refers to a sluggishness with respect to the readers' spiritual progress generally. Their zeal will prevent them from failing to move forward in their spiritual pilgrimage, and this forward movement, in turn, will keep them from the calamitous decision to "fall away."

Making positive moves in the pursuit of holiness is often the best way to avoid negative spiritual outcomes. So, here, the author urges his readers to display zeal as a means of avoiding its opposite, "sluggishness." But there will be a positive consequence to this zeal also: the readers will become "imitators of those who through faith and perseverance inherit what has been promised." The imitation motif is prominent in some Pauline letters (1 Cor 4:16; 11:1; Eph 5:1; Phil 3:17; 1 Thess 1:6; 2:14; 2 Thess 3:7, 9) and is certainly not absent from Hebrews: see, explicitly, 13:7—"consider the outcome of their [the leaders'] way of life and imitate their faith"—and, implicitly, chapter 11. The introduction of the language of "promise" (ἐπαγγελία) and "inherit" makes clear that our author is looking ahead to Abraham as a particularly clear model to imitate. The language of "promise" is associated with Abraham in the immediately following verses (the verb ἐπαγγέλομαι in 6:13, the noun in 6:15, 17), and this association continues in the rest of the letter (see 7:6; 11:9, 11, 17).[94] "Inheritance" language is also used with reference to Abraham (6:17; 11:8, 9).[95] Yet the plural form here ("those") shows that the author is referring to additional Old Testament believers, perhaps especially the other patriarchs, as well. There is a certain tension between the author's claim that these Old Testament figures "inherited what was promised" and his assertion later that the Old Testament saints did *not* receive what was promised (11:13, 39). The point apparently is that Abraham and the others received a kind of "down payment" on the fulfillment of the promises while not, before Christ's coming, being able to experience the full measure of that fulfillment.

It was through (διά) "faith and perseverance" that the Old Testament saints were enabled to inherit what had been promised. The author here anticipates a key focus in the conclusion of his sermon, where he again highlights the vital importance of faith (10:37–39; ch. 11) and perseverance, or endurance (10:36; 12:1–11). "Faith" (πίστις) is strongly oriented to the future: it is the quality people must possess if they are to enter the final rest.[96] "Perseverance" translates μακροθυμίας here, while in 10:36 and 12:1 the word behind "endurance" is ὑπομονή. The two Greek words are sometimes distinguished; the former, it is argued, often connoting the "patience" we show toward others, the latter connoting the "bearing up under" difficult circumstances. However, the two often overlap with each other. The focus on future expectation here suggests that μαρκοθυμία might combine the ideas of "patience" and "endurance." Perhaps "perseverance" is the English word that best captures

---

94. I should note that it is the concept of promise, not the word itself, that forges a connection with the Abrahamic narratives; the Greek word group ἐπαγγ- is absent from these narratives. These words are very often used in connection with Abraham elsewhere in the NT: see Acts 7:5, 17; Rom 4:13, 14, 16, 20, 21; 9:8, 9; 15:8; Gal 3:14, 16, 17, 18, 19, 21, 22, 29; 4:23, 28; Heb 7:6; 11:9, 11, 13, 17.

95. The verb κληρονομέω, "inherit," is used here (see also 1:4, 14; 12:17); the cognate noun κληρονόμος ("heir") refers to Abraham in 6:17 (see also 1:2; 11:7), another cognate noun, κληρονομία, "inheritance," is used with reference to Abraham in 11:8 (see also 9:15); and in 11:9 yet another cognate noun, συγκληρονομία, "fellow heir," refers to Abraham, Isaac, and Jacob.

96. See esp. Grässer, *Glaube*.

the idea (NET; CSB; NJB).[97] It is possible that the two nouns combine in a hendiadys: "faithful perseverance" or "persevering faith." However, while these virtues will obviously have something of an impact on one another, it is better to give each word is own full force here.[98]

Theology in Application

Perseverance

Hebrews 6:4–8 is the best-known "warning passage" in the New Testament—that is, a passage that warns people about the serious consequences of ignoring or turning away from God's grace as it has been climactically manifested in Christ. Many of these texts warn people who have not responded at all to God's gracious offer of salvation in his Son. These texts, while certainly quite sobering, do not offer a challenge to the theological coherence of the New Testament. Jesus and the writers of our New Testament books display a clear consensus about the need for humans to enter into relationship with Christ in order to escape ultimate condemnation. The texts that do create theological controversy are those that issue warnings about judgment to people who are described in language that implies that they are true believers. Hebrews, of course, is famous for these kinds of warning passages (in addition to 6:4–8, see also 2:1–4; 3:12–4:11; 10:26–31; 12:14–17, 25–29). However, it is important to recognize that warning passages of this kind are found throughout the New Testament (see esp. John 15:1–8; Rom 8:13–14; 11:17–24; 1 Cor 9:24–27; 2 Cor 13:5–6; Col 1:21–23; 2 Tim 2:12; 2 Pet 1:5–11; 2:20–22). The "problem" of warnings is not a problem limited to Hebrews.

Why, however, speak about a "problem"? Because these warning texts seem to conflict with other passages that appear to affirm that truly regenerate believers will infallibly attain final salvation. There are many of these texts, and this is not the place to list them. But I might mention by way of illustration Romans 5:9–10, where Paul asserts that those who have been justified and reconciled "will be saved"; or Romans 8:29–30, where the apostle likewise appears to claim that the group of those who have been "justified" is identical with the group of those who will be "glorified."[99] Offering a coherent explanation for these two sets of passages is incumbent on anyone who is serious about reading, applying, and teaching the New Testament as an intelligible and authoritative word from God. Brilliant and serious interpreters of the Scriptures

---

97. Attridge, *Hebrews*, 176. See esp. Jas 5:7–11.
98. I might also note that, while it is doubtful it was intended by the author, we find in vv. 10–12 the familiar trilogy of "love" (v. 10), "hope" (v. 11), and "faith" (v. 12); see Backhaus, *Der Hebräerbrief*, 241.
99. See my exposition of these passages in Moo, *Romans*, 2nd ed., NICNT (Grand Rapids: Eerdmans, 2018), 337–41, 553–58.

have wrestled with this challenge of coherence over the entire lifetime of the church. These interpreters have come, and continue to come, to different conclusions. This lack of consensus means that the "solution" to this problem is not an easy one and that the New Testament evidence does not offer clear-cut evidence for any one view. Whatever conclusion we come to on this matter is a conclusion that we must hold with humility, and we should welcome those with whom we disagree as brothers and sisters in the one body of Christ.[100]

If we formulate the issue in the usual way, then, we are asking what is the New Testament's answer to the question: Can a genuinely regenerate person turn decisively away from Christ and as a result not gain eternal life? Formulated this way, the answer to the question is binary: we must answer either yes or no (or "we can't decide"—see below). Traditionally, we label the people who respond yes to this question as "Arminians," and those who answer no as "Calvinists." Applying these labels to the issue is at least an overgeneralization (some scholars who answer this question would demur from accepting either label) and perhaps misleading. But they are probably nevertheless useful as convenient ways of identifying these views.

As I confessed at the beginning of this exposition, I generally identify as a Calvinist on this issue. To put it in popular terms, I think the New Testament overall probably teaches "eternal security." However, as I noted in the course of my exposition, I struggle to reconcile this warning text (and others both in Hebrews and elsewhere in the NT) with that theological perspective. I have alluded in the course of my exposition to the approaches Calvinists adopt in order to reconcile this text with an "eternal security" view. In approximate sequence from least likely to most likely, these are:

1. The text warns against falling under the Lord's discipline and/or losing a degree of reward in the afterlife.
2. The text warns about judgment that falls on a community; individual salvation is not at issue.
3. The "impossibility" of renewing these Christians to salvation is limited to humans; God is able to restore them.
4. The author's pastoral admonition is issued to a general audience, among whom will be some who are not truly regenerate: the warning applies to them.[101]

---

100. I spent my teaching ministry at two institutions, Trinity Evangelical Divinity School (for twenty-four years) and Wheaton College (for twenty-three years). In both institutions, I was privileged to work with colleagues who held different views than mine on this issue.

101. Many interpreters cite this issue as at least part of the explanation. See, e.g., Laansma, *Hebrews*, 145–47, and esp. Michael S. Horton, "A Classical Calvinist View," in *Four Views on Eternal Security*, ed. J. Matthew Pinson (Grand Rapids: Zondervan, 2002), 23–42. I give this view its own place in this list although, at the end of the day, it appears to be a form of the seventh view. The issue of a "mixed audience" is a relevant one and is certainly a factor in some of the NT warning passages. However, the problem here is that the author goes into considerable detail to describe those who are in danger of falling away; he is not simply referring to a general "church" audience. See, e.g., Schreiner, *Hebrews*, 182.

5. The spiritual state the Christians cannot be renewed to is the initial experience of "repentance" only; they can, however, be renewed to salvation.
6. The Christians cannot be renewed only "as long as" they continue to "crucify Christ for themselves" and "hold him up to public shame."
7. The people our author warns about eternal condemnation are ones who have had significant experiences of God's new-covenant grace but who are not yet regenerate.
8. The author uses hyperbole to warn true Christians what would happen should they "turn away": if they are, indeed, true Christians, they will ultimately not turn away.

I offer a few additional comments on these options, particularly the last two. The recognition that the author speaks mainly about "salvation" as the culmination of the Christian life suggests that it is wrong to even frame the issue in terms of "losing salvation": one cannot lose what one does not have. There is some point to this observation, but 1) the author does sometimes speak of "salvation" as an "already" state (probably 2:3); and 2) the issue we are investigating is conceptual, not linguistic. That is, whatever we call it, our author clearly has a concept of a status conferred on those who have turned to Christ, and it is whether that state can be forever lost that we are concerned about.

One of the reasons that I think one of the last two options is the most promising is because each of them would "work" in the other warning passages in the letter as well. I rate highly the view that this text is referring to people who are not yet saved (view 7) out of respect for the many fine exegetes and theologians who hold it. Regretfully, my exegesis of the text (see above) prevents me from adopting it. At the end of the day, the view I think holds most promise is that the author uses hyperbole as a rhetorical device to stir his readers into moving on to maturity. I noted how the author used hyperbole in 5:11–14 to make his point, and we might expect him to continue to do so. Exegesis of this passage (and other warning passages) has been often treated as if it were a dispassionate theological reflection rather than a passionate call to repentance. In our day, as in the time of Hebrews, pastoral passion often is expressed in exaggerated language. When my five children were small, their playroom was right next to my office. More than once, while wading through the litter of toys (and inevitably stepping in my stocking feet on at least one Lego piece), I would threaten, "If you kids don't clean up these toys, I am throwing them all away!" My children knew that I would not actually do this; but the threat nevertheless spurred them to action. So the author may be warning his audience about the danger of the road they are tempted to take by stating the consequences of that direction in exaggerated fashion.

This "least problematic" view is often labeled the "hypothetical" view, and this language is probably not inappropriate when we think on the level of logic. However, taking into account the author's rhetorical concerns shifts the focus in a healthy direction. Schreiner and Caneday, in their stimulating book on perseverance, stress this rhetorical point: the author (like other NT authors) is using warnings to imprint on the minds of his readers the terrible consequences that he outlines as a means of maintaining and encouraging these Christians in perseverance.[102] In the same vein, Laurie Norris has shown how speech act theory reinforces this approach.[103] This theory focuses not only on what words are communicating but on what authors are "doing" with their words: what their linguistic utterances are designed to accomplish. Thus, for instance, if my wife were to mention to me that "the kitchen garbage bin is full," her utterance is intended not to inform me about the state of the garbage bin but to get me to empty it. So warning passages are intended to motivate those within the community to move on in their faith so that they do not fall prey to the danger of falling away forever. I wholeheartedly endorse this emphasis. However, at the end of the day, at the level of logic and theology, it is difficult to see how this approach avoids the accusation that the warning is merely hypothetical.[104]

Where, then, does that leave us? I would go so far as to say that, were Hebrews the only book in the canon of the New Testament, I would probably adopt the Arminian perspective on this issue. However, I should add very quickly that Hebrews itself does not speak with a single voice on this issue. For alongside the warning passages, the author also issues strong assurances of eventual salvation for those who have embraced God's new-covenant work in Christ (see the "Theology in Application" section after 6:13–20). However, without in any way taking away from the strength of these assurances, they all focus on God's faithfulness in providing all that we need in order to experience final salvation; they do not assert that a person who is saved initially will certainly be saved finally. So, in my view, the strength of the warning passages slightly outweighs the assurances of these texts.

If we continue to think that there are clear texts supporting eternal security, the warning passages in Hebrews leave us (or, at least, they leave me) with two options. First, we could simply admit that we have two sets of texts that we are not able, given our present knowledge, to neatly reconcile. As many have noted, the tension between God's assurance of final salvation and warnings about humans failing to persevere to the end is one example of the pervasive biblical tension between God's sovereignty

---

102. Thomas R. Schreiner and Ardel B. Caneday, *The Race Set before Us: A Biblical Theology of Perseverance and Assurance* (Downers Grove, IL: InterVarsity Press, 2001). Following Schreiner and Caneday is Christopher Cowan, "The Warning Passages of Hebrews and the Nature of the New Covenant," in *Progressive Covenantalism: Charting a Course between Dispensational and Covenantal Theologies*, ed. Stephen J. Wellum and Brent E. Parker (Wheaton, IL: Crossway, 2016), 189–214.

103. Laurie L. Norris, "The Function of New Testament Warning Passages: A Speech Act Theory Approach" (PhD diss., Wheaton College, 2011).

104. See esp. Norris, "Function," 291–300, on the issue of the "integrity" of a speech act in terms of its rhetorical purpose.

and human responsibility. And many interpreters think that biblical fidelity requires us to embrace fully both these points without being able, finally, to explain how they are logically related.[105] Second, we could decide that the overall weight of New Testament teaching falls on the "eternal security" side and offer explanations that can reconcile other texts with this view. I incline to this option. However, I should stress that, while not bypassing the theological issue in our teaching and preaching, it is imperative to allow both sets of texts to have their full rhetorical effect. God's people need to be assured of their standing with Christ, a standing that depends not on their always wavering faith and imperfect works but on the completed work of our great high priest, the Lord Jesus Christ, who constantly intercedes for us. But God's people must also be reminded that their continuing enjoyment of Christ's work for them depends on their persevering in faith. "Comfort the afflicted" and "afflict the comfortable."

No More Repentance?

In the last couple of centuries, the question I addressed above—can genuine Christians lose their place in the kingdom of God?—has dominated the theological discussion of this passage. However, as I mentioned above, the theological issue that early Christians debated was the question of whether lapsed Christians could be restored. And it is, in fact, this issue that our text more directly speaks to. This question became especially pressing in times of persecution, when some believers who had denied their faith sought to be restored to fellowship in the Christian community. The specific locus of the debate was often baptism, to which many early interpreters thought connected the language of being "enlightened" (v. 4).

In our day also, persecution is a sadly widespread phenomenon, and many people and pastors have to deal with church members who have renounced their faith only to seek restoration to Christian fellowship again. However, it is not only persecution that gives rise to this conundrum. Many spiritually sensitive people worry that they have "fallen away" through serious sin and wonder if they are therefore barred forever from enjoying salvation. Some interpreters think the author of Hebrews goes too far here, betraying the gracious gospel of God by an undue rigorism.[106] However, our author is not the only New Testament figure to identify this kind of sin. Most interpreters, probably rightly, associate the falling away here in Hebrews 6 with the sin "against the Holy Spirit" in Mark 3:28–29 (//Matt 12:31–32) and the "sin that leads to death" in 1 John 5:16–17. In all three texts, a certain sin is singled out as putting a

---

105. See, e.g., Grässer's comments on the teaching of 5:11–6:20 as a whole (*An die Hebräer*, 1:388).

106. E.g., Attridge, *Hebrews*, 172; Peter Stuhlmacher, *Biblical Theology of the New Testament* (Grand Rapids: Eerdmans, 2018), 541.

person beyond the reach of God's grace: the person cannot be restored to repentance or be forgiven, and believers should not even pray for this sin. If, as I argue above, the author uses hyperbole for his rhetorical ends, then we perhaps should not conclude that God will never offer grace to a truly repentant sinner.[107] However, the parallel texts I have noted suggest that there is, in fact, a sin that can permanently exclude a person from the realm of God's salvation.

Once we draw this conclusion, however, two important pastoral points become urgent. First, as I have noted in my exposition, the sin of "falling away" here is not an ordinary sin—even a sin of a very serious nature, such as murder, adultery, or excessive greed. The sin the author speaks of here is the open-eyed renunciation of God's gift in Christ. The texts in the Gospels and 1 John appear likewise to be a similar kind of willful rejection of God's grace.[108] Second, the reason that a sin of this nature prevents a person from being renewed again to repentance, as I noted above, lies not in God but in the person. A decision to turn back from God's grace in Christ can be so decisive that they can never regain the spiritual interest or sensitivity that would bring them back to God again. Calvin, commenting on the blasphemy against the Holy Spirit in the Gospels, wisely notes that any person who is worried that they have committed this sin has not done so: their spiritual concern reveals that they have not become forever hardened to spiritual matters.[109]

---

107. E.g., deSilva, *Perseverance in Gratitude*, 244.

108. As R. T. France comments on Matt 12:31–32, the sin is "a complete perversion of spiritual values, revealing a decisive choice of the wrong side in the battle between good and evil, between God and Satan" (*The Gospel of Matthew*, NICNT [Grand Rapids: Eerdmans, 2007], 482). Robert W. Yarbrough understands the "sin unto death" in 1 John as an umbrella term for sinning that fundamentally denies God. Such a person "has a heart unchanged by God's love in Christ" (*1–3 John*, BECNT [Grand Rapids: Baker Academic, 2008], 311).

109. The warning about this sin is like a "wake-up call to the arrogant, not a bogey to frighten those of tender conscience" (France, *Matthew*, 483).

Hebrews 6:13–20

Literary Context

This passage is the third paragraph in the author's long hortatory detour from his exposition of Jesus as "high priest in the order of Melchizedek." The author introduced this theme in 5:10, and he closes this whole part of the letter on this same note (6:20). In this way, he signals his readiness at last to devote concentrated attention to this matter, about which he has "much to say" (cf. 5:11). In the first two paragraphs, the author is scolding (5:11–14), exhorting (6:1–3), and warning (6:4–8) his readers. In the conclusion of the second section (6:9–12), the author shifts gears, indicating his confidence in the readers' spiritual status and future. The assurance our author expresses in these verses dominates this next paragraph (6:13–20). The connection between these two units is forged by means of three "hook words" (or "hook lexemes"): "perseverance" (the noun μακροθυμία in v. 12; the verb μακροθυμέω in v. 14), "inheritance" (the verb κληρονομέω in v. 12; the noun κληρονόμος in v. 17), and "promise" (the noun ἐπαγγελία in v. 12 and vv. 15 and 17; the verb ἐπαγγέλλομαι in v. 13).[1] For the biblically literate reader, this cluster of language brings to mind especially the patriarchal narrative, with its focus on God's promise to Abraham and his descendants that they would receive a rich inheritance. And so we are not surprised at finding our author citing a key promise text from these narratives (Gen 22:16–17 in v. 14) as a basis for his reminder that the God who makes promises is faithful in keeping those promises.

---

1. The author may also focus on "oath" in this section to prepare the way for his elaboration of the oath in Ps 110:4 (see 7:20–28).

I. The Exalted Son and a Rest for the People of God (1:1–4:13)
II. **Our Great High Priest and His Ministry (4:14–10:31)**
   A. Exhortation: Persevere through the Power of Our Exalted High Priest (4:14–16)
   B. Exposition: High Priests and Our High Priest (5:1–10)
   C. Exhortation: Move on to Maturity (5:11–6:20)
      1. Avoiding Spiritual Stagnation (5:11–6:12)
   ➤ **2. The Dependable Promises of God (6:13–20)**
   D. Exposition: A High Priest "According to the Order of Melchizedek" (7:1–28)
   E. Exposition: The Ministry of Our High Priest (8:1–10:18)
   F. Exhortation and Warning: Appropriating the Benefits of Our High Priest's Ministry (10:19–31)
III. Exhortation: Follow and Serve the Pioneer of Our Faith through Endurance and Faith (10:32–13:25)

Main Idea

The hope that believers will inherit the full blessing promised by God is certain and secure because the God who made the promise confirmed it with an oath. We who belong to Christ therefore have this hope as "an anchor for the soul, certain and secure."

Translation

Hebrews 6:13–20

13a	elaboration (of 9–12)	For		
13b	subject (of 13e)	**God, ...**		
13c	circumstance		making a promise to Abraham,	
13d	cause		since he had no one greater to swear by,	
13e	assertion	**... swore by himself,**		
14a	means		saying	
14b	content		"I will surely bless	you and
14c	parallel		I will surely multiply	your descendants." (Gen 22:17)
15a	sequence	And		
15b	manner		in this way,	
15c	circumstance		after persevering,	

Continued on next page.

15d	assertion	**Abraham received**
15e	object (of 15d)	what had been promised.
16a	explanation (of 13–14)	For
16b	assertion 1	**humans swear by someone greater,** and
16c	assertion 2	**the oath**, . . .
16d	manner	beyond all possibility of dispute
16e	sphere	among them,
16f	predicate (of 16b)	. . . **brings confirmation.**
17a	cause (of 17e–f)	Because God wished to show
17b	manner	as clearly as possible
17c	recipient	to the heirs of the promise
17d	content (of 17b)	how unchangeable was his will,
17e	assertion	**he confirmed it**
17f	means	with an oath
18a	purpose (of 17e–f)	in order that, . . .
18b	means (of 18e–g)	by two unchangeable things,
18c	description	in which it is impossible for God
18d	content	to lie,
18e	assertion	. . . we who have fled for refuge might have powerful encouragement
18f	purpose	to hold fast to the hope
18g	description 1	set before us,
19a	description 2	which we have
19b	manner	as an anchor for the soul,
19c	description 3	certain and
19d	description 4	secure, and
19e	description 5	which enters
		into the inner place behind the curtain
20a	description	where our forerunner,
20b	identification	Jesus, has entered
20c	advantage	on our behalf—
20d	description	one who is a high priest
20e	time	forever
20f	identification (of 20e)	in the order of Melchizedek.

Structure

The passage is perhaps best structured in three parts.[2] The first (vv. 13–15) introduces the Old Testament incident that forms the basis for the author's encouragement. God not only made a promise to Abraham, but he confirmed that promise with an oath (citing Gen 22:16–17). And Abraham attained at least some of what God had promised. However, echoing a key focus from the preceding verses (esp. v. 12), the author asserts that Abraham received what had been promised only after he had patiently endured (v. 15). The divine promise motivates and requires human response. The second part of the text (vv. 16–17) picks up the idea of the oath introduced in verse 13. Using language familiar from the legal world of that day, the author asserts that the oath guarantees the fulfillment of his promise. Following a pattern we see so often in Hebrews, the Old Testament text holds significance for the author's new-covenant readers. God's oath-secured promise to Abraham is typologically representative of his promise to Christians. So it is the case that the purpose (ἵνα) of the Old Testament text is to give "us" hope (vv. 18–20: the shift to the first-person plural in these verses signifies that this purpose is where the text has been heading all along). These verses offer to us one of the most beautiful expressions of Christian assurance anywhere in the Bible: we have a hope that is "an anchor for the soul, certain and secure." The author reinforces this assurance with another metaphor, drawn from the world of the Old Testament cult that will be central to the theological argument of 8:1–10:18: we who hope are given entrance "behind the curtain" into the inner sanctum, the holy of holies, where God himself dwells (8:1–10:18). And the one who makes possible this entrance is none other than Jesus, our high priest according to the order of Melchizedek (see ch. 7; 5:10).

Exegetical Outline

- **2. The Dependable Promises of God (6:13–20)**
    - a. God's Oath-Secured Promise to Abraham (vv. 13–15)
    - b. The Confirmatory Power of the Oath (vv. 16–17)
    - c. The Encouragement of God's Promise and Oath (vv. 18–20)

---

2. The paragraph unfolds without obvious breaks, so it is natural that interpreters differ over how to divide it. For the division I suggest, see Bruce, *Hebrews*, 152–54. Others also divide it into three parts, putting the breaks between vv. 15 and 16 and 18 and 19 (Backhaus, *Der Hebräerbrief*, 246) or between vv. 15 and 16 and 16 and 17 (Grässer, *An die Hebräer*, 1:373). Others suggest two sections (vv. 13–15, 16–20; Koester, *Hebrews*, 232).

Explanation of the Text

6:13–14 For God, making a promise to Abraham, since he had no one greater to swear by, swore by himself, 14 saying "I will surely bless you and I will surely multiply your descendants" (Τῷ γὰρ Ἀβραὰμ ἐπαγγειλάμενος ὁ θεός, ἐπεὶ κατ᾽ οὐδενὸς εἶχεν μείζονος ὀμόσαι, ὤμοσεν καθ᾽ ἑαυτοῦ 14 λέγων, Εἰ μὴν εὐλογῶν εὐλογήσω σε καὶ πληθύνων πληθυνῶ σε). The author's stern warning against "falling away" in verses 4–8 gave way in verses 9–12 to reassurance. While the author presents the spiritual catastrophe he outlined in these earlier verses as a genuine danger, the evidence of God's work in his readers is grounds for thinking that they are truly God's people and, by maintaining their zeal to the end, will have that status confirmed in final salvation; they will "inherit what has been promised" (v. 12). The new paragraph elaborates on this language and concept ("for," γάρ) by citing the example of God's oath-bound promise to Abraham.

The specific incident the author mentions comes after Abraham "passed the test" by his willingness to offer his son Isaac. The Lord responds (Gen 22:16–18): "I swear by myself, declares the LORD, that because you have done this and have not withheld your son, your only son, I will surely bless you and make your descendants as numerous as the stars in the sky and as the sand on the seashore. Your descendants will take possession of the cities of their enemies, and through your offspring all nations on earth will be blessed, because you have obeyed me." The author quotes verse 17a in verse 14, following the LXX closely but not exactly.[3] Reiterating the earlier promise texts in Genesis (12:1–3; 15:4–20; 17:1–8), God promises Abraham numerous descendants and that those descendants would possess the "cities of their enemies." The latter note, echoing the promise of land that is a standard element in God's promise to the patriarchs, is naturally omitted by our author, who has no interest in a continuing territorial promise for the people of God. He also abbreviates the promise of descendants by replacing that language with the simple pronoun ("I will multiply *you* [σε]"). As English translations recognize, the language of "multiplying you" implies descendants. However, it is not the content of the promise that interests the author; rather it is the security that God offers for the fulfillment of that promise: the oath.

When God made this promise to Abraham,[4] he "swore by himself."[5] Pledging one's commitment to

---

3. In place of the introductory particle ἦ, which always occurs in combination with μήν in the LXX (meaning "surely"; see LEH), Hebrews uses εἰ, a form of the word current in the first century (G. Guthrie, "Hebrews," 965). The similarity in sound made it easy to confuse the one for the other (the LXX MS A has εἰ; some MSS in Hebrews have ἦ). The author keeps the participle + indicative verb construction of the LXX (εὐλογῶν εὐλογήσω, πληθύνων πληθυνῶ), which imitates the Hebrew infinitive absolute + indicative this text uses to indicate emphasis. See, e.g., Muraoka, *Syntax*, 383–85.

4. The participle ἐπαγγειλάμενος is probably temporal (Turner, *Syntax*, 80). Despite being in the aorist tense, it does not indicate antecedent action—"after promising, he swore"—but contemporaneous action ("when" in almost all the English versions); see, e.g., Turner, *Syntax*, 80. It is possible, though not likely, that we should reverse the semantic force of participle and indicative verb (this does happen occasionally in Greek): "swearing by himself . . . he made a promise" (see Zerwick, *Biblical Greek*, §263; Lane, *Hebrews*, 1:148).

5. The Greek is ὤμοσεν καθ᾽ ἑαυτοῦ. The verb ὀμνύω, "swear," does not mean "use an impolite epithet" but "take a vow." In the NT, taking an oath "by" someone or something (i.e., validating the oath with reference to someone or something) is usually expressed with the preposition ἐν + the dative (e.g., "swearing by the altar" [ὀμόσῃ ἐν τῷ θυσιαστηρίῳ] in Matt 23:18). The author's use of the preposition κατά + genitive to connote this idea follows his LXX source (see Gen 22:16).

fulfill an oath by calling on someone or something else as a "witness" was widespread in the ancient world—including the Jewish world (see esp. Matt 5:33–37; 23:16–22; Jas 5:12). The author points out that God's swearing "by himself" in the Genesis text was the only way God could guarantee his utter commitment to the promise: he has no one "greater" to swear by than himself (see also Exod 32:13; Isa 45:23; Jer 22:5).[6] A rabbinic text says: "Lord of all the world, if you had sworn to them by heaven and earth, I would say that even as heaven and earth pass away, so shall your oath pass away. But now you have sworn to them by your great name, and just as your great name endures forever and ever, so shall your oath endure forever and ever."[7] Of course, there were natural questions raised about why the utterly perfect and truthful God would need to take an oath. The standard answer appears to have been that God's taking of an oath has the purpose of giving humans strong assurance of God's intention to accomplish what he promises.[8]

6:15 And in this way, after persevering, Abraham received what had been promised (καὶ οὕτως μακροθυμήσας ἐπέτυχεν τῆς ἐπαγγελίας). It was, then, "in this way" (οὕτως)[9] that Abraham received "what had been promised." God not only made Abraham a promise of what he would do in and for him, he confirmed the promise with an oath—and this is the reason Abraham "received what had been promised."[10] The claim appears to stand in tension with the author's later assertion that Abraham and the other patriarchs "did not receive the things promised" (11:13; see 11:39). This tension could be resolved if the author is here saying only that Abraham was given a reiteration of the promise.[11] However, this view does not do justice to the strength of "received" (ἐπέτυχεν).[12] Probably, then, the typical biblical "already-not yet" framework better explains the difference. While living in the land as a "stranger," Abraham did live in the land of promise and was given a son, Isaac, as the first stage in the numerous descendants he had been promised (see Heb 11:8–12). Like other Old Testament saints, he did, indeed, receive some elements of what God had promised (see 11:33). However, he did not find a permanent home in this new land, nor did he see the ultimate object of the promise, that single descendant who would bring all the promises to their fruition.

As many interpreters emphasize, the spotlight in this passage is on the God who promises: it is his trustworthiness that gives us hope. This emphasis stands in some contrast to the typical Jewish portrayal of Abraham, which pays great attention to

---

6. The Greek is a bit opaque. The key is to recognize that the verb ἔχω + infinitive means "be able" ("ἔχω," BDAG 421, §5). Therefore here εἶχεν . . . ὀμόσαι means "he is able to swear." The infinitive is completed with the prepositional phrase κατ' οὐδενός, which in turn is modified by μείζονος; hence: "he is able to swear by no one [or conceivably "nothing"—the word could be masculine or neuter] greater."

7. b. Ber. 32a; cf. Koester, *Hebrews*, 325.

8. See esp. Philo, *Sacrifices* 91–94; see also *Alleg. Interp.* 3.203–8.

9. Most translations render οὕτως as "so," an English word that (like οὕτως) can mean either "in conclusion" or "in this way." The latter meaning is probably intended here, since οὕτως, which can mean, "thus," always has this meaning elsewhere in Hebrews: 4:4; 5:3, 5; 6:9; 9:6, 28; 10:33; 12:21. With this meaning, οὕτως could refer forward to μακροθυμήσας: "it was in this way, namely, by persevering, that Abraham gained what was promised." But it more likely refers backward, perhaps especially to the oath in v. 13.

10. The noun ἐπαγγελία can refer in Hebrews to the act of promising (7:6; 8:6; 11:17) but more often refers to "what" had been promised (4:1; 9:15; 10:36; 11:9, 13, 17, 33, 39); it has this meaning in this context (6:12, 15, 17).

11. Lane, *Hebrews*, 1:151.

12. See 11:33, where the author uses this same verb to claim that OT saints "gained [ἐπέτυχον] what was promised" (the verb occurs elsewhere in the NT in Rom 11:7 [twice]; Jas 4:2).

his faithful obedience.¹³ However, this verse reveals that the author's stress on divine faithfulness has not entirely pushed out a concern for human response.¹⁴ The realization of the promise came in the context of Abraham's "persevering." This persevering should probably not be viewed as the *reason* he attained what was promised, for this would unduly minimize God's role in fulfilling the promise. On the other hand, his persevering is not merely incidental to his receiving the promise. We could say, perhaps, that it was the condition necessary for the promise to come to its realization. It is typical of the author's concern that he highlights Abraham's "persevering" rather than his faith (contrast Rom 4; Gal 3:6–9). This concern stands out especially when we note that the language of "persevering" is not used in the Old Testament Abraham narratives.¹⁵ The author is deeply concerned that his readers maintain their spiritual fervor right to the end (3:14; 6:11).

6:16 For humans swear by someone greater, and the oath, beyond all possibility of dispute among them, brings confirmation (ἄνθρωποι γὰρ κατὰ τοῦ μείζονος ὀμνύουσιν, καὶ πάσης αὐτοῖς ἀντιλογίας πέρας εἰς βεβαίωσιν ὁ ὅρκος). This verse is transitional, explaining the significance of God's oath in verses 13–14 (hence the "for," γάρ) and preparing the way for its application to the readers in verses 17–20. The author reminds his readers how oaths "work." When people take an oath, they swear "by someone greater." In the Old Testament, the most binding oath was therefore one that was taken in God's name; see, for example, Boaz's pledge to Ruth: "Stay here for the night, and in the morning if he wants to do his duty as your guardian-redeemer, good; let him redeem you. But if he is not willing, as surely as the LORD lives I will do it" (Ruth 3:13). God had no one greater than himself to swear by, and this is why he solemnizes his promise to Abraham by swearing by himself. But the more important point our author wants to make is the way oaths are intended to guarantee the content of the oath. In this verse, as well as in verses 17–19, the author deploys several words and phrases common in the legal world of his day to make this point.¹⁶ First, the oath puts any matter at issue among humans (αὐτοῖς) beyond dispute.¹⁷ The legal connotation of "dispute" (ἀντιλογία) can be recognized from its use in 2 Samuel 15:4: "Absalom would add, 'If only I were appointed judge in the land! Then everyone who has a complaint [ἀντιλογία] or case could come to me and I would see that they receive justice.'"¹⁸ Second, the oath brings "confirmation" (εἰς βεβαίωσιν, "[the oath] results in confirmation"). As BDAG ("βεβαίωσις," 173) remarks on this verse, the word used here (βεβαίωσις) is "a legal technical term for *guaranteeing, furnishing security*." The word group is one that is natural for our author to use, given his deep concern that his readers finalize and confirm their spiritual standing (see also the use of the adjective

---

13. See, e.g., Jdt 8:25–26; 1 Macc 2:52; Sir 44:19–21; Jub. 17.17–18; Philo, *Abraham* 167–99.

14. As Cockerill rightly notes (*Hebrews*, 286).

15. These narratives do not use μακροθυμία or its cognates or ὑπομονή ("endurance") or its cognates.

16. Lane remarks on "a remarkable concentration of forensic language" (*Hebrews*, 1:149; see also Grässer, *An die Hebräer*, 1:380; Backhaus, *Der Hebräerbrief*, 248).

17. The Greek is πάσης αὐτοῖς ἀντιλογίας πέρας. The word πέρας often has a spatial sense, and it occurs often in the stereotyped phrase "the ends of the earth" (τὰ πέρατα τῆς γῆς, e.g., Pss 2:8; 22:27; Dan 4:22; Matt 12:42; Luke 11:31; cf. Rom 10:18 [= Ps 19:4]). But it also can denote "the end point of a process" (the category of definition for this word in "πέρας," BDAG 797, §2).

18. It should be noted, however, that this word can also refer to a "contradiction" (Heb 7:7) or opposition in general (Heb 12:3; cf. also Jude 11).

βέβαιος, "firm," "secure," in 2:2; 3:14; 6:19; 9:17 and the verb βεβαιόω, "confirm," in 13:9; cf. 2:3).[19]

6:17 Because God wished to show as clearly as possible to the heirs of the promise how unchangeable was his will, he confirmed it with an oath (ἐν ᾧ περισσότερον βουλόμενος ὁ θεὸς ἐπιδεῖξαι τοῖς κληρονόμοις τῆς ἐπαγγελίας τὸ ἀμετάθετον τῆς βουλῆς αὐτοῦ ἐμεσίτευσεν ὅρκῳ). God takes an oath to reassure us that he remains true to his promises. Differences in the way English versions translate the opening of this verse point to a Greek construction that can be interpreted in different ways (the combination is the preposition ἐν + a relative pronoun, ᾧ). Thus, English versions translate variously as "in which case," "in this way" (see NET; NRSV),[20] "and so" (RSV; ESV; NAB),[21] or "because" (NIV; CSB).[22] I think this last option is best.[23] Granted this reading, verse 17 is then an example of asyndeton—that is, it has no explicit word connecting it to what comes before. Asyndeton often marks a mild break in the flow of a discourse,[24] and I think this is the case here. After the author's analysis of the significance of the oath in Genesis 22:17 (vv. 13–16), he now pauses to draw a conclusion about God's purpose in taking an oath.

This purpose is implied by the verb the author uses to connote the "taking" of the oath, μεσιτεύω. This verb often means "mediate" (it is cognate to the word μεσίτης that our author uses in 8:6; 9:15; 12:24),[25] but the author uses it here in a Hellenistic legal sense to mean "guarantee."[26] The point is drilled home with the author's claim that the oath shows "as clearly as possible"[27] to the heirs of the promise "how unchangeable was his will." "Heirs of the promise" could, considering verses 13–15, refer to Abraham and his descendants. However, as with the similar phrase in verse 12, it more likely embraces all Abraham's heirs, including especially the audience of Hebrews, people who "follow in the footsteps of the faith that our father Abraham had" (Rom 4:12).[28] "Unchangeable" (ἀμετάθετον) is a rare word, occurring only here and in verse 18 in the Greek Bible.[29] But the concept of God's dependable will is a rich biblical theme. See, for example, Numbers 23:18–20: "Arise, Balak, and listen; hear me, son of Zippor. God is not human, that he should

---

19. Outside of Hebrews, the noun βεβαίωσις occurs in Phil 1:7; the adjective βέβαιος in Rom 4:16; 2 Cor 1:7; 2 Pet 1:10, 19; and the verb βεβαιόω in Rom 15:8; 1 Cor 1:6, 8; 2 Cor 1:21; Col 2:7.
20. Delitzsch, *Hebrews*, 1:313.
21. BDF §219.2; Turner, *Syntax*, 253.
22. Moule, *Idiom Book*, 131–32; Lane, *Hebrews*, 1:148; D. Harris, *Hebrews*, 150. The "because" in some translations might also reflect a causal interpretation of the participle βουλόμενος ("wishing").
23. The author uses this combination only two other times: in one text it is causal (2:18); in the other it means "in which" or "through which" (10:29). The reason I prefer the causal reading here is because, unlike 10:29, there is no immediately obvious antecedent for the relative pronoun (the best candidate for an antecedent is ὅρκος at the end of v. 16, but the repetition of this word, as the subject of the sentence, at the end of verse 17, makes this connection unlikely [Ellingworth, *Hebrews*, 340–41]).
24. See, e.g., Runge, *Discourse Grammar*, 20–23.
25. The verb occurs in Philo and Josephus with the meaning "mediate." E.g., in *Spec. Laws* 4.31, Philo uses this verb to refer to the unseen God as "intermediary."
26. "μεσίτης," BDAG 634; see Weiss, *Der Brief an die Hebräer*, 362.
27. "As clearly as possible" translates περισσότερον, an accusative neuter singular form of περισσότερος, a comparative adjective that means "greater, more, even more." The neuter singular form functions as an adverb and probably here is equivalent to the superlative, in an "elative" sense (see Lane, *Hebrews*, 1:148; Koester, *Hebrews*, 327). This adverb might modify βουλόμενος (see NASB, "desiring even more"; Weiss, *Der Brief an die Hebräer*, 362), but more likely modifies ἐπιδεῖξαι (see NRSV, "to show even more clearly"; D. Harris, *Hebrews*, 150).
28. Attridge, *Hebrews*, 181; Ellingworth, *Hebrews*, 341.
29. It occurs twice in 3 Maccabees with reference to a king's plan (5:1, 12).

lie, not a human being, that he should change his mind. Does he speak and then not act? Does he promise and not fulfill? I have received a command to bless; he has blessed, and I cannot change it" (see also Pss 89:35; 145:13; Isa 40:8; 45:23).[30]

6:18 in order that, by two unchangeable things, in which it is impossible for God to lie, we who have fled for refuge might have powerful encouragement to hold fast to the hope set before us (ἵνα διὰ δύο πραγμάτων ἀμεταθέτων, ἐν οἷς ἀδύνατον ψεύσασθαι θεόν,[31] ἰσχυρὰν παράκλησιν ἔχωμεν οἱ καταφυγόντες κρατῆσαι τῆς προκειμένης ἐλπίδος). This verse consists of a purpose clause (ἵνα, "in order that") that depends on the main verb in verse 17: "he confirmed it with an oath" (ἐμεσίτευσεν ὅρκῳ). This being the case, it would be natural to see this verse as primarily tied to the verses before it. However, verse 18 also marks a shift from a reminder of past events to direct exhortation of the readers. This shift is marked by the move from third-person verbs—"[God] swore," "Abraham received," "God wished"—to first-person verbs—"we might have," "we have." The author is at his rhetorical best, using vivid imagery as he tries to bring home to his readers the firm ground on which they now stand and the assurance they have for the future.

The "two unchangeable things"[32] through which we find great encouragement are probably God's promise (v. 13) and his oath (v. 17).[33] God's appointment of the Son as a priest in the order of Melchizedek (Ps 110:4; see Heb 5:6, 10) may be in view, in light of verse 20 and the way this text prepares the way for chapter 7.[34] With respect to these matters (ἐν οἷς) it is impossible for God to lie. Of course, God by nature cannot lie; his promise and oath do not change the inherent truthfulness of all that he says. However, as I noted above, in keeping with other Jewish authors in his day, the author sees God's solemn promise and his oath as helping the people he addresses to be all the more certain that what God promises will indeed come to pass. The author uses a surprising image to describe himself and his fellow believers: "we who have fled." The idea of fleeing *from* might be present; for example, believers have fled from the great danger of eschatological judgment.[35] But the focus is probably on fleeing *to*, an idea explicitly added in most translations: "we who have fled for refuge" (RSV; ESV; see also NLT; NET; CSB; CEB).[36] It is possible that the author alludes to those who fled to the "cities of refuge" in Old Testament Israel (e.g., Num 35:25, 26; Deut 4:42; 19:5; Josh 20:9).[37] The form of word the author uses (an aorist tense participle, καταφυγόντες) does not indicate *when* this fleeing for refuge occurred. He may refer to the

---

30. The faithfulness of God to his word was an important theme in Second Temple Judaism also, as Philo's tractate entitled "The Unchangeableness [ἄτρεπτον] of God," suggests.

31. UBS⁵/NA²⁸ read ψεύσασθαι [τὸν] θεόν.

32. The phrase is δύο πραγμάτων ἀμεταθέτων. This last word, "unchangeable," picks up the use of this same word in v. 17. The noun πρᾶγμα often has a very general meaning, "deed, thing, event, occurrence, matter" (BDAG, 858–59, §1; see, e.g., Acts 5:4; 2 Cor 7:11).

33. E.g., Attridge, *Hebrews*, 181; Koester, *Hebrews*, 328; Cockerill, *Hebrews*, 288.

34. However, as Attridge points out, the appointment of the priest in the order of Melchizedek is accompanied by an oath (Ps 110:4a)—a point the author draws attention to in 7:21 (*Hebrews*,

181–82). Suggesting a reference to Ps 110:4 are, e.g., Backhaus, *Der Hebräerbrief*, 249–50; Loader, *Sohn und Hoherpriester*, 143–45. G. Guthrie suggests the reference is to the two parts of Ps 110:4: high priest *forever* and high priest *in the order of Melchizedek* ("Hebrews," 966–67).

35. DeSilva, *Perseverance in Gratitude*, 252.

36. E.g., Delitzsch, *Hebrews*, 1:317: "those who have sought and found a refuge."

37. Philo also uses the language of "fleeing" to describe those who find refuge in God (*Flight* 63; *Dreams* 2.273). See also Ps 143:9 ESV: "I have fled to you for refuge" (κατέφυγον); and also Zech 2:15. The "fleeing for refuge" also reminds us of the "rest" God has promised his faithful people (3:7–4:11; see Ellingworth, *Hebrews*, 344).

whole Christian life, as a time when believers find refuge in God, or it could have a timeless, gnomic force.[38] But the past-time focus found in most translations—e.g., NIV "we who have fled"—is probably justified.

The English versions reveal another key issue in the syntax of this verse. Compare NIV, "we who have fled to take hold of the hope set before us may be greatly encouraged" with ESV, "we who have fled for refuge might have strong encouragement to hold fast to the hope set before us." The issue is how to integrate the infinitive "to take hold of" (κρατῆσαι) into the sentence: Does it indicate the purpose of "we who have fled" (καταφυγόντες) or "we might have powerful encouragement" (ἰσχυρὰν παράκλησιν ἔχωμεν)? An interesting conflict between translations and commentaries is found here: most of the translations take the second option, while most of the commentators argue for the first.[39] Commentators can cite the fact that "flee," used absolutely, is rare: we expect it to be completed with a phrase or verb.[40] Translators, on the other hand, argue that "taking hold of hope," since it expresses the key point of these verses, should be attached to the main verb, "that we might have" (ἔχωμεν). I am very slightly inclined to favor the translations. On this reading, the infinitive κρατῆσαι ("take hold of") expresses the purpose, or result, of the verbal idea expressed by ἔχωμεν παράκλησιν: "in order that we might have powerful encouragement to take hold of the hope set before us." The word παράκλησις has a range of meaning in the New Testament, but here "encouragement" (or even "incentive," "inducement") works well.

In the phrase "hope set before us" (τῆς προκειμένης ἐλπίδος), "hope" might refer to the act of hoping, but more likely refers to "what one hopes for," the content of the hope. This hope "lies ahead of us."[41] Our author has been laser focused on the need for his readers to grasp tightly the spiritual benefits they already enjoy as new-covenant believers so that they can receive the benefits still to come. So here "hope" draws our attention to the future; but that future we hope for even now is "set before us." The necessary response, then, is to keep a tight grip on the promise of that hope.[42]

6:19 which we have as an anchor for the soul, certain and secure, and which enters into the inner place behind the curtain (ἣν ὡς ἄγκυραν ἔχομεν τῆς ψυχῆς ἀσφαλῆ τε καὶ βεβαίαν καὶ εἰσερχομένην εἰς τὸ ἐσώτερον τοῦ καταπετάσματος). In verses 19–20, the author deploys language from three different spheres of life to illustrate the utter reliability of Christian hope. A metaphor describes one thing in terms appropriate to another; for example, "he threw a Hail Mary pass" (speaking of a football play in terms of prayer). So here, our hope is an "anchor" (a nautical metaphor); it penetrates into the very presence of God (a cultic metaphor);

---

38. Ellingworth, *Hebrews*, 344.

39. Translations that take "to take hold of" with "encouragement" are RSV; NRSV; ESV; NLT; NET; CSB; CEB; NAB; NJB; NASB; contrast NIV. A few of the commentators who take the phrase with "flee" are Westcott, *Hebrews*, 162; Attridge, *Hebrews*, 183; Cockerill, *Hebrews*, 288; Massonnet, *L'Épître aux Hébreux*, 168.

40. A probably statistically insignificant observation is that καταφεύγω, "flee," is followed by an infinitive once in the Greek Bible (Isa 10:3); the noun παράκλησις, "encouragement," never is.

41. The participle προκειμένης (functioning as an adjective) comes from the verb πρόκειμαι. This verb can refer to what is "present" (e.g., 2 Cor 8:12) but, arguably at least, always refers to something not yet attained in Hebrews (see also 12:1, 2).

42. The verb κρατῆσαι, from κρατέω, can mean "keep a grip on [what one already has]" (see 4:14) or "seize [what one does not yet have]" (see BDAG 564, §3). Cockerill (*Hebrews*, 288) sees elements of both here; see also Weiss, *Der Brief an die Hebräer*, 365.

it is secured by the one who leads the way (a military/athletic metaphor). The rapid shift from one metaphor to the next creates some unusual word combinations, but the main point is quite clear: Jesus's entrance as our high priest into the presence of God on our behalf gives us unbounded confidence that we will, in fact, enter the final "rest" for which we long.

The relative pronoun at the beginning of verse 19 (ἥν) picks up the reference to "hope" (ἐλπίδος) at the end of verse 18 (both are feminine singular). In verse 18, "hope" refers mainly to what we hope for, but in verse 19 the focus gradually "glides" toward the more subjective *act* of hoping.[43] For hope to be "an anchor for the soul," more than our act of hoping must be intended; our hope is sure and stable only to the degree that "what we hope for" is certain. "Anchor" appears elsewhere in the Bible only with reference to a physical anchor in the narrative of Paul's "shipwreck voyage" (Acts 27:29, 30, 40). However, the anchor is a fairly popular metaphor for stability in secular Greek. The late first-century orator Dio Chrysostom, for instance, says: "Havens free from billows can be found, trusting which men may safely ride at anchor, however high the gale may rise. But with human beings, the most temperate are like our summer anchorages, which afford shelter for the moment only."[44] It is, the author of Hebrews says, our "soul" (ψυχή) that "rides at anchor," indicating that his focus here is on the way hope grounds our eternal, spiritual lives.[45] The imagery of the anchor holding a vessel in place as winds and waves buffet it is powerfully evocative, and interpreters both ancient and modern develop the imagery.[46] Perhaps no modern author has done this more effectively than Koester:

> Travelers lower an anchor when a ship nears land . . . , and Hebrews's imagery suggests that the listeners' hope has already been secured at their port of destination. To be sure, they have not disembarked at God's place of rest (Heb 4:1–11) in the heavenly Jerusalem (12:22–24), but the anchor has been planted, and they are no longer at the mercy of the winds on the open sea. The trouble is that they seem to be in danger of drifting away from their Christian moorings (2:1b) and must therefore hold fast (2:1a).[47]

The author draws out the significance of hope as our anchor with three modifiers: "certain" (ἀσφαλῆ), "secure" (βεβαίαν), and "which enters into" (εἰσερχομένην, an adjectival participle). The first two modifiers are adjectives that are closely joined together (they are linked with the double conjunction τε καί) and are used together elsewhere to convey the idea of certainty or security.[48] The participle, "which enters into," clearly modifies "hope" (via the relative pronoun ἥν): it would stretch the author's figurative language to the breaking point for him to refer to an anchor as entering in.[49] It is harder to know whether the paired adjectives "certain and secure" also modify "hope" or whether they modify "anchor."[50] The issue is

---

43. The word "glide" is Ellingworth's (*Hebrews*, 345). See on this issue esp. Johnson, *Hebrews*, 172.

44. *Orations* 74.24; see deSilva, *Perseverance in Gratitude*, 251.

45. The word "soul" (ψυχή) often refers simply to the "person" in Scripture; but in Hebrews the word focuses on the inner, spiritual dimension of human life (see 4:12; 10:39; 12:3; 13:17; and see also 10:38). See Grässer, *An die Hebräer*, 1:383; contra Lane, *Hebrews*, 1:148.

46. See, e.g., Calvin, *Hebrews*, 86.

47. *Hebrews*, 334.

48. See, e.g., Wis 7:23, where the author characterizes wisdom as being "steadfast" (βέβαιον) and "sure" (ἀσφαλές). Philo uses the adverb βεβαίως in a context where he compares virtue to an anchor (*Sacrifices* 90).

49. Although, see Attridge, *Hebrews*, 184.

50. For the former, see Westcott, *Hebrews*, 163; Montefiore, *Hebrews*, 116; Ellingworth, *Hebrews*, 345 (and see NIV; NET;

somewhat academic: since "anchor" stands in for "hope" in the metaphor, the adjectives end up effectively modifying hope in either case.⁵¹

With a sudden shift of metaphors, the author now claims that our hope is entering "into the inner place behind the curtain." We must make allowance for the author's figure of speech: "hope entering" is a compact and picturesque way of saying "we who hope enter in." The author uses a phrase drawn from LXX Greek to depict what we enter into: the "inner place behind the curtain"—that is, the holy of holies, the inner sanctuary within the temple.⁵² Granted this almost technical use of the phrase in the LXX, translators are entirely justified to render it as, for example, "through the curtain into God's inner sanctuary" (NLT); "the inner shrine behind the curtain" (NRSV); "inner sanctuary behind the curtain" (CSB). The "curtain" (καταπέτασμα) here, then, is "the second curtain" (9:3), the curtain, or veil, that separates the outer part of the sanctuary from the inner part (see also 10:20).⁵³ The entrance of our high priest Jesus into the holy of holies, offering the sacrifice of his own person before the Father's own throne, is the author's chosen means to communicate the significance and finality of Christ's atoning work for his people. The author introduces this imagery here as a kind of foretaste of what is to come.

6:20 where our forerunner, Jesus, has entered on our behalf—one who is a high priest forever in the order of Melchizedek (ὅπου πρόδρομος ὑπὲρ ἡμῶν εἰσῆλθεν Ἰησοῦς, κατὰ τὴν τάξιν Μελχισέδεκ ἀρχιερεὺς γενόμενος εἰς τὸν αἰῶνα). The purpose clause the author began in verse 18 continues: God confirmed his promise with an oath (v. 17b) in order that we might be encouraged to hold fast to our hope (v. 18), which hope is safe and secure and enables us to enter the presence of God (v. 19) where (ὅπου) Jesus, our high priest, has entered on our behalf before us (v. 20).⁵⁴ Characterizing Jesus as our "forerunner" evokes the third metaphor the author employs in these verses. We are not sure which world the author is drawing from, since the word is used in a bewildering number of contexts: "forerunner" (πρόδρομος) refers, among other things, to military scouts, who go ahead and prepare the way for the main army (Wis 12:8; cf. Josephus, *Ant.* 12.372), to advanced ships in a flotilla, to athletes who race ahead of others, and to the "first" of the crops (Num 13:20; Isa 28:4).⁵⁵ It is impossible to know which background the author has in view here, although the use of running imagery for the Christian life, with Jesus as our "pioneer and perfecter of faith" in 12:1–2, might favor the athletic background. What is clear is that the language of "forerunner" here parallels the term

---

CSB; NAB; NASB); for the latter, Cockerill, *Hebrews*, 290; D. Harris, *Hebrews*, 153 (and see RSV; NRSV; ESV; CEB; NLT).

51. Cockerill, *Hebrews*, 290.

52. The phrase is τὸ ἐσώτερον τοῦ καταπετάσματος, which occurs several times in the LXX to describe the holy of holies (e.g., Exod 26:33; Lev 16:2, 12). Elsewhere the word ἐσώτερος is regularly associated with the tabernacle or temple in a variety of expressions (Ezek 8:3, 16; 10:3; 40:17, 23, 27, 28, 34, 44 [twice]; 41:3, 17; 42:3; 43:5; 44:17 [twice], 21, 27; 45:19; 46:1; 1 Macc 9:54). See Roy Gane, "Re-Opening *Katapetasma* ("Veil") in Hebrews 6:19," *AUSS* 38 (2000): 5–8. Contra George Rice, who thinks the reference is to the entire sanctuary ("Hebrews 6:19: Analysis of Some Assumptions Concerning *Katapetasma*," *AUSS* 38 [1987]: 65–71).

53. The word καταπέτασμα also occurs in the Synoptic descriptions of the "rending of the veil" at Christ's death (Matt 27:51; Mark 15:38; Luke 23:45). The technical nature of the phrase makes it difficult to identify the function of the genitive in the phrase; it generally relates the "inner place" to the "curtain," but the exact relationship depends on the imagery it evokes. Translations usually render "within" or "behind."

54. Though impossible to duplicate in English, "Jesus" comes last in the opening clause, reflecting again the author's highlighting of this name.

55. See H. Baurenfeind, "πρόδρομος," *TDNT* 8:235.

"pioneer" (ἀρχηγός) that is applied to Jesus in 2:10 and 12:2. The idea is somewhat similar to Jesus's claim that he is "going . . . to prepare a place for you [his disciples]" (John 14:2)[56] and, perhaps also, to Jesus as the "firstborn of the dead" (1 Cor 15:20, 23; Col 1:18; cf. Heb 1:6). However, it is important to note that the author does not simply present Jesus as one who leads the way; his use of the phrase "on our behalf" (ὑπὲρ ἡμῶν) shows that Jesus prepares the way by acting as our high priest on our behalf.[57]

However, returning to where he left off in his exposition (5:10; cf. 5:6), Jesus is not just any high priest: he is a high priest "in the order of Melchizedek." As, therefore, our entrance, following Jesus, into the holy of holies anticipates 8:1–10:18, so this allusion to Psalm 110:4 prepares the way for chapter 7. A key emphasis in that exposition is Jesus's eternality. It is fitting, then, that the author finishes this section on that note: "forever" (εἰς τὸν αἰῶνα) comes last in this sentence.

Theology in Application

The letter to the Hebrews is famous for its severe warnings about the consequences of failing to persevere in faith. I have explored the significance and implications of these warnings in the "Theology in Application" section after 6:4–12. I also briefly mentioned there another side of the letter: its strong assurances of God's favor and continuing provision for all our spiritual needs. Hebrews 6:13–20 is perhaps the clearest example of those assurances. As was true for Abraham, so for us: God adds to his promise (as if this were not enough!) his oath, manifesting the unchanging nature of his purpose (v. 17). The author goes on to say:

> God did this so that, by two unchangeable things in which it is impossible for God to lie, we who have fled to take hold of the hope set before us may be greatly encouraged. We have this hope as an anchor for the soul, firm and secure. It enters the inner sanctuary behind the curtain, where our forerunner, Jesus, has entered on our behalf. He has become a high priest forever, in the order of Melchizedek. (6:18–20)

This same note of divine provision for all our spiritual needs is sounded elsewhere in the letter:

> Therefore he is able to save completely those who come to God through him, because he always lives to intercede for them. (7:25)

> He did not enter by means of the blood of goats and calves; but he entered the Most Holy Place once for all by his own blood, thus obtaining eternal redemption. (9:12)

---

56. E.g., Weiss, *Der Brief an die Hebräer*, 368.
57. The prepositional phrase could modify either "forerunner" (πρόδρομος, RSV; NRSV; ESV) or "enter" (εἰσῆλθεν, e.g., NIV, NET; CSB; CEB). The difference in meaning is slight.

> For this reason Christ is the mediator of a new covenant, that those who are called may receive the promised eternal inheritance—now that he has died as a ransom to set them free from the sins committed under the first covenant. (9:15)
>
> And by that will, we have been made holy through the sacrifice of the body of Jesus Christ once for all. (10:10)
>
> For by one sacrifice he has made perfect forever those who are being made holy. (10:14)
>
> The Holy Spirit also testifies to us about this. First he says: "This is the covenant I will make with them after that time, says the Lord. I will put my laws in their hearts, and I will write them on their minds." Then he adds: "Their sins and lawless acts I will remember no more." (10:15–17)[58]

As I noted earlier (see again "Theology in Application" after 6:4–12), the author never says God *will* save on the last day everyone who is genuinely regenerate. But he comes close. Christ secures for us "an eternal redemption" (9:12); we have been "made holy . . . once for all" (10:10); through Christ's sacrifice, we are "made perfect forever" (10:14). In these texts the author appears to suggest that the once-for-all acceptance of Christ's once-for-all redemptive work introduces us into a new state that will never change.

At the least, these texts provide great encouragement to us as we move through the difficulties and temptations of this life. God is for us! In his Son, the perfect high priest and perfect sacrifice, he has provided for all that we will ever need to get through these difficulties and inherit the final salvation God has destined us for. True, we need to respond with faith and endurance throughout this pilgrimage (6:12). But our faith is directed to one who has promised on oath to provide for our every need, and we endure knowing that blessing at the end has already been secured for us.

---

58. To be added to this list, from a different angle, would be 3:6 and 14, if these texts mean, as some think they do, that a Christian is defined and known by perseverance: e.g., only those who persevere are truly believers; those who do not persevere reveal the fact that they are not, in fact, regenerate (see our notes on those verses). And see 1 John 2:19: "They [the apostates] went out from us, but they did not really belong to us. For if they had belonged to us, they would have remained with us; but their going showed that none of them belonged to us."

CHAPTER 16

Hebrews 7:1–10

Literary Context

The author begins this chapter with a clear "pick up" of the name Melchizedek from the end of chapter 6. "This Melchizedek" (v. 1) refers back to the reference to Jesus as a "high priest forever in the order of Melchizedek" in 6:20. Of course, this verse in turn picks up the similar reference in 5:10. In that context, the author made clear that he had "much to say" on the topic but that the readers were not in the right frame of mind to understand or appreciate the message (5:11). So our author takes a detour from his exposition to rebuke, warn, and encourage his audience (5:11–6:20). Having done so and, he implicitly suggests, having adequately prepared his readers to listen attentively, he is now ready at last to develop the analogy between Melchizedek and Christ.

Chapter 7 therefore occupies an important place in the author's development of his central theological notion, the high priestly work of Christ.[1] After brief mentions of the idea earlier (2:17; 4:14), he begins developing this point in 5:1–10. In 8:1–10:18, the author argues for the superiority of Christ's priestly work by comparing the nature of that work with that of the Old Testament priests: Christ ministers in a "better" sanctuary, he offers a "better" sacrifice, and his work is validated in the context of a "better" covenant. The author continues in those chapters to refer specifically to the nature of Jesus's high priesthood. But the focus also shifts. In 8:1–10:18, the author also focuses on *what* Jesus our high priest does, *where* he does it, and *how* he does it. Chapter 7, on the other hand, focuses on *who* he is. Christ's eternal and sinless nature qualifies him to be a high priest that secures an eternal salvation.

The argument of chapter 7 follows a clear general trajectory, as the author moves the spotlight from Melchizedek himself (vv. 1–3) to the contrast between Melchizedek and Levitical priests (via Abraham; vv. 4–10) and finally to the contrast between Christ and the Levitical priests (vv. 11–25).[2] This last point is where, rhetorically, the chapter is going, as the author begins developing his case for the superiority of the

---

1. Michel (*Der Brief an die Hebräer*, 255) argues that it is the heart of the letter.

2. Westcott, *Hebrews*, 170.

new order of priestly ministry inaugurated in Jesus. The chapter falls into two basic parts, verses 1–10 and verses 11–25.[3] In the first paragraph, the author uses the story in Genesis 14:18–20 to show that Melchizedek is greater than Abraham and that, accordingly, the priest in his "order" is greater than the priests who descend, via Levi, from Abraham. In verses 11–25, the author then turns to the second Old Testament text that mentions Melchizedek, Psalm 110:4.[4] He quotes this passage twice (vv. 17 and 21b) and alludes to it throughout (vv. 11, 15, 20–21a). Two details in the text are especially important, setting up two key contrasts. First, the "priest in the order of Melchizedek" is appointed with Yahweh's oath, which the author contrasts with the "weak and useless" commandment in the law about the Levitical priests. Second, "the priest in the order of Melchizedek" is appointed "forever," in contrast to the Levitical priests who, being merely human, die. The author roots this latter point in the very person of Christ, whose priestly ministry is eternal precisely because of "the power of an indestructible life" (v. 16; see v. 24).

The last three verses of the chapter (vv. 26–28) both summarize key points from the argument of chapter 7 and anticipate the argument about to begin in chapter 8.

I. The Exalted Son and a Rest for the People of God (1:1–4:13)
II. **Our Great High Priest and His Ministry (4:14–10:31)**
   A. Exhortation: Persevere through the Power of Our Exalted High Priest (4:14–16)
   B. Exposition: High Priests and Our High Priest (5:1–10)
   C. Exhortation: Move on to Maturity (5:11–6:20)
   D. Exposition: A High Priest "According to the Order of Melchizedek" (7:1–28)
➤   **1. Melchizedek's Supremacy over Abraham (Gen 14:17–20) (7:1–10)**
      2. The Supremacy and Sufficiency of Our High Priest (Psalm 110:4) (7:11–25)
      3. The High Priest Who Is Also the Son (7:26–28)
   E. Exposition: The Ministry of Our High Priest (8:1–10:18)
   F. Exhortation and Warning: Appropriating the Benefits of Our High Priest's Ministry (10:19–31)
III. Exhortation: Follow and Serve the Pioneer of Our Faith through Endurance and Faith (10:32–13:25)

Main Idea

Alerted to the idea of Jesus as "high priest in the order of Melchizedek" from Psalm 110:4, the author now turns to the only other Old Testament passage that

---

3. Favoring this division are, e.g., Weiss, *Der Brief an die Hebräer*, 373; Cockerill, *Hebrews*, 294.

4. It is less likely that all of ch. 7 is a "midrash" on Ps 110:4 (as Kurianal thinks [*Jesus Our High Priest*, 85]).

mentions Melchizedek, Genesis 14:18–20. The story about the encounter between Melchizedek and Abraham in this text contains clues to the nature of Jesus's distinctive priesthood. Even as the supriority of Melchizedek to Abraham is indicated in this story, so Christ's priesthood is superior to that of the Levitical priests who are descended, via Levi, from Abraham.

Translation

Hebrews 7:1–10

1a	explanation (of 6:20f)	Now
1b	assertion	**this Melchizedek**,
1c	description 1	king of Salem,
1d	description 2	priest of God Most High,
1e	predicate (of 1b)	met Abraham
1f	time	when he was returning from the slaughter of the kings and
1g	sequence	blessed him,
2a	parallel (to 1e)	and Abraham distributed to him
2b	object (of 2a)	a tenth of everything.
2c	assertion	The name Melchizedek means,
2d	definition 1	first of all, "king of righteousness" and then also
2e	definition 2	"king of Salem," that is,
2f	restatement	"king of peace."
3a	description 1	Without father,
3b	description 2	without mother,
3c	description 3	without genealogy,
3d	description 4	having neither beginning of days
3e	parallel	nor end of life,
3f	description 5	being made like the Son of God,
3g	assertion	**he remains a priest**
3h	time	forever.
4a	inference (from 1–3)	**You see**
4b	content	how great this man was,
4c	description	to whom Abraham the patriarch gave a tenth of the spoils.
5a	background (to 4)	Now,
5b	contrast (with 6)	on the one hand,
5c	assertion	**the sons of Levi . . .**
5d	identification	who received their priesthood
5e	predicate (of 5c)	**. . . had a commandment**
5f	standard	according to the law
5g	content	to receive a tithe
5h	source	from their brothers and sisters—
5i	contra-expectation	even though they came

5j	source	from the loins of Abraham.
6a	contrast (with 5)	However, on the other hand,
6b	assertion	**the one ...**
6c	identification	who does not trace his descent
6d	source	from them
6e	predicate (of 6b)	**... receives a tithe**
6f	source	from Abraham,
6g	sequence	and **he blessed the man**
6h	identification	who was given the promises.
7a	clarification (of 6g–h)	Now
7b	assertion	it is beyond dispute that
7c	content	**the inferior is blessed**
7d	agent	by the superior.
8a	contrast (with 8d)	On the one hand, then,
8b	assertion	**men who die receive tithes**
8c	contrast	but,
8d	contrast (with 8a)	on the other hand,
8e	assertion	**there is testimony**
8f	content	to the effect that he lives.
9a	conclusion (to 1–8)	**It could even be said**
9b	content	that Levi,
9c	description	who receives the tithe,
9d	predicate (of 9b)	paid that tithe
9e	agent	through Abraham,
10a	basis (for 9a–e)	because he was in the loins of his ancestor
10b	time	when Melchizedek met Abraham.

Structure

The passage is in two parts. The first, verses 1–3, provides a brief outline of the story about Melchizedek and Abraham from Genesis 14:18–20. The second, verses 4–10, elaborates on the significance of this story for Christ's priesthood.

As is widely recognized, the passage exhibits a chiastic structure:[5]

---

5. See, e.g., Vanhoye, *Structure and Message*, 125–27; Lane, *Hebrews*, 1:160; Ellingworth, *Hebrews*, 350.

Melchizedek "met" (συναντήσας) Abraham (v. 1a)
　Melchizedek "blessed" (εὐλογήσας) Abraham (v. 1b)
　　Abraham gave a tithe (δεκάτην) to Melchizedek (v. 2)
　　Abraham gave Melchizedek a "tenth" (δεκάτην) of the plunder (v. 4b)
　Melchizedek blessed (εὐλόγηκεν) the one who had the promises (v. 6b)
Melchizedek "met" (συνήντησεν) Abraham (v. 10)

Exegetical Outline

→ **1. Melchizedek's Supremacy over Abraham (Gen 14:17–20) (7:1–10)**
　　a. Commentary on Genesis 14:17–20 (vv. 1–3)
　　b. Application of Genesis 14:17–20 (vv. 4–10)

IN DEPTH: Mysterious Melchizedek

Melchizedek appears in only two Old Testament passages:

> The LORD has sworn and will not change his mind: "You are a priest forever, in the order of Melchizedek." (Ps 110:4)

> After Abram returned from defeating Kedorlaomer and the kings allied with him, the king of Sodom came out to meet him in the Valley of Shaveh (that is, the King's Valley). [18]Then Melchizedek king of Salem brought out bread and wine. He was priest of God Most High, [19]and he blessed Abram, saying, "Blessed be Abram by God Most High, Creator of heaven and earth. [20]And praise be to God Most High, who delivered your enemies into your hand." Then Abram gave him a tenth of everything. [21]The king of Sodom said to Abram, "Give me the people and keep the goods for yourself." [22]But Abram said to the king of Sodom, "With raised hand I have sworn an oath to the LORD, God Most High, Creator of heaven and earth, [23]that I will accept nothing belonging to you, not even a thread or the strap of a sandal, so that you will never be able to say, 'I made Abram rich.' [24]I will accept nothing but what my men have eaten and the share that belongs to the men who went with me—to Aner, Eshkol and Mamre. Let them have their share." (Gen 14:17–24)

Psalm 110:4 appears to be the jumping-off point for our author's comparison of our high priest Jesus to Melchizedek, since the comparison is first introduced via a quotation of that verse (5:6). As I noted in my comments on that text, Psalm 110:4 probably captures the author's attention because it comes only three verses after a text, Psalm 110:1, that is applied to Jesus throughout the New Testament—and not least in Hebrews. Moreover, both these verses appear to address the same person: the "Lord," who is invited to sit at God's right hand, who will subdue enemies, is the one appointed by Yahweh to the role of "priest forever, in the order of Melchizedek."[6] "In the order of" translates a phrase (*al-dibrāti*) that might mean "because of" but probably means "according to the case of," "on the model of."[7] The person addressed in these verses, then, combines the roles of king/messiah and priest—an unusual combination of roles in the Old Testament.[8] Priests had to be from the tribe of Levi, while kings came from the line of Judah. It would, then, have been impossible for a single person to hold both offices, although kings occasionally carried out priest-like duties.[9] Several aspects of Psalm 110 offer considerable interpretive challenges.[10] However, these problems have little or no impact on our author's use of the psalm, so I will not pursue them here.

The situation with respect to Genesis 14:17–24 is quite different. The brief cameo appearance of Melchizedek in these verses is intriguing. As Sarna notes, Melchizedek "suddenly emerges from the shadows and as suddenly retreats into oblivion."[11] Indeed, chapter 14 in general seems at first sight to sit rather awkwardly in the narrative flow of Genesis.[12] In chapters 12 and 13, we find Abram, in obedience to the Lord's call, settling in a new land, along with his nephew Lot. Abram prospers (despite his questionable behavior in Egypt), divides the land with Lot, receives a renewed promise from the Lord, and begins to worship God in this new land. The concern with Lot provides continuity from these chapters into chapter 14, but in other ways the whole "feel" of the narrative shifts. The wider political world, with its territories and rulers, provides the backdrop for Abram's military expedition to rescue captive Lot. Abram and his men win the victory and, as they are returning to their homes, they encounter the king of Sodom in the "Valley of Shaveh" (which possibly is

---

6. The Hebrew behind "my lord" is אֲדֹנִי, which means "my lord," "my master" (in contrast to יהוה, which is the divine name—"the Lord"). Both are rendered in Greek with κύριος.

7. Leslie C. Allen, *Psalms 101–150*, WBC 21 (Waco, TX: Word, 1983), 81. Contra Nancy L. deClaissé-Walford, Rolf A. Jacobson, and Beth LaNeel Tanner, *The Book of Psalms*, NICOT (Grand Rapids: Eerdmans, 2014), 826.

8. See, e.g., Carl E. Armerding, "Were David's Sons Really Priests?," in Hawthorne, *Current Issues in Biblical and Patristic Interpretation*, 75–86.

9. See, e.g., Daniel Estes, *Psalms 73–150*, NAC 13 (Nashville: Broadman & Holman, 2019), 341–42.

10. E.g., Kraus: "no other psalm has in research evoked so many hypotheses and discussions as Psalm 110" (*Psalms 60–150*, CC [Minneapolis: Fortress, 1993], 345).

11. Nahum M. Sarna, *Genesis*, JPS Torah Commentary (Philadelphia: Jewish Publication Society, 1989), 109.

12. Gordon Wenham, *Genesis 1–15*, WBC 1 (Waco, TX: Word, 1987), 305.

to be identified with a location near Jerusalem). Abram's encounter with this king frames the following narrative (vv. 17, 21–24), with his encounter with Melchizedek sandwiched in between.

The sudden shifts in the text have led a number of scholars to propose that the Melchizedek narrative was a late insertion into the text.[13] In fact, however, the contrasting responses of Abram to the king of Sodom on the one hand and to Melchizedek on the other fit well into the narrative flow of the larger passage.[14] Abram refuses to accept gifts and thus become dependent on the king of Sodom, whose very name suggests his ungodly disposition. In contrast, Abram is quite willing to accept food and drink from Melchizedek. Abram signifies his regard for this priest by receiving his blessing and offering him a tithe of the spoils from his military campaign.

Jewish interpreters from the Second Temple period did not display a lot of interest in Melchizedek.[15] The book of Jubilees, a rewriting of Genesis and the early chapters of Exodus, has a lacuna where the Melchizedek story would have appeared (see 13.24–25); speculation about what might have been there is quite useless. Josephus mentions Melchizedek, calling him "righteous king" (based on the etymology of his name) and linking him to Jerusalem (*J.W.* 6.438; *Ant.* 1.181). The Genesis Apocryphon (1QapGen) sticks close to the Old Testament narrative.[16] Philo refers to Melchizedek in three places. In *Preliminary Studies* 99, he claims that Melchizedek had learned the tradition concerning priesthood "from none other but himself" (αὐτοδίδακτον), a reflection on the lack of any mention of Melchizedek before this. In *Allegorical Interpretation*, Philo, following his typical hermeneutical method, allegorizes Melchizedek, associating him with "right reason" and the *logos* (*Alleg. Interp.* 3.79–82; see also *Abraham* 235). Some interpreters think that Hebrews's depiction of Melchizedek has its closest parallel in Philo[17]—but the parallels are not very

---

13. E.g., Fred L. Horton, *The Melchizedek Tradition: A Critical Examination of the Sources to the Fifth Century A.D. and in the Epistle to the Hebrews*, SNTSMS 30 (Cambridge: Cambridge University Press, 1976), 14; Claus Westermann, *Genesis 12–36*, CC (Minneapolis: Augsburg, 1985), 203.

14. See, e.g., Gareth Lee Cockerill, "Melchizedek without Speculation: Hebrews 7:1–25 and Genesis 14:17–24," in Bauckham et al., *Cloud of Witnesses*, 142–43. Tremper Longman notes that the narratives of ch. 14 illustrate the two-sided promise given to Abraham: those who bless him are blessed, while those who curse him are cursed (Gen 12:3) (*Genesis*, Story of God Bible Commentary [Grand Rapids: Zondervan Academic, 2016], 184).

15. For a survey of Jewish interpretations, see Kurianal, *Jesus Our High Priest*, 162–85. Second Enoch contains an elaborate legend about a miraculously born Melchizedek who is taken to heaven and who is the template for the Melchizedek that Abram meets (71.29–72.11). But the probably post-NT date of the book and clear evidence of Christian interpolations mean it cannot be used to fill out the background of Hebrews. See discussion of F. I. Andersen in Charlesworth, *OTP* 1:92–100.

16. See 22.14–17 (*DSSR* 3:32–33).

17. Gerd Theissen, *Untersuchungen zum Hebräerbrief*, SNT 2 (Gütersloh: Mohn, 1969), 26–27, 130–52. Thompson does not focus on the literary parallels but thinks the basic world of thought of Heb 7 is close to that of Philo (*Beginnings of Christian Philosophy*, 116–27).

close. The most intriguing reference to Melchizedek comes in the Qumran document 11QMelchizedek.[18] As the title suggests, this document focuses on Melchizedek. However, its fragmentary nature makes any attempt to determine just what is being said about him very difficult. Most scholars think the document presents Melchizedek as an angelic figure who provides eschatological atonement for "the sons of light" and opposes Belial.[19] Others, however, think that the text does not even refer to the biblical figure of Melchizedek, simply using the language of "righteous ruler" (*malchi tsedek*) to refer to the archangel Michael.[20]

No Second Temple Jewish text cites Psalm 110:4 with reference to Melchizedek. The texts that use Genesis 14 include some points also found in Hebrews—but these common elements have to do with the very basics of the story: the significance of Melchizedek's name, his blessing of Abram, and his receiving of a tithe from Abram. In other words, the elements that are distinctive in these Jewish texts do not show up in Hebrews.[21] The relationship between Hebrews and these texts appears to be indirect, all of them independently drawing out various points of significance from the enigmatic Genesis 14 narrative.[22]

Post-Christian Jewish interpreters did not view Melchizedek as an eschatological figure; they often identified him with Shem (this identification is found in the targums and in, e.g., Pirqe Rabbi Eliezer 8 and 27.3). Indeed, some interpreters think the rabbis may have downplayed Melchizedek's significance in response to the Christian appropriation of him in Hebrews 7. One rabbinic text interprets the Genesis text as suggesting that Melchizedek passed the

---

18. Text and translation can be found in the *DSSR* 2:24–27. Melchizedek is mentioned briefly, but without elaboration, in 4Q401 (4QShirShabb[b] 11.1–3).

19. See esp. A. S. van der Woude, "Melchisedek als himmlische Erlösergestalt in den neugefundenen eschatologischen Midraschim aus Qumran Höhle XI," *OtSt* 14 (1965): 354–73; Yadin, "Dead Sea Scrolls," 36–55; M. Delcor, "Melchizedek from Genesis to the Qumran Texts and the Epistle to the Hebrews," *JSJ* 2 (1971): 115–35; Longenecker, "Melchizedek Argument in Hebrews," 67–69; Eric F. Mason, *"You Are a Priest Forever": Second Temple Jewish Messianism and the Priestly Christology of the Epistle to the Hebrews*, STDJ 74 (Leiden: Brill, 2008), 164–90; Mason, "Cosmology, Messianism, and Melchizedek: Apocalyptic Jewish Traditions and Hebrews," in Mason and McCruden, *Reading the Epistle to the Hebrews*, 54–75.

20. See Cockerill, "Melchizedek without Speculation." 11QMelch always divides "Melchizedek" into two words, *malchi* (probably "my king") and *tsedek* ("righteousness")—as does Gen 14.

21. Thus, for instance, the hypothesis that Hebrews was dependent on the tradition that Melchizedek was the first priest, found in Josephus and Philo (F. L. Horton, *Melchizedek Tradition*, 156–60) is unnecessary; it is simpler to think that all three were working from the OT.

22. A solid majority of scholars therefore conclude that it is unlikely that the author has drawn from Jewish tradition in his portrayal of Melchizedek. See, e.g., Theissen, *Untersuchungen*, 135–43; Deborah W. Rooke, "Jesus the Priest: Reflections on the Interpretation of the Melchizedek Tradition in Hebrews 7," *Bib* 81 (2000): 84; Joseph A. Fitzmyer, "Further Light on Melchizedek from Qumran Cave 11," *JBL* 86 (1967): 31; Grässer, *An die Hebräer*, 2:18–19; Weiss, *Der Brief an die Hebräer*, 383; Lane, *Hebrews*, 1:160–63; Koester, *Hebrews*, 339–41; Hurst, *Epistle to the Hebrews*, 52–60.

priesthood over to Abram (b. Ned. 32b). Early Christians, on the other hand, tended to view Melchizedek as a human figure, the king of Jerusalem, sometimes viewing him as a priest for the gentiles (Justin, *Dial.* 33). The tendency in early orthodox writings to portray Melchizedek as a human figure arose partly in response to heretical interpretations that often portrayed him as a heavenly being. On the other hand, some early Christians apparently viewed Melchizedek as a manifestation of the preincarnate Christ (see Epiphanius, *Pan.* 57.7.3; Ambrose, *Abr.* 1.3.4). Melchizedek's provision of Abram and his army with "bread and wine" was interpreted as an allusion to the Eucharist as early as Clement of Alexandria.[23] Reformation interpreters, following their more textually oriented hermeneutic, shied away from some of the more speculative views of Melchizedek. They generally doubted any reference to the Eucharist and stressed the way the author of Hebrews exploits the silences of the Genesis text as the basis for his comparison with Christ.[24]

In contrast to these interpretations, our author sticks closely to the biblical text he is working with, seeing significance in both what the text says about this mysterious figure and what it does not say. The author again reveals himself to be a creative and deeply informed interpreter of Scripture.

Explanation of the Text

7:1 Now this Melchizedek, king of Salem, priest of God Most High, met Abraham[25] when he was returning from the slaughter of the kings and blessed him (Οὗτος γὰρ ὁ Μελχισέδεκ, βασιλεὺς Σαλήμ, ἱερεὺς τοῦ θεοῦ τοῦ ὑψίστου, ὁ συναντήσας Ἀβραὰμ ὑποστρέφοντι ἀπὸ τῆς κοπῆς τῶν βασιλέων καὶ εὐλογήσας αὐτόν). "This Melchizedek" picks up the reference to this person in 6:20, as the author begins his lengthy explanation of Melchizedek's significance for Christ's high priesthood (the "for" [γάρ] is then explanatory). The sentence that begins in this verse continues right through to the end of verse 3. The subject is "Melchizedek" (which is in the nominative, as the article indicates), and the main verb is "remains" (μένει) at the end of verse 3. Thus the main clause is "Melchizedek remains a priest forever."[26] Verses 1b–3a consist of a series of descriptions of Melchizedek:

---

23. F. L. Horton provides a good overview of the early Christian and later Jewish interpretive landscape (*Melchizedek Tradition*, 87–130).

24. For a survey of Reformation and post-Reformation interpretation, see Bruce Demarest, *A History of Interpretation of Hebrews 7, 1–10 from the Reformation to the Present*, BGBE 19 (Tübingen: Mohr Siebeck, 1976).

25. The author always uses the fuller name "Abraham" (Ἀβραάμ) even when the LXX (following the Hebrew) uses the shorter name "Abram" (Αβραμ), as here.

26. E.g., Westcott, *Hebrews*, 170.

two noun phrases: "king of Salem," "priest of God Most High" (v. 1b)

two participles: "The one who met [ὁ συναντήσας] Abraham" and "the one who blessed [εὐλογήσας] him" (v. 1c)[27]

a relative clause: "to whom Abraham distributed a tenth of all the spoils" (v. 2a)

a participial clause introducing two of Melchizedek's titles: "king of righteousness" and "king of Salem/peace" (v. 2b)

a series of three further descriptions: "without father, without mother, without genealogy" (v. 3a)

two final adjectival participial clauses: "having neither beginning of days nor end of life"; "being made like the Son of God"

The main verbal clause, "remains a priest forever," alludes to Psalm 110:4—"you are a priest forever"—and is perhaps the most important point the author makes about Jesus in this chapter.[28]

The author's first description of Melchizedek, "king of Salem" (βασιλεὺς Σαλήμ), is also the first description of Melchizedek in Genesis 14:18. "Salem" is identified by some early Jewish interpreters as Jerusalem (e.g., the Genesis Apocryphon [1QapGen], Josephus [J.W. 6.438]), and many modern scholars (though by no means all) agree. In any case, the author makes nothing of the place name, so it is irrelevant for Hebrews. Nor does the author even mention the first episode in the Melchizedek narrative: that he "brought out bread and wine" for Abraham. Some early Christian interpreters, as we noted, saw here a reference to the Eucharist, but this is obviously not the author's interest. "Priest of the Most High God" (ἱερεὺς τοῦ θεοῦ τοῦ ὑψίστου, which exactly reproduces the LXX) is basic to the author's argument, the word "priest" (ἱερεύς) occurring also in Psalm 110:4. "Most High God" is almost certainly in Genesis a reference to the one true God—and, of course, it certainly is in Hebrews.[29] After noting another detail from the Genesis narrative—that Abraham was "returning from the defeat of the kings" (Gen 14:17)—the author mentions another detail that becomes important for his argument: Melchizedek "blessed" Abraham.

7:2 and Abraham distributed to him a tenth of everything. The name Melchizedek means, first of all, "king of righteousness" and then also "king of Salem," that is, "king of peace" (ᾧ καὶ δεκάτην ἀπὸ πάντων ἐμέρισεν Ἀβραάμ, πρῶτον μὲν ἑρμηνευόμενος βασιλεὺς δικαιοσύνης ἔπειτα δὲ καὶ βασιλεὺς Σαλήμ, ὅ ἐστιν βασιλεὺς εἰρήνης). The author continues his brief overview of the story about Melchizedek in Genesis 14. Our translation, following most English versions, moves away at certain points from the form of the Greek text in order to adequately capture its meaning. Thus the personal pronoun in the opening clause, "him," translates a relative pronoun, "[to] whom" (ᾧ) (see NASB). The second sentence in our translation is actually a participial clause in the Greek, and its subject is implied (I have supplied "the name Melchizedek"; see also, e.g., NIV; NLT; NRSV).

---

27. The second participle lacks an article. The article before the first participle, then, probably governs both participles, suggesting that they be read together (which is, in any case, obvious here).

28. E.g., Weiss, *Der Brief an die Hebräer*, 372; Grässer, *An die Hebräer*, 2:8.

29. "Most high" (ὕψιστος) often refers to God in the Bible, both alone and with the name of God (θεός). Luke is particularly fond of this title for God: NT occurrences are, without θεός, Luke 1:32, 35, 76; Acts 7:48; with θεός, Mark 5:7; Luke 2:14; 8:28; Acts 16:17. There are almost one hundred occurrences in the LXX; four are in Gen 14 (vv. 18, 19, 20, 22) and over twenty in Psalms.

The indicative verb the author uses in verse 2a— "he distributed" (ἐμέρισεν)³⁰—highlights this clause, suggesting the importance of this point for our author's interpretation of the narrative (vv. 4-6, 8-9). The "tenth" or "tithe"³¹ that Abraham apportioned to Melchizedek came from the plunder he took in his victory over the kings (Gen 14:20b; and see v. 4).³²

The participial clause in the second part of the verse develops the significance of Melchizedek's name and title. The name Melchizedek "means" (ἑρμηνευόμενος) "king of righteousness." Most scholars think that "Melchizedek" in Genesis means "my king" (*malchi*) is "righteousness" (*tsedeq*),³³ but the author agrees with other early Jewish interpreters who took it to mean simply "king of righteousness" (see Josephus, *J.W.* 6.438; Philo, *Alleg. Interp.* 3.79). The author then interprets "king of Salem" (Hebrew *melek Shalēm*) to mean "king of peace" (Hebrew *melek shalom*). It is difficult to know why the author adds these details, since he never comments on their significance. Perhaps, however, "righteousness" and "peace" had messianic overtones that he wanted to introduce into the portrait of Melchizedek (e.g., Isa 9:6; Jer 23:5; 33:15; Zech 9:9-10; the author associates "righteousness" with Christ in 1:8-9 and "peace" in 13:20).³⁴

7:3 Without father, without mother, without genealogy, having neither beginning of days nor end of life, being made like the Son of God, he remains a priest forever (ἀπάτωρ ἀμήτωρ ἀγενεαλόγητος, μήτε ἀρχὴν ἡμερῶν μήτε ζωῆς τέλος ἔχων, ἀφωμοιωμένος δὲ τῷ υἱῷ τοῦ θεοῦ, μένει ἱερεὺς εἰς τὸ διηνεκές). Three adjectives, parallel in form, continue the author's characterization of Melchizedek. All three are formed with an "alpha privative" (the prefix "a-," which functions like our "un-"): ἀπάτωρ ("un-fathered," or "without father"), ἀμήτωρ ("without mother"), ἀγενεαλόγητος ("without genealogy"). The literary quality of this alliteration and the Hellenistic flavor of these words (none of them are used elsewhere in biblical Greek), along with some other stylistic features in verses 1-3, have led some scholars to suspect that the author is quoting or adapting a preexisting hymn.³⁵ However, this hypothesis lacks adequate evidence; our author is clearly a skilled enough stylist to have composed these verses himself.³⁶

These three descriptions are by far the most controversial aspect of our author's depiction of Melchizedek. The language of "without father" and "without mother" in the time of Hebrews was generally applied to one of two kinds of being: a person whose origins were uncertain (e.g., an orphan or one who did know his or her parentage), or a god.³⁷

---

30. The verb in the LXX is ἔδωκεν, "he gave." The verb our author uses, μερίζω, has the sense here of "deal out," "apportion" (BDAG 632, §2.a, b).

31. The Greek word δέκατος means "tenth," and, when used in a context referring to the offering of a "tenth" to someone, takes on the more specific sense "tithe" ("δέκατος," BDAG 216, §2.b). See also vv. 4, 8, 9, and the verbal cognates δεκατόω and ἀποδεκατόω ("apportion a tenth") in vv. 5, 6, and 9.

32. The LXX explicitly names "Abraham" as the subject of the verb, whereas the Hebrew has no specific subject (leading a few interpreters to think that the subject is Melchizedek). The LXX is joined by most early Jewish interpreters in correctly inferring that the subject is Abraham (see, e.g., the Genesis Apocryphon [1QapGen] 22.17; Josephus, *Ant.* 1.181; Philo, *Prelim. Studies* 99).

33. Note the parallel name "Adoni-Zedek" ("my lord is righteousness") in Josh 10:1, 3.

34. E.g., Fitzmyer, "Further Light on Melchizedek," 314; Backhaus, *Der Hebräerbrief*, 260. Fitzmyer has a good overview of the names and their significance (pp. 311-14).

35. Gottfried Schille, "Erwägungen zur Hohepriesterlehre des Hebräerbriefes," *ZNW* 46 (1955): 81-109; Ellingworth, *Hebrews*, 352-53. Theissen offers a good defense of this view along with a reconstruction of the alleged hymn (*Untersuchungen*, 20-28).

36. See, e.g., Attridge, *Hebrews*, 189-90; Lane, *Hebrews*, 1:160.

37. See, e.g., G. Schrenk, "πατήρ, κτλ," *TDNT* 5:1019-20. See Euripides, *Ion* 109, for one of the few places where both ἀπάτηρ and ἀμήτωρ are used together: in this case to describe

Since the generally negative nuance attaching to the former is ruled out by context, some scholars conclude that the author is depicting Melchizedek as a god.[38] Later Christian interpreters sometimes identified Melchizedek with the preexistent Christ (see the "In Depth" excursus), and a few scholars think this may have been the author's intention.[39] However, the author's focus on Christ's descent from Judah in 7:14 makes it awkward for him here to claim he is "without father" and "without mother." Moreover, identifying Melchizedek with Christ would appear to contradict the author's typological view of Melchizedek as being "like" Christ. Other interpreters think the language might be intended to depict Melchizedek as an angel, an interpretation known in the Judaism of that time.[40] However, it is questionable if these terms were used with reference to angels.

The clue to the author's true intention lies in the third term, "without genealogy" (ἀγενεαλόγητος), a word apparently coined by our author. An argument from genealogy plays an important role in the author's argument for the superiority of Christ as "high priest in the order of Melchizedek" over the Levitical priests. "Without genealogy," then, draws attention to the fact that Melchizedek, virtually alone among important early figures in Genesis, is provided with no genealogy—and yet he is "priest of God Most High"! In other words, the author's focus appears to be not on the person of Melchizedek per se but on the depiction of Melchizedek in Genesis. As Bauckham puts it, "It is the textual, not the historical Melchizedek that explains what the Melchizedekian priesthood of the Psalm is."[41]

As we have seen, the author is a careful and attentive biblical interpreter. Having been clued in by Psalm 110:4 that Christ is a priest like Melchizedek, he naturally turns to the only other passage in the Bible about Melchizedek to flesh out what this means. He apparently follows a Jewish interpretive rule that finds meaning in the silences of Scripture—as it is often put, in Latin, *non in tora non in mundo*: "not in Torah, not in the world." The sudden appearance of Melchizedek as a priest (the first one in Genesis), without any indication in the text about his parentage or background, is seen by our author as indicative of his significance as a typological precursor of Christ.[42] As our author will make clear later in the chapter (vv. 13–16), the high priesthood of Christ is not based on his ancestry, as is the case with the Levitical priests.

This direction in our interpretation is confirmed by the next description of Melchizedek, as "having neither beginning of days nor end of life." In its technical sense, this language can only be applied to deity, for even angels are created beings. However, it is much more likely that the author again is simply noting that the Genesis narrative depicts neither Melchizedek's origins nor his eventual destiny.

---

a person whose parentage is unknown. Philo uses ἀμήτωρ eleven times, often to claim that ideal persons or numbers are generated from a father alone.

38. See, e.g., Jerome H. Neyrey, "'Without Beginning of Days or End of Life' (Hebrews 7:3): Topos for a True Deity," *CBQ* 53 (1991): 439–55; Cockerill, *Hebrews*, 300–306. Note, e.g., the Apocalypse of Abraham (first or second cent. AD) 17.10: the "Mighty One, Holy El" is "without father, without mother, self-generated."

39. E.g., A. T. Hanson, *The Living Utterances of God: The New Testament Exegesis of the Old* (London: Darton, Longman and Todd, 1983), 107–8. See, possibly, Georg Strecker: it is not that "Melchizedek was a type of the Son of God but that conversely the preexistent reality of the heavenly high priest is inherent in the priest-king Melchizedek" (*Theology of the New Testament* [Berlin: de Gruyter, 2000], 613).

40. Attridge (*Hebrews*, 191–94) argues that the language depicts Melchizedek either as a divine being or as an angel.

41. Bauckham, "Divinity of Jesus Christ," 30.

42. This view is widely held; see, e.g., Fitzmyer, "Further Light on Melchizedek," 316–17; Grässer, *An die Hebräer*, 2:12; Bruce, *Hebrews*, 159–60.

In all these ways, then, Melchizedek has been "made like" (ἀφωμοιωμένος) the Son of God. This verb is often interpreted to mean simply "resembling" (e.g., NIV; ESV; NLT; CSB), but it more likely has the dynamic sense of "having been made to resemble" (NAB; cf. NASB).[43] The direction here is important: Christ is not "made like" Melchizedek; Melchizedek is "made like" Christ—that is, Melchizedek is portrayed in such a way in Scripture so as to prefigure the Son of God.[44]

The author finally is now ready to finish the sentence he began at the beginning of verse 1: "this Melchizedek... remains [μένει] a priest forever."[45] As I have noted, this focus on an "eternal" priesthood is a key point in our author's argument for the superiority of Christ as "priest in the order of Melchizedek."[46] The phrase meaning "forever" that the author uses here (εἰς τὸ διηνεκές) is not the usual Greek phrase for "forever" (which is εἰς τὸν αἰῶνα). Some interpreters think that the author may use them slightly differently: the latter implying no beginning as well as no end; the former no end but a beginning. However, this difference in nuance between the phrases is not present generally in Greek, and it is not even clear that it holds in Hebrews.[47]

7:4 You see how great this man was, to whom Abraham the patriarch gave a tenth of the spoils (Θεωρεῖτε δὲ πηλίκος οὗτος, ᾧ καὶ δεκάτην Ἀβραὰμ ἔδωκεν ἐκ τῶν ἀκροθινίων ὁ πατριάρχης). In verses 1–3, the author draws attention to characteristics and actions of Melchizedek stated or implied in the Genesis 14 narrative. Now he turns to his audience—"you see" (θεωρεῖτε, a second-plural form)—to draw out their significance for the relationship of Melchizedek and Abraham, and ultimately for the relationship of the priests in their "orders": Christ, on the one hand, and the Levitical priests on the other. In verses 1–3, the author has drawn attention to two incidents in the Melchizedek narrative: Melchizedek "blessed" Abraham (v. 1c), and Abraham paid a tithe to Melchizedek (v. 2a). In his application, the author mentions the significance of the blessing (vv. 6b–7), but especially focuses on the tithe Abraham paid (vv. 4–6a, 8–9).

The act of tithing is, then, where our author begins. The tithe of the spoils[48] Abraham gave Melchizedek is indicative of the "greatness"[49] of the latter. To reinforce his point, the author reminds us that Abraham is "the patriarch," putting the word last in the sentence for emphasis.[50] As Calvin notes, the "more excellent Abraham is, the higher is the dignity of Melchizedek himself."[51]

**7:5 Now, on the one hand, the sons of Levi who received their priesthood had a commandment according to the law to receive a tithe from the their brothers and sisters—even though

---

43. Peterson, *Hebrews and Perfection*, 106; Cockerill, *Hebrews*, 302; contra, e.g., Ellingworth, *Hebrews*, 358–59. The perfect form of the participle hints at the enduring significance of this fact.

44. E.g., Westcott, *Hebrews*, 173; Koester, *Hebrews*, 343; Johnson, *Hebrews*, 177.

45. This is one of the few places where the verb μένω, "remain," takes a predicate noun.

46. This focus on "remaining," which is important in Hebrews (e.g., 10:34; 12:27; 13:14), is sometimes thought to reflect a Middle Platonist approach (see Thompson, "What Has Middle Platonism to Do with Hebrews?," 43–44).

47. Ellingworth, *Hebrews*, 359. The "eternal" (εἰς τὸ διηνεκές) sacrifice of Christ in 10:12 appears to be a claim that no sacrifice before or after it is like it. And Christ's "eternal" (εἰς τὸ αἰῶνα) priesthood, language rooted in Ps 110:4 (see 5:6; 6:20; 7:17, 21), appears to imply an appointment at some point in time to this role.

48. The Gk. word is ἀκροθίνιον, used only here in biblical Greek. It is governed by ἐκ, which has a partitive sense: a "tenth part" (δεκάτην) "from among the spoils" (ἐκ τῶν ἀκροθινίων).

49. The Gk. word is C, which can mean "how large" (Gal 6:11) or, as here, "how great." See "δέκατος," BDAG 811, §2.

50. The NIV captures this emphasis by translating "even the patriarch Abraham" (see also CSB).

51. Calvin, *Hebrews*, 92.

they came from the loins of Abraham (καὶ οἱ μὲν ἐκ τῶν υἱῶν Λευὶ τὴν ἱερατείαν λαμβάνοντες ἐντολὴν ἔχουσιν ἀποδεκατοῦν τὸν λαὸν κατὰ τὸν νόμον, τοῦτ᾽ ἔστιν τοὺς ἀδελφοὺς αὐτῶν, καίπερ ἐξεληλυθότας ἐκ τῆς ὀσφύος Ἀβραάμ). Verses 5 and 6 are joined together by a construction (οἱ μέν ... ὁ δέ) that signifies a contrast: "on the one hand ... on the other hand." The contrast is between the Levitical priests who, by law,[52] collect tithes from the people, and Melchizedek, who received a tithe from Abraham. These verses add background information that helps the readers understand the significance of Abraham's tithe to Melchizedek.[53] The law requiring a tithe to be paid places the Levitical priests "over" the people, in a sense. Yet Abraham paid a tithe to Melchizedek, thereby signifying the "greatness" of the latter with respect to Abraham. The Old Testament sets apart the Levites to be "in charge of the tabernacle" (Num 1:50; see vv. 47–53). They received no allotment of land when the people entered the promised land, and, as Hebrews points out, the law commanded that they be given a tithe. The Old Testament specifies two stages in this tithing: the people give a tithe to the Levites, and the priests (a subgroup within the Levites)[54] receive a tithe in turn from their fellow Levites (Num 18:26–28; see Neh 10:38–39).[55] The author is not concerned with this intermediate stage: for his argument, it is sufficient that those Levites who "received their priesthood" receive a tithe from the people—whether that process is direct or indirect.[56]

The "people" from whom the Levitical priests receive the tithe are, the author points out, their "brothers and sisters" (ἀδελφούς: variously translated "fellow Israelites" [NIV]; "kindred" [NRSV]; "brothers and sisters" is the rendering in CSB and CEB[57]). The author emphasizes this physical connection in a final adverbial participial construction: "even though they came from the loins of Abraham."[58] The word I translate "loins" (ὀσφύος) often refers specifically to the reproductive organs; so the focus here is on physical descent (see also v. 10).[59] The author draws attention in the last part of this verse to the common descent shared by the Levitical priests and the people of Israel. All trace their ancestry back to Abraham and can therefore be set over against Melchizedek when it comes to the significance of priesthood.

---

52. The author stresses the law by mentioning, first, the specific "commandment" (ἐντολήν) about the tithe and then, second, that this command was "in accordance with," or "based on" (Koester, *Hebrews*, 344), or "in" (ESV) the law (κατὰ τὸν νόμον). This is the first occurrence of νόμος in Hebrews. The word almost always focuses on the cultic law and plays an important role in the argument of subsequent verses (see 7:12, 16, 19, 28; 10:1).

53. The καί at the beginning of the verse introduces this "backstory." "Now" in English signals this idea (NIV; NLT).

54. The author recognizes the distinction between the Levites generally and those among them who are appointed priests: he refers to those "from among the sons of Levi" (οἱ ... ἐκ τῶν υἱῶν Λευί, a partitive construction) who "receive the priesthood" (τὴν ἱερατείαν λαμβάνοντες, the participle is adjectival, modifying οἱ, an article functioning as a personal pronoun). For the distinction between Levites and priests, see also Luke 10:31–32; John 1:19.

55. The verb our author uses for "receive a tithe," ἀποδεκατόω, can mean either "pay a tithe" (Matt 23:23; Luke 11:42; 18:12) or "receive a tithe," depending on context ("ἀποδεκατόω," BDAG 109).

56. There is no need, then, to think that our author's generalization about priests receiving the tithe from the people reflects a possible practice of his own day (see Josephus, *Ant.* 20.181, 206–7; see, e.g., Bruce, *Hebrews*, 162–63). There is some uncertainty, leading to scholarly debate, about the relationship of Levites and priests in the OT (see, e.g., D. A. Garrett, "Levi and Levites," under "Priests and Levites," in *Dictionary of the Old Testament: Pentateuch*, ed. T. Desmond Alexander and David W. Baker [Downers Grove, IL: IVP Academic, 2003], 519–22).

57. "Brothers" (ESV; NAB; NASB) is an inaccurate translation because the word connotes males, while the tithe was collected from all the people.

58. The participle is ἐξεληλυθότας, from ἐξέρχομαι, "come out." The perfect tense suggests the emphasis is not so much on the action but on its consequences. The participle, since it is modified by καίπερ ("although"), has a concessive force.

59. See "ὀσφῦς," BDAG 730, §2; and note Gen 35:11 (RSV): "God said to him, 'I am God Almighty: be fruitful and multiply;

7:6 However, on the other hand, the one who does not trace his descent from them receives a tithe from Abraham, and he blessed the man who was given the promises (ὁ δὲ μὴ γενεαλογούμενος ἐξ αὐτῶν δεδεκάτωκεν Ἀβραὰμ καὶ τὸν ἔχοντα τὰς ἐπαγγελίας εὐλόγηκεν). We find here the contrasting part of the author's "on the one hand [μέν in v. 5] . . . on the other hand [δέ]" sequence. Melchizedek, in contrast especially to the Levitical priests, does not trace his descent "from them" (ἐξ αὐτῶν)—that is, from the people of Israel. As the author points out in his brief commentary on the Genesis 14 narrative, Melchizedek is "without genealogy": the inspired text says nothing about this absolute sine qua non for priestly status, suggesting the interpretive significance of the omission. Despite this lack of genealogical qualification, Melchizedek is shown to be superior to Abraham. First, Melchizedek "receives a tithe" from Abraham, and second Melchizedek "blesses" Abraham. The author again goes out of his way to point out the significance of this; Abraham is the one "who was given the promises" (τὸν ἔχοντα τὰς ἐπαγγελίας; see esp. 6:12–20) and who plays such a signal role in salvation history. I translate both this participle as well as the substantival participle at the beginning of the verse (γενελογούμενος) in the present tense because I think the author is not so much relating past history as pointing out the present significance of that story. The perfect form of the indicative verb "receives a tithe" (δεδεκάτωκεν) points in this same direction.[60]

7:7 Now it is beyond dispute that the inferior is blessed by the superior (χωρὶς δὲ πάσης ἀντιλογίας τὸ ἔλαττον ὑπὸ τοῦ κρείττονος εὐλογεῖται). The author now adds background information that buttresses the point he made at the end of verse 6. Melchizedek's blessing of Abraham signifies the former's greatness (see v. 4) because "it is without dispute" (χωρὶς . . . πάσης ἀντιλογίας) that the "inferior" (τὸ ἔλαττον) is blessed "by the superior" (ὑπὸ τοῦ κρείττονος).[61] The author's assertion of this general rule appears to be easily challenged: for instance, servants "bless" kings (2 Sam 14:22; 1 Kgs 1:47) and humans "bless" God (e.g., Deut 8:10—all these Old Testament texts use εὐλογέω, the verb found in this verse). DeSilva, then, suggests that we have here "something of a fallacious argument."[62] We need not be quite so critical, however. The author may simply be stating a general or regular truth, even if there are exceptions—this is a common way for us to speak. Or he may be laser focused on this particular text. But another consideration is that the verb "bless" (εὐλογέω), in fact, has two different senses: "to pronounce a blessing" or "praise."[63] The author may, then, be using the word with this former sense.

7:8 On the one hand, then, men who die receive tithes but, on the other hand, there is testimony to the effect that he lives (καὶ ὧδε μὲν δεκάτας ἀποθνῄσκοντες ἄνθρωποι λαμβάνουσιν, ἐκεῖ δὲ μαρτυρούμενος ὅτι ζῇ). The author has advanced two arguments on the basis of the Genesis 14 narrative for the superiority of Melchizedek to Abraham:

---

a nation and a company of nations shall come from you, and kings shall spring from you [i.e., "from your loins"; LXX ἐκ τῆς ὀσφύος]."

60. On this force of the perfect here, see, e.g., Moule, *Idiom Book*, 14; Wallace, *Greek Grammar*, 582. We should stress that the decision to translate the participles with present tenses is not based simply on the fact that both are in the present tense in Greek, since the tense (especially in participles) often has no bearing on the time of action. However, as Wallace points out, the present tense is sometimes used with substantival participles

when the author wants simply to identify the person with a particular characterization (*Greek Grammar*, 620). I might also point to the contrast with the aorist participle in v. 1—"he met."

61. The Gk. τὸ ἔλαττον is clearly neuter, making it likely that τοῦ κρείττονος should also be read as neuter. The author uses neuter forms to focus on the quality of the persons (BDF §138.1).

62. DeSilva, *Perseverance in Gratitude*, 267.

63. See Takamitsu Muraoka, *A Greek-English Lexicon of the Septuagint* (Leuven: Peeters, 2009), 301; "εὐλογέω," BDAG 408.

Melchizedek received a tithe from Abraham, and Melchizedek blessed Abraham. Now he moves to a third argument, shifting the focus from Abraham to the Levitical priests whom he tied to Abraham in verse 5. As in verses 5–6, the author uses a construction that enhances the contrast he intends to draw: ὧδε μεν ... ἐκεῖ δέ ("on the one hand ... on the other hand").[64] Melchizedek's "greatness" (v. 4) is seen in the fact that "he lives" while the Levitical priests are "men who die." Of the three arguments in verses 4–10, this one becomes the most important. After verse 10, we no longer hear anything about tithes or blessing. Instead, Jesus's eternal nature and unending, unchanging priesthood becomes the key focus (vv. 16–17, 21, 23–25, 28).

"Men who die" refers to the Levitical priests.[65] Their inability to continue in office because of their mortality demonstrates the inferior nature of their priestly order, in contrast to the priestly "order" of Melchizedek. The author's simple claim that "he lives" (ζῇ) invites elaboration. The author's introduction to this claim, as being "witnessed to" (μαρτυρούμενος), points to the scriptural record as the source of this information (see the use of this verb elsewhere in Hebrews: 7:17; 10:15; 11:2, 4, 5, 39).[66] The simple claim here echoes the characterization in verse 3—namely, that Melchizedek has no "beginning of days nor end of life." Those who stress the implications of this language of verse 3 for the divine character of Melchizedek think the author here, likewise, claims that Melchizedek himself had "life without beginning or end."[67] However, in keeping with our interpretation of verse 3, I think it more likely that the author is again thinking not of the "historical" Melchizedek but of the "literary" Melchizedek: the Genesis narrative does not mention his death or cessation from priestly duties. That silence attests to one of the ways he is "made like" the Son of God.

7:9–10 It could even be said that Levi, who receives the tithe, paid that tithe through Abraham, 10 because he was in the loins of his ancestor when Melchizedek met Abraham (καὶ ὡς ἔπος εἰπεῖν, δι' Ἀβραὰμ καὶ Λευὶ ὁ δεκάτας λαμβάνων δεδεκάτωται 10 ἔτι γὰρ ἐν τῇ ὀσφύϊ τοῦ πατρὸς ἦν ὅτε συνήντησεν αὐτῷ Μελχισέδεκ). The author's ultimate concern is not to contrast Melchizedek with Abraham. That contrast is simply the means to make the more fundamental and applicable point that Christ's priesthood is greater than that of the Levitical priests. Whether the author's point is negative as well as positive—cling to Christ, don't go back to your Jewish institutions!—or positive only—cling to Christ, because a comparison with the Levitical priests reveals how great he is—it is this comparison that is rhetorically powerful. In these last two verses in the paragraph, then, the author adds the final step to make this argument "work." Melchizedek received a tithe from Abraham, and the significance of this lies in the priesthood each represents. Christ is in the "order of the Melchizedek." But Levi, and the priests descended from him, was "in the loins of Abraham."[68] It is because of this physical solidarity, then, that it can be said, in a manner of speaking (ὡς ἔπος εἰπεῖν),[69] that Levi, the one who received

---

64. BDAG ("ὧδε," 1101) note that ὧδε, usually translated "here," can mean "in this case"; ἐκεῖ, then (often "there"), by contrast, means "in that case" (RSV preserves the more common meanings: "here ... there").

65. The Gk. is ἀποθνῄσκοντες ἄνθρωποι. The participle, coming before the noun it modifies, functions virtually as an adjective ("mortal men," NET) (see Moule, *Idiom Book*, 104).

66. See Michel, *Der Brief an die Hebräer*, 257.

67. E.g., Cockerill, *Hebrews*, 311.

68. See v. 5b for the meaning of "loins" (ὀφύος).

69. The clause is used widely in non-biblical Greek to mean "so to speak," or "to use just the right word" (see "ἔπος," BDAG 388; and note, e.g., Philo, *Creation* 107; *Worse Attacks the Better* 73). The infinitive εἰπεῖν is an infinitive absolute (Turner, *Syntax*, 136).

the tithe from his fellow Israelites (v. 5), paid a tithe to Melchizedek through Abraham.[70] The author assumes a way of thinking in terms of the interconnectedness of humans that was quite common in the biblical culture (and in many cultures in our own day) but is sometimes quite foreign to certain Western cultures. Suffice to say that the readers of this letter would probably not have batted an eye at this argument.[71] The author then ends the paragraph where he began, with a reminder of the setting: "when Melchizedek met [συνήντησεν] Abraham" (see v. 1: "Melchizedek met [συναντῆσας] Abraham").

Theology in Application

The author to the Hebrews is a careful and creative reader of Scripture. Perhaps nowhere else in Hebrews is this revealed as clearly as in 7:1–10. The author, I have suggested, begins his exploration of the "priest in the order of Melchizedek" theme with Psalm 110:4. For our author, who reads Psalm 110 as a passage about Jesus the Lord, this text also gives him clear biblical basis to regard Jesus as a priest "like Melchizedek." But what does this mean? The author seeks to answer that question on the basis of Scripture. And so he inevitably lands on Genesis 14:18–20, the only other Old Testament text even to mention Melchizedek. As we have seen, then, the author uses both what this text says and what it does not say to shed light on the unique nature of Jesus's high priesthood.

The author's procedure in this text serves to some extent as a model for us. He obviously is reading Scripture very carefully, attending to its details as well as to its overall message. He is reading the Old Testament with a christological lens—meaning not that he is intent on finding Christ *in* every Old Testament verse but that he reads all of Scripture with attention to its ultimate meaning in light of Christ. And, more controversially, he reads Scripture, I argue, on its own terms. In our postmodern environment, we have come to appreciate that every one of us reads from a particular perspective. We cannot shed our context, background, education, or theological predilections when we read Scripture. And this is, of course, true for the author to the Hebrews. Nevertheless, as I have argued in my exegesis, the author shows no indication that his reading of Genesis 14 is influenced by the various Jewish speculations about Melchizedek current in his day.

---

70. "Paid a tithe" translates δεδεκάτωται, another perfect form that puts the stress on the enduring significance of the scriptural account. Likewise, the adjectival participle ὁ . . . λαμβάνων is in the present tense to draw the reader into the biblical narrative (see also the participles in v. 6; and see, e.g., Turner, *Syntax*, 151).

71. Early interpreters were sometimes bothered by the realization that Christ also was "in the loins of Abraham," for he was, of course, a descendant (see, e.g., Matt 1:1–17). Augustine suggested that Christ was "in Abraham" only in his humanity but not in his divinity (*On Genesis Literally Interpreted* 10.19–21; see Erik M. Heen and Philip D. W. Krey, eds., *Hebrews*, ACCS 10 [Downers Grove, IL: InterVarsity Press, 2005], 108–9).

We should imitate the author's attention to the text for its own sake. The many tools we have available today as we read Scripture are without any doubt a great boon (and I certainly don't want to discourage believers from reading my own commentaries!). But it is terribly easy to turn too quickly to these tools and lose sight of Scripture itself.

I say above that "the author's procedure . . . serves to some extent as a model." Why the qualification? Because his drawing of theological conclusions from the silence of the text is a procedure that we would have to use very cautiously. This is not to say that conspicuous silences are not sometimes significant. (One thinks of the Sherlock Holmes story *Silver Blaze* in which the *failure* of a dog to bark in the night is the decisive clue in solving the mystery.) Nevertheless, a "silence" is by definition something that is not *in* Scripture. The issue of authority comes into play here as well. One of my mentors, Dr. Walter Kaiser, was fond of reminding us, his students, that the biblical authors are "inspired" while we are "perspired." Inspired and led by God's Spirit, their interpretations of the Old Testament bear an authority that we don't have in our own interpretations.

Hebrews 7:11–25

Literary Context

In these verses, the author continues and completes his exploration of the theme of Jesus as "a priest in the order of Melchizedek." This language appears in Psalm 110:4, which is the biblical jumping off point for this interpretation of Jesus's priestly ministry. However, one other Old Testament text mentions Melchizedek, and the author chooses to begin his exposition of this theme by drawing out implications from that text: Genesis 14:18–20. Having expounded the meaning of that text (vv. 1–10), he now turns back to his biblical starting point in vv. 11–28, exploiting virtually every word and phrase in Psalm 110:4 in order to develop his teaching. Chapter 7 as a whole, then, contributes vitally to the author's central theological argument that Jesus is our "great high priest" who brings his people into intimate and permanent fellowship with God.[1]

As I noted in the introduction and have alluded to at points since, the specific situation addressed by the author is unclear and debated. Many interpreters, especially recently, think that the author's argument is pretty much entirely positive: he compares Christ with various Old Testament persons and institutions in an effort to convince his audience of the need to move on in their spiritual pilgrimage. In this chapter, then, the contrast between Christ's priesthood and the Levitical priesthood is simply a biblically oriented means of highlighting Christ. Others, however, following a long-standing perspective on the book, think that this positive argument is combined with a negative one: the author urges his audience (Jewish, or mainly so) to appreciate and cling to Christ even as he also implicitly warns them about falling back into reliance on Levitical priests for access to God. A key word in this last sentence is "implicitly": advocates of the first view note that the author never in this chapter makes that warning explicit. However, I think the length and detail of the comparison is best explained if, indeed, there is a negative side to the author's rhetoric.[2]

---

1. Michel thinks ch. 7 is the heart of the letter (*Der Brief an die Hebräer*, 255).

2. On this point, see, e.g., Bruce, *Hebrews*, 166; Koester, *Hebrews*, 357.

I. The Exalted Son and a Rest for the People of God (1:1–4:13)
II. **Our Great High Priest and His Ministry (4:14–10:31)**
   A. Exhortation: Persevere through the Power of Our Exalted High Priest (4:14–16)
   B. Exposition: High Priests and Our High Priest (5:1–10)
   C. Exhortation: Move on to Maturity (5:11–6:20)
   D. Exposition: A High Priest "According to the Order of Melchizedek" (7:1–28)
      1. Melchizedek's Supremacy over Abraham (Gen 14:17–20) (7:1–10)
   ➡ 2. **The Supremacy and Sufficiency of Our High Priest (Psalm 110:4) (7:11–25)**
      3. The High Priest Who Is Also the Son (7:26–28)
   E. Exposition: The Ministry of Our High Priest (8:1–10:18)
   F. Exhortation and Warning: Appropriating the Benefits of Our High Priest's Ministry (10:19–31)
III. Exhortation: Follow and Serve the Pioneer of Our Faith through Endurance and Faith (10:32–13:25)

Main Idea

The author continues to develop his creative exploration of the biblical testimony about Melchizedek to shed light on the meaning and greatness of Christ as our high priest. A comparison between Melchizedek and Abraham, the focus of the Genesis 14 narrative, now gives way to a focus on the priestly "orders" that extend from each of them: Christ, on the one hand, and the Levitical priests on the other. The Levitical priests are mortal, sinful, and carry out their ministry in the context of a "weak" and "earthly" law. Christ, by contrast, has an "indestructible life" and is appointed to his ministry by God's own oath. He, and he alone, is therefore capable of bringing people into the presence of God, saving them to full extent.

Translation

Hebrews 7:11–25

11a	continuation (of 7:1–10)	Now
11b	condition	if perfection had been possible
11c	means	through the Levitical priesthood
11d	parenthesis	(for
11e	assertion	the people were given the law
11f	reference	with respect to the priesthood), then
11g	rhetorical question	**what need was there**

Continued on next page.

11h	content	for another priest to arise
11i	description	who is said to be according to the order of Melchizedek and not
11j	content	
11k	contrast	according to the order of Aaron?
12a	continuation (of 11c–e)	For
12b	time	when the priesthood is changed,
12c	assertion	**of necessity there also is a change in the law.**
13a	explanation (of 12)	For
13b	assertion	**the one . . .**
13c	identification	about whom these things are said
13d	predicate (of 13b)	**. . . belongs to a different tribe,**
13e	description	from which no one has served
13f	sphere	at the altar.
14a	explanation (of 13c)	For
14b	assertion	**it is clear**
14c	content	that our Lord has arisen
14d	source	from the tribe of Judah,
14e	reference	concerning which tribe Moses says nothing
14f	reference	about priests.
15a	series (with 13–14)	And
15b	explanation (of 12)	**this is still more evident**
15c	content	if another priest . . .
15d	standard	according to the likeness of Melchizedek
15e	predicate (of 15c)	. . . appears,
16a	description (of 15b)	who has taken his position
16b	basis	not on the basis of the law,
16c	description	with its fleshly commandment, but
16d	contrast (with 16b)	on the basis of the power
16e	source	of an indestructible life.
17a	verification (of 16d–e)	For
17b	assertion	**it is testified**
17c	content	that "You are a priest forever,
17d	sphere	in the order of Melchizedek" (Ps 110:4)
18a	summary (of 11–17)	So,
18b	contrast	on the one hand,
18c	assertion	**there has been (1) an annulment of the previous commandment**
18d	cause	because of its weakness and ineffectiveness
19a	explanation (of 18c–d)	—for **the law perfected nothing**—
19b	contrast	and,
19c	contrast	on the other hand,
19d	assertion	**(2) an introduction of a better hope**

Hebrews 7:11–25

19e	means		through which we are drawing near to God.
20a	comparison (with 22a)	And to the degree that	
20b	content	**it was not without an oath—**	
20c	elaboration (of 20b)	for, on the one hand,	
20d	assertion	**those . . .**	
20e	identification	who have become priests	
20f	predicate (of 20e)	**. . . became priests**	
20g	manner	without the taking of an oath,	
21a	contrast	but, on the other hand,	
21b	assertion	**this one became a priest**	
21c	agent	by the one	
21d	identification	who said to him,	
21e	content	"The Lord has sworn and	
21f	parallel	will not change his mind:	
21g	content	'You are a priest forever'"— (Ps 110:4)	
22a	comparison (with 20a)	to the same degree	
22b	assertion	**Jesus has become the guarantor**	
		of a better covenant.	
23a	development	In addition,	
23b	contrast	on the one hand,	
23c	assertion	**there are many**	
23d	identification	**who have become priests**,	
23e	cause	because they were prevented	
23f	means	by death	
23g	separation	from continuing,	
24a	contrast	but, on the other hand,	
24b	assertion	**Jesus, . . .**	
24c	cause	because he remains forever,	
24d	predicate (of 24b)	**. . . has a priesthood**	
24e	description	that is perpetual.	
25a	inference (from 24)	For this reason,	
25b	assertion	**he is able**	
25c	content	**to save completely**	
25d	identification/object	those who come to God	
25e	means	through him,	
25f	basis	since he always lives	
25g	purpose	to intercede for them.	

Structure

The use of *inclusio* again suggests the ordering of this text. The implication in verse 11 that "perfection" (τελείωσις) could not come via "the Levitical priesthood" because that priesthood was established by the law is matched by the claim in verse 19 that "the law perfected [ἐτελείωσεν] nothing." An *inclusio* also marks out the second part of the passage: the "oath," which is a focus of the author in verses 20–21, is picked up again in verse 28. At the same time, however, verse 28 (along with vv. 26–27), rings notes found throughout the passage: in addition to the oath, the inadequacy of the law (vv. 11–19), the "perfection" (τετελειωμένων) brought through the Son (in contrast to the law; see vv. 11, 19), and the "eternal" nature of his work (vv. 16, 17, 24, 25). Verses 26–28 are set apart also by the explicit turn to application in verse 26: "it is indeed fitting for *us* to have such a high priest." Probably, then, while we can identify verses 11–19 and 20–28 as two main parts of the passage, verses 26–28 need to be singled out as a brief but rich concluding and transitional unit.[3] As I note above, Psalm 110:4 is the constant reference point in the author's argument (it is quoted in vv. 17 and 21). Indeed, virtually every element of that verse receives attention, in reverse order: "the LORD has sworn and will not change his mind [the oath: vv. 20–22]: 'You are a priest forever [eternal focus: vv. 15, 19, 23–25], in the order of Melchizedek [vv. 11–14].'"[4]

Exegetical Outline

→ **2. The Supremacy and Sufficiency of Our High Priest (Psalm 110:4) (7:11–25)**
    a. Perfection through Our Melchizedekian High Priest, not the Law (vv. 11–19)
    b. The Oath that Installs Our Permanent High Priest (vv. 20–25)

Explanation of the Text

7:11 Now if perfection had been possible through the Levitical priesthood (for the people were given the law with respect to the priesthood), then what need was there for another priest to arise who is said to be according to the order of Melchizedek and not according to the order

---

3. Some commentators therefore divide these verses into two parts, vv. 11–19 and 20–28 (e.g., Lane, *Hebrews*, 1:178; Weiss, *Der Brief an die Hebräer*, 407), while others identify three parts, vv. 11–19, 20–25, and 26–28 (e.g., Attridge, *Hebrews*, 206; Grässer, *An die Hebräer*, 2:35). However, the difference is not great; almost all the commentators who divide the text into two parts also recognize the distinct character of vv. 26–28 within that second part.

4. Cockerill, *Hebrews*, 313–14; Koester, *Hebrews*, 358.

of Aaron?[5] (Εἰ μὲν οὖν τελείωσις διὰ τῆς Λευιτικῆς ἱερωσύνης ἦν, ὁ λαὸς γὰρ ἐπ᾽ αὐτῆς νενομοθέτηται, τίς ἔτι χρεία κατὰ τὴν τάξιν Μελχισέδεκ ἕτερον ἀνίστασθαι ἱερέα καὶ οὐ κατὰ τὴν τάξιν Ἀαρὼν λέγεσθαι;). The two-word combination (μὲν οὖν) that connects this paragraph to verses 1–10 signals "continuation."[6] Our author continues his argument about Melchizedek, but shifts from a contrast between Melchizedek and Abraham to a focus on the priesthood each represents. This contrast is the concern of verse 11. The author uses a "contrary-to-fact" conditional sentence to argue for the inferiority of the Levitical priesthood: if it could have brought "perfection," then God would not have announced the institution of a different priesthood in Psalm 110:4.[7] The provision of a new Melchizedekian priesthood demonstrates the inadequacy of the former arrangement. The author returns to the language of "perfection" that he has used with respect to Jesus (2:10; 5:9; see also 7:28), now for the first time applying it to believers (see also 9:9; 10:1, 14; 11:40; 12:23; and note also 5:14; 6:1).[8] As we noted earlier (see the notes on 2:10), "perfection" language in Hebrews does not refer to moral perfection; nor does it refer to cultic purity. As Johnson puts it, it is "a matter of human transformation rather than cultic transaction."[9] Peterson, whom I follow on this issue, defines the word here as the "consummation of mankind in eternal relationship with God."[10] Only through our high priest Jesus can we be brought near to God (7:19, 25).

The author inserts a parenthetical remark between the protasis and apodosis of the conditional sentence in verse 11: most English versions recognize the interruption by enclosing the clause in parentheses or dashes. The interruption links the priesthood the author is talking about with the law: "the people were given the law [νενομοθέτηται] with respect to [or 'on the basis of' (the preposition ἐπ᾽)] the priesthood [the antecedent of the pronoun αὐτῆς]." The relationship between the law and the priesthood expressed in this verse can be understood in two different ways, which I suggest in my two alternatives for linking "given the law" with "priesthood." The option chosen by almost all the English versions and defended by a sizable majority of the commentators is to translate something like "on the basis of it [the priesthood] the people received the law" (CSB). It is not hard to see why this option is so popular. The normal meaning of the preposition the author uses here (ἐπί) is "upon," and this base meaning is often extended to mean "upon the basis of." The object of the preposition is usually in the dative when it has this meaning, but there are also examples of this meaning when the

---

5. The second part of the conditional sentence (the apodosis) takes the form of a question (τίς ἔτι χρεία—"Why [is there] yet need . . . ?"). The infinitive ἀνίστασθαι ("to arise"; see the note on v. 15) with its subject, ἕτερον . . . ἱερέα ("another priest" [accusative because it is subject of the infinitive]), explicates "need." The infinitive λέγεσθαι at the end of the verse elaborates "another priest": e.g., one "said" (according to Ps 110:4) to be "according to the order of Melchizedek and not according to the order of Aaron" (see, e.g., NET; contra, e.g., ESV, which takes the participle only with the immediately preceding "according to the order of Aaron").

6. "οὖν," BDAG 737, 2.d; it suggests the translation, which I follow, of "now" (see also ESV; NJB; NASB). The other main option is to separate the two conjunctions—μέν and οὖν—and take the latter to mean "therefore" or "so" (Moule, *Idiom Book*, 162–63; see CEB; NET; NLT).

7. The logic of contrary-to-fact conditional sentences is: if X, then Y; not Y, therefore not X. The protasis of such a sentence is often marked with the particle ἄν—but this particle is not required. See, e.g., Wallace, *Greek Grammar*, 694–96. The author neatly balances the two priestly orders: one "according to Melchizedek" (κατὰ τὴν τάξιν Μελχισέδεκ) vs. one "according to Aaron" (κατὰ τὴν τάξιν Ἀαρών—Aaron being, of course, the descendant of Levi who is the progenitor of the Israelite priests).

8. The Greek word here is τελείωσις, its only occurrence in Hebrews (see also Luke 1:45).

9. Johnson, *Hebrews*, 185.

10. Peterson, *Hebrews and Perfection*, 127–30.

genitive case is used (as here).¹¹ On this reading of the clause, the author is highlighting the vital role of the Levitical priesthood in the life of Israel: the whole law, the Torah that stood as their central covenant document, depends on the priesthood. Perhaps, then, the sense is, as Cockerill puts it, that "living under the law was based on and dependent upon its perpetual functioning."¹²

However, it is telling that Cockerill refers to *living* under the law, while the verb the author uses refers to the *giving* of the law—here, in the passive, with the sense "receive the law."¹³ The difficulty of thinking of the priesthood as the *basis* for the *giving* of the law opens the way to consider the alternative meaning: that the author is saying simply that the people of Israel were given a law that "concerned" the priesthood. The NIV reflects this option: "the law given to the people established that priesthood." This meaning for the combination of verb and preposition is attested and makes better sense in this context.¹⁴ Having denied that God's purposes for humanity could have been attained via the Levitical priesthood, the author adds, as an aside, that this priesthood is inextricably tied to the law as a whole. This connection is immediately exploited by the author in verse 12 and ultimately explains the inability of the priesthood to achieve perfection: it is tied to a law that is "fleshly" (v. 16), and it is weak and useless (v. 18). I will comment further on the author's use of "law" below, but suffice to say here that the author probably has in view the Old Testament law (i.e., the law of Moses or Torah) as a whole.

7:12 For when the priesthood is changed, of necessity there is also a change in the law (μετατιθεμένης γὰρ τῆς ἱερωσύνης ἐξ ἀνάγκης καὶ νόμου μετάθεσις γίνεται). In verse 11, the author makes a simple initial point in his elaboration of the biblical claim about Jesus as a high priest in the order of Melchizedek: the very fact that God announces the appointment of a priest in a different order (Ps 110:4) suggests the inadequacy of the Levitical priests. His argument resembles what he has said about the "rest": David's promise of a "rest" in Psalm 95 reveals that the occupation of the promised land by Israel under Joshua could not be considered the final state of rest (4:7–8). In verse 12, the author builds on the inextricable link between the priesthood and the law he established in the parenthesis in verse 11.¹⁵ If, as the need for a new priest in the order of Melchizedek indicates,

---

11. A few MSS, along with the Majority text, read the dative form of the word here, but this reading is pretty clearly secondary.

12. Cockerill, *Hebrews*, 316.

13. The verb νομοθετέω means here "receive law"; it occurs also in 8:6, where it means simply "ordain." See also νομοθεσία, "receiving the law," in Rom 9:4 and νομοθέτης, "lawgiver," in Jas 4:12. The verb occurs ten times in the LXX, where it means "give the law," or "instruct." The usage is similar in Philo, where the verb occurs fifty times.

14. A close parallel to the sense I am arguing for Hebrews is found in Philo, *Special Laws* 2.35: "these are the regulations laid down by law [νομοθετεῖται] in the case of human beings [ἐπ' ἀνθρώπων]." (Note that Philo, like Hebrews, uses the genitive case after the preposition.) BDAG (364, §4.a) comments on the genitive with ἐπί: "marking contact with the goal that is reached, answering the question 'whither.'" For this meaning of the phrase, see H. W. Hollander, "Hebrews 7:11 and 8:6: A Suggestion for the Translation of *Nenomothetetai Epi*," *BT* 30 (1979): 244–47; Filtvedt, *Identity of God's People*, 101; Lane, *Hebrews*, 1:174; Koester, *Hebrews*, 353; G. Hughes, *Hebrews and Hermeneutics*, 18; G. Guthrie, *Hebrews*, 266; Weiss, *Der Brief an die Hebräer*, 395; Backhaus, *Der Hebräerbrief*, 269; Barry C. Joslin, *Hebrews, Christ, and the Law: The Theology of the Mosaic Law in Hebrews 7:1–10:18*, Paternoster Biblical Monographs (Milton Keynes: Paternoster, 2008), 143.

15. D. Harris, *Hebrews*, 170; Ellingworth, *Hebrews*, 373–74. The γάρ in v. 12, then, is probably not explanatory, as we might expect ("for" in many English versions) but, in keeping with the author's promiscuous use of the conjunction, probably indicates continuation of argument (the versions that do not translate it, then, probably make a good decision: NAB; NJB; CEB; see "and" in NLT).

the priesthood is changed (μετατιθεμένης ... τῆς ἱερωσύνης, a genitive absolute),[16] then there must be a change (μετάθεσις) of the law also. The whole notion of a change in the law's rules about the priesthood stands in strong contrast to the Jewish view of the time. In the Jewish view, the Torah was an expression of God's unchangeable will; and that Torah, as the author has noted in verse 11, lays out the rules for the priesthood. Josephus, for instance, in his treatise *Against Apion*, extols the Torah as a "finer and more equitable polity ... which assigns the administration of its highest affairs to the whole body of priests, and entrusts to the supreme high-priest the direction of the other priests" (185–86). The Second Temple Jewish book Jubilees applies language from the Melchizedek texts to Levi: "And Levi dreamed that he had been appointed priest of the Most High God, he and his sons forever" (32.1).[17] To speak, then, of a "change" in the priesthood and "change" in the law would have been a strongly polemical claim. Many interpreters think that the author confines "law" in this passage and in others in this paragraph to the cultic law.[18] However, as we elaborate in the "Theology in Application" section below, it is better to see the law in Hebrews as referring to the whole law of Moses, with particular emphasis on its cultic rules. The author here, then, sounds a clear note of discontinuity in the role of the law in the people of God, a discontinuity that echoes and is part and parcel of his view of the discontinuity in the covenants (see 8:13).

7:13 For the one about whom these things are said belongs to a different tribe, from which no one has served at the altar (ἐφ᾽ ὃν γὰρ λέγεται ταῦτα, φυλῆς ἑτέρας μετέσχηκεν, ἀφ᾽ ἧς οὐδεὶς προσέσχηκεν τῷ θυσιαστηρίῳ). Verses 13–17 illustrate the contrast between the "order" of Melchizedek and that of Aaron (v. 11), negatively in verses 13–14—Jesus is *not* "of Aaron"—and positively in verses 15–17—Jesus *is* "of Melchizedek."[19] In these first two verses, 13–14, the general principle enunciated in verse 12 is now illustrated (the "for" [γάρ] then has a general explanatory function): the descent of Jesus from the tribe of Judah rather than the tribe of Levi is an example of the "change in law."

"The one about whom these things are said" could be Melchizedek, but is probably Jesus.[20] The author is obviously alluding to the verse that underlies all of verses 11–28, Psalm 110:4, and this verse addresses not Melchizedek but one who is in the order of Melchizedek. The Old Testament stipulates that priests should be descended from Aaron (Exod 28:1–5; cf. Lev 8–9), and Aaron was a descendant of Levi (Exod 4:14). While not all Levites were priests, all priests needed to be Levites. Only men from the tribe of Levi were, then, officially qualified to "serve at the altar."[21] Yet, our author

---

16. There is debate about the exact force of this participle, some taking it as conditional ("if" [NLT]; see von Siebenthal, *Ancient Greek Grammar*, 396; Attridge, *Hebrews*, 200), and others as circumstantial ("when" [most versions]).

17. T. Levi 18 refers to the priesthood "lapsing" and God's raising up a new priest. But the Testaments of the Twelve Patriarchs (of which this is a part) is so full of Christian interpolations that it cannot be used as a reliable guide to first-century Jewish thought.

18. E.g., Kurianal, *Jesus Our High Priest*, 109.

19. Lane, *Hebrews*, 1:183.

20. See, e.g., Michel, *Der Brief an die Hebräer*, 270–71; contra, e.g., Cockerill, *Hebrews*, 318.

21. The verb I translate "serve" (along with most English versions) comes from the Gk. verb προσέχω, which has a range of meaning; BDAG (879–80) lists "be concerned for," "care for"; "pay attention to"; "occupy oneself with," "devote or apply oneself to." This last meaning fits well in Heb 7:13. The author ignores the illegitimate seizure of the high-priestly office by Menelaus, who was descended from Aaron, in the pre-Maccabean period (see 4:25–29).

points out, Jesus belonged to a different tribe—a point he will elaborate in verse 14.

7:14 For it is clear that our Lord has arisen from the tribe of Judah, concerning which tribe Moses says nothing about priests (πρόδηλον γὰρ ὅτι ἐξ Ἰούδα ἀνατέταλκεν ὁ κύριος ἡμῶν, εἰς ἣν φυλὴν περὶ ἱερέων οὐδὲν Μωϋσῆς ἐλάλησεν). The "different tribe" (v. 13) to which Jesus belonged was the tribe of Judah. The author treats this fact as well-known ("it is clear," πρόδηλον [elsewhere in the NT only in 1 Tim 5:24, 25]). Jesus's descent from Judah was evident because of the widespread early Christian conviction that Jesus was the "son of David," the heir of the promises made to David and his descendants (see, e.g., Matt 1:1; Luke 1:32; Rom 1:3; 2 Tim 2:8; Rev 22:16; Jesus is "the Lion of the tribe of Judah" [Rev 5:5]). The verb the author uses to refer to Jesus's descent from Judah (ἀνατέλλω) is one that usually means "rise up" or "spring up"; it therefore refers several times in the New Testament to the "rising" of the sun (Matt 5:45; 13:6; Mark 4:6; 16:2; Jas 1:11). More importantly, the verb and its cognate "rising" (ἀνατολή) are used in several Old Testament messianic passages: Numbers 24:17, where Balaam predicts that "a star will come out [ἀνατελεῖ] of Jacob; a scepter will rise out of Israel"; Zechariah 6:12–13, where the Lord announces a "man whose name is Branch [ἀνατολή], for he shall branch out [ἀνατελεῖ] in his place, and he shall build the temple of the Lord. . . . He shall bear royal honor, and shall sit upon his throne and rule" (NRSV); and Jeremiah 23:5: "I will raise up for David a righteous Branch [ἀνατολήν], and he shall reign as king and deal wisely, and shall execute justice and righteousness in the land" (ESV). This same language is given a messianic interpretation in the New Testament as well (Matt 2:2, 9; Luke 1:78). These texts are probably an adequate basis to conclude that our author has chosen this particular verb to connote the messianic status of Jesus.[22] Johnson argues that the specific reference is to the exaltation of Jesus,[23] but it is more likely that the author refers more generally to the coming of Jesus.

7:15–16 And this is still more evident if another priest according to the likeness of Melchizedek appears, 16 who has taken his position not on the basis of the law, with its fleshly commandment, but on the basis of the power of an indestructible life (καὶ περισσότερον ἔτι κατάδηλόν ἐστιν, εἰ κατὰ τὴν ὁμοιότητα Μελχισέδεκ ἀνίσταται ἱερεὺς ἕτερος, 16 ὃς οὐ κατὰ νόμον ἐντολῆς σαρκίνης γέγονεν ἀλλὰ κατὰ δύναμιν ζωῆς ἀκαταλύτου). The "and" (καί) signals a shift to a new argument. Just what this argument supports, however, is not clear. The Greek at the beginning of verse 15 is elliptical: the author says simply "still more evident it is" (περισσότερον ἔτι κατάδηλόν ἐστιν),[24] leaving it unclear what is "still more evident." The author may be going all the way back to the beginning of the paragraph, implying that the argument of verses 15–16 supplies further evidence that perfection cannot come via the Levitical priesthood.[25] But the negative

---

22. Koester, *Hebrews*, 354–55; Cockerill, *Hebrews*, 320; Grässer, *An die Hebräer*, 2:41; Backhaus, *Der Hebräerbrief*, 271. The translation "descended," then, is contextually accurate ("ἀνατέλλω," BDAG 73, §3; most English versions; contra Cockerill, *Hebrews*, 319), but it loses the connection with the "rising up" language: see KJV: "our Lord sprang out of Judah." The perfect form of the verb—ἀνατέταλκεν—probably stresses the implications of Jesus's origins for his continuing status.

23. Johnson, *Hebrews*, 186–87.

24. The author's reason for shifting from πρόδηλον in v. 14 to κατάδηλον in this verse is not clear. Grässer thinks that the latter might be more forceful than the former (*An die Hebräer*, 2:43), but any difference between them is hard to detect. (Josephus provides the best data, using πρόδηλον sixteen times and κατάδηλον four times, and no clear difference in meaning emerges.) Note also the closely parallel definitions offered in L&N ("πρόδηλος," 28.60; "κατάδηλος," 32.20).

25. Westcott, *Hebrews*, 173.

reference to "law" in verse 16 suggests that, like verses 13–14, verses 15–16 provide further evidence that "the priesthood," with its accompanying law, has been set aside (v. 12).²⁶ The fact that Jesus is *not* "according to the order of Aaron," which the law required for priestly status, is one piece of evidence for the change in the priesthood and the law. But an even more convincing piece of evidence is Jesus's qualification, via his "indestructible life," to belong to the contrasting "order of Melchizedek." However, our author does not here use the word "order" (τάξις) of Melchizedek, but the word "likeness" (ὁμοιότης). This may be simply a stylistic equivalent of "order,"²⁷ but more likely suggests more of a focus on personal likeness than the language of "order" conveys.²⁸

The author uses a form of conditional clause (εἰ with a present indicative verb) that assumes the condition is true for the sake of the argument; and in this case the condition is, in fact, true: "another priest" has appeared (see NLT "since"). The author uses the same language he used in verse 11b to initiate the argument of this paragraph: the "appearing" (using ἀνίστημι) of "another priest" (ἱερεὺς ἕτερος). We have then a kind of "reset," as the author reminds his audience of the central matter in this paragraph. The verb the author uses (ἀνίστημι) often refers to resurrection in the New Testament, and it is possible the author intends to allude to Jesus's resurrection here (most explicitly in NAB, "raised up"; see also perhaps NRSV; ESV; NET; NASB, all "arises").²⁹ However, the author does not refer to Jesus's resurrection very often, and the same verb is used in verse 11, where a reference to resurrection is unlikely. Probably, then, the author means simply that "another priest" has "appeared" on the scene (see "ἀνίστημι," BDAG 83, §7; and note NIV and CEB, "appears").

Continuing the theme that is the heart of this paragraph, the author in verse 16 uses a relative clause ("who [ὅς] . . .") to contrast the basis for the priesthood of the Levites, on the one hand, and of the "other priest," on the other hand. This other priest, Jesus, has "taken his position"³⁰ not "on the basis of the law, with its fleshly commandment, but on the basis of the power of an indestructible life." "On the basis of" translates the preposition κατά, which, as a quick perusal of the BDAG entry ("κατά," 511–13) reveals, has a wide semantic range. The versions display a range of options: "by" (NLT; NET; CEB; NAB), "through" (NRSV), "in virtue of" (NJB), "on the basis of" (NASB; ESV; NIV; CSB "based on"). As my translation makes clear, I favor this last option, giving the preposition a causal meaning (though the instrumental meaning expressed with "by" or "through" is close in meaning here).³¹ Christ's priesthood was *not* based on "the law, with its fleshly commandment." The law's provisions for priesthood, requiring descent from the Levite Aaron, cannot serve as the basis for the priesthood of one who is from a different tribe altogether (vv. 13–14). The author characterizes the law in terms of "fleshly commandment" (ἐντολῆς σαρκίνης). Most translations, and many commentators, view this genitive phrase as expressing the content of the "law" (νόμος); see, for example, NAB:

---

26. Moffatt, *Hebrews*, 79; Attridge, *Hebrews*, 202; Cockerill, *Hebrews*, 321.

27. Ellingworth, *Hebrews*, 378.

28. The author has used this same word in 4:15, where he claims that Jesus is "like" other humans (this is its only other NT occurrence).

29. Koester, *Hebrews*, 355; Johnson, *Hebrews*, 186–87.

30. I translate here the colorless verb γέγονεν, from γίνομαι, a very common verb with a large sematic range. Most English translations supply "priest" as the object as their contextual rendering. The perfect form of the verb underlines the permanence of Christ's appointment.

31. BDAG ("κατά," 512–13, §5.a.δ) notes that the idea of "norm," which is a common idea expressed by κατά, merges with the idea of "reason for." See also Moule, *Idiom Book*, 59 ("by virtue of"); Ellingworth, *Hebrews*, 378; Cockerill, *Hebrews*, 322.

"a law expressed in a commandment concerning physical descent." This translation also assumes that the word "fleshly" (σαρκίνης) refers to the issue of ancestry that our author has referred to in verses 13–14. I think this latter decision is, with qualifications, a good one. The word σάρξ and its cognates have a wide semantic range, and it is notoriously difficult to translate them into English.[32] Here the proximate issue of physical descent is the word's likely referent.[33] However, the author uses the cognate noun σάρξ to describe the law on two other occasions, and in both places, while a focus on the physical and external is clear, it is also the case that the author appears to be making a more general comment about the "earth-relatedness" of the law: regulations about food and drink and washings are "fleshly" regulations (9:10); sacrifices of animals only provide for "fleshly" or "outward" cleansing (9:13). I think, then, that the author, while *referring* here to the commandment about priestly physical descent, is also *connoting* this broader "problem" with the law.[34] This being the case, I also think that "law" refers not to a "legal requirement" but to the law as a whole.[35] The author, then, in my view, is saying that Christ's priestly status did not come about on the basis of the law, which, in keeping with its general character, established an earthly qualification for becoming a priest.

In contrast to the law's basis for priesthood, Jesus becomes our priest on the basis of the power of his "indestructible life." The genitive phrase "indestructible life" (ζωῆς ἀκαταλύτου) probably indicates the source of the "power" (δύναμιν). The word translated in most of our versions as "indestructible" (ἀκαταλύτου) is rare, occurring only here in the New Testament, never in Philo and Josephus, and only once in the LXX (4 Macc. 10.11, "unceasing torments" [NRSV]). Many interpreters, noting the importance of Christ's exaltation for his priestly ministry, think that the author refers here to the "unending" life of Christ as a result of that exaltation.[36] Certainly our author emphasizes the superiority of Christ's priestly ministry in terms of his "ever living" to make intercession for his people (7:24, 25). However, while Jesus's exaltation and subsequent ministry are central for our author,[37] I think it likely that the power that enabled that ministry rested in his eternal nature as Son of God/God.[38]

---

32. The problem is especially acute in Paul's letters because of his significant theological use of the terms. See Douglas J. Moo, "'Flesh' in Romans: A Problem for the Translator," in *The Challenge of Bible Translation: Communicating God's Word to the World: Essays in Honor of Ronald F. Youngblood*, ed. Glen S. Scorgie, Mark L. Strauss, and Steven M. Voth (Grand Rapids: Zondervan, 2003), 36–79.

33. There is considerable difference of opinion over whether the adjective σάρκινος differs in nuance from σαρκικός. The author uses only the former and only here. Paul, however, uses both, and it is difficult to see any difference in meaning between them: cf. esp. 1 Cor 3:1 (σάρκινος) and 3:3 (σαρκικός) (for an argument they are parallel in meaning, see, e.g., Wolfgang Schrage, *Der erste Brief an die Korinther*, vol. 1, 2nd ed., EKKNT 7/1 [Zürich: Benziger, 2008], 281–82; as well as Rom 7:14 (σάρκινος) with 2 Cor 1:12 and 10:4 (both σαρκικός).

34. See, e.g., Grässer, *An die Hebräer*, 2:44; Attridge, *Hebrews*, 202. Several interpreters see this "outward," "earthly" focus as an expression of the author's Middle Platonism, with its characteristic dualisms (e.g., Backhaus, *Der Hebräerbrief*, 267, 271–73). However, any influence from Middle Platonism is probably indirect, as some of its dualistic emphases were absorbed into the apocalyptic Judaism that has directly influenced the author (see the introduction).

35. While sympathetic to the challenge of carrying over some of the complex wording of Hebrews into comprehensible English, I think the English translations do us a disservice here by failing to use the word "law," opting instead for "regulation" (NIV), "legal requirement" (NRSV; ESV; CEB), "legal regulation" (NET; CSB). Only the NASB preserves "law," but gives it a specific focus ("a law of physical requirement").

36. E.g., Peterson, *Hebrews and Perfection*, 110–11; Koester, *Hebrews*, 355.

37. Weiss, *Der Brief an die Hebräer*, 400.

38. See esp. Michael Kibbe, "'You Are a Priest Forever!' Jesus' Indestructible Life in Hebrews 7:16," *HBT* 39 (2017): 134–55; idem, "Is It Finished?," 36–38; Bauckham, "Divinity of Jesus Christ," 31; Westcott, *Hebrews*, 185; Spicq, *L'Épître aux Hébreux*, 2:193; Montefiore, *Hebrews*, 125–26; Cockerill, *Hebrews*, 323–24.

Like his forerunner Melchizedek, Christ has neither "beginning of days or end of life" (v. 3), and it is this essential nature of his that qualifies him to be a priest like Melchizedek, appointed "forever."

7:17 For it is testified that "You are a priest forever, in the order of Melchizedek" (μαρτυρεῖται γὰρ ὅτι Σὺ ἱερεὺς εἰς τὸν αἰῶνα κατὰ τὴν τάξιν Μελχισέδεκ). The author's quotation of Psalm 110:4 is a reminder that this text is the jumping-off point for the author's elaboration of Christ's priestly ministry in verses 11–25. In verses 12–16, his focus has been on the phrase "in the order of Melchizedek," but the reference to Christ's "indestructible life" in verse 16b may allude to the "forever" in Psalm 110:4.

7:18–19 So,[39] **on the one hand, there has been an annulment of the previous commandment because of its weakness and ineffectiveness**[40]**— 19 for the law perfected nothing—and, on the other hand, an introduction of a better hope through which we are drawing near to God** (ἀθέτησις μὲν γὰρ γίνεται προαγούσης ἐντολῆς διὰ τὸ αὐτῆς ἀσθενὲς καὶ ἀνωφελές– 19 οὐδὲν γὰρ ἐτελείωσεν ὁ νόμος–ἐπεισαγωγὴ δὲ κρείττονος ἐλπίδος δι' ἧς ἐγγίζομεν τῷ θεῷ). The significance of Christ's unique priesthood is that believers can "draw near" to God—something that the law and its rules for priestly ministry could not accomplish. In chapter 7 thus far, the author has been almost entirely in expository mode, explaining the significance of Jesus being called a priest "in the order of Melchizedek" with reference to Genesis 14:18–20 (vv. 1–10) and Psalm 110:4 (vv. 11–17). Exposition continues in verses 18–25, but the author also turns directly to his audience, showing how this exposition is relevant to their situation. We can discern a rough parallelism between verses 16–19 and verses 20–25. In both texts, the eternal nature of Jesus's priesthood is highlighted: he has an "indestructible life" (v. 16); he "remains forever" (v. 24), he "always lives to intercede for them" (v. 25). In both texts the author points out the significance for his readers, using "drawing/coming near" language: we have a "better hope through which we are drawing near to God" (v. 19); Jesus is able "to save completely those who come to God through him" (v. 25). These verses make explicit what is implicit throughout our author's exposition: Jesus, our priest "in the order of Melchizedek," stands ready forever to intercede on behalf of his people, assuring us that the way to the Father is always open for us through him.

This "introduction of a better hope" in verse 19 stands in clear contrast to the "annulment of the previous commandment" in verse 18. The words "annulment" (ἀθέτησις) and "introduction" (ἐπεισαγωγή) are both anarthrous and come at the beginning of their respective clauses. The δέ in verse 19b answers to the μέν at the beginning of verse 18 (I have reproduced the contrast, in what might be a bit of an overtranslation, with "on the one hand . . . on the other hand"). This is the first of three times our author uses this kind of a construction in this context (see vv. 20b–21 and vv. 23–24), in each case contrasting the old order of priesthood with the new order inaugurated by Christ.[41] The negative side of this contrast reiterates points that

---

39. "So" translates γάρ, which, as we have seen (see the note on 2:10), the author uses often and in many different ways. The logic of the argument suggests that it is not used here to introduce a reason or explanation ("for," as in NASB and ESV) but is rather a summarizing point of application ("so" is used also in CSB; and several translations do not use any conjunction [NIV; NET; NRSV; CEB]).

40. The two words are adjectives in form, but they are governed by a neuter article (τό), which gives them a substantive and abstract force (Weiss, *Der Brief an die Hebräer*, 401).

41. Massonnet draws attention to this structural element (*L'Épître aux Hébreux*, 191).

the author made earlier. The "previous commandment" (προαγούσης ἐντολῆς) refers to the "fleshly commandment" (ἐντολῆς σαρκίνης) that requires priests to be descendants of Aaron (v. 16).[42] And its "setting aside" or "annulment" (ἀθέτησις) is parallel to the "change" of the priesthood and law in verse 12 (μετάθεσις). The word the author uses here, however, is stronger than the earlier one: a legal cancellation rather than a change or transformation.[43]

The previous commandment was annulled because of its "weakness and ineffectiveness." While "commandment" probably refers specifically to the requirement about Aaronic descent for priests, the author's explanation for the annulment of this specific command probably has in view the law as a whole (see v. 19a).[44] The word I have translated "ineffectiveness" (with, e.g., NJB) is often translated "uselessness"/"useless" (NIV; ESV; NLT; NET; CEB).[45] This latter rendering, however, might give the wrong impression, as if the author was dismissing any benefit to the law. His point seems to be, rather, that the law was unable to accomplish the ultimate purpose of bringing humans into an intimate and lasting relationship with God. A second problem is that the law is "weak" (ἀσθενές). Paul claims that the law was "powerless" "because it was weakened [ἠσθένει] by the flesh [τῆς σαρκός]" (Rom 8:3a)—in other words, fallen human inability to fulfill the law is a major reason the law could not bring full and final forgiveness. The author to the Hebrews uses the language of "weakness" elsewhere to refer to human sin, so it is possible that this argument from human inability is implied here.[46] However, in the case of Hebrews, that human inability is focused on the priests, whose mortality kept them from continuing in office (v. 23) and whose sin required sacrifice to be made for them (v. 27).

In any case, the parenthesis at the beginning of verse 19 makes the key point: the law "perfected nothing" (οὐδέν ... ἐτελείωσεν). The author completes an *inclusio* by returning to the point he started with in verse 11—"if perfection [τελείωσις] had been possible through the Levitical priesthood ..." After this aside, he completes the contrast initiated in verse 18b with its positive side: there is "an introduction[47] of a better hope through which we are drawing near to God." "Hope" (ἐλπίς) refers here not to human "hoping" but to "the thing hoped for, its content or ground." Indeed, Johnson suggests that "hope" here is "a way of designating Jesus himself";[48] note that the "through hope" here becomes "through him [Jesus]" in verse 25.[49]

---

42. Another, less likely, option is that ἐντολή refers to the entire law. The adjectival participle προαγούσης is from προάγω, "go ahead."

43. The word ἀθέτησις occurs once elsewhere in the NT, at Heb 9:26, referring to the "abolishing" of sin's power. The cognate verb often means "reject" in a variety of contexts in the NT, but particularly relevant is the legal application of the word in Gal 3:15b: "just as no one can set aside [ἀθετεῖ] or add to a human covenant that has been duly established, so it is in this case." The word is applied to legal situations often in the papyri (see Attridge, *Hebrews*, 203).

44. Contra, e.g., D. L. Allen, *Hebrews*, 425; Joslin, *Hebrews, Christ, and the Law*, 150–51.

45. The word ἀνωφελής is used only once else in the NT, to characterize "foolish controversies and genealogies and arguments and quarrels" as "unprofitable" (Titus 3:9—as BDAG ("ἀνωφελής," 93, §2) notes, the word here could mean "harmful").

46. See, e.g., Cockerill, *Hebrews*, 325–26. The author uses the cognate noun ἀσθένεια in 4:15; 5:2; 7:28 (it also occurs in 11:34 with reference to physical weakness). The author does not use the adjective ἀσθενής elsewhere.

47. The Greek word for "introduction" is ἐπεισαγωγή, used only here in biblical Greek. Some interpreters think it has the connotation of "bring in in place of" (Lane, *Hebrews*, 1:185–86; Ellingworth, *Hebrews*, 382; appeal is made to Josephus, *Ant.* 11.196, where Esther is introduced "in place of" Vashti, and to two other ancient texts).

48. Johnson, *Hebrews*, 189.

49. Weiss, *Der Brief an die Hebräer*, 402.

See also especially "the hope set before us" in 6:18 (see also 3:6; 10:23). The Old Testament people of God, of course, had a basis for hope: God was their "hope" (e.g., LXX Ps 61:9; 72:28; 141:6). But, sounding a note that resounds throughout the letter, the author stresses that new-covenant believers have a "better" (κρείττων) grounds for hope, by means of which "we are drawing near to God." Some interpreters think that "drawing near" has a cultic connotation: as is noted, the verb the author uses here (ἐγγίζω) sometimes refers to priests or the people drawing near to God to offer sacrifice or otherwise minister before him.[50] However, the verb only rarely is applied to the cult; most of the time in the LXX it refers to other matters, and when it is used of drawing near to God, cultic associations are often absent.[51] The present tense of the verb here (ἐγγίζομεν) suggests that this "drawing near" is an opportunity even now open to those who are committed to Jesus as their high priest.

7:20–22 And to the degree that it was not without an oath—for, on the one hand, those who have become priests became priests without the taking of an oath, 21 but, on the other hand, this one became a priest by the one who said to him, "The Lord has sworn and will not change his mind: 'You are a priest forever'"— 22 to the same degree Jesus has become the guarantor of a better covenant (Καὶ καθ' ὅσον οὐ χωρὶς ὁρκωμοσίας οἱ μὲν γὰρ χωρὶς ὁρκωμοσίας εἰσὶν ἱερεῖς γεγονότες, 21 ὁ δὲ μετὰ ὁρκωμοσίας διὰ τοῦ λέγοντος πρὸς αὐτόν, Ὤμοσεν κύριος καὶ οὐ μεταμεληθήσεται· Σὺ ἱερεὺς εἰς τὸν αἰῶνα. 22 κατὰ τοσοῦτο [καὶ] κρείττονος διαθήκης γέγονεν ἔγγυος Ἰησοῦς). The oath referred to in Psalm 110:4 signifies the assurance that Christ's priesthood provides for those who belong to him. In verses 11–19, the author has focused on the change of order that has taken place. Now, in verses 20–28, he focuses on the superiority of the new order.[52] As I noted in the introduction to this section, an *inclusio* marked by the word "oath-taking" (ὁρκωμοσία) encloses verses 20–28 but, within this section, verses 26–28 stand out as a concluding application to the whole chapter.

The framework of verses 20–22 consists of a contrast within a comparison. The comparison is denoted with the paired phrases "to the degree that" (καθ' ὅσον) in verse 20a and "to the same degree" (κατὰ τοσοῦτο) in verse 22a.[53] Most English translations do not attempt to reproduce these complementary phrases, since it is difficult for English readers to follow so long and complicated a sentence. I have offered a translation that preserves the Greek structure (as do also the NASB; NAB; NET). The contrast, then, comes in the somewhat parenthetical verses 20b–21, marked with the correlative particles μέν . . . δέ ("on the one hand . . . on the other hand").

In verses 11–19, the author has used as his base text the final line from Psalm 110:4: "in the order of Melchizedek" (see vv. 11, 15, 17). In verses 20–25 (–28), his attention shifts to the first line in the verse: "the Lord has sworn and will not change his mind."

---

50. Exod 19:22; Lev 21:21, 23; Ezek 42:13; 43:19; 44:13; 45:4; see Ellingworth, *Hebrews*, 382; Cockerill, *Hebrews*, 327; Weiss, *Der Brief an die Hebräer*, 402.

51. Exod 24:2; Ps 148:14; Hos 12:7; Isa 29:13; 41:1, 5; see Lane, *Hebrews*, 1:186. The verb occurs forty-four times in the NT, with a wide range of applications. No other NT text uses the verb with reference to a cultic approach to God. The only other occurrence in Hebrews is in 10:25, referring to the "approaching" of the day of the Lord.

52. Lane, *Hebrews*, 1:180; cf. Vanhoye, *La Structure Littéraire*, 132–33; Peterson, *Hebrews and Perfection*, 104.

53. For the correlative function of these two phrases, see "ὅσος," BDAG 729, §3. Some interpreters, especially in past centuries, connected the former phrase, καθ' ὅσον, with v. 19 (e.g., Calvin, *Hebrews*, 100).

This marks a new stage in the author's creative exploration of this text; he has not yet referred to this line in the psalm—his earlier quotations don't even include it (see 5:6; 7:17). The author has, however, earlier brought up the significance of God's oath-taking, in his discussion of the promises made to Abraham (6:12–20), and this earlier text provides some basis for his analysis of its significance here.[54] In contrast to this earlier text, however, where the author used the word ὅρκος to refer to the oath (6:16, 17), he here uses the word ὁρκωμοσία, which can mean "oath-taking" (see NAB here).[55] However, most English translations render simply "oath," and this would appear to be justified by LXX passages where the word also means simply "oath."[56] What, however, was it that the oath confirmed? Most of our English versions reflect the elliptical nature of the Greek by referring simply to "it" or "this." The author could be referring to the introduction of a better hope (v. 19), but more likely he is reflecting broadly on the point he has made in verses 11–19: "this new system was established with a solemn oath" (NLT).[57]

The author will complete his thought in verse 22: the oath signifies the confidence we can have that Jesus does, indeed, guarantee a whole new-covenant arrangement. Before he completes this thought, however, he takes a slight detour, once again contrasting the Old Testament priests in general with Jesus, the priest "in the order of Melchizedek." Old Testament priests were appointed to their offices without an oath,[58] while, as Psalm 110:4 affirms, an oath was taken by the one who appointed the new priest:[59] "The Lord has sworn and will not change his mind: 'You are a priest forever.'" As I noted above, the author quotes selectively, reproducing the part of the verse relevant to the point he makes here.

Verse 22, as we have seen, correlates with verse 20a: "to the degree that" the new system was introduced with an oath, so, "to the same degree has Jesus become the guarantor of a better covenant." It is possible, indeed, that the construction has a causal nuance: *because* the new system was introduced with a divine oath, with all the assurance that such an oath carries, therefore Jesus is indeed able to guarantee the new and better covenant.[60] The word "covenant" (διαθήκη) occurs here for the first time in Hebrews, although it will become a dominant idea in the next two chapters. Indeed, scholars sometimes refer to a "*diathēkē* theology" in Hebrews: seventeen of the thirty-three New Testament occurrences of the word occur in Hebrews. As he has done before, the author smuggles into his argument a word that anticipates an important theological development to come. The author again here uses the word that evokes a central argument of the letter: the covenant Jesus guarantees is "better" (κρείττων) than the previous arrangement (to which the author has alluded with

---

54. Backhaus, *Der Hebräerbrief*, 278.
55. See, e.g., Westcott, *Hebrews*, 188 ("the whole action, and not simply the oath").
56. The word occurs only three times in the LXX, and the simple translation "oath" seems to be justified in two of them (Ezek 17:18, 19; cf. also 1 Esd 8:93 [NRSV numbering] and Josephus, *Ant.* 16.163). The word does not occur outside of Heb 7:20–28 in the NT. Others think that the author uses the word with the expanded meaning of "the act of taking an oath" (Massonnet, *L'Épître aux Hébreux*, 191). Some interpreters also think the longer word used here is "more solemn" (Attridge, *Hebrews*, 207; D. Harris, *Hebrews*, 179).
57. Most interpreters, however, supply "he became a priest" (Attridge, *Hebrews*, 175; Weiss, *Der Brief an die Hebräer*, 408).
58. The Greek is εἰσὶν ἱερεῖς γεγονότες, the combination of εἰσίν with the participle forming a perfect periphrastic tense (according to Bruce, an "elegant periphrasis" [*Hebrews*, 170]).
59. The author speaks elliptically in v. 21a, and we must supply the verbal idea "become a priest" from v. 20: "but . . . this one became a priest by the one who said [διὰ τοῦ λέγοντες] to him" (διά indicates agent). See also 5:5, "the one who said to him" (ὁ λαλήσας πρὸς αὐτόν).
60. On the causal nuance, see Ellingworth, *Hebrews*, 383.

the language of "law" and "commandment" [vv. 11, 12, 16, 18, 19]). Following a pattern we have seen the author using before (cf. 3:1; 6:20), the author puts "Jesus" (Ἰησοῦς) at the end of the verse for emphasis: the guarantor of this better covenant is none other than Jesus. The word we are translating "guarantor" (ἔγγυος) was a technical legal term, well-attested in popular Greek, denoting a person who put himself or herself forward as a pledge to insure the fulfillment of a contract.[61] The author will characterize Jesus later on as the "mediator" of the covenant, a role that is fundamental to the establishing of a covenant (8:6; 9:15; 12:24; the Greek word is μεσίτης). Here, however, the emphasis is on Jesus's role in completing the covenant promises.[62] We can be confident that God will confer on us every promised benefit of the "better covenant" because Jesus himself, a priest confirmed by God's own oath, stands as its guarantor.

7:23–24 In addition, on the one hand, there are many who have become priests, because they were prevented by death from continuing, 24 but, on the other hand, Jesus, because he remains forever, has a priesthood that is perpetual (καὶ οἱ μὲν πλείονές εἰσιν γεγονότες ἱερεῖς διὰ τὸ θανάτῳ κωλύεσθαι παραμένειν· 24 ὁ δὲ διὰ τὸ μένειν αὐτὸν εἰς τὸν αἰῶνα ἀπαράβατον ἔχει τὴν ἱερωσύνην). Jesus's high-priestly ministry is better than that of the Levitical priests because, unlike them, he lives forever. The author once again frames his argument in terms of a contrast (μέν . . . δέ), a contrast that I once again "overtranslate" to reveal what is going on in the Greek (this same μέν . . . δέ pairing is used also in vv. 18–19 and vv. 20b–21). My translation "in addition" brings out the force of καί here: to introduce a further argument. This argument picks up the important emphasis in this context on the eternal nature of Jesus and his work (vv. 16, 25, 28), an emphasis probably reflecting the "forever" in Psalm 110:4.

Set in contrast to this eternal priesthood are the Old Testament Levitical priests. The author's claim that there have been "many" of them[63] in this context means "many over time," as the reason for these many priests indicates: they were prevented from continuing by death. Following his Psalm 110:4 text, the author continues to speak of priests rather than high priests, although his focus may implicitly be on the high priest. Josephus, a Jewish historian roughly contemporaneous with the author, claims there were eighty-three high priests from Aaron to the fall of the temple in AD 70 (*Ant.* 20.227). The "continuing" (παραμένειν) here refers to their continuing in office, an obvious interpretation that most English versions introduce in their translations.

In contrast to these many (high) priests stands one who has a "perpetual" priesthood. There is considerable debate over the meaning of the word I translate "perpetual" (ἀπαράβατον). The problem in defining it is partly a lack of data: it occurs only here in the NT, never in the LXX, twice in Josephus, and once in Philo. A few interpreters, referring to early Greek interpreters, think it means "cannot be passed on," "without a successor."[64] However,

---

61. H. Preisker, "ἔγγυος," *TDNT* 2:329. The word occurs only here in the NT and only three times in (the latter books of) the LXX (2 Macc 10:28; Sir 29:15, 16).

62. Cockerill, *Hebrews*, 330.

63. The Greek is οἱ μὲν πλείονές εἰσιν γεγονότες ἱερεῖς, which probably should be unpacked as: these (οἱ) became (εἰσὶν γεγονότες, a periphrastic perfect) priests (ἱερεῖς, predicate nominative) as a plurality (πλείονες as a predicative modifier) (see Delitzsch, *Hebrews*, 1:369). The adjective πλείων is technically a comparative ("greater," "more") but is used here with a simple positive sense ("many")—a shift that is found in many NT adjectives (Turner, *Syntax*, 30).

64. P. Hughes, *Hebrews*, 268–69; Bruce, *Hebrews*, 171.

BDAG ("ἀπαράβατος," 97) states bluntly, "This [meaning] is found nowhere else." Based on its use in some secular Greek sources, Attridge thinks it might mean "inviolable"—as part of the eternal realm, it has an absolute, final significance.[65] Most interpreters today, however, think it must mean "permanent" or "perpetual" (see NIV; NRSV; ESV; NET; CEB; NJB; NASB).[66] In contrast to the Old Testament priests, who could not "continue" (παραμένειν) because they died, Jesus, our high priest, holds a perpetual priesthood "because he remains" (διὰ τὸ μένειν αὐτόν). Our author lays stress on the fact that Jesus himself remains "the same" (1:12); he "is the same yesterday and today and forever" (13:8). The author has already in this chapter made the same point about Jesus's priesthood (v. 3), and, as we have seen, he has highlighted Jesus's eternal character as basic to his unique priestly significance (vv. 16, 25, 28; cf. "forever" in Ps 110:4).

7:25 For this reason, he is able to save completely those who come to God through him, since he always lives to intercede for them (ὅθεν καὶ σῴζειν εἰς τὸ παντελὲς δύναται τοὺς προσερχομένους δι' αὐτοῦ τῷ θεῷ, πάντοτε ζῶν εἰς τὸ ἐντυγχάνειν ὑπὲρ αὐτῶν). As a consequence (ὅθεν, "for this reason") of the fact that Jesus "remains forever" (v. 24, reiterated in v. 25b), he is "able to save completely those who come to God through him." This is the first, and only, time that the author uses the verb "save" (σῴζω) to depict the benefit that Jesus wins for his people (the verb is used with respect to Jesus in 5:7; and the cognate σωτηρία, "salvation," occurs in 1:14; 2:3, 10; 5:9; 6:9; 9:28; see also 11:7). The meaning of the phrase that qualifies "save," εἰς τὸ παντελές, is debated. It might have a temporal force, meaning "always" (NAB); "for all time" (RSV; NRSV); "once and forever" (NLT).[67] Or it might be used modally, describing the completeness or perfection of the salvation (see "completely" in NIV; NET; CSB; CEB).[68] I think the evidence points to this latter meaning as the best of these two options.[69] However, granted the author's view of salvation as inaugurated at the point of faith but only finally secured in the future, the "completeness" of the salvation has an inevitable temporal aspect to it as well.[70] I am arguing not for a double meaning but for a single meaning that includes a temporal element in the nature of the "completeness" or "perfection" of our salvation. The idea is somewhat related to the author's famous emphasis on the once-for-all nature of Christ's high priestly atoning work and reminds us again that, while the author warns his

---

65. Attridge, *Hebrews*, 210. The word is translated "inviolate" by the Loeb editors in Josephus, *Contra Apion* 2.293, and Philo, *Eternity* 112 (see also Josephus, *Ant.* 18.266).

66. See, e.g., "ἀπαράβατος," BDAG 97; "ἀπαράβατος," L&N 13.61, "unchanging"; Ellingworth, *Hebrews*, 390–91; Lane, *Hebrews*, 1:176.

67. See, e.g., Moffatt, *Hebrews*, 100; Bruce, *Hebrews*, 173; Ellingworth, *Hebrews*, 391.

68. Lane, *Hebrews*, 1:174; D. Harris, *Hebrews*, 183; Koester, *Hebrews*, 365.

69. The word παντελής occurs only one other time in the NT, in the same construction as here (εἰς τὸ παντελές): Luke 13:11: "she was bent over and could not straighten up *at all/fully*." It is not clear whether the phrase modifies "not" (μή)—"not at all"—or "straighten up" (ἀνακύψαι)—"straighten up fully"—but in either case it is modal.

70. Attridge, *Hebrews*, 210; Grässer, *An die Hebräer*, 2:62; Cockerill, *Hebrews*, 334–35. As J. Preisker puts it, the "totality" "can hardly be expounded in only a single direction" (G. Delling, "τέλος, κτλ," *TDNT* 8:67); France claims "the two senses are not in competition" ("Hebrews," 100). This modal/temporal sense can be seen in the one occurrence of the word in the LXX: "but those who had held fast to God even to death and had received the full [παντελῆ] enjoyment of deliverance" (3 Macc. 7.16 NRSV). Philo uses the word 156 times, usually with a modal force but often in contexts that suggest an additional temporal nuance; e.g., he refers several times to "utter destruction" (*Alleg. Interp.* 2.33; *Drunkenness* 23; *Cherubim* 92; *Worse* 178; *Unchangeable* 16).

readers about failure to persevere, he also stresses the utterly complete nature of the salvation that our high priest secures for us.

The author describes those who experience this "absolute" salvation as "those who come near" (τοὺς προσερχομένους), language that is found in the LXX to describe people who "draw near" to God, sometimes in the context of the cult (see the note on 4:16). The author uses the present tense to indicate this "coming near" to God is a process: by faith we enter his presence through the work of Christ, our high priest, but faith must continue to be exercised (combined with endurance, as the author will emphasize in 10:32–39) as we look to the day when we will be fully and finally in his presence. God's provision of "final and complete" salvation requires humans to respond with continuing faith.

The basis for this complete salvation is the intercessory work of Christ: he "always lives" (πάντοτε ζῶν; the participle is probably causal [NIV; ESV]) to "intercede" for us. The verb the author uses for "intercede" (ἐντυγχάνω) is not applied to the issue of the forgiveness of sins in the LXX, but it is in early Christianity; see especially Romans 8:34: Christ is "at the right hand of God" "interceding for us" (the verb occurs also in Acts 25:24; Rom 8:27; 11:2). The author certainly views Jesus's sacrifice as a basic atoning moment; but, in keeping with his emphasis throughout the letter, he highlights here Jesus's ongoing ministry of intercession as a critical means of ultimate salvation. Jesus, our great high priest, represents us before God, providing access to the Father in prayer and provision for the forgiveness of sins. In this verse, the author begins to close off this chapter by weaving into his teaching some of his characteristic themes and emphases; and, as Backhaus notes, in a general way, the "through him" and "for them" get right to the heart of the author's soteriology.[71]

Theology in Application

The role of the law of Moses in the lives of the new-covenant people of God is a contentious theological issue, with obvious practical implications. As a Christian, how should I read the Old Testament law? How is it still authoritative for me? What parts of it must I obey? These questions are usually debated with reference to the teaching of Jesus (especially in the Sermon on the Mount) and of the apostle Paul. But the letter of the Hebrews has its own contribution to make. However, as is typical for this letter, it comes at this issue from a perspective distinct from that which we find in Paul and, for the most part, the Gospels.

When Paul talks about the law of Moses, he usually has in view what we might call the "moral" dimension of the law: its commandments having to do with the way people are to live. In Hebrews, however, the focus is almost entirely on the ceremonial or cultic law. Indeed, most scholars argue that the author *limits* his focus to this dimension of the law.[72] As we have seen in this passage (vv. 12, 16, 18), the author

---

71. Backhaus, *Der Hebräerbrief*, 280.
72. See, e.g., Alan C. Mitchell, "'A Sacrifice of Praise': Does Hebrews Promote Supersessionism?," in Mason and McCruden, *Reading the Epistle to the Hebrews*, 260 (commenting on 7:12).

views this law as ineffective and no longer in force—a point he reiterates elsewhere (e.g., 10:1–2). This discontinuity in the direct authority of the law would, then, apply only to the cultic law. And this, in turn, would fit into a popular way of thinking about the role of the Mosaic law in the life of believers—namely, that Christ's own sacrifice ends the need to obey the "cultic" law, and the shift from a national focus in the Old Testament to a universalizing one in the New Testament means the "civil" law is no longer applicable, but that the "moral" law continues to have direct authority over the people of God.[73]

However, there are problems with this scenario. First, in general, we have to be cautious about dividing the law up into categories. First-century Judaism emphasized the unity of the law. Dividing it into different types (e.g., "moral," "ceremonial," "civil") in terms of its applicability was unknown: the law was treated as a unity, and people could not "pick and choose" which parts they would obey. This same perspective appears to have carried over into early Christianity: "for whoever keeps the whole law and yet stumbles at just one point is guilty of breaking all of it" (Jas 2:10); "again I declare to every man who lets himself be circumcised that he is obligated to obey the whole law" (Gal 5:3).

Second, and more important, I question if the author's teaching on the law is *confined to* the cultic elements of the law. To be sure, virtually all the author's references to the law are in contexts where Christ's high-priestly ministry is the concern. See, for instance, the first occurrence of "law" (νόμος) in Hebrews (7:5): "the law requires the descendants of Levi who become priests to collect a tenth from the people." The context of the cult is clear in most other uses of "law" as well: 7:12, 16, 19, 28; 8:4; 9:22; 10:8. The author also uses "commandment" (ἐντολή) to denote an individual command within the law; and most of these also are regulations concerning the cult (7:5, 16, 18). Nevertheless, there are also indications that our author uses "law" to refer to the entire body of Mosaic legislation—the Torah. He warns in 10:28 that "anyone who rejected the law of Moses died without mercy"; clearly the entire law is in view here. A general reference to the law as a whole seems to be likely also in 9:19, which refers to Moses proclaiming "every command of the law to all the people." The author's claim in 7:11 that the law was given with respect to the priesthood suggests that "law" there refers to something larger than the priestly law per se. These texts suggest that the author does not *limit* the word "law" to the cultic law. Rather, he thinks of "law" as encompassing the entire Mosaic legislation while focusing on the cultic requirements of that law.[74] The role of the law in anticipating

---

73. E.g., Calvin argues, with respect to 7:12, that it is only the priestly law that is abolished (*Hebrews*, 96). See also Joslin, *Hebrews, Christ, and the Law*, 143–48.

74. See esp. Filtvedt, *Identity of God's People*, 99–112. See also, e.g., Mackie, *Eschatology and Exhortation*, 60–63; Cockerill, *Hebrews*, 317.

Christ's high-priestly mediation, and providing the categories within which it can be understood, is critical for the author.

While focused, then, on the legal provisions for sacrifice, tabernacle, and priesthood—matters that loom so large in chapters 5–10—the author is at the same time making points about the larger body of which those provisions are a part. Like Jesus and Paul, then, the author affirms the divine origin and inherent "goodness" of the law, even as he makes clear that the law and, by extension, the covenant it mediated, was a preliminary stage in God's plan of salvation. God indeed "spoke" in the law, but he has now spoken decisively in the Son (1:1–2). The Son and the new covenant he inaugurates are the "reality" anticipated by the "shadow" of the law (10:1).

In contrast to an influential trend in recent interpretation of Hebrews that downplays any criticism of Judaism or the law per se, the author clearly critiques the law. While it is God's gift to his people Israel, the author makes clear that the law was never adequate in itself to provide intimate and permanent access to God. It was weak and ineffectual (7:18); it focused on the outward ("fleshly": 7:16; see also 9:13) and was unable to cleanse the conscience (9:15; 10:2). To be sure, it is important not to take this criticism too far. The author clearly affirms the divine origin and beneficial purpose of the law (e.g., 1:1–2; 2:2–3; cf. 4:12–13). Moreover, he brings out a certain kind of continuity by placing the "change" in the law (7:12) in the context of the new covenant. An important provision in this covenant was the writing of God's laws in the mind and on the heart (8:10; 10:16; cf. Jer 31:33). The coming of a new covenant, then, means not simply a cancellation or annulment of the law but its internalization and transformation.[75]

If we ask why, according to Hebrews, this "change" had to occur, the answer appears to focus on the inherent weakness of the law. Unlike Paul, who tends to stress *human* weakness, rendering humans incapable of fulfilling the law, the author to the Hebrews focuses on the weakness of *the law itself*. As Backhaus puts it, "For Paul, humans weaken the law because they are flesh; for Hebrews, the law fails to rescue humans because the law is flesh."[76] There is some truth in this observation. Paul, focusing usually on the ethical dimension of the law, argues that the power of sin prevents humans from fulfilling that law, thereby leading to condemnation. Hebrews, focusing on the cultic law, sees that law itself as inadequate to care for the human dilemma. But both authors are united in claiming that the Mosaic law is unable to provide full and final forgiveness of sins or to overcome the power of sin that rules human beings. And both authors agree in treating the law as having lost its direct authority in light of its inextricable connection to the old covenant, a covenant that

---

75. A point that is at the heart of Joslin's book (*Hebrews, Christ, and the Law*).

76. Backhaus, *Der Hebräerbrief*, 274 (my translation).

has been superseded by the new covenant inaugurated by Christ. For both Paul and Hebrews, then, the shift in salvation history is a fundamental reason why there has been a "change" in the law. The age of grace has superseded the age of the law (Rom 6:14, 15; Gal 3:15–29); now that the "reality" has appeared, the "shadow" is no longer the focal point (Heb 10:1).[77]

Our author, then, treats the law as a whole as a constituent part of the old covenant, which is "obsolete and outdated," a covenant superseded by a new covenant, superior to the old, "established on better promises" (8:6, 13). Therefore, while Hebrews comes at the issue of the law from a different angle than do Jesus or Paul, the book appears to be in line with them in treating the law as no longer having direct authority over the people of God.[78] At the same time, the author makes clear that the Old Testament continues to speak directly and meaningfully to the people of God. It is just that the words God speaks in the Old Testament have to be sifted in the hermeneutical filter of new-covenant fulfillment to determine how they now relate to God's new-covenant people.

---

77. See, e.g., Hooker, "Christ, the 'End' of the Cult," 207–10.

78. For this view of the teaching of Jesus and Paul on the law, see Douglas J. Moo, "Jesus and the Authority of the Mosaic Law," *JSNT* 20 (1984): 3–49; Moo, "The Law of Moses or the Law of Christ," in Feinberg, *Continuity and Discontinuity*, 203–18; Moo, "The Law of Christ as the Fulfillment of the Law of Moses: A Modified Lutheran View," in *The Law, the Gospel, and the Modern Christian: Five Views* (Grand Rapids: Zondervan, 1993), 319–76.

Hebrews 7:26–28

Literary Context

As I have noted earlier (see the introduction to vv. 11–28), the last three verses of chapter 7 have a dual relationship to their context. On the one hand, the words "oath" and "made perfect" in verse 28 form *inclusios* with "oath" in verses 20–22 and "perfection"/"made perfect" in verses 11 and 19. These connections suggest that verses 26–28 belong with verses 11–25 (or at least 19–25). On the other hand, these verses also reach back into the letter as far as 4:14 to provide an interim summary of much of the author's teaching about Jesus as our high priest.

"high priest" (v. 26)—see 2:17; 3:1; 4:14, 15; 5:1, 5, 10; 6:20 (not used in ch. 7 until here)
"holy, blameless, pure," "set apart from sinners" (v. 26)—see "yet he did not sin" (4:15); "reverent submission" (5:7)
"exalted above the heavens" (v. 26)—"ascended into heaven" (4:14)
"unlike the other high priests, he does not need to offer sacrifices day after day, first for his own sins" (v. 27); "the law appoints as high priests men in all their weakness" (v. 28)—a contrast hinted at in 5:2, which describes high priests in general as "subject to weakness" (5:2) and as those who have "to offer sacrifices for [their] own sins" (5:3)
the contrast between the law and the oath (v. 28)—see 7:11–25
"the Son" (v. 28)—the key title of Jesus in the early chapters (1:2, 5, 8; 3:6; 4:14; 5:5, 8; 6:6; 7:3)
"made perfect" (v. 28)—"make the pioneer of their salvation perfect" (2:10); "once made perfect" (5:9)
"forever" (v. 28)—"a high priest forever" (6:20); "an indestructible life" (7:16); "you are a priest forever" (7:17, 21 [Ps 110:4]); "Jesus lives forever" (7:24); "he always lives to intercede for them" (7:25)

Some of these points receive continuing emphasis in subsequent chapters; for example, the repeated sacrifices of the Old Testament high priests, in contrast to Jesus's one sacrifice (9:25; 10:11), and the need of Old Testament high priests to offer sacrifice for themselves (9:7). Other points that the author takes up later are introduced here for the first time: Jesus's "offering himself" (9:12, 14, 25–26, 28; 10:10) and the "once-for-all" (ἐφάπαξ) nature of that sacrifice (9:12; 10:10; cf. also ἅπαξ in 9:26, 28). Verses 26–28 form, then, a key transitional point in the author's argument, reiterating key points in his presentation of Jesus as our high priest from earlier passages and introducing new ones that, with others, will become important in what follows.[1]

I. The Exalted Son and a Rest for the People of God (1:1–4:13)
II. **Our Great High Priest and His Ministry (4:14–10:31)**
    A. Exhortation: Persevere through the Power of Our Exalted High Priest (4:14–16)
    B. Exposition: High Priests and Our High Priest (5:1–10)
    C. Exhortation: Move on to Maturity (5:11–6:20)
    D. Exposition: A High Priest "According to the Order of Melchizedek" (7:1–28)
        1. Melchizedek's Supremacy over Abraham (Gen 14:17–20) (7:1–10)
        2. The Supremacy and Sufficiency of Our High Priest (Psalm 110:4) (7:11–25)
→   3. **The High Priest Who Is Also the Son (7:26–28)**
    E. Exposition: The Ministry of Our High Priest (8:1–10:18)
    F. Exhortation and Warning: Appropriating the Benefits of Our High Priest's Ministry (10:19–31)
III. Exhortation: Follow and Serve the Pioneer of Our Faith through Endurance and Faith (10:32–13:25)

Main Idea

Jesus's unique identity as the Son of God qualifies him to be a high priest unlike any other—perfect in himself and perfectly able to take care of the human sin problem.

---

1. A number of interpreters make this point about these verses; see, e.g., Weiss, *Der Brief an die Hebräer*, 407; Cockerill, *Hebrews*, 337; Ellingworth, *Hebrews*, 392 ("a great nodal point in the argument"). G. Guthrie (*Structure of Hebrews*, 82–83) notes the way 7:27–28 picks up key emphases from 5:1–3.

Translation

Hebrews 7:26–28

26a	assertion	**It is indeed fitting for us**
26b	content	to have such a high priest, one who is
26c	description 1	holy,
26d	list	blameless,
26e	list	pure—
26f	description 2	set apart from sinners and
26g	description 3	exalted above the heavens.
27a	assertion	This high priest does not have the need,
27b	comparison	as did the former high priests,
27c	content	to daily offer sacrifices
27d	reference	first for his own sins and
27e	sequence	then for the sins of the people.
27f	assertion	**This high priest offered a sacrifice for sins**
27g	time	once for all
27h	circumstance	when he offered himself.
28a	explanation (of 27)	For
28b	assertion	**the law appoints men**
28c	description	who had weakness
28d	complement (of 28b)	as high priests,
28e	contrast	but **the word of the oath . . .**
28f	description	which came after the law
28g	predicate (of 28e)	**. . . appoints a Son**
28h	description	who has been perfected
28i	time	forever.

Structure

Jesus's superiority, as a high priest "in the order of Melchizedek," is revealed in his own perfect character (v. 26), which means he does not have to offer a sacrifice for his own sins (v. 27a). Indeed, the sacrifice he offers has a definitive and final effect—that sacrifice being himself (v. 27b). Summarizing a key theme from verses 11–25, the author then concludes by contrasting Jesus's method of appointment with other high priests—the oath rather than the law—and Jesus's own nature, as the Son, in contrast to that of other priests, characterized by "weakness" (v. 28).

Exegetical Outline

→ **3. The High Priest Who Is Also the Son (7:26–28)**

Explanation of the Text

7:26 It is indeed fitting for us to have such a high priest, one who is holy, blameless, pure—set apart from sinners and exalted above the heavens (Τοιοῦτος γὰρ ἡμῖν καὶ ἔπρεπεν ἀρχιερεύς, ὅσιος ἄκακος ἀμίαντος, κεχωρισμένος ἀπὸ τῶν ἁμαρτωλῶν καὶ ὑψηλότερος τῶν οὐρανῶν γενόμενος). Further indications of the superiority of Jesus's high-priestly ministry are his sinlessness and his ascension to the highest heaven. The author once again links these verses with their context with the particle γάρ, and, once again, some translations simply default to the standard gloss of "for" here (NRSV; ESV; NET; NASB; CSB).[2] These translations suggest that verse 26, or verses 26–28, explain or ground something in the previous context, perhaps especially explaining why Christ is able to intercede for us and thus save "completely" (v. 25). However, as we have seen, verses 26–28 reiterate points the author has been making as far back as 4:14. Probably, then, the author uses γάρ again here in a "loose" sense, and the transition is more summary than explanation.[3] Word order may suggest a particular emphasis the author intends in verse 26a: "such" (τοιοῦτος) occurs at the beginning of the clause and "high priest" at its end: "such a one is indeed fitting for us, as a high priest."[4] This reading also suggests that "such" does not refer back to what the author had earlier said about Jesus as high priest, but ahead, to verse 26b and following.[5] The colon in, for example, NET, brings out the sense very well: "for it is indeed fitting for us to have such a high priest: holy, innocent, undefiled." The "us" (ἡμῖν) points to a shift from exposition (with implied application throughout) to direct application (note also "*we* draw near to God" in v. 19).

This kind of a high priest, the author is suggesting, is precisely what we need. He begins with the moral qualities of Jesus as high priest, using a rapid-fire series of three adjectives: "holy, blameless, pure."[6] We could analyze the exact nuances among each adjective, but this might miss the point: the author is using them together to create a general picture of a high priest who is morally pure.[7] I think it likely that the next description, in the form of an

---

2. The author also uses a καί, which, as is usually the case when it occurs with another conjunction, is adverbial; perhaps here "indeed."

3. See esp. Attridge, *Hebrews*, 212 (who uses the "loose" description); also D. Harris, *Hebrews*, 184. And see the note on 2:10.

4. I paraphrase Westcott, *Hebrews*, 193.

5. As Lane points out, while τοιοῦτος usually looks back to something before it in the NT, when it is followed by a correlative (in this case the relative pronoun ὅς in v. 27), it refers forward (*Hebrews*, 1:191).

6. This series is similar to the series in v. 3: "without father, without mother, without genealogy," and, as is the case there, some scholars suspect this rhythm might point to an underlying hymn. Older scholars discerned a hymn underlying all of vv. 26–28; more recently, the hymnic background is cited only for v. 26 (e.g., Rissi, *Die Theologie des Hebräerbriefs*, 86–87). However, evidence for a hymn in the writing of an author so obviously skilled in literary art is not so clear. See esp. Weiss, *Der Brief an die Hebräer*, 420, for this conclusion and survey of proposals.

7. We should, however, note that the word I (and most translations) translate as "holy"—ὅσιος—is not the "usual" word

adjectival participial phrase—"set apart from sinners" (κεχωρισμένος ἀπὸ τῶν ἁμαρτωλῶν)—continues this same emphasis.[8] I disagree here with most scholars, who take the phrase with what follows, seeing it as another way of asserting Jesus's physical transition into the heavenly realms.[9] However, I think the author's decision to use "sinners" rather than, say, "humans" (ἄνθρωποι), suggests a moral rather than spatial interpretation. The phrase will then reiterate the point the author has made earlier about the sinlessness of Jesus our high priest (4:15; cf. 5:7).

The final characteristic of Jesus listed in this verse that makes him "fitting" to be our high priest is his elevation "above the heavens." As he regularly does, the author attaches Jesus's high-priestly ministry tightly to his exaltation. As in 4:14, the plural "heavens" is not a stylistic variant of the singular, "heaven," the place of God's presence,[10] but refers to the lower realms of the heavenly world as ancients conceived them.[11] Because he is above these heavens, Jesus—our author may be implying—has indeed entered that highest "heaven," the place where God dwells.[12]

7:27 This high priest does not have the need, as did the former high priests,[13] to daily offer sacrifices first for his own sins and then for the sins of[14] the people. This high priest offered a sacrifice for sins once for all when he offered himself (ὃς οὐκ ἔχει καθ' ἡμέραν ἀνάγκην, ὥσπερ οἱ ἀρχιερεῖς, πρότερον ὑπὲρ τῶν ἰδίων ἁμαρτιῶν θυσίας ἀναφέρειν ἔπειτα τῶν τοῦ λαοῦ· τοῦτο γὰρ ἐποίησεν ἐφάπαξ ἑαυτὸν ἀνενέγκας). This verse continues to spell out the ways in which Jesus is an especially "fitting" high priest for us.[15] In 5:3, the author anticipated the contrast he draws in this verse by noting how the Old Testament high priest had to "offer sacrifices for his own sins, as well as for the sins of the people." In light of the emphasis on Jesus's moral purity in verse 26, the author undoubtedly intends to contrast the efficacy of a sacrifice offered by one who is sinless with one offered by one who is himself beset by sin. Old Testament high priests needed to attend to their own sin as well as the sins of the people; Jesus, on the other hand, could focus exclusively on the needs of others. The particular Old Testament ritual that the author refers to here is hard to identify. On the one hand, it was only on the Day of Atonement that the high priest was required to sacrifice for himself and then for the people (Lev 16:6–16). On the other hand, the Day of Atonement comes only once a year, so the author's claim that this ritual occurred "daily" is obviously problematic. Partly because

---

for "holy" (which is ἅγιος). It might also be noted that the author does not use any of the three words anywhere else, and that none of them occurs with any of the others in another NT text.

8. See also Calvin, *Hebrews*, 102; Westcott, *Hebrews*, 195; P. Hughes, *Hebrews*, 273–74; G. Guthrie, *Hebrews*, 269. The perfect form of the participle connotes the ongoing status of Jesus.

9. See, e.g., Attridge, *Hebrews*, 213; Cockerill, *Hebrews*, 341; Johnson, *Hebrews*, 195; Lane, *Hebrews*, 1:192. Lane, e.g., argues that the combination of the verb χωρίζω with the preposition ἀπό has a local meaning. It is true this combination usually refers to a spatial separation (e.g., Acts 1:4; 18:2), but there are certainly texts in which the phrase does not have a (local) spatial sense: see Rom 8:39—we are not separated "from the love of God"; 1 Cor 7:10—a wife should not "separate from" her husband.

10. Contra, e.g., NLT.

11. Rissi, *Die Theologie des Hebräerbriefs*, 35–36.

12. Cockerill (*Hebrews*, 342) points to the refrain, "be exalted above the heavens," in Psalms (57:5, 11; 108:4, 5; cf. 113:4); see Cockerill, *Hebrews*, 342.

13. The author refers here simply to "the high priests" (οἱ ἀρχιερεῖς), but, in context, the article makes clear that he refers to "the other high priests" (NIV; NLT; CEB).

14. In a typical ellipsis, the author uses the article by itself (τῶν) to refer to "the sins" (τῶν ... ἁμαρτιῶν) mentioned in the previous phrase.

15. A relative pronoun (ὅς) refers to the "high priest" who is fitting for us in v. 26a. I have used the antecedent to translate the relative pronoun for the sake of clarity.

the Day of Atonement ritual is so important in Hebrews, many scholars think this must be the reference and that the author has simply misspoken. Scholars have suggested several other interpretations to avoid this conclusion (which I list from least to most likely): (1) "daily" might refer not to the Old Testament high priest's ministry but to Christ's, who "daily" (rather than once a year) intercedes for his people;[16] (2) the phrase translated "daily" (καθ' ἡμέραν) means "on each successive Day [of Atonement]";[17] (3) the phrase translated "daily" means "regularly," "often";[18] (4) the author is referring generally to Old Testament sacrifices, conflating for the sake of brevity the Day of Atonement with other sacrifices;[19] (5) the author "intends to describe the general state under the old covenant cult."[20] I think one of these last two options is best. In any case, the author's point is clear enough: the need to offer a sacrifice for himself and to make offerings repeatedly demonstrates the inferiority of the Old Testament high-priestly ministry in comparison to Christ's ministry.

Since the context requires that our high priest, Jesus, be the subject of the last sentence in the verse, the context requires that "this" (τοῦτο) should refer to "offering sacrifices for the sins of the people."

Two points that will become basic to the exposition of Jesus's high-priestly work in chapters 8–10 are introduced here: the sacrifice Jesus offers is none other than "himself" (ἑαυτόν); and he offered himself "once for all" (ἐφάπαξ).[21]

7:28 For the law appoints men who had weakness as high priests, but the word of the oath which came after the law appoints[22] a Son who has been perfected forever (ὁ νόμος γὰρ ἀνθρώπους καθίστησιν ἀρχιερεῖς ἔχοντας ἀσθένειαν, ὁ λόγος δὲ τῆς ὁρκωμοσίας τῆς μετὰ τὸν νόμον υἱὸν εἰς τὸν αἰῶνα τετελειωμένον). In this verse, the author explains why the Old Testament high priests had to sacrifice for their own sins—they had "weakness."[23] He makes this point with yet another contrast between the Old Testament high priests and Christ as high priest, picking up key language from earlier in the chapter as he does so—"law" (and related words, vv. 11, 12, 14, 16, 19), "oath" (vv. 20, 21, 22), "forever" (and related words, vv. 16, 17, 21, 24, 25), and "perfected" (vv. 11, 19). The overall sequence of the argument in verses 27–28 is similar (in reverse) to what we saw in 5:2–3.

Here, as in verses 20–22, the author views the "oath" as having greater significance than the law.

---

16. Westcott, *Hebrews*, 195–96.
17. Nigel Turner, *Style*, vol. 4 of *A Grammar of New Testament Greek*, 111–12.
18. Cockerill, *Hebrews*, 343. There is some basis for this view in the NT usage of the phrase καθ' ἡμέραν, where it might be questioned if the reference is strictly to "every day" or whether it means simply "often" (e.g., Matt 26:55; Mark 14:49; Luke 19:47; 22:53; Acts 2:46, 47; 16:5; 17:11; 19:9). Still, it is questionable if "often" could be stretched to mean "once a year."
19. Grässer, *An die Hebräer*, 2:70; Attridge, *Hebrews*, 213; Koester, *Hebrews*, 367–68; Michel, *Der Brief an die Hebräer*, 281–82. The other sacrifices might especially be the daily *tamid* offering (Exod 29:38–41; Num 28:3–8). The OT does not specify that the high priest was to offer these daily sacrifices, but it is certainly possible that he did.
20. Ribbens, *Levitical Sacrifice*, 152; Ribbens, "The Positive Function of Levitical Sacrifice in Hebrews," in *Son, Sacrifice, and Great Shepherd: Studies on the Epistle to the Hebrews*, ed. David M. Moffitt and Eric F. Mason, WUNT 2/510 (Tübingen: Mohr Siebeck, 2020), 101–2.
21. The word ἐφάπαξ could modify ἐποίησεν—"he did this once for all when he offered himself" (ESV)—or the (temporal?) adverbial participle ἀνενέγκας—"he did this in offering himself once for all" (NET).
22. The verb "appoint" (καθίστησιν) in the first clause must be read in this second clause also. The present tense of this verb suggests that the author is focusing not so much on the past act of appointing (NIV "appointed") but on the (enduring) testimony of Scripture (see most versions).
23. The γάρ ("for") here then has its "normal" explanatory force.

5:2–3	7:27–28
because the Old Testament high priests, being human, have "weakness" (ἀσθένειαν)	OT high priests must offer sacrifices for their own sins
↓	↑
they must offer sacrifice for their own sins	because the law appoints to this office men who have "weakness" (ἀσθένειαν)[24]

But he hints also at a further argument for the superiority of the oath: the oath was "after the law" (τῆς μετὰ τὸν νόμον). As he does elsewhere, the author finds significance in the temporal sequence of salvation history, viewing later revelation as the lens through which earlier revelation is to be interpreted (cf. 1:1–2; 4:6–9; 7:11, 18; 8:6–7, 13; 10:9; 12:26–27).[25] The author hints at yet another contrast by referring to Jesus as "Son," the title he has used earlier in the letter to denote the supreme status of Jesus (e.g., 3:6; 5:5; and see above also).[26] The high-priestly work of "one who is a son" has a power and finality that cannot be matched by high priests who are "human" (ἄνθρωποι). Moreover, this "Son" and "high priest" now ministers as one who has attained a state of perfection (the nuance of the perfect τετελειωμένον). In keeping with the application of perfection language to Jesus elsewhere, this "perfecting" refers to his full qualification to serve as a "merciful and faithful high priest" (2:17; and see 2:10; 5:9). Because our high priest has himself been fully qualified, he is able to likewise make the humans he represents fully qualified to enter into final salvation (see v. 11).

Theology in Application

The Person and Work of Christ

The New Testament makes clear that Jesus could do what he does for us only because of who he is. Soteriology—the provision of salvation—depends on Christology—the person of Jesus. Our author makes this point in these transitional three verses. Jesus is "holy, blameless, pure." He is "set apart from sinners," which I have interpreted as a reference to Jesus's own sinlessness. This point about sinlessness is confirmed by the author's going on to say that Jesus did not have to offer a sacrifice for his own sins. Why? Because he had not committed any sins: he did not share the "weakness" of all other human beings, including the Old Testament priests. It is important in this respect to note that the author returns to the title "Son" at the end of this passage. This title is the one the author has used preeminently to refer to the unique status and nature of Jesus (1:2, 5, 8; 3:6; 4:14; 5:5, 8; 6:6; 7:3).

---

24. G. Guthrie (*Structure of Hebrews*, 82) draws attention to this *inclusio*.
25. G. W. Lee (*Today When You Hear His Voice*, 165) notes the frequency of the chronological argument in Hebrews.
26. As in 1:2, it is difficult to decide whether to translate the anarthrous υἱός here as "the Son" (focusing on his uniqueness, see NIV; NJB; NLT "his Son") or as "a S/son" (focusing on his nature, see NRSV; ESV; NET; CSB; CEB; NAB).

CHAPTER 19

Hebrews 8:1–6

Literary Context

The author leaves no doubt about the importance of this new passage: it is the "main point in what we are saying." What is this "main point"? It is that "we have" a high priest who has been exalted to the right hand of God and now therefore ministers on our behalf in heaven itself (8:1–2). The author elaborates this basic claim in 8:3–10:18. He signals the conclusion of this elaboration with an *inclusio*-like return to two features of 8:1–2. "We have such a high priest" and reference to the heavenly sanctuary in 8:1–2 are echoed toward the beginning of the later passage, an exhortation built on the theology of 8:3–10:18: "we have confidence to enter the Most Holy Place" (10:19); "we have a great high priest over the house of God" (10:21).[1] The author's focus on the *who* of Jesus as high priest in chapter 7 now shifts to the *what* he has done and the *how* he achieved it. The author develops his teaching about Christ's high-priestly ministry via a focus on three particular aspects of priestly ministry, as that ministry is described in the Old Testament and practiced in a wide array of religions in the Greco-Roman world of that time.[2] First, priestly acts bear significance only as they are performed in the context of a divinely sanctioned arrangement or system. For the Old Testament and the author, this arrangement is a *covenant*. Second, priests offer *sacrifices*. And, third, these sacrifices are usually required to be offered in a particular place: again, for the author's Old Testament-based presentation, a *tabernacle*. In all three of these aspects, the author affirms, Jesus fulfills and transcends the Old Testament high-priestly ministry: he officiates with a "new" and "better" covenant, and he offers himself as the once-for-all, powerfully effective sacrifice. And he offers that sacrifice in the heavenly sanctuary, before God himself.

These three elements of high-priestly ministry appear singly and in different combinations throughout this section. All three are introduced in 8:3–6, which then

---

1. See, e.g., Ribbens, *Levitical Sacrifice*, 82–83; Weiss, *Der Brief an die Hebräer*, 428.

functions as an introductory overview, an overture to the operatic performance that follows. The last part of chapter 8 focuses on covenant. Tabernacle is the focus in 9:1–10, though sacrifice becomes a significant topic toward the end (vv. 7, 9–10). Tabernacle and sacrifice are woven together in 9:11–14, though sacrifice comes to dominate. The author finally turns back to the issue of covenant in 9:15–22—though sacrifice continues to be referred to (vv. 18–22). In 9:23–28, the author mixes together references to tabernacle and sacrifice, with the latter dominating. Reference to the law and the important hermeneutical claim about "reality" and "shadow" suggest a shift at the beginning chapter 10. Noticing this, and pointing to an *inclusio* with the language of "offer" (προσφέρω; see 8:3 and 9:28), some scholars identify 9:28 as the end of the section beginning in 8:1 (or 8:3).[3] However, there are good reasons, in agreement with most scholars, to set the end of the general section at 10:18.[4] Running throughout 8:1–10:18 is a contrast between "first" and "second," applied to covenants (8:7, 13; 9:1, 15, 18), the chambers of the sanctuary (9:2–3, 6–7, 8), the earthly and heavenly sanctuary (9:8), the two sacrificial systems (10:9), and the two comings of Christ (9:28).[5]

I. The Exalted Son and a Rest for the People of God (1:1–4:13)

II. **Our Great High Priest and His Ministry (4:14–10:31)**

  A. Exhortation: Persevere through the Power of Our Exalted High Priest (4:14–16)

  B. Exposition: High Priests and Our High Priest (5:1–10)

  C. Exhortation: Move on to Maturity (5:11–6:20)

  D. Exposition: A High Priest "According to the Order of Melchizedek" (7:1–28)

  E. Exposition: The Ministry of Our High Priest (8:1–10:18)

  → **1. Overview: Sanctuary, Sacrifice, and Covenant (8:1–6)**

  2. A New and Better Covenant (8:7–13)

  3. The Earthly Sanctuary and Its Regulations: An Illustration of the New (9:1–10)

  4. Eternal Redemption: Heavenly Sanctuary, Decisive Sacrifice, and New Covenant (9:11–28)

  5. The Ultimate Sacrifice (10:1–18)

  F. Exhortation and Warning: Appropriating the Benefits of Our High Priest's Ministry (10:19–31)

III. Exhortation: Follow and Serve the Pioneer of Our Faith through Endurance and Faith (10:32–13:25)

---

2. France, "Hebrews," 103–4.

3. E.g., Vanhoye, *La Structure Littéraire*, 138–40, 161; Lane, *Hebrews* 1:203; Ellingworth, *Hebrews*, 397–98.

4. See, e.g., Westcott, *Hebrews*, 211; Attridge, *Hebrews*, 216; Michel, *Der Brief an die Hebräer*, 286–87; Fuhrmann, *Vergeben und Vergessen*, 184. See the discussion in G. Guthrie, *Structure of Hebrews*, 84–87. An intentional *inclusio* with προσφέρω is hard to maintain because the verb occurs several times in the intervening verses (9:7, 9, 14, 25). Weiss (*Der Brief an die Hebräer*, 428–30) argues for a further main division between 8:1–9:28 and 10:1–18. However, while the latter text does introduce some new emphases, it is better seen simply as the final stage in the exposition that begins at 8:1.

5. DeSilva, *Perseverance in Gratitude*, 297.

Main Idea

The main point of the author's sermon is briefly summarized in 8:1–2: as the one exalted to the Father's right hand, Jesus represents us as our high priest in the very presence of God. As our exalted and ascended high priest, Christ has offered himself as a sacrifice, presented that sacrifice in the heavenly sanctuary, and thereby mediates God's new-covenant blessings to his people.

Translation

Hebrews 8:1-6

1a	assertion	Now the main point
1b	sphere	in what we are saying is that
1c	assertion	**we have such a high priest,**
1d	description 1	who sat down
1e	place	at the right hand of the throne of the majesty
1f	sphere	in heaven,
2a	description 2	a minister of the sanctuary and
2b	restatement	of the true tabernacle,
2c	description	which the Lord, ... not
2d	contrast	a human,
2e	predicate (of 2c)	... set up.
3a	development	Now
3b	assertion	**every high priest is appointed**
3c	purpose	to offer both gifts and
3d	parallel	sacrifices.
3e	basis	For which reason,
3f	assertion	**it is necessary**
3g	reference	also for this one
3h	content	to have something
3i	identification	which he could offer.
4a	development	Now
4b	condition	if he were on earth,
4c	assertion	**he would not be a priest,**
4d	basis	because there are those
4e	identification	who offer gifts
4f	standard	according to the law.

5a	elaboration (of 4c–f)	These priests minister
5b	sphere	in a copy and
5c	parallel	shadow of the heavenly sanctuary,
5d	verification	even as Moses was warned
5e	time	when he was about to finish the tabernacle:
5f	command	"see to it
5g	content	that you make everything
5h	standard	in accordance with the model
5i	identification	which was shown you
5j	place	on the mountain." (Exod 25:40)
6a	development	But
6b	time	now
6c	assertion	**Jesus has obtained a greater ministry—**
6d	expansion	to the degree that he is mediator
6e	comparison	of a better covenant,
6f	basis	which has been founded
6g	comparison	on better promises.

Structure

The opening paragraph in this new major section of the letter (8:1–6) is introductory—and on two levels. The highest level of introduction comes in verses 1–2. In these verses, the author states his "main point."[6] Jesus has been exalted to the "right hand of God" (alluding to Ps 110:1), and because of that he ministers as our high priest in the very presence of God. Jesus's unique access to God, and the access to God he thereby provides for his people, is a motif that runs through all this part of the letter. At a second, more specific level, verses 3–6 introduce the three key elements of Jesus's high-priestly work that dominate 8:7–10:18: the sacrifice he offers (vv. 3–4), the sanctuary in which he ministers (v. 5), and the covenant arrangement that undergirds his high-priestly work (v. 6). The introductory and summative character of these verses means that the attempt to pin down a linear sequence of thought is futile. The logic is not linear but episodic, as the author rapidly surveys these general aspects of Christ's high-priestly ministry. The language of "ministry" (λειτουργός, "minister," in v. 2 and λειτουργία, "ministry," in v. 6) provides the general focus of these verses.

---

6. Recognizing the importance and transitional function of vv. 1–2, some scholars separate them from vv. 3–6 in their own paragraph (e.g., G. Guthrie, *Structure of Hebrews*, 106).

Exegetical Outline

→ 1. **Overview: Sanctuary, Sacrifice, and Covenant (8:1–6)**
   a. Transition and Summary: Jesus, Our Exalted High Priest (vv. 1–2)
   b. The New and Better Ministry (vv. 3–6)

Explanation of the Text

8:1 Now the main point in what we are saying is that we have such a high priest, who sat down at the right hand of the throne of the majesty in heaven (Κεφάλαιον δὲ ἐπὶ τοῖς λεγομένοις, τοιοῦτον ἔχομεν ἀρχιερέα, ὃς ἐκάθισεν ἐν δεξιᾷ τοῦ θρόνου τῆς μεγαλωσύνης ἐν τοῖς οὐρανοῖς). The author reiterates a key claim that resounds throughout his sermon: Jesus is a high priest whose ministry is conducted in the presence of God himself. The important role of this verse and the one following it is signaled by the author's claim that he is here stating his "main point," "the 'crowning affirmation' of the argument."[7] "What we are saying" (τοῖς λεγομένοις, a present-tense participle) probably encompasses both what has come before in 5:1–10 and chapter 7 and what follows in 8:3–10:18.[8] We have the kind of high priest that the author describes in these passages—a high priest, specifically, who has "sat down at the right hand of throne of the majesty in heaven."[9] With this language, the author draws our attention again to one of his seminal Old Testament verses, Psalm 110:1—quoted first in 1:13. The distinguishing characteristic of Jesus's ministry as our high priest is that it involves the presentation of his sacrificial work in heaven, before God himself. This point, already briefly made in 4:16 and 7:26, becomes a recurring motif in 8:3–10:18.

8:2 a minister of the sanctuary and of the true tabernacle, which the Lord, not a human, set up (τῶν ἁγίων λειτουργὸς καὶ τῆς σκηνῆς τῆς ἀληθινῆς, ἣν ἔπηξεν ὁ κύριος, οὐκ ἄνθρωπος). In a move typical of the distinctive shape of the author's soteriology, he is not content to locate Jesus's high-priestly work simply in heaven—he locates it in a divinely fashioned sanctuary in heaven. The language of sanctuary refers in the first place to the "holy place" that God required the Israelites in the wilderness to erect as the locus of their sacrifice and worship. The author follows the lead of the LXX in using the adjective "holy" (ἅγιος) to refer to this structure. In the LXX, this word occurs in both the singular and the plural to refer to the entire structure.[10] Our author, however, usually uses the plural of this word to refer both to the sanctuary as a whole and, more often, to the "inner room," or "holy of holies,"

---

7. See, e.g., Samuel Bénétrau, *L'Épître aux Hébreux*, 2 vols. (Vaux-sur-Seine: EDIFAC, 1990), 2:48.

8. Weiss, *Der Brief an die Hebräer*, 431; Bénétrau, *L'Épître aux Hébreux*, 2:48. Contra, e.g., Michel, who thinks the reference is to the entire letter up to this point (*Der Brief an die Hebräer*, 286).

9. "The throne of the majesty in heaven" (τοῦ θρόνου τῆς μεγαλωσύνης ἐν τοῖς οὐρανοῖς) highlights the exalted nature of God and, by extension, the one who sits at his right hand (Cockerill, *Hebrews*, 351).

10. See, e.g., Num 3:28–38, where the LXX uses both the singular (vv. 31 and 38) and the plural (vv. 28 and 32) of ἅγιος to refer to the entire sanctuary (the Hebrew in each case is singular). The word is used with reference to the sanctuary in only three other NT texts, and in each word τόπος ("place") is added to clarify the meaning (Matt 24:15; Acts 6:13; 21:28).

within the sanctuary.[11] There is some dispute about which of these he might be referring to here, for he goes on to mention also the "true tabernacle" (τῆς σκηνῆς τῆς ἀληθινῆς). The language again follows the LXX, which uses the word "dwelling" (σκηνή), usually a tent or hut, to refer to the same mobile tent-like structure that "sanctuary" (ἅγιος) refers to. Some interpreters think that the whole phrase refers to the inner room, the "holy of holies" (τῶν ἁγίων) as part of the larger structure (τῆς σκηνῆς)—the genitive would therefore be partitive: "the holy of holies, which is a part of the tabernacle."[12] However, in this first mention of this structure in Hebrews, it makes better sense to think that the phrase depicts the sanctuary as a whole, with the genitive being epexegetic: "the sanctuary, the true tabernacle" (NIV; and, similarly, most English versions).[13] As Cockerill suggests, perhaps "tabernacle" pictures the structure from the outside, in a wide-angle view, while "sanctuary" offers a "close up" from the inside.[14] It is in this sanctuary/tabernacle that Jesus serves as a "servant" or "minister": the word the author uses (λειτουργός) refers here to a person who "performs public service" ("λειτουργός," BDAG 591); in the LXX and New Testament this word and its cognates (see λειτουργία, "ministry" in v. 6) generally refer to some kind of religious service.[15]

As verse 1 suggests, it is in no earthly sanctuary/tabernacle that Jesus finishes his high-priestly work. Rather, he offers himself as a sacrifice in "the true" one, the one "set up" by the Lord, not by a mere human being. "True" (ἀληθινῆς) has the sense in these kinds of contexts of "real," "authentic." The word occurs especially often with this meaning in John's writings; see, for example, Jesus's claim to be the "true bread from heaven" (John 6:32; also John 1:9; 4:23, 37; 15:1; 1 John 2:8; see also Luke 16:11 and Heb 9:24). The heavenly tabernacle is the true one because it is one that the Lord himself has "pitched" (ἔπηξεν).[16]

8:3 Now every high priest is appointed to offer both gifts and sacrifices. For which reason, it is necessary also for this one to have something which he could offer (πᾶς γὰρ ἀρχιερεὺς εἰς τὸ προσφέρειν δῶρά τε καὶ θυσίας καθίσταται· ὅθεν ἀναγκαῖον ἔχειν τι καὶ τοῦτον ὃ προσενέγκῃ). Just as Old Testament priests offer sacrifices, so Christ has offered his own unique sacrifice. This verse is connected to the previous context with γάρ, which many versions translate with the customary English gloss "for" (NRSV; ESV; NET; CSB). However, as I have noted, our author uses this conjunction very often and with several meanings (see the note on 2:10). As I argue above, a linear logical development is difficult to identify in verses 1–6. The reference to the priestly ministry of offering sacrifices in this verse, therefore, is not tightly connected to verses 1–2. Rather, the verse simply identifies the

---

11. The plural of ἅγιος refers to the sanctuary as a whole in 8:2; 9:24 (probably). In 9:2 it refers to the outer room in the sanctuary; in 9:8, 12, 25, and 10:19 it refers to the inner room, or the "holy of holies." Only once does the author use the full expression, ἅγια ἁγίων, to refer to this inner room (9:3). The singular ἅγιον occurs once as a reference to the sanctuary as a whole (9:1).

12. Ribbens, *Levitical Sacrifice*, 104–5; Jamieson, *Jesus' Death and Heavenly Offering*, 54; Grässer, *An die Hebräer*, 2:82; Attridge, *Hebrews*, 218; Massonnet, *L'Épître aux Hébreux*, 200.

13. Spicq, *L'Épître aux Hébreux*, 2:234; Lane, *Hebrews*, 1:200–201; Ellingworth, *Hebrews*, 401; P. Hughes, *Hebrews*, 282;

G. Guthrie, *Hebrews*, 279; Koester, *Hebrews*, 375–76; Peterson, *Hebrews and Perfection*, 130–31. As D. Harris notes, the singular relative pronoun in the last clause of the verse somewhat favors a single structure (*Hebrews*, 192).

14. Cockerill, *Hebrews*, 354. I follow the NIV and many other versions in consistently reserving "sanctuary" as a translation for forms of ἅγιος and "tabernacle" for forms of σκηνή.

15. The word λειτουργός occurs in Rom 13:6; 15:16; Phil 2:25; Heb 1:7. It refers to priestly functionaries in Isa 61:6.

16. The verb is from πήγνυμι, "make firm," "build," sometimes specifically "pitch a tent." See, with reference to the tabernacle, Josh 18:1; 2 Sam 6:17; 1 Chr 16:1.

first—and most important—of the functions that priests perform. The most accurate rending of γάρ, then, is either "now" (as I have chosen; see also NAB) or nothing at all (NIV; CEB).

The author repeats what he said earlier about high priests: they are appointed to offer "both gifts and sacrifices" (δῶρά τε καὶ θυσίας; see 5:1).[17] So also in the case of "this one" (τοῦτον)[18]—that is, the high priest we have (v. 1) must also have "something to offer." The sacrifice he offers has already been identified with himself (7:27), and this will become an important component of the author's argument in chapter 9.[19] A question that arises at several points in chapters 8–10 is the timing of this offering. The issue arises in this verse with respect to the time referent implied in the last clause. Does the author say that "it *was* necessary for this one to have something to offer" (e.g., NIV; NET; CSB); or that "it *is* necessary for this one to have something to offer" (NRSV; ESV; CEB; NASB)?[20] In the former case, Christ's offering would at least seem to include his death on the cross. In the latter case, however, the offering might take place only when Christ ascended to enter the heavenly sanctuary. The verb in question must be supplied, so we have no good textual basis to decide one way or the other; the decision will rather have to rest on the overall presentation of Jesus's "offering" in Hebrews. I think that offering at least includes his sacrificial death, so the past tense might be preferred here.[21]

8:4 Now if he were on earth, he would not be a priest, because[22] there are those who offer gifts according to the law (εἰ μὲν οὖν ἦν ἐπὶ γῆς, οὐδ' ἂν ἦν ἱερεύς, ὄντων τῶν προσφερόντων κατὰ νόμον τὰ δῶρα). The heavenly dimension of Christ's work sets him apart from the Levitical priests, whose ministry is confined to this world. I again choose to use the word "now" to connect this verse to its context, and for the same reason that I used it in verse 3. Verse 4 does not carry on a logical

---

17. The similarity in wording suggests that the author alludes back to 5:1 in this verse. Compare 5:1—Πᾶς γὰρ ἀρχιερεὺς ἐξ ἀνθρώπων λαμβανόμενος ὑπὲρ ἀνθρώπων καθίσταται τὰ πρὸς τὸν θεόν, ἵνα προσφέρῃ δῶρά τε καὶ θυσίας ὑπὲρ ἁμαρτιῶν—with 8:3: πᾶς γὰρ ἀρχιερεὺς εἰς τὸ προσφέρειν δῶρά τε καὶ θυσίας καθίσταται. "Appointment" is emphasized in the former text; "offering" in this one.

18. The context suggests that τοῦτον is the (accusative) subject of the infinitive ἔχειν, with τι ("something") being its object.

19. The tense of both occurrences of the verb προσφέρω ("offer") in the verse has attracted speculation. The first, a present tense, is sometimes thought to suggest that the temple is still standing (P. Hughes, *Hebrews*, 292); the second, an aorist, is thought to imply the "once-for-all" nature of Christ's sacrifice (Bruce, *Hebrews*, 182; P. Hughes, *Hebrews*, 291; Ellingworth, *Hebrews*, 404). Both read too much significance into the tense choice.

20. For the the former view, see, e.g., Westcott, *Hebrews*, 213; Montefiore, *Hebrews*, 133.

21. The author uses the verb προσφέρω twenty times, eighteen times with reference to sacrifice (in 5:7, Jesus "offers" prayers; in 12:7, the verb means "deal with"). In addition, he uses the cognate noun, προσφορά, for a particular "offering" (10:5, 8) or for the act of offering (10:10, 14, 18). Some interpreters think that the moment of Jesus's offering is confined to his exaltation (or perhaps his arrival in the heavenly sanctuary (e.g., Jamieson, *Jesus' Death and Heavenly Offering*; Moffitt, *Atonement*). However, while this moment cannot be excluded, there is good reason to think that the author views the "offering" as encompassing the whole scope of Jesus's sacrificial work, from death through presentation in heaven. In the LXX, the language can refer to the presentation of the victim's blood after slaughter (e.g., Lev 1:5, 13; 7:3, 11, 12, 13; 9:18), but in the latter part of the LXX, the language refers to the whole process of sacrifice, considered as a single whole. It is especially interesting to note that, unlike the LXX, where "offering" is often said to be made "to" God, the author does not use this particular language—suggesting, again, that he uses the language of the sacrificial process in general. The author appears to use the language this way when he refers to the ministry of OT priests (5:1, 3; 8:3a, 4; 9:7, 9; 10:1, 2, 8, 11). A similar general focus seems clear in our author's references to Abel's "offering" of a sacrifice (11:4) or Abraham's "offering" of Isaac (11:17).

22. "Because" in my translation reflects the decision to give the genitive absolute ὄντων τῶν προσφερόντων a causal force (see also Zerwick and Grosvenor, *Grammatical Analysis*, 670; Lane, *Hebrews*, 1:201).

progression from verse 3 but introduces yet another aspect of the high-priestly ministry of Jesus.[23] The connection is with verse 2: the sanctuary Jesus ministers in is in heaven, not "on earth." Some interpreters take this to mean that Jesus's ministry on earth was not part of his high-priestly work: his death on the cross was the necessary preliminary step in that work, but not part of the work itself (which is, according to this verse, not carried out on earth).[24] This interpretation, however, insists on too narrow an interpretation of what the author is saying here. Jesus's "offering" of himself, mentioned in verse 3 and in many other texts, includes his death on the cross—a manifestly "earthly" event. It is better, then, to see the author here as claiming that Jesus's high-priestly work is not *confined* to earth—its significance lies in the fact that it carries over into heaven itself.[25] The author here touches again on one of the main emphases in his presentation of Jesus's high-priestly work: it culminates in the presentation of himself before the Father in heaven itself.[26]

8:5 These priests minister in a copy and shadow of the heavenly sanctuary,[27] even as Moses was warned[28] when he was about to finish the tabernacle: "see to it that you make everything in accordance with the model which was shown you on the mountain" (οἵτινες ὑποδείγματι καὶ σκιᾷ λατρεύουσιν τῶν ἐπουρανίων, καθὼς κεχρημάτισται Μωϋσῆς μέλλων ἐπιτελεῖν τὴν σκηνήν, Ὅρα γάρ φησίν, ποιήσεις πάντα κατὰ τὸν τύπον τὸν δειχθέντα σοι ἐν τῷ ὄρει). The sanctuary in which Old Testament priests conduct their ministry is but a shadow of the true tabernacle in heaven. "These priests" translates the indefinite relative pronoun οἵτινες, whose antecedent is "those who offer" in verse 4.[29] These priests "minister," or "serve" (λατρεύω is the verb; see my comments on v. 2), in "a copy and shadow of the heavenly sanctuary." The author uses a plural form (τῶν ἐπουρανίων), but the reference is nevertheless probably to the "sanctuary" (NLT; NET; RSV; CEB; on the use of the plural, see comments on v. 2) rather than to "heavenly things" in general (ESV; CSB). A reference here to the sanctuary appears more likely when we consider the Old Testament quotation the author uses to elaborate the first part of the verse. Exodus 25:40 is one of several texts in which the Lord instructs Moses to construct the earthly tabernacle according to the "pattern" the Lord revealed to Moses during his stay on the mountain (see also Exod

---

23. The οὖν, then, is resumptive (see, e.g., Attridge, *Hebrews*, 219; D. Harris, *Hebrews*, 193).

24. See esp. Moffitt, *Atonement*, 198, 274.

25. See, e.g., Geerhardus Vos, "The Priesthood of Christ in Hebrews," in *Redemptive History and Biblical Interpretation: The Shorter Writings of Geerhardus Vos*, ed. Richard B. Gaffin (Phillipsburg, NJ: P&R, 1980), 159; T. Desmond Alexander, *Face to Face With God: A Biblical Theology of Christ as Priest and Mediator*, Essential Studies in Biblical Theology (Downers Grove, IL: IVP Academic, 2022), 89.

26. This focus is captured by the contrary-to-fact logic of the conditional sentence. The author signals this conditional style by using an imperfect verb in the protasis (ἦν) and the particle ἄν in the apodosis. The logic of this kind of sentence is: (1) if A, then B; (2) not B; (3) therefore not A. So, here: (1) if Jesus ministered solely on earth, he would not be a priest; (2) but he is a priest; (3) therefore he does not minister solely on earth. See, e.g., P. Hughes, *Hebrews*, 291.

27. The compound dative ὑποδείγματι καὶ σκιᾷ could also be the object of the verb λατρεύουσιν (objects of this verb are usually in the dative); see von Siebenthal, *Ancient Greek Grammar*, 450; RSV: "they serve a copy and shadow" (followed by ESV).

28. The verb is χρηματίζω, which refers to divine communications, sometimes in the form of a warning (Matt 2:12, 22; Luke 2:26; Acts 10:22; Heb 11:7; 12:25). The verb can also mean simply "call," "name" (Acts 11:26; Rom 7:3).

29. The indefinite form of the pronoun may suggest a qualitative force—"those who are of the kind that" (Weiss, *Der Brief an die Hebräer*, 436)—but often in the NT the indefinite relative has the same meaning as the definite (on the general issue, see Wallace, *Greek Grammar*, 344).

25:9; 26:30; 27:8; see also Acts 7:44).³⁰ The author, then, altogether, uses three words to describe the earthly tabernacle in its relationship to the heavenly one: "copy" or "sketch" (ὑποδείγμα), "shadow" (σκιά), and "pattern," "type" (τύπος). Some interpreters think these words suggest that the earthly tabernacle was to be constructed according to a mental image or "blueprint" Moses was shown in the heavenly realm. On this view, the "heavenly tabernacle/sanctuary" might refer to heaven, or the presence of God, generally. As Backhaus puts it, the author thinks not of a sanctuary in heaven, but of heaven as a sanctuary.³¹ This way of thinking of the relationship might find support in the view of some Old Testament scholars that the earthly tabernacle was designed to be a kind of "movable Sinai," reflecting in its form the stages of access into the presence of God.³² This would mean that the "model" for the earthly tabernacle is not a discrete structure but the overall pattern of access to God revealed in and on Sinai.

However, while I am sympathetic to this overall approach, it is questionable whether the words the author uses, or the situation in Exodus to which he alludes, can be understood in this way. Neither "copy" (ὑπόδειγμα) nor "pattern" (τύπος) helps much. The former usually refers to a moral example in the New Testament (John 13:15; Heb 4:11; Jas 5:10; 2 Pet 2:6), while only here and in 9:23 does it perhaps refer to a tangible "copy." The word "pattern" or "type" (τύπος) lies at the root of the word *typology*, the designation of the way Old Testament people, places, and events prefigure New Testament realities (see esp. Rom 5:14; 1 Cor 10:6; cf. τυπικῶς in 1 Cor 10:11). However, it is used more often in the New Testament to refer to an "example" generally (Phil 3:17; 1 Thess 1:7; 2 Thess 3:9; 1 Tim 4:12; Titus 2:7; 1 Pet 5:3). The third word our author uses, "shadow" (σκιά), is more revealing.³³ Apart from its references to a physical "shadow" or "shade" (Matt 4:16; Mark 4:32; Luke 1:79; Acts 5:15), this word occurs three times in the New Testament to refer to new-covenant realities that cast "shadows," these shadows then referring to preliminary or partial iterations in God's plan of salvation. In two of these texts, the word refers to the law (Heb 10:1) or matters required by the law (Col 2:17). In both these texts, the relationship is temporal or horizontal, the law being a part of an earlier stage of salvation history. Only in 8:5 is the relationship, at least to some extent, "vertical": a heavenly tabernacle casting a shadow that takes the shape of an earthly sanctuary. Complicating our analysis of this word is its use in philosophical speculations that were current in our author's day. Middle Platonism, derived, as its name suggests, from the insights of the famous fifth-century BC philosopher, viewed earthly matters as copies, or shadows, of the more important and permanent "heavenly" realities.³⁴ The Jewish philosopher and theologian Philo, a rough contemporary of our author, worked extensively with this basic

---

30. The author deviates from the LXX (his probable source) in adding πάντα, "all," after ποιήσεις, "do," and in changing the tense of the participle, "shown," from perfect (δεδειγμένον) to aorist (δειχθέντα). The former change may reflect one of the parallel texts in Exodus, which refer to "all its furniture" (25:9). Philo quotes Exod 25:40 with the πάντα (*Alleg. Interp.* 3.102).

31. Backhaus, *Der Hebräerbrief*, 289. See also, e.g., Johnson: "if what defines a sanctuary is the presence of God, where God essentially and eternally exists must be the real 'holy place'" (*Hebrews*, 198).

32. Richard A. Averbeck, "Tabernacle," in Alexander and Baker, *Dictionary of the Old Testament: Pentateuch*, 824; see also T. Desmond Alexander, *Exodus*, ApOTC 2 (Downers Grove, IL: IVP Academic, 2017), 562–63.

33. A few interpreters think that ὑπόδειγμα and σκιά may form a hendiadys: "shadowy copy" (Attridge, *Hebrews*, 219; Moffatt, *Hebrews*, 205; Lane, *Hebrews*, 2:201). But this view gives "shadow" too little significance.

34. The basic relationship was famously illustrated by Plato in his allegory of the cave (*Republic* 7.515).

conception (see, e.g., *Alleg. Interp.* 3.97–99). The degree to which our author is indebted to Middle Platonism is greatly debated. In my discussion of this issue in the introduction, I take a mediating view. Middle Platonism is certainly not the basic conceptual framework for our author. Yet certain views characteristic of Middle Platonism do show up in Hebrews, probably mediated through Jewish apocalyptic.

The point of all this for the present verse is that this broad conceptual context suggests that the author may indeed be thinking that Moses was shown an actual heavenly structure of which the earthly counterpart was to be a "shadow."[35] Jewish apocalyptic, the conceptual context in which the author appears most at home, often seemed to envisage some kind of structure in heaven.[36] Nevertheless, I reiterate the point I have made earlier: our author, while he may think that Moses copied from a heavenly structure, is especially focused on the heavenly presence of God in which our high priest Jesus brings his atoning ministry to its climax.

8:6 But now Jesus has obtained a greater ministry—to the degree that he is mediator of a better covenant, which has been founded on better promises (νυν δὲ διαφορωτέρας τέτυχεν λειτουργίας, ὅσῳ καὶ κρείττονός ἐστιν διαθήκης μεσίτης, ἥτις ἐπὶ κρείττοσιν ἐπαγγελίαις νενομοθέτηται). In this verse, the author introduces yet another aspect of Jesus's high-priestly ministry. In previous verses in this paragraph, the author has touched on aspects of Jesus's ministry that he will develop in 8:7–10:18. Like other priests, Jesus offers sacrifices (v. 3), specifically, *the* sacrifice of himself (7:27; 9:12–15, 26–28; 10:5–10). Priests minister in a sanctuary, and so Jesus also ministered in a sanctuary, the "true tabernacle" in heaven (vv. 1–2, 5; see 9:11, 23–25; 10:12–13). Now, finally, the author claims that Jesus's atoning work is powerfully effective because it is undergirded and authorized by a new and better covenant, another aspect of Jesus's ministry that is developed in the following verses (8:7–13 and 9:15–20).

I have used "now" to translate the conjunctions in both verses 3 and 4 (γάρ and οὖν, respectively); I use it again here for the conjunction usually translated "now" (νῦν). The word probably conveys both a temporal and logical meaning: the old ministry took place in a tabernacle that was only a "copy" of the true one (v. 5). "But now" (NLT), the ministry of Jesus is authorized by a new and better covenant.[37] The underlying point is that any effective work of atonement can only "work" if it takes place in the context of a divinely authorized arrangement. The old system of sacrifice derived its power from the old covenant, solemnized at Sinai. So also the new system of sacrifice requires

---

35. Stephen Wunrow has provided a helpful outline of views, characterized by two axes: metaphorical vs. tangible and inclusive vs. discrete. Thus, the author may conceive of the heavenly tabernacle as (1) metaphorical and inclusive (the whole sphere of salvation); (2) metaphorical and discrete (the sphere of Jesus's salvific action); (3) spatial and inclusive (the tabernacle is heaven); or (4) the tabernacle is a structure within heaven. As he notes, the third view is the most popular among recent interpreters, while the fourth is showing some increase in popularity (taken from a dissertation at Wheaton College titled, "Heavenly Space in Hebrews and Its Christian and Jewish Environment"). Those who incline to this fourth view include Moffitt, *Atonement*, 221–29; Hofius, *Der Vorhang vor dem Thron Gottes*, 56; Jamieson, *Jesus' Death and Heavenly Offering*, 55–56; Scott D. Mackie, "Heavenly Sanctuary," 82–83; Lane, *Hebrews*, 1:237–38.

36. In Jewish apocalyptic, the structure is usually the temple. In a move typical of his perspective, the author focuses on an earlier stage of Israel's history. See, e.g., 2 Bar. 4.2–6; 1 En. 14.15–20; T. Levi 3.2–5; Sib. Or. 4.10. See also Wis 5:8. For a brief discussion, see G. Guthrie, "Hebrews," 968–69. See also Jonathan Klawans, *Purity, Sacrifice, and the Temple: Symbolism and Supersessionism in the Study of Ancient Judaism* (Oxford: Oxford University Press, 2006), 111–14.

37. The νῦν has a logical/temporal force. Lane, on the other hand, thinks it is purely logical (*Hebrews*, 1:201).

an authorizing framework—and that framework is a "new" (vv. 8, 13) and "better" (v. 6) covenant. "Better" (κρείττων) is one of the key words in Hebrews, expressing the author's drumbeat emphasis on the superiority and climactic significance of what God has done in Christ. The ministry Jesus has "obtained" (τέτυχεν)[38] is "better" (κρείττονος) because the promises on which that ministry is founded[39] are "better" (κρείττοσιν).[40] The author describes Jesus's role in this new covenant as "mediator" (μεσίτης). Three of the six New Testament occurrences of this word come in Hebrews (see also 9:15; 12:24; also Gal 3:19, 20; 1 Tim 2:5). All three of the occurrences in Hebrews describe Jesus's role in the new covenant, suggesting that the author is thinking of Jesus not so much as mediator between two parties (i.e., God and the people) but as the founder or guarantor of the new covenant.[41] The "promises" to which the author alludes probably include especially the several promises included in the new-covenant prophecy of Jeremiah 31:31–34 (vv. 8–12). The word "ministry" (λειτουργία) takes us back to the beginning of the paragraph, where the author introduced Jesus as a "minister" or "servant" (λειτουργός) in the "true tabernacle" (v. 2).

Theology in Application

Avoiding Anti-Material Bias

I have commented above on the difficulty of trying to figure out just what the author may intend by referring, via Exodus 25:40, to a "heavenly sanctuary" (v. 5). The issue is not easy to resolve, and I don't want to suggest that the consideration I mention in this brief note comes anywhere near to solving the matter. But I think it might be important at least to recognize a bias that some of us might bring to this issue.

It is well-known that the Western theological tradition has been marked by a certain kind of dualism, which leads often to a denigration of the material. Certain theological traditions have, for instance, been suspicious of sexual relationships between even married Christians because of the materiality, the "fleshiness," of that relationship. Other Christians have instituted strict rules about what food one should eat. This suspicion of the material certainly carries over into perceptions of heaven. Some believers think of heaven as a state in which disembodied souls float around in the ether. Yet the destiny of humans is to live in resurrected *bodies* forever in a "new heaven and new earth"—a *place* where the resurrected and embodied Jesus also resides.

---

38. The lexical form is τυγχάνω, "attain," "find" (transitive), or "happen" (intransitive). The perfect form highlights the continuing reality of the ministry Jesus has obtained.

39. The verb is νομοθετέω, which here probably means "divinely ordained" (Weiss, *Der Brief an die Hebräer*, 440; contrast 7:11, where the word refers to the giving of the law).

40. I translate "because" since the relative clause introduced by ἥτις (another indefinite relative used with definite force; see the note on 8:5) probably has a causal force (Attridge, *Hebrews*, 215; Lane, *Hebrews*, 1:201).

41. A. Oepke, "μεσίτης, μεσιτεύω," *TDNT* 4:620. See Weiss, *Der Brief an die Hebräer*, 441; Grässer, *An die Hebräer*, 2:93.

This often unconscious bias against the material may subtly effect evaluations of Hebrews 8:5. Surely, we might react, the author of Hebrews—and the author of Exodus before him—could not be thinking of an actual structure in heaven! He must be thinking simply of a blueprint that Moses was shown; or perhaps Moses was given a vision of heaven itself that he sought to reflect in the earthly tabernacle. These are certainly viable options in interpreting this text. But I suspect that the preference for such views sometimes be a product of a suspicion about materiality. A good case can be made that Jewish apocalyptic writers (and perhaps the author of the Revelation as well) envisaged an actual structure in heaven in their visions of the spiritual realm (see my comments above). And this may, indeed, be the way our author also thought about "the heavenly sanctuary."

IN DEPTH: The Heavenly Sanctuary[42]

The author to the Hebrews presents the work of Christ in his own distinctive way. While other New Testament authors use the imagery of sacrifice to describe Christ's death, only Hebrews extends the imagery to include the high priest who offers the sacrifice and the sanctuary in which the sacrifice is offered. Thus, the author describes the sanctuary set up and used by the people of Israel during their peripatetic journey from Sinai to the promised land in 9:1–7. He draws attention to the two "rooms" that made up that sanctuary, an outer room that priests in general could enter and an inner room that could be accessed only once a year by one person—the high priest. Our author, using his preferred method of *syncrisis* ("comparison"), argues that Jesus, our high priest, offered his sacrifice also in the inner room of a sanctuary, securing for us an eternal redemption. Our author locates this sanctuary in which Jesus ministers in heaven.

While this notion of ministry in a heavenly sanctuary is hinted at earlier in the letter (6:19–20), it is in 8:2 that the author first makes this idea explicit: our high priest Jesus ministers in "the sanctuary, the true tabernacle set up by the Lord." Then, in verse 5, he quotes Exodus 25:40 (see also 25:9) to show that the earthly tabernacle was to be constructed "according to the pattern" that God showed Moses during his time on Mount Sinai. This "pattern" may have consisted simply of plans ("blueprints," as it were), but the language in verse 2, "set up by the Lord," suggests rather the existence of an actual structure that Moses used as a model for the earthly sanctuary. The author then follows up

---

42. I thank Stephen Wunrow, a PhD graduate from Wheaton College, for helping me think through this topic.

this imagery by referring to Jesus's ministry in the heavenly sanctuary, or entrance into it, in chapter 9 (see vv. 11, 12, 24).

How are we to understand this language of Jesus's ministry in a heavenly sanctuary?

We might find help in answering this question by considering how other writers at the time used sanctuary imagery. However, to gather enough useful data, we will have to expand our survey to the temple, which was far more often the focus of speculation. And this is quite fair, since sanctuary and temple were viewed as overlapping, even equivalent, entities. Our survey could take us far afield, since temples were the topic of all kinds of speculation in the ancient world. I have argued that the author shows considerable influence from Jewish apocalyptic, along with some minor influence from Middle Platonism. The latter is often thought to inform our author's idea of a heavenly sanctuary, since Middle Platonism tended to regard the spiritual or "ideal" realm as the source of ultimate truth.[43] However, the author's conception of a heavenly sanctuary probably has its deeper roots in apocalyptic (which itself may well be influenced itself by Middle Platonism). To be sure, the Old Testament hints of a heavenly tabernacle: in addition to Exodus 25, see, for example, Exodus 15:17: "you will bring them in and plant them on the mountain of your inheritance—the place, LORD, you made for your dwelling, the sanctuary, Lord, your hands established." The lengthy description of a new temple in Ezekiel 40–48 is probably not relevant to this issue, both because it is not clearly located in heaven and because it probably does not envisage an actual temple structure. But it is in Jewish apocalyptic that the existence of a heavenly sanctuary becomes more prominent.[44] A key characteristic of apocalyptic is the recounting by the seer of a vision into heavenly realities. These realities sometimes include a temple, whether merely mentioned or described in some detail. The temple vision sometimes includes worship (often by angels) in that temple. Key texts that describe a heavenly temple are Testament of Levi 3.4; 5.1–7; 2 Baruch 4.3; 1 Enoch 14:10–20; 71:5–9; Sibylline Oracles 4.10; and especially the Songs of Sabbath Sacrifice (a series of documents from Qumran).[45] Of course, we

---

43. E.g., Thompson, *Hebrews*, 167–70.

44. For surveys of Jewish literature on the heavenly temple, see Martha Himmelfarb, *Ascent to Heaven in Jewish and Christian Apocalypses* (Oxford: Oxford University Press, 1993); Georg Gäbel, *Die Kulttheologie des Hebräerbriefes: Eine exegetisch-religionsgeschichtliche Studie*, WUNT 2/212 (Tübingen: Mohr Siebeck, 2006), 32–111; Barnard, *Mysticism of Hebrews*, 56–60.

45. The documents are designated 4Q400, 401, 402, 403, 404, 405, 406 (4QShirShabb[a–f]). They can be found in *DSSR* 5:357–405. Mason summarizes that the documents feature "descriptions of the angelic priesthood, praise, and liturgy in the heavenly sanctuary around the throne of God" ("Cosmology," 57). For an analysis of the documents, see Carol A. Newsom, *Songs of the Sabbath Sacrifice: A Critical Edition* (Winona Lake, IN: Eisenbrauns, 1985). She dates them to the first century BC or earlier.

need not go beyond the bounds of the canon to discover such references; in Revelation, John several times mentions a heavenly temple (11:1–2, 19; 15:5; 16:1, 7).[46] Appeal to these apocalytic texts is only marginally helpful, however, since it is unclear whether the seer in these texts "actually" saw a temple in heaven or whether the temple language is simply an image or metaphor.

Returning to Hebrews, then, I note first that some scholars think that the imagery of sanctuary and our Lord's entrance into that sanctuary to offer his sacrifice refers to the cross, which these scholars consider the moment of atonement. Under this view, the language of sanctuary is metaphorical, speaking of one thing—Jesus's once-for-all sacrifice on the cross—in terms of another—the high priest entering the Most Holy Place on the Day of Atonement. However, while widespread, this view has difficulty dealing with the author's repeated emphasis on the point of "entering" as critical in securing salvation. The spatial movement suggested by this language is difficult to map onto the offering of Christ on the cross.

As I read Hebrews, then, the author speaks of the resurrected Christ entering into a particular space that the author often describes in the language of sanctuary. However, we are still left with two competing explanations of this language. On the first view, the author is describing heaven *as* a sanctuary: Christ enters the highest heaven, the abode of God, to offer his sacrifice, and the author employs sanctuary language in a striking extended metaphor to depict heaven.[47] The language of sanctuary on this reading no more suggests an actual structure in heaven than references to a "city" that believers long to inhabit (11:10, 16; 12:22; 13:14) suggests a physical city in the heavenly realm. This is probably the majority view among modern scholars. However, a recent trend, growing in popularity, is to view the author's language of sanctuary as more realistic than this: the author is not describing heaven *as* a sanctuary; he is describing a sanctuary *in* heaven—an actual structure of some kind

---

46. The temple in Rev 11:1–2 may indeed be an image of the people of God (G. K. Beale, *The Book of Revelation: A Commentary on the Greek Text*, NIGTC [Grand Rapids: Eerdmans, 1999], 559–62), but this identification does not work as well in some of the other texts. In 15:5–6, for instance, seven angels come out of the temple; in 16:1, 7, a "loud voice" comes out of the temple. In these texts the temple seems to connote the presence of God, an idea that seems to be confirmed by 21:22, which says, in a description of the new Jerusalem, that "I did not see a temple in the city [i.e., the new Jerusalem], because the Lord God Almighty and the Lamb are its temple."

47. Two longer defenses of this widespread view are Philip Church, *Hebrews and the Temple: Attitudes to the Temple in Second Temple Judaism and in Hebrews*, NovTSup 171 (Leiden: Brill, 2017), and Marie E. Isaacs, *Sacred Space: An Approach to the Theology of the Epistle to the Hebrews*, JSNTSup 73 (Sheffield: JSOT, 1992). Schenck (*Cosmology and Eschatology*, 144–81) is difficult to classify. At some points, he seems to argue that the sanctuary represents heaven (e.g., "heaven itself, the highest heaven in particular, is the most literal referent for the heavenly tabernacle" [p. 181]). But he also appears to conclude in favor of viewing sanctuary language as part of the overall high-priestly "metaphor" (p. 181; see also Schenck, *Understanding the Book of Hebrews*, 15).

that Christ enters to offer his sacrifice. While allowing, in different degrees, for metaphor and imagery, scholars who argue this view insist that the author's language points to an actual structure in the heavenly realm, with an outer room that Christ "goes through" in order to enter the inner room where he offers himself as a final sacrifice in the presence of God. If we think, then, of a spectrum of views from "real in every detail" to "purely metaphorical," scholars occupy several different spots on this spectrum. But, as I suggest above, the fundamental split is between those who think the author views the sanctuary *as* heaven or the sanctuary as *in* heaven.

I find it difficult to decide between these options. In favor of the "realistic" view is the way the author not only mentions the heavenly sanctuary but goes into detail about its construction and its use: this sanctuary is something the Lord "set up" (8:2), Christ goes through its outer compartment on the way to its inner compartment (9:11–12), and it needed to be purified by "better sacrifices" (9:23).[48] On the other hand, however, we find indications that heavenly-sanctuary language is simply a vehicle to connote heaven itself as a sanctuary, the locus of God's dwelling place. In 9:24, for instance, the author compares the sanctuary with heaven itself: "for Christ did not enter a sanctuary made with human hands that was only a copy of the true one; he entered *heaven itself*, now to appear for us in God's presence." The author, of course, would be referring to the highest heaven, comparable to the "inner room" of the sanctuary. Another suggestion that the language may function simply at the level of imagery is the fact that believers are said to enter this sanctuary. In 6:19, believers have a "hope" that "enters the inner sanctuary behind the curtain," and in several texts believers are encouraged to "draw near" or "enter" the place where God resides (e.g., 10:19). Believers are not obviously in this life entering a structure in heaven. But they are invited through Christ to enter the presence of God. Moreover, as I note above, the author uses several other sets of imagery without apparently intending that imagery to refer to actual things: in addition to "city" language, see also the "throne" we approach through our high priest Jesus, the "better country" the Old Testament people of God were looking for (11:14–16), "Mount Zion," to which the new-covenant people of God have come (12:22), and the "race" that we run surrounded by a "cloud of witnesses" (12:1–2).

In the last analysis, I am not sure it makes a great deal of difference whether

---

48. For this view, see, e.g., Mackie, *Eschatology and Exhortation*, 157–68; Ribbens, *Levitical Sacrifice*, 94; David M. Moffitt, "Serving in the Tabernacle in Heaven: Sacred Space, Jesus's High-Priestly Sacrifice, and Hebrews' Analogical Theology," in *Hebrews in Contexts*, ed. Gabriella Gelardini and Harold W. Attridge, Ancient Judaism and Early Christianity 91 (Leiden: Brill, 2016), 259–79.

the author thinks of an actual sanctuary in heaven or whether he uses sanctuary language to depict heaven itself. In either case, he uses the heavenly sanctuary to convey what for him is the vital point: our high priest Jesus does not offer his sacrifice in an earthly sanctuary; he offers himself directly before God. He "enters" the heavenly realm, sitting at the right hand of the Father, and is making it possible for those who belong to him to enter as well.[49] At minimum, we must beware of the tendency, endemic in Western ways of thinking, to depreciate the material in our thinking about Christ's work in Hebrews. Our high priest is a real "flesh-and-blood" person (2:14). His sacrifice is a real body (10:5, 10). He represents us in heaven as a resurrected and *embodied* person—surely requiring a real, in some sense material, "place" where he finalizes his work of atonement on behalf of his people.

---

49. See, e.g., Barnard, *Mysticism of Hebrews*, 104–9.

Hebrews 8:7–13

Literary Context

In 8:1–6, the author introduces the next major section of his homily by briefly touching on three key components of priestly ministry, relating each of them specifically to Christ's ministry: sacrifice, sanctuary, and covenant. In this next paragraph the author elaborates this last component, using a lengthy quotation (the longest in the NT) from Jeremiah 31:31–34 to show why the new covenant that Jeremiah predicts is "superior" (v. 6) to the old and why this new covenant cancels out the old one (v. 13).[1] At the same time, the author uses the quotation to spell out the "better" promises accompanying this new covenant: God promises (1) to put his laws in the peoples' minds and hearts, (2) to enable all to know him, and (3) to remember their sins no more.[2]

I. The Exalted Son and a Rest for the People of God (1:1–4:13)
II. **Our Great High Priest and His Ministry (4:14–10:31)**
   A. Exhortation: Persevere through the Power of Our Exalted High Priest (4:14–16)
   B. Exposition: High Priests and Our High Priest (5:1–10)
   C. Exhortation: Move on to Maturity (5:11–6:20)
   D. Exposition: A High Priest "According to the Order of Melchizedek" (7:1–28)
   E. Exposition: The Ministry of Our High Priest (8:1–10:18)
      1. Overview: Sanctuary, Sacrifice, and Covenant (8:1–6)
➡   **2. A New and Better Covenant (8:7–13)**
      3. The Earthly Sanctuary and Its Regulations: An Illustration of the New (9:1–10)
      4. Eternal Redemption: Heavenly Sanctuary, Decisive Sacrifice, and New Covenant (9:11–28)
      5. The Ultimate Sacrifice (10:1–18)
   F. Exhortation and Warning: Appropriating the Benefits of Our High Priest's Ministry (10:19–31)
III. Exhortation: Follow and Serve the Pioneer of Our Faith through Endurance and Faith (10:32–13:25)

---

1. A few interpreters attach v. 7 to vv. 1–6 (Bruce, *Hebrews*, 186), but the wordplay with ἄμεμπτος, "without blame," and μεμφόμενος, "finding blame," suggests v. 7 belongs with v. 8.
2. Bruce, *Hebrews*, 192.

Main Idea

The high-priestly ministry of Jesus is greater than any other priestly ministry because his atoning work is carried out in terms of a new covenant that enables the ultimate fulfillment of God's law and that provides for full and final forgiveness of sins.

Translation

Hebrews 8:7–13

7a	explanation (of 6)	For
7b	condition	if that first covenant had been without fault,
7c	assertion	**there would have been no place**
7d	possession	for a second one.
8a	basis (for 7)	For,
8b	manner	finding blame with it,
8c	assertion	**he says to them:**
8d	address	"Note:
8e	assertion	the days are coming, says the Lord,
8f	description	when I will complete a new covenant
8g	association	with the house of Israel and
8h	parallel	the house of Judah.
9a	expansion (of 8f–h)	It will not be like the covenant
9b	description	that I made
9c	association	with their fathers
9d	time	on the day
9e	identification	that I took them by the hand
9f	purpose	to bring them
9g	separation	out of Egypt.
9h	assertion	I also had no regard for them
9i	cause	since they did not continue in my covenant,
9j	assertion	
9j	speech tag	says the Lord.
10a	contrast	Rather,
10b	assertion	this is the covenant,
10c	identification	which I will enter into
10d	association	with the house of Israel
10e	time	after these days,
10f	speech tag	says the Lord:

Continued on next page.

10g	content (of 10b)	I will place my laws
10h	sphere	in their minds and
10i	parallel	I will write them
10j	sphere	on their hearts.
10k	promise	I will be their God and
10l	parallel	they will be my people.
11a	result (of 10)	And
11b	assertion	each of them will not teach their fellow-citizens or
11c	alternate	say to each other
11d	content	'Know the Lord,'
11e	basis (for 11a–d)	for
11f	assertion	all of them will know me,
11g	expansion	from the least
11h	contrast	to the greatest of them.
12a	basis (for 8–11)	For
12b	promise	I will be merciful
12c	reference	with their unrighteous acts and
12d	parallel	their sins I will remember
12e	time	no more." (Jer 31:31-34)
13a	means	By calling this covenant "new,"
13b	assertion	**God has made the first obsolete.**
13c	inference	And **what is becoming obsolete and**
13d	parallel	**growing old**
13e	predicate (of 13c–d)	**is near to being cancelled.**

Structure

The author establishes the need for a new covenant by arguing that the first was inadequate (vv. 7–8a). He elaborates and explains this point with a quotation of Jeremiah 31:31–34 (vv. 8b–12). He then notes that the prophetic claim about a "new" covenant necessarily implies that the old one has come to an end (v. 13). The reference to a "first" (πρώτη) covenant frames the paragraph (vv. 7, 13).[3]

---

3. Bénétrau, *L'Épître aux Hébreux*, 2:55.

Exegetical Outline

→ 2. **A New and Better Covenant (8:7–13)**
   a. The Inadequacy of the Old Covenant (vv. 7–8a)
   b. The New Covenant Prophecy (vv. 8b–12)
   c. The Obsolescence of the Old Covenant (v. 13)

Explanation of the Text

8:7 For if that first covenant had been without fault, there would have been no place for a second one (Εἰ γὰρ ἡ πρώτη ἐκείνη ἦν ἄμεμπτος, οὐκ ἂν δευτέρας ἐζητεῖτο τόπος). "For" at the beginning of the verse accurately captures the sense of the Greek word γάρ here: the author explains why the new covenant is superior to the old. He begins with a simple point: God's revealing to Jeremiah that a new covenant was coming implies that the old one was not "without fault" (ἄμεμπτος).[4] The second part of the verse is worded in a way that leaves it open to three different interpretations. The author uses a Greek word meaning "place" (τόπος) as the subject of a passive verb (ἐζητεῖτο, an imperfect) that can be translated "was being sought." The agent of the verb (and hence the semantic subject) might be God—"a place for a second was being sought by God"[5]—or Israel—"a place for a second was being sought by the people"—or left deliberately open—"a place for a second would not have been sought." This last view is the most likely, in which case the word for "place" might be translated "occasion," as in the CSB: "there would have been no occasion for a second one."[6]

8:8a For, finding blame with it, he says to them: (μεμφόμενος γὰρ αὐτοὺς λέγει). The author now grounds (γάρ, "for") his claim about the arrival of a new covenant to make up for the deficiencies of the old one, introducing his long quotation from Jeremiah. The participle "finding blame" (μεμφόμενος) picks up the claim in verse 7 that the old covenant was not "without blame" (ἄμεμπτος). Identifying the object of the participle, however, is not easy. Most translators and interpreters think that "the people" (of Israel) is the antecedent of the pronoun "them," and read the verse as does the CSB: "but finding fault with his people, he says . . ."[7] However, a textual variant opens up another option. Many early and good manuscripts read a pronoun in the dative (αὐτοῖς, "to them") rather than one in the accusative (αὐτούς).[8] On this view, the pronoun

---

4. The author uses another contrary-to-fact conditional sentence (imperfect in the protasis, ἄν in the apodosis): "if that first covenant had been without fault, there would have been no place for a second one"; however, as the Jeremiah quote reveals, there was, indeed, a place for a second; so the first must not have been without fault.

5. This is the majority view among commentators, who cite the connection with v. 8a. See, e.g., Ellingworth, *Hebrews*, 412; D. Harris, *Hebrews*, 200; Koester, *Hebrews*, 385.

6. Almost all the English versions adopt a translation like this; and see "τόπος," BDAG 1012, §4.

7. See, e.g., Spicq, *L'Épître aux Hébreux*, 2:240. According to Metzger, the UBS committee favored αὐτούς because of the "direction in which scribal corrections moved" (*Textual Commentary*, 597).

8. External evidence for these two options is evenly split. The original hand of ℵ, A, D, and several other uncials and important minuscules support αὐτούς, while 𝔓⁴⁶, a corrector

could be the object of "he says" (λέγει). Hence NET: "but showing its [the covenant] fault, God says to them . . .".[9] As the translation at the head of this entry reveals, I favor this option. The "people" have not appeared anywhere in this context, while the "blame" in verse 7 is clearly attached to the covenant itself. This must not be taken to imply that God himself was at fault in inaugurating such a covenant, and clearly it was the inherent inability of the people to obey God that rendered the first covenant inadequate. However, inadequate it was, and this is the point the author seems to be making here.

8:8b–12 "Note: the days are coming, says the Lord, when I will complete a new covenant with the house of Israel and the house of Judah. 9 It will not be like the covenant that I made with their fathers on the day that I took them by the hand to bring them out of Egypt. I also had no regard for them since they did not continue in my covenant, says the Lord. 10 Rather, this is the covenant, which I will enter into with the house of Israel after these days, says the Lord: I will place my laws in their minds and I will write them on their hearts. I will be their God and they will be my people. 11 And each of them will not teach their fellow-citizens or say to each other, 'Know the Lord,' for all of them will know me, from the least to the greatest of them. 12 For I will be merciful with their unrighteous acts and their sins I will remember no more" (Ἰδοὺ ἡμέραι ἔρχονται, λέγει κύριος, καὶ συντελέσω ἐπὶ τὸν οἶκον Ἰσραὴλ καὶ ἐπὶ τὸν οἶκον Ἰούδα διαθήκην καινήν, 9 οὐ κατὰ τὴν διαθήκην, ἣν ἐποίησα τοῖς πατράσιν αὐτῶν ἐν ἡμέρᾳ ἐπιλαβομένου μου τῆς χειρὸς αὐτῶν ἐξαγαγεῖν αὐτοὺς ἐκ γῆς Αἰγύπτου, ὅτι αὐτοὶ οὐκ ἐνέμειναν ἐν τῇ διαθήκῃ μου, κἀγὼ ἠμέλησα αὐτῶν, λέγει κύριος· 10 ὅτι αὕτη ἡ διαθήκη, ἣν διαθήσομαι τῷ οἴκῳ Ἰσραὴλ μετὰ τὰς ἡμέρας ἐκείνας, λέγει κύριος· διδοὺς νόμους μου εἰς τὴν διάνοιαν αὐτῶν καὶ ἐπὶ καρδίας αὐτῶν ἐπιγράψω αὐτούς, καὶ ἔσομαι αὐτοῖς εἰς θεόν, καὶ αὐτοὶ ἔσονταί μοι εἰς λαόν· 11 καὶ οὐ μὴ διδάξωσιν ἕκαστος τὸν πολίτην αὐτοῦ καὶ ἕκαστος τὸν ἀδελφὸν αὐτοῦ λέγων, Γνῶθι τὸν κύριον, ὅτι πάντες εἰδήσουσίν με ἀπὸ μικροῦ ἕως μεγάλου αὐτῶν, 12 ὅτι ἵλεως ἔσομαι ταῖς ἀδικίαις αὐτῶν καὶ τῶν ἁμαρτιῶν αὐτῶν οὐ μὴ μνησθῶ ἔτι). The author backs up his claim about the coming of a "second" covenant and the implicit criticism of the first covenant entailed in that coming by citing the famous "new covenant" prophecy from Jeremiah 31:31–34. The covenant, the Lord claims via Jeremiah, will be an improvement on the Sinai covenant. The history of Israel has revealed that the people are simply unable to obey the covenant stipulations, and so they have been sent into exile as judgment. But the new covenant will provide for transformed hearts that will enable obedience and allow the great covenant promise of God being their God and the people being his people to be fulfilled at last. The law will be written on the minds and hearts of God's people, and they will all "know the Lord." Moreover, this new covenant will provide for a full and final forgiveness of sins.

A "new covenant" is explicitly mentioned in three other New Testament texts: in the words of institution at the Lord's Supper in Luke's and Paul's versions (Luke 22:20; 1 Cor 11:25) and in Paul's defense of his ministry in 2 Corinthians 3 (see there v. 6). And while the concept is undoubtedly present in other New Testament texts that do not

---

of א, B, a corrector of D, a few minuscules, and the Majority text read αὐτοῖς. We could translate "find blame with them" with either option, since the verb μέμφομαι can take either an accusative or dative word as its object.

9. Lane, *Hebrews*, 1:202; P. Hughes, *Hebrews*, 298–99; G. Guthrie, *Hebrews*, 281; G. Guthrie, "Hebrews," 971.

use the actual language,[10] "new covenant" plays a more important role in Hebrews than anywhere else in the New Testament (in addition to this text, see 7:22; 9:15–20; 10:16, 29; 12:24; 13:20). In line with the overall argument of the letter, a negative purpose in citing this text is clear: the author wants to remind his readers that the old covenant, with its provisions for sacrifice and earthly tabernacle, was inadequate to deal with the problem of sin.[11] However, we need also to see a positive purpose in the quotation, one that becomes integrated into a key theological theme in this part of the letter: the new covenant provides for the full and free forgiveness of sins through the work of our heavenly high priest.[12] This theme surfaces at the end of the quotation—"their sins I will remember no more" (v. 12; Jer 31:34)—and, with the repetition of this claim in 10:17, becomes an *inclusio* around this section of the letter.

The prophetic book of Jeremiah has come down to us in two versions, one found in the Hebrew Masoretic Text and another in the Greek Septuagint. One of the larger differences between them is the placement of the prophecies against the nations. These prophecies occur at the end of the book in the Hebrew version (chs. 46–51) but are inserted in the midst of the book in the Greek (25:14–31:44). As a consequence, the new-covenant prophecy is moved back in the Septuagint, appearing in LXX 38:31–34. However, the different sequence of material would have had little impact on the author's use of the quotation. As is his habit, the author's quotation is close to the LXX text. There are several minor stylistic differences,[13] with only one difference that may have material significance: in place of the Greek for "I will make a covenant" (διαθήσομαι, Jer 31:31/38:31 LXX), the author in 8:8 uses the verb "I will complete [a covenant]" (συντελέσω). Our author's frequent use of the τελ- root (with verbs, nouns, and adjectives meaning "perfect," "complete") suggests that this change might be made to connote the eschatological "completeness" entailed in the new covenant.[14] There are also differences between the Hebrew version and the Greek version of the prophecy.[15] However, since we cannot know if the author had a Hebrew version to consult, these differences do not point to editorial work on the part of the author.

In either version of Jeremiah, the new-covenant prophecy comes in what is often labeled the "book

---

10. E.g., Matt 26:28; Mark 14:24; Rom 9:4; 11:27; Gal 4:24; Eph 2:12.

11. For this view of the author's use of the quotation, see Weiss, *Der Brief an die Hebräer*, 444–47; Backhaus, *Der Hebräerbrief*, 295.

12. Attridge (*Hebrews*, 226) appropriately notes both the negative and positive function of the quotation in this context.

13. The author in vv. 8, 9, and 10 uses λέγει ("he speaks") in place of LXX φησίν ("he speaks" [Jer 31:31, 32, 33/LXX 38:31, 32, 33]); he uses ἐποίησα ("I made") in place of LXX διεθέμην ("I made a covenant") in v. 9 (Jer 31:32/38:32 LXX); he uses the simple διδούς ("giving, placing") in place of LXX διδοὺς δώσω ("placing, I will place") in v. 10 (Jer 31:33/38:33 LXX); he uses ἐπιγράψω ("I will write upon") in place of the LXX γράψω ("I will write") in v. 10 (Jer 31:33/38:33); and he has ἀπὸ μικροῦ ἕως ("from the least unto") in place of the LXX ἀπὸ μικροῦ αὐτῶν καὶ ἕως ("from the least of them and unto") in v. 11 (Jer 31:34/38:34 LXX). It should be noted that the differences I note here reflect the reading of the standard Ralhfs text; some manuscripts of the LXX offer different readings, which we need not explore here.

14. E.g., Attridge, *Hebrews*, 227. Other interpreters, however, think the change might be simply stylistic (e.g., Lane, *Hebrews*, 1:209).

15. In general, the LXX renders the Hebrew quite faithfully, with two possibly significant exceptions. First, while the Hebrew in v. 32 contrasts the peoples' "breaking" (using the verb פרר) with the Lord's continuing as Israel's "husband" (using בעל, "marry," "rule over"), the Greek contrasts the peoples' "not remaining" (οὐκ ἐνέμειναν) with the Lord's "unconcern" or "lack of regard" (using the verb ἀμελέω) for them. This version, adopted in Hebrews, highlights the Lord's judgmental reaction to the disobedience of the people. Second, the LXX translates the singular תּוֹרָתִי, "my law," with the plural νόμους μου, "my laws." For a careful analysis of the different texts, see Walser, *Old Testament Quotations in Hebrews*, 32–89.

of consolation" (MT chs. 30–31; LXX 37–38). After harsh pronouncements of judgment in the earlier part of the prophecy, this section offers hope to the disobedient and exiled people. Although this is the only place Jeremiah refers to a "new" covenant (indeed, this is the only place in the OT where the phrase occurs), he has condemned the people for failing to keep the original covenant (11:1–10; see 22:9) and predicts at the end of the book that "the people of Israel and the people of Judah together" will seek the Lord and "bind themselves to the LORD in an everlasting covenant" (50:4–5). The prediction that God would shower his grace on Israel even after the exile goes back especially to Deuteronomy. As scholars note, the new-covenant prophecy in Jeremiah has many similarities to Deuteronomic theology. Here, as there, judgment for breaking the covenant is combined with a promise that God himself would renew the hearts of his people and enable them to obey his law (see esp. Deut 6:6; 11:18; 30:5–6, 11–14).[16] Yet Deuteronomy issues this call for "the circumcision of the heart" within the context of the Mosaic covenant. While some scholars think that Jeremiah also predicts that the new covenant will be, in effect, a "renewed" Mosaic covenant,[17] the prophet seems rather to be predicting a really "new" covenant. As Lundbom puts it, "discontinuity gets the accent" in Jeremiah's prophecy.[18] Certainly the author to the Hebrews, with his blunt language of a "second" versus a "first" covenant (v. 7) and his claim that the first covenant is "obsolete and growing old" and "will soon disappear" (v. 13), reads the text as a prediction of a truly "new" covenant.

The author to the Hebrews clearly views the fulfillment of this prophecy to take place among all who benefit from Christ's sacrifice—that is, the church. The move within the new-covenant prophecy from "the house of Israel" and "the house of Judah" (Jer 31:31; see Heb 8:8) to simply "the house of Israel" (Jer 31:33; Heb 8:10) suggests a unifying effect of the new covenant: the division within Israel will be ended. At the same time, there is also in Jeremiah (and in many other OT texts) an indication that this unifying move would be accompanied by a universalizing move, as gentiles are also brought into the eschatological people of God. Several New Testament books focus extensively on this universalizing of the people of God (e.g., Galatians, Romans, Ephesians). In support of this move, the New Testament often announces the fulfillment of Old Testament prophecies directed to Israel as the people of God in the church, the new configuration of the people of God. This is exactly what we find here in Hebrews 8: an Old Testament text that promises a new covenant to Israel is applied in this text to the church.[19] This claim does not hinge on a certain identification of the audience of Hebrews

---

16. See, e.g., Stephen G. Dempster, *Dominion and Dynasty: A Theology of the Hebrew Bible*, NSBT 15 (Downers Grove, IL: InterVarsity Press, 2003), 166.

17. E.g., Graeme Goldsworthy, *According to Plan: The Unfolding Revelation of God in the Bible* (Downers Grove, IL: InterVarsity Press, 1991), 194. One debated matter within this continuity/discontinuity issue is the identification of the "law" that God promises to write on the people's hearts.

18. Jack R. Lundbom, *Jeremiah 21–36: A New Translation with Introduction and Commentary*, AB 21.2 (Garden City, NY: Doubleday, 2004), 465 (see 465–66). See, for this view, especially Peter J. Gentry and Stephen J. Wellum, *Kingdom through Covenant: A Redemptive-Theological Understanding of the Covenants* (Wheaton, IL: Crossway, 2012), 483–530; and also Waltke, *Old Testament Theology*, 439–91. The prophecy about "writing" God's law on the hearts of his people is important in parts of the NT (see, e.g., Rom 8:4; 2 Cor 3:6–18; Jas 1:21) and has implications for the way the Mosaic law is understood to relate to new-covenant believers. However, the author to the Hebrews does not take up this aspect of the prophecy (though note Joslin, *Hebrews, Christ, and the Law*, 208–22).

19. Certain theologians resist this conclusion: for instance, historic dispensational theology, which insisted that OT prophecies directed to Israel must be fulfilled in national Israel. Though moving away somewhat from the older, strict dispensational view, note, e.g., F. B. Huey, who claims that

(e.g., that the author writes to gentile Christians). Rather, it is rooted in the theo-logic of the author's argument. The "new covenant" the author refers to here is the new arrangement by which God relates to humanity. Christological connection, not ethnic identity, is the means by which humans can access and benefit from that arrangement. The author therefore aligns himself with other New Testament writers who proclaim that God's new covenant is open to all who believe, whether Jew or gentile.

A strongly dichotomous claim about the church "replacing" Israel should be rejected, badly missing as it does the organic continuity between the Old Testament and New Testament people of God. At the same time, there can be no doubt that Hebrews reconfigures the people of God around Christ. It is his sacrifice, providing for the fulfillment of Jeremiah's prophecy that God would no longer "remember" his people's sins, that is the defining experience of the new-covenant people of God. While not, therefore, a point that Hebrews explicitly makes, the inclusion of gentiles in that people of God is implicit in its teaching about the finality and ultimate significance of Jesus's sacrifice. And, just as gentiles can now be included in that people, so also, by the logic of the argument, Jewish people who do not take advantage of God's offer of forgiveness in Christ are excluded. (See, further, the "Theology in Application" section below.)

8:13 By calling this covenant "new,"[20] God has made the first obsolete. And what is becoming obsolete and growing old is near to being cancelled (ἐν τῷ λέγειν Καινὴν πεπαλαίωκεν τὴν πρώτην· τὸ δὲ παλαιούμενον καὶ γηράσκον ἐγγὺς ἀφανισμοῦ). The author adds a final comment on the significance of the new-covenant quotation from Jeremiah, making roughly the same point he made in introducing the quotation: the very promise of a new covenant implies the inadequacy and obsolescence of the old covenant (see v. 7). The subject of the main verb in the first clause is not expressed in Greek. However, since the quotation refers three times to the Lord's speaking (vv. 8, 9, 10), we should probably assume that "the Lord" or "God" is the implied subject (most versions use "he," though CEB has "it," referring apparently to Scripture). The author uses a perfect verb to connote the state of "being old" (πεπαλαίωκεν), captured well in the English "obsolete" ("παλαιόω," BDAG 751, §2, and most versions). The same verb is then used in present participial form in the next clause: παλαιούμενον, "that which is becoming obsolete." It is paired with a participle from a verb with a similar meaning, translated "growing old" (γηράσκω—used only once else in the NT, with reference to Peter's growing old [John 21:18]). The two present participles suggest a focus on the process of growing old and becoming obsolete. The old covenant, in fact, concludes the author, is "near to being cancelled" (ἐγγὺς ἀφανισμοῦ). Most versions translate "near to disappearing" or something of the sort (ESV, "ready to vanish away"). However, as a number of commentators point out, the word the author uses here (ἀφανισμός) usually has the stronger meaning "destruction" in the LXX (it does not occur elsewhere in the NT).[21] Yet "destruction" does not make for a good English collocation with covenant: hence my choice of "being cancelled." Several interpreters think

---

Hebrews is teaching that "the blessings of the new covenant are now being experienced in a partial way by the church," with their full experience to come when ethnic Israel is converted (*Jeremiah, Lamentations*, NAC [Nashville: Broadman, 1993], 283–84).

20. The Greek here uses the preposition ἐν with an infinitive, λέγειν, "to say" (the same construction occurs in 3:15). We could translate "in speaking" (BDF §403.3), but an instrumental meaning might be better (Ellingworth, *Hebrews*, 418).

21. See, e.g., 2 Chr 36:19: "every beautiful vessel was [consigned] to destruction" (πᾶν σκεῦος ὡραῖον εἰς ἀφανισμόν).

that "near to being cancelled" refers to the author's own time.[22] However, this underplays the author's strong contention that the once-for-all sacrifice of Christ, already accomplished, has already ushered in the new era. It is better, then, to suppose that "near to being cancelled" refers to the time of Jeremiah: in conveying this promise of a new covenant to the people in his day, the near end of the old covenant is clearly indicated—an end that has now taken place in Christ.[23]

Theology in Application

The Covenants: Continuity and Discontinuity

A long time ago now, when I was first learning theology as a seminary student, I was introduced to two contrasting "systems" of thought: covenant theology and dispensationalism. The former tradition stressed continuity in salvation history, holding to the notion of a single covenant, spanning the time from the fall to the new creation. Dispensationalism, on the other hand, stressed discontinuity, with a salvation history marked by distinct stages in the unfolding of God's redemptive plan.

We live in a time when, thankfully, some of these strong binary options have been at least modified. With the advent of "progressive dispensationalism," dispensational thinkers are often arguing for more continuity than in the past,[24] and a willingness to acknowledge more discontinuity has marked recent covenant theology ("progressive covenantalism").[25] But these movements have not yet met in the middle! One of the continuing points of debate is the degree of continuity in the sequence of biblical covenants. Many interpreters and theologians continue to construe salvation history in terms of one overarching covenant. On this view, the "new" covenant Jeremiah predicts is a "renewed" covenant—a reissuing of the Sinai covenant. While not developed by our author, implications of this way of looking at the covenants often include an emphasis on continuity in the law—the law of Moses continuing to have at least modified authority over the people of God—and a recognition that the "sign" of the covenant, circumcision, has its counterpart in baptism (hence infant baptism).

However, I am not sure that this focus on continuity does justice to the kind of contrast between old and new we see in the New Testament—and in Hebrews 8:7–13 in particular. The strength of the author's comments about the old covenant that frame the quotation from Jeremiah (vv. 7–8a and 13) suggests to me a greater

---

22. E.g., Koester, *Hebrews*, 392. A few interpreters think that the author may be thinking about the imminent destruction of the temple (e.g., Bruce, *Hebrews*, 195). But this is unlikely; as Attridge puts it, "The author argues exegetically, not historically" (*Hebrews*, 229; see also, e.g., Backhaus, *Der Hebräerbrief*, 299).

23. Cockerill, *Hebrews*, 370.

24. See, e.g., Craig A. Blaising and Darrell L. Bock, eds., *Progressive Dispensationalism* (Grand Rapids: Baker, 1993).

25. See Gentry and Wellum, *Kingdom Through Covenant*; Wellum and Parker, *Progressive Covenantalism*.

focus on discontinuity. A movement called "New Covenant theology" rightly, in my view, reflects the biblical *contrast* between old covenant and new—to be sure, located securely in a single plan of God unfolding and playing out in a single people of God.[26] I suggest, then, that new-covenant believers are no longer directly under the authority of the Mosaic law—we are "under" "the law of Christ"—and that the "sign" of the new covenant, baptism, is to be administered to all those who, by faith, belong to that new covenant.

These are controversial conclusions, and I fully respect the many brothers and sisters who equally sincerely come to different conclusions on these matters.

A rather more general manifestation of this same debate can be seen in current academic biblical interpretation. Here the focus is on the word *supersessionism*. McCruden defines supersessionism: "Judaism is annulled or rendered useless because Christianity is placed above it and takes its place."[27] Does Christianity generally or in some sense "supersede" Judaism? Many scholars today would answer no. They point out that the whole issue is anachronistic: when the New Testament documents were being written, the "parting of the ways" between Judaism and Christianity lay in the future. There was no "Christianity" to supersede Judaism. Jewish "Christians," or "Jesus followers," viewed themselves as Jews who recognized Jesus as their Messiah. Advocates of this view explain the inclusion of gentiles in this new movement in different ways, but they generally insist on a great deal of continuity between Judaism and early Jewish Christianity.

The continuity must indeed be recognized. New Testament writers continued to view the Old Testament as their own authoritative "Scripture." Paul, for instance, did not stop thinking of himself as a Jew after his conversion—or, as many would like to insist, his "calling." Hebrews, with its resolute emphasis on the "better" things that have come in Christ, at first sight appears to resist this focus on continuity. Nevertheless, a number have argued that this conclusion is mistaken—Hebrews does not advocate "supersessionism."[28]

I am not convinced. To be sure, the author is wrongly interpreted if we misconstrue his "better" contrast to entail full-scale rejection. The message proclaiming Christ is a "better" word than the Old Testament word—but, as his many appeals to the authority of the Old Testament indicate, the author was by no means abandoning the Old Testament or "replacing" it with the new. The Old Testament word continues to "speak." God himself ordained the cult, the priesthood, the sanctuary—and these

---

26. Tom Wells and Fred Zaspel, *New Covenant Theology* (Frederick, MD: New Covenant Media, 2002). For further arguments in favor of this general way of relating the testaments, see Douglas J. Moo, "Law of Moses or the Law of Christ," 203–18; Moo, "Law of Christ as the Fulfillment of the Law of Moses," 319–76.

27. Mitchell, "'Sacrifice of Praise,'" 252. See esp. R. Kendall Soulen, *The God of Israel and Christian Theology* (Minneapolis: Fortress, 1996).

28. E.g., Richard B. Hays, "'Here We Have No Lasting City': New Covenantalism in Hebrews," in Bauckham et al., *Epistle to the Hebrews*, 151–73; Mitchell, "'Sacrifice of Praise,'" 251–67; Matthew Thiessen, "Hebrews and the Jewish Law," in Laansma, Guthrie, and Westfall, *So Great a Salvation*, 183–94.

were "good" things. In place of "supersessionism" or "replacement," then, we might more profitably follow the lead of the New Testament and speak of "fulfillment." However, the author is also clear that Old Testament institutions and regulations did not ultimately bring about full access to God. Since Judaism, though taking many different forms, derived its religious significance from these Old Testament institutions and forms of worship, a clash with the early Jesus movement, which insisted that the only way to access God was by means of the once-for-all sacrifice and continuing ministry of the high priest Jesus, was inevitable. In this sense, then, I think we can accurately apply the word *supersession* to Hebrews's theology. Hebrews, along with other New Testament writers, claims an ultimacy for Christ that makes relationship to him the sole criterion of covenant membership, thereby removing the standard marks of Judaism—Torah obedience, temple piety, the land—from that role.[29]

---

29. Oskar Skarsaune, "Does the Letter to the Hebrews Articulate a Supersessionist Theology? A Response to Richard Hays," in Bauckham et al., *Epistle to the Hebrews*, 174–82; Filtvedt, *Identity of God's People*; G. W. Lee, *Today When You Hear His Voice*, 189–92. On the larger issue, with particular reference to Paul, see esp. N. T. Wright, *Paul and the Faithfulness of God*, 1428–43.

Hebrews 9:1–10

Literary Context

In the overview of the author's celebration of Christ's high-priestly ministry (8:1–9:28), he introduces three of the key elements of priestly ministry: a sanctuary, a covenant, and a sacrifice (8:1–6). In 8:7–13, the author situates Jesus's ministry within the new covenant prophesied by Jeremiah, revealing the superiority of Christ's high-priestly work. Now, in 9:1–10, he focuses on the sanctuary, arguing that, for all its divinely ordained trappings, it ultimately reveals the inadequacy of providing for a full and final forgiveness of sins.

- I. The Exalted Son and a Rest for the People of God (1:1–4:13)
- **II. Our Great High Priest and His Ministry (4:14–10:31)**
    - A. Exhortation: Persevere through the Power of Our Exalted High Priest (4:14–16)
    - B. Exposition: High Priests and Our High Priest (5:1–10)
    - C. Exhortation: Move on to Maturity (5:11–6:20)
    - D. Exposition: A High Priest "According to the Order of Melchizedek" (7:1–28)
    - E. Exposition: The Ministry of Our High Priest (8:1–10:18)
        1. Overview: Sanctuary, Sacrifice, and Covenant (8:1–6)
        2. A New and Better Covenant (8:7–13)
        ➙ **3. The Earthly Sanctuary and Its Regulations: An Illustration of the New (9:1–10)**
        4. Eternal Redemption: Heavenly Sanctuary, Decisive Sacrifice, and New Covenant (9:11–28)
        5. The Ultimate Sacrifice (10:1–18)
    - F. Exhortation and Warning: Appropriating the Benefits of Our High Priest's Ministry (10:19–31)
- III. Exhortation: Follow and Serve the Pioneer of Our Faith through Endurance and Faith (10:32–13:25)

Main Idea

The various components of the Old Testament sanctuary and the regulations for sacrifice within it reveal that the old covenant could not provide for full and final forgiveness of sins.

Translation

Hebrews 9:1–10

1a	development	Now
1b	assertion	**the first covenant had** regulations for worship and
1c	parallel	an earthly sanctuary.
2a	expansion (of 1b–c)	For
2b	assertion	**a tabernacle was prepared.**
2c	elaboration (of 2b)	In its outer room were the lampstand and
2d	list	the table and
2e	list	the presentation of the loaves.
2f	identification (of 2b)	This was called the Holy Place.
3a	series (with 2b)	And **behind the second curtain is a room**
3b	identification	called the Most Holy Place,
4a	description	having the golden incense altar and
4b	list	the ark of the covenant
4c	description 1	covered on all sides with gold,
4d	contents	in which was found the golden jar
4e	description	containing the manna and
4f	list	the staff of Aaron
4g	description	which budded, and
4h	list	the tablets of the covenant.
5a	series (with 3a)	And over the ark were the cherubim of glory,
5b	manner	overshadowing the atonement cover.
5c	conclusion (of 1a–5b)	But **now is not the time to speak**
5d	reference	about these things
5e	manner	in detail.
6a	circumstance (of 6c)	These things having been prepared
6b	manner	in this way,
6c	expansion (of 1b)	**the priests enter the outer room**
6d	time	regularly,

6e	elaboration		fulfilling their ritual duties,
7a	contrast	but	
7b	location		into the inner room
7c	assertion	**only the high priest goes,**	
7d	time		once a year— and
7e	manner		not without blood,
7f	description		which he offers
7g	advantage		for himself and
7h	parallel		for the sins the people had committed
7i	manner		in ignorance.
8a	implication (of 1–7)	In this way	
8b	assertion	**the Holy Spirit reveals**	
8c	content	that the way . . .	
8d	identification		into the Most Holy Place
8e	predicate (of 8c)	. . . was not yet disclosed,	
8f	circumstance		as long as the first tabernacle still had standing.
9a	elaboration (of 8f)	This is an illustration	
9b	reference		for that present time,
9c	content	when	
9d	assertion		gifts and
9e	parallel		sacrifices were offered
9f	description		that were never able
9g	content		to perfect the worshiper
9h	reference		in terms of their conscience.
10a	expansion (of 9e–f)	[These gifts and sacrifices had to do] only with matters	
10b	reference		of food and
10c	parallel		drink and
10d	parallel		various ceremonial washings—
10e	generic		regulations having to do with the flesh
10f	description		which were imposed
10g	time		until the time
			of the new
			order.

Structure

The passage is divided in two, the first part describing the Old Testament sanctuary (vv. 1–7) and the second (vv. 8–10) drawing out the significance of that description. The first part divides, further, into two sections. Verses 1–5 list various components of the sanctuary, while verses 6–7 briefly overview the sacrificial ministry of the priests in that sanctuary, with a focus on the Day of Atonement ritual. These two parts relate chiastically to the introduction in verse 1:

"regulations" (v. 1)
"sanctuary" (v. 1)
the trappings of the sanctuary (vv. 2–5)
the regulations (vv. 6–7)

An *inclusio* again marks the boundaries of the passage: "the first covenant had regulations [δικαιώματα] for worship" (v. 1); they are . . . external "regulations [δικαιώματα]" (v. 10).

Exegetical Outline

→ 3. The Earthly Sanctuary and Its Regulations: An Illustration of the New (9:1–10)
    a. Old Covenant Sanctuary and Regulations (vv. 1–7)
      i. Sanctuary (vv. 1–5)
      ii. Regulations (vv. 6–7)
    b. The Inadequacy of the Old Sanctuary and Its Regulations (vv. 8–10)

Explanation of the Text

9:1 Now[1] the first covenant had regulations for worship and an earthly sanctuary (Εἶχε μὲν οὖν καὶ[2] ἡ πρώτη δικαιώματα λατρείας τό τε ἅγιον κοσμικόν). The author introduces his description of the Old Testament sanctuary and its ministry. "Covenant" has no corresponding word in the Greek, but the reference simply to "first" (πρώτη) in context (τὴν πρώτην in 8:13 clearly refers to "the first covenant") makes clear that this is what the author intends (so all the English translations).[3] The author's use of the particle μέν suggests that he intends a contrast with something that comes later in the text. This particle is usually paired with δέ, and the content of the verses suggests that this contrast might come in verse 6—"the first covenant had regulations" (v. 1), but, even with "things having been prepared," the covenant was inadequate.[4] However, the intended contrast more likely encompasses the two first parts of chapter 9. In this case, though they are quite far apart, it may be that the μέν in verse 1 is answered by the δέ in verse 11: "on the one hand" (as μέν is often translated), the old covenant had a

---

1. "Now" is a good English equivalent to the use of οὖν to denote the new stage of an argument.
2. The καί here is textually uncertain (NA[28] has brackets around the word, and in the introduction it indicates that brackets "reflect a great degree of difficulty in determining the text" [p. 54]). The word is omitted in some early and very good MSS (e.g., 𝔓[46], B), but it is included in some good ones also (e.g., ℵ, A)—and it is found in a wide spread of MSS. Because of the other conjunctions at the beginning of this verse, its inclusion is probably the more difficult reading. The word is represented in some versions by "even," suggesting a correspondence between the first and second covenants (RSV; NRSV; ESV; NAB; NASB; Weiss, *Der Brief an die Hebräer*, 450). However, it might better be translated "also" (NJB), implying a continuation of discussion of the first covenant from 8:13.
3. See, e.g., Westcott, *Hebrews*, 243; Attridge, *Hebrews*, 231. A few MSS read σκηνή, "tabernacle."
4. Westcott, *Hebrews*, 243.

sanctuary and regulations that were inadequate to take care of sin (vv. 1–10), but, "on the other hand" (the correlative δέ), Christ has obtained an "eternal redemption" (vv. 11–14).⁵ The first covenant had "regulations" to govern its worship and "an earthly sanctuary." The word I have translated "earthly," κοσμικόν, was sometimes applied to the sanctuary or to the worship conducted within it, with a positive sense. Josephus, for instance, refers to "ceremonies of world-wide significance [κοσμικῆς]," which have been "reverenced by visitors to the city from every quarter of the earth" (J.W. 4.324). Other Jewish and patristic writers viewed the tabernacle as a model of the universe.⁶ However, the context of this verse makes clear that the author uses the word in a neutral-to-negative way: the old covenant sanctuary belonged to the earth, to "this world," in contrast to the heavenly sanctuary, where Christ offers himself as a sacrifice.⁷

9:2 For a tabernacle was prepared. In its outer room were the lampstand and the table and the presentation of the loaves. This was called the Holy Place (σκηνὴ γὰρ κατεσκευάσθη ἡ πρώτη ἐν ᾗ ἥ τε λυχνία καὶ ἡ τράπεζα καὶ ἡ πρόθεσις τῶν ἄρτων, ἥτις λέγεται Ἅγια). Following the Lord's instructions about the form of the earthly tabernacle, the author distinguishes between the "outer" room and the "inner" room in that tabernacle. Unfortunately, the author is not completely consistent in the terminology he uses to describe these parts of the tabernacle. In the following chart, I set out my own decisions about the references intended by the various expressions, along with the English I will use to represent those entities:

Hebrews	Reference	Translation
8:2 τῶν ἁγίων	the sanctuary as a whole	sanctuary
τῆς σκηνῆς τῆς ἀληθινῆς	the tabernacle as a whole	true tabernacle
8:5 σκηνήν	the tabernacle as a whole	tabernacle
9:1 ἅγιον κοσμικόν	the sanctuary as a whole	earthly sanctuary
9:2 σκηνή	the tabernacle as a whole	tabernacle
9:2 πρώτη . . .	the outer room in the tabernacle	outer room
9:2 Ἅγια	the Holy Place (= outer room)	Holy Place
9:3 σκηνή	the inner room	room
9:3 Ἅγια Ἁγίων	the inner room of the sanctuary	Most Holy Place
9:6 τὴν πρώτην σκηνήν	the outer room	outer room
9:8 τῶν ἁγίων	the inner room of the sanctuary	Most Holy Place
9:8 τῆς πρώτης σκηνῆς	the first tabernacle as a whole	the first tabernacle
9:11 τῆς . . . σκηνῆς	the first tabernacle as a whole	tabernacle
9:12 τὰ ἅγια	the inner room of the sanctuary	Most Holy Place

---

5. E.g., Attridge, *Hebrews*, 238; Johnson, *Hebrews*, 218. Ellingworth, however, objects, arguing that the δέ in v. 11 is too far from the μέν in v. 1 (*Hebrews*, 420).

6. E.g., Philo, *Moses* 2.48, 81–108; *QE* 2.51–106; Theodore of Mopsuestia (PG 66:694).

7. So most commentators. The word occurs only once else in the NT, with a pejorative sense: "worldly passions" (Titus 2:12). The author may put the adjective here in the predicative position (τὸ . . . ἅγιον κοσμικόν) to highlight this characteristic. Zerwick translates "(the) sanctuary, which (however) was a terrestrial one" (*Biblical Greek*, §187). This word order might also be the basis for the ESV's "earthly place of holiness."

I follow several versions in using the language of "first" versus "second" to refer to the contrast between old and new covenants along with their tabernacles/sanctuaries, and the language of "outer" and "inner" to refer to the two "rooms" within the tabernacle (e.g., RSV; NET). On this view, "first" and "second," when applied to the sanctuary, have a primarily spatial focus, tracing the movement of a person who would move through the tabernacle from its "first," or "outer" room, into its "second," or "inner."[8] I also follow the NIV in referring to the outer room as the "Holy Place" and the inner room as the "Most Holy Place."

One of the debated references occurs here at the beginning of verse 2. On the one hand, "the tabernacle" (σκηνή) that was "set up" could refer to the tabernacle as a whole, in which case "the outer room" (ἡ πρώτη; σκηνή is assumed) refers to a part of that tabernacle. The NIV apparently follows this interpretation: "A tabernacle was set up. In its first room . . ." The other option is to take "the outer" to be in apposition to "tabernacle"; see, for example, ESV: "for a tent was prepared, the first section . . ."[9] As my translation reveals, I prefer the former option. The author begins by referring to the "setting up" of the tabernacle as a whole, elaborating on the reference to the "earthly sanctuary" at the end of verse 1 (the γάρ, as often, introduces an explanation).[10] He then mentions some of the trappings within the outer (v. 2b) and inner (vv. 3–5) rooms.

The author, as we have seen, focuses on the portable "tent" or "tabernacle" (σκηνή) that the Lord commanded the Israelites to construct and carry along during their pilgrimage through the wilderness to the promised land. This concern with the tabernacle, rather than the temple, fits the author's rhetorical framework (see 3:7–4:11). For the most part, his brief inventory of the various trappings of the outer and inner rooms follows the Lord's instructions about how the tabernacle and its furnishings were to be made in Exodus 25–30, along with the description of their construction in Exodus 36:8–38:31. But some of the items and their placement are mentioned in other parts of the Old Testament or in Jewish tradition. The three items mentioned in verse 2b—"the lampstand," "the table," and the "presentation of the loaves"—are mentioned respectively in Exodus 25:31–40//37:17–24; 25:23–29//37:10–16; and 25:30. All three were to be placed in front of the curtain shielding the Most Holy Place (26:33–35). This outer room, the author concludes, is also called the Holy Place (Ἅγια).[11]

9:3–5 And behind the second curtain is a room called the Most Holy Place, 4 having the golden incense altar and the ark of the covenant covered on all sides with gold, in which was found the golden jar containing the manna and the staff of Aaron which budded, and the tablets of the covenant. 5 And over the ark were the cherubim of glory, overshadowing the atonement cover. But now is not the time to speak about these things in detail (μετὰ δὲ τὸ δεύτερον καταπέτασμα σκηνὴ ἡ λεγομένη Ἅγια Ἁγίων, 4 χρυσοῦν ἔχουσα θυμιατήριον καὶ τὴν κιβωτὸν

---

8. Lane, *Hebrews*, 2:216. Josephus uses "first" and "second" in a similar way with respect to the temple (*J.W.* 5.193–94).

9. Most commentators favor this option, e.g., Attridge, *Hebrews*, 232; D. Harris, *Hebrews*, 210.

10. See NLT; CSB; NJB; see the translation in Lane, *Hebrews*, 2:214.

11. With most translations and commentators, I take Ἅγια as a neuter plural, referring, as often in the LXX, to the outer room of the sanctuary, the Holy Place (e.g., Lane, *Hebrews*, 2:215; Koester, *Hebrews*, 394). However, the word could also be a feminine singular, agreeing with πρόθεσις—"the presentation of the bread, which is holy." Some commentators (Attridge, *Hebrews*, 233–34) argue for the variant Ἅγια Ἁγίων, contending it is the more difficult reading (since the phrase usually refers to the "Most Holy Place").

τῆς διαθήκης περικεκαλυμμένην πάντοθεν χρυσίῳ, ἐν ᾗ στάμνος χρυσῆ ἔχουσα τὸ μάννα καὶ ἡ ῥάβδος Ἀαρὼν ἡ βλαστήσασα καὶ αἱ πλάκες τῆς διαθήκης, 5 ὑπεράνω δὲ αὐτῆς Χερουβὶν δόξης κατασκιάζοντα τὸ ἱλαστήριον· περὶ ὧν οὐκ ἔστιν νῦν λέγειν κατὰ μέρος). The author continues a brief overview of the key elements found in the two "rooms" of the Old Testament sanctuary. A fundamental feature of the tabernacle was its division into two sections, a curtain serving to separate the two.[12] The author refers to this as the "second curtain" since another curtain was also fundamental in closing off the tabernacle as a whole (e.g., Exod 26:31–37). The word translated "behind" (μετά), when used with an accusative, has a temporal meaning everywhere else in the New Testament. BDAG ("μετά," 637, §B.1) notes this occurrence as the only place it has a spatial sense. However, if I am right about the way "first" and "second" function in the context to refer to stages of movement, a minor temporal sense might still be present: "after the second curtain, one comes to."[13] In any case, the author's point is clear: in addition to the "Holy Place," the outer room, there is another, inner room, the "Most Holy Place" (ἅγια ἁγίων). A chiastic arrangement of material is evident in verses 2b–5a: components of the outer room (v. 2b)—name of the outer room ("Holy Place") (v. 2c)—name of the inner room ("Most Holy Place") (v. 3)—components of the inner room (vv. 4–5a). The author's list of components of the inner room again depends mainly on Exodus, although the impact of other Old Testament texts and Jewish tradition is more to the fore in this list. First, the author mentions the golden incense altar (χρυσοῦν . . . θυμιατήριον).[14] Specifications for its construction as well as its actual construction are found in Exodus (30:1–6//37:25–28). However, the Exodus accounts strongly suggest that this altar was to be placed in the outer room: "in front of the curtain that shields the ark of the covenant law" (Exod 30:6; see also 40:26). It is not clear why the author locates this altar in the inner room. There are two main possibilities. First, the author may have read his LXX source as indicating the placement of the altar in the Most Holy Place. The three relevant texts are a bit ambiguous: they locate the altar "opposite" (ἀπέναντι) the curtain (Exod 30:6; 40:26) or "opposite" (ἐναντίον) the ark (Exod 40:5). These most likely indicate placement in the outer room, but they are not entirely clear.[15] Moreover, the author may have noted that the incense altar is not mentioned with the other furnishings of the Holy Place (there is no reference to it in Exod 25) and that it is featured in the Day of Atonement ritual (30:10).[16] Second, the author may not locate the altar in the inner room at all. He uses the rather vague verb "having" (ἔχουσα) to describe the altar's placement vis-à-vis the inner room: he might mean that the inner room "has" the altar in the sense that one must approach the inner room by means of it.[17] Neither explanation is altogether convincing, and so we must leave the

---

12. The author's reference simply to another "tabernacle" (σκηνή) could be read as if he were envisaging two separate structures. Clearly this is not his intention. To capture the sense, I have translated σκηνή in these contexts as "room."

13. BDF §226; Turner, *Syntax*, 269 (hesitantly).

14. The word θυμιατήριον means simply "a place or vessel for the burning of incense" and usually refers to a censer ("θυμιατήριον," BDAG 461). Here, however, it is clear the author refers to the altar on which incense was burned (Philo [e.g., *Moses* 2.94] and Josephus [e.g., *Ant.* 3.147] both use the word this way, although it is not found in the LXX with this reference).

15. Texts that might suggest this placement are 1 Kgs 6:22; 2 Macc 2:4–8; 2 Bar 6.7. See, e.g., Attridge, *Hebrews*, 234–35; Grässer, *An die Hebräer*, 2:120–22.

16. As Alexander (*Exodus*, 601–2) points out, the incense altar is first mentioned in the sanctuary provisions that focus on God's "meeting" with the people (Exod 27:20–30:38).

17. The approach to the Most Holy Place by means of this altar is a feature of the Day of Atonement ritual, in which the author is very interested (Westcott, *Hebrews*, 247).

discrepancy unsolved. In any case, the matter does not affect the author's argument.

The second item the author lists is the ark of the covenant, covered on all sides with gold—a standard feature of the Most Holy Place (see Exod 25:10–16//37:1–5). The next two items are located by the author within the ark, although the Old Testament is silent about this placement. The Lord commands that a jar (though not described as "golden" in the OT) filled with manna be put "with the tablets of the covenant law" (Exod 16:33–34). The staff of Aaron, before it budded, was to be placed "in the tent of the covenant law" (Num 17:7 [LXX 17:22]); after it budded, it was placed "in front of the ark of the covenant law" (Num 17:10 [LXX 17:25]).[18] The "tablets [πλάκες] of the covenant" were, on the other hand, clearly required to be placed within the ark (Exod 25:16, 21; Deut 10:1–5; cf. 1 Kgs 8:9; 2 Chr 5:10). The final feature of the tabernacle our author mentions, in verse 5, is "the cherubim of the Glory." I follow several versions and commentators in taking "glory" (δόξα) as a reference to the divine presence (capitalized in the NIV; "divine glory" in NLT).[19] The "cherubim" (a transliteration of Greek Χερουβίν, itself a transliteration of the Hebrew כְּרֻבִים) were "creatures associated with the presence of God."[20] They were, then, naturally associated with the "atonement cover" (ἱλαστήριον), the object within the Most Holy Place where the high priest offered sacrifices for the sins of the people on the Day of Atonement (Exod 25:17–22; 37:6–9; Lev 16). It is fitting that our author should conclude with this item, since the imagery of the Day of Atonement will be important in his description of the work of our great high priest, as verses 6–7 demonstrate. The author concludes this section by noting that he will not say anything about these matters "in detail" (κατὰ μέρος).[21] Indeed, we might wonder why the author goes into as much detail as he does. Unlike many later interpreters, he is not interested in assigning allegorical significance to the various components of the tabernacle. In fact, he does not bring up again in the letter any of the specific trappings of the tabernacle that he lists here. Probably, as verse 8 suggests, the author wants to remind us of the complicated procedures necessary in the Old Testament for anyone to approach God—in contrast, of course, to the access we all now have through the ministry of our high priest Jesus.

9:6–7 These things having been prepared in this way, the priests enter the outer room regularly, fulfilling their ritual duties, 7 but into the inner room only the high priest goes, once a year—and not without blood, which he offers for himself and for the sins the people had committed in ignorance (Τούτων δὲ οὕτως κατεσκευασμένων εἰς μὲν τὴν πρώτην σκηνὴν διὰ παντὸς εἰσίασιν οἱ ἱερεῖς τὰς λατρείας ἐπιτελοῦντες, 7 εἰς δὲ τὴν δευτέραν ἅπαξ τοῦ ἐνιαυτοῦ μόνος ὁ ἀρχιερεύς, οὐ χωρὶς αἵματος ὃ προσφέρει ὑπὲρ ἑαυτοῦ καὶ τῶν τοῦ λαοῦ ἀγνοημάτων). An important feature of worship in the Old Testament sanctuary, one that becomes basic to the author's argument, is the restricted access to the inner room. "These things

---

18. Jewish tradition added various items to the contents of the ark; see Bruce, *Hebrews*, 204.

19. Lane, *Hebrews*, 2:216; Koester, *Hebrews*, 396. Others understand δόξης as a descriptive genitive ("glorious winged creatures," NJB; see Attridge, *Hebrews*, 238).

20. A. Steinmann, "Cherubim," in Alexander and Baker, *Dictionary of the Old Testament: Pentateuch*, 112–13.

21. See "μέρος," BDAG 633, §1.c, on this meaning of the phrase. Von Siebenthal notes that this clause is an example of what he calls "a continuative relative clause" that is conceptually an independent clause (*Ancient Greek Grammar*, 545).

having been prepared" is a transitional clause. The author uses the same verb that occurs in the introductory statement in verse 2 (κατασκευάζω), thereby closing off the first part of the passage with an *inclusio*.[22] At the same time, it prepares the way for the new focus of verses 6b-7. In these verses, the author turns to the "regulations" put into place for ministry in that sanctuary (see v. 1). His concern is with the distinction between the two "rooms" that he briefly described in verses 2-5a. Priests "regularly" (διὰ παντός)[23] enter the outer room (τὴν πρώτην σκηνήν, "the first tent/tabernacle"), where they carry out their ritual duties (τὰς λατρείας; see v. 1). The Old Testament cultic law, of course, specifies that the priests should regularly enter this outer room of the tabernacle, thereby "performing" (ἐπιτελοῦντες) the required "rituals" (τὰς λατρείας).[24]

In strong contrast (the δέ here is adversative) to this cultic ministry in the outer room is the ministry to be performed in the inner room (δευτέραν, "second," with σκηνή assumed, "tent/tabernacle"; here "room"). "Priests" (οἱ ἱερεῖς) in general minister in the outer room, but only the high priest (ὁ ἀρχιερεύς) carries out functions in the inner room. Priests enter the inner room regularly, but the high priest enters the inner room only once a year (ἅπαξ τοῦ ἐνιαυτοῦ[25]). The author says nothing about any ritual that is needed to clear the way for the priests to enter the outer room. But the high priest can enter the inner room only with "blood"—the blood that is obtained from the sacrifice that is offered both for himself and for the "sins the people had committed in ignorance." The author refers here to the high priest's ministry on the Day of Atonement (Lev 16), which furnishes the basic pattern for his description of the ministry of Jesus, our high priest. Indeed, all three elements of the Day of Atonement ministry mentioned in this verse—only the high priest, only once a year, only with blood—feature significantly in the author's description of Jesus's heavenly atoning work.[26] The Day of Atonement ritual emphasizes the need of the high priest to offer sacrifice for himself and his household (Lev 16:6, 11). While the author does not here develop its significance, the fact that the Old Testament high priest had to offer sacrifice for himself stands in implicit contrast to Jesus as high priest who, because he was sinless, has no need to sacrifice for himself (the author develops this point in 7:26-28). Why the author characterizes the sins of the people as "acts of ignorance" (ἀγνοημάτων) is harder to know. The Day of Atonement ritual does not restrict the efficacy of its ritual to these kinds of sins only; indeed, the description of the ritual concludes with a reference to "atonement" being made "for all the sins of the Israelites" (Lev 16:34).[27] Of course, the Old Testament elsewhere does restrict the efficacy of the sacrifices to certain kinds of sins. Three kinds of sin are mentioned in Leviticus

---

22. Massonnet, *L'Épître aux Hébreux*, 222. The verb occurs in v. 6a in a genitive absolute construction: τούτων ... κατεσκευασμένων. The verb κατασκευάζω, which occurs here as a perfect participle, means basically "make ready, prepare," though BDAG ("κατασκευάζω," 526-27, §1) suggests the meaning "furnish" here.

23. The phrase can mean either "always" or, as here, "continually" ("διά," BDAG 224, §A.2.a).

24. The words in quotation marks are from the BDAG entries ("ἐπιτελέω," 383, §2, cf. "λατρεία," 587, which translates with "rites") on this verse.

25. The genitive may signify, as in classical Greek, the time within which something takes place (BDF §186.2).

26. Jamieson, *Jesus' Death and Heavenly Offering*, 38.

27. Rabbinic tradition, however, does sometimes restrict the efficacy of the Day of Atonement ritual to certain kinds of sins, but in a way very different than Hebrews; e.g., m. Yoma 8:9 claims that sins between humans and God are atoned for, but that sins against fellow humans are not (unless restitution has taken place).

and Numbers: unintentional sin, intentional but not defiant sin, and defiant ("high-handed") sin. Forgiveness through sacrifice was available for the first two kinds, but not for the third—although it is possible that this third type of sin could be atoned for by a mediator.[28] However, the word the author uses here—ἀγνόημα—is not the word used in the LXX to refer to "sins of ignorance."[29] It is possible, then, that the author uses the word "ignorance" not to specify a particular kind of sin but to refer to sins in general (see, e.g., RSV "errors"; NAB "sins").[30]

9:8 In this way the Holy Spirit reveals that the way into the Most Holy Place[31] was not yet disclosed, as long as the first tabernacle still had standing (τοῦτο δηλοῦντος τοῦ πνεύματος τοῦ ἁγίου, μήπω πεφανερῶσθαι τὴν τῶν ἁγίων ὁδὸν ἔτι τῆς πρώτης σκηνῆς ἐχούσης στάσιν). After detailing some of the furnishings of each tabernacle "room" (vv. 1–5) and drawing attention to key "regulations" governing the use of each room (vv. 6–7), the author indicates the significance of all of this for his overall argument: the old system of cultic worship is inadequate to take care of the human sin problem (vv. 8–10).

This application is attributed to the Holy Spirit, who "reveals" the meaning of the tabernacle's structure and furnishings.[32] My translation "reveals" is disputed. The verb used here—δηλόω—often has a rather prosaic meaning: "indicate," "point out"; see, for example, 1 Corinthians 1:11, where Paul notes that people from Chloe's household have "informed" [ἐδηλώθη] him that there were quarrels among the Corinthians. However, this verb also has a stronger meaning: "making clear what is otherwise obscure or hidden."[33] It is used, for instance, fourteen times in the LXX of Daniel 2 to refer to the "revealing" or "interpreting" of dreams. This stronger meaning fits well here. The nature of the tabernacle would have made clear to the Israelites that approaching a holy God was a daunting prospect. But only with New Testament revelation was it clear that a new work of God was required to "open the way into the Most Holy Place."[34] The ministry of the Holy Spirit here, then, is not confined to the inspiration of Scripture (see 3:7; 10:15) but includes also the opening up of the meaning of Scripture to the contemporary audience.[35]

As the author has just noted, "the way into the Most Holy Place" was open to the high priest once a year on the Day of Atonement.[36] But the author's point in this verse is that it was not open

---

28. Jay Sklar, "Sin and Atonement: Lessons from the Pentateuch," *BBR* 22 (2012): 467–91. See also Mark J. Boda, *A Severe Mercy: Sin and Its Remedy in the Old Testament*, Siphrut: Literature and Theology of the Hebrew Scriptures (Winona Lake, IN: Eisenbrauns, 2009), 50–67.

29. The LXX usually refers to sinning "unintentionally" (ἀκουσίως). The verb ἀγνοέω does occur twice to refer to "sinning ignorantly" (Lev 4:13; 5:18) in this specific sense.

30. E.g., Koester, *Hebrews*, 397; Cockerill, *Hebrews*, 380. There is some basis for this in occurrences of the word in the LXX (see Sir 23:2; 51:19). Among those who think the word refers to a limited range of sins are Johnson, *Hebrews*, 223.

31. Greek τὴν τῶν ἁγίων ὁδόν. Wallace classifies the genitive as a "genitive of destination" (*Greek Grammar*, 101); von Siebenthal as a "genitive of direction" (*Ancient Greek Grammar*, 243).

32. The author again uses a genitive absolute: τοῦτο δηλοῦντος τοῦ πνεύματος τοῦ ἁγίου—"in this the Holy Spirit is revealing." The τοῦτο may be the object of δηλοῦντος, its content being elaborated in the following infinitive clause (e.g., D. Harris, *Hebrews*, 215–16). However, the word is more likely an accusative of respect, looking back to the previous verses. Most of the English versions take it in this way, translating "by this" (NIV; ESV; RSV; NRSV; NJB) or "with this" (CEB) or "in this way" (NAB); see, e.g., Ellingworth, *Hebrews*, 437.

33. Johnson's wording (*Hebrews*, 223). For this view, see Mackie, *Eschatology and Exhortation*, 89–90.

34. The infinitive πεφανερῶσθαι introduces the noun (object) clause dependent on δηλοῦντος (von Siebenthal, *Ancient Greek Grammar*, 372–73).

35. See, e.g., Lane, *Hebrews*, 2:223; Johnson, *Hebrews*, 223.

36. The phrase τῶν ἁγίων refers here, as the context makes clear, to the Most Holy Place. The author uses the doubled phrase, ἅγια ἁγίων, to designate this "inner room" in v. 3, but

for all worshipers. Access to the Most Holy Place symbolizes access to fellowship with God himself, and the restriction of this access to only the high priest means that the tabernacle has a negative significance for the people of Israel. They learn that their state of unholiness keeps them from approaching the holy God. It is this very access to the holy God that Christ's high priestly ministry makes possible.[37] This way into the presence of God was not "disclosed" (πεφανερῶσθαι) as long as the old tabernacle still had "normative status."[38] In putting matters like this, I make two decisions. First, I think that the author is referring here to the "first" tabernacle as a whole rather than to the "first" or "outer" room within the tabernacle (the Greek is τῆς πρώτης σκηνῆς). The latter is certainly possible in light of the author's use of "first [tabernacle]" in this way in verses 2 and 6.[39] However, the author appears to be returning to the significance of the tabernacle as a whole (see v. 1), and the focus in this context is on the temporal shift in salvation history, as the "present time" (v. 9), "the time of the new order" (v. 10), the time of eschatological fulfillment, has dawned.[40] Second, the author uses a word, "standing" (στάσιν), that refers not to simple physical "standing" but to legal "standing."[41] As long as the first tabernacle had divine sanction for the operation of the cult, a barrier existed that prevented all but the high priest—and he, only once a year—from entering into the Most Holy Place, the place where the magnificent presence of God was to be found.

9:9 This is an illustration for that present time, when gifts and sacrifices were offered that were never able to perfect the worshiper in terms of their conscience (ἥτις παραβολὴ εἰς τὸν καιρὸν τὸν ἐνεστηκότα, καθ᾽ ἣν δῶρά τε καὶ θυσίαι προσφέρονται μὴ δυνάμεναι κατὰ συνείδησιν τελειῶσαι τὸν λατρεύοντα). The author points out a fundamental weakness in the Old Testament sacrificial system: its inability to provide full and final forgiveness of sins. A relative pronoun (ἥτις) connects this verse with the preceding context (with most translations, I begin a new sentence here for clarity). This pronoun might refer back to the argument of verses 6–8.[42] However, this view runs into difficulties with the case of the pronoun, which is feminine; we would expect a neuter if the reference were to the teaching of verses 6–8.[43] Most interpreters think the pronoun refers to the "first tabernacle" (τῆς πρώτης σκηνῆς), which, as we have seen, could refer to the outer compartment of the tabernacle or to the tabernacle as a whole.

---

he uses the single neuter plural here and in v. 12 to refer to this inner room. The author follows the LXX in this inconsistent application of the language (see, e.g., Num 3:28–38). The translation "holy places" in the ESV is accurate in terms of the form of the word but misses the technical sense of the word in this context.

37. Cockerill argues that ἅγια here refers to the heavenly sanctuary (*Hebrews*, 381). I think that goes too far: the word *refers* to the inner room of the OT sanctuary, while it *symbolizes* the presence of God.

38. Attridge, *Hebrews*, 240. See also, e.g., Lane, *Hebrews*, 2:216; D. Harris, *Hebrews*, 216.

39. G. Guthrie, *Hebrews*, 299–300; Lane, *Hebrews*, 2:223; Attridge, *Hebrews*, 240; Cockerill, *Hebrews*, 381–82. RSV, NRSV, ESV, NAB, and NASB follow this meaning.

40. See, e.g., Hurst, *Epistle to the Hebrews*, 26–27; Bruce, *Hebrews*, 208; Ellingworth, *Hebrews*, 438–39; Michel, *Der Brief an die Hebräer*, 306–7; P. Hughes, *Hebrews*, 323; Bénétrau, *L'Épître aux Hébreux*, 2:67.

41. For the phrase "normative status," see, e.g., Attridge, *Hebrews*, 240; Koester, *Hebrews*, 397. Most versions translate simply "[still] standing," suggesting a physical meaning. See, however, NAB: "had its place."

42. Those who hold this view argue that the pronoun's case has been "attracted" to its predicate, παραβολή (Bruce, *Hebrews*, 209; Zerwick and Grosvenor, *Grammatical Analysis*, 673). But, as Cockerill (*Hebrews*, 383) notes, the author is usually careful about his case agreements.

43. E.g., Attridge, *Hebrews*, 241; Lane, *Hebrews*, 2:224; Cockerill, *Hebrews*, 383.

As I explain above, I prefer the second option, in which case the author is claiming in verse 9a that the existence of the old tabernacle as a whole is an "illustration" for the present time.[44] The phrase "present time" (τὸν καιρὸν τὸν ἐνεστηκότα) could refer to the Old Testament era (see NET, "the time then present"),[45] but more likely, in light of parallel New Testament texts, refers to the author's own time. A reference to the author's current time could, in turn, be understood in two ways: the time when the tabernacle is still functioning, which signals, negatively, the continuing inability of people to draw near to God;[46] or the "time of the new order" (v. 10), the time of fulfillment in which people have new and open access to God through Christ.[47] A decision is difficult. On the one hand, the word I translate "present" (from the verb ἐνίστημι) normally refers, as we would expect, to the time at which the writer of the word is living.[48] On the other hand, the second part of the verse, which explicates the first part, refers to the old era. Perhaps this latter point is the most decisive. Moreover, as we have seen (see my notes on 8:13), the author sometimes uses "present" temporal references to refer to the era of "scriptural time." The NET captures the point well: "this was a symbol for the time then present."

In verse 9b, then, the author elaborates on the negative implications of the old system of worship: "when [i.e., in the previous era] gifts and sacrifices were offered that were never able to perfect the worshiper in terms of their conscience." "Gifts and sacrifices" (δῶρά τε καὶ θυσίαι), as we have seen, is the author's standard language for Old Testament sacrifices in general (5:1; 8:3). The claim that these sacrifices could not "perfect" (τελειῶσαι) the worshiper, in terms, at least, of the "conscience," introduces a key point in the author's critique of the Old Testament sacrifices. "Perfection," as we have seen, is an important concept in the author's theology (see the note on 2:10). Here the author repeats a point he made earlier (7:11, 19): the old system of sacrifices was unable to accomplish the full and final "dealing" with sin that Christ, in his high-priestly redemptive work (see vv. 11, 15), has accomplished (see also 10:1, 14; 11:40; 12:23). "Conscience" (συνείδησις) refers in Hebrews to the "inner" person, and especially the faculty of humans that makes them sensitive to their sinfulness (9:14; 10:2, 22; 13:18). It is in respect of the conscience (κατὰ συνείδησιν) that the sacrifices were unable to perfect worshipers.

9:10 [These gifts and sacrifices had to do] only with matters of food and drink and various ceremonial washings—regulations having to do with the flesh which were imposed until the time of the new order (μόνον ἐπὶ βρώμασιν καὶ πόμασιν καὶ διαφόροις βαπτισμοῖς, δικαιώματα σαρκὸς μέχρι καιροῦ διορθώσεως ἐπικείμενα). The subject of this verse is continued from verse 9.[49] Having denied that "gifts and sacrifices" could cleanse the

---

44. "Illustration" translates παραβολή, which does not here refer to the kind of "narrative parable" Jesus frequently used in his teaching but to a "type" or "figure" (see also Heb 11:19; see "παραβολή," BDAG 759, §1). The meaning would not change if the pronoun had as its antecedent στάσιν, "standing," which I think is also a good option.

45. G. Guthrie, *Hebrews*, 300.

46. Koester, *Hebrews*, 405–6.

47. Ellingworth, *Hebrews*, 441; Weiss, *Der Brief an die Hebräer*, 459; France, "Hebrews," 116.

48. See Rom 8:38; 1 Cor 3:22; 7:26; Gal 1:4; 2 Thess 2:2 [probably]; cf. 2 Tim 3:1.

49. I follow most of the translations in starting a new sentence in English here, requiring the restating of the subject and verb. I also view the μόνον clause as a continuation of v. 9, with δικαιώματα . . . ἐπικείμενα ("regulations . . . imposed") as an appositional modifier of the concept inherent in βρώμασιν καὶ πόμασιν καὶ διαφόροις βαπτισμοῖς ("[rules about] food and drink and various ceremonial washings"). Contra, e.g., D. Harris (*Hebrews*, 217), who reverses the relationship.

conscience, the author now indicates what they were concerned with (ἐπί[50]): "food and drink and various ceremonial washings."[51] There is no point in our trying to pin down exactly which sacrifices or texts the author has in view. He intends simply to describe the Old Testament food laws and the various washings of the body prescribed by the law (see, e.g., Lev 11; 15; Num 19; Deut 14).[52] These "regulations" that were "imposed" have "to do with the flesh."[53] "Regulations" brings us back to where this paragraph began (v. 1). Here we come to the central point our author wants to make: the Old Testament sacrifices are effective only for the "outward" person (σάρξ) and not the inner person ("the conscience" in v. 9). Unlike Paul, who often uses "flesh" in a pejorative way, Hebrews uses it simply to denote the earthly (see 5:7) or outer person.[54] This inner/outer contrast is important for the author, as his repetition of the same point in 9:13–14 reveals: Old Testament sacrifices are for "the cleansing of the flesh [σάρξ]," while Christ's sacrifice "cleanses the conscience [συνείδησις]." The author made a related point earlier: Old Testament priests were elevated to their position "according to a law consisting of a fleshly [σαρκίνης] commandment" (7:16). However, equally important for the author is the shift in salvation history that the coming of Christ introduces. The Old Testament sacrifices retained their validity only until "the time of the new order." The word I translate "new order" (διόρθωσις) occurs only here in the New Testament and not at all in the LXX (though a related word with a similar meaning, διόρθωμα, occurs in Acts 24:2). BDAG ("διόρθωσις," 251) defines it as "a process leading to a new order viewed as something yet to be realized." In addition to "new order" (NIV; NET; CEB; NAB), English versions translate "restoration" (CSB), "a better system" (NLT), "the time . . . to set things right" (NRSV; NJB). What the author describes here as "the new order" is what he has referred to as the "present time" in verse 9, the time when "the good things" God has promised come into being (v. 11; see 10:1). These are different ways of referring to the new era of salvation history, "these last days" (1:2). Contextually, as France notes, the phrase "encapsulates the essence of Jeremiah's prophecy" (the "new covenant" prophecy of 31:31–34, quoted in 8:8b–12). The "yet to be realized" part of the definition in BDAG might go a bit further than the lexical evidence allows. Yet the phrase is not inappropriate as a way of characterizing this new era—an era that has been inaugurated but still awaits consummation.

The author's claim about the exclusively material significance of the Old Testament sacrifices stands in some tension with the claims for spiritual

---

50. "ἐπί," BDAG 366, §16: "marker of object or purpose, with dat. in ref. to someth." Contra BDF §235.2, which suggests the paraphrase "by virtue of, in accordance with." See NASB: "they relate only to. . . ." Westcott (*Hebrews*, 254), on the other hand, suggests that ἐπί denotes "accompanying circumstances": "ordinances of flesh, combined with, resting upon, meats and drinks." See also Cockerill, *Hebrews*, 385.

51. The Greek words for "food" and "drink" are plural, but they have a generic sense; the singular in English captures this nuance best.

52. E.g., Bruce, *Hebrews*, 210. The translation "ceremonial washings" (see NIV) is a good contextual rendering of βαπτισμοῖς, "washings," "baptisms"; see also NLT, "cleansing ceremonies"; and CEB, "ritual ways to wash with water." The author uses this same word with the same basic meaning in Heb 6:2; see also Mark 7:4.

53. "Regulations" translates δικαιώματα, a neuter plural that probably refers generally to the Mosaic legislation concerning sacrifices (for occurrences of this word with a similar meaning, see Luke 1:6; Rom 2:26; Heb 9:1). Some MSS (D¹, the Majority text) have a dative form, putting it in agreement with the dative words earlier in the verse (βρώμασιν, πόμασιν, and βαπτισμοῖς; "foods," "drinks," and "washings").

54. E.g., Lane, *Hebrews*, 2:216–17. The author uses the word to refer to Christ's earthly life (5:7) and body (10:20), to fathers who are "human" (12:7), and in the stock phrase "flesh and blood" (2:14).

significance found throughout the Old Testament. On the Day of Atonement, for instance—an institution that our author is especially focused on—the sacrifices are said to make "atonement" for "all the sins of the Israelites" and to make them "clean from all [their] sins" (Lev 16:30, 34). In other texts, the author himself appears to grant some spiritual significance to the sacrifices. Two considerations help ease the tension. First, the author may be referring to the limitations of the sacrifices in themselves, when not offered in the right spirit. The Old Testament is clear that only those with a genuinely repentant heart benefit from the sacrifices. Second, we should recognize a degree of rhetorical hyperbole in what the author says here, as he tries to convince his readers not to imagine that they might find forgiveness in those sacrifices. The basic reason this is the case is the turn in salvation history. Whatever benefit the Old Testament sacrifices once may have conferred—and the author is clear that they could never secure full and final forgiveness—they can do so no longer, now that Christ has come to usher in the era of reformation.

Theology in Application

Approaching God

In Hebrews's distinctive presentation of salvation, the spatial imagery of "drawing near" to God or "entering" into God's presence stands out. Spatial imagery obviously dominates this paragraph, with its overview of the structure of the sanctuary. One aspect of that structure is of special interest to the author: its division between an "outer room" and an "inner room." This structure itself illustrates, as our author concludes in verse 8, that "the way into the Most Holy Place was not yet disclosed, as long as the first tabernacle still had standing." The coming of Christ, however, opens the way to that Most Holy Place, the representation of the presence of God. The "way" into the Most Holy Place has been opened for us (10:20). The solid hope we have because of the work of Christ "enters the inner sanctuary behind the curtain" (6:19); this hope enables us to "draw near" to God (7:19). Believers in Hebrews are therefore described as those who "draw near" to God (7:19; 10:1; 11:6; 12:22; cf. 7:25). At the same time, we are also urged to "draw near" to God. The importance of this call to draw near can be seen in the fact that the two places where the author urges us to draw near occur in the paragraphs that frame the great central section of Hebrews (4:16 and 10:22). Thus, Hebrews 4:16: "let us then approach God's throne of grace with confidence, so that we may receive mercy and find grace to help us in our time of need." Applying this verse to prayer is entirely appropriate. Yet the call to "draw near" applies much more broadly than just to our prayer life. "Drawing near" to God should mark our entire lives. The detailed prescriptions for how to enter God's presence and the dire warnings about seeking to approach him without appropriate measures in the Old Testament testify to the great gap that exists between sinful humans and a holy God.

But the good news that Hebrews broadcasts is that Christ entered into God's presence as our "pioneer" or "forerunner" (2:10; 12:2). He not only enters ahead of us, leading the way, but through his entrance he paves the way for us to enter as well.

Entrance into the presence of the God of this universe is an inestimable privilege and blessing—available for all those who seek to follow our forerunner in faith. We should not take that privilege lightly but treasure it and take advantage of it every day.

Chapter 22

Hebrews 9:11–28

Literary Context

The second part of chapter 9 stands in contrast to the first part. In 9:1–10, the author has given a brief overview of the old-covenant sanctuary (vv. 1–5) and the "regulations" for ministry within it (vv. 6–10). While ordained by God himself and valuable in certain respects for Old Testament worshipers, the old-covenant arrangements were not able to give those worshipers access to God. The sacrifices offered under that first covenant had a limited impact and were not able to cleanse the conscience. The author now contrasts that old-covenant situation with the situation under the "new covenant" (v. 15) that the appearance of Christ (v. 11) has inaugurated. The fundamental structure of chapter 9, then, is marked, as we have seen, by the contrast indicated by the μέν in verse 1 in combination with the δέ in verse 11: "on the one hand" is the old-covenant system; "on the other hand" is the new-covenant arrangement.

The chapter as a whole elaborates the overview of topics found in 8:1–6. The exalted status of Jesus our high priest (8:1) is the key starting point: his unique access to the Father ("at the right hand") means he ministers in the heavenly sanctuary (8:2, 5), offers a uniquely powerful sacrifice (8:3–4), and inaugurates a new and superior covenant (8:6). All these aspects of Jesus's high-priestly ministry are elaborated in 9:11–28. The author does not take a linear approach in developing these aspects of Christ's ministry; rather, they are juxtaposed with one another in various ways throughout the passage. Along the way the author introduces some other perspectives on Christ's ministry. One of these is a focus on the outcome of Christ's work for believers. He secures for us "an eternal redemption" (v. 12), cleanses our conscience, enabling us to "serve the living God" (v. 14), gives us a certain hope of an "eternal inheritance" (v. 15), and will bring us, at his second coming, "salvation" (v. 28). All these blessings are ours because of Jesus's high-priestly sacrifice of himself in the heavenly sanctuary, which provides for full and final forgiveness (v. 15), doing away once and for all with sin's power over us (vv. 26, 28).

Main Idea

The paragraph is the center and climax of the author's detailed description of the high-priestly ministry of Jesus (8:1–10:18). Jesus enters the heavenly Most Holy Place by means of his own sacrifice, securing for believers ultimate cleansing from sin and "eternal redemption."

I. The Exalted Son and a Rest for the People of God (1:1–4:13)
II. Our Great High Priest and His Ministry (4:14–10:31)
   A. Exhortation: Persevere through the Power of Our Exalted High Priest (4:14–16)
   B. Exposition: High Priests and Our High Priest (5:1–10)
   C. Exhortation: Move on to Maturity (5:11–6:20)
   D. Exposition: A High Priest "According to the Order of Melchizedek" (7:1–28)
   E. Exposition: The Ministry of Our High Priest (8:1–10:18)
      1. Overview: Sanctuary, Sacrifice, and Covenant (8:1–6)
      2. A New and Better Covenant (8:7–13)
      3. The Earthly Sanctuary and Its Regulations: An Illustration of the New (9:1–10)
➡   **4. Eternal Redemption: Heavenly Sanctuary, Decisive Sacrifice, and New Covenant (9:11–28)**
      5. The Ultimate Sacrifice (10:1–18)
   F. Exhortation and Warning: Appropriating the Benefits of Our High Priest's Ministry (10:19–31)
III. Exhortation: Follow and Serve the Pioneer of Our Faith through Endurance and Faith (10:32–13:25)

Translation

Hebrews 9:11–28

* note the interleaving of verses 11 and 12 below

11a	contrast (with 9:1–10)	But	
11b	time		when **Christ** appeared on the scene,
11c	description		a high priest
11d	description		of the good things that have come,
12d	assertion		**he entered**
12e	manner		once for all
12f	direct object (of 12d)		the Most Holy Place,
12g	circumstance		securing an eternal redemption.

Continued on next page.

		[He entered]
11e	means	through the greater and more perfect tabernacle,
11f	description	one not made with human hands,
11g	explanation	that is, not of this creation.
12a	contrast (with 12c)	Nor [did he enter]
12b	means	by means of the blood of goats and calves but
12c	contrast	by means of his own blood.
13a	elaboration (of 12)	For
13b	condition (to 14a)	if the blood of goats and
13c	list	bulls and
13d	list	the ashes of a heifer . . .
13e	description	sprinkled on those who are unclean
13f	predicate (of 13a–e)	. . . sanctifies them
13g	purpose	for the cleansing of the flesh,
14a	comparison (with 13a)	**how much more will the blood of Christ, . . .**
14b	description	who
14c	means	through the eternal spirit
14d	predicate (of 14b)	offered himself blameless to God,
14e	predicate (of 14a)	. . . **cleanse our consciences**
14f	separation	from dead works
14g	purpose	so that we might serve the living God.
15a	inference (from 11–14)	And because of this
15b	assertion	**he is the mediator of a new covenant**,
15c	purpose	so that,
15d	time	now that a death has occurred
15e	result	for the redemption of transgressions
15f	identification	under the first covenant,
15g	assertion	those who are called might receive the promise
15h	content	of an eternal inheritance.
16a	illustration (of 15)	For
16b	reference	in the case of a will,
16c	assertion	[it is] necessary . . .
16d	content	for the death of the one who made it
16e	predicate (of 16c)	. . . to be established.
17a	explanation (of 16)	For
17b	assertion	**a will is confirmed**
17c	basis	on the basis of death;
17d	expansion (of 17a–b)	it cannot come into effect
17e	time	while the one who made the will lives.
18a	inference (from 16–17)	For this reason
18b	assertion	**neither was the first covenant inaugurated**
18c	manner	without blood.

19a	illustration (of 18)	For	
19b	time		when Moses had spoken
19c	extent		every commandment of the law
19d	recipient		to all the people,
19e	assertion		he took the blood of calves,
19f	addition		together with water and
19g	list		scarlet wool and
19h	list		hyssop, and
19i	sequence		**sprinkled the scroll itself and**
19j	list		**all the people,**
20a	circumstance		saying
20b	content		"This is the blood of the covenant
20c	description		which God has ordained
20d	advantage		for you." (Exod 24:8)
21a	expansion (of 19–20)	Moreover,	
21b	assertion		**the tabernacle and**
21c			**all its equipment . . .**
21d	description		used in cultic worship
21e	predicate (of 21a–c)		**. . . were similarly sprinkled**
21f	means		with blood.
22a	development (of 21)	And,	
22b	standard		according to the law,
22c	assertion		**scarcely anything is cleansed**
22d	manner		without blood;
22e		and	
22f	circumstance		apart from the shedding of blood
22g	restatement (of 22c)		**there is no forgiveness.**
23a	inference (from 18–22)		**It was necessary, then,**
23b	content		for the copies of the things in heaven to be cleansed
23c	means		by these sacrifices, but
23d	contrast (with 23b)		the heavenly things themselves
23e	means		with better sacrifices
23f	comparison (with 23c)		than these.
24a	elaboration (of 23)	For	
24b	assertion		**Christ did not enter the sanctuary**
24c	identification		made with human hands,
24d	description		a copy of the true one, but
24e	contrast (with 24b–c)		he entered heaven itself,
24f	result		now to appear in the presence of God
24g	advantage		on our behalf.

25a	contrast (with 24e)		Neither did Christ enter
25b	purpose		**to offer himself**
25c	time		many times,
25d	comparison		as the high priest would enter the Most Holy Place
25e	time		every year
25f	association		with the blood of another—
26a	basis		since
26b	circumstance		in that case
26c	assertion		he would have had to suffer
26d	time		many times
26e	time		since the creation of the world.
26f	contrast (with 25)	But,	
26g	time		as it is,
26h	assertion		**he has been revealed**
26i	manner		once for all
26j	time		at the culmination of the ages
26k	purpose		in order to set aside sin
26l	means		through the sacrifice of himself.
27a	development	And	
27b	comparison (with 28)	just as	**it is appointed**
27c	reference		with respect to human beings
27d	content		to die
27e	time		once, and
27f	sequence		after that comes judgment,
28a	comparison (with 27)	so also	
28b	assertion		**Christ, ...**
28c	circumstance		having offered himself
28d	manner		once for all
28e	purpose		to take away the sins of many,
28f	predicate (of 28b)		**...will appear**
28g	sequence		a second time,
28h	purpose		not to deal with sin, but
28i	contrast		to bring salvation
28j	advantage		to those who are eagerly awaiting him.

Structure

Commentators differ over how to outline the second part of chapter 9. The majority do not formally identify 9:11–28 as a block of text, dividing chapter 9 into four parts—verses 1–10, 11–14, 15–22, and 23–28[1]—or three parts—verses 1–10,

---

1. See, e.g., Attridge, *Hebrews*, 230, 244, 253, 260; Ellingworth, *Hebrews*, 445, 459, 474; Grässer, *An die Hebräer*, 2:141, 166, 186. Cockerill divides the chapter into four parts, but groups vv. 1–10, 11–15, and 16–22 into one larger unit and

11–14, and 15–28,[2] or verses 1–10, 11–22, and 23–28.[3] However, a strong case can be made that we should identify verses 11–28 as a discrete unit (with other paragraph divisions within this larger unit).[4] Identifying this entire second part of chapter 9 as a formal unit rests particularly on recognizing the similarities between the opening part of this section (vv. 11–14) and the closing part of the section (vv. 23–28). Note the vocabulary that these texts share (and which is absent in the verses in between):

"enter" (εἰσέρχομαι)—vv. 12, 24, 25
"(Most) holy place" (τὰ ἅγια)—vv. 12, 24, 25
"once for all" (ἐφάπαξ/ἅπαξ)—vv. 12, 26, 27, 28
"offered himself" (προσφέρω + ἑαυτόν)—vv. 14, 25, 28
"[not] made with human hands" (χειροποίητος)—vv. 11, 24

Of course, it is easy to make almost any case one wants by selective appeal to data. However, the data I cite in this case involve words that are central to the arguments in each section. And we can add two significant parallels in content. Both texts set the decisive offering of Christ in an eschatological context: Christ comes as a "high priest of the good things that have come" (v. 11); Christ has appeared "at the culmination of the ages" (v. 26). And both texts refer to various "appearances" of Christ (vv. 11, 24, 26, 28). There are, of course, differences between the paragraphs in both content and emphasis. But each promotes a similar central argument: Christ has appeared at the turn of the ages as our high priest who, entering the heavenly Most Holy Place (the presence of God), offers a definitive sacrifice that deals decisively with the human sin problem.

The *inclusio* I have identified, composed of 9:11–14 and 9:23–28, carries the central point of this section, a point I have summarized above. The passage sandwiched between these paragraphs elaborates one key point that our author makes in these outer sections: the necessity of sacrificial blood, involving the death of the victim, to secure forgiveness. The author has already noted the necessity of blood in the Old Testament economy: the high priest who enters the Most Holy Place once a year can never enter "without blood" (v. 7). The author then highlights Christ's blood as the means of his entry into the heavenly holy of holies in verses 12–14. The contrast in these verses between the blood of animals and Christ's own blood is reiterated in the other half of the *inclusio* (v. 25). "Blood" then becomes the key word in verses 18–22, occurring in each verse, as

---

9:23–24 and 9:25–10:4 into another larger unit (*Hebrews*, 370, 411–12). Bruce divides into five paragraphs: vv. 1–5, 6–10, 11–14, 15–22, 23–28 (*Hebrews*, 197, 205, 211, 218, 227).

2. Koester, *Hebrews*, 416–17; D. Harris, *Hebrews*, 208, 221, 229, 240. Spicq (*L'Épître aux Hébreux*, 2:260) identifies vv. 15–28 as a section, but attaches vv. 11–14 to vv. 1–10 (as also does Westfall, *Discourse Analysis*, 196–97).

3. DeSilva, *Perseverance in Gratitude*, 303.

4. See, e.g., Westcott, *Hebrews*, 255; Lane, *Hebrews*, 2:226–35; Johnson, *Hebrews*, 232–33. G. Guthrie suggests this structure also, pointing to the *inclusio* with "appearances" of Christ in vv. 11 and 28 (*Structure of Hebrews*, 86–87).

the author notes how blood is involved in so many Old Testament rituals. Yet the same basic concept is central also in verses 15–17, only now verbalized in the language of death/dying. The connections between texts using these words make clear that "blood" refers to death; this is why the author, having highlighted the necessity of *death* to ratify a will (vv. 16–17), can conclude, "This is why even the first covenant was not put into effect without *blood*" (v. 18). The author summarizes the significance of this in verse 22: "In fact, the law requires that nearly everything be cleansed with blood, and without the shedding of blood there is no forgiveness." Further, in verses 23–28, the author mixes references to blood (v. 25) and death (v. 27) with references to sacrifice (vv. 23, 25, 26, 28). The way the author interchanges references to blood, death, and sacrifice makes it quite clear that he has in view throughout these verses blood sacrifice, certainly including death but perhaps extended to include also the manipulation of blood after death (see the references to "sprinkling" of blood in vv. 19 and 21).

I noted above the theme of Christ's "appearing" in these verses. These references cover the range of salvation history, from Christ's first appearance, at "the culmination of the ages" (v. 26; see also v. 11) to his present appearing before the Father on our behalf (v. 24) and to his second appearing to bring ultimate salvation to his people (v. 28).[5] Finally, it is worth noting the series of antitheses between old and new that characterize this text:

Old	New
old covenant (v. 1)	new covenant (v. 15)
"first tabernacle still had standing" (v. 8)	"time of the new order" (v. 10); "good things that have come" (v. 11); "culmination of the ages" (v. 26)
"earthly sanctuary" (v. 1)	"greater and more perfect tabernacle" (v. 11); "heaven itself" (v. 24)
"blood of goats and calves" (v. 12); "blood of goats and bulls" (v. 13); "the blood of calves" (v. 19); "these sacrifices" (v. 23)	"the blood of Christ" (v. 14); "better sacrifices" (v. 23); "sacrifice of himself [Christ]" (v. 26)
many/repeated sacrifices (v. 25)	a single "once-for-all" sacrifice (vv. 12, 25, 26, 28)

Exegetical Outline

→ **4. Eternal Redemption: Heavenly Sanctuary, Decisive Sacrifice, and New Covenant (9:11–28)**
    a. The Heart of the Matter: Eternal Redemption through Christ (vv. 11–14)
    b. Securing the New Covenant (v. 15)
    c. Death and Covenant: Illustrated through Will-Making (vv. 16–17)
    d. The Necessity of Blood in the Old Covenant (vv. 18–23)
    e. The Efficacy of Christ's Blood (vv. 24–28)

---

5. See, e.g., G. Guthrie, *Hebrews*, 309.

Explanation of the Text

9:11–12 But when Christ appeared on the scene, a high priest of the good things that have come, he entered once for all the Most Holy Place, securing an eternal redemption. [He entered] through the greater and more perfect tabernacle, one not made with human hands, that is, not of this creation. 12 Nor [did he enter] by means of the blood of goats and calves but by means of his own blood (Χριστὸς δὲ παραγενόμενος ἀρχιερεὺς τῶν γενομένων ἀγαθῶν διὰ τῆς μείζονος καὶ τελειοτέρας σκηνῆς οὐ χειροποιήτου, τοῦτ᾽ ἔστιν οὐ ταύτης τῆς κτίσεως, 12 οὐδὲ δι᾽ αἵματος τράγων καὶ μόσχων διὰ δὲ τοῦ ἰδίου αἵματος εἰσῆλθεν ἐφάπαξ εἰς τὰ ἅγια αἰωνίαν λύτρωσιν εὑράμενος). In contrast to the Old Testament high priests, who entered the earthly tabernacle by means of the blood of animals, Christ our high priest enters the heavenly sanctuary by means of his own blood. As I argued above, verses 11–14, the opening paragraph in this section, form an *inclusio* with verses 23–28. Verses 11–14 are often lauded as "the formal and material center of Hebrews."[6] The paragraph falls into two parts. The first, verses 11–12, is more christologically focused, the second, verses 13–14, more soteriologically focused.[7] While obscured in most English translations, verses 11–12 consist of one sentence, with its subject, "Christ," at the beginning of verse 11 and its verb, "entered," in the middle of verse 12: "Christ... entered [the Most Holy Place]." A series of subordinate clauses describe the nature and circumstances of that entering in verses 11 and 12a. The last clause of verse 12 serves as the transitional point from the first part of the paragraph to the second. Christ's entrance secured "eternal redemption," and this redemption is described in verses 13–14.

My translation, in an effort to put a complex Greek sentence into meaningful English, moves away from the order of the Greek text. My first sentence captures the backbone of the sentence, with "Christ" (Χριστός) at the beginning of verse 11 as the subject and "entered" (εἰσῆλθεν) from the middle of verse 12 as the verb. "Securing an eternal redemption," from the end of verse 12, is then a participial clause modifying this main verb. Two longer clauses further modify this main verb. I have given each of these clauses its own sentence, repeating the main verb "entered" in each one.

The contrast with the old order is marked by the opening participial clause, "when Christ appeared on the scene" (Χριστὸς δέ παραγενόμενος). "Appeared on the scene" translates a verb (παραγίνομαι) that, according to BDAG ("παραγίνομαι," 760, §2), here means "make a public appearance" (it cites also Matt 3:1 and Luke 12:51). Specifically, Christ appeared as a "high priest of the good things that have come" (ἀρχιερεὺς τῶν γενομένων ἀγαθῶν).[8] The identification of Christ as high priest brings us back to 8:1–2, where, as the "main point" of 8:1–10:18, the author says that "we have such a high

---

6. Grässer, *An die Hebräer*, 2:142. See also, e.g., Backhaus, *Der Hebräerbrief*, 314. Vanhoye goes even further, identifying the word "Christ" in v. 11 as the fulcrum point of the whole letter (*Structure and Message*, 79–109). See also Koester, *Hebrews*, 411: "the high point in the central part of Hebrews."

7. Weiss, *Der Brief an die Hebräer*, 463.

8. This translation follows the text adopted by NA²⁸ and represented in most English translations. A variant text has a participle that would be translated "about to come" (μελλόντων; see ℵ, A, D², Iᵛⁱᵈ, K, L, P, 0278, a number of important minuscules, and the Majority text). It is read by NET ("good things to come") and is adopted by a few scholars (e.g., Delitzsch, *Hebrews*, 2:76–77), but it is suspect as being an assimilation to Heb 10:1—"a shadow of the good things to come [μελλόντων]" (Metzger, *Textual Commentary*, 598).

priest." As I noted above, we have to skip over two long qualifying phrases in the Greek before we get to the verb that goes with "Christ": "entered once for all the Most Holy Place" in verse 12. The translation "Most Holy Place" (NIV; NLT) or "holy of holies" (CEB) for τὰ ἅγια is accurate in light of the author's use of this word elsewhere to describe the "inner room" of the sanctuary.[9] The author's whole point is that, as our high priest, Christ was authorized to enter the inner room of the sanctuary, the "holy of holies" that signified the very presence of God. And, unlike the Old Testament high priests who were also authorized to enter but had to do so repeatedly, year after year, Christ has entered "once for all." The decisive nature of Christ's high-priestly ministry is an important strand in our author's attempt to urge his readers to "stay the course" and not abandon the status won for them by this high-priestly act (see 7:27 and 10:10, both using ἐφάπαξ; and also 9:25–28; 10:1–3, 11–15). The basic two-room arrangement of the sanctuary, and its elaborate trappings, signified that free access to God was not available as long as it had "standing" (9:7–8). Christ, our "pioneer" (2:10; see 12:2), has opened the way for those he "leads" to penetrate with him "behind the curtain" (6:19) into the very presence of God.

The author inserts two phrases qualifying this main verb, "entered," between the subject and the verb. But he also adds an adverbial participial modifier after the verb. This clause, "securing an eternal redemption," as I suggested above, creates a transition from the work of Christ, which secured that redemption (vv. 11–12), to the experience of believers, who enjoy that redemption (vv. 13–14). Our author uses two related words in this context to refer to "redemption" (λύτρωσις here and ἀπολύτρωσις in v. 15). The words are probably synonymous in this context, referring not simply to "cleansing"[10] but to the notion of a ransom that is paid for release from sin and its destructive power.[11] Reflecting a repeated theme in Hebrews, the author describes this redemption as "eternal" (αἰωνίαν)—that is, a setting free from sin's penalty and power that lasts forever (see also 7:25; 9:25–28; 10:11, 14). An "eternal" redemption is the logical implication of a "once-for-all" sacrifice.[12]

The significance of the tense of the participle that our author uses here (which we translate "securing") is one important exegetical point within a fierce debate about the theology of atonement in Hebrews. Some recent scholars, rightfully pointing to the significance of the exaltation and of Christ's subsequent entrance into the presence of God, argue that the moment of atonement in Hebrews is the moment when Christ offers himself as a final and definitive sacrifice in the heavenly sanctuary.[13] Jesus's sacrifice follows the pattern established on the Day of Atonement: the priest takes the blood of the animal that has been sacrificed into the Most Holy Place in order to effect atonement. Christ's death is a subordinate moment in the atoning process or even, in a more extreme form of this view, not part of the atonement per se at all. I will be dealing with this issue at several points where the text touches on it, and I devote a long excursus to the matter after my exegesis of this passage. Here I simply evaluate the temporal implications of the

---

9. See comments on 9:2. ESV, again, is puzzling, translating here "holy places."

10. Contra, e.g., Koester, *Hebrews*, 412–13.

11. On the synonymity of the words, see, e.g., Leon Morris, *The Apostolic Preaching of the Cross* (Grand Rapids: Eerdmans, 1955), 40–41. For the meaning "release from enslavement through the paying of a price," see, e.g., Morris, *Apostolic Preaching of the Cross*, 9–59; Ribbens, "Positive Function," 95–114; Douglas J. Moo, *A Theology of Paul and His Letters* (Grand Rapids: Zondervan Academic, 2021), 394–99.

12. E.g., Weiss, *Der Brief an die Hebräer*, 468.

13. See esp. Moffitt, *Atonement*.

construction the author uses: an aorist participle, εὑράμενος, "securing," following the indicative verb it modifies (εἰσῆλθεν).[14] Students sometimes learn in beginning Greek that aorist adverbial participles tend to indicate antecedent action relative to the verb they modify—that is, the action of the participle precedes the action denoted by the main verb. If this is the case here, then we would translate "he entered, *having* secured eternal redemption." Among translations, CSB, NJB, and NASB adopt this interpretation, and it receives support from a number of scholars.[15] However, it often happens in the course of our learning Greek that "rules" we learned early on are substantially modified later on. Especially when aorist participles *follow* the verb they modify, they often denote action taking place at the same time as, or even subsequent to, the verb they modify.[16] Only context, then, can tell us what the temporal relationship might be, and here context suggests a contemporaneous relationship.[17] The author's emphasis on Christ's entry suggests that the final clause is intended to accentuate its significance rather than simply note something that happened before the entry. This does not mean that Christ's death is not, for Hebrews, part of the atoning process. As I will argue, the author takes a broad view of atonement, viewing it as a process that moves from Christ's obedient life, to his death and resurrection, to his exaltation and entrance into the presence of God. But in this text, our author wants to draw attention to the role of entrance in that atoning process.

We can now turn back to look at the two phrases in verses 11b and 12a that modify "entered":

1. through [διά] the greater and more perfect tabernacle,
    one not made with human hands,
    that is, not of this creation.
2. nor by means of [διά] the blood of goats and calves
    but by means of [διά] his own blood.

As I note, the word that links these phrases to the main verb is the preposition διά. A few interpreters think that the preposition has an instrumental meaning in all three occurrences, taking "the greater and more perfect tabernacle" to refer to Christ in some manner.[18] But it is strained to interpret "sanctuary" (σκηνῆς) in this way, and most interpreters (along with the translations) give the preposition in verse 11b a local sense: "through."[19]

---

14. For the meaning "secure" (in the sense of "obtain") for the middle form of εὑρίσκω, see BDAG 412, §3.

15. E.g., Moule, *Idiom Book*, 100; Peterson, *Hebrews and Perfection*, 137; P. Hughes, *Hebrews*, 328, who claims that "the aorist participle . . . plainly means that Christ entered into the heavenly sanctuary *after he had secured* an eternal redemption." A similar issue arises in 1:3; see my note there on the pattern of indicative + aorist participle in Hebrews. Hebrews 6:20 provides some support for the antecedent view: the sequence εἰσῆλθεν (aorist indicative) . . . γενόμενος (aorist participle) seems pretty clearly to mean "he entered . . . having become high priest."

16. Wallace, *Greek Grammar*, 624; Porter, *Verbal Aspect*, 381; David L. Mathewson, *Voice and Mood: A Linguisitic Approach*, Essentials of Biblical Greek Grammar (Grand Rapids: Baker Academic, 2021), 154–60.

17. Most English translations and interpreters take this view; see, e.g., Kibbe, "Is It Finished?," 32–33; Ernest de Witt Burton, *Syntax of the Moods and Tenses in New Testament Greek*, 3rd ed. (Edinburgh: T&T Clark, 1898), 66; Attridge, *Hebrews*, 249; Lane, *Hebrews*, 2:230; Ellingworth, *Hebrews*, 453; Weiss, *Der Brief an die Hebräer*, 468; Grässer, *An die Hebräer*, 2:155; Gäbel, *Die Kulttheologie des Hebräerbriefes*, 286–88. It is also possible that the participle indicates subsequent action (e.g., Porter, *Verbal Aspect*, 387; Moffitt, *Atonement*, 222).

18. See, e.g., Chrysostom, *Homilies*, 15.2; Calvin, *Hebrews*, 120; Spicq, *L'Épître aux Hébreux*, 2:256; Bénétrau, *L'Épître aux Hébreux*, 2:72; Albert Vanhoye, "'Par la tente plus grande et plus parfaite . . . ,'" *Bib* 46 (1965): 1–28; James Swetnam, "'The Greater and More Perfect Tent': A Contribution to the Discussion of Hebrews 9,11," *Bib* 47 (1966): 91–106. Others who take διά in an instrumental sense are, e.g., Koester, *Hebrews*, 409; Montefiore, *Hebrews*, 152–53.

19. The NLT—"he has entered the greater, more perfect Tabernacle in heaven"—appears to assume that διά after

The tabernacle through which Christ traveled to enter the Most Holy Place is described by the author in a way that accentuates its otherworldly character: "not made with humans hands" (οὐ χειροποιήτου; see also Mark 14:58 [referring to the temple]; Acts 7:48; 17:24; Eph 2:11; Heb 9:24); see 8:2, where the author describes the heavenly sanctuary as built by the Lord, not humans.[20] This point is emphasized with the second description, "not of this creation." It is a "greater and more perfect" tabernacle, an obvious reference to the heavenly sanctuary that served as a model for the earthly one (8:5). Since the author does not differentiate between the different "rooms" of the sanctuary (see 9:2–3, 6–7), he may refer to the sanctuary as a whole.[21] Some interpreters think the strong description of this sanctuary as "greater and more perfect" points to a structure that at least includes the inner room.[22] But the apparent contrast between this sanctuary, which Christ went "through," and the Most Holy Place, which he "entered," suggests rather that the author here has in view only the outer room.[23] On this view, the imagery falls neatly into place: as the Old Testament high priests moved through the outer room to enter the inner room on the Day of Atonement to effect atonement for the people, so also Christ. It is possible, then, though not certain, that the "outer room" here might signify the lower "heavens" through which Christ has moved on his way to the highest heaven where God dwells (see 4:14, where Christ "passes through the heavens").[24] This specific issue is bound up with the larger question of whether the author thinks there is an actual sanctuary structure in the heavens or whether he simply uses sanctuary imagery to characterize heaven itself as the abode of God (see the "In Depth" discussion after 8:1–6).

The second modifying phrase of the main clause, "Christ ... entered," uses the key preposition in this text (διά) in an instrumental sense, once negatively and once positively. Negatively, it was not by means of the blood of goats and calves that Christ entered. Both goats and calves are involved in sacrifices in the Old Testament. A (male) goat (τράγος), for instance, is mentioned thirteen times in sacrifices that accompanied the dedication of the sanctuary (Num 7), while a "calf" or "bull" (μόσχος) is sacrificed on the Day of Atonement (Lev 16:3, 6, 11, 14, 15, 18, 27). The two are mentioned together in Ezekiel 39:18. It is unlikely, however, that the author has a particular text of sacrificial ritual in view; the pair is simply a way of referring to the role of animals in the Old Testament sacrificial system generally. The author notes in 9:7 that the high priest could enter the Most Holy Place only with "blood" (αἷμα), and the reference in this verse to blood initiates a series of references to the central role of blood in sacrifice (vv. 13, 14,

---

εἰσέρχομαι can indicate destination (see also CSB, though their translation is not clear). But there is no basis for this in the almost two hundred occurrences of this verb in the NT.

20. Those scholars who find Middle Platonism to be a significant influence on Hebrews attribute the created vs. uncreated distinction to this background (e.g., Johnson, *Hebrews*, 235–37). See also deSilva, who thinks the "perfection" of the heavenly sanctuary is a result of the fact that "it exists in the unshakable, abiding realm" (*Perseverance in Gratitude*, 304).

21. E.g., D. Harris, *Hebrews*, 223; Richard M. Davidson, "Christ's Entry 'within the Veil' in Hebrews 6:19–20: The Old Testament Background," *AUSS* 39 (2001): 175–90.

22. Koester, *Hebrews*, 409. On this reading, then, some see διά as indicating the culmination of movement, or entrance. See, e.g., NLT: "he has entered that greater, more perfect Tabernacle in heaven, which was not made by human hands and is not part of this created world"; CSB: "in the greater and more perfect tabernacle not made with hands (that is, not of this creation), he entered . . ."

23. E.g., Attridge, *Hebrews*, 247; Lane, *Hebrews*, 2:229–30, 236–37; Johnson, *Hebrews*, 237; Weiss, *Der Brief an die Hebräer*, 465–66; Ribbens, *Levitical Sacrifice*, 114–15. Schenck's view is similar, though he takes διά in a modal sense (*Cosmology and Eschatology*, 155–64). It should be noted that the instrumental sense does not necessarily preclude the sense of accompaniment.

24. E.g., Isaacs, *Sacred Space*, 211.

18, 19, 20, 21, 22, 25; see also 10:4, 19, 29; 12:24; 13:11, 12, 20). Based on one's interpretation of the famous claim in Leviticus 17:11 that "the life is in the blood," some interpreters think that the focus in using this word is on life.[25] However, the point of Leviticus 17:11 is that because life is in the blood, the shedding of blood signifies loss of life—death. In the Old Testament rituals, blood is both shed at death and then manipulated by the priest in various ways. Our author refers to both. The "blood" by which Jesus enters the Most Holy Place in verses 12 and 13 gives way to "death" in verses 15–17 (see especially the concluding comment in v. 18), and again in verses 25–27 "blood" is unpacked in terms of suffering and death.[26] At the same time, verses 19–21 refer to the ritual sprinkling of blood. "Blood," then, is shorthand for sacrifice, a sacrifice that takes place in stages—"spilling" of blood followed by "sprinkling" of blood. The author can refer to one stage or another to connote the whole process, in what Michael Kibbe has called "a conflation of moments."[27]

It was not, then, through the sacrifice of animals that Christ entered the Most Holy Place, but through his own sacrifice. A number of interpreters, pressing our author's comments to conform to Old Testament sacrificial practice, argue that Christ brought with him into the Most Holy Place his own blood as the means of access.[28] Other interpreters vociferously reject any idea of Christ entering "with" his blood.[29] They are right to note that the preposition our author uses here does not usually convey the sense of "withness."[30] And they argue that "blood" refers in this context not so much to a substance but to Christ's death generally.[31] Yet the references to the sprinkling of blood in verse 13 and verses 19–21 show that blood as a substance is not absent from the context. And 13:11, where the high priest is said to carry the blood of slaughtered animals into the Most Holy Place, reveals that this image is a "live" one for the author.[32]

9:13–14 For if the blood of goats and bulls and the ashes of a heifer sprinkled on those who are unclean sanctifies them for the cleansing of the flesh, 14 how much more will the blood of Christ, who through the eternal spirit offered himself blameless to God, cleanse our consciences from dead works so that we might serve the living God (εἰ γὰρ τὸ αἷμα τράγων καὶ ταύρων καὶ σποδὸς δαμάλεως ῥαντίζουσα τοὺς κεκοινωμένους ἁγιάζει πρὸς τὴν τῆς σαρκὸς καθαρότητα, 14 πόσῳ μᾶλλον τὸ αἷμα τοῦ Χριστοῦ, ὃς διὰ πνεύματος αἰωνίου ἑαυτὸν προσήνεγκεν ἄμωμον τῷ θεῷ, καθαριεῖ τὴν συνείδησιν ἡμῶν ἀπὸ νεκρῶν ἔργων εἰς τὸ λατρεύειν θεῷ ζῶντι). As I suggested above, the author in this

---

25. E.g., David M. Moffitt, "Blood, Life, and Atonement: Reassessing Hebrews' Christological Appropriation of Yom Kippur," in *Rethinking the Atonement*, 90, 94. (This essay was first published in *The Day of Atonement: Its Interpretation in Early Jewish and Christian Traditions*, ed. T. Hieke and T. Nicklas, Themes in Biblical Narrative: Jewish and Christian Traditions 15 [Leiden: Brill, 2012], 211–24.)

26. On this point, see esp. Jamieson, *Jesus' Death and Heavenly Offering*, 128.

27. Kibbe, "Is It Finished?," 32.

28. Ribbens, *Levitical Sacrifice*, 118; deSilva, *Perseverance in Gratitude*, 305.

29. E.g., Bruce, *Hebrews*, 213–14; Hagner, *Hebrews*, 136; Cockerill, *Hebrews*, 394.

30. Though see Moule, *Idiom Book*, 57, who notes the use of διά to indicate "attendant circumstances" and suggests that the pronoun might mean "with" in Heb 9:12. NRSV and NAB translate "with his own blood"; RSV has "taking ... his own blood." Other texts in Hebrews that refer to the work of Christ with a διά have an instrumental sense (2:10, 14; 7:25; 9:26; 10:10; 13:11).

31. E.g., Lane, *Hebrews*, 2:238.

32. See also 9:25, where the author describes the high priest as entering the Most Holy Place "with [ἐν] blood that is not his own." To be sure, ἐν could have an instrumental sense, but the sense of accompaniment is more likely ("with" is the rendering in all major English translations).

paragraph moves from a focus on what Christ our high priest has done to a focus on what he has accomplished for his people. "Eternal redemption," the link phrase at the end of verse 12, summarizes these benefits, which include sanctification (v. 13) and the cleansing of the conscience (v. 14). At the same time, verses 13–14 also elaborate the means by which Christ secures these blessings, picking up the key word "blood" from verse 12.

The single sentence in these two verses contrasts the old order and the new in a manner typical for Hebrews. And, as is often the case, the comparison favors the new order: see "how much more" at the beginning of verse 14. The old sacrificial system is built on the blood of animals: "goats and bulls" (τράγων καὶ ταύρων) here, replacing "goats and calves" in verse 13.[33] The author adds another ritual involving animals: the "ashes of a heifer." According to Numbers 19:1–10, a "red heifer" is to be slaughtered and its blood sprinkled "toward the front of the tent of meeting" (v. 4). It is then to be burnt, and its ashes mixed with water, to be used for the "purification from sin" (v. 9). We cannot know why our author adds a reference to this ritual,[34] but it does remind us that his sacrificial or ritual imagery is not drawn only from the Day of Atonement ritual. The author apparently wants to compare Old Testament sacrificial rituals generally with the sacrifice of Christ. As he has made clear earlier (v. 10), the Old Testament rituals secure only outward cleansing: they "sanctify" those who are "unclean," but their effectiveness is limited to the realm of the "flesh" (πρὸς τὴν τῆς σαρκὸς καθαρότητα).[35]

Not so the sacrifice of Christ. In verse 14, the author describes the greater effectiveness of the sacrifice of Christ.[36] Echoing the language he used earlier (v. 9), the author in verse 14 indicates that the superiority of Christ's sacrifice lies in its ability to "cleanse our consciences" (καθαριεῖ τὴν συνείδησιν ἡμῶν).[37] The verb translated "cleansing" (cf. NIV; CSB) or "purifying" (ESV; NET) matches well the reference to "those who are unclean" in verse 13: the verb often refers to cleansing from a state of ritual impurity (see Acts 10:15; 11:9). Here the cleansing involved affects the moral sphere (Acts 15:9; 2 Cor 7:1; Eph 5:26; Titus 2:14; Heb 9:22, 23; 10:2; 1 John 1:7, 9). The object of this cleansing is the "conscience," the guilty consciousness of sin which, as we have seen (see v. 9), is uniquely

---

33. It is impossible to know why the author makes the switch from "calves" to "bulls." Goats and bulls are mentioned together in Deut 32:14; Ps 50:13 (49:13 LXX); and Isa 1:11; cf. Odes 2.14.

34. Bruce (*Hebrews*, 215) suggests that the author may mention this ritual because, like the sacrifices on the Day of Atonement, it is called a "sin offering." However, while this connection can be made in the Hebrew, the word used here in the LXX at Num 19:9 (ἄγνισμα) is not used in the description of the Day of Atonement (indeed, the word does not occur elsewhere in the LXX). Since our author is usually working in the Greek, this means the connection is unlikely. P. Hughes, on the other hand, reflecting his view of Hebrews as directed to former Qumran covenanters, thinks the prominence of this rite in that community might explain its mention here (*Hebrews*, 362–64).

35. The verb ἁγιάζω refers in this context to being sanctified not in a moral but in a cultic sense; see, e.g., NET's "consecrated." "Unclean" captures the Jewish cultic sense of the verb κεκοινωμένους (a substantival participle), which means "make common," "defile." See also Matt 15:11, 18, 20; Mark 7:15, 18, 20, 23; Acts 10:15; 11:9; 21:28; also the adjective κοινός, "common," in Mark 7:2, 5; Acts 10:14, 28; 11:8; Rom 14:14; Heb 10:29; Rev 21:27.

36. The author uses the common NT phrase "how much more" (πόσῳ μᾶλλον) to create a contrast between vv. 13 and 14. See Matt 7:11; 10:25; Luke 11:13, 24, 28; Rom 11:12, 24; Phlm 16. The author does not use this phrase elsewhere, but he does use two other synonymous phrases: τοσούτῳ μᾶλλον (10:25); πολὺ μᾶλλον (12:9, 25). The author again uses αἷμα to refer to sacrifice. Some interpreters think the focus is narrowly on Christ's death (Bruce, *Hebrews*, 216), but I think, again, the reference is broadly to the whole process of sacrifice.

37. Or "cleanse *your* consciences": several good manuscripts read ὑμῶν in place of ἡμῶν, including the Majority text, hence KJV's "your conscience" (also RSV).

taken away through Christ's sacrifice. Negatively, this cleansing is "from dead works" (ἀπὸ νεκρῶν ἔργων).³⁸ A few interpreters think the author may refer to the works of the sacrificial cult, which are "dead" in the sense of being "useless."³⁹ But, as in 6:1, where the same phrase occurs, the reference is to those thoughts or actions that lead to death.

The reason that Christ's sacrifice has the power to transform the human conscience is hinted at in the subordinate relative clause that the author tucks in between the verses's subject—"the blood of Christ"—and its verb—"cleanse [our consciences]." Christ is one who (ὅς) "through the eternal spirit offered himself blameless to God." A sacrifice being "blameless" (ἄμωμον) is nothing new: it was regularly stated as a prerequisite for any animal that was to be sacrificed to the Lord in the Old Testament (in the NT, see 1 Pet 1:19). The use of this word further suggests that the moment of death in Jesus's "offering" (προσήνεγκεν, from προσφέρω) is in view here, since animals being prepared for slaughter were required to be "blameless." However, it is the claim that Christ offered himself "through the eternal spirit" that suggests one of the reasons his sacrifice is so powerful. The phrase, which occurs only here in the New Testament, is debated. Many interpreters think that the author is referring to the Holy Spirit.⁴⁰ The long list of respected scholars (see the footnote) who hold this view, along with the many English translations that assume it (by capitalizing "Spirit"), makes clear that this is an attractive option. Nevertheless, I side with a good number of scholars who think the reference is rather to a quality of Christ's own person.⁴¹ I take this view mainly because of what I think is a roughly parallel point that the author makes twice in chapter 7. In this chapter, the author grounds Christ's unique Melchizedekian high priesthood in "the power of an indestructible life" (v. 16) and compares Melchizedek to Christ in not having "beginning of days or end of life" (v. 3). Here the author suggests that the unparalleled power of Christ's sacrifice lay in his own unparalleled—and unparallelable—nature as both divine and human. As Moffatt puts it, "it was because Jesus was what he was by nature that his sacrifice had such final value."⁴² Jesus secures an "eternal redemption" (9:12) and an "eternal inheritance" (v. 15) because he himself is eternal.

We should not overlook the point of application that climaxes this long and theologically dense sentence: all this has happened "so that we might serve the living God." As Peterson points out, the verb our author uses here (λατρεύω) moves beyond the issue of status to include issues of practice: prayer, worship, and ministry to and with others.⁴³

9:15 And because of this he is the mediator of a new covenant, so that, now that a death has occurred for the redemption of transgressions under the first covenant, those who are called might receive the promise of an eternal inheritance (Καὶ διὰ τοῦτο διαθήκης καινῆς μεσίτης ἐστίν, ὅπως θανάτου γενομένου εἰς ἀπολύτρωσιν τῶν ἐπὶ τῇ πρώτῃ διαθήκῃ παραβάσεων τὴν ἐπαγγελίαν λάβωσιν οἱ κεκλημένοι τῆς αἰωνίου κληρονομίας).

---

38. The combination καθαρίζω + ἀπό has the sense "cleanse from [the negative effects] of." See also 2 Cor 7:1; 1 John 1:7, 9.
39. Thompson, *Hebrews*, 187.
40. Bruce, *Hebrews*, 218; Michel, *Der Brief an die Hebräer*, 314; Lane, *Hebrews*, 2:240; Lindars, *Theology*, 57–58; Koester, *Hebrews*, 410; Ellingworth, *Hebrews*, 456–57; Cockerill, *Hebrews*, 398.
41. Westcott, *Hebrews*, 261; Montefiore, *Hebrews*, 154–55; Weiss, *Der Brief an die Hebräer*, 472–73; Massonnet, *L'Épître aux Hébreux*, 241; Bénétrau, *L'Épître aux Hébreux*, 2:75–77; P. Hughes, *Hebrews*, 358–59; Attridge, *Hebrews*, 251.
42. Moffatt, *Hebrews*, 124. Some interpreters think the reference is not so much to Christ's eternal nature but to his ethical nature—his life of willing obedience (see 5:10; 10:5–10). See the outline of views in Small, *Characterization of Jesus*, 172–74.
43. Peterson, *Hebrews and Perfection*, 140.

As the mediator of a new covenant (see 8:7–13), Christ provides for all those called—including the Old Testament people of God—an eternal inheritance. Verse 15 introduces a line of thought that runs through verse 22. Of the several points made in verse 15, it is the connection between covenant and death that dominates these following verses. The connection is illustrated in verses 16–17, leading to the thesis statement in verse 18—the first covenant was inaugurated by means of death ("blood"). This point is then itself illustrated by references to Old Testament sacrificial rituals in verses 19–21, leading again to a summary statement in verse 22: as the law indicates, forgiveness is always in and through blood.

The opening phrase in the verse (καὶ διὰ τοῦτο) indicates that this verse draws a conclusion from something in the preceding argument. The inference drawn in this verse could, then, be the final verse in the paragraph that begins with verse 11.[44] However, the close connection forged between this verse and the verses following with διαθήκη ("covenant," "will") suggests rather that verse 15 belongs in the same paragraph with those verses (almost all the English translations format it this way). The connection to the previous context might, then, be specifically to verse 14,[45] but it seems better to think the author now draws an inference from the argument of verses 11–14 generally.[46] Christ's once-for-all entry into the heavenly Most Holy Place and offering of himself as a sacrifice there establishes a new covenant, securing the promised inheritance for the people of God.

"Mediator of a new covenant" takes us back to the introductory overview of the author's description of Jesus's high-priestly work (8:1–10:18). In 8:6, Jesus is designated "mediator of a better covenant" (author's translation), a claim elaborated in the lengthy quotation from Jeremiah 31 in 8:8b–11. The prominence of "covenant" in 9:16–20 and the repetition of Jeremiah 31 language in 10:16 reveal that "new covenant" remains an important aspect of Jesus's high-priestly ministry throughout this section. As I noted in our comments on 8:6, the word translated "mediator" (μεσίτης) has the nuance of "founder" or "guarantor" (note 7:22). Jesus does not act as a negotiator between two parties. Rather, his sacrificial death inaugurates and thus guarantees that his people will receive the benefits of the new covenant.

Sacrificial death, as we have seen, is a key motif running through verses 15–22. In a sequence typical of the author's Greek, he refers to this sacrificial death in a subordinate clause before he completes the purpose clause he introduces with the word ὅπου.[47] (Many English versions reverse the order of clauses for clarity.) The author refers again to "redemption" (ἀπολύτρωσιν; see λύτρωσιν in v. 12) as the benefit that results from Christ's death.[48] As I noted in my comments on verse 12, where the cognate and probably synonymous word occurs (λύτρωσις), "redemption" often refers to a liberation, a "setting free," by means of a price paid. As elsewhere in the New Testament, Christ's death is pictured as the price the triune God "pays" so that sinners might be released from captivity to

---

44. Cockerill, *Hebrews*, 389. See NLT.
45. Delitzsch, *Hebrews*, 2:99; Attridge, *Hebrews*, 254; Lane, *Hebrews*, 2:241; Weiss, *Der Brief an die Hebräer*, 475.
46. E.g., Backhaus, *Der Hebräerbrief*, 328.
47. This clause is built on the genitive absolute θανάτου γενομένου.
48. Pursuing his overall thesis that Christ's atoning work does not include his death in Hebrews, Moffitt argues that Jesus's death here sets off the series of events that bring redemption (*Atonement*, 290). However, Jesus's death, while perhaps not the only atoning moment in Hebrews, is clearly included as an integral part of atonement—as the series of references to death and blood in this context indicate (see, e.g., Kibbe, "Is It Finished?," 33; Jamieson, *Jesus' Death and Heavenly Offering*, 125–26).

sin and death.⁴⁹ What is particularly interesting about this clause is its focus on old-covenant sins: the redemption in view here is from the "transgressions" committed "under the first covenant." Two considerations may explain this focus. First, the author may be influenced by tradition. The text here in Hebrews has interesting parallels with Romans 3:24–26, including the word "redemption" and a reference to "sins committed ahead of time." Moreover, the text in Romans refers to Jesus's death as a ἱλαστήριον, alluding to the Old Testament cult, a way of thinking about Jesus's death that is rare in Paul (note also that the only other NT occurrence of this word is in Heb 9:5). We have some reason to think, then, that the author to the Hebrews and Paul might be independently reflecting an early Jewish-Christian traditional teaching about Jesus's death.⁵⁰

However, the second reason for the reference to old-covenant sins here is the more important. The author has made clear that old-covenant sacrifices were inadequate to care for the human sin problem: they could not cleanse "the conscience" (9:9), bring "perfection" (7:11, 19; 10:1), or "take away" sins (10:4, 11). Just what the old-covenant sacrifices accomplished is unclear, but, despite what we might infer from some of the strong claims in Hebrews, a good case can be made that old-covenant sacrifices did provide forgiveness to those who offered them with the right spirit. But the point our author is making is that those sacrifices, in and of themselves, could not "redeem"—that is, they were unable to provide the ultimate basis for full and final forgiveness.⁵¹ This basis has been provided in the sacrificial work of Jesus, whose sacrifice works both forward and backward in time. All those who come to him in faith after the time of that sacrifice are "redeemed," set free from sin;⁵² but all those before him who offered the prescribed sacrifices in faith are also redeemed on the basis of the decisive, "center-of-history," once-for-all sacrifice of Christ.

Having interrupted the main clause built on the claim that Jesus is "mediator of a new covenant," the author completes it at the end of the verse: "so that . . . those who are called might receive the promise of an eternal inheritance." The author does not often use the language of "calling" to describe believers (elsewhere only 3:1, "who share in a heavenly calling [κλήσεως]"; see also 11:8, 18)—unlike Paul, who uses it extensively to refer to believers as those whom God has drawn into a relationship with himself (see, e.g., 1 Cor 7:17–24). Our author is undoubtedly using the language in a similar way. What believers are called to here is "the promise of an eternal inheritance." The phrase "eternal inheritance" specifies the content of "what has been promised" (the Greek uses an epexegetic genitive construction—τῆς αἰωνίου κληρονομίας).⁵³

---

49. Occurrences of ἀπολύτρωσις with this sense are found in Luke 21:28; Rom 3:24; 8:23; 1 Cor 1:30; Eph 1:7, 14; 4:30; Col 1:14; Heb 11:35. See also λύτρωσις in Luke 1:68; 2:38; λυτρωτής in Acts 7:35; λυτρόω in Luke 24:21; Titus 2:14; 1 Pet 1:18; and λύτρον in Mark 10:45//Matt 20:28. I should note that many scholars doubt whether these words in "biblical Greek" continue to carry the connotation of a "price paid"—the word group, they argue, denotes simply liberation. However, while some occurrences of these words might lose any obvious sense of a "price paid," verses such as 1 Pet 1:18 show that this aspect of the meaning was still very much alive in the NT period: "for you know that it was not with perishable things such as silver or gold that you were redeemed [ἐλυτρώθητε] from the empty way of life handed down to you from your ancestors."

50. See Moo, *Romans*, 249–64; Benjamin J. Ribbens, "Forensic-Retributive Justification in Romans 3:21–26: Paul's Doctrine of Justification in Dialogue with Hebrews," *CBQ* 74 (2012): 548–67.

51. For this point see esp. Ribbens, "Positive Function," 110–11.

52. Delitzsch rightly notes that, while the focus here is on past sins, the author would intend the redemption to refer to sins universally (*Hebrews*, 2:104).

53. E.g., Zerwick and Grosvenor, *Grammatical Analysis*, 674; Attridge, *Hebrews*, 255; Michel, *Der Brief an die Hebräer*, 317.

The translation "promised eternal inheritance" found in some versions (e.g., NIV; ESV) is probably based on this construal of the syntax.[54] The concept of inheritance is rooted in the Old Testament, where the patriarchs and others were promised an "inheritance," often focused on the promised land (e.g., Heb 11:8). The author has earlier specified "salvation" as the "inheritance" that believers are promised (1:14; see also 6:12, 17). And, as is the case with salvation, the inheritance promised to believers is both a present experience and a future hope.[55] God, by instituting a new covenant through Christ, made it possible for sinful humans to enjoy this inheritance—but the author's frequent exhortations make it clear that future enjoyment of it hinges on continuing, steadfast faith.

9:16–17 For in the case of a will, [it is] necessary for the death of the one who made it to be established. 17 For a will is confirmed on the basis of death; it cannot come into effect while the one who made the will lives (ὅπου γὰρ διαθήκη, θάνατον ἀνάγκη φέρεσθαι τοῦ διαθεμένου· 17 διαθήκη γὰρ ἐπὶ νεκροῖς βεβαία, ἐπεὶ μήποτε ἰσχύει ὅτε ζῇ ὁ διαθέμενος). The author uses the human institution of the will to illustrate the necessity of a death for the ratification of such an instrument. As I pointed out above, the Greek word behind "covenant" and cognates crop up several times in this context: the noun (διαθήκη) in verses 15, 16, 17, and 20; the verb (διατίθημι) in verses 16 and 17. We would naturally expect that the language would continue to have the same meaning in all these verses as it clearly does in verses 15 and 20, namely, "covenant," in the biblical-theological sense of a promissory agreement initiated by God with his people. Several scholars think this is, indeed, the case. However, most scholars, along with virtually all the translations (NASB is an exception), think that the author in verses 16–17 illustrates the necessity of death for the ratification of a *covenant* by noting the necessity of death in ratifying a *will* or *testament*. Three distinct interpretations of these verses therefore emerge, one taking διαθήκη to mean "will," the other two variations taking the word to mean "covenant." The latter is certainly the standard meaning of this Greek word (διαθήκη) in biblical Greek (representing Hebrew *berit*), but it normally refers to a "will" or "testament" in extrabiblical Greek.[56] It will help to get an overview of each view, which I provide here by means of an interpretive translation of each one.

1. Διαθήκη as "Will"

   [16] Let me illustrate. In the case of a will, the death of the one who made the will must be proven if is to come into effect. [17] What I mean is that a will is put into effect only on the basis of death; it cannot be executed if the one who made the will is still alive. [18] Just like a will, then, the first covenant was not put into effect without a death being involved.

2. Διαθήκη as "Covenant"
   a. "Covenant"[57]

   [16] For we know that it is the nature of a covenant that the one who ratifies a covenant cannot do so without a death being set forth. [17]

---

54. A minority view takes τῆς αἰωνίου κληρονομίας as the object of κεκλημένοι: "that those who are called to an eternal inheritance may receive the promise" (NJB).

55. Contra many interpreters who think the inheritance is future only (e.g., Cockerill, *Hebrews*, 402).

56. (G. Quell and) J. Behm, "διατίθημι, διαθήκη," *TDNT* 2:124–26.

57. See esp. John J. Hughes, "Hebrews 9:15ff and Galatians 3:15ff: A Study in Covenant Practice and Procedure," *NovT* 2 (1979): 27–96; and also Westcott, *Hebrews*, 299–302; Lane, *Hebrews* 2:231–32, 242–43; G. Guthrie, *Hebrews*, 313.

We understand that a covenant is in force only on the basis of the death of animal sacrifices; it never takes effect while the one who made it is ritually living. ¹⁸ Therefore it is the case that the first covenant was not put into effect without a death being involved.

b. "Broken Covenant"[58]

¹⁶ For in the case of the Mosaic covenant, broken by the sinful people of Israel, it was necessary that a death, or curse, be inflicted on those who agreed to that covenant. ¹⁷ You see, the validity of the Mosaic covenant is revealed in the death of Israel, as they bore the curse; it could not be seen to be truly valid while one people who entered into it, Israel, was living. ¹⁸ Thus we see that the first covenant had no force until death occurred.

While the evidence is by no means conclusive for one view or the other (and all three have problems), I think interpreting verses 16–17 as referring to a human will makes slightly better sense of the verses. A similar situation occurs in Galatians where Paul illustrates the surety of a covenant with the illustration of a "human will" (ἀνθρώπου ... διαθήκη; Gal 3:15).

One of the debated points in the verses comes up immediately in verse 16a, where the author says that "in the case of"[59] a covenant/will, "it is necessary for the death of the one who made it to be established."[60] On the one hand, it is argued that this language cannot apply to wills, since all the evidence we have from the ancient world suggests that they had binding legal effect when they were drawn up.[61] On the other hand, however, the clause appears to suggest that the διαθήκη could only take effect when the one who initiated the διαθήκη died—obviously not applicable to God, the covenant maker.[62] Defenders of the covenant interpretation respond to this last point by arguing that the Greek the author uses here means something like "it is necessary for a death to be put forth"—that is, "the death of the one who ratifies a covenant" must be "represented by a sacrificial death."[63] Or, on the "broken covenant" view (2.b. above), the clause might mean "in the case of a *broken* covenant, the ones who agreed to the covenant must 'bear a death'"—that is, they are liable to the judgment of death. Neither is a natural reading of the text.[64] The one who "bears a death" more naturally refers to the one who initiated the agreement (τοῦ διαθεμένου). And the singular participle, along with the natural meaning of the word—to *initiate*, not simply to agree to—suggests the reference is to the one who instituted the διαθήκη. Moreover, it is difficult to find justification for taking "covenant" in verse 16 to refer to a "broken covenant." It is easier to think

---

58. See esp. Scott Hahn, "A Broken Covenant and the Curse of Death: A Study of Hebrews 9:15–22," *CBQ* 66 (2004): 416–36; Cockerill, *Hebrews*, 405–6; D. Harris, *Hebrews*, 233–34; Jamieson, *Jesus' Death and Heavenly Offering*, 116–26.

59. The Greek is ὅπου, "where."

60. The Greek represented by the phrase "to be established" is φέρεσθαι, a present middle/passive infinitive from φέρω. Most translations follow BDAG 1052, §8, and render "establish" here.

61. E.g., Lane, *Hebrews*, 2:231.

62. The substantival participial [ὁ] διαθέμενος refers to the one who initiates a covenant; the verb διατίθημι always refers in the NT to one who initiates the διαθήκη (Luke 22:29 [twice]; Acts 3:25; Heb 8:10; 10:16). The verb occurs over eighty times in the LXX, referring to making a covenant or a treaty.

63. Lane, *Hebrews*, 2:231.

64. The key word is φέρεσθαι. Advocates of a reference to covenant here think the word can refer to the necessity of the covenant-maker to "put forward" a death (not his own)—either the death of sacrificial victims generally or the death of Christ himself, as the ultimate covenant guarantor. These scholars cite the fairly frequent use of φέρω in the LXX to denote the "bringing" or "bearing" of something to be sacrificed (e.g., Lane, *Hebrews*, 2:231). However, what is "brought" in these OT passages is always a material object; never is "death" the object of the verb in this sense. It therefore makes better sense to think the "death to be borne" refers to the death of the one who makes the will; only with his death does the distribution of his goods take place.

that the author is pointing out the well-known fact that the death of the testator must occur for the provisions of the will to go into effect. As Johnson notes, the language of "inheritance" in verse 15, naturally related to the idea of a will, may have facilitated the author's move from covenant to will.[65]

Verse 17 emphasizes again the necessity of death to put into effect the provisions of a will. A will is "confirmed" (βεβαία) only "on the basis of deaths" (ἐπὶ νεκροῖς). Two aspects of verse 17a would seem to favor the "covenant" interpretation. First, the idea of a διαθήκη being "firm" or "confirmed" might most naturally point to the inauguration of that arrangement: a will did not wait to "go into force" until the testator died. Second, the plural "deaths" seems unnatural if the passage refers to a single will. Advocates of the "covenant" view claim that they offer more natural readings of this half verse. They argue that the plural form "deaths" only makes sense if the word refers to "dead bodies," presumably of sacrificial victims. Or, for those who hold the alternative "broken covenant" interpretation (2.b. above), the "dead bodies" are those of the Israelites, whose deaths are necessary to demonstrate the validity of the covenant. However, while the plural "deaths" is indeed a problem for the view that the author refers here to a will, this last explanation requires us to read a lot into this text which, in my view, is not there. Moreover, I think evidence from other parts of verses 16–17 strongly favor the "will" interpretation. This way of reading the passage can accommodate verse 17a if the author, as in verse 16, is referring not to the initial drawing up of the will but to its coming into force at the death of the testator. The plural "deaths" might then suggest that the author is referring to the regular experience of wills coming into effect.

The second half of verse 17 provides further reason to think the author is referring to human wills in these verses, since it claims the will does not have "legal validity" (ἰσχύει; see "ἰσχύω," BDAG 484, §4) if the one who made the will is still alive. The text seems again to suggest that the διαθήκη does not come into effect unless the one who initiates it dies. Applying this claim to the covenant requires either that we interpret "not being alive" to imply the need of a ritual death (via sacrifice) to inaugurate the covenant (view 2.a. above) or that ὁ διαθέμενος refers to Israel, God's covenant partner, who must die to carry out the sanctions of the covenant. I find neither of these options convincing.

9:18 For this reason neither was the first covenant inaugurated without blood (ὅθεν οὐδὲ ἡ πρώτη χωρὶς αἵματος ἐγκεκαίνισται). The principle of "death necessary for διαθήκη" (vv. 16–17) is now applied to the old covenant: the "first covenant" (the word διαθήκη is to be supplied with πρώτῃ) was not "inaugurated"[66] "without blood." The author switches in this verse from the language of death (vv. 15–17) to "blood." This switch enables him to widen the perspective to sacrifice—which includes death but goes beyond it to include the manipulation of blood by the priest (see "sprinkling" in vv. 19 and 21). "Blood" is the key word in verses 18–22, occurring in each verse. These verses feature a chiastic structure:

---

65. Johnson, *Hebrews*, 239. As Jeremy D. Otten notes, the author's appeal to "testament" to illustrate the covenant enhances the focus on the importance of death and the gracious nature of the covenant ("Why Do We Study the New *Testament* (and Not the New *Covenant*)? The Translation of *Berit* and Its Impact on the Book of Hebrews," in *Off the Beaten Path: A Festschrift in Honor of Gie Vleugels*, ed. Jacobus Kok and Martin Webber, Beiträge zum Verstehen der Bibel 48 [Zürich: LIT, 2021], 51–53).

66. The Greek is ἐγκεκαίνισται, a perfect form from ἐγκαινίζω (in the NT elsewhere only in Heb 10:20). The verb is used with reference to the "dedication" of the temple/sanctuary in the LXX (1 Kgs 8:63; 2 Chr 7:5; 1 Macc 4:36, 54, 57; 5:1). The author probably again uses the perfect to indicate the ongoing significance of what is recorded in Scripture (Michel, *Der Brief an die Hebräer*, 318).

A "not . . . without blood" (χωρὶς αἵματος)—v. 18
   B "according to the law" (κατὰ τὸν νόμον)—v. 19a
      C "sprinkled" (ἐράντισεν)—v. 19b
         D "This is the blood of the covenant"—v. 20
      C' "sprinkled" (ἐράντισεν)—v. 21
   B' "according to the law" (κατὰ τὸν νόμον)—v. 22
A' "not . . . without the shedding of blood" (χωρὶς αἱματεκχυσίας)—v. 22[67]

9:19–20 For when Moses had spoken every commandment of the law to all the people, he took the blood of calves, together with water and scarlet wool and hyssop, and sprinkled the scroll itself and all the people, saying 20 "This is the blood of the covenant which God has ordained for you" (λαληθείσης γὰρ πάσης ἐντολῆς κατὰ τὸν νόμον ὑπὸ Μωϋσέως παντὶ τῷ λαῷ, λαβὼν τὸ αἷμα τῶν μόσχων [καὶ τῶν τράγων][68] μετὰ ὕδατος καὶ ἐρίου κοκκίνου καὶ ὑσσώπου αὐτό τε τὸ βιβλίον καὶ πάντα τὸν λαὸν ἐράντισεν 20 λέγων, Τοῦτο τὸ αἷμα τῆς διαθήκης ἧς ἐνετείλατο πρὸς ὑμᾶς ὁ θεός). The author illustrates his claim about the signficance of "blood" in the inauguration of the first covenant by briefly summarizing the narrative in Exodus 24:1–8. Moses, Aaron, Nadab, and Abihu, along with "seventy of the elders of Israel" are summoned to "come up to the LORD," although Moses only is invited to "approach the LORD" (vv. 1–2). Moses then "went and told the people all the LORD's words and laws" (Exod 24:3a), the incident our author alludes to in verse 19a. On the next morning, Moses builds an altar at the foot of the mountain, after which young Israelite men offer "burnt offerings" and sacrifice "young bulls as fellowship offerings." The author also refers to the sacrifice of "young bulls" or "calves" (μόσχων), although the LXX uses the diminutive form, "little calves" (μοσχάρια).[69] According to many manuscripts the author of Hebrews here at 9:19 also refers to the blood "of goats" (καὶ τῶν τράγων). Most English versions assume these words were original, though NIV follows many other manuscripts that omit this reference to goats. I slightly favor the omission.[70] What is textually indisputable, however, is that the author refers to two other ritual elements not mentioned in Exodus: (sprinkling with) water, and the use of scarlet wool wrapped around a stick with a bunch or branches of hyssop (a small bush) to sprinkle blood.[71] "Scarlet" or "crimson" (κόκκινος) and "hyssop" (ὕσσωπος) are mentioned together in the description of several Old Testament rituals (Lev 14:4, 6; 14:49, 51–52; Num 19:6; hyssop is also mentioned in Num 19:18 and is used to spread blood on the lintels and doorposts at the time of the exodus [Exod 12:22]). It is impossible to know why the author alludes to these other rituals here, although it is worth noting that he often prefers to

---

67. E.g., Backhaus, *Der Hebräerbrief*, 328.
68. This bracketed reading is found in the NA[28] and UBS[5].
69. See LEH.
70. Versions that include reference to "goats" are ESV; NLT; NET; NRSV; CSB; CEB; NASB; NAB; KJV. Metzger notes that the UBS committee decided to include reference to the goats (attested in ℵ* A C 81. 326. 629. 2464 *al* lat sa[mss]), thinking that the words might have been omitted by accident (homeoteleuton—a scribe becoming confused because of the similarity between τῶν μόσχων and τῶν τράγων) or as an attempt to conform this text to Exod 24:5. However, Metzger also notes that the phrase καὶ τῶν τράγων might have been added to conform this text to 9:12—in my view perhaps a more likely explanation for the text (see also, e.g., Lane, *Hebrews*, 2:232). See Metzger, *Textual Commentary*, 599.
71. Delitzsch, *Hebrews*, 2:114.

conflate Old Testament rituals rather than present them in their exact details.[72]

The Exodus narrative refers to Moses sprinkling the people, but, once again, our author goes outside this text to include the sprinkling of "the scroll" or book (τὸ βιβλίον) also; although, since Exodus 24:7 says that Moses "took the book of the covenant" (λαβὼν τὸ βιβλίον τῆς διαθήκης), it is possible that the author infers from the text that Moses sprinkled the book as well as the people.[73]

The covenant-inauguration ritual in Exodus climaxes with Moses sprinkling blood on the people and then announcing, "Behold the blood of the covenant that the LORD has made with you in accordance with all these words" (Exod 24:8 ESV). The LXX follows the Hebrew closely here. However, the author deviates from the LXX in two places. First, he begins the quotation with "this" (τοῦτο) in place of the LXX's "behold" (ἰδού, which in turn is translating Hebrew *hinneh*). Second, he replaces LXX's "Lord" (κύριος) with "God" (ὁ θεός). This latter change may have been made to clarify that the author was not referring to Jesus, and the former change may reflect the author's acquaintance with the "words of institution," of which the versions found in Mark 14:24 and Matthew 26:28 read, "This is my blood of the covenant" (τοῦτό ἐστιν τὸ αἷμά μου τῆς διαθήκης).[74]

9:21 Moreover, the tabernacle and all its equipment used in cultic worship[75] **were similarly sprinkled with blood** (καὶ τὴν σκηνὴν δὲ καὶ πάντα τὰ σκεύη τῆς λειτουργίας τῷ αἵματι ὁμοίως ἐράντισεν). "Similarly" (ὁμοίως) might signify that the author continues to summarize events at the inauguration of the covenant recorded in Exodus 24 and context.[76] However, since the author speaks broadly about Old Testament rituals in verse 22, he has likely widened his focus to include other Old Testament rituals.[77] The question, however, is just what text or ritual he might have in mind. The Old Testament never refers to the tabernacle being sprinkled with blood, although a few texts refer to various parts of the tabernacle and its "equipment" being sprinkled with blood (e.g., Lev 8:15, 19, 24, 30), and other texts refer to the tabernacle and its equipment being anointed with oil (e.g., Exod 40:9–10).[78] Josephus mentions that the tabernacle was cleansed with blood at its inauguration (*Ant.* 3.206), an inference perhaps drawn from the Old Testament claim that the tabernacle was anointed with oil at its inauguration. The author may be following this same tradition.[79] In any case, the author's intention is clear enough: he "is thus expanding the Sinai event with a broad brush mention of later aspects of Old Testament ritual to produce a more comprehensive account of the importance of blood."[80]

---

72. For this explanation of this text, see, e.g., Attridge, *Hebrews*, 257; Koester, *Hebrews*, 419; Backhaus, *Der Hebräerbrief*, 331.

73. Delitzsch, *Hebrews*, 2:115.

74. See Ellingworth, *Hebrews*, 469; Backhaus, *Der Hebräerbrief*, 332; Michel, *Der Brief an die Hebräer*, 332. Other scholars, however, doubt any allusion to the words of institution (e.g., Lane, *Hebrews*, 2:245).

75. The Greek is πάντα τὰ σκεύη τῆς λειτουργίας. The word σκεῦος often refers specifically to a "vessel" (adopted by several English translations here), but also has a very broad meaning: "thing," "object." I follow the BDAG ("σκεῦος," 927, §1) renderings of the phrase in my translation (taking λειτουργίας—"worship," "liturgical service"—as an objective genitive).

76. E.g., Ellingworth, *Hebrews*, 470.

77. Contrary to Ellingworth's claim that "this [view] places a weight on the Greek text that it can hardly bear" (*Hebrews*, 470), I see nothing in the Greek text that creates a problem for this view.

78. For a full list of texts, with analysis, see Gäbel, *Die Kulttheologie des Hebräerbriefes*, 325–38.

79. Bruce, *Hebrews*, 226.

80. France, "Hebrews," 121.

9:22 And, according to the law, scarcely anything is cleansed without blood; and apart from the shedding of blood there is no forgiveness (καὶ σχεδὸν ἐν αἵματι πάντα καθαρίζεται κατὰ τὸν νόμον καὶ χωρὶς αἱματεκχυσίας οὐ γίνεται ἄφεσις). This verse affirms again the indispensable role of blood, or death, in the Old Testament economy. The author marks continuity in his argument with another καί ("and"), as in verse 21.[81] Sprinkling blood was integral in the covenant-inauguration ritual (vv. 19–20); it was used to "commission" the tabernacle and all its equipment (v. 21), and in fact the law indicates that "scarely anything is cleansed *without blood*." This general claim, as we have noted, matches the similar general opening point of this section in verse 18: "neither was the first covenant inaugurated *without blood*." The author restates this point in the second part of the verse in terms of its consequences: "apart from the αἱματεκχυσίας there is no forgiveness." Many of us will be familiar with this famous summary claim about the importance of "blood" in the specific translation "shedding of blood"—the rendering adopted in virtually all English translations from the KJV on.[82] In fact, however, the meaning of this word is quite debated, and many scholars now think the word refers to the manipulation of blood in a sacrificial rite *after* death.[83] This word itself appears here for the first time in Greek literature, and therefore our only resources to define it are context and etymology. Taking the latter first, the noun is built from the verb ἐκχέω plus the noun αἷμα (see "αἱματεκχυσία,"

BDAG 27). In the LXX, this combination can refer to violent death (e.g., Gen 9:6; 37:22; Num 35:33; Deut 19:10; 21:7; 1 Sam 25:31; 1 Kgs 2:31); and the noun cognate to the verb ἐκχέω, ἔκχυσις, also occurs with αἷμα to refer to the "shedding" of blood (1 Kgs 18:28; Sir 27:15). However, the combination ἐκχέω + αἷμα can also refer to the pouring out of blood in a sacrificial ritual (see, e.g., Exod 29:12; Lev 4:7, 18, 25, 30, 34). Etymology is obviously not decisive. Unfortunately, neither is the context. The author refers in verses 19–21 to the "sprinkling" of blood. However, as we have seen, the "blood" that is sprinkled also refers to, or at least includes, in this context, death (vv. 15–18; and note especially the connections in vv. 25–28 between "blood," "suffering," "sacrifice," and "death"). While I am generally skeptical of "both . . . and" solutions, I suspect it may be appropriate here. As I have argued, the author in this context is not fixated on blood shed in dying on the one hand or on blood poured out after death on the other. His focus rather is on sacrifice; and sacrifice in the Old Testament involves *both* the slaughter of the victim *and* the manipulation of the blood of the victim. In this axiomatic conclusion, then, we might expect that the author would have in view both steps in the sacrificial ritual.[84]

9:23 It was necessary, then, for the copies of the things in heaven to be cleansed by these sacrifices, but the heavenly things themselves with better sacrifices than these (Ἀνάγκη οὖν τὰ μὲν ὑποδείγματα τῶν ἐν τοῖς οὐρανοῖς τούτοις

---

81. For καί marking continuity in argument, see Runge, *Discourse Grammar*, 23–27.
82. And see, e.g., Cockerill, *Hebrews*, 410; Ellingworth, *Hebrews*, 471–72; Grässer, *An die Hebräer*, 2:185; Delitzsch, *Hebrews*, 2:122; Jamieson, *Jesus' Death and Heavenly Offering*, 141–53.
83. E.g., T. C. G. Thornton, "The Meaning of Αἱματεκχυσία in Heb 9:22," *JTS* 15 (1964): 63–65; Ribbens, *Levitical Sacrifice*, 131, 155–56; Kibbe, "Is It Finished?," 34–35; Michel, *Der Brief an die Hebräer*, 321; Lane, *Hebrews*, 2:232; D. Harris, *Hebrews*, 238; Attridge, *Hebrews*, 259.
84. E.g., Westcott, *Hebrews*, 269; Schreiner, *Hebrews*, 279; Ellingworth, *Hebrews*, 474 (?); Ribbens, "Positive Function," 103–4 (a shift from his earlier view [?]). A further reference to the words of institution at the Last Supper is possible (see v. 20): after Jesus refers to "my blood of the covenant," he goes on to say that this blood was "poured out [ἐκχυννόμενον] for the many" (see Ellingworth, *Hebrews*, 474).

καθαρίζεσθαι, αὐτὰ δὲ τὰ ἐπουράνια κρείττοσιν θυσίαις παρὰ ταύτας). Sacrifice (which includes blood/death) cleansed the earthly tabernacle and its worshipers; but the corresponding heavenly tabernacle and its worshipers required better sacrifices for their cleansing. Most scholars identify verses 23–28 as the third section within the larger unit of vv. 11–28.[85] To be sure, a connection to the preceding context is clear: the antecedent of τούτοις ("these") is probably the "sacrifices" connoted by references to blood in verses 18–22. However, this verse initiates a shift in argument and vocabulary, a shift that in many ways returns to the argument of verses 11–14.[86] Note the parallels:

Christ did not "enter" (εἰσέρχομαι—vv. 12, 24, 25)
    a tabernacle "made with human hands (χειροποίητος)" (v. 11)
    the sanctuary "made with human hands (χειροποίητος)" (v. 24)
But he entered the Most Holy Place (vv. 12, 25)
He "offered" [προσφέρω—vv. 14, 25, 28] himself
He entered (v. 12)/appeared (v. 26)/offered himself (v. 28) "once for all" (ἐφάπαξ, v. 12; ἅπαξ, vv. 26, 28)

As I have argued, the leitmotif of verses 15–22 is death/blood. The new covenant is inaugurated through Christ's redemptive death (v. 15). The connection of death with "covenant" is confirmed and illustrated with reference to "will" in verses 16–17. Verse 18 returns to the focus on biblical "covenant," as the author shows that "blood" was instrumental in the inauguration of the first covenant (vv. 19–20)—and indeed, absolutely indispensable for a range of Old Testament rituals (vv. 21–22). This focus on the instrumental power of blood/death continues in verses 23–28 (see v. 25 and v. 27), but the author now draws out their significance by referring to "sacrifice" (θυσία—vv. 23, 26; cf. also "offer" [προσφέρω] in vv. 25 and 28).[87] As I argued earlier, the varied language of "blood," "death," and "sacrifice" denotes a single conception: a sacrificial offering that includes the death of the victim and the manipulation of the blood of that victim.

This last paragraph weaves together two of the most important threads in the author's description of Christ's high-priestly ministry: sanctuary and sacrifice. The general movement of the paragraph is from the former to the latter: sanctuary is the focus in verses 23–24, while sacrifice dominates verses 25–28. The author uses his familiar comparative structure in verse 23: on the one hand (μέν) is the need for the "copies of the things in heaven" to be cleansed; on the other hand (δέ) is the need for those heavenly things themselves to be cleansed. At the same time, however, we find here the equally common contrast: the heavenly things require "better" (κρείττων) sacrifices.[88] "Copies of the things in

---

85. Almost all the translations place a paragraph break between vv. 22 and 23. Some scholars, however, view v. 23 as the conclusion of the second unit (usually identified as vv. 15–23). See, e.g., Weiss, *Der Brief an die Hebräer*, 474; Massonnet, *L'Épître aux Hébreux*, 250—although they also note the transitional character of the verse.

86. E.g., Attridge, *Hebrews*, 260; Lane, *Hebrews*, 2:247. The οὖν that introduces v. 23 (and, by extension, vv. 23–28) is resumptive—captured accurately in English with "then" (NIV) or "so" (NET; CEB).

87. The author uses θυσία thirteen other times: 5:1; 7:27; 8:3; 9:9; 10:1, 5, 8, 11, 12, 26; 11:4; 13:15, 16. It is a general term covering whatever elements of sacrifice might be relevant.

88. The plural θυσίαις is surprising in light of the author's stress on the "once-for-all" singular sacrifice of Christ. As Johnson puts it, "This may be a case where grammatical choice is governed by the logic of the image rather than by the logic of the argument" (*Hebrews*, 243).

heaven" (ὑποδείγματα τῶν ἐν τοῖς οὐρανοῖς) refers to the old-covenant sanctuary and its equipment (v. 21): the word "copy" (ὑπόδειγμα) is the word the author used to refer to the earthly sanctuary as a "copy" of the one shown to Moses in heaven (8:5). Reference to the "cleansing" or "purifying" (the verb is καθαρίζω; see 9:14) of the earthly sanctuary is unsurprising; the cleansing of the sanctuary by means of sacrifices was an important part of Old Testament ritual, including especially the Day of Atonement (Lev 16:16, 18–19, 33). Indeed, some modern scholars argue that cleansing the holy space so that the Lord could dwell there was the focus of the sacrifices.[89] While too extreme, this view does remind us of the importance of "sacred space" in the Old Testament cult.

However, if cleansing of the earthly sanctuary raises no particular questions, the second part of the verse does: Why would the heavenly sanctuary require cleansing? There are three basic answers to this question. First, the text might be referring to the inauguration or initial consecration of the heavenly sanctuary.[90] However, it is difficult to think that the verb the author uses here would mean "inaugurate" without some reference to cleansing as well. Second, then, the implicit reference might be to the people's sins, which must be cleansed if the people are to enter the sanctuary.[91] Third, the focus could be on the sanctuary itself, requiring cleansing because human sin affects all of creation. I prefer this third view with, however, a bit of influence from the second.[92] The "cleansing" of the sanctuary is certainly required because of human sin; see, for example, Leviticus 16:15b–16: "He [Aaron] shall sprinkle it [bull's blood] on the atonement cover and in front of it. In this way he will make atonement for the Most Holy Place because of the uncleanness and rebellion of the Israelites, whatever their sins have been." Yet the author refers to the cleansing of the sanctuary, not of sinners. We must at this point make allowance for the way elements in a comparison will not always line up exactly. In this case, we can presume that elements from the "earthly" side of the comparison have crept into the way the "heavenly" side is depicted.[93]

9:24 For Christ did not enter the sanctuary made with human hands, a copy of the true one, but he entered heaven itself, now to appear in the presence of God on our behalf (οὐ γὰρ εἰς χειροποίητα εἰσῆλθεν ἅγια Χριστός, ἀντίτυπα τῶν ἀληθινῶν, ἀλλ᾽ εἰς αὐτὸν τὸν οὐρανόν, νῦν ἐμφανισθῆναι τῷ προσώπῳ τοῦ θεοῦ ὑπὲρ ἡμῶν). The author now elaborates (γάρ, "for") the contrast between the two sanctuaries with respect to the ministry of Christ. More broadly, as Jamieson has shown, verses 24–26 consist of two major contrasts between old and new:

Christ did not [οὐ] enter an earthly sanctuary (v. 24a)
But into heaven itself (v. 24b)

---

89. See esp. Jacob Milgrom, who argues this view throughout his massive three-volume Leviticus commentary (*Leviticus 1–16*, *Leviticus 17–22*, and *Leviticus 23–27*, AB [New Haven: Yale University Press, 1998, 2000, 2001; see also *Leviticus: A Book of Ritual and Ethics*, CC [Minneapolis: Fortress, 2004]). See also, with a focus on the Day of Atonement, Roy Gane, *Cult and Character: Purification Offerings, Day of Atonement, and Theodicy* (Winona Lake, IN: Eisenbrauns, 2005).

90. E.g., Ellingworth, *Hebrews*, 477; Hurst, *Epistle to the Hebrews*, 38–39; Ribbens, *Levitical Sacrifice*, 122–23.

91. Attridge (*Hebrews*, 262) thinks the author is using the "language of cosmic transcendence" to speak about "human interiority." See also Bruce (*Hebrews*, 228–29) who sees a focus on the cleansing of the conscience.

92. Similar interpretations are found in Lane, *Hebrews*, 2:247; Cockerill, *Hebrews*, 416–17. It should also be noted that early Jewish texts do not hesitate to locate evil or evil beings in the heavenly sphere (e.g., 3 Bar. 2–3; 2 En. 7.1–4; I am indebted to Stephen Wunrow for this reminder).

93. Schenck, *Cosmology and Eschatology*, 168.

Neither [οὐδ'] did Christ offer himself many times (v. 25a)
But he has been revealed once for all (v. 26b)[94]

Resuming the language of verse 11, the author designates the earthly sanctuary as one "made with human hands" (χειροποίητα). It is not clear whether ἅγια refers to the sanctuary as a whole or to the inner room of the sanctuary. As we have seen, the author is not consistent in the language he uses to depict the sanctuary or the two rooms within the sanctuary. The simple plural [τὰ] ἅγια refers to the sanctuary as a whole in 8:2, to the outer room of the sanctuary in 9:2—"the Holy Place"—and to the inner room—"the Most Holy Place"—in 9:8, 12, 25; 10:19; 13:11. The comparison between this ἅγια and "heaven" in this verse and the clear reference to the inner room, "the Most Holy Place," with this word in verse 25 might suggest that this is the referent here also.[95] On the other hand, the "tabernacle" (σκηνή) "made with human hands" in verse 11 is the entire sanctuary, and this might make slightly better sense here.[96]

Echoing the language he used earlier, the author describes this earthly sanctuary as the "copy" (ἀντίτυπα; see τύπον in 8:5) of "the true one" (τῶν ἀληθινῶν; see ἀληθινῆς in 8:2). Many interpreters detect influence from the typical Platonic contrast between the heavenly reality and the shadowy, temporary, earthly counterpart.[97] This influence is certainly possible. But it is not indicated by the vocabulary here,[98] and any such influence is probably both muted and indirect: Jewish apocalyptic, a much more likely source for the author's perspective, has at points been influenced by Platonic ways of thinking. The author abandons sanctuary imagery in his description of the heavenly counterpart to the earthly sanctuary: Christ has entered "heaven itself" (αὐτὸν τὸν οὐρανόν). As I have earlier argued, it is heaven, the highest heaven, the abode of God, that has been the author's focus in his sanctuary imagery (whether he conceives of an actual sanctuary in heaven or not).[99] This is made explicit in this verse.

Christ's entrance into heaven makes it possible for him "now to appear in the presence of God on our behalf."[100] "Now" (νῦν) probably refers to the period of time inaugurated by Christ's initial "appearance" before God at his exaltation and continuing until the present. Some think that Christ's appearance may have been for the purpose of offering his sacrificial blood before the Father to secure atonement. However, the "now" suggests an ongoing activity of Christ in heaven on our behalf, unsuited to the "once-for-all" nature of Christ's sacrifice.[101] Probably, then, the reference here is to the continuing intercessory ministry of Christ (see 2:18; 4:15; 7:25).

9:25–26 Neither did Christ enter to offer himself many times, as the high priest would enter the Most Holy Place every year with the blood of

---

94. Jamieson, *Jesus' Death and Heavenly Offering*, 50.
95. Lane, *Hebrews*, 2:248; Attridge, *Hebrews*, 262.
96. E.g., Rissi, *Die Theologie des Hebräerbriefs*, 38; D. Harris, *Hebrews*, 243; Ellingworth, *Hebrews*, 480.
97. E.g., Grässer, *An die Hebräer*, 2:190; Backhaus, *Der Hebräerbrief*, 336; Johnson, *Hebrews*, 243 (he refers to "biblical Platonism"); cf. Attridge's claim of a "Platonizing motif" (*Hebrews*, 263).
98. The key word ἀντίτυπος does not seem to have been used by Platonists until after Hebrews (L. Goppelt, "τύπος, κτλ," *TDNT* 8:247–48; cf. 258 on Hebrews).
99. Many interpreters continue to deny vociferously any idea that the author might have pictured a heavenly sanctuary (e.g., Schreiner, *Hebrews*, 284).
100. "Appear" translates the infinitive ἐμφανισθῆναι, probably used here to indicate purpose (D. Harris, *Hebrews*, 244).
101. E.g., Gäbel, *Die Kulttheologie des Hebräerbriefes*, 292–308. Attridge (*Hebrews*, 263–64) thinks the reference is both to Christ's sacrificial offering and his ministry of intercession.

another— **26 since in that case he would have had to suffer many times since the creation of the world. But, as it is, he has been revealed once for all at the culmination of the ages in order to set aside sin through the sacrifice of himself** (οὐδ᾽ ἵνα πολλάκις προσφέρῃ ἑαυτόν, ὥσπερ ὁ ἀρχιερεὺς εἰσέρχεται εἰς τὰ ἅγια κατ᾽ ἐνιαυτὸν ἐν αἵματι ἀλλοτρίῳ, 26 ἐπεὶ ἔδει αὐτὸν πολλάκις παθεῖν ἀπὸ καταβολῆς κόσμου· νυνὶ δὲ ἅπαξ ἐπὶ συντελείᾳ τῶν αἰώνων εἰς ἀθέτησιν τῆς[102] ἁμαρτίας διὰ τῆς θυσίας αὐτοῦ πεφανέρωται). The superiority of Christ's high-priestly work is evident in the place of his ministry: heaven itself versus an earthly sanctuary (v. 24). It is also evident, the author now reminds us, in what is sacrificed—"the blood of another" versus Christ himself—and the frequency of the sacrifice—"every year" versus "once for all." The main verb in verses 25–26a is "enter," picked up from verse 24 (εἰσῆλθεν) and repeated in verse 25b (εἰσέρχεται).[103] In 7:27, the author noted that the Old Testament high priest offered sacrifices "day after day." Here, with the Day of Atonement ritual in view, the author makes a similar point: the high priest had to "redo" the atoning sacrifices "every year" (κατ᾽ ἐνιαυτόν). The contrast between the need for repeated sacrifices in the Old Testament and the "once-for-all" (ἅπαξ) sacrifice of Christ is a key theme in 9:25–10:4.[104]

The author's reference to Jesus "offer[ing] himself" (προσφέρῃ ἑαυτόν) raises again the question of the timing of Jesus's sacrifice. Many think that time is the crucifixion, when Jesus died for our sins—a view that can marshal considerable support from other New Testament texts.[105] On this view, the "moments" of crucifixion and entrance are, as it were, collapsed: Jesus's entrance into the heavenly sanctuary is a way of referring to his death.[106] However, other scholars claim that the cultic categories Hebrews is operating with point to the time of Jesus's appearance before God in the heavenly sanctuary as the point when he offered himself.[107] Moreover, entrance into the heavenly sanctuary is hardly a clear way of referring to crucifixion. As I argue at greater length below (see the "In Depth" section), I want to "have my cake and eat it too." The author generally, and in this context specifically, makes unmistakable references to both these moments. He has pointed to the significance of death for covenant making in verses 15–17. In verse 26, the author compares Christ's "offer[ing] himself" to his suffering. And, in verses 27–28, he compares Christ's offering to the death of humans.[108] On the other hand, our author obviously puts great emphasis in this passage on the moment of "entering" heaven and his appearance before the Father. A "sequence" perspective may, then, best represent the author's view of Jesus's atoning sacrifice. His death on the cross is vital, a point that is clear in many New Testament texts. But, drawing on the sacrificial rituals of the Old Testament (and especially the Day of Atonement), our author also sees the resurrected Christ's entrance into the heavenly sanctuary to appear on our behalf before the Father as a further sacrificial, atoning moment.

---

102. NA[28] places brackets around this article, indicating that the reading is uncertain.

103. What the OT high priest enters is τὰ ἅγια. Many interpreters think this refers to the sanctuary as a whole (e.g., D. Harris, *Hebrews*, 245; Ellingworth, *Hebrews*, 482), but the focus here on a once-a-year entrance rather suggests a reference to the Most Holy Place (see, e.g., Lane, *Hebrews*, 2:229; NIV; NLT).

104. For this reason, Cockerill (*Hebrews*, 419–20) isolates 9:25–10:4 as a discrete section.

105. See, e.g., Montefiore, *Hebrews*, 161; P. Hughes, *Hebrews*, 337; Lane, *Hebrews*, 2:249; see also Attridge, *Hebrews*, 264–65.

106. Backhaus, e.g., says that "the pictures of death by crucifixion, exaltation, and entrance into the Most Holy Place— 'Good Friday,' 'Easter,' and ascension—form a soteriological unity in Hebrews" (*Die Hebräerbrief*, 337; my translation).

107. Moffitt, *Atonement*, 280–81.

108. See, e.g., Rissi, *Die Theologie des Hebräerbriefs*, 80–81.

Does this mean that we should conceive of Christ entering heaven "with his blood" and then offering that blood to the Father as the culmination of his sacrifice? Many who consider Christ's appearance before the Father to be part of his sacrificial offering think this is the case, pointing to the procedure on the Day of Atonement, which the author obviously sees as parallel in some ways with Jesus's work. And the author's reference to the Old Testament high priest entering the Most Holy Place "with the blood of another" (v. 25b) might suggest that Christ, likewise, entered with his own blood. However, the phrase "in some ways" I have used two sentences back is important: we should not assume that the author views Christ's sacrificial work at every point as fulfilling the Day of Atonement ritual. In 9:12, where the same issue arose, I argued that the author is claiming simply that Christ entered "by means of" blood (instrumental use of ἐν). While the same preposition here in verse 25b is more likely associative (hence the translation "with" in almost all the translations),[109] the clause in which it occurs does not refer to Christ's ministry. While I don't think the notion is out of keeping with Hebrews's conception of Christ's work, entry into heaven "with" his blood is not clearly indicated anywhere.

In verse 26a, the author details what would be entailed if Jesus, indeed, had had to offer himself "many times" (v. 25a): "he would have had to suffer many times since the creation of the world."[110] As I noted above, the shift from "offering" to "suffering" signals plainly that the author, if not exclusively focused on the cross, includes it in the sacrificial work of Jesus.[111] With the emphatic "but now" (νυνὶ δέ), the author introduces the contrast to the "many times" of the Old Testament high priest's offering: Christ has appeared "once for all" (ἅπαξ)—a recurring motif in this part of the letter.[112] The time of this appearing (the verb is a passive form of φανερόω, "reveal, disclose") is not clear. Since the author has just mentioned Jesus's entrance into heaven (vv. 24, 25a), he might be referring to his "appearance" in heaven.[113] However, I think it more likely that the "appearance" here matches the "coming" in verse 11 (perhaps as an *inclusio*), referring in general to the entrance of Christ on the stage of salvation history.[114]

That appearance, picking up a common New Testament theme, takes place at the decisive moment in salvation history: at the "culmination of the ages" (συντελείᾳ τῶν αἰώνων). A similar phrase occurs five times on Jesus's lips in the Gospel of Matthew (13:39, 40, 49; 24:3; 28:20), referring to the climactic conclusion of salvation history.[115] Here in Hebrews, however, the phrase refers not to the "not yet" of eschatological expectation but to the "already" of eschatological climax. The author refers to this same idea at the beginning of his letter: "in these last days [God] has spoken to

---

109. See also BDF §198.2; Turner, *Syntax*, 241. Attridge (*Hebrews*, 264), on the other hand, thinks the ἐν indicates instrument.

110. The author introduces this clause with ἐπεί, which has a causal sense. The syntax is best explained if the author assumes a protasis whose content is drawn from v. 25a: "since [if he offered himself many times] he would have had to suffer many times" (D. Harris, *Hebrews*, 246).

111. E.g., Cockerill, *Hebrews*, 422.

112. The phrase νυνὶ δέ could have a logical force, "but as it is" (RSV; Attridge, *Hebrews*, 264), but more likely has a temporal nuance, connoting the shift to a new era of fulfillment.

113. E.g., Ribbens, *Levitical Sacrifice*, 126; Kibbe, "Is It Finished?," 43.

114. Koester suggests something like this, suggesting the focus is on the incarnation (*Hebrews*, 422; see also Schreiner, *Hebrews*, 286). Note the use of φανερόω to denote Christ's "appearance" in 1 Pet 1:20: "he was chosen before the creation of the world, but was revealed [φανερωθέντες] in these last times [ἐπ᾽ ἐσχάτου τῶν χρόνων] for your sake."

115. Matthew uses the singular αἰῶνος instead of the plural in Hebrews. See also the use of συντελεία in Daniel (9:27; 12:13).

us in (the) Son" (1:2); see also "the age to come" in 6:5.

An important theological point is the purpose of Jesus's appearance: to "set aside" (ἀθέτησιν) sin through "the sacrifice of himself" (διὰ θυσίας αὐτοῦ).[116] This last phrase could mean simply "his sacrifice" (taking αὐτοῦ as a personal pronoun), but the contrast with "blood of another" and the language of "offer himself" in verse 25 suggests the more emphatic meaning (αὐτοῦ as a "verbal genitive").[117] The word ἀθέτησις often has a legal flavor (see its only other NT occurrence in Heb 7:18): "annulment" ("ἀθέτησις," BDAG 24, §1). While the idea of a cancelling of sin's "legal" hold on people might be part of the picture here, the word here seems to connote a broader "setting aside" or "removal" (CSB) or "putting away" (NET) of sin. The significance of the word here is best determined from parallel assertions of the effect of Christ's sacrifice: "those who draw near" are "made perfect" (10:1, 14), especially with respect to the "conscience" (9:9); sins are remembered "no more" (10:17). What Old Testament sacrifices could not do—"take away" sin (10:4)—Christ's sacrifice has accomplished. Nor should we overlook the author's choice to use the singular "sin" here; as Cockerill says, "Christ had done away with sin as a principle and force, as a source of pollution and separation from God."[118]

9:27–28 And just as it is appointed with respect to human beings to die once, and after that comes judgment, 28 so also Christ, having offered himself once for all to take away the sins of many, will appear a second time, not to deal with sin, but to bring salvation to those who are eagerly awaiting him (καὶ καθ' ὅσον ἀπόκειται τοῖς ἀνθρώποις ἅπαξ ἀποθανεῖν, μετὰ δὲ τοῦτο κρίσις, 28 οὕτως καὶ ὁ Χριστὸς ἅπαξ προσενεχθεὶς εἰς τὸ πολλῶν ἀνενεγκεῖν ἁμαρτίας, ἐκ δευτέρου χωρὶς ἁμαρτίας ὀφθήσεται τοῖς αὐτὸν ἀπεκδεχομένοις εἰς σωτηρίαν). In rough correspondence to the unbreakable sequence of human life—death and then judgment—is the sequence of Christ's first appearance, dealing with sin, and his second, providing for ultimate salvation. The author concludes the long elaboration of the elements of sanctuary and sacrifice in Christ's high-priestly ministry that he began in 9:11 with a final comparison. In this case, however, the comparison is not between the Old Testament priesthood and Christ's—as so often has been the case—but between the sequence of death and judgment for human beings in general and the sequence of Christ's first appearance to deal with sins and his second appearance to convey to his people their ultimate salvation. The comparison is not exact: judgment of humans is compared with salvation for humans. But the point of comparison is nevertheless apt: both judgment and the salvation the author refers to here are aspects of the final culmination of salvation history. The main point of comparison is between the decisive and final "moment" of human death and the equally decisive and final moment of Christ's sacrifice. At the same time, by referring to the "second" appearance of Christ, our author situates his presentation of the work of Christ solidly within the typical "already-not yet" eschatology of the New Testament. As important

---

116. The word θυσία is another indication that the death of Christ is in view throughout this passage. This word, in both LXX and Hebrews (Heb 5:1; 7:27; 8:3; 9:9, 23, 26; 10:1, 5, 8, 11, 12, 26; 11:4; 13:15, 16), is a general term for "the thing that is offered"; it is doubtful if the preparation of that object (slaughter in the case of an animal/Christ) can be excluded.

117. D. Harris, *Hebrews*, 247; see Ellingworth, *Hebrews*, 483.

118. Cockerill, *Hebrews*, 423.

as Christ's initial "appearance" to take care of the human sin problem is, there is, our author suggests, more to be done: ultimate salvation, the "rest" God has promised his people, awaits. It is promised specifically to those who are eagerly "awaiting him"—a brief allusion to the main point of the author's sermon: the need for Christ's people to maintain their allegiance right up to the end.

The conjunction our author uses here (καί, "and") indicates that verses 27–28 continue the argument from the previous context. By using "once for all" (ἅπαξ) on both sides of the comparison,[119] the author makes clear the main line of this development (see v. 26). That humans die only once is a truism obvious to all, and many ancient people believed in a judgment of some kind after death. But the author is reflecting the distinctive biblical perspective, which the New Testament stoutly maintains: all humans, believers included, will have to appear before God in the final judgment. And the reminder about this judgment to come is particularly appropriate for his audience. They need the reminder that God will assess their lives in the end as a stimulus to faithful endurance (see esp. 10:27–31).

Christ has also died once—but in his case, death, while of course personal, had far-reaching significance: he was "offered" or "sacrificed" (προσενεχθείς) to "take away the sins of many."[120] We should probably supply God as the implied subject of the passive verb. "Take away the sins of many" is probably an allusion to the fifth strophe of Isaiah 53:12: "he bore the sin of many."[121] As is the case in the New Testament elsewhere (see esp. 1 Pet 2:24), the servant's death in Isaiah 52:13–53:12 provides a particularly poignant anticipation of Christ's death in terms of taking on and providing forgiveness for the sins of others. A few translations (NIV; NLT; NAB) translate this clause "take away sins," but the verb the author uses here (ἀναφέρω) does not seem to have this meaning. It refers, rather to "bearing" (NET; RSV; NRSV; ESV; CSB; CEB; NASB), or, perhaps better, "taking up [on himself]" (see CEB).[122] In the context, of course, this "bearing" of sins provides for a decisive and final dealing with sins—so "take away" sins might be accurate as the ultimate effect of Christ's "taking" our sins upon himself.

Christ's second appearance, in contrast, will be "without sin" (χωρὶς ἁμαρτίας)—that is, "not to deal with sin." The New Testament often uses the form of the verb we find here (the passive of ὁράω) to refer to the "appearance" of Christ.[123] The force of this verbal form is not so much on the passive idea of "being seen" by someone but on the revealing of oneself, or "appearing" (an intransitive notion).[124] The dative case used in the words following the verb, then, τοῖς . . . ἀπεκδεχομένοις, does not indicate the

---

119. The comparison is introduced by καθ' ὅσον; see 3:3.
120. In order to preserve his thesis that Christ's offering is always associated with his entrance into heaven, Jamieson argues that Christ "offering" and "being offered" are distinct ideas (*Jesus' Death and Heavenly Offering*, 64–65), but this is unlikely.
121. Compare LXX αὐτὸς ἁμαρτίας πολλῶν ἀνήνεγκεν ("he the sins of many took upon himself") with Hebrews's εἰς τὸ πολλῶν ἀνενεγκεῖν ἁμαρτίας ("in order to bear the sins of many"). Most interpreters identify the allusion (e.g., Cullmann, *Christology*, 91; Lane, *Hebrews*, 2:250; Ellingworth, *Hebrews*, 487).
122. See the lengthy note in BDAG ("ἀναφέρω," 75, §4). It claims that the verb never means "bear" or "take away," preferring "take up." However, they also develop this meaning in terms of "give someone to bear," so the distinction is not all that clear. See also Cockerill, *Hebrews*, 427; Ellingworth, *Hebrews*, 487. The verb ἀναφέρω in the NT can mean "lead away" or "lead up" (Matt 17:1; Mark 9:2; Luke 24:51), "offer up [a sacrifice]" (Heb 7:27; 13:15; Jas 2:21; 1 Pet 2:5), or "bear" (1 Pet 2:24).
123. Matt 17:3; 28:7, 10; Mark 9:4; Luke 24:34; Acts 9:17; 1 Cor 15:5, 6, 7, 8.
124. Murray J. Harris, *Raised Immortal: Resurrection and Immortality in the New Testament* (Grand Rapids: Eerdmans, 1983), 46–47.

agent—"by those eagerly awaiting"—but the indirect object—"to those eagerly awaiting." The verb our author uses elsewhere refers to believers' anticipation of their ultimate deliverance (Rom 8:19, 23, 25; 1 Cor 1:7; Gal 5:5; Phil 3:20). My translation, "will appear . . . to bring salvation to those who are eagerly awaiting him" follows most English versions in the way the syntax is read.[125] Our author, as we have seen, views "salvation" as both present and future for believers. Here the focus is on the ultimate salvation on the last day. The appearance of Christ to bring salvation climaxes the series of "appearances" that mark this passage: Jesus's initial "appearance" initiated the era of "the good things," such as the fulfillment of God's promises (v. 11; see also v. 25). In the present time, he has "appeared" in God's presence to complete his atoning work and intercede for us (v. 24). And he will appear a final time to culminate history in judgment and salvation.

Theology in Application

Celebrating the Sacrifice

The contrasting images of the empty cross, displayed in many Protestant churches, and the crucifix, displayed in Roman Catholic churches, suggests two different approaches to the celebration of the sacrifice of Christ. For Protestants, the cross is bare, signifying the final and definitive nature of Christ's work. "It is finished," and we celebrate Jesus's sacrifice by continually appropriating its benefits and by offering ourselves as "living sacrifices" (Rom 12:1; see Heb 13:15). Celebration of the Lord's Supper, while taking distinctive forms in different Protestant churches, often focuses on the subjective "remembering" or "bringing to mind" of Christ's once-for-all sacrifice. For Roman Catholics, on the other hand, the mass is an objective "memorial" of Christ's sacrifice. Protestant interpreters down through the centuries have often cricitized this view of the mass on the basis of Hebrews's insistence that Christ's sacrifice is "once for all" (7:27; 9:12, 26; 10:2, 10; cf. 9:27–28). Yet this criticism might be misaimed. While Roman Catholic views of the mass have differed over the years, and there is often a distance between the "official" view and the views of people or priests "on the street," the authoritative view of the mass, as found recently in the *Catechism of the Catholic Church*, is that the mass does not involve a "re-sacrifice" of Christ but "re-presents" the sacrifice of the cross (*CCC* 1356). "The sacrifice of Christ offered once for all on the cross remains ever present" (*CCC* 1363, 1364). This "re-presenting" is possible because the sacrifice shares the atemporality or eternality

---

125. On this view, the substantival participial clause τοῖς αὐτὸν ἀπεκδεχομένοις depends on εἰς σωτηρίαν: "for the salvation of those eagerly awaiting him." But the participle could also depend on ὀφθήσεται, with εἰς σωτηρίαν functioning as a separate purpose clause: "he will appear to those who are awaiting him; and his appearance will be in order to bring salvation" (see NET; D. Harris, *Hebrews*, 249). The difference between the two in terms of ultimate meaning is negligble.

of the divine nature. By locating Christ's sacrifice "outside of time," "the sacrifice of Christ and the sacrifice of the Eucharist are one single sacrifice" (*CCC* 1367).[126]

It is considerably above my pay grade to comment usefully on the claim that Christ's sacrifice is "atemporal." And, as we have seen, accusations that the view of the mass is a "re-sacrificing" of Jesus are off the mark. However, I still wonder if "re-presenting" Christ's sacrifice might stand in tension with the finality suggested by Hebrews's presentation of Christ's sacrifice. His theology moves in the direction of a past definitive act that we look back to, a perspective that appears to clash somewhat with a constant re-presenting of that sacrifice. Moreover, the author connects the "once-for-all" nature of Christ's own sacrifice with the "once-for-all" nature of our sanctification or perfection. Celebration of the mass may detract from the confidence we should have in our current standing before God, a standing resting on Christ's definitive work for us and our definitive appropriation of that work.

IN DEPTH: Sacrifice and Atonement

Perhaps the most distinctive theological contribution of the letter to the Hebrews is the extensive use of Old Testament cultic language to describe the work of Christ. He is our high priest who enters a sanctuary to offer a sacrifice for our sins. This "entrance" appears to be located in the period of time after Jesus's resurrection and ascension, and the sanctuary in which the offering is made is a heavenly one. The Day of Atonement ritual provides an important template for the author's conceptualization of Christ's high-priestly ministry. In this ritual, it is often argued, the decisive "moment" of atonement is when the high priest, having secured blood from a sacrificial victim, manipulates the blood in the Most Holy Place. In light of this background and the express focus in Hebrews, then, it is no wonder that some scholars insist that the author identifies the "moment" of atonement with Christ's post-ascension offering of his own blood to the Father in the "true" Most Holy Place—heaven itself.[127] Jesus's death, of course, has its place in the author's soteriology. But, these

---

126. References to the *Catechism of the Catholic Church* are taken from https://www.vatican.va/archive/ENG0015/_INDEX.HTM. See also the overview in Gregg Allison, *Roman Catholic Theology and Practice: An Evangelical Assessment* (Wheaton, IL: Crossway, 2014), 299–325.

127. The two clearest and best-argued presentations of this view are Gäbel, *Die Kulttheologie des Hebräerbriefes*; and Moffitt, *Atonement*. In articles written after his book, Moffitt appears to modify this view somewhat, still insisting that Jesus's entry into the heavenly sanctuary is the decisive moment of atonement/sacrifice in Hebrews, but including Jesus's death as part of the process. See esp. Moffitt, "Blood, Life, and Atonement." He asserts that the cross is not "the place or primary means of atonement" (p. 87) and that it is "not the death/slaughter of Jesus that atones" but allows for some kind of (atoning?) significance of the cross by claiming it is "not the great atoning moment" (pp. 87–88) and by stressing that Hebrews views the procuring of salvation as a process that includes death as part of blood sacrifice (p. 98).

scholars argue, Jesus's death is not itself atoning: it is the essential (and of course crucial) preparatory act, by means of which our high priest acquires the blood needed to make atonement before the Father in heaven.

This proposal can appeal to a number of texts in Hebrews. Consider, for instance, 9:12, where the author says that "he [Christ] entered the Most Holy Place once for all by his own blood, thus obtaining eternal redemption." However, as I have argued in my exposition of 9:11–28 (see esp. the notes on vv. 25–26), confining "atonement" or the key moment of sacrifice to the heavenly ministry of Jesus underplays other emphases in Hebrews. The author never loses sight of Jesus's death as being instrumental in securing salvation for his people. Jesus "tasted death" for everyone (2:9); it was "by his death" that he broke "the power of him who holds the power of death" (2:14); Jesus "suffered outside the city gate to make the people holy through his own blood" (13:12). Particularly telling is the way the author interchanges "blood" and "death" in 9:11–28, showing, at a minimum, that Jesus's death is included in his references to blood. At the same time, we should be careful about putting too much stock in the author's employment of Day of Atonement imagery.

Competent Old Testament scholars from a variety of theological traditions are far from agreed on the significance of the Old Testament sacrifices in general or the Day of Atonement ritual in particular. At the risk of transgressing into territory both foreign and dangerous, I would tentatively suggest that the ritual in Leviticus 16, while not highlighting the moment of slaughter, presumes that moment as an important part of the ritual. Several passages in Leviticus appear to envisage a "two-step" process (1:3–9[?]; 3:2–5, 6–11, 12–16; 4:3–12, 15–18, 22–26, 27–31; 9:7–10; 10:17; 14:19–20). The Day of Atonement receives almost no attention outside Leviticus 16 in the Old Testament, but there are many references to sacrifice. And many of these focus attention on the death of the victim. Moreover, the author gives clear indications that he is not limiting the cultic imagery of his teaching to the Day of Atonement ritual. As we have noted, he often introduces details into his description of Old Testament sacrifice that find no place in the Day of Atonement ritual. While this ritual is no doubt basic in some texts, there is good reason for thinking that the author wants ultimately to portray Christ's sacrifice against the broad background of Old Testament sacrificial ritual.[128]

---

128. E.g., George H. Guthrie, "Time and Atonement in Hebrews," in Laansma, Guthrie, and Westfall, *So Great a Salvation*, 211–20.

How, then, should we integrate the moment of Jesus's death with his heavenly offering?[129] One popular option is to think that our author uses the priestly imagery of the heavenly ministry to portray the death of Christ.[130] This option has one undoubted advantage: it enables us easily to integrate the soteriology of Hebrews with that of other New Testament authors who focus attention again and again on the death of Christ as the key "moment" of atonement. Paul, for instance, attributes soteriological meaning to Jesus's death in forty-eight texts. His overview of his gospel in 1 Corinthians 15:1–3 is instructive in this regard: Christ's death, burial, and resurrection are listed, but it is only his death that is said to be "for our sins." Paul, on the other hand, barely mentions Jesus's ascension or post-ascension ministry (although see, e.g., Rom 8:34). Those of us who want to read Hebrews canonically, then, cannot ultimately treat the author's soteriology in isolation from that of the rest of the New Testament. Therefore, a powerful motive (not to be dismissed!) for viewing the author's references to Jesus's heavenly offering as ultimately a way of describing Jesus's death on the cross is precisely this interest in reading canonically.

However, I am not sure that the author's extensive and detailed use of cultic language can be reduced to imagery employed to characterize Jesus's death. Again, while sympathetic with the need to read Hebrews canonically, I am not certain that, if taken on his own terms, we would end up reading the cultic language of Hebrews in this way.

It is necessary, then, to integrate into our overall perspective two lines of evidence. On the one hand, the author does seem to invest atoning significance in the post-ascension ministry of Jesus in heaven. And, on the other, he also views Jesus's death as having atoning significance—a perspective that attains heightened importance in light of the larger New Testament witness. The natural way to integrate these perspectives is to attribute to the author a "two-stage," or "sequence" view of atonement.[131] Jesus's death is the vital and indispensable first stage. In the second stage, Jesus enters heaven and offers

---

129. For a taxonomy of views, see Jamieson, *Jesus' Death and Heavenly Offering*, 4–5; Jamieson, "When and Where Did Jesus Offer Himself? A Taxonomy of Recent Scholarship on Hebrews," *CurBR* 15 (2017): 338–68.

130. E.g., Bruce, *Hebrews*, 213–14; Schreiner, *Hebrews*, e.g., 244; Cockerill, *Hebrews*, e.g., 355; Peterson, *Hebrews and Perfection*, 192; Schelle, *Theology*, 638–39 ("the cross and exaltation, the earthly and the heavenly realms, collapse into each other" [p. 639]); see the extensive review, focused on historical theology, in P. Hughes, *Hebrews*, 329–54; Montefiore, *Hebrews*, 134 (he, however, supports this view by claiming that "a man cannot offer himself after he is dead," apparently ignoring entirely the resurrection of Jesus).

131. See, e.g., Ribbens, *Levitical Sacrifice*, 107–8, 132–36; Rissi, *Die Theologie des Hebräerbriefs*, 80–81; Marshall, "Soteriology," 270–72 (though he hints at the "conflation" view on p. 255); Jamieson, *Jesus' Death and Heavenly Offering* (as I note above, he refines the picture by suggestively arguing that the place and time of Jesus's offering is in heaven, but that *what* he offers is his death); Michael S. Horton, "Atonement and Ascension," in *Locating Atonement: Explorations in Constructive Dogmatics*, ed. Oliver D. Crisp and Fred Sanders,

before the Father the blood of his sacrifice on our behalf. We referred above to Jamieson's illustration, but it is worth mentioning again: the author does not pan *from* Jesus's death *to* his heavenly ministry; he zooms out from his death to include the heavenly ministry. Another way to put the matter is that the author does not hold an exclusive view—heavenly offering *versus* the cross—but an inclusive one—cross *and* heavenly offering.

Such an inclusive view, while creating a bit of dissonance with the wider New Testament testimony to what Paul calls "the word of the cross" (1 Cor 1:18 ESV), can be embraced within the "diversity within unity" that characterizes the New Testament. Perhaps a short step toward explaining the diversity on this point is one observation about the distinct emphases in Paul and Hebrews. While cultic metaphors are more common in Paul than many scholars acknowledge, he never develops that metaphor at any length. He rarely uses priestly imagery, and when he does it is usually to depict his own ministry (e.g., Rom 15:16; Phil 2:17) or the life and ministry of believers in general (e.g., Rom 12:1; Phil 4:18). Paul never calls Jesus a priest or high priest, although he occasionally uses arguably priestly imagery to describe Jesus (see esp. Rom 8:34, where Christ, seated at the right hand of God, "intercedes" for us). Rather, as we have noted, Paul makes sacrifice a central component of his interpretation of Jesus's death.[132] But, in one of the many distinctive facets of a very distinctive book, Hebrews not only portrays Jesus as a priest but arguably makes Jesus's high priesthood the centerpiece of the theology he deploys to exhort his wayward readers. The obvious point, then, is this: the choice of cultic imagery significantly dictates the moment of atonement that Paul and Hebrews focus attention on. Paul focuses on the sacrifice of the human being Jesus, which naturally focuses attention on the willingness of that person to die. But once the focus shifts to the role of the priest, the angle of vision is enlarged: the priest, although he is often involved in the slaughter of the victim, enacts his special role in the manipulation of the blood attained from the sacrifice. The decision of Hebrews to focus special attention on Jesus as high priest inevitably brings into play the priest's role after the slaughter, generating the innovative and striking development of this theme in the central part of Hebrews.

Los Angeles Theology Conference Series (Grand Rapids: Zondervan Academic, 2015), 226 ("Our Lord's entrance into the heavenly sanctuary was not merely a victory celebration but an essential part of the victory itself"). (In articles subsequent to his book, Moffitt also hints at this view [e.g., "Blood, Life, and Atonement," 98]). This "sequence" view is often looked at askance because it was an element in the Socinian theological viewpoint (Socinus was a sixteenth-century theologian whose unorthodox views were strenuously resisted by Calvin—to the extent that Socinus was executed in Calvin's Geneva). However, as Ribbens points out, "sequence" views have been held by a number of orthodox theologians: it was not the sequence view of atonement per se that figured in the heretical Socinian viewpoint (Benjamin J. Ribbens, "Ascension and Atonement: The Significance of Post-Reformation, Reformed Responses to Socinians for Contemporary Atonement Debates in Hebrews," *WTJ* 80 [2018]: 1–23; see also Kibbe, "Is It Finished?").

132. See, e.g., Moo, *Theology of Paul*, 387–403.

CHAPTER 23

Hebrews 10:1–18

Literary Context

Hebrews 10:1–18 is the last stage in the author's elaboration of Jesus's high-priestly ministry in terms of sanctuary, sacrifice, and covenant that he began in 8:1. Indeed, looking at the bigger picture, this section is the last stage in the author's exposition of Jesus as high priest that extends all the way back to 4:14. As I argued earlier, 10:19–25 matches 4:14–16 as an exhortatory *inclusio*. Hebrews 10:1–18, while still focused on exposition, begins to prepare more explicitly for this concluding exhortation.[1] The focus in this section is less on the objective provision for final salvation in the work of Christ and more on the subjective appropriation of those benefits. Lane suggests that the overall focus on 9:15–10:18 therefore reflects the two parts of the seminal text in 9:11–14, with 9:15–28 elaborating the work of Christ described in 9:11–12 and 10:1–18 developing the subjective application of Christ's work from 9:13–14.[2]

These verses both summarize the previous argument and advance it. The focus through most of the passage is on Jesus's sacrifice, although covenant is touched on at the end. (The heavenly sanctuary as the locus of Jesus's ministry is not mentioned.) The author is especially focused on contrasting the repeated sacrifices of the old administration with the "once-for-all," universally effective sacrifice of Christ (vv. 1–3, 11–14)—a point of emphasis in his earlier exposition as well (7:27; 9:25–27). However, Christ's sacrifice is "better" not only because it need not be repeated but also by virtue of its intrinsic nature. Animal sacrifices could never "take away sins" (v. 4). It required the sacrifice of a human, dedicated to doing God's will, to take away sins (vv. 5–10). This focus on Jesus's willing obedience as essential to his high-priestly ministry was hinted at earlier (5:9), but is explicitly enunciated here for the first time.

---

1. Weiss, *Der Brief an die Hebräer*, 498. 2. Lane, *Hebrews*, 2:258.

> I. The Exalted Son and a Rest for the People of God (1:1–4:13)
> II. **Our Great High Priest and His Ministry (4:14–10:31)**
>   A. Exhortation: Persevere through the Power of Our Exalted High Priest (4:14–16)
>   B. Exposition: High Priests and Our High Priest (5:1–10)
>   C. Exhortation: Move on to Maturity (5:11–6:20)
>   D. Exposition: A High Priest "According to the Order of Melchizedek" (7:1–28)
>   E. Exposition: The Ministry of Our High Priest (8:1–10:18)
>   1. Overview: Sanctuary, Sacrifice, and Covenant (8:1–6)
>   2. A New and Better Covenant (8:7–13)
>   3. The Earthly Sanctuary and Its Regulations: An Illustration of the New (9:1–10)
>   4. Eternal Redemption: Heavenly Sanctuary, Decisive Sacrifice, and New Covenant (9:11–28)
> ➡ 5. **The Ultimate Sacrifice (10:1–18)**
>   F. Exhortation and Warning: Appropriating the Benefits of Our High Priest's Ministry (10:19–31)
> III. Exhortation: Follow and Serve the Pioneer of Our Faith through Endurance and Faith (10:32–13:25)

Main Idea

As a human dedicated to doing God's will, Jesus, in his once-for-all sacrifice, enables people to escape the domination of sin and to find a secure standing before God. Old-covenant sacrifices were a mere "shadow" of this enduring reality—as they are repeated year by year and day by day, they serve to remind people of their continuing sinfulness and unworthiness.

Translation

Hebrews 10:1-18

1a	assertion	**The law . . .**
1b	content	is a shadow of the good things
1c	description	that have come,
1d	contrast	not the reality
1e	content	of these things itself.
1f	time	Year after year
1g	illustration (of 1a–e)	the priests endlessly offer the same sacrifices,

Continued on next page.

1h	description (of "the law" in 1a)	. . . which are **never able**
1i	content	to perfect those who draw near.
2a	verification	Otherwise,
2b	rhetorical question	**would they not have ceased being offered,**
2c	basis	since the worshipers, . . .
2d	condition	if they had once for all been cleansed,
2e	predicate (of 2c)	. . . would not have had any longer a consciousness of sins?
3a	contrast (with 1f–2e)	Rather,
3b	means	in those sacrifices
3c	assertion	**there is yearly a remembrance of sins.**
4a	basis (for 1–3)	For
4b	assertion	**it is impossible . . .**
4c	content	for the blood of bulls and
4d	list	goats
4e	predicate (of 4b–d)	**. . . to take away sins.**
5a	inference (from 1–4)	Therefore,
5b	circumstance	when he [Christ] came into the world,
5c	assertion	**he said:**
5d	list (with 5e)	"Sacrifice and
5e	object	offering
5f	assertion	you have not desired,
5g	contrast	but
5h	assertion	you have prepared for me a body.
6a	expansion (of 5c–f)	You are not pleased
6b	reference	with burnt offerings and
6c	list	sin offerings.
7a	sequence	Then
7b	assertion	I said,
7c	command	'See,
7d	content (of 7b)	I have come—
7e	parenthesis	it is written about me
7f	location	in the scroll of the book—
7g	purpose	to do, God, your will.'" (Ps 40:6–8)
8a	application 1	First
8b	assertion	**he said,**
8c	object	"Sacrifices and
8d	series	offerings and
8e	series	burnt offerings and
8f	series	sacrifices for sin"—
8g	description	which are offered
8h	standard	according to the law—
8i	predicate (of 8c–f)	"he did not desire or
8j	parallel	take delight in."

9a	application 2	Then
9b	assertion	**he said,**
9c	content	"Behold I have come
9d	purpose	to do your will." (Ps 40:8)
9e	inference (from 8a—9d)	**He abolishes the first**
9f	purpose	in order that he might establish the second.
10a	circumstance	In conjunction with this will,
10b	assertion	**we have been sanctified**
10c	means	through the once-for-all offering
10d	content	of the body of Jesus Christ.
11a	assertion	**Every priest stands**
11b	time	daily
11c	manner	at his ministry,
11d	specific	offering the same sacrifices,
11e	description	which are never able
11f	content	to take away sins.
12a	contrast (with 11)	But **this priest**, . . .
12b	time	when he had offered one sacrifice
12c	reference	for sins,
12d	manner	eternally valid,
12e	predicate (of 12a)	. . . **sat down**
12f	location	at the right hand of God.
13a	sequence	Since then
13b	assertion	he waits
13c	time	until his enemies are placed
13d	manner	as a footstool
13e	location	under his feet.
14a	summary	For
14b	means	with one sacrifice
14c	assertion	**he has perfected**
14d	time	for all time
14e	object (of 14c)	those who are being sanctified.
15a	verification	**The Holy Spirit also testifies**
15b	recipient	to us
15c	reference	about this.
15d	amplification (of 15a–c)	For
15e	assertion	**he first says,**
16a	content	"'This is the covenant
16b	description	that I am making
16c	reference	with them
16d	time	after these days,'
16e	speech tag	says the Lord:

16f	promise	'I will place my laws
16g	sphere	in their hearts and
16h	parallel	I will write them
16i	sphere	on their minds.'" (Jer 31:33)
17a	sequence (with 15e)	**He then says,**
17b	object (of 17a)	"and
		their sins and
17c	list	lawless deeds
17d	content	I will remember
17e	time	no more." (Jer 31:34)
18a	inference (from 17)	And
18b	basis	since there is forgiveness
18c	reference	for these,
18d	assertion	**there is no longer a place for sacrifice**
18e	reference	for sins.

Structure

With most interpreters, I identify four paragraphs in this section: verses 1–4, 5–10, 11–14, and 15–18. As is so often the case in Hebrews, scholars detect various literary devices. Weiss, for instance, notes that the entire passage is framed by "offering" language: προσφέρουσιν ("they offer") in verse 1 and προσφορά in verse 18.[3] More popular is a chiastic structure, with the two outer paragraphs focusing on the contrast between sins "remembered" in the old system of sacrifice (vv. 1–4) and sins no more "remembered" in the new (vv. 15–18). The two inner paragraphs feature a contrast between the old sacrifices, unable to take care of sin, and the decisive and absolutely effective sacrifice of Christ: note, in this regard, the "once for all" (ἐφάπαξ) in verse 10 and the "eternally valid" (εἰς τὸ διηνεκές) in verse 12.[4] Closely related to the eternal value of Christ's sacrifice is the author's claim that Christ's sacrifices can do what the Old Testament sacrifices never could: "perfect" the worshiper (10:1, 14).

---

3. *Der Brief an die Hebräer*, 497. The likelihood of an intentional *inclusio* here might be undercut by the occurrence of προσφορᾶς in v. 10.

4. E.g., Lane, *Hebrews*, 2:258; Koester, *Hebrews*, 436. Backhaus identifies this "for all time" motif as central to this whole section (*Der Hebräerbrief*, 342).

Exegetical Outline

→ **5. The Ultimate Sacrifice (10:1–18)**
   a. The Inability of the Old Sacrifices to Take Care of Sin (vv. 1–4)
   b. The Efficacy of the Willing Sacrifice of Christ (vv. 5–10)
   c. The Contrast Between the Inability of the Old and the Efficacy of the New (vv. 11–14)
   d. The Upshot: Sins Remembered No More (vv. 15–18)

Explanation of the Text

10:1 The law is a shadow of the good things that have come, not the reality of these things itself. Year after year the priests endlessly offer the same sacrifices, which are never able to perfect those who draw near (Σκιὰν γὰρ ἔχων ὁ νόμος τῶν μελλόντων ἀγαθῶν, οὐκ αὐτὴν τὴν εἰκόνα τῶν πραγμάτων, κατ᾽ ἐνιαυτὸν ταῖς αὐταῖς θυσίαις ἃς προσφέρουσιν εἰς τὸ διηνεκὲς οὐδέποτε δύναται τοὺς προσερχομένους τελειῶσαι). A fundamental salvation-historical perspective that lies behind the author's comparison between old and new is the movement from Old Testament "shadow" to New Testament "reality." One element of that shadow is the need to repeat sacrifices year after year—illustrating their ultimate inadequacy. As so often in Hebrews, the conjunction γάρ (often translated "for"; see ESV; NET) seems to establish only a loose relationship between this new section and what has preceded it; not rendering it at all in English is probably the best option (NIV; NRSV; CSB; CEB; NAB). I have also broken the single Greek sentence in verse 1 into two in English for clarity. The two are often related as cause and effect (giving the participle ἔχων, "having," a causal sense),[5] but it might be better to view the second sentence as a specific illustration of the first: the inability of the "same sacrifices" that are offered "year after year" to perfect worshipers is evidence of the "shadow" nature of the law.

Most interpreters think "the law" (ὁ νόμος) refers narrowly to the cultic law. However, while acknowledging that the focus here is on that part of the law, I suspect the author refers to the law as a whole. This opening sentence in chapter 10, then, is an important claim about the New Testament view of the law in salvation history. The phrase "good things that have come" (τῶν μελλόντων ἀγαθῶν) refers to the new-covenant blessings that Christ's first coming to earth has introduced into that history. These blessings are pictured as a solid reality that casts a shadow back into the old era. The imagery of a shadow cast by solid realities is famous in cultural history. Plato used it in his allegory of the cave as a way of expressing his understanding that earthly realities were only insubstantial and fleeting analogies to the "real" or "ideal" world—just as people chained in a cave are able to see only the shadows cast by unseen realities (see *Republic* 514a–520a). Some interpreters think the author is indebted to some degree to this tradition, represented in his day

---

5. See the "since" in RSV; NRSV; ESV; CSB; NAB; "for this reason" in NIV.

by Middle Platonism.[6] I don't think we can entirely rule out such influence. However, the author does not use key words the same as Plato does. For the latter, "shadow" (σκιά) and "image" (εἰκών) were basically synonymous.[7] The author obviously contrasts them, using εἰκών to mean not "image" (of something else) but "reality."[8] More importantly, the author uses the "shadow"/"reality" contrast not in a philosophical sense but to describe the course of history. As in Colossians 2:17, "shadow" characterizes the law given to the people of Israel in the old era of salvation history, a law that is now relativized in its authority for the people of God in light of the reality of fulfilled promises that Christ's coming has introduced. The idea, then, is somewhat similar to Paul's well-known comparison of the law to the "guardian" who watches over a child—when that child is grown, the guardian gives way to other sources of guidance (Gal 3:24–25).

The "shadowy" character of the law is revealed clearly in the fact that it can "never" (οὐδέποτε) "perfect" (the verb is τελειόω) "those who draw near" (τοὺς προσερχομένους). The inadequacy of the law is seen clearly in the fact that the sacrifices required by the law are offered "endlessly" (εἰς τὸ διηνεκές), year after year.[9] The author may be thinking of the Day of Atonement, with the requirement for yearly repetition, but he more likely refers to the Levitical cult in general.[10] As the author has emphasized already, that cult is fundamentally unable to "perfect" worshipers—that is, to restore them to full and permanent relationship with God (7:11, 19, 28; 9:9; cf. 10:14).[11]

10:2 Otherwise, would they not have ceased being offered, since the worshipers, if they had once for all been cleansed, would not have had any longer a consciousness of sins?[12] (ἐπεὶ οὐκ ἂν ἐπαύσαντο προσφερόμεναι διὰ τὸ μηδεμίαν ἔχειν ἔτι συνείδησιν ἁμαρτιῶν τοὺς λατρεύοντας ἅπαξ κεκαθαρισμένους;). The fact that sacrifices kept being offered is good reason to believe that those sacrifices could not "perfect" worshipers (v. 1b). The "otherwise" I use to introduce this verse reflects the fact that the causal conjunction used here (ἐπεί) often assumes an ellipsis: "for (if it were

---

6. E.g., Thompson, *Hebrews*, 194; Attridge, *Hebrews*, 270–71; Mackie, *Eschatology and Exhortation*, 106–14; deSilva, *Perseverance in Gratitude*, 317.

7. See, e.g., *Republic* 509e–510a: "by images [εἰκόνας] I mean first, shadows [σκιάς], and then reflections in water"; also, e.g., 510e. A textual variant would bring the author's usage more in line with Plato: in place of οὐκ αὐτὴν τὴν εἰκόνα—"not the image itself"—𝔓[46] has καὶ τὴν εἰκόνα—"[the shadow] and/even the image." The variant is too weakly supported to be thought original.

8. The Greek word εἰκών is often translated "image" or "likeness," referring to something that resembles or has the same form as something else. Believers thus in some way are in Christ's "image" (Rom 8:29; 2 Cor 3:18), and, displaying a closer resemblance or even identity, Christ is himself the "image" of God (2 Cor 4:4; Col 1:15). While not clearly attested elsewhere in Greek, our author seems to use εἰκών not so much to describe the "image" of something else but to describe the reality itself (G. Kittel, "εἰκών," *TDNT* 2:395; *NIDNTTE* 2:104; Grässer, *An die Hebräer*, 2:206–7; see also Chysostom, *Homilies on Hebrews* 17.5 [*PG* 63:130]).

9. The phrase εἰς τὸ διηνεκές could modify the main verb (δύναται . . . τελειῶσαι), but it would be awkward for both this phrase and οὐδέποτε (which are virtually synonymous) to modify the same verb. As in v. 11, then, εἰς τὸ διηνεκές modifies "offering" (προσφέρουσιν) (though the connection in v. 11 is also debated). See, e.g., Delitzsch, *Hebrews*, 2:145; Attridge, *Hebrews*, 271; Lane, *Hebrews*, 2:255; contra, e.g., Michel, *Der Brief an die Hebräer*, 331; Westcott, *Hebrews*, 303–4. A number of MSS read δύνανται ("they [e.g., the priests] are unable") in place of δύναται. The difference in meaning is negligible.

10. E.g., Ribbens, *Levitical Sacrifice*, 186–87.

11. Peterson, *Hebrews and Perfection*, 144–53.

12. Most English versions rightly punctuate the verse as a question (for which see Philip Church, "The Punctuation of Hebrews 10:2 and Its Significance for the Date of Hebrews," *TynBul* 71 [2020]: 281–92). Church also argues that the argument of the verse implies that sacrifices were still being offered in the temple.

different")."¹³ If those sacrifices had been ultimately effective, the author says, the "worshipers" (τοὺς λατρεύοντας) would have been "cleansed once for all" (ἅπαξ κεκαθαρισμένους) and would no longer have "consciousness" (συνείδησιν) of sins.¹⁴ The language both of "cleansing" and of "consciousness of sins" goes back to 9:14, a verse that presents the "solution" to the "problem" presented here: Christ's sacrifice can accomplish what the Old Testament sacrifices could not; it can "cleanse the conscience" (καθαριεῖ τὴν συνείδησιν).¹⁵ A number of interpreters think that the "unreal" condition—"they would have ceased being offered"—implies that sacrifices were still being offered. This would suggest that the Jerusalem temple was still standing, meaning that the letter would have been written before AD 70.¹⁶ However, the author's perspective might be narrowly confined to the Old Testament: within the Old Testament, he might be saying, sacrifices were continually being offered.

10:3 Rather, in those sacrifices there is yearly a remembrance of sins (ἀλλ᾽ ἐν αὐταῖς ἀνάμνησις ἁμαρτιῶν κατ᾽ ἐνιαυτόν). Having spelled out what Old Testament sacrifices did *not* accomplish in verses 1b–2, the author now indicates what they *do* accomplish: they bring to mind the sins of people. The focus on a "yearly" (κατ᾽ ἐνιαυτόν) reminder suggests that the author is here thinking specifically of the Day of Atonement (see 9:7, 25). "Remembrance" of sins goes beyond simply bringing to one's attention the fact that one has sinned. "Remembrance" (ἀνάμνησις) and similar words in the New Testament often refer to a "calling to mind" or "taking to heart."¹⁷ The author, then, might be suggesting that the repeated Old Testament sacrifices bring to worshipers a recurrent sense of sinfulness and consequent need for a further act of decisive redemption. Even though the same word that our author uses occurs in the New Testament elsewhere only in the Last Supper "words of institution" (Luke 22:19; 1 Cor 11:24, 25), it is unlikely that our author intends any kind of allusion.¹⁸ A more likely, though still improbable, source is Numbers 5:15, which refers to a particular grain offering as a "sacrifice of reminder, bringing to mind sin" (θυσία μνημοσύνου ἀναμιμνήσκουσα ἁμαρτίαν).¹⁹

10:4 For it is impossible for the blood of bulls and goats to take away sins (ἀδύνατον γὰρ αἷμα ταύρων καὶ τράγων ἀφαιρεῖν ἁμαρτίας). As grounds (the function of γάρ here) for the author's negative evaluation of sacrifices (vv. 1b–3), he ramps up his implicit claim about the inadequacy of animal sacrifices (9:12, 13) with the absolute claim that animal blood cannot "take away" sins. As in 9:13, the author refers to the blood of "bulls and goats"

---

13. "ἐπεί," BDAG 360, §2; Turner, *Syntax*, 318. See also 9:26.
14. The accusative participle [τοὺς] λατρεύοντας is the subject of the infinitive ἔχειν.
15. Schreiner (*Hebrews*, 292) remarks on the linguistic parallels between 9:14 and 10:2.
16. E.g., Bruce, *Hebrews*, 236; P. Hughes, *Hebrews*, 391; Massonnet, *L'Épître aux Hébreux*, 261. Johnson (*Hebrews*, 250) and Ellingworth (*Hebrews*, 494) more cautiously support the idea.
17. See, e.g., μιμνήσκομαι, "remember," in Heb 2:6; 8:12; 10:17; 13:3 ("remember" those in prison); cf. 2 Pet 3:12; Jude 17. The author uses a similar verb, μνημονεύω, to encourage his readers to "remember your leaders" (13:7); and see also "remember the poor" (Gal 2:10); "remember my chains" (Col 4:18); and cf. 1 Thess 1:3; 2 Tim 2:8; Rev 2:5; 3:3; 18:5.
18. Weiss, *Der Brief an die Hebräer*, 504.
19. E.g., deSilva, *Perseverance in Gratitude*, 318. Philo refers to Num 5:15 in *Planting* 108: God takes "no delight in blazing altar fires fed by the unhallowed sacrifices of men to whose hearts sacrifice is unknown. Nay, these sacrifices do but put Him in remembrance of the ignorance and offences of the several offerers; for Moses, as we know, speaks of sacrifice 'bringing sin to remembrance'" (Attridge, *Hebrews*, 272).

(ταύρων καὶ τράγων), though he reverses their order (in 9:12, he refers to "goats and calves"). As is often the case, the author is not interested in pinning down a reference to any particular ritual or text; his concern is ultimately with the Old Testament sacrificial system in general.[20] This verse is the climax in a series of texts that teach the inadequacy of the old-covenant sacrifices. They are unable to "perfect" worshipers (7:11, 19; 10:1); they are entangled with a law consisting in a "fleshly commandment" (7:16), "external regulations" having to do with food and drink and washings (9:10) and bringing only "outward" cleanness (9:13); they cannot clear the conscience (9:9); they bring "remembrance" of sins (10:3). Now the author claims that these sacrifices cannot "take away" sins. The verb used here (ἀφαιρέω) is used with reference to sin in the LXX to refer simply to the forgiveness of sins (e.g., Exod 34:7, 9; Lev 10:17; Num 14:18; Isa 27:9; Zech 3:4; cf. also Sir 47:11). In Paul's quotation of Isaiah 27:9 in Romans 11:27, however, the context suggests a stronger meaning: God decisively removes the sin problem when he fulfills his covenant with Israel. This is clearly the sense the word has here. As I suggested earlier, Old Testament sacrifices, as they looked forward to the climactic sacrifice to come, could bring forgiveness for worshipers. But they could not finally deal with the underlying sin problem.[21] The author repeats this point again in verse 11, using a different verb from the same root (αἱρέω): the old-covenant sacrifices could "never ... take away [περιελεῖν] sins."

10:5–7 Therefore, when he [Christ] came into the world, he said: "Sacrifice and offering you have not desired, but you have prepared for me a body. 6 You are not pleased with burnt offerings and sin offerings. 7 Then I said, 'See, I have come—it is written about me in the scroll of the book—to do, God, your will'" (Διὸ εἰσερχόμενος εἰς τὸν κόσμον λέγει, Θυσίαν καὶ προσφορὰν οὐκ ἠθέλησας, σῶμα δὲ κατηρτίσω μοι· 6 ὁλοκαυτώματα καὶ περὶ ἁμαρτίας οὐκ εὐδόκησας. 7 τότε εἶπον, Ἰδοὺ ἥκω, ἐν κεφαλίδι βιβλίου γέγραπται περὶ ἐμοῦ, τοῦ ποιῆσαι ὁ θεὸς τὸ θέλημά σου). The superiority of Christ's sacrifice is seen also in his freely and willingly offering himself. The logical connection between verses 5–10 and verses 1–4 is easy enough to identify: in light of the inadequacy of the old system of sacrifice, "therefore" (διό), a new system is required.[22] The program for this new system is outlined via a quotation from Psalm 40:6–8a (LXX 39:7–9a). After an introduction (v. 5a), the author quotes from this text in verses 5b–7, after which he comments on it in verses 8–10. The key element in this new system of sacrifice is the fact that the one decisive sacrifice is offered by a human being who aligns his own will with the will of God.

As he has already done in 2:12–13, the author again here puts on Jesus's lips the words of Scripture—"he says" (λέγει—we have to go back to 9:28 to identify the antecedent of the assumed pronoun: "Christ"). According to our text, Christ uttered these words "when he came into the world" (εἰσερχόμενος εἰς τὸν κόσμον). The author here assumes the preexistence of Christ. As the eternal Son of God (e.g., 1:2b–3), he existed for all eternity but entered into our human world, becoming incarnate.[23] It was at that moment that Christ

---

20. E.g., Grässer, *An die Hebräer*, 2:212.
21. On this whole issue, see Ribbens, "Positive Function."
22. Schreiner, *Hebrews*, 295.
23. Most interpreters affirm this (e.g., Michel, *Der Brief an die Hebräer*, 336; Attridge, *Hebrews*, 273; Weiss, *Der Brief an die Hebräer*, 508). Fine-tuning our author's point is perhaps not possible—that is, does he view Christ's affirmation as preceding his incarnation (and thus including it; see, e.g., Bruce, *Hebrews*, 242) or as following his incarnation?

affirmed his desire to do God's will. The author is not claiming that Christ actually uttered these words. Rather, he puts these words on Christ's lips in order to convey the attitude Christ had as he took on flesh. In the words of Paul, he "did not consider equality with God something to be used to his own advantage; rather, he made himself nothing by taking the very nature of a servant" (Phil 2:6b–7a); "though he was rich, yet for your sake he became poor" (2 Cor 8:9b).

The words our author puts on Christ's lips come from Psalm 40 (Ps 39 in the LXX), a psalm that has such a strong and unusual shift that some interpreters think it originally existed as two separate psalms.[24] In the first part, the psalmist (identified as David in the title) proclaims God's goodness in response to God's gracious response to the psalmist's plea for deliverance. The second part (vv. 11–17) turns to lament and urgent request that God rescue the psalmist from people who want to take his life. The words our author quotes come toward the end of the first part where, in typical fashion, the psalmist's thanksgiving gives way to an affirmation of continuing faithfulness to the Lord. The author is no doubt drawn to these verses because of their negative evaluation of Old Testament sacrifices, set in contrast with the personal dedication to God's will on the part of the psalmist. Some of the language surrounding the words our author quotes may have helped lead him to this text. In verse 9b, just after the conclusion of the words he quotes, the psalmist affirms that he has the law "in his inmost being" (LXX ἐν μέσῳ τῆς κοιλίας μου)—reminding us of the new-covenant promise of having the law "in their minds" and written on their hearts (Jer 31:33, quoted in Heb 8:10 and 10:16). And just after these words, the psalmist expresses his intention to "proclaim the good news of righteousness in the great assembly [ἐν ἐκκλησίᾳ μεγάλῃ; my translation]"—language similar to the author's quotation of Psalm 22:22 in 2:12 ("I will proclaim your name among my brothers and sisters; in the midst of the assembly [ἐν μέσῳ ἐκκλησίας] I will sing hymns of praise to you" [my translation]—and it is perhaps significant that these words also are put on the lips of Jesus).[25]

Most of the Old Testament quotations in Hebrews follow the LXX pretty closely, suggesting that the author was dependent on a Greek text close to what is found in the LXX. And, in most cases, the meaning of the Greek the author uses is similar to the meaning of the Hebrew (Masoretic) text. However, the author's quotation of Psalm 40 appears at first sight to be an exception. The text we find in Hebrews 10 varies at places both from the LXX and from the MT. The differences are as follows (the translations are mine):

---

24. Ross, *Psalms*, 1:855; Kraus, *Psalms 1–59*, 423.
25. For these connections, see, e.g., Johnson, *Hebrews*, 251; Moffitt, *Atonement*, 246.

Psalm 40:6–8 in Hebrews 10:5–7: Text Comparison

Hebrew (Masoretic Text)	Greek (LXX)	Hebrews
"**ears** you have dug for me" אָזְנַיִם כָּרִיתָ לִּי	"a **body** you have prepared for me" σῶμα δὲ κατηρτίσω μοι (MSS B, S, A) // "but ears you have prepared for me" ὠτία δὲ κατηρτίσω μοι (MS G)	"a **body** you have prepared for me" σῶμα δὲ κατηρτίσω μοι
"**burnt offering** and sin offering you do not **ask for**" עוֹלָה וַחֲטָאָה לֹא שָׁאָלְתָּ	"**burnt offering** and sin offering you did not **ask for**" ὁλοκαύτωμα καὶ περὶ ἁμαρτίας οὐκ ᾔτησας	"**burnt offerings** and sin offering you are not **pleased with**" ὁλοκαυτώματα καὶ περὶ ἁμαρτίας οὐκ εὐδόκησας
"Then I said, 'Behold I have come—in the scroll of the book it is written about me. **To do your will, my God, I desire'**" אָז אָמַרְתִּי הִנֵּה־בָאתִי בִּמְגִלַּת־סֵפֶר כָּתוּב עָלָי׃	"Then I said, 'Behold I have come—in the scroll of the book it is written about me. **To do your will, my God, I desire'**" τότε εἶπον Ἰδοὺ ἥκω, ἐν κεφαλίδι βιβλίου γέγραπται περὶ ἐμοῦ, τοῦ ποιῆσαι τὸ θέλημά σου, ὁ θεός μου, ἐβουλήθην	"Then I said, 'Behold **I have come**—in the scroll of the book it is written about me—**to do, God, your will. [I desire . . .]**'" τότε εἶπον, Ἰδοὺ ἥκω, ἐν κεφαλίδι βιβλίου γέγραπται περὶ ἐμοῦ, τοῦ ποιῆσαι ὁ θεὸς τὸ θέλημά σου

Of the differences between these texts, two are particularly interesting.[26] First, while the Hebrew MT and Greek LXX connect the clause "to do your will" with the following verb, Hebrews, by omitting this following verb (ἐβουλήθην in the LXX), attaches the clause to the verb "I have come" (ἥκω). This change creates a tighter connection between Christ's coming and the doing of God's will, a change that suits the emphasis of Hebrews. Still, the sense is not basically changed. More striking is the author's use of the word "body" (σῶμα) in the opening sentence: "a body you have prepared for me"—versus the Hebrew "ears you have dug for me." The reading of the Greek Old Testament is unclear here. The most important uncials (B, S, A) read "body" (σῶμα). However, the editors of two of our best-known LXX editions (the Rahlfs "hand" edition and the larger Göttingen edition) have chosen to read the much more poorly attested "ears" (ὠτία), which conforms to the Hebrew. Despite this decision, the original reading of the Old Greek was, in fact, more likely "body," and this was also likely the reading that our author found in his Greek text.[27]

---

26. Three of the differences among these versions are minor: in contrast to the MT and the LXX, the author uses the plural ὁλοκαυτώματα, "burnt offerings"; in place of a verb meaning "ask, request" in MT and LXX (שאל and αἰτέω), the author uses a verb meaning "be pleased, take delight in" (εὐδοκέω); and in place of the sequence "to do your will, God" in MT and LXX, Hebrews has "to do, God, your will."

27. Most scholars now agree that the author probably had the word σῶμα in his text. For a full evaluation of the evidence leading to this conclusion, see esp. Walser, *Old Testament Quotations in Hebrews*, 90–140. However, a few think that ὠτία was in the Greek text the author had before him (e.g., Karen H. Jobes, "The Function of Paronomasia in Hebrews 10:5–7," *TJ* 13 [1992]: 181–91; G. Guthrie, "Hebrews," 977; Weiss, *Der Brief an die Hebräer*, 507). On this view, σῶμα might have found its way into MSS of the Septuagint on the basis of the reading in Hebrews.

We are still left with the problem that the Old Testament our author quotes does not seem to be the actual Old Testament (based on the Hebrew text). This problem crops up in a number of New Testament quotations of the Old Testament: What are the implications for biblical interpretation and authority if New Testament authors "misquote" the Old Testament to ground their teaching? Granted these possible implications, the issue is one we need to address. One option is to argue that, while the wording may differ, the Hebrew text of Psalm 40 and Hebrews's quotation of it are saying essentially the same thing. It is, therefore, frequently argued that the LXX (and Hebrews) "body" simply extends a part of the human body ("ears") to the whole.[28] However, there is still dissonance: the Hebrew imagery suggests that God has opened the ears of the psalmist so that he might hear and obey God. The provision of a body, however, suggests more the means by which that obedience can be carried out—a key point the author makes in this context, coming back to the language of "body" again in verse 10 in his application of the psalm. The difference is not great, but it is real. Our author, then, taking his lead from his Greek Old Testament text, has extended the meaning of Psalm 40 a bit, in a maneuver typical of the way the New Testament authors often give a "fuller" meaning to the Old Testament.[29] The psalmist's emphasis on the doing of God's will, in contrast to the offering of sacrifices, finds its deepest expression in Christ's commitment to do God's will, expressed in his offering of the body God himself prepared for him. God gives not only the "open ear" to hear and obey but also gives the instrument of that obedience. We may identify also a broader "informing theology" or "hermeneutical axiom" that undergirds this application of the language to Christ: the widepread interpretation of Christ as the one who fulfills the prophecies about a greater "David" to come. A psalm uttered by David can naturally be seen to have relevance to his "greater son."[30]

However, as we have seen, another important reason for citing this psalm text is because its criticism of the old-covenant sacrifices dovetails nicely with our author's argument. At first sight, this criticism appears to be absolute: the Lord does not "desire" or "ask for" sacrifices (vv. 5, 6). However, this apparent total rejection of sacrifices is clearly a literary device. As in many other Old Testament texts where sacrifices are criticized, the concern is with sacrifices being offered in the right spirit. Thus, in the well-known Hosea 6:6—"I desire mercy, not sacrifice" (quoted in Matt 9:13; 12:7)—the intention is "I desire mercy in addition to your sacrifice" or "your sacrifice does no good if it is not accompanied by mercy."[31] In Hebrews, though, the criticism of Levitical sacrifices is absolute. The one decisive sacrifice of Christ means there is no more place for any others (vv. 9, 18).

Some explain the reading σῶμα in many Greek versions as a mistake in reading the Greek uncials (Grässer, *An die Hebräer*, 2:216–17; Ellingworth, *Hebrews*, 500), but this is unlikely (Delitzsch, *Hebrews*, 153). Jobes argues that the author has himself introduced changes in order to create assonance ("Function of Paranomasia"; cf. also G. Guthrie, "Hebrews," 977), but this also is unlikely (Jared Compton, "The Origin of Σῶμα in Heb 10:5: Another Look at a Recent Proposal," *TJ* 32 [2011]: 19–29).

28. E.g., Ross, *Psalms*, 1:854; Bruce, *Hebrews*, 240; Attridge, *Hebrews*, 274; Lane, *Hebrews*, 2:255; D. Harris; *Hebrews*, 256; Cockerill, *Hebrews*, 436.

29. See Moo and Naselli, "Problem of the New Testament's Use of the Old Testament."

30. See esp. Walter C. Kaiser Jr., "The Abolition of the Old Order and Establishment of the New: Psalm 40:6–8 and Hebews 10:5–10," in *Tradition and Testament: Essays in Honor of Charles Lee Feinberg*, ed. John S. Feinberg and Paul D. Feinberg (Chicago: Moody, 1981), 19–37; also G. Guthrie, "Hebrews," 977; Delitzsch, *Hebrews*, 152; Schreiner, *Hebrews*, 296–97.

31. See also 1 Sam 15:22; Ps 50:8–10; 51:16–17; Isa 1:10–13; 66:2–4; Jer 7:21–24; Amos 5:21–27.

The quotation of Psalm 40 does not, of course, refer to Christ's sacrifice, but to his commitment to do God's will (v. 7 = Ps 40:7–8a). The reference to this willingness being "written . . . in the scroll of the book" is not clear in either the original psalm or in the author's quotation of it. The Hebrew refers to "the scroll of a book" (*bimgillath-sepher*), perhaps a reference to the Pentateuch or to "the law of the kings" (Deut 17:14–20).[32] The LXX, followed by the author, uses a word that technically refers to the knob of the end of the rod around which a scroll is wound, but it came generally to mean "scroll" (see "κεφαλίς," BDAG 542). The combination here (κεφαλίδι βιβλίου) might, then, mean a "scroll in book form."[33] It is not clear that the author intends the phrase to have particular meaning for his readers; if he does, he probably intends a reference to the Old Testament as a whole, as a testimony of Christ.[34]

10:8–9 First he said, "Sacrifices and offerings and burnt offerings and sacrifices for sin"—which are offered according to the law—"he did not desire or take delight in." 9 Then he said, "Behold I have come to do your will." He abolishes the first in order that he might establish the second (ἀνώτερον λέγων ὅτι Θυσίας καὶ προσφορὰς καὶ ὁλοκαυτώματα καὶ περὶ ἁμαρτίας οὐκ ἠθέλησας οὐδὲ εὐδόκησας, αἵτινες κατὰ νόμον προσφέρονται, 9 τότε εἴρηκεν, Ἰδοὺ ἥκω τοῦ ποιῆσαι τὸ θέλημά σου. ἀναιρεῖ τὸ πρῶτον ἵνα τὸ δεύτερον στήσῃ). In these verses, the author makes clear the application he expects his readers to draw from his quotation of Psalm 40. He explicitly divides this application into two parts: "first he said" (ἀνώτερον λέγων)[35] and "then he said" (τότε εἴρηκεν).[36] In his first application comment, the author strings together the four kinds of sacrifices mentioned in verses 5b (= Ps 40:6a) and 6a (= Ps 40:6c). His intention is, again, to use the series to refer generally to the Old Testament sacrificial system.[37] The two verbs the author uses—"desire" (ἠθέλησας) and "take delight in" (εὐδόκησας)—likewise pick up the two verbs that occur in the author's quotation of Psalm 40 (vv. 5 and 6). The one comment the author adds is that these sacrifices are "offered according to the law" (κατὰ νόμον προσφέρονται).[38] The point is clear enough without this addition, but the author clearly wants to emphasize the intimate connection of the sacrificial system to the overall law of Moses—a point he makes similarly in 7:11b.[39] This addition is therefore far from being parenthetical (contra most English translations); it prepares the way for the sweeping claim that the author makes in verse 9b.

In the second stage of his application of Psalm 40 (v. 9), the author shifts from a negative focus on "desire" or "will"—God does *not* "will" (ἠθέλησας) sacrifices—to a positive focus—Christ comes to *do* God's will (θέλημα). The author's summary of Psalm 40:7–8a (quoted in v. 7) is stripped to its essentials. As Cockerill puts it, the author "would rivet his hearers' attention on Christ's affirmation of perfect obedience."[40]

---

32. Craigie, *Psalms 1–50*, 315.
33. E.g., Cockerill, *Hebrews*, 438.
34. E.g., Attridge, *Hebrews*, 275.
35. The participle λέγων is probably circumstantial (modifying εἴρηκεν in v. 9) and is appropriately rendered in English with an indicative verb (e.g., NIV; NLT; CEB; NAB). The word ἀνώτερον is a comparative form of ἄνω, "high," "up": this first comment is "higher" in the sense of being placed above the second one—hence "first" (Koester, *Hebrews*, 434).
36. Since the words τότε εἶπον occur in Ps 40:7 (LXX 39:8), it is possible that the author intends them as part of his quotation. But the shift in tense probably indicates that this is the author's own comment (e.g., D. Harris, *Hebrews*, 258–59).
37. Attridge, *Hebrews*, 275; D. Harris, *Hebrews*, 258.
38. This clause occurs at the end of the verse in the Greek (perhaps for emphasis); I have moved up the English equivalent of this clause in my translation for clarity.
39. Grässer, *An die Hebräer*, 2:221.
40. Cockerill, *Hebrews*, 440.

The author offers his final summarizing comment on the implications of Psalm 40 for his view of Christ's work in verses 9b–10. The first part of this comment, in verse 9b, has been labeled "one of the epochal formulations of the New Testament."[41] "He abolishes the first in order that he might establish the second." The subject of the verbs in this sentence is presumably "Christ," the speaker of the words of the psalm in the context of Hebrews. It is, as becomes clear in verse 10, by means of his actions, expressed by the words of the psalm, that he "abolishes" the one and "establishes" the other. These verbs have a quasi-legal sense in this context.[42] The half verse is an extremely strong claim for salvation-historical discontinuity. Just how strong it is depends on what "the first" (τὸ πρῶτον) and "the second" (τὸ δεύτερον) refer to. The author has used "first" to describe the Mosaic covenant (8:7, 13; 9:15, 18), so he might be contrasting the old covenant with the new (NLT).[43] Many interpreters think the reference is to the sacrificial system. This is no doubt a primary focus, but the reminder in verse 8 that sacrifices are offered "according to the law" might suggest a broader reference to the "former" system as a whole—priest, sanctuary, sacrifice, administration (e.g., covenant)—a reference that would fit with the neuter form of these words.[44] Johnson argues that the author's comment here must be seen in the context of the Old Testament "prophetic critique" of sacrifices and that he does not intend to argue that a new covenant has "replaced" the old.[45] However, the author's language and overall argument make it difficult to moderate the author's view in this way. "Replacement," to be sure, is not the best word to use here, missing as it does the important organic relationship of old and new. But the author clearly argues that a new and better means of accessing God has been introduced and that this new system invalidates the old—some form of "supersessionism" is indicated (see the Additional Note after 7:25).

10:10 In conjunction with this will, we have been sanctified through the once-for-all offering of the body of Jesus Christ (ἐν ᾧ θελήματι ἡγιασμένοι ἐσμὲν διὰ τῆς προσφορᾶς τοῦ σώματος Ἰησοῦ Χριστοῦ ἐφάπαξ). The author continues to stress the importance of the "will"—here probably a reference to the will of God that Christ acknowledges and commits himself to.[46] I go against almost all the translations in not giving the opening preposition, ἐν, an instrumental meaning. My no doubt awkward rendering is intended to suggest a broadly spatial reading of the preposition. "In" the will of Christ is a way of referring to the new way of accessing God, conceived in terms of our standing or resting "in" that new sphere of salvation.[47] Christ's determination to do God's will is again highlighted. As McCruden puts it, "Hebrews understands the superior nature of Jesus' sacrifice

---

41. Lane, *Hebrews*, 2:265.

42. The first, ἀναιρέω, is used widely in the NT and LXX to mean "kill," "put to death" (e.g., Matt 2:16; Luke 22:2; 23:32; Acts 2:23; 5:33, 36). The legal sense "invalidate," "abolish" is found in extrabiblical Greek; see, e.g., Josephus, who refers to the "abolition of the duties" (*J.W.* 2.4). The second verb, ἵστημι, has the sense "establish," or "give validity to" elsewhere in the NT (e.g., Rom 3:31) and was used with reference to covenant in the LXX (Gen 6:18; 17:7; Exod 6:4). Some interpreters think the two verbs may represent two contrasting Hebrew words (the *piel* forms of בטל and קום); see, e.g., Attridge, *Hebrews*, 276.

43. Koester, *Hebrews*, 434.

44. Lane, *Hebrews*, 2:264; Cockerill, *Hebrews*, 441: "that whole 'first' system as a means of access to God."

45. Johnson, *Hebrews*, 252.

46. Benjamin J. Ribbens, "The Sacrifice God Desired: Psalm 40.6–8 in Hebrews 10," *NTS* 67 (2021): 293–96. As Ribbens points out, the "will" in these verses is God's soteriological will (p. 295).

47. The causal meaning that some interpreters give the preposition (Lane, *Hebrews*, 2:256; Massonnet, *L'Épître aux Hébreux*, 269; Bénétrau, *L'Épître aux Hébreux*, 2:102) moves toward this broader sense.

as arising out of its radically personal quality."[48] Some interpreters think this focus on Christ's will suggests the author's concern is with Christ's obedient life and that his death is not really in view.[49] Others claim that the text moves away from cultic categories.[50] And still others insist that "offering" refers to Christ's offering of himself as a sacrifice before God in the heavenly sanctuary.[51] However, while the focus on Christ's will is obvious, that will is directed ultimately to the "offering" of his body. The language of "offering" (προσφορά) is clearly cultic (see προσφορά in vv. 5 and 8; and also 10:18). And this "offering," as I have argued elsewhere, while not perhaps confined to Jesus's death, nevertheless includes it.[52] The "offering, once for all, of the body of Jesus Christ" is therefore the author's solemn summary of all that the preparation of a body and Christ's willing obedience was directed toward: a final sacrifice, involving his death and his high-priestly presentation of that death before the Father.[53]

This "once-for-all" (ἐφάπαξ) offering[54] is the means by which "we have been sanctified." The author uses a perfect form (ἡγιασμένοι) to connote the "definitive nature and abiding effectiveness of the purification from sin."[55] The author's use of the verb "sanctify" (ἁγιάζω) must be seen in the context of his overall cultic theological framework. It does not, then, refer to moral "sanctifying" or "becoming holy" (as it does sometimes elsewhere in the NT) but to purification from sin and restoration to divine favor.[56]

10:11 Every[57] priest stands daily at his ministry, offering the same sacrifices, which are never able to take away sins (Καὶ πᾶς μὲν ἱερεὺς ἕστηκεν καθ᾽ ἡμέραν λειτουργῶν καὶ τὰς αὐτὰς πολλάκις προσφέρων θυσίας, αἵτινες οὐδέποτε δύνανται περιελεῖν ἁμαρτίας). The definitive "sanctification" referred to in verse 10 is developed in verses 11–14, as the author turns back again to the contrast on this point between the old sacrificial system and the new. The Levitical priests "stand," daily offering their sacrifices—a clear indication they can never solve the sin problem (v. 11). Christ, however, having offered an eternally valid sacrifice, "sits" at the right hand of God, simply waiting to culminate his work in final victory over his enemies (vv. 12–13). Returning to the language of verse 10, the author then brings the paragraph to a close: through one "offering" (προσφορά), Christ perfects those who are being sanctified (using a form of ἁγιάζω) (v. 14). The allusion to Psalm 110:1 in verses 12–13 is a framing device, creating an *inclusio* with the allusion to this text in the starting point of this exposition in 8:1. The whole paragraph has a summary

---

48. Kevin B. McCruden, "Concept of Perfection in the Epistle to the Hebrews," in Mason and McCruden, *Reading the Epistle to the Hebrews*, 224. See also Fuhrmann, *Vergeben und Vergessen*, 226–27.
49. See esp. Moffitt, *Atonement*, 230–56.
50. Gäbel, *Die Kulttheologie des Hebräerbriefes*, 185–96.
51. Jamieson, *Jesus' Death and Heavenly Offering*, 74–81. The genitive is likely objective—i.e., it is not Jesus Christ who is doing the offering, but Jesus Christ who is offered.
52. For a stronger claim about the importance of Christ's death here, see, e.g., Schreiner, *Hebrews*, 301.
53. See esp. Ribbens, "Sacrifice God Desired," 289–93. The author caps off his commentary on his own use of Ps 40 by repeating three of its key words: "will," "offering," and "body."

54. I am taking ἐφάπαξ with προσφορᾶς rather than with ἡγιασμένοι (following, e.g., Lane, *Hebrews*, 2:256; Koester, *Hebrews*, 434; Peterson, *Hebrews and Perfection*, 148; contra Delitzsch, *Hebrews*, 2:157; Cockerill, *Hebrews*, 445; Bénétrau, *L'Épître aux Hébreux*, 2:95).
55. Cockerill, *Hebrews*, 443. The author uses a periphrastic perfect: ἡγιασμένοι ἐσμέν.
56. E.g., P. Hughes, *Hebrews*, 399; Bénétrau, *L'Épître aux Hébreux*, 2:96. See the note on 2:11.
57. The verse opens with a καί, signaling "a new step in the argument" (Ellingworth, *Hebrews*, 507). This function of the conjunction is best expressed in English by not using a conjunction (e.g., NIV; NLT; CSB; CEB; NAB; NASB).

character, as the author begins to transition from exposition to exhortation (vv. 19 and following).[58]

Verse 11 repeats a point the author has already made several times (7:27; 9:25-28; 10:1b-4): the ministry[59] of Old Testament priests[60] is continual, as they daily offer various sacrifices, none of which individually—or altogether as a totality—is capable of "taking away" sins.[61] The one point that is new here is the posture of the priests: they "stand." The author is setting up a contrast with Christ, who, à la Psalm 110:1, "sits" (v. 12). Delitzsch summarizes the point: "the sacred writer does not mean to say that sins were not forgiven to sacrificial worshipers under the law, but that the legal sacrifices had no inward spiritual power to give peace to the conscience, or any assured sense of pardon, purity to the heart, or any really new beginning of spiritual life."[62]

10:12 But this priest, when he had offered one sacrifice for sins, eternally valid, sat down at the right hand of God (οὗτος δὲ μίαν ὑπὲρ ἁμαρτιῶν προσενέγκας θυσίαν εἰς τὸ διηνεκὲς ἐκάθισεν ἐν δεξιᾷ τοῦ θεοῦ). In contrast to[63] the many priests who "stand" at their ministy is the one priest[64] who, having completed his atoning ministry, now "sits." The "offering" that Jesus our priest makes is sometimes thought to refer narrowly to his offering of his own blood before the Father in the heavenly sanctuary. However, as I have argued elsewhere, "offer" (προσφέρω) appears to be used by our author to refer to the entire sacrificial process, including the death of the victim.[65] Here, then, he will be referring to Christ's sacrificial work as a whole, at least including death, resurrection, ascension, and entrance into the heavenly sanctuary. The sequence of events culminates in Christ's sitting down at the right hand of God. As is often noted, the act of sitting suggests the completion of a particular process. "A seated priest is the guarantee of a finished work and an accepted sacrifice."[66] "He sat down" is the equivalent of the Johannine "it is finished" (John 19:30).

The exegete must decide what the phrase "eternally valid" (εἰς τὸ διηνεκές) modifies. The phrase means "continually," "without interruption," "for all time" ("διηνεκής," BDAG 245). It might modify the main verb in this verse, "he sat" (ἐκάθισεν): "he took his seat forever" (NAB).[67] However, it fits better with both the style and content of Hebrews to take the phrase with "offering" (προσενέγκας); so most of the English versions (e.g., NIV: "when this priest had offered for all time one sacrifice for sins, he sat down").[68] In my translation, I have attempted to

---

58. Cockerill, *Hebrews*, 447.
59. I have rendered the participle λειτουργῶν with the expression "at his ministry."
60. A number of MSS (e.g., A C P 0278. 104. 365. 614. 630. 2464) read ἀρχιερεύς ("high priest"), an obvious assimilation to the frequency of this title in this part of Hebrews.
61. The author uses a different verb here (περιαιρέω, "remove," "take off," "take away") than he used earlier (ἀφαιρέω in v. 4), but the meaning is the same (contra Grässer [*An die Hebräer*, 2:227], who thinks περιαιρέω is stronger than ἀφαιρέω). For the former, see Acts 27:20, 40; 28:13; 2 Cor 3:16; the verb is not used with "sins" anywhere else in the NT or LXX.
62. Delitzsch, *Hebrews*, 2:160.
63. The δέ at the beginning of this verse answers to the μέν in v. 11.

64. The demonstrative pronoun οὗτος refers back to ἱερεύς in v. 11. See a similar construction in 8:3.
65. See the note on 8:3; and also on 9:25-26.
66. Bruce, *Hebrews*, 245.
67. Attridge, *Hebrews*, 280; Ellingworth, *Hebrews*, 509-10; Cockerill, *Hebrews*, 449; Massonnet, *L'Épître aux Hébreux*, 272; Bénétrau, *L'Épître aux Hébreux*, 2:96-97.
68. In terms of style, the phrase εἰς τὸ διηνεκές elsewhere in Hebrews appears to modify the preceding rather than the following verb (7:3; 10:1, 14 [though this one is disputed]); and, in terms of content, the author regularly draws attention to the "once-for-all" nature of Jesus's sacrifice.

bring out the meaning and emphasis of the phrase by placing it after the clause it modifies.

10:13 Since then[69] he waits until his enemies are placed as a footstool under his feet (τὸ λοιπὸν ἐκδεχόμενος ἕως τεθῶσιν οἱ ἐχθροὶ αὐτοῦ ὑποπόδιον τῶν ποδῶν αὐτοῦ). The reference to Christ sitting at the right hand of God from Psalm 110:1 is common in the letter (Heb 1:3, 13; 8:1; cf. also 12:2). However only here and in 1:13 do we have a quotation of the verse, or part of the verse.[70] In 1:13, as in the LXX, the words of Psalm 110:1b are addressed to the Son in the active voice: "until he places your enemies as a footstool under your feet." The author now changes the active form of the original into a passive. He provides no contextual clues that would enable us to identify the "enemies." A few interpreters think the author might be implicitly warning the readers: do not turn away from the living God lest you become his enemies (see 10:27).[71] But this is a stretch. The best we can do is surmise that he has in view generally all those powers that oppose God and his purposes. By picturing Christ as both now "seated" and at same time "waiting" to subdue his enemies, the author sets Christ's work firmly in the framework of the typical New Testament "already-not yet" eschatology (see also 9:27–28).

10:14 For with one sacrifice he has perfected for all time those who are being sanctified (μιᾷ γὰρ προσφορᾷ τετελείωκεν εἰς τὸ διηνεκὲς τοὺς ἁγιαζομένους). This verse has a summary character, picking up key vocabulary from the preceding context: "sacrifice" (προσφορά; see vv. 5, 8, and 10), "perfected" (the verb τελειόω; see v. 1), "for all time" (εἰς τὸ διηνεκές; see vv. 1, 12), the description of believers as those "sanctified" (using the verb ἁγιάζω; see v. 10), and the emphasis on the adequacy of the "one" sacrifice (see v. 12). The "for" (γάρ) therefore is probably intended to link this verse to the previous content in general.[72]

The author uses "offering" (προσφορά) here as equivalent to "sacrifice" (θυσία, v. 12). As I have noted before, the cultic imagery of Hebrews does not allow us to confine this sacrifice to his death[73] or to his offering of sacrifice in the heavenly sanctuary. Both moments are included in the process of Christ's sacrifice. The "perfecting" that Christ's sacrifice accomplishes picks up language from verse 1: what the Levitical sacrifices could not do, Christ's one sacrifice has done; i.e., it has taken care of, once for all, the sin problem and enabled worshipers to enter freely into the very presence of God (see also 7:11, 19, 28; 9:9). The perfect form of the verb (τετελείωκεν, "perfected") highlights the finality of the action.[74] As Peterson comments, "The author locates this perfecting *in the past with respect to its accomplishment and in the present with respect to its enjoyment*."[75] As he did in verse 10, the author uses the language of "sanctify," "set apart as holy" (ἁγιάζω) to describe believers. However, in verse 10, he used the perfect tense of the verb

---

69. "Since then" (τὸ λοιπόν) here probably means "henceforth" (Zerwick and Grosvenor, *Grammatical Analysis*, 676). For this use of the phrase, see also 1 Cor 7:29.

70. The wording of the reference to the second half of the verse is the same, with the exception that the author in 10:13 uses τεθῶσιν in place of θῶ.

71. Bruce, *Hebrews*, 246; deSilva, *Perseverance in Gratitude*, 324.

72. Ellingworth (*Hebrews*, 511), by contrast, takes it with v. 12b, while Westcott (*Hebrews*, 315) takes it with v. 13 ("*For by one offering . . . so that no fresh duty can interrrupt the continuance of His royal Majesty*"); cf. also Johnson, *Hebrews*, 253).

73. Contra, e.g., Attridge, *Hebrews*, 280.

74. Koester, *Hebrews*, 435; see also Lane, *Hebrews*, 2:256. Weiss (*Der Brief an die Hebräer*, 514) argues that it stresses the duration of the action.

75. Peterson, *Hebrews and Perfection*, 152 (emphasis original).

(ἡγιασμένοι), whereas here the verb is in the present tense (ἁγιαζομένους). The present tense might connote an ongoing action, the "continuous reception of grace" or "the subjective process by which the perfected work of Christ is realized in believers."[76] However, while it is certainly true that a continuing appropriation of grace is necessary in the Christian life—a point the author emphasizes to encourage his sluggish listeners (12:14)—the cultic connotations of "holiness" language that are to the fore in Hebrews suggest rather that the "being made holy" is, like Christ's own offering, a "once-for-all" action. It is likely, then, that the present tense is used here in a timeless sense, simply describing believers as those who are "holy" or "set apart."[77]

10:15–17 The Holy Spirit also testifies to us about this. For he first says, 16 "'This is the covenant that I am making with them after these days,' says the Lord: 'I will place my laws in their hearts and I will write them on their minds.'" 17 He then says, "and their sins and lawless deeds I will remember no more" (Μαρτυρεῖ δὲ ἡμῖν καὶ τὸ πνεῦμα τὸ ἅγιον· μετὰ γὰρ τὸ εἰρηκέναι, 16 Αὕτη ἡ διαθήκη ἣν διαθήσομαι πρὸς αὐτοὺς μετὰ τὰς ἡμέρας ἐκείνας, λέγει κύριος· διδοὺς νόμους μου ἐπὶ καρδίας αὐτῶν καὶ ἐπὶ τὴν διάνοιαν αὐτῶν ἐπιγράψω αὐτούς, 17 καὶ τῶν ἁμαρτιῶν αὐτῶν καὶ τῶν ἀνομιῶν αὐτῶν οὐ μὴ μνησθήσομαι ἔτι). The author brings his long exposition of the high-priestly work of Christ to a close with a scriptural confirmation of the meaning and finality of the one sacrifice of our great high priest. The text that he quotes is from Jeremiah 31:33a and 34b (LXX 38:33b and 34a), portions of the "new-covenant" prophecy that our author has quoted at length in 8:8b–12. This quotation forms, then, with that earlier quotation, a bookend around the the argument of 8:1–10:18. As he does elsewhere, the author cuts right to the heart of the significance of Scripture for his listeners: it is the Holy Spirit who "testifies" (μαρτυρεῖ, a present tense!) to the significance of Christ's sacrifice (referring back to v. 14 narrowly, but more widely also to the recurring focus on this issue throughout 9:11–10:14).

The author introduces the quotation also with the clause "after saying" (μετὰ γὰρ τὸ εἰρηκέναι), an introduction that obviously requires an equivalent "then he says" clause.[78] Some interpreters think this comes in the middle of verse 16, with the clause "says the Lord" (λέγει κύριος).[79] However, this phrase is part of the Jeremiah text. A more likely place for this continuing clause to be introduced is at the beginning of verse 17, since there is here a break in the Jeremiah quotation: after quoting 31:33a, the author skips some lines in Jeremiah before quoting 31:34b in verse 17. Most English translations therefore introduce here an introductory clause to match verse 15b (e.g., NIV: "then he adds").[80]

The paired introductory clauses (one explicit,

---

76. Respectively, Cockerill, *Hebrews*, 452; Delitzsch, *Hebrews*, 163. See also Attridge, *Hebrews*, 281; Lane, *Hebrews*, 2:256. See NIV; ESV; CEB; NLT; NAB.

77. Bruce, *Hebrews*, 247; Peterson, *Hebrews and Perfection*, 150; Ribbens, *Levitical Sacrifice*, 214; Schreiner, *Hebrews*, 306. See RSV; NRSV; NET; CSB. G. Guthrie suggests a compromise view: seeing the language referring to people who come into the new covenant over time ("Time and Atonement," 225).

78. The author's quotation differs from LXX of Jeremiah (ch. 38) and from his earlier quotation in 8:8–12 in three points. In place of "the house of Israel" (τῷ οἴκῳ Ἰσραήλ, Jer 38:33a; Heb 8:10a), the author here indicates that the covenant is made simply with "them" (αὐτούς)—perhaps to universalize the promise. Second, he reverses the references to "heart" and "mind" in referring to the internalization of the law (Jer 38:33b; Heb 8:10b). Third, he uses the future indicative μνησθήσομαι in place of the aorist subjunctive μνησθῶ (Jer 38:34b; Heb 8:12b).

79. E.g., Attridge, *Hebrews*, 281; Johnson, *Hebrews*, 254; Cockerill, *Hebrews*, 455.

80. Most scholars go this direction: see, e.g., Bruce, *Hebrews*, 244; Moffatt, *Hebrews*, 141; Westcott, *Hebrews*, 318; Koester, *Hebrews*, 435; Lane, *Hebrews*, 2:256–57.

one implicit) make clear where the author's interest lies. He is not now focused on the introduction of a new covenant, with its consequences for the old covenant, as he was in chapter 8.[81] The fact that he mentions the promise about God's laws being "placed in the mind" and "written on the heart" reveals that he wants to remind his readers about this new-covenant internalization of God's laws.[82] However, unlike other New Testament writers, he never develops this point, here or elsewhere. Rather, the author's focus is on God's promise to no longer "remember" sins (ἁμαρτιῶν) and "lawless deeds" (ἀνομιῶν). The author's lengthy discussion of the high-priestly work of Jesus has focused on this "sin issue," so it is unsurprising that it comes up here in his summary. And a key focus of that discussion has been the "once-for-all" nature of our high priest's sacrifice, a sacrifice that therefore brings to worshipers a "once-for-all" experience of forgiveness: "redemption" (9:12, 15) and "perfection" (7:11, 19, 28; 9:9; 10:1, 10).

10:18 And since[83] there is forgiveness for these, there is no longer a place for sacrifice for[84] sins (ὅπου δὲ ἄφεσις τούτων, οὐκέτι προσφορὰ περὶ ἁμαρτίας). We might have expected our author to conclude this long exposition with a triumphant celebration of Christ's work on behalf of believers: sin remembered no more. However, instead he concludes on a more negative note, suggesting that a key focus in all this exhortation is not only to encourage believers about what they have in Christ but also to warn them about seeking forgiveness in any place but the all-sufficient sacrifice of Christ. The word "forgiveness" here (ἄφεσις) is a bit unexpected. We might have expected the stronger words the author has associated uniquely with Christ's sacrifice, such as "putting away" or "redemption" or "perfection." Perhaps, however, he deliberately uses a word that is equally applicable to Old Testament sacrifices and Christ's sacrifice. He provides final and definitive forgiveness; one should not seek forgiveness in any other sacrifice.

Theology in Application

The Benefits of Christ's Sacrifice

With 10:18, we reach the conclusion of the author's exposition of Christ's high-priestly work. Exposition in Hebrews is always tied to exhortation. In 10:19, our author will turn to this mode of teaching, picking up where he left off in 4:14–16. Before we also turn to this explicit exhortation, we would do well to pause and contemplate the many ways in which Christ's high-priestly work transcends the work of Old Testament priests and high priests.

---

81. Weiss, *Der Brief an die Hebräer*, 516.
82. See Jason A. Whitlark, "Fidelity and New Covenant Enablement in Hebrews," in *Getting "Saved": The Whole Story of Salvation in the New Testament*, ed. Charles H. Talbert and Jason A. Whitlark (Grand Rapids: Eerdmans, 2011), 72–91.
83. The Greek word ὅπου, almost universally translated "where" in English versions, might indicate cause or reason (see BDAG 717, §3). See Ellingworth, *Hebrews*, 515.
84. The preposition περί probably means here "on behalf of": περί often takes on the nuance of ὑπέρ in biblical Greek (Zerwick, *Biblical Greek*, §96).

Of course, the contrast between Old Testament priests and Christ's priesthood assumes some commonality between them. The author notes that both Old Testament priests and Christ are "appointed" (5:1, 6) and that one of their main duties is the offering of sacrifices (5:1; 8:3), among which are sacrifices that require blood for them to be effective (9:18–22). Moreover, since they participate in the human experience, both Old Testament priests and Christ are able to empathize with those they represent (2:17; 4:15; 5:2, 7–8).

However, the focus of the author, driven by his hortatory purpose, is on differences between high-priestly ministries and the sacrifices they offer. In keeping with the style of these chapters, the author does not develop each of these contrasts in a self-contained paragraph. Rather, he briefly and repeatedly mentions them, weaving them together in his exposition. By means of this style, the author effectively creates a cumulative effect, leaving us in no doubt about his primary concerns.

The Framework

An implicit contrast is seen in the broad salvation-historical framework the author alludes to in several texts: Christ has "appeared once for all at the culmination of the ages" (9:26), the mediator of a new covenant that takes the place of the old covenant (7:22; 8:6, 7–13; 9:15). The essential "realities," which cast their shadow back into the Old Testament, have come into being (10:1; see 9:10, 11). The references, via Psalm 110:1, to Christ having "sat down at the right hand of God" (8:1; 10:12), also suggest the dawning of a new era. Of course, in keeping with the typical New Testament "already-not yet" eschatological framework, a "second" appearance of Christ to culminate salvation history is also mentioned (9:28)—when he will secure final salvation and subdue all his enemies (10:13).

The Old Testament high priest and sacrificial system is established by the Old Testament law, which is in itself "weak and useless" (7:18), exemplified in a "fleshly commandment" (7:16); Christ is appointed to his position by God's own "oath" (5:6, 10; 6:20; 7:20, 21, 28).

The Priest

The Old Testament system appoints priests who die and have to be continuously replaced (7:23). Christ, however, has an "eternal" existence (7:3, 16; 9:14), meaning that he remains a high priest forever (7:24).

The Old Testament system appoints priests who are "weak" and who need to offer sacrifices for themselves (5:3; 7:28; 9:7); Christ, being sinless, is a high priest who does not need to offer sacrifice for himself (7:27).

Old Testament priests and high priests were appointed based on their Aaronic/Levitical ancestry (7:11, 13–14, 16; cf. 8:4); Christ is appointed as a "priest in the order of Melchizedek" (5:6, 10; 6:20; ch. 7).

The Sacrifice

The Old Testament high priests offer sacrifices repeatedly (9:25; 10:1b–2, 11); Christ offers himself once (7:28; 9:26, 28; 10:10, 14).

The Old Testament priests sacrifice animals, who have no choice in the matter and whose blood can never take away sins (9:12, 13; 10:4); Christ willingly offers himself to take care of the sins of others (10:5–9, 10).

The Sanctuary

The Old Testament high priests enter an earthly sanctuary, a mere copy and shadow of the heavenly sanctuary (8:5; 9:24); Christ enters the heavenly sanctuary (4:14; 7:26; 8:1–2; 9:11–12, 24).

The Effect of the Sacrifice

Old Testament sacrifices, endlessly repeated, bring constant memory of sins (10:3); Christ's once-for-all sacrifice means sins are "remembered no more" (8:12; 10:17).

Old Testament sacrifices have a mainly external impact, affecting the flesh (7:16; 9:10, 13) and failing to still the accusing voice of the conscience (9:9; 10:2, 22); Christ's sacrifice stills the conscience (9:14).

Old Testament sacrifices could never definitively take care of the sin problem ("take away sins"; 9:12–13; 10:4, 11); Christ's sacrifice has "taken away" sins (9:26, 28).

Old Testament sacrifices could not bring definitive forgiveness and access to God ("perfection"; 7:11, 19; 10:1); Christ's sacrifice accomplishes this (10:14; cf. 12:23).

The Old Testament system did not enable worshipers to enter the Most Holy Place, symbolizing the presence of God (9:8); Christ's sacrifice enables his people to "draw near" to God (4:16; 6:19; 7:19, 25; 10:22).

The Old Testament sacrifices conferred a degree of ritual "holiness" on worshipers (9:13); Christ's sacrifice confers true holiness (10:10, 14, 29).

One of the consistent emphases in the author's presentation of the work of our high priest is the language of "forever"/"once" that he uses to depict every stage of this work.

Jesus himself is qualified to be a Melchizedekian high priest because of his eternal nature (7:16; 9:14). He "lives forever" (7:24), "always lives" (7:25), enabling him to fulfill the role of the "priest in the order of Melchizedek," who, according to Psalm 110:4, has an eternal priesthood (5:6; 6:20; 7:3, 17, 21, 24). He is "made perfect forever" (7:28).

Jesus offers his sacrifice "once for all." It is final and complete (7:27; 9:12, 28; 10:10, 12; cf. 9:26).

The blessings worshipers enjoy because of Christ's work also have an eternal quality: Christ "saves completely" (including a temporal aspect, 7:25); he secures an "eternal salvation" (5:9) and "eternal redemption" (9:12; see 9:15), and an "eternal inheritance" (9:15). When people benefit from Christ's high-priestly work, they are "made perfect forever" (10:14), and their sins are "remembered no more" (8:12; 10:17).

> **IN DEPTH: The Timing of Atonement in Hebrews**
>
> In the "In Depth" discussion after 9:28, I explored the relationship between sacrifice and atonement in Hebrews. In this note, I take a slightly different tack on this same fundamental issue.
>
> The New Testament obviously highlights Jesus's death on a Roman cross as the critical moment in salvation history. Paul, the New Testament writer who contributes the most to the issue, locates the work of Christ for us at Jesus's incarnation once (2 Cor 8:9; cf. Gal 4:4 [probably]), to Jesus's resurrection five times (Rom 1:4 [?]; 4:25; 5:10; Eph 1:19–23; Col 2:12), and to Jesus's death twenty-eight times. The implication of these statistics is confirmed by explicit references. In the 1 Corinthians 15 text quoted above, for instance, it is only Jesus's death that Paul claims is "for our sins" (1 Cor 15:3). Paul elsewhere summarizes his message in terms of the "message of the cross" (1 Cor 1:18; see also 1:17; Gal 3:1; 6:14; Eph 2:16; Phil 3:18; Col 1:20; 2:14). Some contexts offer clear rhetorical reasons for this focus on the cross, where Paul is countering a spirit of triumphalism with a reminder of the believer's cruciform existence. And not all these references are connected directly to soteriology. More importantly, other New Testament authors have slightly different emphases when it comes to the location of Christ's work for us. In John, for instance, Jesus's death is integrated into a larger "pendulum swing," beginning with Christ's entrance into the world and culminating in his resurrection. However, when all due allowance has been made for the other "moments" in the atoning work of Christ, the focus on his death remains quite clear. There is a reason many of our churches have the cross as their central symbol.
>
> This cruci-centric view of Christ's work is not as clear in Hebrews. The author's presentation of Christ's work is dominated by cultic categories, as he uses the Old Testament Levitical sacrifices and especially the Day of Atonement ritual as the framework for interpreting Jesus's atoning work. And these rituals, in a point of emphasis for recent study of Levitical sacrifice, often do not focus on the death of the victim so much as on the manipulation of blood by the priest/high priest after death. The author appears to think of Jesus's high-priestly ministry against this backdrop, with his repeated emphasis on the importance of Jesus's entry into the Most Holy Place and his ministry on

our behalf in that place, the "location" of God's own presence.[85] A few scholars have argued in recent years that, in fact, the author to the Hebrews does not view Jesus's death as atoning. His death is a necessary preliminary to the work of atonement, which is carried out by our high priest (appointed to that office after and because of his resurrection) as he brings the blood of his death into the Most Holy Place, there to atone for the sins of the people. Nor is this a new idea. While not identical in all details, the sixteenth-century heretic Socinus and his followers also denied atoning power to Jesus's death—though it is only fair to add that it was their denial of Christ's full deity rather than their view of atonement that put them in the camp of the heretics.

The claim that Jesus's death is not given atoning significance in Hebrews certainly goes too far. As I have noted in my comments on several texts, the author clearly views Jesus's death as a fundamental moment in the atoning process (see esp. 2:14–15 and 9:15–23). The other extreme in the spectrum of views on atonement in Hebrews insists that the death, or even *only* the death, of Christ is the atoning moment in Hebrews. Scholars who adopt this view treat the language of ministry in the heavenly sanctuary as an extended metaphor that portrays Jesus's death as a "heavenly" and therefore ultimately significant event. Sometimes explicitly, perhaps more often implicitly, these scholars are trying to align the soteriology of Hebrews with the stress on the cross as the atoning moment that we find elsewhere in the New Testament. And this motivation is entirely appropriate: we must read Hebrews in a way that brings the theology of this book into line with the theology of the New Testament (and ultimately, of course, the Old Testament) as a whole. However, "bringing into line with" does not mean that we have to make sure that every New Testament author marches in lock step with every other New Testament author. Affirming unity should not come at the expense of the beautiful diversity of New Testament perspectives.

I do not see how a view that atonement in Hebrews is attached to Jesus's heavenly ministry *and not* his death can be integrated into the wider soteriological pattern of the New Testament. I am, however, also convinced that a *prominence* given to Jesus's heavenly ministry in Hebrews does not destroy that unity. And, in fact, as I have argued in comments on many texts, it seems clear to me that the author focuses more on Jesus's heavenly ministry than on his death in his portrayal of Jesus's atoning work. I emphasize again that Jesus's

---

85. Peter J. Leithart (*Delivered from the Elements of the World: Atonement, Justification, Mission* [Grand Rapids: Baker Academic, 2016]), emphasizes this Levitical pattern to argue that the NT as a whole adopts the pattern of the Levitical sacrifices, with Christ's atoning work including his life, death, resurrection, and ascension (e.g., p. 115).

death *is* a crucial moment in that atoning work. But if we ask what stands out as distinctive in Hebrews, it is Jesus's entry into the Most Holy Place, where his sacrificial offering reaches its culmination. I therefore endorse what is called a "sequence" view of atonement in Hebrews. The sacrificial and atoning work of Christ moves from death, through resurrection and ascension, to its climactic moment in the heavenly sanctuary, as Jesus intercedes for us before God himself. Jamieson helpfully uses a photographic analogy: the author does not pan *from* Jesus's death *to* the heavenly ministry; rather, he zooms out to include the heavenly ministry along with the moment of death.[86]

The author therefore, as he does so often, brings his own unique perspective to an aspect of New Testament theology. The author's focus on Jesus as high priest, a distinctive New Testament christological view, inevitably brings with it a distinctive soteriological emphasis. Jesus is now portrayed not only as the sacrificial victim, put to death on the cross for the sins of the world, but also as priest. In portraying Jesus as a priest, the author naturally elaborates on all the stages in the priest's duties, including especially the priest's offering of the slaughtered victim before the Lord.[87] Within the unity of New Testament teaching about Jesus's atoning work, then, the author to the Hebrews draws attention to the critical moment after the resurrection when the ascended Jesus enters heaven on our behalf. His perspective enriches our understanding of Christ's atoning work and, as good theology always does, also speaks to God's people. Contemplating Jesus as our high priest who has offered the final and definitive sacrifice before God himself and who ever lives to intercede for us should give us great confidence in our standing before God and boldness, following our pioneer and forerunner (2:10; 6:19; 12:2), to enter God's own presence.

---

86. E.g., Jamieson, *Jesus' Death and Heavenly Offering*, 99. Jamieson's overall thesis is that the author views the heavenly ascension as the *time* of offering, the heavenly sanctuary as the *place* of offering, but the death of Jesus as *what is offered* (127–79).

87. Other NT authors, while not calling Jesus a priest, also stress the self-surrender of Jesus to the work of the cross.

CHAPTER 24

Hebrews 10:19–31

Literary Context

The tone of the author's sermon shifts dramatically at 10:19. He signals this shift in three ways. First, for the first time since 3:12, the author addresses his hearers, in verse 19, as "brothers and sisters" (ἀδελφοί). Second, while the author uses first-person plural forms occasionally in 8:1–10:18 (8:1; 9:14; 10:10), third-person forms dominate—"the ministry Jesus has received" is better (8:6); "[Christ] entered the Most Holy Place" (9:12); "Christ is the mediator of a new covenant" (9:15); "Christ was sacrificed once" (9:28); "by one sacrifice he has made perfect forever those who are being made holy" (10:14). Third-person forms do not disappear in these next verses (see vv. 28–31), but first-person and second-person forms now dominate (the former in vv. 19–25; the latter in vv. 32–39). Finally, third, the author shifts from the indicative mode to the imperative. Three hortatory subjunctives (which function as imperatives) form the backbone of verses 19–25, and second-person imperatives govern verses 32–39. Clearly, then, the author shifts from the mode of instruction or exposition to the mode of command and exhortation—a shift that characterizes the author's sermon throughout.

Determining the way this larger passage, verses 19–39, fits into the sequence of thought in the author's sermon is challenging. The debate over the way this passage, and its component parts—verses 19–25, verses 26–31, and verses 32–39[1]—should be represented in outlines of the letter betrays a somewhat artificial perspective. After all, our author did not use an outline form in composing his letter: for example, assigning Roman numeral II to one section and labeling paragraphs with the letter A or B. We must always keep in mind, then, that our very method of representing the argument of the letter might lead us to make some decisions that obscure the sequence of thought. Some paragraphs, for instance, will be transitional, in which

---

1. Most English versions and commentaries recognize these paragraph divisions.

case a decision to include the paragraph with what comes before it *or* what comes after it might be misleading. However, we seem to be "stuck" with the method, and it does have the virtue of forcing us to think carefully about the sequence of thought in the letter.

One facet of this passage is clear: verses 19–25 closely resemble 4:14–16, the opening exhortation in the great central section of the letter. We set out the striking parallels between these two texts in our comments on 4:14–16. Scholars routinely note this parallel, but they draw contrasting conclusions from it. Some think that the parallel suggests that verses 19–25, like 4:14–16, open a major section of the letter. They therefore view verses 19–25 as the opening paragraph in the last major stage in the author's argument, a stage dominated by exhortation.[2] Other scholars, however, see the two parallel paragraphs in terms of an *inclusio*, forming bookends around the author's exposition of Christ as high priest. On this view, then, verses 19–25 form the conclusion (or part of the conclusion) to this major section of the letter.[3] I think this connection with what precedes is a bit stronger. However, the connection with what follows should not be neglected. The paragraph may to some extent be transitional, concluding the second section of the letter even as it introduces the third.[4]

The same kind of difficulty arises as we track the sequence of thought to the end of the chapter. The author follows up his exhortation to appropriate the benefits of Christ's high-priestly work in verses 19–25 with a severe warning about the consequences of rejecting these benefits (vv. 26–31). These verses could mark the transition to the last section of the letter, but it is better to attach them to verses 19–25, fitting the pattern of exhortation—followed by a warning that typifies the author's sermonic style. One could then argue, for the same reason, that verses 32–39 (or at least vv. 32–34) belong with verses 19–31, because the assurance that the author offers his readers in these verses completes the sequence of exhortation—warning that we see elsewhere in the letter (see esp. 5:11–6:20). However, the introduction of the key concepts of faith and endurance in verses 36–39 bind these verses closely with what follows (note the focus on faith in ch. 11 and endurance in 12:1–13). Even more than 10:19–25, then, verses 32–39 are transitional, and deciding whether to locate them with 10:19–31 or chapter 11 and following is almost a toss-up. Ultimately, I tentatively put these verses with what follows because the author's reference to the circumstances of the readers, using the second-person plural form of address—"remember those earlier days after *you* had received the light . . . *you* need to persevere"—suggests a shift in perspective, matching what we also find in 12:4–13.

---

2. Delitzsch, *Hebrews*, 2:168; Westcott, *Hebrews*, 317; Spicq, *L'Épître aux Hébreux*, 2:313; Cockerill, *Hebrews*, 460; Weiss, *Der Brief an die Hebräer*, 518; Grässer, *An die Hebräer*, 3:9; Schreiner, *Hebrews*, 313; Westfall, *Discourse Analysis*, 242–43.

3. Vanhoye, *La Structure littéraire*, 173–82; G. Guthrie, *Hebrews*, 340; Michel, *Der Brief an die Hebräer*, 343; Ellingworth, *Hebrews*, 515; Koester, *Hebrews*, 447; Thompson, *Hebrews*, 200–201.

4. G. Guthrie, *Structure of Hebrews*, 102–4; Attridge, *Hebrews*, 283; Lane, *Hebrews*, 2:279.

> I. The Exalted Son and a Rest for the People of God (1:1–4:13)
> II. **Our Great High Priest and His Ministry (4:14–10:31)**
>   A. Exhortation: Persevere through the Power of Our Exalted High Priest (4:14–16)
>   B. Exposition: High Priests and Our High Priest (5:1–10)
>   C. Exhortation: Move on to Maturity (5:11–6:20)
>   D. Exposition: A High Priest "According to the Order of Melchizedek" (7:1–28)
>   E. Exposition: The Ministry of Our High Priest (8:1–10:18)
> ➡   **F. Exhortation and Warning: Appropriating the Benefits of Our High Priest's Ministry (10:19–31)**
> III. Exhortation: Follow and Serve the Pioneer of Our Faith through Endurance and Faith (10:32–13:25)

Main Idea

If I were forced to choose one passage from Hebrews to summarize the message of the letter, it would be 10:19–25. A central theological claim of the letter—that Jesus our high priest has opened the way to the presence of God himself—buttresses the author's call for us to enter that presence in faith, to grasp hold of our confession in hope, and to be active in loving and serving our brothers and sisters. The second paragraph in this section (vv. 26–31) also sounds a note that is characteristic of the author's message: those who decisively reject the grace of God's new covenant will suffer judgment.

Translation

Hebrews 10:19-31

19a	inference (from 5:1–10:18)	Therefore,
19b	address	brothers and sisters,
19c	basis 1 (for 22a)	since we have confidence
19d	content	to enter the Most Holy Place
19e	means (of 19d)	by the blood of Jesus,
20a	means (of 19d)	by the new and
20b	parallel	living way
20c	description	that he inaugurated
20d	purpose	for us

20e	place	through the curtain,
20f	apposition	that is, his flesh,
21a	expansion	and
21b	basis 2 (for 22a)	(since we have) a great priest
21c	reference	over the house of God,
22a	exhortation 1	**let us draw near**
22b	manner 1	with a sincere heart and
22c	manner 2	the full assurance of faith,
22d	manner 3	with our hearts sprinkled clean
22e	separation	from an evil conscience and
22f	manner 4	our bodies washed
22g	means	with pure water.
23a	exhortation 2	**Let us hold**
23b	manner 1	firmly
23c	object (of 23a)	to the confession
23d	content	of our hope
23e	manner 2	without wavering,
23f	basis (for 23a)	for
23g	assertion	**faithful is the one**
23h	identification	who has promised.
24a	exhortation 3	And **let us consider**
24b	object	one another,
24c	goal	with the purpose of stimulating each other
24d	purpose	to love and
24e	parallel	good works,
25a	negative	not giving up meeting
25b	association	with one another,
25c	comparison	as is the habit of some, but rather
25d	positive	exhorting one another and
25e	restatement	doing so
25f	intensification	all the more
25g	circumstance	as you see the day coming near.
26a	basis (for 22–25)	For
26b	condition	if we . . .
26c	manner	deliberately
26d	assertion	. . . keep on sinning
26e	time	after receiving a knowledge
26f	content	of the truth,
26g	assertion	**there no longer remains** a sacrifice
26h	reference	for sins but

Continued on next page.

27a	contrast (with 26g–f)	the fearful expectation
27b	content	of judgment,
27c	description	involving a raging fire
27d	description	that consumes the enemies of God.
28a	assertion	**Anyone who rejected the law of Moses died**
28b	manner	without mercy
28c	basis	on the basis of the testimony
28d	source	of two or
28e	alternative	three witnesses.
29a	comparison (with 28)	**How much worse a punishment is deserved**
29b	disadvantage	for the one
29c	description 1	who tramples underfoot the Son of God,
29d	description 2	considers common the blood of the covenant
29e	description (of 29d)	by means of which they were sanctified, and
29f	description 3	insults the Spirit of grace?
30a	basis (of 29)	For
30b	assertion	**we know the one who said,**
30c	identification	
30d	content 1	"Mine is the vengeance;
30e	parallel	I will exact retribution," and
30f	content 2	"the Lord will judge his people." (Deut 32:35)
31a	assertion	**It is a fearsome thing to fall into the hands**
31b	possession	of the living God.

Structure

The passage falls into two obvious sections: a positive encouragement to take advantage of Christ's high-priestly work in 10:19–25 and a negative portrayal of the fate that will befall those who reject this work for themselves (10:26–31).

The first paragraph exhibits a classic New Testament "indicative leading to imperative" structure. The indicative is found in verses 19–21, which are governed by a causal participle—"since we have" (ἔχοντες). What "we have" are (1) "confidence to enter the Most Holy Place" (vv. 19–20); and (2) "a great priest" (v. 21). It is in light of these gracious provisions of God for us, the author then issues three exhortations, using hortatory subjunctives. Each of these exhortations, moreover, is qualified by one of the three great elements of the early Christian "trinity of virtues":

"Let us draw near [προσερχώμεθα] with . . . full assurance of *faith*" (v. 22)
"Let us hold firmly [κατέχωμεν] to the confession of our *hope*" (v. 23)
"Let us consider" [κατανοῶμεν] how to stir up "each other to *love* and good works" (v. 24)

Three movements make up the second paragraph. The first (vv. 26–27) makes the main point of this paragraph: a deliberate rejection of God's grace in Christ brings God's judgment. The second (vv. 28–30) employs the author's typical "how much more" argument, comparing judgment that befell those who rejected the law of Moses with the greater severity of judgment that comes upon those who reject the new-covenant grace. The author concludes his warning with a solemn reminder of just how serious it is to suffer God's judgment (v. 31).

Exegetical Outline

→ **F. Exhortation and Warning: Appropriating the Benefits of Our High Priest's Ministry (10:19–31)**
    1. Encouragement to Appropriate and Act on Christ's High-Priestly Work (10:19–25)
        a. Recognizing Our New Access to God through Christ, Our Great Priest (vv. 19–21)
        b. A Call to Appropriate the Benefits of Christ's High-Priestly Work (vv. 22–25)
    2. Warning about Rejecting Christ's High-Priestly Work (10:26–31)
        a. Judgment for Rejecting Christ's Once-For-All Sacrifice (vv. 26–27)
        b. A Greater Accountability (vv. 28–30)
        c. The Terrifying Prospect of God's Judgment (v. 31)

Explanation of the Text

10:19 Therefore, brothers and sisters, since we have confidence to enter the Most Holy Place by the blood of Jesus (Ἔχοντες οὖν, ἀδελφοί, παρρησίαν εἰς τὴν εἴσοδον τῶν ἁγίων ἐν τῷ αἵματι Ἰησοῦ). The way into the very presence of God is now open to us. The author turns now to exhortation, suggesting the shift in focus with his direct address of the readers: "brothers and sisters" (ἀδελφοί, a form of address comparatively rare in Hebrews [see also 3:1, 12; 13:22]). In verses 19–21, the author lays the groundwork for his exhortations by citing two foundational blessings God has given his new-covenant people: "confidence" to enter God's presence and a "great high priest" (cf. 4:14) whose work has made that confidence possible. These two blessings provide a good summary of the great central expository section of the author's sermon: the οὖν, "therefore," looks back to this argument, as the author draws an inference from his exposition in 5:1–10:18. Again, as I note above, these verses, 10:19–25, are the second member of an *inclusio* that began with 4:14–16. While, however, these passages are indeed very similar, there are also differences. As Ellingworth puts it, "4:14–16 prepare the presentation of Jesus as high priest, while 10:19–31 draw consequences from it."[5]

---

5. Ellingworth, *Hebrews*, 516; see also G. Guthrie, *Hebrews*, 346.

In keeping with the summary character of this passage, the first benefit the author lists uses the imagery of the cult, which he has extensively used to capture the significance of the work of Christ on our behalf: "confidence to enter the Most Holy Place." "Most Holy Place" translates a phrase (τῶν ἁγίων) that, in Hebrews, refers either to the sanctuary as a whole (8:2; 9:1, 24) or to the inner room of the sanctuary (9:2, 8, 12, 25; 13:11) (see my comments on 9:2). Several English versions, by translating "sanctuary," suggest a reference to the entire structure (e.g., NET; NRSV; CSB; NAB).[6] However, as my translation indicates, I think a reference to the inner room, the "holy of holies," is more likely (NIV; NLT; CEB).[7] It is this inner room that symbolizes the presence of God, and it is into this room that Christ enters (9:11) and, as our forerunner, enables us to enter as well (6:19–20).[8] The way into this inner room was barred to all but the high priest under the old-covenant administration (9:8), but that way is now opened for all who follow their forerunner in faith (see 10:22).

The word I have translated as a verb—"to enter"—is actually a noun, εἴσοδον. It could, therefore, refer concretely to an "entrance."[9] But the other four occurrences of this word in the New Testament (Acts 13:24; 1 Thess 1:9; 2:1; 2 Pet 1:11) have to some degree a dynamic meaning, and this works well in this verse as well.[10] The author's assertion that we have "confidence" (παρρησίαν) to enter brings us back to the "close cousin" of this passage, the introductory exhortation in 4:14–16, where the author encourages us to "come near" God's throne "with confidence." The translation "confidence" is the choice of most English versions, and this choice tends to put the focus on the individual believer's subjective state or attitude. This subjective element is certainly present, but the word also at least implies the objective basis on which that confidence rests. It suggests "both the God-given permission and the personal confidence and frankness arising from it."[11] Finally, picking up a key focus from chapter 9 (see esp. vv. 14d, 18–22), this confidence to enter comes through (taking the ἐν as instrumental) "the blood of Jesus"—that is, his sacrifice, involving both death on the cross and presentation of that sacrifice in the heavenly sanctuary.

10:20 by the new and living way that he inaugurated for us through the curtain, that is, his flesh (ἣν ἐνεκαίνισεν ἡμῖν ὁδὸν πρόσφατον καὶ ζῶσαν διὰ τοῦ καταπετάσματος, τοῦτ᾽ ἔστιν τῆς σαρκὸς αὐτοῦ). Christ has opened the way for us to enter behind the "curtain"—that which symbolized lack of access to God. The imagery of "entering," or a "way into" (εἴσοδον), is continued in verse 20, with the author's reference to "the new and living way [ὁδόν]."[12] Jesus has "inaugurated" this way, which is

---

6. And see Davidson, "Christ's Entry," 180–82; Ellingworth, *Hebrews*, 517.

7. Most commentators agree.

8. A reference to the Most Holy Place in 9:12 is required by the contrast with the OT high priest's ministry on the Day of Atonement (9:7–8).

9. Cockerill, *Hebrews*, 446; D. Harris, *Hebrews*, 272.

10. Michel, *Der Brief an die Hebräer*, 344; Koester, *Hebrews*, 442.

11. N. A. Dahl, "A New and Living Way: The Approach to God according to Hebrews 10:19–25," *Int* 5 (1951): 403; see also Koester, *Hebrews*, 442. Scholars who stress the objective side of the word here include Lane, *Hebrews*, 2:274; Massonnet, *L'Épître aux Hébreux*, 282; Cockerill, *Hebrews*, 446 ("authorization"). In keeping with its use in Greek generally, παρρησία usually refers in the NT to boldness in speech (e.g., Eph 6:19, where Paul requests prayer that he might "fearlessly" [NIV; ἐν παρρησίᾳ] make known the mystery of the gospel). But Hebrews uses the word to refer to "open access" and the confidence to take advantage of that opened access (in addition to 3:6 and 4:16, see also 10:35; and Eph 3:12; 1 John 2:28; 3:21; 4:17; 5:14).

12. As D. Harris (*Hebrews*, 273) notes, ὁδόν is an "object complement," parallel to the relative pronoun at the beginning of the verse, ἥν, which, in turn, has the feminine noun εἴσοδον as its antecedent.

"new" (NIV, ESV) or "fresh" (NET)[13] and "living." The latter word touches on an important theme in the letter: God is himself "living" (3:12; 9:14; 10:31; 12:22), as is his word (4:12). More relevant yet is the author's contrast between the Old Testament priests, who die off one by one, and our high priest Jesus, who always lives to intercede for us (7:8, 25; cf. 9:17). As a modifier of "way" here, the word probably connotes "leading to life" or "life-giving" (see 10:38; 12:9).[14] The translation "inaugurated" does not fit the imagery of a "way" as well as "opened," which most of the translations choose. But this same verb (ἐνεκαινίζω) occurs in 9:18 (its only other use in the NT), with reference to the "inauguration" or "consecration" of the old covenant, and it seems useful to keep the translation the same.[15]

The spatial imagery that our author borrows from the rites in the old-covenant sanctuary continues with the phrase "through the curtain" or "veil." "Curtain" (καταπετάσματος) occurs twice elsewhere in Hebrews. In 9:3, it refers to the "second" veil, the one that separates the Holy Place (the outer room of the sanctuary) from the Most Holy Place (the inner room). It almost certainly has the same reference in 6:19b–20a: "it [our hope] enters the inner sanctuary behind the curtain, where our forerunner, Jesus, has entered on our behalf." These texts create a strong presumption that the author here is also referring to this curtain before the Most Holy Place and that the preposition διά then has a local sense: the way we follow passes "through" the curtain. The imagery is vivid and powerful. As followers of our high priest Jesus, we now have the privilege of standing where once only the high priest could stand: in the very presence of the God who rules the universe.

Thus far the interpretation of this verse is straightforward. But the phrase at the end of the verse creates one of the toughest exegetical nuts to crack in all of Hebrews. The problem is simply stated. The phrase "that is, his flesh" is naturally read as an appositive to "curtain": the curtain "is," or symbolizes, Jesus's own flesh. However, such an appositive reading appears to join two disparate things. The curtain, as our sketch of the imagery above makes clear, has a negative symbolic function in Hebrews: it is what keeps worshipers from accessing God. Yet it appears difficult at first sight to give Jesus's flesh a comparable negative meaning. Solutions to this exegetical difficulty fall into four types.

First, we might give "curtain" a positive significance here. Bruce, for instance, argues that the curtain, rather than being seen as what keeps humans from God, can be seen as the point where we are brought together with God.[16] The problem with this view is that the author does not elsewhere suggest any such positive role for the curtain, and it does not seem naturally to fit the imagery.

Second, Jesus's flesh might be given a negative sense. Some forms of this view assume an almost gnostic-like distaste for "flesh" that stands in tension with Scripture.[17] However, if Christ's "flesh"

---

13. The word the author uses here, πρόσφατος, is rare, occuring only here in the NT and only five times in the LXX (a cognate, προσφάτως, occurs in Acts 18:2). In contrast to καινός and νέος, the more common words for "new," πρόσφατος has a stronger qualitative sense (Weiss, *Der Brief an die Hebräer*, 523; Grässer, *An die Hebräer*, 3:15). The word, e.g., refers to "fresh" grapes in Num 6:3.

14. E.g., Lane, *Hebrews*, 2:275; Ellingworth, *Hebrews*, 519. Cockerill (*Hebrews*, 468) and Schreiner (*Hebrews*, 316) see an allusion to Jesus's own resurrection life.

15. See the note on 9:18 for more data on this verb.

16. Bruce, *Hebrews*, 252; see also D. Guthrie, *Hebrews*, 212.

17. E.g., Grässer, *An die Hebräer*, 3:17–18. He follows Käsemann in seeing this text as reflecting the strong gnostic dualism of spirit and matter, according to which the "curtain" separates earth and heaven, with Jesus's flesh situated on the earthly side of this divison (Käsemann, *Wandering People of God*, 224–25). However, as Koester points out (*Hebrews*, 444), the gnostic texts where these ideas are found postdate the NT.

is viewed as a limitation rather than as a negative thing, this interpretation can perhaps pass muster.[18] Standing on its own, Jesus's flesh, seen in terms of his humanity, is incapable of providing the full and final forgiveness that only one who is resurrected, exalted, and eternally lives can provide. Calvin combines the first and second view: "just as the veil covered the recesses of the sanctuary and yet opened a door to it, so, though his Godhead was hidden in the flesh of Christ, He yet leads us to Heaven."[19] However, the idea that the author might conceive of Jesus's flesh as in any way negative or inferior does not match his use of "flesh" (σάρξ) language elsewhere. The author uses the word with reference to Christ in only two other texts, neither of which suggests the kind of negative or limited nuance this interpretation requires. Indeed, in 2:14 Christ's assumption of the "flesh and blood" that other humans have enables him to die in order to accomplish salvation for humanity.

Third, we could detach the explanatory phrase introduced by "that is" (τοῦτ' ἔστιν) from the curtain and attach it to some other element in the sentence. Thus, for instance, it might modify "way": Jesus's flesh, understood either to refer to his humanity or to his sacrifice, is the "new and living way" inaugurated for us. See, for example, the NEB: "the new living way which he has opened for us through the curtain, the way of his flesh."[20] Or, similarly, the phrase could modify the verb "inaugurated": "he inaugurated by means of his flesh a new and living way through the curtain."[21] The instrumental sense of "by means of his flesh" that this view demands is unobjectionable, for Greek allows us to "carry over" a word from one phrase into another.[22] Thus, it is possible to assume that the preposition "through" (διά) in the first phrase is to be read also in the second: thus "[through] his flesh" ([διὰ] τῆς σαρκὸς αὐτοῦ). The shift in meaning of the preposition, from local—"through the curtain"—to instrumental—"by means of his flesh"—is not a problem either (see, e.g., 9:11–12; Rom 4:25). Attaching this final interpretive phrase to something earlier in the verse yields a good sense and is an attractive way out of our exegetical dilemma. The more serious challenge to this view is whether the language after "that is" (τοῦτ' ἔστιν) can go back to one of these elements earlier in the sentence. This phrase occurs sixteen times in the New Testament, usually introducing an interpretation that refers to the word or phrase immediately before it. In four texts, however, the phrase introduces an elaboration of a word or words from earlier in the sentence (Acts 19:4; Rom 10:8; Heb 7:5; 13:15), which is similar to what this view proposes for 10:20. However, in contrast to this view, the word or phrase introduced by "that is" functions as an appositive, not a descriptor.[23] While not absolutely ruling out this view, this syntactical issue does raise questions about its viability.

Fourth, we could view Jesus's flesh as in loose apposition to curtain, with both key words referring

---

18. See the variants of this view argued for by, e.g., Michel, *Der Brief an die Hebräer*, 345; Delitzsch, *Hebrews*, 2:172; Bénétrau, *L'Épître aux Hébreux*, 2:103; Johnson, *Hebrews*, 257; Dahl, "New and Living Way," 405.

19. Calvin, *Hebrews*, 141.

20. Westcott, *Hebrews*, 320; Backhaus, *Der Hebräerbrief*, 358; Moffatt, *Hebrews*, 173; Weiss, *Der Brief an die Hebräer*, 526.

21. Otfried Hofius, "Inkarnation und Opfertod Jesu nach Hebr 10,19f," in *Der Ruf Jesu und die Antwort der Gemeinde: Festschrift für Joachim Jeremias*, ed. E. Lohse (Göttingen: Vandenhoeck & Ruprecht, 1970), 132–43; Joachim Jeremias, "Hebräer 10:20: τοῦτ' ἔστιν τῆς σαρκὸς αὐτοῦ," *ZNW* 62 (1971): 131; Rissi, *Die Theologie des Hebräerbriefs*, 42–43; Lane, *Hebrews*, 2:275.

22. This rather common phenomenon in Greek is called ellipsis or brachylogy (see von Siebenthal, *Ancient Greek Grammar*, 553).

23. See N. H. Young, "ΤΟΥΤ' ΕΣΤΙΝ ΤΗΣ ΣΑΡΚΟΣ ΑΥΤΟΥ (Heb. X.20): Apposition, Dependent or Explicative?," *NTS* 20 (1973–1974): 100–104.

to the means of access into God's presence.²⁴ In contrast to the first view, this interpretation does not view the curtain positively but rather sees the curtain as that through which one must pass to access God. Jesus's flesh, then, functions similarly: as that through which one accesses God. Some interpreters who advocate this interpretation think that the author may have in mind the incident of the "torn curtain" at the time of Jesus's death (Matt 27:51; Mark 15:38; Luke 23:45). As the curtain was torn to symbolize access to God, so Jesus's flesh is "torn" in death to provide that access.²⁵ The author and his listeners could well have known of this tradition from oral accounts of Jesus's death. However, the curtain in the Gospels is most likely the curtain, visible to all (including the centurion at the cross), that shielded the sanctuary as a whole²⁶—whereas in Hebrews the curtain is the one shielding the Most Holy Place.

This fourth main option, like one variant of the third view, posits a brachylogy, according to which "through" before "curtain" is to be read also before "his flesh." And also, like this variant of the third view, we in this case must assume a shift in meaning in the preposition, from the local to the instrumental. But, as I noted above, neither of these syntactical moves is all that unusual. On this reading, in fact, it is possible to give the second (assumed) preposition (διά) something of a local view: as the curtain was the "place" the high priest came to in order to access God, so Jesus's flesh, given in sacrifice, is the "place" all of us now come to in order to enter God's presence.

While a decision among these options is not easy, I slightly prefer this fourth view, with the third view coming in a close second in my estimation.

10:21 and (since we have) a great priest over the house of God (καὶ ἱερέα μέγαν ἐπὶ τὸν οἶκον τοῦ θεοῦ). "Great priest" (ἱερέα μέγαν) is the second object of the causal participle ἔχοντες in verse 19: as followers of Jesus, we have "confidence to enter" and we have a "great priest." The sequence of these two objects signals the author's focus in this part of the letter. The author's focus has shifted from exposition to application. Having Jesus as our "great priest," as the author has spelled out in 8:1–10:18, is wonderful and foundational. However, he is now especially interested in the opportunity that we have to profit from that reality.

"Great priest" (Heb. הַכֹּהֵן הַגָּדֹל) is a simple alternative to "high priest" (see Lev 21:10; Num 35:25, 28; the NIV translates "high priest" in each of these verses).²⁷ The author here returns to the language of 3:1–6, describing the people of God as "the house of God." Specific reference to those

---

The phrase introduces the explanation of a single word (Mark 7:2; Rom 7:18; Phlm 12; Heb 7:5; 9:11; 11:16; 13:15; 1 Pet 3:20), a phrase or clause (Heb 2:14), an OT quotation (Rom 9:8; 10:6, 7, 8), or a translation (Matt 27:46; Acts 1:19). As an appositive, the words after τοῦτ' ἔστιν are in the same case as the word it modifies. The phrase occurs four times in the LXX and around fifteen in Philo to introduce explanations. See also A. T. Robertson, *A Grammar of the Greek New Testament in Light of Historical Research*, 2nd ed. (New York: George H. Doran Co., 1915), 399.

24. With various emphases, Koester, *Hebrews*, 434–44; Peterson, *Hebrews and Perfection*, 153–54; Ellingworth, *Hebrews*, 520–21; Cockerill, *Hebrews*, 470–71; D. L. Allen, *Hebrews*, 513–14.

25. P. Hughes, *Hebrews*, 409; Hagner, *Hebrews*, 164; France, "Hebrews," 135.

26. See the discussions in R. T. France, *Mark*, NIGTC (Grand Rapids: Eerdmans, 2002), 656–57; James R. Edwards, *The Gospel According to Mark*, Pillar New Testament Commentary (Grand Rapids: Eerdmans, 2002), 478–79. It is also unclear what symbolic significance the Gospel writers give this event: Is the torn curtain a sign of judgment (as France, e.g., argues) or a sign of access to God (as Mark Strauss argues [*Mark*, ZECNT (Grand Rapids: Zondervan, 2014), 705])?

27. Lane, *Hebrews*, 2:285.

over whom Christ presides and for whom he gives himself as a "great priest" again focuses attention on the practical consequences of Jesus's office.

10:22 Let us draw near with a sincere heart and the full assurance of faith, with our hearts sprinkled clean from an evil conscience and our bodies washed with pure water (προσερχώμεθα μετὰ ἀληθινῆς καρδίας ἐν πληροφορίᾳ πίστεως ῥεραντισμένοι τὰς καρδίας ἀπὸ συνειδήσεως πονηρᾶς καὶ λελουσμένοι τὸ σῶμα ὕδατι καθαρῷ). Verses 19-21 are in "indicative" mode, as the author briefly describes the new opportunity for people to access God through the work of our "great priest," Jesus Christ. This verse shifts to imperative mode, with the first of three hortatory subjunctive verbs exhorting us to respond to God's incredible new-covenant offer of grace.

The invitation to "come near" or "draw near" (the verb is προσέρχομαι) aligns with the "theology of access" that characterizes the soteriology of Hebrews.[28] The language of "entering" (v. 19; see also 3:11, 18, 19; 4:1, 3, 5, 6, 10, 11; 6:19, 20; 9:12, 24, 25) or "drawing near" (see also 4:16; 7:25; 10:1; 11:6; 12:18, 22) reflects the dominant cultic imagery of the letter. Following our high-priestly forerunner, we are given the privilege of entering the place of God's presence and drawing near to him. The present tense of the verb steers us away from applying this exhortation to our initial coming into God's presence for salvation. Rather, the author wants us regularly to "draw near": in worship, in prayer, in seeking forgiveness. The focus of the verse, however, is not on "drawing near" per se but on *how* we are to come near. Toward this end, the author qualifies his exhortation with two prepositional phrases and two adverbial participles.

We are to approach God, first, "with a sincere heart." "Sincere" translates a word (ἀληθινῆς) that can mean "true" (as opposed to false) or "real" (see Heb 8:2; 9:24), but which here has the sense "sincere" or "genuine" ("ἀληθινός," L&N 73.2; CEB). This heart is the opposite of the "sinful, unbelieving heart that turns away from the living God" (3:12). Second, we draw near to God in "full assurance of faith" (ἐν πληροφορίᾳ πίστεως). "Faith" probably indicates the source of our assurance (e.g., NIV; NET; CEB).[29] We can then combine it with the other verse in Hebrews that uses πληροφορία (6:11) to summarize the heart of the author's message: on the basis of our faith, we have the full assurance that our hope will be realized (the phrase in 6:11 is τὴν πληροφορίαν τῆς ἐλπίδος).[30] It is not surprising that the word faith appears here in this summary of the author's exhortation, for the posture of trustful commitment connoted by faith is the essential thing Jesus followers need to continue on their path of discipleship (see esp. 4:2; 6:1, 12; 10:38-39; 11:6; 12:2).

Two other qualifications of those who are invited to draw near are mentioned in the participial clauses that conclude the verse. First, those who draw near have their "hearts sprinkled clean from an evil conscience." I add the word "clean" (as also, e.g., NRSV) to convey the intention of "sprinkled" in combination with the phrase that follows (ἀπὸ συνειδήσεως πονηρᾶς—the ἀπό expresses separation[31]). In keeping with the summary nature of this paragraph, the author redeploys language he has already used: "sprinkled" (in a cultic sense, 9:13, 19,

---

28. The phrase comes from Isaacs, *Sacred Space*, 67.

29. Grässer, however, in keeping with his view that πίστις in Hebrews is the virtue of faithfulness, takes the genitive as epexegetic (*Glaube*, 39).

30. See also our comments on πληροφορία in conjunction with 6:11.

31. Comparable elliptical expressions are found in Acts 8:22; Rom 9:3; 2 Cor 11:3; Col 2:20; see "ἀπό," BDAG 105, §1b.

21) and "conscience" (9:9, 14; 10:2; see also 13:18). Having "hearts sprinkled" may also allude to a key Old Testament new-covenant prophecy, Ezekiel 36:25–27:

> I will sprinkle clean water on you, and you will be clean; I will cleanse you from all your impurities and from all your idols. I will give you a new heart and put a new spirit in you; I will remove from you your heart of stone and give you a heart of flesh. And I will put my Spirit in you and move you to follow my decrees and be careful to keep my laws. Then you will live in the land I gave your ancestors; you will be my people, and I will be your God.[32]

Second, we draw near with "our bodies washed with pure water." This description does not have a basis in the author's earlier language; indeed, it is somewhat surprising, since "washing" (using λούω) along with "body" (σῶμα) sounds conceptually similar to the language of "washings" (βαπτισμός) and "flesh" (σάρξ) that the author uses to depict the (merely) external effect of old-covenant sacrifices (9:9; see also 9:13). Here, however, the imagery refers to the cleansing from the impurity of sin secured by the sacrifice of Christ. The language might have a priestly connotation: Aaron and his sons were "washed with water" (LXX λούσεις αὐτοὺς ἐν ὕδατι, Exod 29:4) to prepare them for ordination; they were also sprinkled with blood (Exod 29:21; see also Lev 8:6 and 30).[33] Without dismissing these allusions, the more likely source for the author's "washing" language is the Ezekiel text we quote above,[34] a passage with many parallels to the new-covenant prophecy of Jeremiah 31:31–34 (which plays so important a role in the argument of Hebrews).

A further question is whether this last description (and perhaps the first as well) alludes to the Christian rite of baptism. The verb the author uses—λούω, "wash"—does not allude to baptism in its other New Testament occurrences (see John 13:10; Acts 9:37; 16:33; 2 Pet 2:22), but the cognate noun—λουτρόν—is often thought to refer to baptism in Ephesians 5:26 and Titus 3:5. The argument over this point quickly becomes circular: those who think baptism plays a prominent role in the New Testament assume it is referred to here because, well, baptism is important in the New Testament.[35] Those who doubt a reference to baptism argue just the reverse. I think it is possible that the language alludes to baptism, but more important is the metaphorical use of physical "washing" to connote the forgiveness of sin provided to new-covenant believers.[36]

10:23 Let us hold firmly to the confession of our hope without wavering, for faithful is the one who has promised (κατέχωμεν τὴν ὁμολογίαν τῆς ἐλπίδος ἀκλινῆ, πιστὸς γὰρ ὁ ἐπαγγειλάμενος). The second way we need to respond to God's gracious offer to "enter" is to cling firmly to the hope of salvation that God faithfully promises to us. The lack of any connecting word (the phenomenon called asyndeton) highlights the parallelism between the exhortation in this verse and the one in verse 22. Both are in the form of a hortatory

---

32. Peterson, "God and Scripture," 133.
33. Peter J. Leithart stresses this priestly background ("Womb of the World: Baptism and Priesthood of the New Covenant in Hebrews 10.19–22," *JSNT* 78 [2000]: 49–65).
34. See, e.g., Cockerill, *Hebrews*, 474; Schreiner, *Hebrews*, 318–19.

35. See, e.g., Attridge, *Hebrews*, 289; Lane, *Hebrews*, 2:287; Ellingworth, *Hebrews*, 523; Koester, *Hebrews*, 444–45; Weiss, *Der Brief an die Hebräer*, 530. Dahl ("New and Living Way," 407) thinks both participles refer to baptism, "sprinkling" indicating the inner meaning and "washing" the external rite.
36. See esp. Schreiner, *Hebrews*, 318–19.

subjunctive ("let us . . ."). The author urges his listeners to hold firmly (κατέχωμεν) to the confession "without wavering" (ἀκλινῆ),[37] another parallel to the "bookend" exhortation in 4:14–16: "therefore, since we have a great high priest who has gone through the heavens, Jesus the Son of God, let us hold fast [κρατῶμεν] to the confession" (author's translation). Many interpreters think that "confession" (ὁμολογία) involves public declaration of the faith.[38] While not ruling out a verbal element, I prefer, as in 4:14, to take the word to refer to "the Christian view of reality and the hopes and values it articulates."[39] The author is calling for a constant, tenacious commitment to the truth of the faith that will enable believers to maintain their status as the people of God. If we give the word "confession" a verbal connotation, "the hope" (τῆς ἐλπίδος) can be construed as the object of that word: "the hope we confess/profess" (NIV; NLT; NET; NJB). However, even on my view—that "confession" refers to the faith itself—"hope" could have a loosely objective force: an unwavering commitment to the faith, which the believers have been taught, leads to hope (e.g., NAB: "the confession that gives us hope"). And this hope, the author emphasizes, has a solid basis: "for faithful is the one who has promised" (see 6:13–20; I put "faithful" at the beginning in imitation of the probable emphasis in the Greek word order).

10:24–25 And let us consider one another, with the purpose of stimulating each other to love and good works, 25 not giving up meeting with one another, as is the habit of some, but rather exhorting one another and doing so all the more as you see the day coming near (καὶ κατανοῶμεν ἀλλήλους εἰς παροξυσμὸν ἀγάπης καὶ καλῶν ἔργων, 25 μὴ ἐγκαταλείποντες τὴν ἐπισυναγωγὴν ἑαυτῶν, καθὼς ἔθος τισίν, ἀλλὰ παρακαλοῦντες, καὶ τοσούτῳ μᾶλλον ὅσῳ βλέπετε ἐγγίζουσαν τὴν ἡμέραν). The third exhortation in the series—also in the form of a hortatory subjunctive—shifts to the horizontal dimension of faithful Christian living. The author invites his readers to take advantage of their new-covenant privileges of "drawing near" to God, exhorts them to stick tenaciously to their faith, and asks them, finally, to encourage one another to display the reality of their faith in love and good works. As I note above, the author, perhaps intentionally, follows the famous Christian triad of faith (v. 22), hope (v. 23), and now love. "Consider" translates a word (κατανοέω) that can mean simply "observe" (e.g., Acts 27:39) but often has the stronger sense of "contemplate," "take into consideration." The verb is generally followed by a direct object, and it is therefore probable that "one another" (ἀλλήλους) is the object of the verb, with the final clause (introduced by εἰς) indicating the goal of the believers' consideration of one another (see CSB and CEB). Specifically, the author wants his listeners to "stimulate" one another. The word used here (παροξυσμός), is a strong one, often having a negative connotation: as its transliteration into English suggests ("paroxysm," "a sudden, uncontrollable attack"), it can sometimes refer to an outburst of anger (Deut 29:27; Jer 39:37) or a

---

37. The word ἀκλινῆ is an accusative adjective, which may, then, modify ὁμολογίαν: "unwavering confession" (Thompson, *Hebrews*, 205; Johnson, *Hebrews*, 261). But it makes better sense to think it functions here as an adverb (so all English translations; and see, e.g., Koester, *Hebrews*, 445; D. Harris, *Hebrews*, 276).

38. E.g., Koester, *Hebrews*, 450.

39. DeSilva, *Perseverance in Gratitude*, 179. See also Ellingworth, *Hebrews*, 525; Cockerill, *Hebrews*, 476.

strong disagreement (Acts 15:39, its only other occurrence in the NT). However, without losing its strength, the word can also be used positively: Josephus, for example, refers to those who "stimulate ... good will" (*Ant.* 16.125). So believers are to have such a regard for one another that we do what we can to stimulate, or even provoke, one another to live out our faith in love for others and in good works.

However, we cannot encourage and stimulate one another if we do not regularly gather together. So our author's concern in verse 25 about some who are "giving up meeting with one another" follows naturally from his exhortation in verse 24. "Meeting together" translates a word (ἐπισυναγωγήν) used in 2 Thessalonians 2:1 (its only other NT occurrence) to refer to believers "gathered together" to meet Christ at his coming. Many interpreters therefore think that the word here also has eschatological connotations.[40] However, this is not clear; the fact that the word has eschatological associations in one verse does not necessarily mean that those associations are carried into other texts (though, to be sure, the author goes on in this verse to refer to eschatology). The word appears here simply to refer to Christian "gatherings"—we can assume for worship, teaching, prayer, celebration of the sacraments, and mutual encouragement.

We have no way of determining why believers had fallen into the "habit" (ἔθος) of not meeting together, although one plausible guess is that the persecution being experienced by believers (see vv. 32–34) had led many to avoid being publicly identified with the Christian movement.[41] In keeping with his concern in verse 24, the author contrasts "giving up meeting with one another" with "exhorting [παρακαλοῦντες] one another".[42] This ministry of mutual exhortation—stimulating one another to love and good works—is to be engaged in "all the more" (τοσούτῳ μᾶλλον) in light of the coming eschatological climax. "Day" (τὴν ἡμέραν) refers to the time when God brings to a conclusion his work of saving and judging. This "day" was known as the "day of the Lord" in the Old Testament, but in light of the New Testament understanding of Christ as "the Lord," this eschatological "day" is often associated with Christ. Specifically, this day includes and is focused on the return of Christ in glory—his "second" appearance (Heb 9:28). The many references to this day and the many variations in the way it is qualified indicate how ubiquitous this language was in the early church.[43] Also characteristic of New Testament eschatology is the sense that this day is "imminent." Indeed, the verb the author uses here, ἐγγίζω, occurs elsewhere to express this sense of the "nearness" of

---

40. E.g., Koester, *Hebrews*, 446; Weiss, *Der Brief an die Hebräer*, 534; Grässer, *An die Hebräer*, 3:28; Cockerill, *Hebrews*, 480.

41. See esp. Bruce W. Winter, *Divine Honours for the Caesars: The First Christians' Responses* (Grand Rapids: Eerdmans, 2015), 266–85. He thinks increasing pressure to worship the emperor played a significant role.

42. I translate "exhorting one another" on the assumption that the reflexive pronoun ἑαυτῶν used after ἐπισυναγωγήν should be carried over to this clause as well. Translating this reflexive pronoun (technically, "exhorting ourselves") as "one another" is appropriate, granted the fact that this pronoun often encroaches on the territory of the reciprocal pronoun ἀλλήλων

(see, e.g., von Siebenthal, *Ancient Greek Grammar*, 207). As Ellingworth (*Hebrews*, 528) notes, the participle παρακαλοῦντες (along with its pair, ἐγκαταλείποντες) has an imperatival force (see NAB; CEB).

43. For "day of the Lord" in the OT, see, e.g., Jer 30:8–9; Hos 2:16–23; Joel 1:15; 2:1–2, 31; Amos 9:11; Obad 15–17. For "day of the Lord" in the NT, see Acts 2:20; 1 Cor 5:5; 1 Thess 5:2; 2 Thess 2:2; 2 Pet 3:10; and also, "the day of God" (2 Pet 3:12); also "day of Christ" (Phil 1:10; 2:16), "day of our Lord Jesus" (2 Cor 1:14); "day of Jesus Christ" (Phil 1:16); "day of our Lord Jesus Christ" (1 Cor 1:8). The simple "day" is used in this sense (as here in Hebrews) in Acts 17:31; Rom 13:12; 1 Cor 3:13; 1 Thess 5:4; 1 Pet 2:12; 2 Pet 1:19; see also "that day" in

the day.[44] The language does not mean that early Christians were certain that the Lord would return within a given amount of time but that they were convinced his coming *could* occur at any time. Following the typical New Testament pattern, the imminent appearing of our Lord should stimulate us to be involved in the lives of others, exhorting them to love and good works. The author urges us to draw near to God in light of the day that draws near to us.[45]

10:26-27 For if we deliberately keep on sinning after receiving a knowledge of the truth, there no longer remains a sacrifice for sins 27 but the fearful expectation of judgment, involving a raging fire that consumes the enemies of God (Ἑκουσίως γὰρ ἁμαρτανόντων ἡμῶν μετὰ τὸ λαβεῖν τὴν ἐπίγνωσιν τῆς ἀληθείας, οὐκέτι περὶ ἁμαρτιῶν ἀπολείπεται θυσία, 27 φοβερὰ δέ τις ἐκδοχὴ κρίσεως καὶ πυρὸς ζῆλος ἐσθίειν μέλλοντος τοὺς ὑπεναντίους). Deliberate and willful renunciation of God's grace in Christ will result in judgment. As I noted above, this passage follows the threefold structure the author uses elsewhere: exhortation (vv. 19-25), warning (vv. 26-31), reassurance (vv. 32-39; see esp. 6:1-12). The warning in this paragraph is a strong one, rivaling and perhaps surpassing the strength of the better known warning in 6:4-6 (other warning passages are found in 2:1-4; 3:7-4:11; and 12:14-17, 25-29). The two passages include the same three basic elements:

Bold type: what they have done
<u>Underlined: who they are</u>
<u>Double-underlined: what their fate will be</u>

6:4-6	10:26-31
<u>For it is impossible to renew again to repentance those who have once been enlightened and who have both tasted the heavenly gift and become partakers of the Holy Spirit and who have tasted both the good word of God and the powers of the age to come</u> and **who then fall away, crucifying the Son of God for themselves and disgracing him publicly.**	For if we **deliberately keep on sinning** <u>after receiving a knowledge of the truth, there no longer remains a sacrifice for sins, but the fearful expectation of judgment, involving a raging fire that consumes the enemies of God.</u> Anyone who rejected the law of Moses died without mercy on the basis of the testimony of two or three witnesses. <u>How much worse a punishment is deserved by</u> **the one who trample underfoot the Son of God, considers common the blood of the covenant by means of which they were sanctified, and insults the Spirit of grace?** For we know the one who said, "Mine is the vengeance; I will exact retribution," and "the Lord will judge his people." <u>It is a fearsome thing to fall into the hands of the living God.</u>

Matt 7:22; 24:36; 26:29; Mark 13:32; 14:25; Luke 10:12; 17:31; John 14:20; 16:23, 26; 2 Thess 1:10; 2 Tim 2:12, 18; 4:8; "his day" in Luke 17:24; "last day" in John 6:39, 40, 44, 54; 11:24; 12:48; "great day" in Jude 6; "great day of God Almighty" (Rev 16:14).

See also "day of judgment" (Matt 10:15; 11:22; 12:36; 2 Pet 2:9; 3:7; 1 John 4:17); "day of slaughter" (Jas 5:5).

44. See Luke 21:20, 28; Rom 13:12; Jas 5:8; 1 Pet 4:7.
45. Koester, *Hebrews*, 447.

One difference from the warning in chapter 6 is that the author now brings into play the cultic language with which he has described the work of Christ in 7:1–10:18.[46]

The interpretation of the opening clause in verse 26 is key to rightly understanding the author's warning in this paragraph. The verb "sinning" is a general term, but five considerations enable us to pin down more specifically what is meant. First, the participle the author uses here (ἁμαρτανόντων) probably has a conditional force (hence the "if" in most versions).[47] The author is not condemning those who have committed this sin but warning people not to commit it. Second, the participle is in the present tense, which probably suggests continuity here—hence "keep on" sinning in my translation (most of the English versions do something similar). Third, the sinning is characterized as "deliberate." The Greek word (an adverb: ἑκουσίως) can mean "willingly" (see 1 Pet 5:2, the only other NT occurrence; see also the cognate adjective in Phlm 14) but clearly here means "deliberately" (NIV and most English versions), "willfully" (NRSV). We are naturally reminded of the Old Testament category of the sin committed with "a high hand" (ESV; NIV "defiantly," NLT "brazenly"), contrasted in Numbers 15:24–31 with a sin committed "unintentionally." A person who commits such a sin is to be "cut off from the people of Israel . . . their guilt remains on them" (Num 15:30–31).[48] The author's claim that there remains "no sacrifice" for this sin may, then, reflect some Old Testament passages that likewise claim that no sacrifice can atone for this sin.[49] Fourth, the further description in verse 29 of this sin makes clear it involves a defiant rejection of God's grace in Christ. And this is confirmed by the fifth point: the parallel between "deliberate sinning" here and "falling away" of 6:6. As Cockerill summarizes, then, the sin is "intentional, persistent, and informed."[50]

The deliberate nature of the sin the author refers to is evident from the fact that the sin takes place after receiving the "knowledge of the truth." This phrase regularly refers to conversion, the acceptance of the gospel, in the Pastoral Epistles (1 Tim 2:4; 4:3; 2 Tim 2:25; 3:7). "Knowledge of the truth" matches the fivefold description of the people in danger of apostasy in 6:4–5. And just as those who "fall away" cannot be restored to repentance (6:6), so here those who sin "deliberately" no longer have any sacrifice for sins that will avail for them (see 10:18). As Johnson remarks, this conclusion reflects "the promise and the peril of the priestly work of Jesus."[51] The promise of definitive

---

46. Lane, *Hebrews*, 2:291.
47. See, e.g., Grässer, *An die Hebräer*, 3:36; Weiss, *Der Brief an die Hebräer*, 538.
48. As Roy Gane points out, the Numbers text does not intend to divide all sins into one of these two categories; rather, it notes the extremes on a spectrum (*Leviticus, Numbers*, NIVAC [Grand Rapids: Zondervan, 2004], 624–26). In addition to the Numbers passage, other texts specify that people who sin "unintentionally" can be restored while those who sin intentionally are to be put to death (e.g., Exod 21:12–14; cf. Deut 19:4). Most interpreters think that the author is alluding to this OT category of sin, although others, noting that the Greek word the author uses is not used in the LXX to depict this sin, doubt it (e.g., Cockerill, *Hebrews*, 484). It should also be noted that the distinction between sins committed "in ignorance" and sins entered into deliberately was known in the Greco-Roman world as well (see Koester, *Hebrews*, 451).
49. The issue is complicated because other texts suggest that the Day of Atonement ritual would suffice to cancel the penalty of all sins (Lev 16:16). Jewish tradition was also divided, some Jews claiming that all sins could indeed be taken care of by the Day of Atonement (Philo, *Spec. Laws* 1.234–38), while others argued that the Day of Atonement would not benefit persistent sinners (m. Yoma 8:90). Sklar helpfully suggests that "high-handed" sin cannot be atoned for by ordinary sacrificial rituals but could be atoned for by a mediator's intervention ("Sin and Atonement," 472–76).
50. Cockerill, *Hebrews*, 483.
51. Johnson, *Hebrews*, 261.

forgiveness via the "once-for-all" sacrifice of Jesus means that those who turn their backs on this sacrifice have no other recourse to take care of their sin problem. "If no salvation is to be found apart from Him, we should not be surprised that those who let go of Him of their own accord are deprived of every hope of pardon."[52]

If those who decisively and knowingly spurn Christ's sacrifice have no other sacrifice to turn to, then they are left in their sins—and the prospect can be nothing but judgment (v. 27). Along with early Christians generally, the author carries over from the Old Testament and Judaism the expectation that the last day would be marked by a universal judgment when all humans would stand before the just God to be assessed (6:2; 9:27). That judgment is a "fearful" (φοβερά) prospect for those who have turned away from Christ—they are in effect numbering themselves among God's "enemies" and can expect therefore "a raging fire [πυρὸς ζῆλος] that consumes" them.[53] "Judgment" and "raging fire" are connected by "and" (καί), which might have a simple coordinate significance: the "expectation" (ἐκδοχή) is of both "judgment" and "raging fire" (so most English versions).[54] But I think it is more likely that the conjunction functions epexegetically, introducing "raging fire" as another way of referring to judgment.[55] The language is drawn from the Old Testament, where the image of fire is often used to portray judgment. Particularly relevant here is Isaiah 26:11: "Lord, your hand is lifted high, but they do not see it. Let them see your zeal [ζῆλος] for your people and be put to shame; let the fire [πῦρ] reserved for your enemies [ὑπεναντίους] consume them."[56] The language is metaphorical, the biblical authors depicting the eternal punishment of hell with language connoting a painful and destructive earthly experience.[57]

10:28–29 Anyone who rejected the law of Moses died without mercy on the basis of the testimony of two or three witnesses. 29 How much worse a punishment is deserved for the one who tramples underfoot the Son of God, considers common the blood of the covenant by means of which they were sanctified, and insults the Spirit of grace? (ἀθετήσας τις νόμον Μωϋσέως χωρὶς οἰκτιρμῶν ἐπὶ δυσὶν ἢ τρισὶν μάρτυσιν ἀποθνήσκει· 29 πόσῳ

---

52. Calvin, *Hebrews*, 146. As I noted in my comments on 6:4–8, early interpreters sometimes used these "rigorist" texts to deny the possibility of forgiveness for post-baptismal sin, a view that led to various degrees of pushback from other interpreters (Bruce, *Hebrews*, 262–64).

53. The phrase πυρὸς ζῆλος is probably an example of an "attributed genitive," when the genitive—in this case πυρός—becomes the dominant word, with the "governing" word—in this case the nominative ζῆλος—as the modifier (see Wallace, *Greek Grammar*, 89–91, for this genitive). The word ζῆλος here means "fierce" (see L&N 78.25).

54. The τις before ἐκδοχή has an intensifying force—a "certain" or "definite" expectation (BDF §301.1; Lane, *Hebrews*, 2:277).

55. See also Ellingworth, *Hebrews*, 535.

56. See also, e.g., Pss 11:6; 21:9; 79:5; Isa 26:11; Jer 4:4; Ezek 22:21; 38:19; Zeph 1:18; and, of course, frequently in the NT as well (Matt 5:22; 18:9; 25:41; 2 Thess 1:7; 2 Pet 3:7; Rev 18:8; 20:14, 15).

57. "Fire" is also referred to as a method of refinement in the NT (e.g., 1 Pet 1:7; Rev 3:18), and a few interpreters think that fire here refers to the refining of believers rather than to eternal judgment (Thomas Kem Oberholtzer, "The Warning Passages of Hebrews, Part 4: The Danger of Willful Sin in Hebrews 10:26–39," *BSac* 145 [1988]: 413–14). But the imagery of fire is far more often used to depict eternal punishment, and the author does not use fire for the process of refining anywhere else (see, e.g., Ellingworth, *Hebrews*, 535). It is even more unlikely that the prospect the author warns about is the physical destruction impending for first-century Israel (contra Randall C. Gleason, "The Eschatology of the Warning in Hebrews 10:26–31," *TynBul* 53 [2002]: 97–120; Gleason, "Moderate Reformed View," 363–64). For an effective rebuttal of this view, see Buist M. Fanning, "Classical Reformed Response (to A Moderate Reformed View)," in Bateman, *Four Views*, 402–10.

δοκεῖτε χείρονος ἀξιωθήσεται τιμωρίας ὁ τὸν υἱὸν τοῦ θεοῦ καταπατήσας καὶ τὸ αἷμα τῆς διαθήκης κοινὸν ἡγησάμενος, ἐν ᾧ ἡγιάσθη, καὶ τὸ πνεῦμα τῆς χάριτος ἐνυβρίσας;). In these verses, the author introduces yet another comparison between the situation under the old covenant and the new. As he has done in 2:2–3, he argues that punishment for turning away from the new and decisive revelation in Christ will incur a more severe punishment than was meted out for rejection of the law of Moses. The author refers to Deuteronomy 17:2–7 to make his point with respect to the old covenant. This passage singles out the Israelite who "is found doing evil in the eyes of the LORD your God in violation of his covenant, and contrary to my command has worshiped other gods, bowing down to them or to the sun or the moon or the stars in the sky" (vv. 2b–3). Such a person, "on the testimony of two or three witnesses," "is to be put to death" (v. 6a; see also Lev 24:13–16).[58]

A greater punishment hangs over those who commit the sin the author has in view in this paragraph. The author does not identify that punishment, leaving its identification to the imaginations of his readers in a rhetorically effective strategy.[59] This rhetorical focus suggests also that, with most versions and interpreters, we should punctuate this verse as a question.[60] Those who deserve this "worse ... punishment" (χείρονος ... τιμωρίας)[61] are described in three parallel clauses:

the one who tramples underfoot the Son of God
(ὁ τὸν υἱὸν τοῦ θεοῦ καταπατήσας)

[and the one who] considers common the blood of the covenant by means of which they were sanctified,
(καὶ τὸ αἷμα τῆς διαθήκης κοινὸν ἡγησάμενος, ἐν ᾧ ἡγιάσθη)

and [the one who] insults the Spirit of grace
(καὶ τὸ πνεῦμα τῆς χάριτος ἐνυβρίσας)

These three parallel descriptions (all referring to the same sinner, as the single article governing all three suggests) might depict a single "moment" at which a person renounces Christ and his benefits. Or they might depict the "climax to which uncorrected laxity and neglect of God's provision in Christ will lead" (culminative aorists).[62] More likely they should be seen as characterizing the "persistent attitude" that typifies these sinners (constantive aorists).[63]

"Son/Son of God" is the most important title for Jesus in the first part of the letter (1:2, 5, 8; 3:6; 4:14; 5:5, 8; 6:6; 7:3, 28). The author's return to this title here (in a position of emphasis, coming first in its clause) therefore encourages us to think back to the description of this Son in these earlier verses. The picture of an exalted figure, greater than the angels, who was instrumental in creation (1:2–3) and who is, indeed, himself "God" (1:8) accentuates the seriousness of trampling him "underfoot." The verb the author uses (καταπατέω) occurs elsewhere in the New Testament to depict a physical trampling—as when pigs "trample" pearls under their feet (Matt 7:6; see also Matt 5:13; Luke 8:5; 12:1).

---

58. Reference to the Torah requirement of "two or three witnesses" is applied to other matters in the NT (Matt 18:16; 2 Cor 13:1; 1 Tim 5:19), suggesting it was a well-known stipulation.

59. Philo uses similar rhetorical logic: "if he who swears a wrongful oath is guilty, how great a punishment does he deserve [πόσης ἄξιος τιμωρίας] who denies the truly existing God" (*Spec. Laws* 2.255).

60. Exceptions are NLT and NJB, which punctuate as a statement.

61. The word τιμωρία occurs only here in the NT, but fifteen times in the LXX, in most cases referring to punishment.

62. Cockerill, *Hebrews*, 491.

63. E.g., Lane, *Hebrews*, 2:294.

In the LXX, this verb is used as a metaphor for oppressing the righteous or the needy (Ps 7:5 [7:6 LXX and MT]; 57:3 [56:4 LXX, 57:4 MT]; Amos 4:1; 5:12) or the temple/sanctuary (e.g., Isa 25:10; 63:18; 1 Macc 3:45, 51; 3 Macc. 2.18). To "trample underfoot" the Son of God is not only to reject his benefits and authority but to do so with contempt.

If the first description brings us back to chapters 1–7, the next one reminds us of the argument of 8:1–10:18. Both "blood" and "covenant" are key words in that part of the letter (for the former, see esp. 9:12–25; for the latter, 8:6–13; 9:15–17; 10:16). "Blood of the covenant," then, summarizes the author's teaching on atonement: by means of Christ's "blood," including his sacrificial death and offering in heaven, a new covenant, offering full and final forgiveness, is inaugurated.[64] Moreover, personalizing the point, the author reminds his readers that this blood is the means by which they were "sanctified."[65] In Hebrews this verb refers to the initial cleansing from sin that sets people apart as the people of God (2:13; 10:10, 14; 13:12). The person who considers Christ's covenant-making blood as "common," essentially, as Johnson suggests, "reverses the effect of Christ's priestly works."[66] The word "common" (κοινόν) has the sense of "defiled": it is used in the New Testament in Jewish ritual contexts to denote people or things that are considered "impure" (Mark 7:2, 5; Acts 10:14, 28; 11:8; Rom 14:14; Rev 21:27)—see "unholy" in NIV; "profane" in CSB; "unclean" in NASB.[67] Christ's blood "cleanses" from defilement; now these sinners that our author rebukes are treating Christ's cleansing blood as defiled—something to be ashamed of and avoided.

Third, the "willful sin" that our author warns against in this paragraph involves insulting "the Spirit of grace." The verb the author uses—ἐνυβρίζω—occurs only here in the New Testament, but a simpler form of the verb (ὑβρίζω), with a similar meaning, does occur. It refers to scornful and outrageous treatment of someone—the kind of treatment Paul and his associates receive from the Philippians, who publicly humiliate, mistreat, and imprison them (1 Thess 2:2; see Acts 16:19–24). The author is again pulling out all the rhetorical stops to frighten his readers out of their temptation to fall into the willful sin this paragraph addresses. And this rhetoric is ramped up when the author characterizes the Spirit as "the Spirit of grace": they are tempted to scorn the very Spirit who is involved in freely conferring blessings on them.[68]

10:30–31 For we know the one who said, "Mine is the vengeance; I will exact retribution," and "the Lord will judge his people." 31 It is a fearsome thing to fall into the hands of the living God (οἴδαμεν γὰρ τὸν εἰπόντα, Ἐμοὶ ἐκδίκησις, ἐγὼ ἀνταποδώσω. καὶ πάλιν, Κρινεῖ κύριος τὸν λαὸν αὐτοῦ. 31 φοβερὸν τὸ ἐμπεσεῖν εἰς χεῖρας θεοῦ ζῶντος). In his typical fashion, the author grounds

---

64. We should probably not see a reference to the Lord's Supper in "blood" (P. Hughes, *Hebrews*, 423) or to baptism in being "sanctified" (Grässer, *An die Hebräer*, 3:46).

65. The ἐν ᾧ before ἡγιάσθη has an instrumental force: "by or through which they were sanctified." G. Guthrie (*Hebrews*, 357) suggests that this phrase may not refer to the subject of this clause—"the one who treats as common"—but to a person in general: "by which one is sanctified." But it is more natural to identify the subject of this relative clause with the subject of the sentence as a whole.

66. Johnson, *Hebrews*, 265.

67. The Jewish ritual context shared by these texts and our author strongly points to this meaning of κοινός—rather than to the meaning "common." Gleason adopts this latter meaning, arguing that the issue is that Christ's sacrifice is being treated as equal to other sacrifices ("Moderate Reformed Response," 252).

68. The genitive τῆς χάριτος probably is descriptive—"the Spirit characterized by grace" (e.g., Bénétrau, *L'Épître aux Hébreux*, 2:113–14)—but might then have also the nuance of "the Spirit who gives grace" (Delitzsch, *Hebrews*, 2:190).

(γάρ, "for")—his warning—and implied exhortation—in the Old Testament. The two quotations in verse 30 are taken from the Song of Moses in Deuteronomy 32. The introduction to these quotations with reference to "him who said" is also typical for the author: for him, Scripture is a matter of God (or Christ, or the Spirit—an implicit Trinitarianism) addressing the people of God (see 1:5, 6, 7, 8, 10, 13; 2:12, 13; 3:7; 4:3; 5:5, 6; 6:14; 7:21; 8:8; 9:20; 10:5, 9, 15, 17; 11:18; 12:26; 13:5). The close relationship between this speaking God and the believers is accentuated by the author's claim that "we" (the author and his readers) "know" this God who speaks.

The first quotation comes from Deuteronomy 32:35a, which the author quotes in a form that differs from both the Hebrew and the LXX but that was apparently circulating among early believers—Paul's quotation of this same passage in Romans 12:19 agrees exactly with the text here in Hebrews.[69] The author's citation of this text is contextually appropriate, since Moses at this point in his song is warning Israel about God's judgment for their turning from him to other gods.

It is not so clear that the second quotation maintains the Old Testament sense. As many English versions suggest, Deuteronomy 32:36 is probably a comment from the author that refers positively to the Lord "vindicating" his people (the verb in the MT is דין; the Greek [in both LXX and Hebrews] uses κρίνω).[70] One option is to think that the verb in Hebrews also has a positive sense.[71] While possible, this would represent a sudden shift from the context.

The threat of judgment issued in our author's quotations in verse 30 is brought to a climax in verse 31. "To fall into the hands" of someone is to come under their control, to become entirely subject to them—usually with a negative connotation. Thus Samson worries about falling "into the hands of the uncircumcised" (Judg 15:18). More relevant to Hebrews is David's response to Gad the prophet, who sets before the king the option between Israel being inflicted with three years of famine, three months of defeat from their enemies, or three days of plague. He chooses plague, reasoning that he would rather fall "into the hands of the LORD" than "into human hands" (2 Sam 24:12–14; see also 1 Chr 21:9–13). This episode makes clear that falling "into the hands of the living God" is not entirely negative, but it is, as the author notes, a "fearsome" matter.[72] With this word, the author comes back to where he begins in this paragraph (see "fearful" [φοβερός] in v. 27). The awesome majesty of God stimulates wonder and fear in those who draw near to him. For those who know and seek to follow him, this response can have positive overtones. But for those who are turning away from God and his gracious provision, an encounter with the living God brings pain and punishment.

---

69. The Greek version in Romans and Hebrews ("to me is vengeance, I will repay") faithfully represents the Hebrew (לִי נָקָם וְשִׁלֵּם, "to me is vengeance, I will repay"), so it is possible that one author—or both—are dependent on the Hebrew. But the overall pattern of quotation in Hebrews does not support his use of the Hebrew text. For the view that both Romans and Hebrews are dependent on a variant Greek text, see, e.g., G. Guthrie, "Hebrews," 980; D. M. Allen, *Deuteronomy and Exhortation*, 58–60; Lane, *Hebrews*, 2:295.

70. The same language (both MT and LXX) is found in Ps 135:14 (LXX 134:14). Since the first quotation in v. 30 comes from Deut 32:35, it is overwhelmingly probable that the second comes from that same context.

71. J. Proctor, "Judgement or Vindication? Deuteronomy 32 in Hebrews 10:30," *TynBul* 55 (2004): 76; Cockerill, *Hebrews*, 493.

72. Characterizing God as "the living God" represents a certain focus in Hebrews. Particularly significant is 3:12: "see to it, brothers and sisters, that none of you has a sinful, unbelieving heart that turns away from the living God." See also 9:14 and 12:22.

Theology in Application

The threefold description of the person who is persisting in a willful sin in verse 29 is arguably the strongest evidence from the letter that the author is warning about the serious possibility that a genuine believer might, indeed, suffer final condemnation. This person is one who has been "sanctified": they have been cleansed and brought into God's people by the blood of Christ. Yet this person is in danger of the raging fire of final judgment.[73] Many interpreters, usually those who hold a traditional Calvinist view of perseverance, resist this conclusion. They suggest that the language in this text depicts people who have had significant experience in the church but who have not "crossed the line" into a converted state. They further note the third-person form of address in verse 29, which creates a certain distance from the author's clear references to his readers with the second person (see 10:32–36). The warning in this passage, then, while referring to his audience in language that would normally denote full Christian experience, might have in view some among his readership who may not have appropriated these spiritual benefits for themselves. As Buist Fanning, who argues this view, puts it, "The writer has portrayed the apostates in distinctly Christian terms to emphasize how close they have been to new covenant salvation and what they are spurning if they depart."[74]

I have great respect for this view (having held it myself for many years!), and, with its advocates, I am also concerned to read Hebrews in a way that aligns with what I think is the overall teaching of Scripture of "eternal security." However, as I explain at more length in my comments on 6:4–8, I am finally not sure that the view espoused by Fanning and many others can find adequate grounding in the text. So, I slightly lean here again to the view that the author is engaged in rhetorical exaggeration to reinforce the strength of his warning (see, again, my comments on 6:4–8).

---

73. Among many who make this point, see, e.g., Osborne, "Classical Arminian View," 120–22 (who argues for a "classical Arminian" perspective on perseverance), and Schreiner, *Hebrews*, 327 (who argues for a Reformed view on perseverance).

74. Fanning, "Classical Reformed Response (to Classical Arminian View)," in Bateman, *Four Views*, 137; cf. pp. 132–37.

Hebrews 10:32–39

Literary Context

I analyzed the flow of the author's argument in 10:19–39 in the "Literary Context" section on 10:19–31. I drew attention there to the transitional character of this whole passage and noted that 10:32–39 is especially difficult to locate. It clearly relates to what comes before, providing reassurance to the readers after the strong warning in 10:26–31. The end of chapter 10 then duplicates the sequence of exhortation, warning, and reassurance that we find elsewhere in Hebrews (see esp. 6:1–12).[1] On the other hand, the focus in 10:32–39 on "endurance" (ὑπομένω/ὑπομονή, vv. 32 and 36) and "faith" (πίστις, vv. 38 and 39) appears to introduce the two key concepts that will dominate 11:1–12:14: "faith" in chapter 11 ("faith" occurs twenty-four times, and "believe" once), and "endurance" in 12:1–14 ("endurance" occurs once; "endure" three times).[2]

Reiterating the conclusion I drew earlier, the present paragraph is, then, transitional, a "Janus" that looks both forward and backward. Perhaps, however, it looks forward just a bit more—hence my decision to place it where it is in the outline of the letter.

I. The Exalted Son and a Rest for the People of God (1:1–4:13)
II. Our Great High Priest and His Ministry (4:14–10:31)
III. **Exhortation: Follow and Serve the Pioneer of Our Faith through Endurance and Faith (10:32–13:25)**
    → **A. Introductory Call to Endurance and Faith (10:32–39)**
    B. The Nature and Power of Faith Illustrated in Salvation History (11:1–40)
    C. Run the Race with Endurance, Remembering That You Are Children of God (12:1–17)
    D. Coming to Mount Zion and Inheriting the Unshakable Kingdom (12:18–29)
    E. Letter Closing (13:1–25)

---

1. See esp. Lane, who provides a chart illustrating the parallels between 6:1–12 and 10:19–39 (*Hebrews*, 2:296–97).

2. See, e.g., Vanhoye, *Structure and Message*, 29; Attridge, *Hebrews*, 298.

Main Idea

The believers whom the author addresses can receive the final salvation that God has promised to them if they persevere in faith, rekindling the zeal they showed toward God after they were first converted.

Translation

Hebrews 10:32-39

32a	exhortation	**Remember the days**
32b	time	of a former time,
32c	simultaneous	when,
32d	time	after you were enlightened,
32e	assertion	you endured a great contest
32f	content	of suffering.
33a	elaboration (of 32f)	Sometimes
33b	assertion	you were exposed
33c	manner	publicly
33d	complement (of 33b)	to acts of ridicule and
33e	parallel	tribulations, and
33f	alternative	at other times
33g	assertion	you entered into fellowship
33h	relationship	with those who were being treated
33i	manner	in this way.
34a	amplification (of 33)	For
34b	assertion	**you also suffered**
34c	relationship	with the prisoners
		and
34d	parallel (to 34b)	**welcomed**
34e	manner	with joy
34f	object (of 34d)	the plundering of your possessions,
34g	basis	since you knew
34h	content	that you have a better
34i	object	possession—and
34j	quality	an abiding one.
35a	inference (from 32–34)	Therefore
35b	exhortation	**do not throw away your confidence,**
35c	motivation	which has a great reward.

36a	inference (from 35)	Therefore	
36b	assertion	**you have need**	
36c	content		of endurance,
36d	result		so that, …
36e	time		having done the will of God,
36f	assertion		… you might receive
36g	object (of 36f)		what has been promised.
37a	elaboration (of 36)	For	
37b	time		"in just a little while
37c	assertion	**the coming one will come and**	
37d	parallel		will not delay. (Isa 26:20; Hab 2:3)
38a	contrast (with 37)	But	
38b	assertion	**my righteous one will live**	
38c	means		by faith;
38d	contrast (with 38b–c)	and yet	
38e	condition		if he shrinks back,
38f	assertion	**my soul will not be pleased**	
38g	reference		with him." (Hab 2:4)
39a	contrast (with 38e–g)	But	
39b	negative	**we are not**	among those
39c	identification		who shrink back and
39d	result (of 39b)		are ultimately destroyed but
39e	positive		among those
39f	identification		who have faith and
39g	result (of 39f)		preserve their lives.

Structure

The passage falls into two distinct paragraphs. The first is dominated by indicative verbs and focuses on the past (vv. 32–34). The author recalls the difficult circumstances the readers faced shortly after their conversion. They experienced verbal taunts and physical abuse. Some had possessions snatched from them; some were imprisoned. The general character of these descriptions makes it impossible to pin down the exact situation or circumstances. Some famous persecutions are eliminated from consideration by the fact that their suffering had not included the loss of life (12:4)—this would appear, for example, to rule out the persecution of Christians in Rome under Nero. Perhaps the most likely scenario, especially if, as I think, the letter was addressed to Christians in Rome, is that Christians were caught up in Emperor Claudius's expulsion of Jews from Rome in AD 49 (see Acts 18:2). An ancient historian claims that this expulsion was because of conflict among the Jews over "Chrestus," probably a garbled version of "Christ" (Suetonius, *Claudius*

25). The Roman authorities would not have distinguished between Jews and Jewish-Christians, so it is almost certain the nascent Christian community in Rome would have been affected by this expulsion order and that this legal order would have been accompanied by various other kinds of persecution.[3] In these trying circumstances, the author reminds them, the readers exhibited deep faith, identifying with those who were afflicted and viewing the loss of their earthly possessions as a minor matter in comparison with the great "possession" promised to them in the time of the consummation.

The pattern of "indicative-imperative" is familiar in the New Testament. Usually, however, it is what God has done in Christ that is the focus of the indicative; here, however, the indicative relates to the believers's own faithfulness. This reminder of their faithfulness is the foundation for the author's imperatives in verses 35–39: negatively, they must not "throw away" their confidence (v. 35); positively, they need to persevere (v. 36) and to have faith (vv. 38, 39).[4] Their confidence, perseverance, and faith are what they need to experience the final salvation (v. 39) that God has promised (v. 36) when their Messiah comes again in glory (v. 37).

Exegetical Outline

→ **A. Introductory Call to Endurance and Faith (10:32–39)**
   1. Looking Behind: Encouragement from Past Faithfulness (vv. 32–34)
   2. Looking Ahead: Grasping Final Salvation by Faith and Endurance (vv. 35–39)

Explanation of the Text

10:32 Remember the days of a former time, when, after you were enlightened, you endured a great contest of suffering (Ἀναμιμνῄσκεσθε δὲ τὰς πρότερον ἡμέρας, ἐν αἷς φωτισθέντες πολλὴν ἄθλησιν ὑπεμείνατε παθημάτων). The author shifts from strict warning (vv. 26–31) to reassurance. The conjunction linking this verse to what precedes, then (δέ), may signal either a sequence of thought or be mildly adversative: "you are in danger of the fire of hell if you sin deliberately in rejecting God's grace in Christ, *but* I have better hope for you." The author's call on his readers to "remember" entails

---

3. For this view, see esp. Bruce, *Hebrews*, 268–70, and Lane, *Hebrews*, 2:301. See, again, the introduction. A few scholars think that the author is not referring to any specific situation and is portraying a situation generally applicable to early Christians (e.g., Grässer, *An die Hebräer*, 3:58–65). Others think the author refers to a specific incident but that we can't identify it (Attridge, *Hebrews*, 299; Koester, *Hebrews*, 464).

4. Scholars debate over whether the imperative "do not throw away your confidence" in v. 35 concludes the first paragraph (NIV; Ellingworth, *Hebrews*, 544; Massonnet, *L'Épître aux Hébreux*, 295) or opens the second (NLT; Grasser, *An die Hebräer*, 3:70; Koester, *Hebrews*, 464; Westcott, *Hebrews*, 335; Johnson, *Hebrews*, 272). I slightly favor the second option, keeping all the imperative verbs in the same paragraph.

more than a simple recollection of past events; it is "making present to mind and heart the experiences that shaped and continue to shape their identity."[5] The readers are to call to mind the "days of a former time,"[6] a time when, having been enlightened, or converted,[7] they endured "a great contest of suffering." "Contest" translates ἄθλησιν (*athlēsin*), from which we derive our words "athletics," "athlete." The English derivations in this case provide a clue to the meaning of the word, which referred in ancient Greek to various kinds of athletic contests. However, Jewish literature undoubtedly known to the author had already transferred the language into the realm of spiritual conflict. An especially clear example comes in 4 Maccabees 17, which celebrates the sacrifice of the martyrs at the time of the Maccabean revolt:[8]

> Truly the contest [ἀληθῶς . . . ἀγών] carried on by them was divine, for then virtue, testing them for their perseverance [ὑπομονῆς], offered rewards [ἠθλοθέτει]. Victory meant incorruptibility in long-lasting life. Eleazar contended first; the mother of seven boys entered the fray [ἐνήθλει], and the brothers contended. The tyrant was the antagonist; the world and human society looked on. Godliness won the victory and crowned its own athletes. Who did not marvel at the athletes contending for the divine law code? Who were not astonished? The tyrant himself and all his council marveled at their endurance [ὑπομονήν]. (4 Macc. 17.11–17 NETS)

As this snippet reveals, the language of "endurance" describes the virtue needed to engage successfully in such a spiritual contest: hence the author uses the verb "endure" (ὑπομένω) here. The need for endurance amid affliction is found not only in pre-New Testament Judaism but in the New Testament itself (see esp. Matt 5:11–12; Luke 6:22–23; 1 Pet 1:6; 4:13–17; Jas 1:2, 12). The author, then, commends his readers for their steadfast "bearing up" under the weight of this "contest of suffering."[9]

10:33 Sometimes you were exposed publicly to acts of ridicule and tribulations, and at other times you entered into fellowship with those who were being treated in this way (τοῦτο μὲν ὀνειδισμοῖς τε καὶ θλίψεσιν θεατριζόμενοι, τοῦτο δὲ κοινωνοὶ τῶν οὕτως ἀναστρεφομένων γενηθέντες). In this verse, and in the first half of the next verse, the author elaborates on his general reference to "sufferings" at the end of verse 32. These sufferings, on the one hand, involved public exposure to acts of ridicule and tribulations. "Ridicule," used here in the plural (ὀνειδισμοῖς, hence "acts of ridicule"), connotes verbal abuse: "insults," "reproaches," "scorn." The "righteous sufferer" of the Psalms, a type of Christ, suffers such ridicule (see esp.

---

5. Johnson, *Hebrews*, 268. Note especially the use of the cognate noun (ἀνάμνησις) in the words of institution ("do this in remembrance of me," Luke 22:19; 1 Cor 11:24, 25). The verb (ἀναμιμνήσκω) occurs also in Mark 11:21; 14:72; 1 Cor 4:17; 2 Cor 7:15; 2 Tim 1:6.

6. I translate this way to bring out the (possible) emphasis in the author's use of the singular πρότερον with the plural τάς . . . ἡμέρας (see Westcott, *Hebrews*, 333).

7. As in 6:4, the passive verb φωτισθέντες refers to coming from darkness into light—that is, to experiencing conversion. A secondary reference to baptism is possible (e.g., P. Hughes, *Hebrews*, 427) but by no means certain (Christian Rose, *Die Wolke der Zeugen: Eine exegetisch-traditionsgeschichtliche Untersuchung zu Hebräer 10,32–12,3*, WUNT 2/60 [Tübingen: Mohr Siebeck, 1994], 37; Grässer, *An die Hebräer*, 3:61; Lane, *Hebrews*, 2:298).

8. "ἄθλησις," LSJ 32; E. Stauffer, "ἀθλέω, κτλ," *TDNT* 1:167–68. See the use of the cognate verb, ἀθλέω, in 2 Tim 2:5 and the compound form συναθλέω ("struggle with") in Phil 1:27; 4:3.

9. "Of suffering" translates παθημάτων, which I take to be epexegetic of ἄθλησιν—"a contest consisting in sufferings."

Ps 69:7, 9, 10, 19, 20; and note Paul's application of Ps 69:9 to Christ in Rom 15:3; see also Heb 5:7). The second term (θλίψεσιν—also in the plural) refers to "afflictions" or "distress" of various kinds. Often these stem from the limitations of our mortality and of the fallen world we live in (e.g., John 16:21; Acts 7:11; 1 Cor 7:28; 2 Cor 1:4), but at other times they are the product of persecution, as here (see also, e.g., Acts 11:19; 2 Thess 1:4; Rev 2:10). The pairing of these two words (which occurs only here in the NT) probably covers both verbal and physical abuse.[10] Both these kinds of suffering were public. The author uses a verb from which we derive "theater": θεατρίζω (*theatrizō*), "put on display." The word occurs only here in the New Testament, but Paul uses the cognate noun in a similar way: "for it seems to me that God has put us apostles on display at the end of the procession, like those condemned to die in the arena. We have been made a spectacle [θέατρον] to the whole universe, to angels as well as to human beings" (1 Cor 4:9). It is important to note that a key reason to abuse Christians in public was in order shame them, a devastating blow to these Christians living, as they did, in a society dominated by considerations of honor on the one hand and shame on the other.

Even when the readers were not personally experiencing affliction, they demonstrated the depth of their commitment by coming alongside other believers who were being mistreated.[11] The author uses a word to express this solidarity (κοινωνοί) that can be translated "partners" or "companions" (so most English versions).[12] However, I have chosen (at the risk of overtranslation) to bring out the special Christian nuance of the word here by rendering "entered into fellowship with." The κοιν- root is the basis for words in the New Testament that express the close fellowship, the intimate identifying with one another, that was to characterize believers (see esp. Acts 2:42; Gal 2:9; Phil 1:5; 2:1; Phlm 6; 1 John 1:3, 7; cf. 2 Cor 6:14). The author commends his readers for their "fellowship" with those who were being persecuted. Rather than "keeping their heads down," thankful that they were not being exposed to hardship, these believers went out of their way to express in tangible ways their solidarity with their suffering brothers and sisters.

10:34 For you also suffered with the prisoners and welcomed with joy the plundering of your possessions, since you knew that you have a better possession—and an abiding one (καὶ γὰρ τοῖς δεσμίοις συνεπαθήσατε καὶ τὴν ἁρπαγὴν τῶν ὑπαρχόντων ὑμῶν μετὰ χαρᾶς προσεδέξασθε γινώσκοντες ἔχειν ἑαυτοὺς κρείττονα ὕπαρξιν καὶ μένουσαν). The author here "amplifies"[13] the point he has made in the previous verse by first developing the readers' identification with other suffering believers (see v. 33b) and then elaborating on their own sufferings (see v. 33a), forming a chiastic structure.[14] A prime illustration of the readers' willingness to mark their solidarity with

---

10. D. Harris, *Hebrews*, 290.

11. With the English versions, I am taking the comparative construction τοῦτο μέν . . . τοῦτο δέ to indicate, not a shift in persons—"some were suffering, others were identifying with those who were suffering" (Lane, *Hebrews*, 2:299; Koester, *Hebrews*, 459 [possibly])—but a shift in circumstances (so most interpreters). On the (classical) τοῦτο μέν . . . τοῦτο δέ construction, see BDF §290.5.

12. See, e.g., the use of this word to denote the sons of Zebedee as Simon's "partners" in their fishing enterprise (Luke 5:10).

13. "Amplifies" is Ellingworth's accurate description of the function of γάρ ("for") here (*Hebrews*, 548). The καί perhaps adds a sense of "heightening" to v. 34a: "you identified with those who are suffering; indeed, you even suffered with them."

14. Many interpreters note this chiasm; see, e.g., Lane, *Hebrews*, 2:299.

brothers and sisters is that they suffered along with those who had been imprisoned for their faith.[15] The verb the author uses—συμπαθέω—occurs once elsewhere in the New Testament, in Hebrews 4:15, describing the "sympathy" or "empathy" Jesus our high priest exhibits toward the weak. Christ's solidarity with us is the model and stimulus for us to express radical solidarity with each other.

Returning to the readers' own suffering in verse 34b, the author commends them for reacting to the confiscation of their property with joy. The plundering (ἁρπαγήν) of people's homes and possessions in the context of persecution is a well-known phenomenon, whether such plundering was given official sanction or whether officials simply looked away as it was happening.[16] The readers were able to "welcome" (προσεδέξασθε) the plundering of their possessions (τῶν ὑπαρχόντων) because they knew (γινώσκοντες, a clear causal participle) they had another "possession" (ὕπαρξιν).[17] This latter "possession" is a "better" one, the author using here again his favorite word to compare God's new-covenant provision for his people to the old-covenant provision. Here, however, the author uses it to contrast the possessions of this world with that of the next world. The reason this new "possession" is superior is because it is "abiding" or "remaining" (μένουσαν)—a characteristic the author draws attention to by placing it last in the sentence. The "abiding" and therefore superior character of God's new-covenant provision is a theme throughout the letter (see μένω in 7:3, 24; 12:27; 13:14; see also 1:12; 13:8).[18] The believers imitated Abraham, who was willing to live a nomadic existence in tents because "he was looking forward to the city with foundations, whose architect and builder is God" (11:9–10).

10:35 Therefore do not throw away your confidence, which has a great reward (μὴ ἀποβάλητε οὖν τὴν παρρησίαν ὑμῶν, ἥτις ἔχει μεγάλην μισθαποδοσίαν). This verse is the "linchpin" of this passage.[19] The author's celebration of his readers' past faithfulness in verses 32–34 leads up to it (hence the οὖν, "therefore"). And his call for endurance and faith in verses 36–39 is the means by which the readers will be able to avoid "throwing away" their confidence. My translation of this key imperative (ἀποβάλητε)[20] with "throw away" agrees with most of the English versions and interpreters in giving the verb an active meaning (rather than a passive one; e.g., perhaps NRSV's "abandon"),[21]

---

15. The text adopted by modern Greek New Testaments and supported by almost all commentators is δεσμίοις, "prisoners" (found in, e.g., A D H 6. 33. 81. 1739 and a few others) in preference to δεσμοῖς, "chains" (found on its own or with a pronoun in, e.g., 𝔓46 ℵ D² Ψ 104. 1881). The KJV's "in my bonds" reflects this latter variant.

16. A good example is the events surrounding the persecution of Jews in Alexandria in AD 38. Philo says, about this incident, that once Jews had been taken away by the authorities, "their enemies overran the houses now left empty and turned to pillaging [ἁρπαγήν] them, distributing the contents like spoil of war" (*Flaccus* 56).

17. While the author uses two different words for "possession," the two are obviously related in form and pronunciation. The recipients of the letter would have heard the assonance as this "sermon" was being read to them.

18. Some interpreters here again find evidence for a Middle Platonist perspective on the part of our author, since he appears to denigrate earthly possessions in favor of those that exist in another realm (heaven?), which is the only place where one can find things of lasting value (e.g., deSilva, *Perseverance in Gratitude*, 359). But this is not clear: the contrast could be more between the present era and the future "new heaven and new earth."

19. Cockerill, *Hebrews*, 503.

20. As customary in Greek, the aorist subjunctive is used to indicate a prohibition.

21. The verb is rare in biblical Greek, occurring elsewhere in the NT only in Mark 10:50 ("throwing aside" a cloak). It occurs only five times in the LXX but much more frequently in Philo and Josephus. I can find little basis in these occurrences for the more passive translation. See Ellingworth, *Hebrews*, 550–51, for discussion of this active/passive distinction.

that is, whether the author thinks of this "throwing away" as a single decisive renunciation of Christ or as the culmination of a long process of neglect and "drifting away" (2:1) is difficult to say.

The readers are not to throw away their "confidence" (παρρησία). This word, though not all that frequent in Hebrews, nevertheless beautifully captures the central thrust of the author's sermon. God has provided through the work of his Son, our high priest, the means by which we can enter boldly and confidently into the very presence of God (3:6; 4:16; 10:19). We need to maintain an attitude of confidence and boldness in order to continue to appropriate the benefits of Christ's high-priestly work. In 10:19, the word connotes the objective basis for our boldness: we *have* παρρησία. Here, in an *inclusio*, the word tilts toward a more purely subjective sense.[22] The author seeks to motivate his readers to such resolute boldness by reminding them that their boldness brings "great reward."[23] The word translated "reward" (μισθαποδοσία) is used again positively in 11:26, but negatively in 2:2: the word means "recompense," which can be either favorable or unfavorable ("μισθαποδοσία," BDAG, 653).

10:36 Therefore you have need of endurance, so that, having done the will of God, you might receive what has been promised (ὑπομονῆς γὰρ ἔχετε χρείαν ἵνα τὸ θέλημα τοῦ θεοῦ ποιήσαντες κομίσησθε τὴν ἐπαγγελίαν). In order for us to experience the final salvation God has promised us, we need endurance above all. Many translations connect this verse to verse 35 with "for," suggesting that verse 36 explains or gives a basis for verse 35. However, as we have seen, the conjunction that occurs here—γάρ—has a flexible meaning in Hebrews. Here it makes much better sense to view it as inferential ("therefore").[24] The endurance that the audience exhibited in the past as they "endured" under persecution (v. 32, ὑπομείνατε) is what they need going forward to ensure they do not "throw away" their confidence. "Endurance" (ὑπομονῆς) is placed in the emphatic position at the beginning of the sentence. Encouragement to endure is rooted in the prospect of what that endurance can bring in the future. The result[25] of steadfast perseverance is that believers would receive "what has been promised" (τὴν ἐπαγγελίαν). This promise is elaborated in this context in terms of "a better possession—and an abiding one" (v. 34), a "great reward" (v. 35), and the preserving of one's life (v. 39). As these references make clear, the pattern of present faithfulness leading to eschatological reward is an outstanding feature of this paragraph. If faith*less*ness leads to judgment in the last day (vv. 26–31), so also faith*ful*ness brings reward and blessing. To underscore the connection between present faithfulness and future blessing, the author also mentions that one will receive what has been promised only after "doing the will of God."[26] As Lane puts it, "the measure of endurance is obedience to God."[27]

---

22. See, e.g., Attridge, *Hebrews*, 300; Massonnet, *L'Épître aux Hébreux*, 298.

23. The indefinite relative pronoun (which the author uses interchangeably with the definitive relative pronoun), ἥτις, might have a causal flavor. See, e.g., NET: "so do not throw away your confidence, because it has a great reward." See also Lane, *Hebrews*, 2:278.

24. See, e.g., Lane, *Hebrews*, 2:278; D. Harris, *Hebrews*, 292. For γάρ in Hebrews, see the note on 2:10.

25. The word ἵνα probably signifies result rather than purpose here (Lane, *Hebrews*, 2:278; Ellingworth, *Hebrews*, 553).

26. While the aorist form of the participle does not always indicate antecedent action, ποιήσαντες pretty clearly has this temporal force (e.g., Koester, *Hebrews*, 461).

27. Lane, *Hebrews*, 2:302.

10:37–38 For "in just a little while the coming one will come and will not delay. 38 But my righteous one will live by faith; and yet if he shrinks back, my soul will not be pleased with him"[28] (ἔτι γὰρ μικρὸν ὅσον ὅσον, ὁ ἐρχόμενος ἥξει καὶ οὐ χρονίσει· 38 ὁ δὲ δίκαιός μου ἐκ πίστεως ζήσεται, καὶ ἐὰν ὑποστείληται, οὐκ εὐδοκεῖ ἡ ψυχή μου ἐν αὐτῷ). A quotation from the Old Testament introduces the importance of faith. The author passes seamlessly into a composite quotation from the Old Testament, combining a few words from Isaiah 26:20 with a substantial excerpt from Habakkuk 2:3–4. The author, contrary to his usual practice, does not formally introduce the quotation, but there is no doubt he would expect his readers to identify it as such.[29] The quotation reinforces three of the author's key points in this context. First, he confirms and elaborates (γάρ in an explanatory sense) the eschatological prospect that he has just mentioned. The time when the promises will come to their fulfillment is not far away: "the coming one" is indeed coming "in just a little while" and "will not delay." Second, the quotation elaborates the posture that God's people—"my righteous one"—need to have in the face of this imminent prospect: they must "live by faith." Third, the author uses the quotation to remind his readers of the opposite prospect: God "will not be pleased" with those who "shrink back."

While it is a matter of only three words, the opening of the quotation—μικρὸν ὅσον ὅσον ("in just a little while")[30]—is almost certainly taken from Isaiah 26:20. The combination of these words is not found elsewhere in the New Testament or in the LXX (see, however, Odes Sol. 5.20). In Isaiah, these words refer to the coming of God's wrath to punish people for their sins. The people of God are exhorted to hide themselves until the wrath passes by. The author adds them to "yet" (ἔτι) from Habakkuk 2:3 to heighten the sense of imminence.[31]

Habakkuk 2:2–4 is right at the heart of the prophet's message. In the face of the puzzling ways of the Lord in history, the prophet "stations himself" on the ramparts to see how God would respond. That response comes in verses 2–5: God has a "vision" or "revelation" that speaks to the end he has appointed. Even if that end seems to be delayed, God urges his people to wait for it. God's people need to "live by faith" as they wait patiently and with assurance for the end to come (v. 4b). They must avoid becoming like the "puffed up" person, who is not upright and falls into sin and judgment (vv. 4a, 5). We can understand in general the relevance of this text for the author's audience. Like Habakkuk, his readers also are required to wait, as they see the wicked prosper and the righteous suffer (vv. 32–36). They too need a fresh vision of God's promises to bring all his promises to fulfillment. And, as they wait, they need to endure and have faith.[32]

To appreciate fully what the author intends

---

28. I am using the masculine pronoun in this discussion in what I know to be an outdated generic sense; but there is no other way to convey the specifics of the text for this kind of discussion.

29. Contra, apparently, Grässer, who argues that the text is not a "citation" (*An die Hebräer*, 3:75).

30. The words ὅσον ὅσον are a vernacular idiom that originally meant "how much" or "how little," but came to mean also (as here) "a very little" (BDF §304).

31. Ellingworth (*Hebrews*, 555) notes other possible parallels between Isa 26 and the situation of the author: the warning about judgmental fire consuming Israel even as it consumes the Lord's enemies (v. 11; cf. Heb 10:27); reference to the people's "affliction" in v. 16 (θλῖψις; cf. Heb 10:33); a contrast between the city of the godless and the "strong city" of the righteous (Isa 25:2; 26:1; cf. Heb 11:10).

32. On Habakkuk, see, e.g., F. I. Andersen, *Habakkuk: A New Translation with Introduction and Commentary*, AB (New York: Doubleday, 2001), 198–224; O. P. Robertson, *The Books of Nahum, Habakkuk, and Zephaniah*, NICOT (Grand Rapids: Eerdmans, 1990), 168–85.

with his quotation from Habakkuk 2:3–4 requires an investigation into its textual background—a complicated undertaking in this case because of the variety of textual forms of Habakkuk 2:3–4 apparently in circulation at the time of the author. It will help to set out some of these texts (the translations are my own, with notable variations with each tradition indicated in parentheses):

Habakkuk 2:3–4 in Hebrews 10:37–38: Text Comparison

Hebrew	Greek LXX	Hebrews
³For yet the vision is for the appointed time; it speaks of the end and will not prove false. Though it is delayed, wait for it, for coming, it will come; it will not delay. ⁴See, the one whose soul is puffed up is not upright; but the one who is righteous will live by his [or its] faith/faithfulness (בֶּאֱמוּנָתוֹ).	³For yet the vision is for its time and it will rise up at the end and will not be in vain. If he (or it) is delayed, wait for him (or it), for the one (or it) who is coming will not delay. ⁴If he (or it) draws back, my soul will not be pleased with him (or it), but the one who is righteous will live by my faith/faithfulness (MS B) -or- my righteous one will live by faith/faithfulness (MS A)	The coming one will come and will not delay. But my righteous one will live by faith/faithfulness; and yet if he shrinks back, my soul will not be pleased with him.

While the texts of both the Hebrew and Greek of Habakkuk have a number of issues, two are of relevance for what is happening in Hebrews.³³ First, in the Hebrew text of Habakkuk 2:4b, "faith"/"faithfulness" is probably that of the righteous person (as all the English versions translate).³⁴ The Greek tradition is divided, however. The important manuscript Vaticanus (MS B) attaches a first-person singular possessive pronoun (μου) to "faith" / "faithfulness" (πίστεως), attributing the word to God, presumably requiring the meaning "faithfulness." However, the manuscript Alexandrinus (MS A) attaches this pronoun to "righteous one" (δίκαιος).³⁵ As so often is the case, the author of Hebrews uses a text similar to what is found in Alexandrinus: "*my* righteous one will live by faith/faithfulness." Second, in the Hebrew text, the subject throughout verse 3 appears to be the "vision." This is possibly also the case in the LXX: the NETS translation, for instance, renders the LXX of Habakkuk 2:3 as "for there is still a vision for an appointed time, and it will rise up at the end and not in vain. If it should tarry, wait for it, for when it comes it will come and not delay." However, there is a problem with this rendering. The word "vision" in Greek is feminine (ὅρασις), while key words later in the verse are masculine: "wait for it [αὐτόν]"; "coming [ἐρχόμενος]." This shift in gender suggests that we have in the

---

33. For a more detailed consideration of the complex textual issues, see esp. Joseph A. Fitzmyer, "Habakkuk 2:3–4 and the New Testament," in *To Advance the Gospel: New Testament Studies* (New York: Crossroad, 1981), 236–46; Gheorghita, *Role of the Septuagint*, 170–78.

34. It is also possible, however, that the pronominal suffix on the word refers to the vision: the point would then be the "reliability" of the vision.

35. Scholars debate about which might have been the original reading of the LXX. For an argument for the MS B version, see Gheorghita, *Role of the Septuagint*, 176–77. Barnabas Lindars has suggested (improbably) that the reading in MS A arose from the influence of Hebrews (*New Testament Apologetic: The Doctrinal Significance of the Old Testament Quotations* [London: SCM, 1973], 231). Paul also quotes Hab 2:4b, but he omits any pronoun: ὁ [δὲ] δίκαιος ἐκ πίστεως ζήσεται (Rom 1:17b; Gal 3:11).

Greek an awkward shift in the middle of verse 3 from speaking about a "vision" to speaking about a person (hence our translation above). Moreover, the shift might be owing to a messianic reading of the text by the LXX translators: the "coming one" is the Messiah whose arrival will not be delayed.[36] It seems clear, at least, that the author to the Hebrews read the Greek text this way: in his application of the quotation, "the coming one" is Jesus the Messiah. He might have been influenced to make this identification by the use of "the coming one" to refer to Jesus in early Christianity (Matt 11:3; 21:9; 23:39; Luke 7:19, 20; John 1:15, 27; 12:13; Rev 1:4).

On another textual issue, our author differs from both the Hebrew and the Greek. In both these traditions (and in all the known texts of Habakkuk), the order of the lines in verse 4 moves from condemnation of the wicked—"the one whose soul is puffed up is not upright"—to exhortation of the righteous—"but the one who is righteous will live by his faith/faithfulness." The author of Hebrews reverses this order, accomplishing two things. First, he eliminates the possibility that someone might read the warning about "drawing back"[37] in the LXX as applying to the "vision" (as in the NETS translation) or to "the coming one." This language must now apply to the subject introduced in verse 38a, "my righteous one." Second, the reversal of the lines enables the author to end his quotation with a word of warning, fitting with the rhetoric that has dominated his sermon.

Nevertheless, the point from the Habbakuk quotation that will dominate our author's focus throughout chapter 11 is "faith." I have consistently given the alternate translations "faith" and "faithfulness" for this word throughout my discussion of the textual issue above. Keeping these options before us was important to understand all the options. However, I prefer to translate "faith." To be sure, this word (Heb. אֱמוּנָה) is only infrequently used to depict human response to God (1 Sam 26:23; 2 Chr 19:9; 31:12; Ps 37:3) and generally means to be "faithful." But the cognate verb (particularly in the *hiphil*) is used more often to depict a person's acceptance of God's words and promises and trust in and reliance upon him (Gen 15:6; Exod 14:31; Num 20:12; 2 Chr 20:20; Ps 116:10; etc.). This best captures the nuance our author intends (see further on 11:1).

10:39 But we are not among those who shrink back and are ultimately destroyed but among those who have faith and preserve their lives (ἡμεῖς δὲ οὐκ ἐσμὲν ὑποστολῆς εἰς ἀπώλειαν ἀλλὰ πίστεως εἰς περιποίησιν ψυχῆς). The author once again quickly shifts from warning (v. 38b) to assurance. While the author warns against "shrinking back" (ὑποστείληται in v. 38b), he is confident that he and his readers (ἡμεῖς, "we")[38] are "not among those who shrink back [ὑποστολῆς]." The genitive form of this word, along with the parallel "of faith" (πίστεως), probably depends on an understood "sons" (υἱοί) or "children" (τέκνα)—a common way in Scripture to denote people characterized by a certain feature (see, e.g., Matt 13:38; 23:15; Luke 16:8; John 12:36; 17:12; Acts 4:36; 13:10; Eph

---

36. Most interpreters think such a messianic allusion in the LXX is likely. Some, however, doubt it (Koester, *Hebrews*, 467; Rikk E. Watts, "'For I Am Not Ashamed of the Gospel': Romans 1:16–17 and Habakkuk 2:4," in *Romans and the People of God: Essays in Honor of Gordon D. Fee on the Occasion of His 65th Birthday*, ed. S. Soderlund and N. T. Wright [Grand Rapids: Eerdmans, 1999], 9–10).

37. "Drawing back" or "shrinking back" translates ὑποστείληται, from ὑποστέλλω. The verb occurs only three other times in the NT (Acts 20:20, 27; Gal 2:12). In the middle voice, as here, the meaning is "shrink back" ("ὑποστέλλω," BDAG 1041, §2.a).

38. As Lane notes, the pronoun is "doubly emphatic"—both by occurrence and by position (*Hebrews*, 2:278).

2:2; 5:6; 1 Thess 5:5; 2 Thess 2:3). Those who are characterized by "shrinking back"—that is, those who commit apostasy, are doomed to destruction. The Greek word translated "destroyed" (ἀπώλεια) is regularly used in the New Testament to depict the ultimate fate of those who do not embrace the gospel (Matt 7:13; John 17:12; Rom 9:22; Phil 1:28; 3:19; 2 Thess 2:3; 1 Tim 6:9; 2 Pet 2:1, 3; 3:7, 16; Rev 17:8, 11; cf. also the cognate verb ἀπόλλυμι). While some have taken this language to suggest annihilation as the ultimate fate of the wicked, the language probably should not be taken in such a literal sense.

In contrast to those who "shrink back" are those who are characterized by the "faith" that Habakkuk refers to. Their destiny (indicated by εἰς) is the "preservation of their lives," which, with most translations, is best rendered in a verbal clause: "preserve their lives"; cf. NIV, CSB: "are saved," NAB: "possess life." "Lives" translates a word often translated "soul" (ψυχή). Several versions favor the latter rendering (e.g., ESV; NLT; NASB; NET; NJB). However, ψυχή (under the influence of Hebrew נֶפֶשׁ) often refers simply to a person or "life" in general—and this might be the case here (see NIV; NRSV; CSB; NAB; CEB puts it strongly: "our whole beings are preserved"). The decision here is a difficult one, since the author is clearly referring to a spiritual, not a physical, "preservation," and "soul" may better communicate this idea.[39]

Theology in Application

Readers of Hebrews are often interested in answering the question, "Does the letter teach that a Christian can lose their salvation?" Asking this question is certainly not inappropriate: answering it contributes to our understanding of biblical soteriology and can have important pastoral implications. However, the question the author really wants us to ponder is the reverse of this one: "What does the letter teach about how a Christian can keep their salvation?" The entire argument of the letter is focused on answering this question. But in 10:32–39, the author draws attention to two key means of preserving our spiritual status and vitality: perseverance and faith. These two will dominate the conclusion of the author's sermon, and I will say a lot more about these in the rest of the commentary. Here I draw attention to another means of spiritual vitality the author mentions in this context: memory.

The author begins this paragraph on this note, asking his readers to "remember the days . . . after you were enlightened" (v. 32). They demonstrated the reality of this transformation in a willingness to suffer for their new faith (vv. 32b–34). The author suggests that their remembering of this initial enthusiasm will help them hold on to the "confidence" about their spiritual status and prospects that they now need to have. To "remember" an experience is to do more than mentally recall something

---

39. Some interpreters argue that the author here has adopted a Hellenistic soteriology, one that focuses on inward and immaterial salvation rather than a wholistic salvation (e.g., Grässer, *An die Hebräer*, 3:83). But this is a serious overreading of this text. Even if "soul" is the best translation in English, there is no suggestion that the rest of the person is ignored in salvation.

that we might be in danger of forgetting. As Simon Schama argues in his wonderful book *Landscape and Memory*, "remembering" in its deepest sense means allowing past experiences, which imprint themselves on our minds, to form our thinking and perspectives.[40] All of us have had such experiences of the power of memory. On the flight home after our honeymoon, my wife, Jenny, and I listened to Rachmaninoff's *First Piano Concerto*. Fifty years, five houses, five children, and thirteen grandchildren later, I still cannot hear that piece of music without seeing, in my mind's eye, the Rocky Mountains beneath me, and sensing my wife in the seat beside me, our life together before us.

The writers of the Old Testament constantly urge the Israelites to remember God's great acts of salvation for his people. Neither the writer of Hebrews nor the readers addressed were present to witness those events. Nevertheless, they have become imprinted in the memories of the people, and they need to bring them to mind as a means of maintaining their faithfulness. The best known act of "remembering" in Scripture is the way Christians are called on to eat the bread and drink the wine of the Eucharist "in remembrance of me." So also our author encourages us to "remember" our early days of spiritual passion as a means of keeping ourselves in the faith.

---

40. Simon Schama, *Landscape and Memory* (New York: Alfred A. Knopf, 1995).

CHAPTER 26

Hebrews 11:1–7

Literary Context

The celebration of the "heroes of the faith" in chapter 11 is an obviously discrete stage in the author's sermon. The passage is marked by repeated references to "faith": the verb (πιστεύω, "believe") occurs only once (v. 6), but the noun (πίστις, "faith") appears twenty-four times, eighteen of them at the beginning of sentences in the dative case: "by faith . . . by faith . . . by faith." The author thereby creates a powerfully effective rhetorical emphasis, one that would have been especially striking as the letter was read out in a gathering of believers.

The author signals the beginning and end of his panegyric with similarly worded claims about the "ancients" being commended for their faith:

> 11:2 "This [faith, πίστις, in v. 1] is what the ancients [οἱ πρεσβύτεροι] were commended for [ἐμαρτυρήθησαν]"
> 11:39 "These were all commended [μαρτυρηθέντες] for their faith [διὰ τῆς πίστεως]"

Between these general assertions, the author moves in general chronological order through Old Testament and Second Temple Jewish history:

creation (v. 3)—Genesis 1–2
Abel (v. 4)—Genesis 4
Enoch (vv. 5[–6])—Genesis 5:21–24
Noah (v. 7)—Genesis 6–9
Abraham (and Sarah) (vv. 8–12, 17–19)—Genesis 12–25
Isaac (v. 20)—Genesis 25–26
Jacob (v. 21)—Genesis 27–49
Joseph (v. 22)—Genesis 50
Moses (vv. 23–28)—Exodus 1–13
Israelites (at the Red Sea) (v. 29)—Exodus 14

Israelites (at Jericho) (v. 30)—Joshua 6
Rahab (v. 31)—Joshua 2; 6
judges and prophets (vv. 32–34)
faithful women and martyrs (vv. 35–38)

An obvious dividing point occurs at verse 32, where the drumbeat of "by faith" ceases, to be replaced by a brief overview of later Israelite history and the exploits of judges, prophets, faithful women, and Maccabean-era martyrs.

The first part of the chapter thus falls into five parts: after a brief "definition" of faith (vv. 1–2), the author quickly moves through Israelite history: creation (v. 3), the antediluvian period (vv. 4–7), the patriarchs (especially Abraham) (vv. 8–22), and Moses and the events of the exodus (vv. 23–31). The author's rhetorical strategy is clear: "rapidly listing examples impresses upon listeners the breadth of material that supports the author's point."[1]

Similar lists of people commended for their exemplary lives are found in Second Temple Judaism (e.g., 1 Macc 2:51–60; Wis 10; Sir 44–50; Philo, *Rewards* 11–14; 4 Macc. 16.18–23), the New Testament (e.g., Acts 7), and early Christianity (1 Clem. 17–19).[2] The author has made use of this standard literary form to highlight the indispensable role of faith for those who would be saved and not "shrink back" and be destroyed (10:39). "Faith" plays an instrumental role in the chapter. The focus is not so much on what faith *is* but on what faith *does*.

This celebration of the many saints who exhibited faith in God throughout Israelite history must be set alongside the strongly negative portrayal of Israel in 3:7–4:11, which focuses on a certain moment in Israel's history: the people's failure to "believe" when they were invited to enter into the land of promise. This failure to believe becomes a sad pattern in Israel's history—a pattern that God now invites his people to leave behind by embracing his new invitation to "enter." At the same time, it is important to recognize that the blessings achieved by this faith fall short of what God has ultimately promised his people. These Old Testament saints were looking ahead, not yet having received what ultimately was promised to them by God (vv. 13, 39). Only in tandem with the new-covenant people of God, created in and through Christ's sacrificial work, is this ultimate promise attained (v. 40). Therefore, while

---

1. Koester, *Hebrews*, 470.
2. Johnson (*Hebrews*, 310–12) provides a good overview; see, in more detail, Richardson, *Pioneer and Perfecter of Faith*, 144–59. The lists closest to Heb 11 are 1 Clem. 17–19 (Mary Rose D'Angelo, *Moses in the Letter to the Hebrews*, SBLDS 42 [Missoula, MT: Scholars Press, 1979], 19–24), and Wis 10 and Sir 44–50 (Grässer, *An die Hebräer*, 3:870). There is no reason to think that the author has used a preexisting source as his basis for this passage (Grässer, *An die Hebräer*, 3:88–90; Cockerill, *Hebrews*, 516–17; contra Weiss, *Der Brief an die Hebräer*, 554–58; Attridge, *Hebrews*, 306–7). See also, on these lists of examples, Michael R. Cosby, *The Rhetorical Composition and Function of Hebrews 11 in Light of Example Lists in Antiquity* (Mercer, GA: Mercer University Press, 1988); Pamela Eisenbaum, *The Jewish Heroes of Christian History: Hebrews 11 in Literary Context*, SBLDS 156 (Atlanta: Scholars Press, 1997).

the author does not explicitly link "faith" with Christ in the way, say, Paul does,[3] he nevertheless in his own way makes clear that faith achieves its ultimate goal only as it is linked with the new-covenant promises of God in Christ.[4]

> I. The Exalted Son and a Rest for the People of God (1:1–4:13)
> II. Our Great High Priest and His Ministry (4:14–10:31)
> **III. Exhortation: Follow and Serve the Pioneer of Our Faith through Endurance and Faith (10:32–13:25)**
>   A. Introductory Call to Endurance and Faith (10:32–39)
>   B. The Nature and Power of Faith Illustrated in Salvation History (11:1–40)
>   → **1. The Ancients Commended for the Faith That Sees the Unseen (11:1–7)**
>   2. Faith in the Patriarchal Era (11:8–22)
>   3. Faith in the Era of the Exodus and Conquest (11:23–31)
>   4. The Faith of Judges, Prophets, Women, and Martyrs (11:32–38)
>   5. The Ancients Commended for Faith That Looks to the Future (11:39–40)
>   C. Run the Race with Endurance, Remembering That You Are Children of God (12:1–17)
>   D. Coming to Mount Zion and Inheriting the Unshakable Kingdom (12:18–29)
>   E. Letter Closing (13:1–25)

Main Idea

Those who exercise biblical faith have assurance that what God has promised will come to pass and things that cannot now be seen are, in fact, real. This kind of faith was exemplified by many of the people of God in the Old Testament, including Abel, Enoch, and Noah.

---

3. Unlike Paul, who frequently makes "Christ" (or some such title) the object of the verb "believe" or the noun "faith," the author of Hebrews never does so. See the "In Depth" section on faith in Hebrews below.

4. Contra, e.g., Hays, who suggests that ch. 11 might imply that the author views the people of Israel, after Christ's coming, as still belonging to the people of God ("'Here We Have No Lasting City,'" 151–73). (Markus Bockmuehl, similarly, suggests that ch. 11 reveals that the author is not as supersessionist as many think: "Abraham's Faith in Hebrews 11," in Bauckham et al., *Epistle to the Hebrews*, 365–69.) Filtvedt, e.g., rightly challenges this view (*Identity of God's People*, 219–20).

Translation

Hebrews 11:1-7

1a	development	Now
1b	assertion	**faith gives us confidence**
1c	description	in what we hope for
1d	parallel	and **assures us of the reality**
1e	reference	of things that are not seen.
2a	cause	It is because of this faith that
2b	predicate (of 2a)	**the people of old received commendation.**
3a	means	By faith
3b	assertion	**we understand**
3c	object (of 3b)	that the ages of the world were created
3d	means	by the word of God,
3e	result	so that what is seen did not originate
3f	source	from what is seen.
4a	means	By faith
4b	assertion	**Abel offered a better sacrifice**
4c	comparison	than Cain
4d	indirect object	to God; and
4e	cause	because of it,
4f	response	it was testified
4g	content	that he was righteous,
4h	expansion (of 4f)	God offering this testimony
4i	basis	on the basis of his gifts. And
4j	means	through his gift,
4k	contra-expectation	though dead,
4l	assertion	he yet speaks.
5a	means	By faith
5b	assertion	**Enoch was taken up**
5c	result	so that he did not see death;
5d	verification	"he was not found
5e	cause	because God had taken him." (Gen 5:24)
5f	time	Before he was taken up,
5g	assertion	**it was testified**
5h	content	that he was pleasing
5i	reference	to God.
6a	separation	Without faith
6b	assertion	**it is impossible to please God.**
6c	explanation (of 6a–b)	For

Continued on next page.

6d	assertion	**it is necessary ...**	
6e	subject (of 6f)	for the one who draws near to God	
6f	content (of 6d)	**... to believe**	
6g	content	that he is and	
6h	parallel	that he is a rewarder of those who seek him.	
7a	means	By faith	
7b	assertion	**Noah, ...**	
7c	circumstance	having been warned	
7d	content	about things not yet seen,	
7e	basis (of 7f)	in reverent fear	
7f	predicate (of 7b)	**... built an ark**	
7g	purpose	for the salvation of his house.	
7h	means	Through this he	condemned the world and
7i	parallel		became an heir
7j	content		of the righteousness
7k	standard		according to faith.

Structure

I have already noted that verses 1–2—sharing with the concluding verses, 11:39–40, the theme of the ancients "commended" for faith—stand out as the introduction to the whole series. Verse 3 begins with "by faith" (πίστει), the same form of the word (or phrase in English) that introduces most of the examples of faith in the following series. This similarity suggests verse 3 should be attached to what follows. On the other hand, verse 3 differs from those that follow in having the author and his hearers as the subject of the verse—"we"—rather than a figure from Old Testament history. Moreover, belief that the existing universe arose from what is "unseen" closely matches the characterization of faith in verse 1. I tentatively conclude, then, that verse 3 goes a bit more closely with what precedes than with what follows.[5] Verses 4–7 move in a different direction, initiating the series of commendations of Old Testament "heroes of the faith." However, we can detect framing between verses 1–3 and verses 4–7: both texts focus on the ability of faith to look beyond "what is seen" (βλεπομένων in both vv. 1 and 7); both refer to people being "commended" for their faith (the verb translated "commend" [μαρτυρέω] occurs in vv. 2, 4 [twice], and 5 and not again until v. 39). While, then, verses 4–7 are closely related to what follows, it is not inappropriate to consider them here with verses 1–3.

---

5. The RSV, followed by NRSV and ESV, puts a paragraph break between vv. 3 and 4. Other versions (e.g., NIV; CSB; CEB) put v. 3 in its own paragraph. See, for this structure, Weiss, *Der Brief an die Hebräer*, 559; D. Harris, *Hebrews*, 297; Lane, *Hebrews*, 2:330.

Exegetical Outline

→ **1. The Ancients Commended for the Faith That Sees the Unseen (11:1–7)**
   a. Introductory Characterization of Faith (v. 1)
   b. Introductory Commendation of the "Ancients" for Their Faith (v. 2)
   c. Illustration of Faith's Ability to Penetrate beyond What Is Seen (v. 3)
   d. Commendation of Three Antediluvian Figures for Their Faith (vv. 4–7)

Explanation of the Text

11:1 Now faith gives us confidence in what we hope for and assures us of the reality of things that are not seen (Ἔστιν δὲ πίστις ἐλπιζομένων ὑπόστασις, πραγμάτων ἔλεγχος οὐ βλεπομένων). Faith has both a "forward" look and an "upward" look. This famous "definition" of faith is, in fact, probably not a definition. The author does not focus on what faith *is* so much as on what faith *does*.[6] The author's purpose here and throughout the chapter is to highlight the spiritual benefits, enjoyed both now and in the future, that faith secures for us. The author extensively develops the point he has made in 10:38–39: the righteous "live by faith" (Hab 2:4); it is faith that secures final salvation.

The first characteristic of faith in the verse is its provision of "confidence in what we hope for." The word I translate "confidence" (ὑπόστασις) has a broad scope of meaning, making it difficult to decide just what nuance it might have here. It occurs twenty times in the LXX, translating twelve different Hebrew words. The author uses it elsewhere in 1:3 and 3:14, where I argue it probably means "inner nature" or "essence." Most scholars argue for a meaning something like this here in 11:1 also (cf. KJV "substance"; CSB and CEB "reality"). They claim that the word refers to an "objective" reality: as Johnson puts it, "Faith . . . makes actual, or makes 'real,' for the believers things that are hoped for, as though they were present."[7] However, English translations suggest another option: the more subjective sense of "confidence" (NIV) or "assurance" (RSV; NRSV; ESV; see "being sure" in NET). There is some doubt about whether the word can have this more subjective nuance,[8] but it *may* have this sense in two of its other New Testament occurrences (2 Cor 9:4; 11:17), and Schreiner is right to argue that the current context strongly favors this subjective meaning. Faith does not "make actual" what is future; it assures the believer that those things will indeed come to pass.[9] This

---

6. E.g., Westcott, *Hebrews*, 349; Ellingworth, *Hebrews*, 566–67; Massonnet, *L'Épître aux Hébreux*, 312; S. M. Baugh, "The Cloud of Witnesses in Hebrews 11," *WTJ* 68 (2006): 119. Even though it is not technically a definition, the lack of articles in the verse is typical of what may generally be labeled "definitional style" (Weiss, *Der Brief an die Hebräer*, 559).

7. Johnson, *Hebrews*, 278 (he prefers the sense "pledge," "down payment"). For this objective direction in interpretation, see also, e.g., Cockerill, *Hebrews*, 520–21; Lane, *Hebrews*,

2:326; Backhaus, *Der Hebräerbrief*, 383; Bénétrau, *L'Épître aux Hébreux*, 2:125–26.

8. "ὑπόστασις," BDAG 1041, §3 (in a change from the earlier edition, they now comment that "the sense 'confidence,' 'assurance' . . . must be eliminated, since examples of it cannot be found").

9. Schreiner, *Hebrews*, 339. As possible instances of this meaning, see also Ps 39:7 [38:8 LXX] and Ezek 19:5. Note Ellingworth's comment: "it is difficult to give meaning to faith

forward-looking aspect of faith is frequently singled out in the commendations that follow: Noah based his actions on "things not yet seen" (v. 7); Abraham was "looking forward to the city that has foundations" (v. 10); he and other faithful Israelites were "seeking a homeland" (v. 14); Isaac blessed Jacob "with regard to things to come" (v. 20); Joseph looked forward to the exodus (v. 22); Moses, in faith, was looking forward to his reward (v. 26). In his general description in verse 6, the author includes belief that God is "a rewarder of those who seek him." And in his final comment on the people he has commended in the chapter, the author claims they could not attain what was ultimately promised them until they were perfected along with new-covenant believers (vv. 39–40). Westcott claims that "things which in the succession of time are still 'hoped for' as future have a true existence in the eternal order; and this existence Faith brings home to the believer as a real fact."[10]

At the same time, the author also commends the ancients for a faith that looks beyond the visible world to the invisible spiritual realities beyond this world. Christians believe that the visible universe came into being out of the invisible (v. 3); Moses "persevered because he saw him who is invisible" (v. 27); and, in general, all these heroes of the faith exhibited a bedrock conviction that, as verse 6 puts it, knowing God means believing "that he exists and that he rewards those who earnestly seek him." The author, therefore, celebrates both the "forward" look of faith and the "upward" look of faith. These two perspectives are briefly stated in verse 1, the "forward look" in verse 1a and the "upward look" in verse 1b: "Faith . . . is the conviction about things not seen."[11] Indeed, this is sometimes disputed, as it is argued that "things not seen" is essentially equivalent to "things hoped for": i.e., "things not *yet* seen."[12] However, in light of the concern with the "upward" look we have noted in this chapter, it is better to see the second part of the verse as making a distinct, though related point, with regard to verse 1a. The author's choice to use the word ἔλεγχος to signify this act of convicting is somewhat puzzling: although not used elsewhere in the New Testament,[13] the word occurs in the LXX, Philo, and Josephus, almost always with the negative connotation of "reproof" or "rebuke." The cognate verb, used seventeen times in the New Testament, similarly always has the negative sense of "rebuking," "convicting of doing wrong." There are, however, a few instances of a more neutral meaning, but again many interpreters insist that the word must have the objective sense of "proof" or "test."[14] However, again, a more subjective sense of the word is attested and makes good sense here: faith convicts those who possess it of the reality of the unseen realm—a realm that transcends and gives ultimate meaning and direction to believers.[15] This almost universal negative slant to the word suggests that the author hints at the need for people of faith to be "convicted" of their tendency to unbelief even as their faith positively convicts them about the reality of the unseen spiritual realm.

---

as constituting or even creating substance in things hoped for" (*Hebrews*, 565).

10. Westcott, *Hebrews*, 351.

11. See, e.g., Weiss, *Der Brief an die Hebräer*, 560.

12. E.g., Lane, *Hebrews*, 2:329; Easter, *Faith and the Faithfulness of Jesus*, 89. The reluctance to find in v. 1b a reference to the unseen spiritual realm appears at times to be a reaction to a Middle Platonic reading of Hebrews (suggested here by, e.g., Attridge, *Hebrews*, 311, and Thompson, *Hebrews*, 231). But one does not have to embrace a full-fledged Middle Platonic interpretation of the letter to find reference to the thoroughly biblical notion of an unseen spiritual realm.

13. The noun is found in a variant reading in 2 Tim 3:16.

14. E.g., Attridge, *Hebrews*, 310; Lane, *Hebrews*, 2:326; Michel, *Der Brief an die Hebräer*, 373. Attridge cites Epictetus *Diatr.* 3.10.11 for the neutral sense of proof or test: "here is the proof [ἔλεγχος] of the matter, the test of the philosopher."

15. Bruce, *Hebrews*, 277; Schreiner, *Hebrews*, 340; F. Büchsel, "ἐλέγχω," *TDNT* 2:474. Contra the majority of scholars, who argue for the more objective "proof" or "evidence."

11:2 It is because of this faith that the people of old received commendation (ἐν ταύτῃ γὰρ ἐμαρτυρήθησαν οἱ πρεσβύτεροι). As I noted above, this verse is the "heading" for what follows, and it acts, together with verse 39, as a frame around the list of people who exemplified faith and were rewarded for it. The verse does not develop or provide a basis for verse 1, so translating the connecting word as "for" (the Greek is γάρ) is not the best option (contra, e.g., RSV; ESV; NET; CSB). The word appears to be used simply to create a transition into a new point; perhaps the best way to capture the sense in English is to not translate the word at all (see NIV; NLT; CEB).[16] "People of old" translates a word that means "old ones" or "elders" (πρεσβύτεροι) and in this kind of context refers to "a person who has lived in ancient times, that is to say, at a point long before the point of time of the discourse itself."[17] It is because of their faith[18]—the faith characterized in verse 1—that these people of old received a commendation from the Lord. The idea of commendation or approval (the language used in most of the translations) captures the passive voice of the verb μαρτυρέω, "witness," "testify." "Were witnessed to" or "were testified about" is not natural English, so we have to resort to these other verbal roots to try to bring out the meaning in English. This passive use of the verb occurs also in Hebrews 7:8, 17; 11:4, 5, 39—all with reference to the "testimony" of Scripture.

11:3 By faith we understand that the ages of the world were created by the word of God, so that what is seen did not originate from what is seen (Πίστει νοοῦμεν κατηρτίσθαι τοὺς αἰῶνας ῥήματι θεοῦ, εἰς τὸ μὴ ἐκ φαινομένων τὸ βλεπόμενον γεγονέναι). The conviction that God created the universe out of nothing is a product of faith. The phrase "by faith" (the dative πίστει in an instrumental sense)[19] at the beginning of this verse inaugurates a series of eighteen such occurrences in this chapter, extending right through verse 31. This outstanding example of anaphora (a series of statements that begin the same way) would have made a strong impression on the people to whom this text was read.[20] The similarity between verse 3 and these many following verses naturally suggests that the verse should be attached to what follows. However, the verse also differs from the following examples in having as its subject not one of the "people of old" (v. 2) but rather our author and his readers—"we." The focus in this verse on finding the ultimate origin of the universe in things not seen also appears to connect closely with verse 1.[21] Verse 3, then, is transitional.[22]

It is by faith, then, that we understand "the ages of the world were created[23] by the word of God." "Ages of the world" translates a word (αἰῶνας) that, as we noted in our comments on 1:2, combines the temporal with the spatial.[24] The focus here is clearly on the spatial, so "universe" (as in many

---

16. On the wide range of functions for γάρ in Hebrews, see the note on 2:10.

17. "πρεσβύτερος," L&N 67.27.

18. The ἐν before ταύτῃ (which itself refers to πίστις) is often given an instrumental force (note that most English translations render "by" or "through"). Ellingworth, however, might be right to identify this as a place where the preposition moves toward a causal meaning (*Hebrews*, 567; see NAB: "because of it"; on the causal use of ἐν, see, e.g., M. Harris, *Prepositions*, 120).

19. I favor the instrumental sense here (with, e.g., D. Harris, *Hebrews*, 299) over the causal (see Grässer, *An die Hebräer*, 3:110).

20. Michael R. Cosby, "The Rhetorical Composition of Hebrews 11," *JBL* 107 (1988): 259–61.

21. Lane, *Hebrews*, 2:330; Hagner, *Hebrews*, 181.

22. Massonnet, *L'Épître aux Hébreux*, 316.

23. The author does not use the usual word for "create" (κτίζω), but καταρτίζω, "prepare," "restore." "Create," however, is within its semantic range (see BDAG 526, §2.a).

24. I quoted in those comments Adams's description of the word: "the physical cosmos, with the plural perhaps laying emphasis on the succession of eras allotted to it" ("Cosmology of Hebrews," 125).

versions) is probably accurate enough. The result[25] of God's creation by means of his word alone is that "what is seen did not originate from what is seen." The translation of this clause is debated, the issue being what the particle "not" (μή) negates. Its placement could suggest that it modifies "from the things that appear" (ἐκ φαινομένων): "that which is seen came from those things that do **not** appear."[26] However, it could also negate the whole clause: "that which is seen did **not** come from those things that appear."[27] The latter may be preferable, but the difference between them is small. This text may support the traditional orthodox view labeled "creation ex nihilo"—that is, the belief that God created the universe "out of nothing."[28] Most commentators doubt this, however, pointing out that the author claims only that things that now appear were not created from what can be *seen*.[29] However, the author appears to be using "seeing" in this verse to refer more broadly to whatever can be perceived by the senses—so I think a reference to creation ex nihilo may be suggested. The author's decision to lead off his discussion of faith with this example suggests its importance. As Johnson writes, "This is the most fundamental of insights, the one that distinguishes believers and atheists: this sensory world is not self-contained, self-derived, or self-sufficient, but derives from a power greater than itself, which remains inaccessible to the senses, even as it brings forth everything that the senses encounter."[30]

11:4 By faith Abel offered a better sacrifice than Cain to God; and because of it, it was testified that he was righteous, God offering this testimony on the basis of his gifts. And through his gift, though dead, he yet speaks (Πίστει πλείονα θυσίαν Ἄβελ παρὰ Κάϊν προσήνεγκεν τῷ θεῷ, δι' ἧς ἐμαρτυρήθη εἶναι δίκαιος, μαρτυροῦντος ἐπὶ τοῖς δώροις αὐτοῦ τοῦ θεοῦ, καὶ δι' αὐτῆς ἀποθανὼν ἔτι λαλεῖ). The author now moves into his celebration of the faith of Old Testament and Jewish personages. He begins with the antediluvian ("pre-flood") period, mentioning Abel, Enoch, and Noah. As is typical of the passage as a whole, reference to an example of faith is introduced without the use of any conjunction ("asyndeton"; see also vv. 5, 7, 8, 9, 17, 23, 24, 27, 28, 29, 30, 31). This pattern enhances the sense of repetition. Abel's faith is expressed in the sacrifice he offered—one "better" than the one Cain offered (Gen 4:2b–5). Interpreters have speculated for centuries about what made Abel's sacrifice superior to Cain's; Lane surveys seven popular options in his commentary.[31] Clearly what is important to the author of Hebrews is the faith that accompanied Abel's sacrificial offering. Because of the prominence of faith throughout the chapter, most interpreters think the antecedent of the relative pronoun ἧς ("it" in the prepositional phrase "because of it") is faith.[32] However, the closer antecedent is "sacrifice" (θυσίαν), and it is Abel's sacrifice that the Old Testament commends him for and that the author emphasizes again in

---

25. The construction εἰς τό + infinitive indicates result (Zerwick, *Biblical Greek*, §352). However, it is true that this construction normally indicates purpose in Hebrews (2:17; 7:25; 8:3; 9:14, 28; 12:10; 13:21).

26. Ellingworth, *Hebrews*, 569; Koester, *Hebrews*, 300. See, e.g., NET: "so that the visible has its origins in the invisible" (see also RSV; NRSV; CSB; CEB; NAB; NJB).

27. Most commentators take this view, noting that the placement of the negative particle μή (immediately preceding ἐκ φαινομένων ["from the things that appear"]) does not mean it cannot modify the whole clause (see, e.g., BDF §433.3; Turner, *Syntax*, 287). See, e.g., NIV; ESV.

28. See esp. P. Hughes, *Hebrews*, 443–52; and also Bruce, *Hebrews*, 279–80.

29. E.g., Grässer, *An die Hebräer*, 3:103.

30. Johnson, *Hebrews*, 280.

31. Lane, *Hebrews*, 2:333–34. See also Walter R. Moberly, "Exemplars of Faith in Hebrews 11: Abel," in Bauckham et al., *Epistle to the Hebrews*, 353–63.

32. E.g., Ellingworth, *Hebrews*, 572.

the following clause: "God offering this testimony on the basis of his gifts."[33] More likely, then, the author is claiming that Abel was commended as righteous by God for his faith-generated sacrifice.[34] It is by means of, or because of,[35] this sacrifice that "it was testified that he was righteous." "Testify" translates a word that we have already seen in verse 2 (μαρτυρέω), which, when used in the passive voice, translates awkwardly into English: in verse 2, I translated it as "received commendation." Despite the fact that the Old Testament does not label Abel as "righteous," the testimony is probably that of the Scriptures: it is a fair summary of Genesis 4:4b, which says that "the Lord looked with favor on Abel and his offering."[36]

The author adds that "through his gift, though dead, he yet speaks." Both the source and the content of this "speaking" are uncertain. However, the language of "testimony" or "witness" in the verse points to the Scriptures as the source of Abel's voice: his faith-generated sacrifice stands attested in the word.[37] Some interpreters think that the content of Abel's speaking is a cry for vengeance: see Genesis 4:10b, where the Lord addresses Cain: "Listen! Your brother's blood cries out to me from the ground."[38] And see also Matthew 23:35: "and so upon you will come all the righteous blood that has been shed on earth, from the blood of righteous Abel to the blood of Zechariah son of Berekiah, whom you murdered between the temple and the altar." Another option is to think Abel "speaks" through the intercessory power of his blood, an option grounded in Hebrews 12:24, which claims that new-covenant believers have come "to Jesus the mediator of a new covenant, and to the sprinkled blood that speaks a better word than the blood of Abel."[39] However, the nature of our author's appeal to Abel in this context suggests rather that Abel, though dead,[40] continues to speak in Scripture a word of encouragement and exhortation to the people of God.[41]

11:5 By faith Enoch was taken up so that he did not see death; "he was not found because God had taken him."[42] Before he was taken up, it was testified that he was pleasing to God (Πίστει Ἐνὼχ μετετέθη τοῦ μὴ ἰδεῖν θάνατον, καὶ οὐχ ηὑρίσκετο διότι μετέθηκεν αὐτὸν ὁ θεός. πρὸ γὰρ τῆς μεταθέσεως μεμαρτύρηται εὐαρεστηκέναι τῷ θεῷ). The second exemplar of faith from the pre-flood era mentioned by the author is Enoch. He is given only four verses in Genesis 5 (vv. 21–24), sandwiched among the descendants of Adam. Despite the brief mention, Second Temple Judaism

---

33. As the text is printed in the NA[28], the clause is a genitive absolute, with θεοῦ as the subject and μαρτυροῦντος as the verb. An alternative text reads the dative θεῷ (ℵ A D* 33. 326); if this text is adopted, the subject would be αὐτοῦ (perhaps referring to Abel) and θεῷ would be the indirect object: "he was testifying to God on the basis of his gifts." The NA[28] text, however, should probably be adopted (see 𝔓[13] 𝔓[46] ℵ[2] D[1] K L P Ψ, etc).

34. See, e.g., Westcott, *Hebrews*, 356; Cockerill, *Hebrews*, 527.

35. The preposition διά with the genitive sometimes moves from an instrumental force (usual with this combination) to a causal force (e.g., M. Harris, *Prepositions*, 72–73), and this may be a case in point.

36. Jesus refers to "righteous Abel" in Matt 23:35, John claims that Abel's actions were "righteous" (1 John 3:12), and some Jewish texts use "righteous" language to describe Abel; e.g., Josephus claims that he "had regard for righteousness [δικαιοσύνη]" (*Ant.* 1.53).

37. E.g., Lane, *Hebrews*, 2:335; Cockerill, *Hebrews*, 528.

38. Bruce, *Hebrews*, 283–84; Ellingworth, *Hebrews*, 573.

39. Attridge, *Hebrews*, 317.

40. The participle ἀποθανών is concessive (Zerwick and Grosvenor, *Grammatical Analysis*, 279).

41. Bénétrau, *L'Épître aux Hébreux*, 2:130; Lane, *Hebrews*, 2:335.

42. This clause is introduced with a καί, which signals a close connection with the preceding sentence (see, e.g., Runge, *Discourse Grammar*, 23–26). In this case, the relationship is best communicated in English with no conjunction (see NLT; CSB).

devoted a lot of attention to Enoch: the enigmatic claim that "he was no more, because God took him away" proved an irresistible starting point to all kinds of speculation. Our author, however, shows no interest in these speculations.[43] He is interested only in the biblical testimony to Enoch's faithful walking with God (mentioned in both Gen 5:22 and 24), which the author paraphrases as "pleasing to God." The author, in keeping with the theme of the chapter, further summarizes this faithful walking with God as a matter of faith. As is the case with Abel, the Old Testament does not itself use the language of faith to describe Enoch, but the word accurately captures the fundamental posture of Enoch toward God that enabled him to walk faithfully and to please God.

The author follows his Greek LXX source in the verb he uses to describe Enoch's being "taken up" (μετατίθημι).[44] In fact, as several versions note by the use of quotation marks, the middle sentence of the verse is a quotation from Genesis 5:24.[45] The result of this transfer to heaven is that Enoch did not experience death.[46] It is possible that the author deliberately contrasts two outcomes of faith: Abel suffers with temporal deliverance; Enoch is delivered from death.[47] The verse ends with a further "testimony" from Scripture (μεμαρτύρηται, "it was testified"), continuing the author's emphasis on this point in the opening verses of the chapter (v. 2 and twice in v. 4).

11:6 Without faith it is impossible to please God. For it is necessary for the one who draws near to God to believe that he is and that he is a rewarder of those who seek him (χωρὶς δὲ πίστεως ἀδύνατον εὐαρεστῆσαι· πιστεῦσαι γὰρ δεῖ τὸν προσερχόμενον τῷ θεῷ ὅτι ἔστιν καὶ τοῖς ἐκζητοῦσιν αὐτὸν μισθαποδότης γίνεται). The author interrupts his series of commendations of faithful individuals to cite a general truth. His reason for adding this comment at this point is not clear, but it might be that the link to the context is the word "please" (εὐαρεστέω), which the author has just used to describe Enoch. Verses 5–6 would then form a kind of syllogism: one cannot please God without faith (v. 6); Enoch pleased God (v. 5b); therefore Enoch had faith (v. 5a).[48]

Faith is necessary if one is to live a life pleasing to God because it refers to the fundamental disposition of a person—their posture toward God. The author would agree with James: true faith, a disposition that orients the whole life toward God, produces works pleasing to God (Jas 2:14–26; see also Gal 5:6). In the second half of the verse, the author focuses on the "mental" or "intellectual" aspect of faith. Using language that we have seen often in Hebrews, he refers to "the one who draws near to God"—that is, the one who would experience a genuine and intimate relationship with God.[49] Faith for our author is much more than right thinking, but neither is it any less than

---

43. Ellingworth, *Hebrews*, 574. Ellingworth provides a quick overview of the relevant Jewish texts. Outside of Gen 5 and Heb 11, Enoch is mentioned in the Bible only in genealogies (1 Chr 1:3; Luke 3:37), as well as in Jude 14, where a prophecy from him (found in the Second Temple book 1 Enoch) is recorded.

44. The verb μετατίθημι means basically "transfer," "change" (see Heb 7:12). English versions rightly interpret the "transfer" referred to in Gen 5:21–24 as a transfer from this life to the next.

45. The author's Greek reproduces exactly the Greek of LXX MS A: καὶ εὐηρέστησεν Ενωχ τῷ θεῷ καὶ οὐχ ηὑρίσκετο, διότι [ὅτι in other MSS] μετέθηκεν αὐτὸν ὁ θεός. English versions that mark the quotation include NIV; NLT; NRSV; NAB; NASB.

46. The infinitive clause τοῦ μὴ ἰδεῖν could indicate purpose (Massonnet, *L'Épître aux Hébreux*, 320) but more likely indicates result (as most of the English versions take it; see, e.g., Lane, *Hebrews*, 2:327). As one might expect, Enoch's avoidance of death was regularly mentioned in Jewish literature.

47. Victor (Sung Yul) Rhee, "Chiasm and the Concept of Faith in Hebrews 11," *BSac* 155 (1998): 329–30; Cockerill, *Hebrews*, 526.

48. Ellingworth, *Hebrews*, 576; Cockerill (*Hebrews*, 530) thinks there might also be a reference to Abel.

49. Heb 4:16; 7:25; 10:1, 22; 12:18, 22.

right thinking. Believing that God "is" (ἔστιν) was taken for granted in the Old Testament, with the result that we do not often find texts that assert it. Exodus 3:14 is perhaps the closest: "God said to Moses, 'I AM WHO I AM.'" However, the meaning of the text is debated. A greater influence on the author was his own Greco-Roman environment, where, although certainly not widespread, there were those who denied the existence of any god altogether. It was Jewish responses to this atheism that probably influenced the author: see, for example, 4 Ezra 7.23, which refers to people who "even declared that the Most High does not exist."[50] A second element in the intellectual aspect of biblical faith is a conviction that God is "the rewarder" of those who seek him.[51] It is not clear why the author singles out this matter. However, in a general way, it adds a focus on God's character to the focus on God's existence. The author may also have an eye on his initial description of faith in verse 1. Belief that God exists corresponds to being assured of "the reality of things that are not seen," while belief that God rewards his followers corresponds to those things "we hope for."[52]

11:7 By faith Noah, having been warned about things not yet seen, in reverent fear built an ark for the salvation of his house. Through this he condemned the world and became an heir of the righteousness according to faith (Πίστει χρηματισθεὶς Νῶε περὶ τῶν μηδέπω βλεπομένων, εὐλαβηθεὶς κατεσκεύασεν κιβωτὸν εἰς σωτηρίαν τοῦ οἴκου αὐτοῦ δι' ἧς κατέκρινεν τὸν κόσμον, καὶ τῆς κατὰ πίστιν δικαιοσύνης ἐγένετο κληρονόμος). Noah is the third pre-flood figure that the author commends for his faith.[53] He circles back to verse 1 by focusing again on the way faith enables those who believe to focus on "things not yet seen" (τῶν μηδέπω βλεπομένων; see "things not seen" [οὐ βλεπομένων] in v. 1). Noah was "warned" about these things: in this case, God's prediction of a worldwide flood (Gen 6:6–7, 13, 17; 7:4). And in response to God's command, he "built"[54] an ark "for the salvation of his house."[55] The author hints at Noah's willing obedience to the Lord's command by claiming that he acted on the basis of "reverent fear" (εὐλαβηθείς).[56] This term, along with "by faith" in the opening of the verse, is the author's way of summarizing the Old Testament testimony about Noah: he was "a righteous [δίκαιος; see also 7:1] man, blameless among the people of his time"; he "walked faithfully with God" (Gen 6:9).[57] The LXX renders this last clause as "he was pleasing [εὐρέστησεν] to God." Noah, then, along with Enoch

---

50. See also Philo, *Creation* 170; 4 Macc. 5.24; Wis 13:1. Note also Heb 6:1, where "faith in God" is the first of the series of "elementary teachings."

51. "Rewarder" translates μισθαποδότης, a rare word (this is perhaps its first occurrence). The author uses the cognate μισθαποδοσία, "reward," "recompense," three times (2:2; 10:35; 11:26).

52. Grässer, *An die Hebräer*, 3:115; Cockerill, *Hebrews*, 531.

53. Noah is mentioned in the NT also in Matt 24:37–38; Luke 3:36; 17:26–27; 1 Pet 3:20; 2 Pet 2:5.

54. The Greek verb κατασκευάζω means, basically, "prepare," and is applied to a wide range of semantic situations, including the notion of "bringing a structure into being" (BDAG 527, §2; see Heb 3:3–4; 9:2, 6; 1 Pet 3:20 [also with reference to the ark]).

55. "Salvation" (σωτηρίαν) obviously has a physical reference; but there might be a slight spiritual allusion as well (Ellingworth, *Hebrews*, 579). Peter refers to the family of Noah being "saved" (διασῴζω, 1 Pet 3:20). "House" (οἴκου) refers to Noah's family (see the note on 3:2).

56. The verb εὐλαβέομαι occurs only here in the NT; on the meaning "reverent fear" for this word group, see the notes on 5:7 (where εὐλάβεια occurs). See also εὐλαβής (Luke 2:25; Acts 2:5; 8:2; 22:12); εὐλάβεια (Heb 5:7; 12:28).

57. Noah is often lauded as "righteous" in the OT and Jewish texts (Ezek 14:14, 20; Tob 4:12; Sir 44:17; Wis 10:4; Jub. 5.19; 10.17; 1QapGen 6.2; Philo, *Worse* 105; *Posterity* 48; Josephus, *Ant.* 1.74–75).

(Heb 11:5), can be identified as having faith because "without faith it is impossible to please God" (v. 6).

The author concludes his commendation of Noah with two assertions about the effect of his faith. First, "through this he condemned the world." The question is, what does "this" (ἧς) refer to: the ark, salvation, or faith?[58] Granted its importance in this context, the last is perhaps most likely, but ultimately the author may have in view "Noah's good example," as "a standing judgment on the wicked."[59] Second, Noah's faith and his faithful response to God's command means that he himself becomes "an heir of the righteousness according to faith."[60] Hebrews scholars regularly, and with some justification, protest about interpreting Hebrews in Pauline terms. They therefore insist that "righteousness according to faith" here is not the same as Paul's "righteousness by faith."[61] And it is true that the author does not appear elsewhere to use "righteousness" (δικαιοσύνη) to refer to a righteous status before God, which is the meaning of the word in Paul's phrase. However, the claim that Noah is an "heir" to righteousness points to the idea of status. The author's phrase may not, then, be that distant from the meaning of the language in Paul.[62]

Theology in Application

Faith, according to the author, gives us the ability to "see" things that cannot be seen (11:1). These unseen things may now exist or they may be promised future realities—the author, as I have argued, mentions both in verse 1. Thus, in this chapter, Moses, for example, persevered in the course God chose for him "because he saw him who is invisible" (v. 27); at the same time, he was willing to suffer disgrace for Christ because "he was looking ahead to his reward" (v. 26). This ability of faith to see the unseen bookends the passage we have just exposited (vv. 1, 7).

The importance of seeing the unseen is underscored throughout the New Testament. Paul famously reminds us that "we live by faith, not by sight" (2 Cor 5:7). A key word in Ephesians is "the heavenlies" (NIV "heavenly realms")—the unseen spiritual realm where we, as believers, have our true identity (1:3; 2:6) and where we daily fight a battle with evil spiritual forces (6:12; see also 1:20; 3:10). In Revelation, John is regularly given a vision of the spiritual reality that lies behind the battles we fight in this world. But the need for faithful Christians to see the unseen is especially prominent in Hebrews 11.

---

58. For the first, see Westcott, *Hebrews*, 356–57; for the second, Cockerill, *Hebrews*, 533; for the third, Ellingworth, *Hebrews*, 579; Koester, *Hebrews*, 477. Several versions translate "faith" (NIV; NET; NLT; CSB; CEB).

59. Ellingworth, *Hebrews*, 579.

60. Several commentators (e.g., Grässer, *An die Hebräer*, 3:119) and most English versions (implicitly, by not using a new subject with the second clause) suggest that this final clause is also dependent on δι' ἧς. However, it would be awkward, if the relative pronoun refers to faith, to repeat the word here ("according to faith").

61. E.g., Weiss, *Der Brief an die Hebräer*, 580–81.

62. E.g., Bénétrau, *L'Épître aux Hébreux*, 2:133.

We believers live inescapably in a world that bombards us with its own images, sounds, ideas, values, etc. In a basic sense, a key to leading a faithful Christian life is to keep our gaze focused on the unseen spiritual realm—to constantly remind ourselves that our true identity is found there, not in this world, that the realities of that realm are the ultimate, enduring realities, and that the values of that realm must therefore shape our own lives. To put it another way, we believers are called daily to exercise our imaginations—to live with a vision of a world filled with spiritual beings, both evil and good. It is for their effect in stimulating my imagination in this way that I so appreciate the "space trilogy" of C. S. Lewis (*Out of the Silent Planet*, *Perelandra*, and *That Hideous Strength*). These books do not explicitly teach theology or Christian living. But they have the inestimable value of portraying the unseen spiritual world that has so enormous and decisive an impact on the nature and direction of our mundane, sensory world. It is the vision of that unseen spiritual world that the author presents as a basic effect of genuine biblical faith.

> ### IN DEPTH: Faith
>
> Faith is vitally important to the author's sermon. In his list of the "elementary teachings about Christ," "faith in God" is paired with repentance as of first importance (6:1). Faith is the drumbeat of chapter 11, the noun appearing twenty-four times and the verb—"believe" or "have faith"—once. Lack of faith is what prevented the wilderness generation from attaining the promise (3:12, 19; 4:2). Only those who have faith inherit what has been promised (6:12), draw near to God (10:22), and are saved (10:38–39). Christian leaders and, preeminently, Jesus himself are exemplars and enablers of faith (13:7; 12:2). Altogether, the author uses the noun "faith" (πίστις) thirty-two times, the adjective "faithful" (πιστός) five times, the verb "believe" (πιστεύω) twice, and the noun "unbelief" (ἀπιστία) twice.
>
> Faith in Hebrews, then, describes the fundamental posture that one must have to enter God's presence and, ultimately, his promised rest. In highlighting faith in this way, the author follows Old Testament teaching. Indeed, many scholars argue that the Old Testament calls not so much for "faith" as for "faithfulness." And it is true that the Hebrew noun *emunah* (אֱמוּנָה) and the cognate verb *aman* (אמן) often refer to "faithfulness," "trustworthiness," or "steadfastness." Typical is Deuteronomy 32:4, where Moses confesses that the Lord is "a faithful God." But the verb often refers to a person's fundamental posture or disposition toward God—the basic response to God that leads to, but does not clearly include, faithfulness. See, for example:

Deuteronomy 9:23
> And when the L ORD sent you out from Kadesh Barnea, he said, "Go up and take possession of the land I have given you." But you rebelled against the command of the L ORD your God. You did not **trust** him or obey him.

Isaiah 7:9
> If you do not stand firm in your **faith**,
> you will not stand at all.

Exodus 14:31
> And when the Israelites saw the mighty hand of the L ORD displayed against the Egyptians, the people feared the L ORD and **put their trust** in him and in Moses his servant.

Deuteronomy 1:32
> In spite of this, you did not **trust** in the L ORD your God.

Nehemiah 9:8
> You found his heart **faithful** to you, and you made a covenant with him to give to his descendants the land of the Canaanites, Hittites, Amorites, Perizzites, Jebusites and Girgashites. You have kept your promise because you are righteous.

Psalm 78:37
> Their hearts were not **loyal** to him,
> they were not faithful to his covenant.

Isaiah 28:16
> So this is what the Sovereign L ORD says:
> "See, I lay a stone in Zion, a tested stone,
> a precious cornerstone for a sure foundation;
> the one who **relies** on it
> will never be stricken with panic."

Isaiah 43:10
> "You are my witnesses," declares the L ORD,
> "and my servant whom I have chosen,
> so that you may know and **believe** me

> and understand that I am he.
> Before me no god was formed,
> nor will there be one after me."

Jonah 3:5
> The Ninevites **believed** God. A fast was proclaimed, and all of them, from the greatest to the least, put on sackcloth.

The author follows the Old Testament in singling out faith in this way, although in contrast to the Old Testament, he prefers the noun to the verb. Some argue that this difference is semantically quite important: that the author views faith as a kind of virtue, using the language differently than does Paul, for instance.[63] However, the pattern of usage in Hebrews points instead in a different direction: like Paul, the author has taken the idea found in the verb in the Old Testament and brought it into his use of the noun.

The author's focus on faith as one's basic orientation to God follows Old Testament precedent and is similar to Paul. To be sure, faith, while having a similar semantic significance in Hebrews and in Paul, is set in a different context. Paul often develops his faith teaching in the context of his overall view of salvation history. He therefore focuses on the christological orientation of faith—faith is "in Christ." For the same reason, he also contrasts faith with "works of the law" (Torah adherence) and with "works" in general.[64] Neither of these contextual factors is explicit in Hebrews, although the author clearly expects us to connect faith in chapter 11 with the fully developed Christology of 7:1–10:18.[65] While set in different contexts that focus on different issues, the root idea of faith in Paul and Hebrews is very similar.[66]

Another feature of the author's teaching about faith is its close relationship to hope: faith involves "confidence in what we hope for" (11:1); faith is often directed to receiving what God has promised (see 6:12 and many of the examples in ch. 11).[67] The close relationship of faith and hope is also grounded in Old Testament teaching. The Hebrew verb *btkh* (בטח) often occurs in the sense of "rely on" or "trust in." See, for example, the taunt directed at the Israelite leaders by the spokesperson of the Assyrian king: he warns them not to "depend

---

63. See esp. Grässer, *Der Glaube im Hebräerbrief.*
64. See, e.g., Backhaus, *Der Hebräerbrief*, 381–82.
65. Cockerill, *Hebrews*, 522.
66. See esp. the long excursus in Bénétrau, *L'Épître aux Hébreux*, 2:228–54. On faith in Hebrews, see also Adolf Schlatter, *Glaube im Neuen Testament*, 3rd ed. (Stuttgart: Vereinsbuchhandlung, 1905), 524–39; Victor (Sung Yul) Rhee, *Faith in Hebrews: Analysis within the Context of Christology, Eschatology, and Ethics*, StBibLit 19 (Eugene, OR: Wipf & Stock, 2001); Weiss, *Der Brief an die Hebräer*, 564–66.
67. See, e.g., R. Bultmann, "πιστεύω, κτλ," *TDNT* 6:207; Lane, *Hebrews*, 2:315–16; Michel, *Der Brief an die Hebräer*, 369.

on" the God of Israel to deliver them (Isa 36:4–9). Hezekiah responds by putting his trust in the Lord, displaying the quality for which he is praised in the introduction to his reign in 2 Kings: "Hezekiah trusted in [*btkh*] the LORD, the God of Israel. There was no one like him among all the kings of Judah, either before him or after him" (2 Kgs 18:5). See also, for example, Isaiah 26:4—"Trust in the LORD forever, for the LORD, the LORD himself, is the Rock eternal"—and Jeremiah 17:7—"But blessed is the one who trusts [LXX *peithō*] in the LORD, whose confidence is in him."

Hebrews 11:8–22

Literary Context

No strong break separates this new section from the previous one: the litany of "by faith" continues from verses 3–7 into verses 8–22. Nevertheless, it is convenient to draw a dotted line between verses 7 and 8, recognizing the shift from the pre-flood era to the patriarchal era. Singling out Abraham as a key exemplar of faith is a natural reaction to the Old Testament narrative, especially when Abraham's significance as the ancestor of the nation of Israel is taken into account. In addition to tributes to Abraham in Judaism (where his actions more than his faith are celebrated), Christian writers also focus on Abraham: Luke (quoting Stephen) in Acts 7:2–8, Paul in Romans 4, and James in James 2:21–23. All three of these New Testament writers single out Abraham's extraordinary faith in his willingness to offer up his son, and Luke, as does the author to the Hebrews, also points to Abraham's willingness to leave his home and travel to an unknown land.[1]

---

1. For an exploration of the similarities and differences in the NT appropriation of Abraham, see esp. Richard N. Longenecker, "The 'Faith of Abraham' Theme in Paul, James and Hebrews: A Study in the Circumstantial Nature of New Testament Teaching," *JETS* 20 (1977): 203–12.

I. The Exalted Son and a Rest for the People of God (1:1–4:13)
  II. Our Great High Priest and His Ministry (4:14–10:31)
 III. **Exhortation: Follow and Serve the Pioneer of Our Faith through Endurance and Faith (10:32–13:25)**
     A. Introductory Call to Endurance and Faith (10:32–39)
     B. The Nature and Power of Faith Illustrated in Salvation History (11:1–40)
        1. The Ancients Commended for the Faith That Sees the Unseen (11:1–7)
     → 2. **Faith in the Patriarchal Era (11:8–22)**
        3. Faith in the Era of the Exodus and Conquest (11:23–31)
        4. The Faith of Judges, Prophets, Women, and Martyrs (11:32–38)
        5. The Ancients Commended for Faith That Looks to the Future (11:39–40)
     C. Run the Race with Endurance, Remembering That You Are Children of God (12:1–17)
     D. Coming to Mount Zion and Inheriting the Unshakable Kingdom (12:18–29)
     E. Letter Closing (13:1–25)

Main Idea

The author encourages his readers to have faith by reminding them of the faith of those in the earliest generations of the people of God. The patriarchs and Sarah exhibited a faith that enabled them to look beyond their earthly circumstances to focus on what God had promised. While they enjoyed some of the blessings God promised, they looked ahead with faith to the ultimate fulfillment of those promises.

Translation

Hebrews 11:8–22

8a	means	By faith,
8b	circumstance	when he was called,
8c	assertion	**Abraham obeyed,**
8d	result	leaving for a place
8e	description	that he was to receive
8f	identification	as an inheritance;
8g	parallel	and **he left,**
8h	manner	not knowing
8i	object (of 8h)	where he was going.
9a	means	By faith

9b	assertion	**he lived as a stranger**
9c	place	in the land of promise,
9d	manner (of 9b)	as if in a foreign land,
9e	circumstance	living in tents
9f	comparison	as did Isaac and
9g	parallel	Jacob,
9h	description	fellow heirs of the same promise.
10a	explanation (of 9)	For
10b	assertion	**he was looking forward to the city**
10c	description 1	that has foundations,
10d	description 2	whose designer and
10e	parallel	builder is God.
11a	means	By faith
11b	assertion	**Sarah herself,**
11c	contra-expectation	though she was beyond the usual age
11d	identification	to have children,
11e	predicate (of 11b)	**also received power**
11f	reference	with regard to the deposition of seed,
11g	cause	because she considered the one who had promised
11h	description	to be faithful.
12a	result (of 11)	Therefore
12b	source	from one man, and indeed
12c	elaboration (of 12a)	from one as good as dead,
12d	assertion	**were born descendants**
12e	measure 1	as many as the stars in the sky and
12f	measure 2	as innumerable as the sand on the seashore.
13a	general	All these died
13b	manner	in faith,
13c	circumstance	not receiving
13d	object (of 13c)	the things that had been promised.
13e	assertion	They saw them and
13f	parallel	welcomed them
13g	place	from a distance,
13h	result	acknowledging
13i	content	that they were strangers and
13j	parallel	temporary residents
13k	place	on the earth.
14a	assertion	Those who say such things make clear
14b	content	that they are seeking a homeland.
15a	condition	If they had been focused
15b	reference	on the country they had left,
15c	assertion	**they would have had opportunity to return.**

Continued on next page.

16a	contrast (with 15)	But
16b	assertion	**they were longing**
16c	content	for a better country,
16d	identification	a heavenly one.
16e	cause	Because of this
16f	assertion	**God is not ashamed to be called their God,**
16g	verification (of 16f)	for
16h	assertion	**he has prepared a city**
16i	advantage	for them.
17a	means	By faith
17b	assertion	**Abraham,**
17c	time	when he was tested,
17d	predicate (of 17b)	**offered up Isaac—**
17e	description 1	his only son,
17f	description 2 subj of 17b	**the one who had received the promises.**
18a	elaboration (of 17f)	It was said to Abraham:
18b	agent	"Through Isaac
18c	assertion	your descendants will be traced." (Gen 21:12)
19a	explanation (of 19f)	Abraham considered that God was able even
19b	content	to raise Isaac
19c	source	from the dead and so,
19d	elaboration	in a prefiguration
19e	content	of what was to come,
19f	parallel (to 19a)	**received him back.**
20a	means	By faith
20b	reference	also with regard to things to come
20c	assertion	**Isaac blessed Jacob** and
20d	parallel	**Esau.**
21a	means	By faith,
21b	assertion	**Jacob,**
21c	circumstance	as he was dying,
21d	predicate (of 21b)	**blessed each of the sons of Joseph and**
21e	parallel	**worshiped**
21f	place	over the top of his staff.
22a	means	By faith
22b	assertion	**Joseph,**
22c	circumstance	as his end drew near,
22d	basis (for 22f–g)	**had in view the exodus**
22e	identification	of the children of Israel and
22f	predicate (of 22b)	**gave instructions**
22g	reference	concerning his bones.

Structure

The passage falls into three parts.[2] The first and third are similar, following the chapter's usual "by faith" pattern. The first connects faith with Abraham's leaving his homeland, his willingness to live a nomadic existence in the promised land, and his and Sarah's ability to conceive a son in accordance with God's promise (vv. 8–12). The third section continues the "by faith" sequence, focusing especially on Abraham's "offering" of Isaac and then concluding with brief references to Isaac, Jacob, and Joseph (vv. 17–22). Between these two sections is a reflection on the nature of the patriarchs' faith, the author stressing the forward-looking nature of that faith. Even though they were not receiving what had been promised (at least in full), they were buoyed in their faith and hope by their longing to see those promises finally fulfilled (vv. 13–16).

Exegetical Outline

→ **2. Faith in the Patriarchal Era (11:8–22)**
    a. The Faith of Abraham (and Sarah) (vv. 8–12)
    b. Forward-Looking Faith (vv. 13–16)
    c. The Faith of Abraham, Isaac, Jacob, and Joseph (vv. 17–22)

Explanation of the Text

11:8 By faith, when he was called, Abraham obeyed, leaving for a place that he was to receive as an inheritance; and he left, not knowing where he was going (Πίστει καλούμενος Ἀβραὰμ ὑπήκουσεν ἐξελθεῖν εἰς τόπον ὃν ἤμελλεν λαμβάνειν εἰς κληρονομίαν, καὶ ἐξῆλθεν μὴ ἐπιστάμενος ποῦ ἔρχεται). The author moves now from the pre-flood era to the patriarchal era, using the concept of "inheritance" as a link (see "heir" in v. 7, "inheritance" in v. 8, and "fellow heirs" in v. 9). Abraham now takes center stage in the author's celebration of faith, a position he will hold right through verse 19. Appropriately enough, the author begins with the text that introduces Abraham (or "Abram," as he was at this point) into the drama of salvation history: "the LORD had said to Abram, 'Go from your country, your people and your father's household to the land I will show you'" (Gen 12:1). In the author's restatement of this event, most versions connect "called" (καλούμενος) with "leave" (ἐξελθεῖν); see, for example, ESV: "when he was called to go out" (also NIV; NLT; NET; CEB; NAB). I am reluctant to

---

2. For a similar analysis, see, e.g., Lane, *Hebrews*, 2:321, 347; Weiss, *Der Brief an die Hebräer*, 581.

disagree with so many translations (and the many scholars who have worked on them), but I prefer to connect "leave" (the infinitive ἐξελθεῖν) with the main verb in the clause, "obeyed" (ὑπήκουσεν; see CSB and NASB).³ The infinitive would, then, indicate result: Abraham "obeyed, with the result that he left" ("set out" [CSB]; "obeyed by going out" [NASB]).⁴ The author indicates Abraham's destination only vaguely: "a place that he was to receive as an inheritance."⁵ The uncertain destination of Abraham is explicitly underscored by the author: he "left, not knowing where he was going." The author of Hebrews uses "inheritance" language in chapter 6 in a context focusing on Abraham and the promise (6:12, 17), and the Old Testament frequently uses the language to describe the promised land (e.g., Exod 32:13; Lev 20:24; Ps 37:29).

11:9–10 By faith he lived as a stranger in the land of promise, as if in a foreign land, living in tents as did Isaac and Jacob, fellow heirs of the same promise. 10 For he was looking forward to the city that has foundations, whose designer and builder is God (Πίστει παρῴκησεν εἰς γῆν τῆς ἐπαγγελίας ὡς ἀλλοτρίαν ἐν σκηναῖς κατοικήσας μετὰ Ἰσαὰκ καὶ Ἰακὼβ τῶν συγκληρονόμων τῆς ἐπαγγελίας τῆς αὐτῆς· 10 ἐξεδέχετο γὰρ τὴν τοὺς θεμελίους ἔχουσαν πόλιν ἧς τεχνίτης καὶ δημιουργὸς ὁ θεός). After

Abraham left his homeland, God did not bring him into a secure land that he could possess. Rather, as the Genesis narrative repeatedly makes clear, he traveled in the land from place to place; secure possession of the land remained for him (and for Isaac and Jacob) a promise. See, for example, Genesis 23:4, where Abraham asks the Hittites for some land where he can bury Sarah: "I am a foreigner [πάροικος] and stranger among you." The author of Hebrews attributes Abraham's willingness to live a nomadic existence in the new land to his faith. The opening part of this verse could refer to Abraham's entrance into the land; see ESV, "he went to live in the land of promise." However, it is more likely the author refers to living in the land; see most of the English translations, including CEB: "he lived in the land he had been promised."⁶ Though God promised the land to Abraham, he lived in it as if it were a foreign land (ὡς ἀλλοτρίαν).⁷ The unsettled nature of his residence is underscored by the author's comment that he lived in tents—as did Isaac and Jacob.⁸ The land, then, as the author stresses in this verse, remained a "land of promise"; Isaac and Jacob were "fellow heirs of the same promise." The author again highlights the characteristics of faith he underlined in verse 1: a conviction about things not yet seen.

In verse 10, the author explains (γάρ, "for")

---

3. Scholars who advocate this connection include Grässer, *An die Hebräer*, 3:123; Ellingworth, *Hebrews*, 581; Attridge, *Hebrews*, 322.

4. Wallace, *Greek Grammar*, 594; Lane, *Hebrews*, 2:343.

5. The Greek uses a compound contruction: ἤμελλεν λαμβάνειν. The verb μέλλω sometimes adds a nuance of immediacy—"about to receive"—or certainty—"surely receive." But it probably signals a simple future focus here; von Siebenthal translates "which he would later receive/was to receive" (*Ancient Greek Grammar*, 338), and the English versions agree.

6. The issue is the meaning of the preposition εἰς after the verb παρῴκησεν. This preposition usually suggests movement; hence BDAG ("παροικέω," 779, §2c) suggest the verb here means "migrate" (see also Bruce, *Hebrews*, 292; Lane, *Hebrews*, 2:344). But the verb almost always refers to actual living in a particular place (see Luke 24:18, the only other NT occurrence of the verb), often with nuance of "as a stranger." It makes better sense in this context to give the verb its usual meaning and view the εἰς as being used here as equivalent to ἐν ("in") (e.g., Koester, *Hebrews*, 485).

7. The accusative singular form of the word suggests that it modifies γῆν, "land," rather than Abraham. The word refers to a foreign land also in Acts 7:6.

8. The author uses the simple phrase μετὰ Ἰσαὰκ καὶ Ἰακώβ, which could be translated "with Isaac and Jacob" (so many versions). But this translation suggests that all three inhabited tents at the same time, while the author almost surely means that Isaac and Jacob lived in tents "as did" Abraham (see NIV; NLT; NRSV; CSB).

why Abraham and the other patriarchs were unwilling to settle down in the land: they were "looking forward" (ἐξεδέχετο) to the city of God. The author uses the imperfect form of the verb that highlights the continuing nature of the patriarchs' expectation. Reference to the "city" taps into a rich biblical-theological stream. Jerusalem was the center of the promised land, "the city of God, the holy place where the Most High dwells" (Ps 46:4). When the people of Israel are sent into exile, return to this city is one way that the prophets express hope for future deliverance (Isa 54; Ezek 45:1–8; Zech 8:22–23; and see, of course, the moving poetry in Ps 137). In a development typical of Old Testament prophecies, these hopes for a restored Jerusalem ultimately focus on eschatological realities in the transcendent realm, a "Jerusalem that is above" (Gal 4:26), a "new Jerusalem" that descends from heaven (Rev 21:2). Second Temple Jewish writings continue this theme. In 2 Baruch, for instance, a city will be revealed in the last day, a city that God showed to Abraham ahead of time (2 Bar. 4.1–4; see also 4 Ezra 7.26; 8.52; 10.27). The city of Jerusalem, then, becomes "a symbol of the final and ultimate consummation of Yahweh's plan of salvation."[9]

The author to the Hebrews builds beautifully on this imagery. In this world, God's people have no "lasting city" (Heb 13:14). But God has himself prepared a "city" for his people (11:16), a city to which new-covenant believers now have access (12:22). This contrast between the ephemeral and unsatisfying worldly city and the city that God prepares for his people is indicated by the author's claim that the city that Abraham looked forward to was one with "foundations": securely, even permanently established. And the reason for the established nature of this city is that God himself is its "designer and builder."[10] These descriptions of God fall clearly into the author's pattern of using language drawn from the wider Greco-Roman world of his day to convey thoroughly biblical truth.[11] "Designer" (τεχνίτης) refers to human workers elsewhere in the New Testament (Acts 19:24, 38; Rev 18:22), but refers to God only here. It refers to God (indirectly) once in the LXX (Wis 13:1) but is common in Philo as a description of God. The second term, "builder" (δημιουργός), is not used elsewhere in biblical Greek but was often used in secular Greek (and, later, by the Gnostics) to characterize God as the "architect" or "creator" of the world.[12] As my translation suggests, it is possible that the first description focuses on planning and the second on the execution of that plan.[13]

11:11 By faith Sarah herself, though she was beyond the usual age to have children, also received power with regard to the deposition of seed, because she considered the one who had promised to be faithful (Πίστει καὶ αὐτὴ Σάρρα στεῖρα δύναμιν εἰς καταβολὴν σπέρματος ἔλαβεν καὶ παρὰ καιρὸν ἡλικίας, ἐπεὶ πιστὸν ἡγήσατο τὸν ἐπαγγειλάμενον). This verse continues the sequence of introductory "by faith" (πίστει) references and focuses on the miraculous birth of Isaac to Abraham and Sarah (Gen 21:1–7). God had repeatedly promised that a son would be born to Abraham and Sarah, despite

---

9. B. Arnold, "City, Citizenship," in *New Dictionary of Biblical Theology*, ed. Brian S. Rosner and T. Desmond Alexander (Downers Grove, IL: IVP Academic, 2000), 415. The great theologian of the early church, Augustine, famously appropriated this basic imagery in his *The City of God* (*De civitate Dei*).
10. The relative clause beginning with ἧς, then, has a causal flavor (Lane, *Hebrews*, 2:344).
11. Contra, e.g., Grässer, who thinks the language points to a shift away from typical biblical thinking toward a "cosmological-dualistic" perspective (*An die Hebräer*, 3:128).
12. The word does, however, occur in 2 Macc 4:1. See G. Foerster, "δημιουργός," *TDNT* 2:62.
13. Westcott, *Hebrews*, 360; Massonnet, *L'Épître aux Hébreux*, 324. Ellingworth (*Hebrews*, 585) and Lane (*Hebrews*, 2:352) are not so sure, pointing to texts in Philo where the terms appear to overlap.

their advanced age (Gen 17:17; 18:11, 13; 21:2, 5, 7) and Sarah's inability to conceive (Gen 11:30; 16:2). The author taps into this story—as does Paul in Romans 4:18–21—to highlight the power of faith. Despite the fact that Sarah was unable to have children and that both were "beyond the usual age to have children,"[14] the child Issac was born. Despite moments of doubt (expressed in their laughter [Gen 17:17; 18:10–15]), the patriarchal couple ultimately took God at his word, considering "the one who had promised to be faithful." The faithfulness of God in fulfilling his promises is a recurrent motif in the letter (see 6:12, 13–15; 10:23), with obvious application to the audience: the author's call for them to move forward to the ultimate "country"/"city"/"rest" is grounded in God's promise to bring them to that place.

The main problem is whether Abraham or Sarah is the subject of the verse. The English translations, going back to the KJV, generally prefer Sarah (KJV; CSB; RSV; ESV; NIV; NJB; NASB; NLT; CEB).[15] However, NRSV, NAB, and NET make Abraham the subject, and this option has a slight majority of commentators in its favor. The reason for this difference of opinion is what one might expect: some aspects of the text favor a reference to Abraham, others a reference to Sarah. Making Sarah the subject of the verse would seem to be the obvious way to read the phrase "Sarah herself" (αὐτὴ Σάρρα, a nominative construction).[16] On the other hand, the object of the verb "receive" (ἔλαβεν), "power for the deposition of seed" (δύναμιν εἰς καταβολὴν σπέρματος), strongly suggests that the subject of the verb is Abraham: the phrase used here (καταβολὴν σπέρματος) is used in ancient Greek to depict the male role in procreation. Interpreters have to weigh these conflicting factors.[17] Those who stress the latter point are faced with the problem of integrating the reference to Sarah into a sentence about Abraham receiving the power of procreation. Three options are worth mentioning.

First, we might simply view the entire reference to Sarah as a gloss, a later addition that was not part of the original text.[18] However, while the relevant phrase does have textual uncertainties,[19] no manuscript omits these words. Textual emendation should always be a very last resort, and we do not need to resort to it here. Second, the reference to

---

14. This is my translation of the phrase παρὰ καιρὸν ἡλικίας. The word ἡλικία means, as BDAG ("ἡλικία," 436, §2) paraphrases it, "the age which is sufficient or requisite for certain things." In this context, those "certain things" refer to having children.

15. Most of these translations offer the alternative in a footnote. Note that the NRSV changed the RSV's "Sarah" to "Abraham," while the NIV moved from "Abraham" (1984) to "Sarah" (2011).

16. The αὐτή functions as an emphasizing pronoun.

17. Three other aspects of the text bearing on our interpretation might be noted. Two of them weigh in favor of a reference to Abraham: the masculine forms in v. 12 (ἑνός, "one," and νενεκρωμένου, "as good as dead"), which might point to Abraham as the main focus throughout (Ellingworth, Hebrews, 585), as well as the fact that in the roughly parallel Rom 4:19–21, it is Abraham's advanced age that grounds his inability to have children (hence in Heb 11:11, we might expect that "beyond the age to have children" explains the "deadness" of Abraham in v. 12). One other factor suggests a reference to Sarah: the καί ("and," "also") before παρὰ καιρὸν ἡλικίας ("beyond the usual age to have children"), which suggests that this latter prepositional phrase is paired with "unable to have children" (στεῖρα), obviously referring to Sarah.

18. Günther Zuntz, *The Text of the Epistles: A Disquisition Upon the Corpus Paulinum* (London: Oxford University Press, 1953), 15–16.

19. A few MSS add the participle οὖσα after στεῖρα (P 104. 365. 1505), and others add an article before στεῖρα (D¹ 6. 81. 1241. 1739. 1881). The more difficult decision, however, is whether to include στεῖρα at all. A number of very good MSS (𝔓[13vid], ℵ, A; see also D² K L 33. 630. 1175. 𝔐) omit it, and this is reflected in many English versions (KJV; NIV; RSV; ESV; NASB; and see Attridge, *Hebrews*, 321; Ellingworth, *Hebrews*, 588). However, the modern editions of the Greek New Testament (USB⁵, NA²⁸) include it (following 𝔓⁴⁶ D* Ψ latt), and I tentatively agree (see the discussion in Metzger, *Textual Commentary*, 602; and also, e.g., Lane, *Hebrews*, 2:345; Koester, *Hebrews*, 487).

Sarah could be explained as a nominative absolute clause—a kind of parenthetical remark. The NRSV translation is based on this interpretation: "by faith he received power of procreation, even though he was too old—and Sarah herself was barren—because he considered him faithful who had promised."[20] This is certainly possible, although it is far from the natural reading of the text. Third, the words "Sarah herself" (αὐτὴ Σάρρα) could be understood, not as nominative, but as dative (αὐτῇ Σάρρᾳ): the iota subscripts signaling the dative were not always included in our manuscripts.[21] The phrase might, then, be an associative dative: "by faith, he [Abraham] also, together with barren Sarah, received power to beget."[22] Again, this is a possible reading, but it has one major problem: if, as most assume, the dative is connected with the verb, then we face the problem of associating Sarah with an action that is argued to be one only males can carry out.

On the other side of the situation, interpreters who make Sarah the subject of the sentence have to explain how a phrase that refers to the male role in procreation can be applied to Sarah. The best option is to think that the relevant language means something like "received power with regard to [εἰς] the deposition of seed."[23] In other words, Sarah received from Abraham the "depositing of seed" that enabled her to become pregnant and give birth to Isaac. A decision between these options is very difficult, but I lean ever so slightly to the view that the text is referring to Sarah, concluding that it is slightly easier to stretch the interpretation of "deposition of seed" (καταβολὴν σπέρματος) than to find alternatives to taking Sarah as the subject of the sentence.[24]

11:12 Therefore from one man, and indeed from one as good as dead, were born descendants as many as the stars in the sky[25] and as innumerable as the sand on the seashore (διὸ καὶ ἀφ' ἑνὸς ἐγεννήθησαν, καὶ ταῦτα νενεκρωμένου, καθὼς τὰ ἄστρα τοῦ οὐρανοῦ τῷ πλήθει καὶ ὡς ἡ ἄμμος ἡ παρὰ τὸ χεῖλος τῆς θαλάσσης ἡ ἀναρίθμητος). As a result (διό, "therefore") of "the deposition of a seed" leading to the birth of Isaac (v. 11), God's promise of numerous descendants to Abraham and Sarah is fulfilled. If, as I have tentatively concluded, verse 11 highlights Sarah's faith, this verse returns to a focus on Abraham: from this "one man" (ἑνός) were born innumerable descendants. And not only from one man—but from one man "as good as dead."[26] Paul makes a very similar point, using some of the same language:

---

20. See also KJV; NAB; NET. Matthew Black argues for this option on the basis of Semitic syntax ("Critical and Exegetical Notes on Three New Testament Texts: Hebrews xi.11, Jude 5, James i.27," in *Apophoreta: Festschrift für Ernst Haenchen*, ed. W. Eltester and F. H. Kettler [Berlin: Töpelmann, 1964], 41–44), a somewhat questionable argument in light of the nature of the author's Greek. For this view, see also Lane, *Hebrews*, 2:345; Koester, *Hebrews*, 488; Grässer, *An die Hebräer*, 3:132; Weiss, *Der Brief an die Hebräer*, 587–88.

21. J. H. Moulton and W. F. Howard, *Accidence and Word Formation*, vol. 2 of J. H. Moulton, W. F. Howard, and Nigel Turner, *A Grammar of New Testament Greek*, 4 vols. (Edinburgh: T&T Clark, 1920), 85.

22. Bruce, *Hebrews*, 294–96; Ellingworth, *Hebrews*, 587–88; Attridge, *Hebrews*, 321, 325; Backhaus, *Der Hebräerbrief*, 390–91; BDF §194.1; Turner, *Syntax*, 220.

23. For this rendering, see France, "Hebrews," 153.

24. Calvin, *Hebrews*, 168–69; Moffatt, *Hebrews*, 171; Westcott, *Hebrews*, 360; Cockerill, *Hebrews*, 543–45; Schreiner, *Hebrews*, 351–53; Johnson, *Hebrews*, 291–92; D. Harris, *Hebrews*, 314–15; Bénétrau, *L'Épître aux Hébreux*, 2:136–37; Massonnet, *L'Épître aux Hébreux*, 325.

25. The Greek word οὐρανός here refers simply to "the space above the earth," the "sky" ("οὐρανός," L&N 1.5; so most versions).

26. The Greek is ταῦτα νενεκρωμένου. The plural ταῦτα reflects classical Greek, the word here expressing emphasis: "and indeed" (Ellingworth, *Hebrews*, 590; Turner, *Syntax*, 45). I follow BDAG ("νεκρόω," 668), the English versions, and most commentators in giving the perfect participle νενεκρωμένου the sense of "as good as dead." DeSilva, however, thinks the word should be given its normal sense: Abraham was, in fact,

Against all hope, Abraham in hope believed and so became the father of many nations, just as it had been said to him, "So shall your offspring be." Without weakening in his faith, he faced the fact that his body was as good as dead [νενεκρωμένον]—since he was about a hundred years old—and that Sarah's womb was also dead. Yet he did not waver through unbelief regarding the promise of God, but was strengthened in his faith and gave glory to God, being fully persuaded that God had power to do what he had promised. (Rom 4:18–21)[27]

The author and Paul are united in emphasizing Sarah's inability to have children, the advanced age of Sarah/Abraham, the "deadness" of Abraham, the role of faith, and the conviction, as the expression of that faith, that God would be faithful to accomplish what he promised.

The two images that the author uses to emphasize the great number of descendants are used in the Old Testament in a number of different contexts. Particularly relevant are places where one image or the other is used to characterize the large number of descendants promised to Abraham and the patriarchs. Both are used together in Genesis 22:17a: "I will surely bless you and make your descendants as numerous as the stars in the sky and as the sand on the seashore"; and also, for "stars in the sky," see Genesis 26:4; Exodus 32:13; Deuteronomy 1:10; 28:62, etc.; for "sand on the seashore," see Genesis 32:12. The author may also allude to Isaiah 51:2: "Look to Abraham, your father, and to Sarah, who gave you birth. When I called him he was only one man, and I blessed him and made him many."[28]

11:13 All these died in faith, not receiving the things that had been promised. They saw them and welcomed them from a distance, acknowledging that they were strangers and temporary residents on the earth (Κατὰ πίστιν ἀπέθανον οὗτοι πάντες, μὴ λαβόντες τὰς ἐπαγγελίας ἀλλὰ πόρρωθεν αὐτὰς ἰδόντες καὶ ἀσπασάμενοι καὶ ὁμολογήσαντες ὅτι ξένοι καὶ παρεπίδημοί εἰσιν ἐπὶ τῆς γῆς). The author inserts into the middle of his roll call of incidents demonstrating the faith of Abraham, Sarah, and the other patriarchs (vv. 8–12, 17–22) a general characterization of the orientation of thinking that fed into their faith. Their focus was not on the things of this world but on the realities of the unseen spiritual realm. In a perspective typical of the author, this spiritual realm is both "above" and "ahead." The "country" they long for is a "heavenly" one, a city God has already prepared for them (vv. 16, 17). What is now "above" will one day be revealed here on earth, and the ancestors of our faith eagerly looked forward to that day.

In the context, the people the author now refers to—"all these" (οὗτοι πάντες)—are probably those mentioned in the immediate context: Abraham (vv. 8–10, 12, 17–19), Sarah (v. 11), Isaac (v. 20), Jacob (v. 21), and Joseph (v. 22).[29] None of them received the things that "had been promised."[30] Rather, they "saw them and welcomed them from a distance."[31] As BDAG ("ἀσπάζομαι," 144, §1) nicely puts it, "welcomed" here has the connotation of

---

"dead," when it came to his procreative powers (*Perseverance in Gratitude*, 398–99).

27. It is indeed possible that Paul and Hebrews depend on a common source about Abraham's faith (Ellingworth, *Hebrews*, 590).

28. Michel, *Der Brief an die Hebräer*, 397.

29. Weiss, *Der Brief an die Hebräer*, 589; Lane, *Hebrews*, 2:356. Another, less probable, option is that the reference is to all the "heros of faith" in ch. 11 (Rhee, "Chiasm and the Concept of Faith," 330–31).

30. As is often the case, ἐπαγγελία can refer to the act of promising or, as here, that which had been promised. See "ἐπαγγελία," BDAG 355, §1.b.β.

31. I take the adverb πόρρωθεν ("from a distance") with the first two of three participles ἰδόντες ("saw") and ἀσπασάμενοι ("welcomed"). The three participles in a row reflect typical

"happiness about the arrival of something." While not yet possessing the land or seeing the innumerable multitude of descendants, these ancestors saw and welcomed them by faith. While the reference here to faith (κατὰ πίστιν) technically modifies "died" (ἀπέθανον), it only makes sense to take it as referring to the way these people were living right up to their death; see NIV: "all these people were still living by faith when they died."[32] The author's claim that Abraham and the others did not receive what was promised appears at first sight to contradict the author's earlier claim that Abraham, in fact, "received what was promised" (6:15). As we noted in our comments there, however, reconciliation is not difficult. Abraham (and the others) certainly received a kind of "down payment" on the promise (e.g., the birth of Isaac), but they did not receive the full measure of what God had promised. That ultimate fulfillment would have to wait for the consummation in Christ (11:39–40).

The focus of these ancestors in the faith on what was yet to come had as its corollary a turning away from the things of this world: they "acknowledged"[33] that they were "strangers and temporary residents" (ξένοι καὶ παρεπίδημοι) on the earth. The description probably again reflects the author's knowledge of the Abraham narrative; in Genesis 23:4, in his request for property where he can bury Sarah, Abraham acknowledges that he is "a foreigner and stranger [LXX πάροικος καὶ παρεπίδημος]" among the Hittites.[34] In Abraham's case being a stranger had to do with the land of Canaan, and some interpreters think this might be what our author intends also.[35] But it is more likely that the word γῆ here refers, not to the physical land of Canaan, but to the earth in general (note the possible contrast with "heavenly" in v. 16).[36]

11:14 Those who say such things make clear that they are seeking a homeland (οἱ γὰρ τοιαῦτα λέγοντες ἐμφανίζουσιν ὅτι πατρίδα ἐπιζητοῦσιν). The saints of the patriarchal age exemplified faith in their "forward" look, longing for a true homeland. The Greek begins with a conjunction (γάρ) often translated "for," but which here more likely expresses a continuative or even culminative sense.[37] Those versions that do not directly translate the word (NIV; CEB) or use "now" (CSB) capture the sense well in English. The word translated "such things" (τοιαῦτα) refers back to the acknowledgment of the ancestors that they were "strangers and temporary residents on the earth" (v. 13b). In this verse the author draws out the positive implications of this acknowledgment: they were, in fact, "seeking a homeland." The Greek word for "homeland" (πατρίς) can refer simply to one's "hometown" (e.g., Matt 13:54, 57; Mark 6:1, 4; Luke 4:23, 24) or "home territory" (John 4:44), but it can also convey the richer connotations of one's homeland or fatherland (see NIV and NASB's "a country of their own"). Jeremiah 22:10 illustrates this sense: "do not weep for the dead king or mourn

---

Greek "subordination" style but are better translated in English with a combination of finite verbs and participles.

32. See, e.g., Johnson, *Hebrews*, 292; Grässer, *An die Hebräer*, 3:135. Koester, however, thinks the idea is that "faith shaped the way they dealt with death" (*Hebrews*, 488). The shift from the simple dative πίστει, used throughout the chapter, to the prepositional phrase κατὰ πίστιν may hint at this idea (Cockerill, *Hebrews*, 548).

33. The verb ὁμολογέω usually means to "profess," often publicly (Heb 13:15; and see the note on ὁμολογία in comments on 3:1). Here, however, it probably means "admit" or "acknowledge" ("ὁμολογέω," BDAG 708–9, §§3, 4).

34. The word ξένος, "stranger," is fairly common in the LXX and NT, but παρεπίδημος is more rare: only twice elsewhere in the NT (1 Pet 1:1; 2:11) and once else in the LXX (Ps 39:12 [38:13 LXX]).

35. Lane, *Hebrews*, 2:346, 357.

36. E.g., Ellingworth, *Hebrews*, 595.

37. E.g., D. Harris (*Hebrews*, 321) and Ellingworth (*Hebrews*, 595) argue that v. 14 draws a conclusion from v. 13.

his loss; rather, weep bitterly for him who is exiled, because he will never return nor see his native land [πατρίδος] again."

11:15–16 If they had been focused on the country they had left, they would have had opportunity to return. 16 But they were longing for a better country, a heavenly one. Because of this God is not ashamed to be called their God, for he has prepared a city for them (καὶ εἰ μὲν ἐκείνης ἐμνημόνευον ἀφ᾽ ἧς ἐξέβησαν, εἶχον ἂν καιρὸν ἀνακάμψαι· 16 νῦν δὲ κρείττονος ὀρέγονται, τοῦτ᾽ ἔστιν ἐπουρανίου. διὸ οὐκ ἐπαισχύνεται αὐτοὺς ὁ θεὸς θεὸς ἐπικαλεῖσθαι αὐτῶν· ἡτοίμασεν γὰρ αὐτοῖς πόλιν). These two verses hang together, in one of the the author's many μέν . . . δέ ("on the one hand . . . on the other hand") constructions. His contrast is between the attitude that the patriarchs and Sarah did *not* have—longing to return to their own country—and the attitude they *did* have—longing for a "better country."

Verse 15 is in the form of an unreal condition, which operates according to the logic of "if A, then B—not B—therefore not A."[38] In this case, only the first step in the logic is explicit, while the other two steps are implied: "if they had been focused on the country they had left" (A), "[then] they would have had opportunity to return" (B); [they did not return] (not B); therefore they were not thinking about the country they had left (not A). Abraham's home in Ur of the Chaldees probably offered a much more comfortable life than his nomadic existence in a new and unknown land. He, his wife, and the other patriarchs could have returned to that "homeland." But they were not thinking about, or focused on,[39] the country they had left, and so they never took the opportunity to return.

The argument of v. 15 establishes the negative side of the author's point: Abraham, Sarah, and the other patriarchs were not focused on the country they left. In verse 16a, the positive side of the same point is stated: they were, in fact, "longing for a better country, a heavenly one."[40] The author's key word "better" (κρείττων) appears here again, contrasting the country they had left (Ur) with the one they longed for. But we should also see here a contrast to the land of Canaan itself, where the ancestors were foreigners and resident aliens. The country God promised them was more than Canaan; it was a "heavenly" one. Some interpreters again here detect a strong note of "cosmological dualism characteristic of the Alexandrian approach."[41] However, by labeling the country they longed for as "heavenly," the author is not necessarily claiming that this place is ethereal or unearthly. As P. Hughes puts it, the believer's ultimate "homeland" is "not unearthly, but rather more than earthly."[42] As the author has made clear in 3:7–4:11, the "rest" God promised his people could not be found in its ultimate form in Canaan: "if Joshua had given them rest, God would not have spoken later about another day [of rest]" (4:8)—the rest David refers to much later in Psalm 95. The "country" that God has destined us for is both "above" and "ahead."

---

38. This unreal condition is signaled by the εἰ + past-tense verb in the protasis (ἐμνημόνευον, an imperfect indicative verb from μνημονεύω, "remember," "think of") and the particle ἄν in the apodosis. See, e.g., von Siebenthal, *Ancient Greek Grammar*, 323.

39. The verb μνημονεύω that the author uses here means "remember," but also "think of," "keep in mind" (BDAG 655, §1). The verb often connotes "consider" with the implication of taking something to heart. See the note on 10:3. "Focus on" may be a good contextual rendering in Heb 11:15.

40. The δέ correlates with μέν in v. 15, while νῦν has a logical force (Ellingworth, *Hebrews*, 588).

41. Again, see especially Grässer, who pushes this agenda hard (*An die Hebräer*, 3:142; see also Thompson, *Hebrews*, 238).

42. P. Hughes, *Hebrews*, 478; see also Massonnet: "the perspective of faith is not a negation of the terrestrial, but rather is more than terrestrial" (*L'Épître aux Hébreux*, 327, my translation).

As Rose insightfully notes, we find in Hebrews an "interleaving" of the future-eschatological and transcendent-ontological perspectives.[43]

Because (see the διό, "therefore") the patriarchs had their eyes fixed on God's country, the "better" and "heavenly" one, God in turn "is not ashamed to be called their God." The author probably alludes to the repeated description of God in the Old Testament as "the God of Abraham, Isaac, and Jacob" (Exod 3:6, 15, 16; 4:5; cf. Matt 22:32; Mark 12:26; Luke 20:37; Acts 3:13; 7:32). "Not ashamed" may be a literary device known as litotes, in which a positive point is expressed negatively. Thus "not ashamed" may mean, in effect, "very proud" or "honored." The imagery of "country" in verses 14–15 gives way to the imagery of "city" at the end of verse 16: God "has prepared a city for them." The author referred to this "city" in verse 10 as "the city that has foundations, whose designer and builder is God." Clearly for the author, "country" and "city" are two parallel ways to describe the transcendental and future hope of believers (see also 12:22; 13:14).

11:17–18 By faith Abraham, when he was tested, offered up Isaac—his only son, the one who had received the promises. 18 It was said to Abraham[44]: "Through Isaac your descendants will be traced" (Πίστει προσενήνοχεν Ἀβραὰμ τὸν Ἰσαὰκ πειραζόμενος καὶ τὸν μονογενῆ προσέφερεν, ὁ τὰς ἐπαγγελίας ἀναδεξάμενος, 18 πρὸς ὃν ἐλαλήθη ὅτι Ἐν Ἰσαὰκ κληθήσεταί σοι σπέρμα). After the author's theological commentary on the faith of the patriarchs and Sarah in verses 13–16, he returns to his enumeration of outstanding examples of faith (the dative πίστει again leads off v. 17). While there is no literary indication of a break in verse 23, we should probably, on the basis of content, see a minor shift at that point, from the patriarchal era (vv. 17–22) to the time of the exodus (vv. 23–31).

Continuing to recount the many ways that Abraham expressed his faith in God, the author now comes to the most outstanding example of that faith: his willingness to obey God when he was called to offer his son Isaac as a sacrifice. The author gives this incident more space than any other in the chapter, pointing to its importance.[45] This "testing" of Abaham has fascinated interpreters through the ages.[46] The incident attracted a lot of interest from Jewish authors (1 Macc 2:52; Wis 10:5; Sir 44:20; Jub. 17.15–18:16; LAB 18.5; 32.1–4; 4 Macc. 16.19–20; Philo, *Abraham* 167–99), as well as other New Testament writers (Jas 2:21–23) and modern theologians (e.g., Kierkegaard, *Fear and Trembling*,[47] and R. W. L. Moberly, *The Bible, Theology, and Faith*[48]). Later Jewish writers accorded atoning significance to what they called the Akedah, or "binding" of Isaac.[49] Jewish tradition often focused on Abraham's obedience; see, for

---

43. Rose, *Die Wolke der Zeugen*, 227 (the German word is *Verschränkung*).

44. I am therefore identifying the antecedent of ὅν as Abraham, with πρός meaning "to" (e.g., Cockerill, *Hebrews*, 556). The alternative is that the antecedent is Isaac, "about" whom the text speaks (e.g., NRSV; ESV).

45. Dunnill labels vv. 17–19 the "organizing center" of the chapter (*Covenant and Sacrifice*, 173–81; see also Gareth Lee Cockerill, "The Better Resurrection (Heb. 11:35): A Key to the Structure and Rhetorical Purpose of Hebrews 11," *TynBul* 51 [2000]: 231).

46. The participle πειραζόμενος (probably temporal; so the translations) is from πειράζω, a verb that can mean either "tempt" or "test" (see the note on 2:18). The latter is clearly the meaning here, the author echoing Gen 22:1: ὁ θεὸς ἐπείραζεν τὸν Αβρααμ ("God tested Abraham").

47. S. Kierkegaard, *Fear and Trembling*, ed. C. Stephen Evans and Sylvia Walsh, Cambridge Texts in the History of Philosophy (Cambridge: Cambridge University Press, 2006).

48. R. W. L. Moberly, *The Bible, Theology, and Faith: A Study of Abraham and Jesus* (Cambridge: Cambridge University Press, 2000).

49. James Swetnam, *Jesus and Isaac: A Study of the Epistle to the Hebrews in the Light of the Aqedah*, AnBib 94 (Rome: Biblical Institute Press, 1981), 23–79. For an analysis of the history and date of the tradition, see P. R. Davies and B. D. Chilton, "The

example, James, who cites Abraham's offering of his son as an example of a work that "completed" his faith (Jas 2:21–23). In claiming that Abraham "offered" Isaac, the author means simply that Abraham presented him to the Lord as a sacrifice, not that the sacrifice was completed.[50]

The LXX text of Genesis 22:2 highlights Abraham's love for his son. The author is closer to the Hebrew text in focusing on Isaac as "his one and only" (μονογενῆ) son (the Hebrew uses יָחִיד; see NIV "your son, your only son").[51] However, what particularly distinguishes the author's use of this text is his focus on the salvation-historical significance of Isaac: he was "the one who had received the promises"—specifically, the one through whom the Lord promised to bring into existence descendants for Abraham. God had promised Abraham many descendants, but Sarah's inability to have children and the couple's advanced age seemed to make this impossible. They therefore began to look for other means to fulfill the promise, perhaps through Hagar. In response, however, the Lord insisted that the multitude of descendants he has in view would come through Isaac, a son of Sarah (Gen 17:19, 21). The author of Hebrews quotes Genesis 21:12 to make this point (the same text is quoted for a different purpose in Rom 9:7).

11:19 Abraham considered that God was able even to raise Isaac from the dead and so, in a prefigurement of what was to come, received him back (λογισάμενος ὅτι καὶ ἐκ νεκρῶν ἐγείρειν δυνατὸς ὁ θεός, ὅθεν αὐτὸν καὶ ἐν παραβολῇ ἐκομίσατο). Abraham exhibited faith in his creative insight about how God could fulfill his specific promise to him even as he was asked to kill his son through whom the promise was to be fulfilled. Along with most English translations, I start a new sentence in verse 19. However, in the Greek, verse 19 is tied into verses 17–18 by means of a participle (λογισάμενος, "considering"). The sense might be causal ("because he considered")[52] but is more likely simply explanatory: "in faith Abraham offered Isaac . . . that faith coming to expression in his considering . . ." As we have seen, the author draws attention to Isaac's status as the son of promise, the one through whom Abraham would have innumerable descendants. God's command to sacrifice this son, before he had had any children, appeared to stand in flat contradiction to this promise. Yet Abraham "considered him faithful who had made the promise" (cf. v. 11b). As a result of his faith in his God, Abraham therefore reasoned his way to a solution to this conundrum: God was "able even[53] to raise Isaac from the dead." Belief in the resurrection of the dead was not, of course, widespread among Old Testament believers—making it all the more remarkable that Abraham adopted this explanation.[54]

The word that connects verse 19b to its context (ὅθεν) has two possible meanings, each of which works in this context. On the one hand, the word,

---

Aqedah: A Revised Tradition History," *CBQ* 40 (1978): 514–46; and Geza Vermes, *Scripture and Tradition in Judaism: Haggadic Studies*, StPB 4 (Leiden: Brill, 1961).

50. Contra, e.g., Rose, *Die Wolke der Zeugen*, 234–43; see Cockerill, *Hebrews*, 555. The author actually says twice that Abraham "offered" Isaac: once in the perfect, προσενήνοχεν, and once in the imperfect, προσέφερεν. The latter is probably conative ("Abraham attempted to offer Isaac"—see, e.g., Wallace, *Greek Grammar*, 551), while the former could be another example of the author's penchant for the "scriptural perfect"—that is, a use of the perfect to stress the abiding significance of the action as recorded in Scripture (Moule, *Idiom Book*, 15). The καί that introduces the second occurrence of the verb therefore has an epexegetic function (Lane, *Hebrews*, 2:346).

51. Josephus also uses μονογενής to refer to Isaac (*Ant.* 1.222).

52. D. Harris, *Hebrews*, 327; Cockerill, *Hebrews*, 556.

53. This is the sense καί has here (D. Harris, *Hebrews*, 327).

54. Some interpreters (e.g., Bruce, *Hebrews*, 304) suggest that Gen 22 implies some such solution, since Abraham, on his way to sacrifice Isaac, nevertheless tells his servants that he and "the boy" would come back to them (Gen 22:5).

in its five other occurrences in Hebrews (2:17; 3:1; 7:25; 8:3; 9:18) means "therefore," "and so"—naturally, then, most translations and commentaries give it this meaning here as well. However, in six other New Testament occurrences, the word means "from which" (Matt 12:44; 25:24, 26; Luke 11:24; Acts 14:26; 28:13), and the ESV adopts this meaning: "he considered that God was able even to raise him from the dead, **from which**, figuratively speaking, he did receive him back" (see also NASB; KJV; NKJV).[55] I slightly prefer this option because it fits well with the verb in this half verse (κομίζω), "receive back."[56] Abraham climbed the mountain assuming, right up to the last minute, that he would sacrifice his son. His return down the mountain was virtually like receiving him back from the dead. "Virtually" in this sentence is basically equivalent to the meaning several versions give to the phrase ἐν παραβολῇ (e.g., NIV "in a manner of speaking"; ESV "figuratively").[57] The Greek word, often translated as "parable," is familiar to us from the Gospels, where it occurs forty-six times to denote a special form of Jesus's teaching. But it can also refer to something that points to something else, as the withered fig tree in the Gospels (Matt 24:32; Mark 13:28) or the "first tabernacle" in Hebrews 9:9. Here, however, the "lesson" or "example" of Isaac's "return from the dead" might have a stronger salvation-historical significance: note the translation "symbol" in NAB and "type" in NASB. In this case, Isaac's return from dead would prefigure the resurrection of Jesus[58] or, more likely (see v. 35), the resurrection of believers.[59]

11:20–22 By faith also with regard to things to come Isaac blessed Jacob and Esau. 21 By faith, Jacob, as he was dying, blessed each of the sons of Joseph and worshiped over the top of his staff. 22 By faith Joseph, as his end drew near, had in view the exodus of the children of Israel and gave instructions concerning his bones (Πίστει καὶ περὶ μελλόντων εὐλόγησεν Ἰσαὰκ τὸν Ἰακὼβ καὶ τὸν Ἠσαῦ. 21 Πίστει Ἰακὼβ ἀποθνῄσκων ἕκαστον τῶν υἱῶν Ἰωσὴφ εὐλόγησεν καὶ προσεκύνησεν ἐπὶ τὸ ἄκρον τῆς ῥάβδου αὐτοῦ. 22 Πίστει Ἰωσὴφ τελευτῶν περὶ τῆς ἐξόδου τῶν υἱῶν Ἰσραὴλ ἐμνημόνευσεν καὶ περὶ τῶν ὀστέων αὐτοῦ ἐνετείλατο). Following the general narrative sequence in Genesis, the author now briefly mentions the faith exhibited by the patriarchs of the next two generations—Isaac (v. 20) and Jacob (v. 21)—and by Jacob's son, Joseph (v. 22). In verse 20, the author refers to the well-known story of Isaac's blessing of Jacob, a "blessing" he attained by subterfuge (Gen 27:27–40). Indeed, the only "blessing" Esau receives is a decidedly ambiguous one: he is destined to dwell away from "the earth's richness," to serve his brother, and to ultimately rebel against this servitude (Gen 27:39–40). Perhaps the author of Hebrews mentions Isaac's blessing of Esau as a subtle reminder that blessings can be lost if one does not persevere in faith (see Heb 12:14–17).[60]

I have translated verse 20 in an awkward English word order to bring out the author's focus on "things to come" (μελλόντων). He signals this focus on future realities by putting the prepositional phrase in which "things to come" occurs

---

55. Several versions translate something like "received him back from the dead" at the end of the verse, but it is impossible to know whether they are translating ὅθεν or simply giving a contextual sense to ἐκομίσατο.

56. The verb κομίζω can mean simply "receive" (see, e.g., 11:39), but probably has the stronger sense "receive back" here (BDAG 557, §2).

57. Montefiore, *Hebrews*, 200.
58. Bruce, *Hebrews*, 304.
59. Moffatt, *Hebrews*, 177; Lane, *Hebrews*, 2:363; Koester, *Hebrews*, 492; D. Harris, *Hebrews*, 327; Cockerill, *Hebrews*, 557.
60. Cockerill, *Hebrews*, 560; D. Harris, *Hebrews*, 329.

before the verb and by adding καί, "also," "even."[61] The orientation of faith to the future fulfillment of God's promises has been a persistent theme in this chapter (vv. 1, 7, 10, 11, 13, 14, 16, 22, 26).

Verses 21 and 22 share a deathbed scenario; and verse 21 continues the theme of blessing from verse 20. The story of Jacob's blessing of Joseph's sons, Ephraim and Manasseh, is found in Genesis 48:8–22. The author, however, refers to another incident from this same time period, Jacob's worshiping "over the top of his staff." This incident occurs immediately before Jacob's blessing of Joseph's sons, as the culmination of the narrative of Jacob's request that Joseph bury his body back in the land of promise (Gen 47:31). However, a comparison of the Old Testament verse with Hebrews 11:21 reveals a significant difference: most English versions translate the Old Testament verse "bowed himself on the head of his bed" (NRSV), while Hebrews refers to Jacob "bowing in worship over the top of his staff" (NRSV again). While the meaning is not entirely clear, the Old Testament text probably connotes Jacob's old-age-induced tiredness. The author of Hebrews, however, uses a verb that normally connotes worship, although it sometimes connotes also the physical action of bowing or falling to one's knees (see, e.g., Matt 8:2).[62] The more arresting difference between the Old Testament text and the quotation in Hebrews is the shift from "bed" to "staff." The author is, as usual, following his LXX source. Apparently, the LXX translators read the Hebrew vowel points differently than what we find in the Masoretic Text—a common phenomenon. The MT has *hammittah*, "the bed," while the Greek translators seem to have read this as *hammatteh*, "the staff." The NIV follows the LXX tradition in its translation of Genesis 47:31: "Israel [Jacob] worshiped as he leaned on the top of his staff." Whatever the original Hebrew may have been, the author probably sees theological significance in the reference to a "staff" (ῥάβδος) in the LXX translation. "Staff" can connote both pilgrimage—the pilgrim leaning on his staff as he travels (Gen 32:10; Exod 12:11; Mark 6:8)—and kingship—the staff as a symbol of ruling authority (Ps 110:2; Isa 11:1; esp. Heb 1:8). The author, then, may quote the text with staff to "lay stress on Jacob's faith as a wanderer who longed for the Messianic hope."[63]

The author also focuses on the forward-looking element in Joseph's faith (v. 22). It is for this reason that the author, among all the incidents in the life of Joseph he could have mentioned, singles out Joseph's prediction of the exodus and request that his bones be brought to the promised land (Gen 50:24–25). His request came as he was "nearing his end" (τελευτῶν). The Greek word here comes from a root that has theological significance in Hebrews: τελ-, the basis for words such as "perfect" and "perfection." Here, however, the word is probably simply a stylistic variant for "as he [Jacob] was dying" in verse 21.[64] The translation of many English versions follows the pattern of the NIV in rendering the first

---

61. The author does not usually add a conjunction after πίστει in this series, suggesting that it goes with περὶ μελλόντων rather than the whole clause (e.g., Michel, *Der Brief an die Hebräer*, 404; Ellingworth, *Hebrews*, 604).

62. The Hebrew word translated "head" in Genesis and the Greek word translated "top" in Hebrews both can refer to the "high point," "end," or "top" of something. The Hebrew word is ראש, the Greek ἄκρον (which occurs both in the LXX of Gen 47:31 and Heb 11:21).

63. Moisés Silva, "The New Testament Use of the Old Testament: Text Form and Authority," in *Scripture and Truth*, ed. D. A. Carson and John D. Woodbridge (Grand Rapids: Zondervan, 1983), 155. See the entire article for a survey of options (pp. 147–65; 381–86). See also Walser, *Old Testament Quotations in Hebrews*, 141–83. Cockerill (*Hebrews*, 561) also thinks the author may be connoting the pilgrim status of Jacob. Attridge (*Hebrews*, 360) sees a reference to Jacob's piety and faith.

64. Ellingworth, *Hebrews*, 607. The word is used in this prosaic sense throughout the NT: Matt 2:19; 9:18; 15:4; 22:25; Mark 7:10; 9:48; Luke 7:2; John 11:39; Acts 2:29; 7:15.

main verb in the verse (ἐμνημόνευσεν) something like "spoke about" (e.g., "made mention" in ESV). However, this may be a bit of an undertranslation, since the verb (μνημονεύω) has the sense of "remember" or "bring to remembrance." Joseph did not just "mention" the exodus: he remembered God's promise and his thoughts were directed to it.[65] The clause using this verb, then, might be the basis for the last clause in the verse: it was because Joseph's thoughts were focused on the coming exodus that he "gave instructions" (ἐνετείλατο) about his bones. Joseph's concern about his bones may allude to his hope in resurrection,[66] but more likely simply reflects a concern that, even in death, he be joined with the people of Israel as God's promise to them is fulfilled.[67]

Theology in Application

In the application of verses 1–7, I focused on the way faith enables us to "see the unseen": to look beyond the visible world and direct our gaze to the heavenly realm, allowing that reality to dominate our thinking and form our values. However, as I noted in my comments on verse 1, the author views faith not only in terms of the "upward" look but also in terms of the "forward" look. Indeed, the latter focus dominates the author's rehearsal of the great figures of faith from salvation history. This orientation reflects the fundamental Jewish apocalyptic perspective of the letter, according to which what exists in the unseen spiritual realm, visible only to the eyes of faith, will be manifest one day on earth. A city that Abraham and the others could call "home" had already been prepared by God (v. 16), and it was this city that Abraham was "looking forward to" (v. 10). Abraham, Sarah, Isaac, Jacob, and Joseph all "saw" "the things promised" "from a distance" and looked "for a country of their own" (vv. 14–16). Isaac blessed Jacob and Esau "in regard to their future" (v. 20). Joseph's gaze at the end of his life was directed to the promised return to the land of promise (v. 22).

The importance of the forward look in faith is standard New Testament teaching. We look back to God's inauguration of the new realm through Christ's death and resurrection and the pouring out of God's Spirit. We look back also to our own entry into that realm through God's gracious choice and our faith. However, we have been saved, Paul reminds us, "in hope" (Rom 8:24). We have an "inheritance" that is being "kept in heaven" for us and that we will fully enjoy at "the coming of the salvation that is ready to be revealed in the last time" (1 Pet 1:4–5). The Messiah has come to inaugurate God's kingdom, but he will come again to consummate it. The forward look of

---

65. Grässer, *An die Hebräer*, 3:160; Johnson, *Hebrews*, 296; D. Harris, *Hebrews*, 330. On this verb, see the note on 11:15; and "μνημονεύω," L&N 29.18.
66. Cockerill, *Hebrews*, 561.
67. His motivation is therefore similar to that of Jacob's, who also requested that he be buried in Canaan (Gen 49:29–32; 50:4–14). Mention of Joseph's bones is common in Jewish literature: e.g., Sir 49:15; Jub. 46.5; T. Sim. 8.3–4; T. Jos. 20.6; Josephus, *Ant.* 2.200.

faith, our hope, is vital for many reasons, two of which we mention here. First, as our text in Hebrews particularly emphasizes, looking ahead to "the city with foundations" puts into perspective the very pale imitation that is the "city" of this world. Like the Babylon of Revelation, this city, while superficially alluring, is, in fact, "a dwelling for demons" (Rev 18:2). To be sure, God, in his common grace, gives us gifts to enjoy in this world—family, the beauty and variety of the natural world, friendship. But the temptation is always to view these genuine, yet transient, pleasures as the ultimate pleasure. Keeping a vision of the eternal city, the new Jerusalem, before us will help keep the pleasures of this world in proper perspective.

Second, the forward look of faith enables us to endure the difficulties of this world. This becomes a key focus of the author in chapter 12. He concludes that chapter by reminding us that "we are receiving a kingdom that cannot be shaken" and that we should therefore "be thankful, and so worship God acceptably with reverence and awe" (12:28). In this world, Jesus reminds us, we have "trouble," but, he assures us, he has "overcome the world" (John 16:33). This "overcoming," while secured in principle, is not yet the reality we actually experience. God's people are persecuted, we suffer the ravages of time, we fall ill, we watch loved ones die, and we ourselves die. All these evils will one day be overcome. Until that day, we live "in faith," keeping our focus on the promises that our faithful God will infallibly fulfill on the day when evil is judged and the righteous receive their reward.

CHAPTER 28

Hebrews 11:23–31

Literary Context

The author provides no literary markers that would suggest a break between verses 22 and 23. Verses 20 through 24 all begin the same way, "by faith" (πίστει), and there are no conjunctions or particles. The decision by most commentators and translations, then, to place a weak break at verse 23 rests solely on the substance of these verses: the focus shifts from the patriarchal era, recorded in Genesis, to the era of the exodus. Since verse 22 refers to the exodus, a case could be made for including this verse with what follows. However, Joseph is attached to the Old Testament narratives of the patriarchs, and there are also parallels in wording between verses 21 and 22.

As Abraham dominates verses 8–22, so Moses dominates verses 23–31. Some interpreters further identify a parallel in structure: verses 8–22 include four references to the faith of Abraham, followed by three additions (Isaac, Jacob, Joseph), while verses 23–31 likewise note four instances of faith with respect to Moses followed by three additions (the people, the walls of Jericho falling, Rahab).[1] The parallel is not exact (the first reference is not to Moses but to his parents), and it is difficult to be sure the author intended this parallel.

---

1. Michel, *Der Brief an die Hebräer*, 406; Backhaus, *Der Hebräerbrief*, 397. Cockerill (*Hebrews*, 565) proposes a chiastic arrangement of the references to Abraham and Moses, but the parallels are not close enough to justify the structure.

> I. The Exalted Son and a Rest for the People of God (1:1–4:13)
> II. Our Great High Priest and His Ministry (4:14–10:31)
> III. **Exhortation: Follow and Serve the Pioneer of Our Faith through Endurance and Faith (10:32–13:25)**
>   A. Introductory Call to Endurance and Faith (10:32–39)
>   B. The Nature and Power of Faith Illustrated in Salvation History (11:1–40)
>   1. The Ancients Commended for the Faith That Sees the Unseen (11:1–7)
>   2. Faith in the Patriarchal Era (11:8–22)
>   → **3. Faith in the Era of the Exodus and Conquest (11:23–31)**
>   4. The Faith of Judges, Prophets, Women, and Martyrs (11:32–38)
>   5. The Ancients Commended for Faith That Looks to the Future (11:39–40)
>   C. Run the Race with Endurance, Remembering That You Are Children of God (12:1–17)
>   D. Coming to Mount Zion and Inheriting the Unshakable Kingdom (12:18–29)
>   E. Letter Closing (13:1–25)

Main Idea

After highlighting how key people in the patriarchal era were able, by their faith, to look beyond this world to enduring spiritual realities, the author focuses in these verses on the era of the exodus, drawing attention especially to the way faith led people to resist and overcome unbelievers. Moses's parents hid Moses, ignoring the edict of the king (v. 23); Moses identified with downtrodden Israel rather than with the household of Pharoah (vv. 24–26); he left Egypt, "not fearing the king's anger" (v. 27); the people of Israel passed through the Red Sea, while the Egyptians were drowned (v. 29); the city of Jericho fell to the Israelites (v. 30); Rahab's expression of faith kept her from being killed with the disobedient (v. 31).[2]

---

2. Koester (*Hebrews*, 507) draws attention to these thematic focal points.

Translation

Hebrews 11:23-31

23a	means	By faith
23b	assertion	**Moses,**
23c	sequence	after he was born,
23d	predicate (of 23b)	**was hidden**
23e	time	for three months
23f	agent	by his parents
23g	reason 1	because they saw
23h	content	he was no ordinary child and
23i	reason 2	they did not fear the edict
23j	possession	of the king.
24a	means	By faith
24b	assertion	**Moses,**
24c	time	when he grew up,
24d	predicate (of 24b)	**refused**
24e	content	to be called the son
24f	possession	of the daughter
24g	possession	of the pharaoh,
25a	expansion (of 24b–g)	choosing
25b	content	to suffer abuse
25c	association	along with the people
25d	possession	of God rather than
25e	alternative	to enjoy the short-lived pleasure
25f	source	of sin.
26a	assertion	He considered the reproach
26b	object	of Christ
26c	content (of 26a)	to be greater riches
26d	comparison	than the treasures
26e	possession	of Egypt,
26f	basis (of 26a–e)	for
26g	assertion	**he was focused on the reward.**
27a	means	By faith
27b	assertion	**he left Egypt,**
27c	manner	not fearing the anger
27d	possession	of the king.
27e	explanation (of 27a–d)	For
27f	assertion	**he steadfastly kept his eyes**
27g	reference	on the one who cannot be seen,

Continued on next page.

27h	qualification	as it were.
28a	means	By faith
28b	assertion	**he kept the Passover** and
28c	parallel	**ordered that blood should be sprinkled,**
28d	content	
28e	purpose	so that the destroyer …
28f	object	of the firstborn
28g	predicate (of 28e)	… would not touch them.
29a	means	By faith
29b	assertion	**they passed**
29c	place	through the Red Sea
29d	comparison	as if on dry land, but
	contrast (with 29a–d)	
29e	time	when … the Egyptians attempted to do so,
29f	assertion	… they were swallowed up.
30a	means	By faith
30b	assertion	**the walls of Jericho fell,**
30c	sequence	after being encircled
30d	time	for seven days.
31a	means	By faith
31b	assertion	**Rahab the prostitute did not perish**
31c	association	with those who were disobedient,
31d	reason (of 31b)	welcoming the spies
31e	manner	in peace.

Structure

The author continues to enumerate outstanding examples of faith: the passage is organized around seven occurrences of "by faith" (πίστει), all occuring as the first word in their respective verses. A minor break occurs at verse 29, as the author moves from references to Moses to references to other figures of faith from the general era of the exodus. Lane suggests an *inclusio* in the first paragraph, with references to "not fearing" the king's anger in verses 23 and 27.[3] The author's elaboration of signal instances of faith continues to follow the sequence of the Old Testament narrative.

---

3. Lane, *Hebrews*, 2:375.

Exegetical Outline

→ **3. Faith in the Era of the Exodus and Conquest (11:23–31)**
   a. The Parents of Moses (v. 23)
   b. Moses (vv. 24–28)
   c. The People of Israel (vv. 29–30)
   d. Rahab (v. 31)

Explanation of the Text

11:23 By faith Moses, after he was born, was hidden for three months by his parents because they saw he was no ordinary child and they did not fear the edict of the king (Πίστει Μωϋσῆς γεννηθεὶς ἐκρύβη τρίμηνον ὑπὸ τῶν πατέρων αὐτοῦ, διότι εἶδον ἀστεῖον τὸ παιδίον καὶ οὐκ ἐφοβήθησαν τὸ διάταγμα τοῦ βασιλέως). Moses is the center of attention in verses 23–28, with the phrase "by faith Moses" (πίστει Μωϋσῆς) at the beginning of two verses (vv. 23 and 24) and "by faith he [referring to Moses]" at the beginning of two others (vv. 27 and 28). However, while this opening verse has Moses as its subject, the verb is passive (ἐκρύβη, "was hidden"), so it is actually the parents of Moses who are described as acting in faith. The story is from Exodus 2:1–4. In the Hebrew text, it is Moses's mother alone who hid the child (v. 2b). The author's claim that Moses's "parents" (πατέρων)[4] hid the child comes from the LXX, which uses plural verbs in Exodus 2:2b.

The author also follows the LXX in claiming that Moses's parents acted as they did because the child was *asteion* (ἀστεῖον). Most translations suggest the word refers to outward appearance— "beautiful" is the standard rendering. Some reference to outward appearance seems required by the verb "saw" (εἶδον) and by the early age of the baby. However, this word often connotes moral character so, at the least, the word here probably connotes the idea that Moses's outward appearance gave some clue to his character and significance: hence my translation, following NIV, "no ordinary child."[5] Hiding the child was truly an act of faith because, by doing so, the parents were defying the edict of the king (the pharaoh) that Hebrew boys were to be thrown into the Nile; see Exodus 1:22.

11:24–25 By faith Moses, when he grew up,[6] refused to be called the son of the daughter of the pharaoh, choosing to suffer abuse along with the people of God rather than to enjoy the short-lived pleasure of sin (Πίστει Μωϋσῆς μέγας γενόμενος ἠρνήσατο λέγεσθαι υἱὸς θυγατρὸς Φαραώ, μᾶλλον ἑλόμενος συγκακουχεῖσθαι τῷ λαῷ τοῦ θεοῦ

---

4. While usually meaning "father," πατήρ can also mean "parent."

5. This is Bruce's translation also (*Hebrews*, 309); see also, e.g., D. Harris: "extraordinary" or "unusual" (*Hebrews*, 333). See "ἀστεῖος," BDAG 145. The word occurs only once else in the NT, where it also refers to the infant Moses (Acts 7:20). It is rare in the LXX, but frequent in Philo, who uses the word to refer to noble character.

6. The Greek μέγας γενόμενος ("become great") means "when he grew up" (Zerwick and Grosvenor, *Grammatical Analysis*, 682). The same phrase occurs in the LXX of Exod 2:11.

ἢ πρόσκαιρον ἔχειν ἁμαρτίας ἀπόλαυσιν). Moses exhibited faith in his decision to identify with the suffering people of God rather than to continue to enjoy the wealth and prestige of Pharoah's household. After the baby Moses was hidden by his parents, he was discovered by the daughter of Pharaoh and adopted into the family (Exod 2:5–10). The Exodus narrative says nothing about Moses renouncing his Egyptian status. But the author assumes this must have been entailed in Moses's decision to go out to his own people (ἐξῆλθεν πρὸς τοὺς ἀδελφοὺς αὐτοῦ τοὺς υἱοὺς Ισραηλ, Exod 2:11 LXX). While some interpreters think the author might have in mind a formal renunciation of his legal, adopted status, the issue may have been a simple personal decision.[7] The author may have seen further evidence of Moses's choice to identify with Israel in opposition to Egypt in Moses's killing of an Egyptian overseer who was abusing a Hebrew slave (Exod 2:11–12; cf. Acts 7:24).[8] Egypt, the author says, offered "the short-lived pleasure of sin" (πρόσκαιρον ἔχειν ἁμαρτίας ἀπόλαυσιν).[9] The reference is probably to the life of ease and luxury that a member of the royal household would have enjoyed.[10] By virtue of his faith, Moses looked beyond the obvious "worldly" advantages of aristocratic life in Egypt, choosing (ἑλόμενος) rather to identify with the people of God, even though these people of God were suffering increasing oppression from their Egyptian lords. Perhaps the author sees in Moses's situation a parallel to that of his readers—they are tempted to sever their identity with the messianic people of God in order to avoid the hardships that come with that identification (10:32–35).[11]

11:26 He considered the reproach of Christ to be greater riches than the treasures of Egypt, for he was focused on the reward (μείζονα πλοῦτον ἡγησάμενος τῶν Αἰγύπτου θησαυρῶν τὸν ὀνειδισμὸν τοῦ Χριστοῦ· ἀπέβλεπεν γὰρ εἰς τὴν μισθαποδοσίαν). The inner motivation of Moses's decision recorded in verses 24–25 is now outlined. This verse is closely tied to these two preceding verses, as the author adds a third participial qualifier to the main verb "refused to be called" in verse 24a ("when he grew up... he refused to be called... choosing... considering" [μέγας γενόμενος... ἠρνήσατο λέγεσθαι... ἑλόμενος... ἡγησάμενος]). This third participial clause elaborates on why Moses made the choice to identify with the people of God. Moses "considered" or "regarded" (the verb is ἡγέομαι) "the reproach of Christ to be greater riches than the treasures of Egypt." In this he followed in the footsteps of Sarah, who "considered" (ἡγήσατο) "him faithful who had made the promise" (v. 11) and Abraham, who "reasoned" (λογισάμενος) that God could raise Isaac from the dead (v. 19).[12] "The treasures of Egypt" are another way of describing the "pleasure of sin" from verse 25. As a member of Pharaoh's household, Moses would have had some degree of access to the fabulous wealth accumulated by the royal family. Yet he turned his back on it, considering, with the eyes of faith, that sharing "the reproach of Christ" brought even greater riches.

---

7. Lane, *Hebrews*, 2:371–72; Cockerill, *Hebrews*, 568.
8. See, e.g., Lane, *Hebrews*, 2:371.
9. In the phrase ἔχειν ἁμαρτίας ἀπόλαυσιν, ἁμαρτίας might be a genitive of source—"enjoyment that comes from sin" (e.g., Johnson, *Hebrews*, 300; Cockerill, *Hebrews*, 570)—or descriptive—"sinful enjoyment" (Attridge, *Hebrews*, 340). The word ἀπόλαυσιν is further qualified by the adjective πρόσκαιρον, "temporary" (CEB), "fleeting" (NIV; ESV; NRSV; NET; CSB), "transitory" (NJB).
10. Josephus, in a passage with significant parallels to the one here in Hebrews, refers to Moses's "life of ease" in Pharaoh's household (*Ant.* 4.42; cf. 2.50–51 with reference to Joseph).
11. Grässer, *An die Hebräer*, 3:178.
12. Cockerill, *Hebrews*, 571.

Just how Moses, living many centuries before Christ, shared his reproach (ὀνειδισμός) is quite debated.[13] One option is to understand "Christ" here to refer to "the anointed one" (see NAB; NJB). The author may then have Psalm 89:50–51 in view: "remember, Lord, the ridicule [LXX ὀνειδισμοῦ] against your servants—in my heart I carry abuse from all the peoples—how your enemies have ridiculed, LORD, how they have ridiculed every step of your anointed [τοῦ χριστοῦ σου]" (CSB).[14] Some interpreters then suggest, further, that Moses had a prophetic vision of the Messiah to come.[15] Another interpretation is that the genitive construction used here (ὀνειδισμὸν τοῦ Χριστοῦ) means something like "the kind of reproach that Christ (later) experienced."[16] However, the genitive more likely has a loosely objective sense: "reproach directed toward Christ."[17] The best option is to assume that Moses, in identifying with the people of God, ultimately identified with the Christ who is central to the life of that people. The author anachronistically reads Christ back into Moses's experience in order to emphasize the parallel between Moses and his readers.[18] These readers had already been exposed to "insult" (ὀνειδισμός, 10:33), and the author calls on them to go to Jesus, "outside the camp, bearing the disgrace [ὀνειδισμόν] he bore" (13:13).

The author ultimately grounds (note the γάρ; here "for") Moses's willingness to forego the riches of Egypt for the suffering of God's people in the fact that he "was focused[19] on the reward [μισθαποδοσίαν]." Moses, then, shared a crucial aspect of biblical faith: a conviction that God "rewards [μισθαποδότης] those who earnestly seek him" (11:6).

11:27 By faith he left Egypt, not fearing the anger of the king. For he steadfastly kept his eyes on the one who cannot be seen, as it were (Πίστει κατέλιπεν Αἴγυπτον μὴ φοβηθεὶς τὸν θυμὸν τοῦ βασιλέως· τὸν γὰρ ἀόρατον ὡς ὁρῶν ἐκαρτέρησεν). After his brief commentary on the nature of Moses's faith in verses 25–26, the author here returns to his recitation of examples of faith. The focus remains on Moses, and we would expect, based on the sequence of the Old Testament narrative, that the author now describes the flight of Moses from Egypt after a witness came forward to accuse him of killing the Egyptian who was beating a Hebrew (Exod 2:14–15). This incident occurs in the Exodus narrative just after the incident that probably serves as the basis for the author's commentary in verses 24–26 and before the Passover, which the author refers to in verse 28. However, there is a problem with this identification: whereas the author claims that Moses was "not fearing the king," the Exodus narrative explicitly claims that Moses "was afraid" and that he fled the country when he learned that Pharaoh was trying to kill him (Exod 2:14b–15). Confronted with this discrepancy, some argue that the author does not have any one incident in view.[20] A more popular alternative is to suggest

---

13. Nathan MacDonald surveys patristic and Reformation interpretations ("By Faith Moses," in Bauckham et al., *Epistle to the Hebrews*, 383–404).

14. E.g., Michel, *Der Brief an die Hebräer*, 409.

15. Cockerill, *Hebrews*, 572–73; Attridge, *Hebrews*, 341. See especially God's promise to Moses in Deut 18:15: "The LORD your God will raise up for you a prophet like me from among you, from your fellow Israelites. You must listen to him."

16. Koester, *Hebrews*, 502; Bénétrau, *L'Épître aux Hébreux*, 2:147; G. Guthrie, *Hebrews*, 381.

17. The word refers to "insults" directed toward Christ in Rom 15:3, and the cognate verb is used to describe the mockery of Christ on the cross (Matt 27:44; Mark 15:32). The word ὀνειδισμός also occurs five times in Ps 69 [Ps 68 LXX], a psalm interpreted in terms of Christ's suffering in the NT.

18. Lane, *Hebrews*, 2:374; Thompson, *Hebrews* (2008), 241.

19. The verb ἀποβλέπω means "look," "pay attention"; BDAG 107 suggest here "be intent on."

20. Grässer, *An die Hebräer*, 3:173; Koester, *Hebrews*, 504.

that the author is, in fact, referring in this verse to Moses's departure from Egypt at the time of the exodus (Exod 12:31–14:31).[21] However, the author appears to follow the Old Testament chronology of events in his recitation of examples of faith, and it would be odd, therefore, for him to put the exodus (v. 27) before the Passover (v. 28). Moreover, the author's overview of Old Testament events tracks fairly closely with Stephen's overview in Acts 7:2–47, and Stephen clearly refers to the incident when Moses killed the Egyptian (vv. 23–26). If, then, the author is referring to the story of Exodus 2:11–15, he may be depending on Jewish traditions that minimized Moses's fear and lauded his courage.[22] Perhaps the more likely option, however, is that the author views Moses's leaving Egypt in terms of his overall conviction about God's purposes for him—not as a member of Pharaoh's royal family but as a leader of an insurgent Israel.[23]

Moses, our author explains ("for" [γάρ]), could overcome his fear of the king because he "steadfastly kept his eyes on the one who cannot be seen." My translation follows BDAG ("καρτερέω," 510) and several commentators in recognizing that the indicative verb "persevered" (ἐκαρτέρησεν) functions virtually as an auxiliary verb, with the main idea being expressed in the participle "seeing" (ὁρῶν).[24] That God cannot be seen is a staple of biblical teaching; he is, as the author puts it, "the unseen one" (τὸν ... ἀόρατον). Yet, in a certain manner (ὡς), by the eyes of faith, the unseen God can be seen. That is, one can keep their attention fixed on him so that the reality of his existence and his purposes for his people can determine one's attitude and course of action.[25] By focusing on this aspect of Moses's faith, the author has returned again to his opening characterization of faith, which assures us of the reality of things that are not seen (v. 1; see also vv. 3, 7). Faith means constantly looking beyond the sensory world around us, focusing our attention on and directing our thinking and acting with respect to the unseen, but real and powerful, God.

11:28 By faith he kept the Passover and ordered that blood should be sprinkled, so that the destroyer of the firstborn would not touch them (Πίστει πεποίηκεν τὸ πάσχα καὶ τὴν πρόσχυσιν τοῦ αἵματος, ἵνα μὴ ὁ ὀλοθρεύων τὰ πρωτότοκα θίγῃ αὐτῶν). The author jumps ahead in the Old Testament narrative to one of the climactic moments in Israel's history: when God instituted the Passover, commanding the people to apply blood to their doorframes so that their firstborn would not be slaughtered along with the Egyptian firstborn (Exod 12:1–30). He therefore moves from a focus on Moses's faith with respect to his own life (Heb 11:24–27) to his faith in his "official" capacity as a key instrument used by God to deliver his people—a focus that continues as the author broadens the scope of faith in verses 29–31. Also running through verses 28–31 is a contrast between deliverance (by faith) and destruction (for unbelievers and the disobedient).[26] While Moses is not named in this verse, it is clear that he is the implied subject

---

21. Calvin, *Hebrews*, 178; Westcott, *Hebrews*, 373; Montefiore, *Hebrews*, 204; Hagner, *Hebrews*, 201; Cockerill, *Hebrews*, 574–75.

22. See Josephus, *Ant.* 2.254–57; Philo, *Alleg. Interp.* 3.11–14. See Weiss, *Der Brief an die Hebräer*, 608; Attridge, *Hebrews*, 342.

23. See esp. P. Hughes, *Hebrews*, 498–99; also Delitzsch, *Hebrews*, 2:265–67; Lane, *Hebrews*, 2:375; Schreiner, *Hebrews*, 364–65; Gray, *Godly Fear*, 170–75.

24. "καρτερέω," BDAG 405; Lane, *Hebrews*, 2:367–68. The reverse of this view of the verbs is advocated by others, yielding the translation "he perservered as if seeing the one who cannot be seen" (so most translations; see, e.g., Koester, *Hebrews*, 504).

25. The author is probably not, then, referring to any particular incident in Moses's life, such as the burning-bush encounter.

26. Koester, *Hebrews*, 510.

of the verb "kept" (πεποίηκεν).²⁷ The same verb governs the phrase "sprinkling, or application, of blood" (πρόσχυσιν τοῦ αἵματος), though now the semantic force shifts a bit: "kept" does not fit, and Moses himself did not sprinkle the blood.²⁸ Perhaps, then, as I translate, the meaning is something like "ordered." The reference is to God's command that the Israelites apply blood to their doorframes "so that the destroyer of the firstborn would not touch them" (see Exod 12:7, 22). The language of "the destroyer" (ὁ ὀλοθρεύων) comes from Exodus 12:23 LXX: "when the LORD goes through the land to strike down the Egyptians, he will see the blood on the top and sides of the doorframe and will pass over that doorway, and he will not permit the destroyer [τὸν ὀλεθρεύοντα] to enter your houses and strike you down." It is God himself (v. 27), perhaps through the agency of an angel (v. 23; cf. 2 Sam 24:16), who destroys the firstborn. It is possible that the word "firstborn" (πρωτότοκα) goes with the main verb "touch" (θίγῃ): "in order that the destroyer could not touch their firstborn children" (CEB; see also NLT).²⁹ But it makes better sense to attach the word to the participle—"destroyer"—and assume that it carries over as the implied object of the main verb also. See NIV: "so that the destroyer of the firstborn would not touch the firstborn of Israel."

11:29 By faith they passed through the Red Sea as if on dry land, but when the Egpytians attempted to do so, they were swallowed up (Πίστει διέβησαν τὴν Ἐρυθρὰν Θάλασσαν ὡς διὰ ξηρᾶς γῆς, ἧς πεῖραν λαβόντες οἱ Αἰγύπτιοι κατεπόθησαν). Faith enabled Israel to pass through the Red Sea, even as the Egyptians were destroyed. As Lane notes, we find a transition at this point in chapter 11 from "exemplary people" to "exemplary events."³⁰ At the same time, the author "quickens his pace and increases emotional intensity."³¹ The Israelites' passing through the "Red Sea" (τὴν Ἐρυθρὰν Θάλασσαν) is the high point of the people's exodus from Egypt (Exod 12:31–14:31).³² This miraculous deliverance from the pursuing Egyptians was fundamentally an act of God. At another level, it was the result of "a strong east wind" (Exod 14:21). And at still another level, it was an act of faith on the part of the people of Israel (the implicit subject of the verb διέβησαν, "pass through"; see "Israel" [NIV, Greek αὐτῶν] in v. 28). This faith of the Israelites was not constant. When they saw the armies of Pharaoh pursuing them, they were "terrified" and regretted that they had ever left Egypt (Exod 14:10–14). Yet they overcame this fear when God opened the way for them, daring to enter the path between the "wall of water on their right and on their left" (Exod 14:22). It is this moment that the author appears to have in mind when he refers to their faith. He appears to moderate the straightforward claim in Exodus 14:22 that the people crossed on dry land by qualifying the phrase "on dry land" (διὰ ξηρᾶς γῆς)³³ with the particle ὡς, "as," "as if." Probably what he

---

27. The verb ποιέω has a wide semantic range and can therefore be translated in many different ways to suit the contexts in which it occurs. The author may use the perfect tense to imply the continuing observance of the rite (BDF §342.4).

28. The word πρόσχυσιν is rare, occurring only here in the NT and never in the LXX, Philo, or Josephus. It is derived from the verb προσχέω, "to pour forth" (Muraoka, *Greek-English Lexicon of the Septuagint*); see, e.g., Exod 24:6; 29:21.

29. Ellingworth, *Hebrews*, 618.

30. Lane, *Hebrews*, 2:376.

31. Cockerill, *Hebrews*, 582.

32. The author's reference to the "Red Sea" follows the LXX, which consistently refers to this body of water with this language. The Hebrew, "sea of reeds" (יַם־סוּף), probably refers to a northern extension of the Gulf of Suez, but the precise location continues to be debated (see Peter E. Enns, "Exodus Route and Wilderness Itinerary," in Alexander and Baker, *Dictionary of the Old Testament: Pentateuch*, 273–76).

33. As Moule (*Idiom Book*, 55) notes, διά with the genitive here denotes "extension through" an area.

means is that the people crossed the sea as easily as they would have crossed dry land.³⁴

The deliverance the Israelites experienced by faith stands in stark contrast to the destruction suffered by the armies of Pharaoh. When they "attempted"³⁵ to do what the Israelites had done, they were "swallowed up" (κατεπόθησαν) by the waters of the sea. The deliverance the ancient Israelites experienced has obvious significance for the readers. They, like the Israelites of old, have been rescued from bondage and now face further obstacles. Like the Israelites, the author urges his readers to overcome the obstacles they face by faith and so also experience the full salvation God has promised them.

11:30 By faith the walls of Jericho fell, after being encircled for seven days (Πίστει τὰ τείχη Ἰεριχὼ ἔπεσαν κυκλωθέντα ἐπὶ ἑπτὰ ἡμέρας). The author's focus on events rather than people continues in this verse. He does not mention who it was who had faith, although it is natural to pick up the implied agent of that faith from verse 29: the Israelites. Of course, these were (with a couple of exceptions) not the same Israelites who passed through the Red Sea. Forty years have gone by and, as punishment for disobedience, that earlier generation has died off. It is natural, granted the author's emphasis on the lack of faith of the exodus generation (3:7–4:11), that he skips over this phase in Israel's history. It might be thought mildly surprising that the author does not mention Joshua explicitly, but his focus is on the "encircling" (κυκλωθέντα) of the city, which was carried out by the people generally.³⁶ The author undoubtedly sees the Israelites' faith manifested in what seems to be this very foolish way of conducting the seige of a city. It took faith in the unseen God and his promises for the people to continue doing this for seven days.

11:31 By faith Rahab the prostitute did not perish with those who were disobedient, welcoming the spies in peace (Πίστει Ῥαὰβ ἡ πόρνη οὐ συναπώλετο τοῖς ἀπειθήσασιν δεξαμένη τοὺς κατασκόπους μετ' εἰρήνης). The story of Rahab (Josh 2) comes before the story of the seige and fall of Jericho (Josh 6), but the author probably orders the two events in this sequence because his focus is on Rahab's escape from the fallen city.³⁷ Our author justifiably infers that Rahab's welcoming of the Israelite spies who had entered the city was stimulated by her faith (Josh 2:9–11). Although James does not explicitly credit Rahab with faith, the context in which he mentions her shows that he, also, sees evidence of her faith in her actions (Jas 2:25). The fact that both these authors mention Rahab (as does the early Christian document 1 Clement [12:1–8]; cf. Matt 1:5) suggests that her example was commonly cited among early Christians. This may have been partly because she was a woman, but far more important, as our text makes clear, is her status as a (pagan) prostitute.³⁸ While not a member of the people of Israel, Rahab had heard about the things God had done in and for his people. She inferred from these events that God did, indeed, exist (Heb 11:6), and put her faith in this God.

---

34. Ellingworth, *Hebrews*, 619.
35. "Make an attempt" is the sense of the phrase πεῖραν λαβόντες ("πεῖρα," BDAG 792, §1; Koester, *Hebrews*, 505). The antecedent of the relative pronoun ἧς is probably θάλασσαν, but, more widely, it picks up all of v. 29a (Grässer, *An die Hebräer*, 3:180): "which [passing through the Red Sea] attempting to do, the Egyptians were swallowed up."
36. Pursuing her general thesis that the author "denationalizes" the people of God in ch. 11, Eisenbaum argues that Joshua is omitted because he is too closely associated with national Israel (*Jewish Heroes of Christian History*, 172).
37. Ellingworth, *Hebrews*, 621.
38. The word πόρνη means "prostitute" here (BDAG 854, §1). A textual variant softens this claim (Ῥαὰβ ἡ ἐπιλεγομένη πόρνη, "Rahab, who was called a prostitute" [א, etc.]), but it is clearly secondary. Josephus (*Ant.* 5.7–8) calls her an "innkeeper."

Theology in Application

Sometimes we fail in our walk with God not through spectacular sins or outright rebellion but through much more subtle, but equally dangerous, means. In 2:1 the author has warned us about "drifting away." As I note in my comments there, the image is of a boat gradually moving away from its mooring. For many of us, the danger in our spiritual walk comes in barely noticed subtle failures.

Features in the life of Moses that our author draws attention to point, by contrast, to some of these much easier to overlook failures. Moses did not allow "the short-lived pleasure of sin" to distract him from his identification with the people of God. Identifying with God's people is not always easy. We don't always like or even get along well with fellow believers. It may be particularly difficult to identify with God's people when that identification might interfere with the prestige or social position we might otherwise enjoy in this world. Moses must certainly have found a secure position in the court of one of the world's great monarchs, the pharaoh of Egypt, to be an enticing prospect. Yet he gave up this option in order to be mistreated with his fellow Israelites. C. S. Lewis notes that "prosperity knits a man to the world. He feels that he is finding his place in it, while really it is finding its place in him."[39] Of course, we have to live in this world. Most of us will have jobs that require daily interaction with unbelievers. Many of us will go to school with fellow students and teachers who do not share our values. The world and its values will press hard on us. It can be terribly easy, over time, to allow that world to shape us into its image. Like Moses, we need constantly to battle against that pressure and to spend enough time with God's people so that *that* reality of being with people of faith will have the stronger hand in shaping us.

Moses also kept his eyes fixed on the reward (v. 26). Our lives are subtly yet powerfully shaped by our goals. If our ultimate goal is success in this world—a well-paying job, running a marathon, even having a loving and thriving family—it will direct our energy and focus our attention in a certain way. However if, like Moses, we are motivated by the "reward" that God gives his faithful servants, our lives will take a very different shape. Yet keeping our focus on that reward is not easy. It is terribly easy to allow it to gradually fade from our vision.

---

39. *The Screwtape Letters* (New York: Macmillan, 1950), 143.

Chapter 29

Hebrews 11:32–40

Literary Context

The rhetorical question, "What more should I say?" marks the beginning of a new literary unit. The reference to specific acts of faith attached to particular individuals that has marked the chapter so far comes to an end. The particular expression that provides the literary unity for verses 3–31—"by faith" (πίστει)—is replaced with the phrase "through faith" (διὰ πίστεως) (vv. 33, 39). The author is by no means finished with his encouraging catalog of ways in which the ancients exhibited faith. He uses a staccato "list" style, often omitting conjunctions to link items together (part of vv. 32, 33–35a, 37). This style invites readers to add to the list from their own knowledge of Israel's history. As Koester puts it, the author "evokes associations with an ever widening circle of faithful people."[1]

- I. The Exalted Son and a Rest for the People of God (1:1–4:13)
- II. Our Great High Priest and His Ministry (4:14–10:31)
- **III. Exhortation: Follow and Serve the Pioneer of Our Faith through Endurance and Faith (10:32–13:25)**
  - A. Introductory Call to Endurance and Faith (10:32–39)
  - B. The Nature and Power of Faith Illustrated in Salvation History (11:1–40)
    1. The Ancients Commended for the Faith That Sees the Unseen (11:1–7)
    2. Faith in the Patriarchal Era (11:8–22)
    3. Faith in the Era of the Exodus and Conquest (11:23–31)
    → **4. The Faith of Judges, Prophets, Women, and Martyrs (11:32–38)**
    5. The Ancients Commended for Faith That Looks to the Future (11:39–40)
  - C. Run the Race with Endurance, Remembering That You Are Children of God (12:1–17)
  - D. Coming to Mount Zion and Inheriting the Unshakable Kingdom (12:18–29)
  - E. Letter Closing (13:1–25)

---

1. Koester, *Hebrews*, 517. See also Cosby, "Rhetorical Composition," 262. As is the case for vv. 3–31, a number of scholars suspect that the author is citing from an existing catalog of faithful figures and actions (e.g., Weiss, *Der Brief an die Hebräer*, 615).

Main Idea

The author lacks space and time to recount all the deeds of faith exhibited by the people of God in the past, so he quickly mentions additional Old Testament individuals who manifested great faith and various ways in which they, and others, displayed faith. Despite the faith of these people of old, however, they did not attain the fulfillment of God's promise—a fulfillment that awaits the culmination of God's plan in the new covenant.

Translation

Hebrews 11:32–40

32a	rhetorical question	**What more should I say?**	
32b	explanation (of 32a)	For	
32c	assertion	**the time would fail me**	
32d	condition	if I were to go into detail	
32e	list 1.1	about	Gideon,
32f	list 1.2		Barak,
32g	list 2.1		Samson,
32h	list 2.2		Jephthah, and
32i	list 3.1	about both	David and
32j	list 3.2		Samuel and
32k	list 4		the prophets.
33a	assertion		It was through faith that
33b	means	that these people	conquered kingdoms,
33c	list 1.1		administered justice,
33d	list 1.2		obtained things that had been promised,
33e	list 1.3		shut the mouths of lions,
33f	list 2.1		quenched the power of fire,
34a	list 2.2		escaped the edge of the sword,
34b	list 2.3		were strengthened
34c	list 3.1		in the midst of weakness,
34d	circumstance		
34e	list 3.2		became strong in battle,
34f	list 3.3		put to flight foreign armies.
35a	assertion	**Women received their dead back**	
35b	means	through resurrection.	

Continued on next page.

35c	assertion	**Others were tortured,**
35d	reason	refusing to accept release,
35e	purpose (of 35c–d)	in order that they might attain a better resurrection.
36a	list 1	**Some experienced** mocking and
36b	list 2	flogging,
36c	intensification	and even
36d	list 3	chains and
36e	list 4	imprisonment.
37a	list 5	**They were put to death**
37b	means	by stoning,
37c	list 6	**sawn in half,**
37d	list 7	**killed**
37e	means	by the sword,
37f	list 8	**going about**
37g	circumstance 1	in sheepskins and
37h	circumstance 2	goatskins,
37i	list 9	destitute,
37j	list 10	persecuted,
37k	list 11	mistreated
38a	parenthesis	—the world was not worthy of them.
38b	assertion	**They wandered**
38c	place 1	in deserts and
38d	place 2	in mountains, living
38e	simultaneous (to 38c–d)	in caves and
38f	place 4	in holes in the ground.
39a	contra-expectation	**All these, . . .**
39b	concession	although receiving commendation
39c	reason	for their faith,
39d	predicate (of 39a)	**. . . did not obtain**
39e	content	what was promised,
40a	reason (for 39a–e)	God having planned something better
40b	advantage	for us,
40c	purpose (of 39a–e)	so that they might not be perfected
40d	relationship	without us.

Structure

This unit clearly break into two parts: verses 32–38 and verses 39–40. The latter paragraph is a summary reflection that looks back at the whole chapter, with the verb "received commendation" (a passive form) acting as a frame around the chapter (see vv. 2, 39). Verses 32–38, as I note above, continue the author's list of examples of faith, the paragraph being framed by the phrase "through faith" (διὰ [τῆς] πίστεως—vv. 33, 39).² They contain four lists. The first quickly mentions six faithful people, probably to be grouped in three pairs: Gideon and Barak, Samson and Jephthah, and David and Samuel—along with the prophets in general (v. 32b). The second list (vv. 33–34) is also probably to be divided into three parts, with three acts of faith in each:³

"conquered kingdoms"
"administered justice"
"obtained things that had been promised"

"shut the mouths of lions"
"quenched the power of fire"
"escaped the edge of the sword"

"were strengthened in the midst of weakness"
"became strong in battle"
"put to flight foreign armies"

Verse 35 is transitional. The first part is closely tied to verses 33–34, mentioning another "victory" gained through faith: the women who "received their dead" by resurrection. Resurrection binds verse 35b to verse 35a, with now, however, the focus turning to those who looked forward to the "better" resurrection in their death.⁴ Verse 35b is the point, then, where the author shifts from the triumphs won by faith to the suffering that God's people have endured in faith.⁵ Three examples of suffering are given in verse 36, while in verse 37 the author mentions eight more examples of suffering, now using his "list" style (i.e., dropping all conjunctions). Verse 38 concludes with a brief commentary from the author—"the world was not worthy of them"—and the whole paragraph concludes with a reference to the "wandering" lifestyle of those who suffered for the faith.

---

2. Noted by, e.g., Lane, *Hebrews*, 2:322.

3. Michel, *Der Brief an die Hebräer*, 415; Cockerill, *Hebrews*, 588–89.

4. Cockerill ("Better Resurrection," 222) argues that resurrection is therefore the focal point of the section.

5. See, e.g., Koester, *Hebrews*, 517; Grässer, *An die Hebräer*, 3:187. Weiss (*Der Brief an die Hebräer*, 614) suggests the shift is from war to martyrdom.

Exegetical Outline

→ **4. The Faith of Judges, Prophets, Women, and Martyrs (11:32–38)**
  a. The Victories Won by Faith (vv. 32–34)
  b. Resurrection to the Old Life and Resurrection to the New (v. 35)
  c. The Suffering Endured by Faith (vv. 36–38)
5. The Ancients Commended for Faith That Looks to the Future (11:39–40)

Explanation of the Text

11:32 What more should I say? For the time would fail me if I were to go into detail about Gideon, Barak, Samson, Jephthah, and about both David and Samuel and the prophets (Καὶ τί ἔτι λέγω; ἐπιλείψει με γὰρ διηγούμενον ὁ χρόνος περὶ Γεδεών, Βαράκ, Σαμψών, Ἰεφθάε, Δαυίδ τε καὶ Σαμουὴλ καὶ τῶν προφητῶν). The author turns to a quick overview of other Old Testament "heroes" of the faith. The verb in the first clause (λέγω) is probably a (deliberative) subjunctive rather than an indicative; hence, "What more should I say?" rather than "What more am I saying?"[6] The author's claim that time lacks for him to go into detail[7] about the individuals he now lists follows a typical Greek rhetorical pattern; see Philo, *Sacrifices* 27: "the daylight will fail me while I recount the names of specific virtues."[8] The Old Testament heroes the author lists are obviously not in chronological order. The names fall into three pairs, and in each pair, the second listed comes first in the biblical narrative: Gideon (Judg 7–8) and Barak (Judg 4–5); Samson (Judg 13–15) and Jephthah (Judg 11:29–40); David (1 Sam 16–2 Sam 24) and Samuel (1 Sam 1–16). The author may put the more important figure first in each case.[9] We have no way of knowing why the author has chosen these particular individuals to illustrate the power of faith. First Samuel 12:11 may have been an influence on the author: "then the LORD sent Jerub-Baal [another name for Gideon], Barak, Jephthah and Samuel, and he delivered you from the hands of your enemies all around you, so that you lived in safety." Each of these men certainly displayed faith: Gideon defeated the Midianites with a reduced number of soldiers and unorthodox tactics (Judg 7); Barak obeyed the Lord's word to attack the Canaanites (Judg 4–5); Samson, blinded and bound, nevertheless used his strength to kill many Philistines (Judg 15); Jephthah devastated the Ammonites (Judg 11:29–40); and the wise advice of Samuel and many exploits of David are well-known. Each of these figures is also flawed in some way: Gideon used gold to build an ephod used for worship of false gods (Judg 8:22–27); Barak refused to go into battle unless Deborah came with him (Judg 4:8); Samson was a braggart and womanizer; Jephthah made a rash vow that led to the sacrifice of his daughter (Judg 11:29–40); David's sin with Bathsheba is well-known. (Of these figures, only

---

6. The English translations pretty uniformly take it this way; see D. Harris, *Hebrews*, 345.
7. "Go into detail about" is an option for the meaning of διηγέομαι in BDAG 245 that fits this context particularly well. The participial form the author uses (διηγούμενον) has a conditional sense (Turner, *Syntax*, 157).
8. Philo, *Sacrifices* 27 (Colson, Whitaker, and Earp).
9. Ellingworth, *Hebrews*, 623; D. Harris, *Hebrews*, 347.

Samuel has a rather unblemished record in Scripture.) Perhaps the author includes some individuals with obvious flaws to strengthen the rhetorical effect for his readers: "if faith is possible despite Jephthah's rashness and Barak's hesitancy, then faith is also possible for the listeners, despite their shortcomings."[10]

The author ends his list with a vague reference to "prophets." In the Jewish tradition, "prophets" could include both the Latter Prophets as well as Joshua, Judges, and the books of Samuel and Kings—the Former Prophets. Indeed, another reason why the author may put Samuel last in the list is because of his close association with prophets (1 Sam 3:19–20; 19:20). We have no way of knowing which prophets the author might be referring to here.

11:33–34 It was through faith that these people conquered kingdoms, administered justice, obtained things that had been promised, shut the mouths of lions, 34 quenched the power of fire, escaped the edge of the sword, were strengthened in the midst of weakness, became strong in battle, put to flight foreign armies (οἳ διὰ πίστεως κατηγωνίσαντο βασιλείας, εἰργάσαντο δικαιοσύνην, ἐπέτυχον ἐπαγγελιῶν, ἔφραξαν στόματα λεόντων, 34 ἔσβεσαν δύναμιν πυρός, ἔφυγον στόματα μαχαίρης, ἐδυναμώθησαν ἀπὸ ἀσθενείας, ἐγενήθησαν ἰσχυροὶ ἐν πολέμῳ, παρεμβολὰς ἔκλιναν ἀλλοτρίων). The focus shifts from people who exhibited faith to events that were the product of faith. The verse opens with a relative pronoun whose antecedent is the people mentioned in verse 32b. However, since the vague reference to "prophets," verse 32b has already pointed to the inclusion of many more people than those explicitly named in verse 32, and so we are justified in thinking that "these people" (οἳ) may have an open-ended reference to any figure from Israel's history. "Through faith" (διὰ πίστεως) carries a great deal of weight. In addition to its clear syntactical connection to the verbs in verses 33–34, it also governs all that the author says about the accomplishments listed in verses 35–38. It carries on the crucial instrumental role of faith that we have seen throughout the chapter.[11]

The author continues to use the "list" style he employs in verse 32: verses 33–34 are conspicuous for lacking any conjunctions at all. The semantic focus, however, shifts; as Massonnet puts it, there is a shift from subjects without verbs to verbs without subjects.[12] As I note above (see Structure), the exploits the author relates in these verses fall into three series of three each. The first three may pick up the focus on the time of the conquest we find in the mention of "judges" in verse 33. These judges—or, more accurately, "leaders"—did, indeed, conquer kingdoms, administer justice, and obtain the things promised.[13] Of course, as the author elsewhere notes, they did not obtain what had been ultimately promised to God's people (11:13, 39). The promise of rest held out in Psalm 95 makes clear that the people did not experience true "rest" at the time of the conquest (Heb 4:8). The word "justice" [δικαιοσύνην] in the phrase "administered justice" has a wide range of meaning; but here it refers to the leaders' establishing justice for the people. See, for example, 2 Samuel 8:15: "David reigned over all Israel, doing what was just and right [δικαιοσύνην] for all his people."[14]

---

10. Koester, *Hebrews*, 517–18.
11. Ellingworth, therefore, is correct to note that διὰ πίστεως is semantically equivalent to πίστει (*Hebrews*, 624).
12. *L'Épître aux Hébreux*, 343.
13. While the Greek uses the simple ἐπαγγελιῶν—"promises"—the context makes clear it refers to the things promised (a common meaning of the word).
14. See, e.g., Michel, *Der Brief an die Hebräer*, 416; Johnson, *Hebrews*, 306–7.

The next two faith-fueled exploits take us into the time of the prophets. While Samson (Judg 14:5-6) and David (1 Sam 17:34-37) both overcame the power of lions, "shut the mouths of lions" most naturally refers to Daniel's famous deliverance from the lions' den (Dan 6). Daniel was unharmed because "he had trusted in his God" (Dan 6:23). The author then mentions another story of miraculous deliverance from the book of Daniel: the rescue of his three friends from the "fiery furnace" (Dan 3). "Escaped the edge of the sword" probably refers to being preserved safe in battle and is vague enough as to make it impossible to pin down any specific referent.[15] The same is true of the first item in the third series: "[they] were strengthened in the midst of weakness."[16] Many interpreters, though, think of Samson.[17] "Became strong in battle" might refer again to the many victories won by the Israelites at the conquest, but could also refer to the period of the Maccabees, which the author clearly refers to in verses 35b-37.[18] Some interpreters think that the last item may also refer to the Maccabees, who "put to flight foreign armies."[19] Yet the description also fits the time of the conquest and, indeed, many other times in Israel's history.

11:35 Women received their dead back through resurrection. Others were tortured, refusing to accept release, in order that they might attain a better resurrection (ἔλαβον γυναῖκες ἐξ ἀναστάσεως τοὺς νεκροὺς αὐτῶν· ἄλλοι δὲ ἐτυμπανίσθησαν οὐ προσδεξάμενοι τὴν ἀπολύτρωσιν, ἵνα κρείττονος ἀναστάσεως τύχωσιν). The first sentence in the verse adds to the list of victories achieved through faith. But the addition of an explicit subject, "women" (γυναῖκες), suggests a shift. This shift is confirmed by the focus on resurrection, which is set in contrast to the "better resurrection" in the second part of the verse. This verse, then, is the hinge in the paragraph, as the author moves from the victories faith wins (vv. 33-35a) to the trials faith allows people to endure (vv. 35b-38). As Chrysostom notes, faith "both accomplishes great things and suffers great things."[20]

Verse 35a refers to Elijah's raising of the widow of Zarephath's son (1 Kgs 17:17-24) and Elisha's raising of the Shunammite's son (2 Kgs 4:18-37). From the standpoint of biblical theology, these are resuscitations rather than resurrections—both young men were restored to life, only to die again. In contrast is the "better resurrection"—a being raised to life that has no end. The author here uses again the word that captures a central plank in his argument: κρείττων, "better" (see also 1:4; 7:7, 19, 22; 8:6; 9:23; 10:34; 11:16, 40; 12:24). It is this "better resurrection" that the Maccabean martyrs were focused on amid their suffering. The author now clearly moves beyond the canonical Old Testament to books of the Apocrypha. These books describe the attempt, at the beginning of the second century BC, of the Seleucid king Antiochus IV to stamp out the Jewish faith and the heroic resistance led by the

---

15. "Edge of the sword" translates στόματα μαχαίρης; cf. Heb 4:12. The word στόμα usually refers to a "mouth," but the word is applied also to the part of the sword that "devours" a person ("στόμα," BDAG 947, §4). The plural form of the word probably refers to the two sides of the sword (Grässer, *An die Hebräer*, 3:199).

16. "In the midst of" is a bit of a loose translation for ἀπό, but the idea is probably being strengthened "out of [ἀπό equivalent to ἐκ; see BDF §209.4] a condition of weakness."

17. Ellingworth, *Hebrews*, 626.

18. Delitzsch, *Hebrews*, 2:280; Grässer, *An die Hebräer*, 3:201.

19. E.g., Johnson, *Hebrews*, 307. The verb κλίνω in this expression (ἔκλιναν), which means basically "incline" or "bend," can also mean "cause to fall, turn to flight" (BDAG 549-50, §§1, 4; see, e.g., Josephus, *Ant.* 14.416). Likewise, παρεμβολή means "fortified camp," but can be extended to refer to "an army in battle array" (BDAG 775, §3).

20. *Homilies* 27.5; see Koester, *Hebrews*, 519.

Maccabees who resisted the king and ultimately fought a successful guerilla campaign against the Seleucids. Our author in this text refers specifically to the story of the martyrdoms of Eleazer and a woman and her seven sons (2 Macc 6:18–7:42). The story goes into great detail about the tortures inflicted on these martyrs by Antiochus for their refusal to recant their faith.[21] As the second son is dying, he asserts, "You accursed wretch, you dismiss us from this present life, but the King of the universe will raise us up to a renewal of everlasting life, because we have died for his laws" (2 Macc 7:9 NRSV; see also 7:36). These men were "tortured"[22] and, in contrast to the rescues recounted in verses 33–34, did not receive "release."[23]

11:36–37 Some experienced mocking and flogging, and even chains and imprisonment. They were put to death by stoning, sawn in half, killed by the sword, going about in sheepskins and goatskins, destitute, persecuted, mistreated (ἕτεροι δὲ ἐμπαιγμῶν καὶ μαστίγων πεῖραν ἔλαβον, ἔτι δὲ δεσμῶν καὶ φυλακῆς· ἐλιθάσθησαν, ἐπρίσθησαν, ἐν φόνῳ μαχαίρης ἀπέθανον, περιῆλθον ἐν μηλωταῖς, ἐν αἰγείοις δέρμασιν, ὑστερούμενοι, θλιβόμενοι, κακουχούμενοι). As I noted above, verse 35b inaugurates a shift from examples of victories won by faith to examples of suffering endured by faith. In verses 36–37, 38b, the author again moves rapidly through a list of examples of this suffering. His purpose, again, is not to dwell on any one of these examples but to allow the cumulative weight of the list to convey a general sense of the severe affliction that some of the people of God have suffered for their faith. "Some" (ἕτεροι δέ)[24] is probably not intended to introduce a new group to be differentiated from the "others" in verse 35a (as the translation "others" in v. 36 by several versions might suggest); people who were "tortured" probably also endured some of the trials listed in these verses. They experienced[25] "mocking" (ἐμπαιγμῶν) and "flogging" (μαστίγων), two common forms of punishment that the righteous have endured. These terms could describe suffering from many ages, but probably the Maccabean martyrs are particularly in view.[26] At the end of the verse, the author suggests that an even greater punishment was "chains and imprisonment" (δεσμῶν καὶ φυλακῆς).[27] The author could continue to think of the period of the Maccabees, but some interpreters think he might have in view Jeremiah, who was frequently imprisoned (Jer 20:2; 29:26; 37:15).[28]

In verse 37, the author returns to his "list" style, stringing together eight items without any

---

21. "Refusing to accept release" in my translation is based on the Gk. οὐ προσδεξάμενοι τὴν ἀπολύτρωσιν—"not welcoming release." See "προσδέχομαι," BDAG 877, §1.b, for my translation.

22. The verb τυμπανίζω, which is based on the cognate noun τύμπανον, "drum." While the derivation is not certain, it is probable that the idea is that skin is stretched on a rack or wheel, much as a drum is covered by material pulled tight (the noun occurs in 2 Macc 6:19, 28–30 referring to the "rack"; cf. Bruce, *Hebrews*, 325). The verb comes to refer to "torture" ("τυμπανίζω," BDAG 1019).

23. The Gk. word is ἀπολύτρωσις, which often is used in a technical theological sense to refer to the "release" from sin accomplished by the sacrificial, substitutionary work of Christ (see Heb 9:15 and my notes there).

24. In keeping with the tendency in Koine Greek, ἕτερος (here) and ἄλλος in v. 35b are not distinguished in meaning (e.g., Ellingworth, *Hebrews*, 628).

25. The Greek phrase πεῖραν ἔλαβον means "they had experience of" ("πεῖρα," BDAG 792, §2); it is naturally followed by words in the genitive, as is the case here in v. 36.

26. The word ἐμπαιγμός, "mocking," occurs in 2 Macc 7:7, and the word μάστιξ, "flogging," in 2 Macc 7:1, 37; 9:11; 4 Macc. 6.3, 6; 9.12.

27. The construction ἔτι δέ suggests this heightened emphasis.

28. Johnson, *Hebrews*, 308.

conjunctions between them (asyndeton). Some are specific, apparently focused on one particular incident, but most are general, making it impossible to pin down with any certainty what people or events he might have in view. "They were put to death by stoning,"[29] for example, might have in view Zechariah (2 Chr 24:20-22) or Jeremiah (who according to Jewish tradition was executed in Egypt by stoning).[30] Despite the plural form of the verb (ἐπρίσθησαν), "[they were] sawn in half" almost certainly refers to the execution of Isaiah the prophet (his death by this means is recounted in the pseudepigraphical Ascen. Isa. 5.1-14).[31] "[They were] killed by the sword" is often used to refer to those whom the Israelites kill, but it also describes the execution of the faithful prophet Uriah in Jeremiah 26:20-23. "Going about in sheepskins [μηλωτή] and in goatskins" refers to rough clothes that those who live apart from civilization would often wear (e.g., John the Baptist wore clothes made of camel hair [Matt 3:4]). Elijah had a mantle or cloak (LXX μηλωτή) made of sheepskin (1 Kgs 19:13; 19:19; 2 Kgs 2:8), which was passed on to Elisha (2 Kgs 2:13, 14). The Maccabean fighters were also forced to live "in the wild" to escape the Seleucids, and the language of "going about" (περιῆλθον) might apply to them especially. See 2 Maccabees 5:27: "But Judas Maccabeus, with about nine others, got away to the wilderness, and kept himself and his companions alive in the mountains as wild animals do; they continued to live on what grew wild, so that they might not share in the defilement." Rounding off the series are three participles that generally describe the difficult conditions the faithful often had to live in: "destitute, persecuted, mistreated" (ὑστερούμενοι, θλιβόμενοι, κακουχούμενοι).[32]

11:38 —the world was not worthy of them. They wandered in deserts and in mountains, living in caves and in holes in the ground (ὧν οὐκ ἦν ἄξιος ὁ κόσμος, ἐπὶ ἐρημίαις πλανώμενοι καὶ ὄρεσιν καὶ σπηλαίοις καὶ ταῖς ὀπαῖς τῆς γῆς). Before finishing his series enumerating the sufferings of the righteous, the author adds a brief parenthetical comment: "the world was not worthy of them."[33] From the perspective of the "world," people who dress so strangely and live out in the wild (v. 38) are looked on with disdain, even mistreated. Yet those who live apart from this world in order to follow God and as a witness against this world are the ultimately "worthy" people.

The author concludes his long list of sufferings that the righteous have undergone for their faith by noting how many of them were forced to escape from the persecution of worldly people by living apart from civilization: in deserts, in the mountains, in caves and holes (or perhaps crevices) in the ground. The author accentuates their lack of any kind of permanent dwelling by speaking of them as

---

29. I follow NIV in this expansive translation in order to avoid the possible misunderstanding of the simple "was stoned" (possibly interpreted in terms of alcohol or drug overdose).

30. This tradition is found in a work called the Lives of the Prophets (2.1), a first-century, pseudepigraphical Jewish compilation of stories about prophets.

31. Wallace labels this verb a "categorical plural," intended to refer to one incident (*Greek Grammar*, 404-5). Several important manuscripts add the verb ἐπειράσθησαν, "they were tempted," either before ἐπρίσθησαν (e.g., ℵ L P 048. 33), after it (e.g., 𝔓^{13vid} A D$^{(*).1}$ Ψ), or in place of it (e.g., 0150). A number of emendations have also been proposed (see Metzger, *Textual Commentary*, 604). However, the editors of our Greek texts, most commentators, and all the English translations opt for the shorter reading—that is, simply ἐπρίσθησαν (as in, e.g., 𝔓^{46} 1241; see Metzger, *Textual Commentary*, 604).

32. The shift from a series of aorist verbs to present participles signals a focus on ongoing, general circumstances (Lane, *Hebrews*, 2:382).

33. The KJV, NASB, and NET enclose this clause with parentheses.

"wandering" (πλανώμενοι). Israelites hid in caves to escape their enemies on more than one occasion (Judg 6:2; 1 Sam 13:6; 1 Kgs 18:4). David is an outstanding example of a righteous person who had to flee to the wilderness to escape persecution (1 Sam 23:13, 25, 29; 25:1; 26:1). And the Maccabean fighters also "had been wandering in the mountains and caves like wild animals" (2 Macc 10:6, NRSV; see also 6:11).

11:39–40 All these, although receiving commendation for their faith, did not obtain what was promised, 40 God having planned something better for us, so that they might not be perfected without us (Καὶ οὗτοι πάντες μαρτυρηθέντες διὰ τῆς πίστεως οὐκ ἐκομίσαντο τὴν ἐπαγγελίαν, 40 τοῦ θεοῦ περὶ ἡμῶν κρεῖττόν τι προβλεψαμένου, ἵνα μὴ χωρὶς ἡμῶν τελειωθῶσιν). These two verses offer a final comment on "all these" (οὗτοι πάντες)—that is, all those the author has singled out for their faith throughout the chapter.[34] The claim that they were "commended"—or "borne witness to" (μαρτυρηθέντες)—because of their faith[35] brings us back to verse 2 and therefore functions as the second element of a grand *inclusio*. Being commended for faith is the great theme of the chapter and functions as an encouragement to the readers of the letter to follow in the footsteps of these faithful people (12:1–2).

Despite their faith, these people did not receive "what was promised" (the specific sense that ἐπαγγελίαν has here). The author has made this point earlier: "all these" (οὗτοι πάντες)—that is, Abraham, Sarah, and the other patriarchs—did not "receive the things promised" (v. 13). To be sure, the author can also claim that some of the Old Testament people of faith did, indeed, obtain "things that had been promised" (v. 33; see v. 11). But, as I point out in these contexts, the things received on these occasions are preliminary down payments on *the* promise. "The realization of particular promises (e.g., vv. 11, 33) is not to be confused with the definitive fulfillment of the promise."[36] That definitive fulfillment, the goal of salvation history, involves in Hebrews especially the final and full forgiveness of sins, enabling confident access to God himself, in accordance with the terms of the new covenant (8:12; 10:17). This is the "better thing" (κρεῖττόν τι) that God has planned (προβλεψαμένου)[37] for his people. This plan only comes to fulfillment in the new-covenant era, so the "perfection"—full and final forgiveness of sins—could not be attained until that era dawned. It is at that time that the Old Testament people of God join with the new-covenant people of God in experiencing the ultimate fulfillment of God's promise. The author hints here at a vision of a single people of God, fully forgiven together through the "once-for-all" sacrifice of Christ. As the argument of the letter makes clear, it is God's act in Christ that is decisive, working backward in salvation history to enable the old-covenant people of faith to be "perfected" and providing that same perfection, working forward, to God's

---

34. Michel (*Der Brief an die Hebräer*, 418) rightly argues that the reference is to the entire chapter, not just to the people referred to in vv. 32–38.

35. The verb μαρτυρέω means "bear witness to," but using the passive form of this verb in English is intolerably awkward. Therefore options such as "received approval" (CSB; NAB; NASB) or "were commended" (NIV; NET; ESV) are chosen by translators. "To be borne witness to *through* [διά] faith" is equivalent semantically to "being commended *for* faith." The διά is more causal than instrumental; and the article (τῆς) has a possessive force. D'Angelo suggests that the phrase διὰ τῆς πίστεως might modify οὐκ ἐκομίσαντο (*Moses*, 23), but, with the translations and most commentators, it far more likely modifies μαρτυρηθέντες (e.g., Lane, *Hebrews*, 2:382).

36. Lane, *Hebrews*, 2:392.

37. The verb προβλέπω means to "foresee" and then also "make provision for" (BDAG 866). The participial form functions, with τοῦ θεοῦ, as a genitive absolute.

new-covenant people. There is some debate about precisely when this fulfillment comes: Does the author think of the present era of salvation?[38] Or is he looking for the ultimate eschatological perfection (the "rest," which, I have argued, is future focused [3:7–4:11])?[39] The author's exhortaton in 10:36 seems to tip the scales toward this latter view: "you need to persevere so that when you have done the will of God, you will receive what he has promised." Perhaps, however, this is one of those many places where we need to recognize the two poles of salvation history: both the "not yet" and the "now." "Perfection" will reach its culmination when Christ comes again, but his initial coming already provides for an initial fulfillment of that promise.[40]

Theology in Application

In Hebrews 11:32–35a, the author encourages us in our own faith journey by reminding us of some of the spectacular things that faith enabled people in the Old Testament and Maccabean period to accomplish. They "conquered kingdoms." They "shut the mouths of lions." They even had loved ones who had died restored to them through resurrection. These examples of what faith can accomplish join others from earlier in the chapter. Faith enabled Enoch to escape death and to be transferred directly to heaven (v. 5). Faith enabled the aged and barren Sarah to give birth to a child (v. 11). Faith emboldened the people of Israel so that they were willing to march through the opening in the Red Sea (v. 29). Faith caused the walls of Jericho to fall (v. 30).

The Bible is full of stories of victories and blessings that God's people have experienced by God's grace and power. And such victories and blessings are by no means confined to a period of biblical history that is now over. In a famous passage, Jesus promises his followers: "Truly I tell you, if you have faith and do not doubt, not only can you do what was done to the fig tree, but also you can say to this mountain, 'Go, throw yourself into the sea,' and it will be done. If you believe, you will receive whatever you ask for in prayer" (Matt 21:21–22). Such texts have given rise to the "health and wealth" gospel, a worldwide movement that encourages Christians to think that, if their faith is pure and strong enough, they can receive worldly blessings—such as good health and wealth.

There are many faults with this movement. For instance, faith seems to be inteprreted as a purely self-generating "power of positive thinking" rather than as a gift of God, given as he chooses. It neglects to add to these promises of Scripture the always necessary qualification "if it be your will." But this movement also reads

---

38. Bruce, *Hebrews*, 330. It is unlikely that "something better" and "being perfected" refer to different things (as Schreiner suggests [*Hebrews*, 374]).

39. Lane, *Hebrews*, 2:393; Johnson, *Hebrews*, 309.

40. Peterson, *Hebrews and Perfection*, 157; Delitzsch, *Hebrews*, 2:293; Cockerill, *Hebrews*, 599–600; D. Harris, *Hebrews*, 354.

the Bible selectively. Take this passage in Hebrews. Yes, the author reminds us of many victories won by God's people and of many blessings they have received. But it also reminds us that the people of faith, like Abraham, were called by God to live in temporary arrangements while they waited for the promise to be fulfilled—a fulfillment that never came in their lifetimes (vv. 9–10, 13). Moses, because of his faith, was mistreated with the people of God (v. 25). And immediately after the list of great things faith accomplished in verses 33–35a is a list of difficulties—some of them extreme—that the people of God had to suffer for their faith. They were tortured, imprisoned, mistreated, forced to wander out in the hills, even put to death (vv. 35b–38). This, too, is the reality of the faith that God commends.

Christians today should, indeed, earnestly seek God's blessings. He will always answer that prayer, even if its fulfillment takes place in the spiritual sphere. He is working by his Spirit to draw us closer to him. And we should not ignore the times when God chooses to bless us materially. He often gives us good health, adequate resources to live decent lives, jobs, families, etc. However, as many faithful Christians around the world will attest, he does not always so bless us on this earth. Sometimes he calls us to pass through difficult, stressful, and even disastrous times. Sometimes, like the faithful people of God at the time of the Maccabees, he calls us to suffer and even to die for our faith. We cannot control these circumstances. But what we can do, as the author encourages us to do, is to maintain consistent faith in the God who sovereignly controls all the details of our lives and who loves us with a never-ending love.

CHAPTER 30

Hebrews 12:1–17

Literary Context

In this section, the author continues to elaborate his call to faith and endurance in 10:32–39.[1] In chapter 11 he encourages his readers to maintain their faith by surveying key people and events in the history of the people of God. That history reveals many examples of faith accomplishing great deeds. It also reveals many examples of people having to endure great difficulties for their faith. Both sets of examples have direct relevance to the readers. If they remain stable in their faith, they too will accomplish great things: they will inherit the promised blessing, they will enter God's promised rest. However, as 10:32–34 makes clear, the road to this promised rest is not an easy one, as they are facing persecution. They therefore need also to imitate those people of God in older days who, by their faith, remained loyal to God amid severe trial.

If faith, then, is the focus of chapter 11, endurance/perseverance is the author's main concern in 12:1–17 (though faith is not left behind; see v. 2). The command that lies at the heart of verses 1–3, "let us run," takes its main point from the qualifier "with endurance"—the endurance that Jesus himself exhibited in his suffering (v. 3). Similarly, the command that summarizes verses 4–11 comes in verse 7a: "with respect to discipline that you must endure."[2] Faith and endurance (in the context of God's discipline) are what the readers need to exhibit if they are to continue on in their spiritual pilgrimage and reach the goal of "perfection" or "rest." The author has indicated throughout his sermon his concern for them—they are flagging in zeal, perhaps even tempted decisively to reject their Christian status and to turn back to Judaism. This final part of his sermon is therefore a conclusion that appropriately calls for response.

---

1. E.g., Spicq, *L'Épître aux Hébreux*, 2:382.
2. I defend the identification of this verb as an imperative in my notes on that verse.

Scholars debate both ends of this section in terms of their connection with the context. A few attach 12:1–2, or 12:1–3, to the preceding context, viewing Jesus here as the last and climactic example of faith.[3] However, the shift from third person (ch. 11) to first and second person (12:1–3) strongly suggests that an important transition occurs at 12:1.[4] At the other end, a number of interpreters think that the exhortation and warning in 12:14–17 introduce a new section of the letter, extending all the way to 13:25.[5] Finally, some also want to isolate verses 12–17 as a unit parallel to verses 1–11. The several options for explaining the sequence of thought in verses 12–17 and the number of scholars defending various viewpoints indicates that it is not easy to settle on the boundaries of the paragraphs. Of course, we must remember here that the drawing of lines between units might obscure the various connections, moving both forward and backward, that certain paragraphs have in their context. I think it slightly more likely, however, that the imperatives in verses 12–13, using the imagery of preparing body parts for walking a straight path, are closely related (a bit of an *inclusio*) with verses 1–3 and that verses 14–17 make slightly better sense as a concluding series of encouragements and warning than as the introduction to a new section.[6]

I. The Exalted Son and a Rest for the People of God (1:1–4:13)
II. Our Great High Priest and His Ministry (4:14–10:31)
III. **Exhortation: Follow and Serve the Pioneer of Our Faith through Endurance and Faith (10:32–13:25)**
  A. Introductory Call to Endurance and Faith (10:32–39)
  B. The Nature and Power of Faith Illustrated in Salvation History (11:1–40)
  → C. **Run the Race with Endurance, Remembering That You Are Children of God (12:1–17)**
  D. Coming to Mount Zion and Inheriting the Unshakable Kingdom (12:18–29)
  E. Letter Closing (13:1–25)

Main Idea

Followers of Jesus are running a race that requires endurance. We will run well if we put off the hindrance of sin and keep our eyes fixed on the model and sustainer of our faith, Jesus. Endurance in the race is especially needed in the face of persecution.

---

3. DeSilva, *Perseverance in Gratitude*, 445; Schreiner, *Hebrews*, 375, 381. Westfall (*Discourse Anaysis*, 253) views the hortatory subjunctive in v. 2 as the complement to 10:19–25.

4. E.g., Grässer, *An die Hebräer*, 3:225.

5. Attridge, *Hebrews*, 366; Lane, *Hebrews*, 2:431; Ellingworth, *Hebrews*, 661; Bénétrau, *L'Épître aux Hébreux*, 2:159; Massonnet, *L'Épître aux Hébreux*, 351, 371.

6. See, generally, the proposed structures in Bruce, *Hebrews*, 346; Johnson, *Hebrews*, 312; Koester, *Hebrews*, 533–34.

The trials that persecution brings are put in perspective when we view them as discipline sent to us from our heavenly Father. With the right perspective on our trials and our focus firmly on Jesus, we will be able to follow the path God has laid out for us, avoiding the sad fate of those who drop out of the race altogether.

Translation

Hebrews 12:1-17

1a	inference (from ch. 11)	Therefore,
1b	encouragement	surrounded as we are by so great a cloud
1c	content	of witnesses,
1d	exhortation	**let us run the race**
1e	identification	set before us
1f	manner 1	with endurance,
1g	manner 2	putting aside every weight and
1h	example (of 1g)	sin that entangles,
2a	manner 3	keeping our eyes on the pioneer and
2b	parallel	perfecter
2c	object (of 2a–b)	of faith,
2d	apposition (to 2a–b)	Jesus.
2e	reason (of 2f)	For the sake of the joy set before him,
2f	assertion	he endured the cross,
2g	manner	despising its shame, and
2h	sequence (with 2f)	is now seated
2i	place	at the right hand of the throne of God.
3a	exhortation	**Consider**,
3b	inference (from 1–2)	then,
3c	object (of 3a)	him who endured such opposition
3d	source	from sinners,
3e	goal (of 3a–e)	in order that you might not become weary or
3f	parallel	lose heart.
4a	assertion	**You have not yet resisted**
4b	manner	to the point of shedding your blood
4c	circumstance	in your struggle against sin.
5a	development	And
5b	rhetorical question	**have you forgotten**
5c	content	this message of encouragement,
5d	description	which addresses you

5e	manner	as sons?
5f	address	"My son,
5g	exhortation 1	do not think lightly
5h	reference	of the discipline
5i	source	of the Lord and
5j	exhortation 2	do not lose heart
5k	simultaneous	when he rebukes you.
6a	basis (for 5e–k)	For
6b	assertion	the Lord disciplines those he loves and
6c	parallel	punishes the son he accepts." (Prov 3:11–12)
7a	reference	It is with respect to discipline that
7b	exhortation	**you must endure.**
7c	elaboration 1 (of 7a–b)	**God is dealing**
7d	reference	with you
7e	manner	as sons.
7f	basis (for 7c–e)	For
7g	rhetorical question	**what son is not disciplined**
7h	agent	by his father?
8a	condition	If, then, you are without discipline,
8b	description	which everyone partakes of,
8c	negative	**you are not sons but**
8d	positive	**you are illegitimate children.**
9a	development	Moreover,
9b	elaboration 2 (of 7a–b)	**we have our earthly fathers,**
9c	description	who have disciplined us—
9d	result (of 9a–b)	and **we have respected them.**
9e	comparison (with 9a–c)	How much more
9f	rhetorical question	**should we submit** to the father of spirits and
9g	result (of 9e–f)	**live?**
10a	basis (for 9)	For
10b	elaboration 3 (of 7a–b)	**they disciplined us**
10c	time	for a short time
10d	standard	as they thought best,
10e	contrast (10a–d)	but **he disciplines us**
10f	goal	for our good
10g	purpose (of 10d)	in order that we might share
10h	content	in his holiness.
11a	elaboration 4 (of 7a–b)	**All discipline seems,**
11b	time	at the time,

Continued on next page.

11c	negative	a matter not of joy but
11d	positive	of pain.
11e	contrast (with 11a–d)	Later, however,
11f	assertion	**it repays those who are trained by it**
11g	object (of 11f)	with the peaceful fruit
11h	content	of righteousness.
12a	inference (from 1–11)	Therefore
12b	exhortation 1	**strengthen your feeble hands** and
12c	parallel	**your weak knees,**
13a	exhortation 2	and **make straight paths**
13b	advantage	for your feet,
13c	purpose/negative (of 12a–13b)	in order that what is lame may not be dislocated but rather
13d	positive/contrast	healed.
14a	exhortation	**Pursue peace**
14b	reference	with everyone and also
14c	parallel (with 14a)	**holiness,**
14d	description	without which no one will see the Lord,
15a	expansion (of 14a–d)	taking care
15b	purpose 1	so that no one falls short
15c	reference	of the grace of God,
15d	purpose 2	so that no root of bitterness grows up and causes trouble, and
15e	means (of 15d)	through it
15f	parallel (to 15g)	brings defilement
15g	recipient	to many, and
16a	purpose 3	so that no one becomes an immoral and
16b	parallel	godless man
16c	comparison	like Esau,
16d	description	who sold his birthright
16e	exchange	for a single meal.
17a	assertion	**You know**
17b	sequence	that . . . even afterwards,
17c	time	when he wanted to inherit the blessing,
17d	content (of 17a)	. . . he was rejected;
17e	explanation (of 17e)	**he could find no opportunity**
17f	content	for repentance,
17g	contra-expectation	even though he sought it
17h	manner	with tears.

Structure

As I note above, there is considerable disagreement among scholars over the boundaries and internal divisions of this passage. Assuming, as I argue above, that we can identify 12:1–17 as a discrete unit of thought, it can be divided into four units. The opening paragraph looks back to the exemplars of faith in chapter 11 and uses race imagery to exhort the readers to endure as they look to their ultimate exemplar, Jesus (vv. 1–3). The author's reminder that the readers' trials have not yet led to death (v. 4) could be attached to the reference to Jesus's sufferings in verse 3. Yet it makes slightly better sense to see it as the beginning of a section that encourages the readers to put their suffering in perspective (vv. 5–11).[7] This next section is unified around the related themes of "sonship" and "discipline" (παιδεία). Reminding the readers of the way that earthly parents demonstrate love and concern for their children, the author encourages his readers to view their trials in the same light, as their heavenly Father disciplines and trains them for their good. The center of this section is the command: "It is with respect to discipline that you must endure" in verse 7a. Indeed, this short command brings together in the closest relationship the two great themes of verses 1–17: "endurance" (vv. 1, 2, and 3) and "discipline" (vv. 5, 6, 7, 8, 10, 11). The author leads up to the command by introducing the "discipline" concept via a quotation of Proverbs 3:11–12 (vv. 5–6) and then develops the "discipline" concept with reference to its meaning and nature in verses 7b–11. With a strong inferential conjunction—"therefore" (διό)—the author concludes (vv. 12–13) this section of exhortation with a return to the general "traveling a path" metaphor from verses 1–2. Finally, in verses 14–17, the author encourages the readers to pursue faithfulness in their relations with others ("pursue peace") and with God ("pursue holiness"). This latter concern echoes the central thrust of the author's sermon, reinforced as it is with warnings about the consequences of failing to pursue holiness—another keynote of the sermon.

Exegetical Outline

→ **C. Run the Race with Endurance, Remembering That You Are Children of God (12:1–17)**
    1. Run Your Spiritual Race, Looking to the Pioneer of Your Faith (vv. 1–3)
    2. Suffering as the Disipline of a Loving Heavenly Father (vv. 4–11)
    3. Strengthen Yourself for the Race (vv. 12–13)
    4. Seek Holiness and Avoid Sin (vv. 14–17)

---

7. N. Clayton Croy, *Endurance in Suffering: Hebrews 12:1–13 in Its Rhetorical, Religious, and Philosophical Context*, SNTSMS 98 (Cambridge: Cambridge University Press, 1998), 192–93.

Explanation of the Text

12:1–2 Therefore, surrounded as we are by so great a cloud of witnesses, let us run the race set before us with endurance, putting aside every weight and sin that entangles, 2 keeping our eyes on the pioneer and perfecter of faith, Jesus. For the sake of the joy set before him, he endured the cross, despising its shame, and is now seated at the right hand of the throne of God (Τοιγαροῦν καὶ ἡμεῖς τοσοῦτον ἔχοντες περικείμενον ἡμῖν νέφος μαρτύρων, ὄγκον ἀποθέμενοι πάντα καὶ τὴν εὐπερίστατον ἁμαρτίαν, δι᾽ ὑπομονῆς τρέχωμεν τὸν προκείμενον ἡμῖν ἀγῶνα 2 ἀφορῶντες εἰς τὸν τῆς πίστεως ἀρχηγὸν καὶ τελειωτὴν Ἰησοῦν, ὃς ἀντὶ τῆς προκειμένης αὐτῷ χαρᾶς ὑπέμεινεν σταυρὸν αἰσχύνης καταφρονήσας ἐν δεξιᾷ τε τοῦ θρόνου τοῦ θεοῦ κεκάθικεν). One of the fundamental perspectives believers need as they follow their pioneer Jesus is perseverance. The author uses a strong inferential conjunction (τοιγαροῦν)[8] to indicate the transition from exposition to application, from describing faith to urging his readers to exhibit the endurance that faith produces. Specifically, the author exhorts his audience to "run the race set before us with endurance." Athletic imagery was widely used in the ancient world to describe the life of philosophy or religion. Stauffer notes that Greco-Roman authors used the "imagery and terminology of the arena in relation to the heroic struggle which the pious has to go through in this world."[9] Especially influential for our author would have been the athletic imagery used to describe the Maccabean martyrs. A good sample of this language is found in 4 Maccabees 17.10–15 (NRSV; words shared with Hebrews are highlighted):

They vindicated their nation, **looking** [ἀφορῶντες] to God and **enduring** [ὑπομείναντες] torture even to death.

Truly the **contest** [ἀγών] in which they were engaged was divine, for on that day virtue gave the awards and tested them for their **endurance** [δι᾽ ὑπομονῆς]. The prize was immortality in endless life. Eleazar was the first contestant, the mother of the seven sons entered the competition, and the brothers contended. The tyrant was the antagonist, and the world and the human race were the spectators. Reverence for God was victor and gave the crown to its own athletes.

Early Christians took over the imagery (see, e.g., Rom 15:30; 1 Cor 9:24–27; 2 Tim 2:5). The word for "race" (ἀγών) and its cognates (e.g., ἀγωνίζομαι) can refer generally to a "contention" or "struggle," such as athletes, especially boxers or wrestlers, are engaged in (e.g., John 18:36; 1 Cor 9:25). These words then become appropriate metaphors for strenuous prayer (Phil 1:30; Col 2:1; 4:12; 1 Thess 2:2; 1 Tim 6:12; 2 Tim 4:7). In the context of Hebrews 12:1, however, the reference is obviously to a "race." The need to run this race "with endurance" (δι᾽ ὑπομονῆς) makes clear that this race is not a sprint but a marathon. What is needed is not a quick burst of speed that may equally quickly fade or disappear but a concentrated, continuing effort. A course of life from conversion to glory has been "laid out" or "prescribed" (προκείμενον) for us, and most of us will be required to run well for many years before that course is finished.

---

8. This conjunction, which occurs only here and in 1 Thess 4:8 in the NT, is made up of three conjunctions joined together: τοί, γάρ, and οὖν.

"Let us run the race set before us with endurance" is the main point in verses 1–3. The author qualifies this exhortation with three participial clauses:

Let us run,
> surrounded as we are by so great a cloud of witnesses,
> putting aside every weight and sin that entangles,
> keeping our eyes on the pioneer and perfecter of faith, Jesus.

The first clause gives us encouragement as we run. "Cloud of witnesses"—that is, "a host of witnesses"[10]—naturally draws our attention back to the "heroes of the faith" in chapter 11. Those who are there "witnessed about" (the verb is passive; cf. vv. 2, 4, 5, 39) are now those who, in turn, "bear witness." But in what sense are they "witnesses" (μαρτύρων)? In general, as Croy puts it, a "witness" "refers to anyone who observes some activity or event and is able, or obligated, to testify to it."[11] A "witness" in the New Testament is sometimes, as in modern English, one who testifies to what they have seen in a law court or equivalent setting (Matt 18:16; 26:65; Mark 14:63; Luke 11:48; Acts 6:13; 2 Cor 13:1; 1 Tim 5:19; Heb 10:28). However, a person can bear witness with their lives as well as with their words (see Rev 2:13). It is in this sense that the heroes of faith in chapter 11 can be considered witnesses: their faithfulness to God, sometimes in very distressful situations, "bears witness" to the reality of God and their determination to follow him, whatever the cost. If this is the meaning of "witnesses" in 12:1, then the author is encouraging his readers to look to those who have already run their spiritual races well as a strong incentive for them to run well also.[12] Most interpreters think that "witnesses" has this sense in verse 1. There is disagreement, however, whether the word might have a second nuance, referring to the heroes of the faith in chapter 11 as those now gathered to watch and, in a sense, cheer on, those of us still running the race. The author may suggest this nuance by describing these people as "surrounding" (περικείμενον) us—as if they are gathered on a hillside watching us compete in the arena.[13] And, as the quotation from 4 Maccabees above reveals, this general idea is not at all foreign to accounts of the struggle of faith (4 Macc. 17.14: "the world and the human race were the spectators" [NRSV]). The problem with this attractive and contextually appropriate interpretation is lexical. "Witness," as we have seen, normally combines seeing and testifying, yet it is difficult to see how the heroes of faith would "testify" about us. A number of interpreters, however, argue that the "testifying" element in the word is sometimes lost to the point that it means simply "spectator." But clear examples of the word meaning simply "spectator" are not easy to find.[14]

---

9. E. Stauffer, "ἀγών, κτλ," *TDNT* 1:135.

10. The word νέφος, "cloud," is a metaphor for a "numberless throng" or "host" (BDAG 670). As Calvin notes, "where there is a great crowd we ought to take encouragement" (*Hebrews*, 187).

11. Croy, *Endurance in Suffering*, 169.

12. For this emphasis, see esp. Bruce, *Hebrews*, 333 ("it is not so much they who look at us as we who look to them for encouragement"); Hagner, *Hebrews*, 211. The transliteraed μάρτυς, "martyr" (Acts 22:20; Rev 1:5; 2:13; 3:14; 17:6), is a natural extension of this meaning: one who "testifies" to the point of death.

13. Delitzsch, *Hebrews*, 2:297. Interpreters who see a dual meaning here include Westcott, *Hebrews*, 391; P. Hughes, *Hebrews*, 519; Attridge, *Hebrews*, 354; Bénétrau, *L'Épître aux Hébreux*, 2:160; Thompson, *Hebrews*, 247; Cockerill, *Hebrews*, 602–3; H. Strathmann, "μάρτυς, κτλ," *TDNT* 4:491.

14. The texts sometimes cited for the simple meaning "spectator" (e.g., Wis 1:6; Josephus, *J.W.* 6.134; *Ant.* 18.299; see Attridge, *Hebrews*, 354) seem rather to have the usual sense of "witness": one who sees something and testifies about that thing to others. Croy (*Endurance in Suffering*, 59) also registers skepticism about Attridge's examples. Croy himself goes on to cite texts where "witness" is used alongside "spectator," but

Perhaps it is best to conclude, then, that the notion of faithful people from the past watching us run our spiritual race *might* be present. What is clearly present, however, is the encouraging reminder that people who loved and sought to follow God have shown us the way by their willingness to suffer for their faith and by the rewards of faithfulness that they have reaped.

The second participial clause indicates the manner of running: "putting aside every weight and sin that entangles."[15] The verb "put aside" (ἀποτίθημι), which can refer to taking off clothes, is often used in the New Testament with reference to putting off sinful desires and behavior (Eph 4:22, 25; Col 3:8; Jas 1:21; 1 Pet 2:1). The participial form here (ἀποθέμενοι) takes on something of an imperatival force because it modifies the hortatory subjunctive "let us run" (τρέχωμεν).[16] The imagery is clear: a runner can succeed in the race only if they rid themselves of any excess baggage that might get in the way of their running. "Weight" (ὄγκον) could also be translated "burden" or "that which hinders" (see NIV; CSB; see "ὄγκος," BDAG 689, §2). The second object of the participle, "sin that entangles," could be a further definition of this burden: "the burden that is entangling sin."[17] But it is perhaps better to see it as one of the possible hindrances; see NLT: "let us strip off every weight that slows us down, especially the sin that so easily trips us up." Sin is, to be sure, a serious hindrance to our spiritual race. But other things, not strictly sinful, can also impede our race. A few interpreters think the author might have a particular sin in view—perhaps apostasy, since this has been a concern of the author's.[18] However, the author more likely thinks of sin as a kind of category that can take many different forms in the lives of God's people.

The third participial modifier of "let us run the race with endurance" comes in verse 2: "keeping our eyes on the pioneer and perfecter of faith, Jesus." This clause is the positive counterpart to the "putting aside" clause in verse 1. To run the race well, we need, negatively, to rid ourselves of hindrances and sins. But more important, positively, we need to keep our eyes on Jesus. The verb the author uses (ἀφορῶντες) can be translated simply "looking" (NRSV; ESV), but it may have a stronger meaning: BDAG ("ἀφοράω," 158, §1) suggests "to direct one's attention without distraction," and "ἀποβλέπω, ἀφοράω," L&N 30.2 offers "to fix one's attention on."[19] English versions therefore have "fix[ing] our eyes" (CEB; NIV; NASB); "keeping our eyes on" (NLT; CSB); "keeping our eyes fixed on" (NET; NAB).

Jesus is described here as "the pioneer and perfecter of faith." The word "faith" (πίστεως) goes with both "pioneer" and "perfecter": it is almost certainly an objective genitive.[20] The author here returns to a word he introduced all the way back in 2:10 where Jesus is described as the "pioneer [ἀρχηγός] of their salvation."[21] "Perfecter"

---

his examples don't make it clear whether the two words are semantically equivalent (*Endurance in Suffering*, 59–62).

15. The versions translate variously "entangles" (NIV; NASB), "clings so closely" (NET; NRSV; ESV; cf. NAB), "ensnares" (CSB), "trips us up" (CEB), all of which are attempts to translate the rare word εὐπερίστατον (nowhere else in the NT; not found in LXX, Josephus, or Philo). Some MSS offer the alternative εὐπερίσπαστον (𝔓46 1739), "easily distracting" (it is favored by Bruce, *Hebrews*, 336; Lane, *Hebrews*, 2:398). Arguments for the usual Greek text are given by Ellingworth, *Hebrews*, 638–39.

16. Wallace, *Greek Grammar*, 644.

17. On this view, the καί connecting the words is epexegetic (see P. Hughes, *Hebrews*, 520; Grässer, *An die Hebräer*, 3:231).

18. E.g., Käsemann, *Wandering People of God*, 25–27.

19. The verb ἀφοράω occurs elsewhere in the NT in Phil 2:23 and in the LXX in Jonah 4:5; 3 Macc. 6.8; 4 Macc. 17.10, 23. The verb is formed from the root ὁράω, "look," "see," with the preposition ἀπό, "away from." The form of the word, then, might connote the idea of "look away to" (France, "Hebrews," 168).

20. The word order, with a single article (τόν) governing both "pioneer" (ἀρχηγόν) and "perfecter" (τελειωτήν) and τῆς πίστεως following the article, makes clear that "faith" modifies both accusative nouns.

21. For this translation of the word, see the notes on 2:10.

(τελειωτής), on the other hand, is a rare word,[22] although it clearly taps into an important theological theme in Hebrews: as Jesus is "perfected" in his vocation as high priest (2:10; 5:9; 7:28), he is able to secure "perfection" for those who belong to him (10:14; 11:40; 12:23). The significance of these descriptions of Jesus in this context depends considerably on how we understand "faith." A number of versions (KJV; NRSV; ESV; NET; NLT; CSB) and a few commentators think the reference is to "our" faith—that is, the faith of the author and his readers and, by extension, of Christians generally.[23] On this reading, the author might be saying something very similar to what Paul says in Philippians 1:6— that "he who began a good work in you will carry it on to completion until the day of Christ Jesus." Christ, by his sacrificial work, initiates our faith, and through his heavenly ministry he also completes it. Other interpreters, however, think that Jesus is presented here not as the one who enables others to believe but as the one who has himself, through his faith-filled and faithful life, paved the way for others to follow.[24] However, while this idea does justice to "pioneer," it does not so adequately explain "perfecter." The locution "perfecting faith" is difficult to ascribe to Jesus personally; it much more likely refers to Jesus bringing the faith of others to its perfect end. It seems, then, that the author combines here the image of Jesus as the example who shows the way with the image of Jesus who, in his high-priestly work, provides for others to find that way—all the way to the end of the road.[25] "Jesus accomplished the perfection of our faith by his sacrificial death on the cross. In keeping with the race imagery, he has cleared the path of faith so that we might run on it. The way is open, and although hurdles exist, the roadblocks have been removed."[26]

One reason for thinking that Jesus as example is at least a prominent part of the reference in this verse is the subsequent focus on Jesus's own attitude toward his suffering: "for the sake of the joy set before him, he endured the cross, despising its shame, and is now seated at the right hand of the throne of God."[27] It is possible to translate the opening part of this sentence as *in place of* the joy set before him, he endured the cross." The idea would then be similar to what we find in the famous christological passage in Philippians 2: Jesus, "being in very nature God, did not consider equality with God something to be used to his own advantage; rather, he made himself nothing" (vv. 6–7a).[28] At issue is the meaning of a preposition (ἀντί), which usually indicates the idea of substitution or exchange. However, the preposition at times becomes weakened, taking on the sense simply of "on behalf of" or "for the sake of." This seems to be the meaning in its one other occurrence in Hebrews (12:16), and makes

---

22. The word τελειωτής has not been found in Greek predating Hebrews.

23. There is no possessive pronoun with τῆς πίστεως, but the article can sometimes function as a possessive. For this view, see, e.g., France, "Hebrews," 168; Ellingworth, *Hebrews*, 640; Bénétrau, *L'Épître aux Hébreux*, 2:164.

24. On this view, "faith" refers to faith in general or, perhaps especially, to Jesus's own faith. See, e.g., Peterson, *Hebrews and Perfection*, 172; Easter, *Faith and the Faithfulness of Jesus*, 149–51; Cockerill, *Hebrews*, 606; Bruce, *Hebrews*, 337; Grässer, *An die Hebräer*, 3:237; Lane, *Hebrews*, 2:412; Thompson, *Hebrews*, 248; R. J. McKelvey, *Pioneer and Priest: Jesus Christ in the Epistle to the Hebrews* (Eugene, OR: Pickwick, 2013), 186.

25. Richardson, *Pioneer and Perfecter of Faith*, 95–105; Schreiner, *Hebrews*, 378; Koester, *Hebrews*, 523; Weiss, *Der Brief an die Hebräer*, 635–37; Grässer, *An die Hebräer*, 3:237–38.

26. G. Guthrie, *Hebrews*, 399.

27. This sequence is attached to its context with a relative pronoun (ὅς), and some versions preserve this connection (e.g., ESV). I start a new sentence to break up the long Greek sentence.

28. M. Harris, *Prepositions*, 55–56; Lane, *Hebrews*, 2:399–400; Montefiore, *Hebrews*, 215; Calvin, *Hebrews*, 188.

better sense in verse 2 because the focus is not on a status Jesus already has but on an experience yet before him ("joy set before him").²⁹ On this view, "the joy" would be the prospect of his exaltation as, in a sense, the "reward" for this faithful obedience. As martyrs endured torture in view of the reward (note the 4 Maccabees text quoted above), so Jesus "endured the cross, despising it shame." As is well-known, Romans used crucifixion to execute certain kinds of offenders not only as a means of inflicting physical pain, but especially as a means of shaming the victim.³⁰ P. Hughes comments that "the shame of the cross, where Christ bore the sins of the world, is something infinitely more intense than the pain of the cross."³¹ For Jesus to "despise" (καταφρονήσας) this shame is, as deSilva argues, tantamount to disregarding public opinion—for it is popular beliefs that make things shameful in a culture. As deSilva then further remarks, this note about Jesus is extremely relevant to the readers, who may be in danger of forfeiting their faith because of the way it is perceived in their culture.³² As so often in the New Testament, Jesus's exaltation is presented as the outcome, or reward, of his obedience to the Father in going to the cross (cf., e.g., Phil 2:6–11). For our author reference to Jesus's sitting at the right hand of the Father brings him, via allusion to Psalm 110:1, back to his key christological theme. I have translated the verb here "is seated" to bring out the likely force of the author's choice to use a perfect form of the verb (κεκάθισεν)—the perfect tense often connotes a continuing state of affairs. As Cockerill nicely puts it, "The suffering, although necessary, was temporary. The triumph is forever."³³

12:3 Consider, then, him who endured such opposition from sinners, in order that you might not become weary or lose heart (ἀναλογίσασθε γὰρ τὸν τοιαύτην ὑπομεμενηκότα ὑπὸ τῶν ἁμαρτωλῶν εἰς ἑαυτὸν ἀντιλογίαν, ἵνα μὴ κάμητε ταῖς ψυχαῖς ὑμῶν ἐκλυόμενοι). Jesus, our pioneer, sets an example for us in terms of enduring opposition. I have chosen to translate the conjunction that links this verse with its context (γάρ) with "then," recognizing the inferential sense it appears to have here.³⁴ The readers of this letter are going through some tough times, so the author seeks to keep them from flagging in zeal or giving up on their faith by giving attention to (ἀναλογίσασθε) the one who endured the cross and despised its shame. Like the readers, Jesus experienced opposition from sinners (ὑπὸ τῶν ἁμαρτωλῶν εἰς ἑαυτὸν ἀντιλογίαν),³⁵ but disregarded it in order to be faithful to God's calling. The readers are to follow his example.

The goal of the readers' consideration of Jesus ("in order that," ἵνα) is that they would not become weary or lose heart.³⁶ The author continues to use

---

29. Most commentators interpret it this way; see esp. Croy, *Endurance in Suffering*, 177–85; and also, e.g., Michel, *Der Brief an die Hebräer*, 434–35.
30. See esp. Martin Hengel, *Crucifixion* (Philadelphia: Fortress, 1977), 22–63.
31. *Hebrews*, 525.
32. *Perseverance in Gratitude*, 435.
33. *Hebrews*, 610. See also Ellingworth, *Hebrews*, 642.
34. As we have seen, this conjunction, often translated "for" or "because," has a wide semantic range, especially in Hebrews (see the note on 2:10; on this verse, see Weiss, *Der Brief an die Hebräer*, 641). Margaret E. Thrall (*Greek Particles in the New Testament: Linguistic and Exegetical Studies* [Leiden: Brill, 1962], 45) on the other hand, suggests v. 3 might give the basis for v. 2a.
35. The phrase εἰς ἑαυτόν emphasizes the idea of opposition: "against himself." A textual variant has the plural ἑαυτούς, a reading that has very strong external support (e.g., ℵ* D*). It is also the more difficult reading, since it is hard to make sense of it here (what would "opposition against themselves" mean?). Some interpreters therefore think it was original (e.g., Ellingworth, *Hebrews*, 643–44; Lane, *Hebrews*, 2:400). However, most interpreters agree that this plural reading is too hard and reject it in favor of the singular (e.g., Grässer, *An die Hebräer*, 3:245–46).
36. The main verb, the subjunctive depending on ἵνα, is κάμητε, which is used once elsewhere in the NT with reference

race imagery: the two verbs the author uses here are used in other contexts for the physical collapse of runners after a race (Aristotle, *Rhetoric* 3.9.2).

12:4 You have not yet resisted to the point of shedding your blood in your struggle against sin (Οὔπω μέχρις αἵματος ἀντικατέστητε πρὸς τὴν ἁμαρτίαν ἀνταγωνιζόμενοι). As I argued above (in "Structure"), verse 4 is transitional. It continues the focus on the readers' suffering that verse 3 plainly hints at and also continues to use the athletic imagery of verses 1–2 ("struggle"). At the same time, the verse introduces explicitly the focus on suffering that will dominate verses 5–11. From what the author says in verse 4, we can imagine that the readers were complaining about the persecution they were enduring, using it perhaps as an excuse for their "losing heart" (v. 3). We are probably, then, justified in seeing a minor break in the author's argument at verse 4 (following NA[28]; NIV; NASB). The author begins chapter 12 with two exhortations directed to the readers: "run . . . with endurance" and "consider [Jesus]." He uses Christ's example and provision to ground these exhortations. Verses 4–11 introduce the crucial idea of "discipline" as a way of interpreting suffering, with verse 7a as the center of the unit: "you must endure" hardship as discipline.

The issue the author touches on in verse 4 is the persecution that the readers are experiencing at the hands of unbelievers.[37] The progress of argument strongly suggests that the scenario of persecution the author introduces in 10:32–34 is still dominating his focus. Certainly the language of "struggle" (ἀνταγωνιζόμενοι)[38] points to external conflict, and while the Greek is not as clear as English translations, resisting "to the point of shedding your blood" points in the same direction.[39] To be sure, the reference to sin calls this interpretation into question: struggling against "sin" is an unusual way to describe persecution. But perhaps the author, as Paul often does, is picturing sin as a power that battles against God's people.[40] The author is drawing a contrast between Jesus's suffering and death and the readers' milder experience. As Peterson puts it, the author is not "blaming" them but "shaming" them: when they compare their suffering to that of their pioneer, Jesus, they should be ashamed of making too big a deal of it.[41]

12:5–6 And have you forgotten this message of encouragement, which addresses you as sons?[42] "My son, do not think lightly of the discipline of the Lord and do not lose heart when he rebukes you. 6 For the Lord disciplines those he loves and punishes the son he accepts" (καὶ ἐκλέλησθε τῆς παρακλήσεως, ἥτις ὑμῖν ὡς υἱοῖς διαλέγεται, Υἱέ μου, μὴ ὀλιγώρει παιδείας κυρίου μηδὲ ἐκλύου ὑπ' αὐτοῦ ἐλεγχόμενος· 6 ὃν γὰρ ἀγαπᾷ κύριος παιδεύει,

---

to physical illness (Jas 5:15). This verb is modified by a participial clause, ταῖς ψυχαῖς ὑμῶν ἐκλυόμενοι, which indicates that the problem here is spiritual, not physical. I take the dative phrase to modify the participle (with, e.g., Grässer, *An die Hebräer*, 3:246), although it could modify the main verb. The verb ἐκλύω means "become weary" or "give out" (Matt 15:32; Mark 8:3; Gal 6:9); the dative modifier ταῖς ψυχαῖς indicates the sphere in which the weariness occurs.

37. Most interpreters agree. A few, however, think the issue might be sin within the church (Koester, *Hebrews*, 525–26) or the basic sin of apostasy (Grässer, *An die Hebräer*, 3:259).

38. The verb occurs only here in the NT, but in keeping with the passage as a whole the author may allude to the Maccabean martyrs; see 4 Macc. 17.14: "the tyrant was the antagonist [ἀντηγωνίζετο]."

39. The Greek simply has μέχρις αἵματος, "until blood," which could be an idiom for something like "to an extremity" (Weiss, *Der Brief an die Hebräer*, 646–47). But English translations and most interpreters think, rightly, that the phrase is short for "to the point of shedding blood," i.e., martyrdom.

40. Bénétrau, *L'Épître aux Hébreux*, 2:168.

41. Peterson, *Hebrews and Perfection*, 170.

42. With ESV, NIV, NLT, and NET, I take the opening clause of this verse as a question (see also, e.g., Lane, *Hebrews*, 2:401; Johnson, *Hebrews*, 320). It could be a statement (NRSV; NASB).

μαστιγοῖ δὲ πάντα υἱὸν ὃν παραδέχεται). As he so often does, the author uses an Old Testament quotation to ground his exhortation. The quotation comes from Proverbs 3:11–12.[43] In the original Hebrew of Proverbs, the son's relationship to his father is compared to his relationship to the Lord: verse 12b reads "as a [human] father [disciplines] the son he delights in." In Hebrews, however, following the Greek Old Testament, the person being addressed as "son" becomes explicitly a son of the Lord: "he punishes every son he [the Lord] receives." The notion of being "sons" or "children" of God is fundamental to the author's argument in these verses.[44] But there is another word in the quotation that becomes equally important for the argument in verses 7–11: "discipline." The Greek word—παιδεία—refers to a concept that was central to the Greek worldview, which prized the development of character through the training of athletic endeavor.[45] The author, therefore, has not moved very far away from the imagery of athletics in verses 1–2.[46] Like the Hebrew word it translates in Proverbs 3:11 (מוּסָר), παιδεία can refer, rather neutrally, to "instruction" but also to "chastisement" or "rebuke." Indeed, it is perhaps typical of the word to include some reference to both of these ideas: hence, "discipline" is a good English equivalent.[47] Croy has argued strongly for an educational nuance of the language in chapter 12, and he is certainly correct that the author gives no hint that the "discipline" is punitive, as if the readers are being punished for specific sins.[48] However, he probably errs too far in this direction. First, while we should not press the parallelism in Hebrew poetry to the extent that words in parallel lines must have the same meaning, it is nevertheless significant that the parallel to "discipline" (παιδεύει) in Proverbs 3:12 LXX is "punish," "chastise" (μαστιγοῖ). Second, a "disciplinary" sense of the word seems to be required in verse 11, where the author says that "no [παιδεία] seems pleasant at the time" (v. 11).[49] And, third, this sense of "educate by means of punishment [when needed]" is suggested by the author's portrayal of parental guidance of children in verses 7–10. It is not surprising, then, that almost all the English versions adopt "discipline" as the default translation of παιδεία in these verses.

It is the positive purpose in "discipline" that leads the author to characterize his quotation from Proverbs as a "message of encouragement."[50] The text from Proverbs urges the people of God not to "think lightly" (ὀλιγώρει) of the Lord's discipline and not to lose heart (ἐκλύω is the verb, as in Heb 11:2b) when

---

43. The author again follows the Old Greek, which differs at only two points from the Hebrew: in the last line in v. 12, in place of "**as a father** [he disciplines] the son in whom he **delights**," the Greek has "he **punishes** every son whom he **receives**." The former difference probably arises from a misreading of the Hebrew כְּאָב, "as a father," as if it were from the verb כָּאַב, "cause sorrow" (see, e.g., G. Guthrie, "Hebrews," 987). Bruce K. Waltke explores whether the Greek might represent the original Hebrew text—a theory he ultimately rejects (*The Book of Proverbs, Chapters 1–15*, NICOT [Grand Rapids: Eerdmans, 2004], 237–38). The second difference is a minor one—if, indeed, it is a difference at all. The Hebrew verb רצה can mean "accept favorably" ("רצה I," *DCH* 7:540, §1), and the Greek verb παραδέχομαι can have the same sense (BDAG 761, §2).

44. I have elected to translate υἱός as "son" throughout this text to maintain continuity and to reflect the ANE and Greco-Roman focus on the "son." Reference throughout is obviously to men and women equally.

45. "The word group [παιδεία and cognates] characterizes Gk. culture" (G. Bertram, "παιδεία, κτλ," *TDNT* 5:597; see the survey of Greek usage on pp. 597–606).

46. Johnson, *Hebrews*, 319; Croy, *Endurance in Suffering*, 158–59.

47. As *DCH* ("מוּסָר," 177, §1) notes, מוּסָר can refer to "instruction," "training" and to "discipline (as correction)," "chastisement."

48. Croy, *Endurance in Suffering*; see also deSilva, *Perseverance in Gratitude*, 448–49.

49. Schreiner, *Hebrews*, 384.

50. The Greek has simply "encouragement" (τῆς παρακλήσεως), but the context requires that it refers to something like "the word or message of encouragement."

he rebukes them.[51] The reason why they should take this attitude ("for," γάρ in v. 6) is because discipline is a mark of God's fatherly love for his children—a key point the author will develop in verses 7–11.

12:7–8 It is with respect to discipline that you must endure. God is dealing with you as sons. For what son is not disciplined by his father? 8 If, then, you are without discipline, which everyone partakes of, you are not sons but you are illegitimate children (εἰς παιδείαν ὑπομένετε, ὡς υἱοῖς ὑμῖν προσφέρεται ὁ θεός. τίς γὰρ υἱὸς ὃν οὐ παιδεύει πατήρ; 8 εἰ δὲ χωρίς ἐστε παιδείας ἧς μέτοχοι γεγόνασιν πάντες, ἄρα νόθοι καὶ οὐχ υἱοί ἐστε). The author brings together here the two key focal points of his exhortation in this section: endurance and discipline. The opening clause in this verse is the center of verses 4–11, bringing together the key exhortation from verse 1—"let us run the race with endurance"—with the key word in verses 5–11—"discipline." The author may be claiming that his readers are enduring, his point being the purpose or nature of that endurance—"for discipline" (this view takes the verb ὑπομένετε as indicative—see NLT; NASB[52]). But it is perhaps more likely the author is exhorting his readers to endure and encouraging them toward that end by reminding them of the benefit their endurance brings: "discipline," the kind of discipline a father imposes on his son to foster his son's development (on this view the verb is imperative—so most versions[53]). Whether indicative or imperative, the thrust of the clause comes in the prepositional phrase (εἰς παιδείαν), placed first for emphasis (hence the order of words in our translation). The preposition might indicate purpose—"endure trials for the sake of discipline" (NRSV)—but more likely indicates that the readers are to endure "with respect" to discipline—that is, their endurance should be fueled by their recognition that God is working in that process to discipline them as his beloved sons and daughters.[54]

In verses 7b–11, the author appeals to the discipline that earthly parents use to form their own children to explain further the discipline that God uses to form his sons and daughters into his own image. He makes four points, the first here in verses 7–8 and then three more in verses 9–11.[55] First, the author reminds us that discipline is a sign of parental love (vv. 7b–8). A son is "disciplined by his father" (v. 7); to be without discipline can then be a sign that one is not a true son (v. 8). The culture in which Hebrews was written often rather harshly distinguished between legitimate and illegitimate children. A parent would often spend little time caring for an illegitimate child (νόθος)—so, the author reasons, to be without discipline would be an indication that one is not truly a child of God.[56] In fact, however, the suffering the readers are undergoing shows that God is treating them as sons (v. 7).[57] Chrysostom comments, "See, from that from which they supposed they had been deserted [by God], from these he says they may be confident, that they have not been deserted."[58]

---

51. The Greek is ὑπ᾽ αὐτοῦ ἐλεγχόμενος: "when being rebuked by him."

52. See also, e.g., Westcott, *Hebrews*, 400; Ellingworth, *Hebrews*, 650; Johnson, *Hebrews*, 320.

53. And see Lane, *Hebrews*, 2:401; D. Harris, *Hebrews*, 367; cf. Weiss: indicative with an imperative flavor (*Der Brief an die Hebräer*, 649).

54. For εἰς meaning "with respect to," "with reference to," see "εἰς," BDAG 291, §4.

55. Johnson, *Hebrews*, 321–22.

56. It is odd, given this argument, that the author would say here that "everyone has become partakers" (μέτοχοι γεγόνασιν πάντες) of discipline. The author perhaps indicates that his argument about illegitimacy is more theoretical than real.

57. The verb here, προσφέρεται, means "deal with" here ("προσφέρω," BDAG 886).

58. Chrysostom, *Homilies*, 12:7.

12:9 Moreover,[59] **we have our earthly fathers, who have disciplined us—and we have respected them. How much more should we submit to the father of spirits and live?** (εἶτα τοὺς μὲν τῆς σαρκὸς ἡμῶν πατέρας εἴχομεν παιδευτὰς καὶ ἐνετρεπόμεθα· οὐ πολὺ δὲ[60] μᾶλλον ὑποταγησόμεθα τῷ πατρὶ τῶν πνευμάτων καὶ ζήσομεν;). In this second elaboration of the author's call for the readers to "with respect to discipline . . . you must endure," he urges them to submit to the Father's loving discipline. The Greek παιδ- root continues to bind these verses together: here the author uses a word meaning "one who exercises discipline" (παιδευτής). This exhortation takes the form of a comparison between "earthly fathers"[61] and "the father of spirits." This latter description of God is unusual: only here in the Greek Bible do we find a reference to the "father of spirits." "Spirits" (πνευμάτων) might denote spiritual beings (Heb 1:7, 14),[62] but a reference to God's relationship to spiritual beings does not fit the context well. More likely, the reference is to the spirits of human beings (Heb 12:23; cf. 4:12).[63] The comparison would then be between fathers in terms of the flesh and *the* Father who oversees and cares for the inner spiritual aspect of people. We "respect" (ἐνετρεπόμεθα) those earthly fathers; how much more (πολὺ δὲ μᾶλλον) should we "submit" (ὑποταγησόμεθα) to this father who creates and watches over our inner being? In this context, the submission is obviously to the course of discipline that our Father sets out for us in his love and care for us. And that submission should be all the more important when we recognize that the purpose of that discipline is that "we might live" (ζήσομεν)[64]—that is, enjoy eternal life.[65]

12:10 For they disciplined us for a short time as they thought best, but he disciplines us for our good in order that we might share in his holiness (οἱ μὲν γὰρ πρὸς ὀλίγας ἡμέρας κατὰ τὸ δοκοῦν αὐτοῖς ἐπαίδευον, ὁ δὲ ἐπὶ τὸ συμφέρον εἰς τὸ μεταλαβεῖν τῆς ἁγιότητος αὐτοῦ). This verse explains why ("for," γάρ) believers should submit to the Lord's discipline (v. 9): as the "father of our spirits," he is lovingly and insightfully disciplining (ἐπαίδευον, an imperfect form stressing duration) us for our good, specifically that we might share in his holiness. At the same time, this verse serves as the third elaboration of the author's basic exhortation to "endure" with respect to discipline in verse 7a. As in verse 9, the contrast is between earthly fathers and our heavenly Father.[66] Our human fathers have only so long to discipline their children (πρὸς ὀλίγας ἡμέρας),[67] and they act with limited understanding ("as they thought best," κατὰ

---

59. The Greek word εἶτα that opens this verse means "then" or "next" and can therefore signal the move to a new point; translations such as "furthermore" or "moreover" capture the sense (BDAG 295, §§1, 2; see also Westcott, *Hebrews*, 401; Ellingworth, *Hebrews*, 652).

60. ZGNT does not include δέ; NA[28] has this reading but places the word in brackets to indicate its uncertainty.

61. The Greek is τοὺς . . . τῆς σαρκὸς ἡμῶν πατέρας, "our fathers characterized by flesh."

62. Ellingworth (*Hebrews*, 653–54) thinks such a reference is possible.

63. Interpreters often point to Num 16:22 as a possible parallel: the LXX refers to "God, the God of spirits and of all flesh" (θεὸς θεὸς τῶν πνευμάτων καὶ πάσης σαρκός).

64. The καί before the verb probably has a final meaning here (Zerwick and Grosvenor, *Grammatical Analysis*, 685).

65. Oddly, this is the only use of ζάω (or ζωή) to refer to eternal life in Hebrews (unless the quotation from Habakkuk in 10:38 has this sense).

66. Neither are named in this verse, but the plural article οἱ picks up "earthly fathers" from v. 9, while the singular ὁ picks up "the father of spirits." The two are placed in contrast by the μέν . . . δέ construction.

67. The Greek could be translated "for a few days"; it might refer to the limits of human life or to the time of a child's minority (for the latter, see Bénétrau, *L'Épître aux Hébreux*, 2:171). The use of πρός to indicate extent of time is rare (von Siebenthal, *Ancient Greek Grammar*, 282).

τὸ δοκοῦν).⁶⁸ While not explicit in the comparison, the author may imply that the heavenly Father, by contrast, has a longer time to discipline his sons and daughters. Earthly fathers often are motivated by what is good for their children in their exercise of discipline. So also our heavenly Father: he engages in discipline for our good (ἐπὶ τὸ συμφέρον). The difference is that the heavenly Father disciplines with infinite knowledge and complete control of the circumstances. His purpose is that we, his children, might come to share in his holiness. God's demand of his people is that they be holy, as he is holy (e.g., Lev 11:44–45). That demand has not disappeared with the arrival of the new covenant (1 Pet 1:16), but that covenant brings with it a new enabling power to achieve that holy status—to be set apart from this world, wholly dedicated to God. "Holiness" in Hebrews usually refers to the status of those who have been cleansed and forgiven through the sacrifice of Christ.⁶⁹ Here, however, as well as in verse 14 (where ἁγιασμός is used), the language takes on some degree of moral connotation.⁷⁰

12:11 All discipline seems, at the time, a matter not of joy but of pain. Later, however, it repays those who are trained by it with the peaceful fruit of righteousness (πᾶσα δὲ⁷¹ παιδεία πρὸς μὲν τὸ παρὸν οὐ δοκεῖ χαρᾶς εἶναι ἀλλὰ λύπης, ὕστερον δὲ καρπὸν εἰρηνικὸν τοῖς δι' αὐτῆς γεγυμνασμένοις ἀποδίδωσιν δικαιοσύνης). The author's fourth and final elaboration of "with respect to discipline . . . you must endure" (v. 7a) is a reminder of the essential nature of discipline. As I noted above, this verse makes clear that the author's concept of "discipline" (παιδεία) includes a punitive element. Discipline in this context is not simply "instruction" or "education"—it is a process of education, or of moral formation, that includes an element of rebuke and even physical "correction." Such discipline seems "at the time" (πρὸς . . . τὸ παρόν)⁷² to be a matter of "pain" rather than of "joy."⁷³ Running every day becomes tedious and sometimes painful, but it pays off when one is able to run the marathon. Aristotle is claimed to have said "the roots of discipline are bitter, but its fruit is sweet."⁷⁴ So in the spiritual realm. The suffering the readers are experiencing, because they belong to a Father who cares for and watches over them, is a form of discipline that will ultimately yield a valuable reward. The particular time of this "ultimately" is not clear. Does the author think of the payoff in this life of a closer walk with God? Or is he thinking of the eschatological reward?⁷⁵ The former is more likely since "peaceful fruit of righteousness" probably can be interpreted to mean something like "the fruit that consists of peace and righteousness."⁷⁶ Discipline produces both a peaceful disposition in relationship to others (see v. 14) and, in general, a lifestyle that pleases God. James 3:17–18, using the same three key words as we find here in Hebrews, makes clear that the

---

68. The Greek word δοκοῦν is an infinitive from δοκέω, "think," "seem."

69. See ἁγιάζω, "sanctify," "make holy," in 2:11; 9:13; 10:10, 14, 29; 13:12. The Greek word for "holiness" here comes from ἁγιότης, which occurs only here in the NT (though it is a strong textual option in 2 Cor 1:12).

70. Peterson, *Hebrews and Perfection*, 151.

71. Several manuscripts read μέν (ℵ* P 33. 1739. 1881), which makes good sense in light of the δέ that introduces the second clause. However, it is suspect for just this reason. The particle δέ is the more difficult reading and should be preferred.

72. The word παρόν is a participle from πάρειμι, "be present."

73. The author contrasts two words in the genitive to make this point: χαρᾶς and λύπης. Both modify a word to be supplied from the context, which I have rendered "matter."

74. The saying is credited to Aristotle by Diogenes Laertius (*Lives and Opinions of Eminent Philosophers* 5.1.18 [cited from the Perseus Digital Library]).

75. As Ellingworth suggests (*Hebrews*, 656).

76. The Greek word for "peaceful" (an adjective: εἰρηνικόν), then, is equivalent to an epexegetic genitive (Lane, *Hebrews*, 2:403; Ellingworth, *Hebrews*, 656), while δικαιοσύνης is an epexegetic genitive, referring, as usually is the case with this word in Hebrews (1:9; 5:13; see also 7:2; 11:7, 33), to behavioral righteousness.

author reflects a widespread Christian perspective: "but the wisdom from above is first of all pure; then peaceful [εἰρηνική], considerate, submissive, full of mercy and good fruit, impartial and sincere. And the fruit [καρπός] of righteousness [δικαιοσύνης] is sown in peace [ἐν εἰρήνῃ] by those who make peace [εἰρήνην]" (author's translation).

12:12–13 Therefore strengthen your feeble hands and your weak knees, 13 and make straight paths for your feet, in order that what is lame may not be dislocated but rather healed (Διὸ τὰς παρειμένας χεῖρας καὶ τὰ παραλελυμένα γόνατα ἀνορθώσατε, 13 καὶ τροχιὰς ὀρθὰς ποιεῖτε τοῖς ποσὶν ὑμῶν, ἵνα μὴ τὸ χωλὸν ἐκτραπῇ, ἰαθῇ δὲ μᾶλλον). In these two verses, the author draws an inference ("therefore," διό) from what he has said in verses 1–11. The verses employ the analogy of walking or traveling on a path, imagery that is obviously similar to what we find at the beginning of the passage, where we are urged to "run the race" well (vv. 1–2). The author then appears here to circle back to where he began, and verses 12–13 should be seen as the conclusion of the author's appeal in 12:1–13.[77]

We will not be able to progress very far or very well on the path God has set out for us if we have "feeble hands" and "weak knees." They therefore must be strengthened, or "straightened."[78] The author borrows imagery from the wisdom literature, which often presents people with a choice of roads or paths to take and uses language about physical infirmities to warn of spiritual neglect and failure. Sirach 25:23b is a particularly clear parallel: "drooping hands and weak knees [χεῖρες παρειμέναι καὶ γόνατα παραλελυμένα] come from the wife who does not make her husband happy" (NRSV). The author uses the same two physical features—hands and knees—and the same adjectival participles to describe them—feeble/drooping and weak—as does Sirach.[79] A text using three of these four terms is Isaiah 35:3 LXX: "strengthen the feeble hands [χεῖρες ἀνειμέναι], steady the knees that give way [γόνατα παραλελυμένα]."[80] The general picture is clear: the readers are like runners in a race, whose hands (or arms)[81] are beginning to droop and whose knees are beginning to give way.[82]

Another hindrance to the runner is a path that is strewn with obstacles or is winding and unpredictable. Thus, the author urges his readers also to "make straight paths for their feet."[83] The wisdom background is again evident. In Proverbs 4:26, the father urges his son to "mark out a straight path for your feet" (my translation; ὀρθὰς τροχιὰς ποίει σοῖς ποσίν). This same context in Proverbs furnished the author with his quotation that introduces the filial "discipline" motif (Prov

---

77. As I noted above, a few scholars (e.g., Michel, *Der Brief an die Hebräer*, 447; Westfall, *Discourse Analysis*, 266–67) think that v. 12 inaugurates a new stage in the author's argument.

78. The verb is ἀνορθόω, which refers in Luke 13:13 to Jesus's miraculous "straightening" of a woman with a medical condition that caused her to be "bent over." In Acts 15:16 (= Amos 9:11), the verb means simply "restore."

79. See also Sir 2:12; Jer 50:43 [27:43 LXX]; Zeph 3:16; Philo, *Prelim. Studies* 164. The participle modifying "hands" (παρειμένας) comes from παρίημι, "slacken," "weaken" (only elsewhere in the NT in a different sense in Luke 11:42), while the participle modifying "knees" (παραλελυμένα) comes from παραλύω, which refers to "paralyzed" people in its other NT occurrences (Luke 5:18, 24; Act 8:7; 9:33; cf. 1 Macc 9:55; 3 Macc. 2.22).

80. Only the NIV among English versions marks these words as a quotation.

81. The NIV alone among translations renders χεῖρας as "arms" rather than "hands." This translation is chosen because (1) the equivalent Hebrew word, *yad*, can mean either "forearm" or "hand"; and (2) it is the arm rather than the hand that droops when running. BDAG ("χείρ," 1082, §1) note that the word might mean "arm" in two other NT texts (Matt 4:6 and Luke 4:11).

82. Some interpreters (e.g., Ellingworth, *Hebrews*, 657–58) suggest that the author is referring to "weak" members of the community.

83. Some interpreters think the language refers to a "level" path (Delitzsch, *Hebrews*, 2:326); see NIV. Others think that the phrase τοῖς ποσίν might be a dative of instrument: "make

3:11–12 in vv. 5–6). The word "straight" in Greek (*orthos*, ὀρθός) is the basis for English words such as *orthopedic* ("straightening feet"); and because what is "straight" often connotes what is "right" and "true" ("he was straight with me"), words such as *orthodoxy* ("right thinking") are also based on it. A "straight" path, then, is one that becomes, metaphorically, the right path. The purpose of creating such a straight path is that "what is lame may not be dislocated but rather healed." The verb I have translated "dislocated" (see also NIV; CSB; NAB) means basically "turn" or "turn away," but there is evidence for the more technical medical meaning I have chosen.[84] The ultimate goal is positive: healing. A number of interpreters see a reference to the life of the community here: the stronger members, spiritually, are to carve out straight paths for the weaker members.[85] This is certainly possible, but I suspect the focus remains on the individual throughout verses 12–13. Each believer needs to strengthen themselves for the spiritual marathon they are running, seeking to find the straight and level path that God has marked out for them.

12:14–16 Pursue peace with everyone and also holiness, without which no one will see the Lord, 15 taking care so that no one falls short of the grace of God, so that no root of bitterness grows up and causes trouble, and through it brings defilement to many, 16 and so that no one becomes an immoral and godless man like Esau, who sold his birthright for a single meal (Εἰρήνην διώκετε μετὰ πάντων καὶ τὸν ἁγιασμόν, οὗ χωρὶς οὐδεὶς ὄψεται τὸν κύριον, 15 ἐπισκοποῦντες μή τις ὑστερῶν ἀπὸ τῆς χάριτος τοῦ θεοῦ, μή τις ῥίζα πικρίας ἄνω φύουσα ἐνοχλῇ καὶ δι᾽ αὐτῆς μιανθῶσιν πολλοί, 16 μή τις πόρνος ἢ βέβηλος ὡς Ἠσαῦ, ὃς ἀντὶ βρώσεως μιᾶς ἀπέδετο τὰ πρωτοτόκια ἑαυτοῦ). A shift occurs between verses 13 and 14. The athletic and filial discipline motifs that dominate verses 1–13 are dropped. At the same time, the author's tone turns from positive encouragement to negative warning. In verses 1–13, he urges his readers to participate energetically in the spiritual race with a view to receiving benefits, among them that we will "share in his [God's] holiness" (v. 10). In verses 14–17, on the other hand, the author urges his readers to pursue holiness because, without it, a person cannot "see the Lord." This warning note continues to be sounded throughout verses 15–17. After being absent for a couple of chapters, then (see 10:26–31), the warnings that punctuate the author's sermon surface again. This shift of focus might suggest that verse 14 initiates a new major section in the progress of the sermon, as the author grounds his warning in verses 14–17 with a fresh reminder of the new-covenant benefits God is making available to the readers.[86] Other interpreters, however, think that verses 14–17 are more directly connected with what comes before than with what follows. They see the warnings in these verses as the rhetorical climax to the exhortation in verses 1–13.[87] It is noted, for instance, that the call to "peace" and "holiness" in verse 14 echoes verses 10 (sharing God's holiness) and 11 ("peaceful fruit of righteousness"). These opposing indicators reveal that verses 14–17 are transitional. If forced to put the verses in one

---

straight paths with your feet" (Lane, *Hebrews*, 2:403; Cockerill, *Hebrews*, 630). But a dative of advantage—"for your feet"—fits the imagery much better.

84. See "ἐκτρέπω," BDAG 311.

85. Montefiore, *Hebrews*, 222; Ellingworth, *Hebrews*, 659; Lane, *Hebrews*, 2:428; Cockerill, *Hebrews*, 630.

86. Attridge, *Hebrews*, 366; Lane, *Hebrews*, 2:431; Ellingworth, *Hebrews*, 661; Bénétrau, *L'Épître aux Hébreux*, 2:159; Spicq, *L'Épître aux Hébreux*, 2:398; Massonnet, *L'Épître aux Hébreux*, 351, 371. These interpreters agree in extending this section to the end of ch. 12 but disagree about whether ch. 13 should be included as well.

87. See, generally, the proposed structures in Bruce, *Hebrews*, 346; Johnson, *Hebrews*, 312; Koester, *Hebrews*, 533–34.

section or the other, I lean slightly to including them with verses 1–13.

This brief paragraph of exhortation and warning begins with a dual command: to seek "peace with everyone" and "holiness." The "everyone" probably has particular reference to fellow believers,[88] although an extension of the command to people in general cannot be ruled out.[89] It is not clear why the author urges his readers to pursue peace (see also v. 11): the letter gives no reason to think the community was divided or quarreling with one another. Perhaps, however, the author is influenced by a passage from the Septuagint, which adds the following after Proverbs 4:26 (the verse the author alludes to in v. 13): "For God knows the ways on the right, but those on the left are twisted. But it is he who will make your tracks straight [αὐτὸς δὲ ὀρθὰς ποιήσει τὰς τροχιάς σου], and he will guide your journeys in peace" (Prov 4:27; NETS).[90] Along with the horizontally oriented "peace with all," the readers are also to pursue the vertically oriented "holiness." As in verse 10 (where ἁγιότης is used), "holiness" (ἁγιασμός) will refer to the need to live out in experience the cleansing from sin that has been definitively given to believers through Christ's sacrifice (10:10).[91] As Peterson notes, the author is not calling on his readers to achieve peace and holiness on their own but rather "to realize the practical benefit of what has been made available for them in Christ."[92] The author underlines the importance of "holiness" by reminding the readers that a person cannot "see the Lord" without it. Only "holy," "set apart" people can stand in the presence of the "holy" and "set apart" God. "Seeing God" is held out as the promise that will come to pass for God's people on the last day (Matt 5:8; 1 John 3:2; Rev 22:4; see 1 Cor 13:12). In keeping with his regular emphasis, the author encourages his readers to maintain their zeal for the Lord so that they might enjoy the fullness of God's promises to them.

The main verb in verses 14–16 is the imperative "pursue" in verse 14. Verse 14b is somewhat parenthetical. The author resumes his main point in verse 15, using a participle—"being careful" (ἐπισκοποῦντες)—to introduce three parallel negative purpose clauses (vv. 15b–16):

1. "so that no one [μή τις] falls short of the grace of God,
2. so that no [μή τις] root of bitterness grows up and causes trouble, and through it brings defilement to many,
3. and so that no one [μή τις] becomes an immoral and godless man like Esau, who sold his birthright for a single meal."

Each member of the community is responsible for constantly "being careful" or "watching over" other members of the community. The three dangers the author is concerned about are presented in climactic order: from falling short of God's grace to allowing defilement to stain the community to being removed from God's covenant community.

"Grace" is another way of referring to the

---

88. Ellingworth, *Hebrews*, 661–62; Weiss, *Der Brief an die Hebräer*, 661.

89. DeSilva, *Perseverance in Gratitude*, 458. A few interpreters think that the "with all" (μετὰ πάντων) means "pursue along with all" rather than "peace with all" (Lane, *Hebrews*, 2:438; Cockerill, *Hebrews*, 633–34; Massonnet, *L'Épître aux Hébreux*, 376; see CEB). But it is more natural to attach the phrase to "peace." See Rom 12:18: "if it is possible, as far as it depends on you, live at peace with everyone."

90. Lane, *Hebrews*, 2:432–33. It is also possible that the author alludes to Ps 34:14 (LXX 33:15): "Depart from evil, and do good; seek peace [εἰρήνην], and pursue [δίωξον] it" (NRSV; see Cockerill, *Hebrews*, 633).

91. Cockerill, *Hebrews*, 634.

92. Peterson, *Hebrews and Perfection*, 74–75.

eschatological salvation that God has made available through his Son. The author's concern that some might "fall short" (ὑστερέω is the verb; cf. 4:1) of this grace mirrors warnings that he issues elsewhere in the letter; see especially 3:12: "see to it, brothers and sisters, that none of you has a sinful, unbelieving heart that turns away from the living God." The second and (probably) the third clause in this series depend on Deuteronomy 29:18–21 (29:17–20 LXX):

> [18] Make sure there is no man or woman, clan or tribe among you today whose heart turns away from the LORD our God to go and worship the gods of those nations; make sure there is no root among you that produces such bitter poison [*μή τίς ἐστιν ἐν ὑμῖν ῥίζα ἄνω φύουσα ἐν χολῇ καὶ πικρίᾳ*]. [19] When such a person hears the words of this oath and they invoke a blessing on themselves, thinking, "I will be safe, even though I persist in going my own way," they will bring disaster on the watered land as well as the dry. [20] The LORD will never be willing to forgive them; his wrath and zeal will burn against them. All the curses written in this book will fall on them, and the LORD will blot out their names from under heaven. [21] The LORD will single them out from all the tribes of Israel for disaster, according to all the curses of the covenant written in this Book of the Law.

The verbal parallel, as I note in the italicized Greek in the quotation above, comes in verse 15b, which clearly alludes to Deuteronomy 29:18 (29:17 LXX).[93] In that text Moses warns about the danger posed to the community by an unfaithful Israelite who goes astray to worship the gods of the nations. The author of Hebrews repeats this warning to his own community: a rebellious community member is a "root of bitterness,"—that is, a "bitter root"—who endangers the community. The author names that danger as being "defiled" (μιανθῶσιν)—the opposite of the holiness the author has exhorted his readers to pursue in verse 14.[94]

Cockerill and others attractively suggest that the third warning the author issues (v. 16) may also reflect Deuteronomy 29:18–21. The example of Esau, who loses his birthright and is unable to get it back again, is similar to the rebellious Israelite who suffers the covenant curses and whom the Lord vows never to forgive.[95] In painting such a dire portrait of Esau, the author goes further than the Old Testament does. The claim that he was "profane" (βέβηλος) has a solid basis in Genesis, which portrays him as too willing to surrender his birthright (Gen 25:27–34), claiming that he "despised his birthright" (v. 34b).[96] But the text does not accuse him of being a "sexually immoral person" (πόρνος).[97] This description of Esau might be an inference from his marrying foreign women (Gen 26:34).[98] Or the author may be using "sexually immoral" in the metaphorical sense such language has in the Old Testament, referring to a person's spiritual "adultery" with respect to the Lord.[99] It is perhaps most likely, however, that the author is

---

93. The Greek fragment I quote is what is found in a majority of LXX manuscripts. However, in place of ἐν χολῇ, "in bile," the uncials A and B both read ἐνοχλῇ, "trouble," "annoy." As he usually does, the author follows manuscript A.

94. Attridge, *Hebrews*, 368.

95. E.g., Cockerill, *Hebrews*, 636.

96. The Greek word βέβηλος in this context means "being worldly, as opposed to having an interest in transcendent matters" (BDAG 173, §2; see also 1 Tim 1:9).

97. A few interpreters have suggested that "sexually immoral person" (πόρνος) does not directly modify Esau (they translate "do not be a sexually immoral person or a profane person, like Esau") (Westcott, *Hebrews*, 407; Bruce, *Hebrews*, 350), but this is not the most natural way to read the Greek.

98. P. Hughes, *Hebrews*, 540; Michel, *Der Brief an die Hebräer*, 457.

99. Lane, *Hebrews*, 2:439; deSilva, *Perseverance in Gratitude*, 461.

basing this accusation on Jewish tradition, which went much further than Scripture in its bleak portrayal of Esau.[100] In any case, it is not Esau's sexual immorality that the author emphasizes but his "profane" attitude, which he illustrates by citing the famous incident of Jacob's taking his brother's birthright (πρωτοτόκια; cf. Gen 27:36) in exchange for a "single meal" (βρώσεως μιᾶς).

12:17 You know that even afterwards, when he wanted to inherit the blessing, he was rejected; he could find no opportunity for repentance, even though he sought it with tears (ἴστε γὰρ ὅτι καὶ μετέπειτα θέλων κληρονομῆσαι τὴν εὐλογίαν ἀπεδοκιμάσθη, μετανοίας γὰρ τόπον οὐχ εὗρεν καίπερ μετὰ δακρύων ἐκζητήσας αὐτήν). The author adds a further critical note about Esau: "later on" (μετέπειτα; see Gen 27:30–41) Esau wanted to inherit the blessing (θέλων κληρονομῆσαι τὴν εὐλογίαν), but he was "rejected" (ἀπεδοκιμάσθη). The author appears to view this "blessing" as equivalent to the "birthright" that Esau scorned, even though they are not equated in the Genesis narrative. The author then adds an explanation (γάρ): Esau could find no "opportunity for repentance" (μετανοίας . . . τόπον),[101] "even though he sought it with tears." The antecedent of the pronoun "it" in this last clause is unclear. As a feminine pronoun, it could refer either to "blessing" (εὐλογίαν) or to "repentance" (μετανοίας). Several English versions (NLT; ESV [apparently]; CEB) and a few interpreters think that the reference is to repentance.[102] However, the Old Testament portrays Esau as passionately seeking the blessing from his father, so more likely the author is following that storyline.[103] The Greek word "repentance" could refer more generally to a "change of mind," and the author may, then, mean that Esau sought to change his father's mind without success.[104] However, "repentance" has a stronger theological meaning elsewhere in Hebrews (6:1, 6), and this is probably the case here also. The author's emphasis on the finality of Esau's decision to reject his birthright/blessing fits with his concern elsewhere in the letter to underline the serious nature of the decision the readers are faced with. His warning in 6:4–6 is an obvious parallel: those who spurn God's good gifts after experiencing them cannot be brought back again to repentance.

Theology in Application

Scripture frequently uses the literary device of metaphor to communicate spiritual truth. Indeed, some argue that metaphor is a fundamental mode of all communication. With metaphor, we speak of one thing using language and imagery drawn from a different thing. If I say, for instance, that a football quarterback threw a "Hail Mary" at the end of the half, I am using the imagery of prayer and devotion to refer

---

100. So, e.g., Philo claims Esau was "an unrestrained, lecherous, impure and unholy man" (*QG* 4.201), while the Palestinian targum on Gen 25:29 claims that Esau had committed adultery before his encounter with Jacob (see Bruce, *Hebrews*, 350).

101. For the Greek τόπος in the sense of "opportunity," see BDAG 1012, §4.

102. E.g., Ellingworth, *Hebrews*, 665–69.

103. See NIV; NRSV; NET; CSB; NAB; and most commentators (e.g., Westcott, *Hebrews*, 409; Lane, *Hebrews*, 2:440; Koester, *Hebrews*, 533). A possible syntactical point in favor of this view is the fact that "repentance" comes in a phrase that has a masculine lead word: μετανοίας τόπον. A masculine pronoun might therefore have been expected (though it certainly would not have been required).

104. E.g., Bénétrau, *L'Épître aux Hébreux*, 2:180.

to an athletic play. Metaphors can be simple (as in this example) or complex. The author uses two extended metaphors in 12:1–17 to communicate spiritual truth to us.

The Race

In verses 1–2 and then again in verses 12–13, the author uses the widespread ancient activity of running a race to teach about the importance of dedicated application in living the life God has called us to. This focus dovetails with the author's central concern in his sermon, as he writes to believers who are flagging in zeal, tempted even to give up their rich spiritual position in Christ. This being the case, it is not the sprint that the author is thinking of, but the long-distance race. The author commends his audience for starting the race well (10:32–34). And, indeed, we often find that people who come to Christ display an initial burst of enthusiasm. But can they sustain it? This is what the author is worried about. The metaphor of the race he employs for these ends is not simple but complex, as the author touches on various specific comparisons of athletic competition and spiritual pilgrimage. Keeping our eyes fixed on the goal keeps runners on track: looking to the side or behind is often disastrous. So believers are to keep focused on Jesus, turning away from all the distractions that so easily creep in and put us off course. We will only run well if we divest ourselves of extraneous burdens. When I competed in track many years ago, we would often train with weights affixed to our ankles—but we did not compete in meets with those weights on!

Athletes are spurred on by the example of those who have competed successfully. Coaches often bring star athletes from the past into the locker room to provide an example of what competing well looks like. And so we also run our race surrounded by a "cloud of witnesses." As we noted in the exposition, these believers from the past "witness" *to* us through their unbreakable faith, even when faced with overwhelming pressure. If they can trust in these circumstances, our author is saying, surely you can trust too!

The Family

The earthly family provides the writers of Scripture with perhaps the most fruitful metaphor for the new-covenant people of God. Early Christians commonly addressed each other in terms drawn from family life, as is clear from the common New Testament address of fellow Christians as "brothers and sisters" (3:1, 12; 10:19; 13:22). The author to the Hebrews, following the lead of other early Christians (e.g., Rom 8:29), extends that "siblingship" to include Jesus Christ himself. A central argument of the author in 2:10–18 is that Jesus has fully identified with humans and is therefore part of the same family. He has been "made like them" in every way (2:17) and is not ashamed to address humans as "brothers and sisters" (2:11). The author draws out the spiritual implications of this identification: Jesus can be a merciful high priest, able to identify with every human weakness and challenge (2:17–18; see also 4:15; 5:7–8).

However, perhaps the most evocative application of the family metaphor to spiritual matters in all the New Testament comes in Hebrews 12:5–11. Here the author presents our awesome God as the loving father who disciplines his sons and daughters—always perfectly and wisely and always with our best interests in view. It is hard to imagine any greater encouragement than knowing that, in whatever I face, I am being directed and supported by the loving God who sovereignly controls every aspect of this world.

Hebrews 12:18–29

Literary Context

The body of the author's "word of exhortation" ends appropriately with the three components that have been the building blocks of his sermon throughout: exposition of the superiority of the new economy over the old (vv. 18–24), exhortation (vv. 25a, 28), and warning (vv. 25b–27, 29). This whole section has both a specific and general connection with its context. In the narrow perspective, this passage, especially verses 18–24, grounds the exhortations and warnings in verses 14–17.[1] A close relationship of verses 18–29 with 14–17 is implied by the many scholars who think that verse 14 opens a new section of the letter.[2] Even if we include verses 14–17 with what precedes (as I do), a connection between those verses and verses 18–24 is probable: this latter text provides reasons why it is so important to seek peace and holiness (v. 14) and to avoid neglecting God's grace and falling into defilement and immorality, as Esau did (vv. 15–17).

At the same time, however, the stark comparison between the two mountains in verses 18–24—and, derivatively, the covenants they represent (see v. 24)—serves as a rhetorically powerful summing up of similar comparisons between old and new throughout the sermon. The final occurrence of the key word "better" (κρεῖττον) occurs here (v. 24). Indeed, some scholars identify 12:18–24 as the "rhetorical climax of the epistle."[3] This being the case, we are also justified in finding a more general connection between verses 18–29 and the author's sermon as a whole. The author here returns to a theme that has characterized the early part of his sermon: the significance of God's final "speaking" in his Son and the imperative need to pay the closest attention to that message in order to avoid judgment (see 1:1–2a; 2:1–4; 4:12–13).

---

1. E.g., Lane, *Hebrews*, 2:459; Ellingworth, *Hebrews*, 670. Attridge (*Hebrews*, 372) posits a connection specifically with v. 17.

2. See my comments on v. 14 above.

3. Ellingworth, *Hebrews*, 669; see also Koester, *Hebrews*, 548; Grässer, *An die Hebräer*, 3:302. Weiss (*Der Brief an die Hebräer*, 669), however, questions this.

I. The Exalted Son and a Rest for the People of God (1:1–4:13)
II. Our Great High Priest and His Ministry (4:14–10:31)
III. **Exhortation: Follow and Serve the Pioneer of Our Faith through Endurance and Faith (10:32–13:25)**
    A. Introductory Call to Endurance and Faith (10:32–39)
    B. The Nature and Power of Faith Illustrated in Salvation History (11:1–40)
    C. Run the Race with Endurance, Remembering That You Are Children of God (12:1–17)
→   **D. Coming to Mount Zion and Inheriting the Unshakable Kingdom (12:18–29)**
    E. Letter Closing (13:1–25)

Main Idea

God spoke to the people of Israel from Sinai, but his voice was muted by phenomena that brought terror to the people. In contrast, God speaks in his new-covenant word a message offering access to God and from a mountain characterized by joy and celebration. Those who hear that message must respond properly, recognizing that God's new-covenant message also comes with warning about failure to obey it.

Translation

Hebrews 12:18-29

18a	negative (to 22a)	**You have not come**
18b	description 1	to something that can be touched and
18c	description 2	a blazing fire and
18d	description 3	darkness and
18e	description 4	gloom and
18f	description 5	storm and
19a	description 6	the blast
19b	source	of a trumpet and
19c	description 7	the sound
19d	source	of words,
19e	description	which those who heard asked
19f	content	that no word be added to them.
20a	reason (for 19e–f)	For
20b	assertion	**they could not bear**
20c	object	what was commanded,
20d	condition	"If even an animal touches the mountain,

20e	content (of 20b)	it will be stoned." (Exod 19:12–13)
21a	intensification	Indeed,
21b	reason (for 21c–e)	so terrifying was the sight that
21c	assertion	**Moses said,**
21d	content	"I am trembling
21e	manner	with fear" (Deut 9:19)
22a	positive (to 18a)	But **you have come**
22b	description 1	to Mount Zion and
22c	restatement	the city of the living God,
22d	apposition	the heavenly Jerusalem, and
22e	description 2	to myriads of angels,
22f	description	in festal array, and
23a	parallel (to 22f)	to the assembly
23b	content	of the firstborn enrolled in heaven, and
23c	description 3	to the judge,
23d	identification	God over all, and
23e	parallel (to 23c)	to the spirits
23f	possession	of righteous people
23g	description	who have been perfected, and
24a	description 4	to Jesus,
24b	description	the mediator
24c	object	of a new covenant, and
24d	parallel (to 24a)	to the sprinkled blood
24e	description	that speaks better than Abel.
25a	exhortation	**See to it that you do not refuse**
25b	object	him who is speaking.
25c	basis (for 25a–b)	For
25d	condition	if they did not escape
25e	time	when they refused
25f	object	the one who warns
25g	place	on earth,
25h	rhetorical question	**how much less will we,**
25i	condition	if we refuse
25j	object	the one who speaks
25k	place	from heaven?
26a	assertion	His voice at one time shook the earth,
		but
26b	time	now
26c	assertion	he has promised that
26d	sequence	"Yet once more
26e	content (of 26c)	I will shake

26f	negative		not only the earth but also
26g	positive		the heavens." (Haggai 2:6)
27a	assertion		**The words "once more" indicate the removal**
27b	content		of the things that are shaken,
27c	apposition		things that have been made,
27d	purpose (of 27c)		in order that the things not shaken might remain.
28a	inference (from 25–27)	Therefore,	
28b	basis		since we are receiving an unshakeable kingdom,
28c	exhortation 1	**let us be thankful** and	
28d	means (of 28d)		through it
28e	parallel (to 28c)	worship God	
28f	manner		acceptably
28g	association		with reverence and
28h	parallel		awe,
29a	basis (for 28d–g)	for	
29b	possession		**our**
29c	assertion		**"God is a consuming fire."** (Deut 4:24)

Structure

The passage falls into two obvious parts: a comparison between two mountains and their respective covenants in verses 18–24, and an exhortation and warning in verses 25–29. The first section divides, in turn, into two parts, marked by the strong adversative "but" (ἀλλά) in verse 22 and the repetition of the verb "have come": "you have not come" to Sinai (v. 18), but "you have come to Mount Zion" (v. 22). Scholars often suggest that the author has carefully composed his comparison between Sinai and Zion so that each section (vv. 18–21, 22–24) has seven basic descriptions.[4] However, while verses 18–21, indeed, have seven clearly identifiable parts, the same is not true in verses 22–24. One can come up with seven elements in these verses only by counting the three descriptions of Mount Zion in verse 22 as one (since they all refer to the same entity). However, while the three are indeed referring to the same thing, the structure of the author's list suggests they should be counted as two separate components: "Mount Zion," on the one hand, and "the city of the living God, the heavenly Jerusalem," on the other.[5] A more satisfactory arrangement, then, is to find in verses 22–24 four pairs:[6]

---

4. E.g., P. Hughes, *Hebrews*, 545; Lane, *Hebrews*, 2:464; D. Harris, *Hebrews*, 382; Cockerill, *Hebrews*, 650.

5. The καί—"and"—between "Mount Zion" and "city of the living God" points strongly in this direction. This word is used in the rest of the list to demarcate new items.

6. See esp. Backhaus, *Der Hebräerbrief*, 443; and also Michel, *Der Brief an die Hebräer*, 462–63; Attridge, *Hebrews*, 372; Grässer, *An die Hebräer*, 3:311; Kibbe, *Godly Fear*, 189.

"Mount Zion"	and	"the city of the living God, the heavenly Jerusalem"
myriads of angels in festal array	and	the assembly of the firstborn enrolled in heaven
the judge, who is God of all	and	the spirits of righteous people who have been perfected
the mediator of a new covenant, Jesus,	and	the sprinkled blood that speaks better than the blood of Abel

The author obviously intends to contrast the terror-inducing phenomena of Sinai with the welcoming and joyful, celebratory aspects of Zion. The two mountains ultimately contrast two covenants; indeed, we might say, in Pauline terms, law and gospel. However, as Kiwoong Son notes, the obvious contrast between Sinai and Zion rests on an important degree of correspondence.[7] God "speaks" from each "mountain"; indeed, he "warns" from both mountains. As he has emphasized throughout his sermon, the author does not see a simple antithetical relationship between old and new but one of salvation-historical progress. "Better" (see again 12:24) is again the key word.

The second paragraph, verses 25–29, develops through a series of "hook words" or "hook concepts." The key warning about not refusing "him who speaks" in verse 25 (which ties into the "speaking" blood in v. 24) merges into a reminder that the Old Testament people of God did not escape when they "refused" to hear God's voice. This warning was issued "on earth," but a new warning now comes to the people of God "from heaven." The author uses a quotation from Haggai 2:6 to illustrate the contrast between earth and heaven (v. 26). This quotation, in turn, furnishes the author with the language of "shaking" to depict the great culmination in salvation history yet to come (v. 27). In verse 28, the author picks up the "shaking" language to affirm that the kingdom that God's people now receive is stable and unchanging, providing the basis for an attitude of thankfulness.[8] And yet, coming back to the note of warning he has sounded in verse 25, the author reminds his people that God is a "consuming fire" and needs therefore to be approached with "reverence and awe" (vv. 28b–29).

Exegetical Outline

- **D. Coming to Mount Zion and Inheriting the Unshakable Kingdom (12:18–29)**
    1. The Contrast between Mount Sinai and Mount Zion (vv. 18–24)
    2. The Promise of the Unshakable Kingdom (vv. 25–29)

---

7. Kiwoong Son, *Zion Symbolism in Hebrews: Hebrews 12:18–24 as a Hermeneutical Key to the Epistle*, Paternoster Biblical Monographs (Waynesboro: Paternoster, 2005), 78–82.

8. The "therefore" (διό) that introduces v. 28 might signify that a new paragraph begins here (e.g., Koester, *Hebrews*, 554, who identifies 12:28–13:21 as the "peroration").

Explanation of the Text

12:18–20 You have not come to something that can be touched and a blazing fire and darkness and gloom and storm 19 and the blast of a trumpet and the sound of words, which those who heard asked that no word be added to them. 20 For they could not bear what was commanded, "If even an animal touches the mountain, it will be stoned" (Οὐ γὰρ προσεληλύθατε ψηλαφωμένῳ καὶ κεκαυμένῳ πυρὶ καὶ γνόφῳ καὶ ζόφῳ καὶ θυέλλῃ 19 καὶ σάλπιγγος ἤχῳ καὶ φωνῇ ῥημάτων, ἧς οἱ ἀκούσαντες παρῃτήσαντο μὴ προστεθῆναι αὐτοῖς λόγον, 20 οὐκ ἔφερον γὰρ τὸ διαστελλόμενον, Κἂν θηρίον θίγῃ τοῦ ὄρους, λιθοβοληθήσεται). The author quickly mentions aspects of Sinai that together convey a rather gloomy picture of that experience. As I note above, the first paragraph in this section is clearly marked out by the contrast between "you have not come" in verse 18 and "you have come" in verse 22. The place the readers have not come to is Mount Sinai—although the author never mentions "Sinai" and only refers to a mountain later in verse 20. Nevertheless, the implied contrast with Zion in verse 22 along with the description in verses 18–21 makes clear that the author refers to the place where Moses met with God and received his law for the people of Israel (Exod 19; cf. Judg 5:5; Neh 9:13; Acts 7:38; Gal 4:24, 25). For rhetorical effect, however, the author leaves the place unspecified, allowing the readers to "discover" the reference by means of the descriptions he offers. He provides seven descriptions, drawn from Old Testament passages about Sinai. The language of "come to" or "come near" (the verb is προσέρχομαι) reflects Deuteronomy 4:11: "You came near [LXX προσέρχομαι] and stood at the foot of the mountain while it blazed with fire to the very heavens, with black clouds and deep darkness."[9] "That can be touched" (ψηλαφωμένῳ) is not used in any narrative about Sinai. It may reflect, however, Exodus 19:12–13, a passage the author clearly alludes to in verse 20:[10]

> [12] Put limits for the people around the mountain and tell them, "Be careful that you do not approach the mountain or touch the foot of it. Whoever touches the mountain is to be put to death. [13] They are to be stoned or shot with arrows; not a hand is to be laid on them. No person or animal shall be permitted to live." Only when the ram's horn sounds a long blast may they approach the mountain.

The prominence that the author gives to this first description suggests to many scholars that a basic contrast in this passage is between the material, or physical, realm and the realm of the spirit. This contrast is said to be rooted in Neoplatonism, of which Philo is a key representative.[11] This dualistic way of thinking appears to be reinforced in verse 27, where the author looks to the day when "created things" will be "shaken"—that is, the physical realm will be destroyed so that what remains—the "unshakable kingdom"—is the spiritual. This perspective, which elevates the spiritual or heavenly, and deprecates the physical or earthly, is claimed to lie at the heart

---

9. The listener to Hebrews's sermon will also have heard cultic allusions to this language throughout.

10. See, e.g., D. M. Allen, *Deuteronomy and Exhortation*, 589. The word is a passive participle of the verb ψηλαφάω, "touch" (in the NT elsewhere, Luke 24:39; Acts 17:27; 1 John 1:1). Lane thinks the reference might be to Exod 10:21, which uses a cognate word (ψηλαφητός) to describe the "darkness that can be felt" (*Hebrews*, 2:460).

11. Key advocates of this way of reading the text, whom we have often cited as exponents of this dualism in Hebrews,

of the author's way of thinking and to permeate his sermon. As I have argued before when this issue has arisen, I join those many interpreters who argue that our author is not fundamentally dualistic in his approach. However, I also disagree with many of those same interpreters who deny virtually any influence from Neoplatonic dualism. I think the evidence suggests that our author is mildly influenced by this movement—and his description here of Sinai as "something that can be touched" may reflect this.

The remaining four descriptions in verse 18 pick up language used in several texts that depict Sinai in the Old Testament: for "blazing fire" (κεκαυμένῳ πυρί),[12] see Exodus 19:18; 24:17; Deuteronomy 4:11, 36; 5:23, 25; for "darkness" (γνόφῳ) see Exodus 20:21; Deuteronomy 4:11; 5:22; for "storm" (θυέλλῃ), see Deuteronomy 4:11; 5:22. The only word in Hebrews that does not also appear in the LXX accounts is "gloom" (ζόφῳ), but it certainly and accurately captures the atmosphere of those narratives.[13]

In verse 19, the author turns his attention to the auditory aspects of the Sinai event. The people heard "the blast of a trumpet" and "the sound of words." The former apparently echoes Exodus 19:16: "On the morning of the third day there was thunder and lightning, with a thick cloud over the mountain, and a very loud trumpet blast. Everyone in the camp trembled." The Lord's voice is featured in Deuteronomy 5:22-28, but the author's language is closer to Deuteronomy 4:12: "Then the LORD spoke to you out of the fire. You heard the sound of words but saw no form; there was only a voice."[14]

One might think that the people would welcome the opportunity to hear the voice of God. But this would underestimate the awesome nature of God, attested by the phenomena that both the Old Testament and Hebrews mention. The people who heard God's voice,[15] in fact, "asked"[16] that no word be added to those words God had already spoken. Verse 20 supplies the reason for this request (γάρ): the people could not handle the terrifying nature of the Sinai experience. To be sure, the author does not say exactly this. But his reference to the specific warning about touching the mountain, with its serious consequences (Exod 19:12-13), seems to have this general purpose in view. And, as the language "even if" (κἄν [καί plus ἐάν]) makes clear, the author wants his readers to recall that the prohibition of touching applied to humans as well as animals.

12:21 Indeed,[17] so terrifying was the sight that Moses said, "I am trembling with fear" (καί, οὕτως

---

are Grässer, *An die Hebräer*, 3:313; Thompson, *Hebrews*, 267; Thompson, *Beginnings of Christian Philosophy*, 45–47; Weiss, *Der Brief an die Hebräer*, 671–72; cf., in milder form, Johnson, *Hebrews*, 329.

12. With most versions and interpreters, I take the participle κεκαυμένῳ as a modifier of πυρί. An outlier is Ellingworth (*Hebrews*, 672), who thinks the participle is independent. The series of words in vv. 18–19 are in the dative, either because they are in apposition to ψηλαφωμένῳ or because they depend on the verb προσεληλύθατε.

13. The word does not appear in the LXX, but appears four other times in the NT: 2 Pet 2:4, 17; Jude 6, 13. The author may add it for its rhetorical effect: *gnophō* ("darkness") and *zophō* ("gloom") sound alike.

14. The author's phrase "sound of words" (φωνὴ ῥημάτων) is virtually identical to the LXX (φωνὴν ῥημάτων).

15. The relative pronoun ἧς at the beginning of this clause refers back to φωνῇ, yet the use of the genitive suggests the author is thinking about God as the person heard (the verb ἀκούω [οἱ ἀκούσαντες] is followed by a genitive when the focus is on the person who is heard).

16. The verb παρῃτήσαντο, from παραιτέομαι, almost certainly here means "request" or "ask," and not, as in v. 25, "refuse" or "reject" (contra Ellingworth, *Hebrews*, 673; Koester, *Hebrews*, 543). However, the syntactical argument for a difference in meaning (that the verb followed by μή with an infinitive means "request" and the verb followed by an accusative means "refuse"), mentioned in BDAG (764, §1.b) and picked up by several scholars, does not hold (Kibbe, *Godly Fear*, 12–13).

17. The καί lying behind "indeed" has an ascensive meaning (Ellingworth, *Hebrews*, 675), identifying this verse as the high point of the author's description of the terror evoked by Sinai.

φοβερὸν ἦν τὸ φανταζόμενον, Μωϋσῆς εἶπεν, Ἔκφοβός εἰμι καὶ ἔντρομος).[18] The author appropriately caps off his description of the terrifying Sinai event by noting that even Moses, that great man of God, was overwhelmed by the "sight" (φανταζόμενον). The words the author attributes to Moses do not match any Old Testament text. The closest is Deuteronomy 9:19: "for I was afraid [ἔκφοβός εἰμι] that the anger that the LORD bore against you was so fierce that he would destroy you" (NRSV).[19] Moses is here recounting to Israel his response to discovering that the people of Israel had made for themselves a golden-calf idol while he was on Sinai receiving the "ten words" from the Lord. His terror is caused by the impending wrath of God against the people, not by the phenomena of Sinai themselves. For this reason, many interpreters are convinced that the author here is attributing to Moses his overall response to the various theophanies on Sinai,[20] perhaps under the influence of Jewish tradition.[21] However, a reference to Deuteronomy 9:19 may make sense if the author is deliberately fusing the initial Sinai theophany with the subsequent disobedience of the people. By doing so, he hints at the ineffectiveness of Sinai: God gave his people a good law, but they revealed almost immediately their inability to fulfill it. What Sinai failed to accomplish, Zion has: securing access to God.[22]

12:22–24 But you have come to Mount Zion and the city of the living God, the heavenly Jerusalem, and to myriads of angels, in festal array, 23 and to the assembly of the firstborn enrolled in heaven, and to the judge, God over all, and to the spirits of righteous people who have been perfected, 24 and to Jesus, the mediator of a new covenant, and to the sprinkled blood that speaks better than Abel (ἀλλὰ προσεληλύθατε Σιὼν ὄρει καὶ πόλει θεοῦ ζῶντος, Ἰερουσαλὴμ ἐπουρανίῳ, καὶ μυριάσιν ἀγγέλων, πανηγύρει 23 καὶ ἐκκλησίᾳ πρωτοτόκων ἀπογεγραμμένων ἐν οὐρανοῖς καὶ κριτῇ θεῷ πάντων καὶ πνεύμασιν δικαίων τετελειωμένων 24 καὶ διαθήκης νέας μεσίτῃ Ἰησοῦ καὶ αἵματι ῥαντισμοῦ κρεῖττον λαλοῦντι παρὰ τὸν Ἄβελ). In strong contrast to the rather foreboding picture of Sinai, a joyous and positive picture of Zion is now drawn. The strong contrast with verses 18–21 is indicated with the opening words of this verse: "you have not come [προσεληλύθατε] to [Sinai] . . . but you have come [προσεληλύθατε] to Mount Zion." As I noted above, the author's choice of the verb "come to" (προσέρχομαι) may have been influenced by Deuteronomy 4:11. But also influential in his choice may have been the use of the verb elsewhere in Hebrews to refer to that central concern of the author's—namely, "coming near" to God (4:16; 7:25; 10:1, 22; 11:6). These parallels make clear that "coming to" Zion cannot be confined to any one experience (such as worship); it is a way of referring to the believer's privilege of entering into God's presence, manifest on Zion.[23] Moreover, the author has depicted the spiritual life as

---

18. Most English versions rightly view ἔκφοβος . . . καὶ ἔντρομος as a hendiadys, according to which two terms joined by καί are mutually interpreting, pointing to one idea.

19. The word ἔκφοβος, "terrified," occurs only in this verse and in 1 Macc 13:2 in the LXX (see also Mark 9:6 in the NT). The word ἔντρομος, "trembling," occurs elsewhere in the LXX only in Pss 18:7 [17:8 LXX]; 77:18 [76:19 LXX]; 1 Macc 13:2; Wis 17:9 (and in Acts 7:32; 16:29). Worth noting is 1 Macc 13:2, since it is the only verse where both words occur: "Simon heard that Trypho had assembled a large army to invade the land of Judah and destroy it, and he saw that the people were trembling with fear [ἔντρομός ἐστιν καὶ ἔκφοβος]" (13:1–2a).

20. Ellingworth, *Hebrews*, 676.

21. Koester, *Hebrews*, 544; Westcott, *Hebrews*, 412; P. Hughes, *Hebrews*, 543; D. Harris, *Hebrews*, 386.

22. For this view, see esp. D. M. Allen, *Deuteronomy and Exhortation*, 65–66; and also G. Guthrie, "Hebrews," 988; Schreiner, *Hebrews*, 398.

23. Weiss, *Der Brief an die Hebräer*, 675.

a journey, and we here reach the culmination of that journey.[24] Indeed, the idea of Mount Zion as the goal of pilgrimage resonates with many Old Testament passages. According to Jeremiah, the people of the Lord in the last day will cry out, "Come, let us go up to Zion, to the LORD our God" (Jer 31:6; cf. 3:14); they will "enter Zion with singing; everlasting joy will crown their heads" (Isa 51:11; cf. 35:10; Jer 50:5). These verses reflect the powerful symbolic significance of Zion. Originally a hill in the area of Jerusalem (controlled by the Jebusites), Zion was incorporated into the city that David conquered. "Zion," then, sometimes refers to a mountain within Jerusalem (where the temple was built), but it more often refers to Jerusalem itself. Zion is "the city of David" (2 Sam 5:7; 1 Kgs 8:1; 1 Chr 11:5; 2 Chr 5:2) but, more importantly, "the City of the LORD" (Isa 60:14; see also Ps 48:2), the place where the Lord dwells (Isa 8:18; Jer 8:19; Joel 3:17; see also Pss 74:2; 76:2; 132:13). The exile signaled God's departure from Zion, but in the last days he will return to Zion (Isa 52:8; 59:20) and bring deliverance to his people (Obad 17).[25] This rich theological tradition about Zion was surely enough to trigger the author's reference here. But he may also have been influenced by two texts that are found right next to passages our author quotes. Psalm 110:1, as we have seen, is basic to the author's argument; and verse 2 reads, "The LORD will extend your mighty scepter from Zion, saying, 'Rule in the midst of your enemies!'" Likewise, the author of Hebrews quotes Psalm 2:7 in 1:5 and 5:5; and Psalm 2:6 reads, "I have installed my king on Zion, my holy mountain." Put simply, "Mount Zion" becomes a symbol of the fulfillment of God's promises to his people. One can even see a basis for the contrast with Sinai that our author emphasizes: "in the last days" when many people groups say "let us go up to the mountain of the LORD," "the law will go out" not from Sinai but "from Zion" (Isa 2:2–3; cf. Mic 4:2).[26]

The descriptions of Zion we have noted above explain why the author goes on to describe Zion as "the city of the living God."[27] The next phrase, which stands in apposition to "city of the living God," both replicates and goes beyond Old Testament teaching: "the heavenly Jerusalem." Zion and Jerusalem are identified in many Old Testament texts, but the qualification "heavenly" (ἐπουρανίῳ) introduces the author's distinctive take on Zion. He is not the first, or only, interpreter to qualify Zion in this way. Paul links believers with "the Jerusalem above," in contrast to "the present city of Jerusalem" (Gal 4:25–26). John identifies believers with "the city of my God, the new Jerusalem, which is coming down out of heaven" (Rev 3:12; see also 21:2, 10; and 2 Bar. 4.2–6; 4 Ezra 7.26).

At the end of the verse, the author shifts imagery to focus on the various persons, or beings, that are present at the heavenly Zion: angels, believers generally, God himself, and the spirits of dead believers (vv. 22b–23). As I argued above, these should be grouped into two basic pairs: angels and believers, on the one hand, and the judge, God, and the spirits of dead believers on the other hand. "Myriad" (μυριάς) can mean, precisely, ten

---

24. Koester, *Hebrews*, 548.
25. See, e.g., H. A. Thomas, "Zion," in *Dictionary of the Old Testament: Prophets*, ed. Mark J. Boda and J. Gordon McConville (Downers Grove, IL: IVP Academic, 2012), 907–14; Son, *Zion Symbolism*, 41–63.
26. These passages lead Hartmut Gese to develop the notion of a "Zion torah," to be distinguished from the "Sinai torah" ("The Law," in *Essays on Biblical Theology* [Minneapolis: Augsburg, 1981], 60–92). See also Stuhlmacher, *Biblical Theology*, 123–24, 287–88.
27. I have included the "and" (καί) that the author uses to connect this phrase to "Mount Zion" to make clear the underlying structure. The conjunction suggests that, while in substance the phrase is in apposition to "Mount Zion," stylistically it is a separate element. "Mount Zion" and "city of the living God" constitute, then, the first of four pairs of descriptors in vv. 22–24.

thousand, but usually refers, as BDAG ("μυριάς," 661, §2) suggests, to "a very large number, not precisely defined": "innumerable" (ESV); "thousands upon thousands" (NIV); "countless" (CEB).[28] The "cloud" of human witnesses involved in our earthly race of faith (12:1) is joined by a cloud of angelic beings who inhabit the new Jerusalem. As most translations and interpreters recognize, "in festal array" (πανηγύρει) goes with the previous phrase, referring to the angels.[29] Paired with the angels in their celebratory gathering is a human gathering: "the assembly of the firstborn enrolled in heaven." It is not easy to decide whether to render the Greek word here (ἐκκλησία) with "assembly" or with the more theologically technical word "church" (NIV; NJB). I slightly prefer the former, which establishes greater continuity with the Old Testament "assembly" of the people of God (e.g., Deut 4:10; 9:10; cf. Acts 7:38).

A few interpreters think the author might be adding a further description of the angels,[30] but the language of being "enrolled" usually refers to humans in Scripture.[31] Some think that the author intends this group to be restricted to those on earth,[32] but he does not suggest such a limitation: the reference is probably to the people of God both still on earth and those who have finished their race and are now in heaven.[33] The author calls them "firstborn" (πρωτοτόκων) in order to highlight their special status before God (see 1:6 with respect to Christ). Neither the New Testament nor the LXX anywhere else uses the plural as a description of the people of God; but the singular occurs in Exodus 4:22–23: "Then say to Pharaoh, 'This is what the LORD says: Israel is my firstborn son, and I told you, "Let my son go, so he may worship me." But you refused to let him go; so I will kill your firstborn son." To be "enrolled in heaven" refers to the divine recognition (or even creation) of one's spiritual identity: it suggests a book in which God records the names of those who belong to him and is a variant of the more common expression, to have one's name written in a book (Phil 4:3; Rev 3:5; 13:8; 17:8; 20:12, 15; 21:27).

The fifth aspect of the eschatological Mount Zion is "the judge, God over all." This translation reflects the sequence of words in the Greek and is adopted in RSV and CSB and by many commentators.[34] However, most versions reverse the sequence, and many other commentators prefer that arrangement.[35] There is no doubt that "God, who is judge over all" makes somewhat better sense. And, while the difference is slight, more of emphasis than substance, putting "judge" first gives the word greater prominence—a prominence that may not sit comfortably with the author's positive portrayal of Zion. Indeed, in order to preserve this positive focus, a few interpreters suggest that "judge" may have here the sense it sometimes has in biblical Greek of "vindicate."[36] I suspect that

---

28. See also Luke 12:1; Acts 21:20; Jude 14; Rev 5:11; 9:6.

29. See, e.g., Westcott, *Hebrews*, 414. The other option is to take the word with what follows, as does NET: "to the assembly and congregation of the firstborn" (see also NASB). The word πανήγυρις means "festal gathering"; it occurs only here in the NT and only four times in the LXX, each time referring to one of Israel's sacred assemblies (Hos 2:13; 9:5; Amos 5:21; Ezek 46:11).

30. Montefiore, *Hebrews*, 231; Spicq, *L'Épître aux Hébreux*, 407–8.

31. The verb the author uses is ἀπογράφω, which refers to being entered into a list, such as a tax record (Luke 2:3, 5) or, in the spiritual realm, being entered into the list kept by God. The concept, though not this particular word, occurs often (see, e.g., Exod 32:32; Dan 7:10; 12:1; 1 En. 47.3; Jub. 19.9; 30.22; 36.10).

32. Michel, *Der Brief an die Hebräer*, 465; Delitzsch, *Hebrews*, 2:361.

33. E.g., Bruce, *Hebrews*, 359; Cockerill, *Hebrews*, 655.

34. Montefiore, *Hebrews*, 231; Lane, *Hebrews*, 2:442; Cockerill, *Hebrews*, 656.

35. E.g., Weiss, *Der Brief an die Hebräer*, 680; Bénétrau, *L'Épître aux Hébreux*, 2:187.

36. See, e.g., Ps 75:7 [LXX 74:8]; Isa 33:22; and see Delitzsch, *Hebrews*, 2:352.

the idea of judging here includes this notion (see the next description), but it probably cannot be confined to it. The author has repeatedly warned his readers that they will have to answer to God for their stewardship of his gifts in this life (e.g., 10:30), and this assessment can result in condemnation as well as vindication. Moreover, the focus on the universality of God's judging also suggests an all-inclusive notion of judging here.

The next description of Zion, "the spirits of righteous people who have been perfected" does not seem at first sight to be a natural pairing with "the judge, God over all." However, the language of "righteous" (δικαίων) often has a judicial flavor: we might paraphrase "those who have been declared right in the judgment." Referring to them as "spirits" limits this group to those who have already died (see also 12:9). They have experienced the "perfection" that marks the ultimate work of God in the lives of his people (see 11:40).[37]

The two final items in the author's description of Mount Zion provide an appropriate climax to the list (v. 24), tapping into the central teaching of the letter as well as providing a pointed contrast with the conclusion of the author's description of Sinai. Moses and Jesus are juxtaposed as the two great representatives of their respective mountains and as mediators of their respective covenants. The author has highlighted the gift of the new covenant, a covenant that is "better" than the one that Sinai represents (8:7–13).[38] Ultimately, then, as in Galatians 4:21–31, Sinai represents the old covenant and Zion the new. Again picking up language from earlier in the letter, the author presents Jesus as the "mediator" (μεσίτης) of that new covenant (8:6; 9:15; cf. also 7:22, with a different Greek word). By referring to this mediator as "Jesus" (which, typically, the author puts last in the clause for emphasis), the author suggests the manner in which Jesus mediates that covenant.[39] Indeed, this becomes clear in the final descriptor: believers have come "to the sprinkled blood that speaks better than Abel."[40] "Sprinkled blood" reminds us of the author's heavy emphasis on the ultimate and once-for-all sacrifice of Jesus as the means by which God brings full and final forgiveness.[41] With most translations, I view the contrast in the last part of the verse to be between Christ's blood and *the blood* of Abel. (The author does not explicitly refer to the blood of Abel, but Greek style does not require that the word be repeated in a comparison of this sort.) If we read the verse this way, the question becomes: What is Abel's blood "speaking"? One option is to think the author is tapping into a Jewish tradition that highlighted Abel as the first martyr, and since the blood of martyrs was viewed in Judaism as having atoning significance, the contrast here could be between the limited effectiveness of Abel's atonement and the completely sufficient atonement provided

---

37. The plural "spirits" usually refers to evil spiritual beings in the NT, but this meaning clearly does not fit in this verse. The closest NT parallels to this usage are Luke 24:37, 39; Acts 23:8.

38. In 8:8 and 9:15, the author uses καινός to designate the "new" covenant. His choice here of νέος signals no difference in meaning. The two words are interchangeable in NT Greek (Ellingworth, *Hebrews*, 681).

39. Bénétrau, *L'Épître aux Hébreux*, 2:189.

40. A few interpreters have thought that "the one speaking" (λαλοῦντι) might refer to God, as a separate item in the list (e.g., Gene Smillie, "'The One Who Is Speaking' in Hebrews 12:25,"

TynBul 55 [2004]: 275–94). But this is unlikely (see Cockerill, *Hebrews*, 659).

41. The word "sprinkled" (ῥαντισμός) here is cognate to the verb ῥαντίζω, which referes to the sacrificial manipulation of blood in 9:13, 19, 21, 22. The author probably does not allude narrowly to the inauguration of the first covenant (as Bruce thinks [*Hebrews*, 360]) but to sacrifice in general (Kibbe, *Godly Fear*, 199). There is no basis to think "sprinkled blood" refers to Jesus's own fidelity (contra Kevin B. McCruden, "The Eloquent Blood of Jesus: The Neglected Theme of the Fidelity of Jesus in Hebrews 12:24," *CBQ* 75 [2013]: 504–20).

by Jesus's blood.[42] However, in 11:4, as I argued, Abel's continuing to speak probably refers to his call for vengeance. The contrast in verse 24, then, is probably between Abel's blood, crying out for vengeance, and Christ's blood, providing full atonement for sin.

12:25 See to it that you do not refuse him who is speaking. For if they did not escape when they refused the one who warns on earth, how much less will we, if we refuse the one who speaks from heaven? (Βλέπετε μὴ παραιτήσησθε τὸν λαλοῦντα· εἰ γὰρ ἐκεῖνοι οὐκ ἐξέφυγον ἐπὶ γῆς παραιτησάμενοι τὸν χρηματίζοντα, πολὺ μᾶλλον ἡμεῖς οἱ τὸν ἀπ' οὐρανῶν ἀποστρεφόμενοι;). The author abruptly turns from encouraging exposition—you have arrived at the eschatological Zion! (vv. 18–24)—to severe warning.[43] However, while quite general, a connection with the preceding context is forged with the hook word "the one who is speaking" (λαλοῦντι [v. 24]; τὸν λαλοῦντα) and with the allusion to the phenomena of Sinai in verse 26a ("his voice at one time shook the earth"). Verses 25–29, then, should probably be seen as loosely related to verses 18–24. The move from assurance to warning is quite common in Hebrews—although the sequence is more often from warning to assurance.

The warning in verse 25 picks up language and concepts from earlier such passages in Hebrews. The introductory "see to it" (βλέπετε) reminds us of 3:12: "See to it [βλέπετε], brothers and sisters, that none of you has a sinful, unbelieving heart that turns away from the living God." The focus on the God who speaks reminds us of 1:2 and 2:3. And the comparison between the voice of God in the Old Testament and the decisive "speaking" of God in the New Testament reminds us of 2:1–4 and 10:28–29. It is also typical of the author's portrayal of the word of God that he refers, in the present tense, to the one "who is speaking": God's word directly addresses his people. "Those" (ἐκεῖνοι) who "refused the one who warns on earth"[44] might be specifically the wilderness generation, which the author has held up as a negative example for the readers (3:7–4:11). But the Sinai incident continues to reverberate in the background here, so the reference is probably more broadly to the old-covenant people of God.[45] God's "warning" on earth refers in this context, then, specifically to Sinai (see v. 20) but also to the continuing authority of Sinai, with its threats of punishment for disobedience (see 2:2). The contrast between "earth" and "heaven" is another connection between verses 18–24 and verses 25–29. Sinai is a place that "can be touched," while Zion is the "heavenly Jerusalem" (vv. 18, 22). So God once warned "on earth" (ἐπὶ γῆς), but he now warns "from heaven" (ἀπ' οὐρανῶν). God warned "on earth" at Sinai; he now warns from his heavenly abode, the "city of the living God" (v. 22), the "place" into which Christ has entered to complete his work of redemption and to sit at the right hand of the throne of God. The author invites us to imagine the consequences of refusing to respond to the one who speaks from this location.

---

42. E.g., Grässer, *Der Brief an die Hebräer*, 3:323.

43. The abruptness of the shift is accentuated by the lack of any connecting word (asyndeton).

44. The word behind "refuse" is παραιτέομαι (used twice in this verse), the same verb that means "beg" or "ask" in v. 19. "The one who warns" translates τὸν χρηματίζοντα, a substantival participle from χρηματίζω. This verb can mean generally "speak" (Luke 2:26; Acts 10:22; 11:26; Rom 7:3), but it often has the sense "warn" (as elsewhere in Hebrews: 8:5; 11:7; see also Matt 2:12, 22). A few interpreters think "the one who warns" might be Moses (e.g., Montefiore, *Hebrews*, 234) or even the author of the letter (Smillie, "'One Who Is Speaking,'" 292–94), but it pretty clearly refers to God (e.g., Bruce, *Hebrews*, 363; Grässer, *An die Hebräer*, 3:328).

45. Ellingworth, *Hebrews*, 684.

12:26 His voice at one time shook the earth, but now he has promised that "Yet once more I will shake not only the earth but also the heavens" (οὗ ἡ φωνὴ τὴν γῆν ἐσάλευσεν τότε, νῦν δὲ ἐπήγγελται λέγων, Ἔτι ἅπαξ ἐγὼ σείσω οὐ μόνον τὴν γῆν ἀλλὰ καὶ τὸν οὐρανόν). The contrast between earth and heaven is taken here a step further, with the help of a quotation from Haggai 2:6 (see also Heb 12:21). The "shaking" of the earth mentioned in the first clause refers again to the phenomena of Sinai. Referring to Sinai, Exodus 19:18 claims that "the whole mountain trembled violently," and in the Song of Deborah and Barak in Judges 5:4–5, the speakers remind the people of the Lord's past acts: "When you, Lord, went out from Seir, when you marched from the land of Edom, the earth shook [ἐσείσθη], the heavens poured, the clouds poured down water. The mountains quaked before the Lord, the One of Sinai, before the Lord, the God of Israel" (see also Pss 68:8; 77:18).

This "shaking" of the earth at Sinai will be no match for the ultimate shaking that Haggai promises, for at that time the Lord will shake "heaven" as well as earth. As I noted, this promise is taken from Haggai 2:6: "This is what the Lord Almighty says: 'In a little while I will once more shake the heavens and the earth, the sea and the dry land. I will shake all nations, and what is desired by all nations will come, and I will fill this house with glory,' says the Lord Almighty" (2:6–7). The introductory words in the Hebrews quotation—"yet once more" (ἔτι ἅπαξ)—make clear the author is quoting this passage rather than the generally parallel Haggai 2:21–22: "Tell Zerubbabel governor of Judah that I am going to shake the heavens and the earth. I will overturn royal thrones and shatter the power of the foreign kingdoms. I will overthrow chariots and their drivers; horses and their riders will fall, each by the sword of his brother." The author of Hebrews focuses all attention on the contrast between earth and heaven by omitting reference to "the sea and the dry land" and by introducing the words "not only . . . but also" (οὐ μόνον . . . ἀλλὰ καί). He also focuses attention on "heaven" by putting it in a climactic position at the end.

A key question here is what "heaven" (οὐρανόν) refers to. As I note elsewhere, the author uses this language to refer both to the (created) lower "heavens" and to the (uncreated) highest "heaven," the abode of God. We have also pointed out the difference in meaning does not rest on whether the word is singular or plural (the author uses the plural in v. 25; in v. 26, following his LXX source, he uses the singular). While it might be overinterpreting to suggest that the choice of singular or plural in English translations points to a decision about meaning, it is worth noting that they are quite divided at this point: the plural occurs in NIV, ESV, NLT, and CSB, while the singular is used in the RSV, NRSV, NET, CEB, NAB, and NASB. Since "heaven" in verse 25 refers to the ultimate, highest heaven, this may be the reference here as well. However, in Haggai, as the context I have quoted reveals, the "shaking" has in view the overthrow of kingdoms hostile to Israel, with the end goal that the rebuilt Jerusalem temple might be filled with the "spoils" of those kingdoms.[46] While any reference to nations is far from the context of Hebrews,

---

46. The language of "shaking" in the OT often apparently refers to cosmic upheaval; see, using σείω (as in Hag 2:6): Isa 13:13; Jer 8:16; 28:29; 30:15; Dan 2:40; Joel 2:10; 3:16 (4:16 LXX). See also Matt 27:51. The verb that the author of Hebrews uses to introduce and comment on the quotation (at 12:27) is σαλεύω, which he probably uses because it is much more common in the LXX with this kind of meaning: see Judg 5:4–5 (quoted above); Job 9:6; Pss 18:7 [17:8 LXX]; 46:5 [45:6]; 77:18 [76:19]; 82:5 [81:5]; 97:4 [96:4]; 99:1 [98:1]; Amos 9:5; Mic 1:4; Nah 1:5; Hab 3:6. In the NT, it refers to the shaking of earthly things in Acts 4:31; 16:26 and to heavenly things in Mark 13:25; Luke 21:26.

the author may view the overthrow of hostile kingdoms as generally indicating God's victory over evil forces, whatever they may be. If this is so, "heavens" may be the best translation here, as the author looks forward to the day when spiritual powers hostile to God and his people are vanquished along with all that is evil on this earth.[47] The reference in verse 27 to the shaking of the "things that have been made" could also suggest a reference to the lower heavens. Some interpreters who follow this general line of interpretation then conclude that the author is using the language of cosmic upheaval to refer to God's victory over evil.[48] However, it is unlikely that we can remove all reference to cosmic upheaval in this text.[49] The author appears to be predicting some kind of cosmic catastrophe, not as a way of referring to judgment but as a necessary step toward that judgment.

12:27 The words "once more" indicate the removal of the things that are shaken, things that have been made, in order that the things not shaken might remain (τὸ δὲ Ἔτι ἅπαξ δηλοῖ τὴν τῶν σαλευομένων μετάθεσιν ὡς πεποιημένων, ἵνα μείνῃ τὰ μὴ σαλευόμενα). While the author refers explicitly only to the opening words of the text from Haggai,[50] the logic of what he says in this verse requires that they be a shorthand for a reference to the quotation from Haggai as a whole. The author interprets the shaking of "things that have been made" as a "removal" (μετάθεσιν).[51] The word is rare, occurring only here and in Hebrews 7:12 and 11:5 in the New Testament, once in the LXX (2 Macc 11:24), and a few times in Philo and Josephus. It can mean either "change" or "removal." The former appears to fit Hebrews 7:12 and 2 Maccabees 11:24. "Removal" is more likely in Hebrews 11:5, while most interpreters also think this is the meaning required here, since there is nothing in this context suggesting what the cosmos might be changed into.[52]

Some interpreters insist that the language the author uses here points to a total destruction of the physical universe. Those who think the author is indebted to Neoplatonic dualism further argue that the author reflects here the antagonism to the material world per se that is typical of that approach—the material must be removed so that an eternal spiritual kingdom can take its place.[53] This widely argued view is succinctly stated by Schenck: "Hebrews is interested in the *removal* of the created realm rather than its liberation."[54] However, the language of "removal" is nuanced enough to allow for the idea that the

---

47. See, e.g., Ellingworth, *Hebrews*, 687; deSilva, *Perseverance in Gratitude*, 471; contra, e.g., Filtvedt, *Identity of God's People*, 295–301; Koester, *Hebrews*, 547; Cockerill, *Hebrews*, 666; Lane, *Hebrews*, 2:480.

48. See, e.g., Lane, *Hebrews*, 2:480; Laansma, "Cosmology of Hebrews," 12–14. G. K. Beale stresses the reference to temple in Haggai, viewing the author here as suggesting the coming of a new temple, which will take the form of the people of God (*The Temple and the Church's Mission: A Biblical Theology of the Dwelling Place of God*, NSBT 17 [Downers Grove, IL: InterVarsity Press, 2004], 304–5).

49. See esp. Adams, *Stars Will Fall*, 185–94.

50. The Greek uses the neuter article (τό) with the phrase from Haggai, "once more" (ἔτι ἅπαξ), to refer to it as a whole: hence "the words" in NIV, etc.; "this expression" in NASB, CSB; "this phrase" in ESV, NET.

51. "The things that have been made" (πεποιημένων) is introduced with ὡς, a word that could indicate a degree of difference: "as if." Here, however, it functions basically as a marker of apposition: "the things that have been made" = "the things that are shaken" (see D. Harris, *Hebrews*, 396–97). Those who see Neoplatonism here are inclined to translate it causally: the "things are shaken" are removed *because* they belong to the created world (so, in effect, Grässer, *An die Hebräer*, 3:333).

52. E.g., Ellingworth, *Hebrews*, 688; Cockerill, *Hebrews*, 667; Grässer, *An die Hebräer*, 3:335–36. "Removal" or "removing" is the choice of almost all the English versions. Weiss, however, argues for "change" (*Der Brief an die Hebräer*, 691–92), while Jeffrey S. Lamp argues for "transformation" (*Hebrews: An Earth Bible Commentary: A City That Cannot Be Shaken* [London: T&T Clark, 2023], 145).

53. E.g., Thompson, *Beginnings of Christian Philosophy*, 48–49; Schenck, *Cosmology and Eschatology*, 124–32.

54. Schenck, *Understanding the Book of Hebrews*, 37.

physical universe will be completely renovated, or transformed, and not simply destroyed. To be sure, the author gives us little indication of any such continuity in the material world. However, his claim that Jesus is the "heir of all things" (1:2) and the one who will subject the "world to come" (2:5) might point in this direction.[55] More importantly, some degree of continuity between this creation and the new creation is required by other New Testament texts. The important point here, then, is that this text need not be interpreted in a way that contradicts those texts.[56]

The purpose of the shaking of all "things that have been made" is that "the things not shaken might remain." We might see here again a simple dualism between the material and the spiritual: the entire created world is shaken, removed, and destroyed, so that what is left is only the spiritual or heavenly realm—"the things not shaken."[57] However, the line between what is "shaken" and what is "not shaken" need not run between the material and the spiritual. Indeed, granted the author's inclusion of quite material things, such as "sprinkled blood" (v. 24) in the "heavenly Jerusalem" (v. 22), this cannot be the distinction the author intends. Rather, as the passage from Haggai suggests, the line runs between that which is evil and unredeemable and that which is good and subject to the redemptive work of Christ.[58] It is overwhelmingly likely, for instance, that our author buys into the typical New Testament perspective on resurrection (see 6:1): Jesus and those who belong to him will enter the final kingdom in resurrected, material bodies. The author, then, anticipates the day when God will "shake up" his entire creation—both earth and "the heaven"—in order to strip from it all that is evil, and preserve (and if needed, transform) what belongs to the new covenant, enacted on Mount Zion.

12:28–29 Therefore, since we are receiving an unshakable kingdom, let us be thankful and through it worship God acceptably with reverence and awe, 29 for our "God is a consuming fire" (Διὸ βασιλείαν ἀσάλευτον παραλαμβάνοντες ἔχωμεν χάριν, δι' ἧς λατρεύωμεν εὐαρέστως τῷ θεῷ μετὰ εὐλαβείας καὶ δέους· 29 καὶ γὰρ ὁ θεὸς ἡμῶν πῦρ καταναλίσκον). In verses 28–29 the author draws out an inference from his argument in verses 25–27 (the verses are introduced with the strong inferential conjunction διό, "therefore").[59] Before he spells out that inference, however, he briefly recapitulates in positive terms the key point he develops in verses 25–27: we are receiving an unshakable kingdom.[60] The author elsewhere refers to God's kingdom only in a quotation from the Old Testament in 1:8. He is perhaps led to use the language here because the quotation from Haggai in verse 26 comes from a context that declares judgment on the kingdoms of this world.[61] In contrast to those kingdoms, which will be "shaken" in God's cosmic and judging intervention, stands

---

55. Adams, "Cosmology of Hebrews," 135–38; see also Stephen R. Holmes, "Death in the Afternoon: Hebrews, Sacrifice, and Soteriology," in Bauckham et al., *Epistle to the Hebrews*, 244–45; Laansma, "Cosmology of Hebrews," 12–14; Kibbe, *Godly Fear*, 175–81; Schreiner, *Hebrews*, 406.

56. See esp. Rom 8:19–22; Col 1:20; and the implications of Revelation's claim that God is "making everything new" (21:5).

57. The interpretive gloss of the NIV, which renders "what can be shaken" and "what cannot be shaken," is a possible interpretation of ὡς πεποιημένων.

58. See, e.g., Lamp, who thinks "things created" might refer to those things "made with human hands" (*Hebrews*, 146–47).

59. As I noted above, Koester (*Hebrews*, 554) thinks that v. 28 opens a new section of the letter. See also Westfall, *Discourse Analysis*, 283.

60. Most English versions are on the right track when they render the participle παραλαμβάνοντες as causal: "since we are receiving" (e.g., NIV; NRSV; NET; CSB; CEB; NASB). Some others take the participle as the object of "thanks" (χάριν); e.g., "let us be grateful for receiving" (RSV).

61. Johnson, *Hebrews*, 335.

the kingdom of God. The author might also be influenced by texts such as Psalm 125:1, which refers to "Mount Zion, which cannot be shaken [οὐ σαλευθήσεται] but endures forever." The temporal focus of the verb "receiving" is not clear, but the present tense might suggest that this kingdom is one believers already begin to enter and yet will have to wait to enter fully. We already have access to God himself through the ministry of our high priest, Jesus (e.g., 10:19–20), but there is yet coming a day when he will "bring salvation to those who are waiting for him" (9:28).

Our response to this amazing gift of the kingdom should be thanksgiving[62] and worshipful service. The verb "worship" that occurs here (λατρεύω) is widely used to refer to cultic service in the Old Testament; the author applies it to the "worship" or "service" of new-covenant believers (9:14). Our author further adds that this worship needs to be accompanied by "reverence and awe" (εὐλαβείας καὶ δέους). The author uses the former word in 5:7 to denote Jesus's "reverent submission" to the Father in his earthly life.[63] The latter occurs only here in the New Testament, and it occurs five times in 2 Maccabees to denote the fear or terror in response to worldly threats and dangers.[64] At the same time, then, as the author invites us to celebrate our enjoyment of God's unshakable kingdom, he also implicitly warns us about the need to worship with appropriate respect for the God who is king of this kingdom and with recognition of his awesome character. Verse 29, quoting Deuteronomy 4:24, reinforces this point: "our God is a consuming fire."[65] The author has used the imagery of fire to refer to God's judgment earlier (10:27; see 12:18). This somber conclusion to a passage that celebrates God's new-covenant purposes shows that the author's overall hortatory concern is never far from his purview. His readers are in danger of "falling away," or at least of a failure to progress in their Christian walk, and their negligence of God's blessing means they are threatened with judgment.[66]

Theology in Application

The ultimate fate of the world we now live in is presented in different ways in Scripture. Some texts appear to teach what we might label a "replacement" model: this world will be totally destroyed and replaced with a "new creation," "a new heaven and new earth." Passages such as 2 Peter 3:10–13 are often cited to support this view:

> But the day of the Lord will come like a thief. The heavens will disappear with a roar; the elements will be destroyed by fire, and the earth and everything done in it will be laid bare. Since everything will be destroyed in this way, what kind of people ought you to be? You ought to live holy and godly lives as you look forward to the day of God

---

62. The word χάρις that the author uses here often has the sense "thankfulness," "gratitude" ("χάρις," BDAG 1080, §5); and see, e.g., Rom 7:25; 1 Tim 1:12; 2 Tim 1:3.

63. For more on this word, see the note on 5:7.

64. See 2 Macc 3:17, 30; 12:22; 13:16; 15:23.

65. As usual, the author's wording closely follows the LXX. The only difference is his shift from "your" (σου) to "our" (ἡμῶν) to fit his context. The reminder of God's "consuming fire" grounds Moses's warning about falling into idolatry.

66. Following his usual approach to the warnings of Hebrews, D. L. Allen (implausibly, in my mind) argues that the warning is about God's discipline, not his (condemnatory) judgment (*Hebrews*, 598–99).

and speed its coming. That day will bring about the destruction of the heavens by fire, and the elements will melt in the heat. But in keeping with his promise we are looking forward to a new heaven and a new earth, where righteousness dwells.

On the other hand, we also encounter texts that suggest some degree of continuity between this world and the next. In Romans 8:21, for instance, Paul predicts that "the creation itself will be liberated from its bondage to decay and brought into the freedom and glory of the children of God." Liberation does not suggest destruction and replacement but transformation. The same perspective of continuity between the present creation and the future world is suggested by Paul's claim that God in Christ is working "to reconcile to himself all things, whether things on earth or things in heaven" (Col 1:20). And transformation is hinted at also in the divine pronouncement that "I am making everything new" (Rev 21:5; not, "I am making new things").

We face here then the challenge that our long and complex scriptural record often poses to us, of finding the unified perspective amid diversity. I am convinced that the better option on this issue is the transformation model. On the one hand, negatively, we need to appreciate the way in that Scripture often uses strong language about cosmic catastrophe to refer to God's decisive intervention to judge his enemies and rescue his people. Our translations can fail sometimes to reflect this. For instance, in the 2 Peter text cited above, the word translated "destroy"/"destruction" in verses 11 and 12 is used just before these verses to refer to the "destruction" of the world in Noah's day (v. 6). Yet that world was not "destroyed" but cleansed. Positively, the fundamental Christian teaching about the resurrection of the body also suggests a transformation model: our bodies will be raised and "changed" (1 Cor 15:51). The biblical vision for the future, then, is not a replacement of this world with a new one but its transformation into a "new heaven and new earth" where we will live eternally in resurrected bodies.

I have argued in my exposition of Hebrews 12:25–29 above that this passage, while certainly susceptible to a "replacement" interpretation, does not clearly teach it, and that the witness of Scripture broadly points us in the direction of a "transformation" model. The fate of the created world has implications for the way we as Christians view creation. One too often hears believers rejecting any need for environmental concern with the refrain, "It's all going to burn anyway." Accompanying this view of creation's future is a view of its present: the created world simply does not matter to God—so why should it matter to us? However, if the transformation model is correct, then we have powerful evidence that the creation God brought into being and pronounced "good" is still significant in the divine plan for the universe. And God's continuing care for our world means we, his followers, created to steward that world (Gen 1:26–28), need to care for it also.[67]

---

67. For a fuller exploration of these issues, see D. Moo and J. Moo, *Creation Care*; and, without endorsing all the hermeneutical moves he makes, see also, on Hebrews, Lamp, *Hebrews*.

Chapter 32

Hebrews 13:1–17

Literary Context

The style of Hebrews shifts dramatically at 13:1. In place of extended theological arguments interspersed with exhortations, we find a series of brief and apparently unrelated exhortations (at least in vv. 1–6). So abrupt is this shift that a few scholars have concluded that chapter 13 does not really belong with chapters 1–12 and that this last chapter was added by another author after the bulk of Hebrews had been completed.[1] Bruce's judgment, however, is on target: these theories have "no higher status than that of literary curiosities."[2] A milder form of this thesis is that the author added chapter 13 as a kind of postscript, a section not carefully integrated into the body of the sermon.[3] There is more to be said for this thesis. Yet, if the specific exhortations in verses 1–6 do not clearly pick up anything in the earlier chapters, the claims that Jesus is "the same yesterday, today, and forever" (v. 8) and that new-covenant believers have an "altar" (v. 10) that supersedes the Old Testament sacrifices (see vv. 9–14) carry on central themes from the sermon.[4] Several scholars attractively suggest that chapter 13 acts as the "peroration" (Latin *peroratio*), a conclusion that both selectively reminds listeners of key themes and that seeks to move the listeners to response.[5] In this sense, then, the peroration is "a movement distinct from but continuous with" what has preceded it.[6] As many commentators note, chapter 13 can be seen as a kind of elaboration of the central call in 12:28: "let us be thankful, and so worship God acceptably with reverence and awe."[7]

---

1. See, e.g., Buchanan, *Hebrews*, 243–45; A. J. M. Wedderburn, "The 'Letter' to the Hebrews and Its Thirteenth Chapter," *NTS* 50 (2004): 390–405.

2. Bruce, *Hebrews*, 368.

3. Spicq, *L'Épître aux Hébreux*, 2:415; Moffatt, *Hebrews*, 224.

4. See esp. the thorough study of Jukka Thurén, *Das Lobopfer der Hebräer: Studien zum Aufbau und Anliegen von Hebräerbrief 13*, Acta Academiae Aboensis, Series A, 47/1 (Åbo: Åbo Akademi University, 1973); and also Floyd V. Filson, *"Yesterday": A Study of Hebrews in the Light of Chapter 13*, SBT 2/4 (Naperville: Allenson, 1967), 15–26.

5. Cockerill, *Hebrews*, 675; Laansma, *Hebrews*, 321; Witherington, *Letters*, 351.

6. Laansma, *Hebrews*, 321.

7. E.g., Weiss, *Der Brief an die Hebräer*, 697; Grässer, *An die Hebräer*, 3:347; Lane, *Hebrews*, 2:496–97; deSilva, *Perseverance in Gratitude*, 484; Thurén, *Das Lobopfer der Hebräer*, 234–37.

If a major break can be assumed at 13:1,[8] it is not at all clear where the next break should come. As we will see, internal evidence suggests that there is a break between verses 6 and 7 and that the unit beginning at verse 7 continues at least through verse 17. However, there is debate about whether there is a break in the sequence between verses 17 and 18[9] or between verses 19 and 20.[10] In favor of the latter is the obvious shift from exhortation (vv. 17–19) to the doxology in verse 20. However, I am persuaded that a more important consideration is that the request for prayer in verses 18–19 is typical of letter conclusions. I therefore view verses 18–25 as having a degree of internal coherence related to the standard letter conclusion "form."

I. The Exalted Son and a Rest for the People of God (1:1–4:13)
II. Our Great High Priest and His Ministry (4:14–10:31)
III. **Exhortation: Follow and Serve the Pioneer of Our Faith through Endurance and Faith (10:32–13:25)**
   A. Introductory Call to Endurance and Faith (10:32–39)
   B. The Nature and Power of Faith Illustrated in Salvation History (11:1–40)
   C. Run the Race with Endurance, Remembering That You Are Children of God (12:1–17)
   D. Coming to Mount Zion and Inheriting the Unshakable Kingdom (12:18–29)
   E. **Letter Closing (13:1–25)**
      1. **Concluding Exhortations and Encouragement (13:1–17)**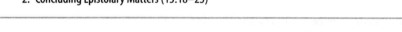
      2. Concluding Epistolary Matters (13:18–25)

Main Idea

New-covenant believers are called to "worship God acceptably" (12:28). This worship will take form in many specific ways (vv. 1–6). It rests on the unchangeable Jesus Christ (v. 8), whose once-for-all sacrifice continually provides the grace we need to serve God (vv. 9–14). Our own sacrifices, then, are of a different nature: praise of God and doing good to others (vv. 15–16). Obedience to leaders who exemplify Christian living is expected (vv. 7, 17).

---

8. As I note, however, a few interpreters attach 12:28–29 to what follows (e.g., Koester, *Hebrews*, 562).

9. E.g., Johnson, *Hebrews*, 351; Schreiner, *Hebrews*, 426–27; Laansma, *Hebrews*, 321.

10. This paragraphing is followed by NIV, NLT; and see, e.g., Attridge, *Hebrews*, 390–91; G. Guthrie, *Hebrews*, 434.

Translation

Hebrews 13:1–17

1a	exhortation	**Continue to love each other as brothers and sisters.**
2a	exhortation	**Do not forget to show hospitality,**
2b	basis	because
2c	means	by doing so
2d	assertion	**some have entertained angels**
2e	manner	without knowing it.
3a	exhortation	**Remember the prisoners**
3b	manner	as if you were imprisoned
3c	association	with them, and
3d	exhortation	**remember also those who are being mistreated**
3e	basis (for 3d)	since you also are in the body.
4a	exhortation	**Let marriage be held**
4b	manner	in honor by all and
4c	parallel (to 4a)	**sexual relations be kept**
4d	manner	unstained,
4e	basis (for 4a–d)	for
4f	assertion	**God will judge** those who commit sexual sin and
4g	parallel (to 4f)	adulterers.
5a	exhortation	**Let your manner of life be free from the love of money;**
5b	exhortation	be content with what you have.
5c	basis (for 5a–b)	For
5d	assertion	**he has said,**
5e	content	"I will never leave you,
5f	restatement	neither will I ever forsake you." (Deut 31:6)
6a	result (of 5d–f)	So
6b	assertion	**we confidently say,**
6c	content	"The Lord is my help, and
6d	result (of 6c)	I will not fear—
6e	rhetorical question	what can a human do to me?" (Ps 118:6–7)
7a	exhortation	**Remember your leaders,**
7b	basis	those who spoke
7c	recipient	to you
7d	object (of 7b)	the word of God.
7e	exhortation	Consider the outcome
7f	source	of their conduct and
7g	parallel (to 7e)	imitate their faith.

8a	assertion	**Jesus Christ, the same**
8b	time	yesterday,
8c	sequence	today, and
8d	sequence	forever.
9a	exhortation	**Do not be carried away**
9b	means	by different kinds of
9c	content	strange teachings.
9d	reason (for 9a–c)	For
9e	assertion	**it is good for the heart to be strengthened**
9f	means	by grace, not
9g	contrast	foods,
9h	description	which do not bring profit
9i	advantage	to those who walk in them.
10a	basis (for 9e)	**We have an altar**
10b	description	from which those who minister . . .
10c	place	in the tabernacle
10d	predicate (of 10b)	. . . have no right to eat.
11a	development	Now
11b	assertion	the blood of the sacrificial animals is **brought**
11c	destination	into the Most Holy Place
11d	agent	by the high priest
11e	manner	as a sin offering, but
11f	contrast (with 11a–e)	the bodies of the animals are burned
11g	location	outside the camp.
12a	comparison	So
12b	assertion	**Jesus also,**
12c	purpose (of 12f)	in order that he might sanctify
12d	object	the people
12e	means	through his own blood,
12f	predicate (of 12b)	**suffered**
12g	location	outside the city gate.
13a	inference (from 12)	Therefore,
13b	exhortation	**let us go out to him**
13c	location	outside the camp,
13d	manner (of 13b)	bearing his reproach.
14a	basis (for 13)	For
14b	location	here
14c	assertion	**we do not have a lasting city,**
14d	contrast	but
14e	assertion	**we are seeking the one to come.**
15a	means and cause	Through him,
15b	inference (from 9–13)	therefore,

Continued on next page.

15c	exhortation	**let us continually**	**offer up a sacrifice**
15d	content		of praise
15e	recipient		to God—
15f	apposition (to 15c)		that is, the fruit of lips praising his name.
16a	exhortation	**Do not neglect**	
16b	object		**to do good and**
16c	parallel		**share with others,**
16d	basis (for 15a–16c)	for	
16e	means		with such sacrifices
16f	assertion	**God is pleased.**	
17a	exhortation	**Obey**	**your leaders**
17b	connection	and	
17c	parallel	**submit**	**to them**,
17d	reason (for 17a–c)	for	
17e	assertion	**they are watching**	
17f	reference		over your souls
17g	standard		as people who will have to render an account.
17h	continuation (of 17a–c)	[Obey them]	
17i	purpose		so that they might do their work
17j	manner		with joy and not
17k	contrast		with groaning—for
17l	elaboration		this would be unprofitable
17m	advantage		for you.

Structure

This section of chapter 13 has two basic parts. The author begins with a series of brief exhortations focused on quite general Christian behavioral issues (vv. 1–6). While not entirely clear, these exhortations seem to be structured as four pairs, with a final pair of Old Testament quotations grounding them (my translations are awkward, in an attempt to reflect the Greek syntax):[11]

sibling love (φιλαδελφία)—let it continue (v. 1)
hospitality (φιλοξενία)—do not forget it (v. 2)

remember the prisoners (v. 3a)
[remember] those being mistreated (v. 3b)

---

11. Several scholars note these series of pairs: Michel, *Der Brief an die Hebräer*, 479; Lane, *Hebrews*, 2:501; Cockerill, *Hebrews*, 677–78. Others prefer a simpler division between concerns for community life (vv. 1–3) and for private life (vv. 4–6; so Grässer, *An die Hebräer*, 3:353; Bénétrau, *L'Épître aux Hébreux*, 2:199; Attridge, *Hebrews*, 385).

honored be marriage by all (v. 4a)
sexual relations—unstained (v. 4b)

not having love of money (ἀφιλάργυρος)—manner of life (v. 5a)
being content with what you have (v. 5b)

"never will I leave you or forsake you" (v. 5c)
"I will not be afraid" (v. 6)

As the bold font above reveals, the author encloses these eight exhortations within references to "love" (φιλ-). The passage begins by exhorting the readers to "brotherly love" (φιλαδελφία) and to "love of the stranger"—that is, "hospitality" (φιλοξενία); it ends with a warning about "love of money" (ἀφιλάργυρος). The exhortation to "remember" leaders (τῶν ἡγουμένων) in verse 7 resumes the exhortatory mode of verses 1–5a. Yet the similar command to "have confidence in your leaders" (τοῖς ἡγουμένοις) in verse 17 works with verse 7 as a framing device, suggesting that verses 7–17 should be seen as a second paragraph within this section. The material enclosed by these two verses falls into three parts. In verse 8, the author enunciates a key christological claim that relates both to what comes before it and what comes after it. Verses 9–14 are a complex combination of warning, encouragement, and exhortation, using cultic language that clearly picks up key themes from chapters 1–12. The cultic motif continues in verses 15–16, as the author encourages his new-covenant listeners to offer sacrifices appropriate to that new state of affairs: praise and good deeds.

Exegetical Outline

➡ **1. Concluding Exhortations and Encouragement (13:1–17)**
   a. The Worship of God in Everyday Life (vv. 1–6)
   b. The Shape of New-Covenant Life (vv. 7–17)
      i. Obey Your Leaders (v. 7)
      ii. The Stable Foundation: Christ (v. 8)
      iii. Warning, Encouragement, and Exhortation (vv. 9–14)
      iv. Sacrifices Pleasing to God (vv. 15–16)
      v. Obey Your Leaders (v. 17)

Explanation of the Text

13:1–2 Continue to love each other as brothers and sisters. 2 Do not forget to show hospitality, because by doing so some have entertained angels without knowing it (Ἡ φιλαδελφία μενέτω. 2 τῆς φιλοξενίας μὴ ἐπιλανθάνεσθε, διὰ ταύτης γὰρ ἔλαθόν τινες ξενίσαντες ἀγγέλους). A notable shift in style occurs at 13:1 with the next several verses containing a rapid-fire series of exhortations, not always clearly related to each other or to material earlier in the letter. The passage is typical New Testament paraenesis and resembles passages such as Romans 12:9–21, 1 Thessalonians 5:12–22, and 1 Timothy 6:17–19.[12] Some of the concerns in these verses, such as love for others, avoiding sexual sin, and avoiding the love of money, echo issues we find in these other passages. Following a now generally discredited view of "paraenesis," some scholars see little relationship between this passage and the rest of the letter. However, while several of the matters the author raises here have not appeared earlier, each of them expresses a natural and well-attested component of Christian obedience. To put it another way: while it would be difficult to demonstrate from chapters 1–12 that the believers to whom the author is writing were struggling with these particular issues, it is also likely that virtually any early Christian congregation would need to be exhorted in these terms. Moreover, we should not overlook connections with earlier material that are present here. The concern for love (v. 1) has been expressed in 10:24. Concern for those mistreated or imprisoned (v. 3) is mentioned in 10:33–34.[13]

Early Christians considered themselves to be members of the same spiritual family: addressing believers as "brothers and sisters" is common throughout the New Testament. It is not surprising, therefore, that believers would be called to have "sibling love" (φιλαδελφία) for one another (see also Rom 12:10; 1 Thess 4:9; 1 Pet 1:22; 2 Pet 1:7). No sharp distinction between this "sibling love" and the more common expression of love in the New Testament (ἀγάπη) can be drawn.[14] The former word simply forefronts the implication of deep family ties often implied in the call for *agapē* (ἀγάπη). The author urges his listeners to let sibling love "continue" (using the third-person imperative μενέτω). The implication is that the author knows or assumes that the community to which he writes is already doing well at loving one another. It is not clear whether the author's choice of the verb "continue," "remain" (μένω) reflects the theological significance of this language elsewhere in the letter (7:3, 24; 12:27; 13:14).[15] As seems to be the case in 1 Thessalonians 4:9, the call to "sibling love" probably governs or at least qualifies the exhortations that follow.[16]

As my outline above indicates, verses 1 and 2 are roughly parallel, each forefronting a word from the *phil-* (φιλ-) stem: "sibling love" (**phil**adelphia [**φιλ**αδελφία]) in verse 1, and "hospitality" (**phil**oxenia [**φιλ**οξενία]) in verse 2. Hospitality (the root of the word suggests "love of the stranger") was an important expression of love for others in the ancient world—hotels, motels, and Airbnb did not exist. The author does not want his listeners to "forget" or "neglect" (good translations of the verb used

---

12. Weiss, *Der Brief an die Hebräer*, 704; Grässer, *An die Hebräer*, 3:347; Thurén, *Das Lobopfer der Hebräer*, 57–70.
13. Lane, *Hebrews*, 2:509–10.
14. E.g., Ellingworth, *Hebrews*, 694.

15. D. Harris (*Hebrews*, 402) thinks it is a "hook word," binding this text together with 12:25 (see v. 27).
16. Lane, *Hebrews*, 2:510.

here) it (this concern is another interesting parallel with Rom 12:9–21: see v. 13; and see also 1 Tim 3:2; Titus 1:8; 1 Pet 4:9).[17] The author grounds his exhortation (see the γάρ, "for") in the experience of some who "entertained angels unawares" (KJV). While somewhat stilted now, this KJV translation is hard to better (it is followed by RSV; ESV).[18] The Old Testament and Jewish literature contain several accounts of people dealing with angels disguised as humans, but most think the episode of the "men" who visit Abraham and Sarah in Genesis 18:1–15 is the most likely source for the author's illustration.

13:3 Remember the prisoners as if you were imprisoned with them, and remember also those who are being mistreated since you also are in the body (μιμνῄσκεσθε τῶν δεσμίων ὡς συνδεδεμένοι, τῶν κακουχουμένων ὡς καὶ αὐτοὶ ὄντες ἐν σώματι). While we cannot be sure that all the issues the author raises in verses 1–6 were pressing problems among his listeners, mistreatment and imprisonment because of one's faith clearly were. In 10:32–34, he reminds them of the persecution they endured after their conversion and commends them for suffering with those in prison. The author returns to this issue in these verses, exhorting his listeners to "keep on remembering" (the present imperative μιμνῄσκεσθε has an iterative force)[19] both those who are in prison (τῶν δεσμίων) as well as those being "mistreated" (κακουχουμένων) in some way. (The verb governs both "prisoners" and "those mistreated.") This "remembering" is not simply a mental exercise or even only a matter of praying for them. It would often take the form of practical acts, such as bringing food for prisoners. Each exhortation—"remember the prisoners" and "remember those being mistreated"—is elaborated with a word (ὡς) that has a different sense in each case. The first occurrence means "as if": the listeners are not actually in prison, but they are to imaginatively enter into the situation of the prisoners. The second occurrence of the word, however, means simply "as": it posits a real situation. We are able to sympathize with brothers and sisters being mistreated when we realize that we "also are in the body."[20] The author's dependence on early Christian paraenesis might be seen here again: Jesus, in his parable of the sheep and goats, urges his followers both to "invite" the stranger in and to visit and "look after" those in prison (Matt 25:42–43).[21]

13:4 Let marriage be held in honor by all and sexual relations be kept unstained, for God will judge those who commit sexual sin and adulterers (Τίμιος ὁ γάμος ἐν πᾶσιν καὶ ἡ κοίτη ἀμίαντος, πόρνους γὰρ καὶ μοιχοὺς κρινεῖ ὁ θεός). The author continues to move rapidly through a series of issues, and attempts to trace a continuity of theme in these verses are doomed to failure.[22] As many

---

17. Bruce (*Hebrews*, 371) wonders if a situation mentioned in other early Christian literature might have been the root of the problem: people masquerading as Christians in order to secure lodging with believers.

18. The Greek behind this expression uses a construction unparalleled in the NT but common in other forms of Greek, whereby the indicative verb becomes the modifier of the participle (which expresses the main idea). Here, then, we would normally translate something like "they escaped notice" (ἔλαθον), "entertaining" (ξενίσαντες). In fact, however, as all the translations recognize, the relationship is just the reverse. See on this, e.g., von Siebenthal, *Ancient Greek Grammar*, 402, 458.

19. Lane, *Hebrews*, 2:508.

20. A few interpreters think that "body" (σῶμα) might be a reference to the church, the body of Christ (e.g., Calvin, *Hebrews*, 205), but this is unlikely.

21. Lane, *Hebrews*, 2:511.

22. Bruce notes, for instance, that "chastity" is "part of charity" (v. 1; *Hebrews*, 372); Lane thinks that reference to the "body" in v. 3 might have led the author to move on to sex (*Hebrews*, 2:516).

New Testament books make clear, early Christians called to lead lives of holiness were often challenged by the different and often loose morals regarding sexual conduct in the Greco-Roman world. So it is certainly not surprising that the author includes this issue in his "checklist" of what worship of God looks like (12:28). The author shifts style here, abandoning the series of imperative verbs in verses 1–3 in favor of very short verbless clauses, consisting essentially of a subject and predicate adjective. Nevertheless, the intent is clearly hortatory, and we rightly supply an imperative verb in English.[23]

"Marriage" translates a word (γάμος) that usually refers in the New Testament to a "wedding feast" or celebration (e.g., John 2:1, 2; Rev 19:9), but the translation here reflects the meaning of the word in a few LXX texts (Wis 13:17; 14:24, 26). To hold marriage in "honor" (τίμιος) is to respect its sanctity and live within the ethical boundaries implied by the intimate union of man and woman.[24] The sanctity of marriage is to be respected "by all" (ἐν πᾶσιν; the pronoun is probably masculine rather than neuter [note CEB's "in every respect"]).[25]

With a syntactical structure parallel to the first part of the verse, the author adds a second exhortation related to sexual conduct: "[let] sexual relations be kept unstained." The almost universal decision of English translations is to translate "marriage bed," and one hesitates to buck this consensus. Yet the word in question (κοίτη) does not refer to "marriage bed" anywhere else in the New Testament, while it does refer to sexual intercourse in general at least once (Rom 13:13; cf. 9:10). Usage in the LXX also provides some basis for a general reference to sexual relationships.[26] Moreover, if these two exhortations refer, respectively, to sex within marriage and sex generally, we would have a nice match with the author's reminder that God will judge both "sexual sinners" (πόρνους) and "adulterers" (μοιχούς) at the end of this verse (in chiastic order). On the whole, then, I slightly favor the translation "sexual relations" here.[27]

13:5–6 Let your manner of life be free from the love of money; be content with what you have. For he has said, "I will never leave you, neither will I ever forsake you." 6 So we confidently say, "The Lord is my help, and I will not fear—what can a human do to me?" (Ἀφιλάργυρος ὁ τρόπος, ἀρκούμενοι τοῖς παροῦσιν. αὐτὸς γὰρ εἴρηκεν, Οὐ μή σε ἀνῶ οὐδ᾽ οὐ μή σε ἐγκαταλίπω, 6 ὥστε θαρροῦντας ἡμᾶς λέγειν, Κύριος ἐμοὶ βοηθός, [καὶ][28] οὐ φοβηθήσομαι, τί ποιήσει μοι ἄνθρωπος;). The author's series of brief exhortations ends with verse 5a, which is cast in the same form as the exhortations in verse 4a (predicate adjective + subject, with no verb). The shift from concern about sex in verse 4 to money in verse 5 seems abrupt, but in fact these concerns were often joined in ancient paraenetic texts. The Decalogue forbids stealing just after it forbids adultery (Exod 20:14–15).

---

23. That verb in Greek would be ἔστω (Ellingworth, *Hebrews*, 697). The KJV translates with an indicative verb: "marriage is honourable in all."

24. The meaning "respected" for τίμιος here (which usually means "precious") is suggested by BDAG (1006, §§1.c, 2).

25. Among those who argue for the neuter are Westcott, *Hebrews*, 432; Ellingworth, *Hebrews*, 697.

26. The translation "marriage bed" reflects the use of the word in nonbiblical Greek (see, e.g., Josephus, *Ant*. 2.55). The word usually means "bed" in the LXX, and a few texts seem to suggest the notion of "marriage bed" (e.g., Gen 49:4; 1 Chr 5:1). Several passages use κοίτη with other words to connote sexual relations (e.g., "lie in bed," "give one's seed"), and the word also occurs on its own in this sense (note the expression "to know κοίτην" in Num 31:35; Judg 21:11, 12; Wis 3:13).

27. "κοίτη," L&N 23.62, translate "sexual life should be undefiled"; "κοίτη," BDAG 554, §2, note this meaning as a possibility.

28. NA[28] reads the καί with brackets, which indicate its uncertainty.

And see, for instance, Testament of Judah 18.2: "guard yourselves, therefore, my children, against sexual promiscuity and love of money" and, in the New Testament, Ephesians 5:3–5:

> But among you there must not be even a hint of sexual immorality, or of any kind of impurity, or of greed, because these are improper for God's holy people. Nor should there be obscenity, foolish talk or coarse joking, which are out of place, but rather thanksgiving. For of this you can be sure: No immoral, impure or greedy person—such a person is an idolater—has any inheritance in the kingdom of Christ and of God.[29]

The believer's manner of life (τρόπος) should be "free from the love of money." The Greek word has three components: the alpha privative (α-), which negates what follows; "love" (φιλ-, see the two words in v. 1); and "money" (ἄργυρος, lit. "silver"): "not having a love for money" (ἀφιλάργυρος). This word occurs only once elsewhere in the New Testament (in the list of qualifications for overseers in 1 Tim 3:3), but the concern is widespread. In contrast to an inordinate and destructive love of money, believers, the author says, should be "content with what you have." Stoic philosophy was a popular movement at the time that Hebrews was written, and the Stoics made contentment a key focus of their teaching. However, as Cockerill notes, "Divine steadfastness provides a much more certain foundation for contentment than Stoic appeals to self-sufficiency."[30]

"Divine steadfastness" is, indeed, the point of the Old Testament quotation that follows in verse 5b. The source of the quotation is not clear, since the wording in Hebrews does not correspond exactly to any Old Testament text. Three passages, however, are similar: God's reassurance of his faithfulness to Jacob (Gen 28:15), God's promise of his enduring presence with the people of Israel as they are about to enter the land (Deut 31:6), and God's promise to Joshua as he leads the people into the land (Josh 1:5).[31] An exact parallel to the form of the text in Hebrews is found, however, in Philo (*Confusion* 166). It is unlikely that Hebrews depends directly on Philo. Rather, Hebrews is probably drawing on a Hellenistic Greek summary of Old Testament teaching that may depend on two or more of these Old Testament passages.[32] The author echoes Jesus's teaching from the Sermon on the Mount: we need not be anxious about material matters because, for those who seek God's righteousness, "all these things will be given to you" (Matt 6:33).[33]

The response appropriate to the divine promise of enduring faithfulness comes in verse 6, in the form of another Old Testament quotation: "The Lord is my help, and I will not fear—what can a human do to me?" The author introduces this quotation with a construction that normally signals result (ὥστε with an infinitive). However, this result is one that the readers are to appropriate for themselves. A number of translations catch this nuance by translating "so we **can** confidently say. . . ."[34] The words the readers

---

29. See also Col 3:5.
30. Cockerill, *Hebrews*, 686.
31. Gen 28:15, with only one clause (οὐ μή σε ἐγκαταλίπω), is less similar to Hebrews than the other two texts, each of which has (like Hebrews) two clauses: οὐ μή σε ἀνῆ οὔτε μή σε ἐγκαταλίπη (Deut 31:6); οὐκ ἐγκαταλείψω σε οὐδὲ ὑπερόψομαί σε (Josh 1:5). Only in Hebrews do we find the rare (and unclassical) triple negation: οὐδ οὐ μή (see von Siebenthal, *Ancient Greek Grammar*, 420). Some scholars think Deut 31:6 is the primary basis (e.g., D. M. Allen, *Deuteronomy and Exhortation*, 68–71; Michel, *Der Brief an die Hebräer*, 483–84; Attridge, *Hebrews*, 388–89; Koester, *Hebrews*, 559). Others prefer Josh 1:5 (Bruce, *Hebrews*, 369; Cockerill, *Hebrews*, 686–87).

32. Calvin calls the saying "common teaching of Scripture" (*Hebrews*, 206). See, for this view, G. Guthrie, "Hebrews," 992.

33. Bruce, *Hebrews*, 374.

34. "Confidently" comes from the participle θαρροῦντας (from θαρρέω, "be confident"), which modifies λέγειν.

are to adopt are in the form of a quotation from Psalm 118:6 (LXX 117:6).[35] The author's attention may have been directed to this text because Psalm 118 is widely quoted in the New Testament. The rhetorical question, "What can a human do to me?" must be interpreted in the light of broad scriptural teaching. Humans do harm God's people, as the audience of Hebrews knows from personal experience (10:32–34; 12:3; cf. 13:3). However, no human can bring any *ultimate* harm to God's people (see also Rom 8:31–39). The two quotations together echo the words of the Lord to the people of Israel as they were about to enter the land: "Be strong and courageous. Do not be afraid or terrified because of them, for the LORD your God goes with you; he will never leave you nor forsake you" (Deut 31:6).

13:7 Remember your leaders, those who spoke to you the word of God. Consider the outcome of their conduct and imitate their faith (Μνημονεύετε τῶν ἡγουμένων ὑμῶν, οἵτινες ἐλάλησαν ὑμῖν τὸν λόγον τοῦ θεοῦ, ὧν ἀναθεωροῦντες τὴν ἔκβασιν τῆς ἀναστροφῆς μιμεῖσθε τὴν πίστιν). The exhortation in this verse could be seen as continuing the series that begins in verse 1. However, the Old Testament quotations in verses 5b–6 break that series. More importantly, the exhortation to "remember your leaders [ἡγουμένων]" finds a close parallel in verse 17: "obey your leaders [ἡγουμένοις]." These texts are probably to be seen as an *inclusio*, marking out verses 7–17 as a separate paragraph.[36] Here I follow, then, the NA[28] Greek text along with most English translations in putting a break between verses 6 and 7.

As I have noted earlier, "remember" in Scripture means not just to "recall" something in an intellectual sense, but to "take to heart" with a view to affecting one's thinking and conduct.[37] "Leaders" (ἡγουμένων) refers in a general sense to those who have spiritual oversight in the community.[38] The word is not a technical one in the New Testament, so the passage does not suggest a developed church organization.[39] The leaders are to be honored because they "spoke" the word of God to them.[40] The aorist form of the verb (ἐλάλησαν) probably refers at least mainly to past "speaking": the author may imply that these people were the founders of the church.[41] However, these leaders are to be commended not only for their faithful teaching of the message from God (τὸν λόγον τοῦ θεοῦ) about Christ but also for their exemplary lifestyle. When the author urges his readers to "consider the outcome [ἔκβασιν] of their conduct [ἀναστροφῆς],"[42] he is probably implying that these leaders have died. The "outcome of their conduct," then, is the record they have left of lives faithfully lived. The author is saying that they finished well.[43] As we run

---

35. The author, as usual, follows the LXX closely; the only possible difference is the addition of καί in the third clause ("possible" because it is textually uncertain).

36. See esp. Vanhoye, *Structure and Message*, 211; and also, e.g., Westcott, *Hebrews*, 433; Michel, *Der Brief an die Hebräer*, 485; Cockerill, *Hebrews*, 688.

37. The verb is μνημονεύω (used also in 11:15, 22); see also μιμνῄσκομαι in 2:6 (= Ps 8:4); 8:12; 10:17; 13:3. On these verbs, see, e.g., O. Michel, "μιμνῄσκομαι, κτλ," *TDNT* 4:675–83.

38. The verb from which this participle is taken is ἡγέομαι, which usually means "consider" in the NT. It also, however, means "lead," and in this sense is used generally (Matt 2:6; Luke 22:26; Acts 7:10) or of those who lead the church (Acts 15:22; Heb 13:17, 24). Note Sir 33:19: "leaders of the congregation [ἐκκλησίας]" (though, obviously, not "the church").

39. Contra., e.g., Weiss, *Der Brief an die Hebräer*, 710.

40. The relative clause introduced by οἵτινες ("who") probably has a slight causal flavor.

41. Cockerill, *Hebrews*, 690.

42. The participle ἀναθεωροῦντες takes on an imperatival sense from its dependence on the imperative μνημονεύετε (and perhaps also μιμεῖσθε at the end of the verse).

43. Some scholars think ἔκβασιν refers to the "end" of life (Delitzsch, *Hebrews*, 2:376; Attridge, *Hebrews*, 392; D. Harris, *Hebrews*, 410), perhaps a martyr's death (Moffatt, *Hebrews*, 230; Westcott, *Hebrews*, 434). However, the author's use of "conduct" (ἀναστροφή) points to an emphasis on quality of life (Montefiore, *Hebrews*, 242; Bruce, *Hebrews*, 374–75; P. Hughes, *Hebrews*, 569; Ellingworth, *Hebrews*, 703).

our own race, we are to look to those "witnesses" who have come before us, leaving an example of faithful Christian living. We are, as the author concludes this topic, to "imitate their faith."

13:8 Jesus Christ, the same yesterday, today, and forever (Ἰησοῦς Χριστὸς ἐχθὲς καὶ σήμερον ὁ αὐτὸς καὶ εἰς τοὺς αἰῶνας). This famous christological statement appears suddenly and unexpectedly in the midst of the author's closing exhortations. It is not explicitly linked to what precedes or follows: no conjunction or other syntactical feature introduces it, nor is there such a connection in verse 9. However, parallels in content between this verse and both the immediate and wider context are evident. In terms of the wider context, the assertion of Christ's changelessness reminds us of the similar assertion about Jesus the Lord in 1:10–12: "In the beginning, Lord, you laid the foundations of the earth, and the heavens are the work of your hands. They will perish, **but you remain**; they will all wear out like a garment. You will roll them up like a robe; like a garment they will be changed. But **you remain the same** [ὁ αὐτός], **and your years will never end**" (the text is quoting Ps 102:25–27). The phrase "the same" (ὁ αὐτός) in 1:12 creates an obvious verbal link with the same phrase here in 13:8.[44] It would be a stretch, but not out of the bounds of possibility, to see these verses as a grand *inclusio* in the sermon. In terms of the immediate context, the author's Old Testament quotation referring to God's enduring faithfulness in verse 5b is a point of obvious connection: God will "never leave" or "forsake" his people, and the changelessness of Christ, the "pioneer" and high priest of the people, embodies that dependable constancy. It is also possible that the author intends to compare the changelessness of Christ with the faithful lives of the leaders (v. 7) and to set this orthodox teaching in contrast to the varied false teachings of verse 9.[45] The author does not give us the kind of data we would need to decide among these contextual connections, but, in my view, at the risk of a questionable "both/and" approach, each of them has merit.

The sequence of words that the author has arranged in this verse gives us a clue to his emphasis. Woodenly carried over from Greek to English, the verse reads "Jesus Christ yesterday and today the same and forever." The emphasis therefore falls on "forever": as Jesus Christ has been, so he will forever be. Believers need not fear that the one who intercedes for them as high priest before the throne in heaven will suddenly cease to carry out his ministry for us. "Yesterday and today" is a customary biblical locution; see, for example, 1 Samuel 20:27: "But the next day, the second day of the month, David's place was empty again. Then Saul said to his son Jonathan, 'Why hasn't the son of Jesse come to the meal, either yesterday or today [ἐχθὲς καὶ σήμερον]?'" (see also, e.g., 2 Sam 15:20). Many scholars stress that the author is not here engaged in theological ontology; he is practically oriented, with "yesterday" referring to Jesus's historical ministry and "today" to his current ministry as our high priest.[46] However, we should perhaps not shy away from recognizing the claim about ontological status that the author might be making here. As Koester points out, the language is similar to Greco-Roman descriptions of the gods. In an ancient Greek hymn, we read that "Zeus was, Zeus

---

44. See, e.g., Massonnet, *L'Épître aux Hébreux*, 409. For this connection, see also, e.g., Bauckham, "Divinity of Jesus Christ," 32–35.

45. See, for the connection with v. 9, Cockerill, *Hebrews*, 691; Ellingworth, *Hebrews*, 706.

46. See, e.g., Filson, *Yesterday*, 30–35; cf. Lane, *Hebrews*, 2:258–59.

is, and Zeus will be."⁴⁷ This language is echoed in Revelation 1:4b: "Grace and peace to you from him who is, and who was, and who is to come" (see also 1:8 and 4:8).⁴⁸ As Richard Bauckham points out, we need not choose between a practical focus on Christ's enduring presence and a theological statement about his ontological status: the one is the necessary basis for the other.⁴⁹

13:9 Do not be carried away by different kinds of strange teachings. For it is good for the heart to be strengthened by grace, not foods, which do not bring profit to those who walk in them (Διδαχαῖς ποικίλαις καὶ ξέναις μὴ παραφέρεσθε· καλὸν γὰρ χάριτι βεβαιοῦσθαι τὴν καρδίαν, οὐ βρώμασιν ἐν οἷς οὐκ ὠφελήθησαν οἱ περιπατοῦντες). The author's conclusion to his sermon takes another sharp turn at verse 9, as he warns about false teaching. However, some continuity in the context can be identified: the commendation of the leaders who taught the word of God faithfully in verse 7 and the succinct summary of orthodox Christology in verse 8 can be seen as preparing the way for this negative thrust. Christ, indeed, might remain "forever," but false teaching has the power to deflect or twist that truth.⁵⁰ The focus on false teaching and the necessary response to it continues through verse 14. The sequence of thought, however, is not immediately clear, and more fundamentally the author refers to the false teaching in such an allusive way that identifying the teaching becomes a challenge. For sequence of thought, I suggest the following outline:

> Avoid false teaching of whatever kind (v. 9a),
>> because (γάρ) at least some of these teachers are arguing for spiritual benefit in the Old Testament cult, and this emphasis conflicts with the bedrock provision of grace (v. 9b).
>> (asyndeton) That grace is found at the "altar," the system of sacrifice and its application that is available to Christians—but not available to those who persist on seeking spiritual benefit from the Old Testament cult (v. 10).
>> [γάρ, signaling a minor break]
>> Like the Old Testament sin offering, which was burnt "outside the camp" of Israel, Jesus, therefore (διό), also suffered outside the city gates (vv. 11–12) in order to (ἵνα) sanctify his people.
>> We therefore (τοίνυν) need to follow him, our pioneer, "outside the camp"—that is, we need to be willing to leave the apparent security of existing religious institutions—in order to gain the benefit of Jesus's sacrifice for our sins (v. 13),
>> because (γάρ), as the author has said before, our focus should be not on the "city" of this world, but on the city of the next world (v. 14).

My outline implicitly addresses also the second point, the nature of the teaching: while verse 9a is a general warning about false teaching, the author quickly hones in on what must have been a particularly attractive form of that teaching for his readers—that is, they were tempted to adopt the Old Testament cultic system as a means of solving the sin problem. Cockerill provides a balanced perspective on this debated question. Responding to the question of why the author delays so long to make this point about teachers who are maintaining the continuing validity of the Old Testament cult, he answers that (1) it is rhetorically powerful

---

47. Pausanias, *Description of Greece* 10.12.10, quoted in Bauckham, "Divinity of Jesus Christ," 35.
48. Koester, *Hebrews*, 560.
49. Bauckham, "Divinity of Jesus Christ," 34–35.
50. On this connection, see, e.g., Ellingworth, *Hebrews*, 705–6.

to wait until the full argument has unfolded before making application; and (2) while the temptation to regress into a form of Judaism is clearly referenced here, this must not have been the most pressing issue the author deals with in his sermon. Rather, the heart of his concern is the failure to move ahead and therefore "drift away" (2:1).[51]

In an exhortation that resembles the author's warning about "drifting away" in 2:1, the author urges his readers not to be "carried away" (παραφέρεσθε) by "different kinds of strange teachings."[52] The plural "teachings" makes it unlikely that the author refers to a single teaching, such as something related to the Jewish cult—and the claim that it is "strange" would also be a bit over-the-top for teaching that God himself instituted in the Old Testament.[53] Probably, then, the author begins with a warning about false teaching of whatever kind. The author's reason (γάρ) for avoiding these teachings is that they seek to "strengthen the heart" by means of "foods" rather than by means of grace.[54] To have the heart "strengthened" (βεβαιοῦσθαι) means to empower the inner person so that one can follow Christ all the more faithfully. Paul uses the same verb in a similar way in 2 Corinthians 1:21: "it is God who makes both us and you stand firm [βεβαιῶν] in Christ."

The reference of the word "foods" (βρώμασιν) is a key factor in determining the direction of this whole passage. Apart from occurrences of the word in general contexts, "food/s" takes on religious significance in several New Testament texts. The appropriateness of eating meat sacrificed to idols divides believers in Corinth (1 Cor 8:8, 13). Many ancient religions advocated abstaining from certain kinds of food as a spiritual discipline. Paul criticizes this in 1 Tim 4:3. And the Old Testament features many prohibitions of eating certain kinds of food. Jesus implicitly released his followers from these laws (Mark 7:19), and Paul made a similar point in Romans 14 (see vv. 15, 20).[55] Particularly interesting, however, is the only other occurrence of the word in Hebrews, where the author claims that "gifts and sacrifices" are "only a matter of food [βρώμασιν] and drink and various ceremonial washings— external regulations applying until the time of the new order" (9:9–10). While, therefore, some interpreters think the reference is quite general,[56] the prominence of "food" in debates about the Jewish law, the reference in 9:9–10, and the obvious Jewish allusions in the context ("altar," "tabernacle," Day of Atonement sacrifice) make it almost certain that the author's polemic against "foods" is a polemic against the continuing observance of Jewish rituals (note NIV "ceremonial foods"; NET "ritual meals"; CSB "food regulations").[57] The reference may not be directly to sacrifice. Although the text in 9:9–10 suggests a connection with "foods" and sacrifices,

---

51. Cockerill, *Hebrews*, 692–94. For this second point, see also Lane, *Hebrews*, 2:536.

52. The two adjectives, ποικίλαις and ξέναις, might form a hendiadys (NIV "all kinds of strange teachings"; see Lane, *Hebrews*, 2:522). The verb παραφέρω occurs three other times in the NT: in Jesus's Gethsemane prayer—"take this cup from me" (Mark 14:36; Luke 22:42)—and in Jude's comparison of false teachers to clouds "blown along" by the wind (Jude 12).

53. Delitzsch, *Hebrews*, 2:381–82.

54. The datives βρώμασιν and χάριτι are instrumental in force—although βρώμασιν also has a local sense in its secondary connection with περιπατοῦντες at the end of the verse: "those who walk *in* foods"; that is, those whose spiritual lives are focused on foods (Ellingworth, *Hebrews*, 708).

55. A few interpreters think the problem in Hebrews is also an insistence on avoiding certain kinds of food (asceticism) (e.g., Bruce, *Hebrews*, 376–77). However, as P. Hughes notes, it appears that "eating," not "non-eating," is the issue (*Hebrews*, 572).

56. According to Thompson, the reference is to "all the earthly alternatives that do not bring stability" (*Hebrews*, 281). See also Hays, who thinks that "foods" may simply refer to the "strange teachings" ("'Here We Have No Lasting City,'" 154).

the word "food" is not a normal way of referring to sacrifice.[58] Lane, however, argues persuasively that regular Jewish meals at that time had a cultic character and that the author may be warning his readers about relying on Jewish customs and laws to find spiritual benefit. While given by God and valid for their time, these laws and customs are no longer applicable (8:13; 9:19), and to revert to them would be to fall away from the grace available in the new-covenant era.

13:10 We have an altar from which those who minister in the tabernacle have no right to eat (ἔχομεν θυσιαστήριον ἐξ οὗ φαγεῖν οὐκ ἔχουσιν ἐξουσίαν οἱ τῇ σκηνῇ λατρεύοντες). Despite the lack of explicit connection (asyndeton), verse 10 follows closely on verse 9.[59] The "grace" by which we are strengthened rests on the provision that God makes for his people in the new-covenant "altar." This altar is sometimes thought to be the heavenly sanctuary or a more-or-less allusive reference to the Lord's Supper,[60] but it more likely depicts in a single image the sacrifice of Christ and the benefits we continue to receive from that sacrifice.[61] Polemic against Jewish ritual becomes especially clear in the author's claim that "those who minister in the tabernacle" have no "right"[62] to eat from the altar. The word "tent" (σκηνή) refers to the Old Testament "tabernacle"; the prominence of this word in chapters 8 and 9 (where it refers to the "tabernacle" or parts thereof [Most Holy Place (9:3) or "outer room" (9:6)] eight times) explains why the author can use "minister in the tabernacle" as shorthand for the Old Testament cultic ritual in general.[63]

13:11 Now the blood of the sacrificial animals[64] is brought into the Most Holy Place by the high priest[65] as a sin offering,[66] but the bodies of the animals are burned outside the camp (ὧν γὰρ εἰσφέρεται ζῴων τὸ αἷμα περὶ ἁμαρτίας εἰς τὰ ἅγια διὰ τοῦ ἀρχιερέως, τούτων τὰ σώματα κατακαίεται ἔξω τῆς παρεμβολῆς). As I have argued, the language of verses 9–10 brings us into the world of the Old Testament cult, a matter that has played a central role in the author's argument. The author's point is one of contrast: Christians have an "altar," a means of atonement, that replaces the old-covenant altar and its provision for sacrifice.

---

57. Most interpreters agree, though differing at times on the specifics. See, e.g., Calvin, *Hebrews*, 209–10; Westcott, *Hebrews*, 436; Lane, *Hebrews*, 2:523; Cockerill, *Hebrews*, 695; Ellingworth, *Hebrews*, 708; P. Hughes, *Hebrews*, 572–74; Mackie, *Eschatology and Exhortation*, 141–42. Koester thinks that Jewish meals may be included but that the basic reference is wider (*Hebrews*, 560–61).

58. The LXX is not very helpful. Most occurrences of the word βρῶμα, "food," are simply in reference to regular eating. Two references refer to OT/Jewish food laws (1 Macc 1:63; 4 Macc. 1.34). The closest we come to an association of the word with sacrifice is in Mal 1:7, 12, where there is reference to "food" for the Lord's table.

59. Contra, e.g., Koester (*Hebrews*, 574–75) and Lane (*Hebrews*, 2:500), who put a break between the verses.

60. For the former, see, e.g., Filson, *Yesterday*, 48–54; deSilva (*Perseverance in Gratitude*, 499–500) is one of many who detects a eucharistic allusion (for this view in the early church, see Grässer, *An die Hebräer*, 3:380–81). Against such an allusion, see esp. Weiss, *Der Brief an die Hebräer*, 725–29.

61. E.g., Bénétrau, *L'Épître aux Hébreux*, 2:210; Westcott, *Hebrews*, 438; Koester, *Hebrews*, 568–69; Cockerill, *Hebrews*, 697; Lane, *Hebrews*, 2:538; Isaacs, *Sacred Space*, 212–17; Small, *Characterization of Jesus*, 224. If I am right in seeing Christ's sacrificial work being culminated in the heavenly sanctuary, this sanctuary is also part of the picture here.

62. Greek ἐξουσίαν. For this meaning of the word, see "ἐξουσία," BDAG 353, §3.

63. Cockerill, *Hebrews*, 697.

64. I have added the qualifier "sacrificial" to make clear which "animals" (ζῴων) the author is referring to.

65. I take διά here to signify agency (see Turner, *Syntax*, 267).

66. The Greek of this clause is rather convoluted; I have taken the liberty of shifting the order to make better sense in English. The problem is obvious from the fact that all the English translations do something similar. Particularly puzzling is the relative pronoun that opens the verse (ὧν). Probably we should construe this with "animals" in the sense of "those animals whose [ὧν] blood . . ." (Zerwick and Grosvenor, *Grammatical Analysis*, 688).

Now, in verses 11–13, the author seizes on a similarity between the Old Testament sin offering and Jesus's sacrificial death to make a different point.[67] "Outside the camp" (vv. 11, 13) and "outside the city gate" (v. 12) are phrases that carry this argument. Verse 11 provides the background for the argument. The author reminds his readers that the regulations for the Day of Atonement stipulated that the bodies of the animals—the bull and the goat—whose blood was sprinkled on the atonement cover should be burned "outside the camp [LXX ἔξω τῆς παρεμβολῆς]" (Lev 16:27). The word for "camp" (παρεμβολή) is very common in the LXX, where it often refers to "a temporary residence for a group of people."[68] It therefore is used to denote the temporary encampment of the Israelites as they traveled through the wilderness on their way to the promised land. The requirement that various ritual acts be carried out "outside the camp" is frequently repeated in Leviticus (Lev 4:12, 21; 6:4; 8:17; 9:11; 10:4, 5; 13:46; 14:3; 16:27; 17:3; 24:14, 23). The concern was that certain purification rituals be performed away from the camp so that it would not be defiled.

13:12 So Jesus also, in order that he might sanctify the people through his own blood, suffered outside the city gate (διὸ καὶ Ἰησοῦς, ἵνα ἁγιάσῃ διὰ τοῦ ἰδίου αἵματος τὸν λαόν, ἔξω τῆς πύλης ἔπαθεν). As the sin offerings of the Day of Atonement, burnt up outside the camp, "sanctified" the people (Lev 16:19), so also (διὸ καί) Jesus suffered "outside the city gate,"[69] that he might sanctify the people. That Jesus was crucified outside Jerusalem is clear from John 19:17–20 and follows common Roman practice. The parallel with the Day of Atonement ritual is not exact; the sacrificial blood was sprinkled on the altar inside the camp before the carcass was burned outside, while Jesus died outside the city and ascended to heaven to complete the sacrificial ritual in the heavenly sanctuary. But the author is not interested in an extended parallel. He draws attention to one point of correspondence: as P. Hughes puts it, sanctity is secured in an unsanctified place.[70] The author implies that the city of Jerusalem, and especially its temple, was, like Israel's camp, "sacred space." Jesus accomplished full and final sanctification of the sins of humankind outside that sacred space. The very location of his sacrifice, then, suggests that God is no longer working within the boundaries set by the Old Testament cultic law.[71]

13:13 Therefore, let us go out to him outside the camp, bearing his reproach (τοίνυν ἐξερχώμεθα πρὸς αὐτὸν ἔξω τῆς παρεμβολῆς τὸν ὀνειδισμὸν αὐτοῦ φέροντες). The idea that Jesus accomplished new-covenant atonement apart from the traditional

---

67. The substance of these verses suggests that the γάρ at the beginning of the verse signals a shift to a new topic (the word is left untranslated in many versions [e.g., NIV; NLT; CEB; NAB]). It probably does not mean "for" here (contra NRSV; ESV; CSB; NASB; NET)—the attempts to justify an explanatory sense of the word (e.g., Cockerill, *Hebrews*, 698, Lane, *Hebrews*, 2:539–400) are not convincing. See the note on 2:10.

68. Lisa Michele Wolfe, "Camp," in *The New Interpreter's Dictionary of the Bible*, vol. 1, ed. Katharine Doob Sakenfeld et al. (Nashville: Abingdon, 2006), 531. In the LXX, the word often refers to an army "encampment," and this meaning is reflected in most of its NT occurrences (Acts 21:34, 37; 22:24; 23:10, 16, 32; in Heb 11:34, it refers to "armies").

69. The Greek is simply πύλη, but the word on its own often referred to the gate, or gates, of a city (BDAG 897, §a; see Acts 9:24; 16:13).

70. P. Hughes, *Hebrews*, 597.

71. Another OT passage that refers to "outside the camp" may play a role in the author's thinking. After the golden-calf incident, Moses pitches his tent "outside the camp [ἔξω τῆς παρεμβολῆς]" where people are invited to come to him in order to meet with God (Exod 33:7–10). See, e.g., Lane, *Hebrews*, 2:544; P. Hughes, *Hebrews*, 581; Backhaus, *Der Hebräerbrief*, 472.

laws and rituals of Judaism is taken further and applied in verse 13. The reference at the end of this verse to "bearing his reproach"—that is, "bearing the reproach that he also experienced"[72]—suggests that Jesus's death outside the city was the product not only of Roman practice but also of human rejection, especially on the part of the Jewish leaders of the time. As the suffering servant, Jesus was "despised and rejected by mankind" (Isa 53:3). So, for the Christians whom the author is addressing, the benefits of Jesus's death and his ongoing ministry of intercession can be enjoyed only "outside the camp." The application of this metaphorical call to "leave" has been variously identified. Rissi thinks the author might be calling his readers to abandon the spiritual lethargy that is holding them back.[73] Some think the reference is to the need to leave this world, with its material security, to identify with our heavenly identity.[74] P. Hughes speaks of the need to leave "the fallen values of an unregenerate society."[75] However, the Jewish imagery that pervades this passage, along with the notion of sacred space that is basic to the "outside the camp" idea, suggests rather that the author is calling his readers to leave the security of the Jewish system of sanctification.[76] This is where Jesus is, as it were, "located": to come to him demands renouncing the apparent security offered by the old cultic system. This exhortation provides, then, some basis for thinking that at least one of the problems the author addresses in his sermon is the temptation facing probably particularly Jewish Christians to abandon their distinctive Christian identity and profile and find their spiritual security in Jewish ritual.

Koester draws our attention to the contrast between the author's insistence that his readers "go out" and his usual exhortation to them to "go in" or "enter." The language of entering is usually used with entrance into the sanctuary in view: "going in" where God's presence is to be found. This entering, the author suggests here, involves a corresponding need for "exiting": leaving the confines of Judaism and its rituals, where the presence of God is no longer manifest.[77]

13:14 For here we do not have a lasting city, but we are seeking the one to come (οὐ γὰρ ἔχομεν ὧδε μένουσαν πόλιν ἀλλὰ τὴν μέλλουσαν ἐπιζητοῦμεν). The author grounds (γάρ, "for") his imperative in verse 13 in the contrast between the "city" of this world and the "city" of the next. The author uses the image of the "city" earlier to refer to the hope of the believer. Abraham was willing to live a nomadic existence in the land of promise because "he was looking forward to the city with foundations, whose architect and builder is God" (11:10). Other believers of his time joined him in this perspective: "God is not ashamed to be called their God, for he has prepared a city for them" (11:16). And in 12:22, the author calls Mount Zion to which believers have come "the city of the living God." The author

---

72. "Reproach" or "disgrace" (ὀνειδισμός) was something the audience had experienced in their early days as believers (10:33); and Moses demonstrated his faith by regarding "disgrace for the sake of Christ as of greater value than the treasures of Egypt" (11:26).
73. Rissi, *Die Theologie des Hebräerbriefs*, 23.
74. E.g., Thompson, *Hebrews*, 283; deSilva, *Perseverance in Gratitude*, 501.
75. P. Hughes, *Hebrews*, 580 (he sees a reference also to leaving Judaism).
76. This is the view of the majority; see, e.g., Westcott, *Hebrews*, 442; Lane, *Hebrews*, 2:545; D. Harris, *Hebrews*, 416; Schreiner, *Hebrews*, 422; Filson, *Yesterday*, 60–65. It is unlikely that the author is calling on his audience, resident in Jerusalem, to leave the city (contra Carl Mosser, "Rahab outside the Camp," in Bauckham et al., *Epistle to the Hebrews*, 397–403).
77. Koester, *Hebrews*, 576. He distinguishes between "entering" as a theological movement and "leaving" as a social movement. But the leaving involves more, I have argued, than the social—it, too, has a religious component.

may introduce this imagery here because he is thinking of an implicit contrast between the city of Jerusalem and the city to come.[78] With this allusion to Jerusalem, the author appears, then, to include in the city that does not "last" or "endure" (οὐ ... μένουσαν) the ritual performances centered in that city. However, by reverting to the language of "city," the author also here alludes to all the values, institutions, and concerns that belong to the kingdom of this world—to that which will be "shaken" (12:27), in contrast to the kingdom that is coming, the kingdom over which Jesus, the one who is "the same yesterday, today, and forever" (v. 8), rules. This verse is therefore the final statement of this key motif in the author's sermon.[79]

13:15–16 Through him, therefore,[80] let us continually[81] offer up a sacrifice of praise to God—that is, the fruit of lips praising his name. 16 Do not neglect to do good and share with others, for with such sacrifices God is pleased (δι' αὐτοῦ οὖν ἀναφέρωμεν θυσίαν αἰνέσεως διὰ παντὸς τῷ θεῷ, τοῦτ' ἔστιν καρπὸν χειλέων ὁμολογούντων τῷ ὀνόματι αὐτοῦ. 16 τῆς δὲ εὐποιΐας καὶ κοινωνίας μὴ ἐπιλανθάνεσθε· τοιαύταις γὰρ θυσίαις εὐαρεστεῖται ὁ θεός). After the author's warning about false teaching in verse 9a, the next verses are bound together by references to and allusions to the Old Testament cultic system. The various Jewish rituals involving "foods" are no longer the source of grace (v. 9b); that grace is now tied to the definitive sacrifice of Christ (our "altar"; v. 10). Jesus's death "outside the city gate" does not follow the pattern of the Day of Atonement sin offerings, suggesting that his sacrifice cannot be linked to the old ritual system. In order, then, to follow their "pioneer" and benefit from his sacrifice, the readers need to go to him "outside the camp" (v. 13)—even if that means facing the ostracism and persecution that comes with identifying with one who was "scorned and rejected." This renunciation, however, does not mean that the readers are done with sacrifices. The author exhorts them in verses 15–16 to offer a very different kind of sacrifice.

The language of "sacrifice" (θυσία) frames verses 15–16, with the identification of those sacrifices coming between (vv. 15b and 16a).[82] It is "through and because of"[83] Jesus that we are now able to offer sacrifices with which "God is pleased" (εὐαρεστεῖται ὁ θεός at the end of v. 16). Those sacrifices consist of praise (αἰνέσεως),[84] which the author further describes as "the fruit of lips [or "the words produced by lips"][85] that consist in praising[86] the name of God."[87] The author here joins other

---

78. Lane, *Hebrews*, 2:546.
79. Ellingworth, *Hebrews*, 718.
80. "Therefore" translates οὖν. This word is omitted in some good MSS ($\mathfrak{P}^{46}$ ℵ* D* P Ψ), and one can understand how a scribe, sensing its appropriateness, might have added it. But the word is also found in many good MSS, and might have been accidentally omitted (Metzger, *Textual Commentary*, 605; Lane, *Hebrews*, 2:524; Ellingworth, *Hebrews*, 720).
81. For the meaning "continually" for διὰ παντός, see Weiss, *Der Brief an die Hebräer*, 740 (he suggests that the phrase follows LXX usage).
82. E.g., Cockerill, *Hebrews*, 704; Thurén, *Das Lobopfer der Hebräer*, 105.
83. Grässer (*An die Hebräer*, 3:390) perceptively notes that the preposition δι' before αὐτοῦ (a pronoun referring to Jesus; cf. v. 13) blends instrumental and causal nuances.

84. The genitive form of the word is used to indicate apposition: the sacrifice that is praise (Lane, *Hebrews*, 2:524).
85. The author may allude to Hos 14:2b, which speaks of "offering" "the fruit of our lips" (καρπὸν χειλέων ἡμῶν).
86. The author uses the verb ὁμολογέω, which, as we have seen, with its cognate ὁμολογία, has a varied semantic range in Hebrews (see the note on 3:1). One of its meanings is "praise" (see "ὁμολογέω," BDAG 708, §4; although this is the only NT verse it includes with this meaning; see also Lane, *Hebrews*, 2:524; Ellingworth, *Hebrews*, 721). English versions translate "confess" (RSV; NRSV; NAB; CEB; CSB), "profess" (NIV), "acknowledge" (ESV; NET), "give thanks" (KJV; NASB).
87. Cockerill suggests that the antecedent of αὐτοῦ, the pronoun that depends on "name," is the Son of God (*Hebrews*, 706), but θεός, "God," occurs just before this pronoun in v. 15 and again at the end of v. 16.

early Christians in shifting the focus of "sacrifice" from what priests do in the tabernacle or temple to what ordinary believers do in their daily lives. This application is not a "spiritualization" of sacrifice, since the sacrifices that are now pleasing to God are still often quite concrete; for example, our "bodies" (Rom 12:1) or a gift of money (Phil 2:17; 4:18). To be sure, Peter calls them "spiritual sacrifices" (1 Pet 2:5), but this means sacrifices suitable to those who are governed by the Spirit of God.

The author identifies two other kinds of general sacrifice with which God is pleased in verse 16a: "to do good" (εὐποιΐας)[88] and to "share with others" or "generosity" (κοινωνίας).[89] He urges us not to "neglect" or "forget" (μὴ ἐπιλανθάνεσθε) them. The language and substance of this verse may take us back to verses 2–3, where the author urged his readers not to "forget" (μὴ ἐπιλανθάνεσθε) hospitality and to remember prisoners and those being mistreated.

13:17 Obey your leaders and submit to them, for they are watching over your souls as people who will have to render an account. [Obey them] so that they might do their work with joy and not with groaning—for this would be unprofitable for you (Πείθεσθε τοῖς ἡγουμένοις ὑμῶν καὶ ὑπείκετε, αὐτοὶ γὰρ ἀγρυπνοῦσιν ὑπὲρ τῶν ψυχῶν ὑμῶν ὡς λόγον ἀποδώσοντες, ἵνα μετὰ χαρᾶς τοῦτο ποιῶσιν καὶ μὴ στενάζοντες· ἀλυσιτελὲς γὰρ ὑμῖν τοῦτο). As I noted above, the call to obey leaders in this verse forms an *inclusio* with the exhortation to "remember your leaders" in verse 7. The author therefore signals that he is wrapping up this particular series of exhortations. The focus in verse 7 seems to have been on the community leaders who had been active in the past, perhaps in founding the community. Now the focus is on the present. It is not entirely clear how strong the author's exhortation is. Almost all the versions translate "obey," but the word used here could also have a slightly milder flavor, "have confidence in" (NIV).[90] The author pairs this command with another, calling on his readers to "submit" (ὑπείκετε) also.[91] These commands probably arise from a concern that the audience of the letter is in danger of succumbing to many kinds of "strange teachings" (v. 9), partly because they were paying insufficient attention to the faithful teaching of their spiritual leaders.[92] These leaders are worthy of following, because (γάρ) they are "watching over" the souls of the people entrusted to them; they are being alert and attentive to the people's needs.[93] Moreover, they are leading the flock that God has entrusted to them "with the thought that"[94] they will one day have to give an account for their stewardship of these souls.[95]

---

88. This is a comparatively rare word, occurring only here in the NT and never in the LXX. A papyrus uses it in its obvious meaning of "doing good deeds" (*New Documents Illustrating Early Christianity*, vol. 4, ed. Stephen Llewelyn and G. H. R. Horsley [Grand Rapids: Eerdmans, 1997], 83).

89. See Lane for the meaning "generosity" (*Hebrews*, 2:524). For κοινωνία in this practical sense, see also Acts 2:42; Rom 15:26; 2 Cor 8:4; 9:13; and see also the use of the cognate verb in Rom 12:13; Gal 6:6; Phil 4:15.

90. The verb is πείθεσθε, a present middle/passive (here middle) imperative form of πείθω. The verb can mean "obey" ("πείθω," BDAG 792, §3b; see also "πείθω," *NIDNTTE* 3:688–89), but its basic sense is "to be persuaded by" someone and thus "follow" them. Johnson translates "depend on," "trust" (*Hebrews*, 350).

91. The verb ὑπείκω is rare in biblical Greek: only here in the NT and once in the LXX, at 4 Macc. 6.35 (with a greater number of occurrences in Philo).

92. For ἡγουμένοις in the sense of "spiritual leaders," see the note on v. 7.

93. The verb ἀγρυπνέω refers to spiritual alertness elsewhere in the NT: Mark 13:33; Luke 21:36; Eph 6:18.

94. This is how Turner paraphrases the sense of ὡς here (*Syntax*, 158).

95. "Give account" is expressed in a rare future participle: ἀποδώσοντες. Lane suggests that the future might convey a note of purpose, "those who intend to give an account" (*Hebrews*, 2:525), but this is not clear.

The second part of the verse might be a command issued to the leaders; see ESV: "let them do this with joy and not with groaning, for that would be of no advantage to you." This translation rests on taking the conjunction here (ἵνα) as introducing an imperative. More likely, however, we should give this word its normal telic meaning and translate, as I have above, "obey them *so that* they might do their work[96] with joy and not with groaning." On this view, the point is that the ready and willing, submissive spirit of the congregation as a whole will make the leaders' work a joy for them and not a burden or matter of "groaning."[97] If, on the other hand, the congregation resists wise and biblically oriented leadership, the leaders will suffer, as will the congregation itself: "this" situation (τοῦτο) will be "unprofitable" (ἀλυσιτελές) for them.

Theology in Application

It is almost expected that one will cite the title of Charles Dickens's novel *A Tale of Two Cities* when considering Hebrews's use of the "city" theme. And, as 13:14 makes clear, the reference is indeed an apt one: "here we do not have a lasting city, but we are seeking the one to come." This verse is the climax to this theme in Hebrews, which the author first introduces in his "heroes of the faith" chapter. Abraham left his homeland to live a nomadic existence in Israel because "he was looking forward to the city with foundations, whose architect and builder is God" (11:10). Similarly, the patriarchs and Sarah were not looking back at their home country but "were longing for a better country—a heavenly one," which is further described as a city prepared for them by God (11:16). Then, in the sweeping salvation-historical comparison in 12:18–24, Mount Sinai is contrasted with Mount Zion, which is further described as "the city of the living God, the heavenly Jerusalem" (12:22). This last verse reveals a salvation-historical framework for the contrast between two cities. As the people of Israel sink deeper and deeper into sin and idolatry, the earthly city of Jerusalem becomes a symbol, not of God's blessing and the people's covenant status, but of their failure (e.g., Lam 1:8, 17). The prophets then begin to predict that God's new work in Israel would bring about a transformation in the city or even a new Jerusalem with a new temple (e.g., Isa 44:28; 65:18; Jer 33:16; Joel 3:1; Ezek 40–48). This theme was picked up and advanced in Jewish literature, where (especially in apocalyptic-oriented material) the idea of a heavenly Jerusalem becomes popular. Paul picks up this idea in Galatians 4:21–31, where he contrasts the "present Jerusalem" with "the Jerusalem that is above." And, of course, the future blessed state that will mark God's new heaven and new earth is pictured as the "new Jerusalem, coming down out

---

96. The verb ποιῶσιν (dependent on ἵνα) could refer to the "giving of an account" (Koester, *Hebrews*, 572) but more likely refers to ministry.

97. The word is στενάζοντες, from στενάζω, "groan."

of heaven from God" (Rev 21:2, cf. vv. 10–27). In typical fashion, then, our author combines a "vertical" dimension—"above" or "heavenly" versus earthly—with a horizontal one—past versus future.

Pinning down the exact meaning or significance of this "city" concept is difficult. This is partly because it is a broad concept: the author uses the "city to come" as shorthand for the entire new state of affairs that God is inaugurating. As the future focus of verse 14 reveals—"we are looking for the city that is to come"—this city is to some extent a future hope for Christians now. Yet we may also assume, granted the typical New Testament eschatological perspective, that this "city" is even now being inaugurated. "City" language suggests an organized center of activity. This becomes especially clear in the way Revelation uses "Babylon" in chapters 17 and 18 to depict the systemic evil that typifies the "world" in opposition to God and his kingdom. The "city" we Christians look for, then, is the "place" where the values of God's kingdom rule. We are "citizens" not of Rome or of the city of this earth, but of the city to come (Phil 1:27; 3:20–21). The author adds a further nuance to the "city" concept in 13:12–13 by adding to his conceptual reference the idea of a "camp." As the sacrifices in Leviticus were burned "outside the camp," so Jesus suffered outside the city gates. And we are invited to follow Jesus out of the camp/the city.

The contrast between the two cities, then, evokes the fundamental contrast between God/Satan, God's kingdom/the kingdom of this world, Spirit/flesh, etc., that marks the reality of our fallen world. In one of the greatest works of Christian philosophy and theology, Augustine appropriates the imagery of two contrasting cities to urge believers in his day to align themselves with the "city of God" and resist the pull of "the earthly city." So, in our day also, faced with the powerful lure of the earthly city, we need consistently to orient ourselves to the city that God is building by renewing our minds (Rom 12:2)—that is, reprogramming our fundamental mind-set in accordance with kingdom values. Kingdom thinking and kingdom living are not always easy. To turn our backs on the city that does not endure entails "bearing [Christ's] reproach."

Chapter 33

Hebrews 13:18–25

Literary Context

Hebrews begins with high theology and without the usual elements that mark the beginning of a letter (identification of author and addressees, greeting, etc.). Without downplaying the sermonic nature of this book, the ending of Hebrews marks it out as a "letter," as the author rapidly moves through a series of topics that are typical of letter closings.[1] As I noted above, there is some disagreement about where this formal "letter closing" begins, a number of translations and commentators identifying verse 20 as the place where the closing begins. However, a request for prayer for the author often marks letter closings (e.g., Rom 15:30–32; Eph 6:18–20; Col 4:3–4; 1 Thess 5:25; 2 Thess 3:1–2; Phlm 22), and this suggests that the letter closing begins with verse 18. A few scholars think the epistolary closing material was added to the sermon at a later time.[2] However, there is no evidence for this; it is more likely that the author added it himself to prepare his sermon for dispatch to his readers.

---

1. For the form of the letter closing (with reference to the letters of Paul), see esp. Jeffrey A. D. Weima, *Neglected Endings: The Significance of the Pauline Letter Closings*, JSNTSup 101 (Sheffield: JSOT Press, 1994).

2. William Wrede, for instance, argues that a "deutero-Pauline" author added the epistolary ending (*Das literarische Rätsel des Hebräerbriefes*, FRLANT 8 [Göttingen: Vandenhoeck & Ruprecht, 1906], 39–73). Rothschild, somewhat similarly, argues that the epistolary ending has a clear Pauline flavor and was added to suggest the letter was written by Paul (*Hebrews as Pseudepigraphon*). However, while sharing some features with Paul's endings, there is no reason to think the author has deliberately sought to imitate Paul (Dyer, "Epistolary Closing of Hebrews and Pauline Imitation," 269–85). See the introduction, pp. 3–5.

I. The Exalted Son and a Rest for the People of God (1:1–4:13)
II. Our Great High Priest and His Ministry (4:14–10:31)
III. **Exhortation: Follow and Serve the Pioneer of Our Faith through Endurance and Faith (10:32–13:25)**
   A. Introductory Call to Endurance and Faith (10:32–39)
   B. The Nature and Power of Faith Illustrated in Salvation History (11:1–40)
   C. Run the Race with Endurance, Remembering That You Are Children of God (12:1–17)
   D. Coming to Mount Zion and Inheriting the Unshakable Kingdom (12:18–29)
   E. **Letter Closing (13:1–25)**
      1. Concluding Exhortations and Encouragement (13:1–17)
      2. **Concluding Epistolary Matters (13:18–25)**

Main Idea

The author puts his sermon into the form of a letter in order to dispatch it to his readers, who live at a distance from him. At the same time, he establishes or reinforces his relationship to his readers by requesting prayer and, in turn, praying for them.

Translation

Hebrews 13:18-25

18a	exhortation	**Pray for us.**
18b	development	For
18c	assertion	**we are persuaded**
18d	content	that we have a good conscience,
18e	elaboration (of 18c)	desiring to live
18f	manner	honorably
18g	circumstance	in all circumstances.
19a	specific	**I especially encourage you to pray**
19b	purpose	that I might be restored to you
19c	time	soon.
20a	development	Now

20b	desire	**may the God**
20c	attribute	of peace,
20d	apposition	the one who brought up
20e	source	from the dead
20f	object (of 20d)	the great shepherd of the sheep,
20g	apposition	our Lord Jesus,
20h	association (with 21a)	in conjunction with the blood of the eternal covenant,
21a	predicate (of 20b)	**equip you**
21b	means	with every good thing
21c	purpose	so that you may be able to do his will,
21d	clarification (of 21a)	doing what is pleasing
21e	recipient	among us
21f	standard (for 21d)	before him
21g	means (of 21d)	through Jesus Christ,
21h	doxology	to whom be the glory
21i	time	forever.
21j	conclusion	**Amen.**
22a	exhortation	**I urge you,** brothers and
22b	parallel address	sisters,
22c	content	to bear with this word
22d	description	of exhortation,
22e	basis (for 22a–d)	for
22f	assertion	**I have written to you**
22g	manner	quite briefly.
23a	assertion	**I want you to know**
23b	content	that our brother Timothy has been released.
23c	condition (for 23d)	If he arrives soon,
23d	promise	I will come with him to see you.
24a	greeting	**Greet** all your leaders as well as
24b	parallel	all the holy people of God.
24c	greeting	**Those from Italy greet you.**
25a	blessing	**Grace be with all of you.**

Structure

The final verses of Hebrews move quickly through a number of matters that often appear at the end of New Testament letters:

A request that the readers pray for the writer (vv. 18–19)
    (Rom 15:30–32; Eph 6:18–20; Col 4:3–4; 1 Thess 5:25; 2 Thess 3:1–2; Phlm 22)
A prayer, in turn, for the readers (vv. 20–21a)
    (Rom 15:33; 2 Cor 13:11c; Gal 6:16; Eph 6:23; Phil 4:9; 1 Thess 5:23; 2 Thess 3:16; 2 Pet 3:18a; 3 John 14)
A doxology (v. 21b)
    (Rom 16:25–27; Phil 4:20; 2 Pet 3:18b; Jude 24–25)
A reference back to the letter itself (v. 22)
    (1 Pet 5:12 ["briefly"]; 1 John 5:13–15; 3 John 13)
Information about fellow workers (v. 23)
    (Rom 16:1–2; 1 Cor 16:10–12, 15–18; Eph 6:21–22; Col 4:7–9; 2 Tim 4:20; 1 Pet 5:12)
Greetings (v. 24)
    (Rom 16:3–15; 1 Cor 16:20b; 2 Cor 13:12; Phil 4:21a; Col 4:15; 1 Thess 5:26; 2 Tim 4:19; Titus 3:15b; 1 Pet 5:13–14a; 2 John 13; 3 John 14)
A grace and/or peace wish (v. 25)
    (Rom 16:20b; 1 Cor 16:23; 2 Cor 13:14; Gal 6:18; Eph 6:24; Phil 4:23; Col 4:18c; 1 Thess 5:28; 2 Thess 3:18; 1 Tim 6:21b; 2 Tim 4:22b; Titus 3:15b; Phlm 25; 1 Pet 5:14b)

Exegetical Outline

   → **2. Concluding Epistolary Matters (13:18–25)**
       a. Request That the Readers Pray for the Writer (vv. 18–19)
       b. Prayer for the Readers (vv. 20–21a)
       c. Doxology (vv. 21b)
       d. Reference Back to the Letter (v. 22)
       e. Information about Fellow Workers (v. 23)
       f. Greetings (v. 24)
       g. Grace and/or Peace Wish (v. 25)

Explanation of the Text

13:18–19 Pray for us. For we are persuaded that we have a good conscience, desiring to live honorably in all circumstances. 19 I especially encourage you to pray that I might be restored to you soon (Προσεύχεσθε περὶ ἡμῶν· πειθόμεθα γὰρ ὅτι καλὴν συνείδησιν ἔχομεν, ἐν πᾶσιν καλῶς θέλοντες ἀναστρέφεσθαι. 19 περισσοτέρως δὲ παρακαλῶ τοῦτο ποιῆσαι, ἵνα τάχιον ἀποκατασταθῶ ὑμῖν). The present tense of the verb for "pray" suggests that the author is encouraging regular prayer.[3] The plural object of the preposition following the verb (ἡμῶν, "us") may be a genuine plural, encompassing the author and others with him, or a "literary" plural, referring to the author only. The claim to have a "good conscience" later in the verse might suggest an individual focus, and the shift to first-singular forms in verse 19 also suggests that the author is requesting prayer for himself.[4] Why the author feels the need to assert that he has a "good conscience" is unclear, but it is possible that he is responding to some kind of accusation. His further reference to his intention to live "honorably" (so most English translations) or "well" (καλῶς) reinforces the point.[5]

In verse 19, the author specifies a particular purpose in his request for prayer: that he might "soon," or "quickly" (τάχιον), be restored to them. The language of restoration clearly implies that the author had been part of the community of believers whom he addresses in this letter. Cockerill suggests the further implication that the author had himself been imprisoned for his faith.[6] However, this might be going further than the text allows. As is generally the case when trying to piece together the situation in which a letter was written, we have to exercise humility and recognize that we just don't have the data we need to say much very specifically.

13:20–21 Now may the God of peace, the one who brought up from the dead the great shepherd of the sheep, our Lord Jesus, in conjunction with the blood of the eternal covenant, 21 equip you with every good thing so that you may be able to do his will, doing what is pleasing among us before him through Jesus Christ, to whom be the glory forever. Amen. (Ὁ δὲ θεὸς τῆς εἰρήνης, ὁ ἀναγαγὼν ἐκ νεκρῶν τὸν ποιμένα τῶν προβάτων τὸν μέγαν ἐν αἵματι διαθήκης αἰωνίου, τὸν κύριον ἡμῶν Ἰησοῦν, 21 καταρτίσαι ὑμᾶς ἐν παντὶ ἀγαθῷ εἰς τὸ ποιῆσαι τὸ θέλημα αὐτοῦ, ποιῶν ἐν ἡμῖν τὸ εὐάρεστον ἐνώπιον αὐτοῦ διὰ Ἰησοῦ Χριστοῦ, ᾧ ἡ δόξα εἰς τοὺς αἰῶνας τῶν αἰώνων, ἀμήν). As I note above, letter closings in the New Testament often include a prayer for the intended audience, and some also include a doxology. In verses 20–21, we find both, as the author's prayer morphs into a concluding doxology. The author prays to "the God of peace." This "peace" (εἰρήνης) might refer to harmonious relationships among believers,[7] but more likely is a general reference to *shalom* (the OT Hebrew word), the new state of affairs in which God brings all creation under his rule (see "God of peace" in this sense in Rom 15:33; 16:20; 2 Cor 13:11; Phil 4:9; 1 Thess 5:23).[8] One of the main

---

3. See BDF 336.3; Turner, *Syntax*, 75.
4. E.g., Attridge, *Hebrews*, 402; Johnson, *Hebrews*, 353; Bruce, *Hebrews*, 386; Massonnet, *L'Épître aux Hébreux*, 419. Contra, e.g., Westcott, *Hebrews*, 446.
5. BDAG ("καλῶς," 505, §2) suggests that καλῶς here refers to living "in a manner free from objection."
6. Cockerill, *Hebrews*, 713–14.
7. Bruce, *Hebrews*, 387; see 1 Cor 14:33.
8. Bénétrau, *L'Épître aux Hébreux*, 2:223.

instruments that God has used to inaugurate his reign of "peace" is the resurrection of Christ from the dead. The author does not use the normal New Testament language for resurrection, but refers to God "bringing up" (the verb is ἀνάγω) Christ from the dead. The closest parallel to the author's language is Romans 10:7: "'Who will descend into the deep?' (that is, to bring Christ up [ἀναγαγεῖν] from the dead)." The author may choose this word because it can readily encompass both Jesus's resurrection and his ascension. He may also use this language to create an allusion to Isaiah 63:11, particularly when we note that he identifies the one whom God brought up from the dead as "the great shepherd of the sheep": "Then the one who brought up [ἀναβιβάσας] from the land the shepherd of the sheep [τὸν ποιμένα τῶν προβάτων] remembered the days of old: Where is the one who put within them his holy spirit, who led Moyses with his right hand?" (Isa 63:11–12a NETS). Letter closings will often reprise certain key themes from the letter as a whole. We might here, then, see a reference back to the key idea of Jesus as the "pioneer" who, as Moses brought the people to the verge of the promised land, now brings God's people to the rest he has destined them for (2:10; 12:2; see 3:7–4:11).[9] The closest New Testament analogy to the author's language is 1 Peter 2:25 and 5:4 which, respectively, describe Christ Jesus as "the Shepherd and Overseer of your souls," and "the Chief Shepherd."

The author's prayer devolves into what we would label in English a run-on sentence (as my rather wooden translation above reveals). He adds at this point a phrase governed by the preposition ἐν. Most translations give this word an instrumental sense and attach the phrase to God's "bringing up"; for example, NIV: "may the God of peace, who *through* the blood of the eternal covenant brought back from the dead . . ."[10] However, I prefer to take the ἐν as denoting "accompaniment" or "attendant circumstances."[11] In this case, "in/through the blood of the eternal covenant" has a more general connection to the prayer, pointing to the larger set of circumstances in which God's raising of Christ takes place. The NLT captures this idea well: "now may the God of peace—who brought up from the dead our Lord Jesus, the great Shepherd of the sheep, and ratified an eternal covenant with his blood. . . ." Of course, the author here again refers back to a central theme in his sermon: the new covenant that God has instituted through the once-for-all sacrifice of Christ.[12]

The author prays that this God of peace might "equip" (καταρτίσαι)[13] his readers "in every good thing" (ἐν παντὶ ἀγαθῷ),[14] an equipping that is designed to enable them "to do his will." One attractive option is to take "good thing" as focusing on the inner disposition that is needed so that the will of God can be done.[15] The author makes clear that this ability to do the will of God depends on him by adding the clause "doing [ποιῶν] what is pleasing among us [or "in us"][16] before him"—all enabled and continually empowered by Christ ("through Jesus Christ").[17] The word "pleasing" (εὐάρεστον)

---

9. E.g., Cockerill, *Hebrews*, 715–16; Koester, *Hebrews*, 573.
10. See, e.g., Ellingworth, *Hebrews*, 728.
11. Moule, *Idiom Book*, 78.
12. The combination "blood of the covenant" occurs also in the words of institution (Matt 26:28; Mark 14:24; cf. Luke 22:20 and 1 Cor 11:25, "new covenant in my blood") and in Heb 9:20 and 10:29. Hebrews 9:20 quotes from Exod 24:8, which might be a key OT text informing all these NT passages. See also Zech 9:11.
13. The verb is a rare NT optative, used to express a wish.
14. A large number of manuscripts, including the Majority text (see the KJV translation here) add ἔργῳ ("work") before ἀγαθῷ. This is almost certainly a secondary addition.
15. Lane, *Hebrews*, 2:564.
16. The phrase ἐν ἡμῖν might have a distributive sense—"in each one of us" (NIV; ESV; NET; CSB; CEB; NAB; NASB)—or a collective sense—"among us" (NRSV).
17. Some manuscripts add a pronoun here: αὐτοῦ αὐτῷ

might take us back to the use of the closely related adverb in 11:28 (εὐαρέστως), in a kind of *inclusio*.[18] At the end of his prayer, the author appends a brief doxology. It is not clear whether the doxology ascribes glory to God or to Christ—or perhaps to both together.[19] "Jesus Christ" is the closest reference, but "him" in the phrase "pleasing . . . before him" is undoubtedly God, and the entire prayer is directed to the "God of peace."

13:22 I urge you, brothers and sisters, to bear with this word of exhortation, for I have written to you quite briefly (Παρακαλῶ δὲ ὑμᾶς, ἀδελφοί, ἀνέχεσθε τοῦ λόγου τῆς παρακλήσεως, καὶ γὰρ διὰ βραχέων ἐπέστειλα ὑμῖν). As most English versions recognize, a minor break comes between verses 21 and 22. The prayer and doxology in verses 20–21 appear to be a fitting conclusion to the sermon, with more obviously personal and logistical issues taken up in verse 22 and following.[20] In urging his readers to "bear with" (ἀνέχεσθε) his "word of exhortation," he implies perhaps that his sermon has addressed some serious matters in a serious tone—as indeed it has.[21] The severe warnings the author feels he needs to issue to his readers are the clearest evidence of this tone. The phrase "word of exhortation" (τοῦ λόγου τῆς παρακλήσεως) occurs once elsewhere in the New Testament, in Acts 13:15, referring to an address delivered by Paul in the synagogue at Pisidian Antioch. This parallel suggests that the author views his own work as a sermon that, because of the distance between them, he puts into the form of a letter to his audience (see the introduction, pp. 2–3). We might wonder about the claim that the author has written "briefly," granted the length of Hebrews. But, of course, brevity is always a relative matter (I could have gone on a lot longer!), and the phrase the author uses can refer to a pretty long document (see Josephus, *Ant.* 20.266; and see the parallel in 1 Pet 5:12).

13:23 I want you to know that our brother Timothy has been released. If he arrives soon, I will come with him to see you (Γινώσκετε τὸν ἀδελφὸν ἡμῶν Τιμόθεον ἀπολελυμένον, μεθ' οὗ ἐὰν τάχιον ἔρχηται ὄψομαι ὑμᾶς). The author's reference to "our brother Timothy" suggests that, whoever our author was, he had some connection with the Pauline circle—because Timothy, of course, is closely identified with Paul in the New Testament. The verb translated "has been released" (ἀπολελυμένον) could rather be translated "has gone away," but the verb often refers to release from judicial confinement (e.g., Matt 18:27; 27:15, 17, 21, 26; Mark 15:6, 9, 11, 15; Luke 23:16, 18, 22, 25; John 18:39; 19:10, 12; Acts 3:13; 4:21, 23; 5:40; 16:35, 36; 17:9; 28:18).[22] The New Testament does not elsewhere mention any imprisonment of Timothy. As far as his movements in the later phase of his ministry, he was with Paul in Corinth (Rom 16:21), traveled back to Palestine with Paul (Acts 20:4), and was in Rome with Paul during Paul's first imprisonment there (Col 1:1; Phlm 1; Phil 1:1; cf. Phil 2:19, 22). He then spent some time ministering in Ephesus

---

ποιῶν. While certainly the more difficult reading, it is almost too difficult; as Metzger comments, it is "unintelligible." With the NA committee, then, we should probably view it as added by dittography from the previous pronoun (Metzger, *Textual Commentary*, 606).

18. Cf. Lane, *Hebrews*, 2:498.

19. Those favoring a reference to God include Westcott, *Hebrews*, 449; Ellingworth, *Hebrews*, 731; Lane, *Hebrews*, 2:559; Schreiner, *Hebrews*, 430. For a reference to Jesus, see Attridge, *Hebrews*, 407; Bénétrau, *L'Épître aux Hébreux*, 2:224. For a reference to both, see Cockerill, *Hebrews*, 718; D. Harris, *Hebrews*, 425.

20. See, e.g., Koester, *Hebrews*, 580.

21. Note the use of the verb ἀνέχομαι elsewhere in the NT: Matt 17:17; Mark 9:19; Luke 9:41; Acts 18:14; 1 Cor 4:12; 2 Cor 11:1, 4, 19, 20; Eph 4:2; Col 3:13; 2 Thess 1:4; 2 Tim 4:3.

22. For this meaning, see, e.g., Koester, *Hebrews*, 581; Ellingworth, *Hebrews*, 733–34.

(1 Tim 1:2). Only this last reference is possibly relevant to the situation supposed in Hebrews. As with so many background matters in Hebrews, we simply cannot know the specifics of Timothy's situation or relationship to the author of Hebrews. All that is clear is that the author hopes that Timothy will come to him quickly, and if so that he "with him" (μεθ' οὗ at the beginning of the clause) will be able to "see" (i.e., visit in person) the Christians to whom he writes.

13:24 Greet all your leaders as well as all the holy people of God. Those from Italy greet you (Ἀσπάσασθε πάντας τοὺς ἡγουμένους ὑμῶν καὶ πάντας τοὺς ἁγίους. ἀσπάζονται ὑμᾶς οἱ ἀπὸ τῆς Ἰταλίας). As I note above, a request to greet others and the passing on of greetings from others are typical elements in New Testament letter closings. What is not always featured is the focus on "leaders" (ἡγουμένους) that we find here. The author has stressed the importance of recognizing and paying heed to leaders (13:7, 17), so his specific greeting here is probably a last-minute further endorsement of their leadership role. I have translated the common word for Christians, τοὺς ἁγίους, as "the holy people of God" in order to bring out the biblical-theological connotations of the word as well as to avoid a misunderstanding that can easily arise from our usual translation "saints." Note NIV, "the Lord's people"; CEB, "God's holy people."

In addition to requesting that his readers pass on his greetings, the author also passes on greetings from another group: "those from Italy" (οἱ ἀπὸ τῆς Ἰταλίας). "Italy" occurs only three other times in the New Testament. In Acts 18:2, we learn that Aquila and Priscilla had come "from Italy"; and in Acts 27:1, 6, Paul and his companions prepare to "sail for Italy" (the word "Italian" also occurs once [Acts 10:1]). The word often referred to the center and capital of Italy, Rome.[23] The phrase here is ambiguous as to what it implies about the people identified in this way. Is the author implying that "people who are now located in Italy send you greetings" (with the possible implication that the author therefore writes from Italy)? Or is he suggesting that "people who have come from Italy [but are now at the place from which the author writes] send you greetings"? Most interpreters think the latter reading is a bit more likely—and, if so, it may provide a clue to the destination of the letter, since the particular mention of "people from Italy" could naturally suggest that the believers whom the author addresses are also in Italy (perhaps specifically in Rome).[24] As with so many other issues relating to the background of this letter, however, we cannot be certain of this reading.

13:25 Grace be with all of you (ἡ χάρις μετὰ πάντων ὑμῶν). A "grace wish" is a standard component of Paul's letter closings (Rom 16:20b; 1 Cor 16:23; 2 Cor 13:14; Gal 6:18; Eph 6:24; Phil 4:23; Col 4:18c; 1 Thess 5:28; 2 Thess 3:18; 1 Tim 6:21b; 2 Tim 4:22b; Titus 3:15b; Phlm 25). The language was therefore somewhat standardized, but this should not take away from its significance. "Grace" is not a particularly prominent word in Hebrews (2:9; 4:16 [twice]; 10:29; 12:15; 13:9; cf. 12:28), but the author uses it often enough to show that, with Paul and other New Testament authors, he views "grace," the free and loving initiative of God that establishes the pattern and context in which we now live, as basic to what it means to be and live as a Christian.

---

23. See, e.g., Donald A. D. Thorsen, "Italy," *ABD* 3:579.
24. See, e.g., Attridge, *Hebrews*, 410; Lane, *Hebrews*, 2:571; Ellingworth, *Hebrews*, 735–36. See also the introduction, pp. 5–6.

Theology in Application

The words of verses 20–21 are familiar to many of us. We may not be able to identify the source, but we have heard them used as the doxology at the end of church services. This is an entirely appropriate use of this text. However, the doxology is embedded in the particular "word of exhortation" we call Hebrews. In its original context, it not only closes off the argument on a majestic note, but it also touches on many of the key themes of the letter. Briefly:

God is the source of all the blessing we enjoy.

Christ, raised from the dead and installed in the heavenly realm, is the one through whom God acts. The author stresses this point by referring to Jesus twice in this brief doxology: as the one "brought up from the dead" in verse 20 and as the one through whom God acts in verse 21.

Among his many roles in Hebrews, Jesus is a "pioneer" (2:10; 12:2), the one who leads his people, as "the great shepherd of the sheep."

All that God accomplishes through this great shepherd is done in the context of a new covenant, a covenant that through divine enablement provides for the full and final forgiveness of sins that the old covenant could not secure.

The efficacy of the new covenant rests on the once-for-all sacrifice of Jesus, whose shed blood fills up and brings to a conclusion the sacrificial rites of the Old Testament.

All of these great acts of God through his Son, our high priest, have a practical end: to "equip" God's people to become the kind of people who can carry out God's will.

All this is ultimately, however, not about us—it is about God, to whom is due "glory forever." And, indeed, "Amen!"

Some Theological Emphases in Hebrews

Hebrews, like every other New Testament book, is written in particular circumstances for particular purposes. These purposes are not to impart theological knowledge per se; theology in Hebrews is very much in service of the practical message the author seeks to convey. We are therefore unable to describe in general "the theology of Hebrews"—that is, how the author might have summarized his beliefs were he writing his own "confession of faith" apart from specific circumstances. The best we can do is summarize some of the key theological emphases that come to expression in this "sermon within a letter."

Such a summary must respect the author's own way of conceptualizing and organizing his theological teaching. It would obviously distort the author's teaching were we to seek to squeeze his teaching into a framework alien to his own way of thinking. Avoiding this error might, then, suggest that we use Hebrews's own language as the hooks on which to hang his theological teaching—for example, "rest," "high priest," "sanctuary," etc. And some of these terms are, indeed, appropriate as labels to organize the author's theology. Yet any summary of the theology of Hebrews must also be attentive to the location of this letter within the canon of Scripture and seek to integrate the teaching of this book with the later formulations of the church. As *Christian* interpreters, we necessarily approach Hebrews with certain presupposed commitments—that Scripture is ultimately a unity that speaks, though with diverse tones, in one voice and that the teaching of scriptural books has valid connections with the confessional teaching of the early church. Recognizing these competing realities, I have organized my overview of the theological emphases of Hebrews within traditional theological categories at the same time as I try to let the author have his own voice in what he ways about these categories.

Salvation History

Scholars agree that any fair interpretation of the theology of the New Testament must begin by recognizing the salvation-historical framework within which the early

Christians formulated their thinking. Systematic categories, while fair to use ultimately to organize their theological teaching, were not their own framework. Rather, they saw themselves enmeshed in a history of God's redemptive activity extending from the life of Israel into their own time. Specifically, they viewed the events of Jesus's death, resurrection, and the gift of the Spirit as marking the beginning of the "last days," with a second coming of Christ expected to culminate those last days. This inaugurated-eschatology framework is evident in Hebrews. Our author begins by celebrating the fact that God has now spoken to his people "in these last days" (1:2). This focus on the "already" of redemption is reflected elsewhere, as he speaks of the "good things" that are now already here (9:11; cf. also, perhaps, 10:1). The "not yet" side of eschatology is also clear enough: Christ will "appear a second time . . . to bring salvation to those who are waiting for him" (9:28) on the day that is approaching (10:25). Psalm 110:1, a key verse for the author, summarizes his eschatological perspective: Jesus has already sat down at the right hand of the Father, initiating the new era (e.g., 1:13; 8:1), but he awaits the day when all his enemies will be "made his footstool" (10:13).

The author's view of the covenants and the law fit within this salvation-historical scheme. The covenant that God made with the people of Israel belongs to the old era; it is "obsolete and outdated" and "will soon disappear" (8:13). God has instituted a new covenant with his people, in fulfillment of Jeremiah 31:31–34 (8:7–12; 10:15–17; see also 7:22; 9:15; 10:29; 12:24; 13:20). The law of Moses, our author explains, is inextricably tied to this old covenant and to the priesthood that it institutes (7:11). Although our author does not develop the point, the writing of the law on the heart predicted by Jeremiah (8:10; 10:16) would appear to mean that the old-covenant law is no longer binding on the new-covenant people of God (e.g., 7:19; 10:1). The note of discontinuity that our author sounds in these texts cannot be missed: there is some degree of what is today called *supersessionism* in his theology. Yet his respect for the Old Testament and its continued application to the people of God warns us against extending this discontinuity to all aspects of the Old Testament. There is continuity as well as discontinuity in our author's conception of salvation history.

The author's basic message to his readers takes form against this salvation-historical background. They have enjoyed the inauguration of the new age, experiencing the full and final forgiveness of sins that their high priest has provided for them. Yet they have not yet attained the culmination of their experience; ultimate "rest" (3:7–4:11), the "city that is to come" (13:14), and final salvation (9:28) are promised by God but will be attained only by those who persevere in faith to the end (3:6, 14). The key word "better" (used eleven times in the letter) captures this argument, as the author repeatedly urges his readers to give careful attention to the new salvation-historical realities that the coming of Christ has inaugurated.

Vertical Typology and the Importance of the Unseen Realm

In the New Testament generally, what we call typology functions within this salvation-historical framework: what is hidden or hinted at in the Old Testament "type" becomes clear when the New Testament "antitype" appears. Typology functions in a horizontal zone. This horizontal focus is certainly not absent in Hebrews, as when the author describes the law as "only a shadow of the good things that are coming" (10:1). Likewise, the arrangement of the Old Testament sanctuary acts as a parable or illustration of what is necessary to draw near to God, with application to the New Testament work of Christ (9:9).

Distinctive to Hebrews, however, is the addition of a vertical element to this typological scheme, seen most clearly in the author's claim that the earthly tabernacle was constructed according to the pattern that God showed to Moses on the mountain (8:5). As I note in my commentary on the relevant passages, it is not completely clear what the author means by this: Did God show Moses a "blueprint" for the tabernacle? Or was there an actual tabernacle structure in the heavenly realm? The latter is, perhaps, a bit more likely in light of the way Jewish apocalyptic regularly portrays a temple in the heavenly realm (see also Revelation). It is this heavenly tabernacle that Jesus entered to perform his high-priestly ministry, "the greater and more perfect tabernacle that is not made with human hands, that is to say, is not a part of this creation" (9:11). This language, along with texts that appear to disparage this world and to locate true realities in the heavenly realm (1:11–12; 12:27–28), has led many interpreters to detect in Hebrews a Middle Platonic way of thinking about cosmology. The Middle Platonists in Hebrews's time inherited a cosmology according to which material realities were insubstantial and ephemeral, with true realities located in an unseen spiritual realm. Other interpreters have reacted strongly against this claim, denying any real influence from Middle Platonism on our author's thought. The truth lies somewhere in between, though closer to the latter view. The generally Platonic way of looking at reality had an influence on various forms of ancient thinking—including, for instance, Jewish apocalypticism. Probably, then, any Platonic influence on Hebrews—which is minimal—comes via the author's indebtedness to this apocalyptic way of thinking.

Whatever its source, however, there is no question that the author locates ultimate reality in the heavenly realm. Faith, the author repeatedly points out in chapter 11, involves "assurance about what we do not see" (11:1). It would be natural to conclude, then, that the "kingdom" the author looks forward to is an entirely spiritual reality, with no material or earthly aspect (see 12:27–28). I think, however, that this is an overinterpretation of this passage (and others). The author, to be sure, envisages an eternal kingdom that has a thoroughly heavenly quality. But, in light of the broad biblical expectation of a "new heaven and new earth," where redeemed humans will live in resurrected bodies in communion with the resurrected Christ, this kingdom should not be viewed as purely spiritual.

The Old Testament

The author opens his sermon by highlighting the vital significance of God's ultimate "speaking" in and through his Son (1:1–2), a point he uses to exhort his readers to careful and reverent "listening" (2:1–3; 12:25). However, while God's Old Testament revelation, which comes to his people via prophets (1:1) and angels (2:1), does not have the ultimacy that his New Testament word has, it would be a serious misunderstanding to think the author in any way disparages the Old Testament—indeed, it is basic to his argument. He quotes from it around thirty-five times, with over half of the quotations coming from Psalms. His quotations regularly agree with the Old Greek (which morphed later into the Septuagint); and, as we note below, the author gives every evidence of being a careful and creative interpreter of Scripture. Three aspects of the author's view of Scripture are particularly striking.

First, in place of the "it is written" formula so familiar in other parts of the New Testament, the author regularly introduces his quotations with the language of speaking. Second, those who speak the words of Scripture are God (1:5a, 6, 7, 8, 10, 13a; 4:3, 4, 6, 7; 5:5, 6; 6:13–14; 7:21; 8:8; 10:30; 12:26; 13:5), the Spirit (3:7; 10:15), and Christ himself (2:12–13; 10:5). Third, the author reflects his conviction that the word of God is "living and active" by often using the present tense in his introductory formulas: not "God spoke" but "God speaks" or "is speaking." The author views Scripture as addressing the people of God of his own time. This does not mean the author thoroughly "de-historicizes" Scripture. He knows that the warning about entering God's "rest" (Ps 95:7–11) had its background in the wilderness wandering of the Israelites (3:16–18) and that it came long after God's original "rest" (Gen 2:2; see 4:3–4, 7); he knows the history of the promise given to Abraham (6:13–14); he refers to the narrative context of the Melchizedek story (Gen 14:18–20; see 7:4–10); he notes that Exodus 25:40 (8:5) was a warning to Moses; and, of course, he goes into great detail in describing the Old Testament heroes of the faith (ch. 11).

Of course, the author does not exegete Scripture as a modern interpreter would do—he reads it in light of its ultimate meaning given in and through Christ. At the same time, he gives little evidence of being influenced in his interpretations by other Jewish interpreters of his day—his attention appears to be riveted on the text itself.

God

As is the case with most New Testament books, Hebrews does not set out to provide direct teaching about the nature of God. The author assumes the reality of God and balances in typical New Testament fashion the majesty of God with the reality of God's intervention in our world. On the one hand, then, God is "the Majesty in heaven" (8:1), whose appearance at Sinai was accompanied by terrifying phenomena (12:18–21, 29), and who breaks out in judgment against his people's sin (3:17–18; 10:27–31). Yet God also graciously stoops down to involve himself with this world. He is its creator (11:3); he enters into a particular relationship with the people of Israel (6:13–15; 9:18–21); he makes and keeps promises to that people (6:10, 13–20; 10:23; 13:5–6), rewarding those who exhibit faith (11:6) and acknowledging that he is their God (11:16). Indeed, he treats his people like his own children, disciplining them for their good (12:5–11). Moreover, he speaks to them in the words of Scripture (4:3, 7; 5:5–6; 7:21; 8:8–12; 12:26; 13:5). Faith in this God is part of the "elementary teaching" (6:1).

Many interpreters, wanting, appropriately, to recognize the author's place at the very beginning of the church era, deny that the author can be seen as providing fodder for later theological developments. Of course, the author does not engage in philosophical speculation about the nature of God. However, his clear locating of Christ within the divine identity at least takes some initial steps toward the later Chalcedonian definition of the Trinity. In keeping with the New Testament as a whole, the author is clearer about what we might call *Binitarianism* than *Trinitarianism*. Yet his association of the Spirit, along with the Father and the Son, in the speaking of Scripture (see below) might at least gesture toward a more robust Trinitarian understanding.

The Spirit

The Holy Spirit is not prominent in Hebrews—only six (or possibly seven)[1] references and no developed teaching. The little our author does say, however, jives generally with other New Testament teaching. Thus, the Spirit is active in testifying, by means of miracles and other signs, to the reality of God's work in Christ (2:4). Possession of the Spirit is a key marker of Christian identity (6:4; see 10:29). The only other role for the Spirit in Hebrews is as one of the "speakers" of Scripture (3:7; 10:15; cf. 9:8).

---

1. The reference to the "eternal spirit" in 9:14 is debated. Many think the author has in view the Holy Spirit; I have argued for a reference to Jesus's own eternal spirit (see comments there).

The Person of Christ

Teaching about Jesus is central to the argument of Hebrews, and it is clearly on this topic that the author makes his most important theological contribution. The author uses at least thirteen names and titles of Christ. Many of them are typical of New Testament teaching—"Jesus," "Christ," "Jesus Christ," "Lord," "Son"/"Son of God," "heir," "shepherd," "God," "mediator"—but some of them are distinctive—"pioneer," "forerunner," "sanctifier," "apostle," "guarantor," and "priest"/"high priest." Several of these deserve some comment.

The name "Jesus," used absolutely, occurs eight times, often in emphatic position (2:9; 3:1; 6:20; 7:22; 10:19; 12:2, 24; 13:12). The name, as we might expect, often focuses on Jesus in his humanity, referring to his suffering and death and to his role as our leader and forerunner. Moving beyond the name per se, we might add here that the author goes out of his way to indicate the full humanity of Jesus. He was "made like [us], fully human in every way" (2:17) and, as a result, has been "tempted"/"tested" in every way as we are (4:15; see 2:18). During his time on earth, he experienced the deepest level of testing, during which he cried out to God in fervent prayer (5:7–8).

A well-known christological point in Hebrews is the author's combination of some of the strongest assertions of Jesus's full humanity alongside claims of deity. In one of only a few New Testament passages where this occurs, the author calls Jesus "God" (1:8), a status also indicated by his being "the radiance of God's glory and the exact representation of his being" (1:3). He was instrumental in bringing the world into being (1:2, 10; cf. 3:3–4), and is worshiped by angels (1:6). He shares with God the status of "remaining" (1:12; 13:8), of having an eternal nature that uniquely qualifies him to act as our high priest (7:16; 9:14).

Some of the titles the author uses for Jesus do not fall neatly on one side of the divine/human interface. Two of these that allude to a central idea in Hebrews are "pioneer" (2:10; 12:2) and "forerunner" (6:20), which picture Jesus as the one who blazes a trail for others to follow. Christians are pictured as pilgrims traveling a potentially dangerous path but who have the assurance that Jesus has gone before us, preparing the way.

The two most important titles in Hebrews are "Son"/"Son of God" (twelve occurrences) and "priest"/"high priest" (sixteen occurrences). The places where these titles occur signal one of the fundamental movements in the letter: from Jesus as "Son" (1:5a, 5b; 3:6; 5:5, 8) to Jesus as "priest"/"high priest" (2:17; 3:1; 4:14, 15; 5:1, 5, 6, 10; 6:20; 7:15, 17, 21, 26; 8:1; 9:11; 10:21). The hinge of this sequence comes in 5:5–6, via two Old Testament quotations: Psalm 2:7—"you are my Son; today I have become your Father"—and Psalm 110:4—"you are a priest forever, in the order of

Melchizedek." The eternal Son, God himself, is also, the author emphasizes, a "priest forever." Jesus is, of course, frequently referred to as the Son in the New Testament, with the title often connoting his unique intimate relationship with the Father. Only in Hebrews, however, is Jesus called a "priest" or "high priest" (although other NT texts occasionally use priestly language to depict Christ's person and work). The author has almost certainly derived his teaching about Jesus as a priest from Psalm 110:4. Psalm 110:1 is both the most-quoted Old Testament verse in the New and fundamental to the author's whole argument. We can well imagine, then, that he would have read further in this psalm, arriving at verse 4 and concluding that this verse also must be characterizing Jesus. From there he would then naturally have inquired about the point of referring to Melchizedek—leading him to the only other Old Testament text that mentions this figure, Genesis 14:18–20.

This focused and intense concentration on the Old Testament marks the author's argument in general, so it is no surprise to find him in chapter 7 drawing out the implications of these two key texts for the nature of Jesus and his ministry (Gen 14 is prominent in vv. 1–10; Ps 110:4 in vv. 11–28). The author pays careful attention to what the Genesis 14 passage says about Melchizedek—as well as what the passage does *not* say. Following the Jewish interpretive principle that "what is not in Scripture is not in reality," the author notes that the text says nothing about Melchizedek's ancestry, nor about the end of his life (7:3). From these omissions, he concludes that Melchizedek's priesthood was not based on his ancestry, nor does his priesthood have any end. He is thus made, in Scripture, to resemble the Son of God. The author draws out these points further in 7:11–28. Jesus, descended from Judah, could not be a priest on the basis of ancestry; rather, he is a priest on the basis of divine appointment, as the psalm verse indicates (7:13–15). Further, the "forever" language of Psalm 110:4 further emphasizes that Jesus is a high priest whose ministry continues into eternity—a point the author repeatedly emphasizes to contrast Jesus with the Levitical priests, whose deaths required a constant change in the priestly cadre (7:23–24).

The Work of Christ

The identification of Jesus as high priest flows seamlessly into the author's conception of Christ's work, which is dominated by cultic categories. While cultic language certainly occurs elsewhere in the New Testament to characterize Christ's work on our behalf, it does not dominate as it does in Hebrews. The author frequently uses the Day of Atonement ritual in Leviticus 16 as his backdrop for explicating Christ's sacrificial work. It is important to note, however, that Leviticus 16 is not the only passage our author has in view. He clearly makes allusion to other cultic texts in the Old Testament in building his picture of Jesus's sacrificial work.

Particularly distinctive to our author's presentation of this work is his focus on Christ's exaltation and session at the right hand of the Father as basic to this work. Psalm 110:1, as we have noted, plays a critical role in the argument of the book. Even more striking, in some ways, is what our author does *not* say. He mentions the cross only once, and attributes to it no redemptive significance (12:2). Likewise, Jesus's resurrection is mentioned only once, at the end of the letter, and again without explicit redemptive significance (13:20). The paucity of references to death and resurrection is striking when contrasted with Paul, who repeatedly makes these two events the fundamental bases for the work of Christ in securing salvation. This focus on exaltation to the relative exclusion of cross and resurrection has led some interpreters to view atonement in Hebrews as wholly bound up with the exalted Jesus's entrance into the heavenly realm and his offering of himself there as a sacrifice. This picture is reinforced, it is argued, by Leviticus 16, where the manipulation of the blood after the victims are slaughtered is given great attention.

Relative to other New Testament authors, the author of Hebrews no doubt focuses considerable attention on the exaltation as a crucial step in securing the forgiveness of sins. However, it is going too far to suggest that the author does not view Jesus's death as having atoning significance. In chapter 2, for instance, he reminds us that Jesus tasted death for everyone (2:9); that God made "the pioneer of their salvation perfect through what he suffered" (2:10); and that the Son became fully human so that "by his death he might break the power of him who holds the power of death—that is, the devil—and free those who all their lives were held in slavery by their fear of death" (2:14–15). References to blood (9:14, 18–22; 10:29; 12:24; 13:12) may allude to the presentation of blood after the death of the victim, but they appear to include death also (see 9:16–17 in comparison with 9:18–22; and the move from "blood" to "suffered" in 9:25–26). Similarly, references to Jesus's sacrifice or offering probably include reference to his death (7:27; 8:3; 9:25, 28; 10:10, 12, 14).

Faced with this data, some interpreters think that language of Jesus "entering" the heavenly realm or "moving through the heavens" (4:14; cf. 9:11) is metaphorical, a way of portraying the work on the cross. But it makes better sense of all the data in Hebrews to think that our author operates with a two-stage understanding of atonement. The death of Jesus on the cross is the essential first step and, in many ways, the decisive moment, since all else flows from that act. But the completion of the atoning act takes place once the exalted Jesus enters the heavenly sanctuary with his blood. We should, then, not view Hebrews's presentation of the work of Christ as in any way in competition with, for example, Paul's focus on death and resurrection. Rather, Hebrews complements the usual New Testament focus, reminding us that the work of atonement is final and decisive precisely because it is in the very presence of God that the ultimate, "once-for-all" sacrifice is offered.

Reference to the language "once for all" brings to our attention another emphasis in Hebrews's presentation of Christ's work. Jesus's sacrifice takes place "once" or "once for all" (7:27; 9:12, 26, 28; 10:10)—in contrast to the repeated old-covenant sacrifices—and procures for worshipers what we might call "full and final forgiveness," which the author refers to in several ways: cleansing the conscience (9:14 [contrast 9:9]; 10:2, 22), taking away sins (9:28; 10:11–12 [contrast 10:4]), and perfection (10:14; 11:40; 12:23 [contrast 9:9; 10:2]).

The Pilgrimage of the Christian

One of the most evocative and significant of the Old Testament images that the author uses to engage his readers is the wilderness wandering of the people of Israel. While "wilderness wandering" is the traditional way of referring to the generation of Israelites (and the alliteration works nicely), it might be better, from the author's perspective, to refer to the "pilgrimage" of the Israelites. While ultimately condemned to "wander," God's original intention for them had been to move quickly from their bondage in Egypt, through the wilderness, and on to the promised land. This imagery provides a kind of template for the author's address of his readers. They also have been rescued from slavery (to sin and death; see 2:14–15); they too are destined for a blessed "rest"; and they too face a moment of testing. For the readers, this testing takes the form of persecution (10:32–34; 12:4–5). Their goal is not a terrestrial possession but an eternal kingdom (12:28). The author is clearly worried that his audience is flagging in their zeal to attain this ultimate goal (e.g., 2:1–2) which, if left unchecked, will lead to renouncing their faith altogether (6:4–6; 10:26–31).

Given this situation, the author is laser focused in his sermon on getting the believers he addresses moving again, seeking to renew their commitment to finish their pilgrimage. Negatively, the author famously warns his audience about the danger of "falling away" (6:4–8; 10:26–31). These warnings are some of the most controversial passages in Hebrews, generating endless discussion and diverse interpretations. As I suggest in my comments on these passages, a neat conclusion that does justice to these texts and dovetails with larger biblical teaching about perseverance eludes us. I conclude that these texts do not necessarily overturn the "eternal security" that other New Testament passages appear to teach once we recognize the author's rhetorical strategy. However, it is also important to respect the strength of these texts and allow them to have their intended effect of motivating us to renewed zeal for Christ.

Positively, the author closes his sermon by stressing two basic virtues these pilgrims need as they move down the road of discipleship: faith (10:37–39; ch. 11) and perseverance (10:36; 12:1–14). Faith, for the author, has both a forward look (confidence in what has been promised) and an upward look (assurance of what is now unseen, 11:1; these are fleshed out in specific examples throughout ch. 11).

Some interpreters think the author operates with a fundamentally different notion of faith than what we find, for instance, in Paul. For example, the author never refers to faith "in Christ" specifically, and only once does he refer to faith in God (6:1). Absent also is any contrast between faith and "works." However, while he is focused on a different issue than Paul often is, their basic conceptions of faith are similar. If faith in Paul is often explicitly faith in God or Christ, faith in Hebrews is oriented toward a firm grasp on the promises of God and toward a conviction about the unseen spritual realm. Both view faith as the fundamental disposition required to please God and to reach the end of our pilgrimage.

Scripture Index

Genesis

1 . . . . 73, 75
1–2 404
1:26 . . . . 73, 76
1:26–28 501
1:28 73
2 . . . . 130, 131
2:2 . . . 57, 58, 124, 125, 128, 129, 130, 131, 134, 135, 139, 536
2:3 129
3:17 198
3:17–18 197
3:18 197
4 404
4:2b–5 412
4:4b 413
4:10b 413
5 414
5:21–24 . . . . 404, 413, 414
5:22 414
5:24 . . . . 407, 414
6–9 404
6:4, 6 44
6:6–7 415
6:9 451
6:13 415
6:17 415
6:18 359
7:4 415
9:3 333
11:30 428
12 229
12–25 404
12:1 425
12:1–3 214
12:3 230
13 229
14 . . . . . 229, 231, 233, 236, 238, 240, 243, 539
14:17 233
14:17–20 . . . . . 17, 225, 228, 243, 264
14:17–24 . . . . 228, 229
14:18 233
14:18–20 . . . . . . 57, 58, 225, 226, 227, 240, 242, 253, 536, 539
14:19 233
14:20 233
14:20b 234
14:22 233
15:4–20 214
15:6 401
16:2 428
17:7 359
17:1–8 214
17:17 428
17:19, 21 434
18:1–15 509
18:10–15 428
18:11, 13 428
21:1–7 427
21:2, 5, 7 428
21:12 . . . . 424, 434
22 434
22:1 433
22:2 434
22:5 434
22:16 214
22:16–17 . . . . 210, 213
22:16–18 214
22:17 . . . . 211, 217
22:17a 430
23:4 . . . . 426, 431
25–26 404
25:27–34 481
25:29 482
26:4 430
26:24 87
26:34 481
27–49 404
27:27–40 435
27:30–41 482
27:36 482
27:39–40 435
28:4, 13 87
28:15 511
32:10 436
32:12 430
35:11 237
37:22 333
43:19 152
47:31 436
48:8–22 436
49:4 510
49:29–32 437
50 404
50:4–14 437
50:24–25 436

Exodus

1–13 404
1:22 443
2:1–4 443
2:2b 443

2:5–10....444	24:1–18....331	34:29–35....98
2:11....443, 444	24:2....255	34:32....152
2:11–12....444	24:3a....331	36:8–38:41....302
2:11–15....446	24:5....331	37:1–5....304
2:14–15....445	24:6....447	37:6–9....304
2:14b–15....445	24:7....332	37:10–16....302
3:6....433	24:8....315, 332, 528	37:17–24....302
3:14....415	24:17....491	37:25–28....303
3:15....433	25....282, 303	39:12....53
3:16....433	25–30....302	40:5....303
4–14....100, 115	25:9....277–78, 281	40:9–10....331
4:14....249	25:10–16....304	40:26....303
4:22....46	25:16....304	
4:22–23....494	25:17–22....304	**Leviticus**
4:25–29....249	25:21....304	1:3–9....343
6:4....359	25:23–29....302	1:5, 13....276
10:21....490	25:30....302	3:2–5....343
12:1–30....446	25:31–40....302	3:6–11....343
12:7....447	25:40....57, 273, 277, 278, 280, 281, 536	3:12–16....343
12:11....436		4:3–12....160, 343
12:22....331, 447	26:28....143	4:7....333
12:23....447	26:30....278	4:12....517
12:31–14:31....446, 447	26:31–37....303	4:13....306
14....404	26:33....221	4:15–18....343
14:10–14....447	26:33–35....302	4:18....333
14:21....447	27:8....278	4:21....517
14:22....447	27:20–30:38....303	4:22–26....343
14:31....401, 418	28:1....160	4:25....333
15:7....282	28:1–5....249	4:27–31....343
16:4....192	29:4....381	4:30....333
16:9....152	29:12....333	4:34....333
16:33–34....304	29:21....381, 447	5:18....306
17:1–7....109	29:38–41....268	6:4....517
19....490	30:1–6....303	7:3, 11, 12, 13....276
19:12–13....487, 490, 491	30:6....303	8–9....249
19:16....491	30:10....303	8:1–36....160
19:18....491, 497	31:10....53	8:6....381
19:22....255	32:13....215, 426, 430	8:15....332
20:14–15....510	32:32....494	8:17....517
20:21....491	33:1....87	8:19....332
21:12–14....385	33:7–10....517	8:24....332
24....332	34:7....354	8:30....381
24:1–2....331	34:9....354	8:33....81

9:7 . . . . 152, 160	**Numbers**	15:24–31 385
9:7–10 343	1:47–53 237	15:30–31 385
9:11 517	1:50 237	16:22 476
9:18 276	3:10 160	17:5 152
10:4, 5 517	3:28 274	17:7 [LXX 17:22] 304
10:17 . . . . 343, 354	3:28–38 . . . . 274, 307	17:10 [LXX 17:25] 304
11 309	3:31 274	18:3, 4, 22 152
11:44–45 477	3:32 274	18:26–28 237
13:46 517	3:38 274	19 309
14:3 517	4:12, 26 53	19:6 331
14:4, 6 331	5:15 353	19:9 324
14:19–20 343	6:3 388	19:1–10 324
14:49, 51–52 331	7 322	19:19 331
15 309	7:5 53	20:1–21 109
16 . . . . 304, 305, 343, 539, 540	8:6 159	20:12 401
16:2 221	11:20 119	23:18–20 217
16:3 322	12–14 92	24:17 250
16:6 . . . . 160, 305, 322	12:7 . . . . 94, 97, 100, 101, 105	28:3–8 268
16:6–16 267	13:2 82	31:35 510
16:11 . . . . 160, 305, 322	13:3 82	32:13 . . . . 109, 118
16:12 221	13:20 221	35:25 . . . . 217, 379
16:14 322	13:26–14:35 . . . . 109, 111, 118	35:26 218
16:15 322	13:30 111	35:28 379
16:15b–16 335	14 . . . . 114, 118, 119	35:33 333
16:16 . . . . 335, 385	14:2 111	**Deuteronomy**
16:18 322	14:4 82	1:8 87
16:18–19 335	14:7b–8 127	1:10 430
16:19 517	14:9 . . . . 111, 115	1:32 418
16:27 . . . . 322, 517	14:11 . . . . 111, 120	2:7 118
16:30 . . . . 35, 310	14:18 324	3:20 . . . . 119, 120, 131
16:32 81	14:21 114	4:10 494
16:33 335	14:22–23 118	4:11 . . . . 152, 490, 491, 492
16:34 . . . . 305, 310	14:28 114	4:12 491
17:3 527	14:29–30 119	4:24 . . . . 488, 500
17:11 323	14:30 111	4:31 200
20:24 436	14:40 119	4:34 66
21:10 379	14:41–43 119	4:36 491
21:17 152	14:33 118	4:42 218
21:21, 23 . . . . 152, 255	14:34 118	5:22 491
22:3 152	14:40 119	5:22–28 491
24:13–16 387	14:43 142	5:23 . . . . 152, 491
24:14, 23 517	14:43b 119	5:25 491

6:6 292
6:22 66
8:2, 4 118
8:10 238
9:10 494
9:19 . . . . 487, 492
9:23 418
9:23–24 119
10:1–5 304
11:11 197
11:18 292
11:26–28 197
12:9 . . . . 119, 120, 131
12:10 . . . . 119, 120, 131
14 309
14:11 120
17:2–7 387
17:14–20 358
18:15 445
19:4 385
19:5 218
19:10 333
21:7 333
25:19 . . . . 119, 120, 131
28:62 430
29:5 118
29:17 (LXX) 481
29:18 481
29:18–21 481
29:17–20 (LXX) 481
29:18–28 198–99
29:27 382
30:5–6 . . . ., 11–14 292
31:6 . . . . 504, 511, 512
31:27 118
32 . . . . 46, 47, 389
32:3 36
32:4 417
32:14 324
32:35 . . . . 374, 389
32:35a 389
32:36 389
32:43 . . . . 41, 46, 47
32:46 62
33:2 63

Joshua
1:5 511
1:13 119
1:15 . . . . 119, 130, 131
2 . . . . 405, 448
2:9–11 448
6 . . . . 405, 448
7:1 199
10:1, 3 234
18:1 275
20:9 218
21:44 133
22:4 133
22:24 164
23:1 133
23:7 133
23:12–13 133

Judges
3:16 142
4–5 454
4:8 454
5:4–5 497
5:5 490
6:2 459
7 454
7–8 454
8:22–27 454
11:29–40 454
13–15 454
14:5–6 456
15 454
15:18 389
21:11, 12 510

Ruth
3:13

1 Samuel
1–16 454
2:35 97
3:19–20 455
12:11 454
13:6 459
14:36 132
15:22 357
16–2 Sam 24 454
17:34–37 456
19:20 455
20:27 513
23:13, 25, 29 459
25:1 459
25:31 333
26:1 459
26:23 401

2 Samuel
5:7 493
6:17 275
7:4–16 45
7:9 45
7:13 43
7:13–14 . . . . 43, 46
7:14 . . . . 41, 45, 49
7:16 49
8:15 455
14:22 238
15:4 216
15:20 513
22:3 84
24:12–14 389
24:16 447

1 Kings
1:47 238
2:10 130
2:31 333
6:22 303
8:1 493
8:9 304
8:56 130
8:63 330
17:17–24 456
18:4 459

18:28....333	**Esther**	22:18....83
19:13....458	1:14	22:22....79, 83, 84, 355
19:19....458	**Job**	22:24....164
21:13, 22, 28....152	1:6....44	22:27....216
2 Kings	2:1....44	25:11....89
2:8....458	9:6....153, 407	29:1....44
2:13, 14....458	26:6....144	33:13–15....143
4:18–37....456	28:24....144	33:15....480
18:5....420	38:7....44	34:6....163
1 Chronicles	41:3 [LXX 40:27]....163	34:8....193
1:3....414	**Psalms**	34:14....480
5:1....510	2....32, 43, 51, 52	37:3....401
11:5....493	2:2....43, 44	37:29....426
16:1....275	2:6....43, 493	38:8 (LXX)....409
17:3–14....41	2:6–7....43	38:13 (LXX)....431
17:13....41	2:7....32, 38, 41, 43, 44, 45, 51, 157, 161, 162, 493, 538	39 (LXX)....355
17:19....36	2:8....216	39:2....194
21:9–13....389	2:8–9....52	39:7....409
28:2....130	2:9....49	39:12....431
29:11....36	7:5....388	40....355, 357, 358, 359, 360
2 Chronicles	7:6 (LXX)....378	40:5....358
5:2....493	8....16, 57, 58, 68, 69, 71, 72, 73, 74, 75, 76, 78, 86, 87	40:6....173, 358
5:10....304	8:4....73, 512	40:6–8....348, 356, 359
6:41....130	8:4–6 (8:5–7 LXX)....58, 70, 71, 72	40:6–8a....354
7:5....330	8:5....72, 74, 161	40:6a....358
19:9....401	8:6....72	40:6c....358
20:20....401	8:6a....75	40:7....358
24:14....53	8:7....68	40:7–8a....358
24:20–22....458	8:9....68	40:8....349
31:12....401	9:12, 17....200	40:9....358
36:19....293	11:6....386	42:9....200
Nehemiah	13:1....200	45....43, 48, 49
9:8....418	17:8 (LXX)....492, 497	45:6....43, 497
9:12....190	18:7....492, 497	45:6–7....43, 48
9:13....490	19:4....216	45:7....43, 49
9:15–17....119	21:9....386	46:4....427
9:19....190	22....164	46:5....497
9:19b–20....192	22:1....83	48:2....493
9:21....118	22:16....83	49:13 (LXX)....324
10:38–39....237		50:8–10....357
		50:13....324
		51:16–17....357
		56:4 (LXX)....388

57:3....388
57:5, 11....267
61:9....255
65:3....89
65:3b....89
68 (LXX)....445
68:8....497
69....445
69:7....396
69:9....396
69:10....396
69:19....396
69:20....396
72:28....255
74:2....493
74:8 (LXX)....494
74:19, 23....200
75:7....494
76:2....493
76:19....492, 497 (LXX)
75:3....153
77:9....200
77:18....492, 497
78:3–6....83
78:8....118, 121
78:8–64....121
78:11....36
78:24....192
78:37....418
78:38....89
79:5....386
79:9....89
81:1–16....121
81:5 (LXX)....497
82:5....497
89:7....44
89:20–29....46
89:35....218
89:50–51....445
93:1....46
94 (LXX)....108
94:1 (LXX)....133
94:7b–11 (LXX)....105

95....108, 109, 111, 113, 114, 115, 116, 117, 118, 119, 122, 125, 128, 129, 130, 131, 133, 141, 191, 248, 432, 455
95:7–8....57, 116, 124
95:7–11....57, 58, 536
95:7b....108
95:7b–11 105, 107, 111, 112, 121, 122, 133, 139
95:8....111, 118, 133
95:10....111, 114
95:11....119, 124, 125, 126, 128, 129, 130, 131
96:4 (LXX)....497
96:7 (LXX)....46
96:9–10....46
97:4....46, 497
97:7 46–47
98:1 (LXX)....497
99:1....497
101 (LXX)....50
102....50
102:24....43
102:25–27....43, 513
102:27....44
103:4 (LXX)....47
103:5....194
104:4....47, 53
104:30....194
105:6....87
105:28....118
105:39....190
105:40....192
106:7....118
106:13–33....121
106:24–27....121
106:33....118
106:24–26....119
106:43....118
108:4, 5....267
110....35, 51, 52, 161, 229, 240
110:1....35, 36, 38, 41, 42, 43, 45, 52, 69, 71, 72, 86, 161, 162, 229, 273, 274, 360, 361, 362, 365, 472, 493, 534, 539, 540

110:1b....362
110:2....436, 493
110:4....17, 35, 58, 157, 161, 162, 210, 218, 222, 225, 228–29, 231, 233, 235, 236, 240, 242, 243, 244, 245, 246, 247, 248, 249, 253, 256, 257, 258, 263, 264, 366, 538, 539
110:4a....218
110:13....45
113:4....267
116:8....163
116:10....401
117:6 (LXX)....512
118....512
118:6....512
118:6–7....504
118:22....84
119....174
125:1....500
132:8....130
132:13....493
132:14....130
134:14 (LXX)....389
135:9....66
135:14....389
137....427
141:6....255
143:9....218
144 (LXX)....88
144:3, 6....36
145....88
145:8....88
145:13....88, 218
148:14....255
149:6....142
150:2....36

Proverbs

3:11....474
3:11–12....465, 467, 474, 478–79
3:12 (LXX)....474
3:21....63
4:26....478, 480
4:27....480

Scripture Index

5:4 142
28:14 164

Isaiah

1:10–13 357
1:11 324
2:2–3 493
5 . . . . 196, 197
5:1–7 196
5:25 199
7:9 418
8:12 84
8:13 84
8:17 79
8:17c 84
8:18 . . . . 79, 493
8:18a 84
9:6 234
10:3 219
10:15–19 199
11:1 436
12:2 84
13:13 . . . . 199, 497
25:2 399
25:10 388
26 399
26:1 399
26:4 420
26:11 386
26:18 418
26:20 . . . . 393, 399
27:9 354
28:4 221
28:16 84
29:13 255
30:27 199
33:14 199
33:22 494
34:4 50–51
35:3 (LXX) 478
35:10 493
36:4–9 420
40:8 218
41:1, 5 255
41:8–10 87
42:25 199
43:10 418
44:4 63
44:28 521
45:17 166
45:23 . . . . 215, 218
49:15 200
50:4–5 173
51:2 430
51:11 493
52:8 493
52:13–53:12 340
53:3 518
53:12 340
54 427
55:11 142
59:20 493
60:14 493
61:6 275
63:11 528
63:11–12a 528
63:17 115
63:18 388
64:10 198
65:18 521
66:1 130
66:2–4 357
66:24 199

Jeremiah

3:14 493
4:4 . . . . 199, 386
7:21–24 357
8:16 497
8:19 493
11:1–10 292
14:9 200
17:4 199
17:7 420
20:2 457
21:12 199
22:1 292
22:5 215
22:9 292
22:10 431
23:5 . . . . 234, 250
23:20 31
25:14–31:44 291
25:19 31
26:20–23 458
27:43 (LXX) 478
28:29 497
29:26 457
30–31 (MT) 292
30:8–9 383
30:15 497
31 326
31:2 130
31:6 493
31:31 . . . . 97, 291
31:31–34 56
31:32 . . . . 87, 291
33:15 234
31:31 . . . . 291, 292, 309
31:31–34 . . . . 280, 286, 288, 290, 309, 381
31:32 291
31:33 . . . . 97, 261, 291, 292, 350, 355
31:33–34 534
31:33a 363
31:34 . . . . 291, 350
33:16 521
37–38 (LXX) 292
37:15 457
38 (LXX) 363
38:31 (LXX) 291
38:31–34 (LXX) 291
38:32 (LXX) 291
38:33 (LXX) 291
38:33a 363
38:33b 363
38:34b 363
38:34 (LXX) 291
39:37 382

46–51 291
50:4–5 292
50:5 493
50:34 130
50:43 478

Lamentations

1:8, 17 521
5:20 200
5:21 194

Ezekiel

1:15, 19 200
2:3, 5, 6, 7, 8 118
3:9, 26, 27 118
8:3, 16 221
10:3 221
10:9 200
14:13 194
14:14, 20 415
15:8 194
17:18, 19 256
18:24 194
19:5 409
20:27 194
22:4 194
22:21 386
36:24–32 192
36:25–27 381
38:19 386
39:18 322
40–48 . . . . 282, 521
40:17 221
40:23 221
40:27 221
40:28 221
40:34 221
40:44 221
41:3, 17 221
42:3 221
42:13 255
43:5 221
43:19 255
44:13 255
44:16 152
44:17 221
44:21 221
44:27 221
45:1–8 427
45:4 255
45:19 221
46:1 221
46:11 494

Daniel

2 . . . . (LXX) 306
2:20 36
2:40 497
3 456
4:22 216
6 456
6:7, 13 152
6:23 456
7:10 494
9:27 338
10:14 31
12:1 494
12:13 . . . . 306, 338

Hosea

2:13 494
2:16–23 383
3:5b 31
6:6 357
9:5 494
10:8 197
12:7 255
14:2b 519

Joel

1:15 383
2:1–2 383
2:10 497
2:31 383
2:28–32 192
3:1 521
3:16 497
3:17 493
4:16 (LXX) 497

Amos

2:10 118
5:25 118

Obadiah

15–17 383
17 493

Jonah

3:5 419
4:5 470

Micah

1:4 497
4:2 493

Nahum

1:5 497

Habakkuk

2:2–4 399
2:2–5 399
2:3 . . . . 393, 399, 400, 401
2:3–4 . . . . 399, 400
2:4 . . . . 393, 401, 409
2:4a 399
2:4b 399, 400
2:5 399
3:6 497

Zephaniah

1:18 386
3:16 478

Haggai

2:6 . . . . 488, 489, 497
2:6–7 497

Zechariah

2:15 218
3 134

Scripture Index

3:4 354
6:12–13 250
8:13 198
8:22–23 427
9:9–10 234
9:11 528

Malachi

1:7, 12 516

Matthew

1:1 250
1:1–17 240
1:5 448
2:2 250
2:6 512
2:9 250
2:12 . . . . .277, 496
2:16 359
2:19 436
2:22 . . . . .277, 496
3:1 319
3:4 458
3:7 180
3:8, 11 194
3:17 44
4:6 478
4:16 278
5:8 480
5:11–12 395
5:13 387
5:22 386
5:33–37 215
5:45 250
5:48 181
6:33 . . . . .5:11
7:6 387
7:11 324
7:13 402
7:22 384
8:2 436
9:4 143
9:13 357
9:18 436
10:15 384
10:25 324
11:3 401
11:10 98
11:22 384
11:28, 29 131
12:7 357
12:25 143
12:31–32 . . . . .208, 209
12:32 33
12:36 384
12:42 216
12:43 131
12:44 435
13:6 250
13:35 128
13:38 401
13:39, 40, 49 338
13:54, 57 431
15:4 436
15:11, 18, 20 324
15:32 473
16:17 85
16:28 181
17:1 340
17:17 529
17:3 340
18:9 386
18:16 . . . . .387, 469
18:27 529
19:8 115
20:28 327
21:9 401
21:21–22 460
21:25 180
21:42 84
22:15–40 52
22:25 436
22:32 433
22:43 108
22:41–46 52
23:15 401
23:16–22 215
23:18 214
23:23 237
23:35 413
23:39 401
24:15 274
24:32 . . . . .198, 435
24:33 198
24:36 384
24:37–38 415
25:24, 26 435
25:34 108
25:36 176
25:41 386
25:42–43 509
26:18 198
26:28 . . . . 291, 332, 528
26:29 384
26:45 131
26:55 268
26:64 52
26:65 469
27: 15, 17, 21, 26 529
27:35a 83
27:44 445
27:46 . . . . .83, 379
27:51 . . . . 221, 379, 497
28:7, 10 340
28:18 65
28:20 338

Mark

1:1 127
1:4 .180, 194
1:11 44
1:15 179
2:23–28 137
2:28 137
3:1–6 137
3:28–29 208
4:1–8 197
4:6 250
4:32 278

4:35....149	14:36....515	5:18, 24....478
5:7....233	14:41....131	5:32....194
6:1, 4....431	14:49....268	6:22–23....395
6:5....180	14:58....322	7:2....436
6:8....436	14:62....52	7:19, 20....401
6:21....153	14:63....469	7:29....180
6:25....201	14:72....395	8:5....387
6:31....131	15:6, 9, 11, 15....529	8:18....114
7:2....324, 379, 388	15:24....83	8:28....233
7:4....180, 309	15:32....445	9:27....191
7:5....324, 388	15:34....83	9:41....529
7:10....436	15:38....221, 379	9:47....87
7:15....324	16:2....250	10:6....131
7:18....324		10:12....384
7:19....515	**Luke**	10:31–32....237
7:20....324	1:1....202	11:13....324
7:23....324	1:6....309	11:24....131, 324, 435
8:3....473	1:32....233, 250	11:28....324
8:23....87, 180	1:33....45	11:31....216
9:1....191	1:35....233	11:36....191
9:2....340	1:39....201	11:42....237, 478
9:4....340	1:45....247	11:48....469
9:6....492	1:68....327	11:50....128
9:19....529	1:76....233	12:1....387, 494
9:48....436	1:78....250	12:6....200
10:5....115	1:79....278	12:51....319
10:27....189	2:3, 5....494	12:58....86
10:30....33	2:7....46	13:10–17....137
10:45....327	2:14....233	13:11....258
10:50....397	2:15....149	13:13....180, 478
11:21....395	2:25....415	15:7....194
11:30....180	2:26....277, 496	16:8....401
12:10....84	2:38....327	16:11....275
12:26....433	3:3....180, 194	17:24....384
12:35–37....52	3:8....194	17:26–27....415
12:36....108	3:22....44	17:31....384
13:25....497	3:36....415	18:12....237
13:28....198, 435	3:37....414	18:13....89
13:29....198	4:11....478	18:14b....74
13:32....384	4:23, 24....431	18:30....33
13:33....520	4:40....180	19:1....149
14:24....291, 332, 528	5:7....95	19:47....268
14:25....384	5:10....396	20:4....180

20:17....84
20:37....433
20:41–44....52
21:20....384
21:26....497
21:28....327, 384
21:30, 31....198
21:36....520
22:2....359
22:19....353, 395
22:20....75, 290, 528
22:26....512
22:29....329
22:42....515
22:53....268
22:69....52
23:4, 14....166
23:16....529
23:18....529
23:22....166, 529
23:25....529
23:32....359
23:34b....83
23:45....221, 379
24:18....426
24:21....327
24:25–27....65
24:34....340
24:37....495
24:39....83, 490, 495
24:46–47....65
24:47....194
24:51....340

John

1:1....142
1:1–18....27, 38
1:3....32, 50
1:9....190, 191, 275
1:12....201
1:15....401
1:17....192
1:19....237

1:27....401
2:1, 2....510
4:2....129
4:23....275
4:37....275
4:44....431
5:1–17....137
5:17b....129
5:28–29....181
6:4....198
6:32....275
6:39, 40, 44....384
6:51....75
6:53....103
6:54....384
6:63, 68....142
8:31....103
8:33....87
8:52....191
9:1–31....137
11:1....6
11:24....384
11:39....436
11:50–51....75
12:13....401
12:31....86
12:36....401
12:48....384
13:8b....103
13:10....381
13:15....136, 278
13:17....103
14:2....222
14:20....384
15....117
15:1....275
15:1–8....204
15:14....102, 103
16:21....396
16:23, 26....384
16:33....438
17:12....401, 402
17:24....128

18:36....468
18:39....529
19:10, 12....529
19:17–20....517
19:24....83
19:30....361
19:37....46
20:25....83
21:18....293

Acts

1:2....96
1:4....267
1:16....108
1:19....379
1:22....180
1:26....96
2:5....415
2:16–21....192
2:17....31
2:20....383
2:22....66, 193
2:23....359
2:29....436
2:30....31
2:33–34....52
2:38....179
2:42....396, 520
2:43....66
2:46, 47....268
3:13....433, 529
3:15....82
3:19....179
3:21–22....31
3:24....31
3:25....329
4:21, 23....529
4:25....108
4:25–26....44
4:30....66
4:31....101, 497
4:36....4, 401
5:4....218

5:12............................66	10:23..............................6	17:30........................179
5:15..........................278	10:28....................324, 388	17:31........................383
5:31.....................52, 194	10:37........................180	18:2........5, 6, 267, 377, 393, 530
5:33..........................359	10:38........................193	18:14........................529
5:36..........................359	11:8.....................324, 388	18:24...........................4
5:40..........................529	11:9..........................324	18:25........................180
6:6...........................180	11:18........................194	19:1..........................149
6:13..........................274	11:19........................396	19:3..........................180
6:13..........................469	11:26....................277, 496	19:4..................180, 194, 378
7 405	12:10........................149	19:5b–6......................180
7:2–8.........................421	13:3..........................180	19:9.....................115, 268
7:2–47........................446	13:6..........................149	19:11........................193
7:5...........................103	13:10........................401	19:12.........................86
7:6...........................426	13:15......................2, 529	19:16........................176
7:10..........................512	13:18........................118	19:21........................149
7:11..........................396	13:24.................180, 194, 376	19:24, 38....................427
7:15..........................436	13:33.........................44	19:40........................166
7:17..........................203	14:3..........................66	20:2..........................149
7:20..........................443	14:17........................129	20:4..........................529
7:24..........................444	14:18........................131	20:7..........................137
7:32.....................433, 492	14:24........................149	20:20........................401
7:35..........................327	14:26........................435	20:21....................179, 194
7:36......................66, 118	15:3..........................149	20:27........................401
7:38..............142, 174, 490, 494	15:9..........................324	21:20........................494
7:42..........................118	15:12.........................66	21:28....................274, 324
7:44..........................278	15:16........................478	21:34, 37....................517
7:48.....................233, 322	15:22........................512	22:12........................415
7:49.....................130, 131	15:39........................383	22:20........................469
7:51..........................115	15:41........................149	22:24........................517
7:53...........................63	16:5..........................268	23:8..........................495
7:55–56.......................55	16:6..........................149	23:10........................517
8:2...........................415	16:13........................517	23:16........................517
8:6............................62	16:17........................233	23:19.........................87
8:13...........................66	16:19–24.....................388	23:32........................517
8:17..........................180	16:26........................497	24:2..........................309
8:22..........................380	16:29........................492	25:24........................259
9:17.....................180, 340	16:33........................381	26:20........................194
9:24..........................517	16:35, 36....................529	27:1, 6......................530
9:37..........................381	17:9..........................529	27:15, 17....................178
10:1..........................530	17:11........................268	27:20........................361
10:14....................324, 388	17:24........................322	27:29, 30....................220
10:15........................324	17:27........................490	27:39........................382
10:22....................277, 496	17:29........................143	27:40....................220, 361

28:13. . . . . .361, 435
28:18. 529
28:25. 108

Romans
1:3. 250
1:3–4. . . . . .45, 162
1:4. 367
1:16. 127
1:17b. 400
1:28. 198
2:4. 194
2:23. 63
2:25. 103
2:26. 309
3:2. 174
3:5. 200
3:8. 63
3:24. 327
3:24–26. 327
3:25. . . . . .88, 89
3:31. 359
4 . . . . .30, 87, 216, 421
4:1–8. 175
4:5. 63
4:12. 217
4:13. . . . . .87, 203
4:14. 203
4:16. . . . . .203, 217
4:18–21. . . . . .428, 430
4:19–21. 428
4:20. 203
4:21. . . . . .202, 203
4:25. . . . . .367, 378
5–8 115
5:8. 75
5:9–10. 204
5:10. 367
5:12–21. 76
5:14. . . . . .63, 278
5:19. 63
6:1–6. 117
6:4. 180
6:6. . . . . .76, 85
6:14, 15. 262
7:3. . . . . .277, 496
7:11. 115
7:14. 252
7:18. 379
7:25. 500
8:3a. 254
8:4. 292
8:5–11. 192
8:9. 103
8:13–14. 204
8:19. 341
8:19–22. 499
8:21. 501
8:23. . . . . .327, 341
8:24. . . . . .53, 437
8:25. 341
8:27. 259
8:29. . . . . .46, 352, 483
8:29–30. 204
8:31–39. 512
8:34. . . . . .52, 75, 259, 344. 345
8:38. 308
8:39. 267
9:3. 380
9:4. . . . . .248, 291
9:7. 434
9:7–8. 87
9:8. . . . . .203, 379
9:9. 203
9:10. 510
9:14. 200
9:18. 115
9:22. 402
9:33. 84
10:6. 379
10:7. . . . . .379, 528
10:8. . . . . .378, 379
10:17. 127
10:18. 216
11:2. 259
11:7. 215
11:11. 136
11:12. 324
11:17–24 204
11:22. .103, 136
11:24. 324
11:27. .291, 354
11:29. 95
11:36. 81
12:1. . . . . .341, 345, 520
12:2. 522
12:8. 201
12:9–21. . . . . .508, 509
12:10. 508
12:11. 201
12:13. .509, 520
12:18. 480
12:19. 389
13:6. 275
13:11. 198
13:11b. 53
13:12. .383, 384
13:13. 510
14 515
14:1. 177
14:1–15:13. 137
14:4. 136
14:5. . . . . .137, 202
14:14. .324, 388
14:15. 515
14:20. 515
15:3. . . . . .396, 445
15:8. . . . . .203, 217
15:10–12 46
15:16. .275, 345
15:19. 66
15:26. 520
15:30. 468
15:30–32 . . . . .523, 526
15:33. .526, 527
16 6
16:1–2. 526
16:3–15. 526
16:20. 527

16:20b............526, 530
16:21..............6, 529
16:25–27.............526

1 Corinthians

1:6..................217
1:7..................341
1:8.............217, 383
1:11.................306
1:17.................367
1:18............345, 367
1:20..................33
1:26..................95
1:30.................327
2:7...................33
3:1..................252
3:2..................174
3:13.................383
3:20..................46
3:22.................308
4:5.............144, 191
4:9..................396
4:12.................529
4:16.................203
4:17.................395
5:5..................383
7:10.................267
7:17–24..............327
7:20..................95
7:26.................308
7:28.................396
7:29.................362
8:6...........32, 38, 50
8:8..................515
8:8b.................103
8:13.................515
9:24–27.........204, 468
9:25.................468
9:27.................198
10:5.................119
10:6........119, 136, 278
10:11................278
10:12................136

11:1..................203
11:24...........353, 395
11:25...290, 353, 395, 528
12:10............177, 193
12:28................193
12:29................193
13:12................480
14:20................181
14:23–25.............193
14:33................527
15...................367
15:1–3...............344
15:3..........75, 90, 367
15:5, 6, 7, 8........340
15:20................222
15:20–28.............180
15:23................222
15:24–28..............72
15:25.................52
15:25–28..............72
15:26.................85
15:27.................52
15:39–50..............76
15:50.................85
15:51................501
16:2.................137
16:5.................149
16:9.................142
16:10–12, 15–18......526
16:20b...............526
16:23...........526, 530

2 Corinthians

1:4..................396
1:7..................217
1:10..................64
1:12............252, 477
1:14.................383
1:21............217, 515
3....................290
3:4...................87
3:6..................290
3:16.................361
3:16–18..............292

3:18.................352
4:4.............191, 352
4:6..................191
5:7..................416
6:14.................396
6:18..................45
7:1.............324, 325
7:10.................194
7:11............201, 218
7:12.................201
7:15.................395
8:4..................520
8:7, 8...............201
8:9..................367
8:9b.................355
8:12.................219
8:16.................201
8:23..................96
9:4.............117, 409
9:13.................520
10:4.................252
10:6..................63
11:1.................529
11:3.................380
11:4.................529
11:17...........117, 409
11:19................529
11:20................529
12:2............150, 153
12:12............66, 193
13:1............387, 469
13:5.................198
13:5–6...............204
13:5b................103
13:6.................198
13:7.................198
13:11................527
13:11c...............526
13:12................526
13:14...........526, 530

Galatians

1:4.............33, 308

Scripture Index

2:9 396
2:10 .... 136, 353
2:12 401
2:14 144
2:19–20 117
2:20 75
2:21–3:5 10
3:1 367
3:1–5 192
3:2 127
3:5 .... 127, 193
3:6–9 216
3:8 127
3:10 198
3:11 400
3:13 198
3:14 203
3:15 329
3:15–29 262
3:15b 254
3:16 .... 87, 203
3:17 203
3:18 203
3:19 .... 63, 203, 280
3:20 280
3:21 203
3:22 203
3:24–25 352
3:29 203
4:3 174
4:4 367
4:9 174
4:21–31 .... 495, 521
4:23 203
4:24 .... 291, 490
4:25 490
4:25–26 493
4:26 427
4:28 203
5:3 260
5:5 341
5:6 414
6:6 520

6:9 473
6:11 236
6:14 367
6:16 526
6:18 .... 526, 530

Ephesians

1:3 416
1:4 128
1:7, 14 327
1:18 .... 95, 191
1:19–23 367
1:20 .... 52, 416
1:21 33
1:22 72
2:2 401–2
2:6 416
2:11 322
2:12 291
2:15 76
2:16 367
3:9 .... 33, 191
3:10 416
3:12 .... 101, 376
4:1 95
4:2 529
4:3 136
4:4 95
4:5 180
4:11 96
4:13 76
4:19–25 76
4:22, 25 470
4:30 327
5:1 203
5:3–5 511
5:6 402
5:26 .... 324, 381
6:12 .... 85, 416
6:17 142
6:18 520
6:18–20 .... 523, 526
6:19 376

6:21–22 526
6:23 526
6:24 .... 526, 530

Philippians

1:1 529
1:5 396
1:6 471
1:7 217
1:10 383
1:16 383
1:27 .... 395, 522
1:28 402
1:30 468
2 471
2:1 396
2:5–11 38
2:6–7a 471
2:6–11 .... 27, 74, 472
2:6b–7a 355
2:9 75
2:16 383
2:17 .... 345, 520
2:19, 22 529
2:23 470
2:25 .... 96, 275
3:10–11 117
3:14 .... 95, 96
3:17 .... 203, 278
3:18 367
3:19 402
3:20 341
3:20–21 522
3:21 72
4:3 .... 395, 494
4:5 198
4:9 .... 526, 527
4:15 520
4:18 .... 345, 520
4:20 526
4:21a 526
4:23 .... 526, 530

Colossians

1:1 529
1:14 327
1:15 . . . . 46, 352
1:15–20 . . . . 27, 38
1:16 . . . . 32, 50
1:17b 34
1:18 . . . . 46, 222
1:20 . . . . 367, 499, 501
1:21–23 204
1:22–23 103
1:26 33
1:28 182
2:1 468
2:2 202
2:7 217
2:8 174
2:12 . . . . 180, 367
2:14 367
2:14–15 154
2:15 86
2:16 137
2:17 . . . . 137, 278, 352
2:20 . . . . 174, 380
3:1 52
3:5 511
3:8 470
3:13 529
3:9–10 76
4:3–4 . . . . 523, 526
4:7–9 526
4:12 . . . . 202, 468
4:15 526
4:18 353
4:18c 526, 530

1 Thessalonians

1:3 353
1:5 202
1:6 203
1:7 278
1:9 . . . . 179, 376
2:1 376
2:2 . . . . 388, 468
2:13 . . . . 127, 142
2:14 203
2:17 136
4:8 468
4:9 508
5:2 383
5:4 383
5:5 402
5:12–22 508
5:23 . . . . 526, 527
5:25 . . . . 523, 526
5:26 526
5:28 . . . . 526, 530

2 Thessalonians

1:4 . . . . 396, 529
1:7 386
1:10 384
1:11 95–96
2:1 383
2:2 . . . . 308, 383
2:3 402
3:1–2 . . . . 523, 526
3:7 203
3:9 . . . . 203, 278
3:16 526
3:18 . . . . 526, 530

1 Timothy

1:2 . . . . 153, 530
1:9 481
1:12 500
2:4 385
2:5 280
2:14 63
3:2 509
3:3 511
3:15 104
4:3 . . . . 385, 515
4:7 176
4:8 176
4:12 278
4:14 180
5:19 . . . . 387, 469
5:24, 25 250
6:9 402
6:12 . . . . 150, 468
6:13 150
6:17–19 508
6:21b 526, 530

Titus

1:4 153
1:8 509
1:16 198
2:7 278
2:12 301
2:14 . . . . 75, 324, 327
3:5 381
3:9 254
3:12 136
3:15b 526, 530

Philemon

1 529
6 . . . . 142, 396
12 379
14 385
16 324
22 . . . . 523, 526
25 . . . . 526, 530

Hebrews

1 . . . . 56, 60, 62, 63, 69, 84, 99
1–2 . . . . 36, 96, 118
1–5 195
1–7 388
1–12 . . . . 502, 507, 508
1:1 . . . . 30–31, 37, 38, 63, 100, 536
1:1–2 . . . . . . 59, 96, 139, 261, 269, 536
1:1–2a 60, 139, 141, 146, 173, 485
1:1–4 . . . . 16, 28, 29, 40, 41, 58, 60, 69,
 . . . . 78, 93, 106, 112, 123, 140
1:1–14 . . . . 27–39, 105
1:1–2:18 . . . . 92, 94, 95, 105
1:1–3:6 150

Scripture Index

1:1–4:11 140
1:1–4:13 . . . . 16, 27, 28, 41, 60, 69, 78, 93, 106, 112, 140, 147, 148, 156, 170, 185, 211, 225, 243, 264, 271, 286, 297, 313, 347, 372, 391, 406, 422, 430, 450, 463, 486, 503, 524
1:2. . . 14, 31–33, 37, 43, 92, 97, 99, 118, 133, 150, 165, 203, 263, 269, 309, 339, 387, 411, 496, 499, 534, 538
1:2–3. . . . . 166, 387
1:2a 62, 63
1:2b 32, 37
1:2b–3 . . . . 27, 32, 38, 42, 354
1:2b–4 29
1:2b–13 62
1:2c 50
1:3 . . . . 32, 33–36, 39, 52, 83, 98, 117, 193, 321, 362, 409, 538
1:3–13 . . . . 68, 100
1:3c 34
1:3d 36
1:4 . . . . . . 29, 36, 37, 43, 131, 203, 456
1:4–13 . . . . 68, 92, 71
1:4–14 87
1:5 . . 32, 36, 37, 40, 43, 44–45, 46, 56, 161, 162, 263, 269, 387, 389, 493
1:5–7 44
1:5–13 . . . . 43, 45, 47, 68, 139
1:5–14 . . 16, 28, 40–59, 60, 69, 78, 84, 93, 106, 112, 123, 140
1:5–2:18 68
1:5–4:13 106
1:5a . . 42, 49, 51, 56, 84, 150, 536, 538
1:5b 43, 49, 132, 150, 538
1:6 . . . . 36, 40, 45–47, 56, 71, 84, 132, 222, 389, 494, 536, 538
1:6b 46
1:7 . . . . .47–48, 56, 97, 275, 389, 476, 536
1:7–9 . . . . 36, 40
1:7b 53
1:8 . . . . . 37, 43, 47, 49, 50, 56, 99, 150, 166, 263, 269, 387, 389, 436, 499, 536, 538
1:8–9 . . . . 43, 44, 48–49, 56, 234
1:9 . . . . 92, 95, 175, 477

1:10 . . . . 50, 56, 99, 389, 536, 538
1:10–12 . . . . . . 43, 44, 49–51, 56, 513
1:11 51
1:11–12 . . . . 51, 535
1:12 . . . . 44, 51, 258, 397, 513, 538
1:13 . . . . 35, 43, 44, 47, 51–52, 68, 69, 70, 71, 86, 129, 284, 362, 389, 534
1:13–14 . . . . 36, 40
1:13a 56, 536
1:14 . . . 44, 48, 52–53, 54, 60, 68, 131, 203, 258, 328, 476
2 . . . . 40, 540
2–4 122
2:1 . . . . . . 6, 61, 62–63, 110, 115, 118, 131, 133, 178, 398, 449, 515, 536
2:1–2 541
2:1–3 536
2:1–4 . . . 16, 28, 32, 40, 41, 60–67, 68, 69, 78, 93, 96, 105, 106, 112, 123, 139, 140, 141, 145, 169, 204, 384, 485, 496
2:1a 220
2:1b 220
2:2 . . . . 60, 65, 217, 398, 415, 496
2:2–3 . . . . 36, 40, 61, 183. 387
2:2–3a 62, 63–64
2:3 . . . . . 3, 6, 35, 53, 54, 60, 64, 65, 92, 131, 178, 217, 258, 496
2:3b 65
2:3b–4 . . . . 62, 64–66
2:4 . . . . 65, 131, 191, 192, 193, 537
2:5 . . 36, 40, 46, 53, 68, 70, 71–72, 499
2:5–6 129
2:5–9 . . . 16, 68–76, 77, 78, 80, 81, 87, 100
2:5–18 . . 16, 28, 40, 41, 60, 68, 69, 78, 93, 105, 106, 112, 123, 140, 151
2:6 . . . . 56, 72, 129, 353, 512
2:6–8 . . . . 57, 139
2:6–8a 71
2:6–8c 72–73
2:6–9 58
2:7 . . . . 36, 40, 161
2:8 86
2:8b–9 71

2:8d 74
2:8d–9 73–75
2:9 . . . . . 36, 40, 69, 73, 80, 81, 82, 92, 96, 98, 150, 152, 161, 191, 343, 530, 538, 540
2:10 . . . . 35, 53, 54, 69, 75, 78, 79, 80, 81–82, 86, 88, 92, 98, 110, 131, 134, 135, 166, 176, 178, 181, 222, 247, 253, 258, 263, 266, 269, 275, 308, 311, 320, 323, 369, 398, 411, 470, 471, 472, 517, 528, 531, 538, 540
2:10–16 . . . . 79, 88
2:10–18 . . . 16, 68, 69, 77–91, 106, 483
2:11 . . . . . 82–83, 92, 95, 96, 116, 191, 360, 477, 484
2:11–13 80
2:11b 78, 83
2:11c 78
2:12 . . . . . 56, 83–84, 92, 95, 355, 389
2:12–13 . . . . 56, 139, 354, 536
2:13 . . . . 46, 84–85, 388, 389
2:13a 34, 88, 92
2:13a–b 84
2:13c–e 84
2:14 . . . . .64, 85, 173, 224, 285, 309, 323, 343, 378, 379
2:14–15 . . . . . .75, 80, 85–86, 122, 368, 540, 541
2:14–16 80
2:14d–15 85
2:15 85
2:16 . . . . 36, 40, 68, 80, 86–87
2:17 . . . 75, 80, 87–89, 91, 92, 96, 120, 131, 146, 147, 149, 151, 159, 263, 269, 365, 412, 435, 483, 538
2:17–18 . . . . 80, 88, 165, 167, 484
2:18 . . . . . . 89, 151, 217, 336, 433, 538
3 92
3–4 131
3:1 . . . . 49, 74, 82, 92, 95–96, 97, 114, 116, 146, 147, 149, 150, 257, 263, 375, 431, 435, 483, 519, 538
3:1–2 94
3:1–6 . . . . . . .16, 28, 41, 60, 69, 78, 88, 92–104, 105, 106, 112, 123, 140, 379

3:1–4:11 105
3:2 . . . . 92, 97, 99, 100, 101, 106, 120, 415
3:2–6a 95
3:3 . . . . 92, 98, 99, 106, 340
3:3–4 . . . . 94, 98, 415, 538
3:3b 98
3:4 . . . . 98–99, 106
3:4b 98, 99
3:4c 99, 99
3:5 . . . . . 92, 94, 99–100, 106, 120, 139
3:5–6 95
3:5a 97, 100
3:5b 101
3:6 . . . . 92, 100–103, 106, 108, 116, 117, 121, 150, 152, 178, 255, 263, 269, 387, 398, 534, 538
3:6–18 57
3:6b 95, 103, 106, 116, 150
3:6d–f 107
3:7 . . . . . . .56, 117, 118, 192, 306, 389, 536, 537
3:7–11 . . . . 16, 105–10, 112, 123
3:7–15 116
3:7–19 122
3:7–4:11 . . . . 16, 28, 41, 58, 60, 69, 78, 82, 93, 105, 106, 111, 112, 120, 123, 131, 139, 140, 141, 183, 218, 302, 384, 405, 432, 448, 496, 528, 534
3:7–4:12(13) 92
3:7–4:13 . . . . 105, 169, 190
3:7a 108
3:7b–11 . . . 107, 108–9, 111, 118, 122
3:8 89
3:9 89
3:9b 109
3:10 118
3:10a 109
3:10b 109
3:11 . . . . 131, 380
3:12 . . . . 10, 114–15, 116, 117, 120, 121, 126, 142, 194, 375, 377, 380, 389, 417, 481, 483, 496
3:12–13 113

3:12–14 . . . . 118, 121
3:12–19 . . . . 16, 105, 106, 111–21, 123
3:12–4:11 204
3:13 . . . . 96, 115–16, 117
3:14 . . . . 49, 63, 95, 101, 102, 103, 106, 116–17, 120, 150, 178, 192, 202, 216, 217, 409, 534
3:14a 113
3:14b 102
3:15 . . . . 105, 115, 116, 117, 118, 119, 293
3:15–19 145
3:16 . . . . 93, 97, 116, 117–18, 119
3:16–18 . . . . 113, 116, 536
3:16b 119
3:17 . . . . 109, 118–19, 121, 136
3:17–18 537
3:17b 119
3:18 . . . . 119–20, 131, 380
3:19 . . . . 114, 119, 120, 123, 126, 380, 417
3:22 . . . . 4, 322
3:29 (LXX) 98
3:30 (LXX) 98
3:35 (LXX) 98
4 . . . . 123, 137
4:1 . . . . . 121, 125, 126, 131, 136, 215, 380, 481
4:1–2 132
4:1–3 178
4:1–3a 125
4:1–5 125
4:1–8 124
4:1–11 . . . . 16, 105, 106, 111, 112, 119, 122–38, 220
4:2 . . . . 127–28, 380, 417
4:2–5 124
4:2–10 125
4:2–13 28
4:3 . . . . 56, 105, 128–29, 131, 380, 389, 536, 537
4:3–4 . . . . 57, 536
4:3b 130
4:3b–5 130
4:3b–10 125

4:3c 130
4:4 . . . . 56, 125, 128, 129–30, 131, 135, 215, 536
4:4a 130
4:4b 130
4:5 . . . . 105, 125, 130–32, 380
4:6 . . 125, 127, 132, 134, 136, 380, 536
4:6–7 132–33
4:6–9 269
4:6–11 . . . . 125, 126
4:7 . . . 56, 57, 105, 115, 132, 536, 537
4:7–8 248
4:8 . . . . 131, 133–34, 432, 455
4:9 . . . . 134–35, 136
4:10 . . . . 131, 135, 380
4:11 . . . . 103, 121, 125, 126, 131, 135–36, 141, 178, 201, 278, 380
4:12 . . . . . . 57, 140, 141–43 144, 181, 191, 220, 377, 456, 476
4:12–13 . . . . . 27, 28, 41, 60, 69, 78, 93, 106, 112, 123, 139–45, 146, 173, 261, 485
4:13 . . . . . . 105, 141, 142, 143–44, 176
4:14 . . . 74, 96, 146, 147, 149–50, 151, 219, 224, 261, 263, 267, 269, 322, 366, 375, 382, 387, 538, 540
4:14–16 . . . . 16, 146–54, 155, 156, 170, 178, 183, 185, 211, 225, 243, 264, 271, 286, 297, 313, 347, 364, 371, 372, 375, 376, 382
4:14–10:31 . . 16, 28, 41, 60, 69, 78, 93, 106, 112, 123, 140, 147, 156, 170, 183, 185, 211, 225, 243, 264, 271, 286, 297, 313, 347, 372, 391, 406, 422, 440, 450, 463, 486, 503
4:14a 149
4:14b 149
4:15 . . 89, 146, 148, 149, 150–52, 153, 156, 159, 163, 165, 167, 251, 254, 261, 263, 267, 336, 365, 397, 484, 538
4:15–16 151
4:16 . . . . . 101, 149, 152–53, 158, 259, 274, 310, 366, 380, 398, 414, 492, 530
5–7 155
5–10 261

Scripture Index

5:1 ... 87, 146, 158–59, 160, 162, 163, 191, 263, 276, 308, 339, 365, 538
5:1-3 264
5:1-4 157
5:1-10 .. 16, 77, 88, 147, 155–68, 169, 170, 183, 185, 211, 224, 225, 243, 264, 271, 274, 286, 297, 313, 347, 372
5:1-10:18 .... 147, 372, 375
5:2 ...... 151, 159–60, 163, 165, 180, 194, 254, 263, 365
5:2-3 268
5:2-4 158
5:3 ...... 160, 215, 263, 267, 276, 365
5:4 .... 96, 157, 160, 161, 162
5:5 .. 32, 56, 145, 161, 215, 256, 263, 269, 387, 389, 536, 538
5:5-6 .... 160–62, 537, 538
5:5-10 158
5:5b-6 161
5:6 .... 35, 56, 155, 161, 166, 169, 183, 218, 222, 229, 236, 256, 365, 366, 389, 536, 538
5:7 .... 53, 162–65, 191, 258, 263, 267, 276, 309, 396, 415, 500
5:7-8 .... 365, 484
5:7-10 165
5:8 .... 31, 151, 162, 165, 166, 263, 269, 387, 538
5:9 .. 35, 53, 54, 81, 82, 162, 181, 247, 258, 263, 269, 346, 367, 471
5:9-10 .... 35, 165–66
5:10 .... 35, 145, 147, 155, 162, 165, 166, 169, 210, 218, 222, 224, 263, 325, 365, 538
5:11 ..... 169, 171, 172–73, 178, 202, 203, 210, 224
5:11-14 171, 172, 177, 183, 202, 206, 210
5:11-6:3 .... 17, 169–82, 185
5:11-6:12 .... 17, 170, 183, 211
5:11-6:20 ..... 16, 147, 155, 156, 158, 169, 170, 181, 183, 185, 208, 211, 224, 225, 243, 264, 271, 286, 297, 313, 347, 371, 372
5:12 .... 172, 173–75, 176
5:12-14 .... 173, 175
5:13 .... 175–76, 477

5:14 ... 81, 176–77, 178, 181, 191, 247
5:14-16 158
5:14b 175
5:15 158
6 ... 155, 183, 191, 208, 224, 385, 426
6:1 ..... 11, 35, 81, 135, 175, 177–79, 181, 193, 194, 197, 247, 325, 380, 415, 417, 482, 499, 537, 542
6:1-3 .... 172, 183, 186, 188, 210
6:1-12 .... 384, 391
6:1b-2 178
6:2 .... 179–81, 191, 192, 309, 386
6:3 .... 101, 169, 181, 188
6:4 ...... 11, 49, 95, 96, 116, 188, 191, 194, 395, 537
6:4-5 .... 66, 385
6:4-6 .... 145, 184, 185, 186, 187, 188–96, 384, 389 482, 541
6:4-8 ... 183, 184, 186, 187, 199, 204, 210, 214, 386, 390, 541
6:4-12 .... 17, 170, 183–209
6:4b-5 .... 192, 195, 197
6:5 .... 53, 71, 192, 193, 339
6:6 .... 10, 115, 179, 188, 190, 256, 263, 269, 385, 387, 482
6:6a 196
6:7 .... 196–97, 198
6:7-8 .... 188, 196, 197
6:8 .... 145, 197–99, 200
6:9 .... 53, 54, 166, 169, 187, 199–200, 215, 258
6:9-12 ...... 187, 188, 210, 211, 214
6:10 .... 82, 200–201, 204, 537
6:10-12 204
6:11 ... 169, 187, 201–2, 204, 216, 380
6:11-12 201
6:12 ..... 126, 169, 173, 202–4, 215, 217, 223, 328, 380, 417, 419, 426, 428
6:12-20 .... 238, 256
6:13 .... 35, 56, 126, 203, 213
6:13-14 .... 57, 212, 213–14, 216, 536
6:13-15 .... 217, 428, 537
6:13-20 .... 17, 170, 185, 201, 210–23, 382, 537

6:14 .... 210, 214, 389
6:15 .... 35, 126, 203, 215–16, 431
6:16 216–17
6:17 .... 126, 203, 215, 217–18, 256, 328, 426
6:17-18 51
6:17-19 216
6:17-20 216
6:17a 214
6:18 ..... 150, 189, 217, 218–19, 220, 221, 255
6:18-20 222
6:19 ...... 51, 63, 191, 217, 219–21, 284, 310, 320, 366, 369, 380
6:19-20 .... 219, 281, 376
6:19b-20a 377
6:20 .... 35, 74, 146, 169, 210, 218, 221–22, 224, 232, 236, 257, 263, 321, 365, 366, 380, 538
6:20f 226
7 ... 58, 138, 155, 166, 169, 173, 183, 218, 222, 224, 225, 230, 231, 242, 253, 263, 270, 274, 325, 365, 539
7:1 .... 232–33, 236, 238, 415
7:1-3 .... 226, 227, 234, 236
7:1-8 227
7:1-10 ..... 17, 35, 161, 224–41, 243, 247, 264
7:1-28 .... 17, 147, 156, 170, 185, 211, 225, 243, 264, 271, 286, 297, 313, 347, 372
7:1-10:18 .... 385, 419
7:1a 228
7:1b 228
7:1b-3a 232
7:2 .... 175, 228, 233–36, 477
7:2a 234
7:3 .... 35, 51, 146, 166, 232, 236, 239, 266, 268, 269, 361, 365, 366, 387, 397, 508, 539
7:4 .... 234, 236
7:4-6 234
7:4-10 .... 57, 227, 228, 239, 536
7:4b 228
7:5 ...... 227, 234, 236–37, 239, 260, 378, 379

7:5–6 239
7:5b 239
7:6 . . 126, 203, 215, 226, 234, 238, 240
7:6b 228
7:7 . . . . 216, 238, 456
7:8 . . . . 234, 238–39, 377, 411
7:8–9 234
7:9 234
7:9–10 239–40
7:10 . . . . .228, 239
7:11 . . 81, 146, 178, 181, 246–48, 249,
   251, 254, 260, 263, 269, 308, 327,
   352, 354, 362, 364, 365, 366, 534
7:11–17 244
7:11–19 . . . . 246, 255, 256
7:11–25 . . . . 17, 225, 242–62, 263,
   264, 265
7:11–28 .249, 539
7:11b 251, 358
7:12 . . . . . 237, 244, 248–49, 254, 259,
   261, 414, 498
7:12–16 253
7:13 249–50
7:13–14 . . . . 249, 251, 252, 365
7:13–15 539
7:13–17 249
7:14 . . . . 146, 235, 250
7:15 . . . . 247, 250, 538
7:15–16 .250–53
7:15–17 .146, 249
7:16 . . . . . . 51, 166, 237, 251, 260, 263,
   309, 354, 365, 366, 538
7:16–17 239
7:16–19 253
7:16b 253
7:17 . . . . . . 56, 236, 239, 253, 256, 263,
   366, 411, 538
7:18 . 246, 253, 260, 261, 269, 339, 465
7:18–19 . . . . 11, 253–55
7:18–25 253
7:18b 254
7:19 . . . . . . 81, 237, 246, 247, 253, 254,
   255, 263, 308, 310, 327, 352, 354,
   362, 364, 366, 456, 534
7:19b 253

7:20 . . . . .256, 365
7:20–21 .146, 246
7:20–22 . . . . 255–57, 263, 268
7:20–25 . . . . 246, 253, 255
7:20–28 . . . . 219, 256, 255
7:20a 255, 256
7:20b–21 255
7:21 . . . . . . 56, 218, 236, 239, 263, 365,
   366, 389, 536, 537, 538
7:21a 256
7:22 . . . . . . 74, 256, 291, 326, 365, 456,
   495, 534, 538
7:22a 255
7:23 . . . . .146, 365
7:23–24 . . . . 257–58, 539
7:23–25 . . . . .51, 239
7:24 . . . . . . 51, 166, 245, 252, 263, 365,
   366, 397, 508
7:24–25 97
7:25 . . . . . 53, 54, 152, 222, 247, 252,
   254, 258–59, 263, 310, 320, 323,
   336, 366, 377, 380, 412, 414,
   435, 492
7:26 . . . . . 36, 246, 263, 266–67, 274,
   366, 538
7:26–28 . . 17, 146, 155, 225, 243, 246,
   246, 255, 263–69, 305
7:26a 266, 267
7:26b 266
7:27 . . 35, 160, 263, 265, 266, 267–68,
   276, 279, 320, 337, 339, 340, 341,
   346, 361, 365, 366, 540, 541
7:27–28 . . . . 268, 264, 269
7:27b 190
7:28 . . . . . . 81, 147, 151, 166, 181, 237,
   239, 246, 247, 254, 263, 268–69,
   352, 362, 364, 365, 366, 387, 471
8 . . . . 225, 271, 292, 364, 516
8–10 . . . . .268, 276
8:1 . . . . 35, 36, 52, 146, 149, 155, 271,
   274, 275, 312, 346, 360, 362, 365,
   370, 534, 537, 538
8:1–2 . . . . 270, 272, 273, 274, 275, 366
8:1–6 . . . . . . 17, 58, 270–85, 286, 297,
   312, 313, 347
8:1–9:28 297

8:1–10:18 . . . . 17, 58, 147, 156,
   170, 185, 211, 213, 224, 225,
   243, 264, 271, 286, 297, 313, 319,
   326, 347, 363, 370, 372, 379, 388
8:2 . . . . . 274, 275, 277, 281, 284, 312,
   322, 336, 376, 380
8:3 . . 146, 159, 191, 270, 271, 275–76,
   277, 279, 308, 339, 361, 365,
   412, 435, 540
8:3–4 . . . . .273, 312
8:3–6 . . . . .273, 274
8:3–10:18 . . . . .270, 274
8:3a 276
8:4 . . . . 86, 146, 276–77, 279, 365
8:5 . . . 1, 13, 53, 57, 96, 136, 277–79,
   280, 281, 322, 335, 336, 366,
   496, 535, 536
8:6 . . . . . 126, 215, 217, 248, 257, 262,
   279–80, 312, 326, 365, 370,
   456, 495
8:6–7 269
8:6–13 388
8:7 . . . . 281, 286, 289, 290, 359
8:7–8a 289
8:7–12 534
8:7–13 . . . . 17, 271, 279, 286–96, 297,
   313, 326, 347, 365, 495
8:7–10:18 279
8:8 . . . . 56, 97, 286, 291, 292, 389,
   495, 536
8:8–11 288
8:8–12 .363, 537
8:8a 289–90
8:8b–11 326
8:8b–12 . . . . . . 289, 290–93, 309, 363
8:9 . . . . .30, 87, 291
8:10 . . . . . . 97, 261, 288, 291, 292, 329,
   355, 534
8:10a 363
8:10b 363
8:11 . . . . .289, 291
8:12 . . . . 200, 353, 366, 367, 459
8:12b 363
8:13 . . . 7, 11, 198, 249, 262, 269, 271,
   293–94, 300, 308, 359, 516, 534
9 . . . . . . 276, 282, 300, 312, 316, 317,
   376, 516

9:1 . . . . . 271, 275, 299, 300–301, 302, 309, 312, 318, 376
9:1–5. . . . . 299, 300, 317
9:1–7. . . . . 281, 299, 300
9:1–10. . . . . . . .17, 271, 286, 297–311, 312, 313, 316, 317, 347
9:1a. 298
9:2. . . . 98, 191, 275, 301–2, 305, 307, 320, 336, 376, 415
9:2–3. .271, 322
9:2–5a. 305
9:2b. 302
9:2b–5a. 303
9:3. . . . . 221, 275, 306, 377, 516
9:3–5. 3024
9:5. . . . . 88, 95, 304, 327
9:6. . . . . 215, 300, 307, 415, 516
9:6–7. . . . . . 271, 299, 300, 304–6, 322
9:6–8. 307
9:6–10. 317
9:6a. 305
9:6b–7 305
9:7. . . . . 146, 160, 190, 264, 271, 276, 322, 353, 365
9:7–8. .320, 376
9:8. . . . . . .56, 108, 192, 271, 275, 304, 306–7, 310, 318, 336, 366, 376, 537
9:8–10. 300
9:9. . . . . . .81, 159, 178, 181, 191, 247, 271, 276, 307–8, 309, 327, 339, 352, 354, 362, 364, 366, 381, 435, 535, 541
9:9–10. 515
9:9a. 308
9:9b. 308
9:10. . . . . . 11, 179, 180, 252, 308–10, 318, 354, 365, 366
9:11. . . . . .81, 146, 279, 282, 300, 301, 312, 313, 317, 318, 319, 326, 336, 338, 339, 365, 376, 379, 534, 535, 538, 540
9:11–12. . . . . . . .35, 284, 319–23, 346, 366, 378
9:11–14. . . . .271, 314, 316, 317, 318, 326, 334, 346
9:11–15. 316
9:11–22. 317

9:11–28. . . . . . . .17, 35, 271, 286, 297, 312–45, 347
9:11–10:14. 363
9:11b. 321
9:12. . . . . .35, 190, 222, 223, 264, 275, 282, 313, 314, 317, 318, 319, 320, 323, 324, 325, 326, 334, 336, 338, 341, 343, 353, 354, 364, 366, 367, 370, 376, 380, 541
9:12–14. 317
9:12–15. 279
9:12–25. 388
9:12a. .319, 321
9:12b. 35
9:13. . . . . .82, 252, 261, 318, 322, 323, 324, 353, 354, 366, 381, 477, 495
9:13–14. . . . . . 309, 319, 323–25, 346
9:14. . . . 114, 135, 142, 179, 192, 264, 271, 308, 318, 322, 324, 326, 335, 365, 366, 370, 377, 381, 389, 412, 500, 537, 538, 540, 541
9:15. . 63, 96, 126, 203, 215, 217, 223, 257, 261, 271, 280, 314, 318, 325–8, 328, 330, 359, 364, 365, 367, 370, 457, 495, 534
9:15–17. . . . . 318, 323, 337, 388
9:15–20. . . . . .279, 291
9:15–22. . . . . 271, 316, 317, 326, 334
9:15–23. . . . . .324, 368
9:15–28. . . . . .317, 346
9:15–10:18 346
9:16. . . . . 178, 314, 328, 329, 330
9:16–17. . . . . .314, 318, 326, 328–30, 334, 540
9:16–20. 326
9:16–22. 316
9:16a. 329
9:17. . . . . 63, 217, 328, 330, 377
9:17a. 330
9:18. . . . 271, 315, 323, 326, 330, 331, 333, 334, 359, 377, 435
9:18–21. 537
9:18–22 . . 315, 317, 330, 334, 365, 540
9:18–23. 318
9:19. . . . . .35, 191, 260, 318, 323, 331, 495, 516
9:19–20. . . . . 315, 331–32

9:19–21. . . . . 323, 326, 333
9:19a. 331
9:19b. 331
9:20. . . . . 323, 328, 331, 333, 389, 528
9:21. . . . . 315, 323, 331, 333, 495
9:22. . . . 318, 323, 324, 326, 331, 332, 333, 334, 495
9:23. . . . . .96, 136, 273, 284, 315, 318, 333, 334, 339, 456
9:23–24. . . . . .317, 334
9:23–25. 279
9:23–28. . 271, 316, 317, 318, 319, 334
9:24. . 13, 275, 282, 284, 317, 333–35, 336–37, 341, 366, 376, 380
9:24–26. 335
9:24–28. 318
9:24a. 335
9:24b. 335
9:25. . . . 146, 264, 271, 275, 316, 317, 318, 323, 334, 336, 339, 341, 353, 366, 376, 380, 540
9:25–26. . . 264, 336–37, 343, 361, 540
9:25–26a. .337
9:25–27. . . . . 181, 323, 346
9:25–28. . . . . 320, 334, 361
9:25–10:4 .317
9:25–12:4 .337
9:25a. .335, 338
9:25b. 335, 337, 338
9:26. . . . . .14, 128, 190, 254, 264, 317, 318, 323, 334, 337, 339, 341, 353, 365, 366, 541
9:26–28. 279
9:26a. 338
9:27. . . . . 190, 316, 317, 386
9:27–28. . . . . 337, 339–41, 362
9:28. . . . . .14, 35, 45, 53, 54, 166, 190, 215, 258, 264, 271, 316, 317, 318, 334, 365, 366, 370, 383, 412, 500, 534, 540, 541
10 . . . . 147, 271, 351, 355, 391
10:1. . . . . .11, 53, 71, 81, 100, 152, 178, 181, 237, 247, 261, 262, 276, 278, 308, 309, 310, 319, 327, 339, 350, 351–52, 354, 361, 362, 364, 365, 366, 380, 414, 492, 534, 535

10:1–2 260
10:1–3 .320, 348
10:1–4 . . . . 348, 350, 351, 354
10:1–18 . . . . . . .17, 271, 286, 297, 313, 346–69, 347, 351
10:1a–e 315
10:1b–2 . . . . .353, 366
10:1b–4 361
10:2 . . . . .190, 261, 276, 308, 341, 352–53, 366, 381, 541
10:3 . . . . 353, 354, 366, 432
10:4 . . . . 178, 189, 323, 327, 329, 353, 361, 366, 541
10:3 . . . . .353, 432
10:4 . . . . 323, 353–54
10:5 . . 56, 173, 276, 285, 339, 389, 536
10:5–7 . . . . 56, 354–58
10:5–9 366
10:5–10 . . . . 279, 325, 351, 354
10:5b 358
10:5b–7 354
10:8 . . . . 276, 339, 359
10:8–9 358–59
10:8–10 354
10:9 . . . . 269, 271, 358, 359, 389
10:9b 355, 358, 359
10:9b–10 359
10:10 . . 74, 77, 82, 190, 223, 264, 276, 285, 320, 323, 341, 350, 357, 359–60, 360, 362, 364, 366, 370, 388, 477, 480, 540, 541
10:11 11, 264, 276, 320, 327, 339, 349, 352, 354, 360–61, 366
10:11–12 . . . . .146, 541
10:11–14 . . . . .351, 360
10:11–15 320
10:11f 350, 362, 365, 366, 540
10:12 . . . . 35, 52, 236, 339, 361–62
10:12–13 . . . . .279, 360
10:12b 362
10:13 . . . . 362, 365, 534
10:14 . . . . .77, 81, 82, 166, 181, 223, 247, 276, 308, 320, 339, 350, 352, 361, 362–63, 366, 367, 370, 388, 471, 477, 540, 541

10:15 . . . . .56, 108, 192, 239, 306, 389, 536, 537
10:15–17 . . . . 223, 363–64
10:15–18 351
10:15b 363
10:15e 350
10:16 . . . . .261, 291, 326, 329, 355, 363, 388, 534
10:17 . . . 200, 291, 339, 350, 353, 363, 366, 367, 389, 459
10:18 . . . . 271, 276, 350, 360, 364, 385
10:19 . . . . .74, 101, 114, 152, 270, 275, 284, 323, 336, 364, 370, 375–76, 379, 380, 398, 493, 538
10:19–20 . . . . .374, 500
10:19–21 . . . . 374, 375, 380
10:19–25 . . . . . .17, 146–47, 152, 183, 370, 371, 374, 375, 463
10:19–31 . . . . .17, 147, 156, 170, 185, 211, 225, 243, 264, 271, 286, 297, 313, 347, 370–90, 391
10:19–39 391
10:20 . . . . .221, 330, 309, 310, 376–79
10:21 . . . . .146, 149, 270, 379–80, 538
10:22 . . . . .202, 308, 310, 366, 376, 380–81, 414, 417, 492, 541
10:22–25 . . . . .373, 375
10:23 . . . . .96, 101, 126, 150, 255, 381–82, 428, 537
10:24 . . . . .96, 383, 508
10:24–25 . . . . 35, 382–84
10:25 . . . . 179, 255, 324, 383, 534
10:25–31 14
10:26 . . . . 194, 195, 339, 385
10:26–27 . . . . 375, 384–86
10:26–31 . . . . .17, 145, 147, 183, 204, 370, 374, 375, 391, 394, 479, 541
10:27 . . . . 53, 198, 362, 399, 500
10:27–31 . . . . 181, 340, 537
10:28 . . . . 35, 260, 374, 469
10:28–29 . . . . 386–88, 496
10:28–30 375
10:28–31 . . . . .64, 370
10:29 . . . . . . .10, 77, 82, 152, 192, 217, 291, 323, 324, 366, 374, 385, 390, 477, 528, 530, 534, 537, 540

10:30 . . . . 46, 56, 389, 495, 536
10:30–31 388–89
10:30a 56
10:31 . . . . 114, 142, 375, 377, 389
10:32 . 6, 35, 89, 147, 191, 193, 394–95
10:32–34 . . . . .10, 392, 394, 397, 473, 483, 509, 512, 541
10:32–35 . . . . 69, 179, 372, 444
10:32–36 390
10:32–39 . . . . .17, 147, 259, 370, 371, 391–403, 406, 422, 440, 450, 462, 463, 486, 503, 524
10:32–13:25 . . . .17, 28, 41, 60, 69, 78, 93, 106, 112, 123, 140, 147, 156, 170, 185, 211, 225, 243, 264, 271, 286, 297, 313, 347, 391, 406, 422, 440, 450, 463, 486, 503, 524
10:33 . . . . .191, 215, 392, 395–96, 399, 518
10:33–34 508
10:34 . . . . . . 51, 151, 236, 396–97, 456
10:34a 396
10:34b 397
10:35 . . . . .63, 101, 115, 152, 376, 393, 394, 397–998, 415
10:35–39 394
10:36 . . . . .35, 89, 126, 203, 215, 393, 398, 541
10:36–39 . . . . .371, 397
10:37–38 399–401
10:37–39 . . . . .203, 541
10:38 . . . . 220, 377, 476
10:38–39 . . . . 380, 409, 417
10:38a 401
10:39 . . . . 220, 401–2, 405
11 . . . . . . .57, 203, 371, 391, 401, 404, 405, 414, 416, 417, 419, 447, 462, 467, 469, 535, 541
11:1 . . . . . 117, 401, 408, 409–10, 411, 415, 416, 419, 426, 427, 437, 535, 541
11:1–2 408
11:1–3 408
11:1–7 . . . . .17, 404–20, 422, 437, 440, 450
11:1–40 . . . . . . .17, 391, 406, 422, 440, 450, 463, 486, 503, 524

Scripture Index

11:1–12:14 391
11:1a 410
11:1b 410
11:2 . . . . .239, 404, 409, 411, 413, 453, 459
11:2b 474
11:3 . . .33, 193, 408, 409, 411–12, 537
11:3–7 421
11:3–31 450
11:4 . . . . . . .65, 239, 276, 339, 408, 411, 412–13, 496
11:4–7 .408, 409
11:5 . . . . .239, 411, 412, 413–14, 416, 498
11:5–6 414
11:6 . . . . .152, 189, 310, 380, 410, 414–15, 445, 448, 492, 537
11:7 . . .35, 53, 98, 203, 258, 277, 411, 412, 415–16, 421, 477, 496
11:8 . . . . .53, 96, 203, 327, 328, 412, 421, 425–26
11:8–12 215
11:8–22 . . . . . . .17, 406, 421–38, 439, 440, 450
11:9 . . . . . . 35, 126, 203, 215, 412, 423
11:9–10 . . . . 397, 426–27, 461
11:10 . . . .283, 399, 426, 433, 518, 521
11:11 . . . . . 126, 128, 203, 423, 427–29
11:12 . . . . 87, 428, 429–30
11:13 . . . . . 35, 126, 203, 215, 430–31, 455, 461
11:13–16 . . . . .425, 433
11:14 . . . . 254, 431–32
11:14–15 433
11:14–16 284
11:15 . . . . 424, 432, 437, 512
11:15–16 432–33
11:16 . . . . . . .13, 96, 131, 283, 379, 427, 433, 456, 518, 521, 537
11:16a 432
11:17 . . . . . 89, 126, 203, 215, 276, 412
11:17–18 433–34
11:17–19 . . . . .35, 433
11:17–22 425
11:18 . . . . .96, 327, 389
11:19 . . . . 180, 308, 425, 434–35
11:19b 434
11:20 .53, 435, 436
11:20–22 435–37
11:20–24 439
11:21 . . . . .436, 439
11:22 . . . . 436, 439, 512
11:23 . . . . . 35, 412, 433, 439, 442, 443
11:23–28 443
11:23–31 . . 17, 406, 422, 439–49, 450
11:24 .35, 412, 443
11:24–25 . . . . 35, 443–44
11:24–26 445
11:24–27 446
11:24–28 .98, 443
11:24a 444
11:25 444
11:25–26 445
11:26 . . . . 398, 415, 444–45, 518
11:27 . . 35, 412, 416, 442, 443, 445–46
11:27h 435
11:28 . . . . . 412, 443, 445, 446–47, 529
11:28–31 446
11:29 . . . . 35, 412, 442, 447–48
11:29–30 443
11:29–31 446
11:30 .35, 412, 448
11:31 . . . . 35, 411, 412, 443, 448
11:32 . . . . 3, 170, 191, 405, 454–55
11:32–34 454
11:32–35a 460
11:32–38 . . . . .17, 406, 422, 440, 450, 452, 453, 459
11:32–40 450–61
11:32b 455
11:33 . . . . .126, 175, 215, 450, 453, 455, 477
11:33–34 . . . . 455–56, 457
11:33–35a 456, 461
11:34 . . . . .151, 517
11:35 . . . . 180, 327, 433, 453, 454, 456–57
11:35–38 455
11:35a 453, 456, 457
11:35b 453, 457
11:35b–37 456
11:35b–38 461
11:36 . . . . 63, 453, 457, 460
11:36–37 457–58
11:36–38 454
11:37 . . . . .453, 457
11:38 . . . . 453, 458–59
11:39 . . . . .35, 126, 203, 215, 239, 404, 411, 435, 450, 453, 455
11:39–40 . . . . .17, 406, 408, 422, 431, 440, 450, 452, 454, 459–60
11:40 . . . . .81, 178, 181, 247, 308, 456, 471, 495, 541
12 . . . . 438, 473, 474
12:1 . . . . .35, 159, 203, 219, 463, 468, 469, 470, 475, 494
12:1–2 . . 221, 284, 459, 463, 464, 467, 468–72, 473, 474, 483
12:1–3 . . . . 371, 462, 463, 467, 469
12:1–11 . . . . 203, 463, 466, 478
12:1–13 . . . . 478, 479, 480
12:1–14 .391, 541
12:1–17 . . . . . . .17, 391, 406, 422, 440, 450, 462–84, 486, 503, 524
12:2 . . . . .35, 36, 52, 74, 77, 81, 82, 89, 93, 182, 219, 222, 311, 320, 362, 369, 380, 417, 463, 470, 472, 528, 531, 538, 540
12:3 . . . . . . 216, 220, 467, 472–73, 512
12:4 . . . . 6, 179, 393, 473
12:4–5 541
12:4–11 . . . . 10, 462, 467, 475
12:4–13 .69, 371
12:5–6 . . . . 473–75, 479
12:5–11 . . . . 473, 475, 484, 537
12:7 . . . . .276, 309
12:7–8 475
12:7–10 474
12:7–11 . . . . 474, 474, 474
12:7a 462, 467, 473, 476
12:7b–11 . . . . .467, 475
12:8 .49, 95, 116
12:8–21 58
12:9 . . . . 324, 377, 476–77, 495

12:9–11. 475
12:10. . . . . 82, 126, 412, 476, 479, 480
12:11. . . . 126, 175, 176, 474, 477–78, 479, 501
12:12. 501
12:12–13 . . . . . 463, 467, 478–79, 483
12:12–17 463
12:12b. 474
12:13. 479
12:14. . . . . .82, 363, 477, 479, 480, 481, 485
12:14–16 479–82
12:14–17 . . . .183, 204, 384, 435, 463, 467, 479, 485
12:14b. 480
12:15. . . . . 152, 480, 530
12:15–17 479
12:15b. 481
12:16. 471
12:16–21 145
12:17. . . . . 179, 194, 203, 482
12:17a. 35
12:17b. 35
12:18. . . . . .13, 152, 380, 414, 490, 491, 500
12:18–19 491
12:18–21 . . . . 488, 490, 492, 537
12:18–24 . . . . 485, 488, 489, 496, 521
12:18–29 . . . . .17, 391, 406, 440, 450, 463, 485–501, 524
12:19. 193, 491
12:19–20 490–91
12:20. .490, 491
12:21. . . . . 215, 491–91, 497
12:22. . . . .96, 114, 142, 152, 283, 284, 310, 380, 389, 414, 427, 433, 488, 490, 518, 521
12:22–24 . . . . 220, 488, 492–96
12:23. . . . . .81, 84, 149, 178, 181, 247, 308, 366, 471, 476, 541
12:24. . . . . . .65, 74, 217, 257, 280, 291, 323, 413, 456, 489, 496, 534, 538, 540
12:25. . . 114, 145, 149, 183, 277, 324, 489, 496, 497, 508, 536
12:25–27 . . . . .488, 499

12:25–29 . . . . .13, 204, 384, 488, 489, 496, 501
12:25a. 485
12:26. . . . . .56, 126, 190, 389, 489, 497–98, 499, 536, 537
12:26–27 269
12:26a. 496
12:27. . . . . .51, 56, 190, 236, 397, 489, 490, 497, 498–99, 508, 519
12:27–28 535
12:28. . . 131, 164, 415, 438, 485, 489, 502, 503, 510, 530, 541
12:28–29 . . . . 422, 499–500, 503
12:28b–29 489
12:29. . . . . 198, 500, 537
13 . . . . .502, 506
13:1. . . . . 502, 503, 506, 508, 512
13:1–2. .508–9
13:1–3. . . . . .506, 509
13:1–5a. 507
13:1–6. . . . . 502, 507, 509
13:1–17. . . . . 17, 502–22, 524
13:1–25. . . . . .17, 391, 406, 422, 440, 450, 463, 486, 503, 524
13:2. . . . . 35, 36, 506, 508
13:2–3. 520
13:3. . . . . 353, 509, 512
13:4. . . . . 181, 509–10
13:4–6. 506
13:4a. .507, 510
13:4b. 507
13:5. . . . . 56, 389, 510, 536, 537
13:5–6. . . . . 510–12, 537
13:5a. .507, 510
13:5b. 507, 511, 513
13:5b–6 512
13:5c. 507
13:6. . . . . 503, 507, 511, 512
13:7. . . . . .65, 353, 417, 503, 507, 512–13, 514, 520, 530
13:7–17. . . . . .507, 512
13:8. . . . . . .51, 74, 166, 258, 397, 502, 507, 513–14, 538
13:8–25. 526

13:9. . . . . .11, 30, 152, 217, 513, 514–16, 530
13:9–10. 516
13:9–13. 505
13:9–14. . . . . .502, 507
13:9a. 505, 514, 519
13:10. .501, 516
13:11. . . . . 146, 323, 336, 376, 516–17
13:11–13 517
13:12. . . . . . .74, 77, 82, 323, 343, 388, 477, 505, 517, 538, 540
13:12–13 522
13:12b. 522
13:13. . . . . 12, 445, 517–18
13:14. . . . .53, 72, 131, 236, 283, 397, 428, 433, 508, 514, 518–19, 522, 534
13:15. . . . 339, 340, 341, 378, 379, 431
13:15–16 . . . . 507, 519–20
13:16. 339
13:16a. 520
13:17. . . . . .220, 503, 507, 512, 520–21, 530
13:18. . . . . 170, 308, 381, 503, 523
13:18–19 . . . . 503, 526, 527
13:18–25 . . . . . 3, 17, 27, 503, 523–31
13:19. .503, 527
13:20. . . . .74, 234, 291, 323, 503, 523, 531, 534, 540
13:20–21 . . . . 527–29, 531
13:20–21a 526
13:21. . . . . 74, 412, 529, 531
13:21b. 526
13:22. . . . . 114, 375, 483, 526, 529
13:23. . . . . 3, 6, 526, 529–30
13:24. 530
13:24. . . . . . 26, 82, 512, 525, 526, 530
13:24b. 5
13:25. . . . . 152, 463, 526, 530

James

1:2. 395
1:4. 182
1:11. 250
1:12. 395

Scripture Index

1:21 . . . . 292, 470
2:10 260
2:14–26 414
2:21 340
2:21–23 . . . . 421, 433, 434
2:25 448
3:4 64
3:10 198
3:17–18 477
4:2 215
4:12 248
4:15 181
5:3 31
5:5 384
5:7–11 204
5:8 384
5:10 . . . . 136, 278
5:12 215
5:15 473

1 Peter

1:1 431
1:4–5 437
1:6 395
1:7 386
1:11 108
1:13 178
1:16 477
1:18 327
1:19 325
1:20 . . . . 128, 338
1:22 508
1:23 142
2:1 470
2:2 174
2:2–3 193
2:3 191
2:4 152
2:4–8 84
2:5 . . . . 340, 520
2:11 431
2:12 383
2:24 340

2:25 528
3:8 151
3:14 84
3:20 . . . . 98, 379, 415
3:21 180
3:22 . . . . 52, 72
4:1 143
4:7 384
4:9 509
4:11 174
4:13–17 395
4:14 131
5:2 385
5:3 278
5:4 528
5:12 . . . . 526, 529
5:13–14a 526
5:14b 526

2 Peter

1:5 201
1:5–11 204
1:7 508
1:10 . . . . 96, 136, 217
1:11 376
1:15 136
1:17 44
1:19 . . . . 62, 217, 383
2:1, 3 402
2:4 491
2:5 415
2:6 . . . . 136, 278
2:9 384
2:14 . . . . 176, 198
2:17 491
2:20–22 204
2:22 381
3:3 31
3:7 . . . . 384, 386, 402
3:9 194
3:10 . . . . 174, 383
3:10–13 500
3:12 . . . . 174, 353, 383

3:14 136
3:16 402
3:18a 526
3:18b 526

1 John

1:1 . . . . 142, 490
1:1–4 27
1:3 396
1:7 . . . . 324, 325, 396
1:9 . . . . 324, 325
2:2 88
2:8 275
2:18–19 102
2:19 223
2:24 117
2:28 . . . . 117, 376
3:2 480
3:12 413
3:21 376
4:10 88
4:12 103
4:17 . . . . 376, 384
5:13–15 526
5:14 376
5:16–17 208

2 John

3 153
13 526

3 John

13 526
14 526

Jude

3 201
5 119
6 . . . . 384, 491
11 216
12 515
13 491
14 . . . . 414, 494
17 353

24–25 526

Revelation
1:3 198
1:4 401
1:4b 514
1:5 . . . . 46, 469
1:6 142
1:8 514
1:10 137
2:5 353
2:7 173
2:10 396
2:11 173
2:12 142
2:13 469
2:16 142
2:17 173
2:29 173
3:3 353
3:5 494
3:6 173
3:12 493
3:13 173
3:14 469
3:18 386
3:22 173
4:8 514
5:5 250
5:11 494
9:6 494
11:1–2, 19 283
12:5 . . . . 44, 49
13:8 . . . . 128, 494
13:9 173
14:11 131
14:13 . . . . 131, 135
15:5 283
15:6 283
16:1, 7 283
16:14 384
16:18 64
17 522
17:6 469
17:8 . . . . 128, 402, 494
17:11 402
18 522
18:1 191
18:2 438
18:5 353
18:8 386
18:22 427
19:9 510
19:15 . . . . 44, 49, 142
19:21 142
20:10 85
20:12 494
20:14 386
20:15 . . . . 386, 494
21:2 . . . . 427, 493, 522
21:5 . . . . 499, 501
21:7 45
21:10 493
21:10–27 522
21:23 191
21:27 . . . . 324, 388, 494
22:4 480
22:5 191
22:10 198
22:16 250

Other Ancient Literature Index

Old Testament Apocrypha

Tobit
4:12..........................415

Wisdom of Solomon
1:6...........................469
2:14..........................143
3:13..........................510
5:8...........................279
6:9...........................194
7:23..........................220
7:26...........................33
10............................405
10:4..........................415
10:5..........................433
12:2..........................194
12:8..........................221
13:1....................415, 427
13:17.........................510
14:24, 26.....................510
15:7..........................179
17:8..........................164
17:9..........................492

Sirach
2:12..........................478
21:3..........................142
23:2..........................306
25:23b........................478
27:15.........................333
29:15, 16.....................257
33:19.........................512
44–50.........................405
44:17.........................415
44:19–21......................216
44:20.........................433
47:11.........................354
49:15.........................437
51:19.........................306

Susanna
28............................143

1 Maccabees
1:63..........................516
2:51–60.......................405
2:52....................216, 433
3:45, 51......................388
4:36, 54, 57..................330
5:1...........................330
6:9...........................194
9:54..........................221
9:55..........................478
13:1–2a.......................492
13:2..........................492
13:42.........................149

2 Maccabees
2:4–8.........................303
3:17, 30......................500
3:38..........................101
4:1...........................427
5:27..........................458
6:11..........................459
6:18–7:42.....................457
6:19..........................457
6:28–30.......................457
7:1...........................457
7:7...........................457
7:9...........................457
7:36..........................457
7:37..........................457
9:11..........................457
10:6..........................459
10:28.........................257
11:24.........................498
12:22.........................500
13:16.........................500
15:23.........................500

1 Esdras
8:93..........................256

Old Testament Pseudepigrapha

1 Enoch
14.10–20......................282
14.15–20......................279
47.3..........................494

2 Enoch
7.1–4.........................
..............................335
71.29–72.11...................230

2 Baruch
4.1–4.........................427
4.2–6....................279, 493
4.3...........................282
6.7...........................303

3 Baruch
2–3 335

4 Ezra
4.23 415
7.26 .... 427, 493
8.52 427
10.27 427

3 Maccabees
1.16 163
2.18 388
2.22 478
5.1, 12 217
5.14 152
6.8 470
7.16 258

4 Maccabees
1.34 516
5.24 415
5.25 151
6.3, 6 457
6.35 520
9.12 457
10.11 252
13.23 151
15.4 34
16.18–23 405
16.19–20 433
17 395
17.10 470
17.10–15 468
17.11–17 395
17.14 .... 469, 473
17.23 470

Apocalypse of Abraham
17.10 235

Jubilees
1.27, 29 63
2.1 63
5.19 415
10.17 415
13.24–25 230
17.15–18.16 433
17.17–18 216
19.9 494
30.22 494
32.1 249
36.10 494
46.5 437

Lives of the Prophets
2.1 458

Odes of Solomon
2.14 324
2.43b 46
5.20 399

Psalms of Solomon
17.24–30 44
18.7 44

Sibylline Oracles
4.10 .... 279, 282

Testament of Abraham (A)
16.8 33

Testament of Judah
18.2 511

Testament of Levi
3.4 282
5.1–7 282

Dead Sea Scrolls and Related Texts

1QapGen
6.2 415
22.14–17 230
22.17 234

1QS
9.11 161

4Q174/Flor
1.10–11 .... 44, 45
1.18–19 44

4Q401 (4QShirShabb[b])
11.1–3 231

CD A
3.6–9 119

Philo

Abraham
167–99 .... 216, 433
235 230

Agriculture
9 174
101 200

Allegorical Interpretation
2.3.3 258
2.254–57 446
3.79 234
3.79–82 230
3.102 278
3.203–8 215

Cherubim
26 132
92 258

Confusion
166 511

Creation
107 239

132 197
146 33
170 415

Dreams
1.188. 173
1.214, 219. 149
2.183. 149
2.273. 218

Drunkenness
23 258
61 72

Eternity
112 258

Flaccus
56 397

Flight
63 218

Heir
14–29. 163
204 197

Moses
2.48. 301
2.81–108 .301
2.94. 303
2.160–86 .100

Planting
50 33
108 353

Posterity
48 415

Preliminary Studies
99 . . . . .230, 234

164 478

QE
2.51–106 .301

QG
4.201. 482

Rewards
11–14 405

Sacrifices
8 132
27 454
90 220
91–94 215

Special Laws
1.234–38 .385
2.35. 248
2.255. 387
4.31. 217
4.123. 33

Unchangeable
16 258

Virtues
74 53

Worse
66 176
73 239
105 415
178 258

Josephus

Against Apion
2.293. 258
185–86 249

Jewish Antiquities
1.53. 413
1.74–75. .415
1.181. . . . . .230, 234
1.222. 434
2.50–51. .444
2.55. 510
2.200. 437
2.554–57 .446
3.147. 303
3.206. 332
4.42. 444
5.7–8. 448
11.196. 254
11.270. 86
12.128. 159
12.372. 221
13.96. 142–43
3.363. 86
14.416. 456
16.125. 383
16.163. 256
18.266. 258
18.299. 469
20.181, 206–7 237
20.227. 257
20.266. 529

Jewish War
2.4. 359
4.324. 301
5.193–94 .302
6.134. 469
6.438. . . . . .233, 234
6.468. 230

Mishnah, Talmud, and Related Literature

Mishnah

m. Yoma
8:9. 305
8:90. 385

Babylonian Talmud

b. Ber.
   32a 215

Other Rabbinic Works

Pirqe Rabbi Eliezer
   8 231
   27.3 231

Sifre Numbers
   110 100

Apostolic Fathers

1 Clement
   12.1–8 448
   17–19 405
   36.1–5 5

Didache
   7.3 180

Classical and Ancient Christian Writings

Ambrose
Abraham
   1.3.4 232

Repentance
   2.2 184

Apostolic Constitutions
   2.36.2 134

Aristotle
Rhetoric
   3.9.2 473

Augustine
On Genesis Literally Interpreted
   10.19–21 240

Dio Chrysostom
Orations
   74.24 220

Diogenes Laertius
Lives and Opinions of Eminent Philosophers
   5.1.18 477

Epictetus
Diatr.
   2.16.39 174
   3.10.11 410

Epiphanius
Pan.
   30.2.2 134
   57.3.3 232

Euripides
Ion.
   109 234

Gregory Nazianzus
Epistle
   101 167

Jerome
Against Jovinian
   2.3 184

John Chrysostom
Homilies
   12.7 475
   15.2 321
   27.5 456

Justin Martyr
1 Apol.
   61.12 191
   65.1 191

Dial.
   23.3 134
   33 232

Pausanias
Description of Greece
   10.12.10 513–14

Plato
Republic
   7.515 278
   509c–521nb 13
   509e–510a 352
   514a–520a 351

Timaeus
   27C–29D 13

Plutarch
Mor.
   166A 134

Quintilian
Institutes
   5.11.24 197

Rhetorica ad Herennium
   4.37.39 187

Seneca
Epistles
   33.9 174

Suetonius
Claudius
   25 393–94

Tertullian
Against Praxeas
   26.9 180

Subject Index

Abel, 65, 276, 404, 406, 412–14, 489, 492, 495–96

Abraham
    (and Sarah), the faith of, 425–31
    Melchizedek's supremacy over (*see in general chapter 16* [224–41])

Alexandrinus (MS A), 55, 400

ancients, commendation of the faith of the. *See chapter 26* (404–20)

angels
    on meanings of the word, 47–48
    as "ministering spirits," 43, 48, 52–53
    comparisons of the Son to the, 36, 40, 51, 68, 71, 95, 100, 105, 387
    humans, Jesus, "a little lower than the," 72–74, 76
    the role and status of, 52–53
    worship the Son, 45

Antiochus IV (king), 456–57

Apollos (apostle), as possible author of Hebrews, 4–5

apostasy, 67, 196, 385, 402, 470, 473

appropriating the benefits of our High Priest's ministry, on. *See chapter 24* (370–90)

Arminians, 184, 205

ascension. See under *Jesus Christ*

atonement
    classic view of, 77 (*see next subentry*)
    an in-depth look at sacrifice and, 342–45
    theories of 77, 90–91
    "penal substitution" view, 77, 90
    the timing of, in Hebrews, 367–69

Attridge, Harold W., 3–4, 30, 84, 150

Barak, 453, 454, 455, 497

Barnabas (apostle), as possible author of Hebrews, 4

benefits of our High Priest's ministry, on appropriating the. *See chapter 24* (370–90)

"better hope," introduction of a, 11, 253–54, 256

Binitarianism, 537

blasphemy against the Holy Spirit, 209

brothers and sisters, the purpose of Christ being made by his, 88

Cain, 412, 413

"calling," a heavenly, 95–96, 327

Calvin, John, 4, 57–58, 87, 115, 143, 163, 201, 209, 236, 260, 345, 378, 469, 511

Calvinists, 205

Catechism of the Catholic Church, 341

Chalcedonian definition of the Trinity, 537

chiasm(s), 1, 16, 29, 32, 33–35, 37, 38, 42, 51, 130, 158, 396

Christ. See Jesus Christ

Christian
    life, the key to living a faithful, 417
    the pilgrimage of the, 541–42
    truth, the foundation of basic, 178

Christology, high, 27, 32, 34, 49

Christus Victor view of atonement, 77, 85, 90, 91

church councils, 3–4

city
    earthly and heavenly contrasted, 521–22
    "of the living God," 488–89, 492–93, 496, 518, 521

Clement of Alexandria, 4, 232

concurrence, 38

"confession," 95, 96, 150–51, 381–82

covenant(s)
    on continuity and discontinuity between the, 294–96 (*see also* new covenant)
    a new and better (the new covenant) (*see chapter 20* [286–96])
    overview of the sanctuary, sacrifice, and (*see chapter 19* [270–85])

danger of falling away, 205, 207 (*see also next*)

danger of falling back, 8–9, 12

Daniel and the lions, 456

David (king of Israel), 31, 43, 45, 46, 52, 55, 108, 125, 132, 133, 163, 248, 432, 453, 454, 455, 456, 459, 513
    the faith of, 454
    Hebrew's citation of, 355
    identification with Jesus, 163–64, 250
    response to Gad the prophet, 389
    son of, and a "greater" son, 45, 357
    and Zion, 493

Dead Sea Scrolls, 12–13, 25, 55–56, 58, 161

death, the means by which it is defeated, 86

devil, 78, 80, 85, 90, 540

discipline, the purpose of God's, 476

"divine hero," 82

doxology, 527–29, 531

drifting away, 62–63, 66–67, 110, 131, 220, 398, 449, 515
    the remedy for, 67

Elijah (prophet), 456, 458

Elisha (prophet), 456, 458

endurance
    and faith, call to (see chapter 25 [391–403])
    the measure of, 398
    on running the "race" with endurance (see chapter 30 [462–84])
Enoch (OT saint), 404, 406, 407, 412, 413–14, 415–16
Esau (son of Jacob), 179, 194, 435, 437, 479, 4810, 481–82, 485
eschatology, 2, 53, 71, 339, 362, 383, 534
Essenes, 13
eternal inheritance, 223, 312, 325–36, 327–28367
eternal redemption, 35, 222, 223, 281, 301, 312, 313, 319, 320–21, 324, 325, 343, 367
eternal security, 184, 190, 208, 390, 541
    approaches Calvinists adopt to reconcile Hebrews 6 with the view of, 205–6
eternal spirit, 192, 323, 325, 537n
exodus and conquest, faith in the era of the. See chapter 28 (439–498)
exodus generation, 131, 132, 448. See also wilderness generation
failure to move ahead, 8–9, 11, 12, 170, 177, 515
faith
    of Abraham (and Sarah), 425–31
    the ancients commended for their (see chapter 26 [404–20])
    call to endurance and (see chapter 25 [391–403])
    in the era of the exodus and conquest (see chapter 28 [439–98])
    exhortation to follow Jesus through endurance and (see in general chapters 25–33 [391–531])
    forward-looking, 430–33
    heroes of the, 57, 404–5, 408, 410, 454, 469, 521, 536
    on the importance of forward-looking, 437–38
    an in-depth look at, 417–20
    of judges, prophets, women, and martyrs. See judges, prophets, women, and martyrs, the faith of
    in the patriarchal era (see chapter 27 [421–38])
family (earthly), as a metaphor for the new-covenant people of God, 483–84
fate of the world, on the ultimate, 500–501
Father's right hand, the Son's exaltation to the, 29, 32, 35, 98, 272
firstborn
    on calling the Son the, 46
    enrolled in heaven, 492, 494
flogging, 457
forty years, 108, 109, 118, 122, 448
foundation of basic Christian truth, the 178
Gad (prophet), 389
gathering together, on, 382–83
gezerah shawah, "equal or similar decision" (hermeneutical procedure), 129
Gideon, 453, 454
Gnosticism, 12, 82, 130
God
    on the dependable promises of (see chapter 15 [210–23])
    the household of, 102, 103, 104
    the "rest" of, 129, 133, 137
    Son of (see Jesus Christ / Son of God)
    speaking, 30–33, 37–38
    will of, 354, 359, 398, 460, 528
good works, 382, 383, 384, gospel, law and (contrasted), 144–45
growing by feeding on solid food (see in general chapter 13 [169–82])
hardening, warning against, 115
"health and wealth" gospel, 460–61
"heart"
    scriptural meaning of, 114
    "unbelieving," 10, 114–15, 116, 197, 380, 389, 481, 496
heavenly Jerusalem, 220, 488–89, 492, 493, 496, 499, 521. See also new Jerusalem
heavenly sanctuary, an in-depth look at the, 271–75
heavenly Zion, 493. See heavenly Jerusalem

heavens, the, 149, 153–54, 267, 322, 497
Hebrews (book)
    audience and occasion of, 7–12
        an alternative view, 10–11
        mirror reading, 7–9
        "traditional" view, 10
    authorship of, 3–5
    closing of the letter
        concluding exhortations and encouragement (see chapter 32 [502–22])
        concluding epistolary matters (see chapter 33 [523–31])
    date of, 6–7
    destination, 5–6
    distinctive features of, 1
    genre of, 2–3
    interpretive assumptions: canonical constraints, 15
    exhortations and warnings in (list), 8
    negative factors of, 1–2
    number of uses of the name "Jesus" in, 538
    Old Testament in, 54–59
    structure and outline, 16–17
    theological emphases in, 533–42
        God, 537 (see also God)
        Old Testament, 536 (see also Hebrews: Old Testament in)
        the person of Christ, 538–39 (see also Jesus Christ: the person of)
        the pilgrimage of the Christian, 541–42
        salvation history, 533–34 (see also salvation-historical framework)
        the Spirit, 537 (see also Holy Spirit)
        vertical typology and the importance of the unseen realm, 535–36
        the work of Christ (see under Jesus Christ: work of)
    the timing of the atonement in, 366–69
    traditional title, 10
    the two most important titles in, 538
    worldview, 12–15
        most significant factor in the author's, 15

Subject Index

heroes of the faith, 57, 404–5, 408, 410, 454, 469, 521, 536
  acts of faith by the, 453

high priest
  "according to the order of Melchizedek," exposition on the (see chapters 16–18 [224–69])
  a call to persevere through the power of our exalted (see chapter 11 [146–54]
  on high priests and our great (see chapter 12 [155–68])
  ministry of our great (see chapters 19–23 [270–369])
  person and (see in general chapters 11–24 [146–390])
  the supremacy and sufficiency of our (see chapter 17 [242–62])
  verses providing an interim summary of Jesus as our, 263
  who is also the Son (see in general chapter 18 [263–69])

Holy Spirit
  blasphemy against the, 209
  as a theological emphasis in Hebrews, 537
  a warning from the, 108
  (see also eternal spirit)

"house," New Testament meaning of, 104

household
  in the ancient world, 104
  of God, 102, 103, 104

human beings, on Jesus Christ's identification with. See in general chapter 5 (77–91); also 150–52, 168

humanity of the Son, and its significance. See in general chapters 4 and 5 (68–91)

human nature, twofold purpose of the Son's assumption of, 85

imprisonment, 6, 177, 457, 509, 529

incarnation, 35, 45, 46, 65, 74, 76, 90, 91, 338, 354, 367

inclusio, 1, 42, 45, 51, 68, 82, 94, 113, 114, 125, 139, 146, 147, 169, 246, 254, 255, 263, 269, 270, 271, 291, 300, 305, 317, 319, 338, 346, 350, 360, 371, 375, 398, 442, 459, 463, 512, 513, 520, 529

inheritance, eternal, 223, 312, 325–36, 327–28367

Isaiah, execution of, 458

Jephthah, 453, 454, 455

Jeremiah (prophet), 30, 286, 289, 290, 292, 293, 294, 297, 309, 457, 458, 493, 534

Jesus Christ / Son of God
  "achieved cleansing for sins" 32, 33, 34–35
  ascension, 90, 153, 266, 337, 342, 344, 361, 368, 369, 528
  assumption of human nature, the twofold purpose of, 85
  death of, 10, 329, 339, 342, 344, 368, 369, 540
  description of the one who is Son, 38–39
  elevation to the Father's right hand, 29, 32, 35, 98, 272
  on the exalted Son and rest for the people of God (see in general chapters 1–10)
  on the exalted status of the Son (see chapter 2 [40–59])
  the faithful Son, exhortation to focus on (see chapter 6 [92–104])
  as "firstborn," 22, 45, 46
  greater than the angels, 36, 40, 95, 100, 105, 387
  greater than/worthy of greater glory than Moses, 98–99, 100
  on his deity/divinity and his humanity, 166–67
  incarnation, 35, 45, 46, 65, 74, 76, 90, 91, 338, 354, 367
  as mediator of the new covenant, 325–26, 327, 365, 370, 413, 492, 495
  ministry of (see under subentry our high priest)
  number of uses of the name "Jesus" in Hebrews, 538
  our high priest, 147, 149–51
    a call to persevere through the power of (see chapter 11 [146–54])
    compared with the Old Testament priest, 365
    ministry of (see chapters 19–23 [270–369])
    appropriating the benefits (see chapter 24 [370–90])
    person and (see in general chapters 11–24 [146–390])
    the supremacy and sufficiency of (see chapter 17 [242–62])
    verses providing an interim summary of, 263
  the person of, 34, 225, 269, 285, 538–39
  priesthood, compared/contrasted with the Levitical priests/priesthood, 239, 249–58
  the purpose of his appearance, 339
  the radiance of God's glory, 33–34, 98, 538
  the representation of God's essence, 33, 34
  as representative human, 75–76
  resurrection, 32, 35, 45, 65, 90, 98, 137, 162, 165, 180, 251, 321, 342, 344, 361, 367, 368, 369, 435, 437, 528, 534, 540
  sacrifice of (see sacrifice: the ultimate)
  speaking, 31–32
  work of, 34–35, 82, 85–86, 90, 152, 224, 259, 269, 276, 281, 285, 310, 320, 323, 338, 339, 342, 346, 359, 362, 363, 364, 366–69, 385, 457, 499, 535, 539–41
    encouragement to appropriate and act on the high-priestly, 375–84
    the eternal quality of the blessings of, 366–67
    the outcome of, for believers, 312
    the requirement for Christians' continued enjoyment of, 208
    significance of the cross to, 341
    warning about rejecting the high-priestly, 384–89

Judaism, 10–11, 12, 45, 149, 179, 180, 181, 235, 260, 261, 295, 386, 395, 421, 462, 495, 515, 518
  apocalyptic, 153, 252
  continuity between early Christianity and, 295
  Second Temple, 405, 413
  standard marks of, 296

Judas Maccabeus, 458. *See also* Maccabean martyrs; Maccabees

judges, prophets, women, and martyrs, the faith of, 453–59
- the victories won by their faith, 454–56
- the faith/exploits of judges, 405, 454, 455
- the faith/exploits of martyrs, 405, 456–58, 468
- the faith/exploits of prophets, 405, 454, 455
- the faith of women, 405, 456

lassitude, a rebuke for spiritual, 172–77

"last days," 14, 27, 31, 96, 181, 192, 309, 338, 493, 534

law and gospel (contrasted), 144–45

Levitical priests/priesthood, the inferiority of the, 246–56

lions, 460, 455, 456

love for one another, 508

Luke, as possible author of Hebrews, 4

Luther, Martin, 4, 144–45, 184

Maccabean martyrs, 456–57, 458, 468, 473

Maccabees (Jewish rebel warriors), 180, 456–58, 461

marriage, Hebrews's advice on, 509–10

martyrs, the faith/exploits of, 405, 456–58, 468

mass (Roman Catholic), 341–42

Massah ["testing"] and Meribah ["quarreling"], 109

maturity
- exhortation to move on to (*see in general chapters 13–15* [169–223])
- on the call to move on to, 181–82

mediator of a new covenant, Jesus as, 325–26, 327, 365, 370, 413, 492, 495

meeting together, 382–83

Melchizedek
- exposition on a high priest according to the order of (*see chapters 16–18* [224–69])
- on Hebrews's controversial description of, 234–35

an in-depth look at the mysterious, 228–32
- and Levitical priests/priesthood, contrasted with Jesus and/or, 236–37, 239, 246–56
- meaning of the name, 233
- meaning of the phrase "in the order of," 229
- Old Testament story of, told in Hebrews, 232–34, 236
- supremacy over Abraham (*see in general chapter 16* [224–41])

"Messiah," meaning of, 43

metaphors, on the use of, 482–84

Middle Platonism, 3, 13–15, 130, 131, 236, 252, 278–79, 282, 322, 352, 397, 535

mirror reading, 7–8

mocking, 457

Moses
- on the faithfulness of, 97
- Jesus greater than/worthy of greater glory than, 98–99, 100
- service of, 100

Most Holy Place, 34, 146, 222, 270, 283, 301–4, 306–7, 310, 313, 317, 319–20, 322–23, 326, 334, 335, 336–38, 342, 343, 366–70, 374, 375, 376, 377, 379, 516

Mount Sinai, the contrast between Mount Zion and, 489–93

Mount Zion, 284, 488–89, 492–95, 499, 500, 518, 521

myriad(s), 492, 493–94

Neoplatonism, 13, 490–91, 498

Nero (emperor), 6, 393

new covenant, 11, 81, 127, 135, 192, 262–63, 287, 288, 289–95, 297, 302, 312, 327, 328, 359, 363, 364, 372, 388, 456, 459, 486, 495, 499, 531, 534.
- the "better" promises of the, 286
- on eternal redemption, the heavenly sanctuary, decisive sacrifice, and (*see chapter 22* [312–45])
- inaugurated through Christ's redemptive death, 334
- Jesus's role in the, 280
- Jesus as mediator of the, 325–26, 327, 365, 370, 413, 492, 495

a new and better (*see chapter 20* [286–96])
- prophecy (of Jeremiah 31), 280, 291–92, 363, 381
- what its coming meant, 261
- (*see also* covenants)

new Jerusalem, 283, 427, 438, 493, 494, 521–22. *See also* heavenly Jerusalem

Nicene Creed, 33

Noah, 98, 175, 404, 406, 410, 412, 415–16, 501

Old Testament
- in Hebrews, 54–59
- as a theological emphasis in Hebrews, 536

order of Melchizedek. *See* Melchizedek

parousia, 45

partakers of Christ, 103, 116–17

patriarchal era, faith in the. *See chapter 27* (421–38)

Paul (apostle), as possible author of Hebrews, 3–4

"penal substitution" view of atonement, 77, 91

people of God, the most fruitful metaphor for the new-covenant, 483–84

"perfection," 77, 176, 178, 181, 182, 188, 197, 246, 258, 263, 322, 327, 364, 459, 462, 495
- Christ is able to secure believers', 471
- meaning in Hebrews, 81, 247
- Old Testament sacrifices could not bring, 366

perseverance
- through the power of our exalted high priest, a call to (*see chapter 11* [146–54])
- warning regarding, 204–5
- of the saints, 102

person of Christ, the, 34, 225, 269, 538–39

Philo of Alexandria. *See* author and ancient sources indexes
- on "milk" and soul nourishment, 174
- portrayal of Moses, 100

pilgrimage of the Christian, 541–42

Subject Index

Plato, 13, 278, 351–52

priest
- Christ compared with the Old Testament, 365
- "in the order of Melchizedek" (*see* Melchizedek)

promise(s)
- of God, on the dependable (*see chapter 15* [210–23])
- warning and (*see chapter 14* [183–209])

prophet, on the biblical meaning of the word, 30–31

prophets, the faith/exploits of, 405, 454, 455

"purification of sins," 27, 35

race, on running with endurance. *See chapter 30* (462–84)
- on the metaphor, 483

radiance, 33–34, 98, 538

rebuke for spiritual lassitude, a 172–77

redemption, eternal, 35, 222, 223, 281, 301, 312, 313, 319, 320–21, 324, 325, 343, 367

repentance, on there being "no more," 208–9

"replacement" model of the end of the world, 500–501

"rest," on entering God's. *See chapter 9* (122–38)
- "Sabbath" (*see* Sabbath rest)

resurrection
- "a better," 180, 456
- of the body/the dead, 179–81, 251, 434, 437, 453, 456, 460, 499, 501, 528, 540
- of Christ, 32, 35, 45, 65, 90, 98, 137, 162, 165, 180, 251, 321, 342, 344, 361, 367, 368, 369, 435, 437, 528, 534, 540
- of the righteous/believers, 180, 181, 435

Roman Catholics, 341

Sabbath rest, 134–35, 136–38

sacrifice
- and atonement, an in-depth look at, 342–45
- and covenant, an overview of the sanctuary, covenant, and (*see chapter 19* [270–85])
- the benefit of Christ's, 364–67
- Christ's sacrifice contrasted with the Old Testament priests', 366
- the effects of Christ's, 366–67
- the ultimate (*see chapter 23* [346–69])

saints, on perseverance of the, 102

salvation
- "already" and "not yet" 53–54
- on neglecting "such a great," 64
- on taking hold of our great (*see in general chapter 3* [60–67])
- three stages in the transmission of, 65–66
- on whether a Christian can lose their, 402–3

salvation history
- the nature and power of faith illustrated in (*see in general chapters 26–29* [404–61])
- as a theological emphasis in Hebrews, 533–34 (*see also* next entry)

salvation-historical framework, 365, 521, 533–35

Samson, 389, 453, 454, 456

sanctuary
- earthly and heavenly, 366
- an in-depth look at the heavenly, 271–75
- and its regulations, the earthly (*see chapter 21* [297–311])
- new, an illustration of the (*see* previous subentry)
- overview of the sacrifice, covenant, and (*see chapter 19* [270–85])

Scripture
- on the careful reading of, 240–41
- on the "living" and "active" nature of, 57
- (*see also* Word of God)

second person of the Trinity, 32

Seleucids, 457, 458

Septuagint, 55, 291, 356, 480, 536

shaking of all things made, the purpose of the, 499

Shunammite's son, 456

"signs and wonders," 64, 66

silence (by definition), a, 241

sin(s)
- "purification of," 27, 35
- the Son's "cleansing for," 32, 33, 34–35
- threefold description of the person persisting in a willful, 387
- (*see also* Jesus Christ)

Sinaiticus (א, 55)

sluggishness, 173, 202–3

"solid food," 172, 173, 174, 176, 177, 183

Song of Moses, 47, 389

Son of God. See Jesus Christ / Son of God

Son of Man
- of Psalms, 71–75
- "sons of God," 44

stagnation, on avoiding spiritual. *See chapters 13–14* (169–209)

stoning, 457, 458

stories, on the power of, 120–21

straight paths, 478–79

supersessionism, 295–96, 359, 534

sword, the word of God as a, 142–43

tabernacle
- various terms the author uses for all or part of the earthly, 301

Ten Commandments, 138

temple, destruction of the (AD 70), 7, 10, 294

theological emphases in Hebrews. *See under* Hebrews

theories of atonement, 77, 90–91

"thorns and thistles," 196, 197–98

timing of the atonement in, 366–69

"today," 115–16, 125, 132

torture, 468, 472

Trinitarianism, 389, 537

Trinity, 32, 50, 537

"trinity of virtues," early Christian, 374

truth, the foundation of basic Christian, 178

two things that believers must hold on to, 101

typology, 57, 278
- "Joshua," 134
- vertical, 58, 535

unbelief, on the disaster of. *See chapter 8* (111–21)

"unbelieving heart"
   the opposite of an, 380
   the result of an, 115

unseen world, on vertical typology and the importance of the, 535–36

Uriah (prophet), 458

Vaticanus (MS B), 55, 400

"vertical typology," 58, 535

walls of Jericho, 439, 448, 460

"wandering" versus rest for Christians, 110

warning(s)
   best-known New Testament passage of, 204
   and exhortations in Hebrews (list), 8
   from the Holy Spirit, 108–9
   and promise (*see chapter 14* [183–209])
   from Scripture (*see in general chapter 7* [105–10])

washings (ritual/ceremonial), 179, 180, 252, 308–9, 354, 381, 515

weaknesses, our, 150, 151, 167

widow of Zarephath, 456

wilderness generation. 106, 109, 111, 113–14, 118–19, 122, 125, 126, 127, 135–36, 142, 190–92, 417, 496
   exhortation to avoid the fate of the (*see in general chapters 7–9* [105–38])
   the root cause of judgment on the, 120

wilderness wandering, 57, 93, 105, 108, 109–10, 118, 125, 131, 139, 536, 541

will (legal declaration), 318, 328–30

will of God, 354, 359, 398, 460, 528

women, the faith of, 405, 456

Word of God, exposition on the power of the. *See chapter 10* (139–45)

world, different perspectives on the ultimate fate of the, 501–2

Zechariah (prophet), 413, 458

Author Index

Adams, Edward, 15, 33, 51, 411, 498, 499
Alexander, T. Desmond, 237, 277, 278, 303, 304, 427, 447
Allen, David L. (D. L.), 4, 164, 193, 194, 199, 254, 379, 500
Allen, David M. (D. M.), 47, 58, 389, 490, 492, 511
Allen, Leslie C., 229
Allen, Michael, 143
Andersen, F. I., 230, 399
Armerding, Carl E., 229
Attridge, Harold W., 4–5, 6, 30, 31, 32, 34, 37, 46, 48, 49, 63, 71, 72, 73, 75, 81, 82, 83, 84, 85, 87, 89, 96, 98, 99, 101, 116, 117, 125, 126, 128, 130, 131, 132, 133, 134, 139, 147, 150, 151, 158, 159, 160, 162, 163, 164, 172, 173, 175, 177, 178, 179, 180, 188, 189, 192, 194, 195, 197, 198, 202, 204, 208, 217, 218, 219, 220, 234, 235, 246, 249, 251, 252, 254, 256, 258, 266, 267, 268, 271, 275, 277, 278, 280, 294, 300, 301, 302, 303, 304, 307, 316, 321, 322, 325, 326, 327, 332, 333, 334, 335, 336, 337, 338, 352, 353, 354, 357, 358, 359, 361, 362, 363, 371, 381, 391, 394, 398, 405, 410, 413, 426, 428, 429, 436, 444, 445, 446, 463, 469, 479, 481, 485, 488, 503, 506, 511, 512, 527, 529, 530
Averbeck, Richard A., 278

Bacchiocchi, Samuele, 134, 137
Bachmann, E. Theodore, 145, 184
Backhaus, Kurt, 32, 65, 69, 99, 130, 133, 139, 147, 152, 158, 162, 169, 170, 172, 190, 191, 195, 204, 213, 216, 218, 234, 248, 250, 252, 256, 259, 261, 278, 291, 294, 319, 326, 331, 332, 336, 337, 350, 378, 409, 419, 429, 439, 488, 517

Baker, David W., 237, 278, 304, 447
Barnard, Jody A., 14, 282, 285
Barrett, C. K., 14, 132
Bateman, Herbert W., IV, 102, 190, 193, 386, 390
Bates, Matthew W., 56
Bauckham, Richard, 3, 10, 15, 36, 42, 46, 49, 52, 57, 85, 99, 134, 164, 165, 230, 235, 252, 295, 296, 406, 412, 445, 499, 513, 514, 518
Baugh, S. M., 409
Baurenfeind, H., 221
Beale, G. K., 37, 283, 498
Beilby, James, 90
Bénétrau, Samuel, 274, 288, 307, 321, 325, 359, 360, 361, 378, 388, 409, 413, 416, 419, 429, 445, 463, 469, 471, 473, 476, 479, 482, 494, 495, 506, 516, 527, 529
Bertram, G., 474
Black, David Alan, 4
Black, M. 36
Black, Matthew, 429
Blaising, Craig A., 294
Blocher, Henri A. G., 91
Bock, Darrell L., 294
Bockmuehl, Markus, 406
Boda, Mark J., 306, 493
Brown, Raymond E., 7
Bruce, F. F., 7, 10, 11, 33, 37, 45, 46, 49, 73, 88, 102, 135, 136, 144, 159, 161, 164, 180, 181, 192, 213, 235, 237, 242, 256, 257, 258, 276, 286, 294, 304, 307, 309, 317, 323, 324, 325, 332, 335, 344, 353, 354, 357, 361, 362, 363, 377, 386, 394, 410, 412, 413, 426, 429, 434, 435, 443, 457, 460, 463, 469, 470, 471, 479, 481, 482, 494, 495, 496, 502, 509, 511, 512, 515, 527

Buchanan, George Wesley, 502
Büchsel, F., 410
Bultmann, R., 419

Caird, George B., 44
Calaway, Jared C., 97
Calvin, John, 4, 57–58, 87, 115, 143, 151, 163, 164, 178, 184, 201, 209, 220, 236, 255, 260, 267, 321, 345, 378, 386, 429, 446, 469, 471, 509, 511, 516
Carson, D. A., 5, 11, 37, 38, 59, 102, 132, 137, 138, 436
Caneday, Ardel B., 46, 207
Chilton, B. D., 433
Church, Philip, 283, 352
Clark, William R., 4
Cockerill, Gareth Lee, 5, 12, 16, 32, 33, 36, 47, 48, 64, 65, 73, 74, 82, 84, 87, 89, 96, 98, 99, 100, 102, 103, 105, 109, 114, 117, 120, 125, 128, 129, 130, 132, 135, 139, 142, 144, 147, 162, 164, 165, 175, 178, 181, 191, 192, 195, 197, 198, 200, 216, 218, 219, 221, 225, 230, 1231, 235, 236, 239, 246, 248, 249, 250, 251, 252, 254, 255, 257, 258, 260, 264, 267, 268, 274, 275, 294, 306, 307, 309, 316, 323, 325, 326, 328, 329, 333, 335, 337, 338, 339, 340, 344, 357, 358, 359, 360–61, 363, 371, 376, 377, 379, 381, 382, 383, 385, 387, 389, 397, 405, 409, 413, 414, 415, 416, 419, 429, 431, 433, 434, 435, 436, 437, 439, 444, 445, 446, 447, 453, 460, 469, 471, 472, 479, 480, 481, 488, 494, 495, 498, 52, 506, 511, 512, 513, 514, 515, 516, 517, 519, 527, 528, 529

Cole, Graham A., 91

Compton, Jared, 35, 52, 357

Cosby, Michael R., 405, 411, 450

Costley, Angela, 99

Cowan, Christopher, 207

Craigie, Peter, 44, 358

Croy, N. Clayton, 467, 469, 472, 474

Cullmann, Oscar, 50, 340

D'Angelo, Mary Rose, 405

Daube, D., 14

Davies, P. R., 433–34

Davies, W. D., 14

deClaissé-Walford, Nancy L., 229

Delcor, M., 231

Delitzsch, Franz, 4, 5, 34, 37, 72, 87, 127, 150, 158, 159, 188, 217, 218, 257, 319, 326, 327, 331, 332, 333, 352, 357, 360, 361, 363, 371, 378, 388, 446, 456, 460, 469, 478, 494, 512, 515

deSilva, David A., 10, 34, 80, 83, 96, 102, 117, 131, 150, 163, 173, 175, 177, 178, 179, 180, 209, 220, 322, 323, 352, 353, 362, 397, 472, 474, 481, 498, 502, 516, 518

Demarest, Bruce, 232

Dempster, Stephen G., 292

Docherty, Susan E., 55

Dodd, C. H., 44–45, 55, 56, 84

Doyle, Arthur Conan, 5

Dunbar, David G., 5

Dunnill, John, 133, 433

Dyer, Bryan R., 3, 10, 81, 523

Easter, Matthew C., 73, 131, 164, 410, 471

Ebert, Daniel J., IV, 29

Eddy, Paul R., 90

Eisenbaum, Pamela, 405

Ellingworth, Paul, 10, 31, 45, 46, 47, 48, 50, 63, 64, 65, 66, 68, 71, 83, 84, 87, 89, 92, 95, 96, 98, 99, 108, 116, 118, 125, 126, 127, 128, 130, 132, 134, 135, 136, 144, 150, 151, 158, 159, 161, 164, 165, 172, 173, 175, 176, 177, 178, 179, 180, 181, 184, 192, 195, 202, 217, 218, 219, 220, 227, 234, 236, 248, 251, 255, 256, 258, 264, 271, 275, 276, 289, 293, 301, 306, 307, 308, 316, 321, 325, 332, 333, 335, 336, 337, 339, 340, 353, 357, 360, 361, 362, 364, 371, 375, 376, 377, 379, 381, 382, 383, 386, 394, 396, 397, 398, 399, 409, 411, 412, 413, 414, 415, 416, 426, 427, 428, 429, 430, 431, 432, 436, 447, 448, 454, 455, 456, 457, 463, 470, 471, 472, 475, 476, 477, 478, 479, 480, 482, 485, 491, 492, 495, 496, 496, 498, 508, 510, 512, 513, 514, 515, 516, 519, 528, 529, 530

Elliott, J. K., 195

Eltester, W., 429

Eisele, Wilfried, 13, 14

Enns, Peter E., 109, 447

Estes, Daniel, 229

Evans, C. Stephen, 433

Fanning, Buist, 102, 103, 190, 386, 390

Feinberg, John S., 138, 262, 357

Feinberg, Paul D., 357

Fewster, Gregory P., 3

Filson, Floyd V., 502, 513, 516, 518

Filtvedt, Ole Jakob, 2, 87, 248, 260, 296, 406, 498

Fitzmyer, Joseph A., 231, 234, 235, 400

France, R. T., 68, 73, 105, 116, 161, 209, 258, 271, 308, 309, 332, 379, 429, 470, 471

Fuhrmann, Sebastian, 75, 86, 89, 163, 271, 360

Gäbel, Georg, 282, 321, 332, 336, 342, 360

Garland, David E., 68

Garrett, D. A., 237

Gelardini, Gabriella, 3, 284

Gentry, Peter J., 292, 294

Gheorghita, Radu, 47, 54, 58, 400

Gleason, Randall C., 189, 190, 199, 386, 388

Goldingay, John, 43, 44, 47, 48, 49, 51, 108

Goldsworthy, Graeme, 292

Goppelt, Leonard, 57, 58, 336

Gordley, Matthew E., 27

Grässer, Erich, 5, 6, 12, 30, 40, 47, 63, 65, 68, 82, 92, 96, 100, 106, 127, 130, 133, 139, 158, 162, 172, 173, 174, 175, 180, 188, 190, 191, 192, 201, 202, 203, 208, 213, 216, 220, 231, 233, 235, 246, 250, 252, 258, 268, 275, 280, 303, 316, 319, 321, 333, 336, 352, 354, 357, 358, 361, 371, 377, 380, 383, 385, 388, 394, 395, 399, 402, 405, 411, 412, 415, 416, 419, 426, 427, 429, 431, 432, 437, 444, 445, 448, 453, 456, 463, 470, 471, 472, 473, 485, 488, 491, 496, 498, 502, 506, 508, 516, 519

Gray, Patrick, 165, 184, 446

Griffiths, Jonathan I., 57, 139, 144

Grosvenor, Mary, 34, 64, 99, 108, 159, 160, 276, 307, 327, 362, 413, 443, 476, 516

Grudem, Wayne, 190, 193

Gundry, Stanley N., 138

Guthrie, Donald (D.), 10, 126, 127, 377

Guthrie, George H. (G.), 16, 37, 54, 68, 73, 83, 84, 102, 110, 118, 125, 143, 155, 161, 164, 175, 177, 179, 190, 192, 196, 197, 198, 214, 218, 248, 264, 267, 269, 271, 273, 275, 279, 290, 295, 307, 308, 317, 318, 328, 343, 356, 357, 363, 371, 375, 388, 389, 445, 471, 474, 492, 503, 511

Hagner, Donald A., 179, 323, 379, 411, 446, 469

Hanson, A. T., 134, 235

Harder, G., 136

Harris, Dana M. (D.), 54, 83, 117, 129, 136, 143, 151, 158, 173, 180, 193, 217, 221, 248, 256, 258, 266, 275, 277, 289, 302, 306, 307, 308, 317, 322, 329, 333, 336, 337, 338, 339, 341, 357, 358, 376, 382, 396, 398, 408, 411, 429, 431, 434, 435, 437, 443, 454, 460, 475, 488, 492, 498, 508, 512, 518, 529

Harris, J. Rendel (J. R.), 55, 134

Harris, Murray J. (M.), 49, 68, 160, 164, 340, 411, 413, 471

Hawthorne, Gerald F., 190, 229

Hay, David M., 52

Hays, Richard B., 295, 296, 406, 515

Heen, Erik M., 75, 240

Author Index

Helm, Paul, 57
Hengel, Martin, 472
Hermann, Markus-Liborius, 54, 57
Himmelfarb, Martha, 282
Hofius, Otfried, 12–13, 130, 131, 132, 279, 378
Hollander, H. W., 248
Holmes, Stephen R., 499
Hooker, Morna, 10, 262
Horsley, G, H. R., 520
Hort, F. J. A., 182
Horton, Fred L., 230, 231, 232
Horton, Michael S., 205, 344
Hossfeld, Frank-Lothar, 52, 108
Howard, W. F., 33, 196, 429
Huey, F. B., 292–93
Hughes, Graham (G.), 11, 57, 58, 69, 71, 84, 177, 208
Hughes, John J., 328
Hughes, Philip Edgcumbe (P.), 5, 12, 13, 33, 34, 37, 50, 75, 87, 132, 135, 164, 175, 180, 190, 194, 257, 267, 275, 276, 277, 290, 307, 321, 324, 325, 337, 344, 353, 360, 379, 388, 395, 412, 432, 446, 469, 470, 472, 481, 488, 492, 512, 515, 516, 517, 518
Hurst, Lincoln D., (L. D.) 13, 14, 36, 44, 231, 307, 335
Hurtado, Larry W., 49

Isaacs, Marie E., 283, 322, 380, 516

Jacobson, Rolf A., 229
Jamieson, R. B., 35, 37, 45, 73, 81, 85, 86, 162, 275, 276, 279, 305, 323, 326, 329, 333, 335–36, 340, 344, 345, 360, 369
Johnson, Luke Timothy, 3, 4, 7, 12, 14, 83, 87, 96, 97, 100, 106, 115, 116, 120, 127, 129, 135, 143, 151, 152, 163, 164, 165, 173, 201, 202, 220, 236, 247, 250, 251, 254, 267, 278, 301, 306, 317, 322, 350, 334, 336, 353, 355, 359, 362, 363, 378, 382, 385, 388, 394–95, 405, 409, 412, 429, 431, 437, 444, 455, 456, 457, 460, 463, 473, 474, 475, 479, 491, 499, 503, 520, 527
Joslin, Barry C., 248, 254, 260, 261, 292

Käsemann, Ernst, 12, 105, 110, 130, 377, 470
Kettler, F. H., 429
Kibbe, Michael, 46, 54, 58, 86, 197, 252, 321, 323, 326, 333, 338, 345, 488, 491, 495, 499
Kierkegaard, S., 433
Kistemaker, Simon J., 47, 50, 51
Klawans, Jonathan, 279
Koester, Craig R., 2, 3, 6, 10, 15, 32, 35, 36, 37, 47, 48, 49, 63, 65, 72, 73, 77, 82, 83, 86, 87, 89, 108, 115, 116, 117, 118, 122, 125, 126, 128, 130, 132, 135, 142, 143, 144, 147, 150, 151, 152, 159, 164, 165, 172, 175, 176, 177, 179, 180, 190, 191, 192, 195, 202, 213, 215, 217, 218, 220, 231, 236, 237, 242, 246, 248, 250, 251, 252, 258, 268, 275, 289, 294, 302, 304, 306, 307, 308, 317, 319, 320, 321, 322, 325, 332, 338, 350, 358, 359, 360, 362, 363, 371, 376, 377, 379, 381, 38/2, 383, 384, 385, 394, 396, 398, 401, 405, 412, 416, 426, 428, 429, 431, 435, 440, 445, 446, 448, 450, 453, 455, 456, 463, 471, 473, 479, 482, 485, 489, 491, 492, 493, 498, 499, 503, 511, 513–14, 516, 518, 521, 528, 529
Kraus, Hans-Joachim, 43, 49, 72, 229, 355
Krey, Philip D. W., 75, 240
Kurianal, James, 155, 165, 225, 230, 249

Laansma, Jon C., 2, 8, 14, 39, 55, 73, 92, 97, 99, 110, 111, 114, 127, 129, 130, 131, 143, 184, 205, 295, 343, 498, 499, 502, 503
Lamp, Jeffrey S., 498, 499, 501
Lane, William L., 10, 29, 31, 33, 37, 46, 48, 49, 51, 63, 66, 68, 73, 74, 75, 82, 83, 85, 86, 87, 92, 96, 98, 99, 100, 102, 106, 115, 116, 118, 125, 128, 132, 133, 134, 136, 142, 144, 150, 151, 158, 163, 164, 177, 178, 179, 180, 193, 195, 198, 201, 214, 215, 216, 217, 220, 227, 231, 234, 246, 248, 249, 254, 255, 258, 266, 267, 271, 275, 276, 278, 279, 280, 290, 291, 302, 304, 306, 307, 309, 317, 321, 322, 323, 325, 326, 328, 329, 331, 332, 333, 334, 335, 336, 337, 340, 346, 350, 352, 357, 359, 360, 362, 363, 371, 376, 377, 378, 379, 381, 385, 386, 6387, 389, 391, 394, 395, 396, 398, 401, 408, 409, 410, 411, 412, 413, 414, 419, 425, 426, 427, 428, 429, 430, 431, 434, 435, 442, 444, 445, 446, 447, 453, 458, 459, 460, 463, 470, 471, 472, 473, 475, 477, 479, 480, 481, 482, 485, 488, 490, 494, 498, 502, 506, 508, 509, 513, 515, 516, 517, 518, 519, 520, 528, 529, 530

Lee, Gregory W. (G. W.), 57, 269, 296
Lee, John A. L., 177
Leonard, William, 4
Levinsohn, Stephen H., 143, 166
Lewis, C. S., 67, 417, 449
Lincoln, A. T., 132, 135, 137
Lindars, Barnabas, 7, 10, 12, 180, 325, 400
Llewelyn, Stephen, 520
Loader, William R. G., 45, 164, 165, 177, 218
Longenecker, Richard N., 172, 231, 421
Longman, Tremper, 49, 68, 230
Lundbom, Jack R., 292
Luther, Martin, 4, 144, 145, 184

Macaskill, Grant, 37
MacDonald, Nathan, 445
Mackie, Scott D., 132, 152, 260, 279, 284, 306, 352, 516
Manson, T. W. 36
Marshall, I. Howard, 38, 85, 344
Mason, Eric F., 3, 10, 14, 231, 259, 268, 282, 360
Massonnet, Jean, 75, 82, 92, 147, 162, 180, 194, 195, 196, 219, 253, 256, 275, 305, 325, 334, 353, 359, 361, 376, 394, 398, 409, 411, 414, 427, 429, 432, 455, 463, 479, 480, 513, 527
Maston, Jason, 73
Mathewson, David, 190, 192, 197, 321
McAfee, Matthew, 191, 193, 197
McConville, J. Gordon, 493
McCormack, Bruce L., 165
McCruden, Kevin B., 3, 10, 14, 82, 151, 231, 259, 359–60, 495

McDonough, Sean M., 15, 33, 50, 98
McKay, J. Michael, Jr., 134
McKay, Kenneth L., 98
McKelvey, R. J., 471
McKnight, Scot, 183
Meier, John P., 29
Metzger, Bruce M., 33, 51, 100, 127, 128, 180, 289, 319, 331, 428, 458, 519, 529
Michel, Otto, 35, 75, 136, 141, 147, 194, 224, 239, 242, 249, 268, 271, 274, 307, 325, 327, 330, 332, 333, 352, 354, 371, 376, 378, 410, 419, 430, 436, 439, 445, 453, 455, 459, 472, 478, 481, 488, 494, 506, 511, 512
Mitchell, Alan C., 259, 295
Moberly, R. W. L., 433
Moberly, Walter R., 412
Moffatt, James, 5, 32, 62, 117, 126, 134, 164, 174, 180, 251, 258, 278, 325, 363, 378, 429, 435, 502, 512
Moffitt, David M., 73, 82, 83, 268, 276, 277, 279, 284, 320, 321, 323, 326, 337, 342, 345, 355, 360
Montefiore, Hugh, 43, 116, 127, 128, 134, 164, 220, 252, 276, 321, 325, 337, 344, 435, 4496, 471, 479, 494, 496, 512
Moo, Douglas J. (D.), 11–12, 51, 59, 83, 89, 138, 204, 252, 262, 295, 320, 327, 345, 357, 501
Moo, Jonathan A. (J.), 51, 501
Mosser, Carl, 518
Moule, C. F. D., 31, 127, 160, 161, 193, 217, 238, 239, 247, 251, 321, 323, 434, 447, 528
Moulton, J. H., 33, 196, 429
Muraoka, T. (Takamitsu), 108, 214, 238, 447

Naselli, Andrew, 59, 357
Newsom, Carol A., 282
Neyrey, Jerome H., 235
Nicklas, Tobias (T.), 54, 323
Nicole, Roger, 190
Norris, Laurie L., 207

Oberholtzer, Thomas Kem, 64, 189, 199, 386

O'Day, Gail R., 184
Oepke, A., 280
Oropeza, B. J., 103
Osborne, Grant R., 73, 193, 200, 390
Owen, John, 190
Owens, H. P., 176

Parker, Brent E., 207, 294
Peeler, Amy L., 34
Pelikan, Jaroslov, 144
Pennington, Jonathan T., 14–15
Perry, Peter S., 173
Peterson, David, 57, 81, 162, 164, 179, 236, 247, 252, 255, 275, 321, 325, 344, 352, 360, 362, 363, 379, 381, 460, 471, 473, 477, 480
Philo of Alexandria, 13–14, 34, 51, 58, 198, 231, 252, 257, 278–79, 410, 427, 443, 447, 470, 490, 498, , 520, et al. See ancient sources index under Philo of Alexandria
Pierce, Madison N., 46, 56, 109
Pinson, J. Matthew, 205
Pitkänen, Pekka M. A., 133
Porter, Stanley E., 3, 117, 321
Preisker, H., 257, 258
Proctor, J., 389
Proulx, Paul, 195

Quinn, Russell D., 73

Rabin, Chaim, 13
Rhee, Victor (Sung Yul), 45, 46, 414, 419, 430
Ribbens, Benjamin J., 14, 35, 54, 89, 150, 159, 160, 268, 270, 275, 284, 320, 322, 323, 327, 333, 335, 338, 344, 345, 352, 354, 359, 360, 363
Richardson, Christopher A., 75, 88, 164, 405, 471
Rice, George, 221
Rissi, Matthias, 12, 36, 65, 75, 92, 191, 192, 266, 267, 336, 337, 344, 378, 518
Robertson, A. T., 379
Robertson, O. P., 399
Rooke, Deborah W., 231
Rose, Christian, 395, 433, 434

Rosner, Brian S., 427
Ross, Allen P., 72, 355, 357
Rothschild, Clare K., 3, 523
Runge, Steven E., 47, 143, 196, 217, 333, 413

Sabourin, Leopold, 195
Sakenfeld, Katharine Doob, 517
Sarna, Nahum M., 229
Schama, Simon, 403
Schenck, Kenneth L., 7, 10, 12, 14, 45, 51, 73, 283, 322, 335, 498
Schille, Gottfried, 234
Schlatter, Adolf, 419
Schmidt, K. L., 115
Schmidt, M. A., 115
Schnelle, Udo, 58
Schöckel, Alonso, 195
Schreiner, Thomas R., 83, 102, 103, 164, 190, 190, 191, 192, 195, 205, 207, 333, 336, 338, 344, 353, 354, 357, 360, 363, 371, 377, 381, 390, 409, 410, 429, 446, 460, 463, 471, 474, 492, 499, 503, 518, 529
Schrenk, G., 234
Schröger, Friedrich, 47
Schröter, Jens, 54
Scorgie, Glen S., 252
Seitz, Christopher R., 2
Silva, Moisés, 436, 463
Skarsaune, Oskar, 296
Sklar, Jay, 306, 385
Small, Brian C., 96, 325, 516
Smillie, Gene R., 31, 57, 142, 144, 495, 496
Soderlund, S., 401
Son, Kiwoong, 489
Soulen, R. Kendall, 295
Spicq, Ceslas, 4, 12, 14, 45, 63, 92, 127, 128, 252, 275, 289, 317, 321, 371, 462, 479, 494, 502
Stackhouse, John G., Jr., 91
Stauffer, E., 395, 468, 469
Steinmann, A., 304
Steyn, Gert J., 55
Strauss, Mark L., 252, 379

Author Index

Strecker, Georg, 235
Stuhlmacher, Peter, 208, 493
Swetnam, James, 321, 433
Synge, F. C., 55

Tanner, Beth LaNeel, 229
Theissen, Gerd, 230
Thiessen, Matthew, 295
Thomas, H. A., 493
Thomas, K. J., 83
Thompson, James W., 10, 14, 49, 51, 52, 131, 172, 230, 236, 282, 325, 352, 371, 382, 410, 432, 445, 469, 471, 491, 498, 515, 518
Thorsen, Donald A. D., 530
Thrall, Margaret E., 472
Thurén, Jukka, 502, 508, 519
Treat, Jeremy R., 91
Treier, Daniel J., 2, 39, 57, 110
Trotter, Andrew H., Jr., 10, 54
Trueman, Carl R., 57
Turner, Nigel, 33, 74, 133, 136, 173, 174, 196, 214, 217, 239–40, 257, 268, 303, 338, 353, 412, 429, 454, 516, 520, 527

van der Woude, A. S., 231
Vanhoye, Albert, 16, 34, 36, 40, 68, 87, 88, 92, 166, 169, 227, 255, 271, 319, 321, 371, 391, 512
van Neste, Ray, 73
Verbrugge, Verlyn D., 196, 197
Vermes, Geza, 434
von Siebenthal, Heinrich, 62, 102, 115, 249, 277, 304, 306, 378, 383, 426, 432, 476, 509, 511
Vos, Gerhardus, 58, 277
Voth, Steven M., 252

Wallace, Daniel B., 31, 47, 65, 99, 102, 103, 115, 117, 128, 133, 135, 170, 187, 193, 195, 197, 201, 238, 247, 277, 306, 321, 386, 426, 4345, 458, 470
Walser, Georg A., 56, 291, 356, 436
Walsh, Sylvia, 433
Waltke, Bruce K., 133, 292, 474
Ware, Bruce A., 102, 190
Watts, Rikk E., 401
Webster, John, 3, 31, 32, 34, 37, 39
Weima, Jeffrey A. D., 523
Weiss, Hans-Friedrich, 2, 7, 10, 14, 16, 31, 32, 40, 46, 50, 55, 77, 82, 88, 91, 92, 96, 101, 105, 126, 147, 149, 162, 172, 179, 184, 190, 193, 217, 219, 222, 225, 231, 233, 246, 248, 252, 253, 254, 255, 256, 264, 266, 270, 271, 274, 277, 280, 291, 300, 308, 319, 320, 321, 322, 325, 326, 334, 346, 350, 353, 354, 356, 362, 364, 371, 377, 378, 381, 383, 385, 405, 408, 409, 410, 416, 419, 425, 429, 430, 446, 450, 453, 471, 472, 473, 475, 480, 485, 491, 492, 494, 498, 502, 508, 512, 516, 519
Wells, Tom, 295
Wellum, Stephen J., 207, 292, 294
Wenham, Gordon, 229
Westcott, Brooke Foss, 5, 31, 45, 48, 49, 69, 126, 136, 152, 159, 167, 179, 180, 194, 198, 219, 220, 224, 232, 236, 250, 252, 256, 266, 267, 268, 271, 276, 300, 303, 309, 317, 325, 328, 333, 352, 362, 363, 371, 378, 394, 395, 409, 410, 413, 416, 427, 429, 446, 469, 475, 476, 481, 482, 492, 494, 510, 512, 516, 518, 527, 529
Westermann, Claus, 230
Westfall, Cynthia Long, 16, 110, 143, 295, 317, 343, 371, 463, 478, 499
Whitfield, Brian J., 16, 82, 92, 127, 128, 131, 134, 135
Williamson, Ronald, 14
Witherington, Ben, III, 27, 83, 173, 175, 177, 180, 187, 195, 502
Wolfe, Lisa Michele, 517
Woodbridge, John D., 5, 436
Wrede, William, 523
Wright, N. T., 44, 49, 296, 401
Wunrow, Stephen, 279, 281, 335

Yadin, Yigael, 13, 161, 231
Yarbrough, Robert W., 209
Young, Frances M., 39
Young, N. H., 378
Yu, Charles. 133

Zaspel, Fred, 295
Zenger, Erich, 52, 108
Zerwick, Maximilian, 34, 64, 81, 99, 108, 159, 160, 214, 276, 301, 307, 327, 362, 364, 412, 413, 443, 476, 516
Zuntz, Günther, 428